TRADIVOX

VOLUME XI

TRADIVOX

CATHOLIC CATECHISM INDEX

VOLUME XI

Jean-Joseph Gaume

Edited by
Aaron Seng

SOPHIA INSTITUTE PRESS
MANCHESTER, NEW HAMPSHIRE

South Bend, Indiana
www.Tradivox.com

This book is an original derivative work comprised of newly typeset and reformatted editions of the following Catholic catechisms, once issued with ecclesiastical approval and now found in the public domain:

Gaume, Jean-Joseph. *The Catechism of Perseverance*. 2nd English ed., translated from the 10th French ed. Vol. 2. Dublin: M. H. Gill & Son, 1883.

Scripture references follow the Douay-Rheims Bible, per the imprint of John Murphy Company (Baltimore, 1899).

Cover and interior design by Perceptions Design Studio.

Sophia Institute Press
Box 5284, Manchester, NH 03108
1-800-888-9344

www.SophiaInstitute.com

ISBN 978-1-64413-370-5

LCCN: 2022943974

Dedicated with love and deepest respect
to all the English Martyrs and Confessors.
Orate pro nobis.

CONTENTS

ACKNOWLEDGMENTS

THE publication of this series is due primarily to the generosity of countless volunteers and donors from several countries. Special thanks are owed to Mr. and Mrs. Phil Seng, Mr. and Mrs. Michael Over, Mr. and Mrs. Jim McElwee, Mr. and Mrs. John Brouillette, Mr. and Mrs. Thomas Scheibelhut, Mr. and Mrs. Kyle Barriger, as well the visionary priests and faithful of St. Stanislaus Bishop and Martyr parish in South Bend, Indiana, and St. Patrick's Oratory in Green Bay, Wisconsin. May God richly reward their commitment to handing on the Catholic faith.

FOREWORD

The Catholic faith remains always the same throughout the centuries and millennia until the coming of our Lord at the end of the time, likewise "Jesus Christ is the same yesterday, today and forever" (Heb 13:8). The Catholic faith is "the faith, which was once delivered unto the saints" (Jude 1:3). The Magisterium of the Church teaches us solemnly the same truth in the following words of the First Vatican Council: "The doctrine of the faith which God has revealed, is put forward not as some philosophical discovery capable of being perfected by human intelligence, but as a divine deposit committed to the spouse of Christ to be faithfully protected and infallibly promulgated. Hence, too, that meaning of the sacred dogmas is ever to be maintained, which has once been declared by holy mother Church, and there must never be any abandonment of this sense under the pretext or in the name of a more profound understanding. May understanding, knowledge and wisdom increase as ages and centuries roll along, and greatly and vigorously flourish, in each and all, in the individual and the whole Church: but this only in its own proper kind, that is to say, in the same doctrine, the same sense, and the same understanding (cf. Vincentius Lerinensis, *Commonitorium*, 28)."[1]

An authentically Catholic catechism has the function of learning and teaching the unchanging Catholic faith throughout all generations. The Roman Pontiffs indeed, taught: "There is nothing more effective than catechetical instruction to spread the glory of God and to secure the salvation of souls."[2] Saint Pius X said, that "the great loss of souls is due to ignorance of divine things."[3] Therefore, the traditional catechisms have enduring value in our own day and age, which is marked by an enormous doctrinal confusion, which reigns in the life of the Church in the past six decades, and which reaches its peak in our days.

I welcome and bless the great project of the "Tradivox" in cataloguing and preserving the hundreds of long-lost Catholic catechisms issued with episcopal approval over the last millennium. This project will convincingly show the essentially unchanging nature of the apostolic doctrine across time and space, and so I invite the faithful of the entire world to support this historic effort, as we seek to restore the perennial catechism of the Church. The project of a catechism restoration on behalf of "Tradivox" will surely be of great benefit not only to many confused and disoriented Catholic faithful, but also to all people who are sincerely seeking the ultimate and authentic truth about God and man, which one can find only in the Catholic and apostolic faith, and which is the only religion and faith willed by God and to which God calls all men.

+Athanasius Schneider, O.R.C.,
Titular Bishop of Celerina
Auxiliary Bishop of the Archdiocese of Saint Mary in Astana

SERIES EDITOR'S

PREFACE

SOME are surprised to find that when a given Catholic is asked to "look something up in the catechism," he may well respond: "Which one?" The history of the Catholic Church across the last millennium is in fact filled with the publication of numerous catechisms, issued in every major language on earth; and for centuries, these concise "guidebooks" to Catholic doctrine have served countless men and women seeking a clear and concise presentation of that faith forever entrusted by Jesus Christ to his one, holy, Catholic, and apostolic Church.

Taken together, the many catechisms issued with episcopal approval can offer a kind of "window" on to the universal ordinary magisterium—a glimpse of those truths which have been held and taught in the Church *everywhere, always, and by all.* For, as St. Paul reminds us, the tenets of this Faith do not change from age to age: "Jesus Christ yesterday and today and the same for ever. Be not led away with various and strange doctrines" (Heb 13:8-9).

The catechisms included in our *Tradivox Catholic Catechism Index* are selected for their orthodoxy and historical significance, in the interest of demonstrating to contemporary readers the remarkable continuity of Catholic doctrine across time and space. Long regarded as reliable summaries of Church teaching on matters of faith and morals, we are proud to reproduce these works of centuries past, composed and endorsed by countless priests, bishops, and popes devoted to "giving voice to tradition."

In This Volume

Abbé Gaume's monumental *Catechism of Perseverance*[4] continues in the present volume, which encompasses the largest portion of its credal and moral content. Beginning with several lessons on the life and public mission of Jesus Christ as the archetypical new Adam, it moves into a consideration of union with Christ through the familiar threefold structure employed in the catechisms of Canisius and Bellarmine: faith (the Apostles' Creed), hope (grace, prayer, and the sacraments), and charity (commandments, precepts, counsels, virtues, and vices). Newly typeset from the second English edition of 1883, the only changes we have made to the body text have been to simplify the Table of Contents and section headers, remove the appended summary questions and litany, and abbreviate one overlong footnote.

In his typical flowing style, Gaume holds up to his contemporaries the witness of an unbroken continuity of Catholic belief and praxis in this volume, using a rhetorical device so similar to the vision behind the Tradivox project that it warrants a longer quotation:

> Suppose that, at this very hour, we could call from the grave a Catholic belonging to each of the eighteen centuries that have preceded us, and that we should ask these children of the Church—one from the East, another from the West, this man from Asia, and that man from Europe—who lived without knowing or seeing one another, and who died a hundred, a thousand, fifteen hundred, or eighteen hundred years ago: "What is your faith?" Each one in particular would recite the Symbol, that Symbol which we recite every day, and which is recited in the selfsame terms at the four ends of the earth.
>
> This perfect harmony, this perpetual unity, filled even the early fathers of the Church with admiration, and furnished them with an excellent proof to show heretics that they were in error. "Though spread over the whole world," said St. Irenaeus, "the Church preserves the apostolic faith with the utmost zeal, as if she dwelt in only one house. She believes it in the same manner, as having only one mind and one heart; and, with admirable accord, she professes and teaches the same faith, as if she had

> only one mouth. For, although the languages of the world are different, faith is everywhere one and the same. The Churches of Germany, of the Gauls, of the East, of Egypt, do not think or teach in different manners." How proud we ought to be to profess the faith of so many generations, the faith of the apostles and martyrs, the faith of the flower of the human race, the faith of the greatest geniuses that the world has ever known! What consolation! What security!

Now, nearly two centuries since the French monsignor first set pen to paper, we find his catechism joining the very chorus of voices that he once brought to witness to "this perfect harmony, this perpetual unity" in faith and morals; offering yet another generation that consolation and security enjoyed by all those who profess the faith of the apostles and martyrs.

Editorial Note

Our *Catholic Catechism Index* series generally retains only the doctrinal content of those catechisms it seeks to reproduce, as well as that front matter most essential to establishing the credibility of each work as an authentic expression of the Church's common doctrine, e.g., any episcopal endorsement, *nihil obstat*, or *imprimatur*. However, it should be noted that especially prior to the eighteenth century, a number of catechisms were so immediately and universally received as reliably orthodox texts (often simply by the reputation of the author or publisher), that they received no such "official" approval; or if they did, it was often years later and in subsequent editions. We therefore include both the original printing date in our Table of Contents, and further edition information in the Preface above.

Our primary goal has been to bring these historical texts back into publication in readable English copy. Due to the wide range of time periods, cultures, and unique author styles represented in this series, we have made a number of editorial adjustments to allow for a less fatiguing read, more rapid cross-reference throughout the series, and greater research potential for the future. While not affecting the original content, these adjustments have included adopting a cleaner typesetting and simpler standard for

Woodcut depicting an early method used in the production of Catholic catechisms, circa 1568.

capitalization and annotation, as well as remedying certain anachronisms in spelling or grammar.

At the same time, in deepest respect for the venerable age and subject matter of these works, we have been at pains to adhere as closely as possible to the original text: retaining archaisms such as "doth" and "hallowed," and avoiding any alterations that might affect the doctrinal content or authorial voice. We have painstakingly restored original artwork wherever possible, and where the rare explanatory note has been deemed necessary, it is not made in the text itself, but only in a marginal note. In some cases, our editorial refusal to "modernize" the content of these classical works may require a higher degree of attention from today's reader, who we trust will be richly rewarded by the effort.

We pray that our work continues to yield highly readable, faithful reproductions of these time-honored monuments to Catholic religious instruction: catechisms once penned, promulgated, and praised by bishops across the globe. May these texts that once served to guide and shape the faith and lives of millions now do so again; and may the scholars and saints once involved in their first publication now intercede for all who take them up anew. *Tolle lege!*

Sincerely in Christ,
Aaron Seng

TRADIVOX

VOLUME XI

THE

CATECHISM OF PERSEVERANCE;

OR,

AN HISTORICAL, DOGMATICAL, MORAL, LITURGICAL, APOLOGETICAL, PHILOSOPHICAL, AND SOCIAL EXPOSITION OF RELIGION,

FROM THE

BEGINNING OF THE WORLD DOWN TO OUR OWN DAYS.

BY MONSIGNOR GAUME,

APOSTOLIC PROTHONOTARY, DOCTOR IN THEOLOGY, VICAR-GENERAL OF MONTAUBAN AND AQUILA, KNIGHT OF THE ORDER OF ST. SYLVESTER, MEMBER OF THE ACADEMY OF THE CATHOLIC RELIGION (ROME), &c.

Jesus Christ, yesterday, and to-day; and the same for ever.—*Heb.* xiii. 8.
God is charity.—1 *John*, iv. 8.

Translated from the Tenth French Edition.

IN FOUR VOLUMES.

VOL. II.

Second Edition.

DUBLIN
M. H. GILL & SON, 50 UPPER SACKVILLE STREET
1883

THE

CATECHISM OF PERSEVERANCE;

OR,

AN HISTORICAL, DOGMATICAL, MORAL, LITURGICAL, APOLOGETICAL, PHILOSOPHICAL, AND SOCIAL EXPOSITION OF RELIGION.

FROM THE

BEGINNING OF THE WORLD DOWN TO OUR OWN DAYS.

BY MONSIGNOR GAUME,

APOSTOLIC PROTHONOTARY, DOCTOR IN THEOLOGY, VICAR-GENERAL OF MONTAUBAN AND AQUILA, KNIGHT OF THE ORDER OF ST. SYLVESTER, MEMBER OF THE ACADEMY OF THE CATHOLIC RELIGION (ROME), &c.

Jesus Christ, yesterday, and to-day; and the same for ever.—Heb. xiii. 8.
God is charity.—1 John, iv. 8.

Translated from the Tenth French Edition.

IN FOUR VOLUMES.

VOL. II.

Second Edition.

DUBLIN
M. H. GILL & SON, 50 UPPER SACKVILLE STREET
1883

Nihil Obstat:
THOMAS O'SULLIVAN,
Censor Deputatus

Imprimatur:
+ PAULUS CARD, CULLEN,
Archiepiscopus Dubliniensis

Catechism of Perseverance

Lesson 1: State of the World at the Coming of the Messias

We have left the old world: today we set foot on the new, in which are to be accomplished, verified, and completed the promises, the figures, the prophecies, the teachings, whose history has for so long a time occupied our minds and made our hearts throb. Before going further, let us pause a moment to learn a little of this new world, the scene of so many wonders.

Political and religious state of the Gentiles: Roman domination.—The Roman Empire, which, according to the prophecy of Daniel, should overthrow and absorb all other empires, was come to its highest degree of glory: it embraced in its vast bosom nearly all the known nations of the world. After a long and bloody warfare against his numerous rivals, Augustus, victorious by land and sea, was tranquilly seated on the throne of the Caesars. The whole earth rested in peace: if we may be allowed to speak of peace in reference to the momentary calm of a brutalized and manacled slave.

Idolatry.—In effect, all the nations, having become tributaries of the Romans, were groaning under the most cruel despotism that ever weighed upon the world. Three-fourths of the human race were slaves, that is, little more than beasts. With the exception of the Jewish people, all mankind were plunged in the darkness of idolatry. The universe was only an immense dungeon, a vast temple of idols; never was corruption deeper or more general. To say everything in a word: it was the reign of the devil, present under a thousand obscene and senseless forms.

Here, the wicked spirit was adored in the elements, the sun, the moon, the earth, water, fire; there, in animals; and man prostrated himself before oxen, cats, crocodiles, serpents, and even before the vegetables of the kitchen-garden. It was not enough to change beasts into gods, but gods should also be changed into beasts, since the most beastly passions were attributed to them. Olympus was peopled with inhabitants so detestable that among us they would be treated as the vilest ruffians. Their example, far from leading to virtue, only offered, as the sum of human happiness, crimes to be committed and inclinations to be indulged. By what ceremonies the different peoples were accustomed to honor the immortal gods, we shall not say: every modest soul knows the reason.

Roman gravity did not treat religion more seriously. On the one hand, it consecrated to the honor of the gods the impurities of the theatre and the bloody combats of the gladiators, that is, whatever can be imagined most corrupt and barbarous; on the other, it adopted all the divinities of the nations that its generals had chained to their chariots. No idol so infamous, no worship so absurd, as not to find an asylum with the queen of the world; so that she ended by counting eighty colleges of priests and priestesses, and thirty thousand gods. Sages and philosophers were powerless to withdraw the peoples from this profound abyss; they were more frequently the accomplices in their errors and disorders. Not one of those men, so highly lauded, that did not profess maxims which it would be impossible to repeat without a blush!

The human race, says Bossuet, was come to that point when it could no longer endure the least idea of the true God. If anyone dared to teach that statues were not gods, as the common people understood it, he was obliged to make a recantation of his doctrine; then, after so much amends, he was banished as an impious wretch. The whole earth was possessed by the same error; truth durst not appear. The Creator of the world had no temple or worship but in Jerusalem.

Such was the state of the nations at the moment when God was about to accomplish the oft-repeated promise of a restorer, appointed to deliver men from their darkness and their vices.

Political and religious state of the Jews: Jewish sects.—As for the Jewish people, the only one that had preserved the knowledge and worship of the true God, it also had great need of the Messias. For a long time it had begun not to forget the God of its fathers, but to blend with its religion superstitions unworthy of him. Four principal sects were formed in Israel: the Pharisees, the Sadducees, the Essenes, and the Herodians. As there is frequent reference to them in the life of our Lord, we shall give a short account of them. Without this knowledge, it is difficult to understand the gospel.

Pharisees. Under the reign of the Machabees—from the time of Jonathan, son of Mathathias—the sect of the Pharisees appeared among the Jews. The Pharisees pretended that God had added to the law, given on Mount Sinai, a great many rites and dogmas, which Moses had transmitted to posterity without any written record. They therefore joined to the text of the law the traditions of the ancients which were preserved unwritten. Thus, with much good doctrine, they mingled a heap of superstitions, for which their conduct gained belief among the people.

Closely united among themselves, they led in the midst of the world a life that seemed at once simple and severe; yet the majority of them were deeply attached to their own interests, ambitious, proud, and avaricious. They gloried in the extreme exactness with which they attended to the external observance of the law. They gave tithes, not only of the larger fruits, but of the least herbs—of cumin and mint and anise.

They observed the sabbath so scrupulously that they pronounced it a crime in our Lord to have moistened a little clay on the end of his finger, to cure a blind man; and, in his disciples, to have plucked a few ears of wheat, to eat the grains. They all fasted frequently: many of them even twice a week, on Mondays and Thursdays. They gave alms in public, so as to be seen; they discolored their faces, so as to appear great fasters; they seduced, by their fine discourses, the ignorant and the simple, whose contributions went to enrich them. They persuaded the Jews that to be descended from Abraham according to the flesh was a distinction which naturally placed them above all other peoples.

Hence, their disdain and contempt for Greeks, for Romans, for foreigners in general. As they only thought of distinguishing themselves from other men, they multiplied external practices beyond all bounds; but they neglected what is most essential in religion, and uttered all their fancies, however ridiculous or contrary to the law of God, as authentic traditions.

We find these pretended traditions, which the Pharisees surrounded with so much mystery, in the books of the Jews that were written about a hundred years after our Lord's resurrection. It is impossible to conceive any questions more frivolous than those with which these books abound. Let us give a few of them: Is it permitted on the sabbath day to ride an ass to drink, or should it not be led along with a halter? Is it permitted on the sabbath day to walk through freshly-sown land, since one runs the risk of carrying off some grains with his feet, and consequently of sowing them? Is it permitted on the sabbath day to write as many letters of the alphabet as would form sense? Is it permitted to eat an egg laid on the sabbath day? Is it necessary—referring to the purification of the old leaven before the Pasch—to immediately purify a house when a mouse has been seen running through it with some crumbs of bread?

We might give a thousand other cases of conscience like these: the Talmud and its commentaries are full of them.[5] Such were the Pharisees. Our Lord, who, on every occasion, unmasked their hypocrisy, had no more bitter enemies.

Sadducees. The second sect was that of the Sadducees. To all appearance, they rejected the traditions of the ancients and attached themselves only to the written word, or scripture, which they interpreted after their own manner. They admitted that God had created the world by his power, and that he governs it by his wisdom; that he had wrought a countless number of prodigies in favor of his people, and, to govern them, had established rewards and punishments: but they believed that these rewards and punishments were purely temporal. Accordingly, they denied the future resurrection and the immortality of the soul, served God only in consideration of the good things of this world, and gave themselves much to the pleasures of the senses.

They had little union among themselves and little authority over the people: their number was not great, but they stood in the front rank of the nation, and some of them were even sacrificators. Our Lord, by putting to them a question which they could not answer, confounded them. This is the meaning of his words: "You believe in scripture, and yet you deny the immortality of the soul; how, then, does it come to pass that God is called in scripture the God of Abraham, Isaac, and Jacob, long after the death of these patriarchs? God is not the God of nothingness, the God of that which no longer exists. Conclude, therefore, that these patriarchs are not quite dead; for God is not the God of the dead, but of the living."

Essenes. The third sect was that of the Essenes. Honoring Moses as the first of legislators, they regarded those who spoke ill of him as so many blasphemers, and condemned them to death. They were opposed to the Pharisees, inasmuch as they rejected traditions, and to the Sadducees, inasmuch as they believed in the immortality of the soul. They principally erred in denying the resurrection of the body, and in regarding the soul as an extremely subtle matter, which, having been attracted into the body by some natural charm, was shut up there as in a prison.

The Sadducees lived only for the body. The Essenes, on the contrary, judging that whatever flattered the body only more and more enslaved the soul, professed an extremely severe morality. They avoided large cities; their property was held in common; their food was most simple. They devoted much time to meditation on the law and to prayer. Their manner of life bore some resemblance to that of the prophets. There were even some among them who observed continence, and led a life wholly contemplative.

Herodians. The fourth sect was that of the Herodians. Their name shows that they had made their appearance in the reign of Herod. The Jews knew that the coming of the Messias was at hand, and Herod was not ignorant of it. To put the nation out of its course in reference to the traditions of the Messias, Herod caused the genealogical books of the Jews to be burnt. He was not content with this. In order that he might himself pass for the Messias, he caused the Temple of Solomon to be, at least in part, rebuilt. The work being finished, his flatterers exclaimed that Herod, the incomparable prince, must be the Messias.

Gross as this flattery was, it met with the happiest success. It gave birth to the sect of the Herodians, the followers or adorers of Herod the Messias. In the same manner do we see, a little later on, a Jewish priest apply to Vespasian and Titus the prophecies that relate to the Desired of Nations. The greater number of the Herodians were ambitious courtiers, members of the prince's suite, his officers and soldiers. They were associated with the Pharisees, for we always meet them together in the gospel. It is needless to add that they taught very dangerous errors, since our Lord considered it necessary to warn his disciples against their leaven.[6]

The Pharisees, the Sadducees, the Essenes, and the Herodians were then the four sects that existed among the Jews on the arrival of the Messias. They falsified religion, whose true spirit was almost extinct. On the other side, the expiring truth would undoubtedly have succumbed among the nations, if God had not hastened to its relief. Never had the world stood more in need of a new revelation: it was not long delayed. At this supreme moment, the Desired of Nations came down, beaming with light, from the summit of the eternal hills.

Scribes. Among the Jews there was yet another class of men, to whom there is frequent allusion in the gospel: I mean the scribes. Such was the name given to those clever men, the doctors of the law, whose ministry it was to copy and explain the holy books. By some, the origin of their profession is attributed to the time of Moses; by others, to that of David; and by others again, to that of Esdras, after the captivity. These doctors were very much esteemed among the Jews: they held the same rank as priests and sacrificators, although their functions were different.

There were three sorts of them—the scribes of the law, whose decisions were received with the utmost respect; the scribes of the people, who were magistrates; and the common scribes, who were notaries public or the secretaries of the Sanhedrim.[7]

To a knowledge of the men in the midst of whom the Son of God should pass his life, let us add a few details on the country which he was about to sanctify by his presence.

Division of Jewish territory.—At the time when the Messias was born, the territory of Palestine was divided into three provinces—Samaria, Galilee, and Judea properly so called. We have seen that the nation of the Hebrews, composed of twelve tribes, was divided into two kingdoms under Roboam, the son of Solomon. The ten schismatical tribes took the name of the Kingdom of Israel, of which Samaria became the capital. In punishment for its idolatry, this kingdom was ravaged by the kings of Assyria, and changed into a solitude. To fill up the places of the ancient inhabitants, led away captive to Ninive, Salmanasar sent some foreign colonies into the country. For having brought their idols into the Holy Land, these new arrivals were almost entirely destroyed by lions.

Samaria. On the news of this catastrophe, Asarhaddon, king of Ninive, sent a Jewish priest, with a fresh colony, to restore the worship of the Samaritans. This colony embraced the Jewish religion, and the new Samaritans were called the "Proselytes of the Lions," because the fear of these animals had determined them to follow the religion of the Jews, from which, however, they wandered in three vital points: a) of all the holy scripture, they received only the five books of Moses; b) they rejected the traditions of the Jewish doctors, and held to the written word alone; c) they maintained that it was necessary to render worship to God on Mount Garizim, where the patriarchs had adored, while the Jews desired, and justly too, that no sacrifices should be offered except at the Temple of Jerusalem.

The Jews, therefore, regarded them as schismatics, and carried their hatred so far against them that they imagined themselves defiled by intercourse with them. In their language, to call a person a Samaritan was an exceedingly gross insult. Such were the Samaritans, the inhabitants of a portion of the ancient kingdom of Israel.

Galilee. The second province of Palestine in the time of the Messias was Galilee. About the half of the ten tribes, led away captive to Ninive, profited of various circumstances to return successively and in large companies to a portion of the lands of the kingdom of Israel, their ancient abode. They rebuilt a sufficiency of cities, and the country which they occupied was termed Upper and Lower Galilee: here was situated the little city of Nazareth.

As for the part of Galilee adjoining Decapolis or Syria, it also bore the name of Galilee of the Nations, because the Israelites there were confounded with the Gentiles as far as civil society was concerned, though there was no communication between them in religion.

Judea. The third province of Palestine was Judea, properly so called. Formed of the territory of the tribes of Juda and Benjamin, it was occupied by such remains of these tribes as had returned from the captivity of Babylon. The Hebrews, who dwelt in this part of Palestine, and who owned the city and the Temple of Jerusalem, were properly called Jews. The high priests bore one after another the title of chief of the holy nation, until the Romans, possessing themselves of Palestine, obliged the Jews to receive a master from the hands of their conquerors.

Dependence on the Romans.—Now that Judea was reduced to a province for the benefit of Augustus and his successors, the Jews themselves had no alternative but to recognize the Caesars as their sovereigns. They could no longer execute the criminals whom they had condemned without first obtaining permission from the emperor, or from the president who commanded in his name. Nothing shows better that the scepter had passed from their hands. The children of Jacob, instructed by the celebrated prediction of their father on his deathbed, might then promise themselves that the kingdom of the Messias was not far distant. We shall see in the next lesson that their expectations were well founded.

PRAYER

O my God! who art all love, I thank thee for having thyself come in Person to the relief of truth, about to perish on the earth, and for having drawn us from the darkness of paganism into the admirable light of the gospel. Grant, O divine repairer of the world! that we may never follow any other master than thee.

I am resolved to love God above all things, and my neighbor as myself for the love of God; and, in testimony of this love, I will take the greatest care to study this second part of the catechism.

Lesson 2: Birth of the Messias

Since the time of Alexander's visit to the East, the Jews had been subject to various princes, although their high priests retained the title and authority of chiefs of the nation. These foreign rulers had shown themselves in turn avaricious, cruel, impious, and tyrannical. They had plundered the treasures of the Temple, ravaged the country, encouraged the worship of idols, and put to death the holy old man Eleazar, and the mother of the Machabees, with her seven sons. In fine, the Romans, not content with requiring a tribute from the Jews, who believed themselves free by nature, had deprived them of the sovereign power.

General expectation among the Jews.—The Pharisees, and the multitude who gave ear to their sentiments, endured this state of affairs with impatience. The heavier they felt the yoke of the Gentiles, the greater were their disdain and hatred for their oppressors. They no longer desired any other Messias than a warrior, who should be terrible to the powers that were the objects of their aversion. Forgetting the numerous prophecies which spoke so expressly of the humiliations of the Redeemer, they had neither eyes nor ears for any but those in which his triumphs were mentioned. Besides, they mistook the nature of these triumphs, which were very different from those that they desired—a fatal error! which eventually led them to deicide.

Let us not forget that this blindness is an additional proof in favor of the prophecies. As a matter of fact, it had been predicted that the chosen Jewish people would be indocile, ungrateful, incredulous; that they would deny the Christ, and put him to death; and that, in consequence, they would be rejected by God, and would become wanderers, without a king, without a sacrifice, without an altar, without a prophet, expecting salvation and not finding it.[8]

Nevertheless, instructed by the prophecy of Jacob, which marks the coming of the great liberator at the moment when the scepter of Juda shall be borne by a foreigner, they are in expectation of his approaching arrival. Their ears are open to every impostor who, calling himself the Messias, promises to deliver them from the yoke of nations: they attach themselves to him with unexampled facility.[9] History attests that the principal motive of the astonishing war which they maintained at this time against the Romans was an oracle of the sacred scripture, announcing that about this period there would arise in their country a man who should rule over the whole earth.[10]

General expectation among the Gentiles, in the East and West.—This expectation of the approaching arrival of the Messias was not confined to the Jews: all the nations of the world shared in it. And very properly so; for, otherwise, how could the prophets have called the Messias the "Desired of all Nations"? The Gentiles were indebted for this knowledge of the future Redeemer either to the primitive tradition, or to their intercourse with the Jews, scattered during several centuries over a great portion of the world. A general impression prevailed, says Tacitus, that the old books of the priests announced: that, at this period, the East would prevail, and that from Judea should come forth the masters of the world.[11] All Asia was moved. A grave and celebrated historian of the Roman Empire, Suetonius, who lived in these ancient times, positively attests it. All the East, he says, resounded with an old and constant rumor, that the fates had decreed to send forth from Judea at this period the masters of the world.[12]

In the West, Virgil, the interpreter of the general expectation, sang the approaching arrival of the Son of God, who, descending from heaven, was about to bring back the golden age on earth, to efface crime, and to destroy the serpent. In a word, this lively expectation of the Messias was to be found among all peoples, however disfigured the primitive religion had become among them.[13] Immemorial traditions, says a learned Englishman,[14] derived from the patriarchs and scattered throughout every part of the East, in reference to the fall of man and the promise of a future mediator, had taught the whole pagan world to expect, about the time of the arrival of the Messias, the appearance of an illustrious and sacred personage.

The greatest enemies of religion have been unable to deny this universal expectation of a liberator. Sacred and mythological traditions of the times prior to the destruction of Jerusalem, says a celebrated unbeliever, had spread through all Asia a dogma perfectly analogous to that of the Jews regarding the Messias: there was nothing spoken of but a great mediator, an absolute judge, a future Savior, who, as King, God, conqueror, and legislator, would bring back the golden age to earth, deliver it from the empire of evil, and restore to men the reign of peace and happiness.[15] This belief was so strong that, according to a tradition of the Jews, given in the Talmud and many other ancient works, a considerable number of Gentiles made their way to Jerusalem about the period of the birth of Jesus Christ, in order to see the Savior of the world, when he should come to redeem the house of Jacob.[16]

It is therefore a fact, as certain as the existence of the sun, that before the coming of our Lord, not only the Jews, but all the other peoples of the world, were anxiously expecting a liberator; it is equally certain that, since the coming of our Lord, this general expectation has ceased. What is the conclusion to be drawn? Either that all mankind, instructed by primitive traditions and by prophecies, were deceived, both in expecting a Messias and in recognizing Jesus Christ as such; or that Jesus Christ is truly the Desired of Nations. There is no middle course.

The annunciation.—The world was rapt in this religious expectation: its looks were turned toward Judea. There was a great silence. For about four hundred years the voice of a prophet had not been heard in Israel. Suddenly, a prince of the celestial court, the archangel Gabriel, is sent by God to a little city of Galilee, called Nazareth: he comes to a Virgin, who is espoused to a man named Joseph, of the house of David, and the

Virgin's name is Mary. The angel, entering the house, says to her: "Hail, thou who art full of grace! the Lord is with thee; blessed art thou among women."

At these words of the angel, Mary is troubled, and, in her humility, endeavors to discover the reason for this respectful salutation. "Fear not, Mary," says the angel to her, "for thou hast found grace with God. Thou shalt bring forth a Son into the world, and thou shalt give him the name of Jesus. The Holy Ghost shall come upon thee, and the power of the Most High shall overshadow thee. Wherefore, the Holy One who shall be born of thee shall be called the Son of God. The Lord shall place him on the throne of David, his father: he shall reign forever in the house of Jacob, and his kingdom shall have no end." The humble Virgin answers: "Behold the handmaid of the Lord; be it done unto me according to thy word." At this moment the angel leaves her, and the man-God is formed by the Holy Ghost in the chaste womb of Mary.

Such is the sublime simplicity with which the gospel relates the greatest of mysteries. The supreme object of forty centuries of the ancient world, the incarnation of the Word, is the starting point of all succeeding centuries, even to eternity. In this culminating event may be found the explanation of all other events, the reason for the rise and fall of empires in the East and the West, the last word of God's action in regard to the human race.

We have said that the Blessed Virgin and St. Joseph dwelt at Nazareth. Yet it was written that the Messias should be born at Bethlehem: his birth in the city of David was a sign by which he should be recognized. God, who makes even the passions of men concur to the accomplishment of his designs, avails himself of the vanity or the avarice of the emperor Augustus to bring Joseph and Mary to Bethlehem; and the haughty emperor becomes, without knowing it, the humble minister of the great King, who, from the summit of heaven, rules the world.

Edict of the emperor Augustus; journey to Bethlehem.—Just at this time, in effect, appeared an edict of Caesar Augustus, ordering a general census to be made. All the subjects of the Roman Empire went accordingly to be enrolled, every one in the city to which he originally belonged. As Joseph belonged to the house and family of David, he went from Galilee to Judea, from the city of Nazareth to that of David, otherwise called Bethlehem, to be enrolled there with Mary his wife. Arrived on the soil of their ancestors, they travel through all the streets in search of a lodging. You imagine, perhaps, that in a city full of their relatives they shall soon meet with a generous hospitality. Alas! no. It was thus that the Savior began to suffer, even before his entrance into the world.

Birth of the Messias.—Joseph and Mary were therefore obliged to leave the city, and to seek an asylum in the country. They found a grotto, which served as a refuge for cattle, and there they resolved to spend the night. It was, according to the vulgar era, the year of the world 4004;—1,000 years after the dedication of the Temple of Solomon, 752 years after the foundation of Rome, the 25th day of December, about midnight. The times being accomplished, the hour of the redemption of the human race struck, and the eternal Word, incarnate in the womb of the purest of virgins, made his entrance into the world.[17]

Scarcely was he born when Mary, his Mother, wrapped him in swaddling clothes and laid him in the manger. Meanwhile, the Son of God did not desire that his birth should remain a secret to men, for whom he had descended from heaven; but it was to the poor and simple, rather than to the rich and learned, that he chose to manifest himself.

There were in the neighborhood some shepherds, keeping watch over their flocks. Suddenly an angel of the Lord appeared to them: a great light shone round about them, and they were very much afraid. But the angel said to them: "Fear not, for I bring you tidings that will be a subject of great joy to all the people: today a Savior is born to you in the city of David; he is Christ the Lord. And this is a sign by which you shall know him: you shall find the infant wrapped in swaddling clothes, and laid in a manger."

Immediately a multitude of the heavenly army joined with the angel in praising God, and saying: "Glory be to God in the highest heavens, and peace on earth to men of good will!" Oh, yes! to God, glory; to men, peace: this is the reason why the divine infant has just been born, this is the grand object of Christianity. To attain it, what must be done on our part? Wealth and learning are unnecessary: it suffices to have a good will.

When the angels had left the shepherds, the latter said to one another: "Let us go over to Bethlehem, and see that which has come to pass." They went thither in all haste, and found Mary and Joseph, together with the infant, which lay in the manger. The first apostles of the newborn Savior—they published the wonders which they had seen. All who heard of them were filled with admiration, while the holy Virgin forgot none of these things, but meditated on their every circumstance in her heart. Thus passed this ever-memorable night.

Circumcision.—At the end of eight days the child was circumcised; for circumcision took place eight days after birth. On this occasion the Messias, shedding the first drops of his divine blood, received the name of *Jesus*, which means "Savior." A mysterious name! which had been given him by the angel even before he was conceived in his Mother's womb; an adorable name! at which every knee in heaven, on earth, and in hell, should bend; an incommunicable name! which no other than the Messias has verified in all its extent.

It had been borne, indeed, by two men, who were celebrated in sacred history: Josue, the successor of Moses, and Jesus, the son of Josedech. But what an immense distance between these two figurative saviors and him whom they represented! As the promised land, into which Josue led the Israelites, was only an imperfect image of heaven, and the reestablishment of legal observances by the son of Josedech, on the return from captivity, a shadow of evangelical perfection, of adoration in spirit and in truth, so the name of *Jesus*, given to these two great men, was a mere symbol of the omnipotent name by which we should be reconciled with God and restored to the inheritance of the saints.

Adoration of the Magi.—Joseph and Mary were still at Bethlehem, when God, wishing to show that his Son was really, according to the predictions of the prophets, the Desired of Nations and the Savior of mankind, caused an extraordinary star to appear in the heavens. This miraculous star had been announced to the Gentiles, more than twelve centuries previously, under the name of the Star of Jacob. It appeared in the East: the Magi recognized it, and understood that the Messias, so long desired, had entered the world. A constant tradition teaches us that the Magi were kings, and three in number: the name *Magi* means "great and learned." Scarcely had they seen the star, when, docile to grace, they began their journey to Judea.

Led along by this heavenly guide, they at length reached Jerusalem. It was in the time of King Herod. "Where is the King of the Jews, who has just been born?" they asked, "for we have seen his star in the East, and we are come to adore him." On hearing this news Herod was troubled, and all Jerusalem with him; and, having assembled the chief priests and the scribes of the nation, he inquired of them where the Christ should be born. Instructed by the prophecies, they had not a moment's hesitation, but immediately answered him: "At Bethlehem of Juda; for so it is written by the prophet: 'And thou, Bethlehem of Juda, thou art not the least among the principal cities of Juda, since from thee shall come forth the leader of my people, Israel.'"[18]

Then Herod, in whom the cruelty of a tiger was blended with the craftiness of a fox, resolved to rid himself of this new King. He called the Magi privately to him, learned from them the exact time at which they had seen the star, and, sending them to Bethlehem, said: "Go and inquire diligently concerning the child, and, when you have found him, bring me word of it, that I also may come and adore him."

Herod reasoned thus: "If the inquiry be made in my name and by my officers, suspicion will cause the child to be concealed, while every one will hasten to show him to these good Easterns, whom no person can doubt." This was to reason cunningly; but Herod did not reason when he ordered the massacre of the children. As a matter of fact, this massacre was useless if the Messias was not born; and if he was born, God, who had promised him to the world, would not allow him to be included in the general slaughter. Accordingly, when Herod was cunning, God sported with his cunningness; and when he raved, God allowed him to commit, without deriving any benefit therefrom, a crime, which rendered him the execration of all succeeding ages. Ye sage and powerful of the world, what fools ye are, when ye dare to oppose the designs of the Lord!

Meanwhile, the Magi, having heard what Herod said to them, went away without suspicion and with the intention of satisfying him. The star, which they had seen in the East, now reappeared, and continued its course before them, until it stopped over the place where the child reposed. On beholding the star, they were filled with a great joy; and, entering the house, they found the child with Mary, his Mother, and, prostrating, they adored him. Then, having opened their treasures, they offered him a present of gold, frankincense, and myrrh. And thus the predictions of the prophets regarding the Messias were verified in the babe of Bethlehem: "The kings of Tharsis and Saba," they said, "shall offer him presents, shall bring him the gold of Arabia."[19]

These gifts were mysterious: by the gold, the Magi recognized the royalty of Jesus Christ; by the frankincense, his divinity; and by the myrrh, which was used to embalm bodies, his humanity, in mortal and passible flesh. We imitate them, says one of the fathers of the Church, by offering to God the gold of charity, the frankincense of prayer, and the myrrh of mortification. The Magi were the first fruits of the Gentiles, and our vocation began with them. Hence proceeds that more than ordinary joy with which we celebrate the feast of the Epiphany. We are not astonished that the wise men of the East, enlightened by faith, should have recognized, without difficulty, in the little babe of Bethlehem, the Redeemer of the world. His sufferings, his humiliations, his absolute want, were glorious proofs of his divinity. "I require," says Bossuet, "a Savior who, by his example, shall trample underfoot the pomps and vanities that deceive the children of Adam: this is the mark by which I shall recognize him."

In effect, to comprehend the state of wonderful abasement in which the Messias presents himself to our eyes, it suffices to recollect the object of his coming on earth. The Savior came to take away the sins of the world, that is, to reconcile man with God, to satisfy the justice of his Father, and to deliver the human race from the evils that had been the consequence of sin. To expiate, it was necessary that the Messias should suffer, for there can be no expiation without suffering, without the effusion of blood. This is the reason why Jesus Christ suffers from his entrance into the world; why his life is only one long pain; why, in fine, he is born in a crib and dies on a cross.

The consequences of sin in regard to man are: ignorance of that which he ought to love; and concupiscence, or a blind, irregular, tyrannical love of creatures. To deliver him from these evils, the Messias should teach him to despise all earthly things, and to direct his love toward God. Behold the reason why the Messias tramps on honors, riches, and pleasures—why he is born, why he lives, why he dies in poverty and humiliation. Hereby he shows himself the true physician of fallen man; and this is the cost at which he shall be our Savior.

PRAYER

O my God! who art all love, I thank thee for having sent us the Savior, so often promised and so ardently desired: do not permit that we should despise him, as the Jews; grant us rather the docility of the shepherds and the faith of the Magi, to enable us to understand, like them, that it is to take away the sins of the world that he lives and dies in poverty, suffering, and humiliation.

I am resolved to love God above all things, and my neighbor as myself for the love of God; and, in testimony of this love, I will imitate the meekness and humility displayed by Jesus in his birth.

Lesson 3: Hidden Life of the Messias

Purification.—Herod was expecting the return of the Magi; and, as he relied on them, did not seek any further information regarding the new King of the Jews. But the Magi, being warned in a dream not to visit this perfidious prince again, returned into their own country by a different way. Joseph and Mary profited of the quiet which they enjoyed, to comply with two new articles in the law of Moses. One commanded that all women who had brought forth children should be purified at the Temple after a certain number of days; the other, that every firstborn son should be offered to the Lord.

Mary, who had not been rendered less pure or virginal by her divine childbearing, went nevertheless to the Temple, to associate herself with the generality of women. A grand example of humility and obedience! which teaches us to follow in every point the order established by God, without seeking for a dispensation from it. Jesus Christ, on his side, being God, was far above the reach of the Mosaic law, by which it was necessary to offer all firstborn sons to the Lord. Nevertheless, he submitted to this law, and was carried to Jerusalem forty days after his birth. By the hands of his parents, he offered himself to his Father, presenting, for the first time, in the Temple, a victim worthy of him. God did not permit this sublime offering to take place unobserved.

Simeon.—There was in Jerusalem, at this time, a holy old man, named Simeon. He was a just man, who looked with eagerness for the consoler of Israel. It had even been revealed to him that he should not die before seeing the Christ of the Lord. Guided by a divine inspiration, he came to the Temple when the father and Mother of the infant Jesus were bringing him to fulfill in his regard that which was the custom according to the law, namely, to offer him to the Lord, and afterward to redeem him by the payment of five sides of silver, as is laid down in the book of Numbers:[20] the offering of a lamb or of turtles being intended only for the purification of the mother.

Not only had the holy old man the happiness of seeing the Redeemer of the world, but he was even allowed to hold him in his arms. Then, transported with a pious joy, and animated by the Spirit of the prophets, he returned thanks to God, and foretold the future victories of this divine infant: "It is now, O Lord!" he exclaimed, "that, according to thy word, thou dost allow thy servant to die in peace, because my eyes have seen the salvation which comes from thee, and which thou hast manifested to all nations, to be the light of the Gentiles and the glory of thy people, Israel."

While the holy Virgin and St. Joseph admired the words of the good old man, as he entertained them on the future destiny of the infant-God and on the sorrow with which Mary's heart should be pierced, a holy widow, named Anna, came also into the Temple. A true daughter of Jacob, she earnestly longed for the coming of the Messias. A widow after seven years of marriage, she had reached the age of eighty in fasting and prayer: the Temple seemed to be her home. Scarcely had she known the Savior when she united her voice with that of Simeon, and gave expression to her gratitude and joy in canticles of praise.

How delightful it is to see these two venerable old persons—the only confidants of Joseph and Mary regarding the birth of the Redeemer—render testimony to his divinity, and die without regret, because they have seen him who is the resurrection and the life! Worthy children of Abraham, happier than your father, you have contemplated with your eyes him, whose day, foreseen in the distance of ages, rejoiced your illustrious ancestor! After this you desire to see no more, and you are right. When one has seen Jesus Christ, what more remains to be seen? And as for us, Christians, what further have we to desire, when, happier than Anna or Simeon, we receive, not into our arms, but into our hearts, the Desired of Nations and the glory of Israel? What canticle can then resound through the sanctuary of our souls, if not that of the holy old man: "Now, O Lord! thou dost dismiss thy servant in peace; I have lived long enough, my desires are satisfied!"

Flight into Egypt.—Forty days at least had rolled away since the birth of the Messias. Herod, seeing that the Magi did not return, fell into a violent rage. He resolved to free himself at any cost from the presence of an infant whose birth had occasioned him so many apprehensions, and, for this purpose, to plunge his cradle into a river of blood. But how vain are the counsels of men against God! The angel of the Lord appeared in a dream to Joseph, and said to him: "Arise, take the child and his Mother, flee into Egypt, and do not return until I tell thee; for Herod will speedily seek the child to put him to death."

Joseph arose, and that very night, taking the child and the Mother, set out for Egypt.

The conduct of St. Joseph on this occasion has ever been regarded as the model of a perfect obedience.[21] His obedience was simple and blind. He did not allege that God, in order to preserve his Son from the fury of Herod, had an infinity of means much less painful for the child, for the Mother, and for himself. His obedience was prompt. Warned during the night, he did not await the break of day to depart. It was generous—full of confidence in providence. He set out without preparations or provisions. He was poor—everything was wanting to him; but, possessing Jesus and Mary, how rich he was! The Holy Family arrived safe in Egypt, where it remained as long as it pleased God to leave his Son in this kind of exile.[22]

Massacre of the Innocents.—Herod, who believed him to be still in Bethlehem or its neighborhood, had not forgotten that, by the account of the time when the star was first seen by the Magi, the child whom it announced might be about two years of age. On this calculation, he assembled a sufficient number of soldiers, and dispatched them to kill in Bethlehem and its neighborhood all the male children of two years old and under.

The command of the new Pharao was executed, and the territory of Bethlehem ran with innocent blood. Nothing was to be heard but the lamentations of afflicted mothers on the death of their poor little children. Their tears did not restore to them the dear victims whom a barbarous king had sacrificed to his jealousy, and they were inconsolable.

Then were fulfilled these words, which God had spoken by the mouth of the prophet Jeremias: "A voice was heard in Rama, great lamentation and weeping; it was Rachel bewailing her children, and refusing to be comforted, because they were not."[23]

Meanwhile, Herod had gained nothing by pouring out streams of blood, unless to awake against himself the wrath of heaven, and to merit for his name the execration of earth. A short time after this barbarous execution, he lost, together with his life, the throne which he had endeavored to secure at such vast expense.

Return to Nazareth.—Scarcely was he laid in the tomb when the angel of the Lord appeared in a dream to Joseph, and said to him: "Take with you the child and the Mother, and return into the Land of Israel, for they who sought the child's life are dead." Joseph at once disposed himself for obedience. Taking Jesus and Mary with him, he left Egypt for the land of his fathers, thus verifying the word of the Lord, spoken by the prophet Osee, in reference to the Messias: "Out of Egypt I have called my Son." But, having learned that Archelaus reigned in Judea, as the successor of his father Herod, he did not venture to appear there. Under a new command from heaven he withdrew to Galilee, and settled at Nazareth, in order to accomplish the oracle of the prophet according to which the Son of God should be called a Nazarean. This is a word which at once expresses the perfect sanctity and consecration of the Savior, and the place where he should spend the greater portion of his life.

Jesus should one day leave the city of Nazareth, to make himself known throughout the extent of his mission, and to lay, by his labors, the foundations of the Church. In the meanwhile, he should remain there unknown, or at least undistinguished by anything but the gentleness, submission, and docility which rendered him a more amiable child than others, but did not discover him to be a man-God.

What an admirable arrangement of providence, which makes the very inaction of the Messias a truly divine spectacle! The humble house that contained all the treasures of heaven and all the hopes of earth was only, in the eyes of men, the retreat of a virtuous artisan, in which peace, simplicity, and the love of labor dwelt. None of those brilliant traits that enrich the history of profane heroes were to be found there. But it was thus that the kingdom of the Messias should be prepared. It was thus that the Son of God continued the lessons of humility and poverty which he had begun in the manger. It was thus that he showed himself truly the Savior of the world, expiating, by his voluntary humiliations, the guilt of the outrage which the rebellious pride of sin had committed against his Father, and healing, by a solemn contempt of riches and dignities, the wounds of man, smitten with the love of vanity.

Jesus in the Temple.—It is probable that Joseph and Mary did not, during the reign of Archelaus, the son of Herod, conduct the Son of God to the Temple, to celebrate the great feast of the Pasch. There was reason to fear that their presence—especially that of the child, who might be recognized in the capital, as the fame of his presentation had already spread somewhat abroad—would arouse the suspicions and awake the jealousies of the king of Judea.

But, after a reign of about ten years, Archelaus was deprived of his crown by the Romans, and the emperor Augustus reserved to himself the immediate sovereignty of Judea. From this period, the government of the province was confided by the Caesars to a president of their own choice. Galilee remained under the sway of Herod Antipas, the brother of Archelaus. This is the Herod who put St. John the Baptist to death and to whom the Savior was sent during his passion by Pilate.[24]

A change of masters brought some moderation to the restraint in which the Holy Family of Nazareth lived. Joseph profited of the tranquil condition of Judea, to conduct Jesus, with Mary, his Mother, to Jerusalem every year, in order to celebrate at the house of God the feast of the Pasch. During one of these journeys, the divine child was pleased to begin, in a manner proportioned to his age, the exercise of his mission. He had attained his twelfth year, and had accompanied Mary and Joseph to the capital for the Pasch of this year.

The solemnity, which lasted seven days, during which time only unleavened bread was used, being ended, Joseph and Mary took the road again for Nazareth. They did not doubt that Jesus, who had never abandoned them, followed close at hand: persons traveled in troops and companies. Although they did not see the child near them, they felt no uneasiness about him, imagining that he had taken an interest in the society of some of their relatives or friends.

It may appear surprising that they made a whole day's journey without showing any extraordinary concern regarding the absence of their dear Son, or rather, nothing can show better how much they relied on his wisdom and on his compliance with their wishes. Toward evening, however, they sought for him among their kinsfolk and acquaintances. It was in vain: no one had any news about him, and the excess of their affliction may be imagined. Finding no consolation anywhere, they decided on returning next morning to Jerusalem, where they supposed the child must have remained.

What place had Jesus chosen for his retreat, what means had he found for his subsistence during the two days that he was separated from Joseph and Mary? This is what no one knows. If it is true that he then honored with his presence some of the inhabitants of Jerusalem, happy was the faithful Israelite who received the divine child into the same house with himself during this brief interval! The Son of God was not without wants, because, of his own choice, he had subjected himself to ours; but he had the power to dispense with the succors that are necessary to us, and, from his most tender age, he was assured that whatever miracles he should ask of God his Father would infallibly be granted to the infinite dignity of his Person. It was only on the third day after the solemnity of the Pasch that the holy Virgin and St. Joseph, having entered the Temple, discovered there the well-beloved Son whose absence had caused them so much grief.

In virtue of a very ancient custom, the masters in Israel, the scribes and the doctors of the law, met on certain days in some of the outer porches of the Temple. There, on elevated seats, they formed a kind of semicircle, in front of which were placed the auditors, to hear their discourses and to learn from their lips the explanation of the sacred scriptures.

Jesus chose this religious assembly-day, and was pleased to be found, among the multitude, at the ordinary instruction. He was then only twelve years of age; but all the treasures of grace, wisdom, and knowledge were hidden in him from the first moment of his conception: though he only allowed that to appear which became his age. If sometimes he went a little further, it was only inasmuch as it was necessary to attract the attention of the Jews to his Person, and to prepare them for the fruits of his gospel. He acted thus on the important occasion of which we now speak.

The master and teacher of all men, he listened with modesty to those disdainful masters whose hypocrisy and ignorance he should, after a few years, unmask and confound. In the meanwhile, that he might teach with an authority very different from that with which the scribes and Pharisees appeared, he profited of the liberty which was granted to every one to interrogate the masters.

A divine wisdom shone in his questions, as well as in his answers. Never had there been seen, at an age so tender, so much maturity and such extensive knowledge. This was what all present thought and said. No one could grow weary of admiring the wondrous child of Nazareth. The Blessed Virgin and St. Joseph, who had themselves come into the Temple, shared in the general admiration.

The instruction being ended, Mary considered that it was her right to complain lovingly to the Savior of the mysteriousness which he had observed in his designs, and of the uneasiness into which his absence had plunged them: "My Son," she said to him, with a respectful tenderness, "why hast thou done so to us? Behold how, sorrowing, thy father and I have sought thee."[25] "Why did you seek me?" answered Jesus. "Did you not know that I must be employed about my Father's business?" Admirable answer! which teaches us all, you and me, that the will of our heavenly Father must be preferred to every human consideration, to all the tenderness of flesh and blood. The apparent rigor which the Savior here manifests might be intended to give strength for the fulfillment of this great lesson.

Then, departing with them, he returned to Nazareth, and was subject to them.

Was subject to them.—These four words contain the history of thirty years of our Savior's life. To be subject to two of his creatures—was this, then, the whole employment of the Son of God, the Savior of the world? And subject in what? In the meanest occupations, in the practice of a mechanical art.[26] Where are those who say that their employments do not suit their capacities, or, to speak more accurately, their pride? Where are the children, the inferiors, the subjects who murmur against obedience? Let them come to Nazareth, to the house of Joseph and Mary, and there behold Jesus Christ. "Pride!" exclaims Bossuet, "come, and be crushed at this sight."

"But," you say, "having only thirty-three years to pass on the earth, to instruct the human race, to found a religion, and spending thirty of them in silence and obscurity: Where is the divine wisdom in this?" I answer you that the divine wisdom shines with as much splendor in the hidden as in the public life of the Redeemer, and that in both he instructs with the same eloquence. Let us fathom the mystery. Let us recollect, once for all, that pride is the source of every evil, that there is no other passion so difficult to uproot, and we shall acknowledge that thirty years of continual obedience and humility, on the part of a God, were not too much to remedy it.

And do you not see that this dependence, this poverty, this obscure and fatiguing labor, prepared the way for the astonishing revolution which has changed the ideas and the sentiments of the world; which has given to dignities the name of burdens, and taught superiors that they are only the chief servants of their subjects; which has sanctified labor, and ennobled the minds of the working classes, that is to say, three-fourths of the human race, by showing them a God, their companion, earning his bread in the sweat of his brow, and bearing without complaint the burdens of the heat and the day?

Do you not also remark with what precision the babe of Bethlehem, the artisan of Nazareth, gradually realizes in his Person the oracles of the prophets regarding the Messias? Could he better prove his divinity, gain the confidence of the world, and establish his religion? Finally, do you not see that at Nazareth, as on Calvary, he fulfilled his mission of victim? His labors and sweat have the same weight in the scales of justice as his sufferings and blood: the value of the one and the other is infinite. Let us reflect on these things, and, penetrated with gratitude, we shall admire how Jesus Christ shows himself, in his hidden as well as in his public life, the Savior of the human race.

PRAYER

O my God! who art all love, I thank thee for having given us, in thy Son, so perfect a model of the virtues of our age.

I am resolved to love God above all things, and my neighbor as myself for the love of God; and, in testimony of this love, I will imitate the obedience of the Child Jesus.

Lesson 4: Public Life of the Messias (1)

Our Lord, who had come on earth to atone for the sins of the world and to apply a remedy to their consequences, struggled for thirty years with the passions of man, by practicing, for the instruction of all ages, the most perfect humility, obedience, and poverty: such was his occupation in the obscure abode of Nazareth. At length, the period arrived when God should manifest him to the world: let us follow him to the new scene of his apostleship.

Preaching of St. John the Baptist.—John the Baptist, his precursor, had dwelt since he was a child in the desert, whither he had been conducted by inspiration. Destined for the most sublime ministry with which a mortal could be honored, he prepared himself for it by the retirement and austerity of his life. He was clothed with camels' hair; he had a leathern girdle around his loins; and his food consisted of locusts and wild fruits.[27] He thus awaited and, doubtless, hastened by his desires the day of his manifestation, which should resemble the aurora of that great light that was to illumine the world. The desired moment came.

During the fifteenth year of the reign of Tiberius, the successor of Augustus in the Roman Empire, of which Judea formed a part—when the affairs of this province were administered, in the name of Caesar, by a Roman president, named Pontius Pilate—Herod being tetrarch of Galilee—under the pontificate of the two high priests, Annas and Caiphas[28]—Jesus having attained his thirtieth year: the voice of God came to John, the son of Zachary, in the desert, and commanded him to leave his retreat, and to prepare the people for the gospel, by exhorting them to do penance. This was to fulfill the word of the prophet Isaias, announcing that the Messias should have a precursor: "Behold, I send my angel before thy face, to prepare the way before thee." Full of the Spirit of God, the new Elias advanced to the banks of the Jordan, where he began his preaching. He spoke of nothing but conversion and penance; for it was by a reformation of hearts that the door should be opened to a belief in the gospel.

As the fame of his preaching spread abroad, sinners flocked to him in crowds, and, confessing their sins, were baptized by him in the river Jordan. The people, struck by the splendor of his virtues, persuaded themselves that John might very possibly be the Christ, and every one was occupied with this thought.

To draw them from an error which might prove dangerous, the humble precursor spoke to them in these terms: "Truly, I give you a baptism of water, that you may do penance; but he who shall come after me is mightier than I. I am not worthy to cast myself at his feet to loose the latchet of his shoe: he shall give you a baptism of the Holy Ghost and fire."

This baptism is the sacrament of regeneration, which should be instituted later on by the Savior. This fire is that which on Pentecost descended on the apostles, the same by which the Holy Ghost continues to purify the hearts of the true faithful. The great humility of John the Baptist did not prevent him from sighing after the Messias, whom he announced so magnificently, but whose countenance he had never yet beheld. His hopes were not long deferred.

Baptism of our Lord.—Jesus set out from Nazareth, about sixty miles distant from the deserts of Judea, where John still preached and baptized. This divine Savior, who did not know sin, but who had been made sin for us, having taken all its debt upon himself, was pleased to mingle among the crowd of sinners, and to enter with them on the career of penance. He came therefore to John, to be baptized by him in the Jordan. But John excused himself, saying: "It is I who ought to be baptized by thee, and yet thou comest to me!" Jesus answered him: "Let it be so now, for so it becometh us to fulfill all justice." Oh, yes, it was proper that, to heal man and to expiate sin, the Savior should continue to give an example of the most profound humility, and that, by a solemn act, he should declare himself the greatest penitent in the world. Then John opposed no further the desire of his divine master, and Jesus was baptized by him in the Jordan.

Jesus came forth immediately, and, while he prayed, the heavens were opened above him, and he saw the Holy Ghost, under the form of a dove, descend and rest upon him. At the same time, a voice was heard from heaven, saying: "This is my beloved Son, in whom I am well pleased." John the Baptist, and all the others who were present, saw the Holy Ghost descend, and heard the heavenly voice; for everything occurred only for them. The mystery of the Trinity began to be declared more distinctly, and minds were prepared for the great truths which Jesus Christ should in a little while reveal to the world.

The baptism which Jesus had just received, was a mere ceremony in his regard. Yet it was a public profession of penance. He desired, by the severities which he exercised toward himself, to show to his Church beforehand that penance which she should prescribe to his children in all ages to come.

Retreat in the desert; temptations.—Full of the Holy Ghost, the Savior left the Jordan, and, under the impulse of this divine Spirit, retired into the desert. There for forty days and forty nights his occupation was one continual prayer, and a fast so rigorous that he did not take the least nourishment. Without a miracle of God's omnipotence, he would have died of exhaustion. But there was no reason to fear that what the sovereign master had, out of his pure mercy, done more than once before for his servants would be refused to the dignity of the Person, and to the merit of the obedience, of his Son.

At the end of the forty days prescribed for his solitude, the Savior chose to experience hunger, and resolved to grant to nature the succors which he had so long withheld from it: but he had not yet reached the term of his trials. After having vanquished hunger he should encounter the devil. The model of all men, our Savior was pleased to experience all our miseries and temptations, that he might teach us how to endure the one and to overcome the other. Now, our temptations may be reduced to three kinds, just as all our passions may be reduced to three kinds, namely: sensuality, pride, and ambition. It was on these three sides that the devil attacked our Lord.

First, sensuality. The tempter, approaching, said: "If thou art the Son of God, command that these stones be changed into bread." Jesus contented himself with answering the seducer: "It is written, 'Not on bread alone doth man live, but on every word that proceedeth from the mouth of God'"—that is, on whatever it pleases God to give him for his nourishment. By which we should understand that, far from sacrificing our souls to the pleasures or even the wants of our bodies, we must have confidence in the providence of God, and expect everything from his goodness.

Second, pride. Satan, although beaten, did not desist. After assailing our Savior on what he imagined the weakest point, namely, hunger, he should also assail him on the strongest, namely, confidence in God. He endeavored to drag him into a proud presumption. Having for this purpose carried him to the holy city, he placed him on a pinnacle of the Temple, and said to him: "If thou art the Son of God, cast thyself down, for it is written, 'He hath given his angels charge over thee, and in their hands they shall bear thee up, lest perhaps thou dash thy foot against a stone.'" "It is also written," said Jesus, "'Thou shalt not tempt the Lord thy God.'"

Third, ambition. After this answer, Satan concluded that delicate measures would any longer be useless. He carried Jesus to a very high mountain, and showed him in an instant all the kingdoms of the world, and the glory of them. Then he said: "I will give thee all these things, if, falling down, thou wilt adore me." The blasphemy was horrible, and the proposal worthy of the prince of devils. Accordingly the Savior, in that tone of voice with which it was becoming to reject the proposal of a crime, answered: "Begone, Satan! for it is written, 'The Lord thy God thou shalt adore, and him only shalt thou serve.'" Then the devil, having ended all his temptations, left him.[29] Immediately angels came to the Savior, and gave him to eat.

It was for our instruction that the Savior was pleased to be tempted. Now, he prepared himself to endure temptations by prayer, fasting, and retirement; and he resisted them by faith and a prompt recourse to God. What success can we expect, if we only present to the most cruel and crafty enemy that ever existed, a dissipated mind, an unmortified flesh, an indulged conceitedness, strong passions, forgetfulness of the truths of salvation? In fine, by this mysterious repast, which the hands of angels serve, he shows us the joy that temptation procures for the soul which is able to overcome it, and for the heavenly court, which witnesses the victory.

The time was come when, according to the will of his Father, Jesus should consecrate himself wholly to the preaching of the gospel, and abandon himself without reserve to the contradictions inseparable from it. The work with which he saw himself charged was great and difficult; Judea, Galilee, Samaria, all the cantons of Palestine awaited his care and invited his culture. This was the field which the Father of the family had destined for him: an ungrateful soil, which should scarcely yield anything to his sweats but thorns and briars—where it would be necessary to sow much and gather little, to prepare for the harvest by excessive fatigues and not to have the happiness of seeing it ripen. The time was short: to complete a laborious career, whose end should be a shameful cross, he was allowed only about three years.

Pains did not terrify him, and the bitter fruits that should be their reward became the object of his desires. In the vista of ages, he saw God his Father honored, man saved, the world Christianized. His life, hitherto so obscure and peaceful, should henceforth be only a series of labors, journeys, and sufferings, until the day when it should be terminated by the horrors of Calvary.

On leaving the desert, he advanced toward the Jordan, where John the Baptist continued to preach penance and the approaching manifestation of the Messias. When the holy precursor saw the Savior coming, he exclaimed in presence of all the multitude: "Behold the Lamb of God, behold him who taketh away the sins of the world."

It was on this memorable occasion that the Savior drew to himself his first disciples: Andrew, Simon Peter, the brother of Andrew, and Philip, all three belonging to the city of Bethsaida. Apostles as soon as proselytes, they entered the suite of the Messias and accompanied him to Cana of Galilee.

Marriage feast of Cana.—Shortly after their arrival in this city, a marriage took place: the Blessed Virgin was present at it. Her manner of life, humble, simple, and modest, without ever being inconsistent, was never singular. She had been asked to assist at the celebration of this marriage, and she was pleased to comply with the request. Jesus was also invited to the feast, with his disciples. It was especially for them, and to sanctify the nuptials by his presence, that he vouchsafed to appear at this banquet, in which, moreover, there was nothing in the slightest degree reprehensible. Religion does not condemn any pleasures of this kind, if they are confined within just bounds. But the misfortune is that men do not know how to observe moderation, and that it is necessary to limit blameless customs in order to prevent abuses.

They were not to be apprehended at a feast where Jesus and Mary were present. But the joy of the occasion happened to be disturbed by a very humiliating accident: toward the close of the repast, the wine began to fail. Mary perceived it, and, without waiting for anyone to have recourse to her mediation, turned and said to Jesus: "They have no more wine." "Woman," answered the Savior, "what is there in common between thee and me? My hour is not yet come."[30]

In reading this short answer which Jesus makes to his holy Mother, we are perhaps struck by the apparent severity which it breathes. But, in point of fact, the Savior could, by his air and the tone of his voice, sweeten that which appears to us hard in these words; and the most tender of sons would not afflict the most beloved of mothers. He wished, however, to teach, not Mary, who was already aware of it, but his disciples and other friends, that he ought not to perform miracles out of considerations of flesh and blood. Mary knew well that her Son would grant her petition, and she said to those who served: "Do all that he shall tell you."

Now, there were there, according to the manner of the purifications of the Jews, six stone pitchers, which held two or three measures each. Jesus said to the waiters: "Fill the pitchers with water"; and they filled them to the brim. Jesus added: "Draw out now, and carry to the chief steward of the feast"; and they did so. When this man had tasted the water changed into wine, he called the bridegroom, and, not knowing whence it came, said to him: "Every one gives good wine in the beginning, and when the guests have drunk well, then that which is not so good; but thou hast kept the good wine until now." Jesus wrought this first miracle at Cana in Galilee. Hereby he manifested his power, and the confidence of his disciples in him was confirmed.

He went next, with his Mother and disciples, to Capharnaum, where he remained only a few days. This opulent and populous city was afterward the place where our Savior usually dwelt, and, as it were, the center of his missions. It was situated on the confines of the tribes of Zabulon and Nephtali, at the opening of the Jordan into the Sea of Galilee or Tiberias.

It was while walking along the shore of this sea, or rather this large lake, that Jesus attracted to himself two new disciples, namely, James and John, the sons of Zebedee. Like Peter and Andrew, they were fishermen by profession. "Come and follow me," said the Savior to them; and, immediately leaving their nets and their father, they joined his suite. What an example of fidelity to grace!

Buyers driven out of the Temple.—Accompanied by his disciples, he set out from Capharnaum for Jerusalem, where he arrived a few days before the feast of the Pasch, intending to celebrate it with the Jews and thereby to give us an example of obedience to law and to legitimate authority. He first caused himself to be remarked by an action that drew upon him the looks of everyone. Having come to the Temple, he was struck by an abuse already old, or rather by a scandalous profanation, which awakened all his zeal. A number of avaricious Jews were holding a kind of market within the enclosure of the Temple, and here they were not afraid to sell oxen, sheep, and doves for the sacrifices.

The Savior could not endure such a scandal. The holy place which they profaned so unconcernedly was the abode of his Father. It was for him to avenge this contempt. Armed with a scourge of little cords, and, still better with that air of authority which an indignant master assumes against insolent slaves, he approached the profaners, drove them shamefully from the Temple, scattered the oxen and sheep, overthrew the tables of the changers, and cast away the money.[31] "Take all these things hence," he said to those who sold doves, "and make not the house of my Father a house of traffic."

The great miracle of this action is that it was performed without being preceded by any miracle. The Jews did not know our Lord, and yet among so many persons interested in opposing him there was not found a single one to utter a word of defense: evidently the influence of the divinity was felt by the profaners. With what terror, indeed, ought they not to be seized, when they heard this unknown man, who treated them with so much authority, call the house of God the house of his Father.

This splendid action not only teaches us the respect that we ought to have for our churches, much holier than the Temple of Jerusalem, but it also shows us the Savior's charity in the midst of his greatest zeal. He tells the sellers of doves to take them away: if he had treated them like the rest, the doves would have flown off and been lost to their owners. Jesus, who wished to terrify all, did not wish to injure any; and, in an action so impetuous, he desired us to learn that zeal ought to be regulated by prudence and moderated by charity.

Our Lord remained for some time at Jerusalem and in Judea. He converted, too, a learned doctor of the synagogue, named Nicodemus, to whom he explained, in a private interview, the whole harmony of Christianity. The splendor of his works soon obliged him to retire from the capital. He took the way back again with his disciples to Galilee, passing through Samaria. The next lesson will contain an account of this journey.

PRAYER

O my God! who art all love, I thank thee for having sent us a Savior so compassionate that he was pleased to experience all our temptations, in order to teach us how to overcome them; grant us the grace to resist them promptly, to pursue like the apostles our vocation, and to manifest toward the Church that respect which thy house deserves.

I am resolved to love God above all things, and my neighbor as myself for the love of God; and, in testimony of this love, I will resist temptations promptly.

Lesson 5: Public Life of the Messias (2)

The Samaritan woman; condescension of the Savior; the water of grace.—It was a very warm season of the year when the Savior left Jerusalem. He had traveled all the morning on foot, and about noon arrived in the neighborhood of a city of Samaria, called Sichar. Weary with the journey, he sat down by the side of a well that was named the Well of Jacob. His disciples left him, and went away together to purchase some provisions in the city.

During their absence, a woman of the district came to draw water, and Jesus said to her: "Give me to drink." "How," answered the woman, who recognized him as a man from Judea, "dost thou, being a Jew, and knowing me to be a Samaritan woman, ask of me to drink?" For the Jews held the Samaritans in horror, regarding them as corrupters of the law of Moses.

The good shepherd, who had drawn near him this poor wandering sheep, and proposed to himself to gain it, was not willing to enter into any contest. "If thou didst know," he said, "the gift of God, if thou didst know who he is that saith to thee, 'Give me to drink,' thou perhaps wouldst have asked of him, and he would not have refused thee a living and life-giving water." The Savior was pleased to speak of the water of grace and the light of the gospel.

The woman of Sichar did not understand, or pretended not to understand, what this water was. "Sir," she said to him, "thou hast nothing wherein to draw, and the well is deep: Whence then hast thou living water? Is it that thou art greater than our father Jacob, who gave us the well, and drank thereof himself, and his children, and his cattle?"

Jesus, who wished to lead this poor stranger gradually to a knowledge of the gospel, observed toward her the utmost condescension, and, without raising any objection to the remark which she had just made about the superiority of Jacob, said to her:

"Is it not true that whosoever drinketh of the water of this well shall thirst again? On the contrary, the water of which I speak to thee is such that he to whom I shall give it, and who will drink of it, shall never thirst again."

The woman appeared to give credit to this information; it was the first step toward her conversion. But, not yet understanding the nature of this wonderful water, she said: "Sir, give me of this water, that I may thirst no more and come hither no more to draw." "Before I satisfy thee," said the Savior to her, "go to Sichar, and call thy husband, and bring him hither with thee." "I have no husband," she replied. This was the acknowledgment for which Jesus waited; mercy, if we may so speak, had caught her in the snare. "Thou hast spoken the truth," he answered, "thou hast no husband, for thou hast already had five husbands, and he with whom thou now livest is not thy lawful husband. Never didst thou say anything more true than that thou hast no husband."

If this woman was not naturally good, she at least had the honesty not to dispute the matter. Instead of giving Jesus the lie, as many others would have done, with so much the more assurance as the reproach would have been better deserved, she said to him with earnestness and shame: "Sir, I perceive that thou art a prophet."

The simplicity of this acknowledgment disposed her for pardon; nevertheless, the sheep still struggled under the hands of the good shepherd. She endeavored to turn the conversation from a subject which naturally ought not to please him, and to introduce again the topic of the controversy which divided the Jews and Samaritans. "Our fathers," she said to the Savior, "adored on Mount Garizim, and all of you say that the Temple of Jerusalem is the place where men must adore."

Whatever was the Samaritan woman's motive in it, this question drew her into a new snare of the divine mercy. The Savior took occasion from her answer to instruct her on the perfect worship which he was come to establish on the ruins of all ancient worships, not excepting even the Jewish, which, although true, was only a preparation for the evangelical worship.

Announcement of a new law.—"Woman," he said to her, "believe me, the hour draws near when you shall no longer adore the Father either on this mountain or in Jerusalem. The time comes, and even now is, when the true adorers shall adore the Father in spirit and in truth." Penetrated with the belief, then universal, that the times were accomplished, the woman answered him: "I know that the Messias is about to come; when, therefore, he comes he will instruct us regarding all things." "This Messias," said Jesus to her, "whom the two peoples expect, who will instruct you regarding all things, and whom you accept as the judge of your differences, is he who is speaking to thee."

Thus, by a marvelous art, the Savior had led this woman so far as to say that she was resigned to the decision of the Messias. There was only one word more required to complete the work of her conversion! And this word the Savior let fall so appropriately that when it was ended his disciples came and interrupted the conversation, as if to take away from the Samaritan woman, shaken a little previously, the temptation of disputing again, and to allow her time to make her reflections in silence.

In effect, when Jesus was just ceasing to inform the woman that he was the Messias, the four disciples whom we saw leave their master at the Well of Jacob, to go to the city for provisions, returned with their supplies. They were surprised that Jesus, contrary to his custom, should converse with a woman. Yet such was their respect for their divine master that none of them durst say to him: "What dost thou ask of this woman of Samaria, or why dost thou allow her the liberty of talking with thee?"

On her side, the Samaritan woman, animated by that divine fire which the conversation of Jesus enkindles in well-disposed souls, went to communicate it to the inhabitants of the city. "Come and see," she said to them, "a man who has told me all things whatsoever I have done: Is not he the Christ?" The Samaritans of Sichar were so deeply convinced that the times of the Messias were at hand that on the mere word of a woman of their country they went forth in a crowd from the city, and, on finding Jesus, besought him to remain with them. He allowed himself to be conducted into Sichar, where he spent two days in instructing and strengthening them in the faith.

The Savior then pursued his journey toward Galilee, whose inhabitants received him eagerly, because they had seen what he had done at Jerusalem during the feast. He began to be spoken of throughout the whole country, and crowds flocked to the synagogues in which he taught. While everyone published his praises, he continued without respite the work for which he had come on earth.

Wherever there was a misery to relieve, there one was sure to see him. It was not man's mind alone, but also his heart and his body that had been affected by the wound of sin. Now, all the discourses, all the journeys, all the miracles of our Lord had for their object the cure of these three parts of our being. This was not all: man was the slave of the devil as well as of sin. He had voluntarily chosen him as his master, by obeying him rather than God. It was also the object of the Messias in coming on earth to deliver man from the humiliating yoke of this cruel tyrant. It would even seem that, in the days of the preaching of Jesus Christ, God gave a more extensive power to the enemy of the human race, in order to furnish more abundant matter for the victories of his Son.

Cure of a man possessed.—One sabbath day he entered the synagogue in which the doctors and people were assembled, when suddenly the devil cried out, with a loud and terrible voice, by the mouth of one possessed: "Let me alone, Jesus of Nazareth! do not disturb me in my possession; what hast thou to do with us? Art thou not come into the world only to declare war against us, and to make the power which we exercise over men cease? I know who thou art, the Holy One of God." It was not from the father of lies that Jesus looked for the truth. In a menacing tone he replied to the wicked spirit: "Be silent, and quit this man's body."

It was a matter of importance for the glory of God that no doubt could be entertained of the possession. To render the miracle incontestable, Jesus permitted the devil to manifest his rage and despair for a few moments on the unfortunate wretch whom he was obliged to abandon. The infernal spirit, departing from him with loud cries, caused him violent pains and terrible convulsions. He cast him down fiercely in the midst of the assembly. But he only showed the impotence of his wrath; for the possessed man soon found himself without ache or wound, as sound in body as free in mind.

The miracle was public, but our Lord had performed it with so calm an air, like one who was certain of success, that the manner in which the prodigy was wrought seemed quite as astonishing as the prodigy itself. Without elation after the event, as he had been without agitation before it, he left the spectators in a surprise so much the greater as he testified none himself.

Accordingly, when the Galileans saw that miracles accompanied the discourses of the Savior, and that nothing whatever cost him the least trouble, they were seized with a respectful fear. "What is the meaning of that which we see?" they said one to another. "What is this new doctrine? Who is this new doctor, that commands unclean spirits, and in a moment they obey him?"

The fame of the deliverance of the possessed man, and admiration for his deliverer, passed quickly from the synagogue to the whole city of Capharnaum, and even to the smallest cantons of Galilee. This was not calculated to procure much rest for the Savior, and he would in a little while have been surrounded by a multitude of the afflicted, if the circumstance of the sabbath had not restrained the more eager in a state of inaction which they thought commanded.

The sabbath began in the evening and ended the following evening. When it was over, a great commotion was visible among the different families that contained sick, infirm, or possessed. Such afflicted persons as were able to walk were led in all haste to Jesus, others were borne to his feet. Their number was so great that the whole city assembled at the door of the house: the Savior cured all without exception. The sufferers blessed him as their deliverer, and the devils, banished from souls and bodies, cried out as they departed: "Thou art the Son of God."

It was thus that the Savior fulfilled the words of Isaias. Speaking of the Messias, the prophet says: "He bore our infirmities, and took upon himself our diseases"; which means: the Messias received power, not only to purify our souls from the stains of sin, but also to heal the infirmities of our bodies, because he undertook to make satisfaction to God his Father, by the effusion of his blood, for all the punishments, whether eternal or temporal, due to sin—among which must be numbered the infirmities of life, the necessity of death, and the attacks of Satan.

Cure of a man paralyzed; the power to forgive sins.—Jesus was not content to heal bodies by driving thence devils and diseases; he also labored for the cure of souls, by freeing them from the darkness of error and ignorance, which are the consequences of sin. To gain credit for his words, he established his divinity by a multitude of the most splendid miracles, and prepared the privileged people to believe in the vocation of all peoples, and to enter a religion which, instead of being confined to the little region of Palestine, should have no other bounds than those of the world. Seating himself therefore one day, he began to instruct the immense crowd that followed him.

Now, there were in the assembly Pharisees, scribes, doctors of the law, come from all parts of Galilee and from Judea, with the design, perhaps, of examining his words and criticizing his actions. The reputation which he had already acquired offended them a good deal. They thenceforth sought every occasion of decrying or destroying him, and their present journey may be regarded as the beginning of that cruel war which they never ceased to wage against his Person, his doctrine, and his disciples until it terminated in the overthrow of their nation. These wicked men were seated by his side, and listening to his words with a malicious attention, when the silence was interrupted by a very singular occurrence, which attracted the eyes of all the spectators.

Four men, who carried a paralytic, stretched on a bed, to present him to the Savior, not being able to make their way through the crowd, decided on bringing the sick man up to the roof of the house, which, according to the custom of the country, was a kind of open platform. They made a large hole in the roof, by which they lowered the paralytic, as he lay in his bed, to the feet of Jesus, in the midst of the assembly. Jesus could not behold the lively faith of the sick man who implored his aid, and the active charity of those who presented him, without being moved thereby. It was an admirable occasion to comfort the miserable, to confound the incredulous, to promote the glory of his Father, and to prove his mission: he availed himself of it. "My son," he said to the paralytic, "have confidence; thy sins are forgiven thee." Mysterious words! which remind us that the infirmities of the body are often the effect of the maladies of the soul.

On hearing these words, the scribes and Pharisees began to reason and to say within themselves: "How can this man use such language? He blasphemes. He arrogates to himself a power which he does not possess. Who can forgive sins but God alone?" Jesus, having read these thoughts in their hearts, said to them: "Why do you form within yourselves these evil suspicions against me? Whether is it easier to say to a paralytic, 'Thy sins are forgiven thee,' or, 'Arise, take up thy bed, and walk?' Now, in order that you may know that the Son of Man has power on earth to forgive sins, hear what I am about to say, and observe the efficacy of my words." Then, looking on the paralytic, he said: "Arise, it is I who command thee, take up thy bed and return home." At that moment the man arose, lifted up his bed on his shoulders, and departed for his house, publishing the praises of God.

The applause of those present was joined to the thanksgiving of the paralytic. "Never," they said, "has the Lord wrought such great wonders in the midst of his people." All together glorified God for having communicated to man a power so divine as that of forgiving sins. Indeed, the power of forgiving sins, much more than that of curing diseases, was the object of the incarnation of the Son of God, the most necessary as well as the most precious benefit which he should procure for human nature. Hence, the surprise, the admiration, the joy of the people, on seeing that God had really been pleased to communicate to mankind a right which of all the rights of the divinity seemed to be the most incommunicable.

After this miracle, Jesus went out. All the people followed him, and he instructed them again according to his custom. It was not without a special design that the Savior had undertaken this little journey. He was meditating a conquest so much the more glorious to grace as the person concerned might appear less disposed to be influenced by its impressions.

Choice of the twelve apostles.—Passing before the customhouse, where payment was received of the taxes levied on the nation, he saw a man named Matthew, seated at the office, and said to him: "Follow me." Matthew arose, and, leaving all, followed Jesus. It is Matthew himself—first a disciple, then an apostle, and then again a historian of his master—who acquaints us with the details of this occurrence. The Son of God, in order to honor human nature, to which he did not disdain to unite himself, constantly chooses men of all conditions to make them his cooperators in the work of the redemption of the world.

He had already a pretty large number of disciples; but heretofore they had been all nearly equal, and he wished to select from them those who should hold the first rank and be the fathers and leaders of the new people whom he was about to create on the earth. The moment was come when he should make this ever-memorable choice. Before proceeding to it, the Savior retired to a mountain, and there spent the night in prayer. He had no need of these preparations; but it was proper that he should give an example to his Church, which has made it a law to imitate him religiously, as we see in the fasts and prayers with which it always approaches the consecration of its ministers.

When day was come, he called his disciples, and chose from them twelve who might accompany him, and whom he might send to preach. He honored them with the name of apostles, which means "persons sent," granting them the power to heal the sick and to cast out devils.

The following are the names of the twelve apostles: Simon (to whom Jesus gave the name of Peter); James and John (the sons of Zebedee); Andrew, Philip, Bartholomew, Matthew (the publican), and Thomas; James (the son of Alpheus) and (his brother) Judas (named Thaddeus); Simon (the Chanaanean, surnamed the Zealot); and Judas Iscariot, who also betrayed our Savior.

PRAYER

O my God! who art all love, I thank thee for having sent us a Savior who at the same time heals our mind by enlightening it, our heart by purifying it, and our body by comforting it: grant us the grace to understand and to practice his lessons.

I am resolved to love God above all things, and my neighbor as myself for the love of God; and, in testimony of this love, I will today pray for sinners and sufferers.

Lesson 6: Public Life of the Messias (3)

Sermon on the Mount: Divided into two parts.—The Savior, having chosen his apostles, came down from the mountain with them and his other disciples. On the plain there stood awaiting him a countless multitude of people from Judea, from Jerusalem, and from the maritime country of Tyre and Sidon, who had come to hear him and to be cured of their diseases. The Savior relieved them all. After healing their bodies, he judged that it was a favorable time to labor for the salvation of their souls. Having gone up again to a height, he seated himself in the midst of his disciples and pronounced, in a tone of voice sufficiently loud to be heard by all the people, that admirable discourse which is termed the Sermon on the Mount. Let us draw nigh, so as to gather up the words of light and salvation which fall from the divine mouth: it is also for us that they are spoken.

The discourse of the Son of God may be divided into two parts. The first chiefly regards the apostles and their successors in the evangelical ministry; the second is addressed to all the people present, and to all Christian people till the end of ages. The founder of a new society, or rather, the restorer of human society degraded by sin, Jesus Christ lays the foundations of the new order of things which he is come to establish; he next traces out the duties of the clergy and the faithful in general.

1. *Foundations of the new society: The eight beatitudes.*—He lays the foundations of the new order of things which he is come to establish. The Prince of Peace, he wishes that peace

should reign in the heart of man, so that it may reign everywhere throughout society, of which he is the founder. But the heart of man is like a troubled sea, because, being made for peace or happiness, it does not seek peace where alone peace is to be found. The Savior came to teach this to man, and at the same time to overthrow all the ideas that had been formed by degenerate reason, by philosophy, and even by Judaism, which hardly imagined any other beatitude possible than the enjoyment of riches, honors, and pleasures.

"Blessed," says the divine preceptor of the human race, "are the poor in spirit, for theirs is the kingdom of heaven." By the poor in spirit are meant those who have left all to follow Jesus Christ; those who, in the midst of riches, have their hearts detached from the goods of earth; and those who are born and who live in poverty, without murmur or complaint. Under the majestic title of a kingdom, eternal felicity belongs to them.

"Blessed are the meek, for they shall possess the land.

"Blessed are they that mourn, for they shall be comforted.

"Blessed are they that hunger and thirst after justice, for they shall have their fill.

"Blessed are the merciful, for they shall obtain mercy.

"Blessed are the clean of heart, for they shall see God.

"Blessed are the peacemakers, for they shall be called the children of God.

"Blessed are they that suffer persecution for justice' sake, for theirs is the kingdom of heaven. You shall be blessed, when, on my account, men load you with opprobriums, persecute you, and speak all that is evil against you untruly. Rejoice, and let your joy appear; for the reward that awaits you in heaven is very great. For so they persecuted the prophets that were before you."

A contempt and even a fear of riches, honors, and pleasures; a love of poverty, humiliations, and sufferings; an ardent, sincere, and efficacious desire of all virtues: behold then the foundations of Christianity and the conditions of happiness! Let all men practice these divine lessons, and society ceases to be a bloody arena in which the unchained passions contend for fleeting enjoyments; heaven comes down on earth; and the world is regenerated. Such was the design of the Savior.

2. *Duties of apostles and priests.*—He traces out the duties of the pastors and the flock. All these truths, so high and so difficult to fallen man, the Son of God himself preached in Judea, and he gave an example of the virtues which they inculcate. After him, these same truths should be announced to the whole world. What fidelity in those who shall be charged with this august ministry, that they may not retrench a single iota from the regenerating code! But, above all, what sanctity, since the example of preachers is the gospel of the people and the sanction of doctrine! The divine master hastens to recommend it to the apostles, and through them to their successors.

"You are the light of the world," he says, "you are the salt of the earth; you are like a city built on a mountain, exposed to the view of heaven and earth." Shine with so much sanctity that all who see you may glorify your Father who is in heaven. The religion of which you are the ministers and the preservers is not new—it is the perfection of the old. Now, if sanctity was required in the ministers of the Mosaic law, with much more reason is it necessary in the ministers of the gospel; and the Savior hastens to show the superiority of the law of grace over the law of fear, as well as its extent and obligation.

After explaining the duties peculiar to the leaders of the new society which he establishes, our Lord next treats of the duties common to all Christians, to the faithful in general, to the shepherds and the sheep. He insists especially on one essential point, which is the abridgment of the gospel and the heroism of virtue: the love of the neighbor, whether a friend or an enemy.

"This is what you have been taught," says the divine legislator: "You shall love your neighbor and hate your enemy. But I say to you: Love your enemies, do good to them who hate you, bless them who curse you, and pray for them who persecute and calumniate you, that you may be the children of your heavenly Father, who maketh his sun to rise upon the good and the bad, and raineth upon the just and the unjust. For if you only love them who love you, what reward do you deserve? Do not the publicans this?[32] And if you only salute your brethren, is there anything extraordinary in it? Do not even the heathens this? Be ye therefore perfect, as your heavenly Father is perfect."

Duties common to the pastors and the flock: Purity of intention.—Such is the perfection to which we are called by Christianity. It is set before us as a model, not that we may equal it—for who can be as perfect as God?—but that we may labor to approach to it, and continually make new progress, for the very reason that we shall never be able to equal it. That we may derive benefit from everything that can lead us toward this sublime perfection, the divine master especially recommends purity of intention, which gives an infinite value to the least actions.

But how is this purity of intention, the necessary basis of true virtue, as well as this divine perfection, to which we are bound, to be attained? Is not the task evidently beyond our strength? The Savior, who foresaw the objection, took care to answer it. With that tender goodness which characterizes him, he places in our own hands an infallible means of arriving at the sublime end to which he calls us: it is prayer.

Prayer, fasting, alms. "Be not afraid," he says. "Ask, and you shall receive; seek and you shall find; knock, and it shall be opened to you. For which of you, if his son ask for bread, will give him a stone? Or, if he ask for a fish, reach him a serpent? If then you—foolish, imperfect, wicked as you are—know how to give good things to your children, how much more will your Father who is in heaven give good things to those who ask him? Now, this is the manner in which you shall pray. You shall say: Our Father, who art in heaven, hallowed," etc.

To prayer, the divine legislator wishes fasting and alms to be joined. He thence takes occasion to condemn avarice, and, according to his custom, attacks this passion at its very root, that is, in the human heart. "Beware," he says, "of anxiety to accumulate riches on earth—gold, silver, costly garments. Rust consumes metals; moths destroy garments; robbers, accustomed to break through everywhere, carry off both. Place your treasures in heaven, even in the bosom of your heavenly Father. The good works which you deposit there, will be secure; your treasures will not there be exposed to the covetousness of robbers, the waste of rust, or the hunger of worms. Having nothing valuable anywhere but in heaven you shall become heavenly men, for everyone is attracted to and, as it were, possessed by that which he possesses: where a man's treasure is, there is his heart also."

Unbounded confidence in providence. "Do not flatter yourselves that you can make a division on this point any more than on the others, or that you can at the same time serve two masters, God and mammon. It is on this account that I forbid you to think with anxiety on the means of procuring the food with which to nourish and the garments with which to clothe yourselves. Is not the life more precious than the meat? Is not the body more precious than the raiment? How, then, shall he who gives you the life and the body fail to give you nourishment and clothing?

"Behold the birds of the air: they do not sow, they do not reap, they do not gather into barns; yet your Father who is in heaven, who is their Creator and not their Father, takes care to nourish them. Are not you of much more value than they? Moreover, what good is there in disquieting yourselves? Which of you can add a single inch to his height? That which I say to you regarding nourishment, applies also to clothing.

"Consider the lilies of the field; see how they grow and flourish; they labor not, neither do they spin. Yet I only speak the truth when I say that Solomon, in all the splendor of his majesty, was not so magnificently arrayed as one of these lilies. Now, if a lily, which after all is only a common flower that one day is seen in the field and the next is cast into the fire, God doth so adorn, how much more care will he not have of you, O men of little faith?

"Beware, then, of allowing yourselves to be tormented by anxieties of this kind, and of saying to yourselves with fear and distrust: 'Where shall we find what we require to eat and drink? Who will supply us with clothing?' These are heathen solicitudes. Your heavenly Father knows well that you have need of all these things: he can and will supply them. Seek ye therefore first the kingdom of heaven, and the virtues which it requires. Everything else will then be added to you."

Let us not, however, run into extremes with the words of our divine master. He who forbids us to be solicitous commands us to labor; he who prohibits any fear regarding the wants of life orders us to be attentive enough to represent them every day to God; he who is so indignant at our concern about the necessities of the body as to consider worthy only of pagans the extent of our forebodings regarding days that may perhaps never shine on us, has at the same time in the hands of his disciples a supply for days to come. The words of God cannot be belied by his actions.

What, then, did he mean by this kind of excess, which we seem to discover in the letter of his instructions? To make us perceive the monstrous excess of our attachment to the things of earth; the excess of the forgetfulness in which we live regarding the cares of providence; the excess of the preference which we give to our temporal over our spiritual wants; the excess of the discouragement which, on account of the inadequacy of our own labors, prevents us from discovering a resource in the sovereign master whom we so many times every day call "Our Father."

He wishes, indeed, that we should endeavor to maintain ourselves in the state in which he has placed us, but without making ourselves the adorers of the god of riches. He consents that we should have foresight for the wants of ourselves and our families, but without giving to this care an attention that would exclude the care of our salvation or lead us to neglect the relief of the poor. He permits that we should reserve something for the morrow, but with so little attachment that in conjunctures where the glory of his name, the good of the neighbor, and the progress of the gospel require great sacrifices from us, we should know how to forget ourselves, and, if necessary, even to lay down our lives.

Contempt of earthly and love of heavenly things: such is the divine basis on which our Lord establishes his religion. Behold how, with one stroke, he cuts off in the heart of man the irregular love of riches, honors, and pleasures—revenge—hatred—all wicked passions, the sad fruits of sin and the causes of the innumerable evils that deluge the world! Behold how, recalling man to his primitive perfection, he secures his happiness even in this life, and shows himself truly the Savior!

Accordingly, the Son of God concludes this admirable discourse with these admirable words: "Every one that hears these my words and leads a life in conformity with them shall be likened to a wise man who built his house upon a rock. The rains fell, the floods came, the winds blew: all united in a mighty effort to overturn the building; but it did not fall, because it was founded on a rock. Every one, on the contrary, that hears these my words and does not profit of them or put them in practice shall be likened to a foolish man who built his house upon sand. The rains came, the floods rolled, the winds blew; and the house fell. And its scattered ruins announced to travelers the folly of its master."

After this discourse, the most beautiful that the ear of man had ever heard, the listeners, filled with admiration, cried out more earnestly than they had done before: "No! our doctors and our scribes are nothing in comparison with the master whom we have just heard."

Leper cured.—On his side, the Savior, who, for the consolation of those who heard him, usually accompanied his discourses with some extraordinary act, which served as a confirmation of his doctrine, had so disposed of things that, at the close of his preaching, he had brought about the occasion of a miracle. When he was come down from the mountain, he found himself surrounded by an innumerable multitude that had been waiting for him.[33]

A leper now came, and adoring, prostrate on the ground, said to him: "Lord, if thou wilt, thou canst heal me." Jesus had pity on him, and, stretching forth his hand, touched him, saying: "I will; be thou healed." When he had spoken, the leprosy disappeared. Jesus made the man withdraw immediately, and said to him: "Beware of telling this to any person."

You ask, perhaps, why the Savior from time to time required secrecy regarding the miracles which he wrought. Of the many reasons that are given for it, the only one that has any probability is that he wished to teach his disciples and all those to whom he should communicate the gift of miracles to conceal them as much as possible, in order to protect themselves from the applause of men and the assaults of vanity. For the rest, let us be content to know that he had reasons most worthy of his wisdom, suited to circumstances of time, place, and person.

"But go, show thyself to the priests," continued Jesus, addressing the leper, "and offer them the gifts required by the law of Moses, as a proof of thy cure." It was out of deference to the law that the Savior obliged him to make this journey; for he himself observed the law in every point.

It was a difficult task for a poor sick man, suddenly delivered from pain and confusion, not to make known the kindness of his benefactor. The leper was so transported with joy that either he did not understand the command of Jesus Christ or he did not suppose himself bound to obey it. In truth, he withdrew from the Savior; but he published the affair everywhere. This imprudence or gratitude drew on our Lord an increase of trouble. The multitude of those who besieged him, as if in spite of him, interfered with him so much that, unable to show himself in the city, he was compelled to hide himself in desert places, where he might be at liberty to devote himself to prayer. His tender charity soon obliged him to come forth again, and to return to the places which he had avoided with so much care. He came, therefore, to Capharnaum, where he found that which his preventing goodness brought him thither to seek.

A centurion's servant cured.—A centurion, that is, an officer in command of a hundred soldiers, came to implore his aid. He acted as military men, when they are religious, always act, in that simple and open manner which gains all hearts, and which obtains from God a favorable reply to their petitions. "Lord," he said to Jesus, "I have a servant at home who is sick of the palsy, and he endures bitter pains." "Well," said the Savior, "I will go and cure him."

"Ah! Lord," answered the centurion, "I am not worthy that thou shouldst come into my house. Without leaving the place where thou art, only say one word,[34] and my servant shall be cured. I know that the most obstinate evils obey thee, just as soldiers do their commander. Now, I am only an inferior officer, subject to the authority of another: I have only a hundred men at my orders. Yet my soldiers are so dependent on my will that I have only to say a word to set them in motion. When I say to one, 'Go to such a place,' he goes; to another, 'Come,' he comes; and to my servant, 'Do this,' he does it. How much more, then, canst thou, whose power is supreme and independent, secure the obedience of all creatures by one of thy commands?"

This profession of faith, nobly and simply expressed under a military figure of speech, was doubtless very affecting from the mouth of a Gentile. The Savior, without being surprised at it, because he could not be surprised at anything, did not fail to show the admiration which it afforded him. He profited of it to give the Jews a very useful lesson.

"I assure you," he said to them, "that since I began to preach among you, I have not found so great faith in Israel. Thus shall a multitude of Gentiles come from the East and the West, and be admitted into the kingdom of heaven. There they shall be seated at the eternal banquet with Abraham, Isaac, and Jacob, as legitimate children of those holy patriarchs, whose faith they will have imitated. As for the children of the kingdom, that is, the Israelites, children of the patriarchs according to the flesh, and destined to be the first subjects of the Church, they shall be abandoned to the darkness of their unbelief, from which they shall pass into eternal darkness: there shall be weeping and gnashing of teeth." Then the Savior said to the centurion: "Go, and be it done unto thee according to thy faith." At the very moment when Jesus spoke these words, the servant was healed.

PRAYER

O my God! who art all love, I thank thee for having sent us a Savior to instruct us, and to deliver us from all the consequences of sin. Grant us the grace to love, as he recommended, poverty, humiliations, and sufferings. Grant us also the spirit of prayer, that we may arrive at the perfection which thou dost require of us.

I am resolved to love God above all things, and my neighbor as myself for the love of God; and, in testimony of this love, I will pray for those who injure me.

Lesson 7: Public Life of the Messias (4)

After the cure of the centurion's servant, the Savior performed many other miracles. He restored health to a woman that had suffered from loss of blood for twelve years, and he raised a young girl to life. He gave the people many instructions. His apostles were sent to the places which he could not visit, in order to preach the kingdom of God, to restore health to the sick, and to cast out devils. During their absence, he was pleased himself to make a mission. He associated to himself a certain number of disciples destined for an inferior ministry and to labor under the direction of the first ministers. It was thus the Savior laid the foundations of the ecclesiastical hierarchy. With a view to train them to their employments, he wished at that time to have them as cooperators in his works and witnesses of his miracles.

The widow of Naim's son is restored to life.—One day, as he traveled in their company, surrounded by a countless multitude of people, he took the way toward a city called Naim. As he drew near the gate of the city, he found, by one of those arrangements apparently accidental but never such to the Savior, that a dead man was being carried out to the place of burial.

The deceased was a young man, the only son of a widow. The mother followed, and there were along with her a great number of persons from the city. She wept bitterly. When the Savior saw her, he was moved with compassion, and said to her: "Weep not." Then, coming near, he touched the bier. The few words which the man-God had spoken meant much: they announced a miracle which would speedily be wrought. Those who carried the bier stood still. The Savior, assuming that absolute tone which became the supreme arbiter of life and death, said: "Arise, young man, it is I who command thee." The dead man heard, sat up, and began to speak; and Jesus restored him to his mother.

The spectators were seized with fear. But their admiration suddenly broke forth into thanksgiving. With one voice they exclaimed, blessing the Lord: "The great prophet has appeared among us, and God has visited his people." These words indicated the Messias and the happy time of his coming.

Disciples of John the Baptist.—The fame of this miracle spread through Judea and all the surrounding districts. It reached the ears of John the Baptist, who was at that time in prison, by the command of the guilty Herod. The holy precursor, therefore, sent two of his disciples to Jesus, to put this question to him: "Art thou he who is to come, or are we to expect another?"

It was not difficult to penetrate his design. John, who had made Jesus known to others, could not possibly be ignorant respecting him; nor could he who had recognized him as the Messias before the performance of any of his miracles doubt of this fact when miracles were a matter of daily occurrence with him. But the disciples of John, always too much prejudiced in favor of their master, still doubted whether Jesus was his superior. To complete the work of their conviction, John wished that they should see Jesus with their own eyes.

The two deputies, who seemed the most incredulous, having come therefore to Jesus, they said: "John the Baptist has sent us to thee to inquire: Art thou he who is to come, or are we to expect another?" Before answering them, Jesus did that which John had foreseen. On the spot he called around him the infirm, the sick, the blind, the lame, the possessed, that were in the crowd: he restored health and freedom to all. Then, turning to the two envoys, he said: "Go and relate to John what you have heard and seen: the blind see, the lame walk, the lepers are cleansed, the deaf hear, the dead rise again, to the poor the gospel is preached: and happy is he who shall not be scandalized on my account!"

This answer was addressed to John; because the inquiry had been made in his name; but it was really intended for the disciples, by whom the inquiry had been made. Now, the answer of the Savior left no further room for doubt; for the prophet Isaias predicted that, in the time of the Messias, the eyes of the blind should be opened and the ears of the deaf unstopped, the lame should leap as the hart and the tongue of the dumb should be set free. It is plain that our Lord alluded to these words: so that the disciples of John had a double proof, that which was miraculous and that which was prophetical.

When they had gone away, Jesus took occasion from their message to deliver a splendid eulogy on the precursor. He said that the time of promises had lasted till the coming of John the Baptist; that, after his preaching, realities should follow promises, the substance should succeed to figures; that if the Jews knew John the Baptist well, they would recognize in him the last ambassador of the law, and understand that the kingdom of the Messias was come.

"But," adds the Savior, "you no more know him than you know me: you profit no more of his discourses and example than of mine. John the Baptist came among you austere and mortified, and you said, you Pharisees: 'He is possessed by the devil.' The Son of Man, on the other hand, comes among you eating and drinking, leading a common and ordinary life, and you say: 'This is a man of good cheer, a friend of publicans and sinners.'"

Accordingly, under whatever form wisdom presented itself to the Jews, they found reasons to dispense themselves from attending to it. Alas, how many Jews there are among Christians! The Savior concludes with these touching words: "Come therefore to me all of you that groan under the weight of your miseries, that resist with difficulty the enticements of concupiscence, I will deliver you from your frailty, I will raise you up from your falls. Take my yoke upon your shoulders, and learn of me, because I am meek and humble of heart, and you shall find rest to your souls; for my yoke is sweet and my burden light."

Multiplication of loaves.—A little while after, John the Baptist was put to death by the order of Herod. The Savior, on his side, returned to Capharnaum, where he remained only a few days. Followed by his apostles, he passed over the Sea of Tiberias, and entered a vast solitude; but the people, watchful of all his movements, found means to join him there, in order to hear his discourses and to obtain the cure of their diseases. It was to reward them for their fidelity, by ministering to their wants, that he miraculously multiplied five loaves and two fishes, so that they fed five thousand men, not to count women and children.

Struck by an act of such extraordinary power and goodness, the people wished to make him King. "For," they said, "he is certainly the Christ, the great prophet, so long expected in the world." But as they were falsely persuaded that the Christ should bear the temporal crown of Israel, Jesus, to undeceive them, escaped and fled to a mountain, where alone he spent the whole night in prayer.

Peter walks on the sea.—During this time the apostles were sailing with much trouble across the Sea of Tiberias: a great storm threatened to sink them. Moved by their distress, our Lord descended, toward break of day, and came to them, walking on the waves. This sight filled them with such consternation that they raised a shout of alarm. Jesus reassured them, saying: "Have confidence, it is I, fear not." Peter, according to his custom, more easily excited and inflamed than the other apostles, here gave a signal proof of his love for his divine master. "Lord," he cried out, "if it is thou, bid me come to thee on the water." The Savior said: "Come." And Peter went, walking on the water.

Promise of the Eucharist.—All these miracles, and especially that of the multiplication of the loaves, were only the prelude to and the foreshadowing of another much more admirable. By this wondrous multiplication, the Son of God had been pleased to prepare minds for the great prodigy of the Eucharist. In effect, on that very evening, having returned to Capharnaum, he announced to the people who came, more numerously than the preceding evening, to hear him, that he would give them a bread more excellent than that with which he had fed them, a bread more heavenly than the manna with which their fathers had been fed in the desert.

"I myself," he said to them, "am the living bread that came down from heaven. Your fathers did eat manna in the desert and are dead. But as for this bread from heaven of which I speak to you, it is such that whosoever eats of it shall never die. It is I myself, I repeat to you, who, come down from heaven, am this living bread. Whosoever shall eat of this bread shall receive a germ of immortality and a pledge of an eternally happy life. This bread, which I will give you when the time for it comes, is my flesh, which shall be immolated for the salvation of the world."

The Jews, on other occasions so dull, understood perfectly that the Savior was promising his flesh to be really and truly eaten. If there was any division among them it was not in reference to the manner of understanding the promise, but to the manner in which the promise should be fulfilled. They therefore disputed with one another, saying: "How can this man give us his flesh to eat?"

Far from correcting them of any error, the Savior only disposes of their embarrassments with a new confirmation of his doctrine. "Verily, verily, I say unto you," he replies, "unless you eat the flesh of the Son of Man, and drink his blood, you shall not have life in you. On the other hand, he who eats my flesh and drinks my blood has everlasting life. He carries a pledge of it within himself, and I will raise him up on the last day, to give him possession of a happiness that will never end; for my flesh is meat indeed, and my blood is drink indeed. He who eats my flesh and drinks my blood abides in me, and I in him. And as my Father, who is the living God, sent me on earth, and I live only for my Father, so he who eats me shall live for me. Not as it was with your fathers, who ate manna and are dead: he who eats this bread shall live forever."

Such was the announcement of the great mystery of our altars, a mystery which holds so high a place in the plan of the redemption. What, in effect, was the object of the incarnation, unless to bring man close to God, from whom he had been separated by sin, and to make God and man friends again in a permanent and intimate union? Now, behold the admirable manner in which this deific union is accomplished!

Life resides in God as in its source: thence it flows out over the humanity of Jesus Christ, which is united to the divinity. In its turn, the humanity of Jesus Christ is united to men by Communion, and imparts to them the life with which it abounds. This life is to be understood in the widest and most excellent sense. It is at once a life of grace, a life of glory, and even a natural life, which consists in the eternal union of soul and body.

Seeing the Savior insist so earnestly on the manducation of his flesh, there were some of his disciples who began to say among themselves: "This discourse is hard, and how can it be believed?" They made their remarks in a low tone of voice; but Jesus, knowing within himself that they murmured, said: "This scandalizes you! What, then, will it be when you see the Son of Man ascend to the place from which he came, and it will be necessary to believe that this flesh, even while in heaven, is given away as food on earth?" Thus the Savior did not change in the least the meaning of his words. He promised to give his flesh to eat and his blood to drink: he reasserts it. He declares that it shall be so, even after his ascension into heaven. How is it possible to doubt when a God speaks?

After this discourse, the Savior left Capharnaum and traveled through various cantons of Galilee. It was during this journey that he confounded the Pharisees, by showing forth the hypocrisy of their conduct and the absurdity of their superstitious traditions. He also healed the daughter of a woman of Chanaan, performed many other miracles, and, in particular, announced formally the great miracle of his resurrection.

The scribes and Pharisees came to ask him for some extraordinary sign from heaven and in the air. But Jesus, from whom miracles escaped in crowds, if we may be allowed so to speak, when they were solicited with a humble confidence, took care not to lavish them on a proud curiosity. "This perverse race," he says, "asks a miracle from heaven, and what it desires shall not be granted to it. It shall have no other miracle than that of the prophet Jonas. For as Jonas was three days and three nights in the belly of a whale, so shall the Son of Man be three days and three nights in the heart of the earth. Jonas coming forth from the fish was so great a miracle in the eyes of the Ninivites that they believed his words and did penance; in like manner, the Son of Man coming forth from the tomb, three days after his death, shall be the great miracle reserved for this generation, that it may believe my words."

Peter chosen head of the Church.—In the course of the same journey, Jesus made St. Peter the magnificent promise of establishing him prince of his Church. They had arrived near one of the towns of Caesarea Philippi, when our Lord asked his apostles: "What do men say of the Son of Man?" His disciples answered: "Some say that he is John the Baptist; others, Elias; others, Jeremias; and others again, one of the ancient prophets come back to life." "And you," he continued, "what do you say?" Simon Peter, leading the way, answered without hesitation: "Thou art Christ, the Son of the living God." Jesus replied: "Blessed art thou, Simon, son of John; for flesh and blood have not revealed this to thee, but my Father, who is in heaven."

Then, rendering testimony as it were for testimony, and wishing to teach Peter what he was and what he should always be, the Savior added: "And I say that thou art Peter, which means a rock, and upon this rock I will build my Church, and the gates,[35] that is, the powers of hell shall not prevail against it. I will give to thee the keys of the kingdom of heaven: whatsoever thou shalt bind upon earth shall be bound also in heaven, and whatsoever thou shalt loose upon earth shall be loosed also in heaven."

He next announced to his apostles his passion, with its fearful insults and outrages, and the death which he should soon suffer. The promise of immortality made to the

Church, in spite of all the efforts of hell and human passion leagued together against it, joined with the visible fulfillment of this promise during the last eighteen centuries, suffices doubtless to prove to us the divinity of the Savior, and to remove from our eyes the scandal of the cross; but the apostles were not to be the witnesses of this miracle. To confirm their faith against the scandal of his humiliations, the Savior brought about a new prodigy, whose object was to prove, with irresistible evidence, that he was really the Son of God, that he was God himself, and that if he suffered it was because he chose to do so.

Transfiguration.—In effect, six days afterward, the divine master found himself at the foot of a high mountain in company with his disciples. He was also surrounded by an immense multitude of people, to whom he explained, according to his custom, the truths of salvation. The instruction being ended, he retired to the mountain to pray, taking with him Peter, and the two brothers James and John, the sons of Zebedee. He wished that the three disciples whom he had chosen beforehand to be the only witnesses of the weariness, fear, and sadness of his most bitter agony in the Garden of Olives, on the eve of his passion, should also be the only witnesses of his glory on the part of the mountain whither he was leading them.

It was a high and lonely mountain. When they had completed their ascent, Jesus began to pray; Peter and his two companions, overpowered with fatigue, fell asleep. While the Savior watched and the disciples slept, the figure of the master appeared quite different. His face suddenly shone like the sun and his garments became all radiant and as white as snow; so that the ablest fuller in the world could never attain to the splendor of such a beautiful color. There also appeared two men conversing with him of what he should suffer at Jerusalem.

Meanwhile, the disciples awoke and saw the glory of Jesus and the two personages who were in company with him. Moses and Elias were about to leave him, when Peter, charmed with the glory of his master, and tasting a little of that joy which the saints experience in heaven, said to Jesus: "Master, it is good for us to be here. If thou wilt, we shall make three tents; one for thee, one for Moses, and one for Elias."

The Savior did not answer; but while Peter was still speaking a bright cloud overshadowed them: Moses and Elias disappeared in the cloud. This sight alarmed the apostles, when a voice was heard coming forth from the midst of the cloud. It said: "This is my beloved Son, in whom I am well pleased; hear ye him." At the same moment there was no one to be seen but only Jesus, in order to show beyond all doubt that to him alone there was reference.

On hearing the voice, the apostles, who previously had been somewhat courageous, fell trembling with their faces to the ground; but Jesus, drawing nigh, touched them, and said: "Arise, and fear not." Then, lifting their eyes, and casting them around on all sides, they could not see anyone but Jesus, who had returned to his ordinary state; that is, the Savior had arrested those torrents of light which continually endeavored to burst forth from his divinity on his holy humanity. The glorious state in which he had just shown himself was his natural state; and the miracle was not that he had appeared for a few moments in the glory proper to the only Son of the Father, but that, by an effect of his omnipotence, he should conceal it within himself and prevent it from dazzling all eyes.

PRAYER

O my God! who art all love, I thank thee for having sent us a Savior who, not content with applying a remedy to our miseries, was pleased to communicate to us a divine life, by giving us his flesh and blood as food.

I am resolved to love God above all things, and my neighbor as myself for the love of God; and, in testimony of this love, I will neglect nothing to dispose myself properly for Holy Communion.

Lesson 8: Public Life of the Messias (5)

Deliverance of one possessed.—The Savior, while coming down from the mountain on which he had been transfigured, discoursed with his three apostles of the circumstances of his passion. Arrived on the plain, he found the nine others surrounded by an immense crowd, who, perceiving him from afar, hastened to meet him, and to testify to him the joy which they felt at his return.

No person desired him more ardently than an afflicted father, whose son, possessed by the devil, could not be delivered by the nine apostles. The eagerness of the father was great, but the liveliness of his faith did not seem to correspond with the ardor of his desires. "Believest thou," said the Savior to him, "that I have the power to do that which thou askest? Nothing is impossible to him who believes." "Yes, Lord!" the man answered, "I believe; but, I implore thee, strengthen my little faith." "Unclean spirit!" the Savior then said, "go out of the body of this child, and never again enter into him." At these words, the child was delivered.

Jesus then departed with his twelve disciples, and traveled through a portion of Upper Galilee, directing his steps toward Jerusalem. It was in the course of this journey that he paid tribute to Caesar and gave his apostles some admirable instructions on humility, scandal, and charity.

To make them understand how unworthy is the conduct of him who refuses to pardon, he related to them the following parable.

Parable of the debtor.—"The dealings of God with man may be likened to those of an earthly king, who would take an account from such of his servants as he had entrusted with money. The examination of the accounts began. A servant who owed ten thousand talents was presented to the king: he had not wherewith to discharge his debt. 'Let him be seized;' said the prince, 'let him be sold, himself, his wife, his children, his property, and let the proceeds be applied to the liquidation of the debt.' 'Ah, lord!' answered the unfortunate man, falling at his master's feet, 'have patience, and I will pay thee all that is due to thee.' The king, moved with compassion, graciously acquitted him of the whole debt, and dismissed him free.

"On leaving the king's presence, this servant met one of his companions who owed him a hundred pence—a very trifling sum in comparison with that of which he had just obtained the remission. Nevertheless, he fell upon him, and, catching him by the throat, almost choked him, saying: 'Pay me what thou owest.' This poor debtor fell on his knees, and cried out: 'Have patience, and I will pay thee all that I owe thee.' The other would not, but had him immediately conveyed to prison, where he ordered him to be detained till payment should be made.

"Several other servants, witnesses of this inhumanity, were deeply grieved at it, and, running, they told their master of what had just happened. Then the prince sent for this servant, of whom he had heard such atrocious things. 'Thou wicked servant,' he said, 'at thy mere petition I forgave thee thy whole debt, and thou rememberest the sum which thou didst owe me. Oughtest thou not then, for so very small a sum, to have taken pity on one of thy companions as I took pity on thee?' The prince, indignant, immediately ordered that he should be delivered to the officers of justice till he should have paid his whole debt.

"So," concluded the Savior, "shall my heavenly Father treat you, if you, whom he pardons so many sins, do not pardon with a good heart the offenses that your brethren commit against you."

During the course of this instruction, only one out of many delivered at the same period, the Savior continued his journey toward Jerusalem. Arrived in the neighborhood of Samaria, he sent a few of his disciples on beforehand to announce his coming at the place where he should stop. The envoys found, on reaching the Samaritan city, that the inhabitants would not give him hospitality because he was going to Jerusalem. Returning highly displeased to their master, they said to him: "Lord, wilt thou that we bring down fire from heaven upon them?"

The good master, turning toward them with a severe countenance, and assuming a tone of reproach, replied: "You know not with what spirit you ought to be animated. The Son of Man is not come on earth to destroy but to save souls." Our Lord endured the affront without complaints and sought an asylum elsewhere. We cannot doubt that, however inattentive to his own wants, he was most sensitive to the wants of his disciples, over whom he watched with the tenderness of a mother.

Example of gentleness and charity.—St. Clement the pope, a disciple of St. Peter, relates that this apostle often took pleasure in mentioning to those with whom he conversed some touching incidents that exemplified the goodness of the divine master during his mortal life. He used to tell with special affection how the Savior, traveling with his disciples through the villages and towns of Judea, would often visit them during the night, to see whether they were well covered, whether they were not exposed to the cold. And, when this kind master found them suffering, he would, with the most tender solicitude, spare nothing to comfort them, depriving himself of rest and spending the whole night in attendance upon them.

It was during the journey of which we speak that he sent his seventy-two disciples to preach in Galilee. He himself was not without occupation. One day, he had to confound the malignity of a scribe or doctor of the law, who took it into his head to ascertain what was the exact capacity of this man whose reputation was so great in every part of Palestine. The scribe came and said: "Master, what must I do to obtain eternal life?" The question was very vague, and under its vagueness concealed a snare. But it was a snare in which he who laid it was caught. "Hast thou not read the law?" answered the Savior. "What does it teach thee regarding the things necessary for salvation?"

"The whole law may be reduced," replied the doctor, "to two great precepts, which are the foundation of the others, and, as it were, the summary of them all: 'Thou shalt love the Lord thy God with thy whole heart, with thy whole soul, with all thy strength, and thou shalt love thy neighbor as thyself.'" "Thou hast answered well," said our Lord, "do this, and thou shalt have eternal life." On hearing these words, the scribe was silent. Accordingly, to love God and the neighbor is the sum of religion. Who will dare to say that this duty is impracticable?

One thing necessary.—After this great lesson, the Savior continued his journey toward Jerusalem, and in the evening he arrived at Bethania, a town near the capital. Here he received hospitality from a family always sincerely attached to him. It was the family of Lazarus and his two sisters, Martha and Mary.

Mary, the younger of the two sisters, sat down at the Savior's feet to hear his divine lessons. Martha, on the contrary, busied herself very much in preparing the repast which Jesus was pleased to take with this holy family. Not being able for all the work, she came to the Savior, and said to him: "Tell my sister, Lord, I beg of thee, to help me." The divine master, who never failed to turn the most ordinary discourses toward heavenly things, profited of the occasion to give us all, in the person of Martha, an instruction so much the more useful as it ought to be a matter of daily consideration, even for the most virtuous and zealous souls. "Martha, Martha," he said to her, "thou art troubled; thy mind is occupied with a hundred different things: think, while doing them, that only one thing is necessary. Mary, thy sister, has chosen the better part, which shall not be taken from her." Jesus alluded to the affair of salvation, and this is what he calls the one thing necessary. The labors and cares of Martha were good in themselves, but they did not tend so directly to salvation as the employment of Mary, who was attentive to the word of God: accordingly, the latter is said to have chosen the better part.

Next day, the Savior set out for Jerusalem. He had scarcely arrived there when a multitude of people surrounded him to hear him discourse. The chief priests, jealous of his fame, resolved to arrest him; but the enterprise failed. The hour of the Son of Man was not yet come. He even preached several times in the Temple. His enemies hoped to surprise him in his words, but they were forced to say, like the people: "Never has any one spoken like this man." Alas! this grand homage remained sterile: they were not converted. The Savior did not neglect to announce to them the frightful punishments which their incredulity was drawing down on their heads: it was all useless. Hence, when the feast of Tabernacles was over, the divine master hastened to quit this hardened city, which thirsted for his blood.

What a striking resemblance between the savants of Jerusalem and those of our days! How many men among us that have the praises of Christianity continually on their lips—admire its morality, its instructions, its arts—and yet give themselves very little trouble to regulate their conduct according to its laws! If we venture to tell them that this fruitless testimony will not defend them from the chastisements with which God threatens the violators of his holy precepts, they laugh at our words. What remains but to pray for these willfully senseless men, who have eyes not to see and ears not to hear?

Sight bestowed on the man born blind.—Jesus had just left the Temple, and was retiring with his apostles, without being followed by his enemies, when he met on the way a man who had been born blind. "Master," said the apostles to him, "was it in punishment for a fault that this man should commit, or rather in punishment for the sins of his parents, that he was born blind?" "No," answered Jesus, "it was neither for the sins of this man nor for those of his parents that God permitted him to be born blind."

It is true that diseases, misfortunes, and death entered into the world only in consequence of sin; but God, who employs them when he pleases for the punishment of sinners, employs them often for the perfection of the just and the manifestation of his glory. "It was his own glory alone," added the Savior, "that God proposed to himself in this man's infirmity: he resolved to display in him the wonders of his power." Having said these words, he spat on the ground, and, mixing some clay with the spittle, rubbed the eyes of the blind man therewith. "Go," he said to him, "and wash in the pool of Siloe." The blind man went, washed his eyes, recovered his sight, and returned home full of joy.

Never was a miracle examined with more care: and this was no harm. When the blind man arrived back, the news of his cure spread like wildfire, and people rushed to him from all parts of the city to assure themselves of it. The neighbors, as well as those who had seen him a hundred times asking alms, said to one another: "Is not this the blind man that used to sit at the corners begging?" "It is," declared some. "No," said others, "it is a man like him." "Not at all," said the blind man, "I am the very man." All doubts regarding the individual immediately ceased.

Regarding the cure, it might be judged of by his eyes: the question was how it had been wrought. "How," said the bystanders to him, "were thy eyes opened?" The blind man answered: "That man who is called Jesus moistened some clay with his spittle, rubbed it on my eyes, and said to me, 'Go to the pool of Siloe and wash.' I went, I washed, and I see." "But what is become," said they, "of the man who gave thee this order?" "I know nothing about that," answered the blind man.

These first inquiries being ended, it was still considered necessary to seek further assurances on the matter, and to consult with some persons of experience as to what should be thought of the miracle and what should be concluded from it. The man, previously blind, was therefore led to the Pharisees. They subjected him to a new interrogation, and, granting on the public testimony that he had been born blind, asked him how he had recovered his sight. Innocence and simplicity fear no questions. "He to whom I owe my sight," he answered, "put some wet clay on my eyes; I washed in the pool of Siloe by his orders; and I see." The precision of this declaration raised a division among the judges. All wished to escape from the consequences of this miracle, which so well proved the divine power of him who had wrought it; but they could not agree on the means of doing so. Here is the pitiful artifice to which they were reduced.

It was on the sabbath that Jesus had made the little mixture of clay and spittle; it was on this day that he had sent to the pool of Siloe the blind man whom he wished to cure. There was not the least thing in the world contrary to the law in either of these actions. Nevertheless, some said: "Though he may restore sight to the blind, the man who does not keep the sabbath cannot be sent by God." Others said: "Since this man is a sinner, a violator of the sabbath, he cannot have wrought such an extraordinary wonder." All these reasonings ended in nothing, and the minds of unprejudiced Israelites were still unsatisfied.

The Pharisees, disconcerted, then put to the blind man a second question, quite as proper as their division to manifest their embarrassment. "And thou," they asked, "what dost thou say of this man who opened thy eyes?" "I say that he is a prophet," answered the blind man. Driven to extremities, the Pharisees began to deny that the man had ever been blind, and to assert that the cure was a complete imposture. They called, therefore, his father and mother. "Is this," they said, "your son? Was he born blind? If so, how is it that he now sees with both eyes?" "We know," the parents answered, "that this is our son; we also know that he was blind from his birth; but how it is that he now sees we do not know; neither do we know who it was that gave him sight. Ask our son; he is of an age to answer you."

The parents of the blind man knew well in what manner the miracle had been wrought, but they had not the courage to say so; for the Jews of Jerusalem, that is, the Pharisees and other leaders of the people, had already agreed to banish from the synagogue, as excommunicated persons, all those who should make profession of believing that Jesus was the Christ. It was on this account that the father and mother of the blind man cast on him the danger of the answer by saying to the Pharisees that he was of an age to satisfy them.

The Pharisees therefore called him to them again, and, assuming a very religious air, said: "Beware of what thou art about to do; fear the presence of the sovereign judge who hears thee, and render glory to God: we know that this man is a sinner." "Whether Jesus is a sinner or not," answered the blind man, with great spirit, "I do not know; all that I know is that I was blind and now I see." "How then did he give thee the use of thy eyes?" they asked. "I have already told you," replied the blind man, "why do you ask me a second time? Is it that you also intend to become his disciples? As for me, there is no doubt but I am one." "Be thou his disciple, if thou choosest," said the Pharisees to him, with angry looks and curses, "as for us, we are the disciples of Moses. We know that God spoke to Moses, whilst, with regard to this man, who is called Jesus, we know not whence he is, whether he comes on the part of God or of the devil."

"Why, this is a very singular thing," answered the blind man, "that you, who pride yourselves on being so learned, do not know whence this man is, who has had the power to open my eyes. As for us, poor ignorant people, we know that public sinners have not the power to perform such miracles: those who have this power are the friends of God. And of what miracle is there question here? Of a miracle without an example since the beginning of the world—the cure of a man born blind. If he who gave me the use of my eyes were not sent by God, how could he do such a thing?"

On hearing these words, which were unanswerable, the anger of the Pharisees knew no bounds. "Thou art a wretch," they said to the blind man, "thou art all covered over with crimes. It well becomes thee to give a lesson to thy masters." And they drove him along to the door. The Savior learned that the poor blind man on whom he had had pity had just been shamefully treated by the Pharisees. He hastened to find him, and, on meeting him, said: "Dost thou believe in the Son of God?" "Who is he?" asked the blind man, "that I may make my profession of belief in him?" "I who cured thee, I who speak to thee," said the Savior. "Yes, Lord," answered the blind man, "I believe." And, falling at the Savior's feet, he adored him.

And we, too, born blind and cured by Jesus, let us know how to thank him for having called us into the admirable light of his gospel. Let us imitate the blind man whose history we have just studied: let his simplicity, courage, and gratitude serve as a model to us.

PRAYER

O my God! who art all love, I thank thee for having sent us a Savior whose whole life was only one continual benefit: grant us the faith of the man born blind, and the tender love of Martha and Mary for this divine Savior.

I am resolved to love God above all things, and my neighbor as myself for the love of God; and, in testimony of this love, I will pardon with a good heart those who offend me.

Lesson 9: Public Life of the Messias (6)

Every word, every miracle, every step of the Messias had the same object, the redemption of man. By his discourses he dispelled the darkness of error and ignorance; by his miracles he proved his divinity; and by his journeys he showed his tender compassion for our miseries. In a word, his whole life tended to draw the human race from the deplorable state into which sin had plunged it. By his kindness and familiarity, he wished to banish that servile fear which everywhere prevailed among men toward God. All his movements seemed to say: "Do not tremble—God is appeased; whatever your crimes may be, have confidence—my Father holds out his arms to receive you." It was to show this consoling truth directly that he related the parables of the good shepherd and the prodigal son. Let us recollect ourselves and hear them.

The lost sheep.—"A shepherd," he said, "had a flock of a hundred sheep. He loved them all, and guarded them with care. Notwithstanding his watchfulness, one of his sheep wandered astray. Is it not true that as soon as he perceived this, he left the ninety-nine others amid the rich pasturages of the desert, and ran with speed after the one that had left its shepherd? He searched for it on all sides; he gave himself no rest until he had found it; and, when he had attained this happiness, he made it no reproaches, he did not strike it, but he laid it on his shoulders and bore it back to the fold, so as to spare it the fatigue of the journey. Having arrived home, he gathered together his friends and neighbors. 'Congratulate me,' he said to them, 'and take part in my joy, for I have found the sheep that I had lost.'

"This is a portrait," concluded the Savior, "of your heavenly Father. I say to you, the conversion of one sinner causes a greater and livelier joy in heaven than the perseverance of ninety-nine just, who, never having gone astray, have no need of penance."

And now, what sinner will fear to return to God? But are we to understand that the sheep returned to the fold is more amiable on account of having been a long time a wanderer? Is the sinner more deserving of favors on account of having deserved severe chastisements? No, without doubt; but the joy of recovering is always proportioned to the sorrow of losing. A just man who perseveres attracts to himself a uniform esteem and enjoys the maximum of earthly happiness. A sinner who is converted wipes away tears, banishes regrets, imparts consolation, rekindles a fire that seemed to have been extinguished forever.

To the parable of the lost sheep, the Savior added another still more consoling, and specially intended to make the just humble and the penitent hopeful.

The prodigal son.—Addressing himself to the Pharisees, who reproached him with lavishing on sinners the cares of his tenderness, he said:

"A man had two sons. The younger said to his father: 'Give me the portion of substance that comes to me.' And the father, dividing his substance into two portions, gave to each of his sons the part that belonged to him.

"A young man, with much property and liberty, always runs a great risk: as the younger of the two brothers soon found. A little while after the division, he gathered together all his patrimony; and, that he might never again see his father or the paternal roof, went off into a distant country.

"Far from all inspection, free from all restraint, the young man speedily wastes his property in every kind of luxury and debauchery. To complete his misfortunes, he has no sooner spent the last farthing than a dreadful famine begins to desolate the country to which he has retired. He is in want of the necessaries of life. What must he do to procure bread? He sells himself. He left his father—he must now give himself to a master! And he enters the service of an inhabitant of the country, who sends him into his farm to feed swine. That liberty for which he cast off the amiable yoke of paternal authority is therefore lost. Behold, the child of an honored house is a keeper of swine! Noble youth, into what an abyss art thou fallen!

"All his sacrifices could not procure him a sufficiency of food. He envied the swine the vile husks which he saw them eat, and which he would not be permitted to touch. Reduced to the last extremity, the prodigal enters into himself. 'How many servants,' he says, sighing, 'are there at this moment in my father's house who have an abundance of bread, and I here perish with hunger. I will set out, I will go to my father, and I will say to him: 'Father, I have sinned against heaven and against thee; I am no longer worthy to be called thy child: receive me among the number of thy servants.'

"But how will he dare appear in the presence of a father whom he so ungratefully abandoned? What will his brother and the rest of the household say when they behold his wretched attire?[36] Will not the sight of him in such a state be apt to increase the anger of all against him? Will he not even run the risk of being disowned?

"Nothing deters him. He takes the road to his father's house. He is yet a great distance from it when his father sees him. Tatters and misery cannot prevent a son from being known. This good father's heart is moved: he runs to meet his son, and most tenderly embraces him. 'Father,' says the prodigal, with grief and confusion, 'I have sinned against heaven and against thee: I am no longer worthy to be called thy son.'

"Intoxicated with joy, the good father, without answering his son, without addressing him a single word of reproach, without even allowing him time to finish what he is saying, calls his servants. 'Make haste,' he says, 'and bring the first robe, and put it on him. Put a ring also on his hand, and shoes on his feet. And let the fatted calf be killed, that we may have a great feast. Let us all rejoice, for my son was dead and he is come to life again, he was lost and he is found!' Forthwith, they sit down to table, the musicians are called, and the festivities begin.

"Meanwhile, the elder son was walking in the fields. As he was returning home, he heard the sounds of extraordinary rejoicings. He calls a servant, and asks the meaning of this unexpected display. 'It is,' answers the servant, 'because thy brother is come; and thy father, happy in finding the son whom he never expected to see again, ordered the fatted calf to be killed.' On hearing this news, the elder son is indignant, and determines not to enter the house. The tender father, being informed of what is passing, comes out, and begs him to come in, and, by taking part in the feast, to crown his joy. 'What!' says he to his father in a reproachful tone, 'for so many years have I served thee, without ever violating a single one of thy commands, and thou hast never offered me a kid to make merry with my friends; but when this other son, after squandering his fortune in debaucheries, returns beggared and ruined, thou orderest the fatted calf to be killed, and knowest not what entertainment is too rich for him.'

"The good father replied lovingly: 'My son, thou art always with me; all my property is thine, thou hast every liberty to dispose of it. In comparison with a friendship so constant and liberal, what is a passing feast that the occasion required? It was very becoming to have an extraordinary repast, and to let my whole house share in the joy. Thy brother was dead, and he is come to life again; he was lost to thee and to me, and he is found.'"

Where could we find a parable more affecting, or more fruitful in motives of consolation for sinners who repent, and in useful reflections for the just who would presume? The Savior gives courage to the first by showing them the merciful goodness of the Father who expects them, and assuring them that, whatever may be their condition, they can recover themselves by repentance; for repentance is the brother of innocence. To the second the divine master teaches charity, humility, and the excellence of the favors which they continually enjoy in his service, and for which they do not always show themselves sufficiently grateful.

After this discourse, so worthy of him who had come to save that which was lost, the Savior performed an action which reveals all the gentleness and amiability of his divine heart.

Little children blessed.—One day as he instructed his disciples, and they were listening to him with extraordinary attention, a great number of fathers and mothers came to present their little children to him, beseeching him to lay his hands upon them and to bless them. The apostles, who were very much absorbed in the lessons which their divine master was giving them, and whose hearts were not yet softened to a tenderness like his, endeavored to drive these parents and children away. The Savior perceived it, and, calling them around him, said: "Suffer the little children to come to me, and never prevent them: for it is to these and to such as resemble them in candor, sincerity, and innocence that the kingdom of heaven belongs. Verily, I say unto you, whosoever will not submit to the gospel with the simplicity of a child shall not enter into the kingdom of God."

This amiable virtue must be very pleasing to Jesus Christ, since he loses no occasion of praising it, and recommends it to us as a virtue peculiar to the gospel. Our misfortune is that we every day wander more and more from the spirit of the divine master: the Christian world is filled, not with children, but with philosophers. An evangelical childlike ingenuousness is decried. We no longer desire obscurity or mystery in our faith. We lay aside practices of piety and the external marks of an ordinary devotion. We cease to be simple; that is, in flattering ourselves that we are wise, we cease to be truly reasonable and sensible.

The Savior, therefore, brought close to him all these little children: he embraced them one after another, imposed hands on them, and sent them away laden with blessings. To place their innocence forever beyond the reach of scandal, he declared, with that air of majesty which became a God, that it would be better for a man to be cast into the sea, with a millstone about his neck, than to scandalize one of these little children. Finally, to ensure for them the protection, respect, and care which their age demands, he added: "Verily, I say unto you, whatsoever you do to the least of these my brethren, you do to myself." Thus the great restorer reinstates the child, which he renders sacred, in its proper position—the child which, among pagans, was abandoned to corruption or death, or sacrificed without remorse to infamous deities.

Announcement of the passion.—The mortal life of the Son of God was now drawing near its close. The will of his Father called him to Jerusalem, and he set out with his apostles, scattering along the way his salutary lessons and splendid miracles. To count from the day of his departure, there only remained to him fifteen days of life—fifteen days till the consummation of his sacrifice. "We go to Jerusalem," he said to his apostles. "There shall be accomplished the oracles pronounced by the prophets in reference to the Son of Man. He shall be delivered to the chief priests, the scribes, and the ancients. They will condemn him to death, they will abandon him to the Gentiles, they will load him with insults, they will spit in his face, they will scourge him, they will fasten him to a cross—on which he shall die, and the third day he shall rise again." While saying these things, he was calm and joyous. Traveling along, he cured the pride of the sons of Zebedee, who were ambitious to obtain the first places in his kingdom, and he restored sight to a blind man.

At evening, they reached the neighborhood of Jericho: the Savior remained here for three days. It was at this place that he received a message from Martha and Mary, informing him of the sickness of their brother Lazarus and begging him to come to them. "Go," said Jesus to the messenger, "and say to them from me that this sickness of their brother's is not unto death, but to manifest the glory of God and to prove the divinity of his Son."

Meanwhile, Lazarus died a few hours after the departure of the messenger. The divine master was not unaware of it, and, when postponing his visit to the sisters, knew well the trial to which he was putting their faith. But it is for dearly-beloved souls that the Savior reserves the greatest afflictions, because it is for them that he prepares the greatest favors. On the other hand, resolved to perform, in the resurrection of Lazarus at the very gates of Jerusalem (for Bethania was only two or three miles from the city), such a splendid miracle that the incredulity of the synagogue would be at least confounded if it would not let itself be convinced, he remained where he was a couple of days longer, visiting with his apostles, as tranquilly as previously, the country of Jericho.

Before departing hence forever, he was pleased to bring about one of those singular conversions whose record the evangelists were so much the more careful to preserve as they judged it more proper to be at once an inducement to and a model of penance in a condition wherein opulence makes many sinners.

Zacheus converted.—As Jesus was walking through Jericho, followed by a great multitude of people, a man, who for a long time had been desirous to see the great prophet, was informed of his coming. Not to lose the opportunity, he ran to meet him on the way. This man was called Zacheus: he was the chief publican of the country, and enjoyed a large fortune. But he was of very low stature. The crowd prevented him from seeing Jesus. He left it and ran on a short distance before. Then, perceiving a sycamore tree by the side of the way, he hastened to climb it.

Meanwhile, the Savior continued to advance. Having reached the tree, he stops, raises his eyes to him who is fixed among its branches, and says: "Zacheus, come down immediately, for I desire to abide in thy house this day." Zacheus, who did not aspire to so much honor, came down in all haste. He led the Savior to his house, overjoyed to have at his table the Christ sent by God for the salvation of Israel. Nothing could be more edifying than this sight. But the aversion of the Jews for publicans was so great that even in the presence of the Savior they murmured aloud at his becoming the guest of a publican or sinner; for these two words were used indifferently in the country, one for the other.

Jesus made no answer to the reproaches that were hurled against him by the scribes and Pharisees; but Zacheus, without an effort, confounded their authors. He let them see that a humble and well-disposed publican could merit from God a kindlier greeting than proud doctors and haughty critics. He draws near the Savior, and, standing before him in presence of all, says: "Now that I have the happiness to see and to hear thee, I am no longer attached to my riches. From this moment I give half of my goods to the poor. Moreover, I will examine whether that which remains belongs to me lawfully; and if I have wronged any man I will at once restore him fourfold."

As you see, Zacheus does not speak of abandoning his situation: when one is determined to act like Zacheus, he can retain his employments. Content with the uprightness of this good publican, the Savior turned toward him with much affection, and, showing him to those who had just heard the expression of his sentiments, said: "Today the master of this house and all belonging to it have found the way of salvation. Zacheus is a true child of Abraham. In this manner has the Son of Man come to seek and to save that which was lost."

The raising of Lazarus.—It is supposed that about three o'clock in the afternoon the Savior left the house of Zacheus, and took the road to Bethania with his disciples. "Let us go forward," he said to them, "let us lose no time: our friend Lazarus sleepeth, but I go to awake him from his sleep." "Lord," answered the apostles, "if Lazarus sleepeth, without doubt he shall soon be well." Jesus spoke, under the name of sleep, of the death of Lazarus. The apostles did not understand this. He therefore said to them plainly: "Lazarus is dead; and on your account I am glad that I was not there, that you may be strengthened in your faith: but let us go to him."

On the journey, the Savior cured two blind men; for the miserable asked him for miracles as they would ask others for a slight alms. About nine o'clock in the morning they arrived near Bethania. Lazarus was now four days dead. A considerable number of Jews were come to console Martha and Mary. The house was full of these comforters, often troublesome, always powerless for hearts deeply affected, when the divine master was announced.

Martha had no sooner heard the name of Jesus uttered than she ran to meet him. "Lord," she said to him, "if thou hadst been here, my brother should not have died. But I know that even now whatsoever thou shalt ask of God he will give it to thee." This was to solicit the greatest of prodigies in a manner no less earnest than respectful.

The Savior answered her with a general truth, which gave her a glimpse of his good intentions, without unveiling them altogether. "Thy brother shall rise again," he said to Martha. "I know," she replied, "that my brother shall rise again on the last day, at the general resurrection of all the dead." "Thou also knowest," continued the Savior, "that I am the resurrection and the life. He who believeth in me, although he may experience a passing death on earth, shall live eternally in heaven. Dost thou not believe this?" "Yes, Lord," Martha answered, "for I make profession of believing that thou art the Christ, the Son of the living God, who art come into the world." Martha, full of hope, ran to the house. She drew her sister aside from the midst of their friends and whispered to her: "The master is come; he calls for thee."

The fervent Mary did not require the announcement to be repeated: she instantly stole away, fled to Jesus, and found him at the place where her sister had left him. The Savior had not made another step toward the house; he was still with his disciples at the entrance of the town. It was outside the walls in this direction that Lazarus was buried. He did not wish to enter until the prodigy had been accomplished. The hasty flight of

Mary surprised all the Jews that were engaged in consoling her. Imagining, when they saw her disappear, that in a sudden fit of grief she was running to her brother's tomb to bedew it with her tears, they went out after her and followed her.

It was not to the tomb of a dead man, but to the consoler of all faithful souls, that Mary ran with so much eagerness. She had arrived before the Jews, and, falling at the feet of her divine master, she said: "Ah, Lord, if thou hadst been here, my brother should not have died." Saying these words she began to weep, and the Jews themselves, who were come with her, could not refrain from tears.

This sight touched the Savior: he groaned inwardly and appeared deeply affected. Then he said to those present: "Where have you laid him?" "Come, Lord," they said, "and see." As they drew near the tomb, Jesus allowed his divine tears to flow, he wished to teach us that if, at the death of a friend, resignation is commanded, yet tears are not forbidden. The Jews remarked these tears, so worthy of their attention. "Behold," said some "how he loved him!" "Could not this man of miracles," said others, "he who opened the eyes of one born blind, have prevented his friend from dying?" Jesus groaned a second time and came to the tomb.

It was a cave closed with a large stone. "Take away the stone," he said. "Ah, Lord," exclaimed Martha, "my brother is now four days dead: his body must already stink." "Martha," the Savior answered, "did I not tell thee that if thou hadst faith thou shouldst see God glorified?" The stone that closed the entrance of the sepulchre was taken away. Then Jesus, raising his eyes to heaven, said: "O my Father, I give thee thanks for granting me that which I have been secretly asking of thee in the depths of my heart. As for me, I know well that thou hearest me always; but I say this for the people who surround me, that they may believe that thou hast sent me." Meanwhile, the tomb was laid open: from the top of the opening the body of the man four days dead might be seen extended below. The corpse exhaled through the shrouds in which it was wrapped a sepulchral smell.

The Savior raised his voice, and pronounced these few words distinctly: "Lazarus, arise and come forth from the tomb." Lazarus immediately arises, having his hands and feet bound with winding-bands, his face covered with a napkin, and his whole body wrapped in linen. "Loose him," says Jesus, "and set him at liberty." Jesus is obeyed; and Lazarus joins the assembled crowd to conduct his Savior to his house in Bethania. Who can express the sentiments of the dead man restored to life? Who can tell the joy of the two sisters, the liveliness of their faith, the depth of their gratitude? With regard to the Jews from Jerusalem, the consolers of Martha and Mary, it was a most precious grace for many of them to be chosen as the witnesses of such a prodigy. They thenceforth believed in Jesus Christ as the Son of God foretold by the prophets. Some of them even, thinking that they had at hand a means of overcoming the most obstinate incredulity, went to inform the Pharisees of the miracle which Jesus had just wrought.

They would have convinced honest unbelievers. But they only irritated jealous sectaries, who were determined, by interest as well as passion, to admit no proof, however conclusive, in favor of a man whom they wished to destroy. Astonished at the miracle and affrighted at its consequences, the pontiffs and the Pharisees held a great council, in which the death of Jesus Christ was fully decided on. "What are we doing," they said, "and of what are we thinking? This man performs innumerable miracles, and the whole world is becoming subject to him." They ought to have concluded: "Therefore, we should believe in him." But passion always reasons amiss. "If we allow him to continue thus," they said, "all will soon believe in him: the people will choose him to be their King, and the indignant Romans will come in arms and destroy our city and our nation."

Wicked men! they were much less concerned about the public interest than their own discredit, which they saw increasing with the fame of the Savior's miracles. But, as they durst not avow any personal motive, they sought to hide it under the veil of the public good: they were mistaken in their reckoning. It was not for having acknowledged their true King, but for having obstinately refused to acknowledge him, that they were overwhelmed with all the evils that they pretended to apprehend. To crown their false reasoning, one of the leaders of the council, Caiphas, the high priest of that year,[37] delivered his opinion in these terms: "You are right: Is it not evidently expedient that one man should die for the people and that the whole nation perish not?"

Thus, Caiphas only confirmed what had just been insinuated. His advice merited the applause of all, and it was unanimously resolved to put Jesus of Nazareth to death. When remarking that to save the people it was better for one man to perish, Caiphas gave expression, without knowing it, to a prophecy by which it was announced that the Son of God made man should be immolated for the rest of men. The sentence pronounced by the members of the council was not, however, less unjust: and in their blind fury they thought of nothing but its immediate execution.

PRAYER

O my God! who art all love, I thank thee for having sent us a Savior whose goodness extended to every want and to every age; preserve in me the innocence and sincerity of childhood, or, if I have had the misfortune to lose them, receive back, O tender shepherd, thy wandering sheep.

I am resolved to love God above all things, and my neighbor as myself for the love of God; and, in testimony of this love, I will avoid everything that might scandalize children.

Lesson 10: Public Life of the Messias (7)

Fulfillment of the prophecies.—The council which had just condemned Jesus of Nazareth to death was composed of such men as were celebrated in Jerusalem for their learning and wisdom. They were deeply guilty, but the nation itself was not excusable when it allowed itself to be dragged along blindly by the high priests according to the rage and infatuation of its dying synagogue. Far above its authority there had arisen another much more imposing, which it could not disown: this was the authority of the works of Jesus. They carried with them a divine testimony, which ought instantly to have gained the submission of all minds. Moreover, according to the oracles of the prophets themselves, it was necessary to believe that the Christ should be disowned by the princes of his people, and condemned to death by the senate of his nation. The violent proceedings of the synagogue against its true King, foreseen and foretold as one of the marks by which he should be known, did not therefore justify any prejudice against the mission of Jesus Christ.

Besides, God had neglected nothing to render the divinity of his Son so evidently credible that men of an upright mind and good will could no longer doubt or suspect it. In point of fact, Jesus had come into the world at the precise time when the Messias was expected. He was born at Bethlehem, of the race of David, and of an ever Virgin Mother, according to the prediction of the prophets. For more than thirty-two years he had done nothing else than every day perfect in his Person the portrait of the Christ, by his doctrine, by his sanctity, by his miracles, by the literal accomplishment of the prophecies which concerned him. All, however, was not yet complete. It remains for us to see him consummating the proof of that which the resurrection of a man four days dead had just brought to such a high degree of evidence.

The decisive trait of the divinity of Christ was his death on a cross, decreed by the synagogue, suffered at the hands of foreigners, accompanied by a number of well-known circumstances, followed after three days by his glorious resurrection, and crowned by his ascension to the right hand of his Father. This was the sign of Jonas the prophet, to which the Savior always referred the unbelievers of his nation. For, in fine, if after a birth like that of Jesus, followed by a mission so miraculous—if after a life of thirty-three years so holy and so consistent, Jesus dies on a cross precisely as he has often foretold, in confirmation of the ancient oracles; and if after his death, he rises again on the day which he has publicly announced, it must necessarily follow, let incredulity rave as it may, that he is what he says he is, the Christ, the Son of God.

Things were rapidly hastening forward to this unanswerable demonstration. After the resurrection of Lazarus, the Savior left Bethania and retired to the City of Ephrem, distant about eight hours' journey from Jerusalem. The feast of the Pasch was drawing nigh: from all parts of Judea crowds flocked to Jerusalem for the solemnity. Jesus now directed his steps also toward this city, which should so soon be stained with the blood of its King, its Christ, its God. He passed again through Bethania on his way and stopped at the house of Lazarus: his arrival was quickly known.

The perfumed ointment; murmurs of Judas.—A great number of Jews came from Jerusalem to see not only Jesus but also Lazarus, raised to life after being four days dead. A supper was given him here, at which Mary, the sister of Lazarus, signalized her tender love for the Savior. While Jesus was at table, she drew near him, poured out on his feet an ointment of exquisite perfume, and wiped them with her hair: in a moment the whole house was filled with the perfume.

Judas Iscariot,[38] the traitor who in a few days should deliver the man-God to his enemies, and who was still among the number of his apostles, found fault with this pious generosity. "Why," he said, "was not such a precious ointment sold? It would have brought three hundred pence, and this money might have been given to the poor."

Remonstrances of this kind, which are renewed among Christians in our own days, in reference to the liberality with which some pious persons act in their zeal for the magnificence of public worship, are much more frequently the result of a secret irreligion than a sincere charity. No one reproaches himself, in favor of the poor, with the splendor of his house or the elegance of his dress, and yet it is said that sympathy for the miserable cannot permit one to behold without regret the enrichment of the altar.

Now, Judas spoke in this manner, not because he cared for the poor, but because he was a thief, and carried the alms which the Savior received for the support of himself and his disciples. Jesus knew well the motive which gave rise to the murmurs of his covetous disciple; nevertheless, he did not, to justify the innocence of Mary, reveal the hidden crime of Judas. "Allow her," he said, "to bedew my feet with this sweet ointment; do not take it ill that she has kept it for my burial;[39] because the poor you have always with you, but me you have not always."

Meanwhile, very many Jews, having learned that Jesus was at the house of Lazarus, ran thither in crowds, and believed in him. The chief priests, exasperated at the progress of the faith, determined to cut away every root of it with one stroke. Lazarus, restored to life and showing himself to all that desired to see him, even at the gates of Jerusalem, appeared too convincing a witness: already determined to put Jesus to death, they now decided to rid themselves also of Lazarus.

Such violent resolutions foreshadowed an important event: no moderate measures were any longer respected. The powerful cabal of scribes, Pharisees, doctors of the law, pontiffs, and chief priests, which ruled at Jerusalem, could not fail to arrive speedily at the end of its designs unless Jesus Christ resolved to disconcert it by a miracle. He might easily perform a miracle; but it was far from his intention to do so. He only wished to prove to them that if he one day delivered himself into their hands it was simply a matter of his own free choice.

Entrance into Jerusalem.—The morning after his arrival at Bethania, and having only five days more to pass on the earth, he resolved to go and show himself publicly in the capital. He even wished to enter it in triumph—with a splendor as proper to arouse the courage of his disciples as to put his enemies to the blush. Accordingly, the most remarkable, though perhaps the least remarked, of the miracles which he then performed was to preserve, in the midst of so many conspiracies, his liberty, his independence, his authority, in acting, in speaking, in commanding; to arrest the storm ready to burst over his head, and to hold it there until the precise moment when his Father should abandon him to the powers of darkness.

On the first day of the week, corresponding to our Sunday, he set out from Bethania, accompanied by all his apostles. He advanced with them toward a town named Bethphage, situated on the side of Mount Olivet, very near Jerusalem. Arrived at the outskirts of this place, he called two of his apostles and said to them: "Go into the town that you see before you. On entering it you shall find an ass and her colt on which no one has ever sat: loose them and bring them to me. If any person shall find fault with you, you have only to answer: 'The master has need of them,' and you shall no longer be hindered."

Thus, in the least occurrences, the Savior showed himself the Son of God, able to dispose of hearts and acquainted with their future resolutions. The two apostles went to the little town and found the ass and the colt as Jesus had announced to them. They began to loose them without saying a word to any person. Such an extraordinary action, performed by men who appeared in their right senses, and who behaved with all possible coolness, created much surprise. "Why do you loose the colt?" asked the owners. "Because," answered the apostles simply, "the master has need of it." Thereupon they were allowed to act as they chose. They accordingly led the ass and the colt to the Savior without understanding what all this meant.

But their divine master did nothing without important reasons. As the Messias, he should fulfill all things that were written of him in the scriptures. He therefore acted thus to accomplish that which had been foretold of him by the prophet Zacharias: "Say to the daughter of Sion, 'Behold thy King cometh to thee in the spirit of meekness, seated on an ass's colt.'" The apostles laid their garments on the colt and Jesus mounted it.

In a country where beasts of this kind were used indifferently by little and great there was nothing either mean or superb about the Savior's equipage. He wished to be this day recognized by his people as their peaceful King, and to enter his capital after the manner of the ancient judges or guides of Israel.

Scarcely had he made a few steps toward Jerusalem when a great multitude who were waiting, some in the city, some in the suburbs, for the feast of the Pasch, came forth to meet Jesus. It was at the descent of the Mountain of Olives that the triumph, so to speak, of the procession began. Some took off their garments and spread them on the ground as a carpet for their master. Others cut down the branches of trees and strewed them along the way. All joined together in praising God, and the air reechoed with acclamations: "Glory, honor, and praise to the Son of David! Praise, honor, and glory to the Most High!"

Jealousy of the Pharisees.—At the sight of this general enthusiasm, the Pharisees said to one another: "See! we are making no progress; the whole world is running after him!" Their disappointment was painful, but the occasion was by no means favorable to violence. They therefore engaged some of their party to mix with the crowd; and these agents had the boldness to address the Savior himself. "Master," they said to him, "command thy disciples to restrain themselves." "If they were silent," Jesus answered, "the very stones would speak." In effect, five days afterward his disciples were silent, when, at the death of the Savior, they totally abandoned him; but at this time the rocks spoke, and, by bursting asunder, proclaimed in their language the divinity of the Son of Man. For the moment the acclamations only increased, and whoever was jealous at them had to endure the mortification of hearing them.

Tears of the Savior.—In the midst of so much joy, what did our Lord do? He wept. Yes, this divine conqueror mingled his sighs with the public rejoicings, and watered with his tears the green boughs that were strewn beneath his feet. Arrived close to Jerusalem, and casting his eyes on the great city which he loved so well, as the principal portion of the field which his Father had confided to him, he wept over it. He knew that in a few days it would put the finishing stroke to its crimes by the greatest of offenses—the death of its Messias. Looking a little further into the future, he saw the calamities that would burst upon it, and leave the queen of cities a heap of ashes, red with the blood of its citizens.

Prediction regarding Jerusalem.—Moved by the consideration of so many evils, he said with a sigh: "Ah, if at least on this day, which is still for thee a day of grace, thou didst know the things that are capable of giving thee peace, the salvation which thy Savior brings thee! But no, they are all hidden from thy eyes! And therefore the days shall come upon thee when thy enemies shall make a trench around thy walls; they shall press thee on every side; they shall cast thee to the ground, thee and thy children. They shall not leave in thee a stone upon a stone, because thou hast not known the time of the visitation." A terrible prediction, accompanied by the tears of a God, and only too literally verified in less than forty years afterward!

The Savior ceased to speak when he set foot in Jerusalem. He had no sooner entered than the whole city appeared in motion. Some asked: "Who is this?" The people answered: "Jesus the prophet, of Nazareth in Galilee." The Savior advanced as far as the Temple, where he cured the blind and the lame that presented themselves to him.

While he was instructing the multitude, and beseeching his Father to accept the glory of his humiliations and sorrows, a voice was heard from heaven, saying: "I have already glorified my name, and I will glorify it again." That is: "I have been honored in thee, O my Son! by the obedience which thou hast rendered to me; I shall be yet more so by that which thou art about to render to me." The voice of God coming with so much majesty spread terror among those who heard it. Some said that it was the rolling of thunder, others that it was an angel who had spoken to Jesus. "It was not for my sake," observed the Savior, "that this voice came from heaven, but for yours. Learn that the judgment of the world draws nigh: the prince of this world shall now be cast out." Mighty words! which announce the overthrow of idolatry.

The widow's mite; purity of intention.—Evening being come, the Savior left Jerusalem to spend the night at Bethania. Next morning, he returned to the capital; put a stop to the abuses which reigned in the Temple; reproached the Pharisees for their crimes and incredulity; and announced anew the destruction of Jerusalem. Then, seating himself opposite the treasury, he beheld how persons cast in money there. Now, several rich men cast in a great deal. After them came a poor widow, whose trembling hand dropped in only two little pieces of brass, of the value of a farthing. This slight action served as an occasion for the Savior to give one of the most sublime instructions that are contained in the gospel. Having called his disciples around him, he said: "I assure you this poor widow has cast more than all the others into the treasury." What then, O my God! is the value of a pure intention and a sincere charity?

He again addressed to the Jews the most pressing discourses, illustrated with the most tender and the most terrible parables, exhorting them to be converted and to avoid the evils that threatened them. It was all useless, at least as regarded the scribes and Pharisees, so hard does the abuse of graces and talents render the heart! Having come out with his disciples from Jerusalem, he sat down on the side of Mount Olivet, from which place the city and the Temple might be seen. It was here that he foretold the complete destruction of both, as well as the circumstances of the end of the world and the last judgment. He then encouraged his hearers to bear up against the persecutions which they should have to endure.

The Savior concluded all these lessons by saying to his disciples: "You know that the feast of the Pasch shall take place in two days, and that the Son of Man shall be delivered into the hands of the Gentiles to be crucified." Next day he was invited to eat by an inhabitant of Bethania, named Simon, and surnamed the Leper. While he was at table, a woman came near him; she bore in her hand an alabaster box of spikenard ointment of great price and exquisite perfume. This she poured on the Savior's head.

Judas on a similar occasion had recently given an evil example, which was now followed by some other apostles. "Why," they said, "waste such precious things thus?" The Savior returned the same answer. Only he added this prophetical announcement: "Verily I say unto you, wheresoever my gospel shall be preached, and that shall be throughout the whole world, this action of hers shall be spoken of with praise." The prediction is fulfilled. No person in the world reads the history of the passion of Jesus without admiring the religious prodigality of the woman of Bethania in the house of Simon the Leper.

Hypocrisy and treachery of Judas.—Judas Iscariot was at the repast as well as the other disciples. He heard, like them, what Jesus said. Consumed by avarice, he was not content: he beheld with pain the escape of any occasion on which a sordid gain might be realized. As he knew with what eagerness the pontiffs, the priests, and the princes of the people desired to have Jesus at their disposal, he imagined that he should never find a surer or shorter way to enrich himself than by ministering to the passions of these wicked men.

Such a base greed opened the door of his heart to the devil: the infernal spirit entered it. Judas went straight to Jerusalem. He presented himself to the chief priests and the magistrates, to arrange with them regarding the means of delivering his master into their hands. "How much will you give me," he said, "and I will deliver him to you?" The proposal of Judas was hardly credible, so frightful did it appear from a man of his character. But those who were interested in it risked nothing by countenancing it. They received it with every demonstration of joy. "We will give thee," they answered, "thirty pieces of silver." The sum was very small: it was just the price fixed by law for a slave. Judas accepted it. Possessed by his devil, he returned to Bethania, as calm in his appearance as if he had nothing to reproach himself with. Meanwhile, his only thought was the consummation of his treachery; and, to ensure success, he watched for the moment when Jesus, separated from the people, who honored him as the envoy of God, could be most easily apprehended.

The master and the disciples passed together the greater part of the day without the Savior appearing to have the least suspicion of the horrible intrigue which the wretched man who stood by his side had formed with the synagogue against him, or the traitor seeming embarrassed in the company of a leader whom he had sold for a vile price, whose penetrating glance he understood, and whose terrible justice he should have feared: But, alas! when one commits enormous crimes with an audacity like this, what place is left for repentance?

PRAYER

O my God! who art all love, I thank thee for having sent us a Savior whose tender compassion for sinners made him shed tears over ungrateful Jerusalem, which should soon put him to death. Grant me the grace to weep over my sins.

I am resolved to love God above all things, and my neighbor as myself for the love of God; and, in testimony of this love, I will act with great purity of intention.

Lesson 11: Public Life of the Messias (8)

Whatever debt the Savior owed the children of Jacob, as a teacher sent specially to prepare them for the kingdom of God, he fully acquitted himself of it during the three years of his evangelical journeying throughout Judea, Samaria, Galilee, every part of the ancient territory of the chosen people. His public addresses were terminated. The end of the world was the subject of his last prophecy; charity, that of his last instruction.

But if Jesus was only for a time the pastor of the wandering sheep of the house of Israel, or the apostle of Palestine, he was for all times the Messias of every people, the victim of the world, the Savior of mankind. On this account, he should die for all, to merit for all the graces of salvation and the glory of adoption. Two days more and the great work should be accomplished.

Feast of the Pasch.—Judas, who had sold his master during the night, was next morning in company with him again, seeking an occasion to deliver him. At three o'clock in the afternoon, the feast of the Pasch began at Jerusalem; for all the people, this was the first day of the azymes. The priests were busy during the evening until sunset in killing and stripping, within the enclosure of the Temple, the lambs that every family should come and take, to eat at the time appointed by the law. The disciples, therefore, coming to the Savior, said to him: "Where dost thou wish that we should make our preparations to eat the Pasch?" "Go," said he to Peter and John, "and prepare the Pasch for us, that we may eat it."

"But, Lord!" they answered, "where shall we prepare it?" He said to them: "Go into the city. As you enter it, you shall meet a man carrying a pitcher of water. Follow him into the house which he shall enter, and say to the good man of the house: 'The master says: "My time draws nigh; I have chosen thy house in which to eat the Pasch with my disciples; show me the place where I may do so."' And he will show you a large dining room furnished: there you shall make your preparations." To teach us detachment and humility, the Son of God was pleased to be born in a stable. But when he wishes to accomplish the great mystery of the Eucharist, he asks for a large and ornamented place. A lesson for those who wonder at the richness of our churches!

It was only the man-God, the master of hearts, the searcher of the future as well as the present, who could give such commands and support them with such assurances. The disciples went accordingly to the city, and found everything to happen just as the Savior had foretold. Provided with an apartment, the two envoys thought of nothing more but the completion of their preparations. They had to procure a paschal lamb, lettuces, unleavened bread and wine, and to roast the lamb. All things were ready when the Savior arrived with the rest of his apostles.

Jesus eats of the paschal lamb, and foretells his betrayal by Judas.—It might be about seven o'clock in the evening; for it was at an hour after sunset that the law had appointed the beginning of the ceremony. The Savior took his place at table, and the legal supper, during which the lamb should be eaten, was celebrated with all the usual rites. We know that, from his entrance into the world, Jesus had solemnly engaged himself to observe the law with the utmost exactitude. Addressing his apostles, therefore, he said: "I have an extreme desire to eat this Pasch with you before I suffer; for, I say to you, I will no more eat it until its fulfillment in the kingdom of God." By these words he gave them to understand that figures were about to cease, and that the eating of the lamb, commanded by Moses, should soon be replaced by that of the true Lamb of God, immolated for the salvation of the world.

Then the Savior took a chalice of wine, returned thanks to his Father, and, presenting it to his disciples, said to them: "Take and drink ye all of this; for I say to you again, I will no more drink with you the fruit of the vine until the coming of the kingdom of God." So far, there was only the consumption of the paschal lamb; and the wine of which the Savior speaks here was not that which he changed into his blood.

The moment of working the great prodigy drew nigh. The sight of the perfidious man who should soon deliver him to his enemies now sensibly touched the divine Redeemer. Casting a sad look on his apostles, he said: "Verily, verily, I say unto you, one of you will betray me." At these words the apostles were astounded; and one after another they inquired of him: "Lord! is it I?" The Savior did not choose to name the culprit. He contented himself with this reply: "He who will deliver me is now at table with me. He dips his hand into the same dish. The Son of Man shall go hence, as the scriptures announce; but woe to him by whom he shall be betrayed! It were better for that man that he had never been born."

On hearing these words, the anxiety and uneasiness of the apostles increased. They asked one another who could commit such a monstrous crime. Judas bore this trial with the utmost effrontery. He even dared to turn toward the Savior and to inquire in a low tone: "Lord! is it I?" "Yes," replied Jesus softly, so as not to be heard by the others.

A very deplorable thing it was that the eleven disciples, who were untainted by infidelity, were not free from ambition. They had just heard the Savior say that the kingdom of God was about to be established. Imagining that their master should soon ascend a throne, they began to dispute in his presence as to which among them should occupy the first places in the new kingdom. The Savior was not indignant at their weakness. He knew that in a short time they should be wholly purified by a divine fire, which would consume in their hearts the very roots of all human pretensions; but, until he merited it for them by his death on the cross, and sent the apostolic Spirit upon them from the throne of his glory, he treated them as children, to whom must be given, along with useful lessons, many a salutary example.

Instruction on humility.—"The kings of the nations," he said, "command as masters, and take the name of benefactors, and other pompous titles; you shall not act thus. Let him who will be the greatest among you comport himself as the least. Let him who will occupy the first rank become the servant of the others, that he may be the first of all to perceive and to relieve all wants."

Such is the admirable idea of power which the divine restorer gives us. In it is contained the overthrow of despotism and slavery; in it is found the source of all the heroic deeds with which the histories of Christian peoples shine. "For, I ask you," continues the Son of God, "who is greater and more distinguished, he who sits at table or he who serves? Undoubtedly, he who sits to be served. And yet I, who am your Lord and master, am I not among you as one who serves?"

After this lesson on humility, the Savior spoke to them of the divine dignities which they should enjoy in heaven: the only dignities worthy of our ambition, but to which we shall never attain except by modesty and abasement. These were the maxims which our Lord wished to engrave indelibly on the minds of his apostles and his children.

Washing of the feet.—To make the impression deeper, he added to the strength of his words a force which is always preferable, that of a noble example. The repast was about to terminate. Suddenly, the Savior arose from table, laid aside his garments, and took a towel, with which he girded himself. He poured water into a basin and began to wash the feet of his disciples and to wipe them with the towel. The Son of God at the feet of his disciples—at the feet of Judas! What an example of humility!

He comes, therefore, to Simon Peter. Amazed at this profound humiliation, Peter says: "What! Lord, thou to wash my feet!" Jesus answers: "That which I do thou dost not understand now; but thou shalt understand it hereafter." "Thou shalt never wash my feet," says Peter to him. "If I wash thee not," replies the Savior, "thou shalt have no part with me, that is, thou shalt be eternally separated from me, for disobeying the command which I impose on thee." "Ah, Lord," exclaims the fervent apostle, inflamed with the desire of being forever united to his good master, "wash not only my feet, but also my hands and my head." Jesus says to him: "He who is washed needs but to wash his feet, and he is quite clean. It is so with you: you are clean, but not all." For he knew who it was that should deliver him.

The expression, "he who is washed needs but to wash his feet," was a lesson which the Savior gave his apostles on a purity more perfect than that of a mere exemption from gross faults. Nowhere could it find a better place. It is especially when we prepare ourselves to receive the Holy Eucharist that we must not neglect to remove the least stains received in the wear of human life. This is what is signified to us by the washing of the feet.

The ceremony being ended, the Savior laid the towel aside, put on his garments again, and resumed his place at table with his disciples. Then he said to them: "You see what I have just done to you. When speaking to me, you say 'master' and 'Lord,' and you say well, for so I am. Now, if I, your master and Lord, have washed your feet, you ought also to wash one another's feet; or I have given you an example that you may do as I have done. If you understand this, you shall be happy in doing it." To encourage them in the practice of this humility, he added that, far from degrading themselves in the eyes of men by thus humbling themselves to one another, the honor which they should have in being his apostles would cause them to be respected as himself: "Amen, amen, I say to you, he that receives whomsoever I shall send receives me; and he that receives me receives him who sent me."

These divine lessons on the importance of a profound humility, a perfect purity of heart, and a respectful charity for the neighbor, admirably disposed the apostles for the heavenly banquet which the Savior was desirous to institute. He was about to leave us, in the sacrament of his body and blood, the greatest of his gifts, and to substitute for the ancient sacrifices one perfect sacrifice, which should far excel them all.

Instruction on the Eucharist.—It was night. This very night, so sad for the man-God—this very hour, when one of his associates hastened to deliver him to his enemies, the Savior honored with the institution of his great sacrament. In the excess of his love, he wished to render this night more beneficial to the world than the brightest of his days. The matter came to pass thus:

Supper was not yet over when the Savior took some bread, such as was used at the time, namely, azymous or unleavened bread, and, holding it in his adorable hands, he returned thanks to God his Father for the power which he had received from him over all nature, to change the laws of the universe at his pleasure—a power of which he had no need, if he only purposed to leave his Church some empty symbols. He blessed this bread, broke it, and gave it to his disciples, saying: "Take and eat; this is my body—the body which is about to be delivered for you to death." Adorable words! all powerful words! in virtue of which there remained nothing of the bread but its appearance, and his own body, taking the place thereof, passed into the hands of his disciples to be eaten by them. In regard to God, to speak and to act are the same thing; for he who can do all things does whatever he wishes by a word. Thus, at the beginning of the world God had no sooner uttered the words, *Let light be*, than light was.

Heretofore it was only imperfect victims, figurative sacrifices, that had been offered to God. Henceforth it shall be the body of the Savior alone: for this new sacrifice must last as long as the world. On this account the Savior hastened to communicate to his apostles, and in them to all priests, the power of working the prodigy which he had just wrought himself. "As often," he said to them, "as you immolate this victim, in virtue of the power which I confer on you, you shall do so in commemoration of me: you shall remember the death which I am about to suffer for love of you."

That which Jesus had just done to change the substance of bread into his body he did again to change the substance of wine into his blood. He took a chalice of wine, returned thanks, blessed it, and presented it to his apostles, saying: "Drink ye all of this, for this is my blood, the blood of the new covenant, which shall be shed for you and for many unto the remission of sins." The Savior added: "That which you have now seen me do, do for a commemoration of me." In other words, "Do as I have done, do what I have done." Such is the greatness of his love that he leaves us in perpetuity his body to eat and his blood to drink. Magnificent inheritance from a dying God! He bequeaths to all, by his last will, his body and blood, that we may become one with and in him.

Departure of Judas.—According to the opinion most generally received, Judas communicated like the rest. So black a crime excited in the divine master's soul an emotion which appeared outwardly. "Amen, amen," he said to his disciples, "one of you shall betray me." On hearing these words, the apostles looked at one another again and endeavored to discover by their eyes of whom he spoke. Peter was weary of this distressing uncertainty. It was well known how much he loved his master; but he had not the hardihood to inquire directly on this matter. He made a sign to John, the beloved disciple, whose place was at the very side of the Savior, to ask about it. John, leaning on the Savior's bosom, said in a low tone: "Who is it, Lord?" Jesus answered: "He to whom I shall reach bread dipped." And dipping the bread, he gave it to Judas Iscariot, the son of Simon.

With the fatal morsel the devil entrenched himself in the wretched man's soul. Judas would not be what he considered inconsistent: this was the height of his misfortune. Yet if he had not been the most shameless of all criminals he would not, perhaps, have been the most obdurate. Meanwhile, the Savior said to him: "That which thou hast determined to do, do without delay." He declared by these courageous words that he read in the depth of Judas's heart his dark designs, and that he feared neither the treachery nor the traitor. Judas was insensible to this last warning. He went out without any of the other disciples suspecting whither he went. Alas! whither might a sacrilegious, treacherous, avaricious man go? He went to put the finishing stroke to his frightful crime by making the final arrangements for its execution.

Farewell words of the Savior.—When Judas was gone out, the Savior gave free course to the tender effusions of his charity. He delivered to his apostles that admirable discourse in which his beautiful soul is perfectly mirrored and in which the immense love of a God is really felt. This sweet farewell seems a compendium of his last wishes. He begins by speaking of his passion with transports of joy, viewing it at the moment only in regard to the infinite glory which it should procure for his Father and himself. "Now," he said, "is the Son of Man glorified, and God is glorified in him. My little children, I have only a few hours to remain with you: you cannot follow me whither I go. Love one another. The world shall know that you are my disciples, if you love one another."

Peter could not without grief hear his good master speaking of separation and departure. "Whither then dost thou go, Lord?" he said. The Savior answered him: "Thou canst not now follow me whither I go; but thou shalt follow me one day." "Why, Lord," asked Peter, "can I not follow thee now? I am ready to die for thee." Jesus answered: "Thou art ready to die for me! Verily, I say to thee, the cock shall not this day crow twice till thou deny me thrice."

Peter should have died of sorrow; but he undoubtedly regarded the words of his master as a precaution intended to put him on his guard: he relied no less on his supposed intrepidity. The Savior had sufficiently warned him: he returned to his discourse. He told his apostles that they ought not to fear anything; that he was going to prepare places for them in the kingdom of his Father; that he would come again to them; that in the meantime he would grant them whatever they should ask of him; that he would send the Holy Spirit to console them for his absence; that he would not leave them orphans. Above all, he recommended them to remain closely united to him, and to love one another tenderly. He announced to them that the world would persecute them, but that they should fear nothing; for, one day, their sadness would be turned into joy and their sufferings into immortal crowns. "Fear not," he added once more, "I have overcome the world."

The Savior's prayer to his Father.—At these words, the Savior raises his eyes to heaven; he is about to speak to God for his disciples and for us. These are the last petitions of a Father and a friend. It is impossible to find anything in the world more beautiful, more affecting, more sublime. He enters into a kind of ecstasy: his every motion breathes respect, and confidence, and love. Addressing himself to his Father, the witness of his submission and the rewarder of his merit. He asks that all nations may know him as their Savior.

"Father," he says, "the hour is come; glorify thy Son, that thy Son may glorify thee. Thou hast placed all men under his power, that he may give eternal life to all whom thou hast given him. Now, eternal life is to know thee, the only true God, and Jesus Christ, whom thou hast sent. As for me, I have glorified thee on earth: I have finished the work which thou gavest me to do. Glorify me now, therefore, O my Father!"

After praying for himself, the Savior prays for his apostles. He asks charity, sanctity for them. "I have manifested thy glory to the disciples whom thou hast given me out of the world. They have believed thy word and remained faithful to me. And now I leave the world, but they remain in it. Holy Father! keep for thy name's sake those whom thou hast given me, that they may be one as we also are one. While I was with them, I kept them; but now I go to thee. I ask not that thou shouldst take them out of the world, but that thou shouldst keep them from evil. Sanctify them in truth."

The Savior does not rest here. His tenderness cannot permit him to forget any of his children. After praying for his apostles, he prays for us. He asks charity for us, and heaven, the object of all his labors, the end of all his sufferings. "Not for them only," he says, "do I pray, but also for those who, through their preaching, shall believe in me, that they may all be one, as thou, Father, art in me, and I am in thee. Father, I desire that those whom thou hast given me should be where I myself shall be, that they may be witnesses of the glory which belongs to me, and which I have received from thee, because thou hast loved me before the creation of the world. Just Father, the world has not known thee; but I have known thee, and these my followers have known that thou hast sent me. I have made known thy name to them, and I will make it known to them, that the love wherewith thou hast loved me may be in them, and that I also may be in them."

He goes to the Garden of Olives.—After this divine adieu, the Savior, who had nothing else to do in the world but to suffer and to die, recited the thanksgiving with which the children of Israel were wont to terminate their repasts.[40] He then quitted the hall, passed over the brook Cedron, and retired to the Mountain of Olives to pray. His disciples followed him. Here God the Father awaited the firstfruits of his sacrifice, and here his enemies found him.

PRAYER

O my God! who art all love, I thank thee for having sent us a Savior who gave us so many admirable examples of humility and charity: grant us the grace to imitate him.

I am resolved to love God above all things, and my neighbor as myself for the love of God; and, in testimony of this love, I will prepare myself for Communion with the greatest care.

Lesson 12: Passion of the Messias (1)

Heretofore we have seen the Messias fill town and country with the splendor of his miracles, the edification of his virtues, and the fruit of his lessons. In a word, we have seen him act from his birth as a man-God. It remains for us to see him suffer and die as a man-God, proving his divinity more evidently by his death than by his life. That which we have related of his entrance into the world and the exercise of his ministry astonish incredulity; that which we are about to say of his final humiliations confounds and maddens it.

Reflections on the passion.—It is, therefore, in the arena of his passion and on the altar of his sacrifice that we must now study the conduct of this man who is called the Son and the envoy of God. Hither we invite both the believer and the unbeliever—the one to sympathize, the other to be convinced. We shall present before them a victim who suffers and dies, but who suffers and dies in the midst of so many divine prodigies and other striking circumstances that the Christian, who adores him, finds in this scene the strongest support of his faith, and the infidel, who blasphemes him, if possessed of a spark of rectitude, the most urgent inducement to return to the truth.

Only let one remember, before considering the sufferings and death of the Savior, that it was predicted in all the scriptures that the Christ should be immolated for the glory of God—for the salvation of men—for the establishment of a new worship, founded on the divinity of his Person and the merit of his sacrifice. Let it also be borne in mind that, up to the moment of his death, Jesus had, so far, verified all the oracles of the ancient prophets.

Everything seemed to prepare the way for their full accomplishment: on the side of the eternal Father, who for more than four thousand years sought a victim worthy of him; on the side of the only Son, who, entering the world, offered himself as a substitute for the imperfect holocausts of the law of Moses; on the side of the human race, which longed for its Redeemer, whose blood should reconcile heaven with earth; finally, on the side, if we may venture so to speak, of hell itself, which had unloosed all its powers against the Christ.

The solemn moment was come.

Prayer and agony in the garden.—The Savior, accompanied by his eleven apostles, had entered the Garden of Gethsemani. This lonely garden was situated on the Mountain of Olives, separated from Jerusalem by the Valley of Josaphat, through which ran the brook Cedron. The distance from the city to the mountain was scarcely a thousand steps, so that on sabbaths and feasts this little journey might be performed without any violation of the law. From the village of Gethsemani, to which the garden was convenient, the city and the Temple were plainly visible.

Now, Judas, who betrayed the Savior, knew that it was to this place he was accustomed to retire during the night to pray. Accordingly, the Son of God, far from shunning the traitor, actually went to meet him. As the moment of conflict approached, he said to his disciples: "Remain here, while I go yonder to pray; pray also yourselves, that you enter not into temptation." Then, leaving the rest, he took with him Peter, James, and

John. When he found himself alone with them, and allowed himself to be struck by the horrors of his passion, fear, disgust, weariness, dejection, and sadness took possession of him. "My soul," he said to his apostles, "is sorrowful even unto death; stay you here and watch with me." Then, going forward about a stone's throw from them, he fell on his knees and uttered this prayer: "Father! remove this chalice, if possible, from me; yet not my will but thine be done."

A great struggle begins, as we perceive, in this great soul. To be innocence itself, the only Son of God, the ruler of the universe, and to die, after enduring a thousand outrages, on an infamous cross—what shame! what ignominy! But to save men, his brethren, and to satisfy the justice of God—what joy! what glory!

The apostles sleep.—After his prayer he arose, returned to his three disciples, and found them asleep. He said to Peter: "Simon, why sleepest thou? Couldst thou not watch one hour with me? Watch and pray, that you enter not into temptation. The spirit is willing, but the flesh is weak." He withdrew a second time and made the same prayer: "Father! if I must drink this chalice, thy will be done." He returned a second time to his disciples and found them again asleep. Rely now upon men to console you—you suffer and they sleep! He went away again and made for the third time the selfsame prayer.

The mortal sadness, fear, and weariness which the Savior feels make him fall into a violent agony: to such a degree that a bloody sweat issues from all parts of his body and rolls in large drops to the ground, which is soon wet with it. An angel now comes from heaven to strengthen him. Jesus accepts the cross: and the world is saved. Such are the consolations of heaven: they do not break our crosses, but they free us from the temptation of desiring to come down from them. Henceforth, there is nothing to be seen in the Son of God but courage and intrepidity—yet a modest courage and a calm intrepidity.

He comes, therefore, to his disciples and says to them: "Sleep now and rest: this is the hour in which the Son of Man shall be delivered into the hands of sinners. Arise, he who is about to betray me draws near; let us go to meet him."

Arrival of Judas; fulfillment of the prophecies.—He was still speaking, when the noise of an approaching crowd, led by Judas, could be heard in the distance. The wretch had asked the high priests, the ancients, the scribes, and the Pharisees, for a detachment of soldiers and an officer to command them. The heads of the sacerdotal families, the princes of the people, the magistrates of the Temple, did not blush to join this troop. It was also accompanied by a disorderly multitude of servants, some of whom bore lanterns or torches, others clubs. Now all this was done to fulfill the oracle of the prophet, which had said that the Messias should be treated as ruffians and robbers are treated.

Jesus is betrayed and delivered.—The traitor had given them a sign, saying: "Whomsoever I shall kiss, that is he, arrest him and lead him away cautiously." The sign and the advice were worthy of Judas. When he was come near, he advanced toward Jesus, and, saying "Hail, Master!" kissed him. The Lamb of God did not refuse this kiss, more bitter to his heart than all the other torments of his passion. Instead of being disposed to treat the wretched man according to his merits, he was more affected at his ruin than at his crime, and, seeking rather to save than to confound him, he said to him kindly: "My friend, for what purpose art thou come? It is with a kiss, Judas, that thou dost betray the Son of Man?"

These sweet words would have appeased a tiger and converted an ordinary sinner; but a perverted and sacrilegious apostle should be the most wicked and hardened of criminals. Meanwhile, the Savior was not yet arrested: it was not becoming that he should seem to be taken by surprise, since the matter was altogether one of his own choice. He advanced, therefore, toward the troop, and said to them: "Whom seek ye?" "Jesus of Nazareth," they answered. "I am he," said Jesus. Now, the moment the Savior said these words, *I am he*, the officers and the soldiers, the masters and the servants, the leader of the conspiracy and his supporters, fell suddenly backward to the ground, one on the top of another.

After such a sensible proof of the power of Jesus, they should only have risen to implore pardon on their knees for their base design; but there comes a time of punishment when sinners no longer reason. He who had cast them to the ground permitted them to rise again, and said to them a second time: "Whom seek ye?" "Jesus of Nazareth," they said. By a single word he had made his enemies feel that, alone and unarmed, he was stronger than a whole troop of armed men. After this evidence of omnipotence, he permitted them to do against his Person that which could never have been possible without his permission. They rushed upon him, and made him their prisoner.

Meanwhile, the apostles, seeing plainly what was about to occur, said to their master: "Lord, shall we strike with the sword?" Without waiting for any answer, Simon Peter, who had a sword, drew it, and, striking the servant of the high priest, cut off his right ear: the name of this servant was Malchus. But Jesus said to him, "Cease"; and, touching the servant's ear, he healed it. "Put thy sword into its scabbard," he added, addressing Peter, "dost thou not think that I could ask my Father, and presently he would give me more than twelve legions of angels? But if I exercise my power, how then shall that which the scriptures say be fulfilled, that all things must be done in this manner?"

Led to Annas, and then to Caiphas.—The Jews then seized and bound the Savior: the apostles had fled. The multitude led him first to Annas, the father-in-law of Caiphas, who was the high priest of that year. Annas, satisfied with this deference, sent Jesus, without interrogating him, to the tribunal of Caiphas. To complete a great injustice and consummate a great crime, he could without anxiety rely on his kinsman. They led the Savior, therefore, to Caiphas, at whose house all the priests, scribes, and ancients were assembled.

Now, Simon Peter, ashamed of his flight and somewhat recovered from his alarm, was following Jesus afar off in company with another disciple. This disciple, who was known to the high priest, entered the house while his master was being led into the council-hall. Peter stood outside at the door. The other disciple, coming out, spoke to the portress, and brought in Peter to the court of the high priest. A tumultuous crowd of soldiers, attendants, and officers were there assembled around a fire; for it was cold and they wanted to warm themselves. To his misfortune, Peter drew near, sat down, and began to warm himself with the rest, waiting to see what should happen.

First examination.—The Savior had entered the hall, in which all his enemies were assembled to be his judges. His fate was decided on; but no action of his life could furnish matter for his condemnation. The high priest, therefore, questioned him regarding his disciples and his doctrine. "I have spoken openly to the world," answered Jesus, "I have always taught in the synagogue, and in the Temple, to which the Jews resort, and I have said nothing in secret.[41] Why askest thou me? Ask those who have heard me; there are persons here who know what I have said."

This answer, full of sweetness and modesty, was worthy of that Wisdom which uttered it. An accused man is not permitted to give evidence in his own favor, and if the crime with which he is charged is public, it can easily be proved by witnesses; but no one, opposing judges who are actuated by passion, can ever be right with safety. Accordingly, when Jesus had answered in this manner, a servant, who stood by his side, gave him a blow, saying: "Is it thus thou answerest the high priest?" "If I have spoken evil," answered the man-God, calmly, "show what I have said; but if I have spoken well, why strikest thou me?" In this manner does innocence defend itself: humility does not abate its firmness, and, without ceasing to be respectful, it is noble and intrepid.

The servant of the high priest deserved to be well punished, because it is a matter of paramount importance for the public weal that accused persons should be granted all the liberty necessary to secure, if possible, their full justification. Nevertheless, the judges approved, if not by their commendation, at least by their silence, of this brutal act. What the Savior had said was so reasonable, that they felt themselves obliged to proceed in order against him as he had just pointed out. The chief priests and the whole council sought, therefore, some false testimonies against Jesus, that they might put him to death; but they could not find any that carried with them the least semblance of truth, although many false witnesses came forward. At length there came two false witnesses, who said: "We ourselves heard him say: 'I will destroy the Temple of God, and in three days rebuild it.'"

The deposition was false: it added to the words of the Savior, and it took away from them their natural sense. On no account should it militate against the accused. He had said, in speaking of his body and announcing his death and resurrection: "I can destroy this temple, and in three days rebuild it." If it was supposed that he had spoken of the Temple of Jerusalem, one could, at most, for want of knowing him well, accuse him of presumption.

The resource of witnesses was becoming either exhausted or dangerous. By the fact of listening to false ones, there was a possibility of meeting with sincere ones: the high priest saw through it. This is the reason why, rising in the midst of the assembly, he questioned Jesus himself. He said: "Thou hast heard all the charges that have been laid against thee, and answerest thou nothing?" Jesus made no reply. "Well," added the high priest, "I command thee, in the name of the living God, whose place I hold, to tell us whether thou art the Christ, the Son of God—blessed be his name!"

This time the question was precise and peremptory. The divine Messias awaited this occasion to boldly confess the truth. He knew that it would cost him his life; but he should be the protomartyr of his religion and give an example to millions of his followers. He answered, therefore, without hesitation: "Yes, I am the Christ, the only Son of God; and I inform you, moreover, that you shall hereafter see the Son of Man sitting at the right hand of Almighty God, and coming on the clouds of heaven."

Then the high priest, concealing his joy under the mask of a hypocritical sorrow, and assuming the air of a man zealous for the interests of God, rent his garments, saying: "He has blasphemed. What further need have we of witnesses? You have just heard the blasphemy; what think you?" All answered: "He is worthy of death." The Savior heard this sentence with as much calmness as he displayed courage afterward when he underwent it.

The high priest was a wicked man; but his act always reminds us that the Jews, when they heard a blasphemy, rent their garments, while we behold Christians nowadays who listen without emotion to the blasphemies of the impious. I will not say that they applaud them; for can those who applaud them be still called Christians?

The synagogue was so eager for the blood of its Messias that it would willingly have passed straight from the declaration to the execution of the sentence. But God was not pleased that the event should be so. To verify some prophecies that yet remained unfulfilled, he permitted the leading men of Jerusalem to call to mind that, being reduced to a state of dependence on the Roman governor, they could not dispense themselves from the necessity of obtaining his consent in a case of capital punishment. They should, moreover, enlist the people on their side, and embitter them against Jesus, by representing him to them as an impious blasphemer. These preparations required time. But as they were resolved to anticipate the great paschal solemnity, there was not a moment to lose. They decided to take only a few hours' rest, and accordingly fixed the return of the assembly at break of day. Each one withdrew from the council-hall, and Jesus was left to the care of the servants and attendants.

Outrages during the night.—These degraded creatures imagined that they would ill serve the designs of their masters if they contented themselves with simply guarding their quiet prisoner. Judging that it was their duty to outrage him, they made him suffer everything most atrocious that could be conceived by men without education or honor against a person so unfortunate as to be abandoned to them. There were some who began to spit in his face; others mocked and struck him. Others, again, more wickedly sacrilegious, bandaged his eyes, and slapped him on the face; then, turning into derision his august prerogatives of prophet and King, they said to him: "O Christ, prophesy to us; who was it that struck thee?" Jesus might well have told them, and at the same time have crushed them to atoms; but he suffered more from their blindness than from his own humiliation. This horrible scene continued all the night: Did ever a disciple of the Savior pass through such a night?

St. Peter's denial.—What seemed to crown all the sufferings of the man-God was that, at the very time when he was left to the good-pleasure of his most cruel enemies, the first and most favored of his disciples, the chief of the apostles, Peter, denied him.

He was seated below in the court warming himself with the soldiers and the officers of the palace. One of the high priest's servant-maids came hither, and, seeing Peter, she said, after considering him: "Thou also wast with Jesus of Nazareth." But he denied it before all present, saying: "Woman, I never knew him; I know not what thou meanest." What! is this thy language, Peter? Then, wishing to avoid a second inquiry, he retired to the porch, and the cock crew. Another servant-maid perceived him now, and she said to those near: "This man was also with Jesus of Nazareth." A little while afterward, a third, seeing him, said: "Art not thou also one of these people?"

His fear increased with his danger, and his crime grew worse with his fear. His first renunciation had been a lie; to the second he added perjury. The second time Peter declared with an oath: "I know not the man." He seemed to be believed on his oath, and about an hour's rest was given him. He should have profited of it to leave the place; but Peter still loved him whom he had denied, and could not resolve to separate from him. Meanwhile, one of the high priest's domestics, a kinsman to him whose ear Peter had cut off, said: "Did I not see thee with him in the garden?" Soon the others in the court drew near, and said to Peter: "Surely thou art one of them, for thou art a Galilean: thy speech betrays thee." Assailed on all sides, Peter lost his presence of mind, and denied his master for the third time, declaring with oaths and curses that he knew not the man.

Ye who are slaves of human respect, behold a striking picture of your conduct!

Peter was still speaking when the cock again crew, and the Savior, who was being led back to the vestibule, turning, looked on him. Peter then remembered the words which Jesus had spoken: "Before the cock crows twice, thou shalt deny me thrice"; and, going out, he wept bitterly. His tears ceased only with his life, and St. Jerome tells us that his cheeks were furrowed with them.

It was little for the authorities of Jerusalem to have tortured an innocent man by the hands of a vile rabble, whose fury they had let loose. When day appeared, they returned to the completion in cold blood of the work of darkness which they had begun. In order to give themselves in the eyes of the people an air of calm and mature deliberation, they repeated to the assumed culprit his acknowledgments of the previous night.

They said to him: "If thou art the Christ, tell us." He answered them: "If I tell you, you will not believe me; if I ask you in turn by what signs, according to the scriptures, the Christ should be known, you will not answer me, nor let me go. For the rest, the Son of Man shall hereafter be seated at the right hand of Almighty God in heaven." "Art thou, then, the Son of God?" they asked. He answered: "I am." Immediately they all cried out, like Caiphas: "What need have we of any other testimony, since we have heard it ourselves from his own mouth?"

The sentence of death was pronounced; the only anxiety remaining was to hasten its execution. The judges had condemned the Savior as a sacrilegious impostor, who had usurped the title of the Messias. This accusation, so grave in the eyes of a deceived multitude, was not of a nature to make a deep impression on the mind of a pagan magistrate. They resolved, therefore, to give quite a different turn to their charge on appearing before Pilate. Since Jesus called himself the Son of God and the Messias, he thereby claimed to be the King of the Jews and a competitor with Caesar. Such was the odious light in which it was resolved to represent the pretended blasphemies of Jesus. No time was to be lost: the whole assembly, rising, led Jesus bound, and delivered him into the hands of the emperor's minister.

It was now that, seeing him condemned, Judas began to experience remorse. Unfortunately, he did not feel that, in the eyes of a God dying for the salvation of sinners, the greatest of all crimes was not to have betrayed him, but to despair in his mercies. Driven on by sorrow, he brought back the thirty pieces of silver to the chief priests and the ancients. "I have sinned," he said, "in delivering the blood of the just to you." He was received with that cruel indifference which the wicked always reserve for evildoers whose crimes are useful to them. "What matter is it to us," they said. "It is thy own affair." This dry and contemptuous answer finished the work of plunging him into despair. He threw down the silver in the Temple, and, going out, hanged himself.

It remained to be considered what should be done with this silver: the worst characters are sometimes scrupulous on matters of decorum. They to whom the pieces of silver seemed to belong, taking them up, said: "It is not lawful for us to put them in the treasury, since they are the price of blood." They accordingly bought with them the field of a potter, to be a burial-place for strangers. This field afterward bore the name of *Haceldama*, that is, "the field of blood," as if the Jews had sought to perpetuate the remembrance of their deicide. But God had other views. He wished to fulfill these words of a prophet: "They received thirty pieces of silver, the sum for which he on whom the children of Israel set a price was delivered, as the Lord showed me in my vision."[42]

PRAYER

O my God! who art all love, I now see how much thou hast loved me. I am resolved to love thee with my whole heart, O my God, suffering for me.

Lesson 13: Passion of the Messias (2)

Jesus before Pilate.—We have seen the priests, and the scribes, and all the rest of the multitude assembled at the house of Caiphas, rising up to lead Jesus to the praetorium, that is, the house of the Roman governor. The name of this governor or president, who exercised over the Jews the authority of Tiberias, was Pontius Pilate. It was yet very early in the morning when they arrived in front of the palace: a scruple stayed them at the door. The law, which forbade the murder of the innocent, did not forbid entrance into the house of Gentile; but these men, religious beyond what was prescribed, would not enter the praetorium, that they might not be defiled, but might eat the Pasch.

Pilate came out, therefore, to them, and said: "Of what do you accuse this man?" They answered: "If he were not a malefactor, we would not have delivered him to thee." It was hatred that spoke, as Pilate understood quite well. He said, therefore, to them: "Take him yourselves, and judge him according to your law." But the Jews replied: "It is not permitted us to put anyone to death." They had been deprived of this right by the Romans; and, by the acknowledgment which they made of their loss, they admitted that the scepter had passed from Juda. They ought to have recognized as a consequence thereof that he who should be sent, the Desired of Nations, was come; but, blinded by passion, they could not allow themselves to see that which became, by their own avowal, more visible than ever.

Yielding to their clamor, Pilate at length determined to judge the Savior. God permitted this, in order that the Messias should die on a cross, as had been foretold by him; for, according to the law, the Jews could only condemn a person to be stoned, and they wished him to be crucified. They began, therefore, to accuse him, saying: "We have found this man perverting our nation, forbidding the payment of tribute to Caesar, and giving himself the names of Christ and King."

Declared innocent.—Pilate, hearing mention of royalty, returned into the praetorium, where the Savior was guarded, and called him. Jesus appeared before the governor, who inquired: "Art thou the King of the Jews?" Jesus answered: "Dost thou say this of thyself, or have others suggested the question to thee?" "Am I a Jew?" asked Pilate, "to concern myself so much about the Christ and the King of the Jews? Thy own nation, thy own pontiffs, have delivered thee to me. What hast thou done?" The Savior told him that he was a King, but that his kingdom was not a political one, like the kingdoms of the earth. "If my kingdom were of this description," he added, "my troops and officers would certainly strive that I should not be delivered to the Jews; but my kingdom is not hence."

Pilate said to him: "Art thou then a King?" Jesus answered: "Yes, I am a King. It was to reign that I came into the world, and to render testimony to the truth. Whosoever loves the truth, hears my voice." "What is truth?" asked Pilate; and, without waiting for a reply, he went out again to the Jews, and said to them: "I find no reason for condemning him." Would it not rather appear that he should announce to them that he had found him guilty? Jesus had just admitted that he was a King: this was the crime of which he was accused. But Pilate understood that his royalty was not of a nature to give umbrage to the powers of the earth.

The Jews, after the manner of calumniators, being furious at the thought that their prey might escape them, began to cry out: "He stirs up the people." The Savior kept silence. It was not his duty, but Pilate's, to say: "It is not enough to accuse; it is necessary to prove." However, not to remain quite dumb on an occasion when he ought to take the leading part, Pilate questioned Jesus a second time. "Dost thou not hear," he said, "how many crimes they lay to thy charge?" But Jesus did not utter a word in reply, so that the governor wondered exceedingly.

Pilate had recognized the innocence of the accused. It was his duty to impose silence on the accusers, and to send them away covered with the confusion which they deserved: he did not do so. The enemies of the Savior perceived the weakness of such conduct; they profited of it to obtain by uproar that which conscience did not permit the judge to grant them. Therefore, without adducing any new crimes, they began to cry out louder and louder, saying: "He stirs up the people, spreading his doctrine through all Judea, from Galilee to this place." Pilate, hearing the name of Galilee, asked whether Jesus was a Galilean. He imagined himself freed from his embarrassments on learning that Jesus really came within the jurisdiction of Herod, who had lately arrived in Jerusalem, and to whom he hastened to send him.

Led to Herod.—Herod had not changed his character since the time when he sacrificed the life of John the Baptist to the undisturbed enjoyment of his pleasures. Cunning, wicked, corrupt, inquisitive, he was delighted on seeing Jesus; because, having heard much of him, he was for a long time very desirous to see him, and hoped to witness some miracle wrought by him. Accordingly, he put many questions to him; but Jesus returned no answer. Meanwhile, the chief priests and the scribes, who saw that, if Jesus complied with the desires of Herod, he should probably escape out of their hands, began to renew their accusations with much earnestness. Jesus took no more notice of their calumnies than he had done of the inquiries made by Herod.

The divine master, who communicates himself to pure and humble souls, holds lasciviousness and pride in abhorrence. On this account, there was little likelihood of Herod's obtaining a miracle from him from whom he was not worthy to hear a word. Herod, therefore, despised Jesus, and all his court did the same. The vexation of finding his curiosity disappointed induced him to add ridicule and insult to contempt. He caused the Savior to be clothed with a white garment, and in this dress, which denoted a blockhead, or a visionary, or perhaps a mock king, sent him back to Pilate.

Brought back to Pilate.—Pilate strove to take advantage of the conduct of Herod, to appease somewhat the fury of the Jews. He said to them: "You have presented this man to me as stirring up the people, and I, having examined him in your presence, find no cause of condemnation in him. Nor Herod either. I will therefore release him, after having chastised him." The chastisement which he had in store for the Savior was scourging: an infamous and painful chastisement, which no man of honor could survive. The hope that the enemies of the Savior would hereby be satisfied had led Pilate to the discovery of this admirable expedient. Such was the protection which this lax diplomatist afforded the innocence which he wished to defend.

Meanwhile, whether he perceived that this plan would not yet satisfy these sanguinary men, or that, from some remaining instinct of humanity, he did not wish to have recourse to it except in the last extremity, he bethought himself of another, the success of which appeared certain, but whose only result was to draw upon Jesus the greatest affront and the deepest confusion that ever any man was obliged to endure.

It was a custom that, on the feast of the Pasch, the Roman governor should grant the people the release of one prisoner, whomsoever they might ask. Established in memory of the deliverance from Egypt, this practice had been maintained by the Romans, and Pilate should necessarily conform to it. This is the manner in which he endeavored to reap benefit from it. There was then lying in prison a famous criminal, called Barabbas. Now, Barabbas was a robber, a conspirator, a murderer. Pilate, therefore, addressing the people, said: "It is a custom among you that, at the feast of the Pasch, I should release one criminal to you: Whom do you wish me to deliver—Barabbas, or Jesus, who is called the Christ?"

The Son of God put in comparison with an assassin! How horrible! And yet how many Christians have repeated this conduct! And you, who read these lines, have you never been guilty of it? But the more odious the proposal was, the more suitable did Pilate consider it for his design. He was awaiting the answer of the people, when an unexpected message delayed it for a few moments. His wife sent to him, as he sat in his tribunal, to say: "Have nothing to do with that just man, for I have suffered much this night in a dream because of him."

In giving this dream to Pilate's wife, God intended to raise up an additional witness to the innocence of the Savior, and to give Pilate a new grace that might support him on the brink of the injustice into which he seemed ready to fall. He had also in view this woman's salvation, more dear to Jesus Christ than his own life; for it is believed that Pilate's wife was saved. Very ancient authors name her Claudia Procula: and this is the name which the Greeks give her in their menology, where she is enrolled among the saints.

While Pilate listened to his wife's messenger, the chief priests and the ancients excited the people, persuading them to ask the liberation of Barabbas and the death of Jesus. When, therefore, Pilate said to them: "Which of the two do you wish me to deliver to you?" they all cried out together: "We do not wish for Jesus; we choose Barabbas." Pilate, astonished, and still desirous to save Jesus, said to them a second time: "What then do you wish me to do with Jesus, the Christ, the King of the Jews?" They all began again to cry out, with redoubled fury: "Let him be crucified!" He said to them a third time: "But what evil has he done? I find nothing in him that deserves death. I will have him scourged, and will set him at liberty." At these words the fire of rage was rekindled; the cries burst forth anew: nothing was to be heard but the dreadful shout: "Let him be crucified!"

The aspect of affairs was threatening, and the feeble governor did not consider himself secure. Seeing, therefore, that every effort was useless, and that the tumult went on increasing, Pilate ordered water to be brought to him, and, washing his hands before the people, he said to them: "I am innocent of the blood of this just man; look you to it." But all the people answered: "His blood be upon us and upon our children!" The Eternal heard the imprecation and ratified it. For more than eighteen hundred years this blood has fallen, and still falls, in presence of the whole world, as a curse upon this unfortunate people.

Jesus is scourged.—After the vain ceremony of washing his hands, or rather after rendering this brilliant testimony to the injustice which he was about to commit, Pilate, wishing to satisfy the Jews, decreed that what they had asked should be granted to them. Hereupon, Barabbas was released. As for Jesus, Pilate ordered him to be scourged, either in the hope that this cruel punishment might appease the rage of the people, or because it was directed in the Roman laws that victims should be scourged before being fastened to the cross. This atrocious torture, which was carried to the utmost limits, was immediately followed by another, suggested by the hatred of the Jews, or invented by the brutality of the soldiers: the account of it ought to be read only with a flood of tears.

The soldiers appointed to crucify the Savior, having led him into the court of the praetorium, gathered around him the whole cohort. After having stripped him of his garments, they covered him with a purple cloak, in imitation of a royal mantle, and bound him to a pillar. Then, twining thorns together, they made thereof a crown, which they placed on his head; they also put a reed in his right hand, to serve him as a scepter. Then, drawing near, and bending the knee before him, they said: "Hail, King of the Jews!" Having uttered this salutation, they drove the thorns into his head with heavy strokes of the reed, spat in his face, and buffeted him.

The Savior suffered all these things without complaint, to expiate those sins in particular which are committed against humility and modesty. It was in his bitter flagellation that he became, according to the predictions of the prophets, a man of sorrows, whose body, from head to foot, was only one great wound.

Jesus is condemned to death.—After so many pains and insults, the Jews ought at length to have been content. Pilate, thinking so, came forth again, and said to them: "I am bringing back this man to you, that you may know that I find no cause of condemnation in him." Pilate was still speaking when Jesus appeared, having his reed in his hand, his crown of thorns on his head, his purple cloak on his shoulders, and on his countenance a look of modest, patient, generous sorrow. Pilate said to them: "Behold the man!"

Yes, behold him such as our sins have made him! Behold, in all its misery, that human nature of which Jesus was only the representative; that human nature such as it came from Adam, and such as it should still be if the Redeemer had not laden himself with its crimes and its punishments, to deliver it from them!

At this sight the people were silent, and perhaps compassion began to gain upon them; but the chief priests and their servants cried out: "Crucify him, crucify him!" Pilate, disappointed once more, said to them rather sharply: "Take him yourselves and crucify him; as for me, I find nothing in him to condemn." The Jews answered: "We have a law, and according to that law he deserves death, because he called himself the Son of God."

At the name of the Son of God, Pilate was seized with amazement. Everything appeared so grand and noble in his prisoner that he was afraid to draw upon himself, by abandoning him, the anger of heaven. He returned quickly into the hall and said to Jesus: "Whence art thou?" But Jesus made no reply. "Wilt thou not speak to me?" added Pilate. "Knowest thou not that I have power to crucify thee or to release thee?" "Thou couldst do nothing against me," said the Savior, "if this power were not given thee from above; therefore, he who has delivered me to thee is the more guilty." He alluded in this remark to Judas and the Jews, eager for his life.

The mildness and the firmness of this answer cast the soul of the governor into trouble. He had learned that Jesus was announcing himself to the nation as the Son of God; and Jesus, far from wishing to clear himself of this charge, said nothing but what helped to confirm its truth. From this moment Pilate redoubled his efforts to deliver Jesus; but the Jews began to cry out with increased vehemence: "If thou release him, thou art no friend of Caesar's; for whosoever makes himself a king declares himself an enemy to Caesar."

Alarmed at the name of Caesar, and seeing the chief priests disposed to make his indulgence a state offense, Pilate took his seat on his tribunal, elevated on a pavement of beautiful stones, called in Greek *Lithostrotos* and in Hebrew *Gabbatha*. Having brought Jesus forth, he said to the Jews: "Behold your King!" But they cried out: "Away with him! away with him! crucify him!" "What! crucify your King!" said Pilate. This was the last sigh of expiring justice. "Our King indeed!" replied the chief priests insolently: "We have no king but Caesar." Then he abandoned Jesus to them, to do with him what they wished, that is, he delivered him to them to be crucified. This is the end at which Pilate arrives, after having so many times declared Jesus innocent.[43] This is also the end at which the Christian arrives, who, allowing himself to be overcome by temptation, consents to mortal sin.

Led out to Calvary.—It was about nine o'clock in the morning. Jesus was no sooner condemned than he was seized by the soldiers appointed for his execution, and treated by them as they desired. They took off him the wretched mantle with which they had just insulted his royalty; they put on him his own garments, and led him forth to crucifixion. Jesus, carrying his cross, proceeded to the place called Calvary—in Hebrew, Golgotha. It was a small mountain near Jerusalem; to reach it, it was necessary to pass through the city. Accordingly, the Jews, who since the preceding night had been pursuing the Savior as furious wolves pursue an innocent lamb, had again the satisfaction of seeing him on his way to the most excruciating pains. But Jesus, exhausted with loss of blood, soon fell under the weight of his burden, and the true Isaac seemed unable to bear to the summit of the mountain the wood of his sacrifice.

As his weakness might release him from the necessity of execution, or at least delay the moment which his enemies so much desired, they laid hold of a traveler—an Israelite by religion, originally from Cyrene in Libya, and named Simon—who was coming from the country. They compelled him to carry, after Jesus, the heavy cross which the Son of God could not drag along. Christians! ye who read these lines, is it not true that ye envy the Jewish stranger his honorable commission? Console yourselves: it continues even in our own days. There is no person that has not more than once in the course of his life an opportunity of carrying the cross of his master and accompanying him to Calvary.

The Savior, assisted by Simon, found himself in a condition to continue his sorrowful journey to the summit of the hill. He was followed by a countless multitude of people, among whom were many women, who struck their breasts, and wept with loud lamentations. But Jesus, turning toward them, said: "Daughters of Jerusalem! weep not for me, but for yourselves, and your children; because the time draws near when it shall be said, 'Blessed are the barren, blessed are the wombs that have not borne!' Then shall they say to the mountains, 'Fall upon us,' and to the hills, 'Cover us'; for if the green wood is treated thus, what shall be done with the dry wood?—that is, if you treat the innocent and the holy thus, what must his murderers expect?" Forgetful of his fate, and bewailing the misfortunes of his people, Jesus, having reached the summit of Calvary, delivered himself into the hands of his executioners and presented himself to the cross.

He was accompanied by two criminals, who were to be crucified, one on each side of him. Providence had so arranged it that the prophecies might be fulfilled, and that there should not be wanting to the passion of the Savior any circumstance capable of increasing its ignominy.

On his arrival he was offered wine, mingled with myrrh and gall to drink. It was the custom to act in this manner, that the draught might deaden a little in the sufferer the sense of his pains. The Savior, who endured his pains for the glory of his Father and the salvation of the world, reserved to himself all their anguish. After tasting this wine, so as to feel its bitterness, he refused to drink it, so as to deprive himself of the relief which he might hope to obtain from it.

Jesus is crucified; he prays for his executioners.—The Lamb of God, a willing victim, now extends himself on the cross. Four soldiers drive nails into his hands and feet. They raise the cross, and allow it to fall heavily into the hole prepared for it. The blood of the sacred victim flows in large drops from his wounds. At the same time, they crucify with him two thieves, one on his right hand, the other on his left.

The deicide was consummated; nothing remained but to avenge it. For this purpose, Jesus had only to speak: it even seemed that he had only to be silent, and the fiery bolts of heaven would crush the authors and accomplices of such a monstrous crime. A person would almost say that he feared this occurrence, so quickly did he hasten to avert the stroke. Scarcely was he raised on the cross when he pronounced this tender prayer: "Father, forgive them, for they know not what they do." Such was the first of the seven memorable words which he uttered on the cross.

The soldiers cast lots for his robe.—The soldiers had no sooner finished their barbarous work than they began to think of gathering their spoils. They divided the Savior's inner garments into four parts: each soldier took a part. All that remained of his property was his outer tunic: it was seamless, woven from the top throughout. "It would be an injury to cut it," said the soldiers, "better let us cast lots for it, whose it shall be." Such, in effect, was the resolution taken by them. Thus was the oracle of David literally fulfilled: "They have divided my garments among them, and upon my vesture they have cast lots." During the course of this amusement, so worthy of four pagan soldiers, the proud Jews were occupied with a matter quite conformable to their genius. Pilate had drawn out the inscription which was placed on the upper part of the cross. The cause of the condemnation of Jesus was there indicated in these terms: "Jesus of Nazareth, King of the Jews." The chief priests were offended at it. They said therefore to Pilate: "Write not 'King of the Jews,' but that 'He called himself King of the Jews.'" Pilate answered: "What I have written, I have written," and with this brief reply sent them off.

God had dictated that which Pilate had written, and held his hand that it might not afterward be effaced. It was by the wood that the man-God should reign: by the act of fastening him to the cross he had been placed on his throne, the seat of his royalty. It was also necessary that he should be proclaimed King, and Pilate did so juridically, notwithstanding the opposition and indignation of the Jewish people: an admirable figure of that which happened soon afterward, when, these homicides growing more and more obstinate in the determination that Jesus should not reign over them, all the Gentile peoples might be seen acknowledging him, not only as their King, but as their Savior and their God.

The Jews insult him.—The Jews, repelled by Pilate, avenged themselves on Jesus, making him pay dearly for the title of King which they were obliged to leave him. From this moment the crucified God heard scarcely any other sounds around his cross than those of atrocious railleries and impious blasphemies. His enemies continually passed and repassed under his eyes: it was with the joy of barbarians, brought up in forests, or rather with the ferocity induced by brutal and gratified passions, which render men more savage than the beasts, that they beheld him.

Some loaded him with curses, shaking their head, and saying: "Thou, who destroyest the Temple of God, and in three days rebuildest it, save thyself; if thou art the Son of God, come down from the cross." And what surpasses all imagination, the chief priests, the doctors of the law, the old white-haired men, drew near him with a satisfied look, and regarded him with delight in the midst of his torments. Blending their insults with those of the populace, they said: "He saved others; he cannot save himself. If he is the King of Israel, let him now come down from the cross, and we will believe him. He trusted in God; if God loves him, it is now in his power to deliver him."

Jesus fulfills the prophecies.—The unfortunate men—how grossly they deceived themselves! It was on the cross that a faithful and instructed Israelite ought to recognize his Messias, provided this adorable Messias should remain constant there until death. If Jesus were to descend from the cross, he would render it impossible to recognize him; the prophecies would not be fulfilled in his Person, and this last miracle which they were asking of him would destroy the effect of all the others.

In the absence of this unseasonable miracle, he wrought another before their eyes, sufficient of itself alone to prove the divinity of our Lord; and how astonishing! they themselves were the instruments of it. Their blasphemies, their insults, their shakings of the head, had been predicted by David, and they lent their services to the literal fulfillment of the prediction in regard to Jesus of Nazareth.

"On seeing me," said the holy King, speaking as the future Messias, "they mocked me and wagged their heads at me, saying: 'He put his confidence in the Lord. Let the Lord, therefore, come to his aid, if it is true that he is interested in him, and save him from the hands of his enemies.'" Who would not suppose, on hearing the vile language of the Jews, that they had expressly copied the words of the prophecy, in order to fulfill it in all its extent? Or rather, who could fail to recognize therein the divinity of a prediction so exactly realized?

Jesus converts the good thief.—To this miracle was soon added another, quite as well calculated to prove the divine power of him whom they so unworthily outraged. The thieves crucified by his side were joining with the soldiers and the Jews in insulting him. Now, suddenly, while one of these thieves was uttering his blasphemies against Jesus, the other reprimanded him, saying: "Dost thou not fear God, thou who art so near death? As for us, it is not without reason that we suffer, for we receive the punishment due to our crimes; but he—he has done no evil." Then, turning toward the Savior, he added: "Lord, remember me when thou shalt come into thy kingdom."[44]

This profession of faith was most affecting and courageous: the salvation of the thief was its reward, and he was assured thereof on the spot. "Verily, I say to thee," answered the Savior, "this day shalt thou be with me in paradise."[45]

Jesus entrusts John to his Mother, and his Mother to John.—An object still more interesting to Jesus attracted his attention, and gave him an opportunity of fulfilling one of the first duties prescribed by nature, in order to teach us that he did not come to destroy but to perfect nature. Mary, whom the most dreadful affliction that ever was known did not hinder from following him, even to the last torments—Mary, the Queen of Martyrs, accompanied by her sister-in-law, the wife of Cleophas, and Mary Magdalen, was standing at the foot of the cross. Jesus, therefore, seeing his Mother, and near her the disciple whom he loved, said to Mary: "Woman, behold thy son," and to the disciple: "Behold thy Mother."

The only reply to such adieus is obedience and tears. Mary adopted John as her son, and in his person all Christians as her children; John adopted Mary and honored her as his Mother. Thus was executed the last will, the dying testament, of the Savior.

Jesus dies in the midst of prodigies.—It was about the sixth hour of the day, that is, noon, when thick darkness fell on the whole earth, and covered it until the ninth hour. The sun veiled his face. All nature mourned for the sufferings of its author.

At the ninth hour, Jesus cried out with a loud and strong voice: *Eloi, Eloi, lamma sabacthani:* which means, "My God, my God, why hast thou forsaken me?" It had been foretold that the Messias would pronounce these words. Some of those who were present and who heard them, said: "Behold, he calls Elias." Then the Savior, knowing that all the oracles which referred to the sufferings of the Messias were accomplished in him, excepting one little circumstance, which his infinite penetration was about to extricate from the multitude of prophecies relative to his Person, in order that the scripture might be fulfilled without the failure of a single iota, said: "I thirst." Now there was a vessel there full of vinegar. Immediately one of the bystanders ran for a sponge, steeped it in the vinegar, and, fastening it with hyssop to the end of a long reed, reached it to him to drink. Thus was fulfilled that saying of David, who spoke as the future Messias: "In my thirst they gave me vinegar to drink."

Jesus, having taken this vinegar to drink, and assured himself by a last look that nothing was wanting to his sacrifice, or to the fulfillment of the prophecies, or to his love for mankind, said, "All is consummated!" Then, raising his voice like a man full of health and strength, at liberty either to retain or to surrender life, he cried out aloud: "Father, into thy hands I commend my soul." With these words, he bowed his head and expired.

He is dead! He is dead! And he is our God, our Savior, our father, our friend, our brother. He is dead: and for whom? He is dead: and for what?

PRAYER

O my God! who art all love, it is in tears at the foot of thy cross that I renew with all my heart the resolution which I have taken, of loving thee above all things, and my neighbor as myself for the love of thee.

Lesson 14: Burial and Resurrection of the Messias

The last sigh of Jesus expiring on the cross had just filled up the measure of the glory which God was pleased to draw from the sufferings and humiliations of the Redeemer. But this last sigh, heaved in the exercise of the most exact obedience, ought also to be, according to the engagements of the eternal Father, the beginning of the divine honors reserved for this dear Son, so much abased.

Universal darkness.—With the realization of the conditions followed that of the promises. At the moment when Jesus expired, and, at the cost of his blood, purchased the title of Savior, judge, and ruler of the whole human family, all nature was moved, in recognition of its King, either to lament his death or to prepare the way for his triumph.

The veil of the Temple is rent; the dead rise again.—The darkness, spread for three hours over the face of the earth, rolled away.[46] The veil of the Temple, that is, the veil which separated the part of the Temple called the "holy" from the part called the "holy of holies," was rent through its whole length; the earth trembled:[47] and this last prodigy prepared the way for another, which happened on the third day following. Many saints who were dead rose again; and, leaving their tombs, after the resurrection of the Savior, came into the holy city and appeared in public.

Conversion of the centurion.—The example of inanimate nature produced its effect. First, the centurion or Roman officer, who presided at the crucifixion, who saw what passed, who beheld Jesus expiring with a loud cry, rendered glory to God, saying: "Indeed this man was just; he was truly the Son of God." In point of fact, to die on a cross meant to die from loss of strength, from loss of blood: the cry of the Savior was therefore preternatural. It was at once a miracle and the fulfillment of a prophecy. A miracle of strength in the last degree of weakness! The literal fulfillment of the Savior's own words: "I lay down my life of myself."[48]

Then the soldiers who guarded Jesus, seeing the earthquake and the other things which occurred, were seized with terror, and cried out: "This man was truly the Son of God." So many miracles also gained those among the spectators whose hearts were not wholly contaminated by false principles. The witnesses of all things, and alarmed at the sight of the vengeance of God, the near approach of which they feared, they went away striking their breasts.

Calvary became gradually free from the crowd that had occupied it since noon: everyone departed either more hardened or most happily undeceived. Is it not thus that every day still we leave the august sacrifice of our altars? There remained, however, in the neighborhood of the cross some other persons more afflicted, but not repining, who could not resolve to quit an object so dear to them. These were the acquaintances of Jesus, and several women who had kept aside, beholding from afar all that passed. Among these women were to be seen Mary Magdalen, Mary the mother of James the Less and of Joseph, and Salome the mother of the sons of Zebedee: who were all accustomed to follow him when he was in Galilee, and to take care of him. Let us imitate their example: let us remain, at least in spirit, at the foot of the altar when we have assisted at the adorable sacrifice, the renewal of that of Calvary.

Fulfillment of prophecies.—In all that the Jews had attempted against the Savior, they had only succeeded so far as to fulfill the decrees of the power of God: they could never make a step beyond these limits. Now, as God did not wish that Jesus should suffer another kind of torment which they intended for him, the idea of it did not come into their minds until after his death. It was again zeal for the law that seemed impelling them to act. The law commanded that the bodies of those who died on a gibbet should be taken down before the close of the day. It was necessary to make haste, because the time when a work of this kind was allowed would soon expire. The Jews came, therefore, to ask Pilate's leave to break the legs of the three crucified men and to remove their bodies.

The soldiers, being sent by Pilate, broke the legs of the two thieves. Then, coming to Jesus, and finding that he was already dead, they did not break his legs, but one of them opened his side with a spear, and immediately there came forth from it some blood and water. In each of these occurrences everything was divine. The soldiers had received no command to make any distinction between Jesus and the two companions of his torments. Although he was already dead they might with propriety have broken his bones; but it was necessary that the scripture should be fulfilled.

Moses had said, in speaking of the paschal lamb: "You shall not break a bone of it."[49] God had so ordained because the figure should be realized in Christ, the true Lamb of God, who would conceal the incorruptible divinity under the frail covering of human nature, just as in the body the bones, which are the hardest part of it, are concealed under the flesh. In the same manner it was either contrary to, or in excess of, the command of the officers that one of the soldiers should open the side of Jesus with a spear. But it was again necessary that a prophecy should be fulfilled: "They shall look upon him whom they have pierced."[50]

Joseph and Nicodemus.—Meanwhile, it was time to think of the burial of the Savior, now about an hour dead. At this moment there arrived a rich man, named Joseph, of the city of Arimathea. He was an officer of importance, remarkable for his justice and virtue. Himself a disciple of Jesus, but secretly for fear of the Jews, he had taken no part in their conspiracy or their evil doings, and he looked for the kingdom of God. He went boldly to Pilate and asked him for the body of Jesus. Pilate, astonished that Jesus should be already dead, sent for the centurion, and inquired of him whether it was true that Jesus was dead.

The centurion having assured him of the fact, Pilate gave over the body to Joseph, who came and took it away. But Joseph had not the glory of burying it to himself alone. It would seem that the death of the man-God gathered around him those who durst scarcely approach him during his life. Powerful virtue of the cross, and immediate fulfillment of the saying of the Savior himself: "When I shall be lifted up from the earth, I will draw all things to myself!"[51] Nicodemus, previously a hidden disciple, the same that had gone to consult him during the night, came also with a mixture, about a hundred pounds weight of myrrh and aloes. Joseph bought a shroud, in which he placed the adorable body of Jesus, after taking it down from the cross. They then wrapped it in linen with perfumes,[52] according to the custom which the Jews observed in burying.

It only remained to select a tomb. Now, quite near the place where our Lord had been crucified there was a garden, and in this garden a newly hewed-out sepulchre, in which no person had yet been laid. This sepulchre belonged to Joseph. Pressed for time, for the sabbath was about to begin, and invited by the proximity of the place, Joseph, aided by Nicodemus, laid the body of the Savior in the new sepulchre which he had cut out of a rock for himself; and, having rolled a great stone to the entrance, he went his way.

All that here appeared the effect of chance was arranged by an all-wise providence. It was necessary that the sepulchre should be near Calvary, so that there might be time to carry the body of Jesus thither before the repose of the sabbath would begin. It was also necessary that the sepulchre should be new, and that no one should have been laid in it, that it might represent in its manner the purity of the womb of Mary, and that there should be no question as to whether he who afterward arose from it was any other person than Jesus. In fine, it was necessary that it should be hollowed out of a rock, that no one could suspect it to have been pierced, and the body taken off by stealth.

Meanwhile, Mary Magdalen, and Mary the mother of James and Joseph, who had come from Galilee with Jesus, were there sitting near the tomb. The burial being ended, they returned from the place in order to prepare spices and ointments; but they remained at rest on the sabbath day, according to the precept of the law. The enemies of the Savior did not do so. These strict observers of holy repose, who had so often accused the Savior of violating it by working miraculous cures, now violated it in their own turn, with the intention of burying his religion in the same tomb with himself.

The chief priests and the Pharisees came, therefore, to Pilate, and said: "Sir, we have remembered that this seducer, while yet alive, said: 'After three days I will rise again.' Command, therefore, the sepulchre to be guarded until the third day, lest his disciples come and take him away, and say to the people: 'He is risen from the dead.' This last error would be worse than the first." Pilate answered: "You have a guard; go, guard it as you know." They went, therefore, to the sepulchre, closed it fast, sealed the stone, and appointed guards. All these precautions were necessary to render the miracle of the resurrection incontestable, and never did human passions render more assistance to divine providence; for if, notwithstanding all these things, the body of the Savior disappeared, the power of saying that his disciples had taken him away was at once destroyed.

Limbo.—Yet he who was dead and who was guarded with so much care was free among the dead. In truth, the body of the Savior rested in the tomb, where, according to the prediction of the prophet, the flesh of the holy one of God should not be subject to corruption: but his soul descended into limbo, where all the departed just of ages gone by awaited in peace the coming of the Messias. He allowed himself to be seen by these souls whom he loved, and who had reaped beforehand the merits of his blood. He announced the gospel to them, that is, his life, his death, his approaching resurrection, the speedy accomplishment of all their desires, the consummation of their glory in heaven, of which, as chief of all the saints, he had made the conquest for his members.

Now, the Savior had been laid in the tomb about six o'clock in the evening, a few moments before the beginning of the solemn sabbath of the Pasch. His body remained here until the midnight of this day, which was counted the first of his burial. It remained here during the whole of the sabbath: this was the second day. It remained here from the midnight which ended the sabbath until the dawn of the first weekday, or the day corresponding to our Sunday: this was the third day. Ever-memorable day! on which, for the fulfillment of promises, figures, and prophecies, the Messias should arise victorious from the grave.

It has not pleased God to reveal to us the precise moment at which this great event took place. Everything leads us to believe that it was between the dawn and the sunrise. The Savior arose by his own power, leaving on the floor of his sepulchre the shrouds in which he had been wrapped, to be, as it were, the witnesses both of his death and his resurrection. He arose without noise, without display, and came forth from the tomb as he had come forth from the womb of his Blessed Mother; in other words, he did not remove the stone, but passed through it with his glorious body. The guards did not observe him.

The holy women.—Meanwhile, Mary Magdalen, Mary the mother of James, and Salome, having bought aromatics to embalm the Savior, came out very early in the morning with their sweet burdens, and arrived at the sepulchre a little after sunrise: they were not aware that guards had been placed there. It was on this account that, foreseeing no other obstacle, they said to one another: "Who shall roll away for us the stone that is before the sepulchre?" For this stone was very large. They were thus considering their situation, when the Lord removed all their difficulties in a moment.

Suddenly there was a great earthquake. An angel descended from heaven, and, rolling back the stone, sat upon it. His countenance was as lightning and his raiment as snow. The guards were so terrified that they fell to the ground half dead. As for the holy women, they entered the sepulchre, but did not find there the body of the Lord. Magdalen immediately ran in search of Peter and the disciple whom Jesus loved, and said to them: "They have taken away the Lord out of the sepulchre, and we know not where they have laid him." Hereupon, Peter and John ran to the sepulchre; but they only saw there the linens and the napkin that had been on Jesus's head. They then returned.

Apparition to Mary Magdalen.—Magdalen, detained by her love, could not resolve on following them: she remained at the entrance of the tomb weeping. As she wept, she stooped and looked into the sepulchre. There she beheld two angels, clothed in white, sitting where the body of Jesus had been laid, one at the head, the other at the foot. "Woman," they said to her, "why weepest thou?" "Because," she replied, "they have taken away my Lord, and I know not where they have laid him." After these words, turning back, she saw Jesus standing near; but she did not recognize him. "Woman," he said to her, "why weepest thou? whom seekest thou?" She, supposing that it was the gardener, said: "Sir, if thou hast taken him hence tell me where thou hast laid him, and I will carry him away." Jesus said to her: "Mary." She, turning, said to him: "Rabboni," that is, "Master," and fell at his feet, to embrace them. "Do not touch me," said the Savior, "for

I am not yet ascended to my Father; but go to my brethren, and say to them: I ascend to my Father and your Father, to my God and your God." He did not charge her merely to announce his resurrection to his disciples: he wished her also to teach them that he was risen never to die again, and that he had only a little time to sojourn on earth. Magdalen, overjoyed, set out immediately.

Scarcely was she gone when the other holy women came to the sepulchre. One of the angels said to them: "Fear not, for I know that you seek Jesus of Nazareth, who was crucified. Why do you seek among the dead him who is alive? He is not here, for he is risen, as he said. Remember that, when he was yet in Galilee, he said to you: 'The Son of Man must be delivered into the hands of sinners; he must be crucified; and on the third day he shall rise again.' Come and see the place where the Lord was laid. Go quickly and tell his disciples and Peter that he is risen, and that he goes before you into Galilee. There you shall see him, as he told you." They then recollected what Jesus had said.

Seized with fear and filled with joy, they left the sepulchre, and ran to communicate the good news to the disciples. They said nothing to anyone, so much afraid were they; but their fear soon subsided, and their joy was perfected. Suddenly Jesus appeared to them, and said: "All hail." They came near, and, embracing his feet, adored him. "Fear not," added the Savior. "Go, tell my brethren to go into Galilee—there they shall see me." They announced these things to the eleven apostles and all the other disciples, who looked on what they said as a dream, and gave no credit to their words. Mary Magdalen had no better success.[53]

Conduct of the guards and the leaders of the synagogue.—The incredulity of the apostles did not proceed from an evil disposition. They all ardently desired that their divine master should rise again; but they feared too much that it should not be so to believe easily that it was really so. They had not met with proofs sufficiently strong, because they longed to be convinced and were afraid lest they should only flatter themselves with a vain hope. The case was quite different with the members of the synagogue: they did not doubt the resurrection of the Savior. But these hardened men only sought to stifle proofs, and to prevent, as far as lay in them, the world from believing that which they were obliged to believe. God, who wished to more and more convince them, because he wished to save them, sent them witnesses whom they could not suspect. After the holy women were gone, some of the guards went down to the city and related to the chief priests all that had occurred.[54] Forthwith the council was assembled to deliberate on what should be done. The leaders of the synagogue at once perceived the consequences that would follow in Jerusalem and throughout all Palestine from the testimony of the guards, if liberty were granted them to speak according to their conscience. The following is the scheme to which they had recourse.

Taking the soldiers aside, they gave them a large sum of money and taught them their lesson thus: "You shall say: 'His disciples came by night and took him away while we were asleep.' If the thing should come to the ears of the governor, and he should wish to investigate your carelessness in keeping guard, we will manage the matter so well that he will believe us, and you shall not be disturbed." The soldiers, having received the money, did as they were told; and this report is spread among the Jews to the present day. It was worthy of those who had purchased for money the blood of Jesus Christ to procure also for money this gross imposition, which they opposed to the certainty of his resurrection!

Thus, to pay for having it rumored abroad among the people that the disciples of the Savior took him away under the cover of night and while the guards were sleeping—such was the last resource of a blind hatred: a pitiful resource, which ended only in covering with confusion those who availed themselves of it, and the weakness of which is apparent to all eyes.

Proofs of the resurrection.—1. It has never been known that a number of soldiers, keeping watch in a company on something entrusted to them, for which they should answer on their honor and their life, have all fallen asleep at the same time. Such a fact cannot be found in the military annals of any people.

2. Let us suppose, however, that the soldiers did fall asleep; how could a stone of enormous size be removed, the sepulchre entered, and the body brought out and carried off? It was necessary that all this should be done in a groping way, the time being night, and also that several men should take part in it. How, I say, could it be done without a single one of the soldiers, placed at the distance of a couple of steps, awaking? A fact so devoid of probability would require, as St. Augustine observes respecting it, some better evidence in its favor than that of sleeping witnesses.

3. If the guards were asleep, how did they know that the body was taken away, and how did they know the persons who took it away? If they were not asleep, why did they allow it to be taken away?

4. Who, then, might have taken it away? Undoubtedly, the disciples. But they had no interest in doing so. In point of fact, either the disciples expected to see their master rise again from the dead, as he had foretold, or they did not expect it. If they expected it, they ought to have left to their master the care of verifying his prediction. They had no need to involve themselves in an attempt equally dangerous and criminal. If they did not expect it, no motive, no interest, no hope could engage them to take him away and to make up the story of his resurrection. On the side of the world, they had everything to fear—the hatred, the contempt, all the punishments reserved for forgers, for violators of tombs, for daring breakers of the seal of public authority. On the side of heaven, they could look for nothing but the punishments reserved for impostors and blasphemers, since they would have endeavored to pass off as a God a man who was not God, a man who had grossly deceived them.

5. An unanswerable proof that the Jews themselves, that is, the chief priests and the leaders of the synagogue, did not believe that the apostles had taken away the body of the Savior, is that they never dared to reproach them with this pretended crime. When they imprisoned and scourged St. Peter, St. John, and the other disciples; when they put to death the two Sts. James and St. Simeon, did they accuse them of having taken away the body of the Savior and falsely proclaimed his resurrection? Not they. They only accused them of having preached in spite of a prohibition given them.

It is, therefore, proved beyond question that this pretended stealing away of the Savior by his disciples is only a gross fable invented by the synagogue to deceive the people, and to justify as far as possible its own incredulity and deicide—a fable so absurd that the synagogue itself made no account of it.[55]

PRAYER

O my God! who art all love, I thank thee for having sent us a Savior who was pleased, not only to die in atonement for the sins of the world, but also to die as a God, and to rise again in order to confirm our faith; grant us the grace to die as Christians, that we may one day rise glorious with him.

I am resolved to love God above all things, and my neighbor as myself for the love of God; and, in testimony of this love, I will assist at Mass as I should have assisted at the death of our Lord on Calvary.

Lesson 15: Glorious Life of the Messias

By withdrawing his body from the Jews, the Savior had proved to them his resurrection. This proof was unanswerable; for, since they had made themselves masters of his body, they should either reproduce it after the third day or acknowledge that it was risen. They did not escape from this alternative by bribing sleeping witnesses to say that it had been taken away. Its removal should have been juridically proved and the authors and accomplices of so daring an outrage severely punished. But there was not the slightest desire in the world to enter on such a procedure, the result of which would inevitably have turned to the confusion of the really guilty.

The Savior appears alone to certain witnesses, and why.—Here you ask, perhaps, why the Savior did not after his resurrection show himself to the Jews, to the synagogue, to the whole city of Jerusalem, in order to confound their incredulity. We answer that he was under no obligation to do so. To whom, indeed, is it pretended that he was obliged to manifest himself so evidently? To the lax governor, who had condemned him against his conscience? To the voluptuous Herod, who had mocked him? To the priests, the doctors, the Pharisees, who had never ceased to pursue him with their calumnies and intrigues, until they led him to Calvary? To those furious Jews who, after being laden with his benefits, had asked his death with wild shouts, and prayed that his blood might fall on them and their children?

By what had all these criminals merited the favor of an apparition from him? Had he not, then, done enough for their salvation? Is it reasonable to suppose that God ought to pour out his graces more abundantly in proportion as they are abused, and multiply the proofs of the faith in proportion as they are despised?

Unreflecting men would wish that he had in some manner forced his enemies to silence by the irresistible splendor of his glorious presence: this is precisely what he did not wish. If he wishes that faith should be justified in order to be reasonable, he also wishes that it should be free in order to be meritorious. He owes sufficient proofs to all; but the man who receives fewer has no right to complain, or to imagine that there is an injustice done him, because another receives more. You ask why the Savior, risen again, did not appear to the whole city of Jerusalem, to the synagogue, to all his enemies. And I—I will ask you why he did not appear at Rome, at Corinth, at Ephesus, at every place where his resurrection was preached as the foundation of his religion. In this manner our questions would have no end.[56]

We will add with St. Chrysostom that his manifestation would have been useless to the Jews, and that, if it would have converted them, it would not have been denied them: but that which had followed the resurrection of Lazarus clearly proved the contrary. In point of fact, so striking a miracle as that of bringing forth from the tomb a man four days dead—with all the marks of corruption—and showing him alive before all the people—with his fetters still on him—so far from converting them, only rendered them more furious, since it was for this very thing that they determined to put the Savior to death. They had not pardoned the resurrection of another: Would they have pardoned his own?

Assuredly they could no longer injure his Person, but their implacable hatred would not have failed to prompt them to a new deicide. Their conduct toward the apostles is a proof of it: they scourged them and put them to death whenever they could. If they treated in this manner the disciples, would they have spared the master? Accordingly, where was the good of exposing himself to a new attack? The chastisements which they had already merited were heavy enough: it was a mercy of the Savior to hide himself from their gaze.[57]

We will also add that he sufficiently manifested his resurrection by his disciples. In point of fact, the testimony of the apostles, supported by astounding miracles, furnished an unanswerable proof of it. The apostles, by their miracles, made public the resurrection of their master, and in a manner placed it before the eyes of the whole nation. Did not the risen Savior show himself in the midst of the Jews as often as the apostles wrought, by his power and in his name, some of the miracles of which we read the interesting account in their history? It was by them that he wished to manifest himself to the Jews. It was by them that he manifested himself to the world. It was by them that he converted the nations. It is still by their testimony, continued throughout the course of ages, that he addresses himself to us. What could the Jews require more than all others?

Conclusion: the Savior manifested his resurrection to unexceptionable witnesses; the testimony of these witnesses is known; this testimony has convinced the world: What more is needed to prove that we are wise in our belief, inexcusable in our unbelief?

Meanwhile, the Savior, whose design it was that the apostles should preach his resurrection throughout the whole world, and confirm it by their death, was pleased to convince them of it fully by appearing to them, and, so to speak, delivering himself into their hands, since he even permitted them to touch his sacred members. But it was only by degrees he led them from the state of incredulity in which they at first languished to that immovable faith which they afterward communicated to the whole world, and which they ultimately sealed with their blood.

The first proof that he gave them was the announcement of the holy women and the sight of his open tomb, with the circumstance of the linens thrown aside and the napkin wrapped up, which at once destroyed the idea of a stolen removal. He next appeared to some of them in particular, afterward to the assembled eleven: it was then that he permitted them to touch him, and that he ate with them. Finally, he showed himself to more than five hundred brethren at the same time.[58] We shall now speak of some of these apparitions, beginning with the special ones.

He appears to Simon Peter.—Before all the others, Simon Peter had the happiness of contemplating his risen master.[59] It was on the very Sunday of the resurrection; but we do not know the moment, the place, or the circumstances. His penance caused his fault to be forgotten, and, far from being rejected, he was not less favored on account of it, since he was the first of the apostles to whom the Lord showed himself. God pardons as a God, that is, he pardons fully: he loves and caresses the penitent sinner as if he had never received any insult from him. We do not lose all the fruit of this apparition, whose details are unrecorded, if we gather from it so consoling a truth.

He appears to James the Less.—There was also a special apparition to James the Less, called the brother of the Lord, to whom he was closely related according to the flesh.

He appears to the two disciples of Emmaus.—That which follows was accompanied with circumstances very remarkable. In vain shall we look for anything more simple or touching than the account of this new apparition. Toward the close of the day of the resurrection, two of the disciples were going to a town called Emmaus, distant from Jerusalem some sixty furlongs, about seven miles: they conversed with each other on all that had lately happened. While they spoke and reasoned together, a traveler joined their company. It was the Savior himself; but their eyes were held that they might not know him.

He said to them: "What is this discourse that you hold with each other as you walk, and why are you sad?" One of them, whose name was Cleophas, answered: "What! art thou only a stranger in Jerusalem, and knowest thou not the things that have come to pass there in these days?" "What things?" said he. They answered: "Concerning Jesus of Nazareth, who was a prophet, mighty in work and word before God and all the people. The chief priests and the magistrates delivered him to the Gentiles to be condemned to death, and crucified him. His death surprised and alarmed us; for we hoped that it was he who should rescue Israel from the yoke of foreigners. What fills up the measure of our sadness is that it is now the third day since these things were done. Yea, and some women of those who, like ourselves, had embraced his doctrine, have greatly astonished us. They were at his tomb before day, and not finding his body, returned, declaring that they had seen angels, who say that he is alive. They saw the sepulchre open, and the linens in which the body had been wrapped; but the body itself they found not."

Thus, the two disciples did not yet know what they ought to believe: they wavered between hope and fear. The Savior, who had listened to them so far without any interruption, then replied in a tone which might well have amazed them: "O men of little sense! O men slow to believe the oracles of the prophets! Was it not necessary that the Christ should suffer in this manner, and so enter into his glory?" Then, beginning with Moses, and passing through the rest of the prophets in succession, he explained to them what was written of him in all the scriptures. His reprimand and his teaching ought to have revealed him to them: he did not permit it.

Meanwhile, they found themselves near the town of Emmaus, to which they were going, and he made as though he would pass farther; but they prevailed on him to stay with them, saying: "Remain with us, for it is growing late, and the day is far spent." He therefore entered, and, while he was at table with them, he took bread and blessed it, and, having broken it, presented it to them; that is, he communicated them with his own hand.[60] Then their eyes were opened, and they recognized him; but he disappeared—leaving on their minds the full and entire conviction that this was he, and that he was truly risen from the dead. On which they began to say to each other: "Was not our heart burning within us while he spoke to us along the way, and expounded the scriptures to us?"

Replenished with this sacred fire, they arose the same hour and returned to Jerusalem. Here they found the apostles gathered together with a number of the disciples, who said: "The Lord is truly risen; he has appeared to Simon." They, on their side, recounted what had happened to them during the journey, and how they had recognized him in the breaking of bread. Oh yes, indeed, it is in the breaking of bread, it is at the holy table that we recognize the Savior!

He appears to the assembled apostles.—They were still conversing on the subject when Jesus appeared. The doors were all firmly closed for fear of the Jews, and the Savior, to make his disciples understand that he was truly risen from the dead to die no more, as well as that his body enjoyed all the qualities of a glorified body, passed through the doors without opening them, and was present suddenly in their midst. He saluted them with these tender words: "Peace be to you; it is I, fear not." He reproached them for not having believed those who had seen him risen; but in their trouble and alarm they imagined that they saw a spirit. He then said to them: "Why this fear? Why do these thoughts come into your minds? See my hands and my feet: it is myself. Touch and see: a spirit has neither flesh nor bone, as you see me to have." After saying this, he showed them his hands and his feet and his side.

The disciples, seeing the Lord, were filled with joy; but as in the midst of their joy they had not yet arrived at a fully settled belief, and were wholly astonished, he said to them: "Have you anything here to eat?" They presented to him a piece of broiled fish and a honeycomb. He ate thereof, and, taking the remainder, kindly distributed it among his disciples, as a father and master would. It was thus that he used to act during his mortal life, when he ate and drank with them.

He appears to Thomas.—There still remained one unbeliever to convince: this was Thomas, also called Didymus, one of the twelve apostles. He was not with the others when Jesus came. They said, therefore, to him afterward: "We have seen the Lord." He answered them: "Unless I see in his hands the print of the nails, and put my finger into the place of the nails, and my hand into the wound of his side, I will not believe." This was to make a law for his master, and no one was less worthy of such a favor than he who dared to require it. But this amiable master did not wish at the time to listen to anything but his own goodness, that he might show us the extent of his adorable condescension.

Accordingly, after eight days, as the disciples were again in the house, and Thomas with them, Jesus came, the doors being closed, and stood in the midst, addressing the company in his usual manner: "Peace be to you." Then he said to Thomas: "Place thy finger here, and see my hands; and bring hither thy hand, and put it into my side: and be not faithless, but believing." Thomas exclaimed: "My Lord and my God!" Jesus said to him: "Because thou hast seen me, Thomas, thou hast believed: blessed are they who have not seen and have believed!"[61]

This would seem an excessive condescension; but the Savior did not think that he could do too much to impregnably establish the belief of his resurrection in the minds of those whom he was preparing to be its preachers and martyrs, and to render unquestionable the truth of a mystery without which, as one of his apostles remarks, our faith would be vain and our hope groundless. To more and more demonstrate the certainty of this miracle, which is the very foundation of Christianity, the Savior multiplied his apparitions during the forty days that he yet remained on the earth. His two occupations at this time were to prove to his apostles that he was truly risen and to instruct them thoroughly in his doctrine.

Until the day of his ascension he did not cease to appear to them—now on the shore of the Sea of Tiberias, where he blesses them with a miraculous draught of fishes, and eats with them; again, on a mountain of Galilee; at another time, in Jerusalem; finally, on Mount Olivet, from which he ascends into heaven before their eyes. The apostles did not fail on their side either to raise difficulties or to desire proofs. They yielded only to the most conclusive evidence: God permitting their incredulity for the maintenance of the faith in all succeeding ages.[62]

"Besides these apparitions," says St. John, "the Savior wrought many other miracles, which are not written in this book. But these are written that you may believe that Jesus Christ is the Son of God, and that, believing, you may have life in his name."

He gives them an understanding of the scriptures.—When, therefore, the Savior saw his disciples and apostles fully convinced of the truth of his resurrection, he justly reproached them with their long incredulity. "Is not this," he said, "what I told you while I was yet with you before my passion: that everything written of me in the law of Moses, in the prophets, and in the psalms, should be accomplished to the letter? Is it not written that the Christ should suffer in this manner, that he should rise from the dead on the third day, and that he should enter thus into his glory? Is it not also written that, after his resurrection, the remission of sins should be preached in his name throughout the whole world, beginning at Jerusalem? Now, it is you—who have been the witnesses of my life, my death, and my resurrection—that are appointed for this enterprise." At the same time he opened the minds of his apostles to the understanding of the scriptures.

From all that precedes, we observe that the life of the Savior after his resurrection was very different from that before his death. He was free from the various necessities of the body. He no longer showed himself to the wicked men who had put him to death. The model of man in all conditions, he wished to teach us what our life ought to be after our resurrection to grace. Like his resurrection, ours ought to be perfect, public, and permanent; if it is so, our life, like his, shall be crowned with a glorious ascension into heaven.

Explanation on miracles.—Since the resurrection of the Savior, of which we have just related the history, is the greatest of miracles, and serves not only as a confirmation of all other miracles but as the chief foundation of religion, it seems to us fit to say a few words here on miracles in general. Impiety having done everything possible to confuse this matter, so essentially important, it will be our duty to reduce it to its simplest form. Two or three questions will suffice for this purpose.

1. *What is a miracle?* A miracle is something that is contrary to the laws of nature, and that can only be wrought by the power of God. Thus, to stop the sun in its course; to feed thousands of persons with five loaves and five little fishes; to restore by a word, or merely by a touch, life to the dead, sight to the blind, hearing to the deaf, speech to the dumb, strength to the paralyzed; to walk on the sea; to calm the storm and still the waves: these are miracles, for they are things contrary to nature, and only capable of being brought about by God himself, or by those on whom he confers the requisite power.

2. *Can God work miracles?* This is to ask whether God can depart from the laws which he has established. "This question," replies a celebrated unbeliever, "would be impious, if it were not absurd. It would be doing too much honor to him who should answer it in the negative to punish him: it would suffice to leave him alone. But what man ever denied that God could work miracles?"[63]

3. *Has God wrought miracles to prove the truth of the Christian religion?* Yes, and many, by the ministry of the Savior and the apostles, and we are much more certain of them than of the most remarkable events of antiquity. On the one hand, they are attested by a greater number of ordinary witnesses. The whole world has believed them, since it was by reason of these miracles that the world was converted. On the other, they are attested by witnesses still more deserving of belief: more than eleven million martyrs have died in defense of their truth. Now, who are more worthy of confidence than witnesses that lay down their lives as an evidence of their sincerity? Accordingly, the unbeliever to whom we have just referred could not prevent himself from declaring: "The facts that concerns Socrates, of which no one doubts, are not near so well attested as those that concern Jesus Christ. The gospel has characteristics of truth so great, so striking, so perfectly inimitable, that the inventor thereof would be a more wonderful man than the hero."

4. *Do miracles prove the truth of the religion in whose favor they are wrought?* They do, and in the most unanswerable manner. In point of fact, God alone can work miracles, and God is truth itself; therefore, he cannot work miracles to authorize deceit. Now, God has wrought an immense number of miracles to prove the truth of the Christian religion; therefore, the Christian religion is true, and is alone true, since it alone can bring forward miracles in its support. Therefore, the only means to be saved is to believe what the Christian religion teaches and to practice what it commands.

PRAYER

O my God! who art all love, I thank thee for having sent us a Savior, who, to confirm our faith, was pleased to remain forty days on earth with his apostles after his resurrection: grant that our resurrection to grace may be perfect, public, and permanent, so that we may deserve to ascend to heaven with him.

I am resolved to love God above all things, and my neighbor as myself for the love of God; and, in testimony of this love, I will avoid evil companions.

Lesson 16: The Messias Is the Restorer of the World

Four thousand years of promises, figures, prophecies, and preparations, culminating in our Lord, are the magnificent demonstration that the babe of Bethlehem is truly the Messias, announced to the human race and expected by all nations since the beginning of time. This is what we have seen in the preceding lessons.

To this unanswerable proof must be added a fact as incontestable as it is decisive, namely, that since the coming of Jesus Christ the universal expectation of a restorer has ceased among mankind, for the simple reason that they have recognized in Jesus Christ the object of their hopes and their desires. Whence it must be concluded either that mankind, instructed by ancient prophecies and traditions, have been deceived, or that Jesus Christ is really the Messias expected by the human race. The Jews are the only exception to a full unanimity on the point; but their very incredulity is an argument in our favor. It was written that they would disown the Messias, so that if they had recognized our Lord Jesus Christ as such, he would not have been the Messias promised to their forefathers.

The life, death, and resurrection of Jesus have already shown us with what plenitude, and, so to speak, superabundance, he fulfilled the great mission of the Messias. It is useful, however, to explain this fundamental matter in greater detail. A more enlightened judgment on religion, and, above all, a stronger love and a deeper gratitude toward the Savior will be the fruit of this new study.

What, then, was the mission of this great liberator, so often announced, so magnificently described, so impatiently awaited? Reason, the prophets, John the Baptist (more than a prophet), come together to inform us that the work of the Messias was to take away the sin of the world. All peoples preserved the remembrance of the primitive fault. "God is provoked against us": this was the terrible dogma proclaimed by the expiations of all kinds, even to the inclusion of human sacrifices, which were employed throughout the world. When men desired the distinguished personage, the just man by excellence, the legislator, the Son of God and of the Virgin, who should bring back the golden age, what did they expect from him if not the reestablishment of order, the reconciliation of heaven with earth, the reign of justice—in a word, a deliverance from evil, that is, an atonement for sin, which is the real evil, the cause of all other evils?[64]

The prophets, divinely inspired, picture to us the future Messias bearing the iniquities of the human race, atoning for them by his sufferings, and creating a new world in which justice shall reign.[65] John the Baptist, commissioned to point out the Messias conversing among men, clearly acquaints us with his mission. "Behold," he exclaims, in a transport of joy, "behold the Lamb of God, behold him who taketh away the sin of the world."[66]

Finally, Jesus himself, summing up his various teachings, reveals, by the mouth of the beloved disciple, the nature of his work: "The Son of Man came to destroy the works of the devil."[67] Now, what are the works of the devil? Sin, and the evils that are its consequence. To take away the sin of the world is therefore the mission of the Messias—a grand mission, worthy of God alone. Now that we know the purpose for which the Messias shall come on earth, let us call to mind what has been proved, that Jesus Christ is a man-God, and see this amiable Savior at work.

First, what is the meaning of taking away the sin of the world? It is to atone for sin, to efface and destroy sin and its consequences, and to give to men the means of avoiding sin, so that those who avail themselves of these means shall be forever free from sin and its consequences.

In regard to God, sin was an outrage done his sovereign majesty; and its consequences the anger of God and his punishments.

In regard to man, sin was a disobedience to God; and its consequences all the evils that afflict man: in his mind—ignorance; in his will—concupiscence; in his body—diseases, afflictions, and death, and, after death, everlasting damnation.

In regard to God and man, the consequences of sin were their everlasting separation.

In regard to creatures in general, their ministration to the iniquities of man.

These are the evils which the Messias should repair, the disorders which he should rectify. Let us examine whether our Lord Jesus Christ has done so.

He took away sin in regard to God.—The Messias should take away sin in regard to God, that is, make amends for the outrage done his sovereign majesty, and so appease his anger. How effect this? By offering to God infinite humiliations, and a victim worthy of his wrath; for, since sin is an outrage committed by a rebellious creature against God, there is no reparation possible without humiliations, as there is no remission without shedding of blood.[68]

Infinite humiliations. And, accordingly, our Lord humbles himself even to perfect abnegation, says the apostle St. Paul, "who is equal to God, who has a right to the same adoration as his Father, humbled himself so far as to take the form of a servant, as to become man,[69] as to be made sin,"[70] that is a sin-offering. A God to be made a sin-offering! The highest degree of majesty and the lowest degree of abasement! Follow the Savior from the crib to the cross: Is not his whole life the most wonderful abasement that ever was heard of? Disowned, rejected, despised, confounded with the poor and the sinful. He appeared even in the midst of his disciples as a servant,[71] as the last of men; or, to use his own expressions, as "a worm of the earth" and "the outcast of the people."[72] Do his abasements leave anything to be desired? No: he could not descend lower.[73] Thus does our Lord repair the outrage done to the supreme majesty of his Father.

Let us see how he appeases his Father's wrath. He suffers. By reason of the infinite dignity of his Person, one of his tears, a single drop of his blood, would have sufficed to calm the anger of the Most High, and to efface the iniquities of a thousand worlds;[74] but this was too little for his love. Because he loved men, he wished to inspire them with a great fear of sin, a just esteem for their souls, an ardent love for himself, a profound respect for his Father, and an unchangeable resignation under the pains of life.

Infinite sufferings. For all these reasons Jesus chose the cross, that is, everything that would be most bitter to him, most meritorious for us, and most proper to repair the outrage offered to the Divine Majesty. If you wish to form some idea of the wondrous extent and infinite perfection of his sufferings, consider the answers to the following questions: What did he suffer? From whom did he suffer? How did he suffer? In what character did he suffer?

What did he suffer? The royal prophet informs us, when he calls him a "man of sorrow."[75] This expression includes all that can be said; for it means that all sorrows, all sufferings found their resting place in the Savior Jesus. External pains—poverty, rebuffs, hunger, thirst, calumny, blows, mockery, death on an infamous gibbet between two criminals and amid the insults and outrages of his people; internal pains—heart pangs, sadness, fear, shame, the agony that should be produced in the most loving of souls by the treachery of Judas, the denial of St. Peter, the flight of disciples, the presence of a tender Mother at the foot of the cross, the loss of so many sinners redeemed at so high a price: all these pains vied with one another in tormenting their innocent victim, even from the first moment of his incarnation.[76]

From whom did he suffer? He suffered from those whose abandonment, persecution, and ingratitude were so much the more sensible to him as he had greater reason to expect from them the warmest love and the most profound reverence. From the Jews, his brethren according to the flesh, the people whose sick he had cured and dead he had restored to life; from his disciples, whom, by an unexampled favor, he had chosen in preference to all other men; from his divine Father, who condemned him to drink the bitter chalice of sorrows to the last drop and to suffer all that the sinners of all ages deserved to suffer.

Infinite obedience. How did he suffer? He suffered with the meekness of a lamb, without a word of complaint, without demanding any compensation for the injuries done him. He suffered all that persons desired to make him suffer. See!—one wishes to kiss him, he yields his lips; another wishes to bind him, he presents his hands; another wishes to strike him, he offers his cheeks. They determine to scourge him inhumanly, he resigns himself even to this; they accuse him before Caiphas and Pilate, he is everywhere equally resigned. He is mocked as a fool by the court of Herod, and he is silent; he is abandoned to servants and soldiers, and he abandons himself still more to them. This face, previously so majestic, so beautiful in the eyes of heaven and earth, he exposes without a murmur to the spittle of the mob. His hair is torn. His beard is plucked, he utters not a word, he heaves not a sigh. It is the poor sheep that allows itself to be shorn.

In what character did he suffer? He suffered as the new Adam, representing the whole human race, and as the man-God, taking an immaculate humanity, to which he was personally united, and sacrificing it in adoration, atonement, thanksgiving, and impetration. All his sufferings being of an infinite value, he fully satisfied the eternal justice, and took away sin in regard to God.

He took away sin in regard to man.—The Messias should also take away sin in regard to man. Now, sin in regard to man means man's disobedience to God; and its consequences, all the evils that afflict man: in his mind, ignorance; in his will, concupiscence; in his body, diseases, afflictions, death.

Our Lord repaired all these things.

He took away man's disobedience to God; for in his Person he rendered man obedient to God, obedient unto death, even the death of the cross. "This is the reason," adds the great apostle, "why God, proportioning the glory of his Son to the extent of the sufferings endured by him, has raised him to such a degree of majesty and power that at the name of Jesus every knee bends in heaven, on earth, and in hell."[77] Our Lord, therefore, took away sin in regard to man.

He repaired the consequences of sin:

The first consequence of sin in man is ignorance. In the state of innocence, man knew God and himself; by sinning, he withdrew himself from God, who is the truth. His mind was immediately involved in darkness, as the world is involved in darkness by the setting of the sun. He gradually fell into the grossest errors with regard to the Creator and himself.

With regard to the Creator. You know how much the idea of the Godhead was disfigured among pagans, and how much the Jews themselves were inclined toward idolatry. You know how the most infamous passions were attributed to the divine being, how his adorable name was bestowed on the vilest creatures, and how, in fine, men came to such a degree of blindness that it was thought necessary to offer him human victims in order to appease him.

With regard to himself. Whence do we come? Whither do we go? Why are we on the earth? Have we any duties toward God, and if so, what are they? Have we a soul, and if so, is it spiritual or material, imperishable or perishable? On all these questions, so clear to man before his fall, you soon find nothing but monstrous errors and endless contradictions. Our Lord fully repaired this ignorance. In his sacred Person, man knew God and himself perfectly.

The second consequence of sin in man is concupiscence, that is, a violent inclination to evil, an irregular love of ourselves and other creatures. Before sinning, man was wholly attracted toward God; he loved God above all things, and himself in God and for God: everything coming from God returned to God through the medium of the human heart. Sin disturbed this admirable order. Man desired to become the center of the universe: he referred everything to himself, nothing to God; honors, riches, and pleasures were the only objects of his affections. He loved them passionately, as if to indemnify himself for the God whom he had lost. Hence, all kinds of crimes and disorders. Now, our Lord fully repaired this concupiscence.[78] In his sacred Person, man anew loved God perfectly, and loved himself and all other creatures in God and for God.

The third consequence of sin in man is temporal evils, that is, that afflicts the physical man—as slavery, injustice, violence, poverty, disease, death. Before sin, man was exempt from all these things; but after sin, death entered the world, accompanied by a long and dismal train of scourges, trials, and sufferings. These evils had come to their height when the Messias descended on the earth. Our Lord fully repaired temporal evils. In his sacred Person, man triumphed over slavery, wrongs, pains, death, all that could affect his corporal existence, and became impassible, glorious, immortal, triumphant in heaven for eternity. Our Lord, therefore, took away all the consequences of sin in regard to man.

The Messias should take away sin in regard to God and man together. Now, sin, considered in regard to God and man together, had produced their separation, an infinite eternal separation, which deprived God of glory and man of happiness—what do I say? which condemned man to everlasting torments.

Our Lord put an end to this separation. In the Person of the new Adam, God and man were united in the closest manner that it is possible to conceive, since in our Lord the divine nature and the human nature form only one and the same Person. In him, God and man were perfectly reconciled; for in him God was perfectly satisfied, known, praised, adored, and loved by man, and man perfectly reestablished in his true relations with God.[79]

He took away sin in regard to creatures in general.—The Messias should take away sin in regard to creatures in general. Now, sin, considered in regard to creatures in general, means their subservience to the iniquities of man. In the state of innocence, man turned all creatures to the glory of their author. The consideration of their beauty and their utility served him as a ladder on which to rise toward God in sentiments of praise and thanksgiving; so that all creatures, descended from God, returned again to God through man, their pontiff and their king. Man sinned, and transformed creatures into so many instruments of his sin. He carried his folly so far as to make them serve him as deities: he adored them all, one after another. Hence, the groanings, lamentations, and tears of creatures, according to the energetic expression of St. Paul,[80] to see themselves compelled in spite of themselves to outrage their Creator. Hence, their sighs for a Redeemer to set them free from the slavery of guilty man.

Our Lord put an end to this disorder. In his adorable Person, man used all creatures in accordance with the design of their author. Our Lord, therefore, took away sin in their regard.

We have already seen that he took away sin in regard to God and in regard to man. It is, therefore, a matter of faith that our Lord took away the sin of the world in the widest acceptation of the term. Accordingly, the babe of Bethlehem fulfilled the sublime mission which reason, the prophets, the Jews, and the Gentiles assigned to the great liberator of the universe. He is, therefore, the Desired of Nations, the envoy of God, the Savior, the object of the hopes of all ages that preceded his coming, as he is the object of the faith, the love, and the adoration of all succeeding ages to the end of the world.

But was it for himself alone that our Lord did all these things? Did he only wish to deliver from sin and its consequences, to sanctify, and to glorify one body and one soul, that is, the individual man united to himself? To think so would be to understand nothing of his mission, or of the end of Christianity. It was for us, it was for the whole human race, that he was sent. It was mankind in general that he came to deliver from sin and its consequences, to sanctify, and to glorify.

Necessity of union with Jesus Christ, the new Adam.—The question therefore is, how can we become participators in the fruit of the redemption? This is a fundamental question, containing in itself the whole economy of our salvation. He who does not understand it understands nothing of the work of human redemption. "The whole science of religion," says St. Augustine, "the whole Christian faith, properly consists in a knowledge of the two Adams. That which we have inherited from the first, that which we have gratuitously received from the second—nature fallen in Adam, nature repaired in Jesus Christ: this is the sum of religion."[81]

Now, the way to profit of the mission and the merits of the Savior is to unite ourselves with him. During the course of his public life the new Adam had been careful in his discourses to refer again and again to this important mystery; but it was in taking leave of his apostles that he endeavored to render most evident the indispensable necessity of this salutary union between him and all men. "I am the vine," he said to them, "you the branches. The branch cannot bear fruit of itself when separated from the stock. So with you: you can do nothing toward your salvation unless you are united to me. But he who abides in me, and in whom I abide, will bear abundant fruits. If he abide not thus he shall become a useless shoot, he shall be cut off as a worthless branch, he shall wither, he shall be gathered up for the fire, in which he shall burn without being consumed."[82]

Accordingly, our Lord occupies a place in the midst of the world like that of the tree of life in the terrestrial paradise. To live by his divine strength, to participate in his merits and his glory, it is necessary that we should be united to him, as it is necessary that the branch should be united to the tree, in order to be nourished with its sap and to bear its fruits. St. Paul the apostle admirably develops the doctrine of the Savior on this fundamental point. He sees only two men in the world: the first Adam and the second Adam. The first represents the human race degraded; the second, the human race regenerated. It is the union of the whole human race with its primitive root that renders it guilty and miserable; it is a union with its second root that must render it just and happy.[83] Confirming the doctrine of the apostle, the holy Council of Trent tells us distinctly: "As men, if they were not born by propagation from the blood of Adam, would not be unjust, since it is on account of this propagation that they contract injustice by the very fact of their conception, so, unless they are born again in Jesus Christ, they shall never be justified, since it is in virtue of this new birth that the grace which justifies them is bestowed on them through the merits of the passion of the Savior."[84]

It is, therefore, fully established both that our Lord requires each one of us to be united to him and that this union explains the whole economy of Christianity. Will you now ask what is the object of this union between the new Adam and men? The object is the same as that of the incarnation, namely, the abolition of sin—consequently, the regeneration of the human race and the glory of God. The next lesson will offer you a few details on the ineffable mystery of this union, which we shall develop further afterward.

From all the preceding explanations let us at present conclude, in accordance with the teachings of the Catholic faith: a) that, in the Person of Jesus Christ, man has been and continues perfectly restored; b) that it is necessary for each one of us to share in this restoration—otherwise "Christ will profit us nothing";[85] and c) that the way to share in this restoration is to unite ourselves with him, for, says the apostle St. Peter, "there is no other name under heaven whereby men can be saved."[86]

PRAYER

O my God! who art all love, I thank thee for having sent us a Savior who truly took away the sin of the world; grant us the grace to unite ourselves with him, in order to share in his redemption.

I am resolved to love God above all things, and my neighbor as myself for the love of God; and, in testimony of this love, I will perform all my actions in union with our Lord.

Lesson 17: The Messias Is the New Adam

First end of our union with the new Adam: Restoration of all things in Christ.—To transform all men into so many reproductions, as it were, of himself, by communicating to them his divine life, a life of grace, a life of truth, of sanctity in time, of glory and happiness in eternity: such is the first end of the union which the new Adam desires that we should have with him. To this union is due the wondrous change which, since the coming of the Messias, has been wrought in the ideas, the manners, the actions, and the sentiments of all the peoples that have become Christian. To it is also due the regeneration which has taken place in each one of us, and which is daily repeated before our eyes in every man who comes into this world. Let us make plain by incontestable facts a truth so consoling, yet so little considered.

Descendants of the old Adam, we are born degraded. Every part of our being has its share in the inheritance of paternal misery. In the mind, ignorance; in the will, concupiscence; in the body, disease and death: in the whole man, the absence of sanctifying grace or the supernatural life. Our union with the new Adam heals all these evils.

I. *Ignorance.* This is so true that the Christian child who knows his catechism, that simple abridgment of the new Adam's doctrine, has far clearer ideas regarding God and the perfections of God, man and the duties of man, the world and the uses of the world, than the greatest philosophers of paganism. The more simple and lively our faith in Jesus Christ becomes, that is, the more perfect our union with him becomes, the more fully shall we be freed from ignorance, the first consequence of sin. Do you wish to see this truth in all the splendor of its evidence? Examine it on a vaster scale, and answer the following questions: What was the mind of man before it had faith in Jesus Christ? What is it still among those peoples who have not faith in Jesus Christ? What does it become among those peoples who lose their faith in Jesus Christ?

II. *Concupiscence.* This is so true that the Christian who loves Jesus Christ and what Jesus Christ commands loves all that man ought to love, more perfectly than the most lauded sages of paganism. The more simple and lively our love for Jesus Christ becomes, that is, the more perfect our union with him becomes, the more fully shall we be freed from concupiscence, the second consequence of sin. Hence, those sublime virtues, that heroic devotedness to the relief and welfare of humanity, unknown in pagan ages, and almost incredible to men who do not live by the love of the new Adam. Here, again, it is easy for you to see this truth in all the splendor of its evidence. Merely weigh the following questions, like those above: What was the heart of man before it had the charity of Jesus Christ? What is it still among those peoples who have not the charity of Jesus Christ? What does it become among those peoples who lose the charity of Jesus Christ?

III. *Death and all other corporal miseries.* This is so true that the Christian who is truly united to Jesus Christ shows a resignation, a courage in the pains of life, which astonishes pagans, and amazes men who have become strangers to the life of the new Adam. It is easy for you to acquire evidence of this fact by studying it on a vaster scale, and considering the answers to the following questions, which resemble the previous ones: What were the calmness, the meekness, the dignity, the—I will not say the joy, but the resignation of man, in the pains of life, before the coming of Jesus Christ? What are they still among the nations to whom Jesus Christ is unknown? What do they become among men for whom Jesus Christ is no longer worthy of a thought?

What more shall I say? For the true Christian, death itself becomes sweet and desirable. In the maternal language of religion, a language which is spoken, too, by docile children, death has changed its name. It is called a sleep, and the place where the remains of man are laid, a cemetery, that is, a dormitory. This last word is like a perpetual witness to the prodigious change which Christianity has effected in ideas; for its origin is wholly Christian.[87] On this point, as on the preceding ones, if you wish to open an immense field for your meditations, and to see in all the splendor of its evidence the truth with which we are at present concerned, examine these few questions: What was death in the eyes of the ancient pagans? What is it still in the eyes of those peoples who are strangers to the grace of Jesus Christ? What does it become in the eyes of those peoples who break the tie that holds them to Jesus Christ?

On all the foregoing remarks, and, in general, on all the effects of our union with Jesus Christ, there is an essential explanation to be given. The work of the redemption will be completed only in eternity. There alone it shall bear all its fruits for us, as it bore them for the new Adam, who did not enjoy his glory until after his resurrection.[88] Such is the reason why all the consequences of sin in man—ignorance, concupiscence, temporal evils—did not entirely disappear after the incarnation.

Do you ask why we do not fully enjoy on earth the fruits of the redemption? The answer is easy. Even in the state of innocence, the present life was a trial. Since the time of the original fall, the trial has become more severe. Time is a delay granted in consideration of the merits of the incarnate Word to the guilty human race for the performance of penance and the regaining of heaven.[89]

Since the life of man on earth is a trial, it ought to be meritorious—consequently laborious. This is the reason why the Savior was not pleased that the consequences of sin should entirely disappear.

IV. *Our union with Jesus Christ gives us sanctifying grace and the supernatural life, of which the fault of the first Adam deprived us.* This is a matter of faith, and alone sufficient to make us appreciate the excellence of this deific union, whose end is to render us participators in the divine nature. Here, again, the effect of this union appears by incontestable facts. To what, do you think, are due the prodigies of meekness, constancy, purity, charity, forgiveness, devotedness, atonement, sanctity, that are the exclusive glory of Christianity? And that you may not doubt the reality of so many virtues, there are numerous authentic miracles to confirm them before the eyes of everyone—in other words, to prove the influence of sanctifying grace and the supernatural life in those pious Christians who practiced them while they were on earth, and their still more intimate union with God in the glory of eternity.

Oh, no! whatever you may say, man, abandoned to his own strength—man, deprived of the supernatural aid of grace, which makes us share the strength of God himself—is incapable of so many heroic virtues. Do you wish to have the evidence of this truth? Answer the following questions: What were the virtues of man, in their motive, in their object, before the grace of Jesus Christ? What are they still among those peoples who have not the grace of Jesus Christ? What do they become among those peoples who cast away the grace of Jesus Christ?

Such, in regard to man, are a few of the fruits of that salutary union which the new Adam desires to have with us.

As for irrational creatures, it was our union with the old Adam that subjected them to iniquity; it is our union with the new Adam that sets them free. The more perfect our union with the new Adam becomes, the more free also do creatures become. They are no longer placed—by the Christian—in the rank of gods; they no longer serve debauchery, pride, the indulgence of corrupt inclinations. Far from it, they are in his hands so many instruments of charity, mortification, and every other virtue—means to rise toward God—at most, objects of legitimate enjoyment. If it were necessary to relate the noble use which Christians, faithfully united to the new Adam, make of creatures, we should be obliged to write the history of all the saints and all the religious orders—those glorious contemners of riches, honors, and pleasures—those diligent stewards under the Father of the family—those generous distributors of the gifts of providence.

The deliverance of creatures, like that of man, is doubtless not yet accomplished; but it is begun. There was a time when all creatures—heaven, earth, water, fire, wheat, oil, wine, etc.—were enslaved to idolatry, and thereby even to Satan. But since it was said by the Savior: "I will draw all things to myself," creatures have begun to be delivered from the slavery of vain superstitions. Heaven no longer belongs to Jupiter, the earth to Vesta, the water to Neptune, the wheat to Ceres, the oil to Minerva, the wine to Bacchus: all have recovered the titles of their nobility. The world, become Christian, knows that these things are the works of the supreme God. They are consecrated to his worship. They are made channels of his grace: water, in baptism; wheat, in the most adorable sacrifice; oil, in the sacraments of confirmation, extreme unction, and holy orders.

If, already in time, creatures are so magnificently honored by grace, what will it be during eternity in glory?[90] "Thus," says the apostle St. Paul, "have all things that are in heaven and that are on earth been reestablished in Jesus Christ; for God was pleased to reconcile all things by him and for him, pacifying by the blood of his cross both the things that are in heaven and the things that are on earth."[91] To take away sin from man and creatures—consequently to restore all things: such, you see, is the first end of the union which our Lord desires to have with us.

Second end of our union with the new Adam: The glory of God.—The second is the glory of God.

The source of all truth, of all justice, of all perfections, of all virtues, and as such, the only adorer worthy of God, the new Adam wishes to unite himself with men, as the head with its members, in order to communicate to them his divine life, and to act in them as often as by their actions they glorify their heavenly Father. It was not enough for the Son of God to take a body in the womb of the Blessed Virgin, and to unite himself with one soul there: he wishes to unite himself mystically with all men, in order to make use of them as so many instruments by which he may himself glorify his heavenly Father.

Thus, in virtue of this union, the new Adam is an apostle in the apostles, a martyr in the martyrs, a confessor in the confessors, a virgin in the virgins. He preaches in a thousand places. He sheds his blood in a thousand manners. He endures macerations in the penitent, calumnies in the persecuted. He is poor in the poor, sick in the sick. He is everything that we are. He is wherever we are. He does all that we do. He suffers all that we suffer. And all for the honor and glory of his Father!

This is so true that he regards as done to himself whatever is done to his members. He does not say to Saul, "Why do you persecute the Christians?" but, "Why do you persecute me?"[92] He does not say, "The poor were hungry," etc., but, "I was hungry, and you gave me to eat," etc.[93] It is so true, indeed, that, identifying himself with us, he says in regard to superiors: "He who hears you hears me; and he who despises you despises me";[94] and in regard to the little and the weak: "Verily, verily, I declare that whatsoever is done unto the least of these little ones is done unto me."[95]

In a word, the end which the new Adam proposes to himself in this union is to make the whole human race a kind of second Jesus Christ, a single adorer, of whom the eternal Father, contemplating him from heaven, may be able to say: "This is my beloved son, in whom I am well pleased." See how admirably this sublime union corresponds with the mission of the Messias, by procuring for God the greatest external glory that can be desired.

Nature of our union with the new Adam.—The end, therefore, of the mysterious union which our Lord desires that we should have with him is the happiness of man and the glory of God in time and eternity. Let us make this union known in its nature and its means.

1. The union which the new Adam contracts with us is a supernatural and divine union, founded on a participation in his merits, and maintained by the influence of a head that is glorified in all the members of its mystic body.

2. A powerful and effectual union, in virtue of which men, adopted into Jesus and living by his Spirit, become morally one and the same person with him, are recognized by the Father as members of the only Son, and acquire, by the title of justice, a right to share in the heavenly inheritance.

3. A necessary and indispensable union, out of which the eternal Father, who places all his delights in his beloved Son, sees nothing on earth that is worthy of a reward in heaven.

4. An intimate, though moral, union, and hence as terrible to the wicked as it is advantageous to the just. In point of fact, if the virtues and good works of the adopted just man become, in consequence of the union of the members with their head, the glory and triumph of Jesus Christ, the vices and shameful actions of a Christian sinner become, for a contrary reason, and in a sense that horrifies us, the confusion of Jesus Christ. This confusion in one of his members deserves a new hell.

5. A union which, once contracted, without any preceding merit of ours, rests as firmly on the Son of God as it rests weakly on us, because it is either broken or maintained, enfeebled or restored, according as the adopted believer makes a good or an evil use more or less frequently of the means with which it supplies him and of the liberty which it leaves him. O my God, how great is man in Jesus Christ!

Means of our union with the new Adam.—The nature of our union with the new Adam being fully explained, we come to the means by which it is realized. Let us recollect that the first Adam, representing the whole human race, subjected his mind, his heart, his body, to sin, and so became a man of sin. It is by inheriting his life, his blood, his flesh of sin, that we become sharers in his fault and in the consequences of his fault. The second Adam subjected his mind, his heart, his body, to God: he was a man-God. It is by participating in his life, his blood, his flesh, so divinely holy, that we become heirs to his divinity and his sanctity.

The union of the human race with the first Adam was a complete union, for the whole human race was contained in Adam. This is the reason why we are degraded in all parts of our being—in our mind, in our heart, and in our body.

The union of the human race with the second Adam has been and must ever be a complete union—a union of mind, of heart, and of body. This union took place most excellently in the Person of our Lord. Hence, in the adorable Person of Jesus Christ, man was perfect in all parts of his being—in his mind, in his heart, and in his body.

After these great principles, what must we ourselves do to be regenerated individually? "We must," answers the great apostle, "bear the image of the heavenly man, as we have borne the image of the earthly man."[96] We must become the children of the new Adam by the communication of a heavenly life, as we are born children of the old Adam by the communication of an earthly life.[97] "As the old Adam," says St. Bernard, "is diffused through all parts of man, and has deranged them all, so it is necessary that the new Adam should now take full possession of man—of man, whom he wholly created, whom he wholly redeemed, and whom he shall wholly glorify."[98]

Connection of the Christian doctrine: Faith, hope, and charity.—But how shall we become the children of the new Adam? To attain this most desirable end we must unite ourselves with him by the three mysterious bonds of faith, hope, and charity—that is, by our mind, our heart, and our body.

These three great virtues are, as we have shown in accordance with the teaching of St. Augustine and St. Thomas, and as we shall further show in the course of these explanations, the three conditions on which we enter into the life of Jesus Christ, the three great bases of Christianity, the three sources whence flows and whither returns all religion; for they constitute the three essential acts of our cooperation with grace.[99]

The moment is come to explain the economy of this system, at once so grand, so simple, and so conducive to our deliverance and our happiness. We are therefore about to place here a complete exposition of the Christian doctrine, which we attach in its entirety to the virtues of faith, hope, and charity. Herein we follow the advice of the great doctors whom we have just named, and the example of our divine master himself, who chose the interval between his resurrection and his ascension in which to thoroughly instruct his apostles regarding the mysteries of the kingdom of God, that is, the truths of Christianity. On faith, we have to answer several most important questions.

1. *What is faith?* Faith is a gift of God, a supernatural virtue by which we firmly believe all that the Church teaches, because God has revealed it, and he is truth itself. Let us explain every word of this definition.

A gift of God. Faith is "a gift of God": that is, we cannot have it of ourselves by the resources of our own minds or the efforts of our own wills. Faith is an alms, a benefit, that can proceed only from the liberality of our heavenly Father.[100]

A supernatural virtue. Faith is "a supernatural virtue": that is, a disposition, a habit of the soul, which perfects our nature, or which leads us to good, and this good consists in believing firmly, without a shadow of hesitation or doubt: a supernatural virtue, that is, a virtue which makes us believe truths that we cannot understand by the mere light of reason, and that are intended to conduct us to an everlasting happiness, not our due.

All that the Church teaches. The authority which instructs us on the truths of religion being infallible, good sense points out that we should receive all those truths alike, without its being permitted us to select some and to reject others. We say "all that the Church teaches," because it belongs to the Church alone to propose a truth as an article of faith.

Because God has revealed it. We add: "because God has revealed it." In point of fact, the Church invents nothing; she is content with manifesting to us the truths which God has confided for guardianship and explanation to her.

Because he is truth itself. We end by saying: "because he is truth itself." Thus, the foundation of our faith is the veracity of God, who can neither deceive us nor be deceived himself. It follows hence that we are a thousand times more certain in regard to the truths of faith than in regard to things that we see with our eyes, or touch with our hands, or believe on the testimony of men.

2. *Is faith necessary?* To answer this question clearly, it is necessary to know that there are several kinds of faith.

Habitual infused faith. This is the gift and habit of faith which God pours into the soul at baptism. It does not suffice for adults: who are bound to make express and formal acts on the mysteries of religion. "He who believes not," says St. John, "is already judged."[101] He does not say, "he who has not faith," but, "he who believes not": which denotes a formal act.

Habitual acquired faith. By corresponding with the graces that are granted us after baptism, and frequently repeating our acts of faith, we acquire a new facility in believing, and this disposition is called a habitual acquired faith. Blessed habit! which, distinguishing the Christian from all others, makes him live in a superior world, to which the pagan, the Mahometan, and the heretic are strangers. This precious treasure he preserves as long as he does not commit a positive act of infidelity. Yet this kind of faith no more suffices than the preceding one for the salvation of adults: who are bound to make formal acts.

Actual faith consists in formally eliciting an act of faith on any truth of religion. Theologians teach that we are bound to make formal acts of faith, implicit or explicit: a) on coming to the use of reason; b) once a month afterward, at least; and c) at the close of life. But it is necessary to remark that the sign of the cross, a Mass well heard, the recital of the Lord's Prayer, the acceptance of afflictions, are so many implicit acts of faith, which suffice for the fulfillment of the precept.[102]

Implicit faith consists in believing the truths of religion confusedly and generally; saying, for example, "I believe all that the Church believes." It does not suffice for salvation.

Explicit faith consists in knowing and believing distinctly and in detail the truths of religion: we are not bound to know and believe them all with an explicit faith, but only a few, which we shall mention hereafter.

Interior faith is that which we hide within ourselves, without showing by any sign that we believe. It does not suffice. For we are bound to show our faith by our words and our works.[103] To do so is to have an exterior faith.

Dead faith is that which is not joined to sanctifying grace. We meet with sinners who are deprived of charity without having lost faith: the possession of the latter will not suffice for salvation. "Though I should have faith strong enough to remove mountains," says the apostle St. Paul, "if I have not charity, I am nothing."[104]

Living faith is that which is animated by charity, and joined to the practice of good works.

The foregoing explanations clearly answer the question proposed, and teach us two things. The first is that faith is indispensable to our salvation, that is, to our supernatural union with God in time and eternity. Our Lord himself has said: "He who believes not, shall be condemned."[105] And the apostle St. Paul: "Without faith it is impossible to please God."[106] Accordingly, the first thing that he should do who wishes to be united to the second Adam is to believe in him. He who has faith becomes the child of God and the heir of heaven.[107] As a matter of fact, he who believes submits his reason to the word of Jesus Christ. He receives and holds the truths which the Savior teaches: they become the foundation of his knowledge. The darkness and ignorance which he inherits from the first Adam vanish: light beams on his soul. His thoughts, from being human, natural, imperfect, false, become true, perfect, supernatural, divine. In the same manner, his reason participates in the reason of God himself, and his mind is transformed into the mind of the second Adam. Thus, slowly and gradually the child takes up the ideas of its master, by attending to his lessons and believing his words.[108] On the contrary, he who refuses to believe, refuses thereby to submit his mind to the word of the Savior. He does our Lord the most cruel of injuries, since he looks upon him as either deceiving or deceived,[109] and he remains in the darkness and ignorance of the old Adam. The reason is plain. The truths of religion, being supernatural, are too elevated for us to know them well by the mere lights of our degraded mind. He therefore condemns himself to be forever ignorant of them, who refuses to believe in the Son of God, who came down from heaven expressly to teach us. His refusal is a crime, since he has all the motives that ought to induce him to believe, and no legitimate reason to excuse him for not believing. The second thing that results from the foregoing explanations is that it does not, in order to be saved, suffice for an adult to have human faith, habitual faith, implicit faith, interior faith, dead faith: he must have divine faith—actual, explicit, exterior, living faith.

3. *Is faith reasonable?* This is to ask whether it is conformable to reason to believe in the word of God, who can neither deceive nor be deceived, since he is truth by essence. But if it is not reasonable to believe in God, in whom, then, will it be reasonable to believe? It will be necessary to doubt of everything. Yet unbelievers believe without hesitation in the most remote events of antiquity, on the word of a few historians, on the faith of some

inscription or monument. They would treat as a man of weak and shallow mind him who should call into doubt such facts. Well, is it unreasonable of a Christian to believe, on the testimony of God himself, in events and truths attested by all the sacred writers, unquestioned during so many ages, and confirmed by the blood of so many millions of martyrs, by the miraculous cure of so many diseases, by the conversion of the whole world, and by a thousand other prodigies?[110]

Our faith is therefore reasonable, since it rests on the strongest grounds. It is also reasonable in this sense, that reason can render an account of it with marvelous facility, and, in a few steps, ascend to God. But this is the exclusive privilege of the Catholic. His faith alone is reasonable; that of the schismatic or the heretic is not so. There is nothing easier than to show this. Let us take, for example, a Catholic child, or a grown Catholic, who is simple and ignorant, but who knows his catechism. Here is the analysis of his faith.

This child is a Catholic, and he knows it. He sees his pastor, who teaches him the catechism: this is the first part of his analysis. He knows that the teaching of his pastor is the same as that of his bishop, since it is his bishop who has prepared his catechism: this is the second part of his analysis. He knows by his catechism that the pope is the head of the Church and the vicar of Jesus Christ on earth; hereby, he comes to understand that his bishop is in communion with the pope, and with every other bishop subject to the pope, to whom all the faithful owe respect and obedience: this is the third part of his analysis. Thus, in his pastor the Catholic child beholds his bishop—beholds the pope—beholds every bishop throughout the world who is united to the pope—beholds Jesus Christ himself, true God and true man, teaching by the ministry which he has established, and teaching with a supreme and an infallible authority.

But is it reasonable to say that the sight of his pastor can assure the Catholic of the infallible authority of the whole Church; for the pastor is not the whole Church, and no one attributes to him an infallibility which he certainly does not possess? This is quite true; yet the Catholic child strikes the nail on the head, that is, he arrives at the most just conclusions. A familiar comparison will illustrate my idea. In France, there are collectors of taxes in every district. When the peasant sees the collector coming for the amount that is put down against him in the schedule, does he not behold in his person the comptroller of the taxes in the province, the minister of finance, the sovereign himself, though in reality he has never seen, and in all probability will never see, any of these authorities? This is an analysis of another kind, and the peasant is right, though the collector is not the comptroller of the taxes, nor the minister of finance, nor the sovereign himself. A single glance enables him to perceive in the collector the various degrees of dignity, until he arrives at the supreme degree. So with the analysis of the faith of the Catholic child or the uneducated adult. It is simple and uncircuitous; but how wise it is! how enlightened it is! how demonstrative it is! This arrangement came from the tenderness of our heavenly Father, that all—the ignorant as well as the learned, fools as well as sages—might easily be able to unite themselves with the second Adam by faith.

The schismatic and the heretic have not such an advantage. The schismatic, indeed, sees his pastor and his bishop, but no more. He sees branches, but branches separated from the trunk; he sees a body, but a body without a head; he sees several rings of the chain, but there is one wanting—the one that should attach all the others to Jesus Christ. The heretic is in a still worse condition. The protestant child, for example, sees the minister, just as the Catholic child sees the pastor, but no more. I mistake: his minister sends him to the scripture, to the pure word of God. But the scripture is a sealed book to the poor child. He cannot read, and, since he cannot read, who will set him right if he should understand the scripture amiss? Besides, who will say that the scripture in question is the word of God, and not the word of man? Hence, the Catholic can render an account of his faith; the schismatic and the heretic cannot do so.

4. *What are the characteristics of faith?* Faith should have three great characteristics: firmness, universality, and simplicity.

Firmness. Firmness consists in believing the truths of religion so unhesitatingly and positively that nothing in the world—the objections of the impious, the waverings of our own minds, or the temptations of the devil—may be able to shake it; it ought to be as immutable as God himself, whose Word is its foundation.

Universality. Universality embraces all the truths revealed by God and taught by his Church, without a single exception. This is the place to say: "All or nothing." Since, in fact, there is only one authority that teaches us, we have the same motive for believing all the truths that it proposes to us—those which we do not understand, as well as those which we understand; those which appear less important, as well as those which appear more important, to us; those whose practice is very easy, as well as those whose practice is not so easy.

Simplicity. The simplicity of faith consists in believing without argument, without discussion, because God has spoken. And what is there to examine when God speaks? To give us an idea of this admirable simplicity, the Savior, taking a little child one day, placed it in the midst of his disciples, and said to them: "Amen I say to you, unless you become converted and become as little children, you shall not enter the kingdom of heaven!"[111] This saying expresses all that can be said. But does it not condemn a great number of persons who take the liberty of criticizing and censuring that which, in religion, does not agree with their weak reason, and who aim rather at being philosophers than Christians?

5. *What are the advantages of faith?* The first advantage of faith is that it makes us acquainted with the truths of the supernatural order—of an order which, raising us above the senses and simple reason, makes us live in time the life of grace, to live in eternity the life of glory. Faith rescues our mind from the ignorance into which sin plunged it. It dissipates the clouds of error which the passions continually endeavor to raise around us. It places us beyond the reach of all those cruel doubts and hapless wanderings, into which man's reason invariably falls when abandoned to itself. We should require whole books to narrate the contradictions and absurdities of those who, extinguishing the torch of faith, follow only the uncertain glimmer of their weak reason. Interrogate them on any of those subjects that interest us most deeply: the existence or the providence of God—the nature of our soul—the duties that we owe to God, to ourselves, and to our neighbor. The only answers you may for the most part expect will be doubts, contradictions, and errors.[112]

Faith is, therefore, a torch, placed by the Savior in the hands of erring man, to enable him to find and follow again the way to heaven. It is a double wall, raised along the road of life to prevent us from wandering either to the right or to the left, and from falling into the abysses that lie on each side of us. What more shall we say? Faith is to reason that which the telescope is to the eye: where the naked eye can behold nothing, the telescope discovers worlds. What would the astronomer say if he were told that his lens is contrary to the sight? His answer is ours. Faith, far from being contrary to reason, is its light and its joy.

Another advantage of faith is that it applies a remedy to our pride. By imposing on us the obligation to believe, Jesus Christ showed himself in an admirable manner the Savior of the human race. Man had been ruined by pride. To cure this dreadful passion, and to render it unable to injure, he captivated the mind of man under the yoke of faith, by obliging it to believe truths which it could not comprehend. Making us thereby feel at every moment our extreme weakness, he placed us on the road of humility, which is the proper road for reason. Here God awaits us, to communicate himself to us, and to renew the ancient covenant, broken by original pride.

6. *What are the means to obtain and to preserve faith?* Persons may every day be heard saying: "I wish I could believe, but I cannot." You may answer them thus: "You cannot believe! You have not faith! What a misfortune!

"You have not faith. Your mind is therefore unacquainted with the world of lights and truths in which the patriarchs, the prophets, the apostles, the martyrs, the greatest geniuses of all ages have lived, and in which all the civilized nations of the globe still live! What a misfortune!

"You have not faith. There remains, therefore, nothing certain in your mind! Your soul is inundated with desolating doubts on your duty here and your fate hereafter! What a misfortune!

"You have not faith. There are no real consolations, therefore, for you in the trials of life, in the loss of friends and relatives! What a misfortune!

"You have not faith! You have, therefore, lost it! What a misfortune!

"What have you done with the grace of baptism, the lessons of your mother, the engagements of your first Communion? You have despised them. What a crime!

"When did you lose faith? Was it when you were chaste, modest, far from evil company? Was it not when you ceased to observe this conduct? What a crime!

"To recover faith it is not argument for the mind, but conversion for the heart, that you require. A good confession would be to the eye of your soul that which the operation for the cataract is to the eye of the body: it would in a moment restore to you the light of faith."

Then add: "You desire to believe, you say. He who desires the end desires the means. Now, have you adopted, do you seriously adopt, the means to arrive at faith? These means are known and infallible. They are: a) Prayer: faith is a gift of God. From him, and him alone, it must be asked. He has promised to grant it to humble and persevering prayer: 'Ask and you shall receive.' b) Study: no one can believe that which he does not know. It is, therefore, necessary to read works proper to instruct you on the truths of religion, or to make inquiry of enlightened persons regarding them, just as on a point of equity or medicine we consult lawyers or physicians. c) Fidelity to the duties pointed out by reason: before practicing all the precepts of the gospel, begin by abstaining from the acts which reason condemns, and by performing the other acts which it recommends; above all, earnestly wish to know and do all that God wishes you should know and do to please him. Be faithful to these means, and success will crown your efforts."

As for the manner of preserving faith, it is necessary, on the one hand, to carefully avoid the occasions of losing it, such as the reading of bad books, the society of wicked and irreligious men, etc., and, on the other, to make acts of faith, while carefully practicing all that it directs and shunning all that it prohibits. Let us not forget the saying of Rousseau: "Keep your soul in a state to desire that there should be a God, and you will never doubt that there is one."

7. *What are the sins opposed to faith?* The sins opposed to faith are: a) Infidelity: this is the sin of pagans and Jews, who refuse to believe religion. b) Apostasy, or the outward denial of religion: this is the sin of those who publicly renounce religion, or who pretend not to be Christians. c) Heresy: this is the sin of those who refuse, on grounds that appear good, and with obstinacy, to believe some of the truths of faith. d) Doubt: this is the sin of those who willfully and deliberately waver as to the certainty of any article revealed by God and defined by his Church. e) Ignorance: this is the sin of those who, through negligence, do not know those truths of religion which they are bound to know.[113]

Such, therefore, is faith, considered in itself. It is so precious a treasure, so great a consolation amid the evils of life, that we ought to hold it fast with all our might, and sedulously guard against every danger of losing it. Above all, let us flee from those books and persons that disseminate pernicious doctrines. Let the conduct of our forefathers serve us as an example.

History.—During the violent persecution raised by Hunneric, an Arian prince, against Catholics, the steadfastness in the faith displayed by persons of all ages and conditions was most remarkable. But none afforded greater matter of edification than twelve choir children, who were distinguished above the others by the sweetness of their voices, and who followed the confessors whom Hunneric had banished from Africa. Their talent caused them to be regretted by the enemies of religion, who pursued them in order to bring them back. Vain efforts! These noble-minded children would not leave their holy masters, on whose garments they laid hold; they allowed themselves to be beaten heavily with sticks; they despised the torments that were threatened against them. At length, however, they were carried off by force, and brought back to Carthage; but not one of them could ever be seduced, either by kindness or severity, which were alternately employed for this purpose.

A long time after the persecution, they were still the consolation and glory of the Church in Africa, living together at Carthage, eating together, and singing together the praises of God. The whole province revered these twelve children as so many apostles, who, by the example of their immovable constancy, taught all the faithful that the true Christian ought to sacrifice everything and to suffer everything rather than betray his faith and abandon his true pastors.

These young confessors were not alone in giving a brilliant proof of their attachment to the faith and to its ministers. "The people," says a historian, "followed the exiled bishops and priests with lighted tapers. Mothers bore their children in their arms, and, their eyes filled with tears, laid them at the feet of the confessors, saying: 'To whom do you leave us as you go to martyrdom? Who will baptize our children? Who will give us the sacrament of penance? Who will bury us after our death? Who will offer the divine sacrifice for us? Would that it were permitted us to go with you!'"[114]

It is not surprising that the people of Carthage should have manifested such deep regret on seeing their bishops and priests depart. Those who have any religion, any zeal for the public welfare, are not aware of anything that is more to be dreaded than the extinction of faith and the loss of the salutary helps which it affords. Are we fully convinced of the justness of their views?

PRAYER

O my God! who art all love, I thank thee for having sent us a Savior who vouchsafed to teach us how to reap the fruits of his redemption: it is by uniting ourselves with this new Adam that we shall become his children, and the heirs of his virtue and his glory.

I am resolved to love God above all things, and my neighbor as myself for the love of God; and, in testimony of this love, I will frequently make an act of faith.

Lesson 18: Our Union with the New Adam by Faith (1)

Objects of faith.—After making known faith in itself, it remains for us to show what are its objects—in other words, what are the truths that we must believe.

Faith is called a theological virtue, because it has God himself for its object: it is the first of its class. Hence, God, and all the truths revealed by God and defined by the Church, are the objects of our faith. Among these truths there are some above reason, some that we cannot understand: they are called mysteries.

Mysteries in general.—Is it reasonable, you may ask, to believe mysteries that cannot be understood? This is to ask a) whether God knows more than man, and whether he can oblige us to believe truths that exceed the limits of our understanding. To anyone who knows how to link two ideas together, the answer to this double question is not doubtful. Besides, when we believe mysteries on the word of God, we do not, to speak properly, submit our reason: we only submit our ignorance. We trust to the most ordinary good sense, which tells us that the positive and incontestable proofs of revelation ought to prevail over our ignorance. So astronomy trusts to the telescope for an acquaintance with worlds which the naked eye cannot behold.

It is to ask b) whether we ought to believe anything whatsoever. In point of fact, everything above, below, around, within us, is a mystery: we do not understand the whole of anything. For example, do you know how and why fire burns, air enables us to live, light shines upon us? Do you know how the grain of wheat, cast into the earth, multiplies, or how the wondrous instinct of animals is produced? Yet it has never occurred to any man to entertain the least doubt on these matters. And you believe them, though you do not, however learned you may be, understand them any better than I.

After this, thou weak and proud man! who dost not understand thyself, who dost not understand the grain of dust that thou treadest under thy feet, thou canst with a good grace pretend to admit only that which thou understandest! There are mysteries everywhere in nature, and let us add that, if there were none in religion, religion would be false. Religion is true only because it comes from God. Now, when God vouchsafes to reveal to us what he is in himself, and what he has done and will do for us, it is impossible that these truths should not be mysteries. An infinite being cannot, in his nature, in his decrees, or in his conduct, be comprehensible to a finite being.

Advantages of the mysteries of Christianity.—The mysteries of Christianity, which are the legitimate objects of every reasonable man's faith, deserve our utmost gratitude. Their benefits are innumerable and continual, to society as well as to the individual.

1. They put a rein on the eager curiosity of our minds, and place beyond the reach of investigations and sophisms those truths which serve as a foundation for thought, no less than for conduct. By obliging us to believe certain dogmas, God says to the human mind, as formerly to the mighty ocean: "So far shalt thou come, but here thou must break thy pride."[115] Will anyone say that it was wrong of God to raise barriers against the ocean? Thus, by revealing to us the mystery of one only God—infinite and incomprehensible—the Creator and ruler of the universe, and by obliging us to believe it, Christianity banished from the imagination of men all further regard for those hosts of strange divinities which were supposed to exist everywhere throughout nature. Now, by proscribing idolatry, an end was put to those fears, superstitions, and crimes which were inseparable from it, which still accompany it wherever it is practiced, and which are ever ready to break forth in shallow minds.

2. The mysteries of Christianity serve as a foundation for all virtues. In the most false religions there are, indeed, mysteries; but, far from leading men to virtue, they are only incentives to vice. Those of Christianity, on the contrary, promote virtue and support morality. They suggest motives of love and gratitude toward God, of charity toward our neighbor, of watchfulness over ourselves. Let us render palpable a truth unfortunately so little known.

Three principal mysteries: The Trinity, the incarnation, the redemption.—The august mystery of the Trinity, for example, is the first object of Catholic faith. Now, there is nothing in the world better calculated to elevate our minds than the knowledge of this fundamental dogma, nothing in the world better calculated to inflame our hearts than the lessons of high morality which proceed from it. There is one God; there is only one:

he is infinite, eternal, omnipotent. He created and he governs all that exists. There are three Persons in God, namely, the Father, the Son, and the Holy Ghost. Each of them is God; yet they are not three gods: they are only one God, having but one and the same nature, one and the same divinity. The Father, eternal, Almighty, the Creator and ruler of the world, does not proceed from anyone.

The Son, the eternal Wisdom, the splendor of his Father, proceeds from the Father alone. He is the Son of God, the second Person of the Blessed Trinity, and the only Person who became incarnate. There are in the Son of God made man, whom we name Jesus Christ, two natures—divine nature and human nature; consequently two wills—a divine will and a human will. But there is only one Person in him—the Person of the Son of God: as in every human being, the body and soul make but one person, so in the Son of God, the divine and human natures make but one Person. Jesus Christ suffered in his body and in his soul—that is, in his human nature: he died on a cross to redeem us. His body was enshrouded and buried. He arose on the third day by his own power. He ascended triumphantly into heaven, where he enjoys the same majesty as the Father and the Holy Ghost, and whence he will come at the end of the world to judge the living and the dead.

The Holy Ghost, the third Person of the Blessed Trinity, the substantial love of the Father and the Son, proceeds from them. The Holy Ghost was not made, nor created, nor begotten: faith tells us only that he proceeds from the Father and the Son. He is the Sanctifier. He is the life of our souls, which, without him, are in a state of death—that is, can do nothing meritorious of salvation. He never ceases to assist the Church.

Such is the teaching of faith on the adorable mystery of the Trinity. Let us learn to appreciate the happy influences of this fundamental dogma. Take away the mystery of the Trinity from the Catholic Creed, and the whole edifice of the Christian religion falls to the ground. But there is no religion outside of Christianity. If, therefore; religion is the basis of society, we must conclude that the mystery of the adorable Trinity, which is the basis of religion, is the pivot of the universe.

Then, again, this fundamental mystery is not presented to us as a purely speculative article of faith, but as an object of love and gratitude, as a sublime model of that sublime charity which should reign among us, and which should lead us to unity. Such was the desire of the Redeemer; that they may be one. He says, as the three divine Persons are one.[116] Now, the mystery of the Trinity shows us God always at peace with himself, always happy, in his own happiness, yet always concerned with the happiness of man, which he made the only aim of all his designs and works.

The Father created the world for his glory and our happiness: not one of his innumerable creatures that he did not submit to our empire, and destine for our service or our pleasure. After creating all things for us, he preserves and rules them by the laws of his sweet providence.

The Son, consubstantial with the Father, was pleased to make atonement for guilty man, in order to rescue him from the just punishment which he had deserved, and to restore him the happiness which he had lost. For this purpose our Lord vouchsafed to clothe himself with our flesh, with our weakness, and to dwell among us, so as to serve us as a master and a model. He gave his life for us. O prodigy of goodness! He still gives himself every day under the form of ordinary food, to unite himself more closely with his brethren.

The divine Spirit, the essential love of the Father and the Son, after speaking to us by the prophets, was sent personally to us to enlighten and to instruct us. Communicated by the sacraments, he works in us by his grace, and presides over the teaching of the Church.

These ideas are not only great and sublime, they are affecting and consoling. They elevate and soften the soul. God, great as he is, has occupied himself with me from all eternity: his whole being has been, so to speak, appropriated to my service. Man, however weak and sinful, is therefore precious in the eyes of God. He is not only my Creator and master, my benefactor and Father, in the order of nature; he is also, in the order of grace, my Savior, my consoler under afflictions, the intimate friend of my soul, and my everlasting reward. He demands virtue of me, but he assists me to practice it: he gives me an example of it, and shows me the reward that awaits me in the distance.

Is it surprising that this doctrine should have made saints? Is it surprising that it should have given birth to the purest sentiments of humanity, of charity, toward our brethren? Notwithstanding the fury of the passions, these sentiments still shine in Christianity; they have brought forth a multitude of useful institutions, such as have scarcely been dreamt of in other religions. The impious man,[117] who could ask of what use to the world or to civil society are the dogma of the Trinity and the other truths of Christianity, would give a conclusive proof of his little reflection and narrow judgment.[118]

Sign of the cross.—You have now heard the explanation, not only of the mystery of the Holy Trinity, but also of the mysteries of the incarnation and the redemption, the triple foundation of Christianity. These mysteries it is indispensable to know distinctly and to believe steadfastly in order to be saved. Lest any of his children should ever come to forget them, our Lord established a sign of easy and ordinary use, which is repeated every day by learned and ignorant, old and young. It is the sign of the cross, called with reason the "sign of the Christian," since it distinguishes us from Jews, Mahometans, and idolaters.

Now, everyone knows that there are two modes of making the sign of the cross. The first, by tracing with the thumb a little cross on the forehead, another on the mouth, and another on the heart. The priest and the faithful make it thus at the reading of the gospel during the Holy Sacrifice of the Mass. We impress the sign of the cross on the forehead, to show that we do not blush to be Christians or to perform the works of Christians; on the mouth, to show that we are ready to confess our religion; and on the heart, to show that we sincerely believe and truly love that of which we make profession with the mouth.

The second mode of making the sign of the cross consists in putting the hand first to the forehead, then to the breast, afterward to the left shoulder, and finally to the right shoulder, pronouncing the words: "In the name of the Father, and of the Son, and of the Holy Ghost. Amen." Hereby, we make it understood that we believe in and adore the three Persons of the Holy Trinity, in oneness of nature. The figure of the cross, which we form on ourselves as we pronounce these words, is a mark of our belief that the Son of God was made man; that he died on a cross to redeem us; that we are his disciples, and that we renew our baptismal contract to serve him with love and fidelity.

Hence, this sign must always be accompanied with great respect and recollection, as well as confidence.

In point of fact, the sign of the cross is all-powerful to banish the devil, our chief enemy, and to draw upon us the protection of God. The devil was vanquished by the cross. At the sight of this sign, he flees terrified. This rebellious angel corrupted creatures, and transformed them into so many snares for fallen man. This is the reason why the Church makes the sign of the cross over everything that she wishes to purify and to employ in her service. The devil, like a roaring lion, roams continually around us. It was to guard themselves against his attacks that the early Christians used so frequently to make the sign of the cross. "In action or in rest," says Tertullian, "coming in or going out, putting on our clothes and our shoes, taking our meals, day and night, we make on our forehead the sign of the cross."[119] Nothing is more profoundly philosophical than this practice. Taught by the example of our ancestors, let us therefore often make the sign of the cross, especially when rising and going to rest, before our principal actions, and in dangers and temptations.

To make this holy sign with piety on ourselves is to become inaccessible to the attacks of the wicked one, or to repair the breaches which he has effected in our souls, by renewing there the image of the Holy Trinity, to whose likeness we were created. To form it on creatures is to banish from them the evil influences of the devil. These influences, equally dangerous to the health of soul and body, we have particularly to dread, when we enter into intimate communication with creatures. Hence a fact, otherwise inexplicable: namely, that all peoples, even pagans, instructed by tradition, have never failed to recite prayers over creatures at the moment of coming into immediate relation with them by manducation. Accordingly, not only gratitude toward God who gives us food, but even an intimate acquaintance with the state of fallen nature, should teach us that the sign of the cross before and after meals is a duty.

All that we have said is so true that there are only two kinds of beings in nature who take food without praying, namely, sots and beasts. Ignorant contemners of the wisdom of nations, these sots are a truly pitiful sight to the sensible man. Beasts sometimes excite the innocent astonishment of children. One day a little girl of three years, whom we knew well, entered the kitchen of the convent in which she was being brought up. There she began to play with the cat, which soon left her to go and take some food. Suddenly the child cried out: "Mother, Mother! The cat is eating without saying any *Benedicite*."

The sign of the cross was taught us by the apostles. It was taught the apostles by Jesus Christ himself, as we are assured by a constant tradition. This sign has been in use since the first ages, in all the churches of the world.[120] No one will be surprised at this when he knows the marvelous power which the Savior was pleased to attach to it. There is not the least doubt that the sign of the cross, made with faith and piety, has the power to banish devils and to work miracles. The writings of the fathers of the Church render the matter certain. Let us give a few of their testimonies.

History.—Lactantius relates that the emperor Maximian, while in the East, desired to know the future. For this purpose he caused victims to be immolated, and searched among their entrails for some token of events to come. One day, as he indulged in this diabolical superstition, a few Christian soldiers, who were present, made on their foreheads the immortal sign of the cross. Instantly the devils took to flight, and the sacrifice was deprived of its results. The priests of the idols trembled, but could discover in the bowels of the victims none of the usual signs. They sacrificed new ones, but without any better success.

St. Gregory of Nazianzen, in his discourse against Julian the Apostate, relates the following fact. Julian went down one day into a subterranean sanctuary, inaccessible to the multitude: it was a fearful place to enter. He was accompanied by a famous magician. Scarcely had the emperor entered, when he was struck with terror. Frightful unearthly cries were heard, a black smoke filled the sanctuary, and fiery spectres flitted before his eyes. Shuddering at a sight so new to him, for he was already pretty ripe in years when he embraced idolatry, he had recourse to the sign of the cross. This all-powerful weapon, which he would have wished to destroy, he employed as a safeguard in his danger. The sign of the cross showed its might: the devils fled, the alarms of Julian subsided. But a new miracle follows. He wishes to continue his sacrilegious superstitions: his terrors return, the infernal monsters reappear. He again makes the sign of the cross, and the devils, overpowered and confounded, hasten to take flight a second time.

It is not only to banish devils, but also to cure diseases and to remove dangers which threaten injury to our bodies, that the venerable sign of our redemption has an omnipotent virtue. The fathers of the Church supply us with the most authentic proofs on this point.

A man whom no one will suspect of credulousness or weak-mindedness—St. Augustine—relates that a woman of Carthage, named Innocent, was afflicted with a cancer, which the physicians had declared incurable. "I learned it," says the holy doctor, "from a physician who attended her, and who was an intimate friend of my family. Despairing of the efforts of men, this woman had put all her confidence in God: the Lord vouchsafed to recompense her prayers and her faith. He told her in a dream to present herself at the church on Easter Eve, and, after going to the women's baptistery, to ask the first of the newly-baptized to make the sign of the cross on her cancer. She did so, and was immediately cured. The physician, on coming to visit her, found her in perfect health. Astonished beyond anything that can be expressed, he besought her to tell him what remedy she had employed. She related the occurrence to him with the utmost candor. 'I suspected,' said the physician, 'that you would have something extraordinary to tell me.' Then, in a moment, he added: 'Is it surprising that Christ should cure a cancer when he raised to life a man four days dead?'"[121]

We read in the life of St. Benedict that some wicked men, whose pride and malice could not endure the holy firmness of the saint, resolved to rid themselves of him. With this view, they put poison in a glass of wine, and gave it him to drink. Faithful to the practice of all true Christians, who never partake of nourishment without blessing it and returning thanks,[122] Benedict made the sign of the cross over the glass, which instantly fell in pieces.

St. Antony, though retired into the most remote parts of the desert, often experienced the fiercest attacks of the devils. These malevolent spirits would appear to him under a thousand frightful forms. The saint laughed at their impotence, and, to put them to flight, contented himself with making the sign of the cross. Instructing his disciples on the most effectual means of repelling the temptations of the devil, he said to them: "Believe me, Satan fears prayers, fasts, voluntary poverty, mercy, and humility, but above all an ardent love of Jesus Christ. The mere sign of the cross suffices to disarm and banish him."

Nothing would be easier than to multiply examples of the power of the sign of the cross. Those which we have just given will suffice to arouse our faith and to inspire us with the deepest respect for the august sign of our salvation. Woe to the Christian who makes it negligently! Shame on the Christian who blushes to make it![123]

In a very numerous assembly there was a person who would not dare to make the sign of the cross before a stranger at the beginning of an action when he was accustomed to make it. A zealous priest, observing him, made him blush for his laxity and tepidity. "What!" he says, "Jesus Christ was not ashamed to die on the cross to redeem you, and you are ashamed to form on yourself the sacred sign of your redemption! Take care: if you are ashamed of Jesus Christ before men, he will be ashamed of you before his Father."

Particular truths to be believed.—Besides the three great mysteries of the Trinity, the incarnation, and the redemption, there are other truths regarding which we must have a particular knowledge and an explicit belief: such as the immortality of the soul, and the eternity of rewards and punishments. Faith embraces all the truths revealed by God and defined by the Church, though a clear and distinct knowledge of the other dogmas is not so strictly necessary as it is of those which we have just mentioned. All these articles of faith, explicit or implicit, are contained, at least substantially, in the Apostles' Creed, which we are now about to explain.

General remarks on the Creed.—During the forty days which our Lord spent on earth with his apostles after his resurrection, he instructed them thoroughly regarding the means by which all men should unite themselves with him, to share in the fruits of his redemption. He was not content with saying to them in general: "He who believes, shall be saved." He taught them in detail whatever was necessary to be believed, and charged them to announce it to the nations. Obedient to the orders of their divine master, the apostles composed an abridgment of his doctrine—termed on this account the Apostles' Creed. They committed it to writing before they separated, and each one bore a copy of it with him on his particular mission, so that all Christians might have only one and the same belief, and might in the first place learn the fundamental truths of religion.[124]

Hence, there is really in the Church but one Creed—the Creed of the Apostles. Yet we distinguish four:

1. The Creed of the Apostles, which we are about to explain.

2. The Creed of Nice: it owes its name to a general council held in this city, in the year 325. This Creed is the same as that of the apostles, save a few explanations inserted by the council, to confound the Arians, who denied the divinity of our Lord. For example, in the second article, the council says: "We believe in one only Lord Jesus Christ, the only Son of God, begotten of the Father; God of God, light of light, true God of true God, begotten and not made, consubstantial with the Father, by whom all things were made."

3. The Creed of Constantinople, so called from the general council held in this city, in the year 381. This Creed is also that of the apostles, developed against the Macedonians, who denied the divinity of the Holy Ghost. Accordingly, it is said in the ninth article: "We also believe in the Holy Ghost, the Lord and life-giver, who is adored and glorified with the Father and the Son." The words, "Who proceedeth from the Father and the Son," were inserted by the Church against the errors of the Greeks, relative to the procession of the Holy Ghost. So, too, with the following: "Creator of all things visible and invisible," against the errors of the Manichees. But in all these changes there is nothing additional introduced: it is only an explanation that is given.

4. The Creed of St. Athanasius,[125] a summary of the doctrine of this great defender of the Church, which affords an admirable explanation of the great mysteries of the Trinity and the incarnation.

Division of the Apostles' Creed.—Composed of twelve articles, the Creed may, according to some theologians, be divided into three parts: the first contains that which we ought to believe of the Father; the second, that which we ought to believe of the Son; the third, that which we ought to believe of the Holy Ghost. The work of creation is attributed to the Father: "I believe in God, the Father Almighty, Creator of heaven and earth." The work of redemption is attributed to the Son: "And in Jesus Christ, his only Son, our Lord," etc. The work of sanctification is attributed to the Holy Ghost: "I believe in the Holy Ghost, the holy Catholic Church," etc. Although we attribute different works to the Father, the Son, and the Holy Ghost, these works are, nevertheless, common to the three divine Persons.

According to others, the Creed is divisible only into two parts: the first, composed of eight articles, teaches us to know God our Father; the second, composed of the last four articles, teaches us to know the Church our mother.

The Symbol not only gives us that sublime knowledge of God and the Church which raises the intellect of Christian peoples so high, but it also instructs us in reference to man and the world with a precision which the authors of other systems must ever despair of attaining. As a matter of fact, the Symbol teaches us, in reference to man, that he has been created by God; that he is free in his actions—consequently, that he has a spiritual soul; that he has sinned; that he has been redeemed by God; that, at the end of ages, he must render to the supreme judge a strict account of the means given him to reap the fruits of his redemption; that the sacred bonds of charity unite us, and make all Christians members of one body; that we have every help and facility necessary to preserve our union with the second Adam and with our brethren, and to restore it in case of its being destroyed by sin; that we shall all rise again from the dead, to live in eternal happiness or misery, according to our works.

In reference to the world, the Symbol teaches us that it has been created by God, that it is governed by a universal providence, whose laws are sweet and infallible, and that it shall come to an end.

Advantages and sublimity of the Creed.—To appreciate what is sublime in the Catholic Creed, observe the bold strokes with which it sketches the history of man and the world. Observe also how thoroughly each of its articles pulverizes a whole heap of absurd systems, raved into existence by pagan philosophers, in reference to God, man, and the world, and so shamelessly put forward again in our own days by impious savants. Observe, in fine, how every word is a ray of light, which dissipates some portion of the darkness in which the reason of man has been enveloped since the time of original sin, and that the union of all these rays forms the sun of truth, before which all errors disappear, as the shadows of night before the daystar.

True: in regard to questions on which poor human reason has, in all ages and countries, uttered nothing but miserable rhapsodies and fooleries, the Catholic Symbol leaves no liberty. It is right: this would be the liberty of suicide. What would the human race gain by allowing one senseless man to say freely that there is no God; another, that God and nature are only one being; another, that God exists, but does not concern himself with our affairs; another, that the soul is mortal; another, that there may be a life hereafter, but that the thing is very questionable? No one knows. The human race, on the contrary, gains much from a divine religion, which tells it precisely the why and the wherefore of its existence—which gives it certain, sublime, and consoling views of God and the soul.

Now, these views the Catholic Creed communicates to all the members of the Church. In this manner, it places minds on the same level, treats them with the same consideration, establishes them in the same principles and the same belief. Society no longer travels in divergent lines, in opposite directions. All men act under the impulse of one faith, and, as there is an end to doubt, to hesitation, to resistance, progress is continual.

Thanks to the Creed, the truths of the political order have a solid basis. The forms of government may change; but the change will take place without shock or revolution. It will always gravitate toward justice and charity. As for the truths of the scientific order and the literary order, they meet with no obstacle in Catholic teaching. So far from it, they find therein ideas that render them more and more prolific, ideas that give them a safe and glorious development.

Thus, the Creed is the holy ark which gathers humanity around it during the journey of life. Is it so great a misfortune that no one attempts to destroy it, at the risk of being lost in the desert and buried in the sand? During sixteen centuries Europe has followed it, and during these sixteen centuries has not the Creed produced the most admirable civilization that ever existed? Has it not had the signal honor of seeing assembled around it the greatest geniuses, the most wonderful inventions, the noblest monuments? The Son of God, in giving it to the world, became, as he said himself, the cornerstone of the edifice; his name, a name of universal salvation. Whatever does not rest on this stone has neither grandeur nor durability. There is no other name that can save the individual or society, even temporally.

The peoples may write other names in their records, at the head of their laws, and over the doors of their temples. They may one day celebrate a hero of the sword or of the tongue; another, attach themselves to personages who will be able to excite their enthusiasm by a display of genius, or crime, or folly; but never shall they be able to make a long journey under such guides or to attain to their destiny. They shall always find themselves in the midst of wars and catastrophes; for the only name that carries with it peace, order, harmony, virtue, and prosperity is the name of Jesus.

History.—The truth of the Catholic Symbol makes itself felt so sensibly that, when our forefathers in the faith opposed it to pagan errors, the confounded judges did not attempt to answer it: they contented themselves with the logic of tyrants, that is, they pronounced sentence of death. A child of seven years was led before the prefect Asclepiades, a persecutor of the Christians. "Who are you?" asked the judge. "I am a Catholic Christian." And the child repeated the Creed and other things which had been taught to him from the catechism. This simple profession of faith irritated the tyrant. Moderating his fury, however, he sent for the virtuous mother of the young hero, and, in her presence, had the little child most cruelly scourged. The streams of the youthful martyr's blood filled the eyes of all the spectators with tears.

While his body was being torn, this child of benediction confessed Jesus Christ, to whom his worthy mother offered the sacrifice of her son. Looking tenderly toward his mother, he said: "I thirst." She answered him: "My son, yet a little patience; you shall soon reach the fountain of life, and Jesus Christ will give you to drink a water that will quench your thirst forever." Out of himself with rage on witnessing the heroic firmness of the son and the mother, Asclepiades ordered that the head should be cut off the young athlete, whom he could not otherwise overcome. The mother took the child in her arms, and gave him a last kiss, as religious as it was tender; then, delivering him to the executioner, she uttered these words of the prophet: "Precious in the sight of the Lord is the death of his saints."[126]

Detailed explanation of the Creed: The first article.—It is not enough to admire the Symbol; we must also understand it. We proceed, therefore, to explain its different articles. And, first, the truths contained in the Symbol are called "articles," after a comparison often used by the fathers. As the members of the body are separated and distinguished by "articulations" or joints, so the name of *articles* has, with much reason and propriety, been given to truths which we must believe specially and distinctly in our confession of faith.

I believe in God, the Father Almighty, Creator of heaven and earth. What we have said on the work of the Creation in the first part[127] of the catechism dispenses us from the necessity of making any lengthened observations here. The sense is this:

I believe. To believe is not the same thing as to think, to imagine, to suppose. To believe means, in this place, I hold for certain—I am so sure that what is contained in the Symbol is true that I am ready to lay down my life for it. The word *believe*, which is expressed before the first, is understood before every other article of the Creed.

"*In God,*" *not* "*in gods.*" This brief declaration, by which we profess the unity of God, has overthrown idolatry, and changed the face of the world. *In God:* to believe God is to believe what he teaches, but to believe in God is moreover to confide fully in him, without examination or doubt, and to tend toward him as the sovereign good, with all the power of one's soul.[128] This beginning of the Creed teaches us the excellence of Christian philosophy, which raises us, at the outset, to the highest of all truths, in order that we may thence contemplate the others. It is very different from worldly philosophy, which, depending on natural light alone, raises us only by the help of sensible effects, and comes but very slowly to recognize the author of all things that exist. And yet the knowledge which faith gives us is much purer and more positive than that which comes from the reasonings of human science.[129]

The Father. We give the name of Father to God for three reasons. The first is because he is the Father of all creatures, not by nature, not by adoption, but by creation, and his admirable power and providence extend to all. "Is not the Lord your Father," says the scripture—"He who is your master, who drew you forth from nothingness? Is not he alone your Father?"[130] The second is because he is the Father of all the just, not by nature, but by adoption. "We have not received the spirit of bondage," says the apostle, "to live in fear like slaves, but the spirit of adoption of children of God, whereby we cry: Abba, Father!"[131] As a matter of fact, "God has," says St. John, "shown such a love for us, that we are called and really are the children of God."[132] "And if we are children, we are heirs also: heirs of God and co-heirs of Jesus Christ,"[133] who is "the firstborn of many brethren,"[134] and who is not ashamed to call us his brethren.[135] The third is because he is the beginning without beginning, and, from all eternity, begets his Son, by whom all things have been made.

At the same time, when we say that the Father is the first Person, it is not to be believed that we recognize in the Trinity anything first or last, greater or less. God forbid that such an impious thought should enter the minds of the faithful! The Christian religion teaches that the same eternity, power, and majesty belong to the three divine Persons; that there is no inequality amongst them. The only distinctions of which we are aware, in their regard, are these: the Father is not begotten, the Son is begotten of the Father, the Holy Ghost proceeds from both the Father and the Son. Thus we confess and adore unity in the divine essence, a distinction in the Persons, and equality in the Trinity.

Almighty. By this word we understand that there is nothing, that it is impossible to imagine anything, beyond the power of God. Not only can he do everything that we find it most difficult to imagine—as, for example, to annihilate the universe, or, in an instant, to create far more beautiful worlds than this; but his power extends to things infinitely more exalted, of which our human reason cannot even suspect the possibility. Nevertheless, although he is Almighty, God cannot utter a lie, nor cease to be, nor deceive, nor be deceived, nor commit sin, nor be ignorant of anything: these are things that appertain only to imperfect beings. Thus, while acknowledging the omnipotence of God, we believe that he is totally exempt from all that is not in harmony with his infinitely perfect nature.

Let us here make an important remark. It is not without the wisest reasons that the Symbol begins by proposing to us the omnipotence of God as an object of our faith. Hereby, the apostles desired that we should have no trouble in believing either the wonders of nature or the wonders of grace, of which the following articles contain an abridged account. In fact, when we believe that God is Almighty, we at the same time acknowledge that he knows all things, and that all things are subject to his will. Henceforth, whatever is proposed, no matter how extraordinary, for our belief, our reason will yield its assent without difficulty. Is there question of hoping? Never shall the grandeur of the prospect shake the confidence of the mind; so far from it, we shall find our hopes and desires strengthened by the thought, which we must often recall, that nothing is impossible to an omnipotent God. Let us, therefore, be careful to fortify our faith in the omnipotence of our Father when we have anything difficult to do for the benefit of our neighbor, or anything important to ask in prayer for ourselves.

The Savior himself, to animate our courage, uses these admirable words: "If you have faith as a grain of mustard seed, you shall tell this mountain to pass from one place to another, and it shall pass, and nothing shall be impossible to you."[136] And, to excite our confidence in prayer, he says to us by the mouth of the apostle St. James: "Ask with faith, not wavering; for he that wavers is like a wave of the sea, which is dashed about by the wind on all sides: therefore let not that man imagine that he shall receive anything from the Lord."[137]

The other advantages of this faith in the omnipotence of God are: a) To crush our pride, to lead us to humility, by making us sensible of our weakness. Thus everything, to the least word in religion, tends to repair in man the consequences of sin, and to render him conformable to the second Adam. b) To make us fear God. "I will show you whom you shall fear," says the Savior to us. "Fear him who, after having killed the body, can cast you into hell; verily, I say to you, it is he who should be feared."[138] c) To remind us of the Lord's immense benefits toward us. Whoever reflects on the omnipotence of God would be very ungrateful if he did not often exclaim: "He who is mighty has done great things for me."[139]

Creator. This word signifies that God made all things from nothing, and that it is in his power to annihilate them again. Angels, men, devils themselves, can indeed make and unmake certain things; but they cannot make them without some preexisting matter, nor unmake them unless inasmuch as they may reduce them to something else. Thus, the builder cannot make a house from nothing: he requires stones, mortar, and wood. Nor can he destroy it, so as to annihilate it: he may simply reduce it to stones and dust. God alone is called the Creator, and he is really such, because he alone has no need of matter in the construction of his works.

The word *Creator* does not refer to the Father alone; for the work of the creation is common to the three Persons of the holy and indivisible Trinity. As a matter of fact, if we learn in the Creed that the Father created heaven and earth, we read, in the scripture, of the Son: "All things were made by him";[140] and of the Holy Ghost: "The Spirit of the Lord moved over the waters."[141] "The heavens were established by the word of the Lord," says the psalmist, "and all their beauty is the effect of the breath of his mouth."[142]

Of heaven and earth. By these words we understand not only heaven and earth, but all that they contain: minerals, vegetables, and animals—men and angels—all creatures visible and invisible. It is enough to say, "Creator of heaven and earth," because heaven and earth are the two chief parts of the universe: the one above, where angels dwell; the other below, where men dwell. Now, angels and men are the noblest of creatures, whom all others serve, as angels and men are themselves obliged to serve God.

Such is the simple and literal explanation of the first article of our faith. You may not, perhaps, suspect how profound is all that it contains. Well, this luminous line: "One only God, the Creator and preserver of the whole universe," which appears at the head of the Catholic Creed, is, in the world of spirits, that which the sun is in this world of bodies.

Nations of Europe! know that it is to this first dogma that you are indebted for your enlightenment and your superiority! Who, tell me, scattered that host of absurd deities which received the incense of degraded pagans on the thirty thousand altars of the Rome of the Caesars? Who delivered you from the barbarous dogma of fate, which, bowing down the philosophers of Greece and Italy under the iron scepter of a blind destiny, stifled within them the sentiments of moral liberty, and condemned them either to a Stoic insensibility or to the horrors of despair?

And you, modern savants! so proud of your discoveries, tell me, in your turn, who delivered natural science from the endless cosmogonies of ancient Greece and India? Who put an end to those everlasting surmises about the origin of things, in which the sacred fire of genius was so long and so vainly consumed? With history at hand, run along the chain of centuries, and you will find that science was emancipated on the day when, for the first time, the Catholic Symbol resounded throughout the world. Its first expression is the basis of natural, as well as of divine, science. And that you may never forget it, often call to mind that the last century fell into those errors which excite our pity only from having wished to destroy this necessary basis, the starting point of all investigations.

And you, men! whosoever you are, who suffer, who groan under the burden of life, what shall I say to you? To what source are you indebted for the consoling dogma of a tender providence, attentive to all your desires and sensible of all your misfortunes? How has the sweet word *hope* been restored to human speech for you? Ah! it is again the first article of the Catholic Creed. If you doubt the matter, call to mind the pagan peoples of antiquity, and behold the idolatrous tribes of our own day. Let a glorious concert of praise, therefore, rise from the midst of Christian nations toward God the Creator and Father, who, revealing himself to them, has vouchsafed to lavish so many favors on them. Honor to the heart that is faithful to the Catholic Symbol! Shame on the man who is ashamed of it! Woe to the man who despises it! Anathema to the man who assails it!

Detailed explanation of the Creed: The second article.—The second article of the Creed is expressed thus: "And in Jesus Christ, his only Son, our Lord." We say, "I believe in Jesus Christ," as we say, "I believe in God the Father"; because the Son of God—Jesus Christ—is God as well as the Father. Thus, it is not enough for us to hold as certain what faith teaches regarding Jesus Christ: we must accompany this conviction with sentiments of piety. Our heart must attach itself to Jesus Christ, must find its delight in him, must return him love for love. In this manner, faith, animated by charity, will unite our mind with the mind of the second Adam, will make us live by his life and participate in the fruits of his redemption.

In Jesus Christ. The word *Jesus* means "Savior." It was not by chance, nor by the judgment or will of men that it was given to the Word made flesh, but by the command and arrangement of God himself; for the angel, when announcing to Mary that she should be the Mother of God, used these words: "Behold, thou shalt conceive in thy womb, and shalt bring forth a Son; and thou shalt call his name Jesus."[143]

Without a doubt, several other persons, mentioned in scripture, bore this name, because they were figures of the true Savior; but our Lord alone verified it in its full extent. He, and he alone, saved the world from sin, from the devil, from eternal death. The name of *Jesus*, pronounced with a lively faith, has the power of rendering abortive all the efforts of the enemies of our salvation. It should be often on our lips and always in our hearts.

The name *Christ*, added to *Jesus*, means anointed or consecrated. Among the Hebrews it was a law and a custom to consecrate kings, priests, and prophets with holy oil. On this account they were called "Christs," or "the anointed of the Lord." This consecration was a sign of the particular grace which God communicated to them, to exercise their functions worthily. Now, it is the function of priests to recommend the people to God by assiduous prayers, to offer sacrifices, and to become mediators between God and men. Kings are appointed to govern peoples; to see that good laws are made, and, as far as possible, observed; to protect the rights of the innocent, and to punish the crimes of the guilty.

As these two ministries seemed to represent on earth something of the majesty of God, those who were chosen for royalty and the priesthood should be anointed and consecrated with holy oil.[144] It was also the custom to give the unction to prophets, because they were the interpreters and ambassadors of the immortal God, appointed to correct morals and to announce the future. Now, no one deserved the name of *Christ* better than our Lord. For he was at once a King, a priest, and a prophet; and the unction with which he was consecrated was not a mere participation in divine grace—the divinity itself dwelt within him.

In the first place, he is a King, not only as God, but even as man. So his Father announced him to the world: "He shall be a king in the house of Jacob forever, and of his kingdom there shall be no end."[145] The Savior received from his Father all power in heaven and on earth. He destroyed the empire of the devil, which was idolatry, saved the elect, and made a conquest of the human race, by redeeming all men with his precious blood. Whether they wish it or not, whether they know it or not, it is he who reigns over the nations; his kingdom is spiritual and eternal: begun on earth, it shall be perfected in heaven.

In the second place, he is a priest. He offered a sacrifice with which no other can be compared—a sacrifice of which all those of the old law were only figures—and he continues to offer this sacrifice daily on the altars of the whole world. Strictly speaking, our Lord is the only priest in existence: all others are merely his ministers and representatives. Moreover, he is a priest according to the order of Melchisedech, as the prophets had foretold, since he offered himself once, under the appearances of bread and wine, by his own hands, at the last supper, to God his Father, and he still offers himself daily on the altar, by the hands of his priests, in the same manner.

In the third place, he is a prophet. He received from his Father the knowledge of all things. Everyone else, honored with the name of prophet, was only his disciple—a messenger sent to announce him who should give to men the true knowledge of the mysteries of God. Moreover, he proved himself a prophet. He showed in many circumstances that he was perfectly acquainted with the most secret thoughts of the mind and the most hidden feelings of the heart. He foretold with certainty events that were afterward verified to the letter: the principal circumstances of his passion and death, the destruction of the city and Temple of Jerusalem. So many predictions, exactly fulfilled, are the pledge of the verification of those which are yet unfulfilled: such as his return to earth at the end of time, to judge mankind, and to render to every one according to his works.

His only Son. These words teach us that the Almighty Father, of whom we have spoken in the first article of the Creed, has truly a Son by nature—who is called Jesus Christ—true God as well as his Father, by whom he is begotten from all eternity. Now, when we say that Jesus is the Son of God, let us beware of representing his birth to ourselves in a material and terrestrial manner. If we wish to form any idea of it, let us have recourse to the following comparison. When a person looks into a mirror, he immediately produces there an image so perfectly like himself that it is almost impossible to distinguish between the two. This image resembles him, not only in outline and color, but also in attitude and motion. And it is produced without labor, without lapse of time.

Thus you may imagine that God, contemplating himself, beholds the "splendor of his glory," the figure of his substance—this is the Word; his only Son.

We see hereby how the Son of God is God as well as the Father, and one and the same God with the Father. We also see that the Son of God is not younger than the Father, but has always existed as well as the Father, since he is begotten by the very contemplation which God makes of himself—a contemplation which is as eternal as God.[146]

Let us believe, therefore, with a firm faith, and honor with a profound piety, the mystery by which God the Father begets his Son from all eternity: a mystery which, in spite of all comparisons, remains above reason, and should ever fill us with admiration like that of the prophet. "Who," he exclaims, "shall declare his generation?"[147] Let us believe with joy, and on the testimony of God himself, that the Son has the same nature, the same power, the same wisdom, the same eternity as the Father, according to the more extended explanation of the Council of Trent: "And in Jesus Christ, his only Son, born of the Father before all ages; God of God, light of light, true God of true God, begotten and not created, consubstantial with the Father, by whom all things were made."[148]

Jesus Christ is called the only Son of God, because he is the only true Son of God by nature. We are the sons of God: but it is only by adoption, that is, by the election and grace of God, while Jesus Christ is the true Son of God by nature, and is the only one who can be such.

Our Lord. Jesus Christ is our Lord or master: a) as God, because he created and preserves us; b) as man, because he redeemed us at a great price, and his Father gave him all power in heaven and on earth; c) as the man-God. The admirable union of divine with human nature in one Person rendered him our master, even though he should not have died for us, since by it he is the supreme master of all creatures in general, and especially of the faithful, who are united to him as members to their head, as children to their father, as disciples to their master; for it is from Jesus Christ that we have taken our name of Christians. We ranged ourselves under the banner of his laws on the day of our baptism, and swore an everlasting fidelity to him.

Thus, we belong to Jesus Christ much more than a servant or a slave belongs to his master, than a child belongs to its father. Yet this powerful Lord treats us with so much charity that he vouchsafes to give us, not the name of slaves, but the sweet names of brethren and friends. This is one of the justest reasons, and I know not whether there is any more fitting, to engage us to recognize and honor him as our Lord.

The first two articles of the Creed teach us that we come from God and that we specially belong to God. To what a high degree of virtue are not these few words, well understood, capable of raising us! A Roman emperor had a magnificent stag, which was gradually tamed. The object of its master's tender affection, this beautiful animal was fed in the palace, to which it every day returned after visiting the neighboring forests. Fearing lest in its travels any one should chase or hurt it, the emperor caused the following inscription to be engraved on a collar of gold, which was hung round its neck: "Do not touch me—I belong to Caesar."

We come from God. We belong to God; he has marked us with his seal. Our soul and its faculties, our body and its organs, bear the impress of the divinity. In a word, on our brow shines this sacred inscription: "Do not touch me—I belong to God." Let us know how to respect others. Let us know how to make ourselves respected, by not allowing ourselves to be seduced by evil example, nor ensnared by wicked passions, nor brought into bondage by the spirit of malice, who is our enemy and the enemy of God.

How can we now tell the advantages for which the world is indebted to the second article of the Creed? Considering them merely from an intellectual point of view, it would require whole volumes to recount them. It is to faith in this second article, that is, in the revelation of Jesus Christ which God has made to us, that Christian nations owe their just ideas regarding God, regarding man, regarding the world, regarding the relations of superiors and inferiors. As a matter of fact, Jesus Christ is the keystone of the science of God, of the science of man, of the science of society, of the science of the world. These words, *Jesus Christ* (or "the Son of God made man to redeem the human race"), teach us more regarding the infinite justice, mercy, and wisdom of God, the dignity of the human soul, the enormity of sin, the degradation and restoration of creatures, than all the utterances of prophets, all the traditions of peoples, all the volumes of philosophers.

Jesus Christ! This is the sublime summary of the world's history. The forty centuries that precede his coming lead to him, and all the centuries that succeed it refer to him, that is, to the formation of his mystical body, which is the Church. To this grand design are subordinated all occurrences. The peoples, with their revolutions, gravitate toward this center, as the planets toward the sun. Whoever is not acquainted with this truth, need never expect to understand anything of history: I speak of profane history. But it being given, so simple and so exalted, everything is explained, genius expands, and every people, every event, is exhibited in the clear light of its destiny, and is classed according to the importance which it claims in the general plan.

Let us no longer be surprised to hear the great apostle, so deeply versed in all things, exclaim with a holy enthusiasm: "As for me, I glory in knowing nothing but Jesus, and Jesus crucified."[149] I am no longer surprised to hear one of the most admirable geniuses, and perhaps the strongest-minded man that ever appeared on the earth—St. Thomas—declare boldly that he found all his knowledge at the foot of his crucifix.

PRAYER

O my God! who art all love, I thank thee for having sent us a Savior who has enlightened our minds with the clear and safe lights of faith. From how many errors and disorders has he delivered us by teaching us to know thee, to know ourselves, to know all creatures! Grant us the grace to take advantage of so many lights; for much will be required of him to whom much is given.

I am resolved to love God above all things, and my neighbor as myself for the love of God; and, in testimony of this love, I will listen attentively to the instructions of the catechism.

Lesson 19: Our Union with the New Adam by Faith (2)

Third article of the Creed: Mystery of the incarnation.—The third article of the Creed is expressed in these words: "Who was conceived by the Holy Ghost, born of the Virgin Mary." It teaches us three great truths.

Divinity and humanity of our Lord.—The first, that the Word, the second Person of the Blessed Trinity, the only Son of God from all eternity, was made in time the Son of Mary: so that the same divine Person, remaining God, as he was from all eternity, became man, which he had not been previously. So the apostle St. John explains this profound mystery, of which he derived the knowledge from the very heart of the Savior himself. After declaring the nature of the Word in these words: "In the beginning was the Word, and the Word was with God, and the Word was God," he concludes thus: "And the Word was made flesh and dwelt amongst us."[150] Hence the name *incarnation*, so perfectly appropriate, which is given to this mystery by the doctors of the Church, and notably by the fathers of the First Council of Nice, in their Creed: *Et incarnatus est de Spiritu Sancto ex Maria Virgine.* Let us add that it was congruous in the Son to become incarnate, that all things, in heaven and on earth, might be restored by him through whom they had in the beginning been made.

Who was conceived by the Holy Ghost. These words express the new and miraculous manner in which the incarnation was accomplished. The Holy Ghost, who is the third Person of the Blessed Trinity, and the same God as the Father and the Son, formed by his infinite power, in the womb of Mary, of her most pure blood, the admirably perfect body of a little child. At the same moment, he created a most noble soul, which he united to the body of this little child. The divine Word united his divinity with both, so that in the twinkling of an eye Jesus Christ was perfect God and perfect man; and the most holy Virgin was truly and properly the Mother of a God-man, since at the same moment she conceived a God-man, whose body was formed of her own substance.

As for the Holy Ghost, he cannot be called the Father of our Lord, because to be father it does not suffice to make—it is necessary to make of one's own substance. Thus, we do not say that the mason is father of the house which he builds, because he makes it of wood, stone, etc., and not of his own flesh. Now, the Holy Ghost made, it is true, the body of the Son of God; but he made it of the flesh and blood of Mary, and not of his own substance. This is the reason why our Lord is not the Son of the Holy Ghost. As he is God, he is the Son of God the Father, from whom he holds his divinity, and as he is man, he is the Son of Mary, from whom he holds his flesh.

When we say that the Son of God was conceived by the power and operation of the Holy Ghost, we do not mean that this was the only Person of the Blessed Trinity who concurred to the incarnation. Although the Son alone took human nature, yet the three divine Persons had a share in this mystery. As a matter of fact, it is laid down in the Christian faith that everything is common to the three divine Persons in whatever works God performs outside of himself so that one neither does more than the others nor acts without the others. Now, the mystery of the incarnation is of this description.

Yet it is a usage in scripture to attribute specially to one Person things that are alike common to the three. To the Father, for example, a sovereign dominion over all things; to the Son, wisdom; to the Holy Ghost, love. If, therefore, the scripture attributes the work of the incarnation specially to the Holy Ghost, it is because this supreme mystery is a singular manifestation[151] of God's infinite love toward mankind. It is also because the least shadow of defilement or corruption is banished from this mystery, in which all parties are holy—the Holy Ghost, who operates it; Mary, who remains inviolate; and the infant, who is free from every stain.[152]

But if the three divine Persons concurred to the incarnation, how does it happen that the Son alone became incarnate? The following comparison, which is used by theologians, will give an idea of this mystery. When a prince clothes himself with his purple robes, and two others assist him to do so, three persons concur to the act of robing, and yet only one is robed. In the same manner, the three divine Persons contributed to the incarnation, and the Son alone was robed with human nature.[153]

The second truth which is taught us by the third article of the Creed is that the eternal Word, in taking human nature, united it with the divine nature in one and the same Person. Whence it follows: a) That in this admirable union the two natures preserved every one of their operations and peculiarities, "without the glory of the divinity," says St. Leo, "destroying the humanity, or the elevation of the humanity abasing the divinity." b) That our Lord Jesus Christ is perfect God, since the whole divinity is in him; and, at the same time, perfect man, since he has a body and a soul like ours, and he resembles us in every respect, except that he is sinless. c) That since there are two natures in Jesus Christ, there are also two wills in him: a divine will and a human will; but between these two wills there is never any opposition. The human will being perfect in the new Adam, it always wishes, though most freely, that which the divine will wishes. Nevertheless, as we have already said, there is only one Person in Jesus Christ—a divine Person. The divine and human natures form only one Person in Jesus Christ, almost similarly as the body and soul in us form only one man.[154]

Born of the Virgin Mary. The third truth which this article teaches us is the divine maternity and the perpetual virginity of Mary.

The divine maternity of Mary. To conceive and bring forth constitutes maternity. Now, Mary conceived in her chaste womb our Lord, the only Son of God, true God and true man, uniting divine with human nature in the Person of the Word. Like all mothers, she formed his body of her own substance, of her virginal blood; she bore him nine months; she gave him birth. Mary is therefore truly, and in all propriety of expression, the Mother of God. Mother of God, not as though she gave birth to the divinity, an idea which is too absurd ever to enter the mind of any Christian, nor yet as though she were only the Mother of the flesh of the man-God; for we do not say that other mothers are only the mothers of the bodies of their children, because they do not beget souls: they conceive and bring forth a human being, composed of a body and a soul.[155]

Thus the Blessed Virgin is truly the Mother of God, because she conceived and brought forth a man-God, that is, a real man formed of her substance and personally united to the divinity. Such is the formal teaching of the scripture. "Thou shalt conceive in thy womb," says the archangel to Mary, "and shalt bring forth a Son, and thou shalt call his name Jesus. He shall be great, and shall be called the Son of the Most High... This is the reason why he who shall be born of thee shall be the saint of saints, the Son of God."[156] Instructed by the Holy Ghost, regarding the mystery of the incarnation, St. Elizabeth exclaims on beholding Mary: "Whence is this happiness to me that the

Mother of my Lord should visit me?"[157] Summing up these and other testimonies, St. Paul says in his own energetic language: "The Son of God was made of the substance of the woman."[158]

Such has always been, such is still the faith of the Catholic world—solemnly defined in the Council of Ephesus, which was held in the year 431, against the impious Nestorius. "If any one," says the august assembly, "shall dare to deny that our Lord is true God and true man, and consequently that the holy Virgin is the Mother of God, let him be anathema."[159] Never would an anathema be better deserved. To deny the divine maternity of Mary is to deny the unity of Person in our Lord Jesus Christ. It is to sap the foundations of Christianity; for it is to destroy the work of human redemption.

In regard to the reasons for which the Son of God was pleased to be born of a woman, the fathers and theologians of the Church assign two principal ones: the first, in order to reestablish both sexes, and to show that he was come for the salvation of both; the second, because it was becoming that woman, who had been the author of evil, should be the author of good.[160]

The perpetual virginity of Mary. It is the teaching of the Catholic and apostolic faith that the august Mother of God is the Virgin of virgins; that she has ever been a Virgin—before, during, and after her divine childbearing. The scripture and the fathers are unanimous on this point.[161]

That a virgin should conceive without losing her virginity is doubtless a mystery above the laws of reason and nature; but cannot God, therefore, do anything above these laws, which he has himself established? Do we not say at the beginning of the Creed: "I believe in God Almighty"? The creation of the world furnishes an example which makes the belief of this mystery easy.

According to the ordinary laws of nature, the earth does not produce wheat unless it is first tilled and sown, watered by the clouds, and warmed by the sun. Nevertheless, at the beginning of time, when wheat was first produced, there was no need whatever that the earth should be first prepared by tilling, sowing, rain, and heat—it was completely virginal in its way. At the mere command of an omnipotent God, the great Creator of all things, it suddenly produced wheat and every other description of grain. In the same manner, the virginal womb of Mary, without any regard to ordinary laws, produced, at the command of God and by the operation of the Holy Ghost, the precious wheat of the animated body of the Son of God.[162]

That a virgin should bring forth without losing her virginity is another mystery, no less easy to the omnipotence of God. In connection with this matter, nature itself offers us some examples, which move our reason to bow to the teachings of faith. Do we not every day see the rays of the sun pass through the solid substance of glass without breaking or injuring it?

Thus, but in a far more sublime manner, was our Lord born of his divine Mother without any injury whatever to her virginity. Why refuse the power of working this miracle to him who, later on, came forth from the tomb without breaking its seal, and entered, the doors being closed, the place in which his disciples were assembled? To dispute the omnipotence of God, to deny that which we do not comprehend, is the lowest condition of reason, for it is the plainest evidence of extreme weakness.[163]

It is therefore with the greatest truth that we proclaim, with the most perfect certainty, that we believe the perpetual virginity of Mary, and her absolute integrity in the conception and bearing of her divine Son. Such has been the constant faith of the world, expressed, before the event, among the Jews, by the prophet Isaias, announcing that the divine Emmanuel, the God-man, should be born of an ever Virgin Mother—among the pagans themselves, by their deep and general respect for virginity, and by a tradition which found utterance in the following words engraved on a Druidical stone recently discovered: "The Druids to the Virgin who shall bring forth a Child" (*Virgini pariturae Druides*); and, after the event, proclaimed by all doctors and councils, both of which authorities have not failed to remark, moreover, that perpetual virginity was necessary in the Mother of the Son of God.[164]

As for the name of *Mary*, which means "lady," "queen," "enlightener," it ought, like the prerogatives of the sacred Virgin, to excite in us the deepest sentiments of respect, joined with a filial confidence. It is for us that she is Mary, our Mother and our model. In fact, as our Lord is the second Adam, so Mary is the second Eve. It had been said to Eve: "In sorrow shalt thou bring forth children."[165] Mary, freed from this law, brought forth the incarnate Word without grief or pain.

As the second Adam united himself with human nature and was born in a wholly supernatural manner, so we, to be united to him and to share in his redemption, must be born, not of flesh and blood, but of God: that we may live, in consequence as new creatures, animated by a new spirit.[166] By this means we shall trace in ourselves some image of the spotless virginity of Mary and the most pure birth of the Son of God.

Social advantages of this article.—This thought leads us to speak of the social advantages pertaining to the third article of the Creed. A holy conception, an infant God, a Virgin Mother: in these three dogmas, proposed during the last eighteen centuries for the belief of the world, is found the fruitful germ of the reformation of the family, and thereby of society.

A holy conception. In which carnal and sensual man had no part: this is the model idea which changed all the old ideas on the relations and duties of married persons. To it must be attributed the sanctity of Christian marriage, the angelic manners and heavenly happiness of families, during the long course of the ages of faith. Would you desire a proof of this? Read the history of ancient peoples. What was marriage among them? What respect, what sanctity, what religious fear presided at the fulfillment of the sacred obligations of the married? Behold next what passes at the present day among those peoples who are still seated in the shadow of death; and, even under your eyes, among those communities and families in which the influence of Christian truth is diminished. It is therefore true that the dogma of a wholly spiritual conception of a God made man, the model of men, proposed for the belief of the world, has wonderfully ennobled, because it has greatly sanctified, the family.

An infant God. Tell us: What was the child among the pagan nations of antiquity; what is it still among the idolatrous peoples of our own time; and what is it even among communities and families in which the Christian dogmas lose their influence? Tell us, and you will see what the world owes to the second part of the third article of our Creed. Oh, yes! a God becoming an infant; a God saying, "Woe to him who raises his hand against the life, the innocence, the freedom of the least of these little ones, who are my brethren": this God was the Savior of infancy. It was he, and he alone, who banished the brutal right to kill, abandon, sell, or sacrifice the child.

A Virgin Mother. To these three words woman owes her enfranchisement. Become a dogma of faith, they have totally changed her condition: history is again our witness. What was woman among the ancient pagans? What is she still among modern pagans? Who delivered her from her abjection? Who preserves her from relapsing into it? This Catholic dogma. For you see what she becomes in communities and families which lose their Christianity.

When, therefore, the words "born of the Virgin Mary" were heard throughout the world eighteen hundred years ago, astonished man changed all his ideas and sentiments regarding woman. To the first Eve, the source of all evil, succeeded the second Eve, the source of all good. Seeing now how much God honored woman in Mary, how holy was woman in Mary, how useful to the human race was woman in Mary, man began to respect woman. She ceased to be a slave, a beast of burden, in order to become the noble companion of man, surrounded with affection and consideration. Emancipated by Christianity, woman found again her moral dignity, and at once she turned all the tender sensibilities of her heart and all the activity and ingenuity of her mind to the welfare of man and of society: and the world was transformed.

Behold now the miracle produced by these few words of the Catholic Creed: "Was conceived by the Holy Ghost; born of the Virgin Mary!" O men! how long will you be without a heart to love, without a mind to understand?

Fourth article of the Creed: Mystery of our Lord's passion and death.—The fourth article of the Creed is expressed thus: "Suffered under Pontius Pilate; was crucified, dead, and buried." It teaches us that the Son of God, our Lord Jesus Christ, after having conversed among men for about thirty-three years, was unjustly condemned to death by Pontius Pilate, at the desire of the Jews, and nailed to a cross, on which he died; also that, being dead, he was honorably interred by some of his disciples. There is nothing more necessary than the knowledge of these truths. They are the basis of our salvation; the end of all figures, prophecies, and sacrifices; the term of the wisdom, the mercy, and the omnipotence of God.

Let us penetrate with mingled feelings of respect and fear into the depths of this mystery.

1. *Who suffered?* It was the Son of God himself, made man for love of us. The apostles mention the sufferings of our Lord immediately after speaking of his birth, because our Lord was born to suffer, and he always suffered. Not only had he a deep sense of the pains, fatigues, and privations of his hidden and his public life, but the dolors of his passion were continually before his mind.[167] He suffered all kinds of sorrows, and in the highest degree. He did not suffer in his divine nature, because God, being infinitely perfect, cannot suffer; but as he was our Lord, his divinity gave to the sufferings of his humanity an infinite value.

2. *How did he suffer?* He suffered voluntarily. For God might, without injury to any of his perfections, have left man in the state of sin.[168] He might also have redeemed man by a thousand other means: such as the incarnation alone, or one tear, one prayer, one drop of the adorable blood of his Son, since any of these things, being of infinite value, would have sufficed and more than sufficed to satisfy the divine justice. Finally, our Lord suffered voluntarily in this sense, that he himself gave his enemies the power to make him suffer: otherwise they could have attempted nothing against him.

Hence, all these sayings of the scripture: "It is necessary that the Son of Man should be crucified," "It is necessary that the Son of Man should suffer many things," "It was necessary that Christ should suffer before entering into his glory," merely express a moral necessity.[169] They mean that, taking into consideration the decrees of God, who had chosen the sufferings of our Lord as the most suitable remedy for our evils and the most proper mode of effecting our salvation, it was necessary that our Lord should suffer the torments of his passion and death as he did suffer them.

3. *He suffered through love.* In carrying his sorrows and ignominies to excess, he was pleased to show us the enormity of sin, the terrible rigor of the divine justice, the value of a soul, and consequently the immensity of his love, whose object was to obtain ours and to render us happy in time and eternity.[170]

4. *Why did he suffer?* Our Lord suffered to repair the glory of his Father, to atone for sin, and to be a Redeemer and a model for men. Charity, meekness, patience,

humility, love of enemies, filial piety, obedience: there is not a virtue of which he did not give us an example in his passion; there is not a title to our gratitude left unacquired by him.

5. *For whom did he suffer?* He suffered for all mankind without exception. For all, without exception, he merited the graces necessary to work out their salvation. But if our Lord satisfied for all, if he merited salvation for all, whence does it happen that so great a number are lost, and that every one is obliged to do penance? Without doubt, our Lord satisfied for all, obtained for all the means to be saved; but it is necessary that his merits should be applied to each one of us.[171] They can only be applied by faith, by the sacraments, by good works, and especially by penance. It is therefore absolutely necessary to do penance and to perform good works. The reason why so many are damned is because they do not comply with this condition.

In point of fact, they do not wish to have faith, as the Jews, Mahometans, and heretics; or they do not wish to receive the sacraments—to confess, to communicate—as the indifferent; or they do not wish to make up their minds to live conformably to the law of God and perform some penance for their sins, as bad Christians. A comparison will illustrate this truth.

A man took great pains, and, by unheard-of fatigues, raised a sufficiency of money to discharge all the debts of the inhabitants of a city. He lodged his treasures in a bank, with an order to transfer them to all such persons as should present checks from him. This man would undoubtedly, on his side, have paid all the debts of the inhabitants. Still it might happen that many would remain oppressed with their burdens, because through pride, sloth, or some other vicious propensity, they would not choose to take the trouble of asking a check and presenting it at the bank.[172]

6. *Under whom did he suffer?* He suffered under Pontius Pilate. It was not without good reason that the apostles gave, in this article, the name of the Roman governor who had condemned the Savior to death. On the one hand, they proved that our Lord was truly the Messias, since he died at the time when, according to the prophecy of Jacob, the scepter should have left the tribe of Juda; on the other, they proved their own sincerity and the certainty of this memorable event.

If they had been acting the hypocrite, they themselves would have supplied the surest means of bringing to light their imposture. For this purpose it would have sufficed to prove that Pontius Pilate, the governor of Judea, had never put to death a man named Jesus of Nazareth. The thing would have been quite easy, since in the archives of the Senate, at Rome, was preserved a record of all the events that took place throughout the various provinces of the Empire. It was to this record of Pilate that the first apologists of religion used to refer the pagans, to be enlightened and convinced.

The death of the Savior under Pontius Pilate is accordingly a fact so certain that Tacitus, when speaking of the burning of Rome under Nero, positively asserts that this emperor attributed it to the Christians, so called from *Christ*, who had been put to death during the reign of Tiberius, while Pontius Pilate was governing Judea.[173] The early enemies of the Christian religion never called this matter into question: an evident proof that they looked upon it as incontestable, since, if it were not, they could easily, with their data of time and place at hand, have demonstrated its falsity.

Acts of Pilate.—But we have other proofs of the death of our Lord under Pontius Pilate. It was a usage in the Roman Empire, as it is at present in all the kingdoms of the world, that the governors of provinces should send to the chief authority an account of anything remarkable that occurred in their districts, in order that the prince and the senate should be well informed of the course of events.[174] Now, Pilate, obedient to the law of the Empire, dispatched to Tiberius a full account of all that had taken place in reference to Jesus of Nazareth. His letter was deposited in the archives of the Roman Senate, as is proved by the testimonies which we shall now adduce.

1. *Testimony of St. Justin.* St. Justin the Martyr, who lived a hundred years after the death of our Lord, quotes the following words from the acts forwarded by Pilate to Tiberius: "Jesus was fastened to the cross with nails through his hands and feet, and those who had crucified him afterward cast lots for his garments, which they divided amongst them." He adds: "This is what you can easily know by reference to the acts written under Pontius Pilate...The prophets stated distinctly that Christ should heal all sorts of diseases, and even raise the dead to life, and you may convince yourselves that Jesus did so, by reading the acts which were written regarding him under Pontius Pilate."[175]

2. *Testimony of Tertullian.* Tertullian, who lived fifty years after St. Justin, gives an abridgment of the virtues, miracles, sufferings, condemnation, death, and resurrection of our Lord, and concludes thus: "Pilate, somewhat a Christian in his conscience, wrote a full account of all these things regarding Christ to Tiberius, then emperor. Henceforth, the emperors would have believed in Jesus Christ if the Caesars had not been the slaves of the world or if Christians could have been Caesars. Be that as it may, when Tiberius, under whose reign the Christian name was spread throughout the world, had learned from Palestine all the facts that proved the divinity of Christ, he urged the Senate to place him in the rank of the gods, and gave his own vote for this purpose. The Senate, not admiring the proposal, rejected it. The emperor persisted in his views, and threatened with his anger any one who should accuse the Christians."[176] Then, speaking of the miracles that occurred at the death of our Lord, he says: "You have the account thereof in your archives."[177]

3. *Testimony of Eusebius of Caesarea.* Eusebius of Caesarea, a celebrated historian of the Church, who lived in the third century, speaks thus: "The miraculous resurrection and ascension of Jesus Christ having become famous, and it being an ancient custom that the governors of provinces should send to the emperor an account of anything new that turned up under their administration, so that he might be fully informed of everything that came to pass, Pontius Pilate acquainted Tiberius with the resurrection of the Savior, which was known to everyone in Palestine. He also remarked that he had learned that Jesus had performed many miracles, and had, since his resurrection, been recognized by many persons as a God. Tiberius, having heard these things, mentioned them to the Senate, and proposed that Jesus Christ should be placed in the rank of the gods. The Senate opposed the project under the pretext that there was an ancient law which forbade any person to be admitted into the rank of the gods except by a decree of the Senate; but the real reason of the refusal was that the Christian religion, being divine, should not be established by the authority of men. The Senate having therefore rejected the proposal, the emperor did not cease to maintain his opinion, and attempted nothing against the doctrine of Jesus Christ."[178]

This is what these great apologists of religion used to say to the pagans. If they had forged this testimony of Pilate, would they have dared to offer it as a proof to pagan philosophers? Would they have dared, as St. Justin the Martyr did, to defy the pagans to discuss the Christian religion publicly, in presence even of the Roman Senate, taking as their only basis the acts of Pilate? Or would the pagans have refused to accept the challenge, if they could have triumphed by displaying the falsity of these acts? But we have said enough on a matter that no one can dispute: it is time for us to return to our explanations.

Was crucified. Our Lord was fastened to the cross by four large nails, which pierced his hands and his feet.[179] He chose the punishment of the cross for several reasons, worthy alike of his wisdom and his love. Here are a few of them: to fulfill the figures and prophecies regarding the death of the Messias—the brazen serpent, for example; that death, which had entered the world by the fruit of the forbidden tree, should be banished therefrom by our Lord, the divine fruit of the tree of the cross; that his death should be a notedly incontestable fact, and consequently his resurrection the basis of our faith; that the satisfaction offered to God should be more abundant and our gratitude more lively, in proportion as the punishment of the cross would be more cruel and ignominious.

Dead. We all understand the meaning of this word. It denotes the separation of the soul from the body, not the separation of the divinity from the humanity. For, even after death, the divine nature continued ever united to the body and the soul of our Lord. The death of the Savior took place to fulfill the prophecies and to consummate the work of our redemption.

And buried. Our Lord was wrapped in a winding-sheet, with spices, according to the custom of the Jews, religiously observed by the early Christians, especially in regard to martyrs.[180] He was laid in a new sepulchre, hewn out of a rock, and wherein no person had ever been buried, that the truth of his resurrection might be made more and more apparent. For the rest, the body of our Lord knew no stain of corruption.

Social advantages of this article.—Let us now admire the wondrous influence of the fourth article of the Creed on the whole world. Would that our gratitude were proportioned to its benefits! A God suffering and dying on a cross for all men, and, in the supreme hour of his desolation, pardoning his executioners and praying for them: this is the eternally beneficent dogma which has changed all the relations of men with God and among themselves.

Here we find confidence in God, hope of pardon, peace of conscience, joy in misery, not only during the course of life, but more especially amid the deepening gloom of death. Here we find the grand charter of Christian nations—the great law of universal charity, a law written in the blood of a God, confirmed by his death, and made practicable by the unction of his cross. Man believed in a God dead for love of all men; and the laws of peoples were changed. The stranger was no longer an enemy, nor the prisoner a victim consigned to slavery or death. The atrocious motto, "Woe to the vanquished!" ceased to terrify nations; for war is no longer made to acquire slaves and booty: it is humanized.

A God dead for man: and kings had a sublime example of zeal for the welfare of their peoples; and peoples, a sublime example of obedience to kings; and Christian societies, founded on the spirit of mutual sacrifice, produced miracles of devotedness, as they showed themselves miracles of strength by their duration!

A God dead for man: and hatred, and revenge, and the wicked machinations of rancor became crimes—from being virtues, as they were among the pagans of antiquity, and from being honorable acts, as they are still among the idolatrous nations of our own day, as well as among men who have lost their Catholic instincts!

Fifth article of the Creed: Mystery of the resurrection.—The fifth article of the Creed is expressed thus: "He descended into hell; the third day he arose again from the dead."

The Savior did not for a moment interrupt the work of the redemption, for which he had come on earth. Scarcely had he breathed his last, that is, scarcely had his blessed soul quitted his body, when, in the region of death, he rendered perceptible the salutary influences of his precious blood.

He descended. By these words we make profession of believing that, our Lord Jesus Christ being dead, his holy soul went to visit the souls of the just who had lived before his coming, and his body was laid in the tomb. Although, during this time, the soul of the Savior was really separated from his body, yet his divinity, as we have already said, was not separated either from his body or his soul.

Into hell. The word *hell* has four distinct meanings. It denotes a) that dark and dismal prison in which the souls of the reprobate are tormented in company with the devils, by a fire which is never extinguished: this place, which is hell proper, is also called "Gehenna" and "the bottomless pit"; b) the place in which the souls of the just suffer for some time, in order to be entirely purified, before admission can be granted them into the heavenly country, where nothing defiled can enter: this place is called "purgatory"; c) the place in which are found the souls of little children who die without baptism, and who do not suffer the pain of fire, but only the loss of eternal felicity;[181] d) the place in which were received the souls of the patriarchs, prophets, and other saints, who died before the coming of our Lord: this place is commonly called "limbo," and in scripture it is named the "bosom of Abraham."

To this last-mentioned place went the souls of the just, on leaving this world, if they were free from every stain; otherwise, they went to be purified in the fire of purgatory, as is done today by those who have still some debt to pay on account of their sins. They were not admitted into heaven, because heaven had been closed against the human race since the time of the first Adam's sin, and the second Adam should be the first to reopen its gates. The just souls in limbo were free from pain. They enjoyed a tranquil rest, consoled and supported by the hope of their redemption; but they were deprived of the sovereign felicity, the intuitive vision of God.

It was to these predestined souls that the Savior descended, in order to announce the gospel to them, that is, their redemption and the redemption of the whole world.[182] This was their prison, whose bars and gates he broke. From the moment of his arrival, limbo ceased to exist; for, heaven having been opened to us by our Lord, it is a matter of faith that perfectly purified souls are admitted to its bliss without delay. The presence of the Savior diffused an infinite joy among these holy souls, and they tasted that essential beatitude which is found in the vision of God. Then was verified the promise made to the good thief: "This day shalt thou be with me in paradise."[183] On the day of his ascension, the Savior led with him to heaven this multitude of souls, glorious firstfruits of the human race, noble trophies snatched from death. Thus, not only the just who have appeared in the world since the coming of Jesus Christ, but those who preceded him from the time of Adam, and those who shall enter the arena of life till the end of ages—all are saved by the merits of our Lord's passion. This is the reason why, before his death and resurrection, heaven was not opened to any person.

Throughout the other parts of the infernal regions, the Savior also showed himself: as a conqueror, terrifying the devils; as a supreme judge, threatening the reprobate; as a liberator, consoling the souls in purgatory. So a monarch sometimes visits prisons to cheer and pardon whom he pleases.[184] Such were the motives of our Lord's descent into hell. And now, who will not admire the infinite goodness of God toward mankind and the vast plenitude of our redemption? Who will not be astonished to see the Son of God, after suffering a most sorrowful death for us, penetrate even "to the lowest parts of the earth,"[185] in order to rescue the souls that were dear to him and to conduct them with him to heaven?

The third day he arose again from the dead. As our Lord had spent thirty-three years and some months among the living, he was pleased to spend at least thirty-three hours among the dead: an hour for a year. In effect, the Savior died on Friday, and he arose on Sunday morning: which gives an interval of thirty-three to thirty-five hours. Again, he wished to remain three days in the tomb so as to verify the figure of Jonas and to fulfill a prophecy which he had himself made.[186] He did not, however, remain three whole days in the tomb.

To say with truth that he was three days in the sepulchre and that he arose again the third day from the dead, it sufficed that he should have been there during one whole day, a portion of the preceding day, and a portion of the succeeding day. Finally, to prove that he was God, the Savior did not choose to defer his resurrection till the end of ages. Just as to show that he was man, and that he had really died, he did not return to life immediately after expiring, but on the third day afterward: this interval of time being sufficient to prove that he had truly died.

He arose again from the dead. Coming forth victorious from the tomb, our Lord enjoyed all the qualities that we ourselves shall share if we have the happiness of dying a holy death. His body was impassible, agile, subtle, luminous. Nevertheless, he chose to preserve the scars of his wounds, as we see in the history of the apostle St. Thomas. He wished this that he might eternally retain the emblems of his triumph; that he might prove to his disciples the truth of his resurrection; that he might more effectually obtain from his Father whatever he should ask, by reminding him of the cruel death which he had endured; that he might show men at what a price he had redeemed them; in fine, that he might let the reprobate understand, on the day of judgment, both the greatness of their ingratitude and the justice of their condemnation.

He arose again. We have elsewhere proved his resurrection. As for the causes that rendered it necessary, here are a few of them: that his body, which had undergone so many sufferings, might be admitted to eternal happiness and glory; and that, his divinity being clearly established, our faith might be forever immovable, and our hope of rising again too might acquire a strength capable of consoling us in all our trials, of making us accept every sacrifice and practice every virtue, even those most costly to nature.

He arose again from the dead. When we say that our Lord returned to life, we do not merely understand that he came forth from the dead, as has happened with several others: we mean that he did so by his own power, which no one else could do. In point of fact, the divinity not having been separated either from the body of Jesus Christ in the tomb or from his soul in limbo, there was a divine virtue present both in his body and his soul. It follows hence that the body could rejoin the soul, that the soul could rejoin the body, that Jesus Christ could return to life and arise from the dead by his own power.

In arising thus, the Savior fulfilled, even from the tomb, a prophecy which related to the Messias. David had said: "It was his right hand, his holy arm"—that is, his omnipotence—"that saved him."[187] If we sometimes attribute the resuscitation of Jesus Christ to his Father, we refer to his humanity, as we refer to his divinity when we attribute his resuscitation to himself.[188]

Here several remarks of great importance present themselves. The first, that the resurrection of our Lord was a perfect resurrection, which took away all necessity of dying again, by giving an immortal life...Our Lord was the first who should rise again in this manner. Whence it comes that the scripture calls him the "firstborn among the dead."[189] Whence, also, the saying of the apostle: "Christ, rising again from the dead, dieth now no more; death shall no more have dominion over him."[190]

The second, that the resurrection of the Savior is the principle of the resurrection of all men, whereby it is a resurrection quite peculiar. "By a man came death," says the apostle, "and by a man the resurrection of the dead. And as in Adam all die, so in Jesus Christ shall all live again."[191]

The third, that the resurrection of the second Adam wonderfully advances the work of our redemption. By dying, the Savior had delivered us from our sins; but, by rising again, he restored to us all the goods of which sin had deprived us. That nothing might be wanting to the salvation of mankind, it was necessary that Christ should rise again, as it had been necessary that he should die. Do we desire to share in his resurrection? Let us unite ourselves with the new Adam as we were united to the old; let us believe in him, love him, serve him here on earth, that we may hereafter reign glorious with him in heaven.

Social advantages of this article.—To the explanation of the fifth article of the Creed let us add a few reflections on the lights and advantages which it procures for society. The descent of Jesus Christ into hell—in other words, the universality of his redemption—and his resurrection from the dead shortly afterward, are the two fundamental truths with which the fifth article of the Creed has enriched the world.

The first tells us that all men, from the origin to the consummation of time, are the children of God; that by this title they are dear to his heart; and that the divine blood was poured out to efface their sins and to open for them the gates of the city of the elect. Is not this a magnificent proclamation of the law of universal brotherhood? Is it not effectually to say to every people: "In whatever clime you dwell, to whatever race you belong, love one another, since God has so much loved you?" To publish thus the great law of charity, to show our master and model first fulfilling it in all its extent—is not this a bright ray of light, an unanswerable reply to the objections of selfishness, an immense social benefit?

And do not the words, "He descended into hell," prove, by revealing to us the universality of the redemption of Jesus Christ, that this divine Savior is really the Desired and Expected of Nations, the liberator of all the enslaved? Now, does not this strengthen our faith in him? And is it not on faith in Jesus Christ that, among modern peoples, the whole social fabric rests?

The second truth, contained in the fifth article of the Creed, "He arose again the third day," also confirms, by an evidence as certain as the existence of the sun, the faith of the world in the divinity of our Lord. This article shows us that Jesus Christ is truly the Messias promised to the human race, since he bore all the characteristics and performed all the works foretold of the Messias. Thus, to broaden charity and to deepen faith are the principal advantages which the fifth article of the Creed procures for society.

To understand the extent of these advantages it suffices to ask on what do nations and communities live, if not on faith and charity. Kings and peoples, rich and poor! fall therefore on your knees before the truths of the Catholic Creed, the source of all faith and charity, and, consequently, the principle of all noble, generous, and truly social actions. To suffer, to die, to liberate the souls of the ancient just, to arise again in order to strengthen our faith: these were some of the labors to which the Son of God devoted himself, that he might show his charity for us. Is it possible that there should be men who do not love him—what do I say?—who blush at his name? The following incident will enable us to perceive all the baseness of their conduct.

Historical incident.—A celebrated poet of the last century was the son of an honest artisan. The tender father, at the cost of many severe privations, gave his child a liberal education. For so much kindness the youth made a return of persevering diligence. Brilliant success came at length to crown his efforts and to reveal his talents: a piece of verse especially drew upon him a universal burst of applause. Anxious to be acquainted with its author, one of the court noblemen begged the young poet to come and recite his lines in an assembly composed of all the most distinguished persons in the capital. The proposal was too flattering to be refused. Without the knowledge of the son, the father asked and obtained the favor of admission.

The young poet begins his recitation with great confidence: applause soon interrupts him. He continues: and crowns fall upon his head. He ends: and the nobleman who invited him comes forward and, overjoyed, embraces him in presence of all the illustrious assembly. At the same moment, an old white-haired man, clad in the garments of honest poverty, is seen approaching from the end of the hall: his eyes moistened with tears, and his arms extended, he also wishes to embrace the young laureate. The latter turns away his head, and refuses to recognize him, and yet the old man is—his father!!!

Shouts of indignation break forth from every part of the hall, and nothing is heard but, "Ungrateful son! unnatural son!"

Ungrateful son, unnatural son: these, you say, are the only names that befit a son who is ashamed of his father; what name, then, does he deserve who is ashamed of his God?

PRAYER

O my God! who art all love, I thank thee for having sent us a Savior who acquainted us with all the means of uniting ourselves with him, in order to share in the merits of his redemption. I believe in him. I love him. I will imitate him on earth, in order to become like him in heaven.

I am resolved to love God above all things, and my neighbor as myself for the love of God; and, in testimony of this love, I will never be ashamed of my religion.

Lesson 20: Our Union with the New Adam by Faith (3)

Purgatory.—In the preceding lesson, we have seen that purgatory is a place where the souls of the just that depart out of this world without having sufficiently satisfied the divine justice for their transgressions complete the work of their atonement before being admitted to the enjoyment of eternal happiness; for it is the teaching of faith that nothing defiled can enter heaven. The dogma of purgatory is one of the most consoling truths of religion. To be united to the second Adam, our mind must believe this as well as all the other truths which he has revealed. We are naturally inclined to accept it. It is so sweet to think that death does not break the bonds which attach us to our friends, and that we can be useful to them even after they have quitted life! Hence the proofs that we are about to offer are not intended to remove any repugnance of ours to assent to this truth, but to strengthen and console our belief by showing that it is well founded.

Let us begin by showing what we are to believe regarding purgatory.

Exposition of the Catholic belief.—The Catholic Church, assembled in the Council of Trent, teaches us four truths in reference to this subject. The first, that after the remission of the guilt of sin and the eternal punishment due to it, obtained from God in the sacrament of penance, there still, ordinarily speaking, remains some temporal punishment to be endured for it. The second, that when one has not made due satisfaction in this world, he can and must make it after death in purgatory. The third, that the prayers and good works of the living can be useful to the dead, can soothe and shorten their sufferings. The fourth, that the Sacrifice of the Mass is propitiatory, and consequently has the effect of effacing sins and of satisfying the divine justice for the living and the dead.[192]

It is therefore an article of faith that there is a purgatory, and that we can, by our prayers, by our good works, by the Holy Sacrifice of the Mass, assuage the sorrows of the souls that are undergoing their purification there. Now, in professing this tender truth, we associate our belief with the belief of all ages—an invariable belief, because founded on the word of God, who does not change.

First proof of purgatory: The old testament. A few soldiers belonging to the army of Judas Machabeus had, contrary to the command of God, carried away from the temples of Jamnia some objects consecrated to idols, and hidden them under their coats during the course of a battle, in which they all afterward lost their lives. Their fault, which was looked upon as the cause of their death, was discovered when they were about to be buried. Judas Machabeus, believing that there were grounds for supposing either that they were not sufficiently acquainted with the law to understand the grievousness of their transgression or that they had repented of it in the sight of God before breathing their last, ordered a collection to be made and the silver to be forwarded to Jerusalem, that sacrifices might be offered for their sins. "He considered," says the scripture, "that a great mercy is in store for those who die in piety. It is therefore a holy and wholesome thought to pray for the dead, that they may be loosed from their sins."[193]

Thus, among the Jews, it was believed a pious and salutary practice to offer sacrifices for the dead, that they might be freed from their sins. The historian Josephus indicates plainly enough that this belief existed in his time, when he testifies that the Jews did not pray for those who had taken away their own lives.[194] Now, they certainly did not pray for those who were already in Abraham's bosom, where no one had any need of prayers, nor for those in hell, where prayers could render no service. They therefore believed in a middle state between the two: and this middle state we name purgatory.

Second proof: The new testament. If the custom of offering prayers and sacrifices for the dead, which supposes a belief in purgatory, was only, as Calvin pretends, an invention of Satan, how does it happen that our Lord, finding it established, never said a word against it to the Jews? How is it that he did not warn his disciples against such a false, illusory, and superstitious tradition? Still more: he knew that all Christians would religiously receive this tradition during the ages that were to follow; that, when renewing every day the sacrifice of his body and blood, they would earnestly ask the application of his merits to the suffering souls of their deceased brethren—and yet he took no measures to prevent them!

What do I say? He himself recommended this practice to his disciples, and with his infallible word confirmed their belief in purgatory. One day he said to them: "If any one blaspheme against the Son of Man, he may obtain pardon for his offense; but if he blaspheme against the Holy Ghost, his sin shall not be forgiven him either in this world or in the world to come."[195] Therefore there are sins which are forgiven in the world to come; otherwise, the Savior's expression would be meaningless. Now, as sin cannot be forgiven in the world to come, as regards its guilt and eternal punishment, it can therefore be forgiven as regards its temporal punishment. But this forgiveness does not take place in heaven, into which nothing defiled can enter, nor in hell, out of which there is no redemption. There is therefore a middle place between heaven and hell. This place we call purgatory.

Third proof: The tradition of the Catholic Church. Not only did our Lord confirm the belief of the apostles in purgatory, and approve and recommend the practice of praying for the dead, but he ordered them to preach the same truth and to spread the same usage. The necessity of the matter will be evident if it can be shown that the apostles taught the Church to pray for the dead. Now, the case is really so. It is a fact, as certain as the existence of the sun, that, since the time of the apostles, the Church has never ceased to offer prayers and sacrifices for her departed children. It would be a long task to relate here all the testimonies of the fathers and of ecclesiastical writers, which establish the perpetuity of this touching observance. We shall confine ourselves to a few. "Assemble," say the *Apostolic Constitutions*, "in cemeteries, read the sacred books there, chant the psalms in honor of the martyrs and of all the saints, and for your brethren who have died in the Lord, and next offer the Eucharist."[196]

Tertullian, who lived so near the time of the apostles, speaks frequently of prayer for the dead, and says that this usage was founded on tradition.[197] St. Cyprian, alluding to prayers for the dead, writes these remarkable words: "The bishops, our predecessors, had already ordered that none of our brethren should, in his will, name an ecclesiastic as tutor or guardian, and if he did so, that no one should pray for him or celebrate the sacrifice for the repose of his soul."[198] The decision of the bishops prior to the time of St. Cyprian supposes the practice of praying for the dead established, and thereby points out to us the apostolicity of its origin.

Here it appears in the clearest terms from St. Chrysostom: "It was not without reason that the apostles ordained that, in the celebration of the terrible mysteries, a commemoration should be made of the deceased, for they well knew how useful and profitable it would be to the dead."[199] St. Augustine, who composed a treatise on our duties to the dead, in which prayers for their repose continually occur, expresses himself thus: "Funereal pomp and a gorgeous mausoleum, without being of the least service to the dead, may indeed offer some kind of consolation to the living. But that which cannot be doubted is that the prayers of the Church, the holy sacrifice, alms, bring them relief, and obtain for them a more merciful treatment than they deserved. The whole Church, instructed by the tradition of its fathers, takes care that, at the part of the sacrifice in which the dead are mentioned, a prayer and an oblation are made for all those who have departed this life in the communion of the body of Jesus Christ."[200]

In his work against heresies,[201] the same father ranks Arius among the heretics, as St. Epiphanius did before him, because he denied, in opposition to the doctrine and tradition of all times, the usefulness of prayers for the dead. Both of them also testify to us that this was one of the revealed truths, known by apostolic tradition.

St. Isidore teaches us the same: "Because the oblation of the sacrifice and prayer for the repose of the faithful departed are made in the Church throughout the world, we believe that this custom has come from the apostles. The Church observes it in every place. If the Church did not believe that the faithful might thus obtain pardon for their sins, it would not distribute alms for the relief of their souls, or offer the sacrifice to God for them."[202]

Finally, St. Cyril of Jerusalem, explaining to the faithful the custom of praying for the dead, says: "We pray for our parents and our bishops, and in general for the souls of all our departed ones, in the firm hope that they receive great consolation from the prayers that are offered for them in the holy and awful sacrifice."[203]

It would be useless to multiply testimonies, since the leaders of the pretended Reformation acknowledged the existence of purgatory and the olden practice of praying for the dead. "For more than thirteen hundred years," said Calvin, "the practice of praying for the dead has existed."[204] "As for me, who believe firmly—I even venture to say, as for me who know—that purgatory exists, I am easily convinced that scripture makes mention of it. All that I know of purgatory is that souls suffer there and can be relieved by our works and our prayers."[205]

Fourth proof: Tradition of sects separated from the Church. The liturgies of many of the sects, from which we are about to quote, though not written till the fourth century, date their origin nevertheless from the time of the apostles.[206] The liturgy[207] of the Nestorians of Malabar expresses itself thus: "Let us remember our forefathers, our brethren, the faithful who have departed out of this world in the orthodox faith; let us beseech the Lord to absolve them, to forgive them their sins, their prevarications, and to make them worthy of a share in eternal felicity with the just who are conformed to the divine will."

The liturgy of the Nestorians of Chaldea: "Receive this oblation, O my God!...for all those who mourn, who are sick, who suffer from persecutions, calamities, and afflictions, and for all the deceased whom death has taken from us...Pardon the sins and offenses of those who are dead; we ask it of thee through thy grace and thy eternal mercies."

The liturgy of the Armenians presents some most beautiful prayers for the living and the dead in general. The deacon, addressing all the faithful, exclaims: "We ask that mention should be made, in this sacrifice, of all the faithful in general, men and women, old and young, who have died with faith in Jesus Christ." "Remember them, O Lord, and have pity on them," answers the choir. Then the priest alone: "Give them rest, light, and a place among thy saints in thy heavenly kingdom, and let them be worthy of thy eternal mercy."

The liturgy of the Greeks contains this petition for the dead: "We make our offering to thee also for the repose and the deliverance of the soul of thy servant, N., that it may be admitted into that bright place where there is no weeping or mourning; and that thou mayest grant it rest, O Lord our God! in that place where shines the light of thy countenance."

The liturgy of Alexandria, or of the Jacobite Copts, makes commemoration of the dead in these terms: "Remember, O Lord! those who have fallen asleep and ended their days in the priesthood, as also every order among the laity. Vouchsafe, O Lord! to grant rest to their souls in the bosom of Abraham, Isaac, and Jacob; lead them into the paradise of delights, into that abode from which sadness, grief, and lamentation are banished, and in which shines the light of thy saints." The same sentiments and supplications are found in the liturgies of other sects separated from the Church, as those of the Abyssinians, Syrians, etc.[208]

It is therefore an evident fact, and all the liturgies of the world bear testimony to it, that, since the apostolic times, not only Christians of the Catholic Church, but also those of separated communions, have recited and still recite prayers for the dead in the celebration of the holy mysteries. Now, this unanimous concurrence of all Christians, this perfect uniformity of all liturgies, necessarily supposes a common origin, recognized alike by friends and enemies, by Catholics and dissenters—an authority more sacred, in the eyes of heretics, than that of the Church to which they refuse to submit—an authority, in fine, which it is impossible to find anywhere else than in the teaching of the apostles. It is therefore to their teaching and to that of their divine master that we must refer the universal practice of praying for the dead, and the belief in the utility thereof, as well as in the existence of purgatory, which is inseparable from this belief.

Fifth proof: The tradition of pagans. The dogma of purgatory is one of those essential truths which belong to primitive revelation, and which the tradition of our first parents transmitted to all the peoples of the earth. Plato distinguishes, among the dead, the just who enjoy eternal happiness, the wicked who undergo eternal torments, and the unfortunate whose sins are remediable and who are punished only that they may become better: which is conformable to the belief of Jews and Catholics.[209] We find the same doctrine in Virgil.[210]

According to St. Justin[211] and Tertullian,[212] the ancient pagans offered sacrifices for the dead, and made use of certain expiatory rites to restore them to their first innocence. As the lot of each one departing this life was unknown, all were prayed for in general. In the letters that were sent to announce the decease of any person, care was taken to transmit his eulogy, so as to engage the recipients to pray for him.[213] Besides a liturgy, there were formulas of prayers for the dead. The saints were invoked in their favor, as is proved by various inscriptions found engraven on tombs. Here are some specimens: "O celestial souls! come to his aid; may the gods be propitious to thee!" "O ye holy departed! I recommend my husband to your care; vouchsafe to be indulgent to him!"[214] All pagans in East and West have had these usages.

Thus, pagans, Jews, and Christians agree in recognizing the dogma of purgatory. All nations and all times repeat together in their manner: "It is a holy and wholesome thought to pray for the dead, that they may be loosed from their sins."[215] Now, we ask the protestant and the infidel: Who are you to reject a belief so general and so constant? What can you oppose to the faith of the whole world?

Sixth proof: Reason. If, after so many authorities, it would not be superfluous to add a new proof, we might draw it from the idea which the scripture gives us of the justice of

God, saying that God will render to every one according to his works. We ask whether it is just that a sinner, who lived in disorders during his whole life, but was converted at the hour of death and restored to the state of grace by sincere repentance, should be as amply rewarded and as speedily admitted to the enjoyment of eternal happiness as a just man, who persevered all his life in the practice of virtue and died in the most perfect sentiments of the love of God? Never did it occur to a sound mind to think thus of the divine justice.[216]

Social advantages of this dogma.—Let us add that, whether or not error is ever useful, the dogma of purgatory is certainly a great truth. As a matter of fact, the Savior, by confirming, and the Church, by preserving with so much care this precious dogma and pious usage of praying for the dead, have contributed more than may at first be supposed to maintain charity among the living—that charity which is the root of every other virtue and the basis of public peace. It is well worthy of remark that charity, which is the very soul of Christianity, diminishes among the living in proportion as it is extinguished in regard to the dead.

The custom of praying for the dead brings back to our minds a tender recollection of our parents and benefactors. It inspires us with respect for their last wishes. It contributes to the union of families: it gathers the scattered members of a household around the grave of their ancestors; it recalls a thousand sayings and doings that affect their happiness. Many a time it reconciles them, for we are not far from loving when we weep. In fine, it deadens within us the fever of the passions, by reminding us of the nothingness of everything but God. To resist the most sacred inclination of nature, to despise the spirit of Christianity, to trample underfoot the most general and venerable tradition: this is the aim of heretics and infidels when they endeavor to abolish this holy usage.

Motives to pray for the dead.—1. *The glory of God.* Are we at all sensitive about the glory of our heavenly Father? Are we moved by the outrages, the ingratitude, of which he is the object, on the part of so many men, even of so many Christians? Let us comfort the souls in purgatory, let us hasten the day of their deliverance, let us send to heaven as many as possible of these adorers, of whom the least perfect surpasses in perfection all the saints on earth. They will compensate the Lord for the loss of those innumerable souls that every day dishonor him and ruin themselves. For us, and in our name, they will restore to him that glory of which we have too often deprived him. They will console the new Adam, by uniting themselves with him, as members with their head. He himself only chastises with regret. He looks for someone to disarm his justice. He desires it. Can we doubt of the matter after his complaining in the divine scriptures that there is no one to interpose between his wrath and sinners, who are his enemies?

2. *Charity.* These departed ones belong not only to the Lord, but also to us. They are our brethren in the faith. The same vocation separated them from unbelievers. The same seal of adoption was impressed upon them. They were washed in the same blood, nourished with the same bread, sanctified by the same word and the same sacraments. Though they are gone before us into the house of eternity, they have not ceased to form a portion of the same Church. The sacred bond of Christian charity still continues to unite us with them. This is the reason why every day the tender mother whose children we are recommends them to the Lord in the adorable sacrifice, and makes an application to them of our prayers and good works.

They are our brethren according to the flesh, our parents, our brothers, our sisters, our friends—perhaps our pastors, those spiritual fathers who formed our childhood to piety, who so often broke for us the bread of life, and who, it may be, shortened their days by the activity of their zeal and their solicitude for our welfare. These are the persons who suffer, who suffer much, who perhaps suffer only for having loved us too much, who suffer while we enjoy the life which they gave us, the goods which they left us. These are the persons who, from the midst of flames, raise their suppliant hands toward us, and cry out: "Have pity on us! have pity on us! at least you who were our relatives and our friends."

3. *Justice.* Let us descend into the depths of our conscience and seriously ask ourselves: "Among this multitude of souls is there not one in purgatory through my fault? By my misdeeds did I never give occasion to the impatience that was not justifiable, to the words that were not blameless, to the proceedings that were not irreprehensible—faults that are now being so cruelly expiated by my father, my mother, my brother, my sister, my friend?" Let us think on all the levities, all the scandals more or less grave of our life, and, if we have the courage, let us say: "No, there is no one in purgatory on my account."

4. *Our own interest.* These souls have merely preceded us: What need is there of further warning that we shall follow them? We shall follow them; and is our piety solid enough, is our charity ardent enough, is our life pure enough, will our death be precious enough in the sight of God to permit us to hope that nothing will delay our admission into the realms of eternal bliss? Alas! a long and rigorous term in purgatory is perhaps the most favorable lot that most of us can expect. Let us then have compassion on ourselves, and hasten to make of the souls in purgatory so many protectors around the throne of God.

Delivered by our tender care, these blessed souls will keep our places faithfully in heaven, and, by the power of their intercession, bring near the day of our reception into the eternal tabernacles. Let us have no fear of ingratitude or forgetfulness on their part: such vices are excluded from heaven, the home of charity. Do we wish therefore that, after our death, these happy souls should come to meet us, and to offer us a friendly welcome? Let us now stretch out to them a helping hand in their extreme distress. Let us remember the saying of our divine master: "It shall be done to you as you have done to others."[217]

But these souls will not wait till after our death to show their gratitude to us. During life—in our temptations, under our trials, at our last hour—they will obtain for us assistance proportioned to our wants. What consolation shall we not, from this moment, experience! Ah, if the effect of the prayers and sacrifices of the Church were perceptible to the senses, what joy would be ours on witnessing every day the departure of some of these blessed souls from their fiery prison! And what a consolation it would be if God were to reveal to us that it was to our piety, to our good works, that they were indebted for their deliverance!

Prayer for the dead and confession are two of those things whose loss protestants most regret. "I knew a Lutheran whom our belief in purgatory changed to a Catholic. He had lost a dear brother during a feast; and, as he continually pondered over this sudden step from a joyous hall to a dismal coffin, his heart was tormented. His soul required comfort. He knew all the purity that was needed for heaven, and, in his species of worship, he found no intermediate place between the courts of paradise and the depths of the abyss.

"His fears became agonizing. He lost his rest. His days were without light, his nights without sleep, his thoughts without hope. He was visibly failing, and stooping toward the tomb, toward the tomb of his brother, which he should share as a family bed, he was ordered to travel. But he said: 'I shall not have time to go far—I shall die in some hotel, waited on by hireling strangers…and, when I have closed my eyes, they will be obliged to search among my papers, in order to know the name of the traveler who came to rest among them forever, and who had need of nothing else than a lodging in a cemetery.'

"His friends joined with the doctor, and the young Scotchman came to the Continent. I found myself on board the same vessel with him, and soon we were engaged in deep conversation, for many points of resemblance attracted us to each other.

"When we had disembarked, we stayed at the same hotel. After a few days he revealed to me the cause of all the sadness that had fallen on his young years—the death of his brother, and hiş anxiety regarding the eternal fate of a being whom he so much loved!...'Ah!' he said to me on All Souls' day, 'I wish, for love of my brother, to adopt your rite! Oh! when I can pray for my brother, I shall breathe, I shall live to ask every day some happiness in heaven for him whom I so much loved on earth!...Your worship enables us to help one another after death. Your prayers take away from the grave its horrible silence. You hold converse still with those who have quitted life. You understand the nature of human weakness, that weakness which is not a crime, but which is not purity. And, between the limits of heaven and earth, a place of expiation has been revealed to you by God. Perhaps my brother may be there. I become a Catholic to deliver him, and to console myself, to relieve myself from that weight which oppresses me, that weight which I shall no longer feel when I can pray.' And he became a Catholic."[218]

PRAYER

O my God! who art all love, I thank thee for having revealed to us the consoling dogma of purgatory: grant me a great compassion for the souls whom thy justice purifies there.

I am resolved to love God above all things, and my neighbor as myself for the love of God; and, in testimony of this love, I will every day say a prayer for the souls in purgatory.

Lesson 21: Our Union with the New Adam by Faith (4)

Sixth article of the Creed: The ascension.—After accompanying the Savior to the lowest parts of the earth, we are now about to follow him to the highest heavens, and everywhere we shall behold him accomplishing the great work of the redemption. This is the touching truth which is contained in the sixth article of the Creed: "He ascended into heaven, and sitteth at the right hand of God, the Father Almighty." Reserving the full history of the ascension for a later period, we shall content ourselves with explaining here the dogmatic part of the article.

Now, faith teaches us that after his glorious resurrection from the tomb our Lord remained forty days on earth. In doing so he had a twofold object—to instruct the apostles perfectly in the truths of religion, and by repeated apparitions to confirm their minds fully in the belief of his resurrection. The least reflection enables us to perceive the wisdom of this conduct. On the one hand, the apostles should be the first martyrs for their preaching; on the other, the mystery of the resurrection is the foundation of Christianity, and, as it were, the mighty ring to which all other rings are fastened: for to him who admits it, faith no longer presents any difficulties. As a matter of fact, if I believe that our Lord returned to life, I am forced to admit that he died and that he was born. Moreover, as the earth is not the abode of glorified bodies, if I believe the resurrection of our Lord, I must also believe his ascension into heaven.

He ascended into heaven. We ought therefore to believe firmly and unhesitatingly that our Lord, after completing the work of our redemption on earth, ascended into heaven as man—body and soul. As God, he had never ceased to be there, since by his divinity he is everywhere. He ascended by his own power: not by any extrinsic force, as was the case with Elias, who was carried up to heaven in a fiery chariot; the prophet Habacuc and the deacon Philip, borne by a divine agency a considerable distance through the air; and the Blessed Virgin, raised to the celestial Jerusalem by the omnipotence of her divine Son.

It was not only as God that Jesus Christ ascended into heaven by his own power: it was also as man. It is true that this did not take place by the strength natural to man; but the supernatural might with which his blessed soul was filled could transport his body whithersoever he desired it: for his body, already in possession of glory, obeyed without difficulty the orders and movements of the soul. This is the reason why we say and believe that Jesus Christ ascended into heaven both as God and man.[219]

The expression *he ascended* requires a new explanation. In speaking of the eternal Word we say that to become incarnate he descended from heaven to earth. This is true in the sense that he lowered himself so far as to unite himself with human nature; but it would be false if we meant that by descending he left one place to occupy another, inasmuch as God is everywhere. In the same manner, when our Lord, as God, ascended into heaven, he did not therefore cease to remain as God in this world.[220] But on the day when, as man, he ascended into heaven, he ceased to manifest himself in this world by a visible presence, to remain with us only by an invisible presence in the august Sacrament of the Altar.

We say, "he ascended into heaven," not, "he ascended to heaven," to indicate that our Lord passed through all the inferior heavens, all the lower regions of the air, to go and take his place in the highest heavens, at the summit of glory, in the dwelling place of the adorable Trinity. During this glorious journey, he took possession of the air and all the celestial regions on his way, thus sanctifying the upper parts of the universe as he had sanctified the lower: like a monarch, who, by his solemn entry into his dominions and his cities, fills them all with his fame and his glory.[221]

He sitteth at the right hand of God, the Father Almighty. These words mean that our Lord is in heaven as the place of his rest; that he is there as a King on his throne, to receive the homage and to be the delight of angels and saints. *To be seated* does not refer here to position of body, but means the certain and immutable possession of that royal power and infinite glory which Jesus Christ received from his Father. "It was his Father," says the apostle St. Paul, "who raised him up from the dead, who gave him a seat beside himself in heaven, above all principalities, powers, virtues, dominations, and other dignities that can be named in the world to come, as well as in this world, and who put all things under his power."[222]

At the right hand of the Father Almighty. The eternal Father, being a pure Spirit, has neither a right nor a left hand; but, to accommodate itself to our language, the scripture makes use of this expression to show that Jesus Christ, as God, holds the same rank in glory and majesty as his Father. As man, our Lord is also present at the right hand of his Father, not in the same degree of power, because our Lord as man is inferior to God, but in the same degree of exaltation, on the same throne, because in him the human nature is inseparably united to the divine.

A comparison will illustrate this truth. When a king, clad in his purple robes, is seated on his throne, and all the princes of his court occupy inferior seats, the purple robes of the king shine out above all the princes. Not that they equal the king in dignity, but because they are attached to the king as his garments. In the same manner, the humanity of our Lord Jesus Christ is placed above the cherubim and the seraphim, at the very side of God himself, not by the dignity of its nature, but because it is attached to God—not merely as the purple robes to the monarch, but far and away more strictly, that is to say, by a personal union.[223]

It is a well-known usage among men to give the right-hand place to him whom they wish to honor. The idea has been transferred to spiritual things; and, to explain the glory which Jesus Christ has acquired, and by which he is raised as man above everything created; we say that he sits at the right hand of his Father. We see hereby that there is allusion to a singular and peculiar glory, which belongs to our Lord alone.[224]

Let us sincerely congratulate the Savior on his glorious triumph. And nothing is more proper to make our own hearts beat with gratitude and joy. It was for us that he ascended into heaven. It was we who, in his Person, took possession of this admirable kingdom. It is our regenerated flesh and blood that occupy a place at the right hand of the Father Almighty.

Causes of the ascension.—If we wish to examine further into the causes of the Savior's ascension, faith shows us that the second Adam ascended into heaven for the following reasons:

1. *To open the gates of heaven.* To open its gates, closed since the sin of the first Adam, and to take possession of it in the name of the human race. "That where I am you also may be," he said to his apostles at the last supper.[225] It was to manifest still more clearly the certainty of his promises that he brought with him into the abode of eternal beatitude the souls of the saints whom he had delivered. What more proper to strengthen hope in our hearts? We see the second Adam, our father, our leader, ascend into heaven as man, and place human nature at the right hand of his Father. What more powerful motive to hope that we, who are his members, shall also ascend thither, and be reunited to our head? The Savior ascended into heaven therefore in order to prepare places for us there.

2. *To defend us.* He ascended—O admirable goodness!—to defend us. The apostle St. Paul represents him to us as standing before the throne of his Father, interceding on our behalf, pleading our cause, and obtaining for us by his all-powerful mediation the graces which we require, whether that we may not wander from the road to heaven or that we may return to it when we have had the misfortune to leave it. Hence these touching words of the beloved disciple: "My little children, I write you this that you may not sin; but if any one sin, we have an advocate with the Father: I mean Jesus Christ, who is justice itself, and who is the victim of propitiation for our sins, and not for ours only, but for those of the whole world."[226]

3. *For us to follow him.* He ascended thither to excite in us a desire of following him. In consequence of the sin of the first Adam, the human race had forgotten its true country. That land was looked upon with indifference and disgust. By ascending thither, the new Adam changed our indifference into love and our disgust into desire. It is so natural that high-born children should sigh after the happiness of meeting again a dearly-beloved Father! To maintain this supernatural desire within us he sent us the Holy Ghost, who continually detaches our affections from earth and elevates them toward heaven.

4. *To fulfill and accomplish all things.* The Savior ascended into heaven to put the seal to all the prophecies that concerned his sacred Person, his life, and his actions. "He was raised above all the heavens," says the apostle, "that he might fulfill and accomplish all things."[227] This is the reason why the fathers of the Church call the ascension "the happy end of our Lord Jesus Christ's pilgrimage."[228]

5. *For a proper abode of his glorified body.* He ascended into heaven because his body, become glorious and immortal by his resurrection, required some other abode than this mean and obscure earth: he should dwell in future only on the bright summits of the eternal hills. Still it was not only to enjoy the glory of the kingdom which he had conquered that he ascended, but also to teach us that our bodies, restored on the model of his, should one day share the same happiness. Can we ever forget that the indispensable condition of our being united to him in eternity is to live and suffer like him in time?

Social advantages of this article.—And, now, what need is there of many words to show the social influence of this new article of the Creed? Jesus Christ ascended into heaven; he ascended thither for me: I shall one day ascend thither. Assuredly, this is the consecration of the noblest and strongest incentive to all public and private virtues—hope.

Take away the hope of heaven, and virtue is only a vain word employed by dupes for the benefit of knaves. The goods of the present life are everything to man; and you let loose ambition, cupidity, voluptuousness, all those furious wild beasts that transform society into a bloody arena. No more speak of devotedness, of the spirit of sacrifice: selfishness alone reigns everywhere—hard, pitiless selfishness. Suicide is then a logical act. Society has no other basis than a scaffold, no other protectors than jailers and hangmen.

Bring back, on the contrary, the hope of heaven, and you see a multitude of generous souls exchange the goods of time for those of eternity. A thousand devoted acts break forth on all sides. Every species of human misery is relieved, and society rests in peace: for virtue has a motive—it expects a reward. Among the innumerable prodigies attributable to the hope of heaven, and shining in the annals of the Church as stars in the azure vault above us, we shall select only one, whose date is recent, and at which all Germany was moved.

In 1824, the illustrious countess Welsersheim quitted the society of which she was the ornament, the family of which she was the idol, and an immense fortune, to become a poor and humble religious in a Convent of the Most Holy Redeemer. To the many disapprovers of her conduct, she gaily made reply: "I cannot understand you. Why are you surprised at what I am about to gain by the magnificent promises of him who gives a hundredfold to those who leave all things to follow him? Would it be surprising if a poor man should leave his own fireside for a time that he might go to a distant country for a rich inheritance awaiting him there?"

She did not remain long absent from her true home; for on March 24th, 1841, our Lord came in search of his spouse, to lead her to the eternal nuptials.[229] A moment's reflection suffices to develop the meaning of these hasty remarks, and to show what an important place is held in the world by the sixth article of the Catholic Creed.

Seventh article of the Creed.—We have said in the preceding lessons[230] that, since the time of original sin, life has been a delay granted to man, that he might have an opportunity of doing penance, and that he might be regenerated by uniting himself with the new Adam. We have seen that the new Adam omitted nothing to establish this salutary union between him and us, and to render it permanent. With this view, he became our Redeemer and he continues our advocate in heaven. When, therefore, the period of trial ends, he will come to distinguish those who have profited of it, that is, those who are united to him, from those who are still united to the old Adam: and he will render to everyone according to his works. Such is the solemn truth contained in the seventh article of the Creed: "From thence he will come to judge the living and the dead."

Before explaining the principal truth expressed by these words, we ought to speak of the particular judgment. We must therefore know that there are two judgments, the particular and the general.

The particular judgment; its necessity and preceding signs.—The particular judgment is that which takes place in regard to each one of us the moment that we leave this life. At the very instant that the soul is separated from the body, it stands before the face of God, who, suddenly enlightening its understanding, shows it, as in a mirror, all its works, whether good or evil, and the reward or the punishment which they have deserved. We are judged in the place where we die, for the judge is everywhere. At this judgment, God appears as the judge, the soul as the culprit, the guardian angel as the witness, and the devil as the accuser.

We are judged there, as we have said, on all the thoughts, words, and actions of our lives: on all the evil that was done by us, on all the good that should have been and was not done by us, and on all the good that was ill done by us.[231] As for the sentence, it is executed on the spot. Hell, purgatory, or heaven immediately becomes the abode of the soul, according to its state; and, the judge being infallible, the sentence is irrevocable. It is evident, even to the eyes of reason, that the particular judgment is necessary.

As a matter of fact, God would not be just, God would not be God, if he treated in the same manner those who offend him and those who serve him. It is therefore necessary that the good and the wicked should render an account of their lives, that he may deal with all according to their works. Moreover, this judgment must take place immediately after death, because time, that is, the delay granted to every man for the purpose of gaining heaven, is then at an end. Eternity begins; and eternity is the reward or the punishment that follows life.

The general or last judgment.—Let us now proceed to the literal explanation of the seventh article of the Creed, and speak of the last judgment.

1. *The certainty of the last judgment.* When speaking of the end of the world, our Lord declared that there would be a general judgment.[232] All the occurrences, foretold by the divine master, have been so far literally verified: therefore this shall follow in the same path. The words "from thence he will come" teach us that, according to the scriptures, our Lord will at the end of the world leave the right hand of his Father and come again on earth, that he may receive of all mankind a public and rigorous account of their works, and pronounce in regard to the good and the wicked the sentence that will fix their lot for all eternity. They also warn us not to believe in Antichrist, who will come from the earth, and who will endeavor to persuade men that he is our Lord; for our Lord will not come from the earth, but from heaven.

He will come, body and soul, with great power and majesty—seated on the clouds, preceded by his cross, and accompanied by the angels and the saints. But because our Lord, as man, will be the only judge visible to the eyes of the body, we say of him alone that he will come to judge. The judgment will take place on the earth, and not in heaven. On the one hand, it is on the earth that men earn reward or punishment, it is on the earth that our Lord and his faithful servants are persecuted and outraged; on the other, the judgment is for both the good and the wicked. Now, neither wicked men nor wicked angels can set foot in heaven, where nothing defiled can enter. According to the opinion of many doctors, founded on the prophecy of Joel, the last judgment will take place in the Valley of Josaphat, situated near Jerusalem, between Mounts Olivet and Calvary, that the sight of these holy places may increase the joy of the good and the anguish of the wicked.[233]

From thence he will come to judge. It is our Lord who will be the judge: it is meet and just that he should be. Since there is question of judging mankind, is it not becoming, and even necessary, that they should see their judge with the eyes of the body, hear with their ears the sentence pronounced upon them—in a word, know their judgment through the channels of their ordinary senses? It is also but justice to Jesus Christ. He was, while on earth, unjustly condemned by the wicked: Is it not just that, in his turn, he should appear, seated on his throne, to judge all men? Now, he will judge, not only as God, but as man. He tells us so himself. "The Father," he says, "has given the Son power to do judgment, because he is the Son of man."[234] The prince of the apostles teaches the same truth: "He commanded us to preach to the people, and to testify that it is he who has been appointed by God the judge of the living and the dead."[235]

2. *Necessity of the last judgment.* If the particular judgment is necessary, the general is no less so. In point of fact, it is necessary that justice should be done:

I. *In regard to the Son of Man.* Disowned by the Jews, crucified by pagans, blasphemed by heretics, insulted by infidels, dishonored by Christians, it is necessary that a solemn and splendid act of reparation should be made to him. It is necessary that all mankind should for once fall on their knees before him, who, for love of them, chose to die upon a cross.

II. *In regard to the saint.* Treated now as his divine master, despised, persecuted, mocked, it is necessary that, one day, in the eyes of the world, his crown of thorns should be changed into a crown of glory. It is necessary that all men should see which side was right, and that order, publicly violated in regard to him, should be publicly restored.

III. *In regard to the sinner.* While on earth, crowned with flowers, intoxicated with pleasures, insolently scorning the laws of God, it is necessary that he should one day recognize, with his brow in the dust, the sovereign dominion of him whose commands, and promises, and threats he had the audacity to despise. It is necessary that, in the sight of men and angels, vice should one day be covered with that ignominy and contempt with which it so long endeavored to brand virtue.

IV. *In regard to the whole man.* The soul alone had experience of the particular judgment; it is necessary that the body, in its turn, should also be judged: and that man should receive publicly, in his soul and body, the reward or the punishment of the works which his soul and body accomplished together during their mortal union.

V. *In regard to all mankind.* When dying, men leave children, or disciples, or friends, who imitate their example or follow their advice. This must necessarily increase their reward or punishment for a long time after their death. But this deplorable or beneficial influence, which they exercise over so many persons, can only end with the world. That justice may be perfectly done, it is necessary that there should be a strict and accurate investigation into all the good or evil caused by example till the end of time: this can only be accomplished by the general judgment of all men at the consummation of the world.[236]

VI. *In regard to providence.* Calumniated by blind mortals, it is necessary that the whole world should one day render homage to the wisdom of its counsels, to the sweetness of its ways, to the deep economy of its designs: in a word, it is necessary that all things should return to that order which sin had disturbed. This is not enough. It is necessary that all things should return in a solemn and glorious manner, so as to make due reparation for scandals. Now, a public general judgment of all the nations of the world, assembled together, is the only means of publicly repairing order publicly violated. "For this reason," says the Lord, "I will gather together all the peoples, and I will bring them down into the Valley of Josaphat, and I will enter into judgment with them."[237]

3. *Circumstances of the last judgment.* In his infinite goodness, the Savior was not content with announcing the last judgment: he also pointed out the signs which should precede it. His intention was, first, to keep all men in a state of salutary fear; for we shall all appear at this dreadful judgment—in one sense as near to us as the day of our death.[238] And next, to make known to Christians of the last times the approach of the end of the world and the necessity of their being always in readiness. Now, the signs that will precede this judgment are of two kinds: remote and immediate. The following are, according to scripture and tradition, the remote signs of the judgment, and of the end of the world.

I. *The preaching of the gospel throughout the whole earth.* "The gospel of the kingdom shall be preached in the whole world," says the Savior, "for a testimony to all nations, and then shall the consummation come."[239] The word *then* is well worthy of notice: it seems to indicate that the gospel will no sooner have completed the circuit of the globe than the end of time shall come.

II. *Apostasy.* "The judgment will not come," says St. Paul, "till a revolt precedes it."[240] Hereby we are to understand the revolt of peoples against kings, especially against the sovereign pontiff, and finally against Jesus Christ and his gospel.[241] Since apostasy is one of the signs that are to precede the last judgment, it shall therefore be public, amazing, general. Not only individuals, but even the majority of nations as nations will rebel simultaneously against their princes—against the sovereign pontiff—and against our Lord, both as God and King.

III. *Antichrist.* "The last judgment," continues the apostle, "will not come until the man of sin has first appeared—the son of perdition, who raises himself above all that is called God."[242] Anti-Christian doctrines having perverted the nations, by everywhere diffusing a spirit of impiety and revolt, there will come a man who shall be at once their impersonation and their punishment, and this man shall be in consequence the most frightful tyrant ever known to the world. This man will be Antichrist. He will reign, according to the interpreters, for about three years and a half, and be put to death by our Lord on his arrival. The persecutions that he will wage against the elect will be the last and the most terrible trial of the Church.

IV. *The conversion of the Jews.* This sign is pointed out by a constant tradition, founded on several texts of scripture, and especially on St. Paul's epistle to the Romans.[243] Before being converted, the Jews will begin to quit that immobility in which they have dwelt since the destruction of Jerusalem: they will be emancipated, and will enter into the stream of Christian ideas, until at length they publicly recognize our Lord as the Messias.

V. *The fall of the Roman Empire.* By the Roman Empire we understand the empire perpetuated, in the West, in Charlemagne and the emperors of Germany, who, till the year 1806, always bore the title of Emperor of the Romans, while their empire was called the Holy Roman Empire, and, in the East, in the emperors of Constantinople, whose power was overthrown in the year 1453 by Mahomet II; also, the temporal and spiritual empire of the sovereign pontiff. Now, it is a universal, and we may say an apostolical tradition, that the fall of the Roman Empire will be one of the foregoing signs of the last judgment.[244]

Preceding signs of the last judgment.—As for the immediate signs that shall precede the last judgment, the following are the terms in which the Savior himself announces them to his apostles. When the end of the world and the day of judgment are at hand, there shall be signs in the sun, and in the moon, and in the stars. And on the earth the nations shall be troubled by reason of the roaring of the sea and the waves. Men shall wither away with fear in expectation of that which shall come upon the whole world. The sun shall be darkened, the moon shall not give her light, the stars shall fall from heaven, and the celestial dome shall be shaken. Then shall the sign of the Son of Man appear in heaven. At this sight all the nations of the earth shall manifest their sorrow, and they shall see the Son of Man coming on the clouds with great power and majesty. At the same time, he shall send his angels with a trumpet, and a loud voice, and they shall say: "Arise, ye dead, and come to judgment!" And the graves shall open, and all those who sleep in the dust of the earth shall hear the voice of the Son of God. And they shall come forth, some to eternal glory, some to eternal misery. And the angels shall gather together the elect of God from the four corners of the earth, from one end of heaven to the other.[245]

At the recollection of his beloved ones, whom he has just named, the Savior suddenly softens the tone of this terrible picture. He wishes that whatsoever should make the wicked pine away with grief and terror should be for the elect an occasion of joy and a motive of confidence. In point of fact, the signs which shall announce to the first the unexpected arrival of the avenger of their crimes shall be to the second an infallible presage of the coming of the rewarder of their virtues. This is the reason why he addresses to them, in the persons of the apostles, these consoling words: "Now, when these things begin to come to pass, raise your eyes and lift up your heads, because your deliverance is at hand."[246]

When all these preparations for the judgment are completed, the Son of Man, in all the splendor of his majesty, accompanied by his angels,[247] seated on a bright cloud as on a tribunal, and having by his side his twelve apostles as assessors, with all the nations of the earth assembled before him, shall open the great book of consciences, that is, shall manifest all the secrets of consciences, shall publish the private sentences delivered at the particular judgment, making them known to angels and to men, and the hope of the hypocrite shall perish.[248]

The suit being prepared from documents so convincing that the wicked themselves shall be obliged to acknowledge the justice of their condemnation, he shall command his angels to proceed to the final and most heartrending separation of all the members of the human family from one another, as a shepherd separates the sheep from the goats. He shall place the sheep at his right hand and the goats at his left. Then shall come the eternal sentence, which the King will pronounce in these terms: "Come, ye blessed of my Father," he will say to the just, "possess the kingdom prepared for you from the creation of the world: for I was hungry, and you gave me to eat; I was thirsty, and you gave me drink; I was a stranger, and you gave me lodging; I was naked, and you clothed me; I was sick, and you visited me; I was in prison, and you came to see me."

The just will answer: "Lord, when did we see thee hungry, and give thee to eat; or thirsty, and give thee to drink? When did we see thee a stranger, and give thee lodging? When did we see thee naked, and clothe thee; or know of thy being sick or in prison, and go to thee?" The King will make reply: "Verily I say to you, as often as you did any of these things to one of the least of my brethren, you did it to myself."

Then, turning to the reprobate, he will say in an angry and terrible voice: "Depart from me, ye cursed! Go to that everlasting fire which was prepared for the devil and his angels: for I was hungry, and you gave me not to eat; I was thirsty, and you gave me not to drink; I was a stranger, and you did not lodge me; I was naked, and you did not clothe me; I was sick and in prison, and you did not come to inquire about me."

They also will answer: "Lord, when did we see thee hungry, or thirsty, or a stranger, or naked, or sick, or in prison, and not assist thee?" Then will he make reply: "Verily I say to you, as often as you failed to do any of these things to the least of these little ones, you failed to do it to myself. And you shall go into everlasting punishment; but the just into life everlasting."[249]

At these words, the elect shall rise triumphant toward heaven, singing their eternal hymn of gratitude and love; and the reprobate shall sink into the depths of hell with the devils. An angel shall close the gates of the horrible abyss, and place thereon the seal of God, which shall never, never be broken. Henceforth, eternity shall reign everywhere.

4. *The existence of hell.* As clearly as that there is a God, the last words of the supreme judge teach us that there is a hell, and an eternal hell, that is, a place where the divine justice punishes and shall forever punish those who die in the state of mortal sin. The belief of a future life, in which the good are rewarded and the wicked punished eternally, is as old as the world and as widespread as the human race. We find it among savages, who show hardly any other sign of religion. We all know how Virgil, like an echo of ancient traditions, professed the eternity of hell, how he recognized its justice, how he celebrated its full victory over crime: "The unfortunate Theseus is fixed immovably in hell, and shall be so forever."[250] Before him Plato had said in express terms: "The wicked are plunged into Tartarus, from which they shall never depart."[251] "I am aware," he says in another place, "that little account is likely to be made of what I say; but, after careful examination and mature reflection, I am convinced that nothing is more in accordance with reason, wisdom, and truth."[252]

Whence has come this belief, so contrary to all the passions, if not from a primitive revelation? Yet this dogma, so steadily professed among the Jews, the Sadducees endeavored to obscure. In like manner, pagan philosophers strove, by their false reasonings, to shake it among other peoples. It was therefore most necessary that our Lord should come to confirm it by his lessons. On this account, he declared in express terms that the wicked should go "into everlasting fire prepared for the devil and his angels"; that "the fire which should burn them should never be extinguished"; and that "the worm which should gnaw them should never die."[253]

Let it no longer be said: "No one has seen hell—we speak of what we know not." Our Lord has seen it—he knows what it is, and he has made it known to us. Among all the men that are alive today there is not one who has seen Charlemagne, there are very few amongst us who have seen Pekin; and yet, on the words of those who have at some time or other seen them, we no longer entertain the least doubt of their existence. So the existence of hell, an eternal hell, is a truth which, founded on the words of our Lord, the Catholic Church has always taught, condemning as heretics all those who have chosen to deny it. It is a truth which we cannot, under pain of damnation, call in question.

In point of fact, when our Lord said that the just should go into life everlasting, no one can deny that he referred to a life which should never end. Therefore, when saying in the same passage that the wicked should go into everlasting fire, he referred to a fire which should never end. Otherwise, the Son of God would have led us into error by giving in the same place, and without any warning thereof, a double meaning to a particular term.

At the thought of an everlasting hell, confounded reason is tempted to rebel; but when it returns to itself, it renders homage to the justice of this punishment.

It says, firstly, that at the tribunal of God, which is justice itself, it is indispensably necessary that there should be a due proportion between the crime and the punishment. Now, sin is both finite and infinite. Finite, because it is the work of a finite creature; infinite, because it is an outrage against infinite majesty. It is therefore necessary that the punishment of sin should, in order to be just, be both finite and infinite. But it cannot be infinite in its rigor, since it is to be undergone by a finite creature: it must therefore be infinite in its duration. Thus does reason, when impartial, demonstrate to itself the indispensable necessity of an everlasting hell.

Moreover, what is a reprobate? He is a man who did not profit of the delay which God granted him, that is, the trial of time, or the time of trial. What do I say? He is a man who came out of it more defiled than he entered it, who quitted life with the will of outraging God by sin. Death surprised him in this disposition of mind: it fixed him therein. In this state he fell into the hands of God: time was no more for him. Therefore, as long as he shall have the will of sinning, he must undergo its punishment. But he shall always have this will. Therefore, he must always be punished. This is the unanswerable reasoning of St. Gregory the Great.[254] Let us add, with Catholic philosophy, that the damned themselves, remaining as they are, do not desire to leave hell, so conscious are they of being in their right place and of the necessity of order.

It says, secondly, that if hell did not exist or were not eternal, man would be God's master, society would be an impossibility, and the earth would become a slaughterhouse. The dogma of an eternal hell is, by every title, a social benefit. What! Notwithstanding this dreadful belief, supported by the twofold testimony of divine revelation and human tradition, the earth is deluged with iniquities! Day and night the wicked threaten order, property, honor, innocence, peace, the very existence of the family and society! What would it be, O my God! if thou wert completely to remove from them the salutary fear of an everlasting hell? What would it be if thou wert to say to all men in general that hell should only continue for a limited period, and that annihilation or felicity should succeed to the torments of a few years, or even of a few centuries? Do we wish to know what would then become of society? See what becomes of it, see what is done to it, through the agency of those who say—without, however, believing what they say—"There is no hell."

This is the cry of the brothel-house; it is the motto of assassins, of robbers, of poisoners, of corrupters, of tyrants, of all sorts of criminals. Let this antisocial blasphemy be regarded as a truth, and, man being what he is, the world shall in future be only a den of wild beasts, a gory field of battle.

Is it necessary to remind you of what occurred in France toward the close of the eighteenth century? Was it not amid shouts of "Away with hell!" and "Hell forever!" that all those monsters with human faces, whose name is the name of every crime and the eternal disgrace of humanity, marched to pillage, to murder, to destruction? Even in our own days, what other motto is borne on their cheerless banner by those unhappy men who threaten to bring back the world to barbarism? For the rest, let us beware of accepting the change. The furious declamations of the wicked against hell prove quite the contrary of that at which they aim. They prove that hell annoys them. We do not hate that which we do not fear, and we do not fear that in which we do not believe. But enough! Instead of losing time in arguing on hell, we shall do much better to think of living in a Christian manner, that we may not fall into it.

5. *The pains of hell.* Faith not only teaches us that there is a hell, an everlasting hell, but it also reveals to us the torments that are endured there. These torments are of two kinds: the pain of loss, or the regret caused by the loss of God and eternal happiness; and the pain of sense, or the sorrow caused by the heat of a fire that shall never be extinguished. These two kinds of torments are clearly pointed out in the words of the Savior. "The worm that shall never die" designates the pain of loss; and "the fire that shall never be extinguished," the pain of sense. The gnawing worm here alluded to is conscience.[255] By the conscience of the unfortunate reprobate, we understand his thoughts of the past, which are most sad. They may be summed up in a few words: "I have lost God! I have lost him through my own fault! I have lost him for a trifle! I have lost him beyond recovery!" This pain is the most bitter that a rational creature can endure.

Nothing can be juster than these two kinds of torments; for they correspond with the two kinds of disorders that are to be found in sin. The one is an insolent contempt of the Creator; the other, an irregular love of the creature. All the damned endure this twofold pain, and their sufferings shall be the same in nature and duration, but the severity of them shall be proportioned to the number and enormity of their offenses. Hence, other things being equal, the hell of the Christian shall be far more terrible than that of the pagan.

Moreover, faith teaches us that the wicked shall suffer day and night for all eternity. In fine, it is certain that the fire which shall burn without consuming them is a material fire—but an intelligent fire, says Tertullian, which shall increase or diminish its heat according to the guilt of each of the reprobate. These few words suffice to freeze our blood, and to make us fear, and fear above all things, and fear all the days of our lives, him who has the power at any moment to hurl us into hell. "Oh, yes," says the Savior, "we should fear him, and him alone." Remember well, therefore, that to fear God and to live as a Christian is the only means to avoid hell.

The terms in which our Lord shall pronounce his eternal sentence give occasion to another remark, which bears very seriously on our conduct. Although, in bringing forward the motives of his twofold decree, the Savior does not speak of the practice or the omission of all the duties which religion imposes on us, it is no less certain that they shall all be, as we have seen in speaking of the particular judgment, the subject of his public examination. If he attaches eternal happiness or misery to the practice or the omission of one virtue only—charity—it is to teach us, on the one hand, that charity is the abridgment of all the commandments, and a short way toward the attainment of all the virtues necessary for our salvation; on the other, it is to put us on our guard against the severity of his judgments, for, if eternal torments are prepared for those who neglect to do good, what must they expect who do evil?

The living and the dead. The seventh article of the Creed ends with the words: "the living and the dead." These words have several meanings. Taken generally, they refer to all mankind without exception: those who shall have died at various periods of time, more or less considerable, before the end of the world, and those who shall die immediately before the last judgment. By *the living*, we understand the just who shall have lived on earth the true life, which is the life of grace, and who shall live eternally in heaven the life of glory; by *the dead*, those who shall have spent and ended their days on earth in the state of mortal sin. The true death consists in the separation of the soul from God, and the wicked shall rise again from the dead only to continue this separation or this eternal death in the flames of hell.

We can also include among the living and the dead all the angels, good and bad, who shall be similarly judged on this great day; for the angels form a part of the Church, of which our Lord is the head. They shall be judged by our Lord, the apostles, and the principal saints: such is the excess of honor and power which God reserves for his friends. On the day of judgment, says the Savior to his apostles, "you shall sit on twelve thrones, to judge the twelve tribes of Israel," that is, all nations.[256] "Do you not know," says St. Paul, "that we shall judge the angels?"[257] This judgment will be a true act of judicial power, a judgment properly so called—a judgment of approval, praise, and glorification in regard to the good angels; a judgment of reproach, shame, and condemnation in regard to the bad angels.[258]

Social advantages of this article.—What shall we now say of the influence of the seventh article of the Creed? The dogma of God's judgment of every man at the moment of death, and of all men together at the end of time, followed by an eternity of torments for the wicked, is of a character so social that, on whatever day we should efface this fundamental truth from the tablet of human belief, society must perish. What rein would be left for the passions, continually excited against order, against property, against the authority of superiors, against the honor of families, against the lives and the rights of the weak and the helpless, if you should take away the belief of a God who knows all things, who will judge all things with absolute independence and perfect equity, and who will punish all things deserving of punishment with inexorable rigor?

They are therefore most guilty and most blind who dare to say that God does not concern himself with the actions of men. Guilty, for they encourage all sorts of crimes, by liberating the sinner from the only fear that can restrain him in his deplorable projects, or inspire him with a salutary remorse for them after their execution. Blind, for they do not see that their senseless doctrines must return in calamities on their own heads. If I have nothing to fear from God's judgment, if hell is a mere chimera, why should I hesitate to benefit myself at your expense, when I am able to do so without any apprehension of being visited by human justice? This is the principle of every villain. Ye kings, peoples, and individuals who attack the dogma which is the protection of all your interests! never shall you be fully aware of all that you owe to the belief of a judgment of God, at which everyone shall be dealt with according to his works. As for us, let us allow this great truth to act with all its weight on our conduct, and we shall live not only as good Christians but also as good citizens.

PRAYER

O my God! who art all love, I thank thee for having forewarned me of thy terrible judgments; penetrate my soul with a filial fear and a tender love toward thee, that, keeping myself united to the new Adam during life, I may deserve to be united to him during eternity.

I am resolved to love God above all things, and my neighbor as myself for the love of God; and, in testimony of this love, I will respect and assist the poor as much as I can.

Lesson 22: Our Union with the New Adam by Faith (5)

Eighth article of the Creed: The Holy Ghost.—Sin had separated man from God. Now, in God there are three Persons. The new Adam should, therefore, to repair the consequences of sin, unite us again with these three Persons. We have already seen what we should believe of the first and the second, to unite ourselves with them by faith. It remains to be explained what we should believe to unite ourselves with the third. The eighth article of the Creed contains the object of our faith on this point. It is conceived in these terms: "I believe in the Holy Ghost."

Divinity of the Holy Ghost.—By these words we make profession of believing in the Holy Ghost as we believe in the Father and in the Son. We confess that he is equal to each of them in all things; that he has the same power, the same eternity, the same divinity; in a word, that he is God as well as the Father and the Son, and that he has a right to the same homage and the same adoration.

The divinity of the Holy Ghost is clearly revealed to us in many passages of scripture: it will suffice to quote a few of them. Our Lord, sending his apostles to preach the gospel, said to them: "Go, teach all nations, baptizing them in the name of the Father, and of the Son, and of the Holy Ghost."[259] He evidently recognized in the Holy Ghost the same power as in the other two Persons of the Holy Trinity. He puts them all on the same level. He therefore proclaims that the Holy Ghost is God as well as the Father and the Son. St. Peter, having said to Ananias: "Why has Satan tempted your heart, and moved you to lie to the Holy Ghost?" adds immediately: "You have not lied to men, but to God."[260] In the same breath, we may say, the vicar of our Lord, the infallible oracle of truth, gives the incommunicable name of God to him whom he has just styled the Holy Ghost. Can the divinity of the Holy Ghost be more clearly indicated? St. John, on his side, tells us: "There are three who render testimony in heaven to the divinity of our Lord: the Father, the Word, and the Holy Ghost; and these three are one."[261]

Thus, the same abode, the same attributes, the same natural unity, belong, St. John assures us, to the Holy Ghost as to the Father and the Son. What clearer proof of the divinity of the Holy Ghost can be desired? The same truth is expressed with equal certainty in the formula which, since the time of the apostles, has so often passed from mouth to mouth, which is repeated millions of times a day, as if to render unceasing the profession of the faith of the Catholic world in the divinity of the Holy Ghost: "Glory be to the Father, and to the Son, and to the Holy Ghost, as it was in the beginning, is now, and ever shall be, world without end." But what need is there of further remark, when we have the Apostles' Creed, and the Creeds of Nice and Constantinople, which all teach us the same dogma?

We not only believe that the Holy Ghost is God, but we also believe that he proceeds from the Father and the Son. To proceed means to receive one's being. Not that the Holy Ghost was made, or created, or begotten; but that he necessarily and eternally proceeds from the Father and the Son, by way of spiration, to use the language of theology. The Father eternally contemplates himself, and, in contemplating himself, eternally produces his Word. The Father and the Son eternally love each other, and eternally produce the Holy Ghost, who is their consubstantial love, and who is, like each of them, a divine Person.[262] The Catholic faith on this point is clearly expressed by the fathers and the councils of the East and the West. Take, for example, the words of the General Council of Lyons: "We faithfully and piously confess that the Holy Ghost proceeds eternally from the Father and the Son, not as from two principles, but as from one principle; not by two spirations, but by one spiration."[263]

We give to the third Person of the adorable Trinity the name of the Holy Spirit, although the Father and the Son may receive the same name. All the angels of heaven and all blessed souls may, in like manner, be called "holy spirits." How is this? How does it come to pass that a name common to several should be specially applied to one? Here is the answer. It is true that the Trinity, in its nature, and in its Persons, is a Holy Spirit. Nevertheless, as the first Person has the proper name of Father, and the second that of Son, we leave to the third the common name of Holy Spirit, to distinguish him from the others, and to make his operations understood. It is also true that the angels and blessed souls are holy spirits. But, being simple creatures, they are holy only by grace; whereas, the Holy Spirit is holy by nature, and the very source of holiness. It is therefore with the utmost reason that we name him the Holy Spirit, or the Holy Ghost, the meaning of which is the same.

The name of the Holy Spirit, like the names of the Father and the Son, comes, not from men, but from God. We owe our knowledge of it to the scripture, which repeats it more than three hundred times, as well in the old as in the new testament. Moreover, this name, as we have just pointed out, serves admirably to express the operations of the Holy Spirit. Faith teaches us that all the outward operations of God, with the exception of the incarnation, are common to the three Persons of the Blessed Trinity. Hence, the Father, the Son, and the Holy Ghost are equally the Creators and preservers of the world, the Sanctifiers and rewarders of men. Yet to the Father we specially attribute works of power; to the Son, those of wisdom; to the Holy Ghost, those of love.

His works.—Now, as the sanctification of souls and the Church—which is the visible instrument thereof—are the most splendid works of the love of God toward us, we attribute them to the Holy Ghost, the eternal love of the Father and the Son. In point of fact, if you search the scripture, you will see that in the old and in the new covenant, the Holy Ghost presides over every work of sanctification, as well as over the formation and the government of the Church. To confine ourselves to the law of grace, it is the Holy Ghost who forms the Church, who changes the apostles into new men, who bestows on the faithful a variety of supernatural gifts. He directs the apostles in their travels. He presides over the councils. He strengthens the martyrs, and inspires them with those amazing answers that close the mouths of tyrants. It is he who vivifies souls by the sacraments, and sanctifies them by a communication of his interior graces. This is the reason why the Church, and, in the Church, all Christian nations and associations, never fail to invoke the Holy Ghost on important occasions, when there is question of dissipating the darkness that has been thrown like a pall over our souls by the devil and sin, or of removing the difficulties that interfere with the work of our sanctification.

His apparitions.—The Holy Ghost has appeared several times on earth—under different symbols, according to the nature of the mystery in connection with which he descended. At the baptism of our Lord, he showed himself under the form of a dove, to make known to us the infinite purity and gentleness of the divine master; at the transfiguration, under the form of a cloud, to make known to us that the Savior, though like us, was really the Son of God, and that his divinity was hidden under the veil of his humanity; in fine, on the day of Pentecost, under the form of tongues of fire, to make known to us the unity of love, of belief, and of language which should afterward distinguish the Church, and which should splendidly repair some of the most glaring consequences of sin—division of hearts, confusion of ideas, and diversity of languages.[264]

The views which we have just given, and those which are about to follow, are of the highest importance. In point of fact, there is nothing that concerns each one of us more than to know the Holy Ghost well, so that we may love him ardently and invoke him frequently. First, he is God, like the Father and the Son; next, he is in a particular manner the author of our sanctification—a work which we of ourselves could not accomplish in the least degree, for we cannot even pronounce the name of Jesus to any advantage without the aid of the Holy Ghost;[265] finally, it is most strictly necessary that we should avoid sinning against the Holy Ghost—an offense so grave that our Lord declared that sins committed against the Son of Man might be forgiven, but that sins committed against the Holy Ghost would not be forgiven either in this world or in the world to come.[266]

What can be more terrible than the vengeance which God has taken, and which he still takes, even in this world, on sins against the Holy Ghost? Out of a multitude of examples we shall cite but one: that of the Greeks. From the origin of the Church, the Greeks, driven on by the evil spirit, were continually attacking the third Person of the Blessed Trinity. Macedonius, patriarch of Constantinople, had the audacity to deny his divinity. At a later period this heresy, though condemned by the Church, reappeared under various forms, and attacked the procession of the Holy Ghost. The Latin Church left no means untried to bring back the Greeks to the true faith. After many fruitless endeavors, she at length succeeded in inducing them to accept and sign at Florence the Catholic Creed. But scarcely had they returned to their own country, when they made a retraction of their act, and resumed their old blasphemies against the Holy Spirit.

This last crime fills up the measure of their offenses, and the new deicide shall be punished like the first. Here begins, between the destruction of Jerusalem and the overthrow of Constantinople, a terrible resemblance, which has not escaped the attention of Christian observers.[267] The Jews blaspheme during three years against our Lord; the Greeks, from the close of the Council of Florence, blaspheme during thirteen years against the Holy Ghost. Alarming predictions announce to Jerusalem the chastisements that must soon burst upon it; predictions no less alarming announce to Constantinople the same fate. The Greeks, like the Jews, remain obstinate. Titus, a stranger in race and religion, comes at the head of his victorious legions to besiege Jerusalem; Mahomet II, a stranger in race and religion, appears at the head of a formidable army under the walls of Constantinople.

The Jews, shut up in Jerusalem, are a prey to mutual enmities, and slay one another; the Greeks, shut up in Constantinople, abandon themselves to the same divisions and the same excesses. Jerusalem, fallen into the hands of Titus, is wholly ruined—the empire of the Jews is destroyed, and they themselves are led away into slavery; Constantinople, taken by Mahomet, is surrendered to horrors and profanations greater than those of which Jerusalem has been the scene—the empire of the Greeks is destroyed, and they themselves, sold like vile cattle, are reduced to the most painful slavery. That nothing might be wanting to the resemblance, Titus surrounded Jerusalem about the days of the Pasch, the anniversary of the deicide; Mahomet surrounded Constantinople about the same period, and took the city, May 29, 1453, at one o'clock in the morning, on the second day of the feast of Pentecost.

Thus, while the Latin Church, religiously assembled in its temples, was celebrating the solemn anniversary of the descent of the Holy Ghost, and boldly proclaiming his divinity, the Eastern Church, which blasphemously denied his divinity, was falling under the yoke of the barbarian. What conclusion are we to draw hence, unless that the two most frightful catastrophes of which history makes mention—the ruin of Jerusalem and the sack of Constantinople—are, one, a splendid punishment of crime committed against the second Person, and the other, a no less splendid punishment of a similar crime committed against the third Person of the ever-adorable Trinity?[268]

Having explained that which concerns the personality of the Holy Ghost, it remains for us to speak of his gifts and his fruits, that is, some of his favors to and operations in souls.

His seven gifts.—We distinguish seven gifts and twelve fruits of the Holy Ghost. The former, mentioned by the prophet Isaias, are wisdom, understanding, counsel, fortitude, knowledge, piety, and the fear of the Lord.[269] To be familiar with the order which we are about to follow in the explanation of the gifts of the Holy Ghost, and to appreciate the value of these most excellent gifts, there are four essential things to be remarked.

The first, that the prophet Isaias, in enumerating the gifts of the Holy Ghost, begins with the most noble and descends to the least noble. So that the gifts of the Holy Ghost are like the steps of a ladder, of which the lowest is the fear of God. Beginning there, we ascend to the highest, which is wisdom.[270]

The second, that all the gifts of the Holy Ghost are necessary to salvation, that they are inseparable, that they are lost by mortal sin, and that they are recoverable by penance. This, by the way, is the reason why the number seven is so often repeated in canonical penances and in indulgences granted by the Church.[271]

The third, that the gifts of the Holy Ghost are not passing emotions, but supernatural habits, which render us docile to the inspirations of grace, and advance us to perfection. "Our soul," says St. Thomas, "is only guided by the Holy Ghost inasmuch as it is in some manner united to him. Just as an instrument is only set in motion by the workman inasmuch as it is, by contact, in some manner united to him. The first union of man with God is effected by faith, hope, and charity; so that these virtues are like the roots of the gifts of the Holy Ghost. This is the reason why all the gifts pertain to these three virtues, from which they seem to take their rise."[272]

The fourth, that the seven gifts of the Holy Ghost are opposed to the seven capital or deadly sins. "The seven gifts of the Holy Ghost," says St. Antoninus, "are the seven spirits sent into the world against the seven evil spirits of which the gospel speaks. The gift of fear is opposed to pride; the gift of counsel to covetousness; the gift of wisdom to lust; the gift of understanding to gluttony; the gift of piety to envy; the gift of knowledge to anger; and the gift of fortitude to sloth."[273]

This luminous view of the great doctor acquaints us at once with the deep need that existed for the seven gifts of the Holy Ghost, and the important place that they occupy in the general plan of human redemption. Listen! Since the primitive fall, two Spirits have been flitting over the world, and over every man coming into the world.[274] These two Spirits are the Holy Spirit and the wicked spirit, the Spirit of God and the spirit of evil, God and the devil. Willingly or unwillingly, we must of necessity live under the influence of the one or the other. According as we are guided by the Holy Ghost or by Satan, we shall become saints or reprobates.

Our Lord reveals to us that the wicked spirit is accompanied by seven other spirits more wicked than himself. These spirits are known to us by their names and their works. By their names, they pass in human language as the spirit of pride, the spirit of covetousness, the spirit of lust, the spirit of gluttony, the spirit of envy, the spirit of anger, and the spirit of sloth. By their works, they are the inspirers and abettors of all public and private sins and disorders—consequently, the cause of all the evils of the world. Which of us has not been the object of their temptations? Which of us has not more than once had experience of their malign influence? What crime is there that cannot, that should not, be referred to some one of these seven spirits, whose continual aim is to corrupt the human race? We now behold the spirit of evil who hovers over the world and over every one of us. It is evident that man, left to himself, is too weak to resist this spirit: witness the conduct of individuals and peoples that withdraw themselves from the influence of the Holy Spirit.

Hence, revelation shows us the Holy Spirit coming to the aid of man, with seven powers opposed to the seven powers of the evil spirit. These seven helping spirits are, in like manner, known to us by their names and their works. By their names, they pass in Catholic language as the spirit of the fear of God, the spirit of counsel, the spirit of wisdom, the spirit of understanding, the spirit of piety, the spirit of knowledge, and the spirit of fortitude. By their works, they are the inspirers and promoters of all public and private virtues, the source of everything good in the world, so that there is nothing of any worth which we must not attribute to them.[275] We now behold the Holy Spirit who hovers over the world and over every one of us.

To reduce the whole matter to a few words: fallen man is an invalid suffering from seven mortal ulcers, or a wounded soldier surrounded by seven furious enemies. The Spirit with the seven gifts becomes the great physician of the unfortunate invalid, the powerful helper of the overpowered soldier. How can we convey a clearer knowledge of the seven gifts of the Holy Ghost, inspire a higher esteem for them, and excite in every breast a stronger desire of possessing them and a livelier fear of losing them?

Let us now explain these seven wondrous gifts, and show their opposition to the seven principal sins.

Fear of the Lord. Fear is a gift of the Holy Ghost which impresses on our souls a great respect for God, a great dread of his judgments, and a great horror of sin. It is easy to see that this salutary fear is opposed to pride, for which it is the remedy. What are the effects of pride? It puffs us up, it leads us to the worship of ourselves, it makes us arrogant and presumptuous, and, by diminishing within us the fear of God, it lays us open to every other kind of fear. The gift of fear, on the contrary, moves us to act as little children under the hand of God—to be humble, and modest, and kind to all.

The fear of God, by permitting no other fear to dwell in our souls, delivers us from worldly fear, which often induces us to offend God rather than lose our rank, our employment, our money; from carnal fear, which draws us into sin, to avoid inconveniences, pains, death; from servile fear, which gives us the spirit of the miserable slaves of Sinai instead of that of the joyous children of Calvary. In fine, it regulates natural fear, that is, timidity, pusillanimity, cowardice, shame, and inspires the Christian with that grand independence of character which makes him the lord of the world, enabling him to say with the utmost truth: "I fear God, and I have no other fear."

Counsel. Counsel is a gift of the Holy Ghost which enables us to see the way to heaven and to adopt the safest means of traveling therein. Counsel is opposed to covetousness, for which it is the remedy. What are the effects of covetousness? It spoils the mind, by making us prefer less to more. It blinds us. It enchants us to such a degree as to make us sacrifice eternal for temporal goods, look upon gold as our God, seek our happiness on earth, and waste ourselves in building castles in the air.

The gift of counsel, on the contrary, rectifies the mind, by making us prefer more to less. It shows us, with special evidence, that the goods of time are unworthy of an immortal soul; that, instead of being a means, they are often an obstacle to our salvation; and that we must always, in our calculations, prefer the goods of eternity—never seeking our God on earth or our happiness in riches. By disengaging the soul from all material possessions, it gives us a great firmness and soundness of judgment, to settle doubts for ourselves and others. In fine, it ennobles the heart, by delivering the affections from the tyranny of avarice, which the language of every nation pronounces base and sordid.

Wisdom. Wisdom is a gift of the Holy Ghost which makes us relish the things of God; that is to say, God himself, and everything that leads us to the possession of him. The gift of wisdom is opposed to lust, for which it is the remedy. What are the effects of lust? It spreads a deceitful charm over the pleasures of the senses, toward which it allures us, and in which it teaches us to seek our happiness. It makes the soul the slave of the body. It darkens the understanding, hardens the heart, and reduces man to the level of the beast.

The gift of wisdom, on the contrary, disgusts us with the pleasures of the senses, and, spreading an indescribable charm over goods of a superior order, draws us sweetly toward all that is worthy of an immortal soul. It emancipates the heart from the sway of the senses, and raises us to a level with the angels, in whose inclinations and joys it makes us sharers. It not only delivers us from animal wisdom, but regulates our natural wisdom, that is, it lets us taste the pleasures of earth within their just limits.

Understanding. Understanding is a gift of the Holy Ghost which enables us to grasp with ease, and to comprehend as far as a finite mind is capable of comprehending, the truths of religion. The gift of understanding is opposed to gluttony, for which it is the remedy. What are the effects of gluttony? It endeavors to make the physical life predominate over the moral: it wishes to have the soul the slave of the body. It makes us stupid, and unfit for study. It blunts the edge of the mind, and renders us indifferent to everything that deserves our attention. The more we eat, the less we think; the more daintily we eat, the less sensibly we think.[276] But, above all, gluttony separates man from the true light, and prevents him from understanding things of a spiritual order.[277] Is not this what we see every day on an immense scale? When a relish for material things, or the love of the comfortable, as it is called, governs society, the understanding of truths of a superior order disappears. Man loses his faculty of drawing ideas from facts. In a little while he will only see, even in the natural order, the immediate cause, or, what the irrational animal sees, the plastic manifestation.

The gift of understanding, on the contrary, makes the soul predominate over the body. It leads to sobriety, a necessary virtue for men of study. It enables us to penetrate deeply into the sense of holy scripture, sermons, and explanations of the truths of religion, showing us all the weakness of the errors and objections of the impious. Hereby, it strengthens our faith, the most precious treasure in the world.

Piety. Piety is a gift of the Holy Ghost which teaches us to render a filial worship to God. The gift of piety is opposed to envy, for which it is the remedy. What are the effects of envy? It withers, degrades, hardens the heart. It makes us unjust, fills us with the bitterness of Cain and the jealousy of the devil, and leads us to all the iniquities of selfishness, which is only another name for the hatred of our neighbor.

The gift of piety, on the contrary, communicates to the heart a delightful sentiment of affection, which ennobles it, which refines it, which dilates it, which renders it respectfully filial toward God and toward everything belonging to God—his Church, his word, his temples, his priests, his suffering members—and which makes it lavish on all mankind the generous love of a brother and the tender compassion of a friend.

Knowledge. Knowledge is a gift of the Holy Ghost which imparts to us an acquaintance with the truths of religion, and teaches us to make a holy use of human information. The gift of knowledge is opposed to anger, for which it is the remedy. What are the effects of anger? Anger blinds us. This is so true, that the term *blind* is applied to it in all languages. It hinders man from reasoning, from seeing the light of truth, from distinguishing that which is true from that which is false, and that which is seriously evil from that which is only slightly or apparently so, and spreads over the countenance the furious look of a lunatic or a wild beast. The light of reason vanishes from the angry man, to give place to brute force: death is ready to issue from his hands and feet.

The gift of knowledge, on the contrary, enlightens the soul, and, adjusting our views to a true appreciation of all things, prevents us from being irritated at evils which do not deserve punishment, or stays us before the right of vengeance which God reserves to himself. It gives us the simplicity of the dove and the wisdom of the serpent. It puts us on our guard against purely human science, and establishes in our souls that steadiness of glance, that rectitude of judgment, that practical good sense, at once so precious and so rare.

Fortitude. Fortitude is a gift of the Holy Ghost which, raising us above our natural weakness, makes us do great things for God and our neighbor, and overcome the obstacles that oppose us in the accomplishment of our duties. The gift of fortitude is opposed to sloth, for which it is the remedy. What are the effects of sloth? Sloth enervates the soul, binds it with the chains of the passions, and lulls it asleep in the abominations of sin. Sloth makes us incapable of attempting anything good, and capable of attempting everything evil; for idleness is the mother of all vices.[278]

The gift of fortitude, on the contrary, gives elasticity to all the powers of the soul. It makes us undertake with courage and continue with earnestness things of importance for God, our neighbor, and ourselves, as we see in the examples of our Lord, the apostles, the saints, the martyrs, and missionaries. It makes us reject indignantly the solicitations of the flesh and the devil, and the scandals and maxims of the world; trample human respect under our feet; and endure with sweet and peaceful resignation all sorts of trials in body and soul, contradictions, reverses of fortune, abandonment of friends, and death itself.

Such are the seven great remedies which the Holy Ghost applies to our souls, to heal the seven great wounds which sin has inflicted on them. Or, rather, such are the seven friendly powers with which the Holy Ghost comes to our aid, to combat the seven inimical powers that attack us.

When the soul, assisted by the seven gifts of the Holy Ghost, or, more correctly, by the septiform Spirit, has fought victoriously, it is only proper that it should reap the benefits of its victory. The first of these is order. Order is the parent of peace: peace with God, peace with the neighbor, peace with oneself. Hence come the beatitudes. They, as far as the trial of life permits it, banish from the soul those interior and exterior pains which torment the majority of men.[279]

His twelve fruits.—The second is the enjoyment of the fruits of the Holy Ghost. Glorious is the fruit of good labors, according to the saying of scripture.[280] Now, as there are no better labors than those which take place in the vast field of a spiritual life, to these labors correspond the fruits of the Holy Ghost. We call them so, because they bring to the heart of man the same sweetness and pleasure which the fruit of a good tree brings to the mouth. The fruits of the Holy Ghost are twelve in number, and are pointed out to us by the apostle St. Paul: "Charity, joy, peace, patience, benignity, goodness, longanimity, mildness, faith, modesty, continence, chastity."[281]

These delicious fruits give the soul which nourishes itself with them a foretaste of that which contains them all, the fruit of eternal life. Let the end of life come, and the Christian, deified by the Holy Spirit, enters into the possession of this incomparable fruit, the sight, taste, and enjoyment of which will inundate his faculties with ineffable delights; for this fruit shall be God himself, seen, tasted, and possessed, without a shadow of fear, and with a boundless love. Such is the marvelous intertwinement of virtues, gifts, beatitudes, and fruits, whose end is the deification of man.

Are the perfection and the happiness of a soul, a nation, a society, in which the Holy Ghost dwells and works, now understood? Do we perceive how important it is for individuals and peoples to know the Holy Ghost, to love him, to place themselves under his influence, to yield themselves to his action, and never to contristate him?

The necessity and the importance of these duties will be still more apparent if we reflect on the effects produced in souls, in nations, in societies, by the evil spirit, which flits over the world, and which assumes the sway of it as soon as it ceases to live under the influence of the Holy Spirit? When a soul, a family, a society allows itself to be overcome by the seven powers of the wicked spirit, it is not slow to reap the fruits of its laxity and defeat. These fruits of death, called by St. Paul "the works of the flesh," are very different indeed from the fruits of the Holy Ghost. Let us give, in the words of this apostle, their frightful enumeration: "Fornication, uncleanness, immodesty, luxury, idolatry, witchcrafts, enmities, contentions, emulations, wraths, quarrels, dissensions, sects, envies, murders, drunkenness, reveling, and other like things."[282]

What can become of the soul in which all these ferocious beasts meet, as in their lair? What must become of the nations on which they are let loose? That which we know, because we see it with our eyes, is that the habit of these iniquitous works leads souls, families, societies, to various stages of an indescribable restlessness, the source of monstrous outrages and revolutions, in which the passions find their bloody and ignoble joy. Now, infernal beatitudes of this kind constitute the misery of this world, and prepare the way for the supreme misery of the next. Such are the lines in which men walk, according as they live under the influence of the Holy or the evil spirit.

The beatitudes.—To sum up the whole doctrine of our sanctification by the Holy Ghost, and to show its perfect harmony with the plan of the catechism, we shall avail ourselves of the thoughts of St. Thomas, and say: Far from destroying nature, grace perfects it, by communicating to it faith, hope, and charity. This divine sap is set in motion by the action of the gifts of the Holy Ghost, like the sap of a tree by the heat of the rays of the sun. The result of this supernatural action is the fruits of the Holy Ghost. The possession of the fruits of the Holy Ghost leads to the beatitudes, the foretaste of a blessed eternity, in which deified man becomes happy with the happiness, and perfect with the perfection, of God himself: just as in a tree, the motion of the sap is directed toward the fruit, or, if I may so speak, toward the happiness of the tree, since it attains the end for which it was created.[283] How lovely is this divine vegetation! But what deep thoughts does it inspire! What sort of trees are we? What kind of sap circulates in our souls? What are the fruits we bear? What are we to think of society in general?

If, after considering the various gifts of the Holy Ghost, we reflect on what contains them all—grace: that divine thing which renders us just, which marks us with the seal of adoption, which is the pledge of our inheritance, which unites us so closely with God in the bonds of love, which excites within us the purest sentiments of piety, which makes us embrace a new life, which transforms us into children of God, how can we fail to see that it is with the utmost justice we attribute to the Holy Ghost the work of our sanctification?[284]

Social advantages of this article.—What shall we now say of the salutary influence of this dogma? The preceding articles of the Creed made known to us a God, the Creator and preserver of the world—a God, the repairer of his work, dying to restore to man, with lost innocence, a new title to eternal glory. To complete these teachings, which would have ravished with admiration all the philosophers of antiquity, the Creed introduces you, in its closing articles, to a God, the Sanctifier and Glorifier of man.

Take away the eighth article, "I believe in the Holy Ghost," and the Catholic doctrine regarding God—that doctrine which is the principle of the civilization of modern peoples, because it is the source of their lights and the rule of their actions—is mutilated, incomplete, and, so to speak, lifeless. It is the Holy Ghost who, by his salutary influence, makes us see, relish, and practice the truths that emanate from the Father and that are taught by the Son. A Holy Spirit, God like each of the other two Persons of the adorable Trinity, the father of our souls, the light of our minds, the strength of our hearts, the soother of our sorrows—oh! there is in this faith an inexhaustible fund of courage and devotedness.

In effect, the Holy Ghost, the great Sanctifier, is an express model, as well as the Father and the Son, for every one of us. We ought then to be, in regard to our brethren, so many sanctifiers. And from this thought how many holy souls, a thousand times more useful to society than all our legislators and academicians, have drawn and still draw the principle and the rule of that life of sacrifice and good example which the world so much admires, but of which it does not understand the secret! Let all men believe this article of our Creed, and, in accordance with their faith, allow themselves to be guided by the Holy Spirit; and the world, and society, and families shall be saved. For right reason, soundness of judgment, purity of morals, shall then succeed to the contrary disorders, and the Spirit of goodness shall everywhere take the place of the spirit of wickedness.

PRAYER

O my God! who art all love, I thank thee for having sanctified me by the Holy Ghost; grant me the grace to be ever docile to the inspirations of this Spirit of light and love.

I am resolved to love God above all things, and my neighbor as myself for the love of God; and, in testimony of this love, I will never contristate the Holy Ghost.

Lesson 23: Our Union with the New Adam by Faith (6)

Ninth article of the Creed.—We have just seen that all sanctity proceeds from the Holy Ghost, as water from a fountain. Hence the Church, which, in our regard, is a mother, a dispensatrix of sanctity, can proceed only from the Holy Ghost. This is the reason why the Creed, after speaking of the Holy Ghost, immediately adds: "I believe the holy Catholic Church, the communion of saints." These words express the ninth article of the Creed.

Here begins, according to the division of Bellarmine and St. Augustine, the second part of the Creed. The first, composed of eight articles, made known to us God our Father; the second, composed of four articles, makes known to us the Church our mother.[285]

We say: "I believe the Church," not: "I believe in the Church"; as we say when speaking of the three Persons of the Blessed Trinity. The reason for this difference is that God is our last end and the fundamental object of our faith, while the Church is not. On hearing us say: "I believe the Church," someone may ask how the existence of the Church can be an article of faith, since we do not believe that which we do not see, and we do not see the Church with our eyes.

It is easy to answer that there is in the Church something that we see, and something that we do not see. That which we see is the body of the Church—I mean the congregation of all the faithful subject to the holy father. That which we believe, without perceiving anything with our eyes, is the divine origin of the Church; the soul of the Church, which is the Holy Ghost; the gifts, the powers, the prerogatives, the sacraments of the Church; the graces which it communicates to its children; its stability, its immortality, its sanctity, its supernatural end.

All these things, not being visible to the eyes of the body, are the objects of faith. It was thus that the apostles beheld the humanity in our Lord; but what they believed, though they did not see it, was that the divinity resided in him.[286] We also say, "I believe the Church," not, "the Churches"; because as there is only one God, so there is only one Church, spread over the whole earth.[287]

Definition of the Church.—According to the definition of fathers and doctors, the Church is the congregation of all those who are baptized, and who make profession of the faith and law of Jesus Christ, under obedience to the supreme Roman pontiff; or, again, the Church is the congregation of all the faithful, ruled by our holy father the pope;[288] or, in other terms, the Church is the society of all the faithful, joined together by the profession of one faith, by participation in the same sacraments, and by submission to our holy father the pope.

Church. The word *Church* means "convocation," because we are not born Christians, as we are born Europeans, Asiatics, etc.; but we are called by God to the Church in baptism. It also means "assembly," because it refers to the believing people, scattered over the earth, and bound together by the sacred bonds of one and the same faith and obedience. The Church is also called the "house of God," "the pillar and the ground of truth,"[289] because it is the abode of our Lord, who is its architect and builder; or because it is like a great household, ruled by one father, and having all things in common; or because it is established in the truth by the aid of the Holy Spirit, like a magnificent column on a pedestal, and confirms the faithful in the truth by its teaching.[290]

It also bears the august name of the "spouse of Jesus Christ,"[291] because our Lord made an immutable alliance with it, and washed and purified it in his own blood; because he loves it as a most dear spouse, governs it, protects it, leads it to heaven; and because it loves him as a divine spouse, always remains faithful to him, and gives to him alone the true children of God. In fine, the Church is called the "body of Jesus Christ,"[292] because it is, though not physically and naturally, yet really and properly, the body of our Lord, in a mysterious and supernatural manner.

In saying, therefore, that the Church is the body of Jesus Christ, our language is not mere metaphor, like that of calling a republic or an army a body, because of the unity of its government, spirit, or aim: the Church is really and properly the body of Jesus Christ.[293] He is its head. All the faithful are his members: they are animated by his Spirit, they live by his life, they obey his will.

Of all the faithful. We say, "of all the faithful." Understood in its widest sense, the word *faithful* includes all those who compose the Church. Now, the Church, considered in the full majesty of its dimensions, embraces all times and all places—heaven, purgatory, and earth. Its duration is divided into two grand epochs: from the sin of Adam to Jesus Christ, and from Jesus Christ to the end of ages.[294]

Scarcely had original sin been committed, when God showed mercy to our first parents, by promising them a Redeemer. Through the future merits of this Redeemer men were able, after the primitive fall, to recover the friendship of God, and to regain eternal happiness, on the condition of piously entertaining the hope of this divine Messias. Thus, before Jesus Christ, all those who made profession of living according to the precepts of the natural law, and who looked forward with a lively faith to the redemption of the human race, were truly a portion of the faithful, and consequently belonged to the Church of Jesus Christ.[295] The first Catholic was Adam.

From the time of Moses, the Israelites were obliged to practice everything prescribed by the law. The Church was then composed of two kinds of persons: the Jews, who made profession of living according to the law of Moses, and who alone formed the Judaic Church, which is called the synagogue; and the Gentiles, who expected a Redeemer, and lived according to the principles of the law of nature. When any of the latter embraced Judaism, they were obliged to keep the whole law of Moses, and became members of the Judaic Church. But those who did not make profession of the law of Moses did not cease to be numbered among the true faithful, and to belong to the Universal Church. It was on this account that, in the Temple of Jerusalem, there was a special place for the Gentiles who came thither to offer up their prayers, and this place was separated by a wall from that in which the Jews assembled. Such was the state of the Church militant before the coming of the Savior.

From this happy epoch, there is no longer any difference before God between Jews and Gentiles. These two peoples were reunited in Jesus Christ, who took away, as St. Paul says, the wall of separation, and formed of them a single people, named the Christian people. Thus, the Church embraces all ages. It is from her ever-fruitful womb that all the elect derive their origin; it is with her virginal milk that they are all nourished. When, therefore, we date the foundation of the Church from the day of Pentecost, we mean that to this memorable occasion we trace, not its origin, but its wonderful development throughout the whole earth, its explicit belief in truths that had been hidden under the veil of the old covenant, and a more abundant effusion of divine graces in the hearts of its members.[296]

Extent of the Church: The Church triumphant, suffering, and militant.—It reaches to heaven, purgatory, and earth. Hence, there are three Churches—no, three branches of one tree. The first is the Church in heaven, called the "Church triumphant," because the angels and saints who compose it triumph there with the Savior, after having, by his grace, won a glorious victory over all their enemies. Freed from every kind of danger and misery, they enjoy eternal beatitude. The second is the Church in purgatory, called the "Church suffering," because souls that are defiled with any slight stains go to efface them there by sufferings, whose duration is fixed by the sovereign justice. Their work of expiation being ended, they take their place among the blessed, to share in the felicity of paradise. The third is the Church on earth, called the "Church militant," because it is always at war with its implacable enemies—the world, the flesh, and the devil.

These three Churches are only one and the same Church, consisting of three parts, and existing in different places and conditions. The first precedes the second and third in the celestial country, while the others tend thither every day, until the happy moment when the three, embracing one another in heaven, shall form but one Church eternally triumphant.

In the narrowest sense, the word *faithful* is applied only to the living members of the Church. It means all those who have been baptized; for, since the time of our Lord, baptism has been necessary in order to become a member of the Church.

We shall merely mention here what we shall fully explain elsewhere, that there are three kinds of baptism: baptism by water, baptism by fire, and baptism by blood. The first is the sacrament of baptism; the others hold the place of the sacrament.

Joined together by the profession of one faith. That is, they believe in the same manner and for the same reasons all the truths taught by Jesus Christ.

By participation in the same sacraments. That is, the faithful are hereby incorporated with Jesus Christ; they are united among themselves; they form one visible body.

By submission to our holy father the pope. There is no society without authority on one side and obedience on the other. The Church, being the most perfect society, may boast of its possession of these two conditions in the highest degree. As a celebrated protestant of our day calls it, it is "the grandest school of respect that ever existed." We say "to our holy father the pope," because he is the supreme head of the Church. The Church has two heads: one invisible, our Lord Jesus Christ, who dwells in heaven; the other visible, our holy father the pope, who dwells in Rome. As the supreme pontiff dwells in Rome, and is the successor of St. Peter, the first bishop of Rome, the Catholic Church is called "Roman."

Supreme authority of the Roman pontiff.—St. Peter being our Lord's vicar on earth, it first follows that the Church of Rome, as all ages have admitted, is the mother and the mistress of all other Churches; it next follows that the Roman pontiffs, the successors of St. Peter, have received, like him, "full and entire authority to govern, teach, and rule the Universal Church." Such, too, is the unanimous teaching of all Christian ages.

1. *Full authority to govern.* All other pastors, that is, all other bishops, and all the faithful in general, owe respect and obedience to the Roman pontiff.[297] The supreme power with which he is invested has been conferred on him by the Savior himself. St. Peter having confessed the divinity of his master, Jesus Christ answered him: "And I say to

thee that thou art Peter, and upon this rock I will build my Church, and the gates of hell shall not prevail against it. I will give thee the keys of the kingdom of heaven: whatsoever thou shalt bind or loose on earth shall be bound or loosed in heaven."[298]

By the *gates of hell* we understand the infernal powers, schisms, heresies, scandals. The *keys* are the symbol of authority and government. The power of *binding and loosing* is the characteristic of magistracy. The authority here mentioned is granted without restriction to St. Peter—consequently to the Roman pontiffs, his successors; for it is necessary to secure the unity, the solidity, and the perpetuity of the Church to the end of time.

2. *Full authority to teach.* St. Peter received from our Lord himself full authority to teach both the shepherds and the sheep. Appointed to confirm his brethren, his faith shall never fail, his word shall ever be the oracle of truth. This magnificent prerogative is also founded on these other words of the Savior to Peter: "Feed my lambs, feed my sheep."[299]

Again, speaking to his apostles of the kingdom which he leaves them, and in which they should be established to judge the faithful, he addresses himself particularly to Peter, and says: "Simon, Simon! Satan hath desired to sift you all as wheat; but I have prayed for thee that thy faith fail not; so, one day, turned toward thy brethren, be careful to strengthen and to confirm them."[300] How could he confirm them, if he were himself fallible in his faith? Full authority, that is to say, infallibility, in teaching, has therefore been given to St. Peter—consequently to the Roman pontiffs, his successors; for it is necessary to secure the unity, the solidity, and the perpetuity of the Church to the end of time.

3. *Full authority to rule the Church.* St. Peter received from Jesus Christ himself full authority to rule the Church, that is, to bind and to loose—to make all the laws necessary for the government of the Church. This power is expressed in the words already quoted: "Feed my lambs, feed my sheep"; "whatsoever thou shalt bind or loose on earth shall be bound or loosed also in heaven." The right of supreme jurisdiction, like his other rights, is exercised by Peter without opposition. After our Lord's ascension, what do we see? Peter appears first on every occasion. It is he who, at the head of the apostolic college, proposes and conducts the election of an apostle in the place of Judas. It is he who is the first to preach and announce to the Jews the resurrection of Jesus Christ.

If he is the first to convert the Jews, he is also the first to receive the Gentiles. It is he who is sent by the order of heaven to baptize Cornelius the centurion. It is he who first confirms the truth of the faith by a miracle. It is he who, at the Council of Jerusalem, first declares judgment. Full authority to rule the Church has therefore been given to St. Peter—consequently to the Roman pontiffs, his successors; for it is necessary to secure the unity, the solidity, and the perpetuity of the Church to the end of time.

These powers have been recognized in the successors of Peter by all Christian ages. All the fathers of the Church vie with one another in exalting the dignity of the Roman pontiff, calling him "the head of the episcopate, the center from which the government of the Church radiates"; and his see—that is, the see of Rome—"the principality of the apostolic chair, the chief principality, the source of unity, the only chair, the place where all meet in unity." In these words you hear the voice of St. Optatus, of St. Augustine, of St. Cyprian, of St. Irenaeus, of St. Prosper, of St. Avitus, of Theodoret, of councils, of nations, of East and West.[301]

It is in virtue of their sovereign right to govern, teach, and rule the Church of God that popes preside in general councils, and confirm them. Hence no council can be regarded as ecumenical or infallible unless it is presided over by the supreme pontiff in person or by his deputies, approved or confirmed by him. No other bishop in the world enjoys, like the successor of St. Peter, the privilege of being represented by legates. From the time of the First General Council down to our own day, there is not one in which we do not find marks of the primacy and the universal jurisdiction of the Holy See.

It is on account of the same right that great questions on morals and discipline have always, from the first ages, been referred to the tribunal of the sovereign pontiffs. Also, that they have appointed bishops, confirmed their election, determined their jurisdiction, assigning to them the portion of the fold to be cared for by them: so that bishops are true pastors only because the universal pastor numbers them among the members of his communion.

Having established the supreme head of his Church, the new Adam associates cooperators with him. Approaching his apostles, he says to them with a majesty becoming the dignity of the occasion: "All power is given to me in heaven and on earth."[302] The meaning of these divine words is this: The great monarchy of the universe, which belongs to me as God and man together, belongs to me still more by right of conquest; for it is the price of my sufferings and death. "Go therefore, teach all nations, baptizing them in the name of the Father, and of the Son, and of the Holy Ghost. Teach them to observe all things whatsoever I have commanded you; and behold I am with you all days, even to the consummation of the world."[303] A divine promise, which assures us that our Lord, the Son of God, truth itself, speaks, and always speaks, by the organ of his Church! What rest for the mind of the Christian! What security for his faith! What nobility in his submission! What facility in his obedience!

The Son of God gave to all the other apostles, as well as to Peter, the same mission to preach the gospel, and to found and govern Churches throughout the whole earth; but it does not follow hence that all the episcopal chairs which they founded should be the center of Catholic unity, like the chair of St. Peter. They were not, like him, established the cornerstone of the Church. The power of bishops—successors of the apostles, and selected by the Holy Ghost himself to rule the Church of God—has its limits, while that of the sovereign pontiff reaches even to those who have authority over others of their body. He has the right, for a legitimate cause, to depose a bishop from his see.

Who are they that are not members of the Church?—After the definition which we have just given of the Church, it is easy to distinguish those who belong to it from those who do not belong to it. To be a member of the Church, it is necessary a) to be baptized. Hence, infidels and Jews do not belong to the Church, for they are not baptized. It is necessary b) to believe all that the Church teaches. Hence, heretics, that is, those who remain obstinately attached to any error condemned by the Church, and who refuse to believe that which has been declared an article of faith, do not belong to the Church, for they have not faith. It is necessary c) to obey the sovereign pontiff and lawful pastors. Hence, schismatics, that is, those who withdraw from or refuse to submit to the supreme authority of our holy father the pope over the Universal Church, do not belong to the Church, for they deny lawful authority. It is necessary d) to remain in the Church. Hence, apostates, that is, those who, having made profession of the Catholic faith, outwardly renounce it, to embrace infidelity—Mahometanism, for example—do not belong to the Church, for they do not remain in the bosom of the Church. It is necessary not to be excluded from the Church. Hence, excommunicated persons, that is, those whom the Church cuts off from its body, cease to belong to it as long as they remain in the state of excommunication, for they are castaway members.

Does it follow from what has been said that all the members of the Church are just and holy, so that one cannot be at the same time a sinner, and a child of the Church? Not at all. According to the comparison of the Savior himself, the Church on earth is a barn floor, where the chaff is mixed with the wheat; a net, which encloses fishes good and bad, to be separated from one another only on the day of judgment. Thus, however great a sinner a Catholic may be, he belongs to the body of the Church as long as he is not excommunicated. But, alas! he is like a rotten branch, which, still hanging on to the tree, derives no nourishment from it, is no longer a sharer in the sap communicated by the root to the living branches.

There is, however, a very considerable difference, which leaves a consoling resource for the greatest criminals. A dead branch cannot revive, while a member of the Church, dead by sin, can revive, and receive anew the influences of that divine virtue which Jesus Christ imparts to the just, as a head to its members.[304] How much, therefore, we ought to fear those sins which entail excommunication! How much we ought to pity those unfortunate persons who do not belong to the Church! How much we ought to pray and labor for them, that they may return to its bosom. They are more to be pitied than those who, at the time of the deluge, could not enter the ark. In effect, "out of the Church, no salvation." Nothing is truer than this maxim; nothing is more charitable than to profess it.

Out of the Church, no salvation: Truth of this maxim.—Nothing is truer. Our Lord compares the kingdom of heaven, which is the Church, to a king who celebrates the marriage feast of his son, and who, seeing the invited guests refuse to come, is angry, and swears that not one of those whom he has invited shall taste the meats of his table.[305] Therefore, those who reject the grace offered by the Savior can have no pretensions to reign with him in heaven. Therefore, those who do not enter the Church, to which they are called, remain strangers to Jesus Christ.[306] Besides, the Son of God says to the apostles: "Preach the gospel to every creature; he that believeth and is baptized, shall be saved; he that believeth not, shall be condemned."[307] Our Lord therefore wished, with a most formal wish, that all men should believe the gospel, and should believe it in the Church, of which they become members by baptism. In effect, if all men are bound, as no one can doubt to embrace the Christian religion, they are also bound to enter the Church of Jesus Christ. The reason for this consequence is that the Church has been established only with a view to religion.

Now, he who desires the end desires the means. Therefore a) our Lord, who wishes that by religion all men should arrive at salvation, must necessarily have wished that they should individually form a portion of that society which he himself founded to preserve and teach this religion. Therefore b) all men, being bound to embrace the religion of Jesus Christ, are likewise bound to adopt the means which our Lord established to arrive at a true knowledge of religion and to render to God a lawful and proper worship. Therefore c) the Church is a necessary society, of which all men are bound, by virtue of a natural and a divine right, to form a portion.

As a consequence, he who knowingly and willingly remains out of the pale of the Church cannot expect salvation. "The gates of eternal life," says the Savior, "are open only to those who keep the commandments; he therefore who knows a commandment and refuses to comply with it, shall be condemned."[308]

Inheritors of the doctrine of the Savior and the apostles, the fathers boldly profess the same truth: "No one can have God for his Father," says St. Cyprian, "who has not the Church for his mother. If any one could escape the waters of the deluge without being in the ark, he who lives out of the Church may escape eternal damnation."[309] "No one arrives at salvation," says St. Augustine, "unless he has Jesus Christ for his head; but no one has Jesus Christ for his head unless he belongs to the body of Jesus Christ, which is the Church."[310]

A remarkable thing!—protestants themselves profess the very same maxim. What do I say? This maxim is the very cause of their pretended Reformation. Why did they separate from the Roman Church unless because they did not consider it the true Church, that is, the society to which one ought to belong in order to be saved? Why did they form new Churches unless to belong to societies in which it might be possible for them to be saved? Why did these Churches anathematize one another unless because each one said: "I am the true Church; out of my bosom there is no salvation"? They thought it therefore one and the same thing to be in the true Church and in the way of salvation. Now, the meaning of this, in Catholic terms, is: "Out of the Church, no salvation."

Not only protestants, but the followers of every other religion admit the same principle; and the most ordinary common sense tells us that they are right. In effect, if you suppress the maxim, "Out of the Church, no salvation," you must admit the contrary maxim, "Out of the Church, salvation is possible." Henceforth, there is no longer any difference between truth and error: the heretic, the schismatic, the Turk, the infidel, the Jew, the deist, the atheist, all stand upon the same level, and may be saved with equal facility by professing the most contradictory and outrageous doctrines.[311]

Charity of making this maxim known.—Nothing is more charitable on the part of Catholics than to profess this maxim. Convinced, on the one hand, so deeply as to be willing to shed their blood for it, that there exists a true religion, obligatory on all men, as well as a society charged with the duty of preserving and explaining it; convinced, on the other, that this religion is the Catholic religion, and this society the Roman Church, can they perform a greater act of charity than to say to men: "Join this society, that you may know and practice that religion which alone can make you happy in this world and the next. Beware: what we tell you to do is indispensable; out of the Church, no salvation!"

Is it then to show cruelty toward men, to repeat and publish this maxim everywhere? Is it not, on the contrary, to render them the greatest of services? Was it cruel of Noe, when building his ark, to say to sinners, in order to convert them: "Out of the ark, no salvation"? Did our Lord Jesus Christ fail in charity when he said that whosoever would not enter the Church by faith and baptism should be condemned? Is the physician cruel when he says to a sick patient: "Unless you take this medicine, there is no remedy for you"? I am acquainted with a design that has been formed to set fire to your house, and burn you and your family; I know the only means of averting the calamity, and I say to you: "Beware! Unless you adopt the means which I point out to you, you shall perish!" Am I guilty of cruelty in giving you this advice? Do I not, on the contrary, render you the most signal service?

Well, we Catholics know with a certain knowledge, and all other men may know it as well as we, because the Son of God, truth itself, the supreme judge of the living and the dead, has said it, that out of the society which he has established there is no salvation. We repeat to you what he said; we warn you of what awaits you; we beg you to do what he commands you. We do what apostles, martyrs, missionaries, all the saints did, sacrificing themselves to say again and again to the nations: "Become Christians. Enter the fold of Jesus Christ. Out of the Church, no salvation." Their zeal had but a single motive: Was it a cruel one?

Various modes of belonging to the Church.—Nothing, therefore, is truer than this maxim; nothing is more charitable than to publish it: provided, however, that we understand it aright. We must therefore know that there are several manners of belonging to the Church.

1. A person belongs to the body of the Church, when he lives in the visible society of the faithful, outwardly submissive to its head and doctrine, and, at the same time, chooses to remain in the guilt of mortal sin; but, in this state, he is a dead member, a withered branch.

2. A person belongs to the body and the soul of the Church, when to the outward profession of the Catholic religion he joins sanctifying grace.

3. A person belongs to the soul, without belonging to the body of the Church, when, by good faith or invincible ignorance, he is excused before God for being and persevering

in a society foreign to the Church. In this state, one can arrive at salvation by a true charity, by a sincere desire to know the will of God, and by the faithful practice of all the duties that one knows, or that one could and should know.[312]

Hence, among heretics and schismatics, all the children that have been baptized and have not yet attained the use of reason, as well as many simple persons who live in good faith, and whose number is known to God alone, do not share in heresy or schism. They are excused by their invincible ignorance from the state of things around them, and should not be regarded as not belonging to the Church, out of which there is no salvation.

First, the children: not having yet lost the grace which they received in baptism, they undoubtedly belong to the soul of the Church, that is, they are united to it by habitual faith, hope, and charity.

Next, simple and ignorant people: they may have preserved the same grace. They may, in several of these sects, be instructed in certain truths of faith which are not in the least adulterated, and which absolutely suffice for salvation; they may believe them sincerely, and, with the help of grace, lead a pure and innocent life. God does not impute to them the errors to which they are attached by an invincible ignorance. While in the eyes of men they are members of a sect, they may therefore belong to the soul of the Church, and have faith, hope, and charity.

For the rest, all these children and persons of good faith owe their salvation to the Catholic Church, which they do not know. From it come the salutary truths, as well as baptism, which the sects have preserved in their separation. They, indeed, received them immediately from these sects; but these sects obtained them from the Church to which the Son of God confided the administration of the sacraments and the deposit of faith.[313] Hence, salvation is possible though one belongs outwardly to a strange religion, not because one belongs to it, these two things being very different.

This then is the precise meaning of the maxim so perfectly irreprehensible and yet so often made a subject of reproach to Catholics: "Out of the Church, no salvation." No salvation for any man who, knowing or being able to know the true Church, refuses to enter it. No salvation for any man who, being in the true Church, leaves it to join a sect. All these people put themselves evidently out of the way of salvation; for they render themselves guilty of an inexcusable obstinacy. Jesus Christ only promises eternal life to the sheep that hear his voice. Those that flee from his fold, or refuse to enter it, become the prey of ravenous wolves.

As for us, the children of the Church, let us often awake within us such sentiments of gratitude toward God our Father and the Church our mother as may correspond in some manner with the immense benefits for which we are indebted to them. Whence did it happen that we were not born, like so many others, in the bosom of heresy, infidelity, or idolatry? Whence did it happen that we were nursed and reared, with maternal tenderness, in the arms of the true Church? Let us therefore love this Church, so good, and unfortunately so little loved, nay, so much persecuted.

Let us testify our love for her by receiving her decisions with a filial respect, by observing her laws with a scrupulous fidelity, by sharing her sorrows and her joys, by interesting ourselves in all that concerns her; by ever showing ourselves ready to sacrifice our liberty, our repose, our goods, our honor in the sight of men, our very lives, for the maintenance of her faith, her unity, her discipline, her authority; and by neglecting no means to make her known by those who do not know her, and loved by those who do not love her. In this manner, we shall be the true imitators of our Lord Jesus Christ, who himself loved the Church so much that he delivered himself to death for her.[314]

PRAYER

O my God! who art all love, I thank thee with my whole heart for having established thy Church to perpetuate thy holy religion and our union with thee; grant that I may ever be one of the docile sheep of thy fold.

I am resolved to love God above all things, and my neighbor as myself for the love of God; and, in testimony of this love, I will often pray for the Church.

Lesson 24: Our Union with the New Adam by Faith (7)

Ninth article of the Creed (continued).—God wishes that all men should come to salvation. They cannot come to it except by Jesus Christ, that is to say, by the knowledge and the practice of the true religion, of which Jesus Christ is the soul and the founder.[315] Jesus Christ and the true religion are only to be met with in the true Church. There alone does Jesus Christ teach, dispense his graces, and communicate his Spirit. Henceforth, it is evident that there necessarily exists a true Church, as demonstrated by faith and reason.

1. *Necessity of the Church.* Our Lord solemnly promised to establish a Church with which he should remain all days, even to the consummation of the world. He ordered that those who would refuse to hear the Church should be regarded as heathens and publicans. He died to form this Church, and to communicate to it that sanctity of which it should be the only channel to the end of time. Unless we choose to maintain the frightful blasphemy that the Son of God deceived us, either by not establishing at all or by only establishing for a time the Church which he promised to establish forever, threatening us with hell if we should refuse to hear it, we must admit the existence, the perpetual existence, of one only true Church.

Confirming the lessons of faith, reason teaches us that our Lord, not intending to remain visibly on earth forever, should provide in some manner for the perpetuity of his religion. Now, it would not suffice for this purpose to leave his law in writing. A book, and a code of laws especially, requires to be interpreted. Evidently, therefore, our Lord should establish an authority, that is to say, a Church, charged with the duty of explaining unequivocally his religion and causing it to be practiced. Thus, unless we attribute less good sense to the Son of God than to the most ordinary man of business, we must admit that he established a Church, an infallible Church, to preserve intact the deposit of his doctrine.

2. *Visibility of the Church.* This Church should be always visible. First, for the reason which we have just mentioned, that God wishes the salvation of all men, and salvation is possible only in the Church. It was therefore strictly necessary that the Church should always be visible, that all might be able to know it and to become its members. Next, because God formally declared that it should be visible to all peoples. By his prophets, he compares it to an immense city, built on the summit of a high mountain, exposed to the view of all nations, resplendent with the rays of truth, so that all the tribes of the earth may walk by its light as they walk by the light of the sun.[316] Finally, because the Church being a society of men bound together by the profession of the same faith, by participation in the same sacraments and the same public ceremonies, and by submission to the same leaders, it is impossible that it should not be visible. So all the fathers[317] have understood the matter; so the most ordinary common sense understands the matter.

3. *Infallibility of the Church.* The true Church should be infallible. By infallibility we understand the privilege of being unable to be deceived itself, or to deceive others when teaching them. Nothing is easier than to prove that the true Church is infallible, and ought to be so. Four questions only! Was our Lord a) infallible? No one doubts it. Could he b) communicate his infallibility to those whom he sent to teach mankind? No one

doubts it; for, being God, he could do all things. Did he c) communicate his infallibility to his apostles and their successors? Yes; for he said to them: "Go, teach. I will be with you all days, even to the end of ages." Should he d) communicate his infallibility to his apostles and their successors? Yes, he should; otherwise we should have no means of knowing with certainty the true religion. Yet God wishes that we should know with certainty the true religion, since he wishes that, under pain of everlasting damnation, we should practice it and be ready to die rather than call in question any of the truths which it teaches. The true Church is therefore infallible. It has always been so. It shall always be so.

If it were not, the following are the monstrous consequences which we should admit: a) There would no longer be any means of knowing the true religion; we should all be blown about as children by every wind of doctrine; and in vain would the Son of God have come on earth to teach mankind the way to heaven. Our separated brethren are a striking example in point. Among them nothing is certain. The more heads, the more doctrines: a manifest proof that the Bible alone is not enough. The Bible is a book which requires to be explained, and explained by an infallible authority, that it may become an obligatory rule of belief and conduct. b) Our Lord himself—a most horrible thing to say—would be inferior to any honest man, for he would have failed in his word. He would have promised ever to speak by the instrumentality of his apostles and their successors, and he would have done nothing: he would have left them to disseminate lies. c) Jesus Christ—to use still worse language—would be the most unjust and barbarous of tyrants. He would command us, under pain of being cast into hell, to hear men who could teach us error and lead us straight to the precipice. Behold how many blasphemies they are forced to maintain, how many frightful consequences they are obliged to admit, who dare to deny the infallibility of the Church!

To say, as protestants do, that the Church was infallible in the early ages, but has ceased to be so, is to utter implicitly the same blasphemies—is to pretend that our Lord, contrary to his promises, has withdrawn his assistance from the Church. It is to accuse him of lying, and, consequently, to deny his divinity. But to deny the divinity of our Lord is atheism. This is the logical consequence of protestant principles.

As for us, the docile sheep of the divine fold, let us faithfully follow our pastors. Today more than ever let us profess the most perfect submission toward them. Let us believe what they believe; let us approve what they approve; let us reject what they reject; let us condemn what they condemn. Let us, children of the Church, say like our forefathers: "All that we know is how to hear the Church, and even to die for its faith; we do not know how to dispute."[318] It was by departing from this rule that so many heretics made shipwreck in faith—that so many presumptuous men, imagining themselves capable of discussing the truths of religion, preferred their own judgment to the judgment of the chief pastors of the Church, and, following their private fancies, fell at length into the precipice which they had dug for themselves.

4. *Marks of the true Church.* It now remains to know the true Church. To distinguish it from false churches, it is not enough that it should be visible, since other religious bodies are visible too. It is not enough that it should be infallible, since infallibility is a prerogative which the various sects also attribute to themselves or to each of their members. What then is necessary? It is necessary that the true Church, the lawful spouse of the man-God, should bear upon her brow such splendid signs, such inimitable characteristics, that none of the sects should be able to counterfeit them. Now, these marks cannot be any others than those of truth itself. They are chiefly four: unity, sanctity, apostolicity, and catholicity.

Unity. Unity is an essential characteristic of truth; for God is one, and truth is God revealed to man. Our Savior asked that his Church should be one. He represents it as a fold with only one shepherd, as a house with only one master, as a body whose members are all perfectly united.[319] Hence, the true Church should be one: one in its beliefs, one in its laws, one in its hopes, one in its head.[320]

Sanctity. Sanctity is an essential characteristic, the perfection of the perfections, of God. This sanctity in God excludes the very shadow of evil or error. The true Church should therefore be holy: holy in its maxims, holy in its dogmas, holy in its sacraments, holy in its precepts, holy in the end which it proposes to attain, holy in its members, and with a holiness made visible by miracles, which would enable all persons, learned and ignorant, to know it. It was to obtain such a Church that our Lord laid down his life. "He died," says St. Paul, "that he might form to himself Church without spot or wrinkle."[321]

Apostolicity. To have come from the apostles, to have been preached by them: another characteristic of truth. It was to them that the Savior confided all the truths which he had himself drawn from the bosom of his Father—truths which developed, confirmed, and completed all those which God had revealed from the beginning of the world. It was to them that he gave the commission of announcing these truths to the whole world. The true Church should therefore come from the apostles, and be traceable back to the apostles.

Catholicity. Truth is one and the same in all times and in all countries. Whatever is true in Europe cannot be false in Asia. Whatever is true today cannot be false tomorrow. Moreover, all men being made for the truth, truth ought to be accessible to all men, ought to be found wherever there are men. Therefore, the true Church, in which alone the truth resides, should embrace all times, and all places, and all the truths taught by our Lord Jesus Christ. Such are the marks or notes which necessarily belong to the true Church. They are all necessary that we should be able to recognize it; and, with them, it is impossible that we should fail to distinguish it from every other society.

5. *Truth of the Roman Church*. Let us now make a tour round the world. Let us study all the religious associations that exist among the different peoples, and discover which of them presents us with these four characteristics: it, and it alone, is the true Church. Now, this tour has already been made, not once, but thousands of times; not by one man, but by millions of men; and it has always given this result—the four characteristics of the true Church meet in the Roman Church, and in no other.

I. *Unity*. The Roman Church is one in its faith and in its ministry. In its faith. Suppose that, at this very hour, we could call from the grave a Catholic belonging to each of the eighteen centuries that have preceded us, and that we should ask these children of the Church—one from the East, another from the West, this man from Asia, and that man from Europe—who lived without knowing or seeing one another, and who died a hundred, a thousand, fifteen hundred, or eighteen hundred years ago: "What is your faith?" Each one in particular would recite the Symbol, that Symbol which we recite every day, and which is recited in the selfsame terms at the four ends of the earth.

This perfect harmony, this perpetual unity, filled even the early fathers of the Church with admiration, and furnished them with an excellent proof to show heretics that they were in error. "Though spread over the whole world," said St. Irenaeus, "the Church preserves the apostolic faith with the utmost zeal, as if she dwelt in only one house. She believes it in the same manner, as having only one mind and one heart; and, with admirable accord, she professes and teaches the same faith, as if she had only one mouth. For, although the languages of the world are different, faith is everywhere one and the same. The Churches of Germany, of the Gauls, of the East, of Egypt, do not think or teach in different manners."[322] How proud we ought to be to profess the faith of so many generations, the faith of the apostles and martyrs, the faith of the flower of the human race, the faith of the greatest geniuses that the world has ever known! What consolation! What security!

Not so with the societies that are separated from the Church: there, new variations are unceasingly springing up, endless contradictions. Professions of faith succeed one another, private sects multiply, like the falling leaves of autumn. In the city and environs of London alone there are at present 109 different religions. The same discord is found in Germany, in Switzerland, in America, in all those countries that are supposed to be so highly evangelized. Matters have come to such a pass that a protestant minister declared lately that he would undertake to write on the nail of his thumb all that was still an object of common belief among the reformed.[323] Protestantism, therefore, is not the true Church, since it has not unity of doctrine.[324] So with Mahometanism, Judaism, and all the other religious associations that are scattered over the globe.

The Catholic Church is one in its ministry. This means that all its children, submissive to the same authority, are united in one body by participation in the same sacraments, in the same sacrifice, in the same prayers, in the same worship. Travel all the regions of the earth, and question the Catholics that inhabit them: you shall everywhere find the most perfect harmony. To maintain this divine unity our Lord instituted a ministry, spread over all parts of his Church, the same everywhere, commissioned to preach and teach the faith, to administer the sacraments, to celebrate the holy rites, in a word, to rule the fold. He divided this ministry into various orders, which constitute a hierarchy.

He wished that in every town, village, and hamlet there should be a minister of an inferior order, and in every large district a minister of a superior order, called a bishop, to whom the inferior pastors are subject, and who communicates with the bishops of other regions. All these bishops are subject to the sovereign pontiff, the supreme head of the Church. Invested with the primacy of honor, he is raised above them all, that he may be seen by all as the center of unity; invested with the primacy of jurisdiction, he can by his authority cut off the erring or bring back the strayed. Thus, among all Catholics, spread over the earth, this ministry forms a magnificent bond of union. Thus, being united to their pastors, who are united to the pastor of pastors, they are necessarily united to one another.

Nothing of the kind among separated sects. No general subordination among their ministers: no other center of unity than the temporal power, which holds them under its sway. Thus, the hierarchy, which in the Catholic Church culminates in the pope, the vicar of our Lord Jesus Christ, culminates in protestant countries in a king, sometimes even in a queen, strangers to divine science, and yet supreme rulers of the Church of God and of the human conscience!

More divided among themselves than they are with the Church, they decry, accuse, condemn it. Always at war, they are united only by a common hatred of the true Church, because it strikes them all with the same anathema. Hence, no unity of worship. Some admit two sacraments—others, three; these have a worship with symbols—those, without: so that a protestant, leaving the corner of the world where the sect to which he belongs prevails, finds himself a stranger among the rest of men.

II. *Sanctity*. The Roman Church is holy in its dogmas, in its morality, in its sacraments, in its worship. We may defy the most hostile adversary, provided only that he is impartial, to find in all these things a single iota that is not eminently calculated to enlighten the mind, to purify the heart, to raise man to God. No ancient or modem sect in possession of this first kind of sanctity. All have flattered, all still flatter, some one of the three great human passions: pride, ambition, and sensuality.

The Roman Church is holy in its head—Jesus Christ; in its founders—the apostles. Not so with the founders of heresy. We know what was the sanctity of Arius, Manes, and other heresiarchs in the early ages. In modern times, who present themselves to us as the leaders of protestantism? Luther, Calvin, and Zuinglius, three apostate ecclesiastics, three of the most scandalously debauched men of the sixteenth century: And do you think that God chose such men to reform his Church?

The Roman Church is holy in a great number of popes and bishops; holy, also, in an immense number of its children. It suffices to cast a glance over a martyrology or a calendar to see the hosts of saints that have been formed in the Church, even within the last few centuries. In addition to the wondrous multitude of saints that have excited universal admiration by their heroic virtues, and merited the solemn homage of the world, a still greater multitude have been sanctified by virtues that were hidden from the eyes of men.

The sanctity of the children of the Church is true, since God has performed many miracles to make it known. Miracles have been wrought by the saints in all ages. They take place at the present day, and only in the Catholic Church. The separated sects cannot offer the regular conduct of their members or followers as a mark of the sanctity of their doctrines. God has never confirmed their virtues, much less their doctrines, by any miracles, while protestants themselves admit the truth of miracles wrought by saints of the Catholic Church—for example, by St. Francis Xavier.[325]

That the Roman Church should be holy, the mother of saints, and should have the right to present her sanctity as a mark of her truth, it is not necessary that all her members should be holy. Our Lord himself compares his Church to a net in which there are both good and bad fishes, to a barn floor on which the chaff is mixed with the wheat. It is enough that all the members of the Church should have been holy, and they were so on the day of their baptism; that a considerable number should have continued so, and that God should have manifested their sanctity by miracles.

III. *Catholicity*. The Roman Church is Catholic in a triple sense. First, in regard to doctrine. Inheriting a precious treasure of revealed truths, the Roman Church, conformably to the orders of the divine master, teaches, without distinction, without exception, without increase, without decrease, all those things in which our Lord was pleased to instruct her. She does not, after the manner of heretics, permit a sacrilegious hand to be laid on the scriptures, and a choice made among the truths entrusted to her keeping, so that some may be admitted and others rejected. She receives, preserves, and teaches with equal solicitude the dogmas and the precepts of her divine spouse. Ancient and modern heretics, assisted by philosophers and infidels, have never been able, in spite of all their efforts, to show that the Catholic Church has changed, added to, taken from, much less invented, one of the truths which she proposes for the belief of the world. The apostolic fathers speak as our priests of the present day.[326]

Next, in regard to time. Revealed to our first parents—transmitted by the patriarchs, developed under the law, completed under the gospel, confided to the apostles by the man-God himself and by them propagated through all parts of the earth, conveyed to us by a constant tradition: the truths taught by the Roman Church reach back to the early days of the world, and shall be announced by it to all future generations till the end of ages. Its creed is the creed of the human race, inasmuch as whatever truth we meet with among the various peoples belongs to it as a branch belongs to a tree, a member to a body, a ray to the sun.

Finally, in regard to place. Travel the world, visit every quarter of it, pass from the most remote extremity of Asia to the most remote extremity of America, from the most southern parts of Africa to the most northern parts of Europe: in all places you will find Catholics. By an admirable disposition of his providence, God has been pleased that it should be so, in order that at every hour of the day and night there should be someone reciting the Catholic Creed.

This recital is as free from interruption as the sacrifice of our altars, in virtue of which the divine blood has never ceased for a moment during the last eighteen centuries to flow on some point of the globe. When, in one part of the world, it is night, and the priest descends from the altar, and the Catholic ceases to repeat the Symbol, day dawns on other places, and priests ascend the altar, and Catholics recite their profession of faith. So on in unvarying succession to the end of time.[327] But in all places you will not find heretics or sectaries.

Catholicity in regard to place: the Roman Church, like the sun, has made the circuit of the universe; its light has risen successively on the different countries of the earth. Not so with sectarianism. Catholicity in regard to place: of all societies or churches taken singly, the Catholic is the most numerous. Mahometanism, idolatry, and protestantism are divided into many sects, of which none counts near so many followers as the Catholic Church. Catholicity in regard to place: the Roman Church is one as God is one, and, without ceasing to be one, is everywhere as God is everywhere. Unity in universality is the grand characteristic which distinguishes it, and which obtains for it the title of Catholic.

"As there is only one episcopate," said St. Cyprian, seventeen centuries ago, "so there is only one Church, spread out through the vast multitude of members that compose it. As we see innumerable rays come forth from the sun, though there is only one center of light; as from the body of a tree issue a crowd of little branches, while the body itself is kept steady by a trunk firmly fastened in the ground by the root; as from one source flow many streams, which may be traced back to their common origin, notwithstanding the difference in the quantity of their waters: so with the Church. The divine light which penetrates it illumines the whole world, and, though shining in so many places at the same time, loses nothing in unity; its inexhaustible fecundity sends forth branches over the whole earth, and still it is the same in its principle; it pours out its abundant waters to the most distant regions, and yet remains unchanged in its origin."[328]

IV. *Apostolicity*. The Roman Church is apostolical, that is, it reaches back to the time of the apostles: they were its founders, its masters. We distinguish two kinds of apostolicity: apostolicity of doctrine and apostolicity of ministry. The Roman Church is apostolical in its doctrine, that is, it believes and teaches, it has always believed and taught, the doctrine which it received from the apostles. Pass from age to age to the day when the Son of God said to the twelve evangelical missionaries, "Go, teach all nations," and you will find the same teaching, the same belief, the same Symbol as you find today. You will hear our glorious Creed resounding through the vast basilicas of Nice and Constantinople. You will hear it reverberating along the galleries of the catacombs. The same sacraments are administered there as among us. There, one believes in the same God, in the same Jesus Christ his Son; one hopes for the same heaven; one fears the same hell.[329]

This venerable antiquity, this uninterrupted continuity, is the everlasting confusion of heretics. To convict them of error it suffices to ask them: "What was believed when you came?" There never was a heresy which did not find the Church in actual possession of the doctrine contrary to it: this has been the fact publicly and universally. Hence, the decision is easy. It is only necessary to see what was the faith when heretics appeared, to see in what faith they themselves were brought up by the Church, and to pronounce their condemnation on a fact that can neither be doubted nor concealed.[330]

O my brethren, you who are separated from Catholic unity, you have not then that essential mark of true doctrine—apostolicity! What then is your antiquity? Three hundred years, perhaps? You deceive yourselves: you have only the antiquity of your own opinion. Yesterday you wrote it on paper; today, this morning, you changed it. This is your antiquity.

The Roman Church is apostolical in its ministry. This is a fact as evident as the existence of the sun, and the most palpable proof that the Roman Church is the true Church. Our Lord said to Peter: "Thou art Peter, and upon this rock I will build my Church." To find the true Church, it suffices therefore to discover that which may be traced back to our Lord, and of which St. Peter was the foundation. Now, this glorious privilege cannot be claimed by any sect ancient or modern. Not one ascends to our Lord, or has St. Peter for its founder. The Roman Church alone, and the Churches that have come forth from its womb, can show the order of succession of their bishops as far as the apostles, or as far as the apostolic men sent forth by the apostles. Thus do the Churches that are truly apostolical demonstrate that they are so.

Setting out from our holy father the pope, Pius IX,[331] now reigning, you ascend by an uninterrupted succession of 258 popes, till you reach St. Peter, the founder of the Church of Rome. So with other portions of the Catholic Church. All alike show us at their head an apostle, or an envoy of the apostles, who established them and made a beginning of the chain of tradition. It was from the primitive Churches that others borrowed the seed of doctrine, and the same order is still observed as new Churches are daily founded.

Hence, we justly number them with the Catholic Church, to which they are affiliated. All are apostolical, and all together are only one and the same Church. The sovereign pontiff and the bishops are therefore the successors of the apostles. From these they derive their origin, and the power to preach the doctrine of Jesus Christ.

Not so with heretics. Though in the beginning the gospel was preached in their country by the apostles, or by the representatives of the apostles, they cannot for all that call themselves apostolical. By their act of separation they have broken the chain of succession. No one sends them: they send themselves.

"Who are you?" the Church can say to all these innovators—to protestants, for example. "When or whence did you come? Where were you before the sixteenth century? For hundreds of years no one spoke of you, no one knew so much as your name. What are you doing in my house, not being mine? By what title, Luther, do you cut down my trees? How does it happen, Calvin, that you turn aside my streams? Who authorized you, Zuinglius, to remove my fences? How dare you think to have free quarters in this place? This is my property. I have been a long time in possession of it. I descend from the ancient possessors, and I prove my descent by authentic documents. I am the heir of the apostles, and I enjoy my estate conformably to the terms of their will, and to the oath which I took. As for you, they denounced and disinherited you as strangers and enemies. But why are you strangers and enemies to the apostles? Because they did not send you; because the doctrine which each of you has invented or adopted according to his caprice is directly opposed to the doctrine of the apostles."[332]

Thus the Roman Church alone is one, holy, catholic, and apostolical. It alone therefore bears the marks of the true Church: it alone is the true spouse of Jesus Christ; it alone is the pillar and the ground of truth.

There is yet another mark of the true Church, announced by the Savior himself when he said, "You shall be the continual object of the hatred and persecution of men."[333] Seek therefore among all religious societies that which is most an object of hatred to the rest, most an object of hatred to the world, and you will find it to be the true Church of God. It is by the crown of thorns pressed on her head that we recognize the bride of the Lamb. Now, this crown no sect has ever worn, or even had the least ambition to wear. It is the diadem that adorns the brow of the Roman Church alone.

My Catholic brethren, you sometimes tremble at the roar and the crash of this world's failing elements. Yet, far from being an occasion of alarm, the storms that today assail the Church are marvelously well calculated to confirm your faith. What do these new persecutions, coming in the train of so many others, prove, unless that the Roman Church, your mother, has not ceased to be the faithful spouse of the God of Calvary? While the diadem of sorrow encircles her venerable brow, you may be sure that she has made no adulterous alliance with the world, or with vice, or with error. The more fiercely persecution rages, the brighter shall be the lustre of her inviolable fidelity, and the worthier shall she be of your confidence and your love: *Ecclesia pressa, Ecclesia victrix!*

First advantage of the Church: The communion of saints.—The ninth article of the Creed terminates thus: "I believe the communion of saints." An explanation of what precedes them, these words do not form a special article. Yet they are of great importance. On the one hand, they make known to us the Church in her inner life; on the other, they express the first of the four great advantages which the Church procures for us.

In uttering the words "I believe the communion," our lips reveal the most magnificent, the most beautiful, the only real, the only desirable kind of "Communism"; for we make profession of believing with the same confidence and delight as we believe the existence and goodness of God:

1. That all the members of the Church—those in heaven, those on earth, and those in purgatory—are united among themselves, and to the three Persons of the Blessed Trinity, in a close and permanent manner.[334]

2. That this union consists not only in a community of faith, hope, and charity, but also in a participation in the same sacraments, by which our Lord, the saint of saints, conveys the merits of his life and death to all the members of the Church who receive them worthily; that this fraternal union begins in baptism, by which we are born children of God, and is specially maintained by the Holy Eucharist, wherein the eating of the same bread and the drinking of the same wine make us all one body.[335]

3. That, in virtue of this union, all the spiritual goods of the Church are common among the faithful, as the goods of a family among the children thereof; so that the interior graces and exterior gifts which every one receives, the good works which every one performs, benefit the whole body and each individual member of the Church.

4. That, in virtue of the union which all the faithful on earth have among themselves, the graces with which they are favored, the good works which they perform—as assisting at the Holy Sacrifice of the Mass, confessions, Communions, meditations, pious readings, alms, mortifications, prayers—benefit, to a certain extent, all those who are in the state of grace. We say "to a certain extent," because the fruits of good works are not wholly communicated.

Effects of the good works of the just.—To understand this truth, it is necessary to know that the good works of the just have three effects: merit, satisfaction, and impetration.

Merit. Merit is the effect of a good work inasmuch as it produces an increase of grace, and gives a right to a higher degree of glory in heaven. Merit is personal to him who performs the good work, and cannot be communicated to others. It can only be acquired by man a pilgrim, and in the state of grace. With him only who is in the state of grace can it be increased. The inhabitant of heaven or purgatory, not being a pilgrim, can no longer merit, though in the state of grace.

Satisfaction. Satisfaction is the effect of a good work inasmuch as it obtains the remission of the temporal punishment due to sin. It is only man on earth and in the state of grace that can satisfy. The saints have no more need of satisfaction. The souls in purgatory do not, to speak properly, satisfy: it would be more precise to say they "satis-suffer." Men in the state of mortal sin cannot satisfy, inasmuch as one cannot obtain the remission of the punishment due to sin before having obtained the remission of sin itself. Satisfaction therefore cannot be applied to them; but it can be applied to the just in the state of grace and to the souls in purgatory. This is done by offering the satisfaction or the satisfactory merit of good works in payment for him whose debt one wishes to diminish.

Impetration. Impetration is the effect of a good work inasmuch as it obtains favors from God. Strictly speaking, the just alone can impetrate, because they alone have some right to be heard, inasmuch as it is becoming, it is grounded on reason that God should, according to his promise, comply with the will of his servants, who, on their part, endeavor to comply with that of their master.[336] As for sinners, though God has declared that he does not hear them,[337] yet they can derive benefit from an impetration less strict. Thus, by imperfect movements of faith and hope, they dispose themselves for grace and the friendship of God, and ask him for something good. Their impetration has no other foundation than the infinite mercy of God.

This third effect of good works, impetration, can be communicated not only to all the members of the Church, just and wicked, but also to all those who are not members of the Church—as Jews, heretics, schismatics, infidels, excommunicated persons. We can ask their conversion, and do good works to obtain it.

What difference, therefore, you will perhaps say, is there on this head between the faithful and all others? There is this difference, that the latter are deprived of the benefit of the public prayers of the Church, except on Good Friday, and that they profit of no private good works but such as are offered expressly for them. Whereas, the faithful enjoy the fruits of public prayers, and profit naturally of the private good works of all the members of the Church, even though no one thinks of offering them expressly for this purpose: the reason of which is that they are all living members of one body. As when the mouth eats and the stomach digests, all the other members are benefited thereby; so, when one of the just performs a good work, all the other just find themselves enriched thereby.[338]

We have said "a good work," for everything that has the appearance of being such is not really such. In effect, we distinguish three kinds of works. They are as follows: living works, which are those of man in the state of grace, and which benefit all the living members of the Church; lead works, which are those of man in the state of mortal sin, which neither merit nor satisfy, but only move God to exercise his mercy and to convert him who performs them; finally, amortized works, that is, those which have been performed in the state of grace, but whose merit is covered, and, as it were, extinguished, by subsequent sin: this merit revives when he who performed the works returns to the state of grace.[339]

To complete the preceding explanations, let us add that our Lord, as the source of every blessing, distributes the precious fruit of good works among the different living members of his mystic body in proportion to their wants and their merits. As for sinners, they still hold fast to the Church by faith and hope; but, not having charity, they are dead members, and do not participate in its spiritual goods, except in this sense, that God, having regard to the prayers of the just, sometimes grants to sinners the grace of conversion, or suspends the punishment which they deserve.[340]

5. That, in virtue of the union which the faithful on earth have with the saints in heaven, the former obtain from God, through the intermediation of the latter, many graces for themselves individually and generally, when they invoke, honor, and imitate them.

6. That, in virtue of the union which the saints on earth and in heaven have with the saints in purgatory, these suffering souls are comforted and relieved by the prayers, alms, indulgences, and Masses offered for their intention.[341]

An admirable comparison, employed by the Holy Ghost himself,[342] gives us a magnificent and touching idea of the union that exists among all the members of the Church, so that even children are able to understand this perfect communication of goods among the faithful: it is taken from the nature of the human body.

In the human body there are various members, and yet they all form only one body. All have not the same functions: each has its own. The foot walks, the eye sees, the ear hears. No function is referred directly to the benefit of the member that exercises it, but to the general welfare of the whole body. Accordingly, it is for all the members that the foot walks, that the eye sees, that the ear hears.

So in the body of the Church there are various members. The saints in heaven, the souls in purgatory, the faithful on earth—Catholics in all parts of the world, in Europe, in Asia, in Africa, in America, in Oceanica—are members of the Church, and form only one body. All have not the same functions. Some are bishops, or priests, or religious. Others are doctors, or preachers, or confessors. Others, again, are masters or servants. Every one has his state of life, and its functions are referred to the general welfare of all the members. Accordingly, it is for the whole Church that the priest preaches and administers the sacraments, that the doctor teaches, that the religious prays and makes vows, that the simple faithful acquit themselves of the duties attached by providence to their particular conditions.

In the human body, the members are so united that the moment one of them, even the least, experiences a sensation of pain or pleasure, the others immediately feel the effects of this pain or pleasure, on account of the union and sympathy which nature has established among them.

So in the body of the Church. As we are benefited by the favors granted to each of our brethren, we ought to share the sorrow that afflicts them: we ought to rejoice with those who rejoice and to weep with those who weep. How could it be that the union, established among us by grace, should be less powerful to make us sensible in regard to the sorrows and joys of our brethren than natural sympathy is to make us share with all the members of the body the pain or pleasure experienced by each one of them?

In the human body there is one head, which rules all the other members, which influences each of them by its action. There is one heart, from which the blood goes forth, and to which it returns, that it may be purified, warmed, prepared to go forth again. There is, moreover, one spirit, which animates the body, and gives beauty and vigor to it.

So in the body of the Church. There is one head, our Lord Jesus Christ, who rules the various members, who influences them by his grace. There is one heart, which is the Blessed Eucharist, from which love goes forth, and to which it returns, to be purified, warmed, prepared to go forth again. There is, lastly, one Spirit—we mean the Holy Spirit—who, diffusing himself through all the parts of this admirable body, communicates to it beauty, strength, and life, the life of grace in time and the life of glory in eternity.

At the sight of this magnificent body, there are only three sentiments that can find place in the soul: a sentiment of ineffable gratitude for forming a part of it; a sentiment of exceeding fear of being cut off from it, or of being numbered only among its dead members; and a sentiment of tender and active compassion for infidels, heretics, schismatics, and all other strangers to it.

Saints. To conclude the explanation of the ninth article of the Creed, it remains to give the meaning of the word *saints*, when we say the "communion of saints." All the members of the Church are called saints: first, because sanctity is the end of our vocation to the faith and a strict obligation imposed on us by baptism;[343] next, because the just have a more abundant share in the admirable communion which we have just described; again, because sinners themselves find in this communion a powerful means of sanctification; and lastly, because this communion of saints on earth leads us to the general and eternal communion of saints, angels, and God himself in heaven.

Excommunication.—Woe, therefore, to those who cause themselves to be cut off from the Church, out of which there is no salvation! The Church treats them thus only with regret; but she can do so, invested as she is with the power to excommunicate. Nothing is better established than the legitimacy of this formidable power. The apostles made use of it; councils, popes, and bishops followed their example, in the course of ages, as often as they judged it necessary.[344] Has not the father of a family a right to banish from his house a scandal-giving and rebellious child? Must not the shepherd separate from his flock the infected and perverse sheep? Do not our judges and magistrates every day cut off from society a multitude of dangerous and obstinate criminals? Why then should not the Church, which is the most perfect society, have the same right?

There is nothing, except the sentence of our Lord on the last day, that ought to inspire us with more fear than excommunication. Those who are struck with it are deprived of all the spiritual goods of the Church. They cannot return to her maternal bosom until they have made their submission, given satisfaction to those whom they have offended or injured, and obtained absolution from a superior empowered to grant it to them. If they die without being reconciled to the Church, they are deprived of ecclesiastical burial, and of all share in the suffrages of the Church for the departed. Excommunication has often produced visible effects on the guilty. Hence, in the ages of faith, powers and peoples never feared anything so much as this spiritual thunderbolt.

Napoleon himself, who pretended to despise the one that had fallen on him, was visibly tormented by it: sometimes his exasperation knew no bounds. In his rage, he exclaimed: "And does the pope imagine that his excommunication will make the arms fall from the hands of my soldiers?" Now, all the world knows that it was just after the excommunication that the star of Napoleon grew dim, and that his life became one series of disasters. Moreover, all the historians of the Russian campaign, in relating the particulars of that frightful catastrophe, say expressly: "The arms fell from the hands of the soldiers."[345]

Philosophers will not fail to say that it was the cold, and not the excommunication, that made the arms fall from the hands of the soldiers! How very fine! But the cold—who sent it? Who lowered the thermometer to such a perishing degree? Was it you? Was it not he who commands the elements with greater authority than Napoleon commanded the "Grand Army"? Now, he who thus commands the elements is he who said to the Church and to the pope: "Whosoever despises you, despises me; I will crush as a worm him who dares to resist you." There is no revolution, no civilization, no skill, no might, that can induce him to limit or to abdicate his power.[346]

We shall speak of the social advantages of the ninth article of the Creed when explaining the commandments of the Church.

PRAYER

O my God! who art all love, I thank thee for having made me a sharer in all the spiritual goods of thy holy Church; do not permit that I should ever deserve to be deprived of them.

I am resolved to love God above all things, and my neighbor as myself for the love of God; and, in testimony of this love, I will love the Church as a child loves its mother.

Lesson 25: Our Union with the New Adam by Faith (8)

To put us in communion with our Lord—the saint of saints, with the angels and the other blessed inhabitants of heaven, with the souls in purgatory, and with all the just scattered over the four divisions of the globe; to make us participate in their merits, in their prayers, in their spiritual life, as all the members of the human body participate singly in the life, in the health, in the beauty of the whole body: this, as we have seen, is the first of the four great advantages which we find in the Church.

Tenth article of the Creed: The forgiveness of sins.—The second is no less precious. The tenth article of the Creed is expressed in these terms: "I believe the forgiveness of sins." By these words we proclaim that in the Catholic Church is found forgiveness of sins, that it is found here alone, and that it is so found in virtue of the power which our Lord gave his Church to unbind consciences. Is this power certain? Is it permanent? Is it limited? By whom is it exercised? How is it exercised? By what means can the faithful derive benefit from it? Such are the questions whose development will serve as an explanation of the tenth article of the Creed.

1. *Is the power of forgiving sins, which we attribute to the Catholic Church, certain?* To answer this question, I put three others. I ask first: Can God forgive sins? Everyone recognizes in princes the right to show mercy to criminals; in a father, the right to forgive his guilty child; in a creditor, the right to abandon his claim on a debtor; in the vilest of men, the right to pardon an injury which has been received.

To refuse to God the power of forgiving the offenses committed against him would therefore be to refuse to him a right analogous to that which all the world attributes to the prince in his kingdom, to the father in his family, to the creditor with his debtor, and to the vilest of men with those who have injured them. Evidently, therefore, God has the power to forgive sins. He himself lays claim to this sublime prerogative. "It is I, it is I," he says, "who blot out iniquities."[347] This is the reason why he wishes that we should say to him every day: "Forgive us our trespasses."

I ask next: Can God confide to men the power of forgiving sins in his name? Everyone recognizes in the kings of the earth the power of causing justice to be administered in their name, that is, of confiding to magistrates the right to pardon or to condemn the guilty. For what reason should we deny the same right to God? Is the sovereign master less powerful than his creatures? Evidently, again, God can confide to men the power of forgiving sins in his name.

I ask finally: Has God really confided this power to certain men? The power of forgiving sins, that is, of transforming a guilty into an innocent man, of restoring life to a soul dead by sin, is as great as the power of creating the world, of raising the dead. Hence, during four thousand years, God reserved it to himself alone: no creature was admitted to a share of it. At length, the fullness of the time of grace and mercy came, and our Lord, as man, was the first to receive from his Father this glorious prerogative.[348]

We know the splendid miracle which he wrought to prove that he had this power, not merely as God, since it is inherent to the divine nature, but even as man. The Pharisees, being scandalized at hearing him attribute to himself the power of forgiving sins, said: "He blasphemeth; God alone can forgive sins." "Which of the two is easier," replied the Savior, "to heal a paralytic or to forgive sins? Both alike surpass the power of man. Well, that you may know that this double supernatural power, of healing the sick and remitting sins, has been given to the Son of Man, listen to me." Then, addressing the paralytic, he said: "Arise, take up thy bed, and go into thy house."[349] And the paralytic was healed at the same hour. Our Lord, as man, had evidently, therefore, the power of forgiving sins.

Now, this power he confided to his Church, represented by the apostles and their successors, in these words, which leave nothing to be desired: "Receive ye the Holy Ghost; as my Father sent me, so I send you: whose sins you shall forgive, they are forgiven; whose sins you shall retain, they are retained."[350] It is therefore with good reason that we recognize, and that all bygone ages have recognized, in the Church the power of forgiving sins. We are no less safe in attributing this glorious prerogative to the Church alone. "It alone, indeed," says St. Augustine, "received the Holy Ghost, without whom no sin can be forgiven, so as to open the gates of eternal life, for it alone was represented in the apostles, and in Peter, its head and type, when the Son of God gave to man the power of loosing the fetters of consciences."[351]

2. *Is the power of forgiving sins permanent in the Church?* What end did our Lord propose to himself when giving the power of the keys to the Church, unless to liberate men from the bonds of sin, and to open the gates of heaven for them? Henceforth, it must be evident that this power shall endure as long as there shall be sins to forgive, as long as the Church itself shall endure.

Now, there shall always be sins to forgive. On the one hand, all the members of the human family coming into the world until the end of ages shall bring original sin with them; on the other, all shall contract, during their mortal career, some light or grievous stains. The power of absolving men shall therefore be no less necessary in the last century than it was in the first. Moreover, the Church has promises which guarantee its existence to the consummation of time. Hence, the power which it received of forgiving sins is permanent, and shall end only with the world.[352]

3. *Is this power limited?* This power is unlimited and unbounded, like the mercy of God, of which it is an emanation; for it is intended to remove all the obstacles that sin can oppose to our entrance into heaven. No restriction arises from the gravity of the faults: "All, absolutely all, that you shall loose on earth," said the Savior, "shall be loosed in heaven."[353] Hence, it is a matter of faith that no sin, however enormous, is unpardonable—even the sin against the Holy Ghost, the greatest of all sins. The merits of our Lord, which the Church received the power to apply to the healing of our souls, infinitely surpass the sins of this world and of a thousand worlds.

We except final impenitence, that is, death in the state of mortal sin, without any desire to repent. But if it is not forgiven, the fault does not come from the merits of our Lord nor from the power of the Church. We must attribute it to this: that in impenitence the sin accompanies death, after which there is no more room for repentance. No restriction arises from the number of the sins. St. Peter, having asked our Lord how many times a penitent sinner might be forgiven, received the following reply: "Not only seven times, but seventy times seven times"—that is to say, always.[354]

4. *By whom is the power of forgiving sins exercised in the Church?* It is exercised by those alone whom our Lord appointed to do so, namely, bishops, the successors of the apostles, and priests, their fellow laborers in the service of souls. No sinner, whatever his rank, age, or condition, can obtain pardon for any mortal sin without having recourse to the keys of the Church, that is, to the power of the priest in a confession actually made when it is possible to make it, or sincerely desired when it is impossible to make it.

Let us hear St. Augustine summing up the Catholic faith on this matter, and answering, twelve centuries beforehand, the objections of protestants: "Let no one say: 'I do penance in secret and before God; God, who knows all things, knows what I do in my heart.' It is in vain then that he said: 'Whatsoever you shall loose on earth, shall be loosed in heaven.' It is in vain then that the keys were given to the Church. We thus render the gospel illusory, we render the words of Jesus Christ illusory: we promise what he refused."[355]

5. *How is the power of forgiving sins exercised?* The power of forgiving sins is exercised by the administration of the sacraments. Baptism effaces original sin. Penance remits all actual sins, both mortal and venial. All the sacraments remit, by their own virtue, *ex opere operato*, venial sins for which the penitent retains no affection.

"Venial sin," says St. Thomas, "does not exclude habitual grace, but impedes its action, because man attaches himself inordinately to the creature, without, however, casting away the love of God. Hence, the remission of venial sin does not require a new infusion of habitual grace, but, to effect it, some movement of grace or charity suffices. It is thus that venial sins are remitted by the Eucharist, by extreme unction, and by all the other sacraments of the new law, in which grace is conferred."[356]

The reason is because all the sacraments of the new law were instituted to sanctify our souls by their own virtue, *ex opere operato*, and to perfectly dispose them to enter heaven; consequently, to remove all the obstacles that could, in any manner whatsoever, hinder us from attaining eternal beatitude. Since venial sins delay in our regard the enjoyment of this glory, they should therefore be remitted by sacraments well received.[357]

6. *By what means can the faithful derive benefit from the power granted to the Church to forgive sins?* If the question refers to mortal sin, we have seen that, to remit it, there is the sacrament of penance, which must be received actually when it is possible to confess, or in desire when it is impossible to confess. As for venial sins, three means set us free from them: the sacraments in general, sacramentals, and ordinary good works.

Sacraments. The first and most powerful means of obtaining the remission of venial sins is the worthy reception of the sacraments, which all produce this effect by their own virtue, *ex opere operato.* On which point it is necessary to remark that baptism, administered to adults, requires for the remission of actual sins a hearty repentance; also, that no venial sin can be remitted as long as a person perseveres in the state of mortal sin.[358]

Sacramentals. The second means is the use of sacramentals. We give this name to certain ceremonies, certain prayers, certain things which are employed in the administration of the sacraments and whose virtue imitates in some degree that of the sacraments themselves.[359] The sacramentals remit venial sins, partly by their own virtue, and partly by the dispositions of him who makes use of them. Hence their efficacy, though real, is neither direct nor infallible, like that of the sacraments.[360]

Let us hear the Angel of the Schools on this subject: "For the remission of venial sins there is no need of a new infusion of grace. All that is necessary is an act, proceeding from grace, by which we detest venial sin explicitly, or at least implicitly—as, for example, when we are borne with fervor to God. Hence, there are three modes in which certain things effect the remission of venial sins. The first, when they bring with them an infusion of grace. Such are the sacraments. The second, when they are accompanied with some movement of detestation of sin. It is thus that reciting the *confiteor*, striking the breast, and using the words 'Forgive us our trespasses,' which occur in the Lord's Prayer, remit venial sins. The third, when they are accompanied with some movement of respect toward God and holy things. Thus, the blessing of a bishop, sprinkling oneself with holy water, every kind of sacramental anointing, praying in a consecrated church, and other such things, suffice for the remission of light faults."[361]

Conformably to the doctrine of St. Thomas, which is that of theology, we count six sacramentals, expressed in the following line: *Orans, tinctus, edens, confessus, dans, benedicens.*

1. *Prayer.* It comprises the daily prayer of the faithful, and especially the Lord's Prayer. In effect, the daily prayer of the faithful satisfies for daily sins—sins that are light, momentary, and inevitable in this life—for it is the faithful who are recommended to say: "Our Father, who art in heaven," etc. This prayer totally effaces the little sins of each day. "It is," says St. Augustine, "the baptism of each day." Since then we sin every day, let us be baptized every day.[362]

2. *Unction.* It comprises the sprinkling with holy water, all sacramental anointings, and the application of blessed ashes.[363]

3. *Manducation.* It indicates the pious eating of blessed bread and other sanctified things, assisting at Mass, and hearing the word of God with respect.

4. *Confession.* It refers to the *confiteor*, which, for this purpose, is recited, according to the prescriptions of the Church, at the beginning of Mass, and before receiving the sacrament of penance.

5. *Donation.* It includes alms, and all the works of mercy, spiritual and corporal.

6. *Benediction.* It includes the blessing given by a bishop, by a consecrated abbot, by a priest at Mass—above all, with the Holy Sacrament.[364]

It is well understood that all these things require, on the part of him who avails himself of them, sentiments of contrition, of the love of God, of respect, and of piety. For the rest, any one of them suffices, when we are well disposed, to effect the remission of venial sins. The sacraments and the sacramentals are then two of the most powerful means to obtain the remission of venial sins. It is now enough to say that we should recur to them frequently and with proper dispositions.

Good works. The third means is every other class of good works to which we are accustomed, but which only take effect by reason of the dispositions of him who performs them. Such are acts of contrition, virtuous actions done with a view to God and to obtain the remission of venial sins or at least of sins in general, and formal acts of the love of God, by which we prefer God to everything that displeases him, be it great or little. If we had faith, how zealously would we employ these means, at once so easy and so efficacious, to pay our debts to the divine justice and to deliver our souls from the pains of purgatory! Let us recollect what we have said on the greatness of the torments endured by the poor prisoners who are shut up in that place of expiations, and cease at length to be insensible to our own interests.[365]

Second advantage of the Church.—How is the forgiveness of sins an advantage of the Church? To appreciate the reality and the extent of this benefit, which we find in the Church, there are three things to be considered.

The first, that all men are born sinners, enemies of God, and, as they advance in life, become worse, so long as the grace of God does not remove their sins and make them friends and children of God.

The second, that there is no greater evil in the world than sin; not only because it produces all the other evils of this life and the next, but also because it renders man the enemy of God and brings death to the soul. Among corporal goods the most precious is life, because it is the foundation of all other goods; and the thing most terrible is death, because it is contrary to life. Hence, as sin is the spiritual death of the soul, and the forgiveness of sin is the life and the resurrection of the soul, it is easy to understand what a happiness it is for us to be children of the Church, in which we find the forgiveness of sin.[366]

The third, that this great grace is found exclusively in the holy Catholic Church, wherein are the sacraments, especially baptism and penance, which, like divine remedies, heal all the spiritual maladies of mankind.

In effect, there is no forgiveness for original sin, or mortal sin, or venial sin, outside the Church. As for original sin, the matter is evident, since it is effaced only by baptism. Now, baptism is found only in the Catholic Church, to which it does not cease to belong even when administered by heretics. It is no less evident that mortal sin can be forgiven only in the Catholic Church. Our Lord said that the sacrament of penance, received in reality or in desire, according to the possibility or the impossibility of the case, is the only means of obtaining pardon for it. Like the sacrament of baptism, that of penance is found only in the Church.

The same must be said of venial sin as of original sin and mortal sin. To obtain the remission of venial sin, even the slightest, we must be in the state of grace. No one can be in the state of grace unless he belongs to the Church; for faith teaches, as we have learned from the ninth article of the Creed, that out of the Church there is no salvation. This would be false if one could at the same time be out of the Church and in the state of grace, since the state of grace is the pledge of a blessed eternity. Only let us not forget that one can belong to the Church in several manners.

Children of the Church! have we ever thought of our happiness? Have we ever deplored, as we should, the misfortune of so many persons, strangers to this holy mother, who alone possesses the remedies for the spiritual maladies of the human race?

Let us draw hence the following conclusions: a) the tenth article of the Creed ought to inspire us with a deep sense of gratitude in regard to the infinite mercy of God, who was pleased that in his holy Church all sins, however great or numerous, might be forgiven; b) we ought to live in a manner worthy of the grace of our vocation, by which we were received into the Church, wherein exclusively are found the forgiveness of sins, sanctity, and justice; c) we ought to have a great respect for priests, to whom our Lord confided the keys of heaven, that they might open it for us by the administration of the sacraments; d) we ought to entertain the highest esteem and affection for the sacraments of the Church, and dispose ourselves to receive them worthily and frequently, since they apply to our souls all the merits of the blood of Jesus Christ; e) we ought to manifest a great respect for, and eagerly have recourse to, the sacramentals; f) we ought to perform our ordinary good works with greater perfection, and if possible increase their number, so as every day to discharge the debts which we every day contract.

We shall speak of the social advantages of the tenth article of the Creed when treating of the sacrament of penance.

PRAYER

O my God! who art all love, I thank thee for having given to thy Church the power to forgive sins; grant me the grace always to have recourse to it with proper dispositions, in order to obtain the pardon of my faults.

I am resolved to love God above all things, and my neighbor as myself for the love of God; and, in testimony of this love, I will often pray for the enemies of the Church.

Lesson 26: Our Union with the New Adam by Faith (9)

Eleventh article of the Creed.—The eleventh article of the Creed is admirably associated with the tenth. What, in effect, is more natural than, after having explained the forgiveness of sins, which is the resurrection of the soul, to speak of the resurrection of the body? Could there be any means better calculated to make us acquainted with the plenitude of our Lord's redemption, and the contrast which exists between the first and the second Adam? The first Adam drew upon us by his sin a double death, that of the soul and that of the body. The second Adam obtained for us by his grace the resurrection of the soul, explained in the last lesson, and the resurrection of the body, the subject of this lesson.

This article also manifests most clearly to us the immense goodness of the Holy Ghost, the author of this double resurrection, according to the words of St. Paul: "If the Spirit of him that raised up Jesus from the dead dwell in you, he that raised up Jesus from the dead shall quicken also your mortal bodies, because of his Spirit that dwelleth in you."[367]

Let us now explain the eleventh article of the Creed, and for this purpose let us answer the six questions following: What is the resurrection? Is the resurrection certain? When and how shall it come to pass? Shall it be universal? In what sense is it an advantage of the Church? What shall be the qualities of risen bodies?

1. *What is the resurrection?* The resurrection is a miracle of God's omnipotence, in virtue of which the souls and bodies of men, separated by death, shall be reunited, never more to part again. Hence, by the eleventh article of the Creed, faith teaches us that, on the day of the resurrection, the soul which shall return to our body shall be the same soul, our body shall be the same body, as we have here on earth, with this difference, that our body, which is at present corruptible, shall no longer be so.[368]

The word of God is express on this point.: "Yes, I know it," says the holy man Job, "on the last day of the world I shall come forth from the dust of the tomb, clothed with my skin, and in my own flesh I shall see my God: I shall see him with my own eyes, myself and not another."[369] "It is necessary," says St. Paul, "that this body should be clothed with immortality."[370]

Reason itself tells us that it ought to be so; for, properly speaking, there would be no resurrection if the same man, body and soul, were not restored to life.[371] Besides, why will the general resurrection take place unless that every man may receive in his own body the reward or the punishment which he has deserved—a thing which would be impossible if we did not receive back the same bodies that we have in this life?[372]

The fathers and doctors point out another difference. They say that we shall all rise again in the perfection of human nature, because God, having created it without defect, will reestablish it in like manner without defect. Whence they conclude: a) that men shall rise again, not in childhood, when nature is not yet perfect, nor in old age, when it ceases to be so, but in youth, when it possesses all its beauty;[373] and b) that every man shall rise without corporal defect.

"Nothing defective," says St. Augustine, "will then remain in the body. Those who have been too stout will not take back all their mass of flesh: whatever exceeds a just proportion will be considered superfluous. On the other hand, whatever has been destroyed by sickness or old age will be repaired by the virtue of Jesus Christ. So, too, with bodies naturally lean and thin: the Savior will not only raise them from the dead, but restore to them all things whatsoever of which they had been deprived by the evils of life."[374]

We say, "I believe the resurrection of the body," and not simply, "the resurrection." It may be asked why the resurrection of the dead is called, in the Creed, the resurrection of the body. Here is the reason, worthy of the infinite wisdom that directed the apostles: they intended thereby to teach us the immortality of the soul. As there was reason to fear that it might be supposed to die with the body, and afterward be recalled to life with the body, our masters were careful only to mention in this article the resurrection of the body. Their object was to make us understand that of the two parts which compose man—soul and body—the body alone is subject to corruption, and must return to the dust from which it was taken, while the soul is altogether incorruptible and imperishable.

2. *Is the resurrection certain?* By the eleventh article of the Creed we make profession of believing that, at the end of time, we shall rise again from the dead. To show how well founded is this consoling belief, we shall now proceed to answer the three following questions: Has the resurrection of the dead been always believed? Can God raise us from the dead? Will God raise us from the dead?

I. *Has the resurrection of the dead been always believed?* Immediately after man had fallen into sin, and been condemned to death, God, to console him, announced to him his future resurrection, by promising him a Redeemer, who, crushing the serpent's head, would remedy all the effects of sin, and restore to him all the goods that he had lost—consequently, deliver him one day from death. This consoling promise of the resurrection, coming from the month of God himself, was preserved in the memory of men. We have an illustrious witness hereof in the person of Job.

This just man, in the midst of Gentiles, consoled himself for the unexampled calamities that had overwhelmed him by reflecting on his future resurrection. Here are the sublime words in which he expresses his belief and confidence: "I know that my Redeemer liveth, and that, at the end of the world, I shall come forth from the dust of the tomb; I shall be clothed again with my body, and in my flesh and with my own eyes I shall see my God."[375]

Five hundred years before Jesus Christ, the prophet Daniel announces the general resurrection in these terms: "Those who sleep in the dust of the earth shall awake; some to everlasting life, others to everlasting reproach."[376] This belief was perpetuated without interruption among the Jews to the time of our Lord. Is there any other proof required than the answer of Martha, the sister of Lazarus? The Savior having asked her whether she believed that her brother should rise again, "Yes," she answered, "I know that he shall rise again at the last day in the general resurrection."[377]

Pagans themselves, at least in certain countries, preserved a confused belief of this fundamental truth, as is shown by various passages of their authors, and by the general care which they took of the dead. On this subject we cannot resist the pleasure of quoting from Zend-Avesta, that is, the *Living Word*, or the sacred book of the Parsees. In reading it one would imagine that he was listening to Job or Isaias.

"It is in the law, on the subject of the resurrection of the dead, that in the last year of the world Sosiosch shall appear...that he shall revive the dead, as it is said: Zoroaster consulted Ormuzd, saying: The wind carries away the body, the water carries it away; how shall it be restored, how shall the resurrection be accomplished? Ormuzd answered: It is by me that the brilliant heaven of stars is scattered over space, whose duty it is, by showing its face, to give light from afar. It is by me that the earth exists, the earth on which walks the master of the world. It is by me that the sun, the moon, and the stars rise in the clouds with their luminous bodies. It is I who give the grain, which, sinking into the earth, grows anew and multiplies abundantly. It is I who give veins and roots of various kinds to the trees. It is I who put in all beings the fire that does not burn them. It is I who place the young, according to its species, in her that bears it; and give to every being the skin, the nails, the blood, the eye, and the ear. It is I who give man, whose eye sees, whose strength is in his breath: when he will rise up he cannot be overcome with the arm. It is I who give every one of these beings.

"Let him who only does evil appear, and endeavor to work the resurrection. In vain would he attempt it: he could not raise these things to life. But this resurrection shall certainly be. All the dead shall be resuscitated. The soul shall recognize bodies, and say: This is my father, this is my mother, this is my brother, this is my sister, these are my friends and relations.

"Then shall appear on earth the assembly of all beings with man. In this assembly every one shall see the good or the evil which he has done. Then the just shall be separated from the darvands. The just shall go to Gorotman; the darvands shall be anew precipitated into Douzakh. Then the father shall be separated from the mother, the sister from the brother, the friend from the friend: everyone shall be dealt with according to his works. Those who are pure shall go into the excellent Gorotman. Ormuzd himself shall raise them up on high: they shall walk under his protection as long as they shall continue to be. The strength of Ahriman shall be broken; he shall be plunged anew into thick darkness. This robber-snake shall be burned in flowing metals."[378]

It would be easy to multiply testimonies which prove the same belief, more or less varied, among the principal nations of pagan antiquity.[379]

In the plenitude of time, when the divine light, destined to illumine the whole world, descended beaming from the eternal hills, our Lord boldly proclaimed this truth, and dissipated all the clouds that error had gathered round this capital point. One day, having to confound the Sadducees, who denied the resurrection, he announced the last judgment, and said in express terms: "All the dead shall rise again."[380] The apostles taught the same truth:[381] the Catholic Church, Jews, and heretics make profession of believing it. None deny it but certain degraded beings who would wish that man should be only a beast, because their inclinations are all beastly.

Now, this belief, which we see beginning with the world and continuing throughout the course of ages, can come only from God; and God, when giving it to sinful man, did not wish to sport with him, but rather to console him.[382] In effect, since God said that he would resuscitate man, he shall do so: he has the power and the will to do it.

II. *Can God raise us from the dead?* Here is the manner in which Tertullian answers the question: "God can do all things; and if you are tempted to doubt that, at his voice, this flesh, reduced to dust, devoured by beasts, swallowed up by the waves, scattered by the winds, can become a body again, transport yourself to the moment of the creation, and you shall have no more difficulty in believing. This world, which on the eve of the creation did not exist—how was it produced?...And yourselves, O men! what were you before being men? Nothing.

"Why then cannot he, who called you from nothing into existence, lead you back to it again when he chooses? Will it be anything new? You were not, and you are; you shall not be, and you shall begin again to be. Explain to me, if you can, the mystery of your creation, and I will explain to you that of your resurrection. Will it be more difficult to become again that which you were before than to be that which you had not yet been? Certainly, it is something greater to produce than to repair; to give a being than to restore it; to build a house than to remove the ruins. To repair, you have materials; to produce, you have nothing. God was pleased to begin with that which is more difficult, that it might cost you nothing to believe that which is less so."[383]

Thus, God can raise us again from the dead. The thing is evident. But will he? This is the third question, which we must now answer.

III. *Will God raise us from the dead?* Yes. God will raise us from the dead, and he is so resolved on it that he has promised to do it. "The hour shall come," says the Word made flesh, the Word by whom all things were made, "when all those that are in their graves shall hear the voice of the Son of Man. And they that have done good works shall come forth to a blessed life; and they that have done evil shall come forth to their condemnation."[384] Let us again hear the doctor of nations, St. Paul, instructed immediately by our Lord. "Behold," he says, "I tell you a mystery: we shall all rise again, but we shall not all be changed. In a moment, at the sound of the last trumpet, for the trumpet shall sound, the dead shall rise again, to die no more."[385]

We will go further and say that God owes it to his justice to raise all men from the dead. This justice requires that man should be judged—punished or rewarded—according to his works. But what is man? He is not a soul separated from a body, nor a body separated from a soul: he is the union of both. It is necessary that man, in body and soul, should appear at the judgment, inasmuch as it is by the flesh, with the flesh, and in the flesh that the soul does good or evil. It is therefore most just that the flesh—the companion, the instrument of all his works—should share their punishment or reward during eternity. But, for this purpose, it must be reunited to the soul. In other terms, the body must rise from the dead: this is rigorously demanded by justice. Therefore, the resurrection shall take place.[386]

To help us to believe this mystery, God has multiplied images of the resurrection before our eyes. See: every day the light disappears as if it were destroyed, and every day it comes back again as if it were revived. The plants throw away their greenness, and take it back again, as if they were restored to life. The seeds die in corruption, and are resuscitated in new germs. Every day we have within us a sensible image of our death and resurrection. What is sleep but an image of death, and what is awaking but an image of the resurrection?

Hence, we shall rise again.[387] In vain does pride struggle: it must, under pain of falling into inconsistency and absurdity, admit this mystery. "On the subject of the resurrection," said St. Augustine to some pretended unbelievers of his time, "the Son of God predicted two incredible things, namely, that bodies should rise from the dead, and that the world should believe it; and he predicted both long before either should happen. Of these two incredible things we have seen one already come to pass, namely, that the world believes an incredible thing, the resurrection of bodies. Therefore, we shall see the other, since that which has happened is no less difficult to believe. To these two incredible things add, if you like, a third, which is quite on a par with them, namely, that the world believed an incredible thing on the word of a few rude and ignorant men.

"Here now are three things alike incredible, which nevertheless have occurred: it is incredible that Jesus Christ should have risen again in the flesh; it is incredible that the world should have believed such an incredible thing; and it is incredible that a small number of unlettered and unknown men should have succeeded in persuading the world and the learned of the world to believe such an incredible thing. Of these three incredible things our adversaries will not believe the first; they are obliged to witness the second; and they do not know what to make of the third. As for the first, it is preached and believed from the land of the rising to that of the setting sun. If it is not credible, how does it happen that it is believed throughout the whole earth? If it is credible, why do not a handful of obstinates believe that which the whole world believes?"[388]

3. *When and how shall the resurrection take place?* The resurrection shall take place at the end of the world, immediately before the last judgment. Our Lord tells us in express terms that the dead shall pass from their graves to his tribunal.[389] It shall be done in the twinkling of an eye. At the beginning of the world God said, "Let light be," and light was. This same voice, so powerful as to draw in one moment the universe from nothingness, shall be no less powerful to awake in one moment from their sleep all the generations of men, buried in the silence of the tomb.

However widely the different parts of the same bodies may have been separated, it matters little. He who every day makes the light run in eight minutes a hundred million miles—what do I say?—he who sends the electric spark round the earth with the quickness of thought: Shall not he be able to transport in one moment the elements of bodies from end to end of the world? For the rest, let us hear the apostle St. Paul: "In a moment, in the twinkling of an eye, at the sound of the last trumpet,...the dead shall rise again, to die no more."[390] Then, on all sides, the human race shall rise, like an immense harvest; and the angels of God shall bear these dead, resuscitated, to the place where the sovereign judge shall await them to pronounce their sentence.[391] Great God! what a sight! And we shall be there: both you who read these lines, and I who write them!

4. *Shall the resurrection be universal?* Yes, it shall; that is, all mankind, without exception, shall rise again: and it should be so. Let us hear the supreme Lord: "Verily, verily, I say unto you that the hour cometh when...all that are in their graves shall hear the voice of the Son of God, and those who have done good shall come forth to the resurrection of life, but those who have done evil, to the resurrection of judgment."[392] The great apostle, commenting on the words of the divine master, says with much elegance: "We shall all rise again, all without exception; as in Adam all die, so in Jesus Christ all shall be made to live; the reparation, like the ruin, shall be universal."[393] Moreover, it is necessary, as

we have seen, that the just should receive their reward, and the wicked their punishment. Now, this cannot be but by the resurrection of both.

5. *In what sense is the resurrection an advantage of the Church?* Since all men, good and bad, must rise again, it seems wrong to say that the resurrection is an advantage of the Church. At the first glance, it certainly does seem wrong; but, in reality, it is not so. All men shall doubtless rise again to the natural life. But only the children of the Church, who have died after receiving the forgiveness of their sins, shall rise to the enjoyment of eternal happiness. The wicked, on the other hand, that is, those who leave this world without having been purified from their sins, shall rise to be eternally miserable. This is the reason why their life is called a continual death rather than a true life. Accordingly, the true, the only desirable resurrection shall be the exclusive portion of those who die purified from their sins. Now, this purification from sin, actual as well as original, is found only in the Church. It is in this sense, and with the utmost reason, that the resurrection of the body is numbered among the advantages of the Church.[394]

6. *What shall be the qualities of risen bodies?* The first quality of risen bodies shall be immortality. It is a matter of faith that our bodies, previously subject to death, shall become really immortal after the resurrection, without distinction of good or bad. We are indebted for this glorious privilege to the victory which our Lord gained over death, as we see by the express declarations of scripture.

"He shall cast death down headlong forever," says Isaias, speaking of the Savior.[395] Osee makes him say: "O death, I will be thy death!"[396] On which point, St. Paul assures us that "death was the last enemy vanquished by Jesus Christ";[397] and St. John, that "death shall be no more."[398] It ought to be so. On the one hand, it is becoming that the merits of Jesus Christ, which destroyed the empire of death, should be more powerful than the sin of Adam; on the other, the justice of God demands that the good should rejoice eternally in a blessed life, and that the wicked should suffer eternally in a most wretched life, seeking death without finding it, and desiring it without being able to obtain it.

Accordingly, the first quality of risen bodies shall be immortality. This quality shall be common to the good and the bad. There are others, which shall belong exclusively to the bodies of the saints, and which shall render them incomparably more excellent than they were on earth. The fathers of the Church, resting on the words of the apostle, enumerate four of these qualities as the principal ones: impassibility, splendor, agility, and subtility.

Impassibility. Impassibility will prevent the bodies of the saints from being subject to any grief, pain, or inconvenience. No heat, no cold, no accident can touch them. "The body is sown corruptible," says St. Paul, "it shall rise incorruptible."[399] Now, theologians have applied to this gift the name of impassibility rather than incorruptibility, in order to express that which is peculiar to the bodies of the good. These alone shall be impassible, while the bodies of the reprobate, incorruptible as they shall really be, shall nevertheless be sensible to all the impressions of heat, cold, and other sufferings.

Splendor. Splendor will render the bodies of the saints as bright as the sun. "The just," says our Lord in St. Matthew, "shall shine as the sun in the kingdom of my Father."[400] And to confirm this promise, he wrought before the eyes of his apostles the miracle of his transfiguration. St. Paul, to express this quality, sometimes calls it brightness, sometimes glory. "Jesus Christ," he says, "shall reform our vile and abject body, by rendering it like to his glorious body."[401] This brightness will gush forth from the supreme felicity of the soul, and diffuse itself like light over the whole body. Hence, the body shall be happy with the happiness of the soul, which shall be perfectly happy by its participation in the infinite happiness of God himself. This gift shall not, like that of impassibility, be equally distributed to all. Among the saints there shall be the same difference of splendor and brilliancy as we remark among the stars. "One is the brightness of the sun," says St. Paul, "another the brightness of the moon, and another the brightness of the stars."[402] So shall it be in the resurrection of bodies.

Agility. Agility will deliver the body from the heaviness that now oppresses it, and the soul will be able to pass whithersoever it desires with as much ease as speed. So teach St. Augustine and St. Jerome most clearly.[403]

Subtility. Subtility will render the body perfectly submissive to the soul, which shall always find therein a fitting instrument for the execution of its designs. Wondrous privilege! which St. Paul reveals to us in these words: "That which was laid in the earth a natural body, shall rise again a spiritual body."[404]

Social advantage of the eleventh article of the Creed.—Long developments would be superfluous to show the salutary influence of the eleventh article of the Creed. It is evident that nothing is more useful to society than the belief of a future resurrection. What would become of the world, O my God! if the present life were the end of all things, and nothingness the common lot of just and unjust, oppressed and oppressors? On the other side, the dogma of the resurrection is so consoling to the just, and so terrible to sinners, that we ought, even in consideration of our temporal interests, to thank God with our whole heart for having vouchsafed to reveal this admirable truth to little ones, while he has left the wise in ignorance of it.

If from society you descend to individuals, how can you fail to see that the certainty of the resurrection is the surest means of consoling ourselves and others on the death of those who are dear to us? "Weep for your dead," says the apostle to us, "but do not weep like those who have no hope."[405] Is there anything more efficacious than the thought of our resurrection to encourage us in all the afflictions and miseries of life; and is not this the very lesson that the example of the holy man Job teaches us? How sweet it is for the Christian, when stretched on the bed of sorrow, and beholding himself expire little by little, to be able to say with the utmost confidence: "These members, which this cruel sickness racks, and these senses, which it weakens, shall one day be restored to me impassible and glorious!"

In fine, is there anything better calculated than the thought of the resurrection to induce Christians to lead a pure and sinless life? Is there anything, above all, more proper to inspire us with a religious respect for our bodies? If I make my body an instrument of sin, it shall reappear a vessel of ignominy. If I make it an instrument of virtue, it shall reappear a vessel of honor, to the knowledge of the whole world. How can we be so blind as not to devote ourselves with earnestness to the practice of good works when we seriously reflect on the glory that is to follow the resurrection and repay virtue? How can we be so foolish as not to repress our passions and avoid sin if we call to mind the torments and shame that are reserved for the wicked, when, on the day of the resurrection, they shall make their appearance to be judged?

I am not surprised that this thought should have moved millions of Christians, of every age and condition, to lead an angelic life in mortal flesh, I am not surprised that, from the sole thought of the resurrection, the martyrs should have drawn that courage, that joy even, which they displayed in the midst of their torments.[406]

Out of a thousand examples, let us cite that of the Machabees. The cruel Antiochus, having become master of Judea, issued an edict obliging the Jews to renounce their religion. Those who refused to obey it were treated with the utmost cruelty. Among their number was a family—forever celebrated in the history of martyrs—the family of the Machabees, consisting of a mother and seven sons. Threats, and promises, and all other measures imaginable were employed to induce them to apostatize; but it was in vain.

Then the tyrant ordered them to be put to the most excruciating tortures. They all endured them with a heroic courage, supported by the thought of the resurrection. The second of the seven sons, being on the point of breathing his last, said to the king: "Thou takest away the present life from us; but the King of the world, for whose glory we die, will one day raise us up again to everlasting life." The third added, with admirable confidence: "I received these members from heaven; but I now sacrifice them in defense of the laws of God, because I have the hope that he will one day restore them to me." The rest spoke in the same manner, and showed the same constancy.

The most excellent mother of these pious children had exhorted them to die with courage, saying: "The Creator of the world will restore to you again, in his mercy, both breath and life." She herself suffered death with a firmness that amazed the tyrant. Happy mother of seven martyrs, it was most just that she should share their crown! The condition on which we shall attain to a glorious resurrection is that we suffer in a Christian manner.

PRAYER

O my God! who art all love, I thank thee for having communicated to me, by thy holy grace, the germ of a new life; grant O my God! that I may live and die piously, so as to rise again gloriously.

I am resolved to love God above all things, and my neighbor as myself for the love of God; and, in testimony of this love, I will every day ask the grace of a happy death.

Lesson 27: Our Union with the New Adam by Faith (10)

Twelfth article of the Creed.—The twelfth article of the Creed is the natural consequence of the eleventh, and the glorious crowning of the Catholic faith. After speaking of the resurrection of the true children of the Church, it was necessary that the apostles should make known to us what is reserved for those who shall have the happiness of participating therein. They tell it to us by the immediate mention of life everlasting.

This consoling truth is placed at the end of the Symbol to remind man: a) that heaven is his end—that for it God the Father created him, God the Son redeemed him, God the Holy Ghost sanctified him, the Church nourishes and protects him as a beloved child, so that all the works of the Holy Trinity, explained in the preceding lessons, tend to this same end; and b) that heaven ought to be the object of all his thoughts and actions, the term of his life, as it shall be the reward of his fidelity. May it be so for me, and for all who are dear to me!

Certainty of life everlasting.—We say, "I believe life everlasting," to show that we hold beyond all doubt that after the present life there shall be another without end, which shall be filled with every desirable good for soul and body, and which the just shall enjoy, each one according to his merits. Like a miserable eternity, a blessed eternity has been the object of the belief of all peoples from the beginning of the world. We find the proofs of this in the historians, the poets, the monuments, the religious usages of antiquity.

But, like every other truth, this one had been obscured by the passions. It was necessary that our Lord should proclaim it anew and place it beyond the reach of all human contradiction. He did so by declaring in formal terms that "the just shall go into life everlasting."[407] The apostles continued the teaching of their master by inserting his very words in the Symbol.

Definition of life everlasting.—The words *life everlasting* designate not only the eternity of the existence of the saints, but also the eternity of their happiness. The principal reason why the sovereign happiness was so called was to remove altogether the idea that it should consist in the enjoyment of frail, corporeal, perishable things. The name *life everlasting* tells us also that felicity, once acquired, can never be lost. Now, felicity, properly so called, comprises every good without any mixture of evil. Since it ought to satisfy all the desires of man, it should be eternal; otherwise, fear and anxiety would bring inevitable torments to the elect.

Lastly, the expression *life everlasting* helps us to conceive how great is the happiness of the saints in heaven. Life is the greatest good that we can naturally desire. Happiness is presented to us here under the name of life everlasting, life by excellence, the true life.

"Wherever," says St. Augustine, "you hear the scripture speak of life, banish from your mind every idea of pain or torment. For to be always in torments is an eternal death, and not a life. The sacred books call it the second death, the death which shall succeed that in which we live on earth. It is called the second death, the real death, and yet no one dies therein. It would be better to say that no one lives therein; for, I repeat, to live always in anguish is not to live. This is the reason why the scripture says: 'They that have done good shall come forth to the resurrection of life.' It does not say 'of a blessed life,' but only 'of life'; for the mere name of life implies beatitude."[408]

If then there is nothing more loved than this life, which is so short, so full of miseries, and so worthy of being called a death, with what zeal, with what ardor ought we to seek that everlasting life in which, exempt from every evil, we shall enjoy every good!

Nature of life everlasting.—But how can we explain the nature of the heavenly life? No human tongue can describe it. St. Paul assures us that the eye has not seen, nor the ear heard, nor the heart ever conceived anything like the happiness which God reserves for the just in eternity.[409] Let us content ourselves with stammering over a few words in regard to it, and say in general that the happiness of eternal life comprises, on the one hand, an exemption from every evil, and, on the other, an enjoyment of every good.

An exemption from every evil. It is said expressly in the Apocalypse that the blessed "shall no more hunger or thirst; that neither the sun nor burning winds shall any more inconvenience them; that God shall wipe away all tears from their eyes; that death shall be no more; that sorrows shall be at an end."[410]

An enjoyment of every good. Our Lord reveals it to us in this astonishing expression: "Well done, good and faithful servant!...enter into the joy of thy master!"[411] Accordingly, the joy of the blessed is so great that it cannot enter into hearts, but hearts must enter into it, must be surrounded by and penetrated with it. They shall be lost in its abyss, as fishes in the depths of the ocean. In a word, they shall be wholly satiated with joy. How shall this delightful mystery be accomplished? By participation in two kinds of goods, which form eternal beatitude. These goods are essential and accidental.

Essential happiness of the saints.—True beatitude, that which is called essential, consists in the vision of God and the knowledge of his infinite beauty—the source of all created beauty and amiability. We shall see God face-to-face, such as he is; we shall possess him; we shall love him, without any fear of ever losing him. We shall see the Father, infinitely powerful, who created us; the Son, infinitely wise, who redeemed us; and the Holy Ghost, infinitely good, who sanctified us.[412] We shall not only see God, but we shall love and possess him, without the slightest fear of ever losing him.

Yet the happiness of the saints shall not be equal: it shall be regulated according to the merits of each one. But this inequality shall not be productive of jealousy, nor diminish in the smallest degree the happiness of a single individual. All shall be content, for every saint shall know in the clearest manner that God rewards him proportionally to his merits. It shall be in the blessed house of the heavenly Father as it is among ourselves. When a father provides for two of his sons a coat each of the same cloth, the younger does not envy that of the elder, though it requires more cloth than his; because he knows that it would not fit him. In the same manner, again, the finger is not jealous of the head, though the head wears a diadem; nor is the head jealous of the finger, though the finger wears a ring.

This is not all yet. We shall not only see God, the source of all loveliness; we shall not only possess God, the source of all good; we shall not only love God, the source of all delight: but we shall become like to him.[413] The saints always preserve, it is true, their own substance; yet they receive an admirable, and, as it were, a divine strength, which makes them appear rather gods than human creatures. Though the tongue of man is powerless to explain so great a wonder, yet we see some image of it in sensible things. The iron that is placed in the fire takes the appearance of fire; and though its substance is not changed, yet it seems changed.

Thus the saints, introduced into celestial glory, shall be so inflamed with the love of God that, though their nature remains unchanged, they shall be as different from those on earth as a fire at white heat from pieces of coal. To say all in a word, the sovereign and absolute happiness, which we call essential, consists in the possession of God. What can be wanting to the perfect happiness of him who possesses the all-perfect God?

Accidental happiness of the saints.—As for the accidental goods, to enumerate them would be an endless task. It is even impossible to know them all. We must know, in general, that all kinds of pleasures which it is possible to taste or to desire on earth, whether for the mind or for the body, shall be superabundantly possessed by us in heaven, but in a manner so exalted that, according to the words of the apostle already quoted, "the eye has not seen, nor the ear heard, nor the heart of man ever conceived anything like it."[414]

To give some idea of it, let us say that the accidental happiness of the saints is a consequence of the essential happiness which they enjoy, and this happiness consists in the complete satisfaction of all the desires that man, become like the angels, can have in regard to his body and his soul. Let us add that the blessed soul shall enjoy three gifts, raised to their highest perfection, namely, vision, comprehension (or possession), and fruition—the magnificent reward of the three theological virtues. Vision is the faculty of seeing God face-to-face: it shall be the reward of faith. Comprehension is the faculty of possessing God as the sovereign good: it shall be the reward of hope. Fruition is the faculty of delightfully enjoying God, the beginning and the end of all love: it shall be the reward of charity.[415] These three ineffable felicities shall be so much the greater as we practice with greater perfection the three virtues of which they are the reward.

Aureolas. Let us also add that the body shall enjoy four gifts, namely, splendor, agility, subtility, and impassibility, as we explained in the preceding article. Moreover, the body and soul of certain classes of the blessed shall enjoy a particular glory, which is called an *aureola*. "The *aureola*," says St. Thomas, "is the privileged reward of a privileged victory. As there are three privileged victories in the three great conflicts which man must sustain on earth, there are also three *aureolas*. In the conflict with the flesh, the privileged victory, that is, the most excellent victory, is virginity. In the conflict with the world, the victory which may well be called privileged, since it costs the conqueror his blood and his life, is martyrdom. In the conflict with the devil, the victory which is truly privileged, since it banishes the spirit of darkness and deceit, not only from our own hearts, but also from the hearts of others, is preaching. Hence, three orders of saints in heaven enjoy the *aureola*: virgins, martyrs, and doctors. Among the last-mentioned we must include catechists—in a word, all those who, by their words or their writings, teach the truths of salvation."[416]

Now, what shall this *aureola* be, and what advantage shall it procure the saints who are favored with it? In itself, the *aureola* shall be a more brilliant radiance of the essential glory of the saints. For the soul, it shall be a special felicity, in connection with the victory of which it shall be the reward; for the body, it shall be a peculiar splendor, which shall distinguish virgins, martyrs, and doctors among all the blessed.[417]

Hence, the *aureola* of virgins shall be a light of fairest whiteness, which shall surround them as a diaphanous cloud, through which shall be seen the spotless purity of their souls. It shall draw upon them the admiration and respect of all the heavenly Jerusalem, with the particular love of our Lord, whose illustrious suite they shall form, singing the eternal hymn of their double victory, that is, their integrity of soul and body.[418]

The *aureola* of martyrs shall be a light of rosy purple, which, surrounding them, shall make every cicatrix on their glorious bodies shine with incomparable splendor, shall cause them to be admired as the heroes of the faith, and shall merit special favors for them from the adorable Trinity—above all, from our Lord Jesus Christ, the King of martyrs.[419]

The *aureola* of doctors shall be a light like, according to scripture, by its brilliancy and color, to that of the stars of the firmament, which shall make them known from afar as the beneficent luminaries whose rays dissipated the darkness of ignorance and error, which the devil had spread around the Church militant, and with which he had endeavored to obscure the intellect of every man coming into the world.[420]

Let us also add: as well to show that admirable charity by whose effect all the saints shall have but one heart and one soul, as to console us on the death of our friends, to excite within us a desire of heaven, and to make us rejoice at the approach of death, that the accidental glory of the saints shall continue every day, every hour, to increase from the moment of their entrance into heaven till the end of the world. A simple comparison will enable us better to appreciate this delightful thought.

Suppose that a man enters a pond in which the water comes up to his waist; the greater the number of men that enter with him the higher the water rises, without there being, for all this, any more water in the pond. Thus, although in heaven the essential glory, that is, the happiness of seeing and possessing God, is always the same, yet in proportion as new arrivals take place, the pleasure of seeing new companions in their happiness really increases the felicity of the saints.

Fourth advantage of the Church.—The consideration of the happiness of heaven ought to excite in our souls a gratitude so much the greater as everlasting life is the fourth advantage of the Church whose children we are. Heaven shall be only for the just. The just are those who, before dying, are purified from their sins. Now, the forgiveness of all kinds of sins is found, as we have shown, only in the Catholic Church.

The Symbol terminates with the word *Amen*—"So be it!" Placed on our lips at the end of our profession of faith, the word *Amen* means: "Yes, it is so; all that has been said is true; I believe it without a shadow of doubt or hesitation, and I am ready to seal it with my blood." In effect, we are sometimes obliged to seal the faith with our blood, as happened to the martyrs of the early Church, and as still happens to the Christians of China.

Obligation of professing the faith.—As for us, it is commanded us not only to believe in the depths of our hearts, but also on many occasions to manifest our faith outwardly.[421] This sacred duty was imposed on us by the Savior himself, when he said: "Whosoever shall confess me before men, I will also confess him before my Father who is in heaven; on the contrary, whosoever shall deny me before men, I will also deny him before my Father who is in heaven."[422]

There are three ways in which we make profession of our faith before men: a) by our words and works; b) by the recital of the Creed, if such is necessary; and c) by the sign of the cross, which is an abridgment of our whole belief. One is obliged to profess his faith when interrogated juridically concerning his belief; when, without being interrogated juridically, he knows that his silence would be construed into an act of apostasy, and would scandalize the neighbor; in fine, when he has to fulfill any outward duty of religion. In this last case, one professes his faith by his works. One denies it, on the contrary, in a manner, when through human respect he fails in the duty imposed on him.[423]

The abridgment of what we ought to believe, in order to unite ourselves by faith with the new Adam, and to share in the fruits of his redemption, both for time and eternity, the Symbol is the admirable means by which the Messias has delivered the human mind from its old errors, and placed it beyond the reach of new ones. Whoever believes the Symbol possesses the truth. Whoever refuses to believe it condemns himself to the most humiliating uncertainties.

Hail, Catholic Symbol! source of wisdom, principle of virtue for individuals, thou art no less necessary or useful for society! Ungrateful society!—Why should it despise thy benefits? It was thou, O sun of truth! that, appearing eighteen centuries ago above the horizon of the world, buried under the thick shades of paganism, didst put to flight those hosts of ridiculous divinities before which philosophers, peoples, and princes bowed their heads to the ground. It was thou that didst deliver the human race from the gross superstitions that degraded it: it is thou that dost still deliver it from the same evils! It is thou that, shining on every mind that cometh into the world, dost give it the most just ideas of God and man—man in his origin, his duty, his destiny, and the august society which unites him with the Father of all creatures!

Sublime summary of the doctrine of the legislator who came down from heaven, it is to thee that modern society owes that civilization which is its glory! From ideas and beliefs come the morals, the laws, and the institutions of peoples. It was thou that, substituting Catholic for Jewish and pagan ideas, didst change the face of the earth, and give to Christian nations that brilliant superiority which distinguishes them! It was thou that didst reform the ideas that were anciently entertained concerning the slave, concerning woman, concerning the child, concerning the prisoner, concerning the poor, concerning the powers of kings and the duties of subjects!

Integral part of Christianity, thou art as necessary to society as Christianity itself! Thy twelve articles are like twelve pillars, brighter than gold and stronger than adamant, which raise so high and support so well the social edifice among Catholic nations: let one of them be shaken, and the edifice falls to ruins! Emanation of the divine intelligence, it is thou that dost give the human intelligence that vigor, that elevation, that light which is the principle of its noble success in all the sciences! It is thou that dost supply the sciences with their starting point, and furnish them with the solution of their deepest problems!

O men! O modern nations! so wondrously exalted by the Catholic Creed, why then do you not fall on your knees before this salutary teaching? Why, ye ungrateful! do ye despise it? Search the creeds of non-Catholic peoples, the systems of philosophers, the regenerating schemes of ancient and modern politicians, what will you dare to compare with it, what will you dare to put in its place? Ah! rather cast away those deplorable errors by which you have been too long oppressed, and rally sincerely round the Creed which has civilized the world, that is to say, which has drawn you forth from barbarism and which prevents you from relapsing into that dreadful state.

To love it with your whole hearts, only reflect on the following questions: What were the most celebrated nations of the world in religion, in politics, in true civilization before the promulgation of the Catholic Symbol? What are those that are still unacquainted with it? What becomes of those that despise it? See: the answer to all these questions is before your eyes. And this answer, by showing you the important place which the Catholic Symbol occupies in religion, in politics, in science, will fill you with admiration for a benefit so much ignored, and with gratitude toward the God who vouchsafed to grant it to you.

PRAYER

O my God! who art all love, I thank thee for having given me the Symbol to enlighten my mind, and to show me the way to heaven; grant me the grace never to follow any other light.

I am resolved to love God above all things, and my neighbor as myself for the love of God; and, in testimony of this love, I will always show myself a Christian.

Lesson 28: Our Union with the New Adam by Hope (1)

On hope.—By faith, uniting our mind with the mind of the new Adam, we are healed of our errors and our ignorance: under this first head, we participate in the fruits of the redemption. Yet, important as this union is, it does not suffice. Faith alone cannot save us. The reason is simple: by faith alone our union with the Savior is only begun. Our will must be united to him. It was not merely our understanding that was degraded by sin, and that should be reestablished in the supernatural order, but also our will. If, then, faith rehabilitates our understanding, by delivering it from ignorance, and communicating to it the divine thoughts of the new Adam, hope rehabilitates our will, by the communication of supernatural strength and divine inclinations.

This second manner of uniting ourselves with Jesus Christ will now occupy our attention, and hope will become the subject of our lessons. Now, hope holds a middle place between faith and charity; and faith, hope, and charity are, as we have already said, according to St. Augustine and St. Thomas, the three steps that raise us to a union with the new Adam. Hope depends on faith, because it is supported thereby; it depends on charity, because it finds its perfection therein. "Faith," says Origen, "is the foundation of the edifice; hope, its walls; charity, its roof."[424] It is easy to see by this that these three virtues, like three sisters, assist one another, favor one another, perfect one another.

These essential observations clearly show the usefulness of our plan, and the whole economy—at once so simple and so comprehensive—of the work of the redemption. Let us now study hope in itself, and for this purpose let us answer the following questions: What is hope? What are its foundations? What is its necessity? What are its qualities? What sins are opposed to it? What are its objects? By what means is it obtained?

1. *What is hope?* Hope is a gift of God and a supernatural virtue by which we expect with confidence all that God has promised us. We say that hope is "a gift," that is, a favor gratuitously bestowed—"a virtue," that is, a strength, an aptitude, which disposes the soul to expect with confidence—"supernatural," because it comes from God and has for its object those good things to which man cannot attain of himself, and to which he does not possess any right by his nature.

But, as we explained in the first part[425] of the catechism, God having gratuitously destined man for a supernatural end, he promised him the means to arrive thereat. "All that God has promised us," then, signifies the possession of himself in heaven, and the means to come to this possession; in other terms, grace in this world and glory in the next.

2. *What are the foundations of hope?* The foundations of our hope are the fidelity of God to his promises, and the merits of our Lord. The fidelity of God: nothing more solid than this foundation. God can no more deceive us than he can cease to be God. Now, God would deceive us if he were to fail in his promises; for they are formal, repeated a thousand times, and accompanied with oaths.

Let us add, fully to reassure ourselves, and to make our hope an immovable anchor, that in God these promises are united to all the conditions necessary for their fulfillment, namely, infinite power, wisdom, and goodness. He is infinitely powerful: nothing can prevent him from keeping his promises. He is infinitely wise: nothing can make him forget his promises, or ignore our petitions, or despise our wants. He is infinitely good: he cannot and will not sport with us. As a building on its foundations, so hope rests, in the first place, on the fidelity of God—on the infinite power, wisdom, and goodness of God: immutable perfections, to which it renders a solemn homage.

It rests, in the second place, on the merits of our Lord. On the one hand, these merits are infinite; they suffice, consequently, to obtain for us all that is necessary to our salvation. On the other hand, these merits are ours; we can, therefore, make use of them with confidence. The price of all the graces that we solicit has been paid in advance: God himself has accepted it. He has engaged to grant us all that we shall ask through the merits of his Son.

There is only one thing that can disturb our security; it is the apprehension of our own unworthiness and inconstancy. Hence it is that we cannot have, so long as we are in this world, an absolute certainty. We can indeed have a moral certainty that we are in the state of grace, and this assurance suffices to calm us. The proof that we can have this moral assurance is that the Church commands all her children to communicate. Now, she would guard against imposing such a precept on them, if they could not be assured, as far as it is possible in the actual order of providence, that they are in the friendship of God.

3. *What is the necessity of hope?* Hope is an absolute necessity for salvation. As a matter of fact, we cannot arrive at salvation without fulfilling the will of God. Now, the express will of God is that we believe his fidelity to his promises, and that we confidently expect everlasting beatitude, with all the means to attain it. By not hoping in God, do we not offer him the grossest insult? There is then a formal, a direct precept, which rigorously imposes on all the duty of hoping, and of making acts of hope.[426]

This is intimated to us in every page of the scripture. Among the transgressions with which Saul was reproached, God placed the violation of this commandment. "He did not hope in the Lord: therefore he should die."[427] St. Paul, writing to Timothy, says: "Charge the faithful not to trust in uncertain riches, but in the living God."[428] In his epistle to the Hebrews he seems to express himself in a still more positive manner: "Every one coming to God must believe that he is, and that he is a rewarder."[429] *Must*—behold the precept! *Rewarder*—behold the obligation of expecting eternal beatitude from God!

This duty of hoping is so imperative that it is an indispensable condition of our salvation. "It is by hope that we are saved," adds the great apostle.[430] Not only are we obliged to preserve that habitual hope which we received in baptism, but we are bound to make formal acts of hope. The circumstances in which we ought to elicit them are: a) when we come to the use of reason; b) when we are assailed by any great temptation of despair; c) frequently during the course of life, as we explained in treating of faith; and d) at the point of death.

4. *What are the qualities of hope?* Hope ought to be supernatural, firm, and universal. It ought to be supernatural: it is on the goodness, wisdom, and power of God, and his fidelity to his promises, as well as on the infinite merits of our Lord, that we ought to rely for the obtaining of everlasting bliss. He who would rely for his salvation on his own good works or on the support of any creature, excluding the supernatural and gratuitous help which God gives us by his grace, would not only be wanting in true hope, but would sin mortally against both faith and hope.

Not that we ought not to do good works and rely upon them; but we ought only to regard them as a secondary means, whose value is derived wholly from their connection with grace. In effect, since eternal life is proposed to us as a crown, and no one is crowned unless he fights well, it is evident that, to obtain this crown, good works are required of us, not—to repeat it once more—as they are in themselves and apart from grace, but as done with the help of God.[431]

Hope ought to be firm. We ought to expect with immovable confidence the good things which God has promised us, because nothing can equal the fidelity of God to his promises, or the merits of our Lord accepted by him, as the price of that heaven which is reserved for us, and of that grace which is necessary for us to obtain it. But if, on God's side, our hope ought to be immovable, it ought not to be so on our own, because of our inconstancy. To give it this character, as far as is compatible with human weakness, we must, as St. Peter says, endeavor, by our good works and the faithful performance of our duties, to make our vocation to eternal happiness more and more sure.

Hope ought to be universal, that is, ought to extend to all those things which God has promised, without exception or diminution. To expect the fulfillment of one promise, and not to expect with as much confidence that of another, would be to annihilate hope, whose foundations are ever the same. Like faith, hope cannot be divided. It is whole and entire, complete and universal, or not at all.

5. *What are the sins opposed to hope?* Is it possible to sin against a virtue which ought to be so sweet to us, poor exiles in this valley of tears? Alas, yes! and we sin against it in two manners, by excess and by defect, by presumption and by despair.

Those sin by presumption who flatter themselves with the idea of being able to obtain pardon for their sins without renouncing and detesting them; to live virtuously without controlling their passions, without often reflecting on the truths of salvation, without disposing themselves for a worthy frequentation of the sacraments; to die the death of the saints without living the life of the just, without observing faithfully the commandments of God and the Church.

The presumptuous expose themselves to the greatest danger of losing their souls. Witness the sinner who lived for a long time in forgetfulness of his duties, and who was accustomed to say: "I have plenty of time to be converted; at the end of my life, I will save myself by two or three words." One day, as he is out riding, he wishes to cross a bridge, half broken down. His horse becomes restive, and to make it advance he gives it the spur. But the horse begins to prance and rear, and finally leaps into the water, where the unfortunate man is drowned, without being able to utter anything else than these two or three words of anger and despair: "May the devil take us both!"

To correct oneself of presumption, it is necessary to reflect on this warning of the wise man: "Say not: The mercy of God is great, and he will pardon the multitude of my sins; for mercy and wrath come from him, and his eyes are on the sinner."[432] It is necessary to remember that all the saints made great efforts to be saved; that our Lord said that no one would be crowned who had not fought well; that, to be glorified, we must be in a manner crucified; that the way to heaven is strait, and the gate narrow; that the kingdom of heaven suffers violence, and must be taken by force.

One sins against hope by defect when he neglects to make acts of this virtue at proper times; also, when he allows himself to fall into despair—let the reason be because he looks upon his sins as too enormous or too numerous to obtain forgiveness for them, or because he considers his passions too violent, his evil habits too deeply rooted, ever to be able to set himself free from them, or because he is afflicted and disquieted beyond measure for the least imperfection, after the manner of scrupulous persons, who seem to imagine that God is always on the watch to surprise them, or, in fine, because he does not trust sufficiently in providence and abandons himself to excessive anxieties regarding the wants of life. The state of despair is a frightful state. "Sin," says one of the saints, "brings death to the soul, and despair places an insuperable obstacle to its resurrection."[433]

The remedy for despair is to call before one's eyes the infinite goodness with which God provides for the birds of the air and even for the smallest insects, but especially his mercy, which nothing can weary or exhaust. It must be borne in mind that he has forgiven many great sinners; that he never despises a contrite heart; that there is no sin except final impenitence unpardonable. We must consider the wonderful facility with which he forgave David, Magdalen, St. Augustine, St. Peter, and the good thief.[434] He would have forgiven Judas himself, if Judas had asked forgiveness.

It will encourage one to read the parable of the lost sheep or the prodigal son, or the history of our Lord's passion. In a word, it is necessary to recollect that we have in God a most tender Father, who sincerely desires that all his children should be converted and saved; in Jesus Christ a charitable Savior, who loved us so much as to die for us, and who loves us so much as to give himself to us; in Mary a Mother full of clemency, who is the refuge of all sinners, even the most despairing; in the angels and saints powerful intercessors.[435]

6. *What are the objects of hope?* The first and noblest object of hope is eternal beatitude—in other words, the possession of God and the joys of which he is the source, for all eternity. Such is the sublime degree to which Christian hope elevates us. Bounding through all space, leaving behind it all created goods, however precious, however seducing, it pierces, according to the expression of St. Paul, into the sanctuary where God unveils the wonders of his being. There, attaching itself to the being of beings, it wishes never more to be separated from him, until it has made him its everlasting conquest and possession.[436]

The second object of hope is grace. Hereby we must understand all the means that are necessary to arrive at eternal beatitude. Now, it is during life, while our soul is united to our body, that we must labor to obtain everlasting happiness. Whence it follows that all that is necessary for the life of the soul and the life of the body is the secondary object of hope. God, who desires the end, also desires the means. This is the reason why he commands us to expect and every day to ask of him the possession of his kingdom; afterward, bread, that is to say, all that is spiritually and corporally necessary for us to labor, during the days of our mortal pilgrimage, for the attainment of the beatitude which he has promised us.

It is therefore permitted us to ask of God all the goods that we require for soul and body, but only with a view to our last end. To ask them only to rest in them with complacency, without making them serve as steps to raise us to heaven, is a criminal disturbance of order, is a degradation of the soul.[437] In short, glory, that is, the possession of God for eternity, and, on earth, grace, which is the beginning of glory: these are the objects of Christian hope.[438] What are all other hopes in comparison with this?

On grace.—In the preceding lesson we spoke of glory, and we will speak of it again in the last part[439] of the catechism. It remains to speak of grace, which must conduct us to glory. The answers to the following questions suffice to teach us what we ought to know regarding this inestimable gift of God: What is grace? Is grace necessary for us? Does grace alone save us? Does grace destroy our liberty? Which are the different kinds of grace? Is grace always at our disposal? What are the effects of grace? What is the excellence of grace?

1. *What is grace?* Considered in its essence, grace is a divine principle or element which really makes us the children of God and the heirs of his glory.[440] In its relations with us, grace is defined: a supernatural help or gift which God bestows gratuitously on us, in consideration of the merits of our Lord Jesus Christ, that we may be enabled to work out our salvation.[441] Grace is "a gift," that is, a present which God makes us; a light, a strength, which he diffuses through our souls, and which adds to their perfection; a "supernatural" gift, that is, one which is above the strength of nature, beyond the reach of every creature—which comes consequently from God alone and consists in a certain communication of himself, commenced on earth, to be consummated in heaven.[442] "Which God bestows on us," that is, on men and angels, who, being the only

intelligent creatures in existence, are alone capable of receiving grace. "Gratuitously," that is, without any personal merit on our part, and without any exigency of our nature.

It follows hence that we cannot merit the first grace: it is necessary that God should give it to us in his preventing goodness. The increase of grace which we merit by our good works proceeds from the grace granted gratuitously to us in the first place, so that this increase can be called both a reward and a grace: a reward, since it is procured by merit; a grace, since this merit flows from grace, which, in its principle, its root, its origin, is absolutely gratuitous.[443]

"In consideration of the merits of our Lord Jesus Christ": thus, God is the author or efficient cause of grace. Our Lord, immolated, satisfying, and interceding for us, is the meritorious cause of grace; it is with the plenitude of his merits that we are enriched.[444] On which it is necessary to remark in passing how well the grace of our Lord deserves to be called supernatural and gratuitous, since it is granted, not to man a friend, but to man an enemy of God by sin. "That we may be enabled to work out our salvation": these words indicate the final cause of grace—I mean the supreme end for which God gives it to us. "In effect," says St. Augustine, "it is by grace that, being predestinated, we are called, we are justified, we are glorified."[445]

Grace poured into our souls is therefore the principle of a new being, of a new life which ennobles us, by communicating to us a certain beginning of the substance of God, to conduct us to the consummation of ourselves in him, and to our perfect resemblance with him:[446] so that, if the expression may be permitted us, man replenished with grace on earth is a God commenced, and the saint in heaven is a finite God. What nobility! But what gratitude and what sanctity!

2. *Is grace necessary for us?* To ask whether grace is necessary for us to work out our salvation is to ask whether, by the mere strength of nature, man can do anything above the strength of nature; whether a bird can fly without wings; whether an astronomer can without a telescope perceive the stars that are invisible to the naked eye; in a word, it is to ask whether man, a finite creature, can, by his own unaided resources, arrive at infinite happiness: to place the question thus is to solve it. Here you see the reason why, as God himself struck Lucifer with the thunderbolt of his anger, the Catholic Church strikes with her anathema the man who is so proud as to say that, without the inspiration and the assistance of the Holy Ghost first acting within us, we can believe, hope, love, or repent, as we should, to obtain the grace of justification.[447]

Hence, we cannot of ourselves have faith or the beginning of faith, hope or the beginning of hope, charity or the beginning of charity, contrition or the beginning of contrition; we cannot pray, nor prepare ourselves to receive grace, nor keep the commandments of God, nor do the least good work, nor even pronounce the name of Jesus in a supernatural or meritorious manner, without the help of grace.[448] Let us add that we require, moreover, a special succor from God to persevere in a good course and to die in the friendship of God.[449] Can there be any indigence greater? Can there be any obligation stricter than to humble ourselves and to pray?[450]

3. *Does grace alone save us?* Grace is given us to act, that is, to keep the commandments which God has laid down for us: it would fail in its object if we did not act. It is therefore evident that grace alone does not save us: it requires our cooperation. Accordingly, the apostle St. Paul, speaking of the great actions which he had performed and the prodigies of mercy of which he had been the object or the instrument, did not say, "It was grace alone that did all these things," nor, "It was I alone that did all these things"; but he said, "It is by the grace of God that I am what I am, and grace has not been void in me, but I have labored more than all they—yet not I, but the grace of God with me."[451] In a word, without grace we can do nothing in the order of salvation; with grace, everything. God

commands nothing impossible, but, in commanding, he warns us to do what we can, and he assists us to do what we cannot do.

Now, we cooperate with grace when we act faithfully in accordance with its inspirations, and not in accordance with the foolish suggestions of our inclinations or the simple lights of our minds, without referring what we do to our supernatural end. Nothing is more necessary than to correspond with grace. On our fidelity to this fundamental duty depends our salvation, as well as the degree of glory which we shall enjoy in heaven. Habitual recollection, and the mortification of our interior and exterior senses, are the means to make us alive to the inspirations of grace, as its inestimable value is the strongest motive to induce us to profit by it. [452]

4. *Does grace destroy our liberty?* As happens to all those who abandon the infallible compass of the faith, to guide themselves by the uncertain lights of their weak reason, heretics have run into two opposite extremes regarding the article of grace. Some, like the Pelagians, have exalted man beyond measure, and denied that he has any need of grace; others, like the Lutherans, have degraded him into a mere automaton, and denied that he has free will. Between these two errors, which are equally fatal, since one leads to pride and the other to despair, is found the truth. It utters its anathema against those who deny the necessity of grace, and also against those who deny the liberty of man under the influence of grace.

By sin the free will of man was weakened. Man has therefore need of a remedy, which is grace. Grace no more destroys human liberty than a remedy destroys health, than a staff in the feeble hands of an old man destroys his liberty. On the contrary, it perfects our liberty, by giving us the light and strength which we cannot have of ourselves.[453] Man, fortified by grace, remains free in his will. He can act, he can resist; he can do good, he can do evil: everyone knows it, everyone feels it. It would be folly to think of proving a truth whose negation would instantly justify all sorts of crimes, or rather annihilate every distinction between vice and virtue.[454]

5. *Which are the different kinds of grace?* Grace is divided into:

Exterior grace, which comprises all the exterior means that God gives us to work out our salvation. We explained it when speaking of religion.[455]

Interior grace, which comprises the lights, the inspirations, the facilities which God communicates to our souls, to make them know and do good or resist evil.

Grace gratuitously given, that is, whose principal end is not the personal sanctification of him who receives it, but the sanctification of the neighbor. Under this head are included the gifts of science, prudence, power to forgive sins, and other such favors.[456]

Grace which makes us pleasing to God, that is, whose principal end is the sanctification of him who receives it. Now, grace makes us pleasing to God in two ways: either by making us, sinners as we are, just, that is, by raising us from the state of mortal sin to the happy state of the friendship of God; or by making us still more just, by an increase of the sanctity and charity which it communicates to our souls. We also speak of the wonders thus wrought as the first and the second sanctifying grace. This grace is the most precious of all treasures, since it is the pledge of eternal beatitude.

Sanctifying grace is either habitual or actual. Habitual sanctifying grace is that which, remaining in us after its entrance, whether it has entered by baptism or penance, renders us just before God, by communicating to us something divine, and making us in a certain manner participators in the nature of God himself.[457] To habitual sanctifying grace are referred the infused virtues, that is, ones that we cannot have by the mere strength of our nature, but which are poured into our souls by the goodness of God alone, and of which we receive the first fruits in baptism. They are the three theological virtues (faith, hope, and charity), and the four cardinal virtues (prudence, justice, fortitude, and temperance); also the seven gifts of the Holy Ghost. [458]

Actual sanctifying grace is a passing light which God imparts to our mind, a passing motion which he communicates to our will to make us know and do good. Actual grace is necessary for us to do good, because by it habitual grace is stirred up, as it were, and reduced to acts.[459] "As the eye," says St. Augustine, "however sound it may be, cannot see, unless it is struck by a ray of light, so man, however fully justified we may imagine him, cannot live, that is, cannot act as he should, unless assisted by the grace of God."[460]

"As the head influences the members, and the vine nourishes the branches, so," adds the Council of Trent, "our Lord Jesus Christ pours a sensible virtue into the just themselves, and this virtue always precedes, accompanies, and follows their actions, which otherwise cannot in any manner be agreeable to God or meritorious to them."[461]

6. *Is grace always at our disposal?* On the one side, God wishes that each of us should come to salvation. The way to arrive at salvation is to keep the commandments of God, who never commands anything impossible. On the other side, faith teaches that without grace we cannot keep the commandments of God. Faith therefore teaches that grace is always at our disposal. It is so in two manners: either immediately, in the sense that we can, on the spot and without a new help, overcome a temptation, or do a good work, which presents itself; or mediately, in the sense that we can obtain the grace necessary to overcome a temptation which assails us, or do a good work which is commanded us. It is only necessary to remark that the ordinary just and unjust obtain most easily the grace of which they have need, and that the difficulty is greater for hardened sinners.

Let us say, in conclusion, that infidels themselves obtain in time and place the graces sufficient to avoid evil, and thus to open for them little by little the way of salvation, whatever may be the nature of these graces, the secret of which is reserved to God's infinite wisdom. We know that it is so; because our Lord Jesus Christ died for all men:[462] so that the wicked perish, not because they cannot be good, but because they will not.[463] Let us add that, besides sanctifying grace, we have need of a special succor to persevere to the end.[464]

Hence, you easily conclude that Pelagians, Semi-Pelagians, protestants, and Jansenists were in error, and that the Catholic Church, entrusted with the deposit of the faith, was right in condemning them: the first, because they denied the necessity of grace; the second, because they only admitted the necessity of grace in certain cases; the third, because they denied human liberty under the influence of grace; and the fourth, because they renewed a portion of the preceding errors, and pretended that it is impossible to keep some of the commandments of God, and that grace is wanting to us to render those commandments possible.[465]

We see that all these errors, ignoring the true condition of man, lead to consequences that are no less frightful than absurd: to make man either a god or a machine, and to make God a tyrant.

7. *What are the effects of grace?* Grace produces two great effects: justification and merit. Justification is that effect of grace which makes sinners just. The sinner is he who, putting his own will in the place of God's, takes it as the rule of his thoughts, words, and actions. The just man, on the contrary, is he who, putting God's will in the place of his own, takes it as the rule of his thoughts, words, and actions. The sinner is in a state of rebellion—consequently of crime and disorder. The just man, on the contrary, is in a state of submission—consequently of virtue and order.

Justification consists in bringing the sinner from his state of rebellion against God, of enmity with God, of crime, of slavery to the devil, to the state of obedience to God, of friendship with God, of sanctity, of the liberty of the children of God. It is a renovation and purification of the soul, a restoration of order, a passage from injustice to justice. This mystery of mercy, more admirable than the creation of the world, is wrought in a moment by the infusion of grace, which effaces sin, and remains in us as a principle of sanctity and supernatural life. As conditions, it supposes, on the part of the sinner, faith and a correspondence of will.[466]

Merit is a reward which God owes to man for works done.[467] The sinner, once justified, can perform good actions, which merit new graces, by means of which he arrives at eternal beatitude. Now, to acquire merit, properly so called, that is, something to which an everlasting reward is due, in virtue of the laws of justice and the promises of God, it is necessary a) to be on earth, for the saints in heaven can no longer merit; b) to be in the state of grace; c) to do an action good of its own nature; d) to do it with a good motive; e) to do it with perfect liberty, inwardly and outwardly.[468]

After the example of all the saints, we should continually endeavor to acquire merits; but though we may place a certain confidence in them, it is much better, in order to avoid the temptations of pride and vainglory, to put all our trust in the infinite goodness of God, from whom, after all, come whatever merits we can acquire.

8. *What is the excellence of grace?* "Though I should speak the languages of angels and men, though I should have a knowledge of all the secrets of nature and an understanding of all the mysteries of faith, if I have not charity, I am nothing";[469] the rest would be useless to me. You are right, O great apostle! In the eyes of any man capable of linking two ideas together, it is as clear as day that the least grace, the smallest degree of sanctifying grace, is more precious than all natural gifts—genius, talent, learning, health, riches, dignities, thrones. Hence that admirable saying of the Angelic Doctor, already quoted: "The supernatural good of a single individual is more important than the natural good of the whole universe."[470]

In point of fact, all natural gifts together cannot, without grace, raise us to infinite supernatural happiness, while the least degree of grace, without any uncommon natural gifts whatever, can lead us to it. The reason is simple: grace is a supernatural element or principle which communicates to us something divine, and authorizes us to say with St. Paul: "I live—yet not I, but Jesus Christ himself liveth in me."[471]

Accordingly, to comprehend the excellence of grace, we must know that its benefits are not limited to the brief period of our earthly existence; they embrace the endless ages of eternity: here the foretaste, there the plenitude. It follows that grace—consequently religion itself—is nothing else than a certain beginning of glory in us, and glory nothing else than a consummation of grace. Oh, what esteem we ought to have for grace! what care to preserve it! what anxiety to recover it if we have had the misfortune to lose it!

PRAYER

O my God! who art all love, I thank thee for having diffused hope through my heart; grant that I may strengthen it by faithfully corresponding with grace.

I am resolved to love God above all things, and my neighbor as myself for the love of God; and, in testimony of this love, I will be most faithful to grace in little things.

Lesson 29: Our Union with the New Adam by Hope (2)

First means to obtain grace: Prayer.—Grace is absolutely necessary for salvation, and we cannot have grace of ourselves. Such are the two truths contained in the preceding lesson. In his infinite goodness, God has given us two great means to obtain grace: prayer and the sacraments. We now proceed to speak of these immense benefits.

1. *What is prayer?* In its widest sense, prayer is taken to represent every kind of good work. In its narrowest sense, it signifies praise and thanksgiving to God. Finally, in its proper sense, prayer is a petition made to God for the good things which he has promised

us; or rather, "an elevation of the soul to God, to represent to him our indigence and to offer him our homage."[472] Nothing more noble, nothing more useful, nothing more delightful than this commerce of man with God.

2. *Is prayer necessary?* Prayer is necessary by a natural right, a divine right, and an ecclesiastical right. By a natural right—that is to say, in the common order of providence, we cannot obtain the grace necessary to do good and to avoid evil, consequently to work out our salvation, without prayer. This necessity is deduced most clearly from the words of St. Paul to the Romans: "Whosoever shall call upon the name of the Lord shall be saved; but how shall they call upon him in whom they do not believe?"[473] The apostle places faith and the invocation of the name of God on the same level. If then faith is necessary, as no one can doubt, prayer is equally necessary. The same truth is found in the words of our Lord when he says, "Ask and you shall receive"[474]—as if he should say, "Unless you ask you shall not receive."

Whence it must be concluded that, generally speaking, prayer is a necessary means to obtain grace and to arrive at salvation. Though the divine aid, to overcome temptations and observe the commandments, is sometimes given to those who do not ask it, yet it is usually given only to those who ask it. "You do not receive," says the apostle St. James, "because you do not ask."[475] Moreover, if we consider our weakness, our misery, our innumerable spiritual and temporal wants—if we call to mind that we are like beggars, burdened with a numerous family, without food or shelter, and almost without clothes, we shall understand, no other proof being required, that prayer, and continual prayer, is a most natural and pressing duty on us.

The knowledge of this duty is so deeply rooted in human nature that there is no nation, however barbarous, that does not comply with it. Since the world began, prayer has been continually rising heavenward. The Jews prayed, Christians prayed, pagans prayed, Mahometans prayed, even savages prayed: they still pray, and they pray much.

In the eyes of unbelievers, whoever dispenses himself from this law takes his place among the brute creation. "You dog of a Christian!" a Bedouin, not very long ago, used to repeat daily to one of our French officers who had become his prisoner. One morning the officer, enraged beyond measure to hear himself saluted in this manner by a barbarian, said to him: "Why do you call me a dog? I am your prisoner. I am a man like yourself, and a better man." "You a man!" replied the Arab, coldly, "no, you are a dog. You have now been my prisoner for six months, and I have never seen you pray; and you wish me not to call you a dog!" The barbarian was right. In all nature, it is only the beasts that do not pray.

Prayer is necessary by a divine right. This means that God makes it a formal precept. "You ought always to pray," says our Lord himself, "and never to cease."[476] *You ought:* this is not a counsel, but a command and a necessity. His faithful interpreter, the apostle St. Paul, adds: "Persevere in prayer, be vigilant in prayer,"[477] "pray without ceasing,"[478] "pray at all times."[479] The same command reappears in every page of the divine scriptures. The fathers and the doctors of the Church, who so well understood the gospel, proclaim to us in one voice: "Whoever does not pray assiduously is dead."[480] To corroborate their words, they show us our Lord, the saint of saints, praying and praying much; the saints and true Christians of all times praying and praying much.

Finally, prayer is necessary by an ecclesiastical right; but this command refers only to public prayer, of which we shall speak later on.

3. *When must we pray?* It is difficult to determine with precision when the natural and divine precept of prayer obliges us by itself. Yet all agree that it would be sinful to remain a notable time without praying, and that the direct obligation of praying arises as often as that of making acts of the theological virtues, and that prayer is necessary to maintain us

in a Christian life. Thus, the precept is understood by the generality of the faithful, who make it their duty never to let any day pass without praying, and even several times.[481] Certain heretics once pretended that the obligation of praying, in the proper sense of the word, was continual. They founded their doctrine on the text of the gospel: "We ought always to pray, and not to faint."[482]

But they mistook the meaning of our Lord's words, which signify, in the first place, that it is necessary to pray often, at convenient times, according as the outward duties imposed on us by providence permit it—above all with perseverance, without ever being cast down or discouraged, no matter how long our Lord may appear to delay in complying with our desires.[483]

These words also signify that we ought to refer, with great purity of intention, all our works to God, doing and suffering everything for his glory. "To pray always," says St. Augustine, "is always to desire the accomplishment of the will of God and the attainment of the blessed life which he has promised to us. Let us therefore desire these things, and we shall always pray." "To pray always," continues the Venerable Bede, "is to act always in the presence of God." "He prays always," add the commentators, "who always acts well."[484]

The precept of prayer obliges us indirectly on many occasions, inasmuch as it is bound up with the precept of charity toward ourselves and others. Here are a few of the occasions: a) when there is question of recovering grace; b) when we are liable to lose grace; c) when we are in danger of death; d) when the neighbor is exposed to a great necessity which we cannot remedy by any other means than prayer; e) when the society, the community, the family of which we are members, is threatened with some great spiritual or temporal calamity. In all these and the like cases there is an obligation to pray, under pain of sin, more or less grievous, according to circumstances.[485]

By the side of the strict right of which we have just spoken there exists a general custom of the Church, and on this account a custom worthy of the utmost respect, in virtue of which all true Christians find leisure several times a day for the great duty of prayer. This custom takes its origin in the night of time. A thousand years before our Lord, David observed it amid the splendors of his court. Five hundred years later, Daniel showed himself faithful to it amid the rigors of the Babylonian captivity.[486] Our forefathers made it a law under the sword of persecution. What do I say?—Mahometans themselves have inscribed it among the articles of their religious code, and conform to it with scrupulous exactitude.

Morn, noon, and eve are the three times of the day which custom consecrates to prayer, and of which the Church is careful to remind us by the sound of the bell. At morn, to salute God our Father, to thank him for watching over us during the night, and to ask his blessing on the new day for which we are indebted to his goodness. At noon, to take breath, to purify our intention, and to reanimate our courage. At eve, to offer to God with our thanks our night's sleep, and to express to him our regret for faults committed and our resolution to avoid them on the morrow.

Do you know anything more rational or beautiful than this triple prayer, especially when it is made in common in families by parents, children, and servants? According to the example of every people, it is also necessary to pray before and after meals, and this for reasons of which we shall speak elsewhere.

4. *Where must we pray?* We must pray everywhere. Yet we must seek in preference, according to the counsel of the Savior, a retired place, far removed from noise, where we can more conveniently entertain ourselves with God, and give him those outward marks of respect which are demanded by his holy presence, or inspired by the liveliness of our affection, confidence, and sorrow. The Church is the place which best suits prayer. God

hears us there more easily, as he assures us in express terms.[487] Besides, the very sanctity of the place, the memories which it recalls, the sight of altars and statues and pictures, all are admirably calculated to fix the attention of the mind, to excite the devotion of the heart, and consequently to render our prayers more efficacious.

5. *To whom must we pray?* We must pray to God and the saints. To God—as the absolute master of all things—who alone can grant our petitions. To the saints—as God's friends and our protectors—that, uniting their prayers with ours, we may more easily obtain the graces of which we have need. Among the saints, the greatest—and those who during life occupied a position like our own, in the same state, amid the same temptations—and those whom the piety of peoples invokes for such or such a necessity, ought to be the objects of our special devotion. Moreover, as there are saints on earth, we can also recommend ourselves to their prayers. The apostles taught this practice to the early Christians, as well by engaging them to pray for one another, as by conjuring them not to forget before the Lord those who had announced the gospel to them.

6. *For whom must we pray?* We must pray for the whole Church. For the Church triumphant, to obtain an increase of its outer glory, which consists in a wider manifestation of the power, goodness, and other perfections of God, our Lord Jesus Christ, the Blessed Virgin, and the saints.[488] For the Church suffering, to obtain its consolation or a termination of its pains. For the Church militant, to obtain its triumph over its enemies and the salvation of its children.

As for the order in which we should pray, we shall give it in a few words. We must pray before all a) for our holy father the pope, the supreme head of the Church; b) for prelates and others charged with the care of souls; c) for Christian kings, princes, and magistrates; d) for our parents, and those confided to our care; e) for the just; f) for sinners; g) for those who do not belong to the Church. Do not imagine that in praying for many our prayers become less advantageous: quite the contrary. "If you only pray for yourself," says St. Ambrose, "you alone will pray for yourself; but if you pray for all, all will pray for you."[489]

7. *Why must we pray?* We must pray in order to obtain all that is useful for us, as well in the spiritual as in the material order, to arrive at our last end. Hence, all that directly refers to this supreme end, which is the possession and glory of God, ought to hold the first rank in our prayers. So our Lord himself tells us, as we shall show, when explaining the Lord's Prayer.

In the second rank are placed the graces, virtues, and other spiritual goods which are the immediate means to come to God. Corporal goods, such as health, character, fortune, being remote means, occupy the third rank. We see hereby that these three kinds of goods must be asked in very different manners. We ought to ask in an absolute manner the sanctification of the name of God, the coming of his kingdom, the accomplishment of his holy will, the spiritual goods which may conduct us to the happiness of eternity. As for temporal goods, we ought to solicit them, not as the end of our desires, but as means to reach heaven, either because they maintain our corporal life or they enable us to practice virtue.[490]

8. *How must we pray?* To answer this question, we must speak of the postures of the body and the dispositions of the soul.

Postures of the body. All peoples have taken, and still take, when praying, a particular posture, corresponding to the sentiments of respect, love, and sorrow which bring them before God. There are three different postures in general use among Christians.

We pray on our knees, as criminals and suppliants, who acknowledge in the presence of God their great unworthiness and misery, but at the same time his infinite mercy. Thus, Solomon prayed in the Temple of Jerusalem, St. Peter when raising to life the good widow Tabitha, St. Paul when quitting the priests of Ephesus, and our Lord himself in the Garden of Olives.

We pray on our knees with our hands extended, to show to God and men that they are pure, and that we are the disciples of a crucified Lord, through whose merits we expect to be heard. Thus Moses, a living figure of our Lord, prayed when he besought for Israel a victory over the Amalekites; David, another figure of the Savior; the early Christians; and our Lord himself on the cross. Thus, also, do priests pray at Mass.

We pray standing, particularly on Sundays and during the paschal time, in memory of the resurrection of our Lord Jesus Christ, and to put ourselves in mind of the wholly divine life which we should lead in the midst of the world. Such was the ordinary manner of praying in the first ages of the Church. Thus our Lord himself often prayed, as we see in the gospel. Yet these various attitudes are not obligatory, so that he who does not conform to them does not offend God. It suffices that his demeanor be humble and respectful; for the prayer of him who humbles himself shall pierce the heavens.[491]

St. Paul wishes that men should pray in the church with the head bare, because man is the glorious image of God, and this image shines particularly on his brow. This brow should be uncovered in prayer, to show the most glorious work of the Creator humbled before him. On the other hand, the apostle wishes that women should pray with the head covered. This for three reasons. The first, because, being the glorious image of man, they ought to veil this glory before God, inasmuch as man, when he prays, ought to conceal whatever might be a subject of vanity for him. The second, because, being inferior to man, they ought to acknowledge their inferiority before God, by bearing on their head, in the dress that covers it, the mark of their dependence. The third, because, modesty being their most beautiful ornament, they ought, out of respect for the angels and the ministers of the Lord, to avoid, especially in the temple, everything that could tarnish it.[492]

As for the eyes, they ought either to be cast down to the ground, through respect for the Divine Majesty and confusion for our faults, or raised toward heaven to implore the aid of him whose abode is there—according to the example of the Savior himself. If one prays in a church during the Holy Sacrifice of the Mass, the looks ought to be directed toward the altar, and chiefly toward the East. This usage rests on several reasons, held in deep respect since the times of the primitive Church.

The first, because the terrestrial paradise, the first happy abode of man, was situated in the East. Now, it is fitting that when we pray we should turn our looks toward the place from which we were banished, in order to ask with greater earnestness the grace to enter into the true paradise, of which prayer and penance are the double key. The second, because in the scripture, our Lord is called the Orient and the sun of justice, and nothing is more natural than, when we invoke him, to turn toward that point of the heavens which reminds us of these august titles. The third, because our Lord was crucified with his face turned toward the West, so that when, in praying, we look toward the East, we in some manner contemplate our Lord's countenance. The fourth, in order to distinguish ourselves from the Jews, who pray with the face turned toward the West; for, in the Temple of Jerusalem, the tabernacle was situated at this point.[493]

Nothing is unimportant in these various attitudes. On the one side, all peoples have regarded it as a duty to conform to them; on the other, they are eminently calculated to manifest and foster humility, confidence, sorrow, and all the other sentiments that are proper for man in the presence of God.

Dispositions of the soul. Let us come to the dispositions of the soul. Faith, confidence, devotion, perseverance: such ought to be the dispositions of the soul that takes to heart the duty of prayer—consequently, the qualities that it ought to give to prayer.

Faith. Faith is the principle and foundation of society. This is the reason why nothing is promised to such prayer as does not proceed from faith. Hence it is that this virtue is so strongly recommended to us when we pray. "Whatsoever you shall ask in prayer with faith," says the Savior, "you shall obtain."[494] "Ask with faith," adds the apostle St. James, "and without doubting; for he who doubts is like a wave of the sea, which comes and goes."[495] Such a person fails in steadiness and cannot calculate on success in prayer. "Without faith," continues St. Augustine, "there is no prayer."[496] The faith of which there is question here does not consist merely in a general belief of the power, goodness, and fidelity of God, but also in a special conviction that God will grant us whatsoever we ask, if he judge it expedient for our salvation.

Confidence. It ought to be immovable, since it is founded on the promises of God and the merits of our Lord. It ought to be lively, so as to banish all laxity and tepidity in prayer. It ought to be really present, so as to banish a certain vague uncertainty which cannot be reconciled with simple habitual confidence—so as to exclude every kind of fear arising from the greatness of the favor asked or the unworthiness of the person who asks. "Be assured," says Cassian, "that you shall never be heard, when you doubt of being heard. It is a sign of future success, when one is impelled by the Holy Ghost to ask with great confidence, and a kind of certainty that he shall obtain what he asks."[497]

Devotion. It requires purity of intention in prayer. We ought not to ask anything that we do not intend to turn directly or indirectly to the glory of God, our own sanctification, or the sanctification of our neighbor. It is only for these purposes that our Lord has placed his power at our service. "How," says St. Augustine, "is he called who promised to grant us whatsoever we should ask in his name? He is called Savior. Consequently, anything that is contrary to salvation we cannot ask in the name of the Savior."[498]

It requires humility, which renders prayer omnipotent. "The prayer of him who humbles himself," says the Holy Spirit, "shall pierce the clouds, and shall not return to earth till it meets the kindly glance of the Most High."[499]

It supposes a sincere disposition not to refuse God anything that he asks of us: whether to quit sin, or to make greater progress in virtue.

It supposes attention. "How can you expect God to hear you," says St. Cyprian, "when you do not hear yourself?"[500] "To pray with the mouth and mentally to wander about through houses and public places, to babble over words and to be busied with amusements and trifles: What else is it," asks the Council of Treves, "than to deceive men and to mock God?"[501] As for the means, to have attention at prayer, let us mention some of them: a constant guard on the inward and outward senses; mortification of the passions; the sign of the cross made piously; care to place one's self in the presence of God, considering to whom and of what one is about to speak; a petition for grace to pray well; to renounce beforehand all distractions, and to drive them away gently, but firmly, when they present themselves during prayer.

Perseverance. Our Lord insists very much on the necessity and efficacy of this condition of prayer. We shall just give three proofs hereof. The first is the history of the Chanaanite woman, who was indebted to her perseverance for the cure of her daughter and for our Lord's eulogy of her faith.[502] The second is the parable of the man who, by obstinate begging, finally obtained the three loaves which he wanted from his friend.[503] The third is the formal precept: "We ought always to pray, and not to faint."[504]

God is the master of his gifts. He knows the day and the hour in which he will hear us: it is our duty to be resigned to the arrangements of his tender providence. These salutary delays are a proof of his wisdom and his goodness. They make us esteem what we have obtained with difficulty; they make us grateful for having received it and careful to preserve it. They make us practice a multitude of virtuous acts, on which perhaps we should never have thought, but which we willingly employ in the hope of success: for instance, those of humility, vigilance, mortification, and almsgiving.

To know how long one ought to persevere is a question not easily solved. In the first place, we ought never to abandon prayer through diffidence or discouragement. If there is question of temporal favors—a considerable delay, occurrences that surprise us, particular circumstances that arise, often become signs more or less probable that it is not the good pleasure of God to hear us. In this case, we may cease to make our petition, doing so with a humble submission, a filial conformity to the will of God and an assurance that the refusal is for our greater good. If there is question of spiritual favors, we should be slow to leave off our petitions. In the first place, such a prayer is always useful by itself. In the second, it often arrives at its effect without our knowledge. Thus, you ask deliverance from a temptation, which nevertheless continues to torment you; but it is possible that your prayers keep away others more serious. It is possible also that the temptation will be removed from you after a little; and, if not, why you will be indebted for many victories to your fidelity. It is possible that at the very moment when you are tempted, a soul has need of a special grace to prevent it from sinning, and that you, by virtue of the communion of saints, obtain for it this victorious grace. Finally, if prayer has for its object the grace of perseverance, of course it should be continued till death.[505]

Among the necessary conditions of prayer, we have not numbered charity. This seeming forgetfulness requires a word of explanation. The prayer of a man in the state of grace has a triple effect: it is meritorious, satisfactory, and impetratory. That of a sinner is only impetratory. It is certain that God willingly hears the prayers of the just. Yet he also hears the prayers of sinners,[506] because the impetratory efficacy of prayer does not depend on charity, nor on the dignity of the person who prays, but on the faith and confidence of him who prays and the mercy and promises of God.

Another difference distinguishes the prayer of the just man from that of the sinner. The prayer of the just man, springing from a heart that is vivified by sanctifying grace, is meritorious for eternal life, while that of the sinner is not so.[507] All this shows us the infinite goodness of God, who continually verifies in the fullest sense the saying of our Lord, that he makes his sun to rise on the good and the bad.

9. *What are the effects of prayer?* Prayer being an act of the virtue of religion, it a) ennobles us, raising us up to God, with whom it brings us into close communication; it b) acquits us of our debts, for it is a filial and solemn homage which we render to the power, the wisdom, the goodness, the fidelity, and all the other perfections of God; and, being an acknowledgment of our absolute dependence, it c) places us in our true relations with God, who regards it as omnipotent.

Hence, the surprising word by which the Greeks designate prayer. In their language, *to pray* and *to be well* are expressed by the same term. Hence, also, the celebrated saying of a Roman poet: "To have a sound soul in a sound body, it is necessary to pray."[508] Hence, in fine, the name given to prayer by the Catholic faith, which calls it the "queen of heaven and earth." In effect, prayer controls God, and, through him, all nature, as we see by a thousand examples in the holy books, and in the histories of martyrs, saints, and all peoples. It satisfies for our sins. It merits grace and glory. It obtains all that it desires; for the words of the gospel are most comprehensive: "Whatsoever you shall ask with faith, you shall obtain."

Such is the formal promise of our Lord, which St. Thomas, in harmony with the other great authorities of the Church, explains thus: "The effect of prayer is infallible as often as it is accompanied with these four conditions: that one asks for himself; that he asks things necessary for salvation; that he asks with piety; and that he asks with perseverance."[509] "When these four conditions are present, the success of the just man's prayer is infallible. If success does not come, you may be assured that one or more of the conditions are wanting."[510] "The prayer of the sinner," continues the Angel of the Schools, "is also heard, not in virtue of the laws of justice, but of those of mercy, when it proceeds from a good desire, and is accompanied with the four conditions mentioned above."[511]

As for prayers well made, but which have not for their object things necessary to salvation, they are also infallible in their effect; only, the thing which we ask is not always that which is granted us. Sometimes God hears us by giving us precisely that which we solicit. At other times he hears us by positively refusing it, because he sees, in his infinite wisdom, that what we are pleased to call a good would be an evil for us. Nevertheless, he does not leave our labor without a reward: he grants us something else.

For example, we ask health for a person: God refuses it, but grants him the grace to endure the pains of his illness with great merit. We ask life, and God grants us the grace of a good death, which puts us in possession of eternal life. We ask the conversion of somebody: God delays it, but grants us the graces of perseverance, of which we have the greatest need, though we did not think of asking them. It is therefore true that no prayer, well made, is without its reward. In giving prayer to man, God placed in his hands the keys of heaven and all its treasures. Whose fault will it be if we languish in weakness? But, above all, whose fault will it be if we have the misfortune to be lost?[512]

It would be necessary to quote nearly every page of the old and the new testament if we wished to relate all the occurrences that prove the omnipotent efficacy of prayer. Abraham obtaining pardon for Sodom, if ten just men could be found in it; Moses snatching from the hands of God the sentence of death passed on the people of Israel; the Ninivites saving themselves from destruction; the leper, the centurion, the man born blind, the woman of Chanaan obtaining health; the Church of Jerusalem bursting the gates of the prison in which St. Peter was confined: so on through the course of ages. Now, prayer has lost none of its efficacy. Out of a thousand examples we shall only cite two: that of M. Ratisbonne, converted at Rome in 1842—of which a detailed account is given in our work, the *Trois Rome*, 21st January; the second happened a few years ago.

Historical incident.—In a southern city there lived a pious young girl, as pure as an angel, but so unfortunate as to have a father and mother without religion. "What! to be separated from papa and mamma for all eternity!" would this tender child often say to herself; and this sad thought broke her heart. Every day she would go to the church; and there, prostrate in a chapel of the Blessed Virgin, she would say, raising her eyes, full of tears, to the statue of Mary: "O Mary, Mother of God and my Mother, convert my father and mother!"

A year passes, and she has not the consolation of seeing her petitions heard. At length the day of her first Communion comes, and she prepares for it with the utmost piety. She advances to the foot of the altar. As she returns to her place, she begins to weep: she has seen something, enough to cause her the bitterest grief. Mass and thanksgiving over, she follows her father and mother, who await her at the door of the church. They press her fondly to their bosom, and load her with kisses. She is brought back in triumph to the domestic hearth. A numerous company, invited to celebrate the most beautiful day of her life, assemble in the evening. The little child occupies the place of honor at the banquet. The repast begins: every countenance is radiant with joy.

Suddenly deep sighs escape from the young girl's breast; large tears fall from her eyes: she almost chokes. Her father rises quickly, and hastens to ask the cause of her sorrow. The more he inquires the more she sobs. A long silence is the only reply she makes to all the pressing questions of her father and mother. At length the father, in a solemn voice, says to her: "My daughter, have you had the misfortune to profane the Holy Sacrament, which you received this morning?" "O father, what do you ask me? I trust that, through the grace of God, I have nothing to reproach myself with. My Communion was good: I did the best I could to prepare myself."

"My child, what then is the matter? I command you to tell me." "Well, since you command me, I will tell you. It is this: Mary, the daughter of our porter, is much happier than I." "How so? What has she that you have not? Speak: your mother and I are ready to grant you whatever you wish." "Yes, Mary is much happier than I. This morning, as she was making her first Communion, she had the happiness of seeing by her side her father and mother, while I was all alone like a poor orphan."

She can scarcely finish. Her sighs redouble. The emotion spreads among the guests. The father and mother share in it. At length the father, in a broken voice, says to her: "Console yourself, my daughter; you will soon be as happy as Mary. Who could resist the prayers and tears of such an angel as you?" In effect, a month afterward the child again approached the altar, accompanied by her father and mother, and happier than a queen at the moment of her coronation.

10. *Are there different kinds of prayer?* Prayer, whose necessity, conditions, and general effects we have just explained, is divided into mental and vocal. Mental or interior prayer, to which we properly give the name of prayer, is that which is made in the heart without the motion of the lips. It consists in affectionate meditation on the truths of salvation, in order to make them the rule of our thoughts, words, and actions, and to move us to the praise of God and the imitation of the virtues of our Lord and the saints.

Mental prayer: Its excellence. Mental is much more excellent than vocal prayer. It renders us more like the angels, with whom it is a continual occupation. It can exist without vocal prayer, which without it cannot be good, since attention of the heart is necessary to pray well.

Its necessity. It is impossible to work out one's salvation without thinking thereon. Under one form or another, prayer is therefore an absolute necessity. Meditation, properly so called, is hence morally necessary to all men, inasmuch as it is during meditation alone, in ordinary practice, that we think seriously on our salvation. Accordingly, the Holy Spirit, and all the saints formed in his school, vie with one another in proclaiming the necessity of meditation. "Why is the world covered with iniquities?" asks the Lord by the mouth of the prophet Jeremias. "Why are souls lost by thousands? Why is the earth made desolate?"[513] "Because no one considers in his heart."[514]

All the saints were and are apostles of prayer. "Our whole spiritual progress," says Rufinus, "depends on meditation."[515] Father Suarez, the impersonation of theological science, used to say: "I would give all my books for a quarter of an hour's prayer." "The soul that abandons prayer," adds St. Teresa, "has no need of the devil to take it to hell: it goes there itself." She used also to say: "Promise me a quarter of an hour's prayer every day, and I, in the name of Jesus Christ, will promise you heaven." "Without the exercise of meditation," continues Gerson, "no one can live as a Christian, except by a miracle."[516]

All the holy founders of religious orders prescribed mental prayer as an essential exercise. Indeed, experience proves that those who make mental prayer rarely fall into mortal sin, and if unhappily they sometimes fall into it, they speedily rise again, thanks to mental prayer, and return to God. One may recite vocal prayers and remain in mortal sin; one may assist at Mass—give alms—alas! even communicate, and remain in mortal sin: but mental prayer and mortal sin are incompatible. Such is the thought of St. Liguori: "Many recite the rosary, the office of the Blessed Virgin, and remain in mortal sin; but it is impossible that he who makes meditation should remain in mortal sin: either he will abandon meditation, or he will abandon sin."[517]

Its facility. To meditate, it suffices to love; for we easily think on what we love. The miser thinks willingly on his riches, the merchant on his business, the mechanic on his trade, the magnate on his dignities. Why? Because they love them. Let us love God, let us love our soul, and we shall think willingly on God and our soul. To say that we cannot make meditation is therefore to accuse ourselves of indifference in regard to God and our soul.

"But I cannot fix my mind, I am destroyed with aridities: this is the reason why I do not attempt mental prayer." St. Francis de Sales answers that even though a person occupied himself during the whole time of mental prayer in driving away distractions and temptations, it would be nothing the worse thereof. The Lord will be content with your good intentions, and will reward you for what you endured against your will. An ounce of meditation made in the midst of disgust is worth more than a hundred pounds in the midst of consolation. How many courtiers go a hundred times a year to the chamber of their prince, without any hope of speaking to him, but merely to be seen by him and to pay him their respects! If God does not judge it fit to bring us into his entertainments, let us remain in the antechamber, and offer him our reverence. Motionless statues, ranged along the galleries of princes, do honor to their masters: if, therefore, the Lord wishes that we should be like statues in his presence, let us be content to honor him as statues.[518]

"But I have not time." And yet you have time for everything else—you have time to sleep, to indulge in idle talk, to stroll about, to work; you even find time to commit sin, and you cannot find time to save your soul! *Vacat ut philosophus sis, non vocat ut Christianus sis*, says St. Paulinus! If a poor man saw you throwing a number of golden pieces into a river, would it be unreasonable of him to ask you for the half of one of them? And does our Lord ask too much when he asks you for the half, the quarter of one of those hours which every day you squander so recklessly?

Will you have the goodness to tell me why time has been given you? Do you believe that Jesus Christ died to obtain it for you, that you might not abandon yourself to the pleasures and follies of life? You are not more engaged than those bishops who govern immense dioceses, than those rulers who are charged with the administration of mighty kingdoms, and yet they find time to meditate. If you absolutely cannot meditate in the silence of rest, meditate during your labor. How many poor villagers make a meditation thus every day! A flower, a plant, the least thing, suffices to raise their minds to God: all because they love. Love, therefore, like them, and you will always find time to meditate.

Its practice. The most favorable place for making mental prayer is the church; but it can be made everywhere—in the house or in the field. Still, it is proper to retire to a solitary place, away from noise. The most suitable time is the morning. Meditation is the soul's breakfast. There will be a good deal to blame in the actions of the day if one does not begin it by giving the soul a proper supply of the strengthening food of virtue. The prayer of which we speak consists of three parts.

I. *Preparation.* The first part is the preparation. In the preparation, there are three acts to be made: a) to place one's self in the presence of God, saying: "My God, I believe that thou art here present; it is with thee that I am about to speak: I adore thee from the depths of my nothingness"; b) to humble one's self, saying: "Lord, I ought to be at this moment in hell on account of the sins which I have committed; I repent of having offended thee: forgive me in thy great mercy"; c) to ask the lights of the Holy Ghost, saying: "Eternal Father, grant me, for the love of Jesus and Mary, thy lights during this meditation, that I may profit by it." We next say a Hail Mary to the Blessed Virgin, that she may obtain these lights for us, and a Glory be to the Father in honor of St. Joseph, our guardian angel, and our holy patron. We make these acts with attention, but in a few words, and pass on to the meditation.

II. *Actual meditation.* The second part is the actual meditation. The subject of the meditation is a truth of salvation. We must consider what our Lord and the saints taught us regarding it, and the example that they left us. We must compare their thoughts with our thoughts and their conduct with our conduct, and draw hence practical resolutions for the reformation of our lives. We may avail ourselves with advantage of some books. St. Francis de Sales says that we must imitate bees, which stay on one flower as long as they find any honey in it, and then pass on to another. He who cannot read should meditate on the four last things (death, judgment, hell, and heaven), on the benefits of God, and chiefly on our Lord's passion. The fruit of meditation consists in the resolution that is made during it. A person should never quit it without having said to himself, "In consequence of what I have just meditated upon, I will do such a thing, or I will avoid such a thing." This resolution should be frequently called to mind during the course of the day.

III. *Conclusion.* The third part is the conclusion. It consists of three acts: a) we thank God for the lights and graces which he has granted us during our meditation; b) we promise to keep faithfully the resolution which we have made; c) we ask of God, through the intercession of Jesus and Mary, the grace to be faithful to this promise. At the close we recommend to God the souls in purgatory and the wants of the Church, by saying for this purpose an Our Father and a Hail Mary, which are the two most excellent prayers that God and the Church have taught us.

Vocal prayer. Vocal prayer is that which is made with the mouth—pronouncing the words. Like meditation, it requires a modest and religious demeanor, attention of mind, and devotion of heart. Without these conditions no one prays properly: to neglect them is to merit the reproach addressed by the Lord to the carnal Jews: "This people honoreth me with their lips, but their hearts are far from me."[519]

The attention which we ought to bring to vocal prayer differs somewhat from that which is necessary for mental prayer. This attention is of three kinds: a) attention to the words, which consists in pronouncing the words well, that is to say, fully, gravely, and distinctly; b) attention to the meaning, which consists in penetrating the sense of the words, so as to join to their pronunciation the affection of the heart; and c) attention to God, which is the best of all, and which consists in occupying one's self interiorly with God during the time of prayer, adoring, thanking, and loving him, and asking him for his graces. The first kind of attention suffices to satisfy the precept of prayer; but, with it alone, prayer will be cold and will not produce any great fruits.[520]

Vocal prayer is necessary, as well as mental: a) our Savior commanded it by prescribing for us the Lord's Prayer. The Church gives us an example of obedience on this point, for in all her offices she employs vocal prayer. b) Being composed of body and soul, it is necessary that our senses should concur in their manner to praise and glorify God. c) Our soul is so dependent on the senses, especially since the commission of sin, that we generally have need to pronounce words or to hear them pronounced, as a help to us in forming good thoughts and in raising our minds to God. d) Vocal prayer is necessary to edify the neighbor, and to maintain the external worship of religion.[521]

Public prayer. Vocal prayer is divided into public and private. Public prayer is that which is made by the ministers of the Church, in the name of all the faithful. This prayer must be vocal, that it may be known by all those for whom it is made. Hence the Church directs her ministers to pronounce it in a loud voice.[522] The Holy Sacrifice of the Mass and the divine office are the most excellent of all public prayers. We will speak of them in the fourth part[523] of the catechism.

Private prayer. Private prayer is that which is made by each of the faithful individually or with others, for one or for many.[524] Among the most useful private prayers, we must place ejaculatory prayers. This name is given to those short and fervent prayers which shoot forth from the heart of man, like burning arrows, and go to pierce the heart of God. Being very short, they can be repeated every moment, whether one is alone or in company, at rest or in the midst of business. They are, besides, less subject to distractions and tepidity than others. In fine, they maintain a habitual commerce of the soul with God, form gradually the interior spirit within us, and carry away our conversation to heaven.

Hence all the saints made great account and frequent use of these ejaculations or aspirations. Most of the saints even adopted or composed one in particular, which served as a war cry or motto to encourage them in the battles of virtue, and to cheer them on in their great undertakings for the glory of God. "My God and my all!" would St. Francis of Assisi repeat continually. "I am come to cast fire on the earth, and what will I but that it be kindled?" said St. Dominic. "O glorious Lady, raised above the stars!" used the great Thaumaturgus of Italy, St. Antony of Padua, to repeat almost as often as he breathed. "All for the greater glory of God!" said St. Ignatius. "What is this for eternity, and in comparison with eternity?" asked St. Aloysius Gonzaga. "To suffer or to die!" cried out the angelic Teresa. "O most Holy Trinity!" exclaimed every hour the apostle of the Indies, St. Francis Xavier. "Alleluia!" was the word of a holy soul, stretched for many years on a bed of sorrow.

Such are a few of those excellent prayers, which we cannot do better than take to ourselves. If we be faithful in repeating them often and recollectedly, we shall not be slow to reap the happiest fruits from them.

PRAYER

O my God! who art all love, I thank thee for having taught me the means of obtaining everything from thee; grant me the grace to turn this knowledge to account frequently and well.

I am resolved to love God above all things, and my neighbor as myself for the love of God; and, in testimony of this love, I will every day make at least a quarter of an hour's meditation.

Lesson 30: Our Union with the New Adam by Hope (3)

The Lord's Prayer.—Though the Lord's Prayer becomes a public prayer when it is offered to God by a sacred minister of religion in the name of all the faithful people, yet we place it at the head of private prayers, because our Lord seems to have composed it chiefly for the private use of each individual Christian in those continually recurring cases which oblige us to have recourse to God. "When you are about to pray," he says, "retire into your chamber, and close the door; then, addressing yourself to God, say: Our Father," etc.[525]

Regarded in its author, in its form, or in the depth of its meaning, the Lord's Prayer is evidently the most excellent of all prayers.

1. *In its author.* It was not a saint, nor a prophet, nor an angel, nor an archangel, that composed it. It was our Lord Jesus Christ himself, the Son and the eternal Wisdom of God.

2. *In its form.* The Lord's Prayer is clear. The whole world can understand it—the little child as well as the old man, the peasant as well as the citizen. It is short. Anyone can learn it easily, remember it accurately, and repeat it frequently. Its brevity makes it essentially popular—consequently, worthy of God who came to save all mankind, and of religion which should be preached to the free and the enslaved, to civilized as well as savage peoples. It is persuasive. Nothing can be more humble, more simple, more filial, that is to say, more effectual, than the manner in which it expresses our wants to God.

3. *It is deep in its meaning.* It is complete, for it includes all that we can and should, as children of God, ask for time and eternity, for body and soul, for ourselves and others.

It is wise, for it recalls to our minds and makes us put in practice the three great virtues which are the foundations of religion, society, and salvation, namely, faith, hope, and charity. It is divinely logical, for it regulates the desires of our heart, by teaching us to express first the most noble and most necessary; then, those which are less so.[526]

"In effect," says St. Thomas, "it is manifest that the first object of our desires is our last end; then, the means to arrive at this end. Now, our end is God, to whom our affection tends in two manners: the one consists in desiring the glory of God; the other in wishing to enjoy this divine glory. The first belongs to charity by which we love God in himself; the second to charity by which we love ourselves in God. This is the reason why the first petition, 'hallowed be thy name,' asks the glory of God; and the second, 'thy kingdom come,' asks that we may come to the enjoyment of the glory of God.

"Now, a thing can lead us to our last end either by itself or by accident. By itself and directly, by making us merit eternal beatitude through obedience to the commandments of God. Hence, our third petition, 'thy will be done on earth as it is in heaven.' By itself again, though in a less direct manner, by helping us to merit eternal beatitude. Hence, our fourth petition, 'give us this day our daily bread.' A thing leads us to our last end by accident when it removes the obstacles that would hinder us from arriving at it. There are three obstacles of this class. Sin, which directly closes our way. Hence our fifth petition, 'forgive us our trespasses.' Temptation, which leads us to sin. Hence, our sixth petition, 'lead us not into temptation.' Temporal evils—the consequence of sin—which make the burden of life too heavy. Hence, in fine, our seventh petition, 'Deliver us from evil.'"[527]

The seven petitions of the Lord's Prayer correspond also with the gifts of the Holy Ghost and the gospel beatitudes, so that this admirable prayer is in perfect harmony with everything else in religion, and its tendency is to obtain for us all that can make a Christian perfect in this life and happy in the next. No wonder that St. Augustine should speak of it in these sublime terms: "The Lord's Prayer is the petition given to the faithful by the heavenly lawmaker himself, that they may be able to obtain the accomplishment of all their desires."[528]

In fine, that which adds to the excellence of the Lord's Prayer is that it is the most necessary of all prayers. Various councils—among them the Council of Rome—oblige all Christians to know it by heart, inasmuch as, according to the doctrine of the holy fathers, it is proper that we should recite it every day.[529] "Since we live in the midst of the world," says St. Augustine, "where no one can live without sin, the forgiveness of our faults is found not only in the sacred waters of baptism, but also in the daily repetition of the Lord's Prayer. It is like our daily baptism."[530]

The Lord's Prayer, then, is the remedy for the sins which we commit every day, that is, our venial sins, provided we are animated in reciting it with a true sentiment of contrition. It is proper that every one should know it in Latin and in the vernacular: in Latin, because such is the language of the Church; in the vernacular, or mother tongue, that one may understand what is asked.

Division of the Lord's Prayer.—The Lord's Prayer is divided into three parts: the preface or preparation, the body of the prayer, and the conclusion.

I. *Preface of the Lord's Prayer: Our Father.* The preface consists of these simple but sublime words: "Our Father, who art in heaven." The Savior could have taught us to give God titles more capable of revealing to us his majesty, and of filling us with respect; but these titles would have continued to make us the slaves of Sinai, while we ought to be the children of Calvary. We are therefore instructed to say, not "Our God," "Our Creator," "Our master," but "Our Father." Consider this expression in regard to God, ourselves, and our neighbor.

In regard to God, it wonderfully excites our confidence, by reminding us that, in spite of our nothingness and misery, we are still the children, not of a king, not of an emperor, not of any earthly potentate, but of God himself. On the other hand, it infallibly touches the heart of God, by reminding him that he is our Father—our Father in every manner, by creation, by redemption, by preservation—the Father of our soul, and the Father of our body. As children, the Savior tells us, have recourse with these tender words to their father in all their necessities, not being afraid to acquaint him with the number or the extent of their troubles, so do you in all your wants and trials have recourse to your heavenly Father, who will console you, who will relieve you, who will have pity on you, as a father has pity on his children.

In regard to ourselves, the expression *Our Father* reminds us, more eloquently than the grandest discourse, of the nobility of our origin—consequently, of the respect which we ought to have for our body and soul, and of the care which we ought to take to maintain ourselves in the friendship of God, and to behave ourselves as worthy children, if we wish to be heard by him. Sinners, who, according to the words of the Savior himself, are children of the devil, cannot with any right call God their Father, since they do not obey his commands. Still they ought not to omit the Lord's Prayer, and they do not recite it fruitlessly. If they are truly penitent, they will say "Our Father" like the returning prodigal, to obtain forgiveness for their faults; if they remain obstinate in evil, they will say it at least in the name of the Church, of which they are members by faith and hope.

In regard to our neighbor, the expression *Our Father* brings before our mind the great law which saved and which alone can again save the world—the law of universal brotherhood. It teaches us what the rest of mankind are to us, and what we ought to be to them. In effect, we do not say "My Father," but "Our Father," because we are all brethren, and we ought to pray not only for ourselves but for all men in general—Catholics, heretics, Jews, infidels, friends, and enemies—that is, we ought to love them all with a truly fraternal love.[531]

In the single expression *Our Father* we find the abolition of every species of tyranny, the exaltation of the lowly, the protection of the weak, the generous devotedness of the rich and powerful to the corporal and spiritual relief of those among their brethren who are less favored than they with the gifts of fortune and intelligence—that is, we find charity, the basis of the family, the bond of society, the pledge of future happiness.

In a word, we say "Our Father," on the one hand, to testify that we pray for all and in the name of all; on the other, to engage the Lord to grant us, in consideration of the rest, that which, by ourselves, we do not merit. When we say "Our Father," it is to the three divine Persons that we address ourselves, because all three merit the title of Father, by reason of our creation, our redemption, and our sanctification.

Who art in heaven. The God whom we invoke is everywhere.[532] Yet we say, "Who art in heaven," because it is there that all the magnificence of his glory appears; or because it is there that he reigns over the angels and saints in all the plenitude of his love; or because we should continually remind ourselves that it is there our thoughts, our desires—our conversation, as the apostle says—ought to be.

Our Father, who art in heaven. "Yes, O good Father! thou art in heaven, at the summit of felicity, infinitely rich, infinitely powerful, infinitely bounteous; and we, thy children, are on earth, in a land of exile, far from our country and our family, poor, weak, sick, surrounded by enemies." What more proper to move the heart of God? What more proper at the same time to form in our souls a profound humility, a lively sense of our wants, a filial respect, piety, confidence, purity, and charity toward our brethren? How can a prayer fail to be heard which opens on such kindly terms between him who addresses it and him to whom it is addressed? So much for the preface of the Lord's Prayer.

But what ought we to ask, and in what order ought we to ask? Alas! we are so senseless and blind that often we know neither the nature of our true wants nor the order in which we should ask relief for them. Hence it happens either that we ask nothing or that we ask improperly. To remedy this double evil, the new Adam himself composed a supplication for our use, in which he had regard both to the objects that we should desire and to the order in which we should desire them. Now, reason and religion tell us that well-born and truly intelligent children always prefer their father's interests to their own, the goods of eternity to those of time, the end to the means. All this is taught us in an admirable manner by the second part of the Lord's Prayer.

II. *Body of the Lord's Prayer: Divided into two portions.* In effect, the body of this divine prayer is divided, like the decalogue, into two portions. The first refers to God, and includes three petitions: "Hallowed be thy name"; "thy kingdom come"; "thy will be done on earth as it is in heaven." The second refers to man, and includes four petitions: "Give us this day our daily bread"; "and forgive us our trespasses, as we forgive them who trespass against us"; "and lead us not into temptation"; "but deliver us from evil."

First petition: Hallowed be thy name. The first thing that we ought to ask, because it is the greatest and most excellent of all goods, is the glory of God. Hence, like children desirous to honor their father, we begin by asking in general that the name of our heavenly Father, that is to say, God himself, his majesty, his power, his wisdom, his goodness, his mercy, his justice, may be known, appreciated, honored, revered, loved, sanctified on earth as in heaven.[533] We ask that, in imitation of the blessed inhabitants of heaven, all the inhabitants of the earth may praise, glorify, and exalt, by their words and their actions—by faith, hope, and charity—the adorable name of God.

We ask in particular that infidels, enlightened by a light from on high, may know the true God, and be regenerated in the saving waters of baptism, in the name of the Father and of the Son and of the Holy Ghost; that heresies may be rooted up, and that their followers may own and embrace as their true mother the holy Roman Catholic Church, out of which there is no effusion of the Holy Ghost, no forgiveness of sins, no salvation; that we may no longer see the earth deluged with superstitions, sorceries, perjuries, blasphemies, or any of the other diabolical disorders by which the name of God is despised and outraged; the return of sinners to the amiable and sacred yoke of our heavenly Father—a thorough knowledge throughout the world that all goods of body and soul come from God and ought to be referred to his glory—and a religious care to honor the Blessed Trinity by our conduct, lest our scandals should cause its name to be blasphemed among men. We ask these latter things, not for one day only, but for our whole life: in other terms, we ask perseverance in good to our last breath.[534]

The desire that the name of God should be sanctified is certainly the noblest that can issue from the heart of man, since it was for this that we were created and endowed with reason. It was also the most ardent and constant of those which our Lord himself, and all the saints, after his example, in the course of ages, formed. One day St. Ignatius of Loyola, addressing Father Laynez, said: "If God gave you the choice of going now to paradise, or of remaining still on earth with the prospect of doing something great for his glory, which would you prefer?" "I would prefer to go to heaven," answered Father Laynez. "As for me," replied the saint, "I would prefer to remain on earth, in order to do the will of God and to render him some service. With regard to my salvation, I have no doubt that God would take care of me, and that he would not let one who, for love of him, had voluntarily delayed his entrance into heaven, perish."

Second petition: Thy kingdom come. After asking the glory of God, we ask a participation in this glory, which is the end for which we were created—consequently, the term of religion, of life, of time, of eternity.[535] Observe that we ask the kingdom of God to come to us, and not that we should go to it, because the kingdom of grace must come to us in order that we may be able to go to the kingdom of glory.

To the words *kingdom of God* we attach three meanings: the kingdom of nature, the kingdom of grace, and the kingdom of glory. The kingdom of nature is that by which God rules and governs all creatures, including the human family. Of this kingdom the scripture speaks, when it says: "Thy kingdom, O God! is a kingdom of all ages; O Lord God, Omnipotent King! the whole universe is subject to thee, and nothing can resist thee."[536] We do not ask that this kingdom should come, since it has existed since the origin of the world; and the wicked themselves, whether they like it or not, cannot escape from it. We only ask that it should be manifested, and that all men should recognize, admire, and bless the laws of that tender providence which disposes of everything created in number, weight, and measure, attaining its end sweetly and mightily, and that they should always submit to it with a filial resignation.

The kingdom of grace is that by which God rules and governs the hearts and souls of the faithful children of the Church, by the action of the Holy Ghost, and by the three great virtues of faith, hope, and charity, which lead them to follow his divine precepts and to seek his glory in preference to everything else.

The kingdom of glory shall exist in the other life, after the general judgment. Then God shall reign with the saints, without any kind of opposition; for all power shall have been taken away from the devils and the wicked, chained together in eternal prisons. Then also shall have been destroyed the empire of death and corruption, with all the temptations of the world and the flesh that here afflict the servants of God: so that this shall be a tranquil, peaceful kingdom, abounding in an unmixed and endless felicity.

Of which of these three kingdoms do we solicit the coming in the Lord's Prayer? As we have already said, not the first—it is not to come, it is come: we do not even ask its continuance, for this would interfere with the attainment of our last end, which is to see God face-to-face in eternity. Neither is it the second—since we desired its coming in the first petition, and it is already in great part come. We ask the coming of the third, which must come, and which all those who know the miseries of this life desire with ardor. This kingdom consists in the supreme good and perfect glory of our body and our soul: such cannot be till after the last judgment.

Thus, we daily and earnestly ask the end of the world and the coming of the last judgment. We ask that this world of iniquities and disorders should be speedily replaced by a new earth and a new heaven, in which justice should reign, that so God may be all in all. While the lovers of the world think that they cannot fear any worse news than the announcement of the general judgment, we, the citizens of heaven, who live here like pilgrims and exiles, have not and ought not to have any greater desire than to witness its arrival. Hence the saying of St. Augustine: "As before the coming of the Messias all the supplications of the virtuous of the old covenant had for their object the coming of our Lord, so today all the desires of the saints of the new covenant have for their object the second coming of the Son of God, who will lead us to the height of perfection and felicity."[537]

This is a truth which it is very important that we should often recall to our own minds and to the minds of others. Nothing is more proper to ennoble our thoughts than the recollection of the sublime end for which we are destined. Nothing is more proper to make us endure adversities with patience, resist temptations with fidelity, and trample under our feet the prized things of earth, than the thought of the royal felicity which awaits us in eternity. Yes, we shall one day reign with our Lord. Let us therefore learn to show ourselves masters, by commanding our passions, and by compelling the world to bow before our faith. How shameful, if it were otherwise! Is it in the chains of slavery that we make our apprenticeship to royalty?

Third petition: Thy will be done. In the preceding petition we asked eternal beatitude, which is our last end; in this we ask the chief means to attain it. The grand road to heaven is, according to the words of our Lord himself, the accomplishment of the will of our heavenly Father: "If you will enter into life, keep the commandments."[538] But we cannot, of ourselves, keep these divine commandments.

Accordingly, we ask of God that his will may be done in us, that is, that he may give us a) the grace to accomplish it, by everywhere and always obeying his commandments, after the example of our divine model, who became "obedient unto death, even unto the death of the cross";[539] and b) the grace to accept, at least without murmuring, if not with filial confidence and joy, the spiritual and corporal afflictions that may befall us, such as the loss of relatives, friends, or property. In effect, all these things that God appoints or permits are for our good. If we are just, they give us more ample matter from which to acquire merit; if not, they supply us with an excellent means of attaining to our purification.

Men of little faith! what can we ask more advantageous than the accomplishment of the will of our Father? He loves us more tenderly than we love ourselves. His will is holy, just, and perfect. It was by not accomplishing it that the first Adam plunged himself into the abyss of evils of which we are the sad heirs. It is by accomplishing it that we deliver ourselves from them; and we shall be so much the more exempt from them, or they shall be so much the lighter in our regard, as we shall better accomplish this perfect will.

Hence it follows that the happiness of heaven shall be complete, because the will of God shall there reign alone, fully, and eternally. This happiness shall be proportioned, for each one of us, to the fidelity with which we shall have accomplished the will of God on earth.

On earth as it is in heaven. In asking of God the grace to obey him, we at the same time ask of him to render our obedience worthy of him and meritorious for ourselves, that is, like that of the angels and saints, the blessed inhabitants of heaven. The angels and saints submit to the will of God with a plenitude of love. They obey solely because God wills it, without any self-seeking; they execute his orders with the speed of lightning; they neither argue nor murmur. No matter what they are commanded by God, they answer in a canticle of praise and thanksgiving: "Holy, holy, holy is the Lord God of hosts!"[540]

Thus ought we to obey. Oh how delightful would our sojourn on earth be if all those millions of human wills around us submitted at all times and in all things to the will of God! As for us, at least, let us always have in our hearts and on our lips the saying of the apostle St. Paul: "Lord, what wilt thou have me to do";[541] or that of the royal prophet: "My heart is ready, O God, my heart is ready";[542] or that of the holy man Job: "The Lord gave to me, the Lord hath taken away from me, he hath done that which seemed to him good: blessed be his name!";[543] or, in fine, that of our divine model himself: "Father! if it be possible, let this chalice pass away from me; yet not my will, but thine, be done!"[544]

Such is the first part of the Lord's Prayer. Considered in their object, nothing can be more sublime than the three petitions of which it consists: as nothing can be more logical than the order in which they are expressed.

The second part of the Lord's Prayer contains four petitions, by which we ask the temporal good things necessary to arrive at the eternal. What more wise? As man is referred to God, as his last end; so the goods of this life are referred to those of the next, as means to their end. This is the reason why our Lord wishes that these things should only be asked in the second place. We ought only to solicit them inasmuch as God himself permits it, and as we have need of them to acquire the celestial.

Fourth petition: Give us this day our daily bread. By these words, so touching and simple, we ask all that is necessary for the maintenance of our temporal life. Now, we are composed of two substances, a body and a soul: both have need of nourishment to live. The soul, which is spiritual, requires a spiritual food. For the body, which is material, we must have a material food. The Holy Eucharist, the word of God, holy inspirations; these are the food of the soul: we ask them for the soul. Eating, drinking, clothing, and other such things are necessary for the life of the body: we ask that they may be granted to the body.

Give us. Humble expression, admirably adapted to touch the heart of God! We acknowledge that we have nothing, and that we are beggars. We acknowledge that God alone is rich, and that he alone can give us everything. We acknowledge that we are indebted to him for our very existence, that is to say, for the things most necessary to our spiritual and our corporal life: not to our own labor, not to our own industry, not to our own virtues. Nothing truer. It is not we who make the wheat that nourishes us grow in the earth, nor the wool that covers us grow on the sheep, nor the virtues of faith, hope, and charity that sanctify us grow in our soul.

Hence, rich and poor, we must all say, "Give us"; for we are all, without exception, like beggars who wait at the door of the Father of the family.[545] The rich should say, "Give us," and on their lips these words mean: "My God! vouchsafe to preserve the good things which thou hast confided to me; continue thy liberality. We acknowledge that thou canst at any moment take away all things which we possess; so that, in preserving them for us, thou doest us the same favor as if thou didst give them to us every moment."[546] The poor should say, "Give us," and on their lips these words mean: "My God! we expect from thy liberality everything needful for our life. Send it to us either directly, by thyself, or indirectly, by the rich, whom thou dost inspire to be charitable toward us. Bless our work, and grant that neither private nor public misfortunes may deprive us of the fruits of our labors."

Now, it is to tempt God to imagine that he will send us manna from heaven without our having anything else to do but to ask it. God, who commands prayer, also commands labor, and our petitions should be directed to obtain his blessing on our endeavors. The sweat of our brow is useless, if God, in his goodness, does not render it productive. So that the expression *Give us* is an acknowledgment that we depend more on the providence of God than on our own industry.[547]

In fine, rich and poor, we not only ask that God may give us our daily bread but that he may bless and sanctify it, in such a manner that we may always use it for the advantage of our soul and our body.

We say, "Give us," and not, "Give me," because it is proper that a Christian should not think of himself alone, but also of the neighbor. Another reason is that God does not grant us his benefits in order that we alone may profit of them, or that we may abandon ourselves to intemperance; he wishes that we should share with others what remains to us after providing for our own wants.

This day. This expression has two meanings. In the first place, it means the whole time of the present life; for life is only a day, without a yesterday or a tomorrow. And we ask of God that he may give us, during the term of our pilgrimage, the bread of the soul and the bread of the body, until we arrive in that blessed country where we shall no longer stand in need of sacraments, or instructions, or corporal meats.[548] In the second place, *this day* signifies the present day. And we ask of God that he may give us, even this day, the bread of which we have need, because we do not wish to disquiet ourselves about that of tomorrow, knowing that tomorrow may never dawn for us. Thus, the bread of today we ask today; tomorrow's we shall ask tomorrow.

Was it possible to teach us more eloquently that admirable, that delightful evangelical poverty which consists, on the one hand, in an absolute detachment from all created things, and, on the other, in a filial confidence in providence? Our heavenly Father will not have us rely on our own strength, even for one day, since he wishes that we should every day ask him for our daily bread. He wishes that we should every day cast on his providence the care of providing for our wants. And what uneasiness can we have? If we seek first of all the kingdom of God and his justice, everything else shall be given to us over and above. See! Does not our heavenly Father feed the sparrow, which sows not? Does he not clothe the lily, which spins not? Does he not make his sun to rise on the just and the unjust?

Since we ought only to occupy ourselves with the present, is it not improper to lay up provisions of wheat, wine, and other such things for a whole year? When our Lord teaches us to concern ourselves only with the present, he merely desires to free us from a multitude of superfluous cares that are a very great hindrance to prayer and other occupations of higher importance, by attention to which we must obtain eternal life. Since therefore the thought of the future, as that of laying up provisions, is not superfluous, but necessary, it is not improper. What do I say? Such a thought does not belong to tomorrow, but to today; for if we leave it till tomorrow, it may then be too late.

Our daily bread. Nothing is more natural than to ask bread, which sustains life, after having, in the preceding petition, asked grace, which is life itself. The first thing that he who begins to live desires is food, by which life may be sustained. Let us not forget that we here ask, above all things, that spiritual bread which is the food of the soul; then material bread, which is the food of the body: so reason and faith declare.

By spiritual bread, we understand the Holy Eucharist, which is a divine and heavenly bread, a wondrous support of the life of the soul. We also understand the word of God, which, received through preaching or reading, powerfully assists in maintaining our spiritual life. In fine, we understand holy inspirations, prayer, and everything else that contributes to preserve or to increase grace, which, as we have said, is the life of the soul within us. Accordingly, our Lord wishes that we should every day ask his flesh to eat and his blood to drink. It follows hence that the Holy Eucharist ought to be our daily food, and that we ought to live in such a manner as to be worthy to partake of it every day. What can we think, O my God! of those who only receive it once a year?[549]

He also wishes that we should every day ask his divine word. What must be thought henceforth of those who never hear it, who never read it, or who only give their attention to it to criticize it? In the eyes of the fathers, they condemn themselves to death, and make themselves guilty of the same sacrilege as the profaners of the Eucharist.[550] That which may be positively affirmed is that those who shun the word of God, like those who shun the Blessed Eucharist, do not know what they say when they say the Lord's Prayer.

By material bread, we understand what is necessary for the life of the body, but nothing more: nothing that could flatter sensuality or satisfy luxury. Our Lord makes use of the word *bread*, first, because in the scripture this word expresses all things indispensable to life, as food, clothing, and lodging; and next, to teach us that we ought to be content with a little, and not seek any superfluities, as becomes travelers who only pass through a strange land.

We ask "our daily bread," and the word *our* has a very deep meaning. In effect, if there is question of the Holy Eucharist, it is ours. It was for us that it was formed in the womb of the Blessed Virgin Mary by the operation of the Holy Ghost; that it was fully prepared on the cross in the fire of charity; and that it is served up on the altar by the hands of priests. It is our bread, because it is the bread of true children, and not of dogs, that is to say, of sinners, as the scripture speaks—the bread of Catholics, and not of heretics or infidels.[551]

Is there question of the word of God? We ask, in saying "our daily bread," the sound and pure word of God, which true preachers distribute to the children of the Church, and not the strange, corrupt, poisonous bread, which heretics give to their followers.

Do we refer to our corporal bread? We desire that God may give us our bread, and not that of others: in other words, that he may help us to gain it, by blessing our labors, our fields, our crops, our affairs, so that, without having recourse to fraud, or even to begging, we may be able to procure wherewith to live.[552]

We also say "our bread," not that, properly speaking, it belongs to us, but because God, in his mercy, vouchsafes to give it to us as the food that suits us.[553] In fine, we say "our bread," and not "my bread," because every one of us ought to desire and to ask for his brethren what he desires and asks for himself. Can we say that we act thus, if we refuse to share with others that which God gives us above what is necessary.

The word *daily* warns us that we must not ask exquisite or delicate food, but simple, ordinary food, sufficient for the wants of the day, according to the saying of the apostle: "Having food and raiment, let us be content."[554] To a lesson on frugality, this word adds another, no less eloquent, on humility and detachment: man asks bread only for one day, because he does not know whether he shall see another day.

Fifth petition: Forgive us our trespasses as we forgive them who trespass against us. In the four preceding petitions we besought our Father to grant us eternal as well as temporal goods. In the three following we beg him to deliver us from evils, let them be past, present, or future. Thus, the Lord's Prayer contains all that we can desire. Past evil means sin committed; future evil means temptation, which leads to sin; present evil means the trials and tribulations inseparable from our wearisome pilgrimage. We also understand by the evils from which we ask to be delivered the greatest evils, which are sins, because they separate us from God; moderate evils, which are temptations, because, though they are not sins in themselves, yet they are of a nature to make us fall into sin—(and what is more reasonable than to call evils those things which expose us to so great a danger?); in fine, slight evils, which are temporal and eternal punishments, and are so called, because they really are slight in comparison with the others of which they are the consequence.

Forgive us our trespasses. In this fifth petition, our Lord therefore teaches us to ask the pardon of our sins.[555] He makes use here of the word *debita*, "debts," to denote sins. Why this expression? For three reasons, say the doctors. The first, because every man who offends God becomes a debtor to God for the injury done him. The second, because every man who sins violates the law of God. This law promises rewards to those who keep it, and threatens punishments against those who break it. The breaker, therefore, finds himself, by his own fault, a debtor for the punishment appointed in the law. The third, because every one of us is bound to cultivate the vine of his soul, and to deliver its fruits, which are good works, to God. He therefore who does not devote himself to good works, or, what is worse, who devotes himself to evil works, makes himself a debtor to God, who is the true master of the vine and its fruits. Now, as we all fail very often, either by doing that which we ought not to do or by not doing that which we ought to do, it is proper to say to God many times a day with a profound humility: "Forgive us our trespasses," or, "Pardon us our debts."[556]

Do these words suffice to obtain the remission of sins? If there is question of venial sins, these words, accompanied, as we have said, with true contrition, remit them directly. As for mortal sins, they remit them indirectly, in this sense, that they dispose the heart of our heavenly Father to grant us the grace to receive with fruit the effusion of our Lord's merits in the sacrament of penance.[557]

The just as well as sinners ought to say, "Forgive us our trespasses": a) because there is a very great difference between not knowing one's sins and not having any: my conscience, says the apostle, does not reproach me with anything, yet for all that I am not justified;[558] b) because there are many hidden sins; c) because if we say that we have no sin, we are liars, according to St. John;[559] d) because it is not the forgiveness of sin only that we ask, but also of the punishment due to it; and e) because we ask pardon for our brethren as well as for ourselves.[560]

As we forgive them who trespass against us. By these words we say to our heavenly Father: "To obtain the remission of the debts which we owe thee, we remit those which our brethren owe us." Whoever offends us contracts a debt in our regard, for he violates the law of charity, and sometimes that of justice; consequently, he places himself under the obligation of making satisfaction to us.

We here consent to that which God takes as the rule of his mercy toward us, the mercy which we ourselves display toward our neighbor. If then we forgive imperfectly and by halves, or if we only forgive outwardly, retaining bitterness, rancor, and antipathy in the heart, or, in fine, if we do not forgive everything, we say to God that he may treat us in the same manner.

Yet those who do not forgive their enemies may recite this prayer, not indeed with the intention that God should forgive them as they themselves forgive others; for they would thus condemn themselves. But in this sense, that God may forgive them as they themselves ought to forgive others, and in the name of the Church, which always counts a large number of the faithful who grant pardon to and pray for their enemies. It was thus that the most holy Virgin, though she was exempt from all sin, could say the Lord's Prayer, and even "Forgive us." On her lips, these words meant: "Forgive the sinners who are with me in the Church."

"If those only," says St. Augustine, "who love their enemies can say, 'Forgive us our trespasses as we forgive them who trespass against us,' I do not know what I ought to do or what I ought to say. Shall I tell you not to pray? I dare not. I shall rather tell you to pray, that you may love them. But, in fine, if you do not love them, shall I forbid you to say the Lord's Prayer? If you do not say it, you will not be forgiven. If you say it, and do not that which you say, you will not be forgiven either. What remains, unless that you should both say and do that which is necessary to be forgiven?"[561]

Hence, the words, "as we forgive them," express a condition, attached by our Lord himself to the divine mercy. Why this condition? For several reasons, equally worthy of his infinite wisdom.

The first, that we might well understand the greatness of the favor which God does us in forgiving us our sins—a favor so great that he is not pleased to grant it without annexing to it as a condition that we shall show mercy toward our brethren.

The second, to remove our reluctance, by showing us how very easily we may obtain the immense benefit of the forgiveness of our sins, since he promises to have mercy on us if we have mercy on our neighbor: a thing which entirely depends on our own will.

The third, to maintain charity, which is the grand precept of the gospel, among us, by making this charity the condition and the rule of God's charity toward us.

The fourth, to crush our pride and to show us how criminal and absurd is the conduct of worldly people, who say that it is cowardly to forgive and not to take revenge. In effect, when they shall ask mercy of God, he will condemn them out of their own mouth, saying: "You wish me to forgive you, and you hate mercy. You turn it into ridicule. You call him who exercises it a coward. How dare you then ask me to degrade myself, by hearing you?"

In accordance with what has been said, our duty and our interest command us to pardon both outwardly and inwardly. The words of the scripture are plain: "If you do not forgive others from your heart, neither will your heavenly Father forgive you."[562] And elsewhere: "Let not the sun go down upon your anger."[563] The saints always took these words as the rule of their conduct. St. John the Almoner, patriarch of Alexandria, had once occasion to reprehend a senator, who withdrew very dissatisfied. Evening being come, the saint sent to the senator to say: "The sun is about to set." At these words the senator, touched with regret, runs to the holy bishop. He is received and embraced as a brother, and the last rays of the setting sun illumine this affecting scene of reconciliation.

Let us often meditate on this example, as well as on the fifth petition of the Lord's Prayer. God promises to forgive us, if we forgive our brethren. The offenses that we forgive our neighbor are nothing in comparison with those of which we are guilty against God: we have crucified him! We ask the canceling of a debt of ten thousand pieces of gold, in return for that of two or three pieces of copper. Yet if we renounce our claims to this trifling sum with a good heart, and without waiting for our debtors to entreat us—if we pardon everything wholly and unreservedly, that is to say, if we fully forgive our neighbor—if we prevent him with kindness and charity, instead of abandoning ourselves to a blind revenge, or waiting till he appeases us by his expressions of regret, all our sins will be forgiven us. "If you forgive men their faults against you," says the Savior, "your heavenly Father will also forgive you your faults against him."

It is well understood that this promise supposes in him who forgives his brother the spirit of repentance for his sins. It is a truth of faith that, without the spirit of repentance, no sin can be forgiven.

Let us not content ourselves with meditating on these words—let us put them in practice, like that good religious of whom history speaks. He had lived in his monastery with a negligence that often drew upon him the reprimands of his superiors. Arrived at an advanced age, he fell sick, never to recover. One of the brothers, seeing him draw near his end, without manifesting any signs of fear or uneasiness, asked him how he could die with so much confidence, after having led a life so far from edifying.

"It is true, my brother," replied the sick man, "that I have been very careless, and the angels have shown me a long list of sins that I have committed since my entrance into religion. I acknowledged all. But they were not able to show me a single rash judgment nor the least little revenge of which I had ever been guilty. Then I said to them: 'I trust in the promises of the Lord: Judge not, and you shall not be judged; condemn not, and you shall not be condemned; forgive, and it shall be forgiven you.' At these words, the angels tore up the list of my faults, and hence my confidence." Hereupon, he fell asleep tranquilly in the arms of the Father of mercies, leaving to all his brethren a most edifying and salutary lesson.

Sixth petition: Lead us not into temptation. When well-born children have obtained from their father the pardon of their offenses, what remains but to avoid them ever afterward, and by an irreproachable conduct, to console the dear father whom they have had the misfortune to grieve? It is thus that our Lord would have us to act.

Nothing more natural than the link which joins this petition to the preceding one. In the fifth, we asked deliverance from past evil, which is sin committed. In the sixth, we ask the assistance of God against future evil, which is temptation. Yet temptation by itself is not an evil, except inasmuch as it leads us to a real evil, that of offending God. It is on this account that it is very dangerous, and that we beg of God to deliver us from it.

Here again it is very necessary to explain the meaning of our prayer. In saying, "Lead us not into temptation," we do not ask to be wholly delivered from every kind of temptation. We ask a) that we may not be overcome by temptation; b) that we may be delivered from extraordinary temptations; c) that we may not be exposed to temptations great or little if God sees that the victory will not be ours, but the devil's.[564]

Why do we not ask to be delivered from every kind of temptation? Because it is useful for us to be tempted. Temptation instructs us. It makes known to us, on the one hand, our weakness and our corruption; and, on the other, the power of grace, which enables weak soldiers to gain wondrous victories. Temptation keeps us in humility. "Lest the greatness of my revelations," says St. Paul, "should puff me up with pride, the sting of the flesh, the angel of Satan, was permitted to buffet me, that is, for the purpose of keeping me in humility, watchfulness, and prayer."[565]

Temptation confirms us in virtue. The winds that shake the plants nourish them, says a holy father. Thus do temptations increase the strength of the soul.[566] Temptation enriches us. As often as we resist it, it elicits from us acts of fidelity, which increase our merits. Temptation gives us experience, as well for ourselves as for others. "What does he know who has not been tempted?"[567] asks the wise man. In fine, temptation makes us compassionate in regard to the infirmities of the neighbor, and, according to the apostle St. James, causes the Spirit of the Lord to rest upon us, until the day when we shall receive that immortal crown which is to rest on the brow of the conqueror.[568]

We say to our heavenly Father, "Lead us not into temptation." What is the meaning of these words? Is it that God tempts us? No, properly speaking, God does not tempt us; for, to tempt means to lead to evil.[569] We read indeed in sacred history that God tempted Abraham, but this signifies that he wished to prove the holy man's faith and obedience. Every day God tempts us in the same manner, by sickness, misfortunes, and various other trials, either to convert us, or to increase our merits.

God only permits that we should be tempted, in the strict sense of the term, and this thought ought to console us. On the one hand, the enemies of our soul cannot even attack us without the permission of our heavenly Father. On the other, he never permits them to tempt us above our strength.[570] This, then, is the meaning of the prayer that we address to him: "O Lord! we know our own weakness and frailty, as well as the malice and power of the devil; never permit us to be overwhelmed by temptations, and do not even permit us to be tempted if thou seest that we should not come forth victorious from the conflict."

Now, to come forth victorious from these dangerous conflicts, we must know both our enemies and the arms with which we should oppose them. Three great enemies are leagued against us, and they scarcely ever cease to tempt us: the devil, the world, and the flesh. The devil tempts us by suggesting to us the thought of evil: for instance, the thought of pride, of jealousy, of blasphemy, of revenge. The world tempts us by bad discourses, bad books, and bad examples. The flesh tempts us by bad inclinations. Of these three enemies, the most dangerous is the flesh, because we cannot separate ourselves from it.

As for the arms which we should employ against these three enemies, we must oppose to the devil the sign of the cross, and the invocation of the holy names of Jesus and Mary. To the world—a contempt of its railleries, its threats, and its promises, by considering its impotence, as well as the worthlessness of temporal things, which vanish at death. To the flesh—the avoidance of occasions of sin, the mortification of the senses, and devotion to the Blessed Virgin. So much for particular remedies. The general remedies are: humility, meditation, fasting, consideration of our Lord's passion and our last end, and, in fine, fidelity in acquainting our confessor with the temptations under which we labor.

Seventh petition: But deliver us from evil. This petition confirms the preceding ones, by adding to them something new.[571] In the fifth and sixth, we asked deliverance from sin and temptation. We here again ask the same favor, since we beg a deliverance from every kind of evil; but we add a deliverance from every corporal and spiritual, public and private affliction which could hinder us from arriving at eternal happiness.

Thus, after begging a deliverance from past and future evil, we beg a deliverance from present evil. After asking a deliverance from the evil of guilt, which is sin, the greatest of all evils, we ask a deliverance from the evil of punishment, which is much inferior to the first, and consists in temporal and eternal afflictions, the sad consequences of sin.

Let us here remark the profound wisdom of our Lord. He teaches us to ask deliverance from evil in general, and not in particular, as poverty, sickness, persecution, and other such things. In effect, we often imagine that a thing would be good for us, while God sees that it would be injurious for us, and vice versa. Hence, in accordance with the teaching of the Savior, we ask him to deliver us from everything that he knows would be an evil for us, whether health or sickness, prosperity or adversity.

But was it not superfluous to command us to beg a deliverance from evil, since nature itself teaches us well enough to have recourse to God in our tribulations? We address ourselves, indeed, to God in our sufferings. But, first, many neglect to do so: it was necessary to remind them of this duty. Then, others do so too late—after they have exhausted every human resource. God seems to be the last resource: this is a most unjustifiable want of confidence, against which it was necessary to put them on their guard. Finally, we are nearly all forgetful of the order and the manner in which we should ask a deliverance from evil. Instead of asking, above everything else, a deliverance from sin, we ask a deliverance from punishment. Do we experience a reverse of fortune or the loss of our health? Immediately we ask of God a deliverance from this evil, without even thinking of a deliverance from far more important evils, sin and the danger of committing sin.

Hence it happens that we obtain nothing, because we do not follow the command of our Lord, which tells us to seek above all things the kingdom of God and his justice. Moreover, instead of asking a deliverance from temporal evils conditionally, we often ask it absolutely—without resignation, sometimes even with impatience; allowing ourselves to fall into murmurs and complaints, if we do not obtain it, or even if God obliges us to wait for it. Now, to pray as our Lord wishes, we ought to ask in an absolute manner that God would preserve or deliver us from sin, which is the only real evil; as for other evils, we ought to ask to be delivered from them, insofar as this deliverance may be conducive to our salvation.

Deliver us from evil. It is thus that all the prayers of man since his fall terminate and ought to terminate. Deliverance from evil: this has been the object of all the religious observances, all the sacrifices, all the public and private penances that have come into existence among all peoples since the beginning of the world. In the petition which precedes it we beseech God to deliver us from the evil of sin; in this we ask him to deliver us from the punishment of sin.

Thus we ask him to preserve us from a sudden and unprovided death, from the torments that are reserved for the impious, and from the flames of purgatory, out of which we also entreat him to deliver the souls suffering there. We ask him to preserve us from all evils, interior as well as exterior—evils of water, of fire, of thunder, of hail, of famine, of sedition, of war. We beseech him to keep away from us diseases, plagues, ravages, prisons, exiles, treacheries, ambushes—in a word, all the inconveniences that afflict the human race. We ask, in fine, that riches, honors, health, life itself, may not turn to the ruin of our soul.

In this petition the word *evil* signifies also the wicked one or the devil. We beg of God to deliver us from him; for the devil is the author of all the crimes and all the misfortunes of mankind. We say the "wicked one" and not the "wicked ones," because the evils that come to us from our neighbor ought to be imputed to the suggestions of the devil. Hence, far from being offended with our brother, we ought to turn our anger against Satan, who is the cause of all the evils that men do to one another.

Conclusion of the Lord's Prayer.—The third part or the conclusion of the Lord's Prayer consists of this single word, which is, as it were, its seal: *Amen. Amen* is a Hebrew word, meaning "So be it"—"may it be done as I have now said, may all our petitions be granted: we believe it, we hope it." It is as a souvenir of the primitive Church and of our venerable antiquity that this Hebrew word[572] is preserved, as well as to show respect for our Lord, on whose lips it so frequently rested.[573] *Amen* is also a new request, a more earnest wish to obtain what has been asked. It is proper to pronounce this conclusion with special piety and sincerity, either to supply for the defects of inattention and indevotion that may have glided in during the course of the prayer, or to make a last effort, and give a last knock, as it were, so as to touch our Father's heart.

Such is the Lord's Prayer. What more holy, more touching, more august, more efficacious! It is a golden key with which we can open, whenever we please, all the treasuries of heaven. Let all, then, love and venerate it, attach themselves to it as a most valuable possession, and make frequent use of it. But powerful as it is, this divine prayer remains fruitless if it is not well made. Now, nothing is better calculated to animate our fervor in praying, as nothing is more famous in the history of sanctity, than the vision of St. Bernard. It makes known to us the different classes of persons who give themselves to prayer, and the rewards merited by each.

Historical incident.—One night, the illustrious founder of Clairvaux was in prayer, while all the religious were reciting the office. They were very numerous, and God made known to him that they should all be saved; but, at the moment of the vision, they were not all fervent—far from it. The saint saw, by the side of each religious, an angel writing. Some of the angels wrote in letters of gold; many with water; several with black ink. Our Lord instructed the holy founder on the meaning of this vision. The religious who prayed with fervor were those whose prayers the angels were writing in letters of gold. Water served for writing the prayers of the tepid. Black ink did for those of the brothers who prayed with distractions, and half asleep. He added that the first were meriting a great reward, that the second were meriting nothing or almost nothing, and that the third were deserving of punishment.

You who read this, suppose that you saw what your good angel writes when you pray, morning or evening, in the church or at your work. Would his pen be dipped in gold, in water, or in black ink? It is a question that I leave you to solve.

PRAYER

O my God! who art all love, I thank thee for having composed for me a short, easy, complete, and supremely efficacious prayer; grant me the grace always to repeat it with the dispositions which it requires.

I am resolved to love God above all things, and my neighbor as myself for the love of God; and, in testimony of this love, I will recite with great attention the Our Father in my morning prayers.

Lesson 31: Our Union with the New Adam by Hope (4)

Angelical Salutation.—After the Lord's Prayer, the most beautiful of all private prayers is the Angelical Salutation. In effect, it was composed by God himself, though he did not teach it to us from his own lips, but from the lips of the archangel Gabriel, St. Elizabeth, and the Church, all directed by the Holy Ghost.[574]

It is the universal practice in the Catholic Church to recite it after the Lord's Prayer. Here is the reason: a man who has affairs at court begins by presenting his petition to the prince himself—he next has recourse to the courtier whom he knows to be in highest favor with the monarch, beseeching him to watch over the success of his petition, and to bring it to a happy issue: such is our conduct. After presenting our supplications to the King of heaven, our Father, we conjure the Queen of heaven, his and our Mother, to speak for us, and to help us by her powerful intercession to obtain a favorable answer to our prayers.[575] Such is also the reason why we are now about to explain the Hail Mary.

Division of the Hail Mary.—Like the Our Father, the Hail Mary is divided into three parts, or into four, if we make account of the conclusion, which is the same as in the Lord's Prayer. The first consists of the words of the archangel Gabriel to the Blessed Virgin: "Hail, full of grace, the Lord is with thee, blessed art thou among women."[576] The second comprises the words of St. Elizabeth: "Blessed is the fruit of thy womb."[577] The third is formed of the words of the Church: "Holy Mary, Mother of God," etc.[578]

First part: Hail. According to the most approved calculations, in the year of the world 4004, on the 25th March, which was a Friday, the archangel Gabriel, all radiant with light, descended from heaven as the ambassador of the most Holy Trinity, to a young virgin of the royal race of David, dwelling in a lowly house of the little city of Nazareth in Galilee, and he said to her: "Hail."

This word expresses at once familiarity, respect, and congratulation. Familiarity—when we address the Blessed Virgin we show, like the archangel Gabriel, that we are her friends and acquaintances, and this gives us the boldness to speak to her. Respect—for we salute Mary because she is the most holy, the most exalted, the most powerful of creatures. Congratulation—the word *Hail* means: "Rejoice, be happy; after the happiness of God, there is no happiness comparable with thine."

That it is most agreeable to the Blessed Virgin to hear us frequently repeating this word is evident. How, in point of fact, can it be supposed that she does not hear with pleasure a salutation which reminds her of the most delightful, the most solemn, and the most glorious moment in her life, and of her incomparable dignity as Mother of God, which alone surpasses all the titles and the prerogatives that can be attributed to any other creature? How, again, will it not rejoice her to see us occupied with the thought of her glory, and grateful for the wondrous benefit of the incarnation? Undoubtedly, as often as we pronounce this beautiful word, we render ourselves most pleasing to her maternal heart.

Hence, by the word *Hail*, we testify to the Blessed Virgin the affection which we bear her, and the gratitude with which we are penetrated on account of the blessings which we have received through her, and we renew in her soul that joy which the angel caused her formerly when he addressed her in the same manner. It is for these reasons that, since the early ages of the Church, Christians have never ceased to fill the Blessed Virgin's ears with the sweet sounds of the Angelical Salutation, as with those of a deliciously harmonious concert: the proof of which is to be found in our most ancient documents, such as the liturgies of St. James and St. Chrysostom.

Mary. The archangel did not pronounce this august name. He was content to say: "Hail, full of grace." Why so? Because a) finding himself alone with the Blessed Virgin it was not necessary that he should mention her name, to let her understand that his discourse was addressed to her. Because b) the names of persons who excel in any eminent prerogative are understood well enough when we speak of the prerogative. For example, if we say "the wise man," everyone knows that we refer to Solomon. Thus, when the angel said: "Hail, full of grace," he gave Mary to understand that she alone was meant. Because c) persons of quality are not usually addressed by their proper names. Thus, in speaking to princes of the Church, to kings of the earth, to the sovereign pontiff, we say: "Your Eminence," "Sire," "Your Holiness," without pronouncing the proper names of these exalted personages. It was the Church that placed the name of Mary in the Angelical Salutation, to remind us well of her to whom we speak, and to form in our souls the ineffable sentiments which this blessed name awakes of itself.

Mary is a Hebrew word, which means "lady," "mistress," "enlightener." In its triple signification this name is admirably suited to the Blessed Virgin. She is a Lady, since God established her Queen of angels and men. She is Mistress of all creatures: Did not God give her unlimited sway even over himself? She is an enlightener, since she bestowed upon us the Savior, who is the sun of justice and the light of the world.

Hence proceed the profound respect and the lively confidence which the Catholic Church has always testified toward the name of Mary. In public prayers she orders her ministers never to pronounce it without saluting it by an inclination of the head. Pious Poland delayed more than four hundred years before she would allow her daughters to receive it in baptism. The glorious martyr, St. Gerard, bishop of Chonad, taught the Hungarians to pronounce the name of Mary rarely, and instead to say Our Lady; and, if they pronounced it or heard it pronounced, to uncover the head and bend the knee.[579]

We ourselves show our respect for this glorious name by never pronouncing it with levity, and by carrying or keeping it—written, painted, or engraved—as a religious object, as an instruction, and as a preservative. After the example of the Church, we also invoke it with absolute confidence, in our dangers, in our sicknesses, in our temptations, in our afflictions—above all, at the moment of death; for, says a saint, the name of Mary is a sign of life, a cause of joy, and a source of grace.[580]

Full of grace. These words begin to explain the archangel's profound respect for Mary, and manifest the supreme excellence of the august Virgin. Mary is full of grace, that is to say, she alone has received more graces than all men and angels together. In effect, God always proportions the means to the end which he wishes to attain. Now, having chosen the Blessed Virgin to raise her to the dignity of Mother of God, the most sublime of which a pure creature is capable, he endowed her with a plenitude of grace in keeping with this transcendent dignity.[581]

But what is the precise meaning of the words *full of grace*? We must know that the grace of God produces three great effects in the soul: it effaces sins, which are like so many stains disfiguring the soul; it adorns the soul with gifts and virtues; it gives the soul strength to perform meritorious works, which are very agreeable to the Divine Majesty. The Blessed Virgin is full of grace, because, in regard to the first effect, she was never sullied or tarnished by any sin, original or actual, mortal or venial. In regard to the second, she possessed all the virtues and gifts of the Holy Ghost in the highest degree. In regard to the third, she performed works so agreeable to God and so meritorious for herself as to deserve to be raised in body and soul above all the angelic choirs.[582]

The Lord is with thee. These words express the second prerogative of the Blessed Virgin, and the second praise which we give her. "The Lord," here, means the Holy Trinity in general, and the second Person in particular.

Hence, the archangel says to Mary: "The Holy Trinity has been with thee since the first moment of thy conception, by a perpetual assistance, to preserve thee from all stain, from all imperfection, to direct thee in all thy ways, to protect thee, to load thee with the most excellent graces, in a word, to guard so precious a treasure.[583]

"Not only has the Holy Trinity been with thee heretofore by a special providence, but, from this moment, it shall be with thee in a manner much more admirable. The Father overshadows thee, the Holy Ghost comes upon thee, and the Son descends into thy chaste womb, so that he is with thee not only by his grace, but in Person.[584] Thus, the Father is with thee, by raising thee to the dignity of Mother of his own Son; the Son is with thee, by preserving thy virginity before, during, and after childbearing; the Holy Ghost is with thee, by sanctifying thy body and soul with an incomparable sanctification. In a word, the Holy Trinity is in thee, as its living temple: the Father is in thee, as his daughter; the Son, as his Mother; the Holy Ghost, as his spouse.

"This is not all: the Lord, the divine Word, shall be with thee. He shall live for nine months in thy virginal womb. He shall bestow on thee his divine caresses. For thirty years he shall never leave thee. Like an obedient Son, he will render thee every service that thou desirest of him. By his daily conversation, he will instruct thee, he will console thee, he will load thee with graces. During his public life, he shall no more leave thee than during his hidden life. He shall be with thee at the marriage feast of Cana, to continue to do thy will. He shall be with thee again on Calvary, to give thee a last mark of his tenderness, by confiding thee to the care of the beloved disciple.

"After his resurrection, he will come to see thee first; and, after his ascension, he will fill thee with the gifts of the Holy Ghost more abundantly than all the apostles and saints together. When thou art about to quit the earth, he will run to thee, he will receive thee into his arms to lead thee triumphant in body and soul into the abode of his glory, and to place thee by his side for all eternity: Hail, full of grace, the Lord is with thee."

Blessed art thou among women. This is Mary's third incomparable prerogative, and the third praise which we address to her. With the archangel, we acknowledge that no woman ever received or ever shall receive so many and such great blessings as Mary. In effect, by a singular privilege, she united in herself the blessings of the Virgin and the Mother—the like of which had never been before and shall never be again. Justly, then, does she deserve to be proclaimed blessed among women.

The blessings of the Virgin are a continual and spotless purity of body and soul: a sublime state, which gained for virgins among all peoples, even pagans, the greatest honors and the most religious respect; which still gains for them the same advantages among Christian nations; and which, in the midst of the heavenly court, shall gain for them the exclusive glory of following the immaculate Lamb whithersoever he goeth. Mary enjoyed, still enjoys, and shall ever enjoy, more eminently than any other, the blessings of virginity.

The blessings of the Mother are fruitfulness and the perfection of her children. Mary gave birth to a Son who alone was worth more, infinitely more than all other children together. It may also be said that she is the Mother of a greater multitude of children than her father Abraham, whose posterity exceeds in number the stars of the firmament, since all good Christians are the brethren of our Lord, consequently the children of Mary, not by nature, as the Savior, but by maternal love, by grace, and by inheritance.

Moreover, as the virginity of Mary surpasses in perfection that of all other virgins, so the maternity of Mary surpasses in glory that of all other mothers. All women bring forth in sorrow: Mary alone was exempt from this law. It is therefore with the justest title that we hail her as blessed among women, since others may have the blessing of virginity without fecundity, or the blessing of maternity without virginity, but Mary alone unites in herself the twofold blessing of a perfect virginity and a perfect fecundity.

Second part: Blessed is the fruit of thy womb. These words were inspired by the Holy Ghost to St. Elizabeth. They express Mary's fourth privilege, and the fourth praise which we give her. We have exalted the sacred Virgin by that which she is in herself; here we congratulate her on that which she is by reason of her Son, who is the fruit of her chaste womb.

Though at the first glance this praise seems addressed to the Son, yet it returns directly to the Mother. In effect, the honor of fruit belongs to the tree that bears it, and the glory of a son is reflected on his mother. Now, our Lord, being true God and true man, is blessed, not only among all men, but also, as St. Paul says, above everything that exists in heaven and on earth.[585] He is blessed, that is to say, he is the very source of all the goods which he possesses by nature, and which he distributes to his creatures. Hence, the holy Virgin, his Mother, is blessed, not only among all women, but also above every other creature that exists in heaven and on earth; for, as we have already said, the glory of the Son is reflected on the Mother.

Our Lord is designated by the mysterious name of *fruit*, to show, first, that he was really formed of the substance of Mary; next, that he was formed by the supernatural operation of the Holy Ghost; finally, that he was born without injury to his Mother, as fruit is born, is ripened without injury to the tree.

Jesus. St. Elizabeth did not pronounce this divine name when addressing her cousin, and this for some of the reasons that explain the silence of the angel in regard to the name of Mary. It was the Church that added the name of Jesus to the Angelical Salutation, in order to point out clearly what was the blessed fruit of the sacred Virgin's womb, and thereby to lead us to glorify this most chaste womb, worthy of the eternal praises of heaven and earth. In doing so, the Church entered perfectly into the intentions of the Savior himself, whose desire it is to see everyone praise, exalt, and bless the womb of his divine Mother, which for nine months served him as a tabernacle.

Thus, when a woman, who has been listening to the admirable discourse of the man-God, cries out from the midst of the crowd: "Blessed is the womb that bore thee!"[586] Our Lord identifies himself with this eulogium, and confirms it, saying: "Yes, blessed; but still more happy is my Mother in having heard the word of God!" For many centuries the Catholic Church, after the example of this woman in the gospel, has been daily addressing to Mary the same formula of praise.

Third part. We come to the third part of the Angelical Salutation—composed by the Church. We already find the elements of this prayer in the ages that border on the cradle of Christianity. Thus, the Syrians, who learned their *Ave Maria* from the apostles, and probably from St. Peter, did not end without imploring the intercession of the Blessed Virgin. These are their words: "Peace be to thee, O Mary, full of grace! The Lord is with thee; blessed art thou among women, and blessed is the fruit which is in thy womb, Jesus Christ. Holy Mary, Mother of God, pray for us—for us, sinners. Amen."

As for the present formula, Baronius, relying on tradition, traces it back to the year 431, when, after the Council of Ephesus, it burst forth by acclamation from the mouths of all the faithful, as a reparation for the outrages committed against their Mother by Nestorius, and as an everlasting monument of Mary's victory over that heresiarch.[587]

Holy Mary, Mother of God. Here we sum up the principal glories of Mary, which are contained in the ineffable privilege of the divine maternity; afterward, we express to her both our filial confidence in her assistance, and the pressing need which we have of it. Holy Mary—oh, yes! holy with a holiness unequalled by any other creature; holy in her conception, before her birth, in her birth; holy in life and in death; holy in soul and in body, without the shadow of a stain; all beautiful interiorly and exteriorly, with a beauty surpassing that of angels and men, inferior only to that of God himself!

Nothing is more proper than the words, *Mother of God*, to rejoice the heart of Mary. Nothing is more capable of moving her to compassion for us, and of inspiring us with a boundless confidence toward her. Mother of God! thou art then the most glorious of creatures. Mother of God! thou art then almighty: Can a Mother like thee meet with a refusal from a Son like thine? Mother of God! thou art then compassionate, for these sinners who implore thee are tenderly loved by the Son: they are the price of his blood, they are his brethren, they should be his co-heirs. Since thou lovest thy Son, canst thou fail to love us? Since his most ardent desire is our salvation, wilt thou not help us to attain it?

Pray. After giving Mary the most beautiful praise possible, in naming her the Mother of God, we proceed to draw her attention to two points. The first, how easy it is for her, since she has so much power over the heart of God, to come to the aid of sinners. A look, a sign, a word, the least prayer suffices. Why? Because the request of the best and the most beloved of mothers to the best and the most powerful of sons is always received as a command. So speak all the fathers, all the doctors, all the pious and learned men of every

Christian age, who, not knowing how to characterize the union in Mary of that inferiority which is natural to a creature with that superiority which she enjoys by grace, give her the name of an "omnipotent supplicant."[588] The second, the goodness of her maternal heart. Now, the heart of Mary, always in unison with that of Jesus, loves whatever Jesus loved, loves much those whom Jesus loved much—consequently she loves men, created to his image and likeness; men, whom he called his brethren; men, with whom he really contracted, by taking our nature in the womb of Mary, ties of the closest relationship.

For us. By these words we understand all mankind, and chiefly Christians; for all have need of the assistance of the Blessed Virgin, and she is the advocate of the whole world.

Sinners. Those among mankind whom our Lord loves in a manner most are sinners. It was for them that he became man. "The Son of Man," he says, "is not come to call the just, but sinners; he is come to save all that were lost: they that are well have no need of a physician, but the sick have." It was with them that he became so familiar as to be called, by his enemies, "the friend of publicans and sinners." It was to them that he specially addressed the invitation: "Come to me, all you that are overwhelmed with the weight of your miseries, and I will relieve you!" It was for them that he related the touching parables of the lost sheep and the prodigal son. Since it is so, we are very sure to move the Blessed Virgin's heart when we say: "Pray for us, sinners."

Poor sinners: yes, sin robbed us of all our possessions, and cast us wounded and bleeding at the feet of the devil. The humble acknowledgment of our misery is very proper to touch the heart of Mary. In using the word *sinners*, that is, in acknowledging that we are reduced to our pitiable state through our fault, through our fault, through our most grievous fault, we lay before her our wretchedness in all its extent, and employ the true means to move the bowels of the Mother of mercy. We prove to her that, if she is the Queen of mercy, we are the first of her subjects. She understands this so well that St. Bernard ventures to say to her: "I am willing that no one should ever again speak of thee, if it can be shown that any man ever invoked thee in his necessities, without obtaining thy assistance."[589]

Now. This word means the whole time of the present life, in which we own no yesterday or tomorrow, but only one fleeting moment. Let us be careful to remark how God, in the two most beautiful prayers, the Lord's Prayer and the Angelical Salutation, reminds us of the shortness of time and the frailty of life. *Now* tells us also of our condition on earth, a condition of warfare without truce or respite, so that every day, every hour, we have need of help, inasmuch as there is not a single instant without peril.

And at the hour of our death. The most dangerous and the most decisive hour, consequently that in which we have the greatest need of help is the hour of death. It is the most dangerous, because then the devil, seeing that he has only a few moments more to tempt us, redoubles his fury, and invents new stratagems, to plunge us into evil. The most dangerous, because the past, the present, and the future, with the pains of sickness, all conspire to cast us into discouragement, impatience, and despair, while the exhaustion of nature leaves us less energy to resist, or renders us almost insensible to the state of our soul, and often the persons around us endeavor on their side to lull us asleep in fatal illusions. It is the most decisive, because on the hour of death depends eternity. On whichever side the tree falls it shall remain. Now, the Blessed Virgin is all-powerful to strengthen, console, and defend the sick man; to awake in his heart sentiments of repentance, confidence, perfect conformity with the will of God—in a word, to obtain for those who, like St. Joseph, lived in her company, the grace to die, like him, in her arms and those of her Son.

Amen. May it be done as we have asked! Oh, how admirably placed is this *Amen* at the end of the Angelical Salutation well understood and well recited!

In explaining the Lord's Prayer and the Angelical Salutation, we have made known the two most excellent as well as most venerable of all special prayers. To complete this important lesson, it remains to point out a few other prayers, very much esteemed for their antiquity, or for their intrinsic beauty, or for being in general use among the faithful during many long centuries in every part of the world.

The Angelus.—The first, which flows in a manner from the two preceding ones, is the *Angelus.* Thrice a day, at morn, noon, and eve, the bell is heard, and pious Christians thrice salute the august Virgin. This practice, universal today throughout the Church, has its origin far back in antiquity. In 1262, St. Bonaventure prescribed to the Order of St. Francis, of which he was general, the recital every evening, at the sound of the bell, of three Hail Marys in honor of the mystery of the incarnation.

The diocese of Saintes was the first in France to adopt this practice. By a bull of 15th October, 1318, John XXII approved of it, and encouraged it with indulgences. In 1724, Benedict XIII granted a hundred days' indulgence each time, and a plenary indulgence once a month to those who should recite the *Angelus* in its present form.[590] To gain the indulgence it is necessary to recite the prayer kneeling, even on Saturday at noon. In virtue of a common law, Sunday is excepted from this rule, and during paschal time the *Angelus* is replaced by the *Regina Coeli.*

The triple repetition of this prayer makes us understand the great need we have of frequently recurring to God and the saints, surrounded as we are by visible and invisible enemies. By the usage of ringing the bell thrice a day and reciting the Angelical Salutation, the Church intends to remind us continually of the three great mysteries of our redemption: the incarnation, the passion, and the resurrection. It desires that the Catholic world should salute the holy Virgin in the morning, in memory of the resurrection; at midday, in memory of the passion; in the evening, in memory of the incarnation. In effect, as we are certain that our Lord was placed on the cross at midday, and that he arose from the dead in the morning, so we believe that he became incarnate during the night.[591]

The Salve Regina.—The second is the *Salve Regina.* The pious and learned Hermann Contractus, Count of Veringen, who died in the year 1054, is regarded as the author of the *Salve Regina.* This favorite prayer of St. Bernard is so beautiful, so touching, so well suited to the poor banished children of Eve, pilgrims in this valley of tears, that it is difficult to repeat it without having our heart moved, and without also moving the most tender and compassionate heart of Mary.[592] Precious indulgences are attached to it.

The Litany of the Blessed Virgin.—The third is the Litany of the Blessed Virgin, also called the Litany of Our Lady of Loretto, where it is sung with great pomp on every Saturday of the year. This litany, which all Catholics know by heart and make it a duty to recite daily, is most venerable by the beauty of its petitions; by the titles, at once so gracious and so affecting, which it bestows on the holy Virgin; by the devotion with which so many pontiffs, kings, and scholars in every clime have employed it in their addresses to Mary; finally, by its antiquity.

Everything leads us to believe that it is referable to the apostles.[593] Only we think that the word *Sancta*, "holy," placed before each invocation, is of a later date. An indulgence of three hundred days is granted for each recitation of this devout litany; and a plenary indulgence on the feasts of the Immaculate Conception, the Nativity, the Annunciation, the Purification, and the Assumption of the Blessed Virgin, to those who recite it daily.

The Regina Coeli.—The fourth is the *Regina Coeli*, which was commenced by angels and completed by Pope St. Gregory the Great and the people of Rome on Easter day, April 25, in the year 590, at the time of a terrible pestilence which was desolating the capital of the Christian world, and which ceased immediately.[594] Same indulgences as the *Angelus.*

The Litany of the Holy Name of Jesus.—The fifth is the Litany of the Holy Name of Jesus, in which we remind our Lord of his various titles as man-God, Savior, and model; though less ancient than the Litany of the Blessed Virgin, still it is very beautiful and pious.

The Litany of the Saints.—The sixth is the Litany of the Saints, which is like a long, deep sigh of the Church on earth toward her sister, the Church in heaven. Nothing is more solemn or more touching than those invocations of all the orders of the blessed, whose powerful intercession is implored by representing to them the sad multitude of corporal and spiritual, public and private miseries, which surround us poor exiles in this valley of tears. The origin of this prayer is lost in the distance of ages;[595] and we are forbidden to add anything to it, to take anything from it, or to change it in the least.[596]

Such are the chief formulas of prayer whose use is most general and most ancient in the Church. The faithful cannot do better than recite them in preference to others not so approved: they are the means to pray most properly and most efficaciously.

PRAYER

O my God! who art all love, I thank thee for having inspired thy Church with so many prayers, so powerful over thy heart; grant me the grace to recite them like the saints who have gone before me, and like those who shall come after me.

I am resolved to love God above all things, and my neighbor as myself for the love of God; and, in testimony of this love, I will never fail to recollect myself a moment before prayer.

Lesson 32: Our Union with the New Adam by Hope (5)

The first means to obtain grace is prayer. It is a very easy means. By the word *prayer* we understand not only mental and vocal, public and private prayer, such as we explained in the preceding lessons, but also good works in general, such as mortification, alms, labors, sufferings—in a word, all that we do or endure for the glory of God.[597]

Second means to obtain grace: The sacraments; the Eucharist as chief.—The second means to obtain grace is the sacraments. It is, if we may be allowed the expression, a more efficacious means than the former. "By the sacraments," says the Council of Trent, "all true justice is begun, or increased, or recovered."[598] According to St. Thomas, it is to the Eucharist that all the other sacraments owe their origin and must be referred. Now, the Eucharist contains our Lord Jesus Christ, the very author of grace, personally and continually among us, so that the Eucharistic union is, as it were, the consummation of the spiritual life and the end of all the sacraments.

Baptism renders us capable of this union; confirmation keeps us so, or makes us more worthy of it; penance effaces sin, which destroys it, and thus enables us to form it anew; extreme unction, the admirable supplement of penance, removes all the obstacles that could prevent it, or helps to strengthen it at the moment of death; orders and marriage perpetuate it, by perpetuating the Church, that is to say, priests, who preserve Jesus Christ always present on earth, and the faithful, who receive him. Such are the sacraments in the general plan of religion.[599] It is time to enter into an explanation of these powerful helps to salvation which the new Adam bequeathed us.

General definition of the sacraments.—And first, what is a sacrament? A sacrament, says St. Augustine, "is a sign of a sacred thing; or," what amounts to the same, "a visible sign of invisible grace, instituted for our sanctification."[600] Hence, the definition admitted by the Church: "The sacraments are sensible signs, instituted by Jesus Christ for the sanctification of our souls."[601]

Signs. The sacraments are signs, because they make known to us a thing which does not fall under our senses, that is to say, an invisible grace which they convey to our souls.[602] Thus, when in baptism water is poured on the body, while the appointed words are being pronounced, this means that, by virtue of the Holy Ghost, the soul is interiorly cleansed from all the stains and defilements of sin, and decked with the heavenly ornaments of justice and grace.

Sensible signs. The sacraments are sensible signs, because they consist of words and actions which fall under our senses. In baptism, for example, we see the action of the priest pouring on water, and hear the words which he pronounces. This action and these words signify and produce in the soul of him who is baptized an invisible grace which sanctifies him.

Signs instituted by Jesus Christ. It is a matter of faith that our Lord Jesus Christ instituted all the sacraments. He alone could do so; for a sacrament is not a natural sign of grace, but an arbitrary sign, which only signifies and produces grace dependently on the will of God, who instituted it for these effects. With what respect should this thought inspire us for the sacraments, since the dignity and excellence of him who gives add infinitely to the value of the benefits bestowed! With what piety, what religious fear, what filial confidence, ought we to approach them!

But alas! how much reason there is to be afflicted on beholding the indifference of the generality of Christians toward the sacraments, and considering the levity, the want of care, with which they frequent them! A holy priest remarked on this subject, with a sigh: "How many delicate persons go in summer to the waters of Bourbonne, Vichy, Barèges, etc.! They incur great expense to cure a few bodily infirmities, and it would require much more to cure them all. We have admirable fountains for all the diseases of the soul: the sacraments. These fountains of grace infallibly cure all who have recourse to them, well disposed. How then does it happen that so many sinners neglect to come to these salutary waters? How is it that so many persons come to them without the proper dispositions?"

For our sanctification. The definition of the sacraments terminates with these words: *for our sanctification.* To sanctify men is to render them pleasing to God by a removal of sin or by an increase of grace. Accordingly, there are sacraments which sanctify us by giving us the life of grace, of which we were deprived—as baptism and penance: on this account they are called "sacraments of the dead." Others sanctify us by increasing and fortifying the grace which we already have: they are called "sacraments of the living," because it is necessary to be in the state of grace in order to receive them.

Sacramental grace. Besides habitual and sanctifying grace, which the sacraments produce in the souls of those who receive them worthily, they also confer what is called a sacramental grace, peculiar to each sacrament. This grace is a right to have in case of need the succors actually necessary: a) to acquit ourselves of the obligations to which the sacraments engage us; b) to surmount the obstacles that may oppose us; c) to attain the end of each sacrament.[603]

Sacramental character. We must also know that there are three sacraments—baptism, confirmation, and holy orders—which imprint a character. "This character," says St. Thomas, "is a spiritual power communicated to our soul, and renders us capable of receiving and distributing that which pertains to the worship of God, that is to say, the sacraments."[604] Thus, this character has two effects: by the one it makes us capable of receiving and doing certain things in the order of religion; and by the other, it serves to distinguish those who have received the sacraments which imprint it.

The character of baptism fits us to receive the other sacraments, and at the same time distinguishes Christians from infidels. By the character of confirmation we are armed as the soldiers of Jesus Christ, to proclaim and defend his name, to struggle with our internal and external enemies. Moreover, we are separated from the newly baptized, who are like "newborn babes."[605] In fine, the character of the sacrament of holy orders gives the power to administer the sacraments, and distinguishes those who are invested with this power from the rest of the faithful.

These three sacraments form in the Church the three different states of which society is composed: citizens, who are its members; soldiers, who defend it; and magistrates, who rule it. The character impressed by these three sacraments is indelible, remaining in the saints to increase their glory, and in the reprobate to increase their shame. It follows hence that these sacraments can only be received once, and that it would be a horrible sacrilege to approach them again.[606]

All the sacraments produce effects by "their own virtue."[607] These important words mean: a) that the sacraments produce grace immediately by the action which is done, that is to say, by the application of outward signs which have in them a supernatural virtue proceeding from the institution and the merits of Jesus Christ; and b) that they do not produce grace in virtue of the merits of him who administers them or of him who receives them, but by the merits of Jesus Christ, who instituted the sacraments and communicated their efficacy to them.

It does not follow hence that adults require no good dispositions in order to be sanctified by the sacraments. On the contrary, the Catholic faith teaches that adults do not receive sanctifying grace by the sacraments unless they have the proper dispositions. From the fact that the sacraments produce grace of themselves, we must only conclude therefore that neither faith, nor devotion, nor any other disposition with which one approaches them, is the efficient cause of the grace conferred by the sacraments, but rather a preparation which removes the obstacles to grace. The more perfect our dispositions, the more abundant are the graces received.

How moral is all this! While, on the one hand, the certainty regarding the effect produced by the sacrament, when validly administered, consoles our faith; on the other, the uncertainty regarding our dispositions keeps us in humility and leads us to fervor.

Elements of the sacraments: Matter, form, and minister.—After having defined the sacraments in general, let us pass on to the elements of which they are composed. By what has been said it is shown that, to form a sacrament, several things are necessary: a sensible sign; a sign to which should be attached the virtue of producing grace; finally, some person with authority to make and apply this sanctifying sign. These are called the elements of the sacraments. They are three in number: the matter, the form, and the minister. Such is the doctrine of the Church, formulated by Pope Eugenius IV, in his celebrated decree for the instruction of the Armenians. "Every sacrament," says he, "consists of three parts: certain sensible things as the matter; certain words as the form; and a minister, who confers the sacrament with the intention of doing what the Church does. The three are so essential that any one of them being absent there is no sacrament."[608]

The matter is the element or thing employed in the administration of the sacrament, as water in baptism and holy oil in extreme unction. The form is the words of the minister; and faith teaches that these words being joined to the matter, the sacrament exists.[609] The words should be added to the matter, in order that the meaning of the thing employed might be more clearly and easily understood. If there were no words connected with the sacraments, it would be difficult to divine what was meant by the matter alone. The minister of the sacraments is the person who administers them. That the administration of a sacrament may be valid, the minister must employ the prescribed matter and form, and, moreover, have the intention of doing what the Church does; but it is not necessary that he should be a virtuous man, or even in the state of grace. The validity of the sacrament does not in any manner depend on the qualities of him who confers it.

The reason is easily understood. The principal minister of the sacraments is our Lord, to whom the sacraments belong.

"Now," says St. Augustine, "what evil can a bad minister do to you, since the Lord is good? If he who plants or he who waters a tree with soiled hands cannot injure the tree, since it is God who gives the increase, how can a sinful minister injure a soul which receives a sacrament, since the sacrament belongs to God, and it is God himself who confers the grace? It is certain that those who were baptized by Judas were really baptized; for the baptism of Jesus Christ is really conferred even by a Judas."[610]

All that the personal sanctity of the minister produces is an increase of grace to him—the reward of his virtues—or, as theology speaks, a merit due to the dispositions of him who acts, *ex opere operantis*.

Intention of the Church. But it is necessary that the minister should have an intention of doing what the Church does.[611] This intention may be either actual or virtual. It is actual when one expressly proposes at the time, with attention and reflection, to administer a sacrament. A virtual intention is an impression resulting from an actual intention, which, not being recalled by a contrary act of the will, still morally continues, though, in applying one's self to a sacramental action, something else is thought about. The actual intention is certainly more desirable, but the virtual suffices for the variety of the sacrament.

As a general rule, bishops and priests are the only ministers of the sacraments. Yet, in cases of necessity, it is the right and the duty of the laity to confer baptism. If all Christians were at liberty to meddle with the administration of the sacraments, everything in the Church would be confusion. No person can or should attribute to himself the honor of administering the sacraments unless he is called by God, as Aaron was,[612] to do so. Our Lord did not say to all the faithful, but only to his apostles: "Go, teach the nations." "Baptize them." "Whose sins you shall forgive, they are forgiven." Hence, the Council of Trent struck with its anathema anyone who should dare to say that every Christian has the power to preach and to administer all the sacraments.[613]

Ceremonies.—As for the ceremonies which accompany the administration of the sacraments, they do not belong to the essence of these sanctifying signs: which may exist without them. But they were most wisely established: a) to represent to us the sanctity which the sacraments require of those who administer them and of those who receive them; b) to figure in a more ample manner and render sensible the effects of each sacrament; and c) the better to raise the souls of those who are the witnesses of their administration to a contemplation of divine things and to an increase of faith and charity. Most venerable in themselves, these august ceremonies are no less so in their antiquity: the majority of them ascend to the apostles or to apostolic times.[614]

As a proof of all this, let us adduce the ceremonies of baptism, which we shall explain later on. Baptism is one of the most imposing acts of religion. It bears on the two fundamental dogmas of the fall and the redemption. Nothing more important than to render them sensible and, so to speak, palpable to the weakest minds. How does the Church proceed? By ceremonies. To understand, it suffices to see.

Here is a catechumen, sullied with the stain of that primitive degradation which vitiated humanity in its source. He presents himself to be purified, and to be introduced into the Christian communion, so as to participate in the abundant means of sanctification brought to humanity by the Savior. On his arrival at the baptismal font, the Church announces to him by the somber hue of her ornaments, and by a first exorcism, his original forfeiture and his slavery to the devil. Then she marks his brow with the seal of the cross; places some salt—the emblem of wisdom—in his mouth; and proceeds to exorcisms on his person, a purification preparatory to that of the sacrament.

Next follows the aspirant's profession of faith. The first condition for being admitted into a society is to believe the power which governs it. When he possesses a sufficiency of divine knowledge and understands the full extent of his duties, the aspirant is summoned to make solemnly a triple renunciation of the evil spirit, its maxima, and its works. To prepare him to wrestle well with his implacable enemy, whose attacks shall be incessant, the Church anoints with holy oil the breast and shoulders of the new athlete. Now is poured on his brow the material water, a sensible sign of the divine grace which invisibly purifies his soul.

When he is thus regenerated by water and the Holy Ghost, when he has received the forgiveness of all his sins, the priest pours on his head the holy chrism, a precious balm composed of the most exquisite aromatics of the East, and whose perfume reminds him of the good odor which should henceforth, during the course of his life, exhale from his Christian virtues. Thus purified, enlightened, and fortified, the Church clothes him with a white robe, places in his hand a lighted taper, symbolic of faith and charity, and makes him advance in the way which leads to the eternal nuptials of the Lord.

What do you think of this? Is it not a grand action, made sensible in a grand language? Thanks be to the Church! Oh how well she understood us when she instituted her eloquent ceremonies!

Proofs of the divine institution of the sacraments.—It is now necessary to show you what you already believe with all the sincerity of your soul: that all our sacraments were instituted by our Lord Jesus Christ. The scripture, the holy fathers, the tradition of sects separated from unity, the teaching of the Catholic Church, reason itself—all unite to establish this fundamental and consoling truth.

1. *The scripture.* Who can better inform us whether Jesus Christ instituted the sacraments than Jesus Christ himself? Now, in the following lessons we shall quote the words of the gospel, which attribute to the Son of God in Person the institution of each sacrament.

2. *The holy fathers.* The same truth is unanimously proclaimed by all those great men of the East and the West who are so fitly termed the fathers of the Church. Disciples of the apostles and faithful inheritors of their doctrine, they begin by telling us with St. Paul that the apostles were only the ministers and dispensers of the sacraments which Jesus Christ had instituted.[615] "Who is the author of the sacraments," asks St. Ambrose, "if not Jesus Christ? They all came from heaven."[616] St. Augustine is no less precise. "Jesus Christ," he says, "made a small number of sacraments, very easily received and most excellent in their signification—the bond of his new people."[617]

That you might better know that these sacraments, divinely instituted, were the same as those which we admit, that they are neither more nor less numerous today than formerly, the fathers took care to name them one after another. Tertullian makes mention of baptism, confirmation, and penance.[618] St. Justin gives an admirable description of the Eucharist.[619] Tertullian speaks of holy orders in his celebrated work on Prescriptions.[620] St. Augustine explains baptism and the Eucharist,[621] and shows confirmation to be a distinct sacrament from baptism; a little while afterward, he treats of matrimony.[622] Innocent I and St. Chrysostom make mention of extreme unction.[623] We might here add the other fathers—among them St. Cyril of Jerusalem, who, in his beautiful *Catecheses*, so well explains the ceremonies of our sacraments.

Thus, the testimony of the fathers whom we have just cited establishes the antiquity and the divinity of the sacraments, as the silence of some and the reserve of others on this capital point are proofs of that wise solicitude which never forsakes the Church. Through fear of exposing our mysteries to the contempt of pagans, it was necessary to speak of them with discretion and only when circumstances required it.

3. *The tradition of sects separated from unity*. Even in the first ages, there arose heretics. They formed societies apart, of which some still subsist in the East. When withdrawing from the Church, these prodigal children carried away with them a number of truths—among others, that of the existence of seven sacraments: their liturgies bear witness to it.[624] At a later period, the Greek Church broke with the Latin, toward which it had always showed itself crotchety and captious. Now, the Greek Church preserves the same belief as ourselves regarding the institution and the number of the sacraments.

It furnished a brilliant proof of this in the sixteenth and seventeenth centuries. Protestants, who flattered themselves with the idea of thinking like the Greek Church in denying several of the sacraments, sent a copy of their profession of faith to Jeremias, the schismatical patriarch of Constantinople. He, having examined it, censured it indignantly, and wrote to say that the Greek Church had always admitted and then admitted the same sacraments as the Latin, and concluded his reply by uttering an anathema against protestants.

In 1672, the synod, which was held at Bethlehem, under Dositheus, patriarch of Jerusalem, declared anew that the Greeks (the schismatical ones) believed the same sacraments as the Latins. In fine, the variety of opinion which prevails among protestants regarding the number of the sacraments is also an excellent proof of the truth of the belief of the Catholic Church, which has always been the same. The character of error, the unhappy child of Satan and man, is to vary continually, while the seal of truth, the offspring of God, is unity and perpetuity.

4. *The teaching of the Catholic Church*. We might have dispensed with every other proof, the testimony of the Church alone sufficing to convince us of the truths of faith. The only one who ascends to Jesus Christ, the only keeper of his doctrine, she alone has the right to transmit to us the teachings of her divine spouse. Now, you always see her condemning as heretics those who, during the course of ages, refuse to admit any one of the sacraments. In the third century, she struck with her anathema the Novatians, who did not give confirmation to the newly-baptized; in the fourth, the Manichees, who condemned matrimony; in the fourteenth, Wickliffe and his adherents, who despised extreme unction; in the sixteenth, Luther, Zuinglius, and Calvin, who in turn rejected several sacraments.

Summing up on this point the teachings of scripture and tradition, the holy Church, solemnly assembled in the Council of Trent, speaks thus: "If any one says that the sacraments of the new law were not all instituted by our Lord Jesus Christ, or that there are more or less than seven, namely, baptism, confirmation, Eucharist, penance, extreme unction, holy orders, and matrimony, let him be anathema."[625]

5. *Reason itself*. In harmony with faith, reason tells us that Jesus Christ alone could institute the sacraments. On the one hand, it easily perceives that between a spiritual effect, as grace, and material signs, as the sacraments, there is no natural or necessary connection. On the other, it admits that the sacraments are channels through which the merits of our Savior's passion flow to us. Now, no one can dispense the treasure of our Lord's merits except our Lord himself, or in the manner and by the means which he himself established. Such is the language of plain common sense.

This language is understood by every person capable of joining two ideas together; but it seems to surpass the comprehension of the unbeliever. Ignorant and proud, as the apostle says, he pretends that the sacraments are a human invention—an absurd and gratuitous assumption, whose defense covers it with ridicule!

Absurd. Because it was impossible for men to invent the sacraments. Properly speaking, man invents nothing. Human inventions are only the application, the combination, the result of received ideas, and do not spring from an order of facts naturally inaccessible to our minds. Such, among others, are the inventions of powder, the compass, printing, the steam engine, and the telegraph.

As for the sacraments, where could man have found the first ideas of their invention? From what fact could he have concluded that a little water, joined with two or three words, had the virtue of effacing sin? This is evidently above all combinations, above all calculations, since the first idea is beyond the domain of reason. Yet man believes this, he believes it to the last drop of his blood, he believes it for eighteen centuries, he believes it on the word of a few illiterates. And what do we mean by man? The most enlightened, nay, the only enlightened nations of the globe.

The pretense is absurd, because it was above the power of men to impose the sacraments on the world. Supposing it possible that impostors could have originated our sacraments, their task would only have been begun. It would have remained to cause them to be accepted, and accepted as a solemn duty. But what is the fact? Notwithstanding the splendid proofs which establish the divine institution of the sacraments, notwithstanding the eternal fires of hell with which God himself threatens the contemners of the sacraments, the majority of men despise and reject them. And do you mean to say that impostors, disowned by heaven and earth, could have secured their admission and frequentation in silent acquiescence by millions of men during hundreds of years? No, it is impossible: you must feel it.

Gratuitous. Catholics have shown you the title-deeds of their faith. To oust them it is not enough for you to make an imaginary supposition; you must show that their documents are forgeries, and that the sacraments are really a human invention. Let us reason a little, and support if you can the consequences of your assumption. Men, you say, invented the sacraments. Well, what men? Did Jews, pagans, heretics, Catholics, meet in a general council to announce this grand invention? Who then convoked this admirable assembly? In what place, at what time, was it held? On these points, not a word.

Did the idea of the sacraments arise suddenly in the minds of all the bishops and priests of the Catholic world? If so, it might very properly be recognized as the inspiration of God. Will you say that it was one individual, a bishop, or even a pope, who had the merit of it? But how did he succeed in bringing the whole world to credit his dreams? Was it by force or was it by intrigue? What were the means which he employed to delude the eyes of his contemporaries, and to conceal the wickedness of his imposture from posterity? On these points, not a word.

There were philosophers in those times, as there always are; and did they say nothing? Did they not hold up to scorn either the impostor or the imposture? And those sects, separated from the Church, who always had their eyes upon her teachings, and were always ready to censure them; and particularly that Greek Church—so maliciously watchful and punctilious—which could make an alleluia or a comma a crime in the Latin Church, and which so often discovered a sentimental grievance to lay to her charge; and those numbers of Catholics who were naturally so impatient under the yoke of authority: Did they all keep silence and receive unrepiningly from the hand of an impostor a yoke which the whole authority of God seems scarcely sufficient to recommend?

And was the Catholic Church herself dumb? Yet we see proofs throughout the course of ages of her active and constant solicitude to preserve intact the deposit of faith. We see that the moment any innovator appeared—king, bishop, or priest—he excited a commotion which spread from East to West. The whole Church rose up against him. There were entreaties, there were letters, there were councils, there were anathemas; and if error was not always stifled in its beginning, at least its origin was marked, and its history transmitted to succeeding ages.

Now, tell us, in what century was the heretical originator of the sacraments condemned? In what council? Under what pope? On all this what does history teach us? Nothing. Verily, history is inexcusable. It tells us of the originators of the various arts: it acquaints us with their lives, their countries, their eras, their various inventions and discoveries. Then, unmindful of all its duties, reversing all its habits, it does not utter a single word regarding the author of the most wonderful invention that ever was chronicled—of an invention that exercises so great an influence on society—of an invention that should excite the liveliest remonstrances, since it humbles pride and irritates all the passions!

It is necessary, therefore, to maintain one or other of two things. Either that the inventor of the sacraments was so clever as to secure, without the least opposition, the acceptance of his tyrannical imposture by men naturally averse to every kind of restraint, by the learned as well as the ignorant, by kings as well as peoples, by submissive Catholics as well as the most implacable enemies of the Church—separated from her unity since the first ages; that he was so clever as to stifle the voices of all those who complained, and to efface every record of their complaints; that he was so clever as to rummage all the libraries of antiquity, in the East and the West, in order to tear away every page which exposed his imposture, and, without the least hindrance, to insert passages which made the sacraments the word of God; that he was so clever as not only to close the mouth of every person in the world, but even to make God himself an accomplice in the imposture, since God would have permitted and would still permit the human race to be thus deceived in his name; in a word, that he was so clever as to make heaven and earth conspire to sport with humanity. Or else that he caused his invention to be received suddenly, that is to say, that the Catholic Church fell asleep one day without the sacraments, and on awaking the next she found them established in all the books, in all the liturgies, throughout the East and the West; and, what is still more strange, that, having lost her memory during the night, she imagined that she had always professed a belief which dated only from the morning. Take your choice: there is no other course left. But enough!—do you not see that with all your suppositions you are to be pitied? So much for inventions.

Necessity of their institution founded on the nature of man.—The divinity of the sacraments being established, it is proper to say a word on the necessity of their institution. It was in a certain sense necessary that God should establish the sacraments, and their establishment admirably illustrates the profound wisdom and infinite goodness of our Lord. United in the closest manner to the first Adam, represented by him, contained in him, as children in their father, we all sinned in him.[626] Not only the understanding and the affections, but the flesh and the blood of man were vitiated. To be regenerated in every part of our being, it was necessary that we should be wholly united to the second Adam.

This complete union is accomplished in Communion, to which, as we have seen, all the sacraments refer. There the mind, the heart, the senses of man are so strictly united to the Savior that, so to speak, they are identified with him; so that we become "participators in the divine nature,"[627] being able to say: "I now live no longer; it is Jesus Christ who liveth in me."[628] "In the Eucharist," as Bossuet says, "the Son of God, taking the flesh of each one of us, communicates to our being the divine qualities of his own, and thus attains the final end of religion on earth."

Here you behold one of those numerous paths terminating at that fundamental truth which cannot be too often placed before our eyes, because it is the explanation of all things and the bond of all things, namely, that under the gospel as under the law, in past as in present and future ages, Jesus Christ is always the soul, the center, the Alpha and the Omega of religion: everything refers to him and to our union with him.

Hence, the first reason why our Lord instituted the sacraments was to regenerate our body and soul by communicating grace to us.

The second, he wished to supply man with a means, proportioned to his nature and condition, to work out his salvation. Since his fall, man has been buried in his senses; the weakness of his mind is such that it is next to impossible for him to rise otherwise than by sensible things to a knowledge of spiritual things. It was therefore to help us the more easily to understand what his power works invisibly in our souls that the sovereign master of all things was pleased to figure and represent by signs, taken from among sensible things, this mysterious operation. If man were simply a spirit, he would have communicated immediately with God; but, the soul being united to a body, it was necessary that sensible things should serve it as a means to comprehend invisible things.[629]

The third, he wished to be adored, not only by the internal acts of the spirit, but also by an external worship. The Creator of our body as well as of our soul, he requires the homage of both.

The fourth, he wished to instruct man, and to overcome his pride, by subjecting him to sensible things to which sanctification is attached. It was his object to try the obedience of sinful man, as he had tried that of innocent man.

The fifth, he wished to manifest to men his infinite power and wisdom, by making use of little things to work great things.

The sixth, he wished to maintain among men the sacred bond of charity, by reminding them that their partaking of the same goods, their purification in the same waters and by the same blood, and their presence at the same table, unite them with one another in the closest manner, and make them members of one and the same body.[630]

History.—Penetrated with a profound respect for the sacraments, here is the manner in which a servant of God used to prepare herself to receive them:

"Every day I make a prayer," she said to her director, "in which I ask, through the merits of our Lord and the intercession of the Blessed Virgin and St. Joseph, to be preserved from bad confessions and bad Communions, and to have the happiness of receiving, in the most worthy dispositions, the holy viaticum and extreme unction, if it be the will of God that I should receive them.

"Not to fail in contrition when I am about to confess, I usually make beforehand all the acts of contrition that I form in my morning and evening prayers and during the course of the day. On the eve of my confession I excite myself to sorrow, not only for the faults committed since my last confession, but also for the great sins of my life; and, at the close of my confession, I accuse myself of one or two of these sins. Every day I say an Our Father and Hail Mary for my confessor, that the Lord may inspire him to give me the advice most useful for me, and that my heart may be touched by his words.

"As a preparation for my Communion, I make several times a day a spiritual Communion. When I awake on the morning of the day on which I am to communicate, I consider the happiness which I shall soon enjoy. I say to myself: 'I am today invited to the table of the King of kings.' It is in thanksgiving for the Communion that I endeavor to perform all the actions of the day. I make the last Communion of each month a kind of viaticum, thinking that it may be the last Communion of my life.

"In fine, I often make this reflection: whoever receives the last sacraments ill-disposed shall be lost; whoever receives them well-disposed shall be saved; and the sacraments are usually received at death as they have been received during life."

PRAYER

O my God! who art all love, I thank thee for having been pleased to consummate my union with the new Adam by the Holy Eucharist, and thereby to communicate his divine qualities to me, and to make me his child. Inspire me with a deep love and reverence for this august sacrament, and for all the others, which lead to it.

I am resolved to love God above all things, and my neighbor as myself for the love of God; and, in testimony of this love, I will excite in my soul a great desire of communicating well.

Lesson 33: Our Union with the New Adam by Hope (6)

We have considered the sacraments in their relation with the final end of religion on earth, which is our union with our Lord Jesus Christ by grace; also, in their relation with the Holy Eucharist, to which all the others tend: we must now study them in their relation with society and the wants of man.

Social advantages of the sacraments.—No society without religion; no religion without redemption, because man fell; no redemption applied to man, and by man to society, without the sacraments, since the sacraments are the channels by which the merits of the redeemer flow to us. To ask what is the importance or the necessity of the sacraments in regard to society, its prosperity, its very existence, is to ask what is the importance or the necessity of the soul in regard to the body, of the sap in regard to the tree, of the foundation in regard to the house, of breathing in regard to life. Hence, among all peoples, you will find sacred and mysterious rites, "sacraments" in their way, by which it is believed that man communicates with God.[631]

An essential part of Christianity, our sacraments are therefore necessary to society by the same title as Christianity itself. To comprehend the advantages for which society is indebted to them, it suffices to say that, considered in a merely human light, the sacraments of the new law form the most beautiful social teaching that reason can discover. All the crimes that disturb society, that trouble families, that bring ruin on individuals, proceed from the little respect which man bears to himself. Because he neither knows what he is nor what he is worth, he makes little account of himself, he has no respect for himself; and, accordingly, he lends himself, sells himself, abandons himself to crime—he degrades himself, and, by degrading himself, becomes miserable and wicked. His mind he hands over to error, his heart to beastly affections, and his senses to all the passions that wish to make use of them. Respecting others no more than himself, he makes it a jest, a study, a fiendish pleasure to degrade them, and, by degrading them, he renders them like himself—miserable and wicked.

The original of this picture may be found everywhere. It is man. It is you, it is I, it is every one of us, so long as we do not know what we are. Who will teach us? Polity is dumb, philosophy sick. What then? Religions that are foreign to Christianity? All fail in respect for man. Some have shed his blood; others have placed him trembling on his knees before frightful idols; all have bowed him down under the yoke of the most degrading errors. All have more or less sported with his life, his mind, and his heart.

The only true religion, the universal repairer, teaches man, by teaching him what he is and what he is worth, to respect himself and to respect his kind. "O son of God!" she says to him, "be holy like thy Father; he is thrice holy—be thou thrice holy":[632] holy in mind, holy in heart, holy in body. This triple holiness the Catholic Church is not content merely to preach in words; she impresses it on all the senses of man by the sacraments.

Hence, those exorcisms, those blessings, those unctions, so often repeated on man at the different periods of life. What are we to understand henceforward by our sacraments but a great teaching of sanctity, of virtue, of innocence, of respect for ourselves—a precious teaching, which begins at the cradle to end only at the grave? It is something better still. Not only do the sacraments reveal man to man, but they also show him what he ought to do in order to maintain his dignity in all the circumstances of life: we shall make this clear in the explanation of each sacrament. Yet more: the sacraments are not a fruitless teaching; they give to man the fitness and strength necessary to do what they teach. He who profits by them is a hero.

A hero in youth. He fastens to his chariot his vanquished passions. These are the same passions that enchain the heroes of the world, and drag their brows to the dust in the presence of infamous idols. Alexander, Caesar, Plato—if you could hear me you would blush in the depth of your tombs! But, in your stead, more than one among us may be found who reads here his humiliating history.

A hero in manhood. He is acquainted with the nobility and the capacity of his heart. He has measured the earth, and found it too small for him. He has seen the riches, the honors, the idols of the full-grown man, and he has said: "I am above all these things; I was born for greater things." No one has seen him, descending to base intrigues, quarrel over the blood-stained shreds of a royal mantle, or, false to conscience and honor, attempt to overthrow society by his speeches and writings. No one has heard him, coloring self-interest with the pretext of the public welfare in order to arrive at fortune, repeat, with a threat upon his lips and hatred in his heart against everything above him, that ignoble refrain which is too faithful a summary of the political history of our days: "Away with thee hence, that I may take thy place."

A hero in old age. His great soul expands more and more at the thought of eternity. He beholds with calmness the approach of his last hour: it is he who consoles the bystanders. This is the hero whom Christian ages have seen in every costume, and in every rank of society. Today we meet him again: sometimes in the city; more frequently in the country, under the rough garb of the peasant. Such is man, taught, strengthened, and ennobled by the sacraments in every circumstance of life.

What is your opinion? Would a society composed of such citizens be inferior to ours? Has modern Europe gained much in tranquility, in disinterestedness, in morality, in candor, in sanctity, since the sacraments were abandoned or denounced? Do you now perceive that religion, which seems to have no other object than the happiness of the next life, is also the best means to secure the happiness of this? If you do—and if you are, as you say, the friends of society—then practice religion, receive the sacraments. Believe me, whatever may be your rank, your age, your intelligence, your position, you have no less need of doing so than others. If you will not, why cease to complain of the insubordination, the immorality, the deceit, the misery—what do I say?—all the evils that make social life one long torment: for all these calamities are your work. By your indifference you are the leaders of revolutions; it is you who inspire all those wild utopian ideas that threaten to transform the civilized world into a den of thieves and murderers. The most dangerous sophism is bad example; and the worst kind of bad example is indifference to religion.

By what right do you pretend that others should have recourse to the sacraments and become virtuous if you do not begin by giving them the good example thereof? Do you not perceive that on their lips the following argument must be unanswerable: either it is necessary to frequent the sacraments in order to subdue one's passions, or it is not. If it is, why do you not frequent them? If it is not, why would you impose on us a yoke which you think it well not to bear yourselves? Men like us, you are weak like us: Why would you oblige us to repress our passions for the advantage of yours?

From the social advantages of the sacraments, let us pass on to their touching harmony with all our wants.

Their harmony with our wants.—Relying on the express testimonies of the scripture, the authority of tradition, and the decisions of councils, the Catholic Church recognizes seven sacraments.[633] But why did the new Adam establish seven, neither more nor less? Here is the chief reason: the grand aim of religion, and consequently of the sacraments, is to form, maintain, and perpetuate in us the spiritual life. Now, there are seven things necessary for man to lead the natural life, to preserve it, and to employ it usefully. He must be born, he must grow, he must be fed, he must make use of remedies to recover his health when he falls sick, he must recruit his strength when he is exhausted, he must have magistrates invested with authority to provide for the public weal, and, finally, he must perpetuate himself and the human race by the legitimate birth of children.

Well, all these things are necessary for the spiritual life, and enable us to see the reason why the number of the sacraments is seven.

By baptism, which is the first of all, and, as it were, the door to the others, we are born to Jesus Christ; by confirmation we grow in the spiritual life; the Eucharist feeds us; penance cures us; extreme unction effaces the remains of sin, renews the energies of the soul, and prepares us for everlasting glory; holy orders perpetuate in the Church the ministers of the sacraments; and matrimony perpetuates the faithful.[634]

It was thus that the Savior provided for all the spiritual wants of man from the cradle to the grave, and for the perpetuity of the Christian republic. Let us now come to details. In order to render as clear and complete as possible our explanation of the sacraments, we shall treat of the following points in connection with each of them: a) its definition; b) its elements; c) its institution; d) its efficacy or effects; e) dispositions with which it is to be received; f) its necessity; g) its liturgy; h) the social advantages which result from it.

Definition of baptism.—The first ring in that long chain of benefits which the new Adam prepared to support man along the road of life: baptism is a sacrament which effaces original sin, gives us a divine life, and makes us children of God and of the Church. That baptism is a sacrament of the new law is a truth regarding which an attentive examination of its definition leaves no doubt. We saw in the last lesson that the sacraments are sensible signs, instituted by our Lord Jesus Christ for the sanctification of our souls. Now, baptism brings together these various conditions.

It is a) a sensible sign. The water poured on the head of the person baptized, the words pronounced by the minister: behold the sensible sign. It is b) a sign instituted by our Lord. It is c) a sign which has the virtue of producing grace, that is to say, of effacing original sin, giving a divine life, and making us children of God and of the Church. We shall see the proofs of these things in the course of the present lesson. The belief of the heretics of all ages, as well as that of Catholics, may be added to the reasons given already to prove that baptism is a true sacrament of the new law. On this point there is so much unanimity that the Council of Trent did not consider it necessary to make any particular canon to vindicate the faith of the Church.[635]

Elements of baptism.—The matter of baptism is any kind of natural water—water from the sea, from a river, from a marsh, from a well, from a fountain—every sort that bears simply the name of water. Let us here remark the infinite goodness of our Lord. The sacrament of baptism being absolutely necessary for salvation to all men, he chose as its matter water, which is to be found everywhere and always. Moreover, water represents very well the effect of baptism. It cleans the body, and thereby sensibly expresses the action of baptism on the soul, which by means of this sacrament is purified from sin. Besides, it has the property of cooling the body, as baptism has the virtue of lessening in a great measure the heat of the passions. Finally, water is the mother of the material world: sanctified, it becomes in baptism the mother of the moral world.

To administer baptism validly, it is not necessary that the water should be blessed. Yet, except in a case of necessity, one should only employ the water of fonts, solemnly blessed, according to an ancient tradition, on the eves of Easter and Pentecost. The Church forbids the first of her sacraments to be administered with common water, either the better to express the effects of baptism, or to increase the respect which is due to it.

The form consists of the words which the minister pronounces at the time of pouring the water on the person to be baptized. They are these: "I baptize thee in the name of the Father, and of the Son, and of the Holy Ghost." These words should be pronounced: a) not before or after, but during the ablution; b) by the person who makes the ablution; c) with the intention of baptizing, that is to say, with the intention of giving the sacrament instituted by our Lord and administered by the Church when it baptizes—otherwise, the baptism would be invalid. It is on the head, in preference to any other part of the body, that the water should be poured, because the head seems to be the place in which all the interior and exterior senses meet. In every case the water should touch the skin, and not merely the hair.

Modes of baptism.—The Church admits three modes of administering baptism validly: a) by plunging the person to be baptized in water—baptism by immersion; b) by pouring water on him—baptism by infusion; c) by sprinkling water on him, either with the hand or with a brush—baptism by aspersion.

By immersion. Baptism by immersion was that most used in the early ages of the Church. If the person to be baptized was a man, the priest and the godfather, taking him by the hand, accompanied him down the steps of the sacred font, and plunged him thrice in the salutary water. If a woman, the priest and the godmother acted in like manner. These three immersions, without being necessary to the validity of the sacrament, may be traced back to the first ages of Christianity.[636] They were made in the name and in honor of the three Persons of the Blessed Trinity, and they brought to mind the resurrection of our Lord after having lain three days in the tomb. Baptism by immersion continued in use till the fourteenth century: it is still practiced in several churches of the East.

By infusion. Baptism by infusion is the mode in use among us. It has been known from the apostolic times. It was thus administered in cases of necessity, and these cases were not rare. How, for example, could a sick man, just ready to expire, be immersed in water? Where could a martyr, shut up in prison, find water enough to plunge therein his guards or his jailers, who were converted at the sight of his miracles or by the consideration of his patience and his courage?

By aspersion. Finally, baptism by aspersion takes place in cases of necessity. For the rest, it matters little whether one or three ablutions are made: baptism with one or several ablutions has always been regarded as valid, but it is necessary to observe the rite prescribed by the Church.

Kinds of baptism.—We distinguish three kinds of baptism. The first is the baptism of water: this is the sacrament. The second is the baptism of fire: this denotes a movement of the Holy Ghost which produces faith, charity, and repentance in the soul—consequently a desire, at least implicit, of receiving the sacrament of baptism.[637] The third is the baptism of blood: this is martyrdom. The second and third are not sacraments. We give them the name of *baptism*, because they purify the soul from sin, and supply for the want of the sacrament when it cannot be had.[638]

The ministers of the sacrament of baptism are bishops and priests. Yet, in the first ages of the Church—before the establishment of parishes, which were called titles—as the bishops governed their diòceses immediately and conjointly with their clergy, it was usually the bishop, as chief pastor, who solemnly administered baptism, especially at Easter and Pentecost. This usage was still existing in the sixth century.

In the course of time, when many country people had embraced the Christian religion, the bishops alone no longer sufficed to give baptism. Baptisteries were therefore established throughout the country districts for the convenience of the inhabitants, who would have found it very hard to bring their children a considerable distance to the episcopal city in order to have them baptized, particularly in the large dioceses of France and Germany. Henceforth, priests usually baptized in the little towns and villages where no bishop resided. When there was no priest at hand, deacons conferred this sacrament. Still the deacons could not, they cannot yet, administer baptism without the leave of the bishop or priest.

Formerly the ministers of baptism should be fasting, to confer this august sacrament. Even the whole Church fasted to draw on catechumens the favorable looks of the Lord. The obligation of fasting had to cease when it became the custom to give baptism every day and every hour of the day. The ministers of the Church used to array themselves for this grand ceremony in their most magnificent robes. Constantine the Great made a present to the Church of Jerusalem of a robe woven of gold, that the bishop might clothe himself with it when administering baptism.

Finally, as a mark of his infinite goodness, our Lord wished that, in case of necessity, baptism might be administered, but without ceremony, by any person in the world, man or woman, no matter of what religion, provided the person baptizing had the intention therein of doing what the Church does when it administers this sacrament. Remark, however, that a woman should not baptize in presence of a man, unless she is better instructed on the matter; nor a layman in presence of a cleric; nor a cleric in presence of a priest: for in all these things order should be observed.[639]

Hence, all the faithful ought to know the manner of conferring baptism, since they may find themselves some time or other under the necessity of giving it. Holy water, or, for want of it, natural water from a well, cistern, or fountain, is procured. One pours the water on the head of the child in such a manner as to touch it, saying: "I baptize thee in the name of the Father" (pouring the water in the form of a cross), "and of the Son" (pouring the water again in the form of a cross), "and of the Holy Ghost" (pouring the water a third time in the form of a cross). We must remark hereupon that the signs of the cross are not necessary to the validity of baptism. Let us add that parents are rigorously bound to have their children baptized as soon as possible after birth: if these little ones die without baptism, as often happens at this uncertain age, parents are responsible for the loss.[640]

Godfathers and godmothers; their duties.—Besides the persons who confer baptism, there are others who concur in the ceremony in a different manner: they are godfathers and godmothers.[641] The custom of giving them to those who sought baptism may be traced back to the beginning of the Church.[642] The godfathers and godmothers used to present the catechumens, to watch over them during the time of their instruction, to receive them on coming forth from the sacred font, to answer to the Church for them, and to become guarantees for their faith. It was on this account that they were called bails and sureties. Later, they received the name of godfathers and godmothers, that is to say, other fathers and mothers, because they concur to the spiritual birth of the person baptized.

Nothing wiser than this arrangement. To be convinced of this, it suffices to recollect that baptism is a spiritual regeneration, by which we become children of God. It is thus that St. Peter speaks: "As newborn babes, desire the pure spiritual milk."[643] Beautiful words, which it was usual in the primitive Church to explain to the newly baptized eight days after their great happiness.

Now, when a child comes into the world it has need of a nurse and a master: the former to give it the necessary food; the latter to instruct it in the arts and sciences. Accordingly, those who are born to Jesus Christ by baptism require to be confided to the solicitude and wisdom of someone who may train them to the practice of virtue, by instructing them in the precepts of religion and making them grow up little by little in the new Adam, until, by the grace of God, they become perfect.[644]

Such is the duty, such are the functions of godfathers and godmothers. Here is what they said in the first ages of the Church, and what they still say by the very fact of accepting their title: "I promise to engage this child by careful instruction and exhortation—when it shall be of an age to understand religion—to renounce everything evil, to profess its faith openly, and to fulfill exactly the promises which it now makes to God."[645] Although the majority hardly ever think of it, this obligation subsists in full force; but it lasts only till the time when godchildren are in a state to guide themselves. The case of godfathers and godmothers is the same as that of tutors or guardians: their obligations cease when the persons confided to their care are in a condition to pass from it.

The relations between godfathers and godmothers and their godchildren are therefore very close and sacred. It was accordingly an evidence of deep wisdom in the Church to establish from the beginning a spiritual affinity between the person who baptizes and the person who is baptized—between the godfather or godmother and the godchild and its father and mother. Whence it follows that marriage cannot be contracted between these persons, and, if contracted, is radically null.

From what we have said on the duties of godfathers and godmothers, it is easy to see who those are that should not be entrusted with so holy a function.

Institution of baptism.—Following the order of the words which constitute the definition of baptism, this is the place to speak of the institution of the sacrament. Our Lord instituted it when he was himself baptized by St. John. The fathers of the Church teach us so expressly, when they say that at this moment water received the virtue of regenerating, by giving a spiritual life.[646] Here you find the reason why, during the baptism of our Lord, the whole Blessed Trinity, in whose name baptism is conferred, manifested its presence. The voice of the Father was heard, the Person of the Son was seen, and the Holy Ghost descended under the form of a dove; moreover, the heavens opened, as they open for us at baptism.

Our Lord manifested to Nicodemus the institution of this sacrament when he said: "Unless a man be born again of water and the Holy Ghost, he cannot enter into the kingdom of God."[647] The obligation of receiving baptism in order to be saved began on the day when our Lord said to his apostles: "Go, teach all nations, baptizing them in the name of the Father, and of the Son, and of the Holy Ghost."[648]

Effects of baptism.—All the preparations that formerly preceded baptism, all the solemn circumstances that still accompany its administration, cannot surprise us if we reflect for a while on the greatness of this sacrament. Let us judge of it by its effects.

1. It effaces original sin, and all the actual sins, however enormous, that one may have committed before its reception. Such has been the constant doctrine of the Church, formally defined by the Council of Trent.[649]

2. It remits all the punishment due to sin, so that he who dies immediately after baptism goes straight to heaven.[650] The ignorance and the concupiscence which remain in us after baptism are indeed the consequences of original sin, but they are not sins.[651] The new Adam did not choose to deliver man from them during this life, any more than from corporal infirmities. It was necessary that man should be mindful of his fall; that this earth should be a place of exile to him; that he should live in humiliation and self-distrust; that all these miseries, becoming a continual exercise for his virtue, should give him occasion to merit, and make him sigh after heaven, where his deliverance shall be complete and perfect.

3. Baptism gives us a divine life, and makes us children of God. It is by baptism that we become participators in the life of the new Adam. Hence, the grace of baptism is a grace inherent to our soul, effacing all its stains, cleansing it from all its defilements, and communicating to it all the infused virtues, faith, hope, charity, and the gifts of the Holy Ghost, which render it beautiful and pleasing in the sight of God. We are by this means incorporated with our Lord, as members with their head, and

God adopts us as his children and makes us the heirs of his kingdom and co-heirs with Jesus Christ.[652]

4. Baptism makes us children of the Church. It places us among the number of the faithful, gives us a right to the other sacraments, and enables us to share in all the goods of our mother the Church. Without baptism we are incapable of receiving the other sacraments, so that the ordination of a person who should be ordained priest without having been baptized would be absolutely null, and it should be repeated again after baptizing him.[653]

5. Baptism imprints on the soul an indelible character, which prevents the reception of the sacrament a second time. "As, according to the order of nature," says St. Augustine, "we can be born only once, so there is only one spiritual regeneration, and baptism can never be repeated."[654]

The dispositions with which baptism is to be received and the obligations which it imposes.—The effects of baptism are the same for all, insofar as the virtue of the sacrament is concerned. But if we regard the dispositions of those who receive it, it is quite certain that everyone draws from it more or less abundant fruit according to the state of his soul. The Church does not require any special dispositions from children who have not attained the use of reason, in order to administer baptism to them. She lends them her heart and mouth, because they cannot yet believe with their own heart in order to be justified, nor confess with their own mouth in order to be saved. "As they were wounded by the sin of another," says St. Augustine, "so they are healed by the word of another."[655]

From adults, the Church requires the following dispositions: a) consent; b) faith; c) instruction, that is to say, a knowledge of the things which, by a necessity of means and a necessity of precept, must be believed; d) sincere sorrow for their sins.

As to the obligations that we contract in baptism, they rest, on the one side, on the promises which we therein make to God, and which are called vows, and there are none, says St. Augustine, more sacred; on the other, on the inestimable gifts which God therein bestows on us. "Much shall be required," says the Savior, "of him to whom much is given."[656] These obligations consist in a) remaining steadfastly attached to Jesus Christ, following his gospel as the rule of our principles and morals, because baptism is a solemn profession of Christianity; in b) remaining always united to the Church, obeying it and its pastors, because baptism makes us members of that mystical body whose head is Jesus Christ, that is to say, the Church, out of which we cannot live by the Spirit of Jesus Christ—no one can have God for his Father who has not the Church for his mother; and in c) renouncing everything contrary to that life which the children of God should lead.

It is very proper to renew frequently one's baptismal promises, in order to excite one's self to their fulfillment, to avoid entangling one's self in the pomps of the age, and to repair the faults that one has committed against these solemn vows. This excellent practice is often recommended by the fathers of the Church.[657]

Necessity of baptism for salvation.—Of all the sacraments, the most necessary is baptism. Faith teaches us that no person unbaptized can be saved, that is, can be admitted to the vision of God, face-to-face in heaven. The words of our Savior are formal: "Unless a man be born again of water and the Holy Ghost, he cannot enter into the kingdom of God."[658] Such has been in all ages the invariable doctrine of the Church, solemnly proclaimed by the Council of Trent.

"If any one assert," said this august assembly, "that the sin of Adam, single in its source, but common to all and proper to each person by transmission, and not by simple imitation, is effaced by human effects, or by any other means than the merits of our only meditator, our Lord Jesus Christ, who reconciled us to God in his blood, by becoming our justice, our sanctification, and our redemption; or deny that the said merits of Jesus Christ are applied to children and adults by the sacrament of baptism, conferred according to the forms used in the Church: let him be anathema."[659]

Yet it does not suffice to be baptized in order to be saved. We must fulfill the sacred obligations imposed on us by the august title of children of God, which is given us at baptism. Here is an example of the fidelity with which we ought, in spite of every obstacle, to hold fast to our sacred engagements:

"During the persecution which lately took place," writes a missionary of the Indies, "a little pagan girl, only ten years old, was married to a Gentile. Too young to follow her husband, she remained some years under the guardianship of her mother, a pagan like herself. Suddenly the mother formed the desire of becoming a Christian, and eagerly sought instructions for this purpose. It was I who bestowed the first cares on her. After a sufficient trial, I promised to give her baptism, and fixed the day for doing so.

"The girl, unwilling to remain an idolater without her mother, earnestly asked to be baptized with her. I resisted her solicitations for a long time, as well because she did not appear to me enlightened enough as because I feared that her tender faith would run too great a risk under the roof of a pagan husband, in the bosom of an idolatrous family, in a village where no Catholic might be found to lend her support. My refusals did not discourage her. She associated herself with her mother, and the two overwhelmed me with entreaties to be made together the children of God.

"Meanwhile, the husband of the young pagan returned: he came to bring her away with him. I sent for him, informed him of the wishes and entreaties of his wife, and asked him if he would consent to her becoming a Christian. He consented, assuring me that he would leave his wife free in the exercise of her new faith. On his word, I baptized my two catechumens in 1835. The young woman departed with her husband: she was then thirteen years of age.

"On the first announcement of this baptism, the persecutors wrote a furious letter to the chief men of the village in which this poor neophyte had arrived, and threatened to take vengeance on them if they did not immediately oblige her to apostatize and to sacrifice in the pagoda to the idols which she had cursed. Terrified by these threats, they summoned the neophyte, and commanded her to renounce Jesus Christ and return to the gods of her fathers. 'Neither the one nor the other will I do,' she answered; 'here is my head: it will fall rather than that I should betray my faith.'

"Unable to shake her constancy,'they had recourse to her husband, and imperatively required that he should strive to disengage her from her religion. The husband was only too fit an instrument for their fury. To seduce his young wife from her allegiance, he first employed the arts of insinuation; but, finding them useless, he resolved to try the effects of violence. Such was his brutality that, one day, armed with a huge stick, he beat her for a long time, till her body was one immense wound. 'Renounce your God,' he would say to her, 'or I will kill you.' But she, as strong as he was cruel, made answer: 'Kill me; I will remain faithful to my God.' On hearing this, a kind of frenzy seemed to take possession of the Gentile. He seized a knife, threw his wife on the ground, laid his foot on her breast, held the knife over her face, and said to her: 'Unless you abjure, I will cut off your nose.' 'Do so,' she replied, 'but I will remain a Christian.' A last instinct of humanity, or an irresistible respect for heroic courage, moderated the fury of the pagan. He made a slight wound on her face, instead of disfiguring it; after which he banished her from his house.

"Tender and good at all times, to the highest degree of heroism, the poor woman took in her arms her little child of two months, which she was suckling, and set out on a journey of eighteen miles to seek with her mother that home which her husband denied her. May the Lord bless her courage, and fill the heart of her child with all the generosity of its mother's faith!"

PRAYER

O my God! who art all love, I thank thee for having instituted the sacraments, which are like so many fountains of grace. I thank thee for having given me birth in thy holy Church, and admitted me to baptism.

I am resolved to love God above all things, and my neighbor as myself for the love of God; and, in testimony of this love, I will every year celebrate the anniversary of my baptism.

Lesson 34: Our Union with the New Adam by Hope (7)

Explaining in succession every word of the definition of baptism, we spoke to you in the last lesson of the elements, the institution, and the effects of this sacrament, the dispositions which it requires, and its necessity. It remains for us to explain its liturgy, that is, the ceremonies which accompany its administration, and the social advantages derived from it.

Liturgy of baptism since the times of the primitive Church.—Like the history of all the other sacraments, that of baptism may be traced back to our Lord Jesus Christ. It is he whom we always behold opening to men these fountains of salvation. Before ascending to heaven, he said to the depositaries of his doctrine: "Go, teach all nations, baptizing them in the name of the Father, and of the Son, and of the Holy Ghost." Obedient to the commands of their divine master, the apostles preached throughout the world the necessity of baptism. Since then, the Church has never ceased to baptize.

The vigilant spouse of the Son of God has, in her profound wisdom, surrounded baptism, as well as all the other sacraments, with ceremonies and prayers. Without doubt this majestic apparel adds nothing to the essence of the sacraments, but it is wonderfully well calculated to render them more august in our eyes, by raising our minds to a comprehension of the admirable effects which they produce in our souls. Let us go back in fancy to the early ages of the Church, ages of happy memory, and see what the Church used to do in order to inspire men with a profound veneration for the first of her sacraments.

Catechumens, ceremonies, and preparations.—Before giving baptism to those who sought it, she placed them in the rank of catechumens. The word *catechumen* means "one catechized." This name was given to those who were orally instructed in the truths of religion, to dispose them for baptism. The rites of their reception were simple: the sign of the cross was made on their foreheads, and hands were imposed on them with some suitable prayers. The catechumens were divided into three classes.

The hearers, or first class, were those admitted to hear the instructions which were given in the church. They were permitted to assist at that part of the Mass which derived its name from them, the Mass of the catechumens. It began at the introit, and ended at the offertory. They could also hear the reading of the holy scriptures, and the exhortations or sermons of bishops, which usually followed the reading of the gospel. This advantage was common between them, penitents, Jews, pagans, and even heretics. The discourse being finished, a deacon said in a loud voice: "Catechumens, penitents, Jews, heretics, infidels, depart." And they all went out. The second class were those who had the right of remaining in the church a little while after the departure of the first, and who prostrated themselves to receive the bishop's blessing. When they were found capable of receiving baptism, they gave in their names for this purpose. They were then called competitors, that is to say, persons asking together. When their petition was granted, they were called the elect, because they were destined to receive baptism on the first occasion, that is to say, the following Easter or Pentecost, and formed the third class of catechumens.

Before sending them out of the church, some prayers were recited for them. The deacon, having imposed silence, said: "Pray, catechumens, and let all the faithful pray for them, that the Lord, who is full of goodness and compassion, may hear their prayers and supplications; that he may discover to them the gospel of his Christ; that he may inspire them with a chaste and salutary fear; that he may confirm them in piety, and render them worthy of regeneration, of the robe of immortality, of the true life." After these words, the deacon added: "Arise, catechumens; ask the peace of God through Jesus Christ." The people answered: "Lord, have mercy!"

A very touching incident occurred here, which we should not omit to mention.

After exhorting the people in general, the deacon exhorted the children in particular, because of their innocence, to pray. It was for the same reason that St. Basil and St. Chrysostom desired that children should be asked to pray in all public necessities, their prayers having a special efficacy in appeasing and averting the anger of God.[660] When these human angels had ceased their tender supplications, the catechumens bowed to receive the bishop's blessing. Then the deacon said anew: "Catechumens, depart." Afterward the doors of the church were closed, and the Mass of the faithful, which began with the oblation of the gifts destined for the sacrifice, was celebrated.

The catechumens were instructed with much care. Those who exercised this function were called catechists. The greatest men were often charged with it: witness Pantenus, Clement of Alexandria, Origen, Heraclas, and various others. The period of this instruction was usually two years.[661] It was prolonged for those who fell into considerable faults. When the day of baptism drew nigh, the catechumens fasted and confessed.[662] The faithful themselves fasted for them. The whole Church betook itself to prayer.

There were now held some particular assemblies, which were called scrutinies, because the sentiments and dispositions of those who should be baptized were examined therein. This is the reason why it was not thought enough to explain the Creed and the Lord's Prayer: they were also given in writing, that they might be learned by heart. In the following scrutinies, those who received them were obliged to repeat them word by word, and to give an account of them. They were also bound to bring back the manuscript which contained them, lest it should fall into profane hands. This was called the return of the Symbol. It usually took place eight days after the delivery or exposition of the Creed.

In these assemblies, exorcisms were made on the catechumens, to banish the devil, and to purify those whom sin had subjected to his dominion. The priest made the sign of the cross on their foreheads with his thumb and laid his hand on their heads, saying as he came to each one the prayer of the elect. He next put salt into their mouths—a salt which had been blessed and exorcised in their presence.

Then followed the imposing ceremony of opening the ears, destined to put the catechumens in a state to hear the gospel and the Symbol of the faith, which were about to be explained to them. While the priests were proceeding to touch their ears, two lessons from the scripture were read, asking God to cure the deafness of their hearts. Four deacons were next to be seen coming from the sacristy, bearing the four gospels in separate volumes, and preceded by tapers and censers.

Each deacon went and laid his gospel on one of the corners of the altar. Before any of the gospels was opened the bishop addressed a discourse to the catechumens, to teach them what the gospel was and who were its authors. A deacon then took the gospel of St. Matthew, and, going to the jubé, read the beginning of it there with many ceremonies. The bishop explained that which had just been read before the whole assembly. It was the same with the other evangelists. Attention was drawn to their different characteristics, that the catechumens might better relish the doctrine of our Lord. All these explanations being ended, the Mass of the faithful began.

At length, the much desired moment of baptism arrived. In the primitive Church, baptism was administered on the eves of Easter and Pentecost, because the former of these feasts brought to mind the departure from Egypt, and the latter the abolition of Judaism and the introduction of the law of grace. However, when necessity required it, baptism was administered at all times. It was also permitted to administer baptism to children, even when they ran no risk of life, if the parents presented them and desired that they should be baptized.

It was in the beginning of night that solemn baptism was given, because the baptism and confirmation of neophytes should precede the office, which was very long on the eves of great solemnities, and during which they should participate with the rest of the Christians in the awful mysteries. The practice of baptizing at night was long preserved in the majority of the churches—in some, even to the end of the eleventh century. The reality corresponded perfectly with the figure.

It was during night that the children of Israel crossed the Red Sea, and escaped from the slavery of Pharao: a slavery which was only a shadow of that of the devil, from which we escape by baptism. If in the course of time the Church forbade the administration of baptism at night, it was because the observance of sacred watchings had been done away with for several centuries, and in our days it would be very inconvenient to baptize at this hour.

When then everything was ready, the catechumens, led by their godfathers and godmothers, were presented before the bishop and priests. Three imposing ceremonies immediately took place:

1. *The renunciation of the devil.* The bishop asked the catechumens: "Do you renounce Satan?" Whoever was to be baptized answered: "I renounce him." "And all his works?" "I renounce them." "And all his pomps?" "I renounce them."

2. *The unction.* An unction of exorcised oil was made first on the head, and then between the shoulders and on the breast of the catechumens. This was to denote their union with Jesus Christ, who is a rich olive tree, and their vocation to encounter as athletes the devil whom they had just renounced.

3. *The profession of faith.* The catechumens were asked: "Do you believe in God, the Father Almighty?" "I believe." "Do you believe in Jesus Christ, his only Son, our Lord, who was born and who suffered?" "I believe." "Do you believe in the Holy Ghost, the holy Catholic Church, the forgiveness of sins, the resurrection of the body?" "I believe."[663] Assured of the dispositions and the belief of the catechumens, the bishop and priests proceeded toward the baptistery to open its gates for the new elect.

Baptistery.—The baptisteries were usually buildings of a circular form,[664] apart from the church, and sometimes so spacious that large assemblies might be held in them.[665] The faith of our forefathers was attentive to everything that could add to the embellishment of these places, in which the great mystery of regeneration was accomplished. The purest gold and the most exquisite marbles shone on all sides. But nothing can give us a better idea of the magnificence of early baptisteries than the description of that of St. John Lateran at Rome, built by the emperor Constantine.

It was a magnificent square hall, with walls of marble and porphyry. In the center was to be seen a basin of porphyry, adorned with silver, in which the baptismal waters were preserved; from the middle of the basin rose a column of porphyry, supporting a golden vase 50 pounds weight, which contained the holy chrism for the unctions of the newly baptized. On one side of the basin were steps to descend into it; on the other, a golden lamb, which jetted water into it. At the two extremities were silver statues, one of our Lord, the other of St. John the Baptist, each weighing 170 pounds. Around the sides of the basin were seven large silver harts, emblems of souls that pant after the salutary fountains: each of them weighed 80 pounds, and jetted water into the basin.

Let one imagine that he beholds this superb edifice gloriously lighted up—the gold and silver and marble sparkling in all their dazzling brilliancy; a multitude of the faithful, and of catechumens, in white garments; a venerable pontiff, surrounded by a numerous clergy, presiding at this august ceremony, and he will have a faint idea of the magnificence and solemnity of the nights of Easter and Pentecost.

Administration of baptism.—In the center of every baptistery was the font, into which a descent was made by several steps. It was from the last step that the bishop and the godfather plunged into the sacred bath him who was to be baptized. The immersion was repeated three times in the name of the three Persons of the Blessed Trinity. As soon as the newly baptized ascended from the font, the godfather presented him to a priest, who, taking holy chrism, made therewith the sign of the cross on the top of the man's head with his thumb, saying, "May Almighty God, the Father of our Lord Jesus Christ, who has regenerated thee by water and the Holy Ghost, and who has given thee pardon of all thy sins, anoint thee with the chrism of salvation unto life everlasting." The baptized man answered: "Amen."

The newly baptized were now handed linens by the sponsors, to wipe themselves. They were next clothed with a white dress, which they wore for eight days as a sign of joy. To the white dress was added a chrism-cloth, which has since taken its place. The chrism-cloth was a covering for the head, which, out of respect for the holy chrism, was worn by the newly baptized immediately after the anointing made thereon by the priest.

After baptism, the bishop withdrew to the sacristy, while the neophytes dressed themselves to be confirmed. The white robes in which they were arrayed were a sign of innocence and spiritual liberty. In effect, among the Romans it was usual to clothe in white those slaves who were granted their freedom. It is thus that antiquity, even profane antiquity, reappears in the ceremonies of the Church. The use of these white garments may be traced back to the beginning of Christianity.[666]

When the neophytes were dressed, they were arranged according to the order in which their names were enrolled. Children were held by the right arm, and adults placed one foot on a foot of their sponsors. The choir intoned the litany, and the bishop returned to administer confirmation. The ceremony being over, all the neophytes received a lighted taper, and were led in procession toward the altar singing psalms. St. Gregory acquaints us with the mysterious reasons for this usage, when he says: "After baptism you are led toward the altar. This is a prelude to that glory which is prepared for you. The altar is heaven. The singing of psalms, with which you are received, announces to you beforehand the future praises. The torches which you carry denote the light with which you should go to meet the bridegroom."[667]

Arrived at the altar, the neophytes received the Holy Communion. Milk and honey were next given them, to make them understand that by the sacraments in which they had just participated they were come into possession of the true land of promise, of which Palestine was only a figure.[668] This usage came from the apostolic times.

The eight days which followed baptism were feast days. They were spent in thanksgiving—in prayers and good works. Every day the newly baptized were instructed. It was not thought enough to catechize them, as had been done in their preparation for baptism; more detailed instructions were addressed to them, in order to give them an explanation of mysteries which could be discovered only to the faithful, and to make them understand their virtue and efficacy. These discourses were called "mystagogics," because they contained an explanation of our mysteries. In a word, nothing was omitted to give them a high idea of the dignity of the state to which God had called them, and to excite them to be mindful during their whole lives of the graces and benefits which they had just received. The sanctity with which the Church shone in those happy days teaches us that these cares were not in vain.

The newly baptized were objects of veneration to the whole Church; so much so that when any favor was desired of emperors or kings they were employed to ask it. It was believed, moreover, that God attached special blessings to their presence. In effect, were they not his beloved children, the living temples of the Holy Ghost? It was under this impression that, when Belisarius was setting out with his fleet to recover Africa from the Vandals, the emperor ordered the chief vessel to be drawn up on the shore, near the imperial palace, and there the patriarch Epiphanius, having recited some prayers suitable for the blessing of the ship, put on board a soldier lately baptized, so as to draw upon the fleet the blessings of the God of hosts.[669]

The neophytes wore their white dress for eight days. On the eighth day of this holy octave—when baptism had been given on the eve of Easter—this touching introit was sung at Mass: "As newborn babes, desire the pure milk, whereby you may grow unto salvation."[670] And the greatest doctors of the Church, the Augustines and the Chrysostoms, explained to them the admirable meaning of these divine words.

Such were in the early ages of the Church the ceremonies that preceded, accompanied, and followed the administration of baptism. The happy day on which our ancestors in the faith became children of God and of the Church was in their eyes the loveliest of their life. Every year they celebrated with renewed fervor the feast of their baptism. This was called the annotine Pasch, because those who had been baptized at Easter celebrated the anniversary of their regeneration on the same day the following year. The word *annotine* means "annual."

On this day the baptized, for whom the feast came specially round, put on again their white robes, and made with great solemnity the offering for the sacrifice. They were accompanied by their sponsors and parents, particularly if they were yet children. After the service, all joined together in an innocent feast. This tender custom was still existing in the thirteenth century. It died away in the Church with that of giving solemn baptism on special occasions to adults; but what is there to hinder any of us from reviving and preserving it?

We have seen that the neophytes, children as well as adults, received confirmation and the Eucharist on coming forth from the baptismal font. Thus, they were at the same time put in possession of all the goods and advantages of the Church. This practice, which still subsists in the East, was preserved among us till about the thirteenth century. As for confirmation, when bishops no longer administered baptism by themselves, the increase of their flocks and the extent of their dioceses rendered this function impossible. With regard to Communion, it altogether ceased when, for the wisest reasons, the Church forbade it to be given under the two species: this was done in the beginning of the fifteenth century, at the Council of Constance.[671]

Let us now come to an explanation of the prayers and ceremonies which, at the present day, accompany the administration of baptism. Better than any discourse, they will acquaint us not only with the sad condition in which we are born, but with the dignity of this sacrament, the rank to which it raises us, and the obligation of sanctity which it imposes on us. To render, even in the eyes of reason, the prayers and ceremonies of baptism worthy of respect, it suffices to say that they are the same now as in the early days of Christianity. This venerable antiquity, whose beauty is in our times so much admired, is perceptible through all the ceremonies of baptism that are actually in use. If some, very few indeed, are no longer used, even their suppression is a proof of the wise solicitude of the Church.

Honey and milk.—Here are two new examples of this. The triple immersion was suppressed by Pope St. Gregory in the churches of Spain because certain heretics of that country pretended to authorize their errors regarding the Trinity by this triple immersion, from which they inferred, and endeavored to persuade others, that there were three substances in the Trinity. In like manner, the custom of giving milk and honey to the newly baptized was abolished because in certain places a practice was set on foot of mixing the milk and honey in the chalice with the wine which was to be consecrated—a thing forbidden. The custom of giving milk and honey continued till the ninth century.

Ceremonies and prayers which, at the present day, accompany the administration of baptism.—To understand well the ceremonies of baptism, it must be known that at the present day the Church attaches all those which she has preserved to one occasion. We shall now explain them.

1. *Ceremonies which precede baptism.* These are the ceremonies with which the catechumens were anciently familiar. When a child is born, some humble woman takes it in her arms, and, accompanied by a godfather and a godmother, comes to the church. On the threshold of the sacred edifice stands a priest, who stops it. The priest is robed in a surplice, whose whiteness is symbolic of innocence, and a purple stole. The purple color, employed by the Church on days of sadness and mourning, here points out the miserable state to which sin has reduced guilty man. After the exorcisms, whose object is to banish the devil from this little creature of God, the priest assumes a white stole which reminds one of the innocence conferred by the sacrament.

The priest stops the child at the door of the church, to make known to it that it has no right to enter the house of God. Addressing himself to the godfather and godmother, he asks what name they give the child. A name is bestowed on it *a*) to teach it that by baptism it becomes a new creature, engaged in the service of Jesus Christ, and *b*) to give it a protector and a model in heaven. Wherefore it is only the names of saints that children receive. The custom of giving a name to the newly baptized is most ancient in the Church. Examples of it may be traced down from the first ages.[672] Our ancestors in the faith usually selected for their children the names of the apostles and martyrs, in order to place them under the protection of those saints in whom they had very great confidence.[673]

What would they say if they heard parents asking to have profane or heathen names—formerly unknown among true Catholics—imposed on their children?[674] This abuse has been proscribed by councils. The Church wishes that the names of the saints of the new testament should be given to children, that they may thereby be excited to imitate their virtues, to pray often to them, and to have recourse to them in every difficulty as to so many advocates and patrons around the throne of God. As for each of us, to celebrate with special fervor and gratitude the feast of our holy patron is a duty as sacred as it ought to be pleasant. This duty implies the necessity of knowing his or her life, in order to bear with honor the glorious name that has been given us.

The priest says to the child: "What dost thou demand of the Church of God?" "Faith," replies the child by the mouth of its sponsors. "What does faith procure thee?" "Life everlasting." "If then thou wilt enter into life, keep the commandments." And he adds in a few words the sublime abridgment of all divine and human laws: "Thou shalt love the Lord thy God with thy whole heart, and thy neighbor as thyself."

Satisfied with its dispositions, the priest breathes thrice on the child's face, saying: "Depart, unclean spirit, and give place to the Holy Ghost the Comforter." The breath is employed to banish the devil, in order to show the contempt in which he is held, as well as his extreme weakness, since he is blown away as chaff by a mere breath.

After banishing the tyrant, who holds under his sway every one coming into the world, the priest impresses on the child the seal of a very different master. He makes with his thumb the sign of the cross on its forehead, that it may learn never to be ashamed of Jesus Christ; and on its breast, that it may learn always to love him. At the same time he says: "Receive the sign of the cross on thy brow and in thy heart, attach thyself to the divine precepts, and be such in thy manners that thou mayst become the temple of God."

The representative of God, the priest, then lays his hand on the head of the child, to denote that he takes possession of it in the name of the Almighty, and he addresses to the Lord this touching prayer: "Almighty and eternal God, Father of our Lord Jesus Christ, vouchsafe to look upon this child, which thou hast called to the grace of the faith; take away from it all blindness of mind and heart…that it may be able to shun the pestilential breath of all vices, and, drawn by the odor of thy holy precepts, may joyfully serve thee, and daily grow in virtue, through Jesus Christ our Lord."

The priest then exorcises the salt, that is, disengages it from the malign influences of the devil, diffused since the fall throughout all creatures. He next puts some of the blessed salt into the child's mouth. Salt preserves from corruption, and gives a relish to food. For these mysterious reasons the Church employs it in baptism, and teaches her minister to say: "Receive the salt of wisdom, that thou mayst be pleasing to God, and mayst move him to grant thee eternal life."[675]

The priest has just communicated Christian wisdom, a relish for divine things, represented by the salt, to the child. He now forbids the devil ever to take away this precious gift. "Unclean spirit," he says, "I exorcise thee in the name of the Father, and of the Son, and of the Holy Ghost, that thou mayst go out from the child. He who commands thee, cursed angel, damned angel, is he who walked on the waves of the sea, and held out his hand to Peter when about to perish. Acknowledge then, wicked angel, the justice of the sentence that condemns thee; give honor to the true and living God; give honor to Jesus Christ his Son, and to the Holy Ghost; and withdraw from this servant of God, whom our Lord, by a prodigy of infinite mercy, calls to the grace of baptism, and never have the audacity to insult the sacred sign of the cross which we now impress." At the same time, the priest makes the sign of the cross on the child's forehead, and, in the name of the Holy Trinity, again takes possession of this creature by laying his hand on its head.

Son of man! thou art about to become the child of God, to enter the house of him who shall soon say, showing thee to the astonished and delighted angels: "This is my beloved son."

And the priest lays the end of his stole on the head of the child, and leads it into the church, saying: "Enter the house of God, that thou mayst have part with Jesus Christ unto everlasting life." The priest then makes the child recite, by means of its godfather and godmother, the Apostles' Creed and the Lord's Prayer. This is also what the catechumens used to do before baptism, in order to show their belief and their instruction. After this new initiation, the priest again banishes the unclean spirit, that it may be taught to respect the dignity of sanctity.

Now follows a ceremony equally venerable and mysterious. It is written that our Lord cured a deaf and dumb man by touching his ears and putting a little spittle on his tongue, saying: "Ephpheta, be opened." Here is a new deaf-mute to be cured. The spouse of Jesus Christ, the depositary of his doctrine, the Church imitates this example. The priest, taking his spittle, touches with it the child's ears and nostrils, repeating the miraculous words: "Ephpheta, be opened." Child of Adam, poor slave of the devil! thy hearing is about to be opened to the truth, thy smell to the odor of virtue, and thy mouth to the praise of the Lord. This ceremony may be traced back to the first ages of the Church: St. Ambrose makes express mention of it.[676]

The child is come to the regenerating font. Here are accomplished the last of the ceremonies that were formerly in use with the catechumens.

The renunciation. Thrice the priest inquires of it: "Dost thou renounce Satan?" And thrice it replies: "I renounce him." What an account must be rendered at the judgment if, after this triple renunciation, we return to the yoke of Satan![677]

The unction. The priest, dipping his finger in the oil of the catechumens, makes therewith the sign of the cross on the breast and the shoulders of the child: on the breast, to make it love the yoke of Jesus Christ; on the shoulders, to give it strength to carry this yoke; with oil, to denote the sweetness of this amiable yoke.

The profession of faith. Today as in the early days, the Church is not content with a general profession of faith; she desires an explicit acknowledgment of the fundamental truths confided to her keeping. This is the reason why the priest asks the child: "Do you believe in the Father, in the Son, in the Holy Ghost, the communion of saints, the forgiveness of sins, the resurrection of the body, and life everlasting?" The child answers: "I believe."

2. *Ceremonies which accompany baptism.* All these preparations being completed, the priest puts a decisive question to the child: "Wilt thou be baptized?" A poor blind paralytic is before his eyes. The Church does not pronounce the omnipotent word that shall heal him without imitating the Savior, in whose name she works the miracle. "Dost thou wish to be cured?" said the man-God to the paralytic lying near the pond; and, "What wouldst thou have me to do for thee?" to the blind man begging by the wayside. Such are the memories which the Church awakes by this question. She also declares that her divine spouse desires children, not slaves; and that man, after incurring damnation by obeying the devil, can only be saved by freely and willingly submitting to God. The child answers, by its godfather and godmother: "I will."

Then the holy water of regeneration flows thrice on its head in the form of a cross, with these sacramental words: "I baptize thee in the name of the Father, and of the Son, and of the Holy Ghost." The water is poured on thrice during the invocation of the Blessed Trinity, to show that the three divine Persons concur to the regeneration of man in baptism, and to signify that Jesus Christ, with whom we are buried by baptism, was three days in the sepulchre from which he at length came forth glorious.[678] During baptism, the godfather and godmother touch the child, to denote that they answer for it and that they engage to make it keep its promises: their extended hands express this oath.

3. *Ceremonies which follow baptism.* The miracle is wrought. The child of the old Adam has become the child of the new Adam. The ceremony which follows teaches it the august titles and sublime prerogatives which it has just received. The priest, dipping his thumb in the holy chrism, makes therewith the sign of the cross on its brow, and consecrates it a king, a priest, and a prophet. For it was with holy oil that kings, priests, and prophets used to be consecrated.

The newly baptized is a king—lord of the world and his passions. A priest—he ought continually to offer himself to God as a living and pleasing victim. A prophet—he ought by his life to announce the existence of future goods. The priest then bestows on him the only temporal inheritance which the Savior left to his disciples—peace. "Peace be with thee," he says, and his blessing returns to him. For the answer follows: "And with thy spirit." This is the child's thanksgiving.

The priest puts the chrism-cloth on its head, and pronounces these memorable words: "Receive this white robe, and bear it unspotted to the tribunal of our Lord Jesus Christ, that thou mayst there find life everlasting." The baptized answers: "Amen—be it so!"

Oh, yes, may it be so for me who write these lines, for you who read them, and for all those who receive the sacred garment of baptismal innocence! The chrism-cloth, placed on the child's head, is a substitute for the white garments of the ancient catechumens, and like them denotes innocence, freedom, triumph: white garments used to be worn by the enfranchised and the mighty.

How laudable is the custom of those Christian families in which the chrism-cloth of baptism is respectfully preserved and religiously transmitted from generation to generation! They imitate our forefathers in the faith, to whom everything connected with baptism was dear and sacred. Those fervent Christians preserved with a religious care not only their white garments, but also the linens which their sponsors had presented to them to cover themselves on coming forth from the sacred font.[679] This conduct seemed a monument of the signal benefit which they had received, and a mark of the alliance which they had contracted by baptism with God. History records a memorable example of this religious fidelity.

History. In the fifth century, the Vandals were persecuting the Church of Africa. As all the clergy were being summoned to the torture, the deacon Murita distinguished himself among them. He had led from the font a young man named Elpidiphorus. This unfortunate had apostatized, and was at the time a most bitter persecutor of the Christians. The priests and the archdeacon Salutaris had just been tortured, when the second deacon appeared—a venerable old man, named Murita. Before being stripped that he might be laid on the instrument of torture, he drew from beneath his robe the linens with which he had covered Elpidiphorus on coming forth from the sacred font, and, holding them up before every one, addressed to Elpidiphorus, who sat as his judge, these terrible words: "Behold the witnesses of your apostasy! They will accuse you at the tribunal of the sovereign judge. Look at the white robe with which I clothed you when you came forth from the sacred font: it will be changed into a robe of flames, to devour you for all eternity." At these words, the people raised a shout of horror; Elpidiphorus grew pale—trembling and confused, he dared not so much as open his lips to reply.[680] The executioner put an end to the scene by sending Murita to heaven.

There remains the ceremony of the lighted taper, which the priest places in the child's hand, saying: "Receive this burning taper, and preserve unsullied the grace of thy baptism: keep the commandments of God faithfully, that, when Jesus Christ shall come to celebrate his nuptials, thou mayst go forth to meet him with all the saints in the heavenly court, to enjoy eternal life, to live forever and ever." The child answers, through its sponsor: "Amen—so be it!"

Rejoice now, O holy spouse of Jesus Christ, thou who, though yet journeying on earth, dwellest in heaven—a child is born to thee! And behold! the bells and the organs peal to denote the joy which is given to the Church militant and triumphant by the little stranger's arrival in the great Catholic family. The sacristy is visited. There the names of the child, its father and mother, its godfather and godmother, as well as the date of its baptism, are inscribed on the public register. We should look upon this book as the counterpart of the book of life. At the moment when our names are written therein, God places them with his own hand in the book of heaven. Be it our endeavor to merit, by irreproachable conduct, that they shall never be effaced![681]

Social advantages of baptism.—What shall we now say of the benefits conferred on society by baptism? Where shall we find a grander lesson on sanctity? What a knowledge it gives to man of the enormity of sin, the dignity to which he is raised, and the obligations which are laid upon him! Here he is, a simple mortal, consecrated in all his senses, consecrated as a ciborium or a chalice: what holiness! Do you think that this thought has never restrained man in the time of temptation, and prevented a multitude of secret crimes that would destroy both body and soul, ruin the peace of families, and silently undermine society?

And then, what respect for the life of the child, before as well as after its birth! How many criminal or careless mothers who would have brought and who would still bring temporal death on their child, if they were not withheld by the fear of bringing eternal death on it! And after birth, by what means can the child disappear? Will not the witnesses of its baptism, and the register on which its name is enrolled, be there to give evidence? But, above all, what a guarantee for the moral education of the child, for that education which makes virtuous citizens, in the thought, so clearly presented by baptism, that it is a sacred deposit, that an angel guards it, that a saint protects it, that it is the child of God—the friend of Jesus Christ—the companion of the angels!

Thanks to baptism, from the first step that man makes in life his existence grows nobler in the eyes of his parents, by reason of the august character which religion impresses on him. How many delights does the high idea of a divine regeneration impart to the maternal sentiments! How happy does it make parents to think that they have brought into the world a being who has just acquired a right to the possession of God himself!

Take away baptism, and the birth of man is no longer an event. The child is henceforth only a little one of the human species, that is registered on its entrance into life like an addition of cattle to a city. What a strange kind of dignity!

Take away baptism, and you shall see infanticide and desertion multiply, redden your crossroads with blood, and fill society with alarm. Call to mind what used to occur among the pagans. See what happens at the present day in China. Either the children are drowned by the midwives in a vessel of warm water, and their murderers receive payment for this service, or they are thrown into a river with a hollow pumpkin tied to their backs, that they may float for a long time before expiring. Their infant cries would elsewhere awake the groans of human nature; but in China people are accustomed to hear them, and to let them pass without a sigh. There is a third mode there of ridding one's self of children: it is to cast them out into the street. Rubbish-carts pass along every morning, especially at Pekin, pick up the children thus exposed during the night, and throw them into a huge trench. The helpless infants are not covered with clay, in the hope that Mahometans may come and take some of them. But before the arrival of the tumbrels to convey them to the sewer, it often happens that dogs and pigs, which abound in the streets of Chinese towns, eat them alive.

"I have not found an example of like atrocity even among the cannibals of America. The Jesuits declare that in the space of three years they counted 9,702 children thus destined for the sewer; but they did not count those who had been crushed at Pekin under the feet of horses and mules, nor those who had been drowned in canals, nor those whom the dogs had devoured, nor those who had been stifled on coming forth from the womb, nor those whom the Mahometans had carried off, nor those who had been made away with in places of which Jesuits knew nothing."[682]

What do I say? See what passes among ourselves when a regard for baptism and religion wanes. Is not history, then, hideous enough to prove to you that baptism is even a temporal benefit—a barrier to a multitude of crimes which, directly or indirectly, desolate and degrade society, and shake it to its very foundations?

PRAYER

O my God! who art all love, I thank thee with my whole heart for having adopted me as thy child; do not permit me ever to dishonor so glorious a title.

I am resolved to love God above all things, and my neighbor as myself for the love of God; and, in testimony of this love, I will always have a great respect for the ceremonies of the Church.

Lesson 35: Our Union with the New Adam by Hope (8)

Sacrament of confirmation.—The child of the old Adam has become by baptism a child of the new Adam. The weak branch of a poisonous tree, it is grafted on the tree of life: nourished with the sap of the latter, it will one day bear flowers and fruits of benediction. But it requires to be steadily fixed on the new tree: the young brother of the angels requires to be strengthened, for he is born to be a soldier. The waters of baptism did not extinguish the fires of concupiscence in him, as each one of us knows only too well. His whole life he must fight against numerous, indefatigable enemies, visible and invisible, internal and external: life is a warfare, a trial for eternity. It was to secure him the victory that our Lord instituted confirmation.

Definition of this sacrament.—According to Catholic theology, confirmation is a sacrament of the new law, instituted by our Lord Jesus Christ, which strengthens the divine life in us, and gives to those who are baptized the Holy Ghost with all his gifts.

Named in turn by the fathers of the Church the "imposition of hands," the "holy chrism," the "sacrament of the holy chrism," the "sign by which the Holy Ghost is received," the "seal of the Lord," the "spiritual seal,"[683] this sacrament bears at the present day the name of confirmation. "The reason is," says the *Catechism of the Council of Trent*, "because this sacrament fortifies and perfects the new life which the grace of Jesus Christ communicates to us in baptism."[684]

Confirmation has all the conditions that are required for a sacrament of the new law: a) a sensible sign—the imposition of hands, the unction with holy chrism, and the prayers pronounced by the bishop; b) a sign instituted by our Lord; c) a sign which has the virtue of producing grace. This is so true, as we shall prove in the course of this lesson, that the fathers of the Church do not hesitate to put confirmation on a level with baptism. "Confirmation," says St. Augustine, "is a sacrament; it possesses the virtue of communicating the Holy Ghost, and, as well as baptism, is a sacrament."[685]

In reply to a Spanish bishop, Pope St. Melchiades expressed himself thus: "As for the question which you have addressed to us, whether the imposition of the hands of bishops is a greater sacrament than baptism, you ought to know that each of them is a great sacrament."[686] From the early ages, the sects used to acknowledge, as well as the fathers, the sacrament of confirmation; so that, to deny it, protestants have been obliged to face the brunt of all tradition. It was, therefore, with good reason that the Catholic Church pronounced, in the Council of Trent, this solemn decision: "If anyone say that confirmation is not a true sacrament, let him be anathema."[687]

Elements of confirmation: Its matter.—The matter of the sacrament of confirmation consists in the unction of holy chrism, and the imposition of the hand, which naturally accompanies the unction. "The second sacrament," says Pope Eugenius IV, "is confirmation, of which the matter is chrism, composed of oil and balm, and blessed by the bishop."[688] The word *chrism* is a term employed by the Greeks to express every kind of perfume. But in ecclesiastical authors it means a composition of oil and balm blessed by the bishop. These two things show, by their mixture, the diversity of the gifts of the Holy Ghost, which are communicated to us by confirmation, and also the special excellence of this sacrament.

"It is beyond controversy," adds Benedict XIV, "that in the Latin Church the sacrament of confirmation is conferred by the unction of holy chrism, composed of oil of olives and balm, blessed by the bishop, while the bishop makes this unction with the sign of the cross on the foreheads of the faithful, and pronounces the sacred words which correspond to this unction."[689] Hence, the imposition of hands, which the bishop makes before the unction, is not necessary to the validity of confirmation; and the unction alone, with the imposition of the hand which accompanies it, contains the essential matter of this sacrament.

We said that holy chrism is composed of oil and balm. It is only olive oil that can be employed: a) because it alone, properly speaking, deserves the name of oil; b) because it is more common than other kinds of oil; c) because it better represents the effects of the sacrament; in fine d) because it alone is in accordance with the constant practice of the Church and the invariable teaching of the fathers and doctors.

Balm is an oily substance, more or less liquid, very odoriferous, and endowed with medicinal properties: it flows naturally from certain bushes and trees when an incision is made on them. The word *balm* means the "prince or king of aromatics." Balm-trees are found in Judea, Arabia, Brazil, Canada. Hence, there are different balms: known under the names of the balm of Judea, the balm of Mecca, the balm of Canada, the balm of Brazil, the balm of Carthagena, the balm of Tolu, the balm of Peru. They are distinguished by their color, their greater or less liquidity, their perfume, and their medicinal properties; but they are all true balms.[690]

Oil and balm compose the holy chrism, which, before being used for the sacraments, must be blessed by the bishop. Such is the teaching of all antiquity in the East and in the West.[691] St. Cyril of Jerusalem attributes to it, after it has been blessed by the bishop, such a virtue that he compares it to the Eucharistic bread, and declares that it works by the presence of the divinity. "Do not suppose," says the great doctor, "that this perfume is a common thing. As the Eucharistic bread, after the invocation of the Holy Ghost, is no longer ordinary bread, but the body of Jesus Christ, so this holy perfume is no longer a simple—or, if you wish, a profane—thing, but a gift of Jesus Christ and the Holy Ghost, which has become efficacious by the presence of the divinity."[692]

The bishop consecrates the holy chrism on Holy Thursday, because in the primitive Church it was necessary for the solemn administration of baptism, which took place on Easter night; and also, adds St. Thomas, because it is proper to prepare the matter of the sacraments on the same day as we commemorate the institution of the Blessed Eucharist, to which all the other sacraments refer.[693]

In all ages, among the Greeks as well as among the Latins, the greatest respect has been entertained for the holy chrism. Even not long ago it was the custom to cover the forehead of the person baptized with a white linen bandage, which was worn for three days. In the solemn baptism and confirmation of adults the bandage is still used at Rome. We see that the Church does everything possible to give the faithful a high idea of confirmation. For the rest, the holy chrism admirably expresses the diversity of the gifts which are communicated to us by this sacrament.

The oil, a symbol of sweetness and strength, indicates the twofold character of the new Adam, who is called both the Lamb of God and the Lion of the tribe of Juda. Such is the Christian after confirmation. The balm, whose perfume is most agreeable, denotes the good odor of all virtues which the faithful diffuse after being made perfect by confirmation. They are thus permitted to say with St. Paul: "We are the good odor of Jesus Christ before God."[694]

"In effect," says St. Thomas, "confirmation gives us the plenitude of the Holy Ghost, which communicates to us the plenitude of spiritual strength befitting a perfect age. Now, when man arrives at a perfect age, he begins to dispose of that which he has received; until then he lives only for himself. The grace of the Holy Ghost is therefore represented by oil, which spreads with great facility. Balm is mixed with the oil, on account of the exquisite perfume with which it surrounds itself."[695] In these expressive symbols, what a source of meditation and perhaps of grief for many Christians!

Its form. The form of the sacrament of confirmation consists in the words which the bishop pronounces when making the unction with the holy chrism on the forehead. They are these: "I sign thee with the sign of the cross, and I confirm thee with the chrism of salvation, in the name of the Father, and of the Son, and of the Holy Ghost."[696] These words are the most suitable form of confirmation, for the form ought to express all that is contained in a sacrament. Now, confirmation gives the Holy Ghost to strengthen us in the battles of virtue. There are therefore in this sacrament three necessary things perfectly expressed by the form of which we speak.

a) The cause which gives the plenitude of spiritual strength. This cause is the Holy Trinity—expressed by the words: "In the name of the Father, and of the Son, and of the Holy Ghost." b) The spiritual strength which is communicated to us—expressed by the visible unction of the holy chrism, accompanied with the words: "I confirm thee with the chrism of salvation." c) The sign which is given to the Christian soldier—expressed by the words: "I sign thee with the sign of the cross," an august sign, by which our divine King conquered, and by which we shall conquer.[697]

The unction of the holy chrism is made on the forehead. To understand the reason for this, it must be remembered that in confirmation the Holy Ghost is given to us to strengthen us in the battles of salvation, and to make us confess our Lord boldly in the face of his enemies. It is therefore becoming that the holy unction should be made on the forehead of the person confirmed. First, he should be signed, as a soldier, with the sign of his general, and this sign should be conspicuous. Now, the forehead is the most conspicuous part of the body, that which is most rarely covered. It is therefore signed with the holy unction, that the person confirmed may publicly show himself a Christian, in imitation of the apostles, who, after the descent of the Holy Ghost, showed themselves courageously to the people, though beforehand they remained timidly within doors. Again, two things stand in the way of a manful confession of our Lord: fear and shame. These two sentiments are manifested chiefly on the forehead: fear whitens it, shame reddens it. Hence, the sacred unction is made on the forehead to teach him who is confirmed that neither fear nor shame ought ever to hinder him from appearing a Christian.[698]

Its minister. The minister of confirmation is the bishop alone.[699] This august function is reserved to bishops for several reasons alike proper to show us the dignity of the sacrament. The first, because the administration of confirmation was the exclusive privilege of the apostles, whose successors are the bishops. The second, because it belongs only to superior officers to enroll soldiers who shall fight under their orders in the armies of which they are the generals. The bishops are the generals of the great King. It is by confirmation that, from being the children, we become the soldiers of our Lord. The third, because in the arts it is the business of a master to give the finishing touch to the picture, statue, or other work of his pupil. Now, it is in confirmation that the work begun at baptism is completed, and that we become perfect Christians. The fourth and last, because, according to the expression of the apostle, everyone becomes by baptism a living letter, written with the blood of our Lord, in which all the world may read his benefits, his commands, his promises, his virtues. To be authentic, this letter should be signed. It is in confirmation that this admirable letter receives, through the bishop, the signature and seal of the Holy Ghost.[700]

As to the age for the reception of the sacrament of confirmation, the Church has fixed, by her law and by her general practice, on that of reason. The Christian is then in a state to profess his faith; consequently, he requires to be strengthened and confirmed in the grace of God. Yet confirmation would be given, if not licitly, at least validly, to children under this age. The greatest theologians, following St. Thomas, teach even that it need not be refused, to children under seven years, if they are in danger of death, so that, says the Angelic Doctor, they may enjoy a greater degree of glory in heaven, as they shall have received a greater degree of grace on earth.[701] Such was formerly the custom in the primitive Church—continued in some countries to the thirteenth century.

Sponsor. In many churches, a sponsor is taken for confirmation as well as for baptism. This practice may be traced, as we have seen, to the apostolic times. Young soldiers require a master to put them through their drill, to teach them the arts of attack and defense. With much more reason do the young athletes of the faith require a skillful person to instruct them on the manner of using the powerful weapons which are put into their hands by confirmation. It is of no ordinary conflict, with mere material interests at stake, that there is question here, but of a spiritual warfare, whose recompense is the kingdom of heaven! It is therefore with great propriety that sponsors are taken for confirmation. But they contract the same affinities as the sponsors for baptism, and marriage is forbidden between the same persons.

Its institution.—It is a matter of faith that our Lord instituted confirmation as well as the other sacraments. Let us hear the holy Council of Trent, summing up on this point the belief of the Catholic world. "If any one dare to assert," it says, "that all the sacraments of the new law were not instituted by our Lord Jesus Christ, or that there are more or less than seven of them, or that any one of the seven is not a true sacrament, let him be anathema!"[702] Speaking of confirmation in particular, it adds: "If anyone say that confirmation, given to those who have been baptized, is only an idle ceremony, that it is not a sacrament truly and properly so called, let him be anathema!"[703]

St. Luke reveals the existence of this sacrament to us, when he relates that "the apostles laid hands" on those whom they had baptized, and "these received the Holy Ghost."[704] Notwithstanding the silence that was imposed on them by the discipline of secrecy, all the fathers, from the time of the apostles, speak in a manner more or less explicit of the sacrament of confirmation.[705]

Its effects.—What occasion is there to remind the faithful of the necessity of confirmation? Alas! is it not to be found in their weakness, perhaps in their deplorable falls? The remedy for these evils is the sacrament of strength, which works the following effects:

1. It produces sanctifying grace in us, not that which reconciles the sinner with God, but that which more and more purifies and sanctifies those who are already just. It is an increase of grace, which perfects the grace of baptism, by making us soldiers of the Savior; which gives us strength to confess his holy name openly, never to be ashamed of his religion, and to live as perfect Christians, despite the examples and the railleries of the world.

2. It communicates the Holy Ghost himself to us, with all his gifts.[706] Hence, the three Persons of the Blessed Trinity contribute to our sanctification and our happiness. The Father adopts us in baptism; the Son gives himself to us in Communion; the Holy Ghost gives himself to us in confirmation. Not that the Holy Ghost communicates to us as to the apostles and other early Christians, the gift of tongues, of miracles, of prophecy, or the like, necessary in the beginning for the progress of the gospel; but he lavishes on our souls the same inward graces with which he strengthened them—especially the seven gifts which are attributed to him. "Thou hast received," says St. Ambrose to a person confirmed, "the spiritual seal—the spirit of wisdom and understanding, the spirit of counsel and fortitude, the spirit of knowledge and piety, and the spirit of the fear of the Lord."[707]

3. It imprints on our souls an indelible character, which prevents its reception more than once, and which, during all eternity, will obtain for the person confirmed a greater felicity than that enjoyed by him who has not received this sacrament: a new inducement to prepare oneself well when about to receive it. This character differs from that received in baptism: the latter marks us as children of God; the former, as soldiers of Jesus Christ.

Would you contemplate the sacrament of confirmation in all the grandeur of its effects? Turn your eyes toward the upper chamber in Jerusalem and see what happened to the apostles. At the time of the passion, they were so weak and timid that they took to flight as soon as they saw their good master arrested. Peter himself, the head of the apostolic college, a pillar of the Church, was frightened at the voice of a woman, and denied that he was a disciple of the Savior, not once, not twice, but three times. All the apostles, after the resurrection, shut themselves up in a house for fear of the Jews.

Pentecost comes, and they are so filled with the virtue of the Holy Ghost that, displaying an unparalleled courage, they preach the gospel to Jerusalem, to Samaria, to the ends of the earth. They regard it as their glory and their joy to suffer affronts and torments for the name of Jesus Christ.[708] Well, the Holy Ghost, who is communicated to us by confirmation, is the same today as then.

See all the early Christians! What courage did they derive from confirmation! Daily exposed to the risk of being summoned from the font to the amphitheatre, this sacrament was given to them immediately after baptism. Besides the interior effects of light, strength, and love, confirmation often communicated to them the gifts of miracles, tongues, and prophecy. These wondrous effects were, as we have said, necessary to support the Church, and they continued during the whole time of the persecutions.

The Church being well cemented by blood and miracles, these extraordinary gifts ceased to be common, but they were not altogether discontinued.

On leaving the city, and the ordinary assembly of the faithful, this miraculous grace retired, if we may so speak, to the desert, where solitaries were soon so replenished with it that they seemed to sport with nature. We learn this from St. Athanasius, Cassian, Palladius, St. Jerome, Rufinus, and a multitude of other writers, equally remarkable for their learning and their piety. After showing that the Christian, filled with the Holy Ghost, is master of the devil and the world, God also showed him the master of nature.

Dispositions for the reception of confirmation.—The dispositions for receiving confirmation well regard both body and soul. Those which regard the body are: a) to be fasting, if possible, especially when this sacrament is received in the morning; b) to be modest in one's dress and deportment; c) to have the forehead, on which the bishop makes the holy unction, particularly clean. Those which regard the soul are: a) to be baptized—confirmation necessarily supposes the character of baptism, of which it is the perfection; b) to know the excellence of this sacrament and the graces which it produces; c) to be instructed in the elements of the faith, for this sacrament was established to give us strength to confess our faith before the unbelieving and the impious—consequently one must know the Lord's Prayer, the Hail Mary, the Apostles' Creed, and the decalogue; d) to be in the state of grace, for confirmation is a sacrament of the living.

To receive confirmation worthily, the dispositions which we have just stated are indispensable. In order to participate more abundantly in the precious graces which it communicates, it should also be approached with a tender piety, a profound awe, and a sincere devotion. Were these dispositions ever more necessary than in an age when human respect makes so many apostates among Christians?

Its necessity.—Confirmation is not, like baptism, absolutely necessary for salvation; yet it is necessary in some sense: the fathers and doctors will easily help us to understand this. "The sacraments of the new law," says St. Thomas, "were established to produce special effects of grace. Hence, wherever a special effect of grace should be produced, there we find a sacrament established. Now, to take an example from corporal life, we first find the birth, and then the growth, which leads man to maturity, and this is a special perfection. So, in the spiritual order, man receives life by baptism, and he attains to a certain maturity in the spiritual life by confirmation."[709]

Hence, these beautiful words of Pope Melchiades: "The Holy Spirit, who descends on the sacred font to make it fruitful, who fills it with the plenitude of that grace which gives innocence by effacing sin, also descends in confirmation to increase grace. In baptism, we are born to the spiritual life; in confirmation, we are strengthened for the combat. In baptism, we are washed; in confirmation, we are armed. Though baptism suffices for those who immediately quit this life, the help of confirmation is necessary for those who must make its dangerous journey."[710]

It is therefore manifest that confirmation is a sacrament distinct from the others, since it produces necessary effects which the others do not produce. Remark how well adapted it is to the wants of the Christian soldier. We have to encounter seven enemies, called the seven capital sins. Now, the seven gifts of the Holy Ghost, which confirmation communicates to us, are seven graces, and, as it were, seven powers opposed to these different enemies, over whom they enable us to triumph.[711] Those who have only received baptism are weak, like newborn children. Unarmed soldiers, how can they maintain the spiritual conflict into which they shall be drawn by the devil, the world, and the flesh? On the other hand, fortified by the sacrament of confirmation, they can defend themselves against all these enemies and triumph over them.

Accordingly, Catholic theology teaches that the sacrament of confirmation is necessary for adults by a divine and an ecclesiastical law. By a divine law: God wishes that we should procure, when it is in our power to do so, all the helps of which we have need for our salvation—consequently, it is against his will to deprive ourselves of a succor so powerful as that of confirmation. By an ecclesiastical law: since the Church wishes that all Christians should receive this sacrament.[712]

It follows hence that a person sins most grievously when, through contempt or negligence, he does not receive the sacrament of confirmation. Those are thought to contemn and neglect it, who, living in places remote from the episcopal city whither the bishop travels but rarely, do not dispose themselves to receive it when they know that the bishop is coming to administer it. In the same manner, those are inexcusable who, living in cities in which bishops reside, have attained a competent age and not received confirmation, if they fail to present themselves before their bishop the first time that he administers it: according to St. Charles, they are subject to the penalties imposed by the canons on those who contemn or neglect this sacrament.

Historical fact.—Is it not to this culpable indifference, no less than to the profanation of this sacrament, that we must attribute the shameful falls and the numberless defections which dishonor the Church and cause the impious to blaspheme? Why should it not be the same today as formerly? History has been careful to preserve for us a fact that is very well calculated to instruct us. A man, called Novatian, was baptized in danger of death. He afterward neglected to receive the sacrament of confirmation. A child in faith, a soldier without arms, he soon became the sport of the devil. Impelled by unworthy motives, he found a means to be ordained priest. He gave rise to a schism, which degenerated into heresy, and, for a long time, disturbed the Church. He died miserably, and the fathers do not hesitate to tell us that he fell into all his crimes from neglecting to receive the sacrament of light and strength.[713]

Its liturgy.—Would you in some manner behold with your eyes and touch with your hands the grandeur of this sacrament, the dignity to which it raises us, and the holy dispositions which are necessary for its worthy reception? Be mindful of the various prayers and ceremonies which accompanied from the beginning, and which accompany to the present day, its administration.

Scarcely had the apostles departed from the upper chamber when they conferred the sacrament of strength on the newly baptized. St. Peter and St. John went to Samaria, and confirmed the faithful who had been baptized by Philip the deacon.[714] They imposed hands on them, and the Holy Ghost descended on them. The same practice was observed in all succeeding ages. "When we come forth from the sacred bath," says Tertullian, "we are anointed with blessed oil...This unction is made on the body, but it produces its effect on the soul. Then hands are imposed on us at the benediction, invoking and inviting the Holy Ghost."[715] "This unction is made on the forehead, and the bishop alone has the right to make it."[716]

The imposition of hands and the unction of which we have just spoken were not dumb ceremonies. They were accompanied with sacred words of great virtue, to draw down the blessings of sanctification on those over whom they were pronounced. The first Christians had such a respect for these holy words, as well as for all those that express our mysteries, that they concealed them with great care, lest any of them should come to the knowledge of the profane.[717] By these sacred words or prayers was invoked the Spirit with the seven gifts. Several times during their recitation, *Amen* was added, as is still done at the present day.

Here is a proof of this, taken from a pontifical of the eighth century[718] or thereabouts. The bishop says: "O Almighty and eternal God, who hast vouchsafed to regenerate thy servant by water and the Holy Ghost, pour forth from heaven upon him the seven gifts of thy Holy Spirit. (*Amen.*) Give him the spirit of wisdom and understanding. (*Amen.*) The spirit of fortitude and counsel. (*Amen.*) The spirit of knowledge and piety. (*Amen.*) Fill him with the spirit of the fear of God and our Lord Jesus Christ, and mark him with the seal of thy holy cross unto life everlasting. (*Amen.*)" When making the unction with the holy chrism, the bishop said: "I confirm thee, in the name of the Father, and of the Son, and of the Holy Ghost."[719]

The holy chrism, of which the bishop made use for confirmation, was not ordinary oil, but was blessed and consecrated by prayer on the same altar that witnessed the consecration of the Eucharist. This consecration, which may be traced back to the time of the apostles, like that of the water for baptism, was made in the name of Jesus Christ—that is, "the anointed"—unction itself. Hence came the name of *chrism* after the consecration, for *chrism* and *christ* have the same origin.[720] Such a virtue was recognized in the holy chrism that St. Cyril of Jerusalem compares, as we have seen, this oil mingled with balm, after it has been consecrated, to the Eucharistic bread, and he assures us that it works by the presence of the divinity.[721]

So much for what concerns the matter and the form of confirmation in the early ages of the Church. As for the place in which this sacrament was administered, there does not appear to have been any other rule than the will of the bishop, whether he selected the church or the sacristy.[722] The ancient sacristies were much larger than those of succeeding ages, and were adapted to ceremonies of this kind. That of St. Sophia at Constantinople was so spacious that the Turks made it their arsenal, one of the most important in the world. Sponsors were taken for confirmation as for baptism: this usage ascends to the apostolic times.

According to a custom equally ancient, those who were to be confirmed brought with them a linen bandage to cover their forehead when it had received the unction of the holy chrism. This bandage should be a production of flax, thick, without knot or rent, three fingers wide, of fitting length, white, and clean.[723] It was worn for some time on the forehead out of respect for the holy chrism, and that this sacred mixture might not be touched by profane hands.[724]

So many exterior precautions acquaint us with the interior preparations that were required for the reception of this sacrament. It was desired that those who were about to be confirmed should labor carefully to purify their conscience from every stain of sin, by having recourse to penance and confession. It was desired, moreover, that those who, having attained the use of reason, were preparing to receive confirmation, should be sufficiently instructed in the principal mysteries of the faith. If any suspicion of ignorance existed, questions were put to them to ascertain whether they were familiar with the Lord's Prayer, the Hail Mary, the Apostles' Creed, and the decalogue. They were also required to be fasting; and, on the eve of confirmation, they washed the forehead specially, and cut away any hairs which might fall over the eyes, that nothing should interfere with the application of the holy chrism.[725]

Let us add that the custom of giving confirmation immediately after baptism continued to the ninth century. At this period, its administration began in several churches to be deferred. The reason was because the night of Easter or Pentecost no longer sufficed to confer baptism and confirmation on the multitudes who presented themselves. Here again we see that the changes introduced by the Church on the ancient discipline were demanded by circumstances, and that they show the wisdom of this vigilant spouse of the new Adam. Such is an abridged history of confirmation from the time of the apostles down to our own days. But we must enter into a few details on the ceremonies that at the present day accompany its administration.

The bishop who is to give confirmation puts on his rochet, the symbol of innocence; his stole, the sign of his divine authority; and his cope, whose red color tells us of the burning charity of the Spirit who is about to descend. He washes his hands, to show the great purity required by the august function which he must fulfill. He then approaches the altar, and, turning toward those who are to be confirmed, says these words: "May the Holy Ghost descend on you, and may the virtue of the Most High preserve you from all sin!"

These words express not only the desires of the pontiff, but the wonders which are about to be wrought, and the obligations of those in whose favor they shall be wrought. Then follows the sign of the cross. The bishop makes it on himself to draw down the strength of God; for he says, "Our help is in the name of the Lord." And this help is as sure as it is powerful; for, "It was the Lord that made heaven and earth," answer the assistants. Encouraged by this answer, the pontiff adds, "O Lord, hear my prayer!" The assistants, joining him in this desire, continue, "And let my cry come unto thee."

These touching invocations, the like of which are not to be found in any merely human language, have ascended to heaven. The Church knows the power of prayer. And the bishop also knows his own power; for he has been sent to be the dispenser of the mysteries of God. Extending, therefore, his hands over the persons to be confirmed, as a sign of the overshadowing of the Holy Ghost, he makes this beautiful prayer, already in use in the eighth century: "O eternal and almighty God! who hast vouchsafed to regenerate with water and the Holy Ghost thy servants, and who hast granted them the forgiveness of all their sins, send upon them, from the summit of heaven, thy Paraclete, the author of all gifts." The assistants answer: "So be it—Amen." "The spirit of wisdom and understanding. (*Amen.*) The spirit of counsel and fortitude. (*Amen.*) The spirit of knowledge and piety. (*Amen.*) Fill them with the spirit of fear, and, calling them to eternal life, sign them with the sign of the cross of Jesus Christ. We conjure thee to do so through the same Jesus Christ our Lord, thy Son, who liveth and reigneth with thee, in the unity of the same Holy Ghost, forever and ever. (*Amen.*)"

During this prayer the receivers of confirmation kneel, and endeavor to enter into the sentiments of the apostles in the upper chamber when they were expecting the Holy Ghost. They beseech him to come and change them into new creatures, holy, zealous, and firm in the faith. After the imposition of hands, the bishop approaches each of them, and makes the unction with the holy chrism on the forehead, saying: "I sign thee with the sign of the cross."[726] Then, forming with his hand the sign of the cross three times over the person's head, he adds: "And I confirm thee with the chrism of salvation in the name of the Father, and of the Son, and of the Holy Ghost." The bishop's assistant answers: "So be it—Amen."

Then the bishop strikes gently with his hand the cheek of the person confirmed. Never forget what thou hast just done, and be ready to suffer with invincible courage all kinds of contradictions for the name of Jesus Christ: such is the twofold meaning of this little slap. When giving it, the pontiff says: "Peace be to thee." The reward of thy courage will be peace—the peace of a good conscience—peace with God, which is above every other good—peace in life, at death, for eternity.

While the bishop purifies his hands, an anthem is sung, beseeching the Lord to complete the work which he has begun. The anthem ended, the pontiff, at the altar, offers up the most fervent petitions for the perseverance of the newly-confirmed, and gives them his blessing in these words: "May the Lord bless you from the height of heaven, that all the days of your lives you may see the good things of Jerusalem, and that you may obtain eternal life!"

No human words can translate or convey the maternal tenderness of this blessing, which the Church gives by her minister to her children. The bishop anew desires the confirmed to pray for him, and to recite once the Apostles' Creed, the Lord's Prayer, and the Angelical Salutation: which they do before leaving the Church. The recital of these prayers calls to mind the ancient usage, in virtue of which the bishop warned sponsors of their obligation to instruct their godchildren regarding the truths and duties of religion.[727]

All now depart after singing a psalm, which so well becomes the occasion: "Let all nations praise the Lord, let all peoples bless him, because his mercy rests upon us and his truth remains forever!" Happy the newly confirmed, if the truth of God remains uninjured in their souls to their last breath!

Social advantages of confirmation.—Happy also are families, since it was for the happiness of society that confirmation was established! The social teaching, begun at baptism, continues in confirmation. From her arrival on the earth, the Church said to man: "Be holy—thou art the son of God, the brother of the angels, the temple of the august Trinity." All the virtues that make the age of childhood most amiable are enjoined by baptism. Now that man is about to enter on the rougher journey of life, will the Church leave him without a lesson?

Oh, no! A tender mother, she runs to meet him, bearing strong graces in her hands, and words of heavenly wisdom on her lips. "My son," she says, "understand what thou art. This life is a warfare: thou art a soldier."—Uniting here all the ancient traditions, she sends her pontiff to arm, in the midst of magnificent ceremonies, the young knight of Jesus Christ.—"My son," she exclaims, "thou oughtest to be a conquering soldier: thy career ought to be one long series of victories. Thy enemies are the devil, the world, and the flesh; thy arms, watchfulness, mortification, and faith. Champion of God, descendant of so many heroes, it is under the eyes of these noble conquerors, under the eyes of the angels and thy mother, that thou art about to fight! Be worthy of the name which thou bearest, worthy of the blood which floweth in thy veins!"

And now the holy oil, which flows on the brows of kings, to crown them, flows also on his young brow; for he also must be a king, the lord of himself, a royal conqueror: but it is by severe struggles that he must purchase and defend his royalty. On earth he shall wear a crown of thorns, to wear one of glory in eternity. And a little blow teaches him to endure great affronts with patience!

"Thou art a king": the first declaration which the Church makes to man in confirmation. "Son and brother of Jesus Christ, thou art something still more noble, thou art a priest! Thy altar is thy heart; thy victim is thyself, it is the world, it is all that surrounds thee. Behold the holocaust which thou must offer up every hour of the day and night from this moment till thy last sigh! The fire to consume it must always burn in thy heart. This fire is the Spirit of love, who descends on thee as he descended on the apostles, a consuming fire, a fire whose action cannot be resisted." It is thus that the holy unction of the priesthood flows on the brow of the young Christian.

"Thou art a priest": the second declaration which the Church makes to man in confirmation. "The Son of God was a prophet. Like him, my son, be a prophet. A prophet in thy words, foretell the good things that are to come. A prophet in thy works, bear witness that the earth is a land of exile to thee, that thy home is elsewhere. A prophet in thy sanctity, proclaim to all that thou art the child of a thrice holy God; that thou fearest his terrible judgments, and expectest the reward which he has promised to those who continue faithful to him." It is thus that the sacred oil, which flowed on the brows of Isaias, Jeremias, and Daniel, flows also on the brow of the young Christian.

"Thou art a prophet": the third declaration which the Church makes to man in confirmation. Do you see the light that falls from this triple declaration on the end of life, on the duties of man? Do you understand how noble, poetic, and sublime is this triple declaration? Do you know any means more suitable to teach a young man the nature and the object of his earthly existence, to commend sanctity to him, and to obtain for him that miracle of miracles, chastity in a heart of fifteen years, chastity at a time when the rising passions actually boil, destroying thus in its source that torrent of iniquities which, after degrading the individual and desolating the family, brings trouble and confusion on society?

And then, all those long preparations that precede the reception of confirmation, all those instructions, all those fervent prayers of parents and children; afterward, the arrival of the pontiff, so long announced and so impatiently expected—think you not that all those solemn circumstances exercise some influence on public manners? What will it be if you add that this is not a barren teaching, but a teaching that carries with it the strength to do what it directs? Do you now understand how confirmation tends to ennoble man, and to inspire him with sentiments truly worthy of himself and society, because they are worthy of God and heaven?

PRAYER

O my God! who art all love, I thank thee for having given me thy Holy Spirit with all his gifts; do not permit that I should ever contristate within me this Spirit of sanctity and charity.

I am resolved to love God above all things, and my neighbor as myself for the love of God; and, in testimony of this love, I will never be ashamed to show myself a Christian.

Lesson 36: Our Union with the New Adam by Hope (9)

The sacrament of the Eucharist.—The Eucharist! This is the most august of the sacraments. This is the very source of grace. This is the ineffable mystery in which the most perfect union attainable on earth is effected between God and us. Two pieces of wax melted together represent but faintly, according to the language of the fathers, this deific union.[728] After Communion there is only heaven left: Communion is paradise on earth.

Now, the Eucharist comes naturally after baptism and confirmation. Once entered into the world, the child has need of nourishment proportioned to its weakness, and the soldier in the field of the bread of ammunition. So the Christian, born to the spiritual life by baptism, enrolled under the banner of Jesus Christ by confirmation, has need of food to sustain his life, and to maintain his strength for the battles of virtue. He finds this food in the Eucharist, called the bread of the strong, the wheat of the elect, the wine which produces and preserves virginity, by the energy which it communicates to the soul against all kinds of degrading passions.

Figures of the Eucharist.—The august Sacrament of the Altar is called by David "an abridgment of the wonders of God," and by the fathers, "an extension of the incarnation." It occupies so important a place in religion that, from the beginning of the world, God took care to announce it to men, and to fix their attention on it by a multitude of figures. A few will suffice to render unquestionable the designs of God and to show the excellence of this adorable sacrament.

The first figure of the Eucharist is the tree of life, planted in the midst of the terrestrial paradise. The tree of life was produced by an act of the omnipotence of God from a virgin soil: the body of our Lord was produced immediately by the operation of the Holy Ghost in the womb of the Virgin Mary.

The tree of life was destined to render the body of man immortal: the body of our Lord, far superior to the tree of the terrestrial paradise, gives to the soul the life of grace, to the body the life of the resurrection, to both the immortal life of glory.

The tree of life had the virtues of all plants and trees: the body of our Lord has all the tastes, all the virtues, all the treasures of the divinity itself.

The tree of life was to be found only in the terrestrial paradise: the body of our Lord is to be found only in the Church.

The tree of life existed only in one place: the body of our Lord is offered to us everywhere throughout the earth, and yet it remains eternally in heaven.

The second and third figures of the Eucharist are the sacrifices of Abel and Melchisedech, which we have already explained.

The fourth is the paschal lamb, regarding which it is proper to enter here into a few details. The paschal lamb should be immolated on the fourteenth day of the moon of the March: our Lord instituted the Holy Eucharist and was offered in sacrifice about the same time.

The paschal lamb should be immolated in the evening: our Lord instituted the Eucharist in the evening.

The paschal lamb should be immolated as a sign of the approaching deliverance from the captivity of Egypt: our Lord should be immolated to bury in the merits of his precious blood, as in the waters of the Red Sea, all the sins of the world and the powers of hell.

The paschal lamb should be roasted: our Lord in the Eucharist is consumed by the fire of his charity, to teach us that it is with a heart all burning with love that we ought to receive him.

The paschal lamb should be eaten in every family: by the Eucharist, our Lord is eaten in every family. On Calvary, no person ate, and the sacrifice was offered, not in the interior of a family, but in public; while in the guest chamber, where Jesus Christ instituted the Eucharist, the divine Lamb was distributed by our Lord himself, the true father of the family, to his apostles, representing the whole Church.

The paschal lamb should be eaten only by those who were Jews in blood and religion: our Lord can be eaten only by faithful Christians.

The paschal lamb should not have its bones broken: our Lord in the Eucharist cannot be broken or divided.

The paschal lamb should be eaten in haste: the Eucharist should be received with a lively faith, ready for action.

The paschal lamb should be eaten with unleavened bread and bitter lettuce: the Eucharist should be received with purity of conscience and sorrow for sin.

The Jews should eat the paschal lamb with loins girt, a staff in the hand, and shoes on the feet: Christians, to eat the virginal flesh of the Lamb of God, should be perfectly chaste, bear like pilgrims of eternity the staff of the cross in hand, and for shoes cover their feet with meditation on death and their last end.

The fifth figure of the Eucharist is the manna, regarding which we have entered into all the details necessary.

The sixth is the loaves of proposition. The loaves of proposition, placed on a table in the Temple of Jerusalem, were a perpetual testimony to the dependence of the Jews on God, whose absolute dominion over life, represented by bread, which is a condition of it, they thus acknowledged. The Holy Eucharist is likewise a perpetual evidence of our total dependence on God and of our gratitude for his benefits.

The loaves of proposition were prepared by the priests of the purest unleavened flour: the body of our Lord was formed by the Holy Ghost himself, of the purest blood of the Blessed Virgin, and without any mixture of original sin or corruption.

The twelve loaves of proposition were offered every day in the name of the twelve tribes of Israel: the body of our Lord is offered every day in the name of all Christians.

In the old law, the priests alone had the right to make the loaves of proposition: in the new, to priests alone belongs the power to consecrate the body of our Lord.

On the loaves of proposition rested a golden vase, filled with exquisite perfumes: the end of Communion is to make the soul a golden vase by charity, filled with the perfumes of praise and prayer.

Many other figures of the Eucharist are to be found in the holy scripture. The foregoing suffice to show us the place which it occupies in the plan of providence, and the dispositions which it requires for its worthy reception. But it is time to say what it is in itself.

Definition of the Eucharist.—The Eucharist is a sacrament which truly, really, and substantially contains the body, the blood, the soul, and the divinity of our Lord Jesus Christ, under the appearances of bread and wine.

The word *truly*, employed by the Council of Trent, means that the Eucharist is not a mere figure or a simple sign of the body of Jesus Christ, as Zuinglius would have it. The word *really* means that Jesus Christ is not present in the Eucharist only as an object that faith can conceive there, as Calvin imagined. The word *substantially* denotes that the Eucharist does not contain merely a virtue that emanates from the body of Jesus Christ, as the same Calvin said at a later date. These three terms are directly opposed to the three modes of speaking adopted by the innovators. It was impossible to define better the Catholic belief in regard to the real presence.

As for the various names given to this august sacrament, they remind us of the profound veneration with which Christian ages have surrounded this gift above all other gifts. Thus, we see the apostles at Jerusalem, in the midst of the fervent neophytes whom they had converted on the day of Pentecost, finding time for the "breaking of bread." In the early ages of the Church, these words and others equally mysterious were used to designate the Blessed Eucharist; for it was feared lest a knowledge of a thing so holy should come to the profane. Still, even then, our forefathers in the faith gave this adorable sacrament the same names as we give it at the present day.

They called it "Eucharist," that is, thanksgiving. First, because, when instituting it, our Lord returned thanks to his Father; and, next, because in offering and receiving the body and blood of the Savior, under the appearances of bread and wine, we make a worthy thanksgiving to God for all the benefits that we have received from his infinite goodness, since we present to him a gift which equals all those that he has bestowed on us.[729] The Eucharist is the true expression of man's gratitude to God. Could there be anything more beautiful?

With St. Paul himself, "the table of the Lord, the supper of the Lord," because the Eucharist is a spiritual banquet which Jesus Christ instituted after partaking of the paschal lamb—a banquet to which he invites all the faithful, in order to nourish them with his body and blood.[730]

"Communion," because when we participate in the body and blood of our Lord, we are united to him and the rest of the faithful in a manner so close that henceforth we make with Jesus Christ and among ourselves but one body.[731]

"Viaticum," because it is the spiritual food of the faithful during the pilgrimage of this life.[732]

"The body and blood of the Lord," "the holy of the Lord," or simply the "holy things;" at other times, "the terrible mysteries."[733]

That the Eucharist is a sacrament of the new law is most certain. a) It possesses all the conditions of a true sacrament; a sensible sign, a sign instituted by our Lord, a sign which has the virtue of producing grace: of all which we shall see the proof in this lesson. b) It has been regarded as a true sacrament by the fathers of the Church, and even by separated sects, since the first ages.[734] c) The Catholic Church, the infallible interpreter of scripture and tradition, anathematized the innovators of the sixteenth century, who, scorning the belief of the world, dared to attack this sacrament.[735]

Elements of the Eucharist: Its matter.—The matter of the Eucharist is bread and wine. The evangelists teach us that our Lord took bread in his hands, and blessed it, and broke it, saying: "This is my body"; then a chalice of wine, which he also blessed, saying: "This is my blood." Bread alone properly so called, bread of pure wheat, and wine alone properly so called, wine of the vine, are the matter of the Eucharist. Such is the tradition of the apostles as well as the express teaching of the Catholic Church.[736]

It is also easy to see that the bread should be unleavened, in order to harmonize with the circumstances in which our Lord instituted the Eucharist. He did so on the first day of the Azymes, a time when the Jews were forbidden to have leavened bread in their houses. Yet the quality of being unleavened is not so necessary that one cannot validly consecrate leavened bread. These two kinds of bread are alike real bread. But it is not permitted to any individual to change, on his own private authority, the holy custom of the Church. The priests of the Latin Church are so much the less able to do this, as sovereign pontiffs have forbidden the holy mysteries to be celebrated by them otherwise than with unleavened bread.

Although wine properly so called, wine which comes from the fruit of the vine, is also the matter of the Eucharist, the Church has always been accustomed to put a little water into it. The authority of councils and the testimony of the fathers teach us that our Lord did so himself. Besides, we are thus reminded of the blood and water which flowed from the side of Jesus Christ. In fine, the water, being a figure of the people, as we see in the Apocalypse of St. John, represents, when mixed with the wine of the sacrifice, the union of the believing people with Jesus Christ, their head. This apostolic usage has always been observed in the Church.

We shall now see why our Lord was pleased to give us his body and blood under strange appearances. Here, as elsewhere, his conduct was grounded on reasons worthy of his infinite wisdom and his love for us. The first was not to banish us from his sacred table. We should be horrified to eat his flesh and drink his blood under their ordinary appearances. The second, to increase our merits, by exercising our faith. The third, to remind us that we are strangers and pilgrims here, and ought to sigh continually after our true country, where we shall behold our Lord, no longer under veils, but face-to-face.

Let us admire, moreover, how proper were the symbols of bread and wine to represent to us the nature and the effects of the Eucharist.

1. Bread and wine, being the noblest sustenance and the most excellent nourishment of our bodies, tell us plainly that our Lord in the Eucharist is the firmest support and the most precious food of our souls. He himself explains the matter to us in these terms: "My flesh is meat indeed, and my blood is drink indeed. He who eateth my flesh and drinketh

my blood...shall live forever."[737] The body of Jesus Christ is therefore a food which gives eternal life to those who receive it worthily. Nothing, therefore, could be more natural than to consecrate it with a matter which may be considered the life of the body.

2. The bread and wine have also this advantage, that they serve to convince us of the real presence of the body and blood of Jesus Christ in the Eucharist. In effect, we every day see bread and wine changed into our flesh and blood. What is better calculated than this daily and indisputable fact to produce or to preserve within us the belief that the bread and wine are changed by the words of consecration into the true body and blood of our Lord?

3. This miraculous change serves admirably to express the change which takes place in the soul. As the bread and wine are really changed into the body and blood of Jesus Christ, without any visible change occurring, so when we communicate, though outwardly nothing appears to change in us, yet we are, by the virtue of this august sacrament, renovated, and transformed, and animated with a new life.

4. The bread and wine eloquently recall to our minds the great mystery of love which is accomplished in the Eucharist, and the end which our Lord proposed to himself in its institution. In effect, as wine is made from many grapes, and bread from many grains, so we all, however numerous we may be, form only one body, consisting of various members, but united by the closest bonds, when we participate in the divine mysteries. This is the very language of the apostle St. Paul.[738]

5. The bread and wine, representing most vividly all that our Lord endured for us, are incomparably well adapted to penetrate us with a lively sense of gratitude toward him. To become bread, the grain must first be cast into the ground, from which it will spring up into a stalk and multiply. Before ripening, it endures the wind, the rain, and the hail, the heat and the cold. Then it is threshed in the barn, ground in the mill, baked in the oven. The grape passes through the same trials. After enduring, like the grain, all the inclemencies and vicissitudes of the weather, it is crushed in the press. It must then be left in the vat, and afterward be shut up in the vault, to become good wine. Can anything point out to us better the labors, sorrows, and death which our Lord underwent in order to become our heavenly bread and wine in the sacrament of his love?

Its form. The form of the Eucharist consists in the words of consecration. The Catholic faith teaches that three admirable and miraculous effects are produced by these divine words. The first, that the bread and wine are changed into the true body and blood of Jesus Christ, the same who was born of the Blessed Virgin and who is now seated at the right hand of the Father in heaven. The second, that the bread and wine are so changed, so destroyed, that there absolutely remains nothing of them, though the contrary appears in regard to the senses. The third, the consequence of the other two, that the sensible accidents or appearances which remain are not supported by any matter, and subsist by a miracle wholly incomprehensible.

We see indeed, after consecration, the appearances of bread and wine—the color and the form; we perceive their taste. Yet, the substances of the bread and wine are so changed into the body and blood of Jesus Christ that there absolutely remains nothing thereof, that there is no longer really present either the substance of the bread or the substance of the wine. Such is the doctrine of the Savior himself and the invariable belief of his Church.[739]

It follows hence that our Lord is whole and entire in the Sacrament of the Altar, and whole and entire under the appearances of either the bread or the wine. Under the latter is comprised, not only the blood, but the body whole and entire—Jesus Christ, true God and true man, without division. In like manner, under the former is comprised, not only the body, but the whole Person of the Savior, without division. And not only is Jesus Christ,

God and man, whole and entire under each of the species of bread and wine, but he is likewise whole and entire under the least part of each species, for the fundamental reason that our Lord is living in the Eucharist. Hence, his flesh and blood cannot be separated. This admirable change, by which the substance of the bread and the substance of the wine are each changed into the body and blood of Jesus Christ, is called transubstantiation.

The simultaneous presence of our Lord in a great number of hosts is a wonderful truth, which we must believe without a shadow of hesitation, since it has been attested by God himself, to whom nothing is impossible and who cannot deceive. Yet we find in ourselves something which may help our belief. It is certain that our soul is whole and entire in all our members—whole and entire in the head, whole and entire in the feet, whole and entire in every part of the body. What then is there surprising in the fact that God should render present the body of his Son in many hosts, when he causes our soul to be present whole and entire in so many organs at once?

Bodies differ, doubtless, from souls in their manner of being, but who can say to God, "Thou canst not change the mode of existence peculiar to my body, such as I know it to be?" Is it not well known, and in a manner more certain than the existence of Caesar is known, that several saints—St. Antony of Padua, St. Francis Xavier, and St. Alphonsus, for example—have been seen at the same time in different places, far distant from each other?

Its minister. The ministers of the Eucharist are, to the exclusion of all others, bishops and priests. The Son of God conferred this august ministry on them when, after consecrating his own body and blood, he said to them: "Do this in commemoration of me."[740] Words of ineffable love, which, giving to the apostles and their successors the power to do that which the man-God has just done, bequeath to us in perpetuity the inheritance of his body and blood, that we may be nourished therewith, and become in reality other children of God, new Jesus Christs!

Institution of the Eucharist.—The great God who created and who governs nature was pleased that the sunrise should be preceded by the pale tints of the dawn, then by the bright hues of the morning. This same God, who created and who governs the moral world, was pleased that the appearance of the august Eucharist, the divine sun of the universe, should be preceded by figures; the dim reflex of its splendor; then by promises, which announced it with admirable clearness. We have already explained the figures of the greatest of our mysteries. The solemn promise of it, made to the Jews by our Lord himself, is developed in the life of the Messias: it only remains for us to speak of the accomplishment of this promise. To our foregoing historical details in reference to the institution of the Blessed Eucharist, let us add the following explanations, which will serve to confirm the dogma of the real presence.

The Savior, presenting to the apostles the bread which he had just consecrated, said to them: "Take and eat—this is my body." And, to confound from this moment the innovators of the sixteenth century, he adds: "Yes, my body, which shall be delivered for you." Now, it was not the figure of our Lord's body that was delivered to tortures. In the same manner, when presenting to them the wine which he had just consecrated, he said to them: "Drink ye all of this—this is my blood." And, again to confound heretics, he adds: "Yes, my blood, which shall be shed for you." Now, it was not the figure of our Lord's blood that was shed for us. Since then the body and blood which Jesus Christ gives us in the Eucharist are the same body that was delivered and the same blood that was shed for us, we must conclude that our Lord is really present and is really given to us in the sacrament of our altars.

If Calvinists were sincere, they would have no difficulty in admitting this: as you may judge. Suppose it was said in a will, made in favor of one of them: "I leave my house to such a man," would not that man believe himself the heir to the house? What would he say if some person handed him as the equivalent of his inheritance a picture of the house, under the pretext that the words, "I give my house," meant, "I give the picture or the figure of my house"? He would cry out against the injustice as monstrous. He would appeal to the laws, and, in fact, every court in the world would acknowledge and support his right; for never, among any people, did the words, "I give my house," mean, "I give the figure of my house."

So here. Never, during Christian centuries, among Christians of East or West, have the words, "This is my body, this is my blood," meant, "This is a figure of my body, this is a figure of my blood." Protestants ought to bear in mind that, from every quarter of the globe, even from the midst of sects withdrawn from Catholic unity, there arose a concert of protestations against the delusive interpretation which they had dared to put upon the words of our Lord. This loud voice was, in the sixteenth century, but a faithful echo of the voice of all ages. The limits of this lesson rendering it impossible for us to quote all the testimonies of tradition in reference to the constant belief of our Lord's real presence in the Eucharist, we shall content ourselves with adducing one. It is that of a father who lived in one of those beautiful centuries when, according to the acknowledgment of protestants themselves, the Catholic Church was the infallible organ of truth.

St. Cyril of Jerusalem, instructing the newly baptized on what they ought to believe regarding the Eucharist, speaks to them thus: "The words of St. Paul would suffice to teach you with certainty what you ought to believe regarding the divine mysteries in which you have just participated, and which have made you one body and blood with Jesus Christ. Since Jesus Christ, speaking of what bore the appearance of bread, declared that it was his body, how should anyone afterward dare to doubt it? And since he affirms that this wine is his blood, who shall dare to call the matter in question, and say that it is not his blood? He changed water into wine at Cana in Galilee by his mere will, and does he not deserve to be believed when he changes wine into his blood?

"If, when he was invited to an ordinary marriage feast, he vouchsafed to perform so wonderful a miracle, shall we not with much greater reason admit that he gave his body and blood to the children of his own spouse? We ought to have no difficulty in believing it. Receive then with full certainty the body and blood of Jesus Christ; for, under the species of bread, the body is given to you, and, under the species of wine, the blood is given to you, in order that, having received the body and blood of your Savior, you may bear within you Jesus Christ, whose body and blood you have received, and that thus you may be, as St. Peter says, participators in the divine nature. Regard not then these things as common bread and wine, for they are the body and blood of Jesus Christ, according to the express words of the Lord.

"And although the senses suggest to you that they are bread and wine, faith must confirm you in such a manner that you shall not judge of them by the taste, however much the senses may persuade you to do so, but rest assured that you receive the body and blood of the Lord, and that there is not a shadow of doubt left on the matter...Know and hold for certain that what appears to your sight and taste bread is not bread, but the body of Jesus Christ, and that what appears to your sight and taste wine is not wine, but the true blood of our Lord."[741]

Can any clearer or more formal passage be found? And this, we repeat, is the doctrine of all the fathers.[742] It was not then, as you see, on scripture or tradition that the Calvinists grounded their opinion. On what then? On the difficulty which reason feels in believing this mystery. They said, like the people of Capharnaum, "This is a hard saying; who can understand it?" Let us imagine them there. We might well say to them: "You do not understand it, and you conclude therefore that it cannot be true. Powerful logic! You ought to deny that you exist, since you do not understand how you exist." In condemning the innovators who denied the real presence, the Catholic Church therefore only hurled a thunderbolt at pride. "If anyone," she says, "deny that in the most Holy Sacrament of the Eucharist are contained truly, really, and substantially, the body, blood, soul, and divinity of our Lord Jesus Christ, consequently Jesus Christ whole and entire, let him be anathema."[743]

Effects of the Eucharist.—Who will tell the effects of the Holy Eucharist? Picture to yourself an immense fountain of beautiful spring water on the summit of a high hill. Six large channels carry away its precious treasures to the wide lowlands. Down there you see a very paradise, the softest verdure, flowers and plants and trees of every kind, with abundant fruits. Behold the Eucharist and its effects! This august sacrament is really the source of all graces, since it contains their author in Person. Established on the holy mountain of the Catholic Church, it sends out its salutary waters through six channels, which are the six other sacraments. All that is beautiful and good in the Catholic Church is due to the waters of this vivifying and perennial fountain.

But what in particular are the effects of this divine sacrament, and the end for which our Lord established it? Our Lord established the Holy Eucharist for three reasons: a) to be the food of souls; b) to be the sacrifice of the new law; c) to be at once a memorial of his passion and an everlasting pledge of his love.

I. *Food of souls.* The first end of the Eucharist is to be the food of souls. Under this head, behold some of the effects which it produces. It increases sanctifying grace. The Eucharist, inasmuch as it is food, supposes life in the soul which receives it. It does not therefore, at least directly, give that first grace which makes us pass from spiritual death to life, but it admirably increases this life.[744]

To move us to an ardent desire of this bread of angels and to show us its excellence, our Lord always sets it before us as a principle of life. "This," he says, "is the bread which came down from heaven: if any man eat of this bread, he shall live forever. The bread which I will give is my flesh, for the life of the world. He who eateth my flesh and drinketh my blood hath everlasting life. Verily, if you eat not the flesh of the Son of man and drink not his blood, you shall not have life in you. As the living Father hath sent me, and as I live by the Father, so he who eateth me shall live by me."[745]

As nothing would afford us greater pleasure than to be exempted from the necessity of death, and as the strongest and most general passion is the desire of life, the second Adam repairs the fault of the first, and, in an admirable manner, shows himself our Savior, by delivering us through the Holy Eucharist from the greatest of our fears, that of death, and by restoring to us the greatest of our lost goods, that of life.

But what kind of life does the Savior give us in Communion? His own. In the same manner as we communicate our life to the meats which we eat and which are transformed into our substance, the Savior changes us in Communion into himself, takes away the life of the old Adam from us, and gives us his divine life. The life of the old Adam is a life of pride, of ambition, of love of creatures, of forgetfulness of God, of self-interest—a life of all the passions and of all kinds of sins. The life of the new Adam, communicated by the Holy Eucharist, is a life of meekness, of humility, of patience, of charity—a life of all the virtues and of all kinds of good works. Such is the life that we draw from the Holy Eucharist.

To give it to us, our Lord is not changed into us, because he is more perfect than we; but he changes us into himself, to make us perfect like himself. Hence, those beautiful words which St. Augustine puts into the mouth of the Savior: "I am the food of grown men; grow up, and you shall eat me. You shall not change me into you, as happens with bodily food, but I will change you into me."[746] And the blood of the Savior poured into our veins is like a generous wine which excites all the powers of the soul, ennobles them, and prompts them to deeds of a perfection wholly divine. Of what is the soul not capable in the delightful inebriation of Communion? We shall soon say something hereof.

The natural consequence of this divine life is to give us the most ardent and tender love for our Lord, by uniting us to him in the closest manner. All friendships rest on two foundations. The first is the bond of blood. It is on this account that a father loves his son, that a son loves his father, and that all relatives naturally love one another. The second is the tie of spirit. The Persons of the adorable Trinity love one another infinitely, because they are only one Spirit; and the unity of their nature is one of the chief sources of their happiness.

In order to gain the hearts of all men, the only Son of God was pleased to contract, in the incarnation, a corporal and a spiritual alliance with human nature. But in this mystery, he was united to the body and soul of one man only. He therefore established the sacrament of the Eucharist to unite himself corporally and spiritually with all those who should communicate, and to engage them by this twofold relationship to love him perfectly. O mystery of mercy! O bond of charity! If union is a reason for loving, how deeply should Communion penetrate us with love for our Lord, to whom it unites us so closely that we make with him only one body and one spirit!

Another equally natural consequence of the divine life which the august sacrament communicates to us is the purification of our souls. It effaces venial sins; it preserves us from mortal sins; it indirectly remits the punishment due to both. It is certain that the Holy Communion remits venial sins directly and by its own virtue. "It is an antidote," says the Council of Trent, "which delivers us from daily sins and preserves us from mortal ones."[747] Whence it comes that St. Ambrose said: "I ought often to take the blood of the Lord, so as often to obtain the forgiveness of my sins; since I sin often, I ought often to have the remedy for sin."[748]

As for the preservation from sin of which the holy Council of Trent speaks, the Eucharist produces this admirable effect thus. "Sin," says St. Thomas, "is the death of the soul. Now, our soul is preserved from sin, as our body is preserved from death, in two ways. The first, inasmuch as our nature is fortified against the inward germs of corruption. It is thus that we are preserved from death by food and medicines. The second, inasmuch as it is fortified against outward attacks. It is thus that we are preserved from death by the defensive weapons that protect our body. In both these ways the Eucharist preserves us from death. First, uniting us to our Lord by grace, it strengthens our spiritual life as a food; then, being a sign of the passion of Jesus Christ, by which the devils were conquered, it frustrates all their attacks."[749]

Moreover, the Eucharistic union is effected by charity. Now, charity obtains the forgiveness not only of sin, but also of the punishment due to sin. As a consequence of the chief effect, it follows that, by communicating, we obtain the remission of the punishment due to sin, if not wholly, at least proportionately to the fervor and devotion which we bring to the reception of this august sacrament.[750]

Finally, the Holy Eucharist deadens the fire of the passions, and strengthens and beautifies the soul. It deadens the fire of the passions: "When Jesus Christ is within us," says St. Cyril, "he relaxes the cruel law of our members, abates the ardor of our passions, and heals our wounds."[751] It strengthens the soul: "The man," says St. Cyprian, "who has not been armed by the Church, is incapable of martyrdom, and the soul which has not received the Eucharist falls."[752] It beautifies the soul: "The divine blood," says St. Chrysostom, "causes the image of Jesus Christ to shine resplendently in us. It gives beauty and nobility to the soul. By imparting strength, it prevents the soul from falling into languor. This blood purifies, adorns, and refines the soul, which becomes in consequence brighter than gold or fire. As he who dips his hand or his tongue in liquid gold draws it up all gilt, so the soul plunged in this divine blood becomes as pure and as beautiful as gold."

A new consequence of this divine life is that it deposits in our soul the pledge of an everlasting life, and in our body the germ of a glorious immortality. "If any one eat this bread," says the Savior, "he shall live forever." Now, eternal life is the life of glory; consequently, the effect of the sacrament is to procure this for us, not indeed immediately, but mediately, since it gives us the strength to arrive at heaven. Hence, it is called viaticum, and is figured by the mysterious bread of Elias.[753]

As for the immortality whose principle it communicates to our body, "those who take this meat and drink," says St. Augustine, "become immortal and incorruptible."[754] "In effect," continues St. Thomas, "though the body is not the immediate subject of grace, yet the effect of grace is reflected from the soul on the body, whose members are presented to God as instruments of justice and sanctity; so that our body, become the companion of the soul in its struggles, shall one day share in its incorruptible glory."[755]

For the rest, the Savior himself has said: "He who eateth my flesh and drinketh my blood hath everlasting life, and I will raise him up on the last day."[756] After Communion, the Christian may therefore repeat, with more reason than holy Job, these beautiful words: "I know that my Redeemer liveth, and that I shall rise again on the last day, and that I shall see my God in my own flesh. This hope is laid up in my bosom; it shall sleep with me in the grave."[757] Thus, by Communion, the new Adam repairs in our body as well as in our soul the consequences of original sin, and enriches us with new gifts.

II. *Sacrifice of the new law*. The second end of the Eucharist is to be the sacrifice of the new law. In the explanation of the Mass, we shall enter into full details on this point. We shall only say here that our Lord was not content, when instituting the august sacrament, to give us a divine food. He was pleased also to leave us an all-powerful means of appeasing God and obtaining from him whatsoever we should ask.

III. *Memorial of his passion and everlasting pledge of his love*. The third end of the Eucharist is to be a memorial of his passion, as well as an everlasting pledge of his love. When treating of the Mass, we shall show that the august sacrifice of our altars is a complete abridgment of all the mysteries of the life, death, and resurrection of our Lord.

The Eucharist is therefore a continual pledge of his love—an eloquent pledge, which not only hinders us from forgetting him who so much loved us, but also excites in our souls an ardent affection for him. In the old testament, God was pleased that the Hebrews should eat the manna which he sent them from heaven, and that they should always preserve some of it in a precious vessel, in memory of the benefits with which he had loaded them on their departure from Egypt. Accomplishing this figure, our Lord was pleased that the Holy Eucharist should be not only received and eaten by Christians, but also preserved in our tabernacles.

The Church, his spouse, has ordained that the true manna, come down from heaven, should occasionally be borne in triumph, in order that as often as we see it the remembrance of the Savior and of his infinite love may take possession of our hearts. By these last two ends of the Eucharist, our Lord wondrously continues the work of the redemption. On the one part, he night and day holds up above our heads the great victim, alone capable of appeasing the anger of God: on the other, he keeps continually lighted on the earth the immense furnace of love that saved mankind.

Dispositions for receiving the Holy Eucharist.—That the Holy Communion may produce its admirable effects in us, we must bring to its reception the proper dispositions. Of these dispositions, some relate to the body, others to the soul; some precede, others accompany, and others follow the Holy Communion.

Dispositions of the body: Fasting. The first disposition of the body is fasting. No person is unaware that our Lord instituted the sacrament of the Eucharist after the legal supper, and that he communicated his apostles only after eating the paschal lamb: it was just that the figure should precede the reality. The early Christians followed this example. Met in their holy assemblies, they received the Eucharist after partaking of an ordinary repast styled *agapae*, a name that was given it, as Tertullian remarks, because it was a charitable repast, of which the rich defrayed the expenses and to which the poor were invited.[758]

This usage lasted for a short time. The apostles themselves, for good reasons, ordained, in virtue of power received from our Lord, that no one should communicate otherwise than fasting. Such became afterward the general usage of the Church, so that one would render himself guilty of a great sin if he were to communicate after breaking his fast, unless in case of a last illness. The fast should be absolute, that is to say, a person must have taken nothing, absolutely nothing, from the midnight of the day on which he is to communicate.

Modesty. The second disposition of the body is modesty. It suffices to be deeply convinced that our Lord is personally present in the Holy Eucharist, to teach us that we should not present ourselves at the holy table without a holy fear, a great humility, a perfect modesty. To come to it with wandering eyes, an ill-ordered demeanor, a worldly air, is to give the beholders an occasion of thinking that one has neither faith nor piety.

Men and women ought to receive the Holy Eucharist on their knees, with eyes cast down, their hands covered under the cloth and placed in such a manner as to uphold the sacred host in case it should fall from the hands of the priest. Men should not carry arms at this time, and women should be very modestly attired. It is necessary to avoid spitting for some time after Communion. If this cannot be done, one should use a linen-cloth, and not spit on the ground, for it might happen that one would cast out some particles of the consecrated species. To shun this danger, St. Chrysostom used to exhort the faithful to drink a little water after receiving the Eucharist: this custom still exists in Germany.

Dispositions of the soul. The dispositions of the soul are derived from the very nature of this sacrament. The Holy Eucharist is the food of our souls, and we ought to bring to the reception of this spiritual food the same dispositions as are necessary to derive advantage from corporal food. Now, there are five conditions required to eat with advantage: a) one must be alive; b) one must be hungry; c) one must eat; d) one must digest; e) one must labor—for we do not eat merely to eat. The same conditions are required to receive with advantage the divine food of our souls.

1. *To communicate, one must be alive.* The dead do not eat, life consists in the grace of God, that is to say, in exemption from mortal sin. If a man is not in this state, he must purify his soul by a good confession. Woe—a thousand times—to him who would dare to communicate with a mortal sin on his conscience! He would commit a most horrible sacrilege. Yet if, before communicating, a person calls to mind a grievous fault of which he has omitted to accuse himself through an involuntary forgetfulness, there is an allowance to be made. He would do well to confess it before communicating, when this can be done conveniently, but he is not bound to do so. It suffices that, after asking pardon anew, he should form the resolution of accusing himself thereof at his next confession.

The life of grace necessarily supposes faith, hope, and charity. In their turn, these virtues suppose in adults a knowledge of certain truths that are their object. He who communicates ought therefore to know and to believe the principal truths of religion, and especially what concerns the Blessed Eucharist: so much is strictly necessary. But if this first degree of knowledge, faith, hope, and charity, that is to say, of sanctifying grace, is enough to excuse one from the guilt of communicating unworthily, and even helps one to draw some fruit from the Eucharist, as is proved by the practice of the primitive Church, which gave Communion to infants, they who wish to share abundantly in the graces of which this sacrament is the source must not be content with this feeble preparation. We shall just now show this in speaking of the second condition.

2. *To communicate, one must be hungry.* It is not enough to be alive, to derive great benefit from food: one must have an appetite. To derive great benefit from the Holy Communion, it is not enough to be in the state of grace: one must have a hunger for this divine food. This spiritual hunger consists in an ardent desire of communicating. In giving himself to us under the form of food, our Lord marks sufficiently well the usefulness of this disposition. Nevertheless, he was pleased to give us an example of it in himself. "I have most ardently desired," he said to his apostles, "to eat this pasch with you."[759] This disposition was so common among the early Christians that they called the Eucharist the object of all their desires, *desiderata.*

To excite this hunger within us, it is necessary in the first place to be penetrated with a lively sense of the advantages which the Holy Eucharist procures for us, as well by delivering us from evil as by giving us every real good. To meditation on the advantages of Communion we must join prayer and interior and exterior mortification, so that our heart may be neither divided nor dissipated.

For the rest, it is not necessary that this desire should be sensible: only let it be sincere. It is such if we have a will to amend our faults and to advance in virtue. Nothing is more important than to excite this disposition within us: it will be the measure of the graces that we shall receive in Communion. "Open the mouth of thy heart," says the Savior, "and I will fill it; the more thou shalt open it, the more thou shalt receive. The measure of the favors which thou shalt receive depends not on me, but on thee: if it please thee, thou mayst receive me entirely."[760]

3. *It is not enough to hunger for food: it is necessary to eat.* The manner of eating the bread of angels is to approach the holy table, not only with sanctifying grace, but with a lively faith, a firm hope, an ardent charity, a profound humility, a holy eagerness, in a word, a real devotion, free from tepidity, negligence, and precipitation.[761]

4. *It is not what one eats that nourishes, but what one digests.* As for the manner of digesting the divine food, it may be explained in this wise. Spirits are fed by knowledge and love. In virtue of these two operations, they assimilate to themselves the true and the good. To be assimilated to our Lord in the Eucharist, the soul ought therefore before, during, and after Communion to apply itself to know this divine Savior under his different titles and in his different actions. After thus contemplating him, it appropriates them to itself by imagining, what is moreover perfectly true, that our Lord makes use of all his divine perfections as so many divine meats, and that he says to us: "Eat ye all hereof. Behold my wisdom, *manducate ex hoc omnes.* Behold my patience, *manducate ex hoc omnes.* Behold my love, my meekness, my humility, my zeal, my poverty, my spotless purity, etc., etc., *manducate ex hoc omnes.*"

Thus the soul, by loving his divine perfections, so takes them to itself that it becomes, as St. Peter the apostle says, a participator in the nature of God himself.[762] How useful it is to know these things, in order to correspond with the Savior's intentions, and to communicate with advantage!

5. *We do not eat to eat, but to repair our strength and to labor.* To profit of Communion and to receive it in accordance with the Savior's intentions, we must, after approaching it, resume our labor with new ardor and perfection. If material food communicates its properties to our body, divine food ought to do the same to our soul. Moreover, the labor to which he who has become another Jesus Christ ought to devote himself can only be, under pain of degradation and sacrilege, a labor worthy of Jesus Christ, a divine labor.

Hence, to labor divinely, that is to say, with great perfection of intention, of courage, of sanctity, in a word, to show in our conduct the virtues of our Lord, so as to be able to say, "It is no longer I who live, but Jesus Christ liveth in me," and to labor in things worthy of a soul which has become divine, that is to say, to keep faithfully the commandments of God and the Church, must be the life of the Christian after Communion.

To pursue the analogy still further, when we have labored, and, in doing so, have exhausted our strength, we take food again, and again return to our labor. When, after communicating, we labor for our sanctification, and at length feel our spiritual strength decline, we must anew seat ourselves at the holy table, and then return to our labor. It is easily seen that, as the whole planetary system depends upon the sun, the whole life of a Christian should find its center in the adorable Eucharist.

Necessity of the Eucharist.—Our Lord said, "Unless you eat the flesh of the Son of man, and drink his blood, you shall not have life in you."[763] Taken literally, these words mean that if we do not really receive the body and blood of Jesus Christ, we shall not have life in us. In this sense they are addressed only to adults. If they regarded all men, the Church would not have ceased giving the Eucharist to infants. The real reception of the sacrament is therefore not necessary for children that have been regenerated by baptism and have not lost grace.[764]

Taken spiritually, these words warn us that if we are not incorporated with our Lord as members with their head, we shall have no part in eternal life. In this case, they regard infants as well as adults. Neither the one nor the other can obtain eternal life without being united to Jesus Christ.

Although, then, it is not absolutely necessary for all men to receive the Eucharist really, that is, with the mouth, it is necessary for them to receive it spiritually, that is, to be incorporated with Jesus Christ, and to be members of his mystical body, which is the Church. Now, this spiritual Communion contains the desire of receiving the sacrament of the Eucharist, as St. Thomas teaches.[765] Infants have this desire at baptism by the intention of the Church, as they believe by the faith of the Church, according to the same doctor.[766]

We cannot omit to remark here the striking analogy which exists between the natural and the supernatural order. In the natural order, the child is first fed with the substance of its mother; in the supernatural order, it also begins by being nourished with the belief and life of the Church, its mother.

In the natural order, the child is next fed with a delicate meat provided from without; in the supernatural order, the child has for its second food the divine word, or the Word under the form of the word which comes to it by outward teaching.

In the natural order, the child, having acquired strength, is fed with a more substantial food, which it is obliged to earn by labor, whatever may be its condition; in the supernatural order, the child, having grown up, is nourished with the Holy Eucharist, which is the Word in Person—a powerful food which it is obliged to earn by the labor and struggle of virtue.

How can we fail to see that the laws of the physical and the moral world have for their author the same God, and rest on the same infinite wisdom and goodness?

Besides the ecclesiastical precept of paschal Communion, there is also a divine precept which renders the reception of the Eucharist necessary for all those who have attained to the use of reason. This obligation is founded on the words of our Lord, quoted above. The divine precept obliges at least at the hour of death, and several times during life. To fulfill the divine and ecclesiastical precepts of Communion suffices to escape the guilt of mortal sin. But can Communions so rare suffice for the wants of our soul, or realize the intentions of the Savior? Certainly not. Experience teaches that rare Communions do not produce any fruit. Is it by doing a thing seldom that we learn to do it well?

This is the reason why all Christians who seriously desire their salvation must acquire the holy habit of frequent Communion. Such is the desire of our Lord, who, to manifest it, instituted the Eucharist under the form of our ordinary food. Such was the practice of the early Christians, who used to communicate every day. Such is the desire of the Church, which, in the Council of Trent, expressed a most earnest wish that all the faithful should return to the usage of their ancestors.[767] Such is the advice of all experienced directors of souls.

Let us hear St. Francis de Sales in the name of all: "Among those who wish to serve God devoutly, the greatest distance between Communions is a month...If worldlings ask you why you communicate so often, tell them that it is to learn to love God, to purify yourself from your imperfections, to free yourself from your miseries, to console yourself under your afflictions.

"Let two classes of people communicate often: the perfect, because, being well disposed, they would suffer much by not approaching the fountain of perfection; and the imperfect, in order to aspire rightly to perfection. The strong, that they may not become weak; and the weak, that they may become strong. The sick, that they may be healed; and the healthy, that they may not fall sick. And as for you, imperfect, weak, and sick, you require to communicate often with your perfection, your strength, your physician...

"Those who have not much worldly business ought to communicate often, because they have leisure to do so, and those who have much worldly business, because they have need to do so...Tell worldlings that you receive the holy of holies to learn this exercise well: because an action that is seldom done is scarcely ever well done.

"Communicate often—as often as you can, with the advice of your spiritual father; and, believe me, as hares become white on our mountains in winter by seeing and eating snow, so by adoring and eating beauty, goodness, purity itself, in this divine sacrament, you will become all beautiful, all good, and all pure...To communicate every eight days, it is necessary to be free from mortal sin and from affection to venial sin, and to have a great desire of communicating; but to communicate every day, it is necessary, besides, to have overcome the greater number of one's evil inclinations, and to communicate with the advice of one's spiritual father."[768]

PRAYER

O my God! who art all love, I thank thee for having instituted the adorable sacrament of the Eucharist, to communicate to me thy divine life.

I am resolved to love God above all things, and my neighbor as myself for the love of God; and, in testimony of this love, I will never fail to cast myself on my knees when I see the Holy Sacrament borne to the sick.

Lesson 37: Our Union with the New Adam by Hope (10)

Liturgy of the Eucharist.—If baptism is the most necessary, the Eucharist is the most august of the sacraments, for it contains the very author of grace, the very author of the sacraments. While showing us the profound veneration with which the Christians of the last eighteen centuries have surrounded this august sacrament, the liturgical history of the Eucharist will be a powerful means of awaking our piety toward the Son of God present on our altars, and an illustrious testimony to the perpetuity of the Catholic faith.

As we have seen, the matter of the Eucharist has always been bread and wine. Formerly it was the faithful themselves who offered the bread and wine destined for the sacrifice: the same thing had taken place among the Jews. Nothing more reasonable than that they should supply the matter of a sacrifice to be offered for their benefit. Hence, this offering was made by all—men and women—without distinction. Each person prepared the bread that should be offered. Emperors themselves complied with this duty.[769] Far from imagining that they thereby dishonored the hand that was accustomed to wield the scepter, they believed that they could not employ it for a nobler purpose: and they were right.

St. Radegondes, queen of France, used not only to make with her hands the bread which she would offer at the altar, but also applied herself with much devotion to make other sacrificial breads for distribution among the churches. Before her, Candida, wife of Trajan, commander-in-chief of the emperor Valerian's armies, used to spend whole nights in grinding the wheat whose flour was destined for the Eucharistic bread. "I have seen with my eyes," says a historian of the Church, "this illustrious matron working all night with her own hands at the preparation of the bread for the oblation."[770]

This ancient and holy custom continued in vigor till the ninth century. We still behold some remarkable remains of it at Milan, whose Church maintains a congregation of ten aged men and ten aged women, called the "School of St. Ambrose," to represent the whole people. Two of these aged men, accompanied by the others, and clad in a peculiar dress, present the bread and wine. The first presents three hosts, and his companion a cruet of wine. After them come two aged women, who in like manner present bread and wine. All, both men and women, are followed by the rest of the school, who go in succession to make the oblation of the Eucharistic symbols. The offering is made thus on all solemn feasts.[771]

Apart from this beautiful tradition, we no longer know any Church where the people offer at Mass the bread and wine of the consecration. The change in discipline is owing to two causes. On the one hand, the priests considered it their duty to offer at the altar breads prepared with more care than those which were usually presented by the people. On the other, the faithful made donations or foundations to the Church, charging the sacred ministers with the procurement of all things necessary for the divine service. Thus, although the bread and wine, destined to be the matter of the sacrifice, are no longer offered immediately by the people, yet they may always be regarded as the oblation of the faithful, because they proceed from their gifts. Such is also, at least in part, the object of the collections which are at the present day made in our churches.

The bread and wine destined for the oblation were placed on the altar. The wine was poured into chalices, which usually had two handles, because they were large and heavy, and by this means they were more easily carried and handled when it was necessary to give the people the Communion of the precious blood. The bread was laid on a plate called a paten, a name which it has retained to the present day. But the ancient paten was much larger than ours, and it cannot be doubted that, on great solemnities, there were several of them, as there were several chalices for the wine.[772]

After the consecration of the holy species, the faithful approached the sacred table; but, before the Communion began, a deacon pronounced these terrible words in a loud voice: *Sancta sanctis!*—"Holy things are for the holy!" As if he should say: "Let those who are not holy beware of taking part in these dreadful mysteries." Moreover, when the bishop or priest distributed the body of our Lord, he said: "The body of Jesus Christ!" The communicant answered, "Amen," a word which showed the receiver's faith in the real presence. It was about the eighth century that the above words of the priest were replaced by the more explicit formula which is used at the present day in giving Communion: "The body of our Lord Jesus Christ preserve thy soul to life everlasting. Amen."

History of a Jewish child miraculously preserved in the midst of flames.—In some churches, after the faithful had communicated, the remains of the Eucharist were given to young, innocent children. Let us mention, in connection with this practice, a signal miracle which occurred at Constantinople in 574, under the reign of Justinian. One day, Mass had been said in a church of the holy Virgin, and as there remained several particles of the Blessed Eucharist, a number of little children were brought in to consume them. Among the party was a Jewish child, the son of a glassmaker. He participated like the rest in the body and blood of the Lord, went home very joyful, and related to his father all that had happened. This man, forgetting every sentiment of paternal affection, laid hold of his child, and threw him into the burning furnace where he was making his glass. The mother, becoming aware of the matter, ran to the rescue of her son, but the flames which leaped from the furnace would not permit her to go near him.

Then, tearing away the ornaments of her head, she ran out with disheveled hair, and filled the whole neighborhood with her screams. The Christians came in a crowd, turned aside the fire from the mouth of the furnace, and saw the child as it were reposing tranquilly on feathers. Full of amazement, they brought him out at once, and blessed God on seeing that there was no injury done him. The author of the crime was cast into the furnace, and was immediately consumed. On asking the child how he had been preserved in the fire, he answered: "The woman who holds the child in her arms, and sits in the church where I ate the bread, covered me with her mantle and guarded me from the flames." The mother and child were instructed in the Catholic faith, and were baptized with a large number of other Jews belonging to the city.[773]

The fame of this miracle was such that it reached the Gauls. St. Gregory of Tours refers to it in his book on the *Glory of Martyrs*.[774] Nicephorus, a historian of the Church, who relates the same fact, adds that, when a child, he himself often ate the remains of the Eucharist. From which it is clear that this custom continued in Constantinople till at least the middle of the sixth century, in which the emperor Justinian lived, and elsewhere till at least the fourteenth, which is the time of Nicephorus.[775]

As to the place in which Communion was given, the most general practice was this: the celebrant, as is still done everywhere, communicated at the middle of the altar, the assisting priests in front of it, the deacons behind it, the subdeacon and clerks at the entrance of the sanctuary or in the choir, and the rest of the faithful outside the railing which separated the sanctuary and choir from the nave. Emperors alone were dispensed from this rule. It was permitted them to communicate at the altar, as well as to make their offerings there.[776]

Our ancestors in the faith used to receive the Holy Communion standing. They did so in imitation of the children of Israel, who, with loins girt and pilgrim's staff in hand, used to eat the lamb which was figurative of the Eucharist. Such was the usage, not only of the ministers of the Church, but also of the simple faithful. Yet they bowed the head a little and kept the eyes cast down, to express those sentiments of adoration with which they partook of this divine food—a food, says St. Augustine, which no one ought ever to receive without having first adored.

In our days again, when the sovereign pontiff celebrates Solemn Mass, the deacon communicates standing, doubtless to remind us of the ancient usage.[777] To recall another tradition much more sacred, the holy father, even to this day, communicates sitting at Solemn Masses, when he officiates pontifically:[778] an august spectacle, which naturally brings before our eyes the last supper, when our divine master and the apostles partook sitting of the sacred mysteries.

Formerly, the body of our Lord was left in the houses of the faithful, who communicated themselves. Men received it on their bare hand, which they accordingly washed with great care before entering the church. Women received it on the right hand covered with a white linen cloth. Some accidents having occurred, the Church determined not to lay the Communion any longer thus on the hands of the faithful. This change of discipline took place about the ninth century. Henceforth, priests were directed to bear the species of bread to the mouths of the communicants.

As to the manner in which the faithful took the precious blood, the most ancient was to present them the chalice which contained the consecrated wine, and to let them drink thereof. We shall content ourselves with quoting the words of St. Cyril of Jerusalem, who of all the ancient fathers enters into the fullest details regarding the sacramental rites.

He says: "After thus partaking of the body of Jesus Christ, approach the chalice of the blood, not stretching out your hands, but bowing in adoration to it, and saying, 'Amen.' Be sanctified by the touch of this blood of Jesus Christ which you receive. While your lips are yet wet with it, wipe them with your hand, and bear it, immediately to your eyes, your forehead, and the other chief organs of your senses, as a consecration thereof. In fine, while you await the last prayer of the priest, thank God for having made you worthy to participate in mysteries so great and exalted."[779]

This manner of communicating was still in existence at the close of the sixth century.[780] Then was introduced the custom of taking the precious blood through a pipe: it arose from the fear of accidents and profanations. In the course of time, to make matters doubly sure, the practice of giving the two species together was set on foot: this was done by placing in the communicant's mouth a host dipped in the precious blood.[781] The practice of communicating the faithful under the two species during the celebration of the holy mysteries was observed till the twelfth century: at this period it began to disappear.

Two things contributed to its decline: a) the fear of spilling the divine blood, a woeful inconvenience, which exceedingly alarmed the faithful as well as the ministers of the Church, and to which it was nevertheless difficult to apply a remedy, especially on great solemnities, when all the people communicated; and b) the scarcity of wine in those northern countries which were converted about this time. How, in effect, could people be obliged to communicate under the two species in those icy regions where it was often very difficult and always very expensive to procure a sufficiency of wine, even for the priests at the altar? Finally, the Council of Constance, held in 1414, forbade Communion to be any longer given under the species of wine to the faithful.[782]

This suppression altered in no respect the integrity of the sacrament, for our Lord is wholly and entirely present under each of the species. Nothing whatever was taken from its perfection, for the perfection of the Eucharist does not consist in the use which the faithful make of it, but in the consecration of its proper matter. Hence, there is not the slightest derogation from its perfection when the people take the species of bread without that of wine, provided the priest who consecrates takes both.[783]

The primitive Church itself so little imagined that to give only one species was to divide the mystery, that it had solemn days on which it was content to distribute the sacred body of our Lord. Such were in the Eastern Church all the days of Lent, except Saturdays and Sundays, and in the Western Church Good Friday.[784] We see that the changes made by the Church in regard to discipline are not sudden innovations, but the public sanction of previous acts grounded on the requirements of time and place. That which now engages us is not the first example of a truth too little known; neither is it the last, as we shall just see.

The early Christians had a holy hunger for the Eucharist; but the hatred of their enemies prevented them from coming together as often as they would have desired. As a kind of indemnification for their loss, they partook at one another's houses of the divine banquet. This tender practice may be traced back to the very cradle of the Church. St. Luke acquaints us with it in the Acts of the Apostles.[785] He tells us that the disciples "were going daily to the temple and continuing in prayer": this was their preparation for Communion; "and that then, breaking bread from house to house, they took their meat with gladness and simplicity of heart."[786] By the *houses* here mentioned, the sacred author means the private dwellings of the faithful, as all commentators explain and as the context evidently shows.

The persecutions with which the Church was troubled rendered this custom in some manner necessary. We see it in the course of time becoming general. St. Justin, who lived shortly after the apostles, bears positive testimony to it in the famous apology which he addressed to the emperor Antoninus. "After the celebration of the holy mysteries," he says, "we reserve some particles, which the deacons bear to the faithful who cannot be present thereat."[787] St. Lucian, a priest of the Church of Antioch, who suffered martyrdom at Nicomedia, having no altar in his prison, consecrated the body of the Savior on his own breast. He distributed it to those around him, and sent it to the absent by deacons.[788] Was there ever a sacrifice more touching, a priest more holy, an altar more sacred?

It was especially on the approach of persecution that the faithful made provision of the bread of the strong. They were careful to bring it to their homes, that they might strengthen themselves by receiving it every day, and so prepare for the conflict.[789] After the persecutions, the custom of bringing it to their homes became more rare; yet it continued among many persons and in many churches for more than a century throughout East and West. St. Basil informs us of it in a letter to a lady named Caesarea. "All the solitaries that live in the deserts," he says, "having no priest to give them the Eucharist, keep it always with them, and communicate from their own hands. Moreover, in the city of Alexandria, indeed everywhere in Egypt, each of the faithful has the Communion usually at his own house, and receives it from his own hands."[790] It was the same elsewhere.

Our ancestors in the faith went still further.[791] These early Christians, so worthy of our imitation, loved the Savior to such a degree and felt such a need of his presence that they could not consent to be separated from him for a moment. Hence, they bore the Eucharist with them on their journeys as a defense against every danger of body and soul. In France we see King Robert, who, "whithersoever he wished to go, caused a chariot to be prepared, to carry thither the tent of the divine ministry, in which was laid the sacred body of the Savior, in order that, as the earth with all that it contains is the Lord's, he might render his worship to God in every place." St. Louis, the worthy heir of the throne and the piety of this good king, also took the Eucharist with him in his expedition beyond the sea.[792]

At the present day, the privilege of bearing the Holy Sacrament or causing it to be borne on a journey is reserved to the supreme pontiff. When he undertakes a journey from Rome, the Holy Eucharist, magnificently accompanied, usually precedes him.[793] Not very long ago, Pius IX, when obliged to quit Rome, bore it with him on his way to Gaeta.

For the rest, it was not to be feared that the Savior would meet with any irreverence from those happy Christians whose traveling companion he became. Their deep respect and tender piety in regard to the Holy Sacrament are so well known that they shall ever excite the admiration and the shame of the Christians of these latter times. To heretics alone must be imputed the abolition of this ancient and holy usage. In the fourth century, the Church, wishing to prevent the abuses which the Priscillianists directed against the Eucharist, ordered the faithful to consume it always in the church before departing therefrom, that so these heretics, who neither consumed it in the church nor at home, might not have an opportunity of dishonoring it. This command, which was made by the Church of Spain, became gradually the law of Christendom.[794]

Yet another word on a usage so touching and on the manner in which the Holy Sacrament was preserved in churches. The bishops of the early ages had a custom of sending the Eucharist to one another, no matter how great the distance that separated them. Admirable manner of showing the cordial union which reigned among all the pastors and sheep of the fold![795] This practice having given occasion to some accidents, the Council of Laodicea, held in the fourth century, forbade its continuance. In its stead was substituted the practice of sending ordinary breads, which expressed the same meaning, and which were called "Eulogies," on account of the blessing annexed to them by prayer.

Lastly, the manner in which our forefathers preserved the Holy Sacrament in churches is full of mystery. Two patterns were generally followed for tabernacles: a tower and a dove. The tower tabernacle was suspended above the altar, and symbolized the strength from on high, the bread of the strong, which it contained in its bosom. The dove tabernacle was likewise suspended above the altar: it proclaimed all the mildness, and purity, and excellence that were to be found in the bread of angels. Sometimes the two symbols were combined: the tower rested on a dove with wings extended.[796] The emperor Constantine caused a golden tabernacle, enriched with precious stones, to be made on this last model for St. Peter's Church at Rome.[797]

The Eucharist in its relations with creatures.—Let us now enter into some considerations of another order on the divine Eucharist. With our masters in the faith, we have said that this sacrament is an abridgment of the wonders of the Almighty—the center to which everything else in the body of the Church tends, as everything else in the body of man tends to the heart—the mystery which gives life to society and which brings back the universe to a divine unity.

To understand this last truth, consider what passes around us. All creatures strive to perfect themselves, that is, to pass from a less to a more perfect life; but, to do so, they must lose their own life. Thus, inorganic bodies—air and water, for example—by becoming the food of organic bodies, lose their own life, to take the life of that by which they are assimilated. The vegetable is absorbed in its turn by the animal, which communicates to it a new life by a transformation of substance. The vegetable and the animal, all the species, are absorbed by man, who, assimilating them to himself, communicates to them his life. God at length draws man to himself, assimilates him to himself, and communicates to him his own divine and immortal life. Then, man can and should say, "It is not I who live, but God liveth in me." Possessing man, God possesses the plenitude of his works, of whose life, existence, qualities, man is the summary, as the superior being to whom the rest tend, and God becomes "all in all."[798]

Now, it is in the Eucharist that God changes man thus into himself, and brings back the universe to unity. Hence the divine Eucharist is to the moral world that which the sun is to the physical. And as everything around us gravitates toward this beautiful star, whose light and heat diffuse life and fruitfulness throughout the vast expanse of nature, so in religion everything gravitates toward the august Eucharist.[799] By it the whole creation, which flows incessantly from the bosom of the Creator, incessantly returns thither again.

The Eucharist in its relations with God.—If you consider the Eucharist in its immediate relations with God, what a magnificent idea bursts upon your mind and strikes the tenderest chords of your heart!

The Eucharist, say the fathers and theologians, is an extension of the incarnation. In the incarnation, the eternal Word united himself with only one body and one soul; in the Eucharist, he unites himself with the body and the soul of each one of us. The Eucharistic union does not indeed equal the hypostatic union—such a thing is impossible—but after this, it is the closest that can be conceived. The red-hot iron which assumes all the qualities of fire without losing its own nature, two pieces of wax melted into one, the graft which is nourished by the sap of the tree to which it is attached, the food which is changed into the substance of him who digests it, the very unity which exists between the three divine Persons: these are the sublime types which the fathers give us of man's union with God in Communion.

Its object is to make the whole human race another Jesus Christ,[800] of whom the eternal Father, contemplating him from the highest heavens, may be able to say, "This is my beloved Son, in whom I am well pleased." United to us as a head to its members, so as to act incessantly by us, it is the incarnate Word who adores his Father when we adore him, who praises him when we praise him, who labors and suffers for the glory of God when we labor and suffer for the glory of God. The same Lord, says St. Paul, works in all the faithful. What is done today was done yesterday, and will be done to the end of ages, everywhere over the globe and every hour of the day and night.

The Eucharist in its relations with man and society.—If you consider the Eucharist in its relations with society, your admiration will take a new increase. It would require volumes to explain all the effects of the sun on the rest of the universe, all the influences of the heart on the rest of the human body. Well, what the sun is in the universe, what the heart is in the human body, the Eucharist is in society. Take away the sun, and nature crumbles to atoms; take away the heart, and man falls to decay. Time fails us to speak of the influence of the Eucharist on the arts—on painting, and music, and poetry, and architecture. Yet how much we might say thereon![801] Let us come directly to the point, and see the action of this sacrament on man.

The child of God by baptism, the youth will soon receive a sensible proof of this glorious title. A word, fruitful in angelic virtues, sounds in his ear: "My child," says the Church to him, by the mouth of a pious mother or a white-haired priest, "behold in the distance the period of your first Communion!" "And what is first Communion?" answers the child. "O my child! a day shall come when the God who created you, who consecrated you in baptism, who adopted you as his son, will descend from heaven and solemnly take possession of your mind and your body. The angels shall then be prostrate at your feet. Happier than the beloved disciple, you shall not only rest on the bosom of the Savior, but he himself shall rest on your lips and descend personally into your breast. As happy as Mary, you shall possess him of whom she was the Mother. My child! your first Communion is a solemn contract, a glorious alliance which you are about to make with your God. In exchange, he asks you for all that you have and all that you are. This contract will have as witnesses your father, your mother, your brothers, your sisters, the saints of heaven and earth; it will be written and signed with the blood of your God. The angels will bear it away to heaven, where it will be preserved till the day of your death. They will bring it back again to earth for the last judgment. On the manner in which you shall have fulfilled its conditions, shall be decided the sentence of your eternity."

This announcement fills the soul of the child with an indescribably religious awe, a certain fear mingled with love. And now, to make him worthy of the visit of his God, he has recourse to instructions, to prayers, to alms, to good works of every kind, so much the more meritorious as they are seen only by the angels. Dangerous habits are broken off; the passions are silenced; obedience, piety, and gentleness begin to edify the family and to smooth the way for the alliance. At length arrives the day on which the Creator of worlds is to come down and dwell in the heart of a child. Here I shall pause. It does not belong to any human tongue to tell what then passes between God and his beloved son.

All that I know is that the divine blood which flows through young hearts beautifies and vivifies them: as we see a gentle shower refreshing the lily of the valley, which opens its perfumed cup to the first rays of the sun. "They feel," says the holy and amiable bishop of Geneva, "that Jesus Christ communicates himself to every part of their soul and body. They have Jesus Christ in their brain, in their heart, in their breast, in their eyes, in their hands, in their tongue, in their ears, in their feet. But what does the Savior do hereby?

He rectifies all, purifies all, mortifies all, vivifies all. He loves in the heart, thinks in the brain, sees in the eyes, speaks in the tongue, and so of the rest. He becomes all in all to us; then we live—no, not we, but Jesus Christ lives in us."[802]

Who will tell the deep, sweet, calm, delightful impressions which they experience? What I hear is the seraphic language that falls from one of these innocent mouths: "Heaven is a perpetual first Communion." What I see is the face bedewed with tears of tenderness and brightened with the warm hues of virginal love—the statue-like immobility of recollection—the ecstasy of faith—yea, a divine voluptuousness.

What else do I see? A family in emotion: a mother, who sprinkles with her tears the pavement of the sanctuary, where she kneels to communicate by the side of her child; a sister, a brother, a father, a cousin, a friend, who, on this day feels a new happiness, perhaps regret and remorse, inexpressible sentiments, the germ of a speedy return to the ways of virtue. What I see in particular is a new life which begins for the child; it is an everlasting remembrance of this great day, a barrier against the passions, a salutary remorse after falls, an encouragement in all the trials of life, a supreme consolation at the hour of death.

Oh, how many virtues are sown in the heart by first Communion, how many passions stifled, how many crimes prevented! Consequently, what sorrows in families, what disorders in society, are averted by the omnipotent action of the precious blood the first time that, to destroy the germ of evil, it courses through the veins and penetrates even to the marrow of the bones of the young Catholic! Tell me: Do you know anything so eminently social as the solemn act of first Communion?

The principle of virtue in the individual, Communion is likewise this principle in society. All those miracles of charity that during eighteen centuries have covered the world from pole to pole are the children of the Eucharist: a truth too little known, and which it is now more than ever necessary to repeat. The comparison of Catholicism with protestantism here presents a remarkable phenomenon in the moral world, noticed by Voltaire himself. "The peoples separated from the Roman communion," he says, "have only imperfectly imitated the generous charity which distinguishes it."

Now, as the spirit of a church is eminently manifested in its clergy, let us compare the protestant—I was going to say priesthood—the protestant ministry with the Catholic priesthood. All the examples of individual benevolence that may be adduced in its honor, I admit beforehand. I only ask one question: Can you show me in this clergy, taken all together, the spirit of sacrifice? I have never seen in history that it received, even at the period of its greatest religious fervor, the grace to brave a pestilence in the fulfillment of the first of its duties.

In 1543, the ministers appeared before the Council of Geneva, acknowledging that it was their duty to visit the plague-stricken, but that not one of them had courage enough to do so, and begging the council to overlook their weakness, God not having granted them the grace to confront the danger with the necessary valor, excepting Matthew Geneston, who offered to go in case the lot should fall on him.[803]

It was very different language that Cardinal Borromeo addressed to his clergy about the same period and in similar circumstances: "The most tender cares with which the best of fathers ought to surround the most amiable children in this time of desolation, the bishop ought to lavish by his zeal on his spiritual children, that all other men, inflamed by his example, may embrace the various works of Christian charity. As for all those who have the charge of souls, far from them be the thought of depriving their flocks of the least service at a time when it is so necessary! Let them take a fixed resolution of braving everything, even death itself, with a courageous heart, rather than abandon, in this supreme hour of want and woe, the faithful confided to their care by Christ, who redeemed us all with his blood."[804] It was not he, nor his priests, nor the poor monks whose intrepidity the Geneva pastors found it so easy to ridicule, that waited till the lot fell on them to run to the bed of the plague-stricken.

The case has been the same at all periods. Even recently, when a contagious disease ravaged several cantons of Germany, in which the two forms of worship exist, the contrast was most striking: the public records bear witness to it. Only three years ago, there was a fearful outbreak of cholera in many parts of the Old and the New World. All the newspapers of the time commented on the conduct of the protestant ministers of the United States, who, half opening the doors of their houses, would say to the messengers that called them to the bedside of the cholera-stricken members of their communion: "We cannot go. We have wives and children. Speak to the Catholic missionary."

And the missionary ran to the poor sufferers; and many a time his miraculous charity obtained that sweetest of rewards, the return of a wandering child to the pale of the Church. Here is another fact, which it is well to make known to Europe. In Australia, which England has converted into a vast prison-house, there are fifty thousand convicts. Norfolk Island contains the very worst class of them. Who would believe it?—the protestant bishop and the secretary of the English colonies sought for many years for a protestant minister to take charge of this island; and they could never find one in their communion who would undertake such a mission. These unfortunate criminals have not been visited to this day by any but a Catholic missionary.[805]

The same spirit is found everywhere. "Compare protestant missions with ours: what a difference in the spirit, the means, the success! Where are the protestant ministers who will die to announce to savage Indians or to lettered Chinese the good news of salvation? England can boast to us as much as she pleases about her Lancasterian apostles and her Bible societies. She may, in her pompous reports, describe for us the progress of agriculture among the negroes and of elementary science among the Hindus. All these pitiful civil-service missions, whose only motive is policy, as their only agent is gold, never prove anything else than the incurable apathy of protestant societies in regard to real religion. Whoever knows how to distinguish a noble action, inspired by a sublime motive, from a designing scheme, urged forward by low pecuniary views, will readily perceive that there is an infinite distance between that bishop of Tabraca who lately perished in Su-Tchuen under the sword of persecution, surrounded by the flock of devout Christians whom his courage and labor had won from heathenism to the Church, and the Methodist missionary whose prudent zeal never leads him into places where his life is exposed to any danger, and who, in accordance with a contract made beforehand, is paid so much a head for his converts."[806]

Some remarks, lately dropped by an Anglican bishop, on a solemn occasion, reveal to us the complete failure of protestant missions. "I declare, though with regret," says the bishop of Salisbury, on a solemn occasion, "that our missions have no success. What is the cause? Want of unity. How can we hope to convert infidel nations, when we are not in unity ourselves by Jesus Christ? By whom can the doctrines of Christianity be accepted, when every side presents a scene of the widest division, of heresy and schism?...We have only theories: practice, among us, is dead; religion, among us, nominal! Ah, when will that unity which ought to animate the whole Church of Christ be restored? This is our earnest desire..."[807]

The devotedness of our missionaries has led them to every corner of the world, and taught them to embrace every kind of suffering and death. They have been buried in the foul prisons of Constantinople; they have laid down their lives, singing hymns, under the stone hatchets of savages; they have poured out in large streams on the Calvarys of Japan that blood of the Redeemer which flowed in their veins. Name any desert or any rock in the ocean, despised by rulers and merchants; you will there be shown the tomb of a martyr to Catholic charity.

While it would seem that the love which animates the Church ought to be exhausted by so many losses, I behold it reproduced in the bosom of Christianity under a thousand forms, in that multitude of religious congregations whose members, devoted body and soul to the service of afflicted humanity, give themselves away as an alms: a devotedness more admirable in some respects than martyrdom, for, if it requires an effort of courage to sacrifice one's life, it requires something more to endure a whole life of sacrifice.

And now, what is the source of that Catholic charity which so abounds in wonders and so excels all worldly philanthropy and sectarian benevolence? Ask all those angels of the earth, devoted in person and fortune to the relief of human infirmities. Ask the Catholic missionary, whose home is in the midst of savages. As an answer, every one of them will show you the Eucharist. Oh, yes! the Eucharist—this is the true furnace of the miraculous charity which animates the Catholic Church.

Do you desire a proof of our assertion? Wherever men cease to appreciate this mystery of love, charity becomes extinct, to give place to selfishness or philanthropy. See: except among Catholics who communicate, no more devotedness to the relief of suffering man, no more missionaries, no more Sisters of Charity. The protestant or the philanthropist may indeed give some money, but he will never give himself: his religion does not go so far.[808]

It is otherwise with the Catholic. Mysteriously moved after Communion, he says to himself: "My God, immolated for my salvation, has just given himself to me. In return for his heart, he asks mine; in return for his life, mine. What can I refuse him? As for himself, he has need of nothing. He surrenders his rights to the poor, the sick, the miserable, the unfortunate: they are his brethren. He asks my heart for them, he asks my life for them: I have nothing else wherewith to repay his love, nor does he desire anything else of me."

And a sweet voice is heard in the depths of the soul, a divine joy springs up there, a mighty impulse is felt there; and the Catholic, torn from himself, gives himself away. And now you see, if God wills it, a missionary, a martyr, a Sister of Charity, a servant of the poor: a whole life of devotedness and sacrifice. Should the fire which consumed the holocaust chance to decline, the Catholic knows how to rekindle it at the furnace of love. He returns to the holy table: like the blood which returns from the extremities to the heart, whence it had set out, to depart again, purified, and with warmth and nourishment for all the members.

Such are some of the wonders of Communion in the Catholic world. Shall we not be struck with admiration at the wisdom of the Redeemer, who made Communion a law, and be filled with gratitude toward the Church, which obliges all its members to communicate at least once a year?

PRAYER

O my God! who art all love, I thank thee for all the Communions which I have made during my life; I beg pardon for the faults of which I have been guilty.

I am resolved to love God above all things, and my neighbor as myself for the love of God; and, in testimony of this love, I will every year celebrate the anniversary of my first Communion.

Lesson 38: Our Union with the New Adam by Hope (11)

Sacrament of penance.—A missionary, traveling through the most distant regions of the New World that he might gain souls to Jesus Christ, met a savage of excellent dispositions. He instructed the poor man in the mysteries of faith, and administered baptism as well as the Holy Eucharist to him. The neophyte received these divine sacraments with the liveliest transports of love. In a little while, the missionary was obliged to make other apostolic excursions. The following year he returned to the tribe of the savage who had become a Christian. When the latter heard of the arrival of the missionary, he ran to him and begged that he might be again permitted to receive the Holy Communion. "I will gladly give it to you, my son," replied the missionary, "but first of all you must confess your sins." "I confess, Father?" answered the savage, with amazement, "is it then possible to sin when one has been baptized and has communicated? Thanks to the great Spirit, I do not think that I have been guilty of any willful fault." He confessed, however, and fell into tears as he accused himself of the smallest imperfections.[809]

This affecting error of the virtuous Indian ought to be a general truth. After baptism, confirmation, and Communion, sin, especially mortal sin, ought never more to be known among Christians. But, alas! such is the frailty of human nature that the divine union contracted with the Savior is only too often and too soon broken. What would become of us if this God of goodness had not left us a means of repairing our misfortune? He did so by instituting the sacrament of penance. Let us here admire not only the infinite mercy of the new Adam, but also the profound wisdom with which he provided for the development and maintenance of our spiritual life!

In baptism he gives us life, not a life destined for sloth, but for incessant struggle with the world, the flesh, and the devil. In confirmation he clothes us with a divine armor, summons us to his banner, and writes our name on his army-roll. A kind of farseeing general, he gives us in the Eucharist the bread of the strong, the wine that makes heroes, to support us during the campaign.

But was there ever a war without its wounded and its killed? Or did ever an army enter the field without being followed by its surgeons and its ambulances? The God of armies is not less wise or less compassionate than the kings of the earth. He himself instituted the sacrament of penance. This is the spiritual hospital at which the wounded soldier finds everything necessary for his cure. Such is the bond that unites this sacrament with those which precede it.

Definition of the sacrament of penance.—Penance is defined:[810] a sacrament, instituted by our Lord Jesus Christ to restore us the divine life and forgive the sins committed after baptism. Like the others, the sacrament of penance combines all the conditions necessary for a sacrament of the new law. You find in it a) a sensible sign—the contrition, confession, and satisfaction of the penitent, joined with the absolution of the priest; b) a sign instituted by our Lord; c) a sign which produces grace, that is, the forgiveness of sins. We shall soon have the proof of all this. The holy Council of Trent had therefore good grounds for declaring, with all Christian ages, that penance is one of the sacraments of the new law, and for striking with her anathema anyone who should dare to assert the contrary.

Its elements: Matter.—We say with the Church that the acts of the penitent are, as it were, the matter of the sacrament of penance.[811] Nothing is easier than to understand this truth. The sacrament of penance was instituted by our Lord in the form of a judgment of reconciliation between men and God. Now, in this kind of judgment, it is strictly necessary a) that the culprit should see his fault and be sorry for it; b) that he should confess it; and c) that he should offer to satisfy for it. This is precisely what the sinner does. It is necessary, moreover, that sentence should be pronounced by a competent judge, who can forgive the offense and assure the culprit thereof. This also takes place, as we shall explain further on.

If the Council of Trent says simply that contrition, confession, and satisfaction are, "as it were, the matter" of the sacrament of penance, it does not mean that they are not the true matter. It wished to make us understand that the acts of the penitent do not belong to the same class as the matter of the other sacraments. Not external to him who receives it, like the water in baptism or the chrism in confirmation, the matter in the sacrament of penance is a moral thing, while in the others it is a natural or an artificial thing.[812] Let us now explain each of the penitent's acts, and, first of all, contrition.

Examination of conscience; its qualities. To have contrition for one's sins it is necessary to know them. Hence the indispensable obligation of examining the conscience. The examination of conscience is a diligent search into the faults which one has committed since his last good confession. The chief qualities which it ought to have, and the means to make it well, are the following.

The examination of conscience ought to be exact. We ought to search carefully into all the faults of thought, word, deed, and omission, that we have committed against the commandments of God and the Church, and especially in opposition to the duties of our state of life, since our last confession. We must then see above all whether this last confession was good. It was such, if preceded by a due examination and accompanied with a supernatural sorrow, a full sincerity, and a real firm resolution to amend our conduct.

On the contrary, have we made our examination lightly, in spite of urgent reasons pressing us to do it seriously—contenting ourselves with whatever came spontaneously to our memory? Have we failed in sincerity when declaring any fault that was grievous or that we doubted to be grievous? In fine, have we relapsed into the same mortal sins as before, unresistingly, and as frequently? If so, our confession was bad; for where there is no amendment, says a father of the Church, the repentance is false.[813]

To give the necessary exactness to the examination of conscience, it must be proportioned to the length of time which has elapsed since the last confession, and to the variety and multitude of occasions of offending God in which one has been placed. It is necessary to think on the places which one has frequented and the persons with whom one has associated. We must imitate the woman of the gospel, who, to find her lost groat searches every corner of her house, examines every article of her furniture, and taxes all the powers of her memory; or, to use the expression of St. Francis de Sales, we must take our soul to pieces and consider each portion of it on every side.

The examination of conscience ought to be impartial. We must examine ourselves as if we were examining another; were we unwilling to act thus, our examination would be more or less defective. There are two matters which ought particularly to fix our attention. First, favorite sins, that is to say, sins to which we are most inclined, which seem justified by the prevailing maxims and habits of society, which we commit most frequently and with least remorse—consequently, regarding which it is most to be feared that we form a false conscience. The second, the cause of our sins. Nothing is more important than to know how it happens that we fall into such or such a sin. Does it come from pride? or jealousy? or hatred? or avarice? or sloth? When we want to destroy a tree, we are not satisfied with plucking away its fruits or lopping off its branches: we tear it up by the roots.

May it not be to a want of knowledge of ourselves that we ought to attribute the little fruit derived from our confessions? We must therefore search diligently into the folds of our conscience, study and not hide our case, act the part of a judge and not the part of a barrister, and fear especially not to know ourselves well and not to make ourselves well known; for, unfortunately, that which we fear most is to see or to show ourselves such as we really are. Now to succeed in our examination we must employ the means which faith and reason point out to us.

Prayer. The more our levity, our ignorance, or our passions expose us to the danger of making this examination amiss, the more we ought to feel the necessity of having recourse to God by prayer. As we begin, we may address him with this touching invocation: "O eternal source of light! scatter the darkness which hides from me the enormity and malice of sin. Grant me, O my God! so great a horror of it, that I may hate it if possible as much as thou thyself dost hate it. I ask this favor through the merits of the blood which thou didst shed to atone for it."

Faith. We must keep clearly before our eyes the thought that the examination will decide the confession, that is to say, will decide an action on which perhaps depends our eternal salvation. This thought will help us wonderfully to judge ourselves as if we were about to appear the very same hour before God. After examining yourself, you will actually appear before God, represented by his minister in the tribunal of penance. There a judgment is pronounced for or against you according to your dispositions. If they are sincere and perfect, the sentence is just and is ratified in heaven. If they are false or imperfect, the sentence is unjust, and you profane the blood of Jesus Christ or render it unavailing to you. We must then often recollect that God himself will one day make the examination of our conscience, when he will no longer meet us at the tribunal of his mercy, but at the tribunal of his justice. Happy shall it be for us on that day, if we have judged ourselves according to truth![814]

Recollection. To examine ourselves well, we must withdraw as much as we can to some retired place, far removed from noise and tumult and everything else that could distract us. For the rest, an excellent means of facilitating the task of our examination is to acquire the useful habit of making it every evening. Pagans themselves recommend this practice. What do I say? Herein we follow the example of God himself.

The week of the creation represents the duration of the world as well as of life. God, acting for six days and resting on the seventh, is our model. Now we see that each day of the creation this infinitely perfect God examines the works which he has produced. Then, at the close of this great week, he casts a general glance over all creatures and finds them worthy of him. Could he teach us better that whosoever is anxious to secure his salvation ought to examine his conscience and life daily before going to rest, and also before tasting the repose of the just on the heart of the Savior in Holy Communion?

First act of the penitent: Contrition.—After finding out one's sins, it is necessary to ask God's pardon for them. Contrition is the sentiment which ought to arise in the soul when the examination is ended. This is the first part of the sacrament of penance. Now, according to the Council of Trent: "Contrition is a hearty sorrow for and detestation of sin committed, with a firm resolution of sinning no more."[815]

The word *contrition* means a "bruising of the heart." As material things are broken into little pieces when struck with a hammer, so the word *contrition* teaches us that our hearts, hardened by sin, are struck and broken by repentance. Not that contrition ought to be an external and sensible sorrow: no, it is essentially an act of the will. Hence the saying of Tertullian: "A man who repents is a man provoked against himself."

That contrition is absolutely necessary to obtain the forgiveness of venial or mortal sin is a truth so evident that it is idle to think of proving it. "At all times," says the Council of Trent again, "contrition has been necessary to obtain the forgiveness of sins. It prepares him who falls after baptism to obtain his pardon, if joined with confidence in the divine mercy and a desire to do all that is required to receive well the sacrament of penance. This contrition includes not only the abandonment of sin and the beginning of a new life, but also a hatred of the past life, according to the words so frequently repeated in scripture: 'Cast far from you all your iniquities and make to yourselves a new heart and a new spirit. Against thee alone have I sinned, and done evil in thy presence. I am weary with groaning; I will every night water my bed with my tears. I will recount all my years before thee in the bitterness of my soul,' and many other expressions of the same kind."[816] Such, too, is the unanimous language of the fathers.[817]

Thus, contrition regards at once both the past and the future. For the past, it is the regret of having offended God; for the future, it is the firm will of offending him no more. Everyone knows how ridiculous it would be to say that a man is sorry for an action, if he is not firmly resolved never to commit it again.

Moreover, contrition contains three special acts: a) a sorrow above every other sorrow for having offended the majesty of God, because he is God, and, consequently, worthy of being preferred to everything else; next, for having lost his friendship, the most precious of all treasures; finally, for having deserved hell and the eternal slavery of the devil; b) a firm will never more to offend God, either for the love of any good or the fear of any evil, however great the one or the other—consequently, to repair the injury done to God or the neighbor, to avoid the occasions of sin, and to perform the sacramental penance; c) a great confidence of obtaining from the divine mercy the pardon of all one's sins, with the grace to amend and to persevere to the end: this confidence ought to rest on the goodness of God and the merits of our Lord.

Kinds of contrition. There are two kinds of contrition: perfect and imperfect. Perfect contrition is a sorrow for having offended God, because he is infinitely good. This contrition, joined with the desire of the sacrament of penance, suffices to cancel sins. Imperfect contrition, which is also called attrition, is a sorrow for having offended God, arising from any of the following motives: the loss of heaven, the fear of hell, the supernatural odiousness of sin. This kind of contrition supposes some beginning of the love of God.[818] In order to cancel sins, imperfect contrition must be joined with the reception of the sacrament of penance. If you desire a good understanding of the difference which exists between these two kinds of contrition and purely servile fear, attend to the following parable.

Example. A father had three children, whom he was accustomed to send every day to a meadow to take care of three little lambs which he had entrusted to them. It happened one day that the children fell asleep at their post, and, during their sleep, the wolves of a neighboring forest came forth and bore away the lambs. The children, awakened by the piteous bleating of the lambs, and seeing in the distance the wolves that had carried them off, began to weep most bitterly and to fill the air with their lamentations. They were inconsolable. Now their grief arose in this wise.

The eldest said, "I weep because my father will beat me, and put me to penance for allowing my lamb to be borne off; otherwise I should never weep." The second said, "As for me, I weep because of the penances that will be put on me, and also because of the grief that my father will feel when he hears that the wolves ate my lamb." The youngest, who wept more bitterly than either of the others, said, in a burst of tears, "My poor father will be greatly afflicted; I would rather remain in penance all my life than cause him such grief."[819] The first of these children is the Christian who has only servile fear; the second, he who has imperfect contrition; the third, he who has perfect contrition.

We see hereby that contrition and attrition have this in common, that they are both a supernatural sorrow for having offended God, with a will to offend him no more; but they differ in their motives and in their effects.

In their motives, the first proceeds from a sentiment of love, and refers directly to God without any admixture of self-interest. The second proceeds from a sentiment of fear, and is blended with self-interest.

In their effects, the first justifies the soul, that is to say, puts the soul into the state of grace and effaces sins, provided it is accompanied with a desire to confess, without which it is useless. The second only disposes the soul for justification, since it cannot remit sins but by the help of the sacrament of penance. If then a person should find himself at the point of death without being able to confess, he should make an act of perfect contrition, joining with it the desire of confessing as soon as it may be in his power to do so, and this will suffice for salvation. It would not suffice to make only an act of attrition. See therefore how far perfect excels imperfect contrition!

Qualities of true contrition. Contrition, as we have said, is absolutely necessary: never can a person in any case obtain without it the pardon of his sins. But as there is such a thing as false contrition, apparent contrition, we must beware of deceiving ourselves in regard to this matter. It is to prevent this misfortune that we are about to explain the qualities of true contrition. It must be internal, sovereign, universal, and supernatural.

1. *It must be internal.* How does he act who sins? He prefers the creature to God—his caprice, his pleasure, his will to the will of God. This is a disorder; it comes from the heart or the will: there lies the root of the evil. Hence, contrition, which is the remedy for the evil, ought to exist in the heart, to destroy therein the inordinate love of the creature and to occupy its place with the love of the Creator. Order cannot be reestablished where it continues to be violated. Consequently, tears, protestations, sighs, and all other external marks of repentance are only deceptions and illusions if the will is not changed. God cannot be content with them. What he desires is a contrite and humble heart. "Be converted to me," he says in a hundred places throughout the holy scriptures, "not from the mouth, not from the lips, but from the depth of your hearts."[820] What more just and reasonable?

2. *Contrition ought to be sovereign.* It is necessary that mortal sin should displease us more than any other evil that can befall us, and that we should be more grieved for having committed it than if we had lost whatsoever we hold most dear in the world. The reason is simple. By mortal sin we lose God. God is the greatest of all possessions. It is therefore proper that we should be more grieved at this loss than at any other. And of all evils, sin, which makes us lose God, is evidently that which we ought to fear and to detest most.[821] Were it otherwise with us, our contrition would not be sovereign: we should be preferring the creature to the Creator, Barabbas to Jesus Christ.

How ashamed we ought to be that it costs us so much to excite this sovereign contrition within us! Children of the martyrs, let the example of your ancestors serve you as a lesson! St. Clement, pope, being arrested, was brought before a judge. The latter, hoping to make him apostatize, sent for gold, silver, purple robes, and precious stones, and promised to give them all to him if he would renounce Jesus Christ. The saint, humbled at the idea of God being put in comparison with such things, thought the proposal worthy of no better reply than a sigh and a shrug of his shoulders.

In the ages of faith, great sinners were sometimes seen to fall dead at the feet of the priest to whom they had just confessed their sins. One of these valorous Christians had the misfortune to commit an enormous crime. He came immediately to the archbishop of Sens. Having accused himself of it with many tears, he asked whether he might hope for pardon. "Yes," answered the holy archbishop, "if you are ready to perform the penance which I shall impose on you." "Whatever you wish me to do," answered the penitent, "I am ready, though it were to suffer a thousand deaths." "I give you seven years' penance," said the archbishop. "What is that, father? though I should do penance to the end of the world, it would be too little." "Well, you shall only fast three days on bread and water." "Father, father," said the sinner, sobbing, "give me, I beseech you, a due penance." The archbishop, seeing him so contrite, said to him: "I enjoin you to recite only one Our Father, and I assure you that your sin will be forgiven." At these words, the penitent was so filled with compunction that he heaved a deep sigh and suddenly fell down dead. The holy archbishop, moved to tears, declared with reason that this poor sinner had such contrition that he went straight to heaven without passing through purgatory. That contrition should be sovereign, it is not necessary that it should be the most sensible of all sorrows—in other words, that we should feel the same pain, shed the same tears, and give vent to the same sobs, as, for example, at the loss of our parents. Why? Because, while the soul is united to the body, it is more moved by objects which fall under the senses than by those which do not so fall. It is enough that we should be inwardly disposed, with the help of God's grace, to suffer all kinds of evils rather than commit one mortal sin.[822]

3. *Contrition ought to be universal.* This means that a person must confess all his mortal sins, without a single exception; otherwise, he will not obtain pardon for any, and will, moreover, profane the sacrament of penance. Here is the reason: all mortal sins are the necessary matter of this sacrament, that is to say, they must necessarily be submitted to the sanctifying action of this sacrament, by which alone they can be forgiven. But this sacrament cannot be attended by its action, unless everything is right in regard to the matter, as well as to the form and the minister.

Hence, not to have contrition for some mortal sin is to deprive the sacrament of its necessary matter, that is to say, is to profane it. Besides, we cannot truly hate one mortal sin without hating all the rest with it, because God is offended by all, and a person cannot be both the friend and the enemy of God at the same time. To teach us that we ought to repent of all our sins without any exception, the Savior cured at once both the body and the soul of the paralytic; and, when he cast out devils from the possessed, he cast them all out, even though there were legions of them.[823] Persons enslaved to evil habits ought to fear these dreadful exceptions.

4. *Contrition ought to be supernatural.* To repent of our sins on account of the annoyance which they cause us, or the shame or punishment which they draw upon us in the eyes of men, is to have a sorrow wholly human and natural. Such a sorrow is not enough to obtain forgiveness from God. We must have a supernatural sorrow, that is to say, a sorrow produced by an impulse of grace, and founded on motives which faith reveals to us; for it must have God as its end, and make us detest sin as an offense against God. Hence, contrition is a gift of God; so that man cannot properly repent without the inspiration and assistance of the Holy Ghost. Sin having brought death on the soul, it is impossible that the soul should return to life without the aid of God, who is the author of life.[824]

Firm purpose. We said that contrition referred at once to the past and the future. With regard to the past, it is a regret for having offended God; with regard to the future, it is a resolution never more to offend him. This resolution is called a "firm purpose." The firm purpose is therefore an essential part of contrition. It must accordingly have the same qualities. Or, to speak more correctly, the firm purpose is only contrition itself insofar as contrition refers to the future. It must therefore, according to theologians, be absolute and not conditional; firm and not wavering; efficacious and not speculative; universal, that is, extending to all mortal sins, and not limited to a few; explicit and not indeterminate; formal and not vague.[825]

The disposition to offend God no more and to begin a new life is absolutely necessary. Without it, he who pretends to repent is only deceiving himself and trying to deceive God. His language is this: "I am very sorry for having offended God, and I beg his pardon; but I am not resolved to avoid my old ways." If your enemy were to address you in this strain, would you not look upon his apology as a mockery and his repentance as a sham? Hence, with regard to the future as well as the past, repentance must be internal, sovereign, universal, and supernatural. We may console ourselves with the thought that such has been our contrition, when we take care to shun not only sin, but also the occasions of sin.

As for the motives of repentance, faith proposes two principal ones to us: the fear and the love of God. Let us describe the manner in which a holy bishop of the last century used to excite himself thereto. After finishing his examination of conscience, he had recourse to God with fervent prayers to obtain the grace of contrition. Herein he followed the example of St. Charles, archbishop of Milan, who sometimes passed three hours on his knees before confessing, that he might ask of God a true repentance for his faults. It is by prayer that we also ought to begin. Contrition is a gift of God: if we desire to obtain it, we must ask for it.

After praying, our holy bishop took up a position in three different places: the first in hell, the second in heaven, the third on Calvary. He entered mentally into the place of torments. With the eye of faith he considered the spot which he supposed himself to have deserved, in the midst of devouring and eternal flames, and with no other associates than wretched reprobates. He thanked the Lord for not having cast him into it, and, imploring his mercy, begged the graces of which he had need to preserve him from it. He mounted next to the abode of glory. At the sight of the heavenly Jerusalem, all radiant with light, all overflowing with bliss, he sighed to think that by sin he had closed its gates against himself, and besought the Lord to open them again for him. In furtherance of his petition, he asked the intercession of all holy penitents—David, St. Peter, St. Paul, St. Magdalen, St. Augustine, and the rest.

These two visits were intended to excite in his soul a lively fear of God. From fear he passed on to love, and made his third visit to Calvary. There, considering our Lord crucified, he said to himself: "This is my work. I am the cause of the sorrows which Jesus Christ endured. I joined with all other sinners in covering with bruises and gashes my Savior and father, who never did me anything but good; in crowning him with thorns, and putting him to a most cruel death on the cross. O Jesus! what evil hast thou done to me? How could I treat thee thus, who didst love me to such an excess, and whom I ought to love with an infinite love, if it were in my power to love infinitely? It is because thou art infinitely amiable that I love thee and repent of having offended thee."

In the holy bishop's example, we find together all the motives of contrition and the means to excite ourselves thereto. Let us be faithful to follow them, and we may hope never to fail in a condition that is indispensable for the forgiveness of our sins.

We have spoken in the first place of contrition, not only because it is the most essential, though often the most neglected, part of the sacrament of penance, but also because it must precede the confession, in order to make the latter sorrowful, as theologians say. Still, it is not necessary that a formal act of contrition should precede the confession. It suffices that the confession be made with the intention of obtaining absolution, and that the contrition afterward manifest itself by the asking or the expecting of absolution.[826]

Though it suffices before absolution to have such contrition as we have explained, yet it is dangerous to wait till this last moment to excite it. On the one hand, the penitent may be troubled and cannot think. On the other, it is difficult to arrive at this sorrow in so short a time. It is therefore proper that one should repent immediately after having sinned mortally. Four strong reasons make this a duty on us: a) it is a frightful thing to be in disgrace with God; b) there is danger of falling into other mortal sins, since abyss calls on abyss; c) a person may die suddenly; d) one mortal sin destroys the merit of all the good works that we perform while defiled with it. There is nothing better therefore, when a person desires to confess, than to excite himself to contrition immediately after the examination of conscience.

Second act of the penitent: Confession.—Contrition, then, is the first act of the penitent and the first part of the matter of the sacrament of penance. It is followed by confession, that is to say, an accusation of one's sins, made to an approved priest, in order to obtain absolution for them.

Confession is called an "accusation," and not a recital, to show the dispositions of humility and contrition which must accompany it; "of one's sins," and not of other irrelevant affairs; "of one's own sins," and not of another's; "of one's sins in particular," and not in general: for example, "I have not loved God, I have not prayed to him, as I ought"; "I accuse myself of the seven deadly sins"; "I accuse myself of making an ill use of my five senses." It is necessary to mention in detail all the mortal sins of thought, word, deed, and omission that one has committed; otherwise, the confessor cannot judge of the state of the conscience or apply the proper remedies.

Made "to a priest," and not to a deacon or a layman; "approved," having received from the bishop the power to hear confessions; "in order to receive absolution," not punishment, as before ordinary tribunals. Here we see what distinguishes the tribunal of the divine mercy from the tribunals of human justice and from the tribunal of God's justice after death.

Qualities of a good confession. To effect our reconciliation with God, the confession must be good, that is to say, must have certain qualities or conditions. Among these qualities some are strictly necessary, others are only useful. The confession ought to be simple, humble, pure, and prudent: these qualities are useful for the perfection of the act. It ought to be sorrowful, sincere, and entire: these qualities are indispensable.

1. *The confession ought to be simple.* Simplicity is opposed to duplicity. Now there are three kinds of duplicity which must be carefully avoided in confession: duplicity of mind, duplicity of heart, and duplicity of speech.

Duplicity of mind consists in not receiving as a child that which the confessor says to us for our salvation—in believing only that which pleases us, that which best suits our particular humors, ideas, and inclinations. It teaches us to seek out reasons for not obeying, to discuss, to wrangle. This duplicity is severely condemned in scripture.[827] Simplicity of mind, on the other hand, consists in seeing our Lord himself in the person of the priest, according to the words: "He who hears you hears me"[828]—in receiving with childlike confidence and submission, without discussion or objection, the rules of conduct which he gives us, and conforming ourselves exactly to them.

Duplicity of heart consists in wishing and not wishing, in wishing the end and not wishing the means—in whole or in part; in wishing to go to heaven without renouncing sin and the occasions of sin, without watching over oneself, without controlling one's passions, without doing penance, without practicing virtue. God abhors this duplicity of heart.[829] Simplicity of heart, on the other hand, consists in wishing honestly, firmly, without double-dealing, both the end, which is salvation, and the means, which are the flight of sin and the practice of Christian duties or Christian virtues.

Duplicity of speech consists in having a tongue both to accuse and to excuse. At the end of the confession, you say, "It was through my fault, through my fault, through my most grievous fault." Then, when the confessor addresses some remark or advice to you, you say, "It was my brother's fault"; "it was my sister's fault"; "it was my husband's, my wife's, or my servant's fault." It was everybody's fault indeed but yours! God detests this kind of duplicity no less than the others.[830] Simplicity of speech, on the other hand, consists in accusing without defending oneself—in saying neither more nor less than what is necessary to make known to the confessor the species, the number, and the grievousness of the sins. Far from it are all superfluous details, irrelevant stories, ornamental phrases. The penitent, inspired by it, has no other care than to discover to the confessor the real state of his conscience, without circumlocution or equivocation.

2. *The confession ought to be humble.* What, in effect, is confession? It is no ordinary recital or unimportant narrative: it is a declaration that one is guilty. And guilty of what? Of all that may excite shame and confusion, of the blackest ingratitude, of the most abominable perjury, of the most horrible treachery; for sin is all this. Hence, the penitent ought to be humble in his exterior—ought to appear at the confessional with

plain and modest dress, kneeling as a criminal and supplicant, without arms, without gloves, without gaudy finery.

Humble in the manner of declaring his sins, attributing them only to his malice, and casting himself down before God in the knowledge of his misery, and of the need which he has of the divine mercy. Humble in accepting the directions of the confessor and the penance imposed on him. What pride it is in those penitents who, on hearing the injunctions of the confessor, complain and murmur against him! Offices are exchanged: instead of being a judge, the confessor must become a barrister, and have as many cases to defend as he meets with ill-disposed penitents.

3. *The confession ought to be pure.* Pure in the words which the penitent employs to accuse himself; pure in the intention, that is to say, the penitent ought to approach the holy tribunal only to correct himself of his sins and to change his life—not through custom or merely to relieve his mind; pure in the will, consequently free from those scruples which render it so distressing both to the confessor and the penitent, which trouble the peace of the soul, and which a hundred times over urge the repetition of the same thing. The best remedy for scrupulosity is blind obedience to a confessor. When he speaks, let us say to ourselves, our Lord has told me so and so. Then let us act resolutely, and do quite the contrary to what our scruples suggest. Any person who does not act thus may expect to lose either his head or his devotion.

4. *The confession ought to be prudent.* It is necessary that the penitent, when accusing himself of his faults, should respect the character of the neighbor. Hence, he ought not to discover the faults of another, unless he has shared in them, and cannot otherwise make known his own, such as they are, or unless he thinks that the confessor may give the accomplice some salutary advice, and turn him away from an evil course. Even in the latter case, the name ought never to be mentioned. It suffices, for the integrity of the confession, to state the condition and relationship of the person with whom one has sinned. It is not only an imprudence, but a sin against charity, and a slander, to reveal without necessity the faults of others.

The preceding qualities are useful; the following are necessary.

5. *The confession ought to be sorrowful*, that is to say, accompanied with a true contrition, such as we have explained, and a firm purpose of sinning no more.

6. *The confession ought to be sincere*, that is to say, without disguise, without artifice, without dissimulation, whether employed to make a mortal sin appear venial, or to pass off as doubtful what is certain, or to hide the malice of a sin by not explaining its circumstances with accuracy. It is necessary in confession to tell things as they are and as one thinks of them, without adding to or taking from. Insincerity is of no avail before God, to whom the inmost foldings of the heart are clearer than the sunlight. If we deceive our confessor, we do not deceive Jesus Christ.

7. *The confession ought to be entire.* "The penitent," says the holy Council of Trent, "is obliged by a divine law to confess all and each of the mortal sins which he calls to mind after a diligent examination; also, the circumstances which change the species of sin."[831] Add to this, that the penitent is always bound to answer the confessor truthfully when questioned on any matter of confession. If one cannot know the number of his sins, he must say what he thinks very near it. If nothing certain can be known, he must explain the length of time during which the evil habits lasted, and their strength during that time. Moreover, he must accuse himself of circumstances which are new sins. He, for example, who had stolen out of a church, would not accuse himself sufficiently if he merely confessed that he had stolen. He should add that it was out of a church, because he thereby committed a sacrilege. To conceal a mortal sin in confession is to commit a horrible sacrilege: it is to turn a remedy into a poison.

"But," you will say, "I do not know how to accuse myself of this sin." Ask your confessor then to help you. "But he will grumble at me." A lie! He will love and esteem you more. On the one hand, you will give him a mark of your confidence which will not only honor but rejoice him, since it will make him the instrument of your salvation. On the other, he will perceive in you a noble character, a heroic courage, and a marvelous operation of grace.

"But if I conceal my sin, no one will know anything about it." A lie! For, if you conceal it, your conscience will continually upbraid you with it; you will imagine that everyone reads it on your forehead; and at length it will be made manifest on the day of judgment before all the assembled nations—before your relatives, your friends, your acquaintances. On the contrary, if you tell it, no one will ever know anything about it. God will forget it; your confessor, who can never speak of it, will also forget it; and you will forget it yourself. So that the true means of burying your sin in an eternal oblivion is to accuse yourself of it.

Although venial sins are not necessary matter of accusation, yet it is most useful and safe to tell them as well, because pardon is thus most easily obtained for them, as because one runs the risk of taking for venial what is really mortal. If we have only venial sins to confess, prudence suggests that we should let the contrition and firm purpose fall chiefly on some particular past sin, or on the most notable of our willful venial sins. This is a good means of having the repentance necessary for the validity of the sacrament, which cannot exist without true contrition.

One should accuse himself of this sin at the end of the confession. Thus: "I accuse myself in particular of certain sins which I have committed against charity, or purity, or such a commandment of God or of the Church." It is not necessary to explain more, if all this has been already confessed. For the rest, the true means of never failing in contrition or sincerity is to make each of our confessions as if it were to be the last of our lives. May we never forget this wise rule!

Example. Alas! it was wandered from by a young person of whom St. Antoninus, the illustrious archbishop, leaves us a dreadful history. We offer this example to all as one of the best remedies against shame in confession. A young girl, says this great saint, who had been brought up in the principles of the most edifying modesty, being one day violently tempted, fell into sin. Scarcely had she done so, when she was covered with shame and tormented with remorse. How, she said, shall I have courage to reveal my fault to my confessor? Shame made her fall into a still more frightful crime: she would not venture to acknowledge her sin in confession.

The sacrilege increased her remorse. She fancied that she might be able to appease it by the austerities of penance. She entered a convent, hoping that she would avow her crime in the general confession which is usually made before admission to vows. She did indeed make some efforts to open her heart, but she so veiled her sin that her confessor could not know of what she was guilty. Meanwhile, the superioress of the convent died. This young nun led a life so edifying that the other nuns, deceived by appearances, chose her as the substitute. But it was not for a long time: she soon sank into a mortal illness. She always promised herself that she would declare her sin at the point of death. Shame however, again closed her mouth.

She received the last sacraments with many signs of piety: yet she profaned them. Feeling herself in her death-struggle, she thought of at length explaining herself; but, O terrible judgment of God! raving came on, and she died in her sins. The great austerities which she had practiced, together with her exemplary regularity, left no room to doubt that she had been saved; but, while prayers were being offered for her, God permitted that, as a lesson to all ages, this wretched woman should appear in a state of the utmost consternation to the nuns and say to them: "Cease to pray for me; I am damned for having, in my youth, concealed a sin in confession."[832]

PRAYER

O my God! who art all love, I thank thee for having established the sacrament of penance; I ask pardon for having so often received it with so little preparation and so little profit.

I am resolved to love God above all things, and my neighbor as myself for the love of God; and, in testimony of this love, I will make every confession as if it were to be my last.

Lesson 39: Our Union with the New Adam by Hope (12)

Further remarks on the elements of the sacrament of penance.—In an age of piety, it would be enough to explain the qualities of confession: in our days, this does not suffice. Ignorance on matters of religion, increased by the sophisms of impiety and an unbridling of passions, has become in many a powerful non-conductor against the truth. There being no dogma more galling to haughty minds and corrupt hearts than confession, there is none whose divinity it is more necessary to establish. We proceed to do so, embarrassed only in regard to the selection of our proofs.

In consequence of our Lord's words, "Receive ye the Holy Ghost: whose sins you shall forgive, they are forgiven; whose sins you shall retain, they are retained,"[833] a twofold power was confided to the apostles—the power to forgive sins and the power to retain them.

This awful power should be exercised with great discernment, consequently with a perfect knowledge of the cause. It would be necessary that the apostles, and their successors to the end of time, should know the number and the grievousness of the faults, as well as the dispositions of penitents, in order to decide whether they ought to forgive or to retain, to bind or to loose.

To arrive at this indispensable knowledge, there could be only two ways: either the apostles, and their successors in the ministry of reconciliation, should enjoy the privilege of beholding the inmost folds of the conscience, or penitents should unveil to them all its secrets. Now, it is evident that the judges of consciences have not, any more than public magistrates, the gift of reading the hearts of men. It is therefore necessary that penitents should accuse themselves of their sins. This accusation is called "confession." Hence, confession is a divine institution; consequently, the only means to obtain the forgiveness of sins committed after baptism. It is even absurd to suppose that there is any other.

In effect, if there were any other means in religion than confession by which one could return to the grace of God—if it were enough, for example, to humble oneself in his presence, to fast, to pray, to acknowledge faults in the secret of one's heart—what would be the result? That no one would confess. And who would be such a simpleton, I ask, as to go and suppliantly implore at the feet of a man a favor which he might easily obtain without him and in spite of him? Let us judge by what daily occurs around us. Notwithstanding the certainty that confession is the only means to obtain the forgiveness of sins, a countless number refuse to have recourse to it. What would it be, if there existed a much more convenient and no less efficacious means?

Men always choose of two means that which, being easier, reconciles the interests of salvation with those of self-love. What then becomes of confession, established by Jesus Christ himself? It falls to the ground, and lies unhonored and useless. What becomes of the magnificent power which he gives to his ministers of forgiving and retaining sins? Is it not evident that this power, so surprising, so divine, becomes ridiculous and illusory, since they are never to exercise it?

Hence the dilemma, which admits of no escape: either there is an obligation on all sinners to confess their sins to priests, or else Jesus Christ merely sported with his apostles and his priests when saying to them: "Whose sins you shall forgive, they are forgiven; and whose sins you shall retain, they are retained." He must likewise have sported with their leader, when he said to him: "I will give thee the keys of the kingdom of heaven." Of what use would the keys of the kingdom of heaven be, if anyone might enter without their aid?[834] But if you attribute unmeaning, deceitful, lying words to our Lord, you deny his divinity; you make Christianity a bubble, the Christian world a causeless effect, the human race an ignorant nincompoop—that is to say, you yourself become demented. Here is an end to all discussion. Man reasons no more: he only lives.

But let us leave to the blind the glory of denying the existence of the sun, and the honorable assumption that they alone are enlightened among mortals. It is time to question the Christians of the eighteen hundred years that have gone before us, and to show that, infallible interpreters of the gospel, they have always regarded confession as divine in its origin, and as the only means by which an adult guilty after his baptism can obtain the forgiveness of his sins.

Antiquity and universality of auricular confession.—Impious moderns, following Calvin, have dared to say that auricular confession was unknown in the early ages of the Church, and that it was invented by Pope Innocent III, and published in the General Council of Lateran, held in 1215. Such an assertion does little honor to their learning or their candor. It is true that the Council of Lateran, to raise a barrier against the laxity which was every day becoming more general, ordered that all the faithful who had attained the use of reason should confess at least once a year. That this was very far from an invention of confession is quite plain. The council only fixed the time when it would be necessary, under pain of mortal sin, to comply with a duty that was known, practiced, and taught long before.

In point of fact, St. Bernard, who died in 1153, addressing himself to those who concealed their faults in confession, said: "What will it avail you to tell some of your sins and to hide others? Are not all things open to the eyes of God? What! will you dare to withhold anything from him who holds the place of God in so great a sacrament?"[835]

St. Anselm, archbishop of Canterbury, who died in 1109, speaks thus in his homily on the ten lepers: "Show faithfully to the priests, by a humble confession, all the stains of your internal leprosy, that you may be cleansed from them."[836] In another work, the same doctor adds: "As original sin is forgiven in baptism, so actual sins are forgiven in confession: it is a true judgment. For there are two judgments of God: one is made here below by confession; the other will take place on the last day at that great investigation when God will be the judge, the devil the accuser, and man the accused. But in the judgment of confession the priest, as one who represents Jesus Christ, is the judge; man is both the witness and the criminal; the penance which is imposed is the sentence."[837] See now how confession exists a hundred years before the time of the pope whom the relentless enemies of the Church make its inventor! Let us go back still further.

In the eleventh century, we see that a priest named Stephen, of the diocese of Orleans, was confessor to Constance, wife of the pious king Robert.

In the tenth, St. Uldaric, bishop of Augsburg, confessed the emperor Otho.

In the ninth, Charlemagne had as his confessor Hildebrand, archbishop of Cologne.

In the eighth, St. Martin, a monk of Corbie, rendered the services of confessor to Charles Martel. The First Council of Germany, held in 742, ordered that every colonel should have a priest who might hear the confessions of the soldiers.

In the seventh century, St. Ansberth, archbishop of Rouen, was confessor to King Thierry I. If we were not afraid to tire, we might continue the list, and mention the confessors of Greek and Latin emperors, or other distinguished personages, up to the first ages.[838] It is good, however, to diversify our proofs, so as to show that authorities of all kinds concur in support of the doctrine of sacramental confession.

In the sixth century, St. John Climacus expresses himself thus: "It is unheard of that sins, acknowledged in the tribunal of penance, have ever been divulged. God so directed it that sinners might not be turned away from confession and deprived of the only hope of salvation."[839] In the same century, John, patriarch of Constantinople, composed for the use of the Eastern Churches a ritual in which the priest speaks thus to the penitent: "It is not I, my child, who grant you the forgiveness of your sins. It is God, who absolves you by my ministry, according to his words: 'Whatsoever you shall loose upon earth,' etc. Confess, therefore, and declare to me, without concealing any one of them, and in the presence of the holy angels, all the sins, even the most secret, which you have committed: this is the means to obtain pardon for them."[840]

In the fifth century, we find St. Chrysostom in the East and St. Augustine in the West. The first, who died in 404, says: "Men have received from God a power which has not been granted to angels or archangels. Never was it said to the celestial intelligences: 'Whatsoever you shall loose,' etc. The power of priests reaches even to the soul, which they can cleanse and liberate...Let us then imitate the Samaritan woman, and not be ashamed to tell our sins. He who is ashamed to confess his sins to the priest will hear them published on the day of judgment, not to one or two persons, but to all nations."[841] The second, who died in 430, addresses the faithful thus: "Let no one say: 'I do penance secretly in the sight of God; it is enough that he who will grant me pardon should know what passes in my inmost soul.' If this were the case, then Jesus Christ would have said without reason, 'Whatsoever you shall loose on earth, shall be loosed in heaven,' and would in vain have confided the keys to his Church. It is not enough, therefore, to confess to God: it is also necessary to confess to those who have received from him the power to bind and to loose."[842]

In the fourth century, we have St. Ambrose, who died in 397. His biographer, St. Paulinus, relates that when anyone came to confess to him, he wept in such a manner as to draw tears from his penitent. A person would be inclined to say that, when he heard confessions, he fell with those who had fallen. This writer adds that he spoke of the crimes which had been confessed to him to God alone, with whom he continually interceded for sinners.[843] In the same century, St. Basil, who died in 378, wrote: "It is absolutely necessary to disclose one's sins to those who have received the dispensation of the mysteries, of God."[844] St. Athanasius, who died in 373: "As the man who is baptized by the priest is enlightened by the Holy Ghost, so he who confesses his sins in penance obtains their remission through the priest."[845] At the same period, the celebrated Lactantius was not afraid to say: "The mark of the true Church is the use of confession and penance, by which the sins of our frail nature are forgiven."[846]

In the third century, Origen, that brilliant light of the Eastern Church, taught the same truth: "If we do not repent of our sins, and confess them, not only to God, but also to those who can apply a remedy to them, we shall not be forgiven."[847]

In the second century, Tertullian, that brilliant light of the Western Church, employed language no less formal: "Many avoid declaring their sins, because they are more careful of their honor than of their salvation. Herein they resemble those who, having some secret disease, hide it from the physician and let themselves die. Is it then better to damn yourselves by concealing your sins, than to save yourselves by declaring them?"[848]

In the first century, St. Clement, disciple and successor of St. Peter, wrote to the Corinthians: "While we are yet in this world, let us be converted with our whole heart; for, after we have left it, we can no longer confess or do penance."[849]

We have come at length to those who received religion from the mouth of the Son of God himself. I pass over in silence the texts of St. James and St. John which recommend confession.[850] I shall content myself with the testimony of St. Luke, who tells us that a great number of Christians came to the feet of the apostles confessing and declaring their sins.[851] There is allusion here to a confession made to men, a confession to obtain the pardon of sin: Is not this sacramental confession? The most celebrated protestants have cordially admitted it.[852]

Lastly, the Son of God, who came down from heaven, said to his apostles, and to their successors in the sacred ministry: "Whose sins you shall forgive, they are forgiven; whose sins you shall retain, they are retained." You see then that it is not in the Council of Lateran, nor in any other council, but in heaven, in the bosom of God himself, that we find the origin of sacramental confession.[853] Judge of the honesty and research of those impious men who say that Innocent III was its inventor!

More straightforward than his disciples, Voltaire himself acknowledged that confession reached back even to the origin of the world. "Confession," he says, "is a divine institution, which had its commencement nowhere but in the infinite mercy of its author... The obligation of repenting ascends to the day when man first became guilty; repentance alone could take the place of innocence. When a man repents of his sins, he must begin by acknowledging them."

In harmony with all traditions, he admits, moreover, that confession was practiced among the Jews. "Adam," he says, "was the first penitent: he confessed when he said of the forbidden fruit, 'I did eat.' On every page of the holy books we find confession, either private or public."[854] This same Voltaire declared that the custom of confessing existed also among pagans. "Persons used to accuse themselves," he says, "in the mysteries of Orpheus, of Isis, of Ceres, of Samothrace. History informs us that Marcus Aurelius, when being initiated into the mysteries of the Eleusinian Ceres, was obliged to confess to the hierophant."

It is very remarkable that confession is one of those duties of which we find the most striking traces in paganism. Out of a host of testimonies that we might adduce on the subject and that may be seen elsewhere,[855] we shall content ourselves with a few words on what used to occur among the Parsees. The custom of which we speak is recorded in the *Zend-Avesta*, a work whose antiquity dates, in the judgment of the learned, from more than four hundred years before the Christian era. Among the Parsees were *patets*. This word strictly denotes repentance. The patets are confessions which specify all the sins that man can commit. This is the manner in which the declarations are made: a) the penitent comes before the Destour, that is, the doctor of the law or the priest; b) he begins with a prayer to Ormuzd and to his minister on earth; c) he accompanies this prayer with a resolution of doing all the good possible and of devoting himself entirely to God.

Then he says: "I repent of all my sins. I renounce them. O God! have mercy on my body and soul in this world and the next. I abandon every evil of thought, every evil of word, every evil of deed." Here follows a detailed accusation of the sins that one may commit against God, his neighbor, and himself.

The penitent concludes: "For the sins which Ormuzd has made known in the law, I ask pardon with sincerity of mind, in presence of Ormuzd, the just judge—in presence of Sosiosch—in presence of the doctor of the law." To this confession, the Parsees attached the forgiveness of all their faults: confiding so much in it as to order that, if they should not be able to make it at the hour of their death, it should be made for them afterward.[856]

On reading these and many other testimonies, a person is fully convinced of the antiquity and the universality of confession. But how could all peoples have agreed on this point, if previously it had not been revealed that repentance alone could obtain pardon, and that the essential mark of repentance is confession, that is to say, a sincere and candid acknowledgment of the sins which one has committed?

Divinity and necessity of auricular confession.—Accordingly, when our Lord came on earth, he found confession established. In laying on his disciples an obligation to confess, he did not promulgate a new law; he only perfected and confirmed a law already existing: *Non veni legem solvere, sed adimplere.*[857] As he raised the rite of marriage to the dignity of a sacrament, so he raised the rite of confession to a similar dignity. He attached special graces to confession, by making it an essential part of the sacrament of penance. Hence it came to pass that the precept of confession excited no murmur among Jews or Gentiles. Both were accustomed to it. Nothing seemed more natural. A constant and universal tradition showed them its indispensable necessity.[858]

To dispense oneself from this law, it is therefore necessary to scorn the authority, not only of Jesus Christ and the Church, but also of common sense. It is necessary, moreover, to stifle the voice of nature, which cries aloud to the guilty: "No forgiveness without repentance, and no repentance without the acknowledgment of one's fault."

Third act of the penitent: Satisfaction.—To complete our explanation of the matter of the sacrament of penance, it remains for us to speak of satisfaction. Penance is a second baptism, but a laborious baptism.[859] Different from the first, in which God instantly remits all our debts, this imposes on us an obligation of making satisfaction: nothing more reasonable. Hence, the Catholic faith teaches us that satisfaction is a part of the sacrament of penance.

It is defined: a reparation which the sinner makes to God, by performing the good works laid on him by the confessor. The penitent is bound to perform his penance. He cannot change it in its essence, nor in regard to circumstances of time or place. He should not neglect to perform it at once; otherwise, he exposes himself to the danger of forgetting it or of doing it ill. The penitent ought to accept willingly the penance that is given him. What, in point of fact, is this slight satisfaction, when compared with his faults?

For the rest, let us mention the reason why penances are imposed. In the converted sinner, absolution remits the guilt of his sins, and the eternal punishment due to the mortal sins of which he has been guilty; but there usually remains a temporal punishment. Thus, we see in the holy scripture[860] that, though Moses obtained for the murmuring Israelites the pardon of their revolt, yet they were nearly all punished with death. The eternal punishment was remitted, but the temporal should be endured. David had been pardoned his sins: the prophet Nathan had, on the part of God, assured him of it. Nevertheless, there remained a temporal punishment to be undergone, of which the prophet warned him in these words: "The Lord hath taken away thy sin, and thou shalt not die. Yet, because thou hast given occasion to the enemies of the Lord to blaspheme against him, the child that is born to thee shall lose its life."[861]

Here then is the reason why the Church has always imposed penances on sinners reconciled by absolution. In the early ages, these penances were very long and rigorous, as we shall see elsewhere. It was wished that they should bear some proportion to the outrage which the sinner had offered to God, by rebelling against him.

The obligation to do penance, even after the remission of the eternal punishment, is also a proof of the goodness of God and of his solicitude for our salvation.

1. He wished to inspire us with a horror of sin, and to make us understand the depth of the wound which it inflicts on the soul; for nothing better enables us to know the violence of a disease than the difficulty of obtaining a cure.

2. He wished to put a rein upon the impetuosity of our passions, and to fortify us against the occasions of sin, which are so frequent in this life.

3. He wished to purify us from the remains of sin, that is to say, a certain spiritual tepidity, a sort of disgust for virtue, an irregular attachment to temporal goods, a weariness in well-doing—sad dispositions, which are often left after the remission of the fault.

4. He wished to destroy our evil habits by the practice of the contrary virtues, and to make us pay our debts before being summoned before the bar of his dreadful justice.

5. He wished to make us conformable to our Lord Jesus Christ, whose whole life was spent in labors and sufferings.[862] If we desire to share his glory, we must share his cross.

Its form.—As to the form of the sacrament of penance, it consists in the words of the priest: *Ego te absolvo*, etc. The holy Council of Trent teaches this in express terms, following Eugenius IV, in his decree to the Armenians.[863] On the one hand, these words show perfectly all that Jesus Christ gave his apostles power to do, when he said to them: "Whatsoever you shall loose upon earth, shall be loosed in heaven." On the other hand, they clearly denote the peculiar effect of the sacrament of penance, which is to remove sins, the frightful chains that hold our souls captive.

Its minister.—The minister of penance is therefore exclusively a priest or bishop. Him alone, and not the simple faithful, our Lord had in view when he said to his apostles: "Receive ye the Holy Ghost; whose sins you shall forgive, they are forgiven." Such has been the constant doctrine of the Catholic Church.[864] The administration of the sacrament of penance is a thing so delicate and serious that it evidently requires, apart from legitimate power, such guarantees of virtue, of enlightenment, of discretion, as cannot be expected from men of the world, however honorable we may suppose them. Priests alone, and priests vowed to celibacy, can present these guarantees.

Though the priest is the only lawful minister of the sacrament of penance, he cannot absolve validly unless approved for the hearing of confessions: such has also been the constant doctrine of the Church.[865] Nothing shows us better the divine order which reigns in this holy society. As in an army, officers have authority over their own soldiers only, so in the Church every bishop has his diocese and every priest his parish, that they may cultivate in all its extent the vineyard of the Father of the family, without encroachment or confusion. That the absolution may be valid, it must be received from a priest empowered by a lawful bishop to hear confessions.

Institution of the sacrament of penance.—On the eve of his death, the Savior, as we have seen, had given his apostles power over his natural body, by telling them to consecrate bread and wine like him. Before ascending to the right hand of his Father, wishing to give them power over his mystical body, that is to say, over the faithful, he breathed on them, saying: "Receive ye the Holy Ghost; whose sins you shall forgive, they are forgiven; whose sins you shall retain, they are retained."[866] At this time it was, according to the remark of the Council of Trent, that the Savior instituted the sacrament of penance.[867] It was fitting that he should institute it only after his resurrection, for it was necessary that the Christ should suffer and rise again from the dead, and that penance and the forgiveness of sins should then be preached in his name.[868]

PRAYER

O my God! who art all love, I thank thee for having instituted the sacrament of penance. Without this new means of salvation, what would become of me after the shipwreck of my innocence?

I am resolved to love God above all things, and my neighbor as myself for the love of God; and, in testimony of this love, I will always be faithful to the duty of confession.

Lesson 40: Our Union with the New Adam by Hope (13)

Effects of the sacrament of penance.—Nothing sweeter or richer in its effects than the sacrament of penance. a) It remits all the mortal and venial sins committed after baptism, whatever their number or enormity. b) It remits the eternal punishment which is due to sin, and sometimes the temporal punishment too. c) It causes the merit of good works which have been performed in the state of grace, but which mortal sin has deadened, to revive: they take back their power of conducting to eternal life.[869] d) It restores to man the infused and gratuitous virtues which he has lost by sin: these virtues flow from the sanctifying grace which penance gives us, as the powers of the soul flow, so to speak, from the soul itself.[870] e) It reestablishes us in our dignity of children of God and heirs of the kingdom of heaven.[871] O abyss of mercy!

Dispositions for receiving it.—The dispositions that are essential for the reception of the sacrament of penance are sufficient instruction and the three acts of the penitent, namely, contrition, at least imperfect; confession; and satisfaction, or at least the desire to make satisfaction. As for the dispositions which entitle one to a greater abundance of grace, they may be reduced to a lively faith in the efficacy of this sacrament, a great confidence in the mercy of God, a profound humility, and a heartfelt gratitude.

Its necessity.—The Council of Trent says that penance is no less necessary for salvation to those who fall after baptism, than baptism to those who have not yet been regenerated.[872] Hence also the celebrated saying of St. Jerome, that penance is the "second plank after shipwrecks."[873] Sometimes, when a vessel has foundered, the only chance of escape from death is a plank on which one has the good fortune to lay hold. So, after losing the innocence of baptism, there is no other means of salvation left than the sacrament of penance, to which it is absolutely necessary to have recourse. Such has been, as we have shown, the constant, the universal teaching of the Catholic faith.

Liturgy of the sacrament of penance.—The prayers and ceremonies of confession are a new means to justify what we have said on the efficacy of the sacrament of penance in reforming morals. If any sage of antiquity had invented the tribunal of penance, all our modern philosophers would be lost in admiration of his wisdom: he should be declared the prince of legislators. If he had taught the prayers and ceremonies of confession, it would be the special pride of our classical scholars to tell his genius in prose and verse. These eulogies would be allowable. But no mortal will ever deserve them: it is not thus that man invents.

Search as long as you please through the books of sages and among the customs of nations, never shall you find anything so touching, so paternal, so sublime, so proper to reform morals, as the manner in which the reconciliation of man with God is effected in the sacrament of penance. It is here truly that, according to the words of the prophet, "mercy and truth meet each other," and "justice and peace," like two sisters who have been separated for years, "embrace."[874] Would you like to know well how sweet is this kiss of reconciliation, which the Creator vouchsafes to give his creature? Compare human tribunals with the tribunal of God.

When a man has committed some public crime, human justice dispatches its officers on his track. The day is no longer bright, the night is no longer calm, for this wretched fugitive. He is obliged to hide himself in forests, trembling at the stir of a leaf, till at length he is arrested. Then he is laden with chains. Dragged from prison to prison, he comes to the place where his sentence is to be pronounced. On the tribunal, before which he shall shortly appear, is written the terrible word, *Justice*.

The day of trial arrives. A pompous display is made. In front of the prisoner are the judges, who can punish, but cannot pardon him; around him, jailers and witnesses;

above him, the emblems of death. Everything reminds him of his fate, in case he shall be convicted. Even though he escape the scaffold, he beholds in the dismal future a thousand ignominies, chains that he must wear perhaps as long as he lives, separation from all that is most dear to him in the world. And will this make him any better? Alas, no! Such is human justice.

Very different is divine justice.

When God punishes on earth, he never lays aside his character of Father. Thus, a man, that is to say, one of his children, has offended him. God sends the offender remorse. This messenger enters the culprit's heart, which it bitterly stings. Little by little the rebel grows weary; he stops; he returns to himself. A most sweet voice is heard: it is that of repentance. Tender reminiscences pour in upon his mind, blended with the sad thought of his present condition. Shame and fear divide his soul, and prepare the way for the arrival of hope. Suddenly these sweet words, like those of a mother, a weeping mother, resound through his heart: "Come to me, you who labor; come, and I will refresh you";[875] and it is even from the lips of his judge that these words come. He fears no more; and, guided by remorse, repentance, and hope, he turns his steps toward the house of God.

Before him is a tribunal on which faith reads this consoling inscription, *Mercy*.[876] Here, no ignominious punishment, no chains, no dungeons, no scaffold. At this tribunal is seated a judge who is more than a man, but who is not an angel: he himself requires mercy. He is the vicar of the charity of Jesus Christ. He has the bowels of the Savior's compassion. There is nothing on his lips but blessings, encouragements, and prayers. His eyes will soon flow with tears for the guilty penitent. Here, no strange witnesses, no angry accusers—the culprit will be his own witness, his own accuser: everything is referred to him. If he acknowledges his crime, he will not be punished; he will be forgiven.

His accusation is ready. Behold him as he approaches the sacred tribunal, about to find, in the humble avowal of his miseries, tears sweeter a thousand times than all the joys of sin!

To animate his confidence, he makes on himself the adorable sign of the cross; and his heart tells him that the Son of God died to atone for his sins. Then, addressing himself to the minister of this God of goodness, he says: "Bless me, Father, for I have sinned." Wondrous confidence! He is guilty, and because he is guilty he asks a blessing. Yes, because in the eyes of God the prodigal child who says, "I have sinned," is worthy of a paternal blessing.

He calls the priest his father: this word speaks volumes.[877] Father, you who perhaps gave me the life of grace on the day of my baptism—who perhaps first nourished my life with the bread of angels; Father, you who have the power of restoring me to the life of grace; Father, bless me. And the priest accepts this sweet title, and shows himself truly a father. Moved by the petition of his child, he makes the sign of the cross over him, saying: "May the Lord be in thy heart and on thy lips, that thou mayest make a sincere and full confession of thy sins: in the name of the Father, and of the Son, and of the Holy Ghost. Amen."

The penitent begins by complying with an obligation as old as the world. He makes the confession which Adam, the first of all the guilty, made, and which all the imitators of his wrongdoing in the course of ages have made, and ought to make, in order to be forgiven. He confesses to God: "I confess to Almighty God." He does not confine himself to this. The angels and saints have known his disorders: which he acknowledges to them that he may excite their compassion and increase his own humiliation. He names all that is most amiable, pure, and merciful in heaven—the Blessed Virgin Mary; all that is most terrible to the devil, whose yoke he wishes to throw off—the archangel Michael; all that is most holy among men—St. John the Baptist, whose sanctity, he hopes, may outweigh his iniquity and touch the heart of his judge; all that is most mighty on earth—Sts. Peter and Paul, invested with the power to bind and to loose consciences; in fine, all the saints, his friends and brethren: "to Blessed Mary ever Virgin, to blessed Michael the archangel," etc.

After invoking the whole Church in heaven, he invokes the Church on earth, represented by the priest, and says: "And to you" also, "Father," I confess. And what is he about to confess? What has he so interesting to say that he calls God and creatures, heaven and earth, to hear it? I confess…"that I have sinned": in other words, been a most vile traitor. Has he not at least respected some of the powers of his soul and body? No, he has defiled them all. "In thought, word, and deed": there is nothing in me but has been the slave of iniquity. Was it possible to place in the mouth of a sinner any prayer better calculated to awake in his heart a profound sense of shame and sorrow, with all the other dispositions of sincere repentance?

Then the penitent, as if to show the priest that he has not exaggerated in saying that he has offended God by thought, word, and deed, enters into a circumstantial account of his faults. And what an account! O God, how merciful thou art! If a subject were to acknowledge himself guilty of half the outrages against his king of which man acknowledges himself guilty against thee, the reeking sword of justice would instantly be let fall upon his accursed head; and thou, O my God, dost listen to the confession with patience—what do I say?—with kindness!

Now that the confession is ended, what will the penitent do? What can he do but abase himself, grow angry with himself, acknowledge that he is deeply guilty? He does so by striking his breast and saying: "Through my fault." I had so many motives and so many means not to sin! Was there anything wanting to me? What more could the Lord do for me than he did? "Through my fault." It is not to the occasion, nor to the temptation, nor to the humors of others, but only to my own malice, that I must attribute my iniquities. "Through my most grievous fault." Yes, because I am a Christian, a beloved child of God—laden, in preference to thousands of others, with the richest blessings.

Overwhelmed with the weight of his shame, how shall he act now? Plunge into despair, perhaps? Ah! religion inspires very different thoughts. It tells him to pray, and he prays, saying: "Therefore I beseech the Blessed Mary ever Virgin," etc. He does not dare to address himself to God, but implores all the saints in heaven and on earth, the witnesses of his crimes and his miseries, to become his intercessors with that God whom he has so basely offended. He also addresses himself to his father, the priest. This tender father, this sincere friend, hears the voice of the penitent child. With all the fervor of his love, he says: "May the Almighty God have mercy on you, forgive you your sins, and bring you to life everlasting. Amen." Lest this one prayer should not suffice to appease the Lord, or to reassure the culprit, he adds another: "May the Almighty and merciful Lord grant you pardon, absolution, and remission of all your sins. Amen."

An experienced physician, the priest then points out to the penitent the remedies which he must employ for his cure, the precautions which he must take against a relapse. The priest next imposes a penance on him—a penance very trifling in comparison with his faults: but you must not forget that this is the tribunal of mercy. Yet a moment, and the prodigal son will be restored to all his rights. My child, says the priest, repent—humble yourself—the atoning blood is about to flow upon your soul. The penitent bows his head, and repeats in all the bitterness of his grief the act of contrition. The priest, on his side, invoking the God of goodness, whose place he holds, raises his hand and pronounces the omnipotent words of absolution.

What occurs at this solemn moment? The infernal chains, which bound the sinner, are broken; the devil quits his soul; hell closes beneath him; heaven opens above him;

his name is written anew in the book of life; his robe of innocence is restored to him, with all his past merits; the adorable Trinity looks down upon him with complacency; the angels leap for joy: here is a soul as beautiful and pure as on the day of its baptism. It can expect everything. Already it beholds with its tear-moistened eyes the Eucharistic banquet that awaits it at a short distance, and, further on, the eternal festival of the nuptials of the Lamb.

Happy in having brought back an erring sheep to the divine shepherd, the priest, to secure its perseverance, calls down upon it a strengthening blessing from on high. He says: "May the passion of our Lord Jesus Christ, the merits of the Blessed Virgin Mary and of all the saints in general, all the good that you do, and all the evil that you endure, serve to obtain for you the remission of your sins, to increase grace in you, and to merit for you an everlasting reward. So be it."

What has the priest still to do? He began with a prayer; he ends with a blessing. The penitent, having again become the child of God, has now a right to the earthly inheritance of his heavenly Father. This inheritance is peace—a profound, interior peace—that peace which the world cannot give—peace of conscience, which supplies the place of everything else, and whose place nothing else can supply. The priest says to him: "Go in peace." Yes, all is forgotten; you are a new man: repentance is the brother of innocence.

The penitent withdraws. He knelt down the child of the devil: he rises the child of God, and goes to testify in fervent prayers his gratitude to the God of mercies. Reflecting on the wonders which have just been wrought in him, he swears anew to be faithful to the salutary advice that has been given him.

Jews, pagans, heretics, men of every tongue and tribe! we conjure you to say whether you know anything more divine, anything better calculated to reform the world, than such a tribunal? Add to this that whatever precedes or follows confession contributes to this reformation. Very often, before confessing, the mere thought of doing so becomes a check to sin and an encouragement to virtue. One says: "If I commit sin, I must confess it; I will do such a good work, because I must confess on such a day."

After confession, the thoughts run thus: Yesterday or today I confessed; this is a motive not to relapse, a motive to continue in a good course. The thought that we are in the state of grace gives us strength and courage to lead a new and fervent life. And then the good advice of the confessor on the means of avoiding the occasions of sin, fulfilling the duties of one's state, overcoming temptations, and nourishing piety, has—thanks to the blessing, with which God accompanies the words of the priest, his minister and representative!—a special efficacy in enlightening and encouraging the penitent, long after quitting the confessional.

Its benefits.—It does not suffice to have shown the divinity of the sacrament of penance, the necessity and the spiritual effects of confession: we must show the immense benefits of this institution from a social point of view.

Confession! this is indeed the grand scarecrow for the passions, though the grand object of ridicule for corrupt hearts. Without a doubt there is no better means to reform manners. The proof of this is very clear. When a man wishes to lead a Christian life, or to be converted after a life of sin, he confesses. On the contrary, when he wishes to abandon himself to his passions, he ceases to confess.

It is to confession that we owe in a great measure all the sanctity, the piety, the religion, which it has pleased the infinite goodness of God to preserve still in his Church. Is it surprising that all the passions should have joined in a league with the enemy of the human race to destroy this dogma, which is, as it were, the rampart of Christian virtue? But the very violence of their attacks is the best proof of its necessity, its efficacy, and its advantages.[878]

Its necessity. Yes, confession is necessary for man. It cures him. Pride is the first of our vices, the source of all our misfortunes. Pride cannot be cured but by humility, and humility cannot be acquired but by humiliation. Now the most humiliating act that degraded man can be obliged to perform is to give a full account of his life—of his thoughts, of his desires, of his words: confession is this account. Therefore, of all the means to crush our pride, the most efficacious is confession. The new Adam loved us too well, he had too sincere a desire of our regeneration, to spare us this salutary remedy. This is the reason why he established and commanded confession.

It instructs man. After consecrating him by baptism, confirmation, and the Eucharist, and revealing to him the dignity of his being and the grandeur of his destiny, the Catholic Church continues this teaching in the quiet of the confessional. "My son," she says to him, "you are a mixture of what is noble and what is base. Though you raise your head toward heaven, your feet touch the earth: in you is the germ of every vice as well as of every virtue. You carry two men about with you, or rather within you: they are always at war. I am going to put you on your guard against that enemy who aspires to nothing but to degrade you." How important is this revelation! How many shoals are escaped—how many imprudent steps avoided—how many faults, of which even one suffices to embitter a whole life, are prevented—by confession!

In the retirement of the sacred tribunal you have a wise, firm, incorruptible, experienced friend, who casts a glance, enlightened by faith, into the heart of childhood, of youth, of manhood, of old age. He has lessons of wisdom for all characters and remedies for all evils. He sees, he unveils the hidden artifices of the passions. He points out to the penitent a multitude of little serpents which self-love, inexperience, levity, and preoccupation have hindered him from perceiving, and which nevertheless would very soon attain their full growth and feast themselves on his vitals. He puts him on his guard, whatever may be his rank or condition, against a host of illusions and dangerous maxims. With a steady hand he draws for every state the line of its duties, and makes the steps of man firm in the way of virtue, which even in this life is the way of happiness.

Who else, tell me, could supply these salutary lessons? Not father, nor mother, nor companion. They do not know the heart well enough: there are secrets which man cannot and will not reveal but to God. How blind then, to say nothing more, are those parents who keep their children away from confession, under the pretext of retaining the monopoly of their confidence, of which they imagine themselves in full possession! Ah, they little know how the heart of man is made!

Hence, enchanted with the happy effects of confession, a philosopher of the last century, not likely to be suspected of partiality, exclaimed: "What preservative for the morals of youth like the custom of going every month to confession!"[879] Shall we pass by in silence the touching acknowledgment of a writer brought back to virtue by misfortune? "Oh, yes!" wrote Silvio Pellico, lately, "every time that in my prison I heard the tender reproaches and noble counsels of my confessor, I burned with love of virtue, I hated no one, I would have given my life for the least of my kind, I blessed God for having made me a man. Miserable is he who understands not the sublimity of confession! Miserable is he who, to appear raised above the vulgar crowd, thinks that he is bound to regard it with contempt! We may be acquainted with what is necessary for a virtuous life; but it is no less true that it is useful to hear it repeated to us, and that we should not rely too much on our own studies and reflections. The living speech of one man to another has quite a different effect from that of reading and consideration. The soul is tossed about no more: the impressions which it receives are deeper. In the brother who speaks there is an animation, an appropriateness, which is often vainly sought for in books and in one's own thoughts."[880]

Its efficacy. Confession rehabilitates man. Not only does it instruct him in the art of fighting his enemies, but it establishes him again in the respect of himself and gives him the courage of virtue. See what happens to the young man, especially at the moment when he commits his first sin! How bitter, O great God, is the fruit which he has just tasted! "Behold me a wreck! I have failed in all my promises! My baptismal robe is defiled! The covenant of my first Communion is broken! Jesus Christ is no more in my heart! I am no longer his child! I am disgraced in the eyes of the angels!"

He is so too in his own eyes: he can no more look into the depths of his soul without a blush. And hence he is sad, he is uneasy, he is a burden to himself and to others. Night draws on, and he is afraid to die; day appears, and his conscience is torn with remorse. This is what occurs to man the first time that he falls into a grievous fault, especially after first Communion. Oh, how much he is to be pitied!

What will become of him? The invisible tempter, who promised him happiness, that he might involve him in guilt, suddenly changes his tactics. To hold him fast in evil, he represents to him the enormity of the fault that has been committed by him and the frightful depth of infamy into which it has plunged him. He exaggerates the difficulties of obtaining pardon. Above all, he shows him the absolute impossibility of recovering whole and entire that virtue which has once been lost. A great weariness of heart seizes the unhappy man: he sinks into discouragement.

New falls succeed. He despairs of being able to break his chains. Tired of a cowardly warfare, he abandons himself to all the fury of his passions. And now there are tears in the family, scandals in society, shameful diseases, old age before its time, perhaps one suicide more! Travel through city and country, examine the secrets of life, and say is not this the record of daily history?

Well, this kind of helplessness in regard to virtue, to which man is reduced by vice, ceases the moment you offer him a sure and easy means of recovering himself, a means by which he may find again the olden vigor of his soul. Why do infamous punishments—those of the convict-prison, for example—not make a man better? Because, instead of rehabilitating him, they disgrace him in the eyes of society with an everlasting brand. Now a branded, an irremediably branded life, will always be a useless or a dangerous life. But who will give you the means of rehabilitation? The world? No; for rehabilitation is pardon, is peace with God, sealed and notified: this is not the mission of the world.

Will you find it in religious sects, among whom sacramental confession is suppressed? No likelihood thereof. True: protestants have preserved an acknowledgment of sins, made to God without the aid of a tribunal or of sacramental forms. But there is no longer any efficacious means here which speaks to the senses, which fills the mind and the heart with a religious confidence. There is no longer anything in this avowal of faults but a help which we have already in prayer. An essential thing is wanting—the act of divine jurisdiction to which heaven attaches the grace of pardon. The sentence of remission is not pronounced on the guilty. He cannot, whatever he may do, say to himself: "Today heaven has forgiven me. Today my early errors have been forgotten. Today the life of the immortal man again begins in me; it begins pure and holy; it is given me that I may be able to aspire to a high degree of virtue, beyond the reach of vice." No, he cannot say so.

Hence an expression, which shows well the vanity of protestant confession. "How happy you are," said some of our separated brethren to us lately, "how happy you are to have it in your power to confess!"

The lot of the young Catholic is very different. What do I say—the young Catholic? We must say the Catholic of every age, however guilty he may be. He knows that a tribunal of mercy has been established, where God himself, that God whom he has offended and with whom he must make peace, dwells in the person of his minister. He knows that this God promises him a full and perfect pardon. He has the consoling certainty that the word of peace, which will resound in his ears, will be ratified in heaven. No doubt here, no uneasiness. He will have his pardon, his rehabilitation, all the certainty that he can morally desire. This certainty is his joy. It doubles his strength to begin a new life. And so there is courage in his heart, sweet tears in his eyes, an edifying member in the family, a useful—because a virtuous—citizen in society.

Of these miracles of rehabilitation there is not a priest who in his sacerdotal career does not see and work a great many. The better to appreciate how useful and consoling they are, we shall adduce one instance out of a thousand.

History. An old cavalry officer was one day passing through a place where Père Brydaine was giving a mission. Anxious to hear an orator of such great renown, he entered the church when the missioner, after the evening exercises, was developing in the form of an advice the advantages and the method of a good general confession. The military man, touched, instantly resolves to confess. He comes to the foot of the pulpit, speaks to P. Brydaine, and decides to remain at the mission. His confession was made with all the sentiments of a true penitent. It seemed to him, he said, as if an insupportable burden had been taken off his shoulders. The day on which he had the happiness of receiving absolution, he left the tribunal shedding tears, of which all the people were witnesses. Nothing was so sweet to him, he said, as those tears, which flowed without an effort from love and gratitude. When the holy man withdrew to the sacristy, he followed him, and there, in presence of several missioners, the loyal and edifying officer gave expression to his sentiments thus:

"Gentlemen, be so good as to hear me, and you particularly, Père Brydaine. I have never in my life tasted pleasures so pure and sweet as those which I have found since my return to friendship with my God. I do not believe that Louis XV, whom I have served for thirty-six years, can be happier than I. No: this prince, amid all the splendors that surround his throne, amid all the pleasures that await him, is not so joyous, is not so content, as I have been since I laid aside the frightful burden of my sins."

Here, falling at Brydaine's knees, and clasping his hands, he added: "What thanks I ought to render to my God! He has brought me into this country by the hand. Ah, Father! I thought of nothing less than that which you have made me do. I can never forget you. I beg you to pray to the Lord that he may grant me time to do penance: it seems to me that nothing will cost me anything, if he spares me."

Nothing will cost me anything! Do you see the effects of the words that declare to man his forgiveness? Do you understand the change that is wrought in him by the certainty of his rehabilitation? What energy for virtue! What ardor for piety! This is the point at which the wisdom of the confessor is sometimes obliged to moderate the transports of fervor. Such are the miracles of confession. And these miracles every priest can recount today, occurring in our own century, when confession, despised, is so generally neglected.

Its individual and social advantages. Let us conclude from what has been said that confession, painful as it appears, is nevertheless an immense benefit, and that it is also in perfect harmony with the wants of the human heart in all ages and among all peoples. What more natural, in effect, than the tendency of one heart to communicate a secret to another? The wretched man who is torn with remorse has need of a friend, who will hear him, console him, and sometimes guide him. "A heart in which crime has shed its poison is sickened, is agitated, is narrowed, until it meets with the ear of friendship, or at least that of benevolence."[881] Now, it is confession that, with its divine seal, gives confidence.

Such are some of the benefits of confession in regard to the individual. What shall we say of its advantages relatively to society?

Whence, do you think, come all the crimes that inundate the world, disturb families, and overthrow empires? Is it not from the heart of man? Is it not there that all the offenses of which we are every day the witnesses or the victims are conceived and matured? To save society—to restore sincerity, justice, disinterestedness, purity of manners—it is therefore necessary to begin with making all virtues reign in the human heart. But who will take hold of it? Who will penetrate its inmost depths, to purify and reform it? Human laws may well raise some dikes against the flood, but it is not given them to dry up the very sources of the torrent. They may act on deeds; but desires and thoughts, the principles of deeds, escape them.

To religion alone is reserved this salutary power. But how will she exercise it? How will she go into the recesses of the human heart? Preaching, doubtless, is a means by which religion reaches the conscience of man; but a sermon, being addressed to everyone in general, is addressed to no one in particular. The individual may take it or leave it, according to his temper or his intelligence. Moreover, self-love, so versed in the art of deception, often hinders us from seeing that which precisely suits us. Many a time, even when we see it, we have not courage to make a generous application of it to ourselves. Hence, unfortunately, the general uselessness of a public discourse at the present day to reform manners.

What means, then, is left religion to bring a remedy to our wounds? You have named it. You have named it with trembling, perhaps, since you began to know how efficacious it is. This remedy is confession. There, in that secret and sacred tribunal, the heart wholly discovers itself. There the priest, the man of God, the incorruptible defender of heaven's rights; the priest, the sincere and unchangeable friend of the culprit; the priest, the kind physician, unites with all the means to know the disease all the power to apply a remedy to it. He burns, he cuts, he sweeps away, without human respect or foolish pity, the odious gangrene. Less than anything else does he spare the delicate fiber of the favorite passion, which, to escape destruction, hides itself under the lowest folds of the conscience.

The evil known and acknowledged, the confessor thinks of the cure. For the false thoughts, the irregular—consequently, the anti-social—affections of the old man, he substitutes the true thoughts, the virtuous—consequently, the social—affections of the new man: in a word, he communicates to both mind and heart a new and holy life. It is thus that confession, bringing religion home to the wants of each man, implants a divine life in the very heart of society. It is thus that in the tribunal of penance the priest is the champion of society, the most valuable defender of its interests, the noblest repairer of its wrongs.

Find one public or private, moral or material, interest which confession does not protect, and protect a thousand times better than a powerful magistracy, invested with all the authority of the laws. It protects the holy rights of parents and kings against the insubordination of their children and subjects; the moral, and even the physical, life of children against the negligence and the violence of parents; the innocence, the character, the property, the life, the peace of all, against the guilty passions which threaten them—passions whose germ is found in the hearts of all the children of Adam.

Blind men! who have the misfortune no more to confess—fathers, mothers, rich and poor!—never will you know all that you owe to the tribunal of penance. For a long time, perhaps, dishonor would have rested on all that you hold most dear, calumny would have blighted your name, injustice would have possessed itself of your fortune, a cup of bitterness would have drenched your life with sorrows—had it not been for confession.

To sum up in a few words this evidence on the social necessity of confession, I say: No society without faith and morals, no faith and morals without religion, no religion truly efficacious without application to society, no truly efficacious application of religion to society without confession. We know today what must be thought of the virtues of those "honest" people who do not confess. Those are the honest people who have made society what it is. By the fruits, judge the tree! For the rest, it is very remarkable that all parties—indifferentists, protestants, atheists—have only one voice in rendering homage to confession.

In the eyes of the indifferentists, who do not practice it, it is eminently social. They are quite well satisfied that their wives, their children, their servants, should confess. The distance at which they themselves live from confession is a homage which they render to its excellence. At what period did they dispense with its use? Was it when they became more just and pure? Do we not know that no one quits confession unless when he wishes to abandon himself to his inclinations and to live at liberty?

A man, whom I will not name, said lately in the chamber of the legislature: "The nations no longer confess." You had no need to say so; we know it well enough. The statistics of crime, with which you are better acquainted than anyone else, have taught it to you. This long list of misdeeds of all kinds, becoming more numerous every year, proves today with as much rigor as the cogent reasoning of a geometrical problem, that crimes increase with a nation in proportion as it ceases to confess.

Now that the majority abandon this social duty, what do we see? Disorder everywhere: society on the brink of a volcano. If the world confessed, should we be witnesses of such a spectacle? You raise the cry of lamentation at the thought of the evil which ruins you, and you drive away the remedy, you turn it into ridicule. Suffer, then: you do not deserve to be pitied.

Protestants take the same view of confession as the indifferentists. In the sixteenth century, when their fury against the Catholic Church was just beginning, they abolished this dogma; but in a short time, public order was disturbed by all sorts of crimes. It was then that they besought the emperor Charles V to reestablish confession among them, as the only means to prevent the total overthrow of their republic: and they were right. Even at the present day, Anglican ministers strive to introduce again the practice of auricular confession.

Toward the close of the seventeenth century, an illustrious protestant, Leibnitz, spoke thus of confession:[882] "We cannot deny that this whole institution is worthy of the divine wisdom, and assuredly there is nothing more beautiful or admirable in the Christian religion. Even the Chinese and Japanese were delighted with it. As a matter of fact, the necessity of confession deters many men from sin, especially those who are not quite hardened, and offers great consolation to those who have fallen. Hence, I regard a pious, grave, and prudent confessor as a great instrument of the divinity for the salvation of souls. His counsels serve to regulate our affections, to moderate our passions, to make us avoid the occasions of sin, to make us restore what we have taken unjustly, to make us repair scandals, to dissipate our doubts, to raise the drooping spirit, in fine, to cure or to sweeten all the ills of wounded souls. If, in human affairs, one can scarcely find anything more excellent than a faithful friend, what will it be when this friend is bound by the inviolable religion of a divine sacrament to keep faith with you and to assist you?"

Let us now hear some of the most impious philosophers. "There is perhaps no institution," says Voltaire, "wiser than confession...Confession is an excellent thing, a rein on the worst crimes. In the most remote antiquity, persons used to confess at the celebration of their mysteries...The enemies of the Roman Church, who have risen up against an ordinance so salutary, seem to have taken from men the most powerful check that ever was placed on iniquity."

The author of *l'Histoire Philosophique et Politique du Commerce des Indes*, although a declared enemy of all religion, could not refuse the tribute of his praise to confession.

"The Jesuits," he says, "established in Paraguay the theocratical government, but with an advantage peculiar to that religion which formed its basis, namely, the practice of confession…It alone is a substitute for penal laws and acts as a guard on purity of manners. In Paraguay, religion, more powerful than the force of arms, leads the culprit to the feet of the magistrate. There, far from striving to palliate his crimes, repentance makes him aggravate them; instead of eluding punishment, he comes to ask it on his knees: the more severe and public it is, the more it calms the conscience of the criminal…The best of all governments would be a theocratical, in which should be established the tribunal of confession."

And now, tell me, which is it more necessary to admire—the goodness of our Lord which established confession, or his wisdom which rendered it obligatory? Our gratitude will become still deeper, if we consider how easy confession is. Let us judge hereof by the following parable.

An ordinary citizen was admitted to the court of a mighty prince. Nothing was wanting to his happiness. Honors, riches, pleasures, all were given him by the munificence of the monarch. So many benefits ought to have inspired him with a feeling of boundless devotedness to the king. It was not so. Carried away by some vile passion, the ungrateful man committed against his benefactor a most heinous crime, which did not indeed find its way to the public light, but came nevertheless to the knowledge of the prince, with all the proofs necessary to establish its certainty.

Then the king, using his right to punish, pronounced sentence of condemnation on the guilty. Pale, trembling, with eyes cast down, the wretch is led to the block. Already the executioner holds the axe over his head. There is not a gleam of hope: the ingrate is about to die, and to bear in his death the just chastisement of his offense. Suddenly a loud cry is heard: "Pardon, pardon from the king!!!" Do you see how this man returns as it were to life? He can scarcely believe his ears. His heart overflows with joy.

The king's messenger comes close to the culprit, and says: "My master is good. He grants you pardon, but he wishes that you should make an acknowledgment of your crime to one of his ministers, without omitting the least circumstance concerning it. This is the only condition that his generosity imposes on you: choose between it and death." Hear how the culprit, transported with a new joy, exclaims: "Ah! show me this minister. I am ready to acknowledge all. I have only one fear: it is lest the king should retract what he has done!"

He is still speaking when a second messenger arrives, crying out: "Pardon, pardon from the king!!!" He comes close to the culprit, and says: "My master is good, and, as a proof of his clemency, he permits you to choose among all his ministers the one in whom you feel the greatest confidence." Tender tears fall from the culprit's eyes.

Before he is able to speak, a third messenger arrives, crying out: "Pardon, pardon from the king!!!" He comes close to the culprit, and says: "My master is good. He not only permits you to choose among all his ministers the one in whom you feel the greatest confidence, but he moreover imposes on the minister of your choice an absolute silence regarding all that you shall confide to him, under pain of coming himself to take your place on the scaffold. If you accept the offer, the king forgets your fault forever, restores you to his good graces and your former honors, and fixes your place again in his palace, on the steps of his throne."

Judge of the prisoner's new transports in regard to this generous monarch, and of the blessings that are invoked on him by the multitude. The application is easy. Here you have the whole history of confession. Who will now dare to say that confession is a painful task?

PRAYER

O my God! who art all love, I thank thee for having so often received me to penance with so much mercy. I beg of thee the grace to preserve till my last breath the innocence which I have recovered.

I am resolved to love God above all things, and my neighbor as myself for the love of God; and, in testimony of this love, I will perform my penance with much fervor.

Lesson 41: Our Union with the New Adam by Hope (14)

The number and the enormity of our faults, and the rigor of the penances that should be done to expiate them, would naturally cast us into a state of dejection. Our heavenly Father found a means to suit the weakness of his children, and at the same time to preserve the rights of his justice: we allude to indulgences. Here we meet with one of the most beautiful dogmas of Christianity, and yet one of the least understood, perhaps one of the most calumniated. To vindicate it, we need only tell what it is: we proceed to do so.

1. *What are indulgences?* In a family, a child disobeys. Its father imposes a penance on it. The culprit makes it a duty to perform the penance, when its mother, brother, or sister comes to beg pardon for it. The father is moved, and forgives in consideration of the petition that has been addressed to him: this father grants an indulgence. In a kingdom, a man becomes guilty of a crime. The laws condemn him to death. He is about to mount the scaffold, when some illustrious personage comes to cast himself at the feet of the monarch and to implore pardon for the criminal. The king is moved; the culprit is spared: the king grants an indulgence.

In the person of Adam, the whole human race rebels against God. It is condemned to everlasting death. Immediately the Son of God presents himself and implores pardon, offering to die in our stead. The eternal Father accepts the offer, and man is spared: God grants an indulgence.

Based on this mystery, the whole of Christianity is but one great indulgence, granted to the guilty human race, in consideration of the just man by excellence, who was voluntarily immolated for a sinful world. As we perceive, an indulgence in general is a reversion of the merits of the just to the guilty; it is the source, at once consoling and terrible, of that fraternity which binds all men together; it is the basis of societies, and the very essence of Christianity. Let us now descend from these heights, and see what we must understand by indulgences properly so called, of which we have to speak.

Theology calls an indulgence: the remission of a temporal punishment which remains to be undergone after the remission of the eternal punishment;[883] and tells us that it is granted outside the sacrament of penance by the application of the merits of Jesus Christ and his saints.

To understand the nature and the effects of indulgences, we must remember that every sin must be punished either in this life or in the next. If the sin is mortal, it must be punished in the next life with an eternal punishment, irrespective of all temporal punishments; if it is only venial, it must be punished with a temporal punishment either here or in purgatory. We must also remember that after the remission, in the sacrament of penance, either of venial sin or of mortal sin and the eternal punishment due to mortal sin, there too often remains a temporal punishment to be undergone. This case occurs when a person has not those perfect dispositions of contrition and charity which exclude every affection to sin and fully justify us before God.

That, in remitting sin and its eternal punishment, God does not always remit the temporal punishment which it deserves, is a truth made evident by the conduct of God himself toward the most illustrious penitents. Adam becomes guilty. God remits his fault, and the eternal punishment which it deserves. Nevertheless, he does not exempt Adam from the temporal punishments due to his sin. He lays upon him the hard obligation of eating his bread in the sweat of his brow, as well as the sad necessity of passing on to death through a sea of sufferings.

The Israelites are absolved from their murmurs. Nevertheless, they shall bear the punishment thereof. David is pardoned his double crime. Nevertheless, he shall undergo a temporal punishment. In this conduct, let us recognize the wise solicitude of our heavenly Father. "To show to the sinner," says St. Augustine, "the greatness of the evil which he has committed and of the chastisement which he deserves, to correct a nature always ready to fall, and to exercise that patience which is so necessary for us, God permits temporal punishments to afflict man, even after he has ceased to be given over, for his faults, to an eternity of torments."

2. *Who can grant indulgences?* But these temporal punishments—is it really necessary that we should undergo them, in all their extent and rigor, either here or in purgatory? Faith teaches us that the Church received from our Lord Jesus Christ the power to sweeten them—a consoling power, which we gratefully place among the signal benefits of the divine mediator—a sacred dogma, which rests, like religion itself, on immovable foundations.

The father in his family, the king in his kingdom, enjoys the grand prerogative of showing mercy. Why should not the Church, our mother and our queen, enjoy it with regard to her children? Could the Son of God, who founded the Church, have failed in the power or the will to grant it? In the power? There is nothing to show it. In the will? There is nothing to show it. In point of fact, the Savior gave the Church the power of granting indulgences when he said to St. Peter: "I will give you the keys of the kingdom of heaven: whatsoever you shall bind on earth, shall be bound in heaven; and whatsoever you shall loose on earth, shall be loosed in heaven."[884]

This promise is general, and admits of no exception. Wherefore we reason thus. The Church, in the person of St. Peter, received from the Son of God the power to open heaven to repentant sinners. She has therefore the power to remove all the obstacles that may oppose their entrance. Now, the temporal punishments which remain to be undergone after the remission of the eternal punishment are so many obstacles which prevent converted sinners from entering heaven, whither no one can have access before the payment of the last farthing due to the divine justice. The Church has therefore received the power to remit these punishments; consequently, to grant indulgences. Besides, he who can do more, can also do less. The Church has received the power to remit sins; with much greater reason, therefore, can she remit the punishment due to sins.

Another proof that the Church holds from our Lord the power to grant indulgences is the conduct of the apostles. Instructed by their divine master himself, they made use of this power. St. Paul had preached the gospel at Corinth; he had formed a flourishing church there. Called by his zeal to other provinces, he learns that one of his neophytes has committed a great crime. Immediately he writes to the church of Corinth to cast him out from her pale.[885] He is informed that the culprit repents. Touched with compassion, the apostle writes a second letter, in which he says that he consents to grant an indulgence to this wandering but penitent sheep, lest an excessive sadness should lead it to despair. He adds: "If I do so, it is for your sakes, and as the representative of Jesus Christ."[886]

St. Paul therefore believed that the Son of God had given to his apostles, and consequently to his Church, the power to show mercy to sinners, in consideration of the prayers and merits of their innocent brethren: that is to say, the power to grant indulgences. Do those heretics and infidels who dare to deny this right to the Church flatter themselves that perchance they know the intentions of Jesus Christ better than St. Paul, and can determine with greater precision the extent of the powers which he left to his Church? Did not the great enemy of indulgences in modern times say, before being condemned by the sovereign pontiff: "If any one deny the truth of the pope's indulgences, let him be anathema"?

A third proof is the conduct of the successors of the apostles. From the first ages, bishops have been in the constant habit of granting indulgences. In the third century, the Montanists, and in the fourth, the Novatians, were moved by a false zeal to rise against the facility with which the pastors of the Church received sinners to penance and gave them absolution and Communion. To put an end to their clamors, the rigor of the penances that were imposed on sinners before reconciling them to the Church was carried much further. But the pastors, in spite of the obstinacy of the heretics, continued to use indulgences.[887] The fervor of penitents, the approach of persecution, or the request of martyrs, supplied a motive for their paternal and salutary conduct.

Like Jesus Christ at the moment of expiring, the martyrs, ready to suffer death, turned their tender looks once more toward their brethren, and asked pardon for them. If they knew how to write, they put the names of their friends on a billet, which was called the "Martyr's Billet." If they could not write, they contented themselves with mentioning them to the deacons by whom they were visited in their prisons. The deacons bore these billets or verbal recommendations to the bishops. Whether to honor the constancy of the martyrs, or because all spiritual goods are common among the children of the Church, the bishops judged with reason that the merits of the martyrs might lawfully be applied to the penitents for whom intercession had kindly been made by them, and they shortened the term of their penance.[888]

After the conversion of the emperors, there were no more martyrs to intercede in favor of penitents. For all that, no one supposed that the source of the Church's riches was exhausted or diminished. We shall presently see that this source is inexhaustible. It is therefore a truth of faith, established on the words of our Lord himself, on the example of the apostles, and on the tradition of all ages, that the Church has power to grant indulgences. Hence, the holy Council of Trent pronounces anathema against any one who should dare to say that indulgences are useless, or that the Church has not the power to grant them.[889]

3. *What is the use of indulgences?* It is certain that an indulgence, granted with that discretion which always so eminently distinguishes the infallible spouse of Jesus Christ, turns to the advantage of the faithful. It is for living saints a powerful incentive to multiply their good works; for sinners, a motive of confidence in the communion of saints, and an engagement to avoid all the sins that incur excommunication: for both classes, an admirable bond of fraternal charity.

It would therefore be an error to imagine that indulgences lead to tepidity and depravity. Never have they authorized a penitent to refuse the penance imposed on him by a confessor, or to dispense himself from a restitution or a reparation which he could make. The object of indulgences has always been to supply for penances omitted, ill-accomplished, or too light in comparison with the immensity of faults. Here is the tenor of the Church's words to the sinner on whom she bestows this favor: "You owe much, and you have nothing or almost nothing to pay it; but, if you do such a thing, you shall be acquitted." It is thus that a father or a king commutes the punishment merited by a disobedient child or a rebellious subject.

Acting in this manner, the Church only follows the example of God himself. What, in effect, as we have already said, is Christianity—what is the redemption of Jesus Christ, the first foundation of our faith—but a great indulgence, granted to guilty man in consideration of this innocent victim? Hence, the dogma of indulgences touches the very essence of religion. For the indulgences which the Church grants are only a particular application of that great indulgence which is the basis of Christianity.

4. *Is the dogma of indulgences agreeable to reason?* Nothing can be more agreeable to reason, for nothing reconciles more admirably the rights of the divine justice and mercy. God can no more allow a sin to pass without punishment than a good work without reward; and it is strictly necessary that every sin should be punished as much as it deserves.[890] His mercy therefore does not consist in showing impunity to the culprit, but, as the dogma of indulgences teaches us, in receiving, as a payment of what is due to him, the satisfaction of Jesus Christ and the saints.

5. *What is the treasury of indulgences?* The preceding ideas suppose that there are superabundant satisfactions in the Church, and that these satisfactions may be applied to the faithful: a twofold supposition, a twofold reality.

First, there are superabundant satisfactions in the Church. In effect, all good works performed in the state of grace are at the same time impetratory, meritorious, and satisfactory; they obtain grace, they merit glory, and they expiate sin. The actions of our Lord, who was the model of all the saints, gained him the graces of salvation for mankind and the highest degree of glory for his humanity, while they at the same time effaced the sins of the world.

Similarly, the just man who performs a good work adds another pearl to his crown, receives a new grace, and also atones for some of his sins. But if the just man has no sins to atone for, or if the merit of his good work exceeds his debt, his good action only obtains a part of its reward. Insofar as it is expiatory, it remains deprived of its effect. Before God, who is justice itself, this kind of merit cannot be lost.

So much being laid down, it is certain that the satisfactions of our Lord vastly outweigh the sins of the world. They are infinite: the latter are not so. Hence the memorable words of Pope Clement VI, which so admirably explain the thoughts of the Church on indulgences: "The Savior, immolated on the altar of the cross, did not shed merely one drop of his blood, which nevertheless, on account of the dignity of his Person, would have sufficed for the redemption of the human race, but he shed it all…How great, then, that so many merits should not be useless and unprofitable, must be the treasure of graces which he acquired for the Church militant! This treasure he did not bury in a field: he gave to the prince of the apostles and his successors the power to distribute its riches among the faithful."[891]

It is also certain that the saints made many superabundant satisfactions. Can this be denied of the Blessed Virgin, who, free from every shadow of sin, nevertheless suffered so much? Can it be denied of so many martyrs, who, from the sacred font of baptism in which they had just been purified, only made one step to the scaffold on which they consummated their sacrifice? Can it be denied of so many other saints who, hardly guilty of a few trivial faults, spent their lives in every species of austerity and privation? Such, besides, is the doctrine of the Church.[892] Hence, the treasury of indulgences is filled with the superabundant merits of our Lord Jesus Christ, the holy Virgin, and the saints. It is inexhaustible, since the merits of the Savior are infinite.

We said that these merits might be applied to the faithful, and we have established our statement by showing that the Church has power to grant indulgences. Let us add that justice requires it to be so. Would it not be strange that in so perfect a society as the Church, so rich a treasure should be allowed to lie untouched? Would God leave the immense merits of our Lord and the saints useless? Yet he cannot turn them to the service of his Son or his saints, since they have no personal debts to pay; it is therefore fitting that he should employ them in favor of his needy children: such has been the conduct, from the beginning of the world, of the divine Father of the family.

In the terrestrial paradise, he accepts the mediation of his Son on behalf of guilty man. Under the old covenant, we often see him pardoning the greatest sinners—though they only perform slight penances—when some holy personage offers his satisfactions for them. He pardons the rebellious Israelites for the sake of Moses, his servant. He would have pardoned, at the prayer of Abraham, five infamous cities, if he could only have found therein ten just men. Finally, he pardons the profaner, Heliodorus, in consideration of the high priest, Onias. Under the new covenant, he graciously multiplies the merits of the saints, that they may be applied to us by means of indulgences.

6. *What is to be understood by a plenary indulgence and a partial indulgence?* The remission of the temporal punishment due to our sins is not always granted us in the same measure. Sometimes it is full and entire, at other times it is not so. Hence plenary and partial indulgences.

A plenary indulgence is a remission, not only of all sacramental and canonical penances, but also of all the pains of purgatory.[893] Hence, the Christian who is so happy as to gain a plenary indulgence in all its fullness becomes as pure as the child that is lifted from the baptismal font. If he dies in this happy state, he ascends straight to heaven without passing through purgatory.[894] Do you know any truth more consoling?

But, you will say, he who gains in all its fullness a plenary indulgence for the departed, is therefore sure to deliver from purgatory the soul to which he applies it. No, he is not sure, and here is the reason. A soul may be detained in purgatory either for venial sins that have not been remitted or, if they have been remitted, to undergo the punishments due to them, as well as to mortal sins forgiven in the sacrament of penance. If the soul is detained for venial sins that have not been remitted, the indulgence cannot deliver it. And why? Because an indulgence remits neither mortal nor venial sin, but only the punishment due to sin. When, in the formula or the concession of an indulgence, it is said that he who gains it shall obtain the remission of all his sins, *remissionem omnium peccatorum*, this must be understood of all the temporal punishments due to his sins.[895] If the soul is detained only to undergo temporal punishments, it will infallibly be delivered,[896] unless God, in the counsels of his justice, judges it proper not to apply the whole benefit to it.[897] Let us add that it is very difficult to know whether we have gained an indulgence in all its fullness. Hence, we do well in applying indulgences as often as possible to the souls that are dear to us.

As for partial indulgences—of seven years or seven quarantines, for example—they remit the punishment which would be effaced by seven years or seven times forty days of public penance, imposed in the early ages of the Church; but this does not mean that they diminish by seven years or seven times forty days the pains of purgatory.[898] To excite in us a lively desire of gaining them, it suffices to know that they diminish those pains in the measure fixed by the merciful wisdom of the supreme judge. It is now time to pass on to the seventh question, which we shall answer in a few words.

7. *What must be done to gain indulgences?* As we have just shown, indulgences are an immense benefit, whether for ourselves or for the souls in purgatory. That which enhances their value, while it splendidly manifests the infinite goodness of our heavenly Father, is the facility with which they may be gained.

Facility in the acts that are required of us. Sometimes it is a short prayer; sometimes, a visit to a church. At other times it is the possession of a cross or a medal, accompanied with certain pious acts, which learned and ignorant, old and young, may alike perform. Thus, indulgences are attached to the beads, to the acts of the theological virtues, to the Litanies of the Holy Name of Jesus and the Blessed Virgin, to the *Angelus*, to the sign of the cross, and to a multitude of other prayers, which we know by heart, or which may be found in the most widely-spread books.

Indulgences are also attached to different societies of the Blessed Virgin, the Blessed Sacrament, the Sacred Heart, the catechism, the souls in purgatory, the rosary, the scapular, the Propagation of the Faith. Daily meditation, the pious accompaniment of the Holy Sacrament when it is borne to the sick, as well as the greater number of spiritual and corporal acts of charity toward the neighbor, are other sources of indulgences.

Facility in the manner of performing the prescribed acts. Let us first remark that indulgences are goods which belong to the Church. To enjoy them it is necessary to be a member of this holy association: it is necessary to be baptized. These goods are intended to pay our debts: it is therefore necessary to have contracted some—it is necessary to have committed faults. Hence, children without sin cannot gain them for themselves. The faithful departed, not ceasing to be members of the Church, may also derive profit from indulgences. For this, however, it is necessary that the sovereign pontiff should say that such an indulgence is applicable to the souls in purgatory, because it is his office to regulate the dispensation of the merits of our Lord and the saints. It is necessary, moreover, that the faithful should have the intention of so applying them.

This being settled, to gain indulgences it is necessary: a) to do what is required for the purpose at the time and in the manner appointed, and according to the intention of him who grants the indulgence; b) to do it entirely and by oneself; c) to be in the state of grace, at least when one performs the last action prescribed, because the punishment which is due to sin cannot be remitted before the sin itself is remitted; d) to have an intention at least habitual and interpretative, of gaining the indulgence.[899] To fulfill this last condition, we may direct our intention in the morning thus: "My God! I have the intention of gaining all the indulgences attached to the good works which I shall perform during the course of this day."

Here we must make four important observations—on confession, Communion, prayers, and objects indulgenced.

I. Persons, who are in the holy habit of confessing once a week, may gain all the indulgences that arise during the course of the week, provided they persevere in the state of grace.[900] We must except, however, the indulgences of a jubilee, or those to which confession is attached, as an essential part of the good works to be performed.[901]

II. When Communion is prescribed to gain some plenary indulgence in particular, it may be made on the eve of the feast fixed for the indulgence.

III. Though one is obliged to perform by himself the good works prescribed, yet the Holy See has declared that persons who recite these prayers alternately with others gain the indulgences.

IV. To gain the indulgences attached to beads, crucifixes, medals, it is necessary either to bear these objects on one's person, yet without holding them in the hand,[902] or to have them at home. The prayers, prescribed as conditions for gaining the aforesaid indulgences, ought to be recited while one bears the medals, etc., on him, or, if he does not so bear them, while he keeps them in his bedroom, or in some other decent part of the house; or they may be recited before these objects. Finally, these objects cannot be given, or sold, or lent to others, for the purpose of gaining indulgences, without immediately causing them to lose this power.

What can be simpler or easier than these conditions? To fulfill them, we need only wish it. But, though they were as difficult as they are far from difficult, we ought not to shrink at any sacrifice, considering the immense advantages which indulgences procure us.

8. *What motives have we to gain indulgences for ourselves or for the departed?* Is there anyone among us who, looking over his life with the eye of faith, must not say in the words of the prophet Isaias, "My life is like a piece of dirty linen"—so deeply are all my good works

themselves stained with imperfections?[903] Is there anyone who must not add with David, "My iniquities are gone over my head"?[904] Who will not ask like the same prophet, "How can I find out the number or the greatness of my faults?"[905]

What period of our life had not, has not, its special stains? Of the ten commandments of God, which one have we constantly respected? What do I say? Which one have we not broken—broken often, in thought, word, deed, or omission? Have the commandments of the Church obtained from us a more religious regard? Alas! have we not burst through them with greater facility than those of God? Such is the unfortunately too truthful picture of our life.

On the other hand, what penance have we done for so many sins? With what penance are we at present engaged? Do we impose voluntary mortifications and austerities on ourselves, to satisfy the divine justice? What is the penance given us in the tribunal of reconciliation? Is it proportioned to the number and the enormity of our offenses? With what fervor do we perform it? Do we accept, I will not say with gratitude, but with resignation, the crosses which God in his mercy sends us? Are they not only rendered useless, but even made an occasion of new faults, by the complaints and murmurs, the sadness and impatience, with which we endure them?

All this means that we are laden with debts, that we contract new ones every day, and that we scarcely pay anything of what we owe. Yet God is a creditor with whom no one ever becomes bankrupt. It is in vain for us to think otherwise: every sin will be punished, and punished as it deserves, in this world or in the next.

Hence, as we do nothing or almost nothing to lessen our debt, it is evident that, far from trying to avert or escape them, we labor for public and private calamities in this world, for revolutions, for scourges, for diseases, for afflictions of every kind, which are the wages of sin; it is also evident that we labor for many sorrows in the next world—and the most favorable condition that we can expect is the fire of purgatory, with torments whose duration is unknown to us and whose rigor exceeds imagination. It is ourselves who act in this manner, we who fear so much to suffer anything!

To force ourselves to gain indulgences is useful, not only for the discharge of our old debts, but for the avoidance of new ones; not only to shut the doors of purgatory, but to open those of heaven. You know that, to gain an indulgence, it is necessary to be in the state of grace. Now, what motive so powerful to retain us in or restore us to this happy state, as the salutary thought of obtaining an indulgence? The more value we attach to this favor, the greater efforts shall we make to fulfill its conditions, without which we cannot deserve it.

Far, then, from inducing laxity, as certain heretics have pretended, and as some bad Catholics repeat, the dogma of indulgences, properly understood, is alone sufficient to raise all Christians to the highest degree of fervor, to people heaven with blessed souls. Such are the reasons that urge us to gain indulgences for ourselves: no less powerful are those that urge us to gain them for the souls in purgatory.

"Lord, come and see," said the sister of Lazarus to the Savior, and she led him to the entrance of the sepulchre in which her brother had lain for four days. And the Savior wept, and he raised his friend to life. I will say the same to you, my brother, my sister—*Veni et vide*. Come to the threshold of purgatory, and see in the devouring flames your father, your mother, your brother, your sister, who raise their suppliant hands to you and beseech you to deliver them. They have been there, not for four days, but perhaps for several months, and it may be that they are condemned to remain there, one ten years, another twenty years, others a still longer time.

You may sweeten and shorten their sufferings, reduce them perhaps to nothing. To attain this end, it suffices to gain for them the indulgences which the Church offers you with so much liberality and on such easy terms. And yet you refuse! And after this you will pour out your sighs and lamentations for them, array yourself in garments of mourning, and speak of your affection for those whom you have lost. Pagan sorrow, hypocritical mourning, false affection!

True love, says the Savior, does not consist in vain words. It consists in positive acts. If you love your departed ones, prove it by comforting them. If not, I will not ask you whether you have charity: it is demonstrated that you have not. But I will ask you whether you have faith. When we consider the wondrous influence that the dogma of indulgences exercised on Christian ages; when we see Europe, with its kings, its warriors, its whole populations, rising oftentimes at the announcement of an indulgence; when we reflect that the most splendid temple in the world was built by an indulgence,[906] that all Christian countries are covered with convents, churches, innumerable noble monuments, through indulgences, that St. Francis Xavier knew of no more powerful means to draw the peoples of India from the abyss of vice than the promise of an indulgence: when we ponder over these great truths, and behold the fatal indifference with which so many persons at the present day regard these inestimable favors, a most bitter sorrow fills our souls. We ask, without daring to answer our question, if the world has still any faith.

Let us suppose that we go to visit an immense prison; whose numerous inmates are laden with chains. They are all condemned to dreadful punishments—some for ten, others for twenty, others for forty years. We say to them: "The king, in his bounty, wishes much to lessen your punishments, and even if possible to condone them altogether. He will do so on condition that you say such a prayer, or perform such an act of piety, very short and very easy. If you agree, the gates of the prison will be thrown open to you: you shall again see your parents, your friends, your families."

Would a single one of these prisoners refuse a condition so advantageous? Well, these prisoners are ourselves: we are the debtors of God's justice. The prison is purgatory: the pains of this world are nothing in comparison with what must be endured there. It is proposed to deliver us on very easy terms, and we will not accept the offer! Or if we accept it, we fulfill our part of the agreement with scandalous negligence! Are we in our senses? If hereafter we pine through long years in the flames of purgatory, will it not be through our own great fault?

The meaning of a jubilee.—Let us, in conclusion, speak of the great indulgence of the Catholic Church—the jubilee.

The jubilee is a plenary indulgence to which are added several extraordinary privileges. a) It is given to the universal Church, while other plenary indulgences are only for a portion of the flock of Jesus Christ. b) Approved confessors have the power of absolving from all censures and reserved cases; and of commuting vows, as well as the works prescribed for gaining the jubilee, to those who cannot accomplish them. These works are usually seven in number: procession, visiting of churches, prayer in churches, confession, Communion, fasting, and almsgiving.

During the jubilee, all the ordinary indulgences are suspended, the following and a few others are usually excepted: indulgences granted for the hour of death; those which are attached to the recital of the *Angelus*, to the pious action of accompanying the Blessed Sacrament to the sick, to altars privileged for the departed; and those which are granted directly in favor of the souls in purgatory.[907]

The jubilee, properly so called, or the great jubilee, is that which returns every twenty-five years, and the year in which it occurs is called the holy year. Oh, yes! a holy year indeed, because the Church makes to us therein a singular application of the merits of Jesus Christ, the inexhaustible source of all sanctity, and because it is more than any other time a time of grace, a time of the Lord's clemency and liberality.

The word *jubilee* means dismissal or remission. Among the Jews, it was the name of every fiftieth year. On the return of this happy year, all prisoners and slaves were restored to liberty, inheritances sold were given back to their former masters, debts were annulled, and the land remained uncultivated. It was a year of pardon and rest.[908] Now, the jubilee of the old law was only a figure of that of the new. The jubilee of Christianity forgives the spiritual debts with which sinners are laden; it sets free the prisoners and slaves of the devil; it enables us to recover possession of the spiritual goods which we have lost by sin.

Finally, according to the intention of the Church, this year ought to be a time of holy rest, during which, forgetful of earthly cares, we should occupy ourselves in silence with our eternal years. Thus, the jubilee reminds Christians that their religion dates from the first days of the world, that it is the accomplishment of the Mosaic figures, and that they are the children of the God of Israel, and the true heirs of the promises made to the patriarchs.

It awakes, too, the memory of ancient piety. This admirable institution is derived from a period far more remote than is generally believed. Pope Boniface VIII, to whom it is attributed, in the beginning of the fourteenth century, did but regulate a custom already old. History tells us that, in the first days of the year in which the pope issued his bull on the jubilee, the inhabitants of Rome, and after them strangers, most eagerly visited the basilica of the Vatican, to gain the indulgence which was to be obtained there every hundred years, according to the tradition of the ancients.[909] Clement VIII, judging that the term of a hundred years was too long, because few persons saw the end of the century, and thus the greater number were deprived of this happiness, appointed the jubilee to be held every fiftieth year. For a like reason, Paul II, in 1460, fixed its recurrence every twenty-fifth year.

The great jubilee begins at Rome on Christmas Eve. It has been announced from the preceding Ascension Thursday by the publication of a pontifical bull, which is made with great pomp in the Basilica of St. Peter, after the gospel at High Mass. It continues for a year at Rome, and then extends to the rest of Christendom.[910]

How beautiful, how moral was the sight, which formerly the Catholic world presented on the return of this holy year! Scarcely had the sacred trumpet sounded from the summit of the Vatican, when the words of the common father of Christians, repeated afar off by archbishops and bishops, reached the ends of the earth. Then all hearts beat with joy. Like the children of Israel, the children of the Church rejoiced because it had been told them that they should soon go into the house of the Lord, into the holy places of Rome the eternal, the abode of the vicar of Jesus Christ.

The pilgrim put on his garb, he took down the hereditary staff, and set out on his way to the holy city. From all sides, numerous travelers, quitting their country, their parents, their friends, undertook a long and wearisome journey. An immense deputation, which the Catholic world sent every twenty-five years to the vicar of Jesus Christ, to offer him its homage, to assure him of its faith and its respectful attachment, and to gather up his blessings and bring them back to all the countries inhabited by his large family!

Nothing was more edifying than the pilgrimage of these pious groups. They started at break of day. Hymns were sung to the praise of the Lord, and of the saints, patrons of travelers; or, like mariners tossed about on the wide ocean, they invoked Our Lady of Good Help, addressing to her that angelic prayer whose wondrous charm can only be appreciated by the man who is far from his home. At evening, they knocked at the gate of a monastery. Here they found in their new hosts brethren whom they had never seen before; but religion soon made them known. The most tender and anxious cares relieved the travelers after their fatigues, and seemed to surround them once more with the families whom they had left. Faith made them undertake the journey; charity defrayed its expenses.

At length the end drew nigh. The Eternal City began to appear in the distance: the pilgrims hailed it with their acclamations, until they could kneel and kiss respectfully its sacred monuments. The most cordial welcome awaited them in Rome, the common home of Christians. Immense buildings were set apart for their accommodation: these were the children, the brethren so long expected. What a sight was there! What thoughts crowded in those moments on the excited soul!

Men of all nations sat down at the same table: the European by the side of an African or an Asiatic. Men who had never seen one another, who had not even heard of one another, partook of the same bread gratuitously, loved one another, understood one another, recognized around them only brothers assembled under the paternal roof. The common father of so many Christians made it his happiness to visit this numerous family; and, to recall the example of the divine master, served them with his own hands, gazed on them with love, and pressed to his heart those children whom he had never seen before and might never see again.

In vain shall we search through the history of nations for anything more affecting. What could be better calculated to sanction and proclaim that grand maxim whose observance was the glory of the infant Church and is still the happiness of the world, that all men are brethren; that they ought to have only one heart and one soul, as there is only one God, one baptism, one Church, one visible head of all Christians? What could more properly recall to man the grave and holy thoughts of religion than those examples of fervor and penance which were given him by so many persons of every rank and clime? Above all, what could more naturally reanimate faith than the sight of Rome, the scene of the struggles and the victories of Christianity?

These children, come from afar, did not return till they had received the blessing of their common father. But who can describe the effect which this magnificent ceremony produced on the minds of men unaccustomed to such displays, wherein the heart and the senses found equal satisfaction?

"Let all those," says an author, "who have had the happiness of witnessing them, remember how divine is religion, and how grand is the sovereign pontiff, when, surrounded with all the splendor of a monarch and all the dignity of the chief of the Universal Church, composed of 150,000,000 Catholics, he advances, amid the peals of bells and the roar of artillery, preceded by cardinals and bishops of the Greek and Latin rites, to the spacious portico of the noblest temple in the world, and shows himself to thousands of spectators assembled from all parts of the earth to behold him.

"What a joy it is to see this king, high priest, and father of mankind, appear before so many of his children who are gathered together in the wide court at his feet![911] The vicar of Jesus Christ, the successor of the fisherman of Galilee, now rules in the same circus in which the cruel Nero sacrificed so many victims out of hatred to the Christian name! What a triumph for religion! What a consolation for the faith! Everywhere there reigns a profound silence: then, from the height of the apostolic chair, magnificently upheld, the successor of Peter casts a sweet glance over this numerous family. His heart is moved. He rises majestically, bearing on his brow the triple diadem; and, with the hands of his tenderness and the eyes of his faith, seems to bring down from heaven the treasures of grace which he lavishes on Rome and the world, *Urbi et Orbi*."[912]

One of our philosophers, a witness of this ineffable ceremony, wrote thus: "At that moment I was a Christian." These words convey the highest praise.

We have prolonged our remarks on this subject, to show how unjust are the epithets with which impious men insult the jubilee, the pilgrimages, and the numberless gorgeous ceremonies of the Roman Church.

PRAYER

O my God! who art all love, I thank thee for having left to thy Church a treasury of indulgences in the superabundant merits of Jesus Christ and the saints. Grant me the grace to become worthy of them.

I am resolved to love God above all things, and my neighbor as myself for the love of God; and, in testimony of this love, I will do my utmost to gain indulgences.[913]

Lesson 42: Our Union with the New Adam by Hope (15)

Sacrament of extreme unction.—The union which we contract with our Lord by sanctifying grace may be destroyed; but the sacrament of penance enables us to reestablish it. This sacrament is necessary for us as often as we fall into mortal sin. Hence the Savior, in the person of his ministers, is always present in the tribunal of mercy.

But at the approach of the last moment, our union with Jesus Christ is more than ever exposed to danger. On the one hand, the horror of death, the remembrance of past sins, the fear of the judgments of God, contribute to cast the soul into trouble, impatience, sadness, perhaps despair. On the other, the devil avails himself of this favorable opportunity to lay his most artful snares. Feeling that he has only a few moments more to carry on the war against us, he redoubles his efforts, he multiplies his stratagems for drawing us into mortal sin and separating us eternally from our Lord. Many a time has this roaring lion appeared to the sick, roamed around their bed of sorrow, and employed every means in his power to make them consent to some temptation.

We have an authentic proof on this matter in the history of St. Martin, archbishop of Tours. When he was about to die, the devil appeared to him under a hideous form, striving to terrify him. "What art thou come to do here, cruel beast?" said the saint. "Thou shalt find nothing that belongs to thee in me. The bosom of Abraham is open to receive me." May we be able, at our last moment, to repeat the words of this great saint with as much truth as he did!

It is not only to resist the devil that we require extraordinary succors at the approach of death, but also to overcome the repugnances of nature. All men have a horror of death, as a criminal has a horror of punishment. Its arrival multiplies our fears, our anguish becomes deeper, our weak courage deserts us: it is the most pitiful moment of our painful existence. But let us be reassured: the good shepherd does not forget his sheep. He has found a means of lessening the horrors of our departure for us, of making us accept them even joyfully, of rendering us victorious over the devil, and of eternally confirming our union with himself: this means is the sacrament of extreme unction.[914]

Its definition.—Extreme unction is defined: a sacrament instituted by our Lord Jesus Christ for the support of the divine life, and for the spiritual and corporal relief of the sick. A sensible sign, the anointing and words of the priest; a sign instituted by our Lord; a sign which has the virtue of producing grace, the spiritual and corporal relief of the sick: this is what we find in extreme unction. Justly therefore have the last eighteen Christian centuries transmitted it to us as a sacrament of the new law. The Catholic Church, the infallible organ of truth, only gave expression to their sentiments when it pronounced the following anathema: "If any one say that extreme unction is not a true sacrament, instituted by our Lord Jesus Christ and proclaimed by the apostle St. James, let him be anathema."[915]

It is called extreme unction a) because it is the last unction that we receive through the sacraments,[916] and b) because it is usually administered at the close of life, being given by unctions on the sick person's senses, accompanied with prayers.

Its elements.—Resting on the doctrine of the apostles, the Church has always regarded oil as the matter of this sacrament. This oil is blessed by the bishop on Holy Thursday with a great many ceremonies,[917] to show that it does not derive its sacramental efficacy from nature, but from the power of the Blessed Trinity invoked upon it.

The form of extreme unction consists in the words which the priest pronounces at each of the unctions which he makes on the sick person: "By this holy unction and by his own most sweet mercy, may the Lord forgive thee all the evil that thou hast committed by thy sight," etc. Nothing could be more suitable than the matter and form of this sacrament to signify its admirable effects. Oil sweetens, heals, strengthens, enlightens; and the unction of this oil, joined with the words of the priest, perfectly expresses the internal unction of the Holy Ghost, who, here purifying the soul from the remains of sin, strengthens it against the attacks of the devil, enlightens its faith, sweetens its trials, and sometimes even cures corporal diseases.

In fine, the ministers of this sacrament are bishops or priests, to the exclusion of all others. It must be remembered that in this sacrament the forgiveness of sins finds place. Now priests alone, and not the simple faithful, received from our Lord the power to forgive sins.[918] Such, in regard to the elements of extreme unction, is the doctrine of the Catholic Church, formulated by Pope Eugenius IV in his decree to the Armenians, and by the holy Council of Trent.[919]

Its institution.—It is in the fatherly heart of the new Adam that we must look for the source of this sacrament, destined to purify, comfort, and protect man, arrived at the threshold of eternity. It is therefore true, O my Savior, that nothing escaped thy tender foresight on behalf of thy children! The gospel refers to extreme unction when it says that the apostles "anointed with oil many that were sick, and healed them."[920]

If the institution of this sacrament is not more formally related by the evangelists, we must beware of concluding hence that it is not the work of our Lord. St. John is careful to inform us that our Lord said and did many things of which there is no record in the gospel,[921] especially when he appeared to his apostles after his resurrection. Accordingly, it is the general belief that the Savior instituted extreme unction after penance, of which it is the supplement, during the forty days that elapsed between his resurrection and ascension.[922]

However that may be, the apostle St. James manifests its institution to us in these words: "Is any one sick among you? Let him call in the priests of the Church, and let them pray for him, anointing him with oil in the name of the Lord. And the prayer of faith shall save the sick man; and if he be in sins, they shall be forgiven him."[923] Complying with this precept, the Church has made use of this sacrament since her origin. Perhaps it will be asked why the fathers of the early ages scarcely speak of it, and why there is no mention that the saints who died in the fourth century, immediately after the persecutions, received this sacrament. As these two questions might embarrass persons unacquainted with the real state of affairs and the rules of the primitive Church, we shall here clear them up.

1. As we have already seen, the ancients held it as a maxim that they should not speak of our mysteries unless when necessity compelled them. Now there was no necessity that they should speak of this mystery, since it was unknown to the infidels, and no accusation was raised on it against the Church. If the fathers of these first ages named the other sacraments, it was to refute the calumnies of pagans[924] or to instruct catechumens.

In neither of these two cases had they need to mention extreme unction, of which the pagans had no knowledge, and regarding which there would be ample time to instruct the catechumens, when these should be members of the Church and find themselves under the necessity of receiving it. But it was proper that baptism, confirmation, and the Eucharist should be explained to them, that they might receive these holy sacraments on one day, at their entrance into the Church.

2. It is easy to understand that, in the first three centuries, extreme unction was but rarely given to the sick: this for two reasons. First, it was almost impossible, considering the mixture of Christians with pagans, to administer this sacrament without exposing it to the view of unbelievers, and thus provoking sacrileges and persecutions. There were usually in the same family some members pagans, or at least not yet initiated in our mysteries. If the husband was a Christian, the wife was an infidel, or vice versa. If both were Christians, their children, or their slaves, or their servants, or their neighbors were still pagans. Such was the first obstacle to a ceremony that required time and a certain amount of display. Secondly, the ministers of the Church would be exposed to great danger in passing thus from house to house, and Christian prudence did not permit it. This inconvenience was so great that, as we have seen, the faithful were authorized to carry the Eucharist to their own houses, in order to communicate themselves with their own hands, whether in health or in sickness; but they could not administer extreme unction.

Matters being on this footing for the first three centuries, it is not surprising that in the fourth many still neglected to receive this sacrament, which moreover was not of an absolute necessity, like others. But regular discipline was soon established, and the faithful profited of all the advantages held out to them by the Church, fortifying themselves with extreme unction at the approach of death. Add that all that occurred was not written, and many ancient documents have been lost.

Nevertheless, enough remains to show us that the anointing of the sick has been practiced from the first ages of the Church. Origen speaks of this sacrament as a continuation of penance, and as a means which God has placed in our hands to purify our souls from sin.[925] St. Eusebius, elected pope in 310, speaks of extreme unction in express terms, and points out the time at which it must be received.[926] At the close of the same century, Pope Innocent I, a contemporary of St. John Chrysostom's, was consulted by a bishop as to whether bishops could administer extreme unction, considering that the apostle St. James only designates priests as the ministers of this sacrament.

The holy pope easily removed this doubt, saying that the apostle had mentioned priests only because bishops, being engaged with many other affairs, could not always go to see the sick; "but," he adds, "if the bishop can go, or if he judges it proper to do so, it is permitted him to bless them and to make upon them the unction of holy oil—him to whom it belongs to consecrate it."[927]

Effects of extreme unction.—Nothing can better induce us to adopt all the precautions necessary for the reception of this sacrament than a knowledge of its precious effects: they are three in number.

1. The chief effect of the sacrament of extreme unction, that for which it was primarily and directly instituted, is to support the divine life by cleansing the soul from the remains of sin. "Each sacrament," says St. Thomas, "is chiefly instituted for one particular effect, though by way of consequence it produces many. And because a sacrament operates that which it signifies, it is in the very signification of each sacrament that we must look for its principal effect. Now, extreme unction is employed under the form of a remedy, as baptism under the form of an ablution. A remedy being intended to cure, extreme unction is chiefly destined to cure the infirmities produced in the soul by sin. Baptism therefore is a spiritual birth, penance a resurrection, and extreme unction a cure or remedy.

"But as a corporal remedy supposes the life of the body in him to whom it is given, so a spiritual remedy supposes the life of the soul. Hence, extreme unction is not given against the defects which take away the spiritual life, namely, original sin and mortal sin; but against the defects which make the soul sick, and take away that perfect vigor of which it has need to perform the acts of the life of grace and glory. These defects are nothing else than certain weaknesses, certain unfitnesses, left in us either by original or actual sin. It is against these imperfections that man is strengthened in extreme unction.

"But because it is grace that produces this effect—grace, which is incompatible with sin—it follows that if it finds in the soul any mortal or venial sin, it effaces this sin as to the guilt, provided it meets with no obstacle on the part of him who receives it."[928] It also effaces sin as to the punishment, but only in proportion to the dispositions of the sick person.[929]

Since extreme unction destroys the remains of sin, it follows that it gladdens and strengthens the sick person, either by calming the alarms of his conscience through confidence in the mercy of God, or by increasing his ability to endure more patiently the sufferings of his illness, to resist more easily the temptations of the devil, and to preserve himself from an inordinate fear of the consequences of death.

2. It remits the sins which sometimes remain after the reception of the other sacraments. Such are the sins which the sick person does not recollect or does not know, and which he would willingly and penitently confess, if he recollected or knew them. The words pronounced by the priest when administering extreme unction show most clearly that it remits the sins committed by the senses; for the sacraments operate that which they signify. Hence, the Council of Trent anathematizes those who say that extreme unction does not confer grace or remit sin.[930] It is on account of its efficacy in this respect that the holy fathers style extreme unction the "perfection and consummation of penance," whose property is to remit sin.

It may therefore happen that a person, after receiving absolution and Communion, should fall into a mortal sin, which he either does not know or forgets and consequently will not confess; or that he has received absolution or Communion ill-prepared, which he either does not know or forgets. In these cases, if he receives extreme unction with sorrow, and places no obstacle to the grace of this sacrament, he obtains the remission of his faults.

3. It restores corporal health, when this is expedient for the sick person's salvation:[931] such is the teaching of the Catholic faith. If then extreme unction does not more frequently produce this last effect, we should frequently attribute it to the sick person's little faith and imperfect dispositions. He who is seriously ill should above all be on his guard against the guilty negligence of those who surround him, and who recommend him to delay the reception of this divine remedy till the last moment, when it would require a miracle to restore health. This sacrament was established, not to suspend the laws of nature, but to assist them. The true moment for receiving it is when the physicians judge that the disease is dangerous, and that human remedies seem insufficient.

Hence, we must not ask this sacrament when there is no danger of death, nor, with much greater reason, wait till there is no hope. Here you find the reason why it is not given to criminals sentenced to death: on the one hand, they are not sick, and on the other, they have no longer any hope of life.[932] Let us add that, as this sacrament does not imprint a character, like baptism, it may be received many times, but not in the course of the same sickness, unless the sick person has experienced so great a change for the better that the relapse may be considered a new sickness.[933]

How can we fail to be moved at the sight of the tender care and the powerful assistance which our Lord lavishes on his well-beloved in their last moments? It is at the hour when all, even our kindred, abandon us, that this faithful friend draws nearer to us, and watches with greater solicitude over our wants. Why do the majority repay so much kindness with naught but a guilty repugnance, an anti-Christian terror, which keeps this charitable physician away from their bed of sorrow as long as possible?

Dispositions for receiving extreme unction.—That extreme unction may produce the precious effects of which we have just spoken, it requires several dispositions, remote and immediate. The remote dispositions are: a) to have been baptized; b) to have the use of reason; c) to be dangerously ill; d) to be free from excommunication. The immediate dispositions are both external and internal. The former relate to bodily fitness. It is necessary that the parts on which the unctions are to be made should be washed previously: if the attendants have any zeal for religion, they will never fail in this duty. Of the latter, we count three.

The first, to be exempt from known mortal sin. This disposition is essential, for extreme unction is a sacrament of the living. It is therefore necessary to confess, and to excite oneself to contrition: to confess, because confession is a matter of precept when there is danger of death; to excite oneself to perfect contrition, because, at this last hour, prudence directs us to do everything in our power to secure salvation. Now, there are two cases wherein confession and attrition fail to secure it: the one, when the baptism of the sick person has not been valid; the other, when the priest's absolution has been null.[934]

The second, to make fervent acts of the theological virtues—of a lively faith, like that of the sick persons who were brought to our Lord to be cured; of hope in the mercy of God, expecting the resurrection; of charity, ardently desiring to see God—of perfect resignation to the divine will, making with a good heart the sacrifice of health and life; of sorrow and humility, accompanying in a spirit of penance the prayers of the priest who administers the sacrament to us, and making at each of the unctions an act of contrition for the sins which we have committed by each of our senses.

The third, without which the others are generally useless, consists in receiving extreme unction at the right time, I mean before being deprived of consciousness, before being half dead. A cruel pity, a murderous tenderness, a ridiculous and inexcusable fear, keep people from asking the succors of religion until the sick person is no longer in a condition to profit by them. They even flatter him, lull him asleep with vain hopes, and in a little while he quits them to wake up in hell.

What consolation remains for those guilty relations who allow thus to die, without reconciliation with God, a person who, for many long years perhaps, has neglected the practice of all his duties? A good means of preventing such a misfortune in our regard is to make one of our friends enter into a sacred engagement with us that he will warn us when we shall be in danger of death, and not wait until we shall have lost the use of our senses.

Necessity of extreme unction.—This sacrament is not, with an absolute necessity, necessary to salvation: so that one may be saved without it.[935] Yet, says the Council of Trent, those who, out of contempt, neglect or refuse to avail themselves of it become guilty of a great sin, and do an injury to the Holy Ghost.[936] They deprive themselves of a powerful help, of which they have the utmost need at the hour of death, even supposing that they have received the sacraments of penance and the holy viaticum.

To what, say other councils, does not he expose himself who neglects to receive a sacrament without which it is most dangerous to depart this life?[937] One may therefore be directly obliged to receive extreme unction, on account of the violent temptations by which he may be assailed at the last hour, and the danger of his yielding, if not fortified with this sacrament.

Its liturgy.—Our forefathers in the faith did not wait till they were at death's door before receiving the unction of the sick. They knew that this sacrament was instituted not only to complete the purification of the soul and to fortify it, but also to restore health to the body. It was quite common to have oneself borne to the church, or to walk thither oneself to receive extreme unction.[938] In some churches there was a place set aside for the administration of this sacrament.[939]

We see hereby that the sick did not always receive it lying on their beds; and that, even in their houses, they often received it on their knees.[940] To this practice, so respectful and so conformable to the spirit of the Church, were joined other ceremonies, which breathed all the sentiments of a truly contrite and humble heart. It was believed with reason that the best manner of preparing to appear before the dreadful tribunal of Jesus Christ was penance.

When, therefore, the sick person had received the last sacraments, a haircloth or a kind of coarse rough carpet was stretched out on the ground. The priest sprinkled some ashes over it in the form of a cross, and added some holy water. Then the sick person was laid on it, and the priest made the sign of the cross on his breast, followed by an aspersion of holy water, with the following words: "Remember, man, that thou art dust, and into dust thou shalt return!" This was the ordinary practice.[941]

Already, in the fifth century, St. Martin, who wished to die thus, said to his disciples, "It is not permitted a Christian to die otherwise." Persons of all conditions, kings themselves, conformed to this affecting usage. The lives of St. Louis and Louis the Great, kings of France, and Henry III, King of England, leave no doubt on the matter. This practice lasted in some churches till the sixteenth century.[942]

Though it no longer exists among us, the administration of extreme unction is still sufficiently beautiful to teach us with what profound respect the Church surrounds this sacrament, and sufficiently instructive to give us a salutary lesson. Come, therefore, with me and contemplate the dying Christian; come and assist at a spectacle which we shall ourselves one day present. We behold, on one side, the exile who is about to quit life, and, on the other, religion encouraging the child of her tender care, that she may smooth for him the dreadful passage from time to eternity.

The chamber of the sick person should be decent: the bed should have a white coverlet out of respect for the sacrament. A table should be prepared in a convenient place, and covered with a white cloth. On this table should be set a crucifix, two candlesticks with lighted tapers, holy water in a vessel with a sprinkling brush, a plate containing seven or eight little balls of tow or cotton for wiping away the unctions, some crumbs of bread for cleaning the priest's fingers; finally, a ewer or glass full of water with a white towel and a basin to receive the water and the crumbs when the priest will wash his hands.

On reaching the chamber of the sick person, the priest borrows the sweet words with which our Lord saluted his disciples when he appeared in the midst of them, and says, "Peace be to this house, and to all that dwell therein!" Thou above all, poor sick man, fear not: I am thy friend, thy brother, thy Savior, thy physician! The priest lays the holy oils on the table, and, vested with surplice and purple stole, takes the crucifix to the sick person to kiss. Delicious kiss! which the heavenly friend gives his suffering friend, to reassure him, by placing before him the wounds which he endured for love of him.

Having returned to the table, the priest sprinkles some holy water on the assistants and on the sick person, in whose name he utters the prayer of the penitent king: "Sprinkle me, O Lord, with hyssop, and I shall be cleansed; wash me, and I shall become whiter than snow." Then, turning toward the sick person, the priest beseeches the Lord to banish from him the spirit of darkness and to send the good angels to his assistance. He next asks pardon and mercy for him. After which, the sick person himself makes a general acknowledgment of all his faults by reciting the *confiteor*. The priest does not rest here: he recommends the assistants not to forget their brother. A great conflict has begun: the devil seeks to carry off a soul: it must be saved at any cost.

After purifying the sick person with holy water, and exciting him to sentiments of sincere contrition, the priest proceeds to the sacred unctions. He makes them in succession on the eyes, the ears, the nostrils, the mouth, the hands, the feet;[943] in a word, on all the senses, the organs of our actions, and too often, alas! the instruments of our sins.[944] At each unction he repeats these words: "By this unction and by his own most sweet mercy, may the Lord forgive thee all the sins that thou hast committed by" this sense—sight, hearing, smell, taste, or touch.

All the senses of man, vitiated by the devil, are henceforth purified and sanctified. The sign of the cross, which the priest makes on each of them, is like a seal with which he closes them against the enemy, and marks them in the name of God. Fearlessly may the Christian soldier die who bears thus on all his members the sign that is victorious over the devil, the world, and all the powers of darkness!

The unctions finished, the priest purifies his fingers with the crumbs of bread, washes his hands, and casts the water into the fire, as well as the pellets that served for wiping away the holy oil. Profane hands are not allowed to touch these objects: this is the reason why the Church desires that they should be burned. The priest, turning toward the sick person, says, "The Lord be with thee!"

And he fervently begins a most tender prayer, beseeching the God of goodness to work in his servant all the wonderful effects of this sacrament, whether for soul or body. After this, sweet words, consoling words, words of immortal hope fall from the lips of the priest. He does not retire until he has warned the assistants to come and call him, if the sickness should increase: a devoted friend, he will not leave his friend until he has placed him in the bosom of happiness.

Now is the time when, if it is a father or a mother who is about to die, there occurs in Christian families a ceremony truly patriarchal. Knowing all the value of a father's or a mother's blessing, the children press round the bed of sorrow. With the deepest respect and the most filial piety, they receive the parent's last advice and beg a farewell blessing. And behold how the parent, like a new Jacob, making on their heads the sign of the cross, prays for them, and desires for them all that the fondest love, enlightened by the beams of eternity, can desire for the most dearly cherished beings! Why does not this affecting and solemn act always take place? The Church applauds it; the interest of families demands it. In presenting children to their parents to be blessed, one restores to parental authority, in our days so weakened, its dignity and power.

If God wishes to summon the pilgrim of life to himself, if his last hour is about to strike, the minister of Jesus Christ hastens to him immediately. Prostrate before the sick-bed, surrounded by a weeping family, he makes for his brother the affecting, the sublime prayers of the "recommendation of the soul." Human language is powerless to tell how divine they are; the heart must feel it: listen!

The priest—he who receives man on his entrance into life, who supports him during his career, who raises him up after his falls, who watches over all his steps—does not abandon him at this supreme moment. He sees that the world is about to end for this exile from heaven, and that the gates of eternity are opening before him. He now addresses himself to all the inhabitants of that new world, and, in a most touching litany, conjures them, each by his name, to come to the assistance of their brother.

Assured of their all-powerful protection, he gives the signal of departure in these solemn words: "Depart, Christian soul! out of this world, in the name of the Almighty Father, who created thee, in the name of Jesus Christ, the Son of the living God, who suffered for thee, in the name of the Holy Ghost, who sanctified thee, in the name of the angels and archangels, in the name of the thrones and dominations, in the name of the principalities and powers, in the name of the cherubim and seraphim, in the name of the patriarchs and prophets, in the name of the holy apostles and evangelists, in the name of the holy martyrs and confessors, in the name of the holy monks and hermits, in the name of the holy virgins, in the name of all the saints of God. Even this day mayest thou dwell in the peace of holy Sion, through Jesus Christ, our Lord! Amen."

Such is the mighty and splendid escort that accompanies the Christian across the threshold of eternity. What has he to fear? Then wishes for a happy journey, like those of a mother parting with her beloved son, are addressed to him. All that is most reassuring is said to encourage the sick man. All that is most tender is said to God, to move him to receive mercifully this creature, the work of his hands, who, in spite of the unnumbered frailties and errors of humanity, confesses and adores him.

If the soul still struggles in the fetters of the body and the pains of the agony, one opens the book of great sorrows. As well to support the sick man's courage by the remembrance of a great model, as to touch the divine shepherd with pity for his expiring sheep by the remembrance of his own agony, the sorrowful scene of the Garden of Gethsemani is read…It is over; the conflict is ended: the pilgrim is gone! A lifeless body is all that remains of him in this world. He is dead! Men have nothing to offer but useless tears and unprofitable regrets; but religion has prayers. Borne on the wings of faith, these strong auxiliaries accompany the traveler to the tribunal of his judge. They cease not to raise their suppliant voices until they have obtained his admission into the eternal Jerusalem.

What now remains but to form one desire: that of dying thus amid the prayers and maternal embraces of religion? Is death to be feared when it comes in the arms of a mother, whose last kiss gives immortality?

Its social advantages.—If the sacrament of extreme unction is advantageous for man, it is no less so for society. In the eyes of all it raises the dignity of man, and boldly proclaims the dogma of immortality. The Church had said to the child of Adam on the day of his baptism: "Thou art the child of a thrice holy God; be therefore thrice holy—in thy mind, in thy heart, in thy body." She wrote this lesson on all his senses; then, clothing him with a robe whose whiteness was a symbol of this perfect sanctity, she added, "Receive this white robe, which thou art to carry unsullied to the tribunal of Jesus Christ."

When the moment was come to enter on the career of life, she again stopped the young Christian, to reveal to him a great mystery. "Life," said she, "is every instant a warfare; thou shouldst bear thyself with honor in it!" The unction which made the martyrs then flowed upon his brow, and words like these sank into his heart: "Thou art a king; it is with sword in hand that thou must defend thy royalty; a host of witnesses turn their eyes to thee; be worthy of thy forefathers, worthy of the angels, worthy of thy mother!" Then she made this young king sit down at the holy table; she fed him with the bread of the strong, and gave him to drink the wine which produces virgins. The conflict began. If he received some wounds, she healed them by plunging him into a bath of divine blood, and she sent him back to the battlefield more vigorous and more valiant.

It is thus that, by her sacraments, the Church supplies her athlete with all the weapons of victory, and steadily maintains him in a noble elevation of thought. A profound sense of his dignity is never more necessary for him than at the moment when the conflict is about to end, but to end while becoming more fierce.

At the moment when the greatness of man seems to vanish; at the moment when, exhausted by sickness, his outward being is about to decompose and to become in the tomb something nameless; at the moment when friends and relatives in tears acknowledge their inability to bestow aid, and mourn an approaching and irreparable ruin; at the moment, in fine, when man is only an object of horror and pity, the Catholic Church, displaying all the pomp of her ceremonies and all the richness of her graces, comes to raise in our eyes the dignity of human nature.

In point of fact, everything in the sacramental rites of extreme unction reveals the dignity of man, the dignity of the Christian. Under eloquent symbols shines forth the high destiny which awaits us, if we die in the Lord. The Church reminds us by them that we are wounded, but not vanquished combatants—combatants who may have fallen, but who can rise again, by recovering our natural or our moral strength, and so triumph in the last struggle.

And do you think that this great spectacle is useless to society? But is it not a high lesson that teaches us what life is, what death is; that tells us that man on the bed of sorrow is a sacred being, as he was in the cradle, as he will be in the grave, and how holy he ought to be to appear before him who finds stains in the angels?

And then, is it naught to see man preserving to the end the dignity of his being, keeping the peace of his heart and the calmness of his countenance before the open grave? Yes, this spectacle is eminently social. Social by the serious thoughts which it awakens in the souls of the bystanders, who will themselves too be judged by him who judges justice itself; social by the salutary remorse with which it inspires them; social by the declaration which it summons involuntarily to their lips, "Blessed are the dead who die in the Lord"; social by the warning which it gives them of the shortness of time, the uncertainty of life, the vanity of all that passes away, the reality of all that awaits us. Extreme unction is a solemn proclamation of the dogma of immortality.

What, in effect, are all these prayers, all these ceremonies, all these unctions? They are the authorized profession of a truth which is the principle of virtue and the safeguard of society, namely, that all does not die with the body. What would be the good of all these things, if man were only an animal or a machine? No, no, he is something greater, and by each of her unctions the Church engraves the words, "Thou art immortal!" on the senses of man, as he expires. What a consolation for this frail being, who is about to sink into the darkness of the tomb! What a salutary lesson for his survivors!

Take away extreme unction, and no more of all this! Man dies without dignity, without consolation. You degrade him at the time when he has the greatest need of maintaining a high idea of himself, and death is no longer a school of virtue, and life glides away in forgetfulness of eternity, its dreadful tribunal, its joys, its punishments. Would you like to know what becomes of the world when man no longer reflects on his eternal years? Look around you! And let the horrible sight which meets your eyes teach you how social is that sacrament which reminds all, in a manner so striking, of the dogmas of eternity, judgment, heaven, and hell. Take away extreme unction, and death is nothing more than a scandal or an abomination. A scandal, by the insensibility which accompanies it, and the want of a public reparation after a life of iniquity; an abomination, by the anguish, the terror, and the disgust which it inspires.

Whence, then, proceeds that ridiculous, if it were not shockingly guilty, fear of seeing a man die as a Christian? Do you fear the display of our holy ceremonies? And will you not fear for your father, for your husband or wife, for your child, the torments of eternity? Have our sacraments then caused any one to die? Is not a Christian death rather an effect of the consolation which God brings with him wherever he enters? Are not sweetness and peace so inseparably attached to the worship of our heavenly Father that the sacred minister is sent like a guardian angel to the sick man, to maintain his soul in the love of good and to open his heart to divine consolations?

You are apprehensive lest the display of our ceremonies should bring fear into the soul of the sick man and sadness into the hearts of those who surround him. Fear into the soul of the sick man! But have I not just told you that it is not fear, it is consolation and confidence, that God brings with him? Fear: and after all, who told you that a salutary fear is an evil? A fear which makes one think of eternity, repair injustices and scandals, become reconciled with God, and secure everlasting happiness, was never an evil. Sadness in the hearts of those who surround him! And does not then a death without sacraments, without reconciliation with God, sadden you? Just heaven! What consolation can remain—no, but what cruel remorse, what overwhelming sadness must remain—when one has allowed a dear relative, nay, any person in the world, to cross the dreadful plank from time to eternity, and fall into the hands of the living God, without having made his peace with his judge?

On the other hand, what a source of consolation is a Christian death! If anything can sweeten the pain of separation, is it not the ability to say, my father, my husband, my child, my friend is dead; but he died in the arms of religion, after receiving from God the kiss of reconciliation! He is dead, but he is not separated from those who love him; he is dead to a world of misery and suffering, but he lives in a better world: we shall meet again.

Blessed then are they who procure for their relatives and friends the happiness of dying in the Lord! Blessed, too, are they who die in this manner! They leave indeed their dear ones, their chosen ones, on earth; but they leave them with the hope of seeing them again, never more to part. They leave them with the hope of being always present among them in spirit and in heart, of rendering them greater service amid the various trials of life, and of anticipating them by their desires and supplications. They leave them, in fine, but they do not leave the society of the just, of which all the good form individually a part; they arrive before them at the term of happiness, for which all the just on earth sigh. They go to join the triumphant society of the saints who dwell in heaven. They go to find new friends, who will only increase and purify their love for their friends on earth. They go to be reunited to the head and body of which they are members: and how delightful must be the moment of that reunion![945]

PRAYER

O my God! who art all love, I thank thee for having instituted the sacrament of extreme unction to purify me, to console me, and to strengthen me at my last hour: grant me the grace to receive it worthily.

I am resolved to love God above all things, and my neighbor as myself for the love of God; and, in testimony of this love, I will recite on the last day of each month the prayers for the agonizing.

Lesson 43: Our Union with the New Adam by Hope (16)

The sacrament of holy orders.—The sacraments which we have just explained begin, consummate, repair, and strengthen our union with our Lord. But this divine union should be possible to all the generations that will come into the world to the end of ages. The Son of God establishes the means thereof; for he is the Savior of all men that have been, that are, and that ever shall be. For this purpose, he institutes the sacrament of orders.

Its definition.—By holy orders is meant: a sacrament, instituted by our Lord Jesus Christ to perpetuate the divine life, by giving the power to perform ecclesiastical functions and the grace to exercise them holily. We find in the action by which the ministers of the altar are consecrated all the requisites for a sacrament of the new law: a) an outward and sensible sign—the imposition of hands, the touching of sacred vessels, and the prayers of the bishop; b) a sign instituted by our Lord; c) a sign which has the virtue of producing grace.

Accordingly, the sacrament of holy orders has always been reckoned among those of the new law. The oldest liturgies, even those of sects separated from unity since the first ages,[946] and the most illustrious fathers, such as St. Augustine,[947] St. Chrysostom,[948] St. Jerome,[949] and St. Leo,[950] speak of orders as a true sacrament. In the fourth century lived a holy personage, named Martyrius, who, out of humility, refused to be ordained deacon, and who said to Nectarius, patriarch of Constantinople, lately baptized and ordained, "You have just been purified and sanctified by two sacraments, namely, baptism and orders."[951] It was therefore believed that the latter was a sacrament, instituted by Jesus Christ, and had, as well as baptism, the virtue of conferring grace.

On this point, as on all others, you were then, O Catholic Church, our mistress and our mother! the infallible organ of tradition and scripture when you pronounced against the pride of reason this solemn anathema: "If any one say that orders or ordination is not a true sacrament, instituted by our Lord Jesus Christ, let him be anathema!"[952] It is called "orders," because there are several degrees in this sacrament arranged in order toward one another, and all tending to the same end: as we shall see further on.[953]

Its elements.—The imposition of hands and the touching of sacred vessels are the matter of this sacrament;[954] the prayers of the minister of it are the form.[955] These prayers are among the most venerable in the world; for we find them in use since the beginning of the Church. When the first apostles ordained the first deacons, they imposed hands on them, and at the same time prayed for them. The ministers of the sacrament of holy orders are the bishops: such is the teaching of the Church.

Its institution.—The sacrament of holy orders was promised by the Savior, when he said to his apostles that he would make them his ministers and "fishers of men."[956] He ordained them priests when, after distributing to them his body and blood, which he had just consecrated, he addressed these words to them: "Do this in commemoration of me." Omnipotent and ever-efficacious words, which gave to the apostles and their successors the sublime power of working the same miracle as the Son of God himself had just wrought! From this moment, they were priests like him, according to the order of Melchisedech, that is to say, forever. Here you see the reason why the Church utters her anathema against anyone who should dare to say that the sacerdotal character can be effaced.[957]

Its effects.—The effects of the sacrament of holy orders are: a) to give to him who receives it a grace that sanctifies him and enables him to fulfill its functions, for the benefit of the Church; b) to imprint an indelible character, a character that can never be destroyed, a character that consequently cannot be reestablished by a new ordination; c) to confer the power of consecrating the body of our Lord, and the power of forgiving and retaining the sins of men.

Thus, a twofold power has been given to priests: power over the natural body of our Lord; and power over his mystical body, which is the Church. They beget in a certain manner the first; they are, as it were, the soul of the second. Continuations of the Son of God, they have the power to do all that is necessary in order to preserve this body ever alive, and to conduct it to its eternal union in heaven with the new Adam, who is its head.

Both these powers come from our Lord Jesus Christ himself! First, the power to consecrate his body and blood. He gave it to the apostles and their successors by the words already cited: "Do this in commemoration of me."[958] Next, the power to form and perpetuate his mystical body: "All power is given to me in heaven and on earth. Going therefore teach ye all nations; baptizing them in the name of the Father, and of the Son, and of the Holy Ghost, teaching them to observe all things whatsoever I have confided to you."[959] "As the Father hath sent me, I also send you…Receive ye the Holy Ghost; whose sins you shall forgive, they are forgiven, and whose sins you shall retain, they are retained."[960] "Amen I say to you, whatsoever you shall bind on earth, shall be bound also in heaven, and whatsoever you shall loose on earth, shall be loosed also in heaven."[961]

Dignity of the priest.—Such are the powers, terrible even to the angels, which the new Adam confides to his ministers. What human tongue can tell the dignity of the priesthood or the priest? Great was the first man, who, being established king of the universe, commanded every inhabitant in his wide domain, and was cheerfully obeyed by them. Great was Moses, who with a word separated the waters of the sea, and let a whole people pass over on dry foot. Great was Josue, who said to the sun, "Stand"; and the sun stood, obeying the voice of a mortal. Great were all the kings of the earth who commanded immense armies, and made the world tremble at the very sound of their name.

Well, there is a man still greater. He is a man who, every day, when he pleases, opens the gates of heaven, and, addressing the Son of the eternal, the monarch of worlds, says, "Come down from thy throne; come." Immediately, with quick obedience, the Word of God, he by whom all things were made, comes down from the abode of his glory, and becomes incarnate in the hands of this man, more powerful than kings, than angels, than the august Mary. And this man says to him, "Thou art my Son. This day have I begotten thee. Thou art my victim." And this victim allows himself to be immolated by this man, to be placed where he wishes, to be given to whom he wishes. This man is the priest!

The priest is not alone all-powerful in heaven and over the natural body of the man-God, he is also all-powerful on earth and over the mystical body of Jesus Christ. See: a man has fallen into sin, and is now laden with the chains of the devil; what power can deliver him? Invoke the angels and archangels—St. Michael himself, the chief of the heavenly militia, the conqueror of Satan and his rebellious legions. The holy archangel may indeed banish the devils that surround the unfortunate wretch, but to remove what weighs upon his heart is beyond the power of all the archangels. Never can they burst the fetters of a sinner. To whom then will you have recourse for his deliverance? To Mary, the Mother of God, the Queen of angels and men, the terror of hell? She may indeed pray for this soul, but she cannot absolve it from a single fault, even the smallest: the priest can do so.

Still more: suppose that the Redeemer comes down personally and visibly into a church, and takes up his place in a confessional to administer the sacrament of penance, while there is a priest in another at hand. The Son of God says, "I absolve you," and the priest, on his part, says, "I absolve you"; in both cases, the penitents are alike absolved.

Thus the priest, as powerful as God, can in a moment snatch a sinner from hell, render him worthy of paradise, and from a slave of the devil make him a child of Abraham. God himself is bound to hold to the judgment of the priest, to refuse or to grant pardon, according as the priest refuses or grants absolution, provided the penitent is worthy of it.[962] The sentence of the priest precedes; God only subscribes to it.[963] Can anyone conceive a greater, a higher dignity?

I am no longer surprised to hear the Son of God addressing these sublime words to priests: "He who hears you hears me, he who despises you despises me";[964] and to all the nations of the earth, this solemn warning: "Beware of touching my anointed ones, my christs—he who touches them touches the apple of my eye."[965] I am no longer surprised to see, in the Council of Nice, the great Constantine, the master of the world, unwilling to occupy any other place than one after all the priests, and refusing to be seated until he has obtained their consent. I am no longer surprised to hear St. Francis of Assisi, who, out of humility, all his life declined the honor of the priesthood, say, "If I met an angel and a priest at the same time, I would first bow my knee to the priest and then to the angel." None of these things surprise me. What surprises me is to see men, children even, who despise the priest!

We have just spoken of his power; who will tell his benefits? The priest is the benefactor of humanity by his prayers, his instructions, and his charity.

His prayers. The world is an immense battlefield. Men have to contend there with the powers of hell and their own passions. The victory would be lost to the poor children of Adam, if there were not far more than one fervently interceding Moses on the mountain.

Every priest is a Moses. Day and night the guilty earth sends toward heaven millions of crimes, whose mission is to provoke the vengeance of God. As on a tempestuous day, the thunderbolt would every moment be ready to fall on the heads of these culprits, if priests, by their prayers and their sacrifices, did not extinguish it in the hands of the Almighty. Men, needy and guilty, require the bread necessary for their lives; sinners, how can they have recourse to the goodness of a Father whom they never cease to insult? The priest raises his pure hands to heaven for them, and the beneficent dew comes to fertilize their lands, and abundance succeeds to want.

His instructions. What is the world but a vast desert, over which hangs a perpetual night? A thousand paths cross one another there; travelers go astray, and fall into the abyss. Many are the precipices: at the bottom of which, ravenous monsters, with gaping mouths and glaring eyes, await their prey. Man is a traveler obliged to cross this dangerous territory of life. Whence does he come? He knows not. Whither does he go? He knows not. What course should he take? He knows not. Is he therefore hopelessly lost? No: the priest is there. A faithful guide, he comes to take the young traveler by the hand—shows him the way—travels with him—does not leave him till he has set him in a place of security. This is what the priest does for every man coming into the world.

This is what he has been doing for the whole human race, which, like a blind man, could not do anything during the last eighteen centuries but stumble from abyss into abyss. It was the priest who delivered it from gross, cruel, demoralizing errors, of which it was the shameless and pitiable victim. It was the priest who drew the world from barbarism. It is the priest who prevents it from relapsing into its former state. It is the priest who, at the cost of his blood and his life, still daily civilizes savage peoples, as he formerly civilized our ancestors.[966]

His charity. Travel through cities and countries: ask who was the founder, the supporter, of all institutions truly useful to humanity. A priest will be named for you. Enter the hut of a poor man, and ask him who gave him the bread which he eats: it was a priest, or some person whose zeal was stirred up by a priest. Go to the pallet of the sick man, who is abandoned by everyone, and ask who is the consoling angel that pours over his sad heart the balm of comfort and hope. It is a priest. Make your way even into the dungeon of the prisoner, and ask who lightens the burden of his chains. It is a priest. Ascend the scaffold on which the culprit is about to be executed, and tell me who stands by his side. It is a priest—a priest who with one hand shows him a crucifix, and, with the other, heaven. Investigate all the spiritual and corporal miseries of our poor humanity, and you will not find one that the priest does not every day relieve, without ostentation, without pomp, without the thought or the desire of the slightest human reward.

We are bound to love our enemies as ourselves, and today the priest is not loved! Today the priest is hated: he is the subject of sacrilegious mockery and impious scorn! The priest complains not; for the disciple is not above the master. His mouth opens but to pardon, as his arms rise but to bless. To those who are afflicted on seeing him thus despised, insulted, persecuted, he is content to make reply with his gentle master on his way to Calvary, "Daughters of Jerusalem, weep not for me, but for yourselves and your children."[967]

They who insult priests identify themselves with the crime of the Jews: they shall have a share in their punishments. Meanwhile, as the early Christians delayed by the power of their prayers the fall of the Roman Empire, so the priest appeases by his supplications the fearful storms that are ready to burst upon a guilty world. The imitator of a divine model, he endeavors to go about doing good. His most bitter enemies have a share in his charity. Listen!

History.—One of those wicked men who, during the days of our woes, were stained with the most atrocious crimes and often covered with the blood of priests, fell sick. He had sworn that no priest should ever set foot in his room, or, if any one dared to come in by surprise, he should never permit him to depart alive. Meanwhile, the danger of the sick man became serious. A priest was informed of it, as well as of his hostile dispositions. No matter! The good shepherd knows that he ought to give his life for his sheep. Without a moment's hesitation, he exposes himself to the danger, he ventures to appear. On seeing him, the sick man falls into a fury, and, summoning up all his strength, exclaims in a frightful voice, "What! A priest in my house! Bring me my pistols!"

"Brother," says the priest to him, "what would you do with them? I have more powerful weapons with which to oppose you, God's charity and constancy." "Bring me my pistols! A priest at my very side!" His pistols are refused to him. Then, drawing out his brawny arm from the bed, and threatening the priest, he says, "Know that this arm has slaughtered a dozen of your priests." "You are mistaken, my brother," answers the priest mildly, "there is one less to be counted. The twelfth is not dead: I am he. Here," he adds, showing his breast, "are the marks of the wounds that you gave me. God has preserved my life to save you." At these words, he tenderly embraces him, and helps him to die well. If a thousand priests have not given this example, it is because only one found an opportunity of doing so. Behold the priest!

Dispositions for receiving the sacrament of holy orders.—Besides a sufficiency of knowledge and a more than ordinary virtue, to make them guides and models of the flock, there are several other qualifications to which aspirants to holy orders must attend. a) They must have attained the age required by the canons. For subdeaconship, it is twenty-two; for deaconship, twenty-three; for the priesthood, twenty-five.[968] Can anything be wiser than such discipline? If in the world it is desired that a man should have come to a mature age in order to be fitted for an important employment, with much greater reason should the same recommendation be required in the Church of those who desire to be elevated to the sacerdotal rank. b) They must not be fettered by any censure or irregularity which would render them unworthy of the ecclesiastical ministry or prevent them from exercising its functions. c) They must have a special vocation for this state. It belongs to God to choose his ministers, as to a king to choose his officers and servants.

Necessity of the sacrament of holy orders.—This sacrament is necessary to the Church and to society. Without the sacrament of orders, which gives ministers to the Church and superiors to the faithful, the Church would no longer be a society. Everything about it would be in confusion and disorder; for there is no society without superiors who command, and inferiors who obey. But if the Church did not exist, civil society, of which it is the soul, would no longer exist. No society without religion; no religion without the Church; no Church without bishops and priests; no bishops or priests without the sacrament of holy orders: the sacrament of holy orders is therefore the pivot of Church and state. Will you be surprised if, after this, the new Adam and the Church, his spouse, require a long trial and a laborious preparation before confiding to any one the dignity and the power of the sacerdotal rank? Herein especially must we admire their divine wisdom.

Origin of the tonsure; its meaning.—The first step toward the sanctuary is the tonsure. The fathers of the Church, the most ancient and venerable, say that it comes from the apostles. It is even attributed to St. Peter, who is said to have established it in memory of our Lord's crown of thorns.[969] Be that as it may, the tonsure was already a long time in use in the eighth century. Now, to have the head shaven was considered a disgraceful thing, a thing that rendered a man contemptible, since it was a mark of slavery among the Greeks and Romans.[970] This was the reason why, according to St. Cyprian, it was usual to cut the hair and beard of Christians condemned to the mines.[971]

Hence, the clerical crown is a mark of modesty, of renunciation of the world, and a profession of love for the cross, for the humiliations of Jesus Christ. The Savior triumphed over the world by this means: his successors should have no other arms. To take the ensign of the man-God is therefore the first step to be made by those who aspire to the honor of continuing his mission. All these significations of the tonsure are rendered sensible by the prayers and ceremonies which the Church employs in giving it.

Ceremonies and prayers which accompany its reception.—The bishop, seated on a chair in the middle of the altar, like the Savior himself in the midst of his disciples, calls each of the candidates for the tonsure by name. He shows hereby that no one can enter the holy militia without being called by God as Aaron was.[972] The candidates, after answering that they are present, approach the altar, to show their eagerness to correspond with the grace of their vocation. The soutane which they wear reminds them, by its color and shape, that they ought to be dead to the world and to the desires of the present life. On the left arm they bear a white surplice, an emblem of their innocence; in the left hand they hold a lighted taper, an eloquent symbol of that charity which inflames their hearts, and which impels them to consecrate themselves to God and to consume their lives in his service.[973]

When they are on their knees around the altar, the bishop rises and implores the Lord to purify and inflame the hearts of his new servants. All the people, uniting their prayers with those of the pontiff, intone the psalm which begins thus: "Preserve me, O Lord, for I have hoped in thee." While the choir continues, the bishop cuts with scissors, and in the form of a cross, the hair of those whom he tonsures. "The Lord is my portion and my cup," says each of the tonsured at the same time. "It is thou, O my God, who wilt restore to me my inheritance!"

Then the bishop clothes them with the surplice, which reminds them of the innocence in which they must always live, saying, "May the Lord clothe you with the new man, who is created to the image of God, in a state of perfect justice and sanctity!" It is done. The cleric no longer has part in the world. He belongs to God, whose livery he bears: the new Adam will henceforth be his model.

The tonsure is not an order, but a ceremony established by the Church to separate from the world those whom he calls to the ecclesiastical state. It is a kind of novitiate which leads to the ministry, subjects to the laws relating to the clergy, and serves as a preparation for the reception of orders.

It is not enough to separate from the world those who should compose the holy tribe. To conquer, an army must be well disciplined, must have a regular gradation of officers and men. Hence, different orders among the clergy. "As the priesthood is something all divine," says the holy Council of Trent, "it was meet that, for the good government of the Church, there should be several orders of ministers, who, by various duties, might aid priests in the fulfillment of their functions, and who, being first adorned with the clerical tonsure, might ascend by these different orders, as by so many steps, to the summit of the sanctuary."[974]

Division and number of orders; to what they relate.—In accordance with these words of the council, we may look upon the altar as a holy and terrible mountain, which can only be ascended very slowly, and after long and painful tests. The different orders are steps which lead to the summit of this mysterious mountain. We count seven of them: the four minor orders, those of the doorkeeper, reader, exorcist, and acolyte; and the three major, subdeaconship, deaconship, and priesthood. This distinction dates from the apostolic times.[975] Let us hear on this matter the Angel of the Schools: his words are admirable.

"All the orders," he says, "refer to the Eucharist, and their dignity comes from the relation, more or less direct, which they have with this adorable sacrament. In the highest degree is the priest, because he consecrates the body and blood of the Savior. In the second is the deacon, because he distributes the same. In the third the subdeacon, because he prepares in sacred vessels the matter that is to be changed. In the fourth the acolyte, because he prepares and presents it in vessels not sacred.

"The other orders are instituted to prepare those who shall receive the Eucharist if they are impure or unclean. Now, they may be so in three ways. Some may be baptized and instructed, but if they are energumens, that is, persons demoniacally possessed, they cannot be admitted to the Holy Communion. Hence it follows that in the fifth degree are found exorcists, because they have been established to deliver these persons from the devil and to render them worthy of the holy table. Others are neither baptized nor sufficiently instructed; and in the sixth degree are found readers, charged with the duty of preparing them by instruction for the Sacrament of the Altar. Finally, there are unbelievers, who are consequently unworthy of participating in the holy mysteries; and in the seventh degree are found doorkeepers, whose office it is to remove them from the assembly of the faithful:[976] they must also see that order and propriety reign in the material temple where the adorable sacrifice is offered up..."[977]

Is not this an admirable hierarchy? See how much religion gains by being known!

PRAYER

O my God! who art all love, I thank thee for having established the sacrament of holy orders to perpetuate thy real presence among men and to give ministers to thy Church. I beg of thee a great respect for this sacrament and for those who receive it.

I am resolved to love God above all things, and my neighbor as myself for the love of God; and, in testimony of this love, I will often pray for priests.

Lesson 44: Our Union with the New Adam by Hope (17)

The preceding lesson showed us the relations of the orders among themselves and toward the august Eucharist. It is time to make each of them known in detail.

Doorkeepers: Their functions; ceremonies and prayers of their ordination.—The first of the minor orders, received after the ceremony of the tonsure, is that of doorkeeper. If all employments are honorable in the palace of a king, all ministries are holy in the house of God. This is the reason why the Church consecrates all those who have to fulfill them. The order of doorkeepers was indispensable in the early ages, when the world was not yet Christian. They were charged with the duty of preventing infidels from entering the church, disturbing the faithful, and profaning the holy mysteries.

They were careful to keep everyone in his rank, the people separated from the clergy, the men from the women, and to see that silence and modesty were observed. They should announce the hours of prayer. They should, moreover, guard the church, keep it clean and neatly adorned, see that nothing was lost in it, and open and close the doors belonging to it and the sacristy at suitable hours. Finally, it was their office to open the book for him who preached. We see that, with so many affairs on hand, they had abundance to occupy them. This order was given to persons of a ripe age.

All these functions are called to mind in the prayers and ceremonies of ordination. After the bishop has explained everything to the doorkeepers, the archdeacon leads them to the church door. He makes them open and close it, and presents them with the rope of the bell, which they ring for a moment. He then leads them back to the foot of the altar. All these things, which appear strange to those who neither know their origin nor understand their meaning, are deeply venerable to the pious and enlightened Christian. They remind him of the sanctity of the house of the Lord, of the terrible majesty of the adorable sacrifice, of the glorious antiquity of the Church, and of those beautiful days of faith and innocence which we so much admire and so much regret.

Readers: Their functions; ceremonies and prayers of their ordination.—The order of reader is higher than that of doorkeeper, because it refers more immediately to the Eucharist. The readers acted as secretaries to the bishops and priests, and were instructed by reading and writing under them. Thus were they trained who were best fitted for study and who might become priests. Their function has always been necessary, since the scriptures of the old and the new testament have always been read in the Church, either at Mass or at offices, chiefly during the night. In the early ages, the letters of bishops, the acts of martyrs, homilies or discourses, were also read there, as is still done at the present day. This task was performed by the readers.

Between the nave, which contained the faithful, and the choir, which was occupied by the ministers of the altar, there was a kind of platform, five or six feet high, surrounded with a railing, and capable of accommodating eight persons. This place was called an ambo, because it was reached by two staircases, and looked toward both priests and people. It was used as a stand for preaching and for reading the lessons.[978] It was also called a jube, because the reader, before beginning to read, asked the bishop's blessing thus: *Jube, Domine, benedicere.* From frequent repetition, the first word of this expression came to be applied by the people to the place where the reader stood. Jubes are still to be seen in some old churches.

The readers were also charged with the care of the sacred books. On this account they ran a great risk during times of persecution. The formula of their ordination, which, like those of the other inferior orders, is taken from the Fourth Council of Carthage, held in 398, makes known that they are to read for him who preaches, to chant lessons, and to bless bread and new fruits. The bishop, after asking for the readers the grace to fulfill their holy functions well, makes them touch the book of lessons, and at the same time says, "Receive this book, and be readers of the word of God. If you be faithful to your employment, you shall have part with those who, from the beginning, have wisely delivered this holy word."

Exorcists: Their functions; ceremonies and prayers of their ordination.—The third minor order is that of exorcist. The function of exorcists is to banish the devil. In the early ages, possessions were very common, especially among the pagans. We have authentic proofs on this matter in the gospel, the Acts of the Apostles, and the writings of the fathers. To show the utmost contempt for the power of the devil, the Church gave the office of banishing him to her inferior ministers. In solemn baptisms, they exorcised the catechumens, and caused those who were not to communicate, that is to say, the catechumens and energumens, to leave the church before the oblation of the sacred gifts.

At the present day, the power of exorcising is reserved to priests. Still, they cannot make use of it without an express permission from the bishop. The possessions of the devil becoming rarer as our Lord crushed his power more and more, it was necessary, in order to avoid impostures, to act with the greatest discretion. This is the reason why the Church, adhering to the usages of a venerable antiquity, restrains the power of exorcising, and does not permit its public exercise, except to priests specially authorized, and after the most prudent and circumstantial investigations.[979]

The bishop concludes the prayers of the ordination by making the exorcists lay their hand on the missal. "Receive," he says at the same time, "and study this book, and have the power to impose hands on energumens, whether they are baptized or are catechumens." He then beseeches the Lord in a fervent prayer to protect them, that they may piously fulfill their functions, and that, like physicians without reproach, they may heal others, having first healed themselves.

Acolytes: Their functions; ceremonies and prayers of their ordination.—The fourth minor order is that of acolyte. The word *acolyte* means "one who follows," "one who accompanies." The order of acolytes is the highest of the four minor orders. In ancient times the acolytes were young men, between twenty and thirty years of age, appointed to wait continually on the bishop. They delivered his messages, bore eulogies and even the Eucharist, and served at the altar under the deacons. Now that the times are changed, the Pontifical gives them no other functions than to carry torches, to light candles, and to prepare the wine and water for the sacrifice.

In the ceremony of their ordination, the bishop warns the acolytes that they should shine in the Church as children of light by the splendor of their virtues, so as to edify their brethren; that they should lead a pure life, so as to be worthy of presenting the wine and water at the altar of the Lord. He then makes them touch a candlestick, furnished with a taper, and an empty cruet, saying, "Receive this candlestick and taper, and do not forget that in the name of the Lord you are appointed to attend to the lights of the Church. Receive this cruet; it will serve you for presenting the water and wine in the sacrifice of the blood of Jesus Christ."

Such are the four minor orders, and such were formerly their functions. We need not imagine that the saints who governed the Church in the early ages were only amusing themselves with trifles when they laid down so many external regulations, and established special orders for seeing carefully to the observance of these regulations in every detail. They understood the importance of attending to all that strikes the senses of man: the beauty of places, the order of assemblies, silence, the chant, the majesty of ceremonies. All these things help even the most spiritual to rise toward God. They are absolutely necessary for ignorant people, to give them a high idea of religion and to make them love its exercises.

In consequence of our evil times, it is only rarely that those who are invested with minor orders now fulfill their functions. Waiting for happier days, the Church has preserved the minor orders as a precious monument of ancient discipline, and as so many steps of sanctification which must be ascended by the Levites who aspire to the major orders.[980]

Subdeacons: Their functions; ceremonies and prayers of their ordination.—The first of the major, or sacred, or, strictly speaking, holy orders, is that of subdeacon. It has occupied this rank since the Church attached to it the obligation of chastity.[981] Previously, subdeaconship was reckoned among the minor orders. The subdeacons were the secretaries of the bishops, who employed them on journeys and on ecclesiastical business. They were charged with the bestowal of alms and the administration of temporals. Outside the church, they performed the same functions as the deacons.

It was usually to subdeacons that the Roman Church confided the administration of the "Patrimonies of St. Peter,"[982] in the various parts of Christendom where they were situated. Stewards over these goods, they executed the commands of the popes in regard to the most important ecclesiastical affairs: such as the correction of abuses in the provinces where they were located, the assembling of councils, the warnings which they conveyed to bishops in reference to the conduct of clerics, and the letters which they sent to the pope on events that were occurring in the countries through which they passed.[983]

At the present day, the ministry of subdeacons is reduced to the service of the altar and the assistance of the bishop or the priest on great solemnities. They prepare the ornaments, the sacred vessels, the bread, the wine, the water for the sacrifice. They sing the epistle at Solemn Mass, and carry and hold the book of the gospels for the deacon, whom they serve in all the sacred functions. Hence it comes that they are called subdeacons. They give the book of the gospels to the celebrant and the faithful to kiss, present at the altar the chalice and paten to the deacon, pour water into the chalice in which the deacon has put wine, give water to the priest to wash his fingers, and purify the palls, corporals, and purificators.

Nothing is more imposing than the ceremonies of the ordination of subdeacons. Willing victims, who present themselves to make a heroic sacrifice to God, they wish to renounce forever the world and its hopes: everything about them speaks of the devoted nature of this sacrifice. They are standing, in the attitude of men ready to depart. A white linen cloth, called an amice, covers the head, like the helmet of a warrior. They are robed in a long white alb, the symbol of perfect virtue. A cord encircles the reins, it is the sign of chastity. On the left arm is a tunic, expressive of the joy of their hearts. In one hand they hold a maniple, a figure of the labor which awaits them, and in the other a lighted taper, indicative of their charity. Thus armed, thus arrayed, all the young victims await in silence the moment of the sacrifice.

Suddenly the voice of the pontiff, the representative of Jesus Christ, is heard: "My beloved children," he says to them, "you present yourselves to receive subdeaconship. Think seriously and repeatedly on the heavy burden which you desire. You are still free: it is permitted you to pass to a secular life. But, if you receive this order, you cannot hereafter revoke your decision. You must forever belong to God and serve him. And to serve him is to reign. You must observe chastity and be always ready for the ministry of the Church. There is yet time: reflect...But, if you persevere in your resolution, come near."

After these words, if they feel courage and strength to disengage themselves forever, they make one step forward. An immense step! which places between them and the world a gulf forever impassable. To show that they are forever dead to the world and its hopes, they all prostrate themselves, lying with their faces on the ground, bidding an eternal adieu to the earth which they embrace, to their parents, to their friends, and protesting that they are to be henceforth like Melchisedech, an ancient figure of the Christian priesthood, without father, without mother, without genealogy.

But who will give them that superhuman strength of which they have need, to support during their whole life this heroic sacrifice? The same God who inspired them with the resolution to make it. This is the reason why the bishop and all the people, alarmed as it were at the greatness of their engagements, immediately kneel down and implore on the prostrate the blessing of heaven. Prayers are addressed to the three Persons of the adorable Trinity, to the all-powerful Mary, to the angels, to the patriarchs, to the prophets, to the apostles, to the martyrs, to the confessors, to the whole heavenly court. Then the bishop, rising, blesses and consecrates all these victims by forming thrice upon them the sign of the cross.

All is now over: the victims are immolated. They rise nevertheless, for they must live and continue all the days of their life the immolation which they have just consummated. The bishop conjures the assistants to pray for these new ministers who consecrate themselves to their service. He then ordains them subdeacons, making them touch the chalice and paten,[984] and explains to them the functions which they shall have to fulfill.

Such is an abridged account of the ordination of subdeacons. Do you know anything more proper to inspire the people with a profound respect for the august Eucharist and its ministers, and at the same time more efficacious to teach the latter the virtues required of them by their holy and sublime vocation? We shall find this twofold instruction continued in the ordination of the deacon.

Deacons: Their functions; ceremonies and prayers of their ordination.—The word *deacon* means "servant." The apostles ordained the first deacons on the occasion of some murmurs that arose among the faithful of Jerusalem concerning the distribution of alms. They confided to them the care of tables, around which the poor gathered to eat the bread of Catholic fraternity; for, from the beginning, the poor were the objects of the maternal solicitude of the Church. Their places being taken by the deacons, the apostles could devote themselves entirely to prayer and preaching. Such was not the only, nor even the principal end of the institution of deacons: we soon see them called to functions more exalted.

To the service of the material table was added the ministry of the sacred table. The preaching of the word of God and the administration of baptism were also reckoned among their functions. We learn that St. Stephen and St. Philip gave themselves with much zeal to these employments, which they shared with the apostles. All this did not hinder the deacons from having care of the tables, at which the widows and the poor took their ordinary repasts.

In the primitive times, the deacons always occupied a place in the suite of the bishops. They watched over their safety when preaching, accompanied them in councils, and assisted them in ordinations and in the administration of the other sacraments.[985] The bishops did not offer the sacrifice without being assisted by the deacons, as St. Laurence reminded Pope St. Sixtus, when the latter was being led to martyrdom. "Holy priest!" he said, "whither are you going without your deacon? You used never to offer the sacrifice without him."[986]

To deacons belonged the privilege of reading the gospel at Mass, as they still do at the present day, and of presenting to the priest the bread and wine for the sacrifice.[987] Not only did they administer baptism, dispense alms, and watch over the support of widows and the poor, but they were also charged with the care of the confessors and martyrs who were in prison, and with the duty of encouraging them to suffer for the faith.[988] At present, deacons have usually no other functions than to serve the bishop or the priest at the altar, and to sing the gospel.

We saw that the apostles ordained the first deacons by praying over them and imposing hands on them:[989] this mysterious rite has not changed. When the bishop is seated on his chair in the middle of the altar, the archdeacon says to him, "Most reverend Father! our mother, the holy Catholic Church, asks that you should give the charge of deaconship to these subdeacons." "Do you know whether they are worthy of it?" replies the pontiff. "I know it," answers the archdeacon, "and bear witness to it, as far as human weakness permits me to do so." "Thanks be to God," says the bishop. Then, addressing himself to the clergy and people, he says, "With the assistance of God and our Savior Jesus Christ, we make choice of these subdeacons to raise them to deaconship. If any person has anything to say against them, let him come forward boldly, for the love of God, and say it; but let him be mindful of the seriousness of his act." And he pauses a moment to give the faithful time to answer.

This warning recalls the ancient discipline of the Church, according to which it was usual to consult the clergy and people in reference to ordinations. In our days, ecclesiastical superiors alone are charged with the duty of examining aspirants to holy orders. To preserve as far as possible the ancient usage, and to make sure that the elect are irreproachable, the Church has established the publications which are made at the parish sermon, and the ceremony of which we now speak; as preceding the ordination of deacons and priests.

If the faithful make no complaint, the bishop addresses the candidates and reminds them of the dignity of the order which they are about to receive, the functions which are connected with it, and the virtues which it demands. He then begins a preface—an introduction, as it were, to the grand action which he is about to perform. Suddenly, stopping in the midst of the preface, the bishop lays his right hand on the head of each of the aspirants, and says to him, "Receive the Holy Ghost, that you may have strength to resist the devil and his temptations." He does not lay his two hands on them, to show that deacons do not receive the Holy Ghost with the same plenitude as priests.

This ceremony and the preface being ended, the bishop gives each deacon the stole, the symbol of the power confided to him. "Receive from the hand of God," he says at the same time, "this white stole; fulfill your ministry; God is almighty—he will increase his grace in you." The deacon does not wear his stole in the same manner as the priest, to show that he has not the same dignity. The bishop next clothes him with the dalmatic, pronouncing these words: "May God give you the habit of salvation and the robe of joy, and, by his power, surround you forever with the dalmatic of justice. Amen."

Finally, the bishop presents the book of the gospels to the deacons, saying, "Receive the power to read the gospel in the Church for the living and for the dead. In the name of the Father," etc. The ordination concludes with the prayer of the bishop and people, uniting their hearts and voices to invoke on the newly elected the protection of the Lord.

To the ordination of deacons succeeds that of priests.

Priests: Their functions and powers; ceremonies and prayers of their ordination.—To offer the holy sacrifice; to bless the people at Mass, in assemblies, and in the administration of the sacraments, so as to draw upon them the graces of heaven; to preside at assemblies which are held in the church for the purpose of rendering to God the worship due to him; to preach the word of God, whose ambassadors they are; to administer various sacraments, especially those established for the remission of sins: such have been from the beginning of the Church, and are still today, the functions of priests.

Before confiding the same to them, the bishop, seated on his chair in the middle of the altar, wishes to ascertain whether they are worthy. "Most reverend Father," says the archdeacon to him, "our mother, the holy Catholic Church, asks you to consecrate priests these deacons whom I present to you." "Do you know whether they are worthy of it?" replies the pontiff. And, on receiving a favorable reply from the archdeacon, the bishop says, "God be praised!" Then, addressing himself to the people, and reminding them that it is their interest to have none but holy priests, he asks them, conformably to the ancient usage of the Church, to say what they think of the new deacons.

If no one makes any remonstrance, the pontiff addresses himself to the deacons, and reminds them of the nature, the origin, the sublime functions of the priesthood. He tells them that priests are the successors of the seventy-two ancients, who, according to the command of God, were chosen by Moses to assist him in his ministry, to dispense justice, and to watch over the observance of the ten commandments. These old men were only a figure of the seventy-two disciples, whom our Lord sent two-and-two to preach by their words and their example. "Be worthy, my dear children," adds the pontiff, "to be the assistants of Moses and the twelve apostles, that is to say, of our Catholic bishops, figured by Moses and the apostles, and established to govern the Church of God."

After this discourse, follows the imposing ceremony of prostration. Before being admitted to baptism, man must thrice renounce Satan; before being admitted to the priesthood, the Christian must thrice renounce the earth—flesh and blood. It is only after this triple renunciation that the way to the altar is open to him. Next comes the imposition of hands. The bishop silently imposes his two hands on the head of each deacon. All the priests present at the ceremony, and wearing a stole, do the same thing. The bishop reascends the altar; then, turning toward the persons to be ordained, he stretches out his hands over them—all the priests imitate him—and he recites at the same time a prayer in which he beseeches the Lord to grant them his Holy Spirit and the grace of the priesthood.

The power of conferring holy orders belongs to the bishop alone: he alone can impose hands as a consecrator. If priests, on this occasion, impose them with him, it is to conform to a venerable usage which reminds us that the episcopate and the priesthood are only one sacerdotal body. The bishop next places, in the form of a cross, on the breast of the young Levites, the stole which as deacons they have worn on the left shoulder, and says to them, "Receive the yoke of the Lord; his yoke is sweet, and his burden light."

He clothes them with the chasuble, using these words, "Receive the sacerdotal habit; it denotes charity." And the priest will be a man of charity—charity personified! The chasuble, which the bishop has just given to the priests, is not unfolded behind. They have not yet received all the grace of the priesthood: when the power of forgiving sins is confided to them, the bishop will unloose it.

After a beautiful preface, foreshadowing a sublime action, the bishop intones the *Veni Creator*, to call down upon the ordained the sanctifying Spirit with all his gifts. While the choir sings, the pontiff consecrates the hands of the new priests with a large unction of the oil of catechumens. He says, "O Lord, vouchsafe to consecrate and to sanctify these hands by this unction and this blessing." He makes the sign of the cross, and continues, "In the name of Jesus Christ, our Lord, may all that they bless be blessed, may all that they consecrate be consecrated and sanctified!" Each of the ordained answers, "Amen."

The hands of the new priests being bound with a ribbon, and the consecrated fingers separated with a little bread, the bishop makes them touch the chalice, in which there are some wine and water, and the paten, on which lies a host. He says to them at the same time, "Receive the power to offer to God the sacrifice, to celebrate Mass, as well for the living as for the dead." Behold them priests forever according to the order of Melchisedech! The chief function of the priest is to offer the sacrifice, and on the spot they offer it with the bishop. The Mass thus celebrated, reminds us of what used to occur in the early ages. Then there was only one office in each church: the bishop at the altar and all the priests offering with him.

The Communion being ended, the bishop recites that beautiful anthem, composed of the words which the Savior, in the overflow of his heart, addressed to his apostles, after making them participators in his body and blood: "I will no longer call you servants, but friends, for you know all that I have done in the midst of you. You are my friends—do what I have commanded you." The bishop assures himself of the faith of the new priests by making them recite the Apostles' Creed. They are sent to preach: they should preach the faith in all its purity.

They next prostrate themselves at his feet. He at the same time imposes his hands on them, saying, "Receive the Holy Ghost; whose sins you shall forgive, they are forgiven; whose sins you shall retain, they are retained." To show the plenitude of their power, he unties the chasuble, and prays, "May God clothe you with the robe of innocence!" That is to say, "Be pure and holy, that you may make others holy."

From each of them he asks respect and obedience, for the Church is beautiful and terrible as an army set in battle array. This beauty cannot exist without order, and order cannot exist without subordination. But subordination is sweet in the Church: it only tends to make of all the members and ministers of the Church one heart and one soul, for it is founded on charity. This is the reason why the bishop ends all these affecting and heavenly ceremonies by giving the kiss of peace to each of the new priests.

One glance more. Cast an eye over all those sublime prayers, all those imposing ceremonies, and say whether Catholic worship does not at once satisfy the mind, the heart, and the senses![990]

Social advantages of the sacrament of holy orders.—What shall we now say of the importance of the sacrament of holy orders? Its social necessity is proved in an instant: no society without religion, no religion without priests, no priests without the sacrament of holy orders; therefore, without the sacrament of holy orders, no society.

I say true society, that is, a union of men for the preservation and right development of their physical, intellectual, and moral being. Ancient societies, the Jewish excepted, were rather aggregations of individuals held together by force, and with no other end than material existence and improvement. Protestant societies, if they deserve the name, owe their progress, such as it is, to the Catholic traditions which they have retained among them. For the peoples cannot live without Christian truth, and there is no true Christianity outside the Church, and there is no Church without the priesthood. It is therefore to the Catholic priesthood that our separated brethren are indebted for their social life, that is to say, for whatever remains of faith and morals still exist among them.[991]

PRAYER

O my God! who art all love, I thank thee for having established different orders of ministers in thy Church. This is for thy glory and my salvation. Grant me the grace to be a docile and respectful child of a Church so holy, so beautiful, and so tender.

I am resolved to love God above all things, and my neighbor as myself for the love of God; and, in testimony of this love, I will have the greatest respect for persons consecrated to God.

Lesson 45: Our Union with the New Adam by Hope (18)

The sacrament of holy orders was established to perpetuate the ministers of the Church, and the sacrament of matrimony to perpetuate the faithful. The former keep our Lord Jesus Christ continually present on the earth; the latter come into this world to receive him. Thus, it is to the new Adam and to our union with him that, as we have already said, all the sacraments refer. Matrimony or marriage may be considered in two lights—as a contract and as a sacrament. As a contract, it reaches back to the beginning of the world. As a sacrament, it reaches back to our Lord, who raised the natural contract to the dignity of a sacrament, by giving it the power to produce grace.

Matrimony considered as a contract.—Of all contracts, that of marriage is the most ancient and the most sacred. God himself is its author. He instituted it in the terrestrial paradise, when, after creating Adam and Eve, he blessed them, saying, "Increase and multiply, and fill the earth."[992] Adam, receiving at the moment his inseparable companion from the hands of God, pronounced these mysterious and prophetical words, "This now is bone of my bone and flesh of my flesh; wherefore a man shall leave father and mother, and shall cleave to his wife, and they shall be two in one flesh."[993]

Under the patriarchs, marriage continued the most solemn and venerable contract: witness the history of Isaac and Rebecca, or of Jacob and Rachael. It was the same under the law of Moses. Of which we have examples in the marriages of Ruth and Booz, and Sara and Tobias. But all still occurred, as in the time of the patriarchs, around the domestic hearth, among relatives and friends, amid the prayers which were offered up by the father and the company present to invoke the blessing of God on the newly espoused. It was as yet only a natural or civil contract.

Considered as a sacrament.—The time drew nigh when marriage should be destined to give to the new Adam brethren; to the Church, children; to the world, not Jews, but Christians—not a carnal nation, but a holy nation. It was therefore necessary that marriage, whose end became more dignified and sanctified, should be ennobled and enriched with the graces necessary for the newly espoused. This is what our Lord did, by raising it to the dignity of a sacrament.

Definition.—In the new law, marriage or matrimony is a sacrament instituted by our Lord Jesus Christ to perpetuate the divine life, by giving to those who receive it worthily the grace to sanctify themselves in their state and to bring up their children in a Christian manner, and it represents the union of Jesus Christ with his Church. The marriage of

Catholics contains all the qualities which constitute a true sacrament. We find therein a) a sensible sign—the giving of hands, the mutual consent of the parties, and the blessing of the priest; b) a sign instituted by our Lord; c) a sign which has the power of producing grace, as we shall presently show. Hence the holy fathers, who lived in the times when, according to protestants themselves, the Roman Church was yet the infallible organ of truth, say with St. Paul that marriage is a great sacrament.[994]

Let us mention on this matter a most significant fact. In the sixteenth century, protestants published boldly that the Greek schismatical Church rejected, like them, the sacrament of marriage. During the year 1574, they accordingly sent a copy of the Augsburg Confession of Faith to Jeremias, the schismatical patriarch of Constantinople. He, having assembled a number of Eastern bishops, delivered to them a learned refutation of the protestant creed. He remarked particularly that in the East it was believed and had always been believed that marriage was one of the seven sacraments of the new law.[995] The Council of Trent therefore understood well both the meaning of the scripture and the testimonies of tradition, when it declared its anathema against anyone who should dare to say that marriage under the new law is not a sacrament instituted by our Lord Jesus Christ, and does not confer grace.[996]

Its elements.—We find the matter of the sacrament of marriage in the contract by which the two parties are given power, one in regard to the other. Let us here remark how great is the dignity of this sacrament, so little understood, so little respected in our days, by many of those who receive it. Its matter is not water, as in baptism, nor holy oil, as in confirmation and extreme unction, but the living temples of the Holy Ghost, the sacred members of our Lord Jesus Christ himself.

Its form consists in the words and signs by which the parties to be married express their mutual acceptance and consent. The consent must be clearly expressed by each party, and in terms that denote present time. Marriage is not a mere giving away: it is an agreement, which requires the express consent of both parties; and the words which express this consent must refer to present time: for words relating to future time would not make, but simply promise, a marriage.

The parties themselves are the ministers of this sacrament, which, in virtue of the precept of the Church, ought to be sanctified by the presence of a priest and made valid by his presence. So that a marriage is null if not made in presence of the parish priest of one of the two parties, or another priest representing him. There must also be two or three witnesses.[997]

Its institution.—It is believed that our Lord raised marriage to the dignity of a sacrament on the day when he sanctified by his presence the wedding feast of Cana. Be this as it may, the apostle St. Paul reveals to us the institution of the sacrament of marriage, when he says to us that the union of man and wife is a great sacrament in Jesus Christ and the Church.[998] It is certain that by his words, "This is a great sacrament," the apostle alludes to marriage. In effect, the union of man and wife, of which God is the author, is the sacrament, that is to say, the sacred sign of the bond which unites Jesus Christ with his Church. Such is the meaning attached to these words by all the ancient fathers who have given their explanation, and afterward by the holy Council of Trent.[999]

Its effects and duties.—To make known the precious effects of the sacrament of matrimony, it suffices to explain the concluding words of our definition: it gives the married couple the grace to sanctify themselves in their state, and to bring up their children in a Christian manner, and it represents the union of Jesus Christ with his Church.

Like all the other sacraments of the living, that of matrimony produces, not the first grace, which makes sinners just, but the second, which makes the just still more just. It is only accidentally that it sometimes confers the first, and remits mortal sin.[1000] Matrimony also produces a sacramental grace, which in its turn produces three effects, or, according to the language of the fathers of the Church, three principal goods: the grace of fidelity, the grace of a good education of children, and the grace of indissolubility.[1001] These three characteristics essentially distinguish a Christian marriage, which they raise far above all Jewish and heathen alliances; but they present difficulties to nature. This is the reason why our Lord, the author of all the sacraments, has provided married persons with an abundance of graces to make them worthy of it.[1002]

1. *Fidelity*. The first duty of married persons, as well as the first bond of Christian marriage, is fidelity. The husband and wife give each other a reciprocal power over their bodies, with an oath never to violate the holy alliance of marriage. "A man," says our Lord, "shall leave father and mother, and shall cleave to his wife, and they shall be two in one flesh."[1003] In like manner, the apostle declares that "the wife has not the power of her own body, but the husband"; and "the husband has not power of his own body, but the wife."[1004] The obligation of fidelity is equal on both sides: no distinction between husband and wife.

To make the accomplishment of this fidelity easy, the sacrament of matrimony ennobles, strengthens, perfects the natural love of the married persons, and transforms it into a pure, holy, steadfast affection, like that which exists between Jesus Christ and the Church. A pure affection, which, banishing all that would not be worthy of angels, leads the married couple to live wisely, soberly, and chastely, as children of the saints, friends of Jesus Christ, and heirs of heaven. A holy affection, which, founded on views of faith, makes the yoke which they have imposed on themselves agreeable, and transforms the cares which they lavish on each other into pleasures. A steadfast affection, which, keeping their hearts ever firmly united in spite of the natural changeableness of the mind and the various trials of life, helps them to bear with each other, to excuse each other's faults, and in fine to observe inviolably the promises to which they have sworn at the foot of the altar.

From this mutual affection, formed by grace and commanded by religion, flow the particular duties of married persons toward each other. It obliges the husband to treat the wife with gentleness and honor, remembering that Adam regarded Eve as his companion, since he said to God, "The woman whom thou gavest me as a companion";[1005] and to occupy himself with some honest business. By attention to the latter duty, he will not only avoid idleness, which is the mother of all vices, and the source of innumerable jealousies, tears, and dissensions, but be enabled to provide respectably for the support of his wife and children. He must also govern his family in a Christian manner, correct and steady the habits of those who compose it, so as to keep all to their duties, and thus secure the happiness of the domestic circle entrusted to his care.

The same affection requires of the wife that obedience and kindness which gain the heart of her husband; that modesty which causes him to respect her; that simplicity which, despising the vanities of fashion and disarming jealousy, lets him clearly behold all the inward beauty of her soul. Hear how the prince of the apostles speaks: "Let women," he says, "be subject to their husbands, so that if there are any of them who do not believe the word, they may be won without the word, by the good lives of their wives: considering the purity of your manners, as well as the respect which you entertain for them. Do not adorn yourselves outwardly according to the art of the hairdresser, or with displays of gold, or in splendid attire; but adorn the hidden man of the heart with the incorruptible purity of a quiet and meek spirit, which is a rich ornament in the sight of God. For it was thus that heretofore the holy women, who hoped in God and obeyed their husbands, adorned themselves. Such a one was Sara, who obeyed Abraham and called him her lord."[1006]

A consequence of this Christian affection is the care which the wife ought to take never to love or to esteem any other person so much as she does her husband, according to God, that is, whatever his qualities may be. In effect, respect and affection for superiors ought to be regulated, not according to their virtues, but according to their title of superiors. A last consequence is the vigilant solicitude which the wife ought to have about domestic affairs, so that economy, order, and neatness may always let the husband find happiness within his own doors.

For this purpose a Christian wife ought to remain willingly at home, and not leave it except through necessity and even with the permission of her husband. Let the wife who would maintain domestic union, who would acquire a legitimate ascendancy over her husband and transform her house into a little paradise on earth, make use therefore continually of the following recipe, employed with so much success by all holy women: "Pray, be industrious, suffer, and be silent."

2. *Education of children.* The second duty of married persons, and for the accomplishment of which the sacrament gives them a special grace, is the education of children. This grace leads them first to regard children as a blessing. St. Paul makes so much account hereof that he says, "The woman shall be saved by the children whom she brings into the world."[1007] An expression which is not to be understood only of the bearing of children, but also of their education and the care to form them to piety. The proof of this is that the apostle immediately adds, "if she remain in the faith." Although education is a duty common to both parents, it seems therefore to belong more especially to the mother. On the one hand, she is oftener with the children, particularly at that tender age when impressions are wont to decide the character for the remainder of life; on the other, God has more abundantly enriched her with the means of forming them. The grace of the sacrament is therefore very necessary for her.

It is this that gives her, as well as her husband, a due share of prudence, gentleness, firmness, watchfulness, and patience; and they require a large share, in order to acquit themselves worthily of the kind of priesthood with which they are honored. It teaches them to consider their children as a sacred deposit which God himself has entrusted to their keeping, and of which he will demand an account, blood for blood and soul for soul. It commands them to avoid every action that might scandalize these children. In a word, it teaches them that God has not given them children in order that they may bring up a learned, rich, or happy family according to the world, but a family of saints. Why is it that so many fathers and mothers are ignorant of these first principles of their obligations, and that, instead of following them, they violate them continually?

3. *Indissolubility.* The third duty, or the third effect of Christian marriage, for which the sacrament confers a special grace, is indissolubility. The bond or tie of marriage among the faithful cannot be broken but by death. Founded on the principles of the gospel, the legislation of all Catholic peoples ranks divorce, so fitly termed the "sacrament of adultery," among crimes that deserve punishment.

In effect, indissolubility is one of the greatest benefits of the sacrament of matrimony. Therein are found the honor of families, the protection of the wife, the guarantee of public and private morality, the education and the very life of children, as well as the strength of society. But this everlasting yoke may sometimes become heavy. Accordingly, our Lord prepared for married persons, in the sacrament of matrimony, the graces necessary always to bear it.

The accomplishment of these three duties produces the perfection of Christian marriage, which consists in representing the union of Jesus Christ with the Church. This representation is the glorious privilege, the noblest duty of married persons: a duty which, well considered, includes every other duty, and which, faithfully practiced, secures the happiness of the world. The divine Savior wished that his holy and chaste union with the Church should be copied in every family by husband and wife, that so every family might become a home of saints, and thus society, which is only the assemblage of all families, might become a people of saints. Let us see how married persons represent this union between Jesus Christ and the Church.

The Son of God left his Father to be united to the Church, as a man leaves his father and mother to be united to his wife. The Church was formed from Jesus Christ dead on the cross, as woman was formed from man during his sleep. Jesus Christ is the head of the Church; the husband is the head of the wife. Jesus Christ protects and guides the Church, leads it to heaven; the husband ought to be the protector and guide of his wife, ought to show her the way to heaven, much more by his example than by his words.

Jesus Christ and the Church are but one—one Spirit animates them; so man and wife are but one flesh—one spirit ought to animate them. Jesus Christ loves the Church tenderly, but he loves it with a view to its eternal happiness—and the Church, on her side, respects her divine Spouse, and observes an inviolable fidelity toward him; so the husband ought to love the wife, but with a view to her eternal salvation—and the wife ought to respect her husband, and observe an inviolable fidelity toward him. Jesus Christ is inseparably united to the Church; it is the same with the husband and wife—their union is indissoluble, it cannot be broken but by death.

Hence it follows that the sacred union of marriage can only be contracted between one man and one woman, and that polygamy, that is to say, a plurality of wives, though tolerated in the old law, is absolutely forbidden by the new. If this practice were still allowable, marriage would no longer represent the union of the Savior with the Church, which is the special cause of its dignity as a sacrament.[1008] Such are the effects of Christian marriage.

Dispositions for receiving this sacrament.—To participate in these effects and graces, it is necessary to prepare oneself for marriage with great care. As after first Communion there is nothing more important than the choice of a state of life, marriage is of all acts that which exercises the greatest influence on the destiny of young persons, families, and society. Hence there is no act to which one should bring a more diligent preparation, and yet, by a strange perversion, there is hardly any to which is brought a more negligent.

Vocation. The dispositions for marriage are: in the first place, vocation. When placing us in the world, God destines each of us for a particular state. If we enter it, special graces, proportioned to our duties, are in store for us, and our salvation becomes more easy. Not so, if we take a wrong course. He who is out of his vocation is miserable all his life. He is like a disjointed member, which suffers itself and causes the whole body to suffer; like a straying traveler, who wearies himself much, yet does not reach the end of his journey; like a fish out of water, which writhes, and pants, and dies.

To lead a chaste, pious, and truly Christian life in youth; to ask of God every day, by good works, the grace to know our vocation; to take counsel of parents, of persons fearing God, and especially of our confessor, but long before deciding, and not on the eve say of accepting a situation; to inquire seriously of ourselves what is the state in which, having regard to our dispositions, we can most easily save our souls, and what, at the moment of death, we shall wish to have done; finally, to consider what answer we should give a person who, being in the same position as ourselves, with our qualifications and our defects, came to consult us on the profession that he ought to embrace: such are the means to know our vocation.

Purity of intention. The second disposition for marriage is a great purity of intention. One must only enter this state with a view of God, to accomplish his holy will: not through caprice; not through passion; not through a sordid interestedness, which transforms marriage into a low bargain. Religion recognizes the following motives as just: a) the obtaining of a helper, that one may more easily endure the inconveniences of life, the infirmities and pains of old age; b) the desire of having children, less to leave heirs of one's name and wealth than to give faithful servants to God—such was the intention of the holy patriarchs of the old law;[1009] c) the fear of yielding to attacks of concupiscence.[1010]

State of grace. The third disposition for marriage is the state of grace. The sacrament of matrimony being a sacrament of the living, he who should dare to receive it in the state of mortal sin would render himself guilty of a horrible sacrilege. The better to prepare oneself, it is necessary to avoid dangerous meetings, to give alms, to offer up prayers or other good works, and to redouble one's fervor in the reception of the sacraments of penance and the Eucharist.

It is also recommended, at this important period, to make a general confession of one's whole life, or at least of the portion gone by since the first Communion; but, to do so, one must not wait till the very moment of being married. Oh, how many persons there are who lead in marriage a life of anguish and misery, for having neglected these precautions! How many crimes are the consequences of the profanation of the sacrament of marriage! We do not hesitate to say that herein is to be found one of the greatest wounds inflicted on society.

To avoid so great a misfortune, those who think of marriage ought, as we have just said, to prepare themselves long beforehand by a cessation from sin, by good works, and by fervent prayers. Such, indeed, is the conduct of a number—alas! too small—of young persons truly Christian.

Historical sketch.—A few years ago, a young physician, dwelling in the capital of France, received there the sacrament of marriage with such edifying dispositions that it is most useful to make them known. It was in the month of October, 1829. A friend introduces him at a respectable house, and encourages him to hope for the hand of an only daughter, as pious as the rest of her family. The young lady is soon promised to the doctor, whose modesty is no less remarkable than his learning.

About ten days before the nuptial ceremony, he calls to see the mother of his future wife, and begs to have a private conversation with Miss Amelia. "It is impossible, sir," she answers, very courteously, "my daughter has not been well for the last two days, and she requires rest." "But, madam, it is a great disappointment to me not to be permitted to say a few words to the young lady. I have scarcely had the pleasure of seeing her more than three or four times in society. Until the present moment, I have not had one good opportunity of expressing my sentiments to her and of knowing her." "Your earnestness pains me, sir; my daughter cannot be seen." "And yet I have something very important to communicate to her!" "I will call her, if you like, and you can speak to her in my presence: my daughter has never had a conversation alone with any man."

"But I shall soon be her husband!" "Then, sir, my daughter will no longer belong to me: till that time I must fulfill toward her all the duties of a prudent Christian mother." "Ah! madam," exclaims the physician, "I must acquaint you with my design. Brought up myself by religious parents, I have always remained faithful to that holy religion which dictates to you your admirable conduct. The indifference which unfortunately exists among men of my profession may have inspired you with distrust; but, far from sharing in that indifference, I make it my glory and joy to follow in every particular the practices of the faith: the more I study them, the more venerable they appear to me. If I so earnestly desired an interview with your daughter, it was that I might learn her dispositions on this matter, and beg of her to prepare by a general confession to receive, with the nuptial blessing, all the graces that are attached to it."

The virtuous physician did not rest here. For eight days the Holy Sacrifice of the Mass was celebrated, to draw down an abundance of heavenly blessings. But what was most admirable of all was to see, on the very day of the marriage, the bridegroom and bride approach the holy table, accompanied, the one by his esteemed father and weeping mother, the other by her mother and grandmother. What an example for young people! What a lesson for indifferent or irreligious parents! Is not this your opinion? If all other unions resembled this one, would the world be covered with iniquities, and society shaken even to its foundations?

If young persons could doubt of the care with which they are bound to prepare for marriage, the numerous precautions which both Church and state require to precede its being contracted would suffice to teach them how important is the conjugal union, and with what fear they should burden themselves with the tremendous obligations that are its consequence.

Betrothal.—All peoples, even pagans, have preceded marriage with a betrothal, as a preparation for it. A betrothal means: a mutual promise to marry each other, made by two persons free to do so. That the betrothal may be valid and obligatory, the promise must be true and sincere, given by each party with deliberation, and manifested by words or external signs. The betrothal is intended to afford the parties time to know each other; to consider and examine maturely, before taking a step that must engage them for life, whether they are likely to find in their future marriage that which shall secure their happiness in this world and the next.

The Jews used to celebrate the betrothal with nearly as much solemnity as the wedding.[1011] Among the Romans, it was the custom to send to the future wife an iron ring, without any ornament of precious stones.[1012] The couple to be married pledged their faith reciprocally: one by giving the ring, the other by taking it.[1013] Among the Franks, the man would give his future wife, not a ring, but a few pieces of money. These called to mind the custom established among the different nations, of purchasing those women who were sought in marriage; for paganism regarded woman as man's slave. Thanks to the new Adam! her lot has greatly changed; but the piece of money which is blessed on the marriage day ought to tell her of him to whom she is indebted for this change.

Bans.—The conclusion of the betrothal is followed by the publication of the bans. The word *ban* means "public proclamation."[1014] The Church wishes that marriages about to take place should be announced to the faithful: a) that all may betake themselves to prayer to draw down on the newly espoused the blessings of heaven—never were these blessings more necessary; and b) that the marriage may be contracted without impediment. The bans ought to be regularly published on successive Sundays or festivals, during the solemnity of the Mass, and in one or more parishes according to the age, position, and residence of the parties.

After the publication, the priest says to the faithful, "If you are aware of any impediment to these marriages, you are bound, under the penalties declared by the Church, to reveal it." These penalties are heavy, and it is a mortal sin not to reveal an impediment of which one has a knowledge. The obligation of revealing an impediment extends not only to the inhabitants of the parish in which the bans are published, but to all those who are informed of it. The laws of the Church which enjoin this disclosure are general. They regard everyone; and the matter concerns the public welfare, since its aim is to procure the salvation of souls, the peace of families, and the tranquility of the state, as well as to prevent the profanation of a sacrament.

The publication of the bans is intended, as we have just shown, to bring to light any impediments that may lie in the way of marriage. In point of fact, it is not and never was permitted, among any polished people, that persons should marry one another indiscriminately: nature itself forbids it. Now, there are two kinds of impediments which interfere with marriage. Some render it null: for this reason, they are called "invalidating impediments". Others do not annul it, but prevent its being contracted without sin: they are called "prohibitory impediments."

Invalidating impediments.—The following are the chief invalidating impediments, with which the faithful ought to be acquainted:

1. *Error*. For example, Peter intends to marry Teresa. He is deceived, and gives his consent to Catharine, whom he supposes to be Teresa: the marriage made with Catharine is null. This impediment comes from natural right; for the first condition of an engagement is that the parties should know what they engage themselves to.

2. *A solemn vow of chastity*. A religious man or woman, in the true sense of the word *religious*, or a man who has received holy orders, cannot marry. Such a marriage would be null. Persons who make a vow of chastity form a spiritual alliance with Jesus Christ. They give themselves to him: they can no longer dispose of their body or their heart. This impediment is intended to oblige those who consecrate themselves to God to respect their engagements. Nothing is more sacred than a solemn promise made to God. To violate it would be an exceeding great scandal. To prevent this, the Church has laid down the impediment of which we speak. Do you know any arrangement wiser in itself or more useful to society?

3. *Relationship*. It is forbidden to relations in a collateral line, as far as the fourth degree, inclusively, to marry one another, under pain of the nullity of the marriage. To know what degree of relationship exists between two persons, it is only necessary to see their distance from the common stock. Father and mother are the common stock; their children, that is, brothers and sisters, are in the first degree of relationship; the children of brothers and sisters, that is, cousins, are in the second degree; the children of cousins are in the third degree; the children of these last are in the fourth degree; and so on. The Church extends the impediment of which we now speak to the fourth degree. To prevent numerous grievous maladies,[1015] and to strengthen the bonds of charity among men, are the objects of this law. We cannot fail to admire how well the Church understands the wants of her children, as well as the Spirit of her divine spouse, when she endeavors to make of all mankind but one united family.

4. *Difference of religion*. It is not permitted Christians to marry with infidels, who have not been baptized. If they do so, their alliance is null. It is not the same as that which is contracted with heretics. This is forbidden; but it is not null, unless in consequence of some other impediment. The difficulties opposed by the Church to mixed marriages are a new proof of her maternal solicitude. She knows that the company of heretics is often far more dangerous to Catholics than that of Catholics is useful to heretics. True, in the early ages the Church tolerated the marriage of her children with strangers; but the reasons for this toleration have long ceased to exist. As soon as paganism was nearly destroyed, she forbade her children to contract alliances with infidels, and this under pain of nullity. If she does not forbid marriage with heretics in so absolute a manner, she does all that lies in her power to hinder it. When, for weighty reasons, she thinks well to authorize such a marriage, she annexes to it all the conditions calculated to prevent its being a stumbling block to salvation. It is required a) that all the children born shall be brought up in the Catholic religion; b) that the Catholic party shall not be taken off to a country where he or she cannot practice the Catholic religion; and c) that the Catholic party shall use every effort to convert the other.

5. *Violence*. When the consent of one of the parties is not free, but extorted by force and fear, the marriage is null. This impediment arises from the law of nature: an indispensable condition of every agreement is the liberty of those who subscribe to it.

6. *Public decency*. Should a betrothal come to be broken through by a solemn vow of chastity made by one of the parties before the accomplishment of the marriage, or by mutual consent, or by marriage with another, one of the parties cannot marry the father, mother, brother, or sister of the other. Such a marriage would be null. This impediment does not extend beyond the first degree. It was established by the Church in order to secure for the promise of marriage a due respect, and to prevent a multitude of disorders, including that of a rash betrothal.

7. *Affinity*. There are two kinds of affinity: that which is contracted by marriage, and that which is contracted by the sacrament of baptism or confirmation. The impediment of affinity contracted by marriage consists in this: that the husband is allied to all the relatives of his wife and the wife to all the relatives of her husband. It follows hence that the one of the married persons who survives the other cannot marry with the other's friends to the fourth degree, inclusively, under pain of the nullity of the marriage. The impediment of spiritual affinity consists in this: that it establishes a relationship: a) between him or her who baptizes and the child baptized and its parents, so that the person who baptizes cannot afterward marry the child or the child's father or mother; b) between the child baptized or confirmed and its godfather and godmother in baptism or confirmation, so that the godfather or godmother cannot afterward marry this child; and c) between the godfather and godmother in baptism or confirmation and the father and mother of the child baptized or confirmed, so that, one of the child's parents afterward dying, the godfather or godmother cannot marry the other: all under pain of nullity. It was the Church that established this impediment. She rightly considers those who concur to give the child a Christian life as its spiritual parents. Now, in order to dignify this title and to make those who bear it fulfill the obligations which it imposes, she forbids those who are honored with it to enter into a marriage alliance with their spiritual child, or with the child's father or mother according to the flesh. In the eyes of the Church, both parties are near relatives of the child. Now, near relatives do not marry one another.

8. *Abduction*. This is the carrying away of a person against his or her will, or against the will of his or her parents, tutors, or guardians. Marriage cannot be thus effected without granting to the person so carried away full liberty; this being denied, the marriage is null. Can anything be more moral than such an impediment?

9. *Clandestinity*. That a marriage may be valid, it must be celebrated in the face of the Church—in the presence of the parish priest (or another priest appointed to fill his place), the parties to be married, and witnesses. It was in consequence of monstrous abuses that this impediment was established.

Prohibitory impediments.—There are three prohibitory impediments: a) a simple vow of chastity, of becoming a religious, or of not marrying; b) a betrothal—one cannot, when affianced to a particular person, marry any other in the world without sin, so long as the force of the betrothal subsists; and c) a command of the Church—unless by dispensation, nuptials are forbidden from the First Sunday of Advent to the feast of the Epiphany, inclusively, and from the first day of Lent to the octave of Easter, inclusively, and the reason for this prohibition is because these two seasons of the year being reserved for prayer, recollection, and fasting, Christians ought then to occupy themselves much more with their eternal settlement in heaven than with temporal alliances on earth.

Such are the principal impediments of marriage. They have for their object the good of souls, the advantage of society, and the honor of religion. The Church had a full right to establish them. Her divine spouse, the author of the sacraments, confided the administration of them to her; and the Council of Trent was justly entitled to strike with its anathema anyone who should dare to say the contrary.

Dispensations.—Yet, however wise and necessary these impediments, there may be reasonable motives for dispensing with them. The Church never refuses a compliance in this respect, when the good of her children requires it. But when a dispensation is asked, it is necessary, under pain of nullity, to tell the truth, that is, to state one's motives for seeking it. To obtain it, a person is often obliged to have recourse to Rome, and to give, in compensation, a certain sum. Is it not just that, to maintain the unity of the hierarchy and the authority of his supreme dignity, the sovereign pontiff reserves to himself alone the right of dispensing with the general laws of the Church? As for the sum of money required, is it not also just that he who seeks a dispensation from a law made for all should compensate for this kind of infraction or privilege by a good work? Moreover, the money that is sent to Rome on account of dispensations is not turned to the benefit of the Roman Court. It is employed either in defraying the expenses of excavating the catacombs for the discovery of the bodies of martyrs, or in maintaining missions for the propagation of the faith. In some dioceses, this money is consecrated to local works.

Such is a brief sketch of the Church's legislation regarding marriage. In the eyes of anyone who studies this legislation, it is a masterpiece of wisdom, an admirable collection of guarantees for the fundamental act of the family and society.[1016]

Necessity.—Considered in regard to nature, marriage is necessary to perpetuate the human race. In regard to the Church and Christian society, the sacrament of marriage is necessary to give to those who receive it the graces which they require, that they may fulfill their duties and form saints for heaven. This is the reason why our Lord raised the natural contract to the dignity of a sacrament; but all are not obliged to receive it. Our Lord placed virginity above marriage, and the apostle tells us that the young person who marries does not do ill, but that the one who does not marry does better.[1017] All persons should follow their particular vocation.

Liturgy of matrimony.—What shall we say of the ceremonies that accompany the solemn union of marriage? Their first title to our reverence is their antiquity. From the early ages, Christians have sanctified their entrance into this state by the common prayers of the Church and the blessing of her ministers.[1018] Marriages used to be celebrated publicly before the bishop, who, in the holy sacrifice, recommended to God the parties to be married. These made their oblation on the occasion with the rest of the faithful, and their names were called out. The nuptial blessing was regarded, not as a simple ceremony, but as a source of graces.

To the nuptial blessing was added the blessing of the ring, which the man placed on the woman's finger. The future spouses also presented some pieces of money for the poor: our ancestors always desired that the poor should have a share in their feasts. Children of the same family, they did not think that some ought to suffer while others rejoiced. The man took the hand of the woman, as a sign of that faith which he promised to her.[1019] A veil was stretched out over their heads: a mysterious ceremony, which taught them that modesty was to be the rule of their conduct. The color of this veil was purple, the better to mark a virtue so becoming in married persons, whose chief ornament it is.[1020]

Another ceremony, no less ancient than that just mentioned, was the coronation of the persons to be married. On their young brow the priest placed a crown, which was left in the church as something holy. It was usually formed of an olive branch, with white and purple bands. This usage was intended to denote the virginal innocence with which the young persons came to be married, and the glorious victory which they had won over their passions.[1021] The bride and bridegroom communicated at the Mass of their marriage, in order to cement in the blood of the Savior that union which they were come to confirm, and to draw from this adorable mystery the graces necessary for their new state. Why, alas! do not their successors act thus still? Are their wants less numerous than those of the early Christians, or are they less obliged to aspire to sanctity?

Be that as it may, the most of these venerable ceremonies are still in use among us. The parties to be married, accompanied by their witnesses, place themselves at the foot of the altar, the future husband on the right, the future wife on the left side. The priest causes the couple about to be married to express to each other their mutual consent. They give the right hand to each other, and the minister of the Most High pronounces over them this prayer: "I unite you in marriage in the name of the Father, and of the Son," etc.

At the same time he forms over them the sign of the cross, to remind them that it was in the name of the Blessed Trinity and through the merits of our Lord's death that marriage was raised to the dignity of a sacrament, and that no one can sunder the bond which the Savior establishes between married persons. In order to teach them that their union ought to be sanctified, he sprinkles some holy water over them: and now they are united forever! The angels in heaven and the Church on earth have heard their vows—God himself has received them: they must in future have but one heart.

It remains to give the wife the sign of her alliance, the pledge of her consecration. The priest does so by blessing the ring. The husband presents it to his wife, who receives it as a sign of the chain with which she has just bound herself. She is no longer her own; she belongs to her husband, as the Church does to Jesus Christ. The priest also blesses a piece of money, a figure of the community of goods between the newly espoused.

The Mass begins. After the *Pater*, the priest, turning toward the married pair, his right hand extended over their heads, pronounces an admirable preface in which he invokes on them all the blessings heretofore lavished on the alliances of the patriarchs. He asks all these blessings "through our Lord Jesus Christ," and his most powerful prayer will infallibly produce its effect if the parties in whose favor it is uttered place no obstacle to it.

How grave and solemn is every word in this prayer! What a majestic dignity accompanies it! The man is warned that he begins a new career. The words of the nuptial blessing—words which God himself pronounced on the first couple in the world—tell the husband respectfully that he performs the most important act in his life, that he is about to become like Adam the head of a family, and that he takes upon himself the full burden of our human condition. The wife is no less instructed. The image of pleasures disappears from her eyes in presence of that of her duties. A voice seems to cry to her from the midst of the altar, "O Eve! knowest thou well what thou doest? Knowest thou that there is no longer any liberty for thee, save that of the tomb? Knowest thou what it is to bear in thy mortal womb an immortal man, made to the likeness of God?" Among the ancients a hymeneal celebration was a ceremony full of scandal, a scene of noisy rejoicing, which taught none of the grave thoughts inspired by marriage: Christianity alone gives it dignity.[1022]

After the Mass, there is a visit to the sacristy to write the act of marriage on the parish registers. It was the same with the early Christians: these registers were called the "matrimonial tables." Not only were agreements having reference to material interests recorded thereon, but also the obligations of the married state in general. In assemblies of the faithful, the fathers of the Church often made use of these tables to remind married persons of the sanctity of their duties.

Such are the prayers and ceremonies that accompany the celebration of Catholic marriage. Who will tell the social advantages of this sacrament?

Social advantages of the sacrament of matrimony.—If the family is the basis of society, it is plain that the sacrament which forms the family is the basis of the social edifice. In raising marriage to the dignity of a sacrament, our Lord raised society too, and enabled it to attain that intellectual superiority which distinguishes Christian nations. Unity, indissolubility, and sanctity were the characteristics of the primitive family. Developing itself in accordance with its principles, the family should give birth to a perfect society; but the original disorder overthrew the divine plan. Polygamy and divorce, breaking up primitive unity, introduced jealousy, rancor, and unhappiness into the family.[1023] Concupiscence, shutting out every idea of sanctity, reduced the husband and wife to the level of brutes. And from the domestic hearth came forth swarms of malevolent beings! And degraded society was lost in the cesspool of its own corruption! The father was a despot, the mother a slave, and the child a victim, until it could become the murderer of its guilty parents. In these few words, you have a history of the pagan family.

The Son of God, the Word by whom all things were made, came down from the eternal hills to repair his work. He began by recalling the family to its primitive institution. He proscribed polygamy and divorce, and made the conjugal bond a sacrament of the new law. Numerous graces, suited to the wants of married persons, were attached to it. The family changed its face, and by the family the world was renovated.

Oh, what a difference between the pagan and the Christian father! The first is a despot with a drawn sword. Between him and his children there are no other relations than those of a wild beast with its young ones, of a tyrant with slaves. Paternity, insofar as it is sublime, has no existence for him. The Christian father, on the contrary, is familiar with holy joys. The venerable representative of that beloved Father who is in heaven, the living image of the Creator, he participates not only in his divine paternity, but also in his exhaustless tenderness. The object of respect and love, how sweet does that power become to him which he shares even with his wife and children! Every day, in the most trifling as well as in the most important occurrences, he feels that he is more loved than feared. His authority is even more sacred than if he wielded a sword. On his brow Christianity has placed a ray of the majesty of the Most High, and a voice, resounding through the family, is heard continually to say, "He who hears you, hears me."

What shall I say of the mother? It is to her especially that the sacrament of matrimony is profitable. Paganism only shows me in the wife a slave to be dishonored, to be beaten, to be cast away, to be left to shame and misery; or a beast of burden that is set apart, as is still done in Africa, for the rudest labors.

On the contrary, how beautiful is the place which the sacrament of matrimony assigns to the mother of a family in Christian society! A sacred being, an object of the liveliest affection, of the most tender regard, of veneration to all who surround her, man is no longer a despot for her, but a protector and a supporter. Over his heart she exercises the most powerful of all sways, that of gentleness and patience. Placed between the father and the child, she is a sweet mediatrix of peace—an apostle of that charity which she communicates to every one who comes near her, of that Christian life for which she is so well made. Endowed with an angelic mission, she draws man to God by her virtues, and sows the first seeds of good in the heart of youth. How heavenly is her authority! Today, thanks to the ideas which Christianity has spread among us, a deluge of anathemas would fall upon the head of the child that should cease to love and respect its mother!

And the child itself, what does it not owe to that august sacrament which changed those who gave it existence into new beings? The slave of every caprice, the victim of every tyranny was the pagan child. No respect for its life, for its heart, for its mind. How different is the lot of the Christian child! The son of God before it is that of its parents, the brother of our Lord Jesus Christ, the heir of heaven, the angel of the earth, the living sanctuary of the divinity: this is the child of faith! What a formidable barrier protects its life! Woe to him who should dare to lay hands on its days or its innocence! To touch it is to touch the God of hosts in the very apple of his eye. I am no longer surprised to see cities and countries covered with establishments for the preservation of the child in body and in soul. To do good to this child of the Most High is, as Christianity tells us, to merit the eternal gratitude of its Father who is in heaven.

Such, then, in a few words, is what the sacrament of matrimony has done and still daily does for the family, and for each member of the family, and consequently for society, of which the family is the basis. Take away this sacrament, and the alliance of man and woman is henceforth no more than an ignoble contract; and fortune takes the place of all those genuine qualities which, by securing the happiness of married persons, provide for the order and the repose of society. Take away this sacrament, and the family relapses into that state of degradation from which the gospel drew it forth: the father becomes once more a despot, the mother a slave, the child a victim. Cast your eyes now over the peoples who have not yet heard the good news,[1024] and over those who despise it. What a sight! And yet there are men who ask what is the use of Christianity! And these men are thought great philosophers!

PRAYER

O my God! who art all love, I thank thee for having raised marriage to the dignity of a sacrament; grant to those who receive it the grace to comply worthily with their duties.

I am resolved to love God above all things, and my neighbor as myself for the love of God; and, in testimony of this love, I will often pray for my father and mother.

Lesson 46: Our Union with the New Adam by Charity (1)

Harmony of the three theological virtues.—Faith leads to hope, and hope leads to charity. By faith, the mind enters into possession of a rich patrimony of truths, which enlighten, ennoble, console, and in a manner deify it, by making it participate in the lights of the new Adam himself.

By hope, our will, raised above natural and perishable goods, which it regards only with a noble disdain, is directed to the possession of the goods known by faith, that is to say, supernatural goods, which are felicity, glory, all the advantages—for body and soul—of which God himself is the source, and which he promises to his elect.

Then comes charity, which elevates our heart by filling it with love for God and for the goods that faith reveals to us and hope expects. By these three virtues, which command, require, and perfect one another, our union is brought about with our Lord, and we begin on earth that divine life which shall be consummated in eternity.

Faith, hope, and charity are called theological[1025] virtues, because they have God himself for their object and they lead us directly to him. How sublime they are in their essence! how noble in their effects! Take away faith, and man and society and the world are abandoned to doubts, to perplexities, to errors of every kind. Take away hope, and man cares for nothing but the perishable goods of earth, to the possession of which he is borne with an impetuosity that respects neither acquired rights nor human or divine laws. Take away charity, and man becomes the slave of passions which degrade him, and which render both him and the world supremely miserable. The history of idolatrous peoples, in ancient and modern times, bears witness to this humiliating truth. In Christian nations, the lives of those who are strangers to the faith, hope, and charity of Catholics make it plain to our eyes.

So true is it that the bases of society and religion are united, that the same words serve to name both. The word *credit* comes from *credere*, which means "to believe," "to have faith"; the words *confidence* and *charity* (or *fraternity*) are identical in social language and religious language. Would that this new ray of light might break in upon some of our blind men, and dissuade them from endeavoring to separate what God has indissolubly united: the sun and the sunbeam, the soul and the body, religion and society! Would that it might also show more and more clearly the excellence of the plan that we have followed in the arrangement and development of the Christian doctrine!

We are already acquainted with faith and hope. Animated, fortified, deified by grace, the fruit of prayer, and especially of the sacraments, the chief of which is the Holy Eucharist, the Christian has only one thing more to do, that which man does every day after taking his corporal nourishment—labor. When his strength is exhausted in a glorious labor, he will come to repair it by receiving anew the divine food, the bread of the strong and the wine of virgins, to support him until he reaches the eternal mountain, where God himself, the liberal rewarder of his labor, dwells.[1026]

Now this labor is love, is charity; for no virtue is idle, charity least of all. It is, as the fathers say, essentially active. Under its influence, the mind of man labors continually to know the perfections of God; his heart, to rejoice in them; even his body, to translate them into his acts, by observing, with a fidelity full of fervor, all the commandments of this good God, who is eminently deserving of love. We see then that the explanation of the decalogue follows naturally after the explanation of the sacraments and the other means of obtaining grace. Let us first of all speak of charity in itself, as we have spoken of hope and faith.

1. *Definition of charity*. Charity is a gift of God and a supernatural virtue, by which we love God above all things, because he is infinitely good and amiable, and our neighbor as ourselves for the love of God. When speaking of hope and faith, we explained the words, *gift of God* and *supernatural virtue*. The others, "by which we love God," show that charity is a theological virtue, since it has God himself for its essential object.

Above all things. As God is the being of beings, and our last end, it is clear that we ought to love him above whatever is necessarily inferior to him and only a means to conduct to him.

Because he is infinitely good. These words express two motives for loving God—the goods which he has given us, and those which he has in store for us: this is the love of gratitude and expectation.

Because he is infinitely amiable. This is the special love of complacency, of charity, by which we ought to love God for himself on account of his infinite perfections.

And our neighbor. That is, all men, living or dead, who may be with us in our heavenly country.

As ourselves. We ought to love all men with a love similar, though inferior to that which we are bound to have for ourselves.

For the love of God. That is, with a view to God and to obey God.

Such is an abridged definition of that charity of which this lesson will now proceed to give a development.

2. *Excellence*. "God is charity,"[1027] we are told by the beloved disciple of the Savior. Charity poured forth into the soul is therefore a certain participation of the charity of God himself. It is a wholly divine strength which becomes the life of the soul, as the soul itself is the life of the body; a virtue which makes us think, speak, love, and act divinely, because it effects our close union with God on earth, to consummate the same in eternity. We may say that it is present in all the powers of the soul as the soul itself is present in all the members of the body, imparting life to each; or as fire is present in red hot iron, which at length comes to melt and even to boil.[1028]

As charity is the life of the soul, it follows that it is the soul of all virtues. Without it there is no true virtue, that is, no virtue which can lead us to our true end, the possession of God. It is in regard to other virtues that which the root is to the tree, that which a wise queen is to her subjects. It extends not only to the moral virtues, but also to the other theological virtues, faith and hope.

"Of all virtues," says St. Thomas, "the theological virtues are the most excellent, because they tend directly to God himself, who is the rule of all perfection. Among the theological virtues, the most excellent is that which tends most perfectly to him, and rests in him and for him. This virtue is charity."[1029] In so saying, the Angelic Doctor is the echo of St. Augustine, who defines all virtues by charity. "Faith," he says, "is a love which believes; hope, a love which expects; patience, a love which endures; prudence, a judicious love; justice, a love which gives every one his due; fortitude, a generous love; and so of the others."[1030]

It is charity that gives merit as well as measure to the other virtues. The natural excellence of our actions deserves indeed an accidental reward, which will form the *aureola* of the saints in heaven; but the essential reward is wholly derived from that charity which animates our actions.[1031] While faith and hope pause at the threshold of the heavenly Jerusalem, charity bounds across it and will dwell eternally in that city to form the happiness of the elect. Need we then be astonished at the magnificence of the language employed by St. Paul to celebrate the praises of this queen of virtues? "Though I should speak with the tongues of angels and men," says the great apostle, "though I should have knowledge enough to fathom all mysteries and faith enough to remove mountains, though I should give all my goods to the poor and my body to the flames, and have not charity, I am nothing—everything else is useless to me."[1032]

3. *First object: God.* In order to be as clear as possible, we shall first explain that which regards our charity toward God; we shall then come to that which regards our charity toward the neighbor.

The first and principal object of charity is God himself, considered as the sovereign perfection and the sovereign good. Here again is manifested the excellence of charity. God, that is to say, all that is most beautiful, amiable, and perfect in existence, is presented to us by the divine Redeemer as the banquet on which our love may feast. Oh, how deep ought to be the gratitude of the human heart at the sight of its noble destiny! Oh, how lively ought to be the joy of this heart, which, until the time of the new Adam, nearly always sought in the vilest creatures the food of its affections!

Destined to a place at the table of angels, to be nourished like them with God himself, man's degraded heart besought the meanest animals to share their shameful enjoyments. Vain petitions! Happiness fled from it, for happiness always flees from those who are not moved by the love of the sovereign good. By recalling man to his last end, the new Adam brought him back to peace and glory; for he opened before him a pure and plentiful stream, in which it might quench his loving thirst.

4. *Measure.* "The measure of loving God," says St. Bernard, "is to love him without measure."[1033] We ought then to love God above all things. God should have no superior or equal in our hearts. Riches, honor, fame, relations, friends, health, life, all creatures whatsoever, must be inferior to him.

Is there anything more just than that we should prefer God to everything else? Is not God the sovereign good and our last end? Would it not be a strange disorder to love anything out of God as much as, or even more than, God? The love of God above all things is therefore a most sacred duty. If our charity is not such a love, there is no salvation for us. The Savior explains this matter formally in the gospel: "He that loveth father or mother more than me, is not worthy of me; he that loveth son or daughter more than me, is not worthy of me";[1034] "he that loveth his life in this world shall lose it"[1035]—that is to say, he who loves himself more than God shall be condemned. If then he who loves his relations or his life more than God is in a state of reprobation, with much more reason is he so who loves his character, his pleasures, his money, or his health as much as, or more than, God.

This love of preference, without which no one can be in friendship with God or have a right to heaven, is a love of gratitude, of hope, or of charity.

The loves of gratitude and hope are pointed out in the words of the definition, "because he is infinitely good."

The love of gratitude consists in loving God because he has done us good, because he has been and still is good toward us. How many motives for this love! In the order of nature: the firmament with its stars, the earth with its productions, society with its various advantages; in the order of grace: the angels, our Lord, the Church, all turned to our service: these are a few of the motives that induce us to love God with a love of gratitude.

The love of hope consists in loving God because he loves us so much as to wish to be himself our reward in heaven: this love is most lawful. The greatest saints have had it. "I inclined my heart to the observance of thy commandments," says the royal prophet, "because of the reward."[1036] Moses is highly praised for having denied that he was the son of Pharao's daughter, and this to obtain everlasting life.[1037] Our Lord himself said in reply to the inquiry of one of the doctors, "If thou wilt enter into life everlasting, keep the commandments."[1038] St. Paul exhorts all the faithful so to run in the way of virtue that they may obtain the prize.[1039]

Finally, the Council of Trent utters its anathema against any one who should say that the justified man becomes guilty in the sight of God when he does good to obtain an everlasting reward.[1040] But to love God only as a means to acquire heaven or to escape hell is to make God subservient to our personal interests; to refer him to ourselves, instead of referring ourselves to him; to reverse the order of things, and to violate the precept of charity.[1041]

The love of charity is expressed by the words, *and infinitely amiable*. To love God because he is infinitely amiable is to love him for himself, abstracting from his benefits, and solely because of his infinite perfections. To love God in this manner is to rejoice, to be happy in the thought that he possesses all perfections in the highest degree, without any admixture of imperfection. To have this love of charity is to begin to live on earth the life of the saints, who sing forever in heaven, "Holy, holy, holy is the Lord God Almighty!"[1042]

We ought to regard as a perfect act of the love of God that which is conceived thus, "My God, I love thee above all things, because thou art infinitely good, yea, goodness itself." As a matter of fact, we love God in this case because of his goodness, which is one of his chief perfections, even inasmuch as it is advantageous to us, or as it helps us to accomplish the divine will and to attain our last end, which is to love God for himself.[1043]

5. *Necessity*. The necessity of loving God with a love of preference, as we have just explained, and this under pain of everlasting damnation, rests on the following motives: a) his perfections. Reason and justice oblige us to love specially that which is specially amiable, to love above everything else that which is infinitely amiable. Hence, all our love ought to be referred to the love of God. It is God whom we ought to love in ourselves, in our neighbor, in creatures; for whatever is amiable, good, or beautiful in us or others, comes from God and should return to God. b) His benefits. It would be much easier for us to count the hairs of our head than the benefits of God, whether in the order of nature or in that of grace. c) His promises. St. Paul, having returned from the third heaven, one day took up a pen to describe the wonders of the blessed city; but, unable to convey anything like a full idea of those ineffable delights, he only let these few words escape him: "The eye has not seen, nor the ear heard, nor has it entered into the heart of man to conceive what things God has prepared for those who love him."[1044] d) His command. The command of loving God is not new. It is the first of all by its antiquity, its dignity, and its necessity. It has its foundations in the very nature of man. What indeed is more natural than that man should render to God, as his Creator, a supreme homage

and worship? Now, God being love, the only thing that pleases him, says St. Augustine, is the love of his creatures.[1045]

Without a doubt, God is honored by faith and hope; but our worship becomes perfect only by charity. Hence, the love of God has always been the leading precept in religion. See how it is laid down in the law of Moses: "Thou shalt love the Lord thy God with thy whole heart, and thy whole mind, and thy whole strength. This precept which I give thee today, thou shalt engrave on thy heart. Thou shalt teach it to thy children, and thou shalt meditate upon it sitting in thy house, walking on thy journey, sleeping and rising. Thou shalt bind it on thy arm as a sign."[1046] During more than five hundred years, the prophets never ceased to urge the same precept.

The Savior proclaimed it still louder, and gave it a new extent and perfection. The love of God, he says to all men in general, is the indispensable condition of your salvation: "If you will enter into life everlasting, keep the commandments."[1047] "You shall love the Lord your God with your whole heart and your whole mind: this is the first and greatest of all the commandments."[1048] His whole life is spent in preaching charity. He reduces the gospel, all the teachings of the prophets, all the institutions of the Mosaic law, all the preachings of the apostles, all the exhortations of the Church throughout the course of ages, to these two commandments, which ought to be written in fiery letters on the heart of every Christian and in golden letters on the door of every house: "Love God with thy whole heart, and thy neighbor as thyself." This is the sum of the law and the prophets.[1049]

It is also to engrave indelibly, if possible, on all hearts this divine abridgment of all religion that each of the prayers which terminate our lessons is an act of charity.

The precept of charity, insofar as it forbids us to do anything contrary to the love which we owe to God, obliges all and always. Insofar as it directs us to elicit positive acts of the love of God, it obliges a) when one comes to the use of reason; b) when one meets with a great temptation, which threatens to separate him from God; c) when one is bound to receive or to administer a sacrament, without being able to receive absolution for a mortal sin which burdens his soul; d) often during life, at least once a month; and e) at the hour of death. But it is not necessary that these acts should be made with the intention of fulfilling the precept of charity, nor that they should be expressed in an explicit manner. He, for example, who, in reciting the Lord's Prayer, says devoutly, "Hallowed be thy name, thy kingdom come, thy will be done on earth as it it in heaven," makes an act of the love of God.

Happy is he who observes the sweet law of divine love! Far from him are the dark clouds of terror, the bitter pangs of a deep unrest! St. Francis de Sales used to repose more tranquilly on divine providence than a child on its mother's breast. "God," he would say, "has promised to assist us in all our tribulations. What have we to fear? Nothing happens but by the permission of God." Having been greatly calumniated, he never lost the peace of his soul. He once wrote to the bishop of Belley thus: "I have just been informed from Paris that my robes are being torn up splendidly; but I hope that God will mend them for me, so that they will be better than they were, if this be necessary for his service."

St. Paul was so penetrated with love for God that, even in the midst of the extraordinary labors, fatigues, and persecutions which he underwent, he was filled with consolation, he was inundated with joy. Divine love was so deeply rooted in his heart that he had the hardihood to utter these astonishing words: "Who shall separate us from the charity of Jesus Christ? I am sure that neither life, nor death, nor oppression, nor the sword, nor hunger, nor nakedness, nor the present, nor the future, nor any power whatsoever, shall do so"[1050] and elsewhere: "I live—but no, it is not I who live, it is Jesus Christ who liveth in me."[1051] So speaks love.

6. *Means to obtain this love.* The means to obtain the love of God are: a) to ask it fervently, saying, for example, with St. Ignatius, "O my God! give me thy love and thy grace, and I shall be rich enough"; b) to reflect frequently with admiration and gratitude on the perfections and benefits of God; c) to perform its works, by forcing ourselves to keep religiously the commandments of the Lord, and especially by taking the greatest care to avoid every deliberately willful sin, however slight, and to make much account of little things; d) to accustom ourselves to frequent acts of perfect charity, saying, "O my God! it is for thyself, it is because of thy adorable perfections that I love thee; I love thee because thou art God, because thou art infinitely perfect"—it is only after making many acts of gratitude that, generally speaking, one comes to make acts of pure charity.

7. *Sins opposed to charity.* All sins are opposed to charity: mortal, because they extinguish the life of the soul; venial, because they impede its action. Still there are some sins directly opposed to this virtue: such as hatred of God, and those which attend this hatred. A person hates God when he wishes that God did not exist, or that God should be heedless of the good or bad character of our actions.[1052] The hatred of God is a crime that causes us to shudder: it is the greatest of all.

8. *Second object of charity: The neighbor.* By *the neighbor*, we are not to understand merely our relatives, our friends, our benefactors, the inhabitants of the same city or kingdom, the disciples of the same religion. This tender word, made familiar in human speech by the gospel, comprises all men without distinction or exception: Christians, heretics, Jews, heathens, the living and the dead, and even our enemies. Our charity ought to be universal, that is to say, catholic, like our faith.[1053]

Hence, we ought to regard all men as members of one family, as children of one father, and, consequently, endure one another, forgive one another, help one another, wish well to one another, and do to one another all the good in our power. It is thus that we shall know all, love all, and honor all as the dear children of our Father who is in heaven. Here again, what noble aliment does our Lord Jesus Christ supply on which we may nourish our love! How boldly does he attack the great law of universal hatred, which was the shame and misery of the pagan world, as it is still, in various degrees, the shame and misery of peoples, of families, and of individuals who are unfaithful to the fundamental precept of charity.

9. *Rule.* The rule for loving the neighbor is to love him as ourselves. This rule would alone suffice to prove the divinity of Christianity: never did any legislator propose it—much less dare to impose it. What could be more suited to make earth an anticipated heaven? On the other hand, what rule could be more secure or unequivocal? No one can escape from it, or falsify it with lying interpretations. To love our neighbor as ourselves is to wish and do him all the good that we could reasonably hope anyone would wish and do ourselves, if we were in his place and he in ours.

Since the love of ourselves is the rule and the model of that which we ought to entertain for our neighbor, it follows a) that we are bound to love ourselves. Now, to love ourselves according to the will of the new Adam, we ought on all occasions to prefer our soul to our body, eternal to temporal life. We ought to avail ourselves of every means possible to attain our last end, and shun everything calculated to divert us from it. Hence, to love our neighbor as ourselves is to prefer in all things his soul to his body, his eternal to his temporal life. It is to procure for him, as far as lies in us, the means to be saved, and to avert from him everything calculated to lead him to damnation. It also follows b) that we ought to be the first and dearest objects of our own charity.[1054] Hence, we ought to prefer our own good to that of our neighbor, when these goods are of the same order; for example, our own life to his. Hence also, we are not bound to prefer another's good to our own, unless when the neighbor's good is of a higher order.

Now, the life of the soul is of a higher order than the life of the body; the life of the body, than reputation; reputation, than property. According to this rule, we are bound to prefer the neighbor's salvation to our temporal life, the neighbor's temporal life to our reputation, the neighbor's reputation or honor to our material goods. But this occurs only when the neighbor is in extreme necessity, because then only are we bound, in order to succor him, to renounce our goods of a lower order.

Here then is the admirable order in which reason and faith class the objects of human affections: a) God above all. b) Ourselves, as to the soul and the goods of grace. c) The neighbor, as to the soul and the goods of grace. d) Ourselves, as to the body and the goods of nature: such as life, health. e) The neighbor, as to the body and the goods of nature: such as life, health. f) Ourselves, as to external temporal goods: such as character, fortune. g) The neighbor, as to external temporal goods: such as character, fortune.[1055]

Although we ought to love all men as ourselves, yet there is an order to be observed in our charity toward various persons. Here, again, nature and grace are in perfect harmony: the latter ennobles and consecrates the inclinations of the former. When there is question of procuring the spiritual or temporal good of the neighbor, we ought to relieve our parents, our children, our brothers and sisters, our kindred before others; Christians before infidels; pastors, and such others as act like fathers to us, before the generality of Christians; domestics before strangers.[1056]

Here is the new order of charity, exhibited in different degrees: a) God above all. b) Ourselves. c) Our children. d) Our father. e) Our mother. f) The husband or wife. g) Other relatives. h) Benefactors, friends, inhabitants of the same country.

This order of charity will enter into heaven, of which it will form one of the sweetest joys; for it is founded on nature. "Grace," says St. Thomas, "does not destroy nature, but perfects it. Hence, merits being equal, we shall love our relatives, our friends, more tenderly in heaven than the other blessed; merits being unequal, we shall love those better who are more perfect."[1057] It follows hence that we shall know one another in heaven.

10. *Necessity*. Would you now like to know why we ought to love all men? Because God wishes it. God wishes that we should love all men: a) because all men are created to the divine image and likeness; b) because all men are our brethren in the first Adam, heirs of the same blood and the same miseries; c) because all men are our brethren in the second Adam, heirs of his blood and his merits, redeemed at the infinite price of his death, to form with him and us but one heart and one soul on earth and in heaven—an ineffable union, which, to exist in eternity, must begin in time; and d) finally, because the principal end of the incarnation was to substitute for the law of hatred, which reigned in the world from the time of original sin and divided mankind, the sweet law of charity, which, by uniting all, would henceforth form but one people, one family, as in the days of primitive innocence.

Accordingly, whoever loves not the rest of men, whoever hates one man out of those millions of men who dwell upon the earth, opposes the views of the second Adam, destroys his work as far as lies in him, and consequently resists his will. Hence the sentence that cannot be too often repeated, "If any man say, I love God, and loveth not his brother, he is a liar."[1058]

The love of the neighbor is a necessary consequence of the love of God. Not to love the neighbor is to disobey him who says, "Thou shalt love thy neighbor as thyself."[1059]

Let us here admire the wisdom of the divine legislator, and acknowledge that it was impossible to give to that charity which should unite all men a more solid foundation. Whether the neighbor has virtues or vices, whether he has done us good or evil, he is to have a share in our affection. Our affection ought not to be less generous, or less constant, or less holy, on account of his qualities. God wishes that we should love our neighbor as ourselves, and he wishes it always. We have only to be silent and to submit.

This one commandment, well observed, dispenses with all human laws, as, without it, all human laws are insufficient. We need no longer be surprised that a pagan emperor, Alexander Severus, caused it to be written in golden letters on the walls of his palace. Would that each of us had it written on his heart!

11. *Application.* Charity, to be true, must not only appear in our words: it must exist in our heart and be manifested in our actions. It is of this the beloved disciple reminds us when he says, "My little children! let us not be satisfied to love one another in word, or in tongue, but in deed, and in truth."[1060] To complete the explanation of this commandment, it therefore remains for us to speak of the works of charity toward the neighbor.

Spiritual works of charity.—These works are of two kinds: spiritual and corporal. The spiritual works of charity are seven in number, namely: a) to instruct the ignorant; b) to reprove those who do evil; c) to give counsel to those who require it; d) to comfort the afflicted; e) to bear wrongs, and the defects of the neighbor, patiently; f) to pardon injuries; g) to pray for the living and the dead, especially for those who have persecuted us. By these marks, it may be seen whether our charity is sincere; whether we are truly united to the new Adam; in a word, whether we are the children of our Father who is in heaven.

Among these works, so divine, and so eminently calculated to secure our happiness in this life, there are two, on which it is proper to rouse our faith and to fix our attention: they are the pardoning of injuries and fraternal correction.

Pardoning of injuries. The pardoning of injuries, the loving of enemies, is the great miracle of Christianity, the triumph of Calvary; but it is also the great scandal of fallen man. Puffed up with pride, he wishes to hear no mention of forgetting or forgiving. Hence, those rivers of blood which have deluged the world. Hence, those monstrous hatreds which daily ruin families and which are sometimes perpetuated from parents to children. With degraded man, revenge is glory, pardon is weakness; while in reality pardon is a heroic act of courage and greatness of soul, and revenge a weakness and the proof of baseness.

Accordingly, the new Adam, who came to raise fallen man, by shaping his thoughts and sentiments to the model of his own, never ceased to give him formal precepts regarding pardon, and a cordial pardon. He made the pardon of injuries committed against us the indispensable condition of the pardon of our offenses against him. "If you will not forgive your brethren from your heart," he says, "neither will your heavenly Father forgive you."[1061]

To precept he adds example. He dies forgiving—what do I say? asking mercy for his executioners: "Father, forgive them, for they know not what they do."[1062] He adds, "I have given you an example that you may do as I have done."[1063] Since the time of this great example given to the world on the mountain of sorrows, by a God suffering a most unjust and ignominious death, a look at the cross suffices to disarm the anger of a Christian and to stifle every feeling of resentment in his heart. If this look does not suffice, he is no longer a Christian.

From the foregoing remarks it is easy to understand in what the forgiveness of injuries, so strongly inculcated by the gospel, consists. It consists: a) in not retaining in the heart any sentiment of hatred, any desire of revenge, any bitterness against him who has offended us, but loving him as our brother for the love of God, and proving our love toward him by our works; and b) in giving him outwardly the marks of kindness common among friends and relatives—for example, answering his letters, or his inquiries by word if he makes such, selling to him if he desires to buy, not shunning his conversation if we meet him in company, not depriving him of ordinary service or aid. All this under pain of light or grievous fault, according to circumstances of person, time, and place.[1064]

We are also bound to salute our enemies, or at least to return them a salutation; if they are our superiors, we ought to salute them first. If, without great inconvenience, and by a salutation, we can cure the neighbor of a hatred that he bears us, we are bound to salute him first, because charity obliges us to deliver the neighbor from mortal sin, even though it should be necessary for this purpose to do ourselves some violence.

As a general rule, he who gave the offense ought to be the first to seek a reconciliation. It is enough that he who received the offense forgives inwardly, and is disposed to be reconciled outwardly with the aggressor, when the latter shall come to ask forgiveness. If both are guilty, he who is first touched by grace ought out of charity to make some advances and thus gain his brother to Jesus Christ. Would that man be a Christian who, unwilling to trample underfoot a miserable point of honor, should refuse to save a soul redeemed by the divine blood? How would such a man appear before him who made the first advances to our guilty race, and died for us rather than avenge himself?

Fraternal correction. Another consequence or manifestation of the great precept of charity is fraternal correction.

To correct the neighbor is to reprove and admonish him with prudence and kindness. Every mortal sin into which the neighbor may fall, or into which he has already fallen, without having risen from it, is the matter of fraternal correction. How worthy is this duty of the Christian religion—of a religion which seeks before everything else the eternal happiness of man! In effect, if charity obliges us to withdraw the neighbor from a serious danger that threatens his body, with much more reason does it so oblige us when there is question of his soul.

We are all bound, both by the law of charity and the special command of our Lord, to exercise fraternal correction. Here are the express words of our divine master: "If your brother has committed a fault against you, go and rebuke him between you and him alone. If he hear you, you shall gain your brother. If he will not hear you, take with you one or two witnesses, that everything may be confirmed by the authority of two or three persons. If he will not hear them, tell the Church. If he will not hear the Church, let him be to you as a heathen and a publican."[1065]

The first means to give a fraternal correction well and to obtain the desired success is to say to ourselves, "If it were my case now to receive a correction, what terms, what nice management should I wish to be employed toward me in giving it?—in other words, how should I wish the matter to be done?" This question, attentively considered, may well awake in our souls a proper degree of gentleness and suavity. It will also help us to behave with prudence, that is, to have regard to persons, times, and places: an old man or a superior ought to be reproved far differently from a person of our own age or an equal.[1066] But our invariable rule ought ever to be the greatest advantage of the neighbor.[1067]

The second means to succeed in the correction is to have recourse to God, either before or after giving it, that he may replenish us with his Spirit and dispose the neighbor to profit by it.

Fraternal correction having for its end the amendment of the neighbor, it follows: a) that it is of precept insofar as it is necessary to attain this end; and b) that we are dispensed from giving it when it cannot be of any use—with much more reason when we foresee its consequences to be dangerous to the neighbor's salvation.[1068]

Yet, as fraternal correction is a special duty of superiors, they must have very strong reasons on their side to be able to omit it without sin. The more disagreeable this duty, the more grateful ought we to be to him who is so kind as to acquit himself of it toward us. Under what an obligation should we be to him who would deliver us from a serious illness, or even from some physical defect by which we should be exposed to the railleries of others! What do I say?—we could not be ungrateful to him who would draw our attention to a stain on our clothes. If we are reasonable beings, how exceedingly thankful ought we then to be to him who is so charitable as to warn us of the defilements of our soul, that we may purify it!

The seven spiritual works of charity lay bare, so to speak, the divine heart of our Savior, while they also reveal his infinite wisdom. One might call them so many remedies placed in order along the road of life, either to heal the soul of its diseases or to preserve it from such. It is impossible to imagine any set of helps more fitly arranged, or better calculated to secure the health of the soul—consequently its happiness and that of society; "for by justice are nations exalted, but by sin they are made miserable."[1069]

Corporal works of charity.—No less than the intellectual and the moral, the physical man was an object of solicitude to our Lord. Hence those corporal works of charity which he imposes as a sacred duty on all of us, according to our state and condition. These works are seven in number: a) to give food to the hungry and drink to the thirsty; b) to afford hospitality to strangers; c) to supply clothing to those who need it; d) to visit the sick; e) to visit and comfort prisoners; f) to ransom captives; g) to bury the dead.

In these precepts, so worthy of a God made man, we find the cause and explanation of all those wonders of charity unknown among pagans, but so common among Christians that they are hardly remarked. Here also we find the relief of all the miseries that can beset our frail existence; for these charitable duties embrace the whole life of man from the cradle to the grave. Thanks to them, the swathing bands for wrapping up the newborn babe and the winding-sheet for enclosing the lifeless corpse are equally sure to be provided.

Among these works there is one which holds a very important place in the economy of religion: it is almsgiving. We proceed to show the necessity and manner of almsgiving, and the advantages which flow from it. As long as there have been poor persons on the earth, almsgiving has been commanded. Few other duties are so often repeated in the old testament. "Give alms out of thy substance," said the holy man Tobias to his son, "and turn not away thy face from the poor. Hereby, thou shalt merit that the Lord will never turn away his face from thee. As far as thy means permit thee, be merciful. If thou have much, give much; if thou have little, give willingly out of that little."[1070] The precept of almsgiving, by which we are bound to give away what is superfluous in our goods,[1071] is founded on two reasons, which are very proper to make us love and observe it.

The first is that we may be cured of avarice, or attachment to earthly things. This passion, the sad consequence of sin, is one of the chief sources of the evils that afflict the world. In directing us to keep within the limits of necessity, the new Adam adopted the true means of eradicating it. Avarice once removed, the heart has no further difficulty in rising toward the love of superior goods. Almsgiving is therefore most necessary, and occupies a special place in the plan of our regeneration.

The second, that men may be continually reminded of this touching truth, obscured by sin, namely, that they are all brethren—that the world is only one great family, of which God is the Father. Christian societies are all based on this principle, whose violation brings about the most dreadful revolutions. Need we be surprised if the Redeemer so strongly insisted on the precept of almsgiving, which is the application of this principle, and if our carefulness or carelessness in complying with it shall serve as the leading matter of our judgment and the rule of his sentence?

The precept of almsgiving obliges us to give what is over and above of our goods. The rich are only God's stewards. Is it right that in a family some of the children should have all, and the others be left to gather the crumbs that fall from the table? To justify providence, must not the abundance of one party supply the indigence of the other? Ye rich of the world! hear what St. Augustine says to you: "If you had to remove your treasures to a distant country, and had great reason to fear the attacks of robbers, would you not be delighted if some highly respectable young man came to you and said, 'My father lives in the country to which you are going. He is very rich. Leave your money here with me. I shall have need of it. In return, I will give you a letter of exchange on my father. As soon as you present this letter to him after your arrival, you shall receive the amount.' Well, this highborn youth is the poor man. The country to which you travel is eternity. The rich man is God. Give, therefore, to the poor man, that you may receive from God. If you require guarantees, the poor man will offer you his rags. The more torn they are, the more certain you may be that everything you entrust to him will be restored to you. You say," adds the holy doctor, "'I have children.' Very good! Count one more of them, and give something to Jesus Christ." In fine, he calls the poor *laturarii*, that is to say, "porters": bearers of riches to heaven.

To understand the extent of this precept, so woefully neglected, it must be known a) that by *superfluity* is not meant what is necessary to one's life or state. What is necessary to one's life is that which is required for food and clothing. What is necessary to one's state is that which is required for the decency of one's condition or rank, every species of luxury being retrenched. It must also be known b) that there are three kinds of necessity in which we may find the neighbor. Extreme necessity, when the neighbor is in danger of losing his life. In this case, he ought to be succored even with the goods superfluous to one's life. Grave necessity, when the neighbor is in danger of falling from his justly acquired state or of incurring some other great misfortune. In this case, he ought to be succored with the goods superfluous to one's state. Finally, common necessity, that which is endured by beggars. Those who have goods superfluous to their state are bound, even by a strict obligation, to relieve poor beggars in some manner.[1072]

To be Christian, that is, useful and meritorious, alms ought to be given readily, with a good grace, from a supernatural motive, and without ostentation. Fulfilled thus, the precept of almsgiving not only procures us the sweetest and purest satisfaction, but it also delivers us from sin and damnation. It makes the Lord favorable toward us, atones for our sins, transforms our fleeting possessions into eternal treasures, and gives us the greatest confidence in the divine protection during our trials and especially at the hour of our death.[1073]

Even the temporal advantages of almsgiving it would take long to tell. We shall only say that an alms has been justly compared to a seed. A seed, cast into the earth, seems to be lost; but instead of being lost it multiplies itself, instead of perishing it enriches us. So with an alms, which, according to our Lord, returns a hundredfold even in this life. The history of Tobias, which we related in the first part[1074] of the catechism, is a proof of this, and the history of Tobias will be the history of every other almsgiver to the end of the world. If the poor bless us, it is impossible that God should not bless us. He himself has said, "Whatsoever you do to these little ones, who are my brethren, you do it to me."[1075] "It is Jesus Christ," adds one of the fathers of the Church, "who begs in all the poor: *Christus est qui in universitate pauperum mendicat*."[1076]

Society itself derives the greatest advantages from almsgiving. By it a multitude of passions, roaring like hungry lions around the possessions of the rich, are calmed. The selfishness of the great ends sooner or later by awakening a rebellion among the people.[1077] The best insurance companies are associations of charity.

There is no use in deceiving oneself. It is not philosophy that pipes or dances for the poor man, that calms his passions; it only angers them. Charity alone, Christian charity, she loves and draws near the poor man, weeps with him, smoothes his humble bed, shares all his miseries, she only can calm the desire of having in the heart of him who has not, teaching him by good deeds and kind words that those who have are really his brethren.

This one thought, well considered, ought to be enough to change the mind and conduct of most of the rich of our day.[1078] But must we still be condemned to hear it repeated again and again that alms degrade? Alms degrade! No, they do not degrade; since they are a fundamental precept of Christianity, and the rule on which the sentence of the supreme judge shall be based. Would you dare to say that Christianity is a degrading religion? Cast your eyes over the map of the world.

Alms degrade! No, they do not degrade; since they are a true social bond among Christian nations, and an indispensable condition of liberty. Without alms, be a slave or starve: this is all that is left to the poor man.

Alms degrade! No, they do not degrade; since it is not man who begs, but our Lord himself who makes an exchange with the rich, an exchange wholly for the advantage of the rich. Alms degrade neither him who takes nor him who gives, as a mercantile contract degrades neither of the parties who make it.

12. *Sins opposed to the love of the neighbor*. These sins are: a) hatred, directly opposed to charity; b) jealousy, opposed to the spiritual good of the neighbor; c) envy, opposed to the temporal good of the neighbor; d) discord, opposed to social and domestic union; e) schism, opposed to religious union; f) offense, opposed to beneficence; g) scandal, opposed to fraternal correction.[1079] We shall speak of them further on, when explaining the fifth commandment and the capital sins.

PRAYER

O my God! who art all love, I thank thee for having taught us that the first and greatest of all the commandments is to love thee. May my heart understand this important truth, observe it faithfully, and, by so doing, be united to the heart of the new Adam and freed from concupiscence!

I am resolved to love God above all things, and my neighbor as myself for the love of God; and, in testimony of this love, I will often make an act of perfect charity.

Lesson 47: Our Union with the New Adam by Charity (2)

The decalogue.—To love God above all things, and our neighbor as ourselves for the love of God, is the great precept of the Savior. It is the abridgment of all that God has commanded man—by himself, by the prophets, by the Messias in Person, by the apostles, by the Church. It is the summary of God's law, even to the consummation of ages. Now, we have already remarked that charity is not idle. It manifests itself, not by words, but by works: the works which God prescribes to us in his ten commandments. If we observe these commandments, we may rest assured that we love God. But to observe them, we must know them. The time is come to enter on their explanation.

Let us first of all bear in mind that the decalogue is only the application of the great precept of the love of God and the neighbor. If you examine it attentively, you will see that its only end is to teach us the acts by which we should exercise our charity, and protect this virtue from injury and even from destruction.

Division.—Hence, two kinds of precepts in the decalogue: some positive, commanding certain things to be done; others negative, forbidding certain things to be done. Thus we may consider the great precept of the love of God and the neighbor as a beautiful fountain of living water, which the first Adam closed by sin, but which the second Adam reopened in the midst of the world, to water it, refresh it, and make it bring forth abundant fruits of grace and salvation. The positive precepts of the decalogue are like so many different streams, conveying the riches of this sacred fountain to various parts of the earth. The negative precepts are like banks, which hinder the passions from troubling these limpid waters or turning them out of their course.

It is from this point of view that we must contemplate the decalogue, if we would understand the profound meaning of the Savior's numerous words regarding the sweetness of the divine law; among them, "Take up my yoke upon you, for my yoke is sweet and my burden light." This is the same as to say, "My yoke is love—the only end of all my other precepts is to preserve love; preserve it, and you shall find rest to your souls."[1080]

A few words will make this little-known truth palpable.

The first commandment, which requires us to love God, and to love nothing except for him, delivers us from every affection that could profane and sadden our heart. It preserves us from the misfortune of heathens, who offer their love and incense to demons, as well as from the misfortune of bad Christians, who attach themselves to the perishable goods of this world—deceitful goods, which, after tormenting, vanish without satisfying those who pursue them.

The second, which forbids us to blaspheme the holy name of God, preserves us from the contempt that we might conceive for His Divine Majesty, and so hinders our charity from growing weak; for we soon cease to love those whom we no longer respect.

The third, which prescribes to us the worship that we ought to render to God, preserves us from those shameful and inhuman superstitions with which idolaters used to dishonor and even to this day dishonor themselves. In obliging us to set aside one day every week for him, whether to refresh ourselves after our labors, or to thank him for his past blessings, or to ask him for new blessings, or to acknowledge humbly that whatever we have comes from him and belongs to him: he provides equally for our spiritual and our corporal good, and prevents the love of creatures from acquiring a mastery over our heart.

The fourth, by ordering us to behold and obey God in the persons of our superiors, ennobles obedience, and establishes society on an immovable basis. The Christian obeys not man, but God. He sees God in his superiors: it is the divine voice that he hears when they speak, it is the divine authority that he respects when they command. Hence, obedience is a motive always sacred, because God, whom alone the Christian obeys, is always the same, always infinite in power and goodness, whatever may be the gentleness or the severity, the virtues or the defects of those whom he appoints to command in his stead. If the fourth commandment contains the duties of inferiors, it also contains those of superiors. The lieutenants of God himself, they are his ministers for good. Kind, just, firm, watchful, they ought to command like God himself. Now, the end of obedience and authority is to maintain peace and charity among men on earth, so as to conduct them to their last end, which is the possession of God during eternity.

The fifth places the life of our body and of our soul beyond the reach of murder, scandal, revenge, and hatred. Under all these heads, it prevents an alteration of that charity which should unite men on earth as brethren, as members of the same family.

The sixth and ninth protect the honor of families. They defend our innocence and that of others against our own passions and those of others. Their end is to preserve the union of the domestic hearth, to hinder our love from degrading itself, and to maintain within us a delightful peace, inseparable from the fairest of the virtues.

The seventh and tenth secure our property against the injustice of the wicked. They protect the little and weak against the strength and covetousness of the great and rich. No more efficacious means of preventing cupidity from overcoming charity, and preserving society from disturbances, animosities, and revolutions, the sad consequences of ambition and injustice.

Lastly, the eighth protects our character. In proscribing false testimony, detraction, calumny, lies, it keeps good faith, mutual confidence, and loyalty alive among men. Without these things, there is no longer any union or security; but distrust, imposture, hypocrisy, and dissimulation: odious vices, which make the social life one continual torment.

We see therefore that the decalogue is only the organic law of the great precept of charity toward God and the neighbor. It is wholly for our advantage. All men are supremely interested in the observance of this divine law. They cannot violate a single article of it without offending against their own dearest interests, even in this life. If we have ever looked upon it as a painful yoke, as a shackle on our liberty, we have fallen into a gross error, for which we ought to humble ourselves and to beg pardon. The decalogue is the most admirable present that God could make to us, as the following comparison will show.

A traveler pursues his way toward a magnificent city, where a splendid fortune, as well as a beloved family, awaits him. Between him and the desired city there is a bottomless abyss. The country is shrouded in darkness. The traveler is without a guide or a light. Over the abyss there is only one common, narrow, shaky plank. There he must of necessity pass, and yet he is very liable to make a false step, as experience has too often convinced him.

If a charitable guide were to come and take this traveler by the hand, if he were to erect a strong barrier on each side of the fatal plank and fix thereon a number of bright lights, so that it would be impossible for the traveler to fall into the pit, unless by deliberately pulling down the barriers, could these services be regarded as unkind or unjust? And should this charitable guide be called a tyrant for offering his hand to a stranger, and delivering him from the greatest dangers? The application is easy.

This traveler is man on earth. The city, wherein happiness and a beloved family await him, is heaven. The abyss is hell. The weak, narrow, unsteady plank is life. The charitable guide is God. The barriers erected alongside the plank, and the lamps suspended therefrom, are the commandments of God.

After this, let the worldling who will follow naught but the bent of his passions, let the ill-instructed Christian, say that the ten commandments are unendurable fetters. As for us, O my God! we shall always say that the decalogue is one of thy greatest benefits, and we will take care never to violate it, that so we may not fall, during life, under the heavy yoke of our passions, and, after death, into the eternal abyss. To secure our happiness in this world and the next, to show that he is our master and that we are his servants and children, to teach us that we are free, and to make us acquire merits by the fulfillment of duty: such were God's chief motives in giving us the decalogue.[1081]

History.—This beautiful law of God, so well adapted to form the happiness and the glory of humanity, is nevertheless attacked, despised, calumniated by many; but sooner or later the moment will come when its most implacable enemies must render homage to it. Witness that philosopher of the last century, named Toussaint, whose works were so justly condemned.

This author, invited to Prussia by Frederic, was there attacked by a consumption, of which he died after a year of sufferings. On the eve of his death, he sent to his friends requesting them to be so kind as to come to him next morning at six o'clock, to assist at a religious ceremony which was then to take place in his house. The fact was, says one of them, that next morning we found the Catholic curé there, preparing to give the sick man the holy viaticum; at the foot of his bed were his wife and children on their knees: we put ourselves in the same position.

Then M. Toussaint, having had his pillows raised so that he might almost sit in the bed, requested the curé to wait a moment. Placing his son, who was some fifteen or sixteen years old, before his eyes, he addressed him thus, "My son, hear and remember well what I am going to say to you. I am now about to appear before God and to give him an account of my whole life. I have offended him much: I stand greatly in need of his mercy. For this, my son, are my repentance and confidence enough? Ah! they would doubtless be enough, considering the infinite goodness of God, if I had only to reproach myself with my own weakness and faults! But if I have scandalized, if I have offended other persons, is it not also necessary that they should in some manner intercede for me with God, by forgiving me themselves?

"Well, I rely on this act of charity on the part of those who may have to complain of me. I have been guilty of wrongs against your mother; and her piety, which is known to me, assures me that she will forgive me, as I beg her to do. I have been guilty of many negligences toward your sisters, the second article on which I should have to endure the most gloomy regrets, if I did not reflect that at their age impressions are still weak, and that your mother will be able and anxious to repair the evil by the sound Christian education which she will give them.

"There is only yourself left, my son. But now that I draw near my death, you are the subject of the most dreadful anguish and apprehension to me. I have scandalized you by a conduct anything but religious, and by maxims far from holy. Will you forgive me? Will you do what is necessary that God may forgive me? Can you by yourself attain to other principles than those which I have given you? Weigh well, my son, these late lessons of mine to you: I call to witness that God whom I am about to receive and before whom I am about to appear that if, during the past, I showed little of the Christian in my actions, speeches, and writings, it was never through conviction—it was only through human respect, vanity, and a desire to please various persons.

"If then you have any confidence in your father, employ it solely with the words which I this day utter to you. Would that you could engrave on your soul and ever keep vividly before you this last scene in your father's life! Place yourself on your knees, my son! and join your prayers with those of the other persons who now hear me and see you. Promise God that you will profit of my last lessons, and beseech him to forgive me."

Our own interest and that of the neighbor are powerful motives for observing the decalogue; but, of all motives, the strongest is that God himself is its author. This adorable law is as old as the world, but it was obscured by depravity of manners and a long series of crimes. God resolved to write it on tables of stone, to show that it was as lasting as himself. Hence, in giving the decalogue to Moses, the Lord was pleased rather to renew and revive a law already existing than to issue a new law.

We are bound to observe the decalogue because it is the law of the supreme legislator, the master of the world, the Creator and judge of all men, the immortal King whose wisdom and justice are infinite, whose power is irresistible. The necessity of observing the decalogue regards not only the poor and children, but the rich and the great, kings and nations, because it is by the decalogue that all shall be judged. It is to the observance of this law, given from heaven, that the glory, tranquility, and prosperity of mankind in this world, and their felicity in the next, are attached. Woe to the nations who do not take the decalogue as the basis of their legislation! They either cease to advance, or relapse sooner or later into barbarism.

When God gave the decalogue to Moses, he engraved it on two tables of stone. On one were the first three commandments, on the other the last seven. Thus, the decalogue is divided into two parts: the first contains the commandments which regulate our duties toward God; the second, those which regulate our duties toward the neighbor. What a difference between this code of morality, so short and complete, so wise and fruitful, and those drawn up by legislators and philosophers, who were thought the most wonderful sages in the world!

Evangelical counsels.—Our Lord, being sent by God his Father to instruct us and to guide us to perfection, added to the decalogue some counsels, the practice of which, without being obligatory, is well calculated to secure the observance of the commandments and to promote the happiness of society. In effect, his three principal counsels, opposed to the three great passions of man, are poverty, chastity, and obedience. United voluntarily in immense families, those who engage themselves by vow to follow these counsels become the slaves of Christian society. They renounce all, and, content with poor food and clothing no less poor, establish and maintain, in favor of every species of human misery, those public and gratuitous services of charity which give so much repose to Christian nations, and whose suppression is one of the chief causes of the terrible dangers that threaten us.[1082]

Necessity and possibility of observing the decalogue.—It remains to be known whether we can keep all the commandments of the man-God. The Church, as good sense itself would dictate, condemned those heretics who dared to reply in the negative.[1083] In effect, God, being infinitely wise and good, cannot command anything impossible to us. If the accomplishment of his law is above the strength of nature, he is careful to give us grace by which we may rise to the level of our duty. The example of saints of all ages, conditions, and climes is an unanswerable proof of this truth. Now, grace will no more fail us than it failed the saints: the same faith, the same hope, the same sacraments, the same gospel! We have yet more than they—the help of their example and prayers.

It is not enough to maintain that we can keep the commandments of God: we must also acknowledge that it is easier to keep them than to break them, that it costs more to be damned than to be saved. Besides, it is more honorable to obey God than passion. Further, it is sweeter to have the soul filled with peace than gnawed with remorse. Lastly, it is easier to satisfy God than the world and our own irregular inclinations.

Daily experience shows us that it costs the ambitious, the covetous, or the vindictive man much more to reach his ends than the Christian to reach heaven. This truth, which has been too often surrounded with illusion, will be proclaimed, in tones of bitter despair, by the wicked themselves on the day of judgment. "Fools! we wearied ourselves in the ways of iniquity: what tortuous paths we trod! What disgusts, what deceptions, what disgraces did we not undergo, to reach at length a misery without end and without remedy!"[1084] So much being granted, we come to a detailed explanation of each commandment.

First commandment.—The first commandment, "One only God thou shalt adore and love," commands us: a) to adore God; b) to love him with our whole heart; c) to adore him alone.[1085]

1. *To adore* God. The word *adore* means "to raise the hand to the mouth"—to kiss one's hand out of a sentiment of reverence. Throughout the East, this gesture was one of the greatest marks of respect and submission. It was used toward God and man. Employed toward man, it indicated a deep respect and submission. Thus, Pharao, speaking to Joseph, says, "All my people shall kiss the hand at your command; they shall receive your orders as those of the king."[1086] Employed toward God, it denoted the supreme worship which is due to him alone. This is the reason why Job protests that he never used it toward any creature: "If I beheld the sun in his splendor and the moon in her brightness...if I kissed my hand with a secret joy—which is a very great sin, and a denial of the most high God," etc.[1087] In the third book of Kings, the Lord speaks thus: "I will leave me

seven thousand men..., whose knees have not bowed to Baal, and whose mouths have not worshipped him, kissing hands."[1088] To adore God is therefore to acknowledge him the being of beings, the Creator, the preserver, the sovereign Lord of all things.

2. *To love God.* We already know in what the love which we owe to God consists. It remains for us to show that we fulfill the duty of adoration and love toward His Supreme Majesty by the practice of four virtues, namely: faith, hope, charity, and religion. By faith we acknowledge that God is and alone is the sovereign truth; by hope, that he is and alone is sovereign goodness; by charity, that he is and alone is love itself, the assemblage of all perfections. Such is the homage, in spirit and in truth, which the first commandment obliges us to render to God, considered in himself.

But since God is truth, goodness, love, in a word, infinite perfection, it follows that he is the being of beings, the Creator, the ruler, the absolute master of all things—of man as well as of angels and material creatures. If then the servant owes respect and honor to his master, the subject to his prince, the soldier to his general, the son to his father, it is evident that man also owes respect and honor to God.

Moreover, if the respect and honor due by inferiors ought to be measured according to the greater or less excellence and authority of their superiors, it is also evident that the respect and honor which man owes to God ought to be in proportion to the excellence and authority of God. Now God being, as we have said, the being of beings, the most mighty and perfect of all beings, the absolute master of all things, we owe him the deepest reverence and the highest homage; in a word, we owe him, as Catholic theology speaks, the worship of adoration or *latria*. It is by the virtue of religion that we render to him this necessary worship.[1089]

Virtue of religion.—The virtue of religion is therefore an essential part of justice and the first of moral virtues.[1090] Its acts are internal and external. The chief internal acts of the virtue of religion are devotion and prayer. Devotion is the act of the will which devotes itself, that is, which offers itself to God to perform promptly and joyfully whatever belongs to his service. Nothing more honorable to God than this promptitude. It is a most glorious homage rendered to his supreme authority, justice, and goodness. Nothing more useful to man, whose will is perfected by submission to the infinitely perfect will of God.

They therefore who allow themselves the liberty of turning devotion into ridicule, know not what they do. Not a day passes but they speak of their devotion to their family, to their friends, to their country, to their interests. They glory in it, and yet they will not see that the devotion of a Christian to God, to his service, to the interests of his glory, which are also the true interests of the family and society, is a thing incomparably more honorable and useful.[1091]

Prayer is the second internal act of the virtue of religion. Hereby man acknowledges that he is indigence itself, and that God is the author of every good. This is a sublime act of homage. Prayer therefore, as well as devotion, is honorable to God. It is not only for himself, as a debt of reverence and thanksgiving, that God requires it; but also for man, in order to perfect him by placing him in his true relations of dependence and filial confidence with his heavenly Father.[1092] What concerns prayer having been already treated of, we shall say no more of it now.

The external acts of the virtue of religion are adoration, sacrifice, oblation, and vow.

Adoration. Adoration includes all those external signs by which we acknowledge the supreme dominion of God over us, and the sentiments with which this knowledge inspires us. Such are prostrations, genuflections, and the various other marks of respect and submission that we give to God. Nothing more natural than adoration. It is impossible that the soul, animated with a profound feeling of any truth, should not manifest this feeling outwardly. Nothing more necessary. Man, being composed of a body and a soul, owes to God the homage of his whole being. This is the reason why adoration has been in use at all times and among all peoples. But the body can only adore God by external acts, which are all referable to the internal adoration of which they are the expression, as the body itself is referable to the soul. If it were otherwise, external adoration would be only a mockery and a delusion.[1093]

Sacrifice. Sacrifice is an offering made to God of a sensible thing, which is destroyed or notably changed in his honor, as an acknowledgment of his supreme dominion over creatures. Sacrifice is the essential act of external worship, and it springs from the law of nature. In fact, from the moment man knew God and was himself known, an obligation lay on him to confess, by an external testimony, the absolute right of life and death which God possesses over man and over every other creature in existence. This is the reason why sacrifice is found, from the beginning of the world, among all peoples and in all countries. It is evident that sacrifice is an act of adoration which can be offered to none but God. With greater authority than that of an individual, the Catholic Church so teaches. Heretics are therefore wrong in accusing us of offering sacrifice to the Blessed Virgin and the other saints.[1094]

Oblation. Oblation includes all that is given to God, to be employed in his worship, the ornamentation of his temples and altars, and the maintenance of his ministers. Like sacrifice, oblation comes from the law of nature, in this sense that man is bound to consecrate to the honor of God some part of the goods which he has received from the divine liberality.[1095] In the old law, the Lord required the oblation of the first fruits of the earth. In the new, the Church also appointed certain oblations, and it must be said that Christian ages acquitted themselves magnificently of this debt of gratitude. Witness all the foundations, decorations, sacred vessels, precious stones, riches of every kind, that went to the beauty of God's house, to the support of the poor, and ultimately to the riotous waste of impious plunderers.

Vow. A vow, which consists in dedicating one's person or property to the worship of God, is certainly an act of religion, approved in the old as well as in the new law, and practiced among all peoples. We shall speak of it in our next lesson.[1096]

3. *To adore God alone.* It is evident, after what has been said, that God alone has a right to our adoration, and to our love above all things created. To maintain the contrary would be to defend idolatry or atheism.

Sins contrary to the virtue of religion.—Now that we know the virtues and the acts by which we adore and love God perfectly, it is necessary to point out the sins that are contrary to this obligation, the holiest in the world. The sins opposed to faith, hope, and charity, are all contrary to the first commandment: we have already spoken of them. Those which directly attack the virtue of religion are chiefly three: irreligion, superstition, and unlawful worship.

1. *Irreligion; tempting of God.* The works of irreligion are those by which a wound is inflicted on the honor and respect due to God. Such are tempting of God, sacrilege, impiety, and simony. To tempt God is to make trial, without a just cause, of the power, wisdom, justice, mercy, or any other attribute of God.

Examples: to walk on water, believing that God will uphold us on its surface; to flatter ourselves with the prospect of success in an enterprise, while we neglect the ordinary means established by providence; to seek a miracle without necessity or reason; to expect from God the things necessary for life, while we pass our days in sloth and idleness; not to prepare our soul before prayer, or to pray without attention, while we think to obtain what we ask so negligently; to sin more freely through the hope of pardon, or to imagine that we shall be saved without forsaking sin or observing faithfully the law of God. This last mode of tempting God is very common, and, like the others, a great sin.

Sacrilege. Sacrilege is a profanation of anything holy. Its object may be persons, places, or things. To strike an ecclesiastic or a religious, or to be guilty of an immodest action with a person consecrated by a vow of chastity, would be a personal sacrilege.

To profane holy places is a local sacrilege. By *holy places* are meant churches or chapels, blessed for the purpose of rendering therein the worship due to God; also, cemeteries. Sins committed in these places add to their special malice the guilt of profanation.

Real sacrilege occurs when one profanes holy things. For example, it would be a sacrilege to profane chalices, patens, or altar linens known under the names of corporals, purificators, and palls, which the simple faithful cannot touch after they have been used at the sacrifice. But the most horrible of all sacrileges is to receive the sacraments in a state of mortal sin.

Impiety. Impiety is a formal and affected contempt of religion. Hence, those become guilty of impiety who a) ridicule the practices, ordinances, and ceremonies of the Church, or who outrage crosses and holy images; and those who, b) by their indifference about the duties of religion, preach up a contempt for God and his Church. More dangerous than the former, since the most dangerous sophism is bad example, the latter are often much more guilty, because their conduct is a habitual contempt of authority. For the indifferent, the greatest share in the demoralization of nations, and the most terrible responsibility before God and society!

We cannot be too much on our guard against the writings and speeches of the impious and the pernicious example of the indifferent; for impiety and indifference go hand in hand at the present day to destroy the kingdom of virtue. The faithful ought not to forget that it is rigorously forbidden to print, to sell, to buy, to read, to lend, or to keep impious and heretical books, in which the truths of religion are directly or indirectly attacked; likewise, all works condemned by the Holy See.[1097]

Simony. Simony is the sin of him who traffics in holy things, that is, who sells or buys them for money.[1098] It is reckoned among the most cruel and detestable outrages that can be committed against God.

2. *Superstition.* If irreligion is opposed to the first commandment by defect, superstition is opposed to it by excess. Superstition is a false, exaggerated, superfluous worship. To render to creatures a worship that is due only to God is an abominable superstition: it is the crime of heathens, who adore the devil under the figures of their idols. There is not among Christians any idolatry properly so called; but there is a kind of recourse to the devil which is very common: it is this recourse to the infernal spirit that is properly called superstition. The chief ways in which recourse is had to the devil, are magic, divination, sorcery, and vain observance.

Magic. Magic is an invocation of the devil for the purpose of producing by his help wonderful effects. We see many examples of it in the scripture; among the rest, that of the magicians of Pharao. This diabolical art was widely diffused among the pagans, as all their histories bear witness.[1099]

Divination. Divination is an invocation of the devil for the purpose of knowing things to come. This abominable practice took its rise with idolatry, as both sacred and profane history attest. How often does the Lord reproach his people with their perversity in consulting strange gods![1100] At the present time we find a great number of fortune-tellers, card-drawers, magnetizers, and somnambulists, that is to say, men and women who make profession of knowing the future and revealing the deepest secrets.

Sorcery. Sorcery is an invocation of the devil for the purpose of doing an injury to others, by pronouncing against them certain words, laying certain objects in their house, etc. More criminal than the preceding practices, sorcery is also of very ancient date in the world.

Vain observance. Vain observance is an invocation of the devil for the purpose of doing a service to oneself or to others. It is vain observance when the means that one employs cannot naturally produce what one desires. Hence, all those vain practices which are tried in cities, and still more in the country, to cure the various diseases of men and beasts, are to be condemned. This kind of superstition is as old as the others. The testimonies of scripture and profane history leave us no room to doubt of it.[1101]

You will doubtless ask us what is to be thought of all these superstitious practices, opposed to the virtue of religion. a) It is certain, being formally taught in the scripture, that the devil cannot act on man but by the express permission of God. b) It is certain that God sometimes grants the devil this permission, either to manifest his own glory or to punish those who abandon themselves to their passions: witness the magicians of Pharao, the possessed persons healed by our Lord, and many other examples related in the holy books. c) It is certain that there have always been, even in the bosom of Christianity, occult practices by which man could put himself into communication with the devil. d) It is certain that, taken in their entirety, these occult practices are not juggleries, and that they increase in proportion as faith diminishes. e) It is certain that the devil is most anxious to obtain the honor due to God—on which very account he was cast out of heaven; and that he is most jealous of the good fortune of man in being called to occupy his place in the abode of glory—on which account, as he cannot have the pleasure of injuring God, he does everything in his power to ruin us. He consequently neglects no means of filling the world with darkness and falsehood.

He has succeeded only too well, since all peoples, with the exception of the Jews, adored him at the time of the coming of the Messias. At the present day he is making his greatest efforts to reestablish his kingdom. These efforts are specially manifested in somnambulism, magnetism, and spiritism.

Somnambulism. The somnambulism of which we here speak is an artificial or fictitious somnambulism. It is an intermediate state between waking and sleeping, partaking of the nature of both, and producing phenomena that belong to neither. The person brought into a state of somnambulism by the will of another, obeys him blindly, answers his questions, points out the remedies required by the sick, gives counsel for the direction of conduct, reveals things hidden, makes known events occurring at a distance. He enjoys in this state a degree of lucidity and penetration that is not natural: so much so that, having returned to himself, he remembers nothing of what he has said or done.

Magnetism. Magnetism, which has many points of resemblance with somnambulism, is, according to its partisans, the faculty that man possesses of exercising, by means of a fluid, a secret influence over his fellows and even over other beings. The person on being magnetized acquires an extraordinary power, so as to say and do the most wonderful things. For example, to see with the eyes bandaged; to become insensible to sounds or blows; to speak appropriately on matters never studied; to tell what is passing at an immense distance, and to give information regarding things that cannot be known naturally.

Spiritism. Spiritism is an evocation of the souls of the dead. It is an old superstition, known under the name of necromancy. Sheltering himself under the title of the souls of the dead, it is the devil who answers the callers of the spirits, who deceives them, who entangles them in his snares, and who guides them to folly and suicide. Spiritualism is the religion of the devil: it is a manifest return to idolatry and the latest evolution of the satanic principle in the modern world.

Now somnambulism, magnetism, and spiritism, whose existence and phenomena it is impossible to deny, are guilty practices and are justly condemned. No person therefore can take part in them, or favor them by his presence or advice, or read without permission the works written to propagate them.[1102]

All the superstitious practices of which we have just spoken, and more besides, having become very common in Europe since the Renaissance, tend to restore the empire of the devil, and, under one form or another, paganism. This being their end, we see in the scripture that God has always punished them most severely. The organ of God, the Church herself pronounces the heaviest penalties against those who have anything to do with them. In the early ages she condemned such persons, some to seven, others to five years' public penance.

They who employ practices of this kind need not say, to justify themselves, that they do not intend to have recourse to the devil. It is false. For one has recourse tacitly to the devil as often as, to obtain a desired effect, he employs a cause that cannot produce this effect either in virtue of the promises of God or by the strength of nature. Now, in the occult practices of which there is question, you cannot expect the realization of your desires either from God or nature. Wherefore, it is only from the devil that you can expect it.

Let us give an example. You are sick. A man offers to cure you by means of some strange words or curious signs. He declares that success is certain. It is not from God that he can expect your cure, since both God and the Church forbid the employment of such a means to procure it. Neither is it from nature, since there is no natural relation between certain words or signs and a return of health. If health therefore be restored, it must evidently be attributed to some other power than that of God or nature: which power can only be that of the devil. The spirit of falsehood, he suggests these artifices to deceive men, to win their confidence, to separate them from God, and finally to destroy them.

It is therefore forbidden to have recourse to any of these practices. In vain will a person say that he desires to obtain a cure for himself, or for another, or for beasts, or that he is anxious to know the future or to succeed in some enterprise: the end can never justify the means.

Cards. To draw, or to cause others to draw, cards with a view to divine what will happen is also a sin. "I don't believe them," says one. If so, the sin is less. But is it quite certain that they are not believed? If this were the case, why would they be called into service? "I do it to amuse myself." Is it then quite certain that you have never been delighted or alarmed at the answer of the cards?

Omens. Omens are not superstitions properly so called, because in believing them there is no worship rendered to any other than God—commonly speaking. Hence we cannot regard as sins, at least grievous, the prejudices of persons, more than simple, who fear certain numbers, as to find thirteen sitting at table; certain days, as to begin a work or a journey on Friday; certain occurrences, as the upsetting of a salt-cellar; certain signs, as a knife and fork laid in the form of a cross.

Dreams. As for dreams, which must not be confounded with visions, they may come from God or the devil. Before attaching any credit to them, and especially before acting in consequence of them, it is necessary to make sure of their origin, and for this purpose to submit them to the examination of an enlightened confessor. To believe dreams without this precaution is a weakness of mind, always dangerous, but rarely exceeding a venial fault.[1103]

3. *Unlawful worship.* Unlawful worship is that which is rendered to God otherwise than is due to him, circumstances which cannot be agreeable to him being mixed up with it. The Church has settled all that pertains to the Holy Sacrifice of the Mass, to the administration of the sacraments, to the divine office, to sacred worship in general, whereby men can and should render honor to God and the saints. Hence, we a) ought not to offer to God a worship that the Church does not propose; and we b) ought never to mix up with the worship proposed by the Church anything that the Church cannot approve. The worship of the Catholic Church is beautiful enough, varied enough, proper enough

to speak to the heart and to express all our sentiments in regard to God, without adding any further practices to it. These additions, often ridiculous, are suited more to excite the scorn of the impious than to confer any real benefit on those who make use of them.[1104]

Worship of angels and saints.—The first commandment forbids the rendering of supreme worship to anyone but God. From this our separated brethren have concluded that it is not permitted to render to the angels and saints an inferior and subordinate worship. On this point, as on the rest, they have done violence to logic, and set themselves in opposition to scripture, to tradition, and even to reason. In effect, these three last mentioned authorities teach with one voice that the worship of angels and saints is most ancient, most lawful, most useful, and most consoling.

1. *It is most ancient.*[1105] Abraham prostrates himself before the angels who appear to him. Jacob, having wrestled with an angel, asks his blessing, and will not let him go till it is granted. Josue sees an angel, who says to him, "I am a prince of the host of the Lord." Immediately the leader of the Hebrew people falls on his face to the ground, and exclaims, "What saith my lord to his servant?" The angel replies, "Take away thy shoes from thy feet, for the place where thou art is holy." And Josue does as he is commanded.

Daniel also prostrates himself before an angel who comes to reveal the future to him. The officer sent to arrest Elias prostrates himself before the holy man, and addresses a fervent prayer to him. The Sunamitess, seeing her son restored to life, falls on her knees before the prophet, and adores him. It would be easy to multiply other testimonies from the old testament, which prove that the invocation of angels and saints was a usage in the synagogue.[1106]

In the new testament, we find it from the earliest days of the infant Church. A celebrated protestant, Leibnitz, admits the point candidly. "It is certain," he says, "that in the second century the memory of the martyrs was already celebrated, and that religious assemblies were held around their tombs."[1107] In speaking thus, he is the echo of all the traditions written in books, engraved on monuments, and embodied in the practices of the early Christians.

St. Irenaeus represents the Blessed Virgin as the Mother of all men and the advocate of the human race. "To her," he adds, "we ought to have recourse in all our necessities and afflictions."[1108] "O sacred Mother of God!" cries out St. Ephrem, "we fly to thy protection: guard and shelter us under the wings of thy mercy and goodness. O God! full of compassion, we beseech thee, through the intercession of the Blessed Virgin Mary, and of all the angels and saints, to have mercy on thy creature."[1109]

"We ought to invoke the angels," says Origen, "for God has appointed them to take care of us and to watch over our salvation." "I fall on my knees," he exclaims, "and not daring, because of my sins, to offer my prayers to God, I summon all the saints to my assistance. O all ye saints of heaven! I invoke you with tears and sighs: cast yourselves at the feet of the God of mercy, and pray to him for me, a miserable sinner!"[1110] "In order," writes Eusebius, "to honor the soldiers of true piety, the dear friends of God, we go to their tombs to present our supplications to them, as to holy souls, acknowledging that their intercession with the eternal is in no small degree helpful."[1111] It would be necessary to transcribe the fathers and doctors from beginning to end if we desired to collect all the passages that establish the perpetuity of the worship of angels and saints in the Catholic Church.

2. *It is most lawful.* Even adopting the principles of protestants, who do the Roman Church the honor of regarding her as free from error till the sixth century, it suffices to establish, as we have done, the antiquity of the worship of angels and saints, in order to render its lawfulness unquestionable. Let us, however, give a few direct proofs of this truth. First, we do not act against the first commandment. We know this commandment

as well as our separated brethren, since every Catholic repeats it daily: "One only God thou shalt adore and love." From the fact that a king forbids any of his subjects to assume the dignity of king, and to require the honors reserved for royalty, can you conclude that this king forbids the rendering of honor to magistrates? Protestants are therefore unjust when they accuse us of adoring the saints, and of lessening, by this means, the glory of our Lord. We do not adore the Blessed Virgin, nor the angels, nor the saints: we only honor them with a secondary worship, which is referred to God.

This worship is not the slightest encroachment on the mediation of our Lord. We believe and teach that there is only one mediator, Jesus Christ, and that his mediation is all-powerful. If we invoke the saints, it is to ask them to join their prayers with ours, that we may more effectually obtain from this only mediator the graces of which we stand in need. Such is the sense in which, from the times of the apostles down to our own, the Catholic Church has always honored and invoked the angels and saints.

Far from considering the saints as mediators in the same sense as Jesus Christ, the Church places the mediation of the Savior in his wish to sanctify us and in the infinite virtue of his sacrifice. In the saints she sees mere intercessors, who may ask grace for mankind, without being able to give it. Thus, the saints remain in heaven what they were on earth, creatures, offering to their Creator the worship of thanksgiving and supplication.

Hence the twofold manner of speaking which the Church uses in addressing God and the saints. To God, she says, "Give us." To the angels and saints, "Pray for us." For the rest, protestants are here in contradiction with themselves. They willingly recommend themselves to one another's prayers, and never suppose that they thus weaken the only true and all-powerful mediation of our Lord, or fall into idolatry. Is there any more reason for supposing that one falls into idolatry by recommending himself to the prayers of the saints? The petition that we address to the friends of God who are in heaven is exactly the same as the request that protestants make without scruple to their friends on earth. The only difference about the matter is that we have greater confidence in the prayers of the saints, who, already purified, behold God face-to-face in the abode of bliss. Such is the perfectly lawful worship that we render to the angels and the saints.

3. *It is most useful.* First, they are acquainted with our prayers. God can give them this knowledge, as no one can dispute; that he gives it to them in effect, no one can deny. This belief is the foundation of the invocation of saints, approved in scripture, and always practiced as well in the synagogue as in the Church. What is the use, in point of fact, of invoking angels and saints, if they do not hear us? Moreover, does not our Lord tell us in formal terms that the conversion of one sinner causes more joy in heaven than the perseverance of ninety-nine just?[1112] Therefore the conversion of a sinner in this world is known to the inhabitants of the other. Does he not show us also the rich man speaking from the depths of hell to Abraham, who hears him and answers him? In his answer, Abraham speaks of Moses and the prophets: he knows therefore that they existed.

Besides, many of the saints, while they were on earth, knew hidden things. Eliseus knew the conduct of his servant Giezi; St. Peter, the deception of Ananias and Saphira; St. Benedict, the artifice of Totila. Now that they are in heaven, where they see all things in God as in a mirror, why should they no longer know anything of what occurs on earth? Finally, our Lord said that the saints should have power over the nations, because he himself would associate them to his victory, as they had been associated to his warfare. How do they exercise this power, if they do not know what takes place among men?[1113]

More powerful than we, because more pleasing to God, they can render our prayers more efficacious, by uniting their own supplications with them. It is on account of their merits that God grants us a multitude of graces and benefits. It often happens, says St. Augustine, that God only grants what is asked through the intervention of a mediator.[1114]

We have a proof of this in the friends of Job, who were indebted to the holy man's prayers for the pardon of their sins.[1115]

Here again it would be necessary to cite the whole history of the Church, if one wished to relate the innumerable and, according to the admission of protestants themselves, most authentic facts which establish the power of the angels and saints in bringing our petitions to a successful issue. Hence, the Angelic Doctor does not go too far when he says, "The worship of the saints is one of our duties, since the order of providence requires that inferior beings should attain their end through the intervention of superior beings. God therefore wishes that we who are on earth should go to heaven through the assistance of the saints, obtaining by their intercession the graces necessary for our salvation."[1116] The holy Council of Trent is therefore the organ of the belief of all ages, a belief that neither impiety nor heresy can ever root out of the hearts of the people, when it teaches that the worship of the saints is most praiseworthy and useful.[1117]

4. *It is most consoling.* On the one hand, it is sweet to think that this worship, far from lessening, actually increases the glory of our heavenly Father. In effect, it wonderfully raises the hopes of men, by teaching them how great is the influence enjoyed by the friends of God, and powerfully excites them to walk in the footsteps of the saints. On the other hand, this consoling worship forms the bond that, by a kind of pious commerce in favors asked and obtained, unites the Church militant with the Church triumphant—the pilgrims of life, still exposed to the sorrows and struggles of this land of exile, with those blessed creatures who already rejoice in the unmixed felicity of the heavenly Jerusalem. In vain has a gloomy and withering doctrine striven to represent this worship, cherished by love and hope in the depths of the human heart, as an inexcusable idolatry. It remains alive in every generous soul, even when, by the misfortune of birth, that soul is found torn away from the arms of the common mother of mankind, the holy Catholic Church.[1118]

Worship of relics.—The worship that we render to the relics of the saints is a consequence of that which we render to their persons. We honor the relics of the saints because their bodies were the living temples of the Holy Ghost, and, having been the instruments of all their virtues, will hereafter share in the eternal glory of their blessed souls. This worship has the same qualities as the foregoing, with which it is identified. The scripture is full of facts which show that the worship rendered not only to the bodies of the saints, but also to objects that belonged to them, is most agreeable to God and advantageous to us.[1119]

In the early ages, we see it practiced with a holy enthusiasm by our predecessors in the faith. Who has not heard of the honors rendered to the remains of the first martyrs—St. Peter, St. Paul, St. Ignatius, St. Polycarp; of the oratories, the churches raised over their ashes; of the tears, the prayers poured out at their tombs; of the value attached to their bones, and especially to a few drops of their blood?[1120] Who will venture to blame this homage? Is it not a fact that among all peoples it is the custom to render solemn honors to the remains of great men, of dauntless heroes, of national benefactors? And who are the men or heroes or benefactors to be compared with our saints and martyrs?

Who can doubt of the holiness and usefulness of this worship, when he considers the wonders wrought at the tombs of the saints and by the touch of their sacred remains? There the blind have recovered sight, life has been restored to the dead, and devils have been cast out of the possessed. All these miracles have been attested by witnesses supremely deserving of credit. St. Augustine and St. Ambrose,[1121] among the number, relate many such miracles, not as having read them in histories, or heard them from the lips of others, but as having seen them with their own eyes.

"In the town of Hippo," says the former, "there was a man named Bassus, originally from Syria. This man was one day praying before the relics of St. Stephen the martyr for a daughter of his who was dangerously ill, when some of his people ran to let him know that she had just died. But, being met by a few friends, they were hindered from breaking the sad intelligence to him, lest he should give way to his grief in public. When he had returned to his house, which rang with the cries of its inmates, and had laid a dress belonging to his daughter, which he had borne with him to the church, over the pallid corpse, life was immediately restored.

"Audure," continues the holy bishop, "is a district where there is a church, and in this church a chapel of St. Stephen. Now, it happened that as a little child was once playing in a courtyard, some oxen drawing a wagon came up, and, getting off their track, rolled a wheel over it. The child was killed on the spot. Its mother, taking it up, carried it away forthwith to the saint's shrine, where it not only recovered its life, but there was not the slightest trace of a hurt left on it.

"I might," adds St. Augustine, "relate many other miracles. If I only wished to recount all the cures that have been wrought at Calamus and Hippo by the glorious martyr St. Stephen, they would occupy many volumes. Yet they would only be those of which some brief records have been drawn up for reading to the people. For we have ordered such records to be made, seeing in our own times miracles like those of former times, and considering that the memory of them should not be allowed to perish."[1122]

What is there surprising herein? If the garments of the saints, if their very shadow, before their death, could banish sickness, who will venture to say that God cannot work the same miracles by means of their sacred ashes and bones? Did not the corpse which was laid in the sepulchre of Elias return to life as soon as it touched the remains of the prophet?[1123] Nourished by a multitude of proofs like these, a feeling of confidence in the saints and their relics is too general to be suspected of fraud, and too deeply rooted in the hearts of men ever to be destroyed.

Worship of images.—As for the crucifix, and images of our Lord, of the Blessed Virgin, and of the saints, we honor them because they awaken in our minds the most tender recollections. Here, again, Catholics are the faithful disciples of all antiquity. Do we not find in the scripture that God directs Moses to make a brazen serpent, and to expose it to the view of the Hebrews, that they may be healed of the bite of the serpents? Were there not two golden cherubim above the ark? Did not David, and all the people with him, prostrate before the ark of the Lord? Does not the Lord himself tell us to respect his footstool? Are not all the monuments of the catacombs so many holy images, venerated of old by the faithful, and reminding us to this day of the mysteries of religion?

Not that there is in crucifixes or images any virtue for which they ought to be honored. No, we ask nothing of such things; we place no confidence in them like that which heathens place in their idols. The honor which is rendered to them is referred to the persons whom they represent. In kissing them, in saluting them by uncovering the head, and in kneeling before them, it is our Lord and the saints, figured by them, whom we venerate. Thus, the child that kisses its father's picture does not offer its respect or affection to paint or canvass, but to the dear object brought vividly before its mind thereby.

Such, therefore, is the worship which the Catholic Church renders to the Blessed Virgin, the angels, and the saints. a) She does not adore them. b) She bears toward them that interior respect which is due to the Mother of God and the princes of the heavenly court. c) She honors exteriorly their names, their images, their tombs, their altars, their relics. d) After the example of all antiquity, she authorizes pilgrimages to their shrines. e) She implores their assistance. f) She celebrates their festivals and narrates to the people their admirable deeds. g) She teaches the imitation of their virtues. What is there in all this that is not most ancient, most lawful, must useful, and most consoling?

Enough on this subject. Let us pass to another order of ideas. From the beginning of this work, we have seen that religion, in all its parts, is an immense benefit; and, moreover, that it is as solid as the earth and as bright as the sun: the cause and the end of all events. It follows that religion, instead of being regarded as a nonentity, should enter into all the meditations of men, whether their genius be sublime or shallow, as it enters into all the thoughts of God and all the occurrences of time.

It should enter into all the meditations of politicians, for whom it alone can furnish even the definition of polity; into all the meditations of philosophers, who, without it, can only swell the list of absurdities with which Cicero, two thousand years ago, reproached the philosophers of his period;[1124] into all the meditations of economists, who, without the data which it supplies, can only put forth utopias, whose infallible end is the ruin of the wealthy, the misery of the poor, and social anarchy.

To examine, without further preamble, the first commandment of the decalogue: see what a mighty and salutary influence it exercises on society!

Social advantages of the first commandment.—"One only God thou shalt adore and love." You think, perhaps, that the only result of the observance or the violation of this precept is the eternal happiness or misery of the individual. This would be something, no doubt; but let us not advance to eternity yet, let us delay a while on earth.

"One only God thou shalt adore." It is to this command, Christian peoples! that you are indebted for your intellectual superiority over ancient peoples and over those peoples on whom the light of the gospel has not yet shone! To it you are indebted for the happiness that you do not bow your heads, like the Romans, before Jupiter the corrupt and revengeful; like the Athenians, before Mercury the robber; like the Gauls, before Teutates the eater of children; like the Corinthians, before Venus the prostitute; like the Egyptians, before a crocodile, an onion, or a cat; like the negroes of Central Africa, before a boa-constrictor; like the Hindus and Chinese, before a hundred monstrous divinities; like the savages of America, before the vermilion-dyed trunk of a tree!

That you may be well aware that it is to this command, "One only God thou shalt adore," that you are indebted for a deliverance from those gross idolatries, go back in imagination to the 14th November, 1793, and see what occurred at the Church of Notre-Dame in Paris. A whole people, the leaders of civilization, fell lower than the heathens of old. They prostrated themselves before—what?...I dare not utter it. You must supply the rest.[1125]

Is it all the same to the material well-being of society, whether you adore an infinitely good God, who defends the life of man as the apple of his eye, or divinities that rigorously exact human victims; a thrice holy God, who condemns the very thought of crime, or gods that not only permit all kinds of vice, even adultery and theft, but authorize such things, and make them in a manner divine by their example? "And why should not I do that which the gods permit?" Is not this the everlasting refrain of men whose hearts are corrupt? As you know, their number in our times is great.

"One only God thou shalt adore and love." Take away this commandment, and tell me, I pray, what foundation is left for society? Man can only command his fellow man in the name of God or in the name of force. But the empire of force, applied to free beings, is despotism. Obedience, then, is slavery, and rebellion becomes the holiest of duties in the eyes of the people: I need say no more. Is all this immaterial to society?

"One only God thou shalt adore." Take away this commandment, and do you think that you will be more free? Ye blind! in arrogating to yourselves the right to defy God, you acquire that of bearing the yoke of human passions: this is the right of fools and madmen. What dignity there is in abjuring all that elevates the soul and ennobles life!

"And love." We require another heart. So long as we cannot find it, we are uneasy, consequently unhappy. God offers us his, and he begs—what do I say?—to encourage our timidity, he commands us to accept it. Take away this commandment: What will speedily follow for society? Man will love only himself; for there are two loves—the love of God and the love of oneself. Now, the exclusive love of oneself, or selfishness, is the hatred of everyone else. But universal hatred draws in its train a host of evils—distrust, jealousy, fraud, murder, the blackest crimes—which threaten the complete overthrow of society. Is not modern history at hand, with its soiled and blood-stained pages, to justify this remark?

Take away this command to love, and you degrade man. You make him a beast that ruminates, a plant that vegetates. You compel him to regard riches, honors, and pleasures as his supreme joy: that is to say, you excite all his passions, and all his unchained passions will soon change the dwelling-place of society into a frightful slaughter-house. History is at hand.

Take away this command to love, and you condemn man to the fabulous torments of Tantalus. The phantom of that happiness which you have bidden him to expect, flits before his eyes, but he cannot touch it. When at length he is weary of grasping at it—when he has racked all creatures in his efforts to derive happiness from them, like those idolatrous priests who used to search for the secrets of heaven in the reeking entrails of their victims—surrendering himself to despair, worn out before his time, he puts an end to his days by suicide. Tell me, is this a matter of no importance to society? Tell me again, is it not the record of modern history?

Take away this command to love, and you destroy the spirit of sacrifice. Now, society lives only by the sacrifice of the particular to the general good. Farewell, then, to all those heroic consecrations to the service and solace of humanity! Farewell to all that charms and embellishes life! Farewell to all that ennobles our nature!

It was therefore for us that God gave us his law, as it was for the world he created the sun, and for our soul he created our body. It is therefore most true that religion, that the decalogue especially, is an immense benefit, a fundamental social necessity.

PRAYER

O my God! who art all love, I thank thee for having recalled so forcibly to our minds the great precept of charity toward thee and the neighbor. Charity is our treasure, the source of all our happiness. The devil robbed us of it. Thou hast restored it to us, and, that we may profit by it, thou hast given us the decalogue, which is at once the means of exercising charity toward thee and our brethren, and the safeguard of this admirable virtue against the attacks of the devil and the old man. Grant us the grace to love the decalogue, and to observe it faithfully.

I am resolved to love God above all things, and my neighbor as myself for the love of God; and, in testimony of this love, I will thank God for having given me his holy commandments.

Lesson 48: Our Union with the New Adam by Charity (3)

Second commandment.—"Thou shalt not lightly use the name of God."[1126] The first commandment, which obliges us to honor God in a becoming manner, necessarily contains that which is said in the second. He who wishes that we should adore and love him, undoubtedly wishes that we should speak of him with the greatest respect, and expressly forbids the contrary. Like the first, the second commandment is wholly for our advantage. It is the safeguard of the love which we ought to entertain toward God. Now, this love is the indispensable means of our union with the new Adam, and an essential condition of our salvation.

Division of the second commandment into four parts.—The second commandment treats therefore of honoring and dishonoring the name of God by word; that is to say, it commands us to honor and forbids us to dishonor this holy name. It may be divided into four parts, because there are four ways of honoring and dishonoring the name of God by word.

I. *Respectful and disrespectful use of the name of God.* To honor the name of God is not to respect the letters or sounds of which it is composed, but what is expressed by it, viz., the eternal power, truth, wisdom, justice, and majesty of one only God in three distinct Persons. Hence, we honor God, our Lord, the Blessed Virgin, and the saints when we pronounce their names with respect. "From the abundance of the heart the mouth speaketh."[1127] This is the reason why it is peculiar to those who love God ardently to have the sweet thought of him often in their minds, and his blessed name often on their lips. They always repeat it with a tender devotion, as we see in the epistles of St. Paul, where the sacred name of our Lord Jesus Christ returns at every page. "There is nothing strange in it," says Theodoret. "Paul had Jesus in his heart—could he fail to have him on his lips?"[1128]

Let us conclude, therefore, that we fulfill the first part of the second commandment when in our temptations, our dangers, our trials, our spiritual and temporal difficulties, we call God, the Blessed Virgin, and the saints to our assistance, by piously pronouncing their names. For example: "O my God!" "O Jesus!" "O Mary!"[1129]

But we sometimes meet persons who, out of an evil habit, in moments of impatience or pleasantry, pronounce at every turn the name of God or of some saint, without thinking of what they say. This habit is a very bad one. It shows a contempt, or at least a want of respect, for the names of God and the saints. A comparison, though rather imperfect, will make plain the irreverence of which they are guilty. Let those persons say what they would think if they saw a man to whom they had given a rich garment set to work heedlessly with it on him at some low occupation.

If we are subject to this habit—saying continually, for example, "My God, yes"; "My God, no"; and other such words—let us take the resolution of correcting ourselves from this moment. Do we wish our resolution to be efficacious? Let us call to mind the profound respect which the angels bear toward the name of God, the profound respect which God himself required the Jews to entertain for it, and the no less profound respect with which it was regarded by one of the greatest geniuses of modern times—Newton. This celebrated astronomer never pronounced the name of God, or heard it pronounced, without uncovering his head.

II. *Swearing and perjury.* Swearing, or, to speak more correctly, an oath, is an excellent manner of honoring the name of God.[1130] To swear, or to take an oath, is to call God to witness the truth of what is asserted. Now, to call God to witness the truth is to acknowledge that he knows all things, that he is incapable of lying, that he is truth itself and a zealous defender of truth. This is therefore to honor him, and to honor him with a supreme worship. Hence, in the old as well as in the new testament, we see the holiest personages make use of oaths. God himself, to strengthen our confidence, does not disdain to have recourse to them;[1131] and he encourages us to imitate him: "You shall fear the Lord your God," he says, "and you shall swear by his name."[1132]

To swear, it is not necessary to invoke God himself as a witness. A true oath is taken as often as the holy gospels, the cross, the saints or their relics or their names, heaven, earth, the chief creatures of the universe, are thus invoked. These objects do not, it is true, give any authority of themselves to what is said. It comes from God, whose majesty and sanctity appear with more than ordinary effulgence in them. As for the expressions—"faith," "troth," "my word for it," "the faith of an honest man"—and the like, they are not oaths, the persons who make use of them not intending to take oaths nor to speak of divine things.

Good in itself and honorable to God, the oath is also useful to men. There are many things of great importance to individuals, to families, to society, which no man can affirm with sufficient emphasis by his own testimony alone. This for two reasons: one, through a want of truthfulness, considering that a large number of persons are wont to tell lies; the other, through a want of knowledge, considering that men cannot know the secrets of hearts, nor things to come, nor things remote.

Yet we often speak of things of this nature, and we often require to have a certain knowledge of them. To procure it, to put an end to disputes, and to adjust a variety of interests, it has been found necessary to have recourse to the testimony of God, because God can neither deceive nor be deceived.

Though the manner of honoring God by an oath is good and useful, the frequent use of it is not laudable. "Accustom not thy mouth to oaths," says the Holy Ghost: "This habit draws many evils in its train…The man who swears much shall be covered with iniquity, and a scourge shall not depart from his house."[1133]

St. Augustine and St. Hilary observe that St. Paul, when making use of an oath in his epistles, shows us how we are to understand the injunction of our Lord, "I say to you not to swear at all."[1134] Not that to swear is wrong, but lest one should acquire a facility, a habit of swearing, and so fall into perjury.[1135]

Reason itself condemns this habit. What, in point of fact, is an oath? A remedy against human fallibility, a necessary means of proving what is advanced. Now, remedies are useful only in cases of necessity: their too frequent application is dangerous. Hence, it is not advantageous to swear unless grave reasons require it. To swear often is a pernicious habit. "A great swearer, a great liar," is a proverb not without foundation.

The fathers of the Church remark very justly that the frequent use of oaths cannot be traced back to the beginning of the world. It was introduced at a much later period, when the malice of men had increased amazingly and was spread throughout the whole earth. Corruption and perfidy had arrived at such a height that men, being no longer able to trust one another, were obliged to call God to witness the truth of what they said.[1136]

To lead us back to our primitive perfection, the Son of God gives us this advice: "Let it be enough for you to say, 'It is so,' or 'It is not so'; anything more comes from sin."[1137] Our Lord does not absolutely forbid the use of oaths, as certain heretics, such as the Anabaptists, have pretended: he only condemns the habit of using them. If he adds that every word over and above "yes" or "no" comes from evil,[1138] he wishes to make us understand, as St. Augustine says, that distrust of others is a consequence of original sin and an infirmity of which Christians ought to be healed, since he supplies them with the means of being so.[1139]

Conditions of a lawful and holy oath. An oath being such a dreadful thing, it is a matter of the highest importance to know the conditions required that it may be lawful and holy. They are three in number: truth, judgment, and justice. God himself has declared them to us by the mouth of the prophet Jeremias. "You shall swear," he says, "with truth, with judgment, and with justice."[1140]

1. *Truth.* To swear with truth, it is necessary to swear only in attesting a thing true, which one knows for certain and not from mere guesses. The same rule applies to the formal intention of observing what one promises. They therefore become guilty of one of the greatest sins that can be committed who, on their oaths, affirm things which they

know to be false or which they do not know to be true. In like manner, they who, with an oath, promise things which they have not the intention of performing, or, if they have, which they do not afterward perform in effect.

2. *Judgment.* That is, it is necessary, avoiding rashness and inconsideration, to swear only with great discernment and after serious reflection. Hence, the importance and necessity of the thing alone can render it lawful to take an oath, which must always be accompanied with fear and with a profound respect for the name of God. If a man swears without weighing all things carefully, his oath is rash and precipitate. Such are the oaths of persons who, for slight and often vain causes, swear without any reflection and merely through a most censurable habit, as happens daily among those who buy and sell. The one class to buy at a lower, the other to sell at a higher price, do not hesitate to employ an oath in praise or dispraise of their wares.

3. *Justice.* It is necessary that the thing which one promises with an oath should be just and honest. If a man promises with an oath a thing unjust or dishonest—for example, to take revenge or to commit any action forbidden by the law of God—he renders himself guilty of an enormous sin. Moreover, he incurs the guilt of a new crime, if he fulfills his promise. Such a promise does not in any manner bind: no one can be bound to do wrong. Herod became guilty in this manner by ordering, in fulfillment of an oath which he had taken, that St. John the Baptist should be beheaded.

He who utters an oath in confirmation of a promise which he makes or which is required of him should be sure that this promise is just—in other words, that it contains nothing, obliges nothing, contrary to the commandments of God or the Church, by which we shall all be judged. If the promise includes things permitted at the time, one ought to declare, before taking the oath, that he only engages to respect the promise and oath in things permitted. As for things not permitted, the law of God forbids that they should be promised. If they have been promised, even with an oath, the law of God forbids that they should be done, because an oath, according to the axioms of morality, can never become a bond of iniquity: *Juramentum non est vinculum iniquitatis.*

An oath, taken with the requisite conditions, imposes a serious obligation—grounded on the virtues of religion and justice—to fulfill, in all their extent, the duties contracted by it. This obligation cannot be limited by any mental or inward reserve, but only by reserves clearly and explicitly shown. It loses its force if, after the time of taking the oath, the thing promised becomes impossible or unjust. It likewise ceases by a dispensation of the Church.

Perjury. If to swear with truth, judgment, and justice is an act which honors the name of God, to perjure oneself is an act which greatly dishonors this holy name. In effect, perjury is a lie confirmed with an oath.[1141] Now, he who dares to call God to witness a falsehood does him a monstrous injury. He seems to accuse God of ignorance, as if God could be ignorant of any truth; or of wickedness, as if God could confirm a lie with his approbation.[1142] There is no levity of matter here. It is therefore a mortal sin to swear in support of a lie, however small.[1143]

Perjury is also a social crime. That there may be society, it is necessary that man should have faith in his fellow man. It is necessary that he should believe undoubtingly that another's words and thoughts exactly harmonize. This conviction is the basis of all contracts. But covetousness may lead men to deceive others. To remedy this evil, God permits an oath: it is the highest guarantee of man's promises. Take away oaths from society, let perjury be no longer a crime—in other words, efface the second precept of the decalogue—and you dissolve society.

The life of him who is accused is at the mercy of false witnesses, or a judge, or a jury, interested in seeking his death. The fate of an individual is handed over to a man of bad faith, who laughs at promises.[1144] And thus all your fine speculations, all your industrial associations, fall to ruins, like a house deprived of its foundation, and, falling, crush you to atoms, or rather plunge you into the abyss of misery, despair, and suicide: alas! it is the daily occurrence of our age of progress! So true is it that the oath is the foundation of society that, among the Romans, perjury was declared infamous, and the laws of all peoples have punished it severely. The French Code decrees against perjury the punishment of hard labor.[1145]

III. *Praise of God, and blasphemy.* To praise and bless the holy name of God is an obligation of which it is easy to understand the reasonableness and the extent. Is it not evident that all goods, natural and supernatural, come from God? Is it not equally evident that all the works of God are full of wisdom, justice, and mercy? Henceforth, is it not right that God should be praised and blessed by all and in all? Is it not right that our example should engage other men to praise and bless him? Our Lord laid it upon us a special precept to bless the name of God, teaching us to say daily, "Hallowed be thy name." All the patriarchs, all the apostles, all the martyrs, all true Christians, have joyfully fulfilled this sacred duty, so well that their praises, united with those of angels and saints, form a glorious concert, which will resound eternally throughout the courts of the heavenly Jerusalem.[1146]

We associate ourselves with the magnificent harmony of the universe when we boldly confess that God is our Lord and our Father; when we publish his power, his justice, his mercy; when we proclaim that his only Son is the author of our salvation; when we celebrate his praises, by returning him special thanks for the goods and evils that befall us. Thus Job, that admirable model of patience, having been literally deluged with misfortunes, never ceased to bless God with the utmost courage and magnanimity. Let us strive to imitate this incomparable model of patience. Whether we experience pains of mind or body, let us employ whatever strength remains to us to praise God, saying often with the holy man, "O my God, blessed be thy name!"

To the praise of God, which is enjoined us by the second commandment, are opposed silence and blasphemy. Woe to the mouth that never opens to praise God! Is that a dutiful child which knows not how to thank and honor the author of its existence and happiness? What is to be thought of so many indifferent and ungrateful persons who never have a blessing on their lips for the name of God—who praise and thank creatures for the least benefit, but God, whose creatures are only his instruments, never or seldom? And what is to be thought of so many others who only bless God for form's sake, as a matter of routine, from their lips? Do they keep the second commandment?

Blasphemy. At the present day there is a very large number guilty far otherwise. Not only do they not honor the name of God by praise, but they outrage it by blasphemy. Blasphemy is an expression injurious to God, to the saints, or to religion.

There are six ways in which a person may be guilty of it: a) by attributing to God that which does not belong to him—saying, for example, that God is cruel or unjust; b) by denying to God that which belongs to him—saying, for example, that he is not merciful or that he does not concern himself about what happens on earth; c) by attributing to creatures that which belongs only to God—saying, for example, that the devil knows everything and can work miracles; d) by cursing God, his Church, his saints, or those among his creatures in which his power, wisdom, and goodness particularly shine forth, as man, the soul, heaven, earth; e) by deifying oneself and saying, "Whether God likes it or not, I will do it"; f) by depriving religion or the saints of that which belongs to them—saying, for example, that religion is not true, or that the Blessed Virgin is like any other woman, meaning thereby to attack her divine maternity or her perpetual virginity.

As for the following modes of speaking, "The devil take me if I don't speak the truth!" "May I drop dead this moment if it is not true!" and the like, we cannot but see that they contain imprecations on oneself or others. The corruption of latter times has also introduced among us a number of other expressions more or less opposed to the second commandment: from all which Christians ought to abstain with the greatest care. None ought to avoid this sin with more horror than parents and superiors, whether spiritual or temporal. St. Louis ordered that the tongues of blasphemers should be pierced with a red-hot iron. He was convinced, and properly, that a contempt of the first majesty soon draws in its train a contempt of the second. As for us, when we hear anyone blaspheme, let us inwardly bless the name of God and pray for the blasphemer.

At Namur, where the Brothers of the Christian Schools labor with so much success, as in all other places where they are established, to procure for youth a really virtuous education, one of their pupils, a child of ten or twelve years of age, gave, a few years ago, a most touching proof of his faith and of his horror for blasphemy. He came home one day perhaps a little late from school, and his father scolded him sharply, swearing too by the name of God. The poor child, quite confused at having given occasion to these blasphemies, fell on his knees, and said, "Beat me, father! I beseech you, but do not swear." The father, amazed on beholding the horror with which the blasphemy had inspired the child, profited of the lesson, and never more ventured to blaspheme. How many faults might Christian children, if they wished, cause their parents to avoid![1147]

Blasphemy is an enormous crime, which admits of no levity of matter, that is to say, which is always mortal, when it is committed with full advertence and consent. In the old law, the blasphemer was punished with death.[1148] "Justly," says Theodoret, "since he slays his Creator as far as lies in his power, with the sword of his tongue, not being able to do so otherwise."[1149] According to St. Augustine, the blasphemer who outrages Jesus Christ, now reigning in heaven, is no less guilty than the wretches who crucified him formerly living on earth.[1150] St. Paul excommunicated two blasphemers, Alexander and Hymeneus. On those who render themselves guilty of the same sin, the Church still wishes that heavy penances should be imposed. The ancient legislation of Christian peoples stipulated for the most severe penalties, including that of death, against them.[1151]

To commit it, it is not necessary that one should have a formal intention of insulting God or of lessening the honor which is due to him. It is enough to give utterance to the blasphemy, knowing and perceiving that the words which one permits himself to use are injurious to God.

In outraging God, blasphemy draws down the divine vengeance on the world, and gradually overturns the foundations of society. On what, I ask, does society rest? Is it not on religion? And does not religion itself rest on the love of God? But how shall God be loved, if he is not respected? And what respect is left for God, when he is blasphemed, that is to say, when his holy name is cursed and scorned? What must become of a family whose children daily curse or scorn their father's name? What must become of states in which it is permitted to speak and write all sorts of outrageous things against the name and authority of the prince? History is open before us to give an answer.

It is therefore true that, in forbidding us to blaspheme his name, God looked to the interests of society as much as and even more than his own. St. Louis, in decreeing an exemplary chastisement against blasphemers, showed himself not only a good Christian but a wise politician. He knew that where God has no altar, kings have no throne; where kings have no throne, the wicked have no rein: nothing there but anarchy and chaos. Is it not to innumerable and nameless blasphemies against everything most sacred, pouring forth from tongues and pens during fourscore years, that we must attribute the deep and general throes and convulsions of society, and the streams of blood that not long ago laid Europe waste? "Voltaire," says the infidel Condorcet, "did not see all that he did, but he did all that we see."

IV. *Vows.*—1. *Nature of vows.* By an oath we certify or promise something to men, interposing the name of God. But there are persons who make a promise to God himself of things agreeable to him: this promise is called a vow. A vow is more than a simple resolution: it is a deliberate promise by which a person enters into an engagement with God to perform some good work under pain of sin.[1152]

To understand vows well there are three things to be observed. First, that a vow is an act of supreme worship, and can therefore be made only to God. Accordingly, when you hear mention of vows to the Blessed Virgin and the saints, you must know that these vows are made chiefly to God, in honor of the Blessed Virgin and the saints, in whom God dwells more specially than in other creatures. Hence, a vow made to a saint is nothing else than a promise made to God of honoring the memory of such a saint by an offering, or by any act whatsoever of religion, that is to say, of honoring God in such a saint. I make a vow, for example, to visit the church of Loretto and to bestow an alms there. This is the same as to say, I promise God to honor him in his divine Mother by an alms which I will give at the holy house of Loretto.[1153]

Secondly, a vow is a deliberate promise, that is to say, a promise, and not a simple purpose or resolution, like that of a person who, being sick, should say, "If I recover, I purpose or resolve to make a pilgrimage to such a place, to fast every Saturday, or to confess once a month." These words are not addressed to anyone, and a neglect of their fulfillment, which is simply a resistance to grace or an unsteadiness in well-doing, brings in its train no greater evil than a venial fault.

For a vow, there must therefore be a promise made to God. Example: "I vow to do such a thing." Moreover, the promise must be deliberate—made with knowledge, with freedom of choice, with the perfect use of reason, with the same consent of the will as is necessary for mortal sin.[1154]

Accordingly, the vow of a child not yet arrived at the use of reason, at a degree of intelligence sufficient for the commission of grievous sin, must be regarded as null. In like manner, the vow of a person who, out of ignorance, thought that he only formed a simple resolution. But a vow made under the impression of a purely natural fear is valid. Such is that of the mariner who, threatened by the storm, promises to make a pilgrimage or to send an offering to some sanctuary.

Thirdly, the promise has for its object something agreeable to God, as virginity or poverty. Hence, the person who makes a vow to commit a sin, or to perform any action foreign to the honor of God, or even an action good, but preventive of a better, does not promise something agreeable to God. He offers dishonor instead of honor to him, and sins against the second commandment.

2. *Division of vows.* There are many classes of vows. The absolute vow, or that which is made unconditionally: for example, I make a vow to enter religion. The conditional vow, or that in which a thing is promised only in case of a certain occurrence: "If I recover my health, I will give so much alms." The personal vow is that which regards the person solely. I make a vow to recite a certain prayer, or to go on a pilgrimage somewhere; this is a personal vow. The real vow is that which has for its object something to be given. Hence, to make a vow to give alms, or to have Masses said, is a real vow. The mixed vow is that which is partly real and partly personal: to promise to visit the tombs of the apostles and leave an alms there is a mixed vow.

Vows are still further distinguished into temporary and perpetual. I make a vow to fast every Friday for a year: a temporary vow. I make a vow to observe chastity all my life: a perpetual vow.

Finally, vows are either solemn or simple. Solemn vows are those which are made by profession in a religious order approved by the Church, or by the reception of holy orders. Simple vows are those which are made, either publicly or privately, in congregations which have not been raised to the rank of a religious order. There is this twofold difference between a solemn and a simple vow: the first renders marriage null, while the second only renders it unlawful; and the Church often dispenses from a simple, but scarcely ever from a solemn, vow.

3. *Merit of vows.* As for the merit of vows, it is evident that a good work done in virtue of a vow is much more pleasing to God than if it were done otherwise. In point of fact, is it not more to give the whole tree and its fruit than to give only the fruit? He who does a good work without a vow gives the fruit; he who does it after having vowed it, gives both the tree and the fruit, that is to say, his liberty with his good work. Let us add that a vow testifies better to the Lord our desire to please him, to be wholly his, and to serve him with the utmost perfection. Let us also add that it is a great means of enabling us to advance in virtue, by the holy necessity under which it places us of doing violence to our natural inconstancy and tepidity.

4. *Obligation of vows.* The obligation of fulfilling vows and of fulfilling them promptly is unquestionable. "When thou hast made a vow to the Lord," the scripture tells us, "thou shalt not delay to fulfill it; otherwise, the Lord thy God will require it of thee, and, if thou be slow, thy delay shall be imputed to thee as sin."[1155] Besides, if it is forbidden to fail in our engagements with men, can it be allowable to exhibit faithlessness toward God?

This obligation is serious, so that the violation of a vow in an important matter is a mortal sin; in an unimportant matter, only a venial sin. It extends to all the promised circumstances of time, place, and manner. The obligation of a personal vow extends only to the person who makes it, but that of a real vow passes on to his heirs. Hence, the heirs of him who made a vow to give an alms and to have Masses said, are bound to give the promised alms and to have the promised Masses said, if the vow has not been fulfilled. As for a conditional vow, it binds only when the condition is realized.

5. *Cessation of vows.* Four things cause the obligation of vows to cease.

Change of matter or object. Example: I have made a vow to fast on bread and water every Friday of the year; but I fall sick, and the doctor wishes that I should eat meat: my obligation ceases. I have made a vow to give ten shillings a month to Peter, because he is poor; Peter becomes rich: I am no longer bound to give him alms. I have made a vow to go on a pilgrimage; but, since doing so, I have made another to enter religion: my first ceases.

Annulment. That is, the act by which a superior cancels a vow made by an inferior under his power, as regards the person, or the will, or the things which are the matter of the vow.[1156] Thus, a father, or he who holds the place of a father, can directly annul all the vows, whether real or personal, made by a child that has not yet attained the full age of twelve years if a girl, or fourteen years if a boy. The father being dead or incapable, this power reverts to the mother alone, if she is the guardian, and, in defect of both father and mother, to the tutor.[1157]

Dispensation. It must be received from the sovereign pontiff, or from a bishop, or from him who has received from either of these the power to dispense. Like that of forgiving sins and granting indulgences, this power comes from our Lord, who gave the apostles, and especially St. Peter, authority to bind and to loose consciences. The vows whose dispensation is reserved to the supreme pontiff are, besides solemn vows, the five following: a vow of perpetual chastity, a vow of entering religion, and vows of the three celebrated pilgrimages—to Jerusalem, to the tomb of the apostles in Rome, and to the Church of St. James at Compostella in Spain. Thus, the Church can dispense, in the name of God, from the obligation of performing that which has been promised to God; but she can only do so for strong reasons.

Commutation. Differing from a dispensation, a commutation does not remove the obligation of a vow: it changes the matter to some other of greater, equal, or less value. The surest way, when there is question of changing the matter of a vow, is to submit the affair to one's confessor: just as it is a rule of prudence never to make a vow without having consulted a wise and enlightened director.

6. *Vow of religion.* The vow of religion is a promise made to God to observe voluntary poverty, perpetual chastity, and entire obedience, under a rule approved by the Holy Apostolic See. The religious state, of which this vow is the foundation, is a permanent order approved by the Church, wherein the faithful engage to live in common, and to tend to perfection by the observance of the three vows which we have just named.

To make a vow of these three things is to make a vow of religion, because it is to consecrate oneself perfectly to God, not only as regards the precepts, but also as regards the counsels. Hence it is that those who make such a profession are called "religious," that is to say, persons perfectly dedicated to God, and practicing in a most excellent manner whatever pertains to the Christian religion. It is not the obligation of a religious to be perfect the moment he enters religion, but rather to tend to perfection by the observance of the rules of his order, and especially by fidelity to the three vows which he pronounces.

Vow of poverty. How the three vows of religion lead to Christian perfection, it is easy to show. First, the vow of poverty—which consists in possessing nothing of one's own. He who aspires to perfection must become poor. So our Lord taught. "If you will be perfect," he says, "go and sell all that you have; give to the poor, and you shall have treasure in heaven: then come and follow me."[1158] He himself was the first and most perfect model of voluntary poverty. "The foxes have their dens," he says, "and the birds of the air their nests; as for the Son of man, he has not where to rest his head."[1159] Our Lord being essentially perfect, it follows that whoever makes profession of voluntary poverty imitates him and tends to perfection.

Vow of chastity. Next, the vow of chastity—which obliges one to renounce all sensual pleasures. He who aspires to perfection must vow his virginity to the Lord. Such is also the counsel given by the Savior himself. He never ceased to extol virginity. St. Paul spoke like his divine master. And the Church has condemned the heretics of different periods who asserted that the state of virginity is not more perfect than the state of marriage.[1160] Our Lord being essentially perfect, it follows that whoever makes profession of voluntary chastity imitates him and tends to perfection. Reason itself tells us this, since it is certain that the anxieties of life, the cares of pleasing a husband or a wife, divide the mind and the heart, and slacken one's fervor in the service of God.

Vow of obedience. Lastly, the vow of obedience. By the vow of poverty, the religious gives his property; by the vow of chastity, he gives his body; by the vow of obedience, he gives his soul. The last vow is therefore more excellent than the others and completes the sacrifice. Here again our Lord was the first master and model of this sublime vow. "If you will imitate me," he says, "renounce yourselves and follow me":[1161] and St. Paul says that Christ became "obedient even unto death, and the death of the cross."[1162] Our Lord being essentially perfect, it follows that whoever makes profession of voluntary obedience imitates him and tends to perfection. Reason itself points out that it must be so. In effect, voluntary obedience triumphs over pride, which is the greatest obstacle to virtue. Here you see why the Holy Spirit assures us that the obedient man shall sing of his victories. For who has a better right? To conquer men and vanquish cities—what is all that in comparison with the most difficult of victories, the victory over oneself?

Hence, all religious orders are good and holy; but the most perfect are those which, uniting the active with the contemplative life, copy most exactly the life of our Lord, the pattern of all perfection.[1163]

Social advantages.—If there is nothing more perfect, consequently more glorious to God, than the vow of religion, there is nothing more advantageous to him who makes it, nor more useful to society.

Nothing more advantageous to him who makes it. "In religion," says St. Bernard, "a man lives more purely, falls more rarely, rises more speedily, walks more wisely, rests more securely, is more frequently bedewed with the graces of heaven, dies more confidently, and is rewarded more abundantly."[1164] Absolute obedience, which seems so contrary to nature, is really the greatest consolation of those who have the happiness to make profession of it. "I know of nothing more convenient," said a holy nun, "than to be carried to paradise on the shoulders of a superioress."

Nothing more useful to society. The times in which we live proclaim with a dreadfully eloquent voice the necessity of having religious orders in Christian countries, as well as the guilty imprudence of those who encourage their suppression, and the no less guilty blindness of those who oppose their reestablishment. Vain are the efforts of man to change the bases of society; for society, and especially Christian society, is a divine work. Now, religious orders, coming into existence with society, are among the bases on which it rests, as we shall show in the third part[1165] of the catechism.

On vocation.—It remains for us to say a word on vocation to the religious state. To what we have said on vocation, when speaking of marriage, let us add that, for the validity of a religious profession, it is necessary a) that the subject, no matter which sex, should have attained the age of sixteen years; b) that there should be no impediment essentially contrary to the statutes of the order; c) that the subject should be at liberty to dispose of his or her person; and d) that the profession should be perfectly free from anything like compulsion or fear.[1166]

It is a duty on parents to second the vocation of their children[1167] called by the Lord to a religious life. They may, they even should prove their vocation; but they have no right to oppose it, when it is seen to come from on high. Let children, in taking a step of so much importance, recollect the saying of St. Bernard, "On this occasion only, it is not permitted to obey one's parents."[1168]

PRAYER

O my God! who art all love, I thank thee for having taught me to love my neighbor and to honor thy holy name. I beg pardon for all the faults which I have committed against charity and against that respect which is due to thee.

I am resolved to love God above all things, and my neighbor as myself for the love of God; and, in testimony of this love, I will never take the name of God in vain.

Lesson 49: Our Union with the New Adam by Charity (4)

Third commandment: Its relation with the two preceding ones.—We are the subjects and the servants of God. Now, subjects and servants owe to their princes and their masters three things: fidelity, honor, and service. Fidelity obliges them not to recognize other princes or masters: we fulfill this duty toward God by keeping the first commandment. Next, subjects and servants ought to honor their princes and their masters by words, giving them the titles which become them: the second commandment lays this duty upon us toward God. Lastly, subjects and servants owe external service to their princes and their masters: this duty toward God is prescribed to us by the third commandment. Whence it follows that the first three precepts of the decalogue consecrate in regard to God the three kinds of homage which wholly dedicate man to him: the homage of the heart, the homage of the mouth, and the homage of the body.

St. Thomas points out another connection. He says that in the first two commandments God removes all the obstacles to true religion, and in the third lays its foundation.[1169] As a matter of fact, it is not enough that man should abstain from idolatry and perjury. To this negative worship must be joined a positive, of which God alone can prescribe the acts, the times, and the conditions. Moreover, if the individual ought to honor God, society, which is like one public man, ought also to honor him with a worship befitting his nature, consequently public and solemn. That nothing in an affair of so much importance might be left to the caprice of men, God has been careful to regulate by the third commandment all the details of the public worship which he requires from us,[1170] and to fix the day on which society should render him this public and necessary worship.

This commandment, the last of the first table given to Moses, is expressed thus: "Remember to keep holy the sabbath day. You shall labor, you shall do all your work in six days. But the seventh is the day of the sabbath of the Lord your God. You shall not do any servile work on this day, you nor your son, nor your daughter, nor your manservant, nor your maidservant, nor your beasts of burden, nor the stranger who is staying with you. For in six days the Lord made heaven and earth, and the sea, and all things that they contain, and he rested on the seventh. This is the reason why he blessed and sanctified the day of the sabbath."[1171]

What a noble model is here proposed to us! It is God himself who, creating the world and resting at the end of his work, says, "O man, my child! work for six days like thy Father, with the same holiness, and like him rest on the seventh. The six days of toil are an image of thy life; the seventh is an image of thy eternity: here, sufferings for a moment; there, the repose of endless ages."

Examples from history.—Before explaining the third precept of the decalogue, we shall relate two short examples from history which show its excellence. The first will inspire us with the greatest fear of ever violating this commandment; the second will show us how zealously we should endeavor to prevent our inferiors from violating it.

While the Israelites were in the desert, some of them once found a man gathering wood on the sabbath day. They led him to Moses and Aaron in presence of all the people. The chiefs of the holy nation put him in prison, not knowing as yet what they should decide regarding him. The Lord, being consulted, answered Moses, "Let the man die—let all the multitude stone him outside the camp." The people therefore led him forth and stoned him, and he died according to the order of God.[1172] When we reflect that it is God himself who, infinite in goodness as well as in justice, commands such a punishment, how can we be mistaken concerning the enormity of the evil that is committed by profaning the day which is reserved to him?

The second example. In the fifteenth century there lived in Italy a Camaldolese religious, equally celebrated for his learning and his piety. His name was Angelo Masaccio, of a noble family of Urbino. After a childhood spent in virtue, the young man Angelo resolved to quit the world, and to embrace the institute which we have just referred to, in the monastery of Santa Maria di Serra, near his native city. Having been professed, he consecrated all his abilities to the diffusion of the word of God, to the instruction of the people, to the correction of manners, to the eradication of vice: and he saved many souls. At this time the heresy of the Fratricelli was spreading through the districts bordering on the monastery. The servant of God could not allow himself any peace or rest until the cockle had been removed from the wheat.

In the year 1458, he saw, one festival day, some men belonging to the brood whom we have named cutting down wood in a neighboring forest. Guided by his wonted zeal, he hastened to address a just and strong remonstrance to them. The wretches fell upon the holy religious, struck him with their axes, and killed him in a most savage manner. Meanwhile the monks, uneasy at the lengthened absence of Father Angelo, began to fear some serious evil. A search was made. They were not long in discovering the place where he lay on the ground, covered with blood, and dreadfully cut. In this cowardly murder, it was not difficult to perceive the work of heretics in their hatred of the faith. The people and clergy ran to the spot. Surrounded by an immense concourse, the religious bore to the monastery the lifeless body of the holy apostle, and deposited it under the chief altar of the church. God wrought miracles in honor of his faithful servant, and was pleased to glorify that courageous zeal which led him to the defense of the holy day of prayer and rest.

If the axe of heretics struck in the fifteenth century the defender of divine rights, cupidity, as barbarous as heresy, drags in our day a sacrilegious labor from arms and souls that have need of rest and consolation. Angelo Masaccio! blessed martyr, you see that your murderers have among us but too many and too cruel imitators! May your intercession, sought by the whole Church, reestablish in the bosom of Christian nations a law that is too often sacrilegiously violated![1173]

Necessity.—While the third commandment orders us to reserve a certain time for rendering external worship to God, its necessity comes from the law of nature. What proves this truth is that all peoples have had certain days consecrated to the worship of the divinities which they adored. And as nature has appointed certain times for the functions necessary to the life of the body, such as eating, drinking, sleeping, resting, so religion wishes that there should be certain fixed times in which the soul might recover its strength, by meditating on eternal truths and contemplating the divine perfections.[1174]

The precept of sanctifying one day out of the week, if considered in regard to the precise day, is not immutable. Hence, by the order of God himself, the Israelites sanctified the sabbath day. The Lord chose this day for three reasons. First: in memory of the mysterious rest into which he entered after creating the world, that it might be sanctified by thanksgiving for this great benefit. Second: to confound those senseless men who should in the course of time dare to assert that the world had always existed. A weekly celebration in memory of the creation of the world would proclaim boldly and continually that the world had had a beginning. Third: to remind man that, having made his servants and beasts work for six days of the week, he should allow them to rest on the seventh. God wished hereby that masters should learn to be kind toward their domestics and compassionate toward their poor animals.

But this special command was to be done away with at the time when the other Judaic ceremonies should be rejected, namely, at the death of Christ. These ceremonies were only, as we have seen, a shadow of the truth. They should therefore end on the arrival of the truth—our Lord, as the shadows of night disappear before the rising sun.

Sunday substituted for the sabbath.—The Jewish sabbath gave place to the first of the seven days of the week, called the Lord's day or Sunday. The Lord's day, say the fathers, because we celebrate thereon our Lord's triumph over the world; the Lord's day, because we ought not to find leisure for anything thereon but the Lord's service.[1175] St. John speaks of this day in his Apocalypse,[1176] and the apostle St. Paul desires that the alms of the faithful should be collected on the "first day after the sabbath":[1177] that is to say, as St. Chrysostom explains it, on Sunday. We see hereby that, even in the time of the apostles, Sunday was regarded as holy.[1178]

Would you like to know some of the reasons why the Church transferred the solemnity of the sabbath to Sunday? a) It was on this day that light began to shine on the world. b) It was on this day that our Lord rose from the dead, and caused humanity to pass from a life of darkness and sin to the glorious life of the new Adam. c) It was on this day that the world began to be regenerated by the Holy Ghost, who descended on the apostles.

Thus, in consecrating the Sunday to God, the Church honors God the Father Almighty, as the Creator and preserver of all things; Jesus Christ—the Father's only Son—as our Savior, who, after the labors of his mortal life, entered, by his resurrection, into his eternal rest, figured by God's rest after the work of the creation; and the Holy Ghost, as the principle of a new creation, more wonderful than the first, and through which we receive, after being drawn from the nothingness of sin, a new being and a new life.

Explanation of what is forbidden by the third commandment.—To make us feel the importance of a sacred rest, the expression with which God begins is this: "Remember that thou keep holy the sabbath day." Hereby he reminds us of two things. The first, that there will not be wanting occasions of a nature to cause us to lose sight of this precept, such as the example of those who make no account of it, or that love of amusement which so often hinders us from observing this holy day properly. The second, that while laboring during the week we must always have Sunday in view as the day when we are to render an account of our actions to God, that so we may not perform any work which God would repudiate, and which would be for ourselves, as the scripture says, "a subject of grief and remorse."[1179]

The divine legislator is not content to remind us of the precept: he removes the obstacles to its fulfillment. For the meaning in scripture of the words, "to keep holy the sabbath day," is to abstain from all bodily labor and temporal business. It is necessary therefore to explain what works are forbidden on this holy day.

We distinguish three kinds of works: liberal works, mixed or common works, and servile works.

Liberal works. Liberal works are permitted on Sunday. We call those works liberal which exercise the mind more than the body, which tend directly to the cultivation of the mind, and which are therefore more generally practiced by persons of independent condition. To read, to write, to draw, to perform on musical instruments, to teach, to study, and to do all other things that pertain to the liberal arts, are liberal works, permitted on Sunday, even though done to earn money.

Hence, professors of the arts and sciences may pursue their works and give their lessons. Architects, painters, sculptors, and embroiderers may sketch out their designs. Though it is permitted to paint, yet it is not permitted to grind colors, nor to occupy oneself with certain pictures of a mechanical or coarse description. Such would be servile works, particularly when connected with one's state of life.

Mixed or common works. Mixed or common works are likewise permitted on Sunday, provided one does not run the risk, without good reason, of losing Mass. We call those works common which exercise the mind as much as the body, and which are common to the higher and the lower classes of society: for example, to walk about, to drive, to sail, to hunt, to play, to fish. Hunting and fishing are particularly allowable when they do not require any great labor: such as a mere chase and a simple rod and line. But one ought not to convey wares or provisions from place to place on holy days, unless necessity requires it or custom authorizes it.[1180]

Servile works. Servile works are forbidden on Sunday. We call those works servile which exercise the body more than the mind, which tend directly to the advantage of the body, and which are more generally performed by servants and laborers.[1181] Here are a few of them: to carry on any trade whatsoever, to till the ground, to reap, to gather in fruits, to sew, to knit, to embroider. All these things are forbidden on Sunday, though one should gain nothing by them, and even though one should be working for the poor.[1182] Marketing is also forbidden on Sundays and holidays, particularly such marketing as occurs in public: that is excepted, however, which the custom of places authorizes.

It is a pretty generally received opinion that one may buy and sell on Sunday those things which are necessary for daily life, as bread, wine, meat, vegetables; and what country people may require for one or several weeks, or even for a more considerable time, as victuals, clothes, and other articles of consumption. But it is not permitted to exhibit merchandise for sale publicly. The shop should be closed, or at least the door only should be open.[1183] So much for workpeople and traders.

As for innkeepers, it is forbidden them to supply persons belonging to the place with anything to eat or drink, during the divine offices, especially during the celebration of the holy sacrifice. They cannot do so without being guilty of a grave fault. They are likewise guilty by entertaining young persons, even outside the hours of offices, thus favoring quarrels, blasphemies, drunkenness, and other vices.

The obligation of abstaining from servile works extends from midnight to midnight. It is grave: so that he who, without any necessity, should work on a Sunday or holiday for three hours, consecutively or otherwise, would certainly be guilty of mortal sin. He even exposes himself to the danger of sinning mortally by working two hours.[1184]

There is another kind of works, eminently servile, and much more strictly forbidden than those which we have just mentioned: these works are sins. Now, by a deplorable abuse, a greater number of them are often committed on days consecrated to the divine service than on days devoted to labor. The most ordinary are dangerous walks, dances, shows, and tavern-visiting. Among all Christian nations, these disorders have been forbidden by the civil authority, as essentially contrary to the sanctification of Sunday. Let us take from a multitude of laws that of the emperor Leo V, promulgated in the year of our Lord 469:

"We forbid the profanation, by any amusement, of days consecrated to the Divine Majesty. We forbid that the Lord's day should be profaned by any exaction, by any legal proceedings. Let the harsh voice of bailiffs cease to be heard; let litigants breathe at their case, that they may not seem afraid; let minds be occupied with no foreign thought. Yet, for fear that a holy rest should ever degenerate into sloth, we forbid every kind of dangerous pleasure. Let no theatre, or circus, or spectacle occupy the least part of this day: if such things be due on the return of our birthday, we wish them to be deferred. The loss of their rank for soldiers, the loss of their patrimony for others: such are the punishments which we decree against the violators of this sacred law."[1185]

These prescriptions, which are so easy, and whose profound wisdom and social necessity are demonstrated by experience with the eloquence of thunder, are still, for the most part, observed in Catholic countries—what do I say? in protestant countries, such as England, and especially Scotland.

Refutation of the pretexts for excusing labor.—The profanation of days consecrated to rest, besides being a very great sin, is also a misfortune to operatives and to society. First, it is a sin, a crime of high treason against God—forbidden a hundred times by the supreme legislator, under the most severe penalties.[1186] Unless it is supposed that one can mock God with impunity, it must therefore be admitted that the bold violation of this fundamental law is a continual source of punishments to individuals and to nations.

It is fatal to individuals. Workmen and workwomen, who labor on days consecrated to the Lord, offer as an excuse that their work would be left to them, that they should lose their employment, or that they had promised their work. Frivolous pretexts! The law of

God is above all these reasons. And is it not a want of confidence in God and an insult to his goodness, to pretend that he would fail to supply us with the necessaries of life, because we had kept his law. Let one example, then, only one, be cited of a person who died of hunger or misery, from having been unwilling to work on Sunday! Remember this well: they who work on Sunday are neither happier nor richer at year's end. It is often quite the contrary: God does not bless a work that is performed against his command. "I know two excellent ways to ruin oneself," said the saintly Curé of Ars: "to work on Sunday and to take what belongs to another."

Moreover, is not God the master of your property and your life? Has he not at his beck the lightning, the hail, the frost, the rain, and the heat, to deprive you of the crops that you have tended and gathered in contempt of his prohibition? And is not your health in his hands? Can he not send you a sickness that will cost you a good deal more than you have gained by working on Sunday? In fine, are not revolutions, which disturb public confidence and, for months and years, compel millions of arms to refrain from labor, another means at his disposal to make you bitterly expiate your sacrilegious contempt of his law? I tell you again that no one insults God with impunity.

But this is not all. The profanation of Sunday turns wholly to the spread of disorder: so that habitual labor on Sunday becomes a seed of iniquity and a ticket of recommendation to a workhouse. Ye poor artisans! who all the week go through your functions like machines, in unwholesome atmospheres; ye poor laborers! who bear the burden and the heat of the day, it seems to you that with another day's work you would acquire a new income and better your condition! You are the victims of a sad mistake. First, the man who works on Sunday does not, as a general rule, work on Monday, and thus hope proves deceitful. Secondly, he spends in debauchery a portion of his weekly gain. Thirdly, he wastes his strength by excesses, and, becoming incapable of labor before his time, he goes, a young old man, to die in a hospital. His wife and children, clad in rags, are left dependents on public charity, until philanthropy, weary of meeting them on its path, causes them to be shut up in some depot for waifs. This is the history of our own day.

Ye toilers! undeceive yourselves. That which will procure you ease in your old days is good conduct, and there is no good conduct without religion, because you cannot without religion have strength to subdue your passions and to resist the torrent of evil example. But you can never have religion without instruction and religious practices, and you can never have instruction or religious practices if you do not sanctify the Sunday. So much for working men.

As for working women, the labor of Sunday is no less fatal to them. Without a religious rein, young females abandon themselves to their natural tastes. Passionately attached to toilet and finery, their daily wages soon become insufficient for them...and then comes the barter of innocence. I will say no more: ask public decency. The registries of courts and the statistics of infanticides will acquaint you with the rest.

Do I hear you say that you work on Sunday and every other day without any inconvenience? No, you do not, for the reason which I am about to mention; but if you do, you will not do it long. You have need of rest—continual labor will soon destroy your health. Besides, this continual labor will profit you nothing. You imagine that you can calculate well, but the rich man can calculate still better. He is the master, and you do not see that he makes you submit to a decrease of salary, in such a manner that he only gives you for seven days' work what he would be obliged to give you for six, if it were the case that you only worked for six. It is natural that you should earn enough in a day to enable you and your family to live, without making a present of your arm or your strength to the rich man. Since the practice of working on Sunday began, have you known many persons who made a fortune by reason of this increase of labor?

The violation of Sunday tends wholly, therefore, to the disadvantage of the working classes, who either exhaust themselves before their time by too assiduous labor, or waste themselves in those excesses which are common among the irreligious.

And ye rich! whose cupidity commands this flagrant violation of the law of God, have ye nothing to fear from this crowd of laborers without faith, without morals? Do you think that you can always sleep tranquil, while the passions of the populace, excited by your luxury, insulted by your callousness, unchained by your contempt of the law of God, behold your quickly-made fortune cemented with their sweat, and wish to enjoy it in their own turn? Do you not already see the symptoms of a deep irritation in those plots and riots which physical force may indeed check, but which it cannot hinder from reappearing more desperate and more dangerous?

Social necessity of the third commandment.—The profanation of Sunday is fatal to society, which it disturbs and dishonors.

It disturbs society. Without the rest of Sunday, which, suspending material labor, gives man leisure and imposes on him the obligation to occupy himself with moral labor, every kind of social amelioration is impossible. Why? Because the evils of society are in souls, and Christianity alone can apply a remedy for the evils of souls. Now, without the rest of Sunday, there is neither time nor place left for Christianity to speak to society. Do you yet know the character of a people among whom the voice of Christianity is no longer heard? They are without any religious bridle. They are slaves to passion. They are in a state of continual disquiet. The daily records of events dispense us from the necessity of saying more.

It dishonors society. Let it be well known that the violation of this sacred law of a weekly rest, as old as the world, and so religiously observed in every other region where the sun shines, places us in the lowest degree of public esteem. In Europe it brings us under the ban of civilized nations, and in Africa it teaches savages to rank us with dogs. To the imperative necessity of clearing away such a disgrace, and of settling society here on its proper basis, what is the objection? The interests of industry. For a conclusive answer, I shall be satisfied to say, "Look at England!" Because she religiously observes the sacred law of rest, is her commerce less flourishing, are her manufactures less prosperous, is her agriculture less remunerative than ours? Let society then beware: this is a question of life or death. No society without religion; no religion for three-fourths of the human race without keeping Sunday holy. It is therefore true that the third commandment of God is one of the bases of the social edifice, a guarantee for the rich and a benefit for the poor.[1187]

Reasons which justify labor on certain occasions.—We must now speak of the reasons which justify labor. God is a Father who requires the obedience of his children much more for their own sake than his. In his goodness, he dispenses with his law when sufficient reasons present themselves. There are several which excuse those who employ themselves in servile works on Sundays and holidays:

1. *Dispensation.* It may be granted by our holy father the pope to the Church at large. Thus, at the present day, in France, one can work on the festivals suppressed by the Concordat, though the sovereign pontiff desires that the office should be celebrated as previously. It may be the dispensation of a bishop in his diocese, or, in a few special cases, that of a parish priest in his parish. A person should ask a dispensation when there is any doubt whether the causes that seem to require it are sufficient. If therefore, at the time of gathering in corn, grapes, hay, flax, or the like, one doubts whether there is any necessity for it, that is to say, whether there is any real danger that the goods of the earth should be spoiled by the rain, the parish priest can dispense.

2. *Custom.* Here is the rule on this matter: one may follow the public custom of the places in which he lives, if the bishops and parish priests are aware of it and do not

oppose it. The custom should be public, and followed by virtuous persons. Thus, generally speaking, it is permitted on Sundays and holidays to cook food, even in superfluous quantities; to make the other preparations necessary for repasts, even for banquets; to attend to cleanliness of person and house; and to provide for cattle. Bakers, butchers, and confectioners may also, on these days, sell bread, meat, and confectionery. Usage seems also to authorize barbers, in town and country, to shave on Sunday. There is little difference between their occupation and that of hair-cutters, which is certainly permitted.[1188]

3. *Piety*. It permits the adornment of churches and altars on an occasion of solemnity, when this could not be done on working days. But it does not authorize the making of artificial flowers for the purpose. This is a servile work, which may easily be left to some other time.

4. *Necessity*. That is, when one cannot omit a servile work without incurring a heavy loss, or bringing on oneself or others a serious inconvenience. It is therefore permitted those who burn lime, bricks, or glass, and all those who have begun a work that would entail a heavy loss by its interruption to continue their work. Tailors may work at wedding or mourning suits, or for persons who are going from home and who cannot without much inconvenience delay their departure, or for the poor who have nothing else to put on: but it is necessary that they should not have been able to do so beforehand. Necessity also excuses sailors, boatmen, messengers, and postmen, whose services cannot be interrupted without grave inconvenience. Finally, it excuses wives, children, and servants, who are obliged by their husbands, parents, and masters to work, since they cannot resist without grave inconvenience.

As for persons dependent on others, and so busy during the week that they really have no other day than Sunday to mend their poor clothes, they may labor for a few hours, on condition of obtaining permission from their pastor or confessor to do so, that they may assist at the offices and appear in such a manner as not to give scandal. It is the same with very poor persons, who have to labor to procure the necessaries of life, as well for themselves as their families.

A Christian, who finds himself under the necessity of laboring on Sunday, ought only to do so with regret, and for as short a time as possible. It is little enough to employ one day in the week solely about the great, the only affair for which we have come into existence. What would it avail us to gain the whole world, if we should lose our own souls? Besides, one ought carefully to remember that if it is permitted him to find leisure for servile works, he is not therefore dispensed from the obligation of hearing Mass. It would be a grievous error to imagine those generally exempt from this obligation who, in case of necessity, may work on Sundays and holidays during harvest, vintage, or hay making time.[1189]

Explanation of what is commanded by the third commandment.—After forbidding all works contrary to the sanctification of Sunday, the third commandment prescribes some others which we are to perform. Before speaking of that most sublime act which is commanded us on this day by the Church, under pain of grievous sin,[1190] it is well to bear in mind that to hear the word of God, to assist at catechism with piety and devotion,[1191] to receive the sacraments, to read good books, to visit the Blessed Sacrament, to instruct the ignorant, to console the poor and the sick—in a word, to perform spiritual and corporal works of charity according to one's state and condition, are so many excellent means to sanctify holy days.

Such was the conduct of the early Christians, our ancestors and our models in the faith. We read in history, and we shall see in the third part[1192] of the catechism, that on these holy days they used to listen eagerly to the instructions of the apostles, to receive the Blessed Eucharist, to give alms to the poor, and to offer up fervent prayers to God for themselves and the whole Church. Do we not serve the same God?

If the soul should sanctify Sunday, is it not proper that the body should take part in doing so? In Christian countries, people are careful to sweep the streets on Saturday evening. On the one hand, they wish that no noise should profane the day of rest; and on the other, that everything should be in that state of neatness which delights the beholder, denoting respect for the holy day. So, too, on Saturday, they lay in provisions, as far as possible, for Sunday; and the furniture and the kitchen utensils are cleaned: always through the motives indicated above. Finally, all persons dress themselves on Sunday in their best clothes, not out of vanity, but to do honor to their heavenly Father. Worldlings reserve their costly ornaments and precious garments for vanity, to which they render homage in their balls and other festivities. The Christian does everything for God. On which side is reason?

How admirable was the conduct of the glorious chancellor of England, Thomas More! In the prison to which his love for the faith had led him, he never failed on Sunday to wear his finest clothes. When asked the reason, he replied, "I keep festivals solemnly, and I wear my richest dress in honor of God, who is everywhere, and not to please the eyes of the people, who do not see me." It is also an excellent custom in families to meet on these days around the same table, and to take part in an innocent repast.

Holy Sacrifice of the Mass.—But among all the works of piety, there is one which is prescribed under pain of mortal sin: it is assistance at the Holy Sacrifice of the Mass. Blessed be the Church, which has given us this command! Never did she show herself more a mother toward us. In effect, the Mass being the most excellent act of religion, it is also the most excellent means to honor God and to draw down his sanctifying blessings upon us.[1193]

What is this august sacrifice? Though one should speak the language of angels, it would be impossible for him to tell the excellence of the sublime mystery which is wrought on our altars. The Mass is a continuation of the sacrifice of the cross: the same priest and the same victim. This is the sum of all that can be said. The Mass is, therefore, of all works the most holy, the most divine,[1194] the most pleasing to God; a work which can effectually disarm his anger; a work, says one of the fathers, to which is attached the salvation of the world.[1195]

One single Mass has as much efficacy in promoting the glory of God and the salvation of men as the sacrifice of the cross.[1196]

Conditions for hearing Mass well. In order to hear it well and to satisfy the precept of the Church, there are several conditions necessary: respect, attention, devotion, and entirety.

1. *Respect.* The angels, who surround the altar during the awful sacrifice, are bowed down, their faces covered with their wings. It is the least that we can do, to bring to the holy mysteries a modest demeanor, a profound recollection. A person fails in the respect due to the Mass when he assumes thereat postures which are not allowed in good society; when he appears in attire scarcely deserving the name of decent; when he casts his looks from side to side; when he yields to laughter or conversation; when he kneels at improper times; in a word, when he enters, remains in, or leaves a church, as if God were not there. How reprehensible are those Christians whose behavior during the august sacrifice gives room to doubt whether they have faith, whether it is their object to adore or to insult! If our Lord drove out indignantly the profaners of the Temple of Jerusalem, with what kind of eye does he behold the profaners of a temple a thousand times more sacred?

A young man, belonging to the court of Alexander, was assisting at a sacrifice offered by command of this prince. As he held a censer, a hot coal fell on his arm. He endured the burn without uttering a word of complaint, without so much as stirring the coal. He feared lest the slightest movement should disturb the order of the sacrifice and offend Alexander. This fact, related by St. Ambrose, may well put to confusion a great many Christians, who have so little respect for the Son of God in his temple, even during the adorable sacrifice.

2. *Attention.* It is not enough to assist bodily at Mass: one must assist at it with the intention of hearing it, and of hearing it attentively. The precept would not be fulfilled by him who should assist at Mass merely for the purpose of seeing the church, of waiting for a friend, of meeting some person, or because he had been forced to it by violence. We say "by violence," because the child that should hear Mass just through a fear of its father or mother or superior—if, in addition, it were attentive—would satisfy the precept, even though it sinned by its evil wish to dispense itself from Mass, if in its power. But it is not necessary to have the intention of fulfilling the precept. To satisfy the precept of hearing Mass, it is enough to hear Mass in effect.[1197]

Besides the intention of hearing Mass, there is also need of attention, at least virtual, to what is done during the holy sacrifice. To know whether one has it or not, there are two kinds of distractions to be considered: voluntary and involuntary. To occupy one's mind during Mass with affairs of business, pleasure, frivolity; to fall asleep, to speak, to look about in such a manner as to take no notice of what is occurring at the altar; to perceive all this without making any effort to return to prayer: assuredly there is a voluntary distraction here, which destroys attention.

Such a distraction is sinful, and, if it continues during a notable part of the holy sacrifice, it prevents the fulfillment of the precept. He who renders himself thus guilty is bound to hear another Mass, if in his power. To be voluntarily distracted at Mass, to amuse the mind in those solemn moments with a thousand vain thoughts, is to imitate the pagan soldiers who played their games with one another at the foot of the cross on which the eternal Son of God was dying for their salvation.

Involuntary distractions are those which we experience in spite of ourselves, and which we drive away as soon as we perceive them. Not being culpable, they do not destroy virtual attention, or hinder us from hearing Mass. A means of avoiding distractions is to choose, as well as a person can, a place favorable to recollection; and to follow, in a missal or other such book, the prayers said by the priest, or to accompany him in intention. If one cannot read, it is very good to say the beads. Another means of shunning distractions during the holy offices is to go to them with more recollection, to take holy water with piety, and to say, on entering the church, what St. Bernard used to say to all worldly affairs: "Strange thoughts, thoughts of business, thoughts of amusement, remain outside."

3. *Devotion.* To hear Mass with the desire of going away from it better; with the intention of honoring God; with love for our Lord, with confidence in him, with a wish to be immolated on the altar with him and no longer to live but in accordance with his maxims; in a word, to hear Mass in the spirit of a victim, is to hear it with devotion. How rare is this disposition, and how earnestly we ought to ask it of God! How many go to Mass without any good purpose—through mere routine! Is it surprising that they should depart from the church as little like Christians as they entered it?

The means of exciting this devotion within us is to consider, on the one hand, the number of our spiritual and temporal wants, and, on the other, the infinite goodness of our Lord, who vouchsafes while being immolated, to address us these touching words, "What will you that I should do for you?"[1198] Can he who loved us so much as to shed his blood for us refuse us anything?

4. *Entirety.* It is necessary to hear the whole Mass. They are always guilty who arrive, through their own fault, after it has begun. "But the Mass is too long," said a person

one day in presence of Mgr. de la Motte, bishop of Amiens. "Say rather," answered the holy prelate, "that your devotion is too short." Shame on the child that is weary in the company of its father: shame on the man who is weary in the presence of his God! Out of seven days one day, and out of the twenty-four hours of this seventh day God asks your assistance at the holy mysteries for a couple of hours at most, and you think it too much! If one omits, without reason, a considerable portion of the Mass, he is guilty of a grievous fault; if the omitted portion is but slight, the fault is only venial.

It would be a grievous fault to be absent during all that part which precedes the gospel and that which follows the priest's Communion, or during the consecration and the Communion, or even during the consecration or the Communion under the two species, or finally from the end of the consecration to the *Pater* exclusively.[1199] It is admitted, on the contrary, that the fault is only venial if one omits the offertory, or the preface, or that part of the Mass which follows the priest's Communion.

It appears very probable that one is guilty of a grievous fault by being absent from the beginning of Mass to the gospel, inclusively. St. Alphonsus believes that it is even a mortal sin not to arrive until after the epistle. Yet he admits as "probable" the opinion which holds that the fault is not mortal unless one does not arrive in time for the gospel.[1200] To hear Mass, it is necessary to be in a church or in a place where the holy mysteries are celebrated. He also would hear Mass who should be present behind a partition or a pillar of the church, or even outside the church, if he formed part of the congregation which penetrated into the interior. This case happens often enough on great solemnities.[1201]

Causes which dispense from the obligation of hearing Mass. No one is dispensed from hearing Mass, except in case of physical or moral impossibility. Physical impossibility: one is sick, infirm, or convalescent. If there is doubt, it is necessary to take the advice of a physician or some prudent person: in doubt, the pastor can dispense. Moral impossibility: if, from assistance at Mass, there should result a grievous loss, or a grievous inconvenience, whether spiritual or temporal, to oneself or others.

Thus, those who have to attend on the sick are excused; likewise, those who have to guard a city, a house, little children that cannot be brought to church, flocks that cannot be left without danger, etc. If there are two Masses, these persons may generally hear one of them; if there is only one, they are bound to assist at it in turn. Those also are excused who, on account of distance, can only with great difficulty go to church. In all this, it is necessary to have regard to the age and the condition of persons, and also to times and roads.

They, too, who are in mourning are excused for as long a time as they do not leave their own house, according to the custom of places; the drivers of public coaches, which cannot be stopped; the traveler, who, by delaying, should run the risk of losing his place, or of losing a fellow traveler from whom he could not be separated without grave inconvenience. Lastly, servants, wives, and children are excused, when their masters, husbands, and parents absolutely require them to work during the time of Mass, if they cannot refuse to obey without serious inconvenience. Such would be a well-grounded fear of rage, blasphemy, or cursing; and, in what concerns laborers and servants, a fear of being dismissed, without any good prospect of being able to find speedily or easily another master who would permit them to fulfill their duties of religion. But, O great God! how guilty are they who thus compel their inferiors to profane holy days![1202]

They who cannot assist at Mass pray at home. But what Mass should be heard? To assist at any Mass suffices for the strict fulfillment of the precept. The habit of assisting at late Masses is blamable. It speaks of sloth, of slavery to worldly requirements, and frequently of intentions far from upright. It exposes one to the danger of mistaking the hour, and to the want of all instruction. No one can ever know how injurious to the

Christian spirit—the result of charity and religious instruction—is the habit of being absent from the parish Mass, or how criminal in the eyes of God is that facility with which some persons dispense themselves from the obligation of hearing any Mass.

If Mass were said only once a year, what eagerness would there be to assist at it! But, because it is said many times, is it less precious? Newly-converted savages are found to travel eighteen or twenty miles to be present at the adorable sacrifice. Oh, how loudly does their fervor condemn the wicked indifference of so many Christians, who, having hardly a step to make for the purpose, dispense themselves from attending! But the road is bad, the weather is severe: vain pretexts! If there were question of gaining a sum of money, you would undertake a much longer journey on a worse road and in more severe weather.

The most violent persecutions could not hinder our predecessors in the faith from appearing on Sundays, in the assemblies of religion. A Christian virgin, named Anysia, was once going thither, when she was observed by one of the emperor Dioclesian's guards. He was struck with her modesty. Going up to her, he said, "Stop! where are you going?" Anysia, fearing from the tone of his voice that he meant to insult her, made on her forehead the sign of the cross, to obtain a strengthening grace from God. The soldier was offended that she should not return any other answer than such a sign to the question which he had put to her.

He laid his hand on her, and said angrily, "Speak! Who are you, and where are you going?" She answered, "I am a servant of Jesus Christ, and I am going to the Lord's assembly." "I will take good care to prevent you," he exclaimed, "I will bring you to sacrifice to the gods: we this day adore the sun." At the same moment he endeavored to snatch away the veil that covered her face. Anysia strove to prevent him, and said, "Begone, wretched man, Jesus Christ will punish you!" The soldier, furious, drew out his sword and plunged it into her heart. The young virgin fell, bathed in her blood, a martyr to the observance of Sunday. But while her body lay lifeless, her soul, crowned with glory, went to adore in heaven the Lamb which the priest was about to immolate on earth.

As we have seen, the third commandment, like all the others, is wholly for our advantage. Without this day of prayer and rest, our mind, continually occupied with temporal affairs, would soon forget its last end. Our love, instead of being purified, would become more and more degraded, and we should soon reach the level of pagans. Is not this what occurs among those people who neglect to keep the Sunday holy? Now, our love, by concentrating itself on the goods of time, becomes a source of continual calamities. Avarice, voluptuousness, and ambition are the only rules of those who no longer think of the other life; and these three passions throw the world into confusion.

It is therefore an incontestable truth that the sanctification of Sunday is as necessary to the repose of society as to the salvation of man. May we not henceforth tremble for the future? May we not shed bitter tears on beholding the Lord's day changed, even by the greater number of those who call themselves Christians, into the devil's day? This holy day ought to be consecrated to the service of God and the salvation of our souls. And yet it is the day on which the Lord is most offended, the day on which our souls receive the deepest wounds. Woe be to us! Woe be to us! By a sacrilegious abuse, the festivals of heaven have become the festivals of hell.

PRAYER

O my God! who art all love, I thank thee for having perpetuated the adorable sacrifice of the cross, by daily immolating for us thy divine Son on the altars of the whole world. Reanimate my devotion, that I may always assist at Mass in a Christian manner.

I am resolved to love God above all things, and my neighbor as myself for the love of God; and, in testimony of this love, I will daily assist at Mass either corporally or spiritually.

Lesson 50: Our Union with the New Adam by Charity (5)

We have duties to fulfill toward God and the neighbor, because we live in society with them. The three commandments which we have just explained, and which form the first table of the law, regulate all our duties toward God; and all these duties may be reduced to one—the love of God above all things.

The other seven, which form the second table, treat of our duties toward the neighbor; and all these duties may be reduced to one—the love of the neighbor as ourselves for the love of God. Hence, although the immediate object of these latter commandments is charity toward the neighbor, yet their term is God, since it is for the love of him that we ought to love the neighbor. This is the reason why our Lord said that the commandment of loving God and that of loving the neighbor are like each other, and comprise the whole law and the prophets.[1203]

Fourth commandment: Its meaning and extent.—The fourth commandment is thus expressed: "Thy parents honor, if thou wouldst live long."[1204] If the first table of the law begins with our duties toward God, our Creator, and the source of all paternity, is it not just that the second, which is consecrated to the neighbor, should begin with our duties toward our fathers and mothers. Associated, as it were, to the creative power of God himself, they are the authors of our life, which is the foundation of all temporal blessings.[1205]

The words *fathers* and *mothers* have a very wide meaning.[1206] They regard not only those who have brought us into the world, but also those who hold the place of fathers and mothers toward us, be it from their authority over us, or from their dignity, or from our need of them, or from the excellence of their functions, or from their age. In a word, by *fathers* and *mothers* we here understand all superiors. Of whom there are four classes: our natural superiors—fathers, mothers, old persons; our spiritual superiors—our holy father the pope, bishops, priests, sponsors; our civil superiors—the monarch, princes, magistrates; and our superiors by contract—masters and mistresses.

The word *honor* means in general to have a high esteem for anyone, and to make great account of all that relates to him. It was with reason that God, when imposing this precept, employed the word *honor*, and not *love* or *fear*, although we are bound to love and fear our fathers and mothers. He who loves anyone does not always honor him, and he who fears anyone does not always love him. On the other hand, he who sincerely honors anyone both loves and fears him. Now, the honor which we owe to our parents comprises four duties: respect, love, obedience, and assistance.

Duties of children.—1. *Respect.* Our fathers and mothers hold the place of God himself in our regard. This is the foundation of their dignity, as well as their title to the respect which we owe them. Respect must be internal and external. Internal: children should esteem their father and mother, ask their advice, defer to their opinion, receive their remarks and reproofs with docility and submission. They would be very guilty if they paid no attention to their words; with much greater reason, if they ridiculed them, or, in reply, observed a morose and sullen silence. External: respect should be manifested in looks, words, and actions. Everything should be done in a submissive and humble manner, and this, whatever may be the age, or the poverty, or the infirmity of fathers and mothers.

Thus Joseph, who, after the king, was the mightiest man in Egypt, received his father Jacob with the greatest marks of honor. Solomon, when he saw his mother coming to him, rose from his seat, and, bowing profoundly to her, made her sit down at his right hand on his throne. Among the Persians, children used never to sit in presence of their parents: king as he was, Darius conformed religiously to this practice. How severely do these examples condemn the conduct of Christian children, especially in our day, who sin habitually against the respect due to fathers and mothers! They scoff at them, look askance at them, shrug their shoulders at them, bang doors in their face, address them impertinently, answer them sourly, mimic them, threaten them, decry their character, or expose their faults or their defects. It is also a grievous want of respect toward parents to institute lawsuits against them and drag them before public tribunals.

2. *Love*. It must be acknowledged that the heart of man was very corrupt when God thought it necessary to lay an express command on children to love their parents, and that, to incline them to fulfill it, he added a promise of temporal happiness. Has not nature made it a duty on all beings, even lions and tigers, to love those who have given them birth? And irrational animals are faithful to it. What sorrows, what pains, what labors, what anxieties have we not cost our parents! Is it not to them, after God, that we owe everything? Unnatural children! This is therefore the name that becomes those who do not love their fathers and mothers; who, instead of loving them, grieve them; who entertain for them no other sentiments than those of indifference, bitterness, or aversion.

But, to be Christian, the love of children must partake of a supernatural principle. To love our parents with a view to God and because God commands it; to love them in their soul and in their body; to wish and to do them all the spiritual and temporal good that can reasonably be expected, whatever may be their failings or their virtues: in duties such as these appear the qualities of Christian love. It is a sin, therefore, against filial piety to nourish a hatred of parents in one's heart; to desire that evil may befall them, or to rejoice when it has befallen them; to long for their death; or to sadden them without legitimate cause.

3. *Obedience*. This is the great duty of inferiors in general and of children in particular. Children owe it to their parents, especially in that which concerns good morals and education, and that which concerns the administration and welfare of the family. Obedience ought to be simple, prompt, and constant. Simple: children should not reason about a command. They should hasten to obey as often as the thing commanded is not contrary to the law of God. If it is contrary to this law, they are not only not bound to do it, but they would even sin by doing it. "We must obey God rather than man."[1207] Prompt: scarcely should an order be given when children should have it fulfilled. As soon as they hear the voice of their father or their mother, it should seem to them that they hear the voice of God himself. Constant: obedience should extend to all places; to all circumstances, whether the thing is easy or difficult; to all ages—even after the death of parents, by a faithful execution of their last will.

They are therefore guilty against obedience who oblige parents to repeat over and over again the same command, who only attend to it slowly and with a bad grace, and who thereby cause many sins, such as impatience, and sometimes swearing. It is also a sin against obedience when, in spite of the order of parents, one omits to hear Mass on Sunday, or refuses to approach the sacrament of penance or to assist at instructions; and when, in spite of the prohibition of parents, one frequents suspected houses or meetings, keeps company with dangerous characters, quits the parental roof, or does not faithfully comply with a father's or mother's dying wishes.

Children, to excite themselves to obedience, ought to set before their eyes the examples of the saints. Isaac humbly and unrepiningly submitted to the will of his father, when the latter was about to bind him and to sacrifice him to God. Joseph made a long journey to comply with the last wishes of Jacob, and to convey his bones to the tomb of Abraham and Isaac. But the great example on which they ought always to meditate is that of our Lord. The divine Word, he by whom all things were made, the Son of God, obeyed two of his own creatures! The gospel gives us in five words the history of his childhood and youth: "He was subject to them."[1208] After this, what child will be so bold as to disobey?

4. *Assistance.* Filial piety is not barren: it must manifest itself in works. Children are therefore obliged to assist parents in their temporal and spiritual wants. We should think ourselves happy to have it in our power to return our fathers and mothers a portion of what we have received from them. They nourished us, clothed us, brought us up. In our turn, we ought, when there is occasion, to nourish them, to clothe them, to provide them with all the helps demanded by their poverty, their infirmity, or their old age. We must behave in such a manner that our parents may be able to say to us as the father and mother of young Tobias used to say to their son: "O you, our dear child, the light of our eyes, the staff of our old age, the only consolation of our life!"[1209]

Although the obligation of assisting brothers and sisters is not so rigorous as that of assisting fathers and mothers, yet, by reason of consanguinity, this obligation is much stricter than that of assisting any strangers.

If children owe corporal succor to their fathers and mothers, how much more ought they to procure spiritual succor for them, especially in case of sickness! First, they are bound to pray for them. They ought also, according to circumstances, to remind them of their duties, but with all the respect, prudence, and charity possible. Lastly, they ought to neglect no means of enabling them, if sick, to die well. Thus have truly Christian children acted in all ages. Witness among a thousand instances that of a virtuous Chinee, to whose exemplary zeal we cannot refrain from making reference.

In 1847, this Christian, aged seventy years, and named Peter Amia, dwelt at Singapore. One day, a fellow countryman of his comes and tells him that his mother, whom he left in China many years before and who has reached a very advanced age, is sick, and still unfortunately a pagan. On hearing this news, the good son, the generous old man, makes his preparations for departure, and sets out on a journey of nearly two thousand miles. His faith and filial piety are rewarded. He has the happiness of finding his mother yet alive. He instructs her, baptizes her, and never leaves her till he has the consolation of closing her eyes, that they may open in heaven.[1210]

Children therefore sin grievously if they fail in enabling their fathers and mothers to receive the last sacraments. And yet how many children allow their parents to die without giving themselves the trouble to call the priest, or who only call him when it is too late! Heartless pity! murderous tenderness! whose consequence will be an eternity of torments for the parents, and perhaps for the children! Last of all, this spiritual assistance ought to accompany our father and mother even beyond the grave, that is to say, we ought to continue to pray and to get others to pray for them after their death.

In the midst of his greatest disorders, St. Augustine always honored very much his mother, St. Monica. "In her last illness," he tells us himself, "she assured me that she was well pleased with me, and with the care which I had endeavored to take of her. She called me her 'good son,' and told me that I had never uttered a word to her of which she could complain."[1211]

After losing her, St. Augustine shed many tears, whose flowing he could not prevent, when he thought of her amiable manners, so sweet, so gentle, so full of tenderness, a tenderness wholly Christian. He offered the sacrifice of our redemption for her, and recommended her to the prayers of all the faithful who should read the book of his *Confessions.* A venerable bishop had said to St. Monica before Augustine's conversion, "It is impossible that a mother who asks of God with so many tears the salvation of her son, should have the grief to see him lost." We may add that it was the filial piety of Augustine toward his fond and saintly mother that induced the Lord to grant him the graces by the help of which he broke his chains.

Reward of those who observe it.—As a matter of fact, the fourth commandment promises that those who observe it shall live long. This promise contains a triple blessing: a temporal blessing—a long life; a spiritual blessing—special graces for the attainment of salvation; and an eternal blessing—the blessing of parents reaches even to a good death. Yes, it is of faith that the first fruit of fidelity to the fourth commandment is a long life. What is more reasonable than that those who are mindful of a benefit should be permitted to enjoy it for as long a time as possible? But to make a lengthening of life a reward, it must be happy. Hence, God not only promises length of life, but also the tranquility and health necessary to make it happy. If it were otherwise, God, who desires to reward filial piety, would not be faithful or constant in his promises.

Yet will not one sometimes see die, at an age not very advanced, those who have entertained for their fathers and mothers a deep sense of filial piety? We must answer that, if this is so, there are exceptions which God permits for the greater good of his elect. He calls them to himself before they have abandoned the way of virtue and compromised their eternal honor. At other times he hastens to disengage them from the fetters of the body, that they may not be overwhelmed by the woes which threaten the world; or rather, that they may be spared the sorrow with which they should be filled to see the evils and misfortunes of their relatives and friends. Wherefore, we ought to be seized with an exceeding great fear when good people are taken away by a premature death.[1212]

Punishment of those who violate it.—If God promises a triple blessing to children who honor their fathers and mothers, those who break the fourth commandment deprive themselves of this triple blessing. To die young or to live miserable: such is the fate reserved for them. Terrible are the threats of God in their regard. "He who afflicts his father or mother is infamous and unhappy. Let the eye of him who insulteth his father, and despiseth the labor of his mother in bearing him, be torn out by the ravens of the brook and eaten by the young eagles."[1213] The effect follows the threat, sometimes in an extraordinary manner. Absalom rebels against his father David. God permits that this unnatural child should be pierced with three arrows, and should die miserably, in punishment of his crime.

Duties of parents.—The honor which we owe to our fathers and mothers comprises therefore respect, love, obedience, and corporal and spiritual assistance. These are the things which God requires of children, for their own salvation and for the happiness of families. He is no less just in what he requires of fathers and mothers. They owe to their children: nurture, instruction, correction, good example, and watchfulness.

1. *Nurture.* Parents ought to procure for their children all that is temporally and spiritually necessary for them. This obligation begins even before the child is born. Hence, the mother, under pain of failing in her duty, should wisely take care of her health, in order to preserve that of her child and to give it a strong constitution. To run, to dance, to carry heavy burdens, to yield to anger, to indulge excessively in eating and drinking, would all be reprehensible imprudences. The father who, through a cruelty equally hurtful to mother and child, vexes the former, strikes her, and makes life a kind of torment to her, is exceedingly guilty. In a word, whatever on the part of parents may be notably injurious to the life, the health, or the conformation of the child, is a mortal sin.

When it is born, the father and mother are bound to watch that it meets with no accident which might prove fatal to it, or leave it crippled or deformed. To put a little child in danger of falling into fire or water, or to strike it severely, is mostly a great sin. It is also a guilty imprudence of fathers and mothers to make a child of yet tender age sleep with themselves or with other grown persons.

The father and mother are bound, according to their power, to nourish, clothe, and rear their children according to their state and condition. Nature itself makes this a law. A great many parents are guilty on this point rather by excess than by defect. They supply their children with food that is too delicate, with clothing that is too rich, with pleasures that are not suited to the young. This kind of treatment is not serviceable either to their children or to themselves. For it too often happens that children, brought up in a style above their condition, despise their fathers and mothers. They even become a plague to society.

Besides the maintenance of corporal life, fathers and mothers also owe to their children a preparation for civil life. They are therefore bound to concern themselves about the future of their children, to endeavor to give them a suitable position in life, regard being had to the paternal state and to the inclinations of the children. They sin mortally when, through indolence or extravagance, they render themselves unable to fulfill this duty, one of the most important devolving on parents. "If any man has not care of his own, and chiefly of those of his house," says St. Paul, "he has denied the faith, and is worse than an infidel."[1214]

2. *Instruction.* We have seen that parents owe corporal and civil life to their children. With much greater reason do they owe spiritual life to them. The child is a deposit, of which God shall require an account, blood for blood. They ought therefore to have their children baptized as soon as possible after birth; to instruct them themselves, or to have them instructed by virtuous and capable persons; to send them to catechism and instructions; in a word, to adopt all the means necessary to procure for them a knowledge of religion, and of the duties which it imposes on them.

The neglect of parents to teach their children or to have them taught the elements of the faith, the Apostles' Creed, the Lord's Prayer, the commandments of God and of the Church, and those among the sacraments of which a knowledge is necessary to each of the faithful individually, is a spiritual murder, a very great sin, and an occasion of deplorable disorders in families and in society.

Who will tell the number of parents of all classes that are thus guilty, especially in our day, when so much care is given to profane instruction, and little or none to religious instruction; when parents allow the old customs of faith, such as prayer in common, the daily reading of the *Lives of the Saints*, and the giving an account of sermons and catechisms, to die out: salutary customs, a thousand times more effectual in keeping alive a practical knowledge of religion than all public teachings?

3. *Correction.* This is one of the most important duties in the education of children, and perhaps that in which fathers and mothers fail most frequently. Either they do not comply with it at all, or they comply with it improperly. They do not comply with it at all when they flatter the vices of their children, or reprove them about trifles and neglect to do so about very serious matters. They comply with it improperly when they reprove with bitterness, impatience, or passion.

As a general rule, if one desires a correction to be profitable, it should not be given immediately after the fault. By acting otherwise, a person runs the risk of following his humor rather than his reason, and of scandalizing the child. Besides, the child is too much moved at the moment to derive any benefit from the correction. It is much better, in every way, to wait until souls calm down, so as to show that one is prompted only by a sense of affection and duty. Let parents remember the example of the high priest Heli, who was struck with a terrible punishment for having been too indulgent toward his children.[1215] Correction, to be useful as well as Christian, must be just, firm, mild, prudent, and reasonable.

But let fathers and mothers beware of ever cursing their children: this curse is too often followed by its effect. Passing by the example related by St. Augustine,[1216] and the many others to be found in history, we shall cite one of a very recent date. It was related by a missionary, belonging to the Indies, in 1848. A Malay Christian, named Anna, had lost her husband and had no means of existence left except through an only son, lately married. A frightful occurrence soon deprived her of her son and her daughter-in-law. She was left alone with a grandchild, named Joanni. She sacrificed everything to bring him up, and hoped to establish him well before her death. She cast her eyes on a young Christian, named Bastiana. The marriage was concluded.

In a short time, the young couple began to lose that respect and regard for their old friend which they owed to her age and her kindness. She, exceedingly provoked, brings the children before the missionary, and in the outburst of her anger curses them. In vain the missionary strives to calm this mother's wounded heart. In vain he represents to her that such a curse is never without misfortune, and that she herself may one day bitterly lament having been heard. "Let them disappear from the face of the earth," she replies, "may God strike them, and may their days soon end!"

According to the divine word, the effects of such imprecations are fearful: here, they were not slow to manifest themselves. A few months later, Bastiana dies almost suddenly. Anna begins to weep. Notwithstanding the displeasure that her grandson had caused her, it was he who still provided for her wants; and, besides, the mother's heart had returned to itself. She asks of heaven the preservation of her only child. She goes in search of the missionary, and beseeches him to remove from her Joanni the curse that she has been so unhappy as to utter. God was doubtless pleased to forgive, as regards eternity, both the sin of the son and the sin of the mother, by exercising his justice on them in this world. Joanni falls sick and dies a holy death. "It was on the 16th March," says the missionary, "that I prayed at the church for the poor young man. The funeral service is over, and Joanni's remains are conveyed slowly to the burying-ground. A procession accompanies them from the church...I hear sobs and shrieks. Unfortunate Anna!"[1217]

4. *Good example.* If obedience is the great duty of children, good example is the great duty of parents. Being the vicegerents of God in the family, they ought to be his living images. As far as human weakness permits it, they ought to act, to command, to reprove, to direct, as God himself would do, if he were visibly present at the head of the family. But, of all their obligations the most sacred is that of giving good example by a faithful accomplishment of all the duties of religion.

To pray; to assist at offices; to frequent the sacraments; to observe days of fast and abstinence; to avoid with the utmost care all blasphemous, slanderous, and immodest expressions, in a word, whatever might scandalize children: it is thus that parents ought, under pain of the heaviest guilt, to give good example, not one day, but all the days of their lives. For this purpose they require many graces. No longer, then, should they forget to ask them by prayer, and by prayer in common, which is the true family prayer. In the names of themselves, their children, the Church, and society, let them restore this heavenly and touching custom of our ancestors. Pagans themselves set an example of it.[1218]

5. *Watchfulness.* Parents are bound to watch over the conduct of their children, that is, to see whether they fulfill the duties of Christians, what kind of company they keep, how they make choice of reading. This watchfulness ought to be continual. A moment's sleep is enough to let the enemy sow the cockle in the field of good grain. If parents think that they can lay on others the education of their children, they ought to select persons worthy of their confidence. They sin mortally if they entrust them to persons without faith, without religion, without morals—capable of perverting young people by their principles, or by their evil example, or merely by their indifference.[1219] Parents are also bound to enable their children to enter on their vocation. By prayers and counsels, they should help them to know it; but they commit a very great sin if they force them either to shun or to embrace a state to which God calls them.

Finally, fathers and mothers ought to love their children according to God and for God. If they do so, they will love them equally, without preferring one to another. We know the sad effects that followed Jacob's predilection for Joseph. To conclude what relates to the spiritual life, if children are dangerously ill, parents ought to do everything possible to procure for them a happy death: it would be a grievous fault to let them die without the sacraments.[1220]

In the eyes of religion, society is only one great family: superiors are like parents; inferiors, like children. Hence, the duties of society are only an extension of the duties of the family. This is the reason why inferiors are bound to honor, that is, to respect, to love, to obey, and to assist their superiors—in other words, our holy father the pope, bishops, priests, kings, princes, magistrates, tutors, guardians, masters, old persons. All these deserve to share in the fruits of our charity, our obedience, and our toil, but not in the same degree.

Those whom we ought to honor most of all are our holy father the pope, bishops, and priests, because the first is the vicar of Jesus Christ and the others are his ambassadors, commissioned to perpetuate religion on the earth and to procure for mankind the happiness of eternity.[1221] After them come kings, princes, and our other superiors in the temporal order, because they only concur indirectly to the salvation of our souls.[1222] Finally, old persons, for they are an image of our parents.

Duties of servants, masters, and mistresses.—Servants owe respect, obedience (but a religious obedience), service, and fidelity to their masters and mistresses. Hence, servants sin when they fail in any of these duties. On the other hand, masters and mistresses are bound: a) to instruct servants or to have them instructed in the mysteries of religion and in the duties of Christianity, particularly in the duties of their state; b) to see that they keep the commandments of God and of the Church; c) to watch over their general behavior; d) to reprove them charitably, mindful of that saying which is so true, yet so often forgotten: "If, to be a servant, it were necessary to be faultless, there would be very few masters capable of being servants"; e) to supply them with a sufficiency of food and not to overwork them; and f) to pay them their wages faithfully.

All these duties are founded on this principle: that masters and mistresses hold the place of fathers and mothers to their servants, according to the touching idea which Christianity gives us through St. Paul. Addressing the former, the great apostle says, "Threaten not your servants, but remember that you also have a master in heaven, who has no regard to the condition of persons."[1223]

Conformably to this doctrine, St. Augustine warns masters that they ought to consider themselves as bishops at the head of their houses, and that in this character they ought to watch over the conduct of their domestics, for whose spiritual wants they have to provide.[1224]

Schoolmasters, tutors, governesses, conductors of boarding seminaries, professors, in a word, all those who are charged with the instruction and education of youth, being the depositaries of parental confidence as well as of parental authority, ought to labor constantly to make their pupils advance in piety, virtue, and learning. They become grievously culpable if they abandon them to themselves—without watching over their conduct, without making them fulfill the duties of religion; if they neglect to put them on their guard against anything that might sully their innocence or destroy their health; if they leave in their hands books dangerous to faith or morals: with much more reason, if they give them bad example.[1225]

Duties of superiors in general.—As for the duties of superiors in general, they are like those of masters and mistresses, since every superior is a minister of God for good. Now, the good of man is his end, and his end is his sanctification. Hence, all those who are above others, be they kings or popes, ought chiefly to set before their eyes the glory of God and the salvation of their inferiors. It is a duty on them, whatever may be their form of government, to protect the rights of all, to have justice done, to give their subjects liberty (that is, the opportunity of doing good), to repress licentiousness, to see that the laws of religion are respected, to prevent the publication of wicked books, in fine, to give an example of faith and of an exact observance of the commandments of God and the Church.

Superiors! whoever you are, spiritual or temporal, remember well that you were made for your inferiors much rather than your inferiors for you. Your time, your experience, your health, your care, your vigilance, all belong to them. This is the reason why, in the language of Christianity, power is called a "charge." This is the reason why the greatest of all superiors, the vicar of Jesus Christ, humbly calls himself "the servant of the servants of God."

Social advantages of the fourth commandment.—And now is it hard to understand how advantageous to society is the fourth commandment? Remark in the first place that, under the names of fathers and mothers, God includes all superiors. Profound philosophy of the divine language! It is true, then, that the world is only filled with parents and children, that is to say, that all mankind form but one family! Now, no family without the fourth commandment.

When I say "no family," I mean "no family such as it ought to be," in order to contribute to the happiness and the glory of society—that is, enlightened, moral, tranquil, united; distinguished by the mildness, firmness, and devotedness of fathers and mothers, and the obedience, respect, and love of children. Without the fourth commandment, you may have families of heathens, Turks, or savages, in which the father is a tyrant, the mother a slave, and the child a victim until it grows to be a rebel; but you cannot have a Christian family, the only family worthy of the name. Truly, therefore, it is to the fourth commandment that the Christian family, and consequently Christian society, owe their superiority over all other families and societies that are not acquainted with this precept in its full extent.

O Christian family! O Christian society! why then do you forget, why do you trample underfoot this commandment, the cause of your happiness? Experience, reason, observation, ancient history, modern history—bring all these witnesses to the front, and they will say to you, "Honor your father and your mother: this is the price of your temporal happiness."

History.—Let us finish with a short sketch from history, which will serve as a lesson to children and parents, as well as to inferiors and superiors in general.

Reason points out that an evil should be arrested in the beginning. Fathers and mothers ought therefore to correct their children from an early age, before the passions are strong enough to break the rein. Notwithstanding the precautions of her housekeeper, St. Monica, in her youth, insensibly acquired a relish for wine, as she afterward acknowledged to St. Augustine, her son. It was she that usually went to the cellar, and, when she had drawn the wine, she would sip a few drops. This did not arise from any inclination to intemperance: it was the effect of that levity and impetuosity which everyone remarks in children.

Meanwhile, the quantity of wine which the young Monica was in the habit of taking daily increased, and the aversion with which she naturally regarded this liquor proportionably decreased. She now loved wine, and drank it with pleasure, as often as an occasion presented itself. This propensity was very dangerous, though it was not attended by any considerable excess.

But God was watching over his dear one, and, to correct her, he availed himself of a quarrel that she had with an old servant of the house. The latter, who usually followed her young mistress to the cellar, was aware of all that occurred. She reproached her bitterly with it, and went so far as to give her the title of a "wine-bibber." Monica, deeply pained, reflected on herself, and immediately perceived all the shame of the vice with which she was accused. She labored so effectually to unlearn her bad habit, that, during the rest of her life, the least sign of it never again appeared. The danger that this saint ran ought to make parents exceedingly watchful, and induce them to cut off everything that might lead their children into vicious courses. What would have become of Augustine's mother if she had not taken care to correct herself in time?

PRAYER

O my God! who art all love, I thank thee for having given us this admirable commandment, whose observance is the source of our happiness in this life. Grant us the grace always to keep it faithfully.

I am resolved to love God above all things, and my neighbor as myself for the love of God; and, in testimony of this love, I will obey all my superiors in a Christian manner.

Lesson 51: Our Union with the New Adam by Charity (6)

After establishing, by the fourth commandment, the happiness of the family and society, God forbids, by the six others, everything that might disturb this happiness. As the first of all natural goods is life, the divine legislator begins by placing it beyond the reach of danger: such is the object of the fifth commandment.

Fifth commandment: Benefits of this commandment.—Addressing himself to all mankind in general, and to each person in particular, he opposes to their malicious fury the dreadful barrier of his authority, saying, "Thou shalt not kill."[1226] With what love ought we to receive this commandment! It is a sacred rampart with which God is pleased to surround our days—those of the child yet unborn, those of the poor and the helpless, those of all mankind without exception. A formidable rampart: whosoever dares to pass over it shall receive hell for his reward! "I will require an account of your blood," says the Lord, "from anyone who shall shed it."[1227] This is what God said to men when they had become wicked by sin.

What it forbids.—The chief sin here forbidden is homicide; for it is the end in which all the others alike proscribed by the fifth commandment terminate. Homicide means the killing of a human being. Hence, the fifth commandment does not forbid us to kill animals, because they were made for man, who can, when it is advantageous for him, take away their life. But man having been created for God alone, no one man is master of the life of another man, so as to be able to dispose of it at his pleasure. There are three kinds of homicide, or rather homicide may be committed in three different ways, which are, murder, dueling, and suicide.

Murder. Murder is an action by which one man willfully and unjustly inflicts death on another: assassination or poisoning is murder. To be criminal, homicide must be willful and unjust. Hence a man would not be guilty of homicide if he caused another's death without intending it. Such was the case with the unfortunate man who, while hunting, killed the husband of St. Jane Frances de Chantal, imagining that it was a fallow deer he aimed at. Hence also, princes and soldiers who kill enemies in a just war, as well as magistrates and others who in executing justice put malefactors to death, are not guilty of homicide, because, though their acts are willful, they are not unjust.

In point of fact, they punish with death, not as masters over the lives of men, but as ministers of God, who consecrates the right of legitimate defense, and who commands criminals to be punished, in some cases even with death, that the good may be put in heart again and may live in peace. This is the reason why God himself has placed the sword in the hand of princes and kings.

To constitute a murder, it is necessary that death should be brought about by private authority and without a legitimate motive. Hence, it is permitted to kill an unjust aggressor, in order to preserve one's life, and even, according to the common opinion of doctors, one's chastity, provided that one does not exceed the limits of a just defense, that is, only makes the aggressor experience the evil necessary to avoid one's own evil.[1228] If then one can defend himself without killing, he must not kill; if he can defend himself without wounding, he must not wound.[1229]

The guilt of homicide is incurred, not only by putting a person to death, but also by contributing thereto directly or indirectly. The following contribute directly: those who command it; those who counsel it; those who approve of it; those who encourage it, by exciting hatred, or by reproaching a man with his cowardice if he does not wish to take revenge; and those who facilitate its accomplishment, by supplying arms, etc. They contribute indirectly who omit to do what charity or justice obliges them to do in order to save the neighbor's life. In this class we must number persons who, being aware of a plot against any one's life, do not warn him of it; persons who, being able to save the life of one falsely accused, neglect to do so; physicians and surgeons who, through a gross ignorance of their profession, or through a gravely culpable negligence or imprudence, let sick persons, of whose health they have undertaken the treatment, die; apothecaries who, through great inexperience or inattention, depart when preparing remedies from the prescriptions of physicians; nurses who, instead of watching assiduously over persons dangerously ill, take little or no care of them, leaving them to themselves; and fathers and mothers who take little children, that may easily be smothered, to sleep with them. It is expressly forbidden parents to have children sleep in their bed before they are one year old, and after they are three years old.

Dueling. The second kind of homicide is dueling. The duel is a combat between two or more persons, who meet after having arranged the place, the hour, and the mode of combat. It is a great crime. Like murder, it violates divine and human law, by substituting private authority for the authority of society and of God himself. Hence, the heaviest penalties have always been proclaimed against duelists. French legislation long condemned them to the same punishment as murderers. And the Catholic Church, assembled in the Council of Trent, inflicts the following penalties on them: infamy, and loss of goods; no burial for him who dies in the combat; and major excommunication—which is incurred not only by the duelists, but also by the witnesses, those who counsel or favor it, and those who come expressly to see it, and who encourage it by their presence, even though it does not eventually take place.

The Council of Trent strikes duelists with infamy, so that they are irregular, and can never receive orders without a dispensation. They are indeed infamous, for they are cowardly, bad citizens.

Cowardly citizens. They bow their haughty heads under the yoke of a barbarous prejudice, which they dare not despise.

Cowardly citizens. They fail in that courage which does man the highest honor—the courage to forgive.

Cowardly citizens. They show themselves slaves to the vilest passions—pride, rancor, and cruelty.

Bad citizens. To satisfy personal revenge, they sport with a good which is not theirs—their life, which belongs to society, to their wives, to their children.

Bad citizens. They boldly violate the first law of every society, which forbids the individual to take justice into his own hands.

Bad citizens. They trample underfoot every kind of morality, in order to identify themselves with nothing but the brutal right of adroitness in killing, and to establish as a principle that honor lies at the point of a sword or in the ball of a pistol.

Is it not with ample justice that the Church declares those infamous who are guilty of such a crime? Reason itself, applauding her sentence, exclaims, "Yes, most infamous!" Even infidelity raises its voice to condemn this barbarous prejudice.

"Beware," says Rousseau, "of confounding the sacred name of honor with that fierce prejudice which places virtue at the saber's point, and is calculated only to make brave scoundrels. But, again, in what does this frightful prejudice consist? In the most extravagant idea that ever entered the human mind, namely, that all the duties of society may be supplied for by gallantry; that a man is no longer a knave or a calumniator, but civil, humane, and polite when he knows how to fight; that a lie may be turned into truth; that robbery becomes lawful, perfidy honest, infidelity laudable, as soon as a man can defend his cause with weapons; that an affront is well repaired by the stroke of a sword, and that no man ever wrongs another by killing him. There is another kind of affair, I acknowledge, in which gentleness is blended with ferocity—in which people are only killed by chance: it is that in which the fight continues till the first blood is drawn. The first blood! O great God! What do you want with this blood, you wild beast? Do you want to drink it?

"Will it be said that a duel shows a man to have spirit, and that this suffices to efface the shame and reproach of every vice? I ask, what honor can dictate such a decision, and what reason can justify it? By this account, if you were accused of killing a man, you would kill another to prove that the charge was not true. Thus, virtue and vice, honor and infamy, truth and falsehood, all would take their rise from a hand-to-hand engagement. A fencing-school becomes the court of justice. No other right is left than strength; no other issue than murder. The only reparation due to those who have been injured is to kill them, and every offense is well washed away in the blood of the offender and the offended. Tell me; if wolves could reason, would they be guided by other maxims?

"Let all those people (those wicked subjects) fight one another, nothing is less honorable than that honor about which they make so much noise; it is only a false imitation of virtue, under which are hidden the greatest crimes. The honor of a man who thinks nobly does not lie within the power of another: it is in himself, not in the opinion of the people. Honor does not defend itself by the sword or the shield, but by an upright and irreproachable life, and this conflict is worth much more than the other in point of courage. To be brief, the courageous man scorns dueling, and the good man hates it. I place duels in the lowest degree of brutality that man can reach. In my eyes, he who with gaiety of heart enters a deadly struggle is only a wild beast that strives to tear another to pieces."

Suicide. The third kind of homicide is suicide. Suicide is the killing of oneself. The new Adam, not content with guarding our days from the violence of others, shelters them from our own fury. Could he carry his paternal solicitude further, or can our gratitude toward him be ever deep enough?

Suicide is a crime. Not being masters of our life, we are not at liberty to throw it away. Life is a deposit which providence has entrusted to us, and of which we should take care as long as providence chooses. As sentinels, it is treason to quit our post without an order from the general who has placed us at it. This is the reason why the decalogue does not say, "Thou shalt not kill others," but absolutely, "Thou shalt not kill."[1230] "If he who kills a man," says Lactantius, "is a villain and a wretch, because he takes away the life of a man, how can he who takes away his own life be innocent, since it is a man that he puts to death? His crime, on the contrary, is so much the greater as he escapes from the vengeance of human law. As it was not by our own will that we came into this world, so we ought not to leave it but by the order of God, who placed us in it."[1231]

Suicide, which cannot be permitted on any account, is the most fatal outrage to him who commits it: by taking away his temporal life, he brings on himself eternal death. To the voice of the fathers of the Church is joined that of modern philosophers in branding and dishonoring it. Hear again the impious Rousseau:

"You would wish to be done with life, but I should like to know whether you have begun it. What! were you placed on the earth to do nothing? Does heaven not impose with life a task to be fulfilled? If you have finished your appointed portion, rest for the remainder of the day—you may do so; but let us see your work. What answer have you ready for the supreme judge, who will call you to an account for your time? Wretch! find me the just man who boasts of having lived long enough, and I will teach him how he should have borne his life to have a right to lay it down.

"You count over the miseries of humanity, and say, 'Life is an evil.' But look around you—search through the order of things, and see whether you can find any goods that are not mixed with evils. Is it then to be said that there is no good in the world, and can you make no distinction between that which is evil by nature and that which is evil by accident? The passive life of man is nothing—it only concerns a body from which he shall soon be delivered; but his active and moral life, which ought to influence his whole being, consists in the exercise of his will. Life is an evil for the wicked man who is prosperous; it is a good for the honest man who is unfortunate. For it is not its transitory modification, but its relation with its object, that makes a thing good or evil.

"You are weary of life, and say, 'Life is an evil.' Sooner or later you shall be comforted, and shall say, 'Life is a good.' You will speak more truthfully, but will not reason more correctly; for nothing will have changed but yourself. Change then from today, and since it is in the perverse disposition of your soul that everything is an evil, correct your irregular affections, and do not burn your house to save yourself the trouble of setting it in order.

"What are ten, twenty, or thirty years to a being that is immortal? Pain and pleasure pass away like a shadow. Life flows by in a moment: it is nothing of itself; its value depends on its employment. The good done alone remains, and thereby makes it something. Say not then that it is an evil for you to live, since it depends on yourself alone to make it a good, and if it is an evil to have lived, this is one reason more for living longer. Neither say that it is permitted you to die; for you might as well say that it is permitted you not to be a man—that it is permitted you to rebel against the author of your being, and to make false your destiny.

"Suicide is a shameful and clandestine death. It is a theft from the human race. Before you leave men, repay them for what they have done to you.—'But I care for nothing; I am useless to the world.'—One day's philosophy! Are you not aware that you cannot make a single step on the earth without finding some duty to fulfill, and that every man is useful to humanity by the very fact that he exists?

"Senseless youth! if there is yet left in your heart the least sentiment of virtue, come and I will show you how to love life. Every time that you are tempted to quit it, say within yourself, 'I must do one good action more before I die.' Then look about for some needy person to help, some unhappy person to console, some injured person to defend. If this consideration holds you back today, it will hold you back tomorrow, the day after tomorrow, your whole life. If it does not hold you back, die, you are a monster!"[1232]

The Church forbids burial to be given to suicides, as well as to duelists who die in the combat. What is more just than to deprive of the honors of religion those who die in the act of mocking its laws? They denied their mother: she refuses to bless their ashes or to watch over their graves. Again, what is more just? After this, how dare anyone annoy priests by striving to drag prayers from them, or to make them assist at the funerals of those who, if they could return to life, would perhaps be the first to resent such attentions? Intolerance, therefore, has no place in the priest who refuses his ministry, but in those who require it.

Murder, dueling, and suicide have always been regarded as enormous crimes. In point of fact, they attack both the Creator and the creature: the Creator, by destroying his work and violating his law; the creature, by depriving it of the greatest of natural goods—life. They inflict a very severe injury on society, by depriving it of one of its members, and by overthrowing the reign of justice in order to substitute that of brute force. Hence, these three crimes are chiefly forbidden by the fifth commandment. Those who have killed or wounded a neighbor are bound to repair the injury that they have caused. But how? We shall show this when treating of the seventh commandment.

Hatred, violence, and anger. Homicide is the chief sin forbidden by the fifth commandment. Blows, wounds, all attempts on the life or the health of the neighbor, are likewise forbidden. Still more, our Lord prohibits whatever may lead to these different sins, which all tend to homicide, and he hereby raises the new law far above the old. It is in the heart that homicide is born; it is also in the heart that the divine legislator endeavors to stifle it. "You know," he said to the Jews, "that it was said to them of old, Thou shalt not kill...As for me, I say to you, Whosoever is angry with his brother shall deserve to be condemned by the judgment, and whosoever shall say to his brother, Thou art a fool, shall deserve to be condemned to the fire of hell."[1233]

Hence, the fifth commandment forbids not only killing, wounding, and striking, but also every sentiment of anger, hatred, envy, and contempt toward the neighbor, the very desire of revenge, injurious words, curses, violence, ill treatment: because all these things are like the seeds of homicide. This is the crime to which they may lead, if not suppressed. The God of society shows himself so delicately affected on this point, that he does not hesitate to place our interests before those of his glory. "If you bring your gift to the altar," he says, "and there you remember that your brother has something against you, leave your gift before the altar, and go and be reconciled to your brother. Then coming you shall offer your gift."[1234]

What else it forbids: Scandal.—Let us now speak of another sin, also forbidden by the fifth precept of the decalogue—scandal. If our Lord is so anxious to protect the life of our body, how much more so is he to protect the life of our soul! If homicide, which destroys a mortal body, is one of the greatest crimes, because it attacks the Creator's masterpiece, what shall be said of scandal, which destroys an immortal soul, infinitely more precious than the body, since it was for the soul that the body was made?

Hence, there is no sin against which the Son of God has uttered more terrible anathemas. "Woe to the world because of its scandals."[1235] And again: "Whosoever shall scandalize even the least of men, it were better for him to be cast into the depths of the sea, with a millstone round his neck."[1236] The severity of these expressions cannot surprise us, if we consider that scandal is a sin which makes a direct attack on the work of the incarnation, and which outrages every law of nature and friendship.

Why did our Lord die on the cross? To save souls. And scandal tends directly to ruin them, to rob Jesus Christ of the fruit of his death. To whom is scandal addressed? Not to the strong, but to the little and the weak: scandal comes from above and not from below. Again, to whom? To persons who have the nearest relations with scandal-givers: to children, to domestics, to friends, and not to strangers. Can anything be more opposed to the love of God and the neighbor?

The word *scandal* properly means something against which one strikes when walking. It also means an obstacle or impediment to anything. It is on this account that we call scandal whatever prevents us from arriving at eternal life, by giving us an occasion to sin. Hence, with the fathers and theologians, we here understand by *scandal*, "a word or an action which has not all the rectitude that it ought to have, and which in consequence gives others an occasion of offending God."[1237] An explanation of this definition is important.

I. We say "a word or an action." Though a man should have the will to cause others to fall into sin, if this evil design does not appear outwardly, he does not cause scandal, since he does not give a proximate occasion of sinning. Under the terms *word* and *action* is included the omission of either. He who neglects to do or to say what he ought to do or to say—for example, he who neglects to assist at Mass on Sunday, or to reprove a blasphemer over whom he has authority—gives scandal.

II. Which "has not all the rectitude," that is, which is bad in itself, or which has the appearance of being bad, though it should not be really bad.

III. Which gives "an occasion of falling into sin." That an action may be the cause of scandal, it is not necessary that the neighbor should fall into sin; it is enough that an occasion of falling into it should be given him—in other words, that he should be put in danger of sinning. Hence, the guilt of scandal is incurred only when, having regard to the position of him who does what is wrong and to the dispositions of those in whose presence he does it, there is reason to fear that the latter may be drawn into sin. A blasphemy, for instance, uttered in presence of a priest, could not be regarded as a sin of scandal.[1238]

If a sin was committed publicly, before persons of various ages and conditions, one ought then to accuse himself of it as of a sin of scandal, by reason of the danger to which he exposed himself of scandalizing at least a portion of those who were aware of it. Such is the meaning of the words of St. Augustine: "Whoever," he says, "leads, in sight of the people, an evil life, causes death as often as he can to those who see him. Let him not therefore flatter himself that he who has been a witness of his evil life is not dead. The witness may indeed be alive, but, for all that, the scandal-giver does not cease to be a murderer."[1239]

How scandal is given. There are ever so many ways of being guilty of scandal. Here are a few: to command, to advise, or to request a person to do what he cannot do without sin, or to dissuade him from doing what he is bound to do. It is scandal to solicit any one to tell lies, to steal, to take revenge, to get drunk, to stop from Mass on days of obligation or from annual confession. Likewise, to utter blasphemous or immodest words; to sing bad songs; to print, to sell, or to lend dangerous books or pictures, or to have them exposed before the eyes of others; to eat flesh meat on forbidden days in presence of the neighbor; to prepare flesh meat for libertines on days of abstinence. As for women, to dress immodestly, uncovering the shoulders or throat; to persecute pious persons, to ridicule their devotion, to treat them as simpletons or bigots, to despise their modesty, to give an ill turn to their religious practices: so many scandals.

When one has committed a fault which gives the neighbor an occasion of falling into sin, it is not enough to mention the fault alone in confession; one must also declare that it scandalized the neighbor, because the scandal which is joined to a sin is a distinct sin and of a different species. It is necessary, moreover, to specify the number of persons to whom this fault was an occasion of sin, because the sin of scandal is multiplied in proportion to the number of persons who are led by it to do evil.

Obligation and mode of repairing scandal. It is a duty of justice to repair the scandal which one has caused. If God requires, before granting pardon, that the temporal goods taken from the neighbor by injustice should be restored to him, as well as the character ruined by detraction or calumny, will he not require that the scandal-giver should make every effort to withdraw from the brink of the eternal abyss those who have been led thither by him? But how difficult is this reparation!

The consequences of scandal are beyond number. One improper act which you have done, one improper word which you have spoken, may cause thousands of persons, of whom you know nothing, to sin. How can so much evil be repaired? a) By praying for the persons whom you have scandalized directly or indirectly. b) By setting an example in every respect contrary to that with which you have to reproach yourself. Hence, a person who has taken part in licentious or irreligious conversation, who has sung immodest songs, who has supported by voice or pen maxims opposed to faith or morality, is bound to disavow his conduct in whatever way is best calculated to efface its effects from the minds of those who have been scandalized by it. Women who have wounded the consciences of others by their luxury or immodesty ought to condemn luxury and immodesty, and give an example of modesty and humility. As for the scandal which results from immoral behavior, it is necessary that he who has been its author should repair it by truly Christian behavior. He who has done nothing and is unwilling to do anything to repair the scandals which he has caused is unworthy of absolution. c) By doing a penance proportioned, as far as possible, to the number and enormity of the scandals given. The scandal-giver, having robbed God of his glory, by tearing away souls from him, is bound to do the most he can to restore it to him—contributing to the salvation of as many souls as possible. Acting thus, he will not indeed rescue from hell the souls which he has cast into its depths, but he will do all that lies in his power and all that God requires of him. Let us be more afraid of giving scandal than we are of falling into the fire, and let us with our whole heart bless the new Adam, who has vouchsafed to surround the life of our body and the life of our soul with so many and such sacred barriers.

Example. Nothing causes greater uneasiness at the moment of death than the remembrance of the scandals that one has given. Beranger, archdeacon of Angers, had the misfortune to spread far and near the poison of heresy. He seduced a great many souls. At the close of his days, he was touched by God: he abjured his errors and was converted. Suddenly, when about to die, he is troubled, he is terrified. "Why, brother, these troubles and terrors?" asks the assisting priest, "God is mercy itself—hope in him." "I know that God is mercy itself," answers the sick man, "and I sincerely trust that he will have regard to my tears, and that he will forget my own sins; but the sins that I have made others commit—will he forgive me them? Wretch that I am! It seems to me that the souls which I have destroyed await me at the tribunal of God to invoke his vengeance on me. It seems to me that I hear the voice of Jesus Christ resounding through my frightened heart and asking me, 'Where is such a one whom thou didst destroy?'" It was only with the greatest difficulty that he could be calmed: happy if his patience and his sorrow were enough to make the supreme judge forget the loss of souls which he had caused!

"Thou shalt not kill." That is to say, thou shalt not kill either the body or the soul of thy brother; thou shalt not even admit into thy mind the thought of murder or of scandal. Such is the fifth precept of the decalogue, and, we may add, the fifth pillar of the social edifice.

Social advantages of the fifth commandment.—Take away this commandment: What security exists among mankind? Will you say that human laws are a sufficient guarantee? But the man who is stronger than the law may sport with your life, the man who can flatter himself with a prospect of escape from the scaffold may sport with your life, and how many malefactors so escape![1240] Has not fifty years' experience taught us that human laws are mere spiders' webs, fit only for catching flies?[1241] The small flies are caught by them, but the big ones break them and get away.

And then, without this commandment, what becomes of the life of souls? What becomes of innocence? What becomes of the honor of families? Scandal, having no rein, will multiply its victims with impunity. Who is the man that, reading these lines, can say, "I owe nothing to this commandment—no, neither myself nor mine—neither my father nor my mother, neither my brother nor my sister, neither my son nor my daughter; human laws alone have preserved our lives, and, what is more precious than our lives, our honor"?

But if no man can use such language, neither can society. Thanks, therefore, on the part of man and on the part of society, to the divine legislator; a profound respect for his law; a love for what he has done, and for what he will yet do! We allude to a new benefit, that is, a new commandment: the sixth.

PRAYER

O my God! who art all love, I thank thee for having so carefully guarded the life of my soul and the life of my body; grant me the grace always to respect each of these lives in my neighbor.

I am resolved to love God above all things, and my neighbor as myself for the love of God; and, in testimony of this love, I will always take care not to give the least scandal.

Lesson 52: Our Union with the New Adam by Charity (7)

Sixth and ninth commandments: What they forbid.—After having, by the fifth commandment, placed the first of natural goods, our life, in security, the divine legislator protects our honor, which holds the second rank. Though here, as in the other commandments, he only mentions the chief sin, yet he forbids all other sins which are of a character to lead to it—consequently, whatever may sully the purity of body or soul.

We have nothing, after our soul, more precious than our body. A vessel of honor, consecrated by baptism and Communion, a member of Jesus Christ, a temple of the Holy Ghost, destined to rise glorious and to share in the everlasting joys of the soul, we ought to treat it with deep respect. To profane a chalice would be a sacrilege; to profane our body would be a greater sacrilege.

Enormity of the sin against these commandments.—Who will tell the enormity of the sin forbidden by these commandments? It is a sin which the language of every people terms shameful and infamous; it is a sin which buried the world beneath the waters of the deluge; it is a sin which drew down fire from heaven on five whole cities, and changed their situation into that of an unclean lake; it is a sin which draws in its train all other sins—injustice, murder, perjury, sacrilege, suicide; it is a sin which extinguishes faith, ruins soul and body, degrades man to the level of the brute; it is a sin which daily causes souls to fall into hell like the flakes of snow fall to the earth on a winter's morning; it is a sin which the Lamb of God had to expiate by a special torture; a horrible sin, which it is even forbidden to name. For the very name is capable of sullying the lips that pronounce it and the ears that hear it. This is the sin forbidden by the sixth and ninth commandments.[1242]

The two following principles must be carefully borne in mind:

First principle. In all sins contrary to the sixth and ninth commandments, there is no levity of matter; that is, everything which occurs with full liberty, full knowledge, and full consent, is mortal.

Second principle. Since there is no levity of matter, it is necessary to tell at confession everything of which one has been willfully guilty against these two commandments.

Different species. That which renders this sin most dreadful is that it may be committed in many different ways: by thoughts, by desires, by looks, by words, by actions. But to make it a mortal sin, there must be, as we have said, full liberty, full advertence, and full consent. A thought or an action, however bad in its nature, is not imputable to us but insofar as it is voluntary. Now, to judge whether it is voluntary, there are three things to be distinguished: suggestion, delectation, and consent.

Suggestion, delectation, and consent. Suggestion is nothing else than the idea of evil which is presented to the mind. It is not in itself a sin. Delectation is the carnal pleasure which is occasioned by the thought of evil. It is culpable if it is not renounced as soon as one perceives that it cannot be rested on without sin. If one takes pleasure in it with full advertence and deliberate intention, there is perfect consent, and, consequently, mortal sin. If the will only half consents, the sin is only venial. If the will does not consent at all, there is no sin at all. Care must be taken not to confound the consent of the will with the evil thought, or with the pleasure which may accompany the evil thought. The thought and the pleasure may exist without in the least affecting the will; and, so long as the will takes no part in them, or does not adhere to them, there is no sin. This is only a temptation, which becomes a subject of merit for us.[1243]

To encourage timid souls, and to give rules of conduct for penitents in their confessions, it is useful to present the same question from another point of view. Accordingly, we may distinguish four kinds of thoughts: rejected thoughts, dismissed thoughts, morose thoughts, and consummated thoughts.

Rejected thoughts. Rejected or abhorred thoughts are thoughts which, as soon as we perceive them, we banish with horror and indignation, just as we should chase a dog that tried to bite us. These thoughts are not culpable, however wicked their object. Though they should return a hundred times a day, if you reject them a hundred times in order not to offend God, you make a hundred acts of virtue for which you will be rewarded in heaven. The soldier who a hundred times drives back the enemy gives his prince a hundred proofs of his courage and his fidelity. Wherefore, it is by no means necessary to speak of these thoughts in confession. Only, it may be useful to mention them in general, in order to make known the assaults of the devil, and to learn the method of resisting these assaults.

But someone may say, "I can never know whether I have consented." To quiet your mind, judge by the habitual tenor of your dispositions. A soul that is sincerely resolved never to commit a sin deliberately, ought, in case of doubt, to pronounce that it has not consented. The same, when these thoughts displease, and when one has promptly recommended himself to our Lord, the Blessed Virgin, or the saints. "If they displease you," says St. Francis de Sales, "it is a proof that you do not love them; and, if you do not love them, how could you have consented to them?"[1244]

Dismissed thoughts. Dismissed thoughts are thoughts which one drives away indeed, but with a degree of negligence. The heart, charmed with voluptuousness, is dulled, as it were, and slow to remove from the imagination that on which it dwells, be it ever so little, though not with full deliberation. The soul acts like a man who, being visited by an importunate creditor, does not push him out roughly, but gets rid of him quietly, accompanying him to the door, and looking after him for some time. These thoughts are only venial sins, even though in their kind they should be mortal. To confess them, it is enough to say, "I have had immodest thoughts, on which I did not dwell much; yet I did not reject them with all the promptitude that was befitting."

Morose thoughts. Morose thoughts are thoughts which are allowed to remain in the mind, or on which the mind rests voluntarily, without, however, having the will to do the evil of which one thinks. You have, for example, a thought of impurity, revenge, or envy, and you would rather die than carry it into effect; but you willingly occupy yourself with this thought, you bathe as it were in it, you delight in it, knowing well that you do wrong. Such a thought is a mortal sin, if the matter is grave. A person must confess it, and tell a) what the thought was about, and b) how often it was entertained.

That the simple thought of evil, when voluntary, is a sin, is a thing certain, which cannot be denied without renouncing the faith. "The wicked man," says the Holy Ghost, "shall be questioned on his thoughts."[1245] "It is from the heart," adds our Lord, "that evil thoughts come forth."[1246] There are, therefore, guilty thoughts which defile the soul, as external actions defile the body. "Perverse thoughts separate man from God."[1247] Now, mortal sin alone separates man from God. There are therefore thoughts which are mortal sins.

Consummated thoughts. Lastly, consummated thoughts are thoughts which are accompanied with a desire to put them in execution. Though a person should not proceed so far, the crime is nevertheless committed in the will: this is clear, and needs no explanation. In confessing them, it is necessary to tell what action has been desired, with whom it has been desired, and how often it has been desired.[1248]

We must remark that a thought may be voluntary in itself or in its cause. It is voluntary in itself when one admits it, occupies himself with it, and takes pleasure in it, knowing that he does wrong. It is voluntary in its cause when, willfully and unnecessarily, one looks at, says, reads, listens to, or does anything that is of a nature to raise an evil thought.

Occasions.—Not only are thoughts, desires, and actions contrary to modesty forbidden us, but also the occasions of the sin of which we speak, that is, everything calculated to lead us to it. Unfortunately, these occasions are very numerous. We shall mention a few of them.

1. *Feasting, tavern-visiting, good-cheer, tippling.* All these things tend to nourish concupiscence, and to favor liberty in words, looks, and actions. "Beware of taking wine in excess," says the apostle, "it is mixed with luxury."[1249] And elsewhere he says, "Warn young people to be sober."[1250]

2. *Engravings, paintings, fashion-patterns, statues, books, and songs that treat of profane love.* Persons who have such things cannot, as a general rule, keep them, or sell them, or make a present of them, or lend them: they ought to burn them. Let no one say that they are under lock and key. First, I ask, what is the good of this, since one ought not to make any use of them? I will next tell you that the key may fall into strange hands. We know the example of a child that became, at an age which is usually considered that of innocence, a scandalous libertine, in consequence of having read some books which its father kept hidden "under lock and key."

3. *Shows, dances, balls, meetings among persons of different sexes, dangerous company, that is, the company of persons who, by themselves, by their words, or by their actions, lead to this sin.* It is here that we must observe in all its rigor the prescription of our divine master: "If your right eye scandalize you, pluck it out; if your right hand, cut it off and cast it from you: it is better for you to go into heaven having lost an eye or a hand, than to descend into hell with all your members."[1251] The meaning of these words is that, however dear or useful anything may be to us, we must, as soon as it becomes an occasion of sin for us, part with it at all costs.

Among the chief occasions of sin forbidden by the sixth and ninth commandments, it has always been usual to number dances and plays in which the world says that there is no harm. Well, here is your choice: either the world deceives itself, or the Church of Jesus Christ makes a mistake, for there is no council that does not number dances and plays among the occasions of this sin. In the third part[1252] of the catechism, you will find all the details necessary to form a judgment on plays and shows.[1253] Toward the close of the present lesson, we shall enter into some further particulars regarding dances.

4. *Curiosity.* A hunger for seeing everything and a neglect of guarding one's eyes are nearly always the beginning of evil. "It is my eye that ruins my heart";[1254] "it is by the windows that death enters the soul":[1255] these are the truthful words which are read in the holy scripture.

5. *Dress.* The dress of persons belonging to that sex which is more inclined to vanity and to the desire to please is often, not only for those who wear it, but also for those who see it, an occasion of sin. Let us hear the recommendations which the princes of the apostles, Sts. Peter and Paul, address to women on this subject. The first says, "They ought not to beautify themselves outwardly according to plaiting of hair, or ornaments of gold, or elegance of attire; but let them adorn themselves according to the hidden man of the heart, in the incorruptible purity of a soul full of meekness and peace, which is a glorious ornament in the sight of God."[1256] And the second, "Let women be clad as humility requires; let them adorn themselves according to modesty and chastity, not with curled hair, or gold, or pearls, or costly garments."[1257]

Faithful to the teaching of the apostles, the Christian females of the early ages, those heroines of the faith, who made the astonished barbarians exclaim, "What women there are among the Christians!" were distinguished by the modesty and simplicity of their apparel. Let not worldly women, to justify the indecency of their costume, say, "It is the fashion." We shall answer them, with Tertullian, that Jesus Christ calls them to the truth, and not to the fashion; that it is not according to the fashion which changes, but according to the truth which never changes, that they shall be judged; that the gospel ought not to be reformed by the fashion, but the fashion by the gospel.

Neither let them say, "My rank in life requires it." We shall answer them, "Though you were a queen, your rank would not place you above the gospel."

We take this reply from a holy bishop, addressing some observations to a queen of France on her too elegant attire. Bathilds thought that she could justify herself by answering, "I am not too elegantly attired for a queen." "I admit that," replied the saint, "but you are for a Christian." And the pious princess profited so well of the advice, that ever afterward she dressed in a most simple style.[1258] Seamstresses ought to be very careful not to contribute to scandal, by making garments whose shape is evidently contrary to decency.

After so much has been said, what rule must be followed to place one's conscience in security? We must conform to the manners of really good Christians of our own condition and age, and of the country in which we live. Let us remark, in passing, that the most silly of all vanities is the vanity of dress; hence, it is properly called *vanity*. To triumph over it, it is enough to have a little judgment, and to bear in mind this saying of a great queen: "The head is not valued by that which is around it, but by that which is in it." We should also bear in mind that raiment being a consequence of sin, the person who draws vanity from it is like a sick man who glories in the bandages that hide his wounds.

6. *Idleness.* Our mind cannot remain inactive. If we do not occupy it with good thoughts, it will occupy itself with evil thoughts. Experience proves, and the Holy Spirit speaks the truth in telling us, that idleness teaches all sorts of wickedness. St. Jerome adds, "Let the devil always find you engaged."[1259] He who is busy is tempted only by one devil: he who is idle has legions of them around him.[1260]

Remedies.—It is not enough to have made known the sin opposed to the sixth and ninth commandments; we must also point out the remedies. These remedies are internal and external.

1. *Internal remedies.* The internal remedies are: a) to reflect on the enormity of this sin, which effaces in us the image of the Blessed Trinity—which defiles the members of Jesus Christ, for our members are his members—which crucifies the Savior anew, after covering him with infamous spittle—finally, which profanes the temple of the Holy Ghost, for our bodies are the living temples of the Lord; b) to think of the punishment which God inflicts on this sin—here, the deluge, the burning of Sodom, the curse of Chanaan, blindness of mind, hardness of heart, final impenitence, and, hereafter, the

eternal torments of hell; c) to strive to become humble—the humbler we are, the freer shall we be from this sin: the august Mary was the purest of virgins, because she was the humblest of creatures.

2. *External remedies.* The external remedies are, according to our Lord himself, a) watchfulness and b) prayer. Watchfulness over our inward senses, our memory, our mind, our imagination, our heart. Woe to us if we give them free course! Watchfulness over our outward senses, over our sight and taste and touch. Woe again if we permit ourselves to look at whatever presents itself, or to procure whatever flatters us: dainty food, long sleeps, rich clothes and furniture! Vocal and mental prayer—aspirations; a tender and persevering devotion to the Blessed Virgin—faithfulness in reciting three Hail Marys morning and evening in honor of her spotless purity; above all, frequent use of confession and Communion—without which, all other means will be ineffectual.

What is commanded by these commandments: Purity of body and soul.—The precepts of which we treat command, according to the conditions of persons, either perfect chastity or conjugal chastity. The sin forbidden by the sixth and ninth commandments is as horrible as the contrary virtue prescribed by them is beautiful. It is a virtue which the language of every people terms angelic, and which made God himself come down on earth, so powerful are its charms. It is a virtue which the new Adam loved with a love of predilection, and which gives to those who practice it a delightful peace, as well as a right to see God and to follow everywhere the immaculate Lamb. It is a virtue which makes the countenance shine with the soft fresh colors of the lily and the rose, and which raises man above the angels. It is a virtue to which society is indebted for the greatest assistance in the paths of science and the works of charity. It is a virtue so delicate, though so amiable, that the human tongue can scarcely pronounce its name for fear of profanation. This virtue is that which is prescribed by the sixth and ninth commandments.[1261]

History.—It so ennobles human nature by the heroism which it supposes, that heathens themselves used to profess a religious veneration for it. Witness the conduct of the ancient Romans in regard to the vestals. This name was given to six young girls who used to vow, till the age of thirty years, their virginity to the goddess Vesta, whose priestesses they became. Charged with the preservation of the sacred fire, and of the palladium, on which it was supposed that the safety of the empire depended, they enjoyed the highest honors.

The first places were reserved for them at the theatre, at the amphitheatre, at the circus, and at all public amusements. Like the consuls, they were preceded by lictors, when they appeared in the streets; and, if on their way they met a man condemned to death, they saved his life by the very fact of meeting him. The respect of the Romans for faithful vestals was as profound as the punishment which they inflicted on her who tampered with the most beautiful of virtues was severe: she was buried alive.[1262]

Social advantages of these commandments.—And now let us fall on our knees before our heavenly Father, the author and preserver of society, who never forgets any of our interests. In his infinite goodness. He was not content to protect the life of our body and the life of our soul from the violence and the scandal of others. By the sixth and ninth commandments, he was pleased to secure the peace of society, by securing the peace of the family, which is its basis. For this purpose, he forbids, under the heaviest penalties, not only the sin winch disturbs, divides, and dishonors the family, but also whatever may lead to this sin. A searcher of reins and consciences, the supreme legislator knows that adultery comes from the heart, and he proceeds to stifle the crime in its first breath, in the least thought against purity. He only mentions adultery, though he forbids all other sins contrary to that virtue which is specially amiable: just as in the fifth commandment he only mentions homicide, though he forbids everything hurtful to our life.

He was pleased also to preserve us from our own passions, and from the horrible consequences, as well for soul as for body, of the sin of immodesty. These consequences are remorse, shame, despair, disease, and sudden and premature death. It was thus that our Lord vouchsafed to prevent our love from again degrading itself, after recalling it to its true object.

How plainly do these two commandments reveal the goodness of God toward us! If, in spite of these formal precepts, in spite of the dreadful scourges with which those who abandon themselves to their passions are threatened and punished; if, I say, in spite of all this, the shameful sin occasions such fearful ravages on the earth, if it is the cause of a multitude of crimes that tear families and society to pieces as it were, what would it be, O great God! if thou hadst not forbidden it, and forbidden it so severely?

Oh, how much wiser does religion here show herself than the world! The world ensnares us in all the allurements to this sin. It boasts of dances, plays, obscene books and songs; and it brands with dishonor those who commit the shameful sin. Full of cruelty, it pushes its followers into the abyss, and scorns them in their fall. It drives them into raging flames, and mocks them while they burn.

Religion, on the contrary, much more careful of our honor and our peace, withdraws us from the abyss, by obliging us to avoid all occasions of falling into it. If, in spite of her maternal warnings, we plunge into it, she hastens to reach us a helping hand, addressing us in these touching words, "Courage, my child! all is not lost; repentance is the sister of innocence."

On dances in particular.—Let us conclude with the details which we promised regarding dances.

"Uncle, is it permitted to dance?" This was the question which a young lady of eighteen lately addressed to one of my venerable *confréres.*

"You ask my opinion about dancing," he replied: "I shall be happy to give it to you. We must first of all set aside religious dances, of which we meet a few examples in the scripture. There is nothing in common between the holy enthusiasm of Moses' sister, Mary, or of the royal prophet, and the vain joy of fashionable dances; between the lively flight of gratitude and the love of worldly pleasure. Nor do you consult me regarding those modest, though profane, dances which take place between persons of the same sex: the Church has not condemned them.

"The question then between you and me is about balls and soirees—in other words, about worldly dances, in which the sexes are confusedly assembled together: profane circles, summoned by vanity, animated by the desire of pleasure, in which the passions dispute for empire, in which it is so rare that modesty has not cause to blush, by reason of the nature of the dances, or the shamelessness of dress, or the freedom of manner and speech. These preliminaries being disposed of, I proceed to answer your question whether it is permitted to dance.[1263]

"Innocent of itself, sometimes used on religious festivals to honor God, dancing was afterward degraded by the passions and employed in the worship of idols. The pagans used to honor their wicked deities by licentious dances. This, my niece, was the origin of dancing, such as it is practiced at the present day: history leaves no doubt on the matter."

"But, uncle, it is not the history of dancing that I am asking you about; it is your opinion on the question whether it is permitted to dance."

"I understand quite well, as I shall soon show you. Cicero, having to defend the consul Lucius Morena, who was accused of dancing, exclaimed, 'Such a thing cannot be believed, especially in regard to a consul, without making known the vices to which he was subject before giving himself over to this kind of excess. For no person dances, either in private or in public, unless he is a drunkard or a fool. Dancing is the last of vices, and includes them all.'[1264]

"Demosthenes, the prince of Greek orators, wishing to cast odium on persons belonging to the train of Philip, king of Macedon, accuses them publicly of dancing. At Rome, to describe a woman without morals, it was enough to say that she danced more elegantly than became an honest woman. Ovid, that voluptuous poet, so little acquainted with severity in his morality, calls dancing-places places of shipwreck for modesty, and dances themselves the seeds of vices. I shall spare you the words of Aristotle, Plato, Seneca, and Scipio."

"And you do well, uncle. It is not the opinion of Cicero and the others that I am asking: it is your own. Is it permitted to dance?"

"Since you don't like the pagans, we shall say no more about them. Though I should not have been sorry to tell you also that, in the time of Tiberius, the Roman Senate banished all dancers out of Rome; and that Domitian even excluded from the Senate some members who were attached to licentious dances. But, as I promised you, we shall say no more about the pagans. The Holy Ghost warns us expressly not to be found with a dancer, and to beware of lending an ear to her words, lest we should be overcome by the force of her charms.[1265] And elsewhere, speaking, as you need have no doubt, of what occurs in our balls, he says, 'The daughters of Sion are haughty; they have walked with their heads aloft; they have made signs with their eyes and their hands; they have given themselves vain airs in their stiff and studied steps: wherefore, the Lord will cover them with shame and confusion.'"[1266]

"But, pardon me, uncle, you are not answering me, or rather I have only a glimpse of your answer."

"You may easily be mistaken."

"Be so good then as to keep me from the possibility of any mistake, by telling me plainly whether it is permitted to dance."

"His soul nourished with meditation on holy writings, a father of the Church, St. Ephrem, exclaims, 'Who ever could show from the scripture that it is permitted to Christians to dance? Which of the prophets taught it? Which of the evangelists authorizes it? In what book of the apostles do we find a single text favorable to dances? If such a diversion is to be permitted to Christians, it must be said that everything is full of errors—in the law and in the writings of prophets, apostles, and evangelists. But if all the words of these holy books are true and inspired, as they really are, it is incontestable that Christians are forbidden to seek diversions of this kind.'[1267] Tertullian represents the place of worldly dances as a temple of Venus or a sink of impurity.[1268] St. Basil pictures it as a shameful market for obscenity.[1269] St. Chrysostom regards dances as a splendid school for impure passions.[1270] St. Ambrose calls them a choir of iniquity, the rock of innocence, the grave of shame.[1271] St. Augustine says that it would be better to till the ground on Sunday than to dance."[1272]

"Well now, uncle, I don't know what you are coming to. You give me every one's opinion in general, about which I am not asking at all, and you don't tell me a word about your own opinion, the only thing I wish to know. It is to yourself, to yourself only, that I address this question: Is it permitted to dance?"

"In modern times I hear two illustrious bishops express themselves in very clear terms. 'The worldly dance,' says St. Charles Borromeo, 'is nothing else than a circle of which the devil is the center and his slaves the circumference; whence it hardly ever happens that a person dances without sin.'[1273] 'The custom of balls,' says St. Francis de Sales, 'is so directed toward evil by circumstances, that the soul is therein exposed to great danger...These are dangerous recreations, foolish pleasures, from which arises a strong disposition to evil affections. They are like mushrooms: the best of them are worth little. As certain plants draw to themselves the venom of serpents that come near them, so balls collect the venom of human passions, the poison of a general contagion.'"[1274]

"You are then determined, uncle, to make me submit to all the testimonies of tradition from Adam down to ourselves. There is no necessity for so much. Answer me, I beg of you; it is yourself, and not the others, that I want to hear: Is it permitted to dance?"

"The Council of Constantinople forbids public dances under pain of anathema.[1275] The Councils of Laodicea and Lerida forbid them even at weddings. The Council of Aix-la-Chapelle terms them infamous things; an African Council, very wicked actions; the Council of Rouen, diversions full of folly; the Council of Tours, snares of the devil."

"After the fathers of the Church, there was nothing wanting but the councils! Without exaggeration, uncle, I think that you would like to make me a theologian by one conversation. But I am afraid that you will find it rather tedious work; so tell me: Is it permitted to dance?"

"Make your mind easy. I will say no more of the scripture, or of fathers, or of councils. 'Dancing,' says the poet Petrarch, whose testimony you cannot challenge, 'is a frivolous performance, unworthy of men, hateful to chaste eyes; a prelude to the indulgence of the passions, the source of a multitude of infamies, from which nothing ever comes but irregularity and impurity.'[1276] The father of modern atheists, Bayle, expresses himself thus, 'Dancing is good for nothing but to corrupt the heart and to bring a dangerous war on chastity.' A worldly man, the celebrated Bussy-Rabutin, who had tasted all sorts of pleasures, wrote thus to Mgr. the bishop of Autun, 'I have always considered balls dangerous. It was not only my reason that led me to think so, but also my experience. And, though the testimony of the fathers is very weighty, I hold that, on this point, that of a courtier ought to be regarded as much weightier. I know well that there are some people who run less risk than others in pleasures of this kind; but the coldest natures grow warm in them. It is mostly young persons that make up these assemblies; and if it costs their ardent souls trouble enough to resist temptations in solitude, what will it be in the midst of a fascinating crowd? Accordingly, I maintain that whoever is a Christian should not go to a ball.'"

"Really, uncle, it is too strong. I shall only ask you once more; tell me, yes or no: Is it permitted to dance?"

"I hope you will not be vexed, my dear niece. I promise to give you my advice, when you yourself have answered the questions which I am about to put to you. 1) On the day of your baptism, you renounced the devil, with all his pomps and works: If you do not meet again what you renounced in balls, be so good as to tell me where else? 2) Would you like to die at a ball without having a moment to recollect yourself? 3) Would you appear at the holy table in ball dress? 4) Do you find in the gospel one morality for eight o'clock in the morning and another for ten at night?"

"But, uncle…uncle! we are not speaking, if you please, about that at all. The question is not of my opinion, but of yours."

"Well, I shall excuse you from an answer to these questions, but at least give me an answer to what I am going to ask now. Is it true that a ball is thought of many days before it occurs, and even during one's prayers? Is it true that whole hours are given to one's adornment, hours which are sometimes due to one's family or to religion? Is it true that days consecrated to the Lord, sometimes even to penance, are often chosen for dances? Is it true that at a ball one is stormed by vanity, and that there is as great a parade as possible of ornaments and too often of indecent attire? Is it true that no means are left untried to please others and to attract applause? Is it true that persons do not fear to veil without covering themselves, and that immodest artifices are employed to show off dangerous charms, and to supply for those which nature has refused or time has faded?

"Is it true that at a ball jealousy is enraged with merit, and that the success of one is the anguish of another? Is it true that, to have a triumph over one's rivals, there is little account made of pleasantries no way courteous, of whispers significantly mysterious, of allusions more or less malicious? Is it true that all this is sometimes matter of conversation for many days after a ball?

"Is it true that at a ball everything contributes to awake the senses, to soften the heart, to excite the imagination? Is it true that one finds there a brilliant circle, whose members vie with one another in displaying the most captivating ornaments of fashion; a mixture of the sexes, a confusion of persons whose age alone would point out that they ought to be kept separate, and both parties comporting themselves in a manner very proper to cast into each other's hearts the most fatal sparks: with all this, the gay steps of an effeminate dance, the exquisite harmonies of seducing music, the gorgeous illusions of decoration, and the dazzling beams of light?

"Is it true that at a ball one spends what would feed a great many poor persons, who, while you are inebriated with pleasures, tremble with cold; who are in want of clothes to cover them, of straw on which to sleep, and of bread to eat; and whose tears and sobs ascend to the ears of God with your laughter and song? Is it true that, during the ball, that is, during the greater portion of the night, servants of both sexes remain without any watch over them, and are exposed to the danger of permitting among themselves that which a more careful education forbids to their masters and their mistresses?

"Is it true…"

"Ah! uncle, I have heard enough. I pray you, no more at present. To be candid with you, I would rather, instead of answering all these questions, tell you that I shall never dance: so clearly do I see that you would not permit me to dance."

"You are mistaken now. I tell you in plain terms that I permit you to dance. Do you hear that?"

"You permit me, uncle!"

"Yes, I, an old man with gray hairs, I permit you to dance on one slight condition."

"What is it?"

"Will you promise me to observe it?"

"Certainly."

"Well, listen. You know, my niece, that the most general and unassailable principle of Christian morality is that which obliges us to refer to God everything we do; and God is so good that he accepts the offering of our most common and indifferent actions, such as our meals, our recreations, our sleep, because all these things enter into the order of his providence. When therefore you have arranged your toilet for a ball, you shall retire to your room. There, alone, without any other witnesses than God and your conscience, you shall place yourself on your knees at the foot of your crucifix, and make the following prayer, 'O my God! my model and my judge, I am about to do freely and willingly a thing which thy gospel and thy Church declare to be most dangerous, a thing which has brought shipwreck to the piety, the humility, the innocence of an immense number. To do it well, I have spent a long time in adorning myself: I am crowned with roses, the better to please. I offer thee therefore my ball and my toilet, to imitate thee, O my God! who wast crowned with thorns, and to fulfill the promises of my baptism, by which I renounced the devil, with all his works and pomps; also, for the edification of my neighbor and the salvation of my own soul. Vouchsafe to accept my offering and to give me thy blessing.'"

"Why, uncle, your condition is impossible. There is no baptized person that would dare to make such a prayer: it is a mockery."

"As you like, my niece; take it or leave it: this is the price of my permission."

"Let others avail themselves of it; as for me, I renounce it."

"Since dances and balls cannot, without mockery, be offered to God, you see, my child, that they are not so innocent as the world pretends. Yet, I repeat, dancing is not a sin in itself: it only becomes dangerous and criminal by the circumstances which accompany it, at the present day more than ever before. In consequence, if you wish to know the conduct that is to be observed on this matter, I shall tell you in a few words; but take care to understand them well, and do not afterward imagine me to have said something that I never said: Dances, being an occasion of sin, ought to be avoided. However, as dancing is not an evil practice in itself, a case may sometimes arise when a person doubts whether it is lawful to go to a place where it will be introduced. What is then to be done? Let us consult our confessor, that is to say, the true friend of our soul, who will decide for us, not according to the maxims of the world, but according to the maxims of the gospel, by which we shall be judged."

The decision at which we have arrived regarding dances, may also be applied to shows or plays.[1277]

PRAYER

O my God! who art all love, I thank thee for having protected my body from homicide and my soul from scandal, but I thank thee no less for having protected my affections from everything that might degrade them; give me a pure heart, that I may love thee alone.

I am resolved to love God above all things, and my neighbor as myself for the love of God; and, in testimony of this love, I will always be on my guard against giving scandal.

Lesson 53: Our Union with the New Adam by Charity (8)

Superiority of the law of God over human laws.—God shows himself, in his commandments, much more wise and powerful than human legislators. These only forbid the guilty action: murder, for example, or theft. They only punish the evil when it has been committed; here their power is limited. The thought, the desire, the will to commit crime, escape them. They cut down the evil tree, but it does not pertain to them to tear up the root; for this root is hidden in the heart of man. God does much more. Not satisfied with forbidding the guilty action, the searcher of reins and hearts penetrates into the lowest depths of the soul, and crushes evil in its germ—the desire, the thought. His commandments are intended much rather to prevent than to punish crime. It is by thus acquainting men with the decalogue, that our Lord shows himself to be truly our physician and our Savior.

As in the preceding commandments God does not confine himself to a prohibition of the guilty action, but also includes everything likely to lead to it; so, in the seventh and tenth, he forbids not only stealing, but even the desire, the thought of appropriating to oneself the goods of another. The end, therefore, of these two precepts is to regulate our conduct, our desires, and even our thoughts, in regard to justice.

The seventh and tenth commandments are expressed thus: "Another's goods thou shalt not take nor keep. Another's goods unjustly wish not thine."[1278]

Nothing is more natural than the connection of the seventh and tenth commandments with those which we have explained in the last two lessons. In effect, after life and honor, which hold the chief rank among natural goods, comes property or fortune; and God places it in security by the two commandments which we are now about to explain.

Basis of the right of property.—"Thou shalt not steal." These words are the only true basis of the right of property. On the one hand, possession, even immemorial possession, is but a fact, which alone cannot constitute a right, inasmuch as it may be destroyed by another fact; on the other, all human laws protecting property are but the expression of human wills, which alone do not and cannot constitute a right, inasmuch as one man has not of himself a right to command another man. The right of property, like every other right, is divine in its essence.[1279]

This is a thing which ought not to be forgotten by those who, at the present day, defend the right of property. What they ought to be no less mindful of is that all the rights of God are inseparable: to deny one is to deny them all. To defend some and reject others is to weaken all arguments; for it is to enter into a contradiction with oneself, it is to stand upon ground from which one will infallibly be driven by a charge of vigorous logic.

Object of the seventh and tenth commandments.—The right of property is therefore divine. From this right flows the obligation of respecting it. That virtue which, in the face of this right, imposes silence on our cupidity, and makes us render to everyone his due, is called justice. Justice therefore forbids us to injure the neighbor in his property, and obliges us to repair the harm that we have done him: such is the twofold object of the seventh commandment.

Definition of stealing.—It forbids stealing. To steal means not only to take, but also to keep a thing against the will of him to whom it belongs. Wherefore theologians define stealing: the unjust taking or keeping of the goods of another against his will, when he rightly wishes not to be deprived of them. By the goods of another we understand whatever belongs to the neighbor—whether he has the ownership or the use of the thing, whether it lies with him as a deposit or as a pledge. Hence, one is guilty of stealing, either by unjustly wishing, against the will of the neighbor, to usurp the dominion of that which belongs to him, or by unjustly wishing to acquire merely the use and possession of it.[1280]

It is proper to explain in detail the definition of stealing.

1. Stealing is a taking or a keeping; for the neighbor may be wronged in the one way as well as in the other. He therefore who retains unjustly what belongs to the neighbor, though it originally came into his hands without injustice, is guilty of stealing.[1281]

2. Stealing is an unjust action; for stealing is a vice opposed to justice, which desires everyone to have his own. Accordingly, it is not stealing to take or to keep another's property for some good end; for example, if one takes a sword from a man who wishes to kill himself or his enemy, or if one hides something belonging to a man with a view to preserve it for him, or to prevent its being stolen from him, or to have a little amusement with him in order to make him more cautious. This last method might be criminal: suppose one foresaw that it would occasion quarrels, rage, or rash judgments.

3. Stealing is an appropriation of the goods of another. If a man takes back on his own authority a thing which he knows for certain to belong to him, and which is unjustly withheld from him, he does not steal. But a man is considered guilty of stealing, if he takes away secretly a thing which belongs to him, but which he has given as a pledge to his creditor.

4. Stealing is a laying hands on the goods of another against his will. If a man takes or keeps what belongs to the neighbor, honestly and reasonably believing that the owner would not be offended thereby, but would gladly agree to it, and yet his consent cannot be asked before making use of his property, this is not stealing.

5. Stealing is a detention of the goods of another against his will, when he rightly wishes not to be deprived of them. In effect, one may, without sin, take possession of the goods of another against his will, by legitimate authority. For this reason, the Israelites did not steal when, by the order of God, they carried off the gold and silver vessels borrowed from the Egyptians. In the same manner, whoever takes or keeps the goods of a man, foreseeing that he is about to make a bad use of them: for example, the person who takes

a bottle of wine from a drunkard that is on the point of drinking it and being intoxicated; the person who takes bad books from another that makes guilty use of them; the wife who, seeing that her husband wastes the goods of the house in debauchery, takes his money artfully to employ it in the support of her family—none of these sin.

Species of stealing.—There are so many species of stealing that it is almost impossible to enumerate them. Let us confine ourselves to the principal ones: they are three in number. The goods of another may be taken secretly, and this kind of stealing is called theft or larceny; openly and violently, as is done by highwaymen, and this kind of stealing is called robbery or rapine; and by deceiving the neighbor, and this kind of stealing is called fraud or cheating.

Theft. Not only are they guilty of theft who secretly take the neighbor's goods, but also those who buy stolen things, or who keep things which have been taken in an unlawful manner. When a person finds anything, he should endeavor to discover the owner. If this is impossible, the value of the article must be applied to the benefit of the poor or to other good works. Such is the safest course. Is there question of a treasure, that is to say, of something hidden or buried, which no one can prove to be his own property, and which has been discovered by mere chance? It belongs to him who finds it on his own ground. If it is found on another's ground, one half belongs to the finder of the treasure, and the other to the proprietor of the place.

What is to be thought of tame or quiet animals, that is to say, those which, although of a wild nature, have acquired the habit of retiring to a home prepared for them—as pigeons, rabbits, bees? According to our French laws, pigeons which pass into another cote—rabbits into another warren—fish into another pond, belong to the proprietors of these retreats, if they have not been drawn thither by wrongful artifices.

They are also guilty of theft who take fruit from gardens, or wood from national or baronial forests or private demesnes. In like manner, laborers and tradespeople, who, not having worked as they should, claim nevertheless their full wages. And tailors, who keep pieces of cloth, given them to make garments, under the pretext that the terms to which they have agreed are too moderate.

The same is to be said of children who take anything without the permission of their parents, or who apply improperly that which they have received from their parents for the purpose of defraying the expenses of their education or supplying their real wants. And of servants, who take things from their masters in order to indemnify themselves for the smallness of their wages, or who keep some of the money given them to go to market with, or who secretly make away with wine or meats not usually allowed to them, or who have not that care in their masters' service which they ought to have, or who dispose of their masters' property without permission, or who are otherwise unfaithful.

The husband is guilty of injustice by taking from his wife, against her will, the property which she is entitled to the full and free administration of, or by disposing of common property without the knowledge or the consent of his wife. It is almost needless to say that he can no more employ property so obtained in making reparation for his own personal injustices, than he can squander it in the excesses of a dissolute life. The wife sins against justice when, notwithstanding the opposition of her husband, she takes a considerable amount either of common property or of property which she does not enjoy solely, in order to spend it in superfluous expenses—in dress, in furniture, in pleasure—whether to gratify herself or her children. But she may, when she has no property of her own, take out of the common property some alms—moderately, however—to help a father, a mother, a brother, or a sister in want.

We must regard as guilty of the same sin those who, filling some public or private office, neglect its obligations, and yet continue to receive its emoluments.

Robbery. The goods of another may also be taken by robbery, that is to say, openly and violently. Besides the injustice which is common to it with simple theft, robbery includes a personal injury, which changes the species of the sin.[1282] One is guilty of this sin by refusing to pay, either in whole or in part, the wages due to laborers or servants. This is a great sin in the sight of God. "Know," says the apostle St. James, "that the hire which you have kept back from those who have reaped down your fields, cries against you, and their complaints have ascended to the ears of the God of hosts."[1283]

Those who embezzle in the management of public revenues, who exact what is not due, or who retain for themselves or for their friends a portion of that which ought to enter the state treasury; those who lend money at an exorbitant rate of interest, and thus ruin poor persons by their usury; those who, sitting on the bench of justice, let themselves be corrupted by bribes, and occasion the loss of the most rightful causes; those who deceive their creditors, who deny their debts, or who, having obtained a time for payment, buy on trust and afterward refuse to pay—all those are guilty of robbery.

Fraud. In fine, the goods of the neighbor may be taken by fraud, that is to say, by deceiving him. A man deceives his neighbor by selling him as good, and without any diminution of price, articles that are damaged or adulterated. It is also fraud to use false weights or measures. Cupidity thinks every kind of ruse lawful for its own advantage. Hence, in some places, traders are said to have three different measures: a small one for selling, a large one for buying, and a correct one for showing to inspectors. Though they may succeed in imposing on men, let them remember that they cannot deceive God. This God of all justice says to them in the scripture, "You shall not have two different measures; let your scales, your weights, your bushels, be just, for a double weight is an abomination in the eyes of God, and a deceitful balance is an iniquity."[1284]

Stealing is a great sin, since it is opposed to natural, divine, and human laws. It is opposed to the natural law, which forbids us to do to another that which we would not wish another to do to us. Now, no one is satisfied that another should take or keep his goods against his will. It is opposed to the divine law, which says, "Thou shalt not steal,"[1285] and which threatens those who are guilty of this sin with hell: "Neither thieves, nor covetous, nor liars, nor extortioners shall possess the kingdom of God."[1286] It is opposed to human law, which, among all the peoples of the world, punishes in a most severe manner, sometimes even with death, those who steal. And it ought to be so; for it is necessary that everyone should be allowed to possess in peace whatever belongs to him. Otherwise, society would be out of the question. The unhappy consequences of this sin are another proof of its enormity, and of the horror with which it should be regarded. It is the source of innumerable hatreds, enmities, murders, and riots.

Yet stealing is not always mortal: it is a sin that admits of levity of matter. But what value is required that the matter may be grave—sufficient for a mortal fault? This affair cannot be decided mathematically. Wherefore, doctors do not agree concerning it. Some think that the value corresponding to the day's wages of a workman who earns what is necessary for his support is enough to make a mortal sin. Others, a pretty numerous class among the ancients, teach that the value of half-a-crown is grave matter in itself, whether the person from whom it is taken is rich or poor. But, at the present day, considering the depreciation in the value of money, it would require a larger sum.[1287]

Let us add that stealing ought also to be regarded as mortal as often as the owner is greatly or reasonably offended, if not on account of the worth of the thing stolen, at least on account of the injury sustained; for example, if one stole from a workman a very cheap tool, without which, not being able to work, he should have to suffer a notable loss. In this case, one would be bound not only to restore the tool to the workman, but also to indemnify him for his loss if it was foreseen.[1288] He who makes in succession a number of little thefts from the same or from different persons, with the intention of enriching himself and attaining gradually to a considerable amount, sins mortally at each of these little thefts; for, as often as he steals, he renews and realizes an intention extremely culpable.[1289]

Restitution: Its necessity.—The enormity of the sin of stealing is also proved by the obligation to restore. In order to obtain the pardon of other sins, it is enough to repent of them and to confess; while the pardon of this sin cannot be obtained, unless one restores the things stolen. Hence, the saying of St. Augustine, which has become an axiom of public: "The sin is not forgiven, unless the thing stolen is restored, when possible."[1290] Now, what a difficulty it is for a man who has enriched himself with the goods of others, to make restitution! Everyone may form an idea of it. We may also judge of it by the words of the prophet Habacuc: "Woe to him that heaps together what is not his own, and loads himself with thick clay!"[1291] The prophet calls the possession of another's goods "thick clay," to show the difficulty of freeing oneself from it, that is, of making restitution. Yet it must be done. Let us see, then, who are bound to make restitution.

Who are bound to make restitution.—It is certain that all those who effectually concur in stealing, or who, by a serious fault, cooperate in an injury done the neighbor, are bound to restitution.

Among the number we may count him who commands stealing; him who counsels it; him who gives it that consent without which the offense would not be committed—for example, a judge, who by his influence ruins a good cause; and those who receive or sell stolen goods, as well as those who afford shelter or protection to thieves, in order to favor them in their misdeeds.

Also, those who share in the fruits of plunder, that is to say, those who obtain a part of the booty or derive advantage from the injury; those who lend their aid to the commission of a crime—as he who holds a ladder for a thief, opens a door for him, supplies him with false keys, keeps watch for him while he perpetrates a burglary, or accompanies him by way of encouragement; and those who drive off persons that wish to prevent a robbery.

Finally, those who, being bound by a title of justice, say by their office or employment, to protect public or private property, are silent at a time when they could by some warning prevent a robbery or an injury; who raise no opposition to it, at a time when they could hinder it; or who do not inform on an evildoer that would be obliged to make restitution, if known.

See how the law of God pursues injustice in all its windings, and demands reparation from it! This law even prescribes the order in which persons should restore. The unjust retainer of a thing stolen is the first bound. The retainer may be the person himself who stole, or his heir, or someone else. An heir is therefore bound to restore the goods wrongly acquired—by fraud, usury, or theft—which he finds in the succession. If the retainer does not restore, the duty falls on him who commanded the theft; if the latter does not restore, it falls on him who executed the theft; if this last does not restore, it falls on those who cooperated in the theft.

It is to the person from whom goods have been stolen, or to his heirs, that restitution must be made, and not to the poor or to the Church. It is not permitted to give alms out of the goods of another. Restitution must be made as soon as possible; otherwise, a person continues to offend against the seventh commandment, and, if there is question of an important restitution, to live in the state of mortal sin. Unless there is a real impossibility, it is not permitted to leave this care to heirs. On the one hand, they are not always faithful in fulfilling the wishes of the dying; on the other, a person may cause the neighbor a new and heavy loss, by retaining for a period more or less protracted that which belongs to him. After delays of this kind, it is not rare to see wills made totally void.

If a person wrongs a number of others in the same locality, without knowing exactly who they are, restitution must be made for the benefit of the poor in the same locality. A dealer who has sold with false weights or measures to all those purchasing at his shop, must, if he continue in business, dispose of his wares at a lower price than they are worth for as long a time as is required to repair the frauds of which he has been guilty toward his customers. If he retires from business before having complied with this duty, he should make restitution to the poor of the place where the injustice was committed.[1292]

If it is impossible to make the restitution reach those to whom it is due, either by reason of the distance of places or because the parties are not known, the amount must be expended in good works. If a man finds it out of his power to make restitution, he must have the will to make it as soon as he can; and, if he die before doing so, God, who requires nothing impossible, will be satisfied with his good will. If he is afraid of being defamed on account of making restitution, he must beg his confessor or some other prudent person to take the affair in charge. See how much God loves us, and how careful he is even of our temporal interests!

What is to be said of the things that are to be restored? It is necessary to return another his goods, and to repair the loss which he has suffered. Now, the neighbor has four kinds of goods: the goods of the soul, the goods of the body, the goods of honor, and the goods of fortune. If one has robbed the neighbor of the goods of the soul, either by evil counsel or by evil example, it is necessary to restore to him other spiritual goods, by wise counsel, edifying example, and fervent prayer. We spoke of this kind of restitution when treating of scandal. If one has injured the neighbor in the goods of the body, by wounds, murder, or any other sin, it is necessary to repair as far as possible all the losses that proceed from this injury. If one has lessened the neighbor's goods of honor, that is to say, the neighbor's reputation, it is necessary, as we shall soon show, to repair this reputation, and to compensate the neighbor for all the material losses that he has sustained in consequence of its being injured. The goods of fortune, as money, beasts, property in general, it is necessary to restore such, if possible, as they were taken; otherwise, their value. Moreover, it is necessary that the losses which have been caused by stealth should be repaired, and the profits which would have arisen from the things stolen restored: all according to the judgment of enlightened and impartial men.

So many cares are not enough for the tender solicitude of our heavenly Father. To the seventh commandment he joins the tenth. The one regulates our actions, the other our thoughts, in regard to justice; and both, united, form a piece of the most perfect legislation.

Tenth commandment in particular.—The tenth commandment then forbids us to desire the neighbor's goods, whatever they may be—gold, silver, raiment, fruit, cattle, lands, houses. He who desires to obtain possession of any of these things by unjust means is guilty of stealing in his heart, and of mortal sin if the object of his desire is considerable; only, he is not bound to restitution, since he does not really steal.

Social advantages of these commandments.—The first advantage of this commandment is that it prescribes the true means of keeping the seventh. As a matter of fact, it is from the desire that the action proceeds. He therefore who is careful to stifle in his heart the desire of that which belongs to the neighbor will not inflict an injury on him. A second advantage is that it makes us observe a course of perfect justice, by teaching us that external acts are not sufficient for the accomplishment of the divine law, but that the internal sentiments of the heart are also necessary. Hence arises the immense superiority of the law of God over all human laws.

A third advantage is that of showing us the infinite goodness of God toward us. Could this goodness go further? The seventh commandment places our property beyond the reach of the violence of others. The tenth defends us from ourselves—from those irregular appetites of ours which would prove so disastrous to us if we permitted ourselves to desire whatever we like. In laying upon us a prohibition against cupidity, God blunted, so to speak, the spurs of the passions, which excite us to all sorts of evil actions. Hence comes another advantage. Delivered from the importunate pursuits of cupidity, we have more leisure to occupy ourselves with true goods, and to discharge the important duties which religion prescribes.

Summing up, to stifle in the heart of man an irregular desire of earthly things—consequently, to prevent him from degrading himself and making himself miserable; to preserve society from the innumerable injustices, frauds, evils, that flow from this irregular desire; to establish justice and charity on earth, by causing them to reign in the affections of man: these are the advantages of the seventh and tenth commandments. Let all observe them, and prisons become useless.

But take them away from the decalogue, and you will see what must become of society: nothing left but a forced confidence, an armed security. In vain will you have thousands of legal statutes as a protection for your property! Frail barriers! Chicaneries and stratagems of every kind will soon find a means of eluding your laws. And then how many secret extortions, frauds, injustices, which your laws can never reach! Tell me: What are most of those scandalous fortunes which we see rising so often at the present day as if by enchantment, but a bitter mockery of your laws and a proof of your impotence? Assuredly, they proclaim a truth as old as the world: without the law of God, no honesty.

Though you have thousands of laws, was there ever a century more remarkable for its injustices—a century in which there were louder complaints of bad faith? No one knows what man to trust: Is not this the daily refrain? Why these unceasing murmurs? Because you despise a law, the only law, the law without which all others, supported by police, jailers, and dungeons, cannot defend your fortune. Cease then to complain, or observe the law which alone can put an end to your complaints, the divine law, the safeguard of all interests. I know that you require others to observe it strictly; but, if you wish to succeed, begin by setting the example. You ought to hold to this law, that is, to the seventh and tenth precepts of the decalogue, as you hold to your property: it is a question of life or death.

Cupidity, the cause of all injustices, and thereby the greatest obstacle to restitution! Unfortunate slaves of this blind passion, hear what you may expect from those for whom you sacrifice your souls, by amassing riches for them!

Example. A very rich man, who owed a portion of his fortune to crying injustices, found himself dangerously ill. He knew it. Mortification had already entered his wounds, and yet he could not decide on making restitution. As often as the matter was mentioned to him, he replied, "What would become of my three sons? They would be left to misery." This reply was borne to an ecclesiastic. "If someone," says he, "were to tell him that I have an excellent remedy for stopping mortification, he would ask to see me, and I hope that I might induce him to restore." The news soon reached the ears of the sick man, who sent at once to the ecclesiastic, begging him to come as speedily as possible. The latter did not delay, and, on his arrival, was very kindly welcomed.

"The remedy is unfailing," says the Abbé, "it is simple, and will not cause you any suffering; but it is dear, very dear."

"Though it should cost two thousand, nay, ten thousand francs, no matter," says the sick man, "In what does it consist?"

"The whole remedy consists in this: in melting over the mortified parts some human fat belonging to a person alive and in good health. Much is not needed. If you can find any person who, for ten thousand francs, will let his hand be burned during the space of a quarter of an hour, it will be enough."

"Alas!" says the sick man, "I greatly fear that we cannot find any person."

"Have courage," says the ecclesiastic, "you do not know the devotedness of your children toward a father who leaves them such immense riches. Send for your eldest son. He loves you. He is to be your heir. Say to him, 'You may save your father's life, if, in order to cure me, you consent to let your hand be burned.' I have confidence in him: he may agree. If, however, he should refuse, make your proposal to the second, promising to make him your heir. If the second should refuse, surely the third will accept the offer, in order to have the inheritance."

The three sons are called. The proposal is made to them one after another. All three reject it. "Let not my father think of it," says each of them, as he withdraws.

"I am sure of nothing in the world," says the ecclesiastic now to the sick man, "if it is not this, that you are very foolish indeed to consent to lose your body and your soul, and to be tormented in the fires of hell, for the sake of children who, to obtain your cure and to save your life, are unwilling to suffer the pain of an earthly fire for the short space of a quarter of an hour. What madness!"

"You are right," answers the sick man. "You have opened my eyes. Let someone go for a notary. Meanwhile, I beg you to hear my confession."

And with the assistance of his confessor, he took the means of repairing his injustices as well as he could, having no regard to the enrichment of his children.

PRAYER

O my God! who art all love, I thank thee for having taken so much care to protect our temporal goods; remove from my heart every irregular desire of earthly things.

I am resolved to love God above all things, and my neighbor as myself for the love of God; and, in testimony of this love, I will give alms as often as I can.

Lesson 54: Our Union with the New Adam by Charity (9)

Eighth commandment.—One of the most admirable gifts that God has bestowed on man is speech. By it, man is essentially distinguished from all other terrestrial creatures; by it, he publishes the praises of his Creator; by it, he forms and maintains with his kind those relations, at once so sweet and so useful, which are the glory of the human race and the happiness of families. These are the noble ends for which God endowed man with speech.[1293]

But since the sin of the first Adam, how many abuses of this divine gift! The tongue is the chief instrument of the iniquities that defile the earth and disturb society. By it, man blasphemes his Creator, and diffuses, among his kind, error, impiety, libertinism, hatred, discord, and all those evils which make life in this world a long torment.

Social advantages of this commandment.—To remedy these disorders, by bringing back speech to its primitive use, God has given us the eighth commandment. By this salutary precept, he places in security our honor and reputation—goods often dearer than life; goods whose loss is capable of poisoning all the enjoyments of earth; goods without which dignities, riches, talents even, are a burden. By it, he clears society from suspicion, dissimulation, hypocrisy, lying, which, when they are permitted to reign, occasion so much confusion that men hardly differ from devils. By it, he restores truth, a deep confidence, good faith, which make earth an anticipated paradise. Accordingly,

O truly paternal goodness! there is not one of our interests that the decalogue does not surround with a sacred barrier! Where is there another code of morality, so complete, so wise, so beneficent?

Its object and what it forbids.—The scripture expresses the eighth commandment thus: "Thou shalt not bear false witness against thy neighbor."[1294] Though false witness alone is mentioned, it is certain that this precept forbids whatever may lead to it.

The eighth precept then forbids all the injustices that can be done the neighbor in word or in thought, because the thought is the internal word, according to the royal prophet.[1295]

It follows hence that not only is false testimony forbidden us by this precept, but also detraction, calumny, lies, evil reports, injurious words, pointed railleries, mockeries, flatteries, rash judgments, and whatever else may wound in word or in thought the justice and charity which are due to the neighbor.

Let us become well acquainted with the chief sins that violate the eighth commandment, and entertain for them all the horror that they deserve.

1. *False testimony.* By false testimony is understood a deposition made against the truth before a legal officer, after taking the oath which is usually required of witnesses. It was God who appointed judges to terminate differences: they have a right to summon witnesses and to examine them. Witnesses are bound to appear before judges, and to answer, according to the truth, the questions which they are asked. They ought to tell "the truth, the whole truth, and nothing but the truth," without having regard to the interests of their relatives, or to their own interests: this is their duty, under pain of mortal sin.

St. Thomas says that a false witness commits three sins: perjury, since he utters a falsehood after having sworn to speak the truth; injustice, since he wrongs the neighbor, toward whom he is bound to observe charity and justice; lying, since he asserts or denies a thing contrary to the truth of which he is aware.[1296] Moreover, the false witness sins against God, whose presence he despises, by calling him to give evidence in favor of a falsehood; against the judge, whom he insults by his deception; against the opposite party, whom he endeavors to have unjustly condemned.

Hence, God regards false testimony with horror. "There are six things," the scripture tells us, "which the Lord hates": among them is false testimony.[1297] "Wherefore, the false witness shall perish."[1298] To banish forever this abominable crime, so fatal to society, the Church excommunicates false witnesses, and the civil laws inflict the heaviest penalties on them. Such persons were formerly punished with death.[1299]

The false witness is bound to repair all the injury that he has maliciously caused the neighbor, and even to retract what he has said at the peril of his own life, if the reparation cannot be made in any other way, and if there is reason to hope that the accused will be acquitted from blame and acknowledged innocent: other things being equal, the condition of the innocent must be preferred to that of the guilty. That which we say of the false witness is applicable to those who effectually cooperate in doing an injury, by engaging someone to give false testimony. Witnesses in general who are cited to a court of justice are bound to appear. If they refuse, they are culpable, but it would seem that they are not bound to repair the loss which befalls the interested parties in consequence of this refusal.

If lying and perjury are forbidden to witnesses, they are no less so to the accusers and the accused, to attorneys and barristers, and in general to all persons who are involved in matters of judgment. Hence, judges, who, committing a grievous fault in the sight of God, deliver a sentence contrary to justice, or who, without reason, put off the conclusion of a trial when everything is sufficiently plain, are responsible for the loss which is the result.

The same obligations on lawyers who take charge of suits which they regard as unjust. In case of their client's neglect, they are bound to repair all the injury that they cause to the opposite party. It is the same if, through ignorance, negligence, unfaithfulness, or very censurable indolence, they lose just suits which have been entrusted to them: they are bound to indemnify their client for the wrongs which they have inflicted on him. See in how many ways God protects innocence, even at the tribunals of men!

2. *Lying.* This is one of the most odious and disgraceful vices, one of those which cause the greatest mischief on the earth. To lie is to speak in a manner contrary to one's thoughts, with the intention of deceiving the neighbor.[1300] A person may lie by word, by writing, by gesture, by action. There are three kinds of lies: the jocose, which is told for amusement, as if Christians might take pleasure in that which offends their heavenly Father; the officious, which is told to procure the good of the neighbor, or to prevent an evil from happening him; and the malicious, which is told with the design of raising a prejudice against the neighbor.

All these lies are sins. It is never permitted anyone to lie, even though it were to avoid the most severe tortures; to preserve life, honor, or riches for oneself or others; to save an innocent person unjustly accused; or to promote the neighbor's salvation. It is likewise forbidden to use dissimulation, properly so called, which of itself tends directly to deceive. This is a lie in action, which is no less to be condemned than a lie in word.

But how are we to act on some pressing occasions when questions are put to us? We cannot tell the truth that is asked of us, but still we should not falsify or disown it. We may turn aside the mind of the inquirer to something else. If it should happen that he deceives himself by his own imprudence, or that he gives a wrong meaning to our words, we are not bound to disabuse him of his error. Moreover, it is permitted to avail oneself of some expressions which, without being literally true, are not lies, because the meaning of these expressions may easily be understood according to usage. A beggar asks you for alms; you tell him that you have no money, though you really have some: you do not lie. The beggar understands quite well that you have no money that you can give him. Finally, he who knows something under the seal of a secret may say that he is ignorant of it, as our Lord himself said to his disciples regarding the last judgment: "No person knows the day or the hour of it."[1301]

To have that horror for lies which they deserve, let us make the following considerations:

I. *A lie is an abuse of a most admirable gift of God.* Speech was given us only to manifest our thoughts, not to deceive one another. Besides, it was by speech that God chose to have society maintained among men. But if society cannot subsist without the commerce of language, this commerce necessarily requires that he who speaks should speak conformably to his thoughts, and that he who is spoken to should believe. The belief of the one rests on the truthfulness of the other.

II. *A lie attacks God, who is truth itself.* Every lie is a contradiction offered to God, who knows our thoughts. This is the reason why he tells us that "lying lips are an abomination"[1302] to him. He is the Father of truth. When we speak the truth, we are his children. When we utter a lie, we cast from ourselves this sacred character, and become the children of the devil, "who is a liar and the father of liars."[1303] It was the devil that told the first lie ever told in the world.

III. *A lie dishonors him who is guilty of it.* It shows him to have a base soul, a wretched character, a shameful proneness to vice: it exposes him to the greatest danger of being lost. It is, alas! very easy to bring the habit of lying, even in little things, to the most important occasions. Not a perjury, not a sacrilege, that has not begun by one's being a liar. A person does not arrive suddenly at enormous crimes: lying is usually the apprenticeship.

Henceforward, therefore, let us hold every kind of lie in horror. Let us love the truth; let us love it as we love God himself, its only source and principle; let us love it more than our interests, more than our relatives, more than our friends, more than our life.[1304] To give proof of our love for it, let us imitate, if necessary, the conduct of a holy bishop mentioned in ecclesiastical history.

The emperor Maximian sent some soldiers to arrest St. Antony, bishop of Nicomedia. It happened that the soldiers, not knowing whither they had come, entered the house of the venerable old man, and asked him for something to eat. The saint received them very kindly, and gave them wherewith to appease their hunger. The repast being over, they asked him where they might be able to find Bishop Antony. "I am he," answered the saint. The soldiers, recognizing him, said, "We will take good care not to arrest you; we will say that we did not find you." "God forbid!" replied the saint. "I do not want you to tell a lie: I would rather die than advise you to commit a sin." And he set out with them to be lodged in prison.[1305]

3. *Detraction.* To detract is to speak unjustly of the wrongdoings of the neighbor in his absence. If the person is present, the sin of speaking thus unjustly or insultingly is called contumely. Is the person innocent of the evil charged against him?—the offense becomes calumny. To exaggerate the evil of which a person has been guilty is a species of calumny. If a person has been guilty of a fault, real but hidden, which charity ought to cover, the sin of him who reveals this fault retains the name of detraction. This wicked sin is so easily committed that perhaps there is no other sin more common.

We may be guilty of it in six ways: a) by revealing, without necessity, the hidden faults which the neighbor has committed, or by exposing defects which were unknown; b) by interpreting his good actions in a wrong light; c) by seeking to lessen the merit of his good actions or qualities; d) by maintaining that he does not deserve the praises which are given him—and this is done either by showing impatience or by smiling maliciously when one hears him praised, nodding the head or making some other sign to show that one does not approve of what is said; e) by making a display of reserve—for example, when, after praising some person's good qualities, one adds, "What I have said is quite true, but...if I liked to tell all...," in order to convey that this person is not all that he is supposed to be; f) by keeping silence, not praising the neighbor for his good actions when one ought to do so, or praising him so coldly that it is easy for those present to see that the person to whom such praises are given is thought little deserving of praise.

We have said that it is detraction to reveal the hidden faults or defects of the neighbor; for he is not guilty of detraction who speaks of anyone's vices or disorders to persons acquainted with them, or who speaks of them in a place where they are public. No injury is then done to the character of the person mentioned if at the same time no exaggeration is permitted. But one would sin by revealing hidden faults, without a lawful reason, to a single individual, though this individual might be supposed discreet, and might be recommended to keep the affair secret. Still, if he who thus renders himself guilty does not act through malice, with the intention of defaming his neighbor in the mind of him to whom he reveals a hidden fault, it is very probable that he only sins venially, even in a grave matter.[1306]

It is also forbidden, when a crime has been forgotten, to awake any recollections of it in the place where it was committed, and where the guilty party has recovered the esteem of his fellow citizens, unless that, in speaking of it, one speaks also of the consideration which he has acquired since his change of conduct. It is also forbidden to detract corporations and communities, and even the dead, either because their memory ought to be respected, or because, while reviling them, one may injure their relatives.[1307]

If you would be convinced of the enormity of detraction, first attend to the manner in which the Holy Ghost speaks of the detractor. He calls him "the abomination of men,"[1308] and forbids communication with him.[1309] He says that "the teeth of detractors are like arrows, and their tongues like sharp knives."[1310] St. Paul declares that they shall not inherit the kingdom of God.[1311] In effect, the detractor is a thief, who steals from the neighbor a good more precious than anything that can be the matter of ordinary theft. In the judgment of God himself, "a good name is better than great riches."[1312]

Consider detraction next in its principle, and you will see that it is a most odious vice. Whence does it come? From the passions. A person detracts through interest, through pride, through jealousy, or through hatred. Do you know any causes more contemptible? What shall we say of its consequences?

St. Bernard, who compares the detractor to a viper, tells us that with a stroke of his tongue he kills three persons.[1313] He gives death to himself by the sin. He gives death to him whom he detracts, either because he robs him of his character, which is his civil life, or by the hatred which he raises in his heart, and which deprives him of the spiritual life of his soul. Finally, he gives death to those in whose presence he detracts, by the part which they usually take in the detraction. Ah! with how much reason does the Holy Ghost forbid us to keep company with detractors![1314]

Yet there are some cases in which it is permitted to discover the defects and vices of the neighbor. Thus, we may speak ill of one person for the good of another, who deserves to be preferred to him who is spoken ill of. Let us give a few examples. It is not detraction to discover to a superior the faults of his inferiors, that he may apply a remedy to them, and prevent further disorders.[1315] It is not detraction to tell the truth to a man who comes to acquire some information regarding a servant whom he wishes to engage; regarding laborers whom he wishes to employ; regarding traders who ask the loan of capital; or regarding a person who seeks to form an alliance with another.

In like manner, it is not detraction to declare the hidden defects of the neighbor, if one does so only through necessity, having no other means to defend his own character or to avoid a notable evil; as, if one cannot justify himself from a crime but by making known that the witnesses have given false testimony on a previous occasion. But here, above all, one ought to be most careful to observe the rules of justice and charity. It is necessary, therefore, to say nothing but what is true; to speak without exaggeration; to add no malicious interpretations; to blend no corrupt intention with that which is upright; to utter no evil but with regret and circumspection, and only to reasonable persons, interested in the affair of which there is question, and engaged to keep it secret. Holy religion! with what solicitude dost thou watch over our name!

4. *Calumny.* This solicitude defends our character not only against detraction, but also against calumny. Calumny is the sin of him who imputes to the neighbor an offense of which he is innocent. It is calumny to attribute to the neighbor faults which he has not committed or defects from which he is free; to exaggerate his real faults or defects; to deny his good qualities or actions. All divine and human laws unite in condemning the calumniator: the world itself puts a brand upon him. It would be useless to say more regarding calumny, in order to inspire us with a horror of it. Better occupy ourselves with the line of conduct which we are to pursue when we hear a detraction or a calumny, and with the means of repairing the consequences of either, when we have had the misfortune to incur its guilt.

First, it is never permitted to take pleasure in detraction or calumny; with much greater reason, to applaud by words or gestures the speaker. If a person shows his approbation outwardly in such a manner as to lead the speaker to continue the detraction or calumny, he becomes an accomplice therein, and contracts a joint obligation to repair the injury done the neighbor.

A person would not be bound to this reparation if, while listening with pleasure to detraction or calumny, he did not say or do anything that might induce the offender to believe his words approved. In this case, a person only sins against charity: mortally, it is true, in a grave matter, and venially in a light matter. But it is important to remark that the person who listens to detraction, because he gladly hears something new, without rejoicing at the wrong done to him who is its object, only commits a venial fault, though the detraction may be grave; unless that he is bound, under pain of mortal sin, to prevent it.[1316]

If he who detracts is a superior, it is necessary to testify by our silence, or by our looks, that his discourse displeases us.[1317] If he is an equal, we must strive with tact to change the conversation, or beg him to leave off, or defend the neighbor. If he is an inferior, we are bound to impose silence on him. It is amid delicate circumstances like these that we are especially called upon to put in practice the great precept, "Do to others as you would wish that they should do to you." Now, if we were absent, how would we wish others to defend our reputation?

The illustrious chancellor of England, Sir Thomas More, is a perfect model on this point: his conduct shows us clearly how we may prevent detraction. When any ill was spoken of the neighbor in his presence, he immediately broke out gaily with this reply, "Let everyone say what he likes; as for me, I say that this house is well built," or something else of the same kind, which, while amusing the detractors, put a stop to their guilty conversation.

Detraction and calumny being thefts, one cannot obtain pardon for them without restoring the good which they take away. Now, they take away the character, which is a good sometimes dearer than life. At other times, they cause a real loss to the neighbor. If there is question of character, the matter stands thus: one has either calumniated or detracted.

If one has calumniated, it is necessary to say so, and to remedy the evil as soon as possible, morally speaking. It is with this obligation as with that of making restitution under the seventh commandment: it is founded on justice, and the sin cannot be remitted unless it is fulfilled. A person may avail himself of this mode of speaking, "In saying such a thing of such a man, I was deceived, or I was in error; there was nothing of the sort."

If one has detracted, the obligation is the same, but the difficulty is much greater. Since the evil imputed to the neighbor is true, one cannot say that it is false: this would be a lie. A person should therefore make use of a general phrase: saying that "we need not believe everything we hear"; that "people often exaggerate"; that "it was wrong to speak ill of such a person"; or that "the defamation was unjust."[1318]

At other times it will be more to the purpose simply to speak well of the injured person, especially if there is reason to believe that this method would be more agreeable to him, or that the detraction is forgotten. If the detraction or the calumny, besides the wrong which it has done to the character of the neighbor, has caused him any other hurt—for example, if it has made him lose his employment—one is bound to reparation.[1319] This last obligation passes to the detractor's heirs.

5. *Tale-bearing*. There is another sin opposed like the preceding ones to the eighth precept: it is tale-bearing. This is a very great sin: "The whisperer," says the scripture, "raises trouble among those who were at peace: therefore he shall be accursed."[1320] "It is greater," adds St. Thomas, "than detraction or contumely; for a friend is better than honor."[1321] A person is guilty of it when, without intending to defame anyone, he issues reports capable of destroying or diminishing affection among relatives, confidence among friends, or order between superiors and inferiors. Hence arise quarrels, hatreds, divisions, and a multitude of other evils.

Reports, whether true or false, even in a light matter, are mortal: a) when a person makes them with the intention of dividing families or friends; and b) when, without having this criminal intention, a person foresees in any way that these reports, by being spread abroad, will cause disputes, enmities, or other like effects. We cannot therefore too carefully avoid stories that may be followed by such sad consequences. "If you chance to hear a word spoken against your neighbor, let it die in your bosom, and be sure that it will not kill you."[1322]

6. *Contumely*. This is a new sin committed by the tongue. It means an injury done to the neighbor in his presence by word or deed. Mockeries, sarcasms, jokes, disgraceful or ridiculous titles, are contumelies. To reproach anyone with his hidden defects or faults is at once a contumely and a detraction. This sin is mortal or venial according to circumstances. It binds one to a reparation of the injury, and, if it has been public, the reparation must likewise be public.

7. *Violation of secrets*. A thing is secret when it is known only to two or three persons, or at least to such a small number that it cannot be regarded as notorious. We sin by violating a secret deliberately without a legitimate cause. This violation may be mortal or venial, according to the importance of the secret. If any damage results to the neighbor, one is bound to reparation. The law of secrecy also forbids us to extort secrets from another; consequently, to read letters not addressed to us. A person should not even gather up and fix together the parts of a torn letter, in order to discover its contents. Finally, it is not permitted to read an unsealed letter which falls into our hands: it must be given to the person to whom it is addressed. Circumstances determine whether the indiscretions of which we have just spoken are grave or light.

8. *Rash judgment*. It is not only words, but even thoughts, disadvantageous to the neighbor, that are forbidden by the eighth commandment: such are doubts, suspicious, and rash judgments. Doubt is a suspension of the judgment regarding the goodness or the badness of an action performed by the neighbor. Voluntary doubt is a sin, because charity and justice oblige us to interpret favorably the actions of the neighbor, who has a right to our esteem as long as the contrary is not sufficiently established. Suspicion is a weak persuasion of the malice of the neighbor's action, resting on light foundations. By reason of the imperfection of the act, suspicion is mostly venial. But it would become mortal if, on slight appearances, one voluntarily suspected adultery, atheism, or heresy.

Rash judgment is a firm persuasion or an inward admission of the malice of the neighbor's action, grounded on weak motives. Hence it is called rash. To represent the state of our mind in these various acts, it may be said that in doubt our mind is like a balance whose scales are even; in suspicion, like a balance of which one of the scales goes down a little; and in rash judgment, like a balance of which one of the scales sinks altogether.

A mortal sin of its nature, rash judgment is really so when, accompanied with perfect advertence and full consent, a judgment is formed on an important matter against some individual; also when, the matter being again important, the signs are so uncertain that they cannot support a prudent judgment.

What peace, what union should reign in the world, if everyone, a conscientious observer of the commandments which we have just explained, would imitate the conduct of St. Monica! St. Augustine relates that when persons who were at enmity with one another told her such outrageous things as are usually said in the first heat of anger, she never alluded to what she had heard but insofar as it might serve to reconcile them, for which purpose she labored her utmost. An imitator of the virtues of his holy mother, Augustine held detraction in horror. It was this that led him to keep exhibited, in the room where he usually took his repasts, these two Latin verses, written in large letters:

Si quis amat dictis absentum rodere vitam
Hanc mensam vetitam noverit esse sibi.

"If anyone wishes to speak ill of the absent, let him know that this table is forbidden him." If it happened that one of his guests began to detract, the worthy bishop interrupted him, saying, "Read these verses; do you wish to place me under the necessity of having them removed?"

The decalogue and modern society.—We have now explained the ten precepts of the decalogue. Our explanation, imperfect as it is, is nevertheless sufficient to render palpable these two truths: that every commandment of God is an immense benefit, and that the decalogue is the pivot of society.

An immense benefit. Let men hate one another; cut one another's throats; rob one another of honor, fortune, or character: Will God be anything the less happy? No. Happiness is essential to his being; it does not depend on us. But he has taken our cause in hand. He has said to the wicked, "Whatever you do to the least of your kind I will regard as done to myself; if you escape human laws, you shall not escape my justice." What security in this promise! To know all that we owe to the decalogue, we should know all the guilty thoughts—the projects of robbery, murder, injustice, and every other crime—that it stifles in a single day among those millions of men who exist throughout the world.

The pivot of society. Take away the decalogue, the law of God and God himself may be scoffed at with impunity, the passions would be left without a rein, virtue and vice are the same. No rest but universal disorder.

Take away the decalogue, and the family is left without a foundation. The wife becomes a slave, and the child a victim, because the father is a brutal and fickle tyrant.

Take away the decalogue, and society is forever dissolved. Might is the supreme law: you have despotism, slavery, and anarchy.

Take away the decalogue, and your life and honor—as well as those of your wife and children—your fortune and character, are at the mercy of the murderer, the seducer, the robber, and the calumniator, artful or strong enough to escape the prison or the scaffold: and how many so escape!

Say not that you can replace the decalogue. With what, I ask, can you replace a law which, entering consciences, seizes and crashes crime in its very germ—the desire, the thought? Is it with instruction? This, assuredly, is not what we want. It is said that we know more now at fourteen years of age than used to be known at twenty-five: on which very account our century is termed a century of enlightenment.

Still, if facts prove anything, it is certain that godless instruction, which is offered everywhere at the present day, has solved one problem; but it must be said that it has done so with a desperate perfection, namely, how to corrupt the greatest possible number in a given time. Instruction! Was it needed by the Greeks and Romans, who were never more corrupt than when they were most highly instructed, and who, in spite of all their enlightenment, ended by plunging into a sink of iniquities? Instruction gives ideas; it does not give morals. It may make scholars; it cannot make good men nor good citizens.[1323]

Again, with what will you replace the decalogue? With politico-philosophical systems? But I will say to you with the father himself of all these systems, "O philosopher! your systems are very admirable; but be so kind as to show me their sanction." And then, all these reforming, healing, saving systems—have they not had a trial one after another during the last fifty years? What social evil have they remedied? Have they strengthened power; have they made obedience more exact, devotedness more earnest, society more moral or more tranquil? What people have they delivered?

Again, with what will you replace the decalogue? With new constitutions? But it would seem that, under this head, there is little left to desire. Since 1789, we have had at least a dozen new constitutions. Society has been subjected to all sorts of treatment imaginable, and the poor sick man still lies trembling and gasping on his weary bed, expecting his cure.

With what, then, will you replace the decalogue? With laws? But if laws are enough, without religion, to rescue a people and to consolidate society, we ought to be more moral, tranquil, and contented than any other people that ever was or ever will be; for, thanks be to God! we have no want of laws. During forty-six years, there have been 76,756 of them manufactured for us: which, by a little calculation, gives nearly four a day!

Let us acknowledge then once for all that the decalogue alone can save society, and defend it from the evils that threaten it. Let us love the decalogue; let us observe it faithfully, if we wish that others should observe it: these are the only terms on which we can purchase happiness.

PRAYER

O my God! who art all love, I thank thee for having placed my reputation beyond the reach of every word, and even of every thought disadvantageous to me; grant me the grace always to respect that of my neighbor.

I am resolved to love God above all things, and my neighbor as myself for the love of God; and, in testimony of this love, I will never speak ill of anyone.

Lesson 55: Our Union with the New Adam by Charity (10)

Commandments of the Church.—To love God, consequently to unite ourselves with our Lord by charity, it is not enough to observe the decalogue: we must also observe the commandments of the Church. In effect, our Lord himself said to the heads of the Church, "As my Father sent me, I also send you. All power is given to me in heaven and on earth: go ye, therefore, teach all nations. Whatsoever you shall bind on earth, shall be hound in heaven; and whatsoever you shall loose on earth, shall be loosed in heaven. He who hears you, hears me; and he who despises you, despises me; and he who despises me, despises him who sent me. If any one will not hear the Church, let him be regarded as a heathen and a publican."[1324]

Legislative power of the Church: Certainty of it.—In the persons of St. Peter and the other apostles, consequently in the persons of our holy father the pope and the other bishops, the Church therefore received divinely the power to make, in the order of religion, laws strictly binding on all Christians—priests or bishops, rich or poor, learned or ignorant, kings or subjects—without any exception. In what kingdom of the earth can be found an authority more sacred, a legislative power better established?

Moreover, the Church is a society established by our Lord Jesus Christ himself, in order to lead men to heaven, by making them obedient to religion. Now, every society has the power to make such laws and regulations as it judges necessary for its preservation, its prosperity, and the end for which it was instituted. The most perfect of all societies, the Church, has therefore the power to make laws. It has accordingly made them from its origin; and, up to our age of pride and impiety, all Christians have considered themselves bound to submit thereto. During the first three centuries, in the height of persecution, there were more than fifty councils held, throughout East and West, for the internal and external government of the Church.

Independence of this power. The Church has never ceased to make use of this legislative power, and to make use of it with a sovereign independence. "There are, O august Emperor," wrote Pope St. Gregory to the emperor Anastasius, "two authorities by which this world is governed: the sacred authority of pontiffs, and the authority of kings. The sacred authority of pontiffs is so much the more terrible, as they must render an account to God, at the last judgment, even of the salvation of kings. You are not ignorant that, although your dignity raises you above other men, you ought to piously bow your head before pontiffs, charged with the dispensation of divine things, and that you ought to be devoted to them in everything pertaining to the order of religion and to the administration of the holy mysteries; you know that, in reference to these things, you depend on their judgment, and that you have not the right of subjecting them to your will. In everything pertaining to public order, these same bishops obey your laws. In your turn, you ought to obey them in whatever concerns holy things, of which they are the dispensers; and, as it would be a crime on their part to be silent regarding the worship which is due to God, so it would be no less a prevarication if, instead of obeying them, as is meet, one should despise their instructions."[1325]

There would be no ending, if we wished to cite all the testimonies of the fathers and all the facts that establish, through the course of eighteen centuries, the perfect independence of the Church in the matter of spiritual government. Let us only hear the immortal archbishop of Cambrai:

"It is vain," exclaims Fenelon, "of anyone to say that the Church is in the state. The Church, it is true, is in the state to obey the prince in everything temporal; but, although she is present in the state, she never depends on it for any spiritual function. She is in this world, but to convert it; she is in this world, but to govern it with regard to salvation. The world, by submitting to the Church, does not acquire the right to control her. Princes, in becoming the children of the Church, do not become her masters: they must serve her, not rule her; they must kiss the dust of her feet, not lay a yoke upon her.

"To disturb the Church in her functions is to attack the Most High in the object dearest to him, namely, his spouse; it is to blaspheme against his promises, it is to rebel against his eternal reign. Not only are princes unable to do anything against the Church, but they cannot even do anything for her, in spiritual matters, beyond obeying her. It is true that a pious and zealous prince is called 'an outside bishop,' and 'a protector of the canons,' expressions which we continually repeat with joy in the moderate sense of the ancients who made use of them. But an outside bishop must never undertake the functions of an inside one. He stands, sword in hand, at the door of the sanctuary; but he takes care not to enter.

"While he protects, he obeys; he protects decisions, but he does not make a single one. He confines himself to two functions: the first is to maintain the Church in full liberty from all her enemies without, that she may be free within to pronounce, to decide, to approve, and to correct, as well as to beat down every kind of haughtiness that rises up against the knowledge of God; the second is to support her decisions, never permitting himself, under any pretext, to become their interpreter."[1326]

Summarizing all these authorities, Pius VI wrote: "We admit, we even desire, that, in political government, there should be laws wholly distinct from those of the Church—laws belonging to the civil power. But, while claiming obedience for some laws, we do not permit that others, which fall within the province of the spiritual power, should be violated by lay authority. What jurisdiction can laymen have over spiritual things? By what right can they expect ecclesiastics to submit to their decrees? Every Catholic knows that Jesus Christ, when founding his Church, gave to the apostles and their successors a power independent of all other powers."[1327]

This power extends to whatever relates, by its nature, to religion, to the divine worship, to the salvation of souls. Hence, the teaching and the preaching of the gospel; the administration of the sacraments; the liturgy; the sanctification of Sunday; the establishment and the sanctification of holidays and of days of fast and abstinence; vows;

religious orders, and their approbation; the interpretation and the dispensation of oaths; the institution of the ministers of the Church, with their jurisdiction, canonical punishments, and irregularities: in a word, all that pertains to ecclesiastical government or discipline enters into the domain of the spiritual power, which, so far as its own affairs are concerned, is absolutely independent of the temporal power.[1328]

Object of this power. Among the laws for which the world is indebted to this power of the Church, at once so sacred, so wise, and so gentle, there are six principal ones, which are called, by excellence, the commandments of the Church. Their end is to explain and to apply the laws given by Jesus Christ himself, and to secure the observance of them. This is the place to make known two of these laws; the others are explained elsewhere.[1329]

Third commandment of the Church.—The first of these two commands us to confess our sins at least once a year. It follows hence that we are bound, by two different precepts, to confess mortal sins, committed after baptism, to a priest. One comes from divine, the other from ecclesiastical law. It is certain: a) That if a person has fallen into any mortal sin, he is bound by the divine precept to confess when he is in danger of death. b) That persons who sin mortally are bound to confess many times during life, by the same divine precept. Hence those who, after sinning mortally, pass several years without confessing, sin not only against the ecclesiastical, but also against the divine precept. c) That a person is bound by the same precept to confess when guilty of mortal sin, and when obliged to receive a sacrament of the living.

In the beautiful ages of the Church, the faithful did not confine themselves to the letter of this commandment: they often had recourse to the sacrament of penance. It was with a purification of their souls in this salutary bath that they began their chief undertakings. They were accustomed to confess before setting out on a journey, before entering the religious state, before making a pilgrimage, even before enlisting in the army. "It was the custom in England," says an ancient author, "that he who was about to dedicate himself to a military life should come the evening before to some bishop or priest, that he might make to him a confession of all his sins with sentiments of compunction, and that, having been absolved, he might pass the night in the Church, praying and devoutly afflicting himself before God. Next morning, before hearing Mass, he laid his sword on the altar, and the priest, after the gospel, placed it on his neck with a blessing. He then communicated at the Mass, and became a soldier."[1330]

The same thing used to be done in France.[1331] If our ancestors were so religious when there was question of taking up arms, they were not less so when there was imminent danger of losing their lives in the service of their country. On the eve of a battle, they would spend the whole night in going to confession.[1332] Good Christians make good soldiers. The illustrious marshal De Turenne had communicated during the night before the day on which he was killed.

Our ancestors, therefore, in the faith had recourse often, freely, joyfully, to the tribunal of reconciliation; but, fervor diminishing in the course of ages, confessions became more rare. To put a barrier to laxity, the Fourth Council of Lateran, held in 1215, ordered that all Christians, of both sexes, arrived at the use of reason, should communicate at least once a year, under pain, during life, of being refused admission to the Church, and, after death, of being deprived of ecclesiastical burial.

As may be seen, children themselves are bound, from the moment they can distinguish between good and evil, to observe this precept. The giving of absolution to them should not be deferred till the time of first Communion. It is not enough for parents to send them to the tribunal of penance; they ought to prepare them carefully, by teaching them the meaning of this act, by reminding them of their principal faults and exciting them to conceive a lively sorrow for all their faults, and by recommending them to confess everything with much sincerity.

After confession, they should induce them to perform, as soon and as devoutly as possible, the penance which has been imposed on them by the confessor, and to put his good advice in practice. If there are so many children who do not know how to confess, and who are not sufficiently sincere in confession, it is often the fault of fathers and mothers, who neglect to prepare them to acquit themselves properly of so important a duty.

Fourth commandment of the Church.—The other precept of the Church on which we have to give a few words of explanation is that of receiving the Blessed Eucharist at Easter. For Communion, as well as for confession, there is a divine precept. The early Christians were faithful observers of it. What do I say? They loved the Savior so tenderly, they felt their need of him so deeply, that they used to communicate daily. Admirable custom! whose reestablishment the Church desires at the present day with all the ardor of her maternal charity.[1333]

For a long time it was unnecessary to engage the faithful to communicate. Alas! who would have told our ancestors in the faith that a time should come when their children would regard this heavenly food with so much indifference that the Church should be obliged to employ all her authority to make them approach the holy table? Yet such is the hard and humiliating necessity to which she has been reduced.

At the same General Council of Lateran, therefore, she ordered all Christians, come to the age of discretion, to communicate at least once a year, during Easter time. A pretty general custom authorizes some delay in the Communion of children. The Church says "at least," showing by this expression that though paschal Communion suffices to prevent one's being excommunicated, yet it is far from satisfying the desires of her maternal tenderness, the longings of the Savior, or the pressing demands of our own necessities. Hence, all persons who have at heart their salvation communicate much more frequently. There is not a single saint who does not earnestly recommend frequent Communion.[1334]

Take their maxims as the rule of your conduct, and experience will quickly teach you that all virtues spring up in the heart under the influence of this divine sacrament.

Meanwhile, let us admire the wisdom of the Church in her twofold law of annual confession and Communion. Undoubtedly there exists a divine precept regarding confession and Communion; but to leave its accomplishment to the choice of every individual would be to render it illusory. The passions, which it opposes, would always find a thousand pretexts for dispensing themselves from a compliance with it, and the influence of Christianity would be lost; for, without confession, Christianity is nothing more than justice without a tribunal.

Social importance of these two commandments.—It was therefore necessary that a competent authority should determine the meaning of the precept, and fix the period of its observance. The Church has done so, and her law of annual confession and Communion is the strongest basis of society. Who tells you all this? A priest? No. A Catholic? No; but a protestant. Behold how Lord Fitswilliam reasoned, a few years ago, in his celebrated *Letters of Atticus*:

"All nations have their religions and their laws: their religion to inculcate virtue and morality, and their laws to punish crimes. Herein, Roman Catholic and all other states have the same end. But in the Roman Catholic religion alone, there exist laws of a much more imperative nature—laws which no art or sophism can render nugatory—laws which are calculated not alone to inspire a love of virtue but also to oblige one to its pursuit—laws which are not confined to the punishment of crimes but are directed to their prevention. These laws consist in the obligation which they lay on all Roman

Catholics to communicate at least once a year; or, in other terms, in their belief of the real presence, in confession and Communion.

"And let no one say that this belief is false and deceitful. Nothing could be more absurd than to suppose that any man should have dared to present it out of his own head to other men. If one of the apostles had proposed it to his fellow laborers, they would have thought him mad or laughed at him. Since it cannot have come from men, it is therefore evident that it must have come from God; and, as divine, it loses all its absurdity, however incomprehensible it may be.

"We may say that, in Roman Catholic states, the whole economy of social order turns on this pivot. It is to this wondrous arrangement that they owe their solidity, their durability, their security, and their tranquility. Hence arises an indisputable principle, a precious maxim, the last ring in the long chain of arguments which we have just laid down, namely: that it is impossible to form any system of government which may be permanent or advantageous, unless it is founded on the Roman Catholic religion. Every other system is deceptive.

"The precepts and the prohibitions which this religion imposes on its children are so little known by the sectaries who attack them, that they have scarcely the faintest idea of them. Some, out of ignorance, turn away their eyes from them; others, out of prejudice, treat them with scorn. In order, therefore, to instruct the former and to undeceive the latter, I will repeat that all Roman Catholics are bound to communicate at least once a year—always, however, according to the state of their conscience; and I will add that, before receiving this august sacrament, in presence of which even the boldest Catholic is seized with fear and awe, it is necessary that all, without distinction or exception, should confess their sins in the tribunal of penance: and that they cannot obtain from any minister in this tribunal, which they look upon as so dreadful, permission to approach the holy table, before they have first purified their hearts with all the dispositions necessary for this purpose.

"Now, these indispensable dispositions are contrition for and a full and precise acknowledgment of all faults committed, atonement for all injustices, restitution of all goods unlawfully acquired, pardon of all wrongs, the breaking asunder of all criminal and scandalous bonds, and the renunciation of envy, pride, hatred, avarice, ambition, dissimulation, ingratitude, and every other sentiment contrary to charity. It is necessary, at the same time, to enter into a sacred engagement before God to avoid even the smallest faults and to observe all the sublime laws of the gospel with the greatest exactness.

"Such is, such has always been during the last eighteen centuries, the fundamental and immutable doctrine of the Roman Catholic Church. And if any one dares to say that her children are wicked and perverse, in spite of the bonds with which she holds them fast and the duties which she lays upon them, what shall we say of men free from these salutary restraints? The inhabitants of the happiest and most flourishing monarchy that ever shone in history were suddenly delivered from them. What was the consequence? These senseless wretches, being no longer afraid of any rein, dared everything. Their crimes, like a raging sea, swept away dikes which God alone could restore, desolated Europe, and left on the French name a most disgraceful, an indelible stain.

"What a pledge is thus required from every individual for the accomplishment of his social duties; for the exercise of all virtues—honesty, benevolence, kindness, mercy! Can the like be found anywhere else? Here, the conscience is regulated by the tribunal of God alone, not by that of the world. Here, the culprit is his own accuser, and not his judge. While the Christian of every other communion examines himself lightly, pronounces on his own cause, and absolves himself easily, the Catholic Christian is scrupulously examined by another, looks for his sentence from heaven, and sighs after that consoling absolution which is granted, refused, or deferred in the name of the Most High.

"What an admirable means of establishing among men a mutual confidence, a perfect harmony in the exercise of their functions! The authority of the prince cannot degenerate into tyranny, nor the freedom of the people into licentiousness: the magistrate is impartial; the legislator, upright and disinterested; the priest, pure and zealous; the soldier, loyal; the subject, faithful; the sovereign, just.

"To pronounce on all questions of general importance, it is necessary and proper to take general effects as their bases: this is what I have done. But alas! such is human frailty that all Roman Catholics do not, I admit, profit of the opportunities afforded them. It is therefore a matter of duty, as it is undoubtedly a matter of the greatest interest, for wise and watchful governments to oppose every relaxation in the principles which I have developed. If, in a Roman Catholic state, no person ever went astray, the question would not be, 'What is the best government,' but rather, 'In such a government, what need is there for other laws?' Perhaps all human laws would there be as superfluous as they are powerless wherever the Roman Catholic religion does not serve them as a foundation.

"Summing up, virtue, justice, morality, ought to serve as the basis of all governments.

"It is impossible to establish virtue, justice, morality, on any good foundation, without the tribunal of penance, because this tribunal, the most terrible of all tribunals, takes hold of the conscience, and directs it in a more effectual manner than any other tribunal. Now, this tribunal belongs exclusively to Roman Catholics.

"It is impossible to establish the tribunal of penance, without the belief of the real presence, the principal basis of the Roman Catholic faith, because, without this belief, the sacrament of Communion loses its value and importance. Protestants approach the holy table without fear, because they only receive a commemorative sign of the body of Jesus Christ. Catholics, on the contrary, only approach it trembling, because they receive there the body itself of their Savior.

"Hence, wherever this belief has been destroyed, the tribunal of penance has ceased with it: confession has become useless; as, wherever this belief exists, confession becomes necessary: and this tribunal, which is necessarily established with it, renders indispensable the exercise of virtue, justice, morality. Therefore, as I have already said, it is impossible to form any system of government which may be permanent or advantageous, unless it is founded on the Roman Catholic religion."

To interpret a divine precept and to secure its observance, as well as to raise a barrier against the inconstancy of man, to assist his weakness, to effect his sanctification, and thus to promote the happiness of families and of society: such are the general ends of the commandments of the Church.

PRAYER

O my God! who art all love, I thank thee for having inspired thy Church to give us commandments so exceedingly useful, and yet so easy to observe; grant me the grace never to violate them.

I am resolved to love God above all things, and my neighbor as myself for the love of God; and, in testimony of this love, I will daily pray for the indifferent.

Lesson 56: Our Union with the New Adam by Charity (11)

Life of sanctity in time; life of glory in eternity; conformity with our Lord Jesus Christ.—After teaching his apostles all the secrets of our union with him, the new Adam made known to them what the fruit of this union ought to be. Now, the fruit of our union with our

Lord is to make us live by his life in time and in eternity—to make us lead here on earth a holy life, and hereafter in heaven a glorious life.[1335] "In the Person of Jesus Christ," says St. Augustine, "a great physician came down from heaven, because a great invalid lay suffering on earth."[1336] This invalid was the human race.

The Savior was not satisfied with applying balm to his wounds. He was not satisfied with placing him on the right way, and saying to him, "Walk!" He himself would walk before him, in order to teach him how to walk. He vouchsafed to travel every road, to appear in every state by which we have to pass, that he might sanctify all as he sanctified all the elements, and that he might teach us to sanctify them ourselves.

He left on his divine footprints graces which enlighten and quicken the feet of those who touch them.[1337] After finishing his course, he turned toward man, and cried to him from the summit of the cross, "Follow me. I am the way, and the truth, and the life. He that followeth me, walketh not in darkness. I have given you an example, that you may do as I have done." Then he ascended glorious and triumphant into heaven, and from the summit of his eternal throne he cries to man, stretching out his arms and holding in his hand a crown, "Follow my steps, and thou shalt come to the place where I am myself."[1338]

Let us now learn to know this model of all ages, of all conditions, of all states; for our Lord is man!

Jesus Christ, the model of our interior life.—A Christian is another Jesus Christ. Such is the sublime definition which the fathers of the Church give us of ourselves.[1339] This resemblance between us and the new Adam ought to be such that the eternal Father, contemplating each of us from the summit of heaven, may be able to say what he heretofore said of our Lord: "This is my beloved Son, in whom I am well pleased." That it may be so, our resemblance must be inward and outward.

1. *In our thoughts.* Our thoughts will be conformed to those of Jesus Christ when we judge like him of all things—of God, ourselves, creatures, time, eternity.

What did the new Adam think of God? His examples and words will answer us. He thought that God is the being of beings —an infinitely wise, good, powerful, holy, just, and merciful being—alone worthy of the adoration, homage, and attention of men. To teach us this, he humbled himself before God so far as to annihilate himself, by taking the form of a servant; he was consumed with zeal to make him known; he at length died on a cross to repair his glory outraged by sin. God was everything to Jesus Christ: he should be everything to us.

This is what the new Adam thought of God during his mortal life. Is it thus that we think of him?

Afraid lest men should forget his lessons or falsely suppose that they only regarded certain periods or certain places, he established himself in the Eucharist. Dwelling in town and country, an inhabitant of every region, he repeats and will continue to repeat to all generations passing over the earth till the end of time those lessons which he gave in Judea. He offers the same examples now as he then offered.

Ask him in the Eucharist what he thinks of God, and his lowly state of a victim will answer you that God is everything, that creatures ought to annihilate themselves in the divine presence. He says to you, "You shall love the Lord your God with all your heart, with all your mind, and with all your strength: this is the first and greatest of all the commandments." And he gives you an example of its observance by daily annihilating himself on our altars, as on the cross, for the glory of his Father.

What does the new Adam think of man? The new Adam regards man as the most precious of visible creatures and the most worthy of the divine care. It was for man that he came into this world, that he lived poor, that he died in the midst of torments. He regards our soul as more precious than his own blood, since he did not hesitate to lay down his life to save it. So much for what he thought of us during his mortal life: now for what he thinks of us in the Eucharist. Ask him why he displays such goodness, such patience, in the midst of the outrages and irreverences committed against him during the last eighteen centuries, on those millions of altars where his love holds him captive; and he will answer you, "Because there is only one thing necessary in my eyes—the salvation of man." Is it thus that we think?

What does the new Adam think of creatures? The new Adam regards creatures as means by which we may rise toward God, but to which we must be on our guard against attaching our heart. He said, "Blessed are the poor; woe to you, rich!" He said, "Blessed are they who suffer and mourn; woe to you who laugh and rejoice!" He said, "Blessed are the humble; learn of me, because I am meek and humble of heart." He said, "Woe to the proud! God resists them, and gives his grace to the humble." All these anathemas, uttered against riches, honors, and pleasures, he still utters from the depth of his tabernacle. His state of poverty and humility says to all, "Woe to the rich, the proud, and the happy of this world!"

What does the new Adam think of sin? The new Adam thinks that sin is the most dreadful evil, the only evil in the world. A bloody sweat, a mortal agony, shameful spittle, a crown of thorns, a contemptible reed, a robe of scorn, a cruel scourging, nails, a cross, gall, death—all these pains he endured to atone for it. "Go, ye cursed! into everlasting fire": this is the punishment of those who commit it. What he thought of it during his mortal life, he still thinks of it in the Eucharist. He there exposes himself to a renewal of all the horrors of his passion, in order to expiate it; for the Eucharistic state is permanently that of a victim. Every day, too, from his altar as well as from his tribunal, he says to the sinner who dies impenitent, "Go, you cursed! into everlasting fire."

2. *In our affections; he loved God.* Our Lord had only two affections, which he expressed in these words. "Thou shalt love the Lord thy God with thy whole heart, with thy whole soul, and with thy whole strength: this is the first and greatest of all the commandments. And the second is like the first: thou shalt love thy neighbor as thyself for the love of God." His mortal life was only one long act of love toward his Father. It is the same with him in his Eucharistic life. So obedient is he for the love of his Father, that he daily renews before the door of his tabernacle the sacrifice of his cross. He always does what pleases his Father: dwelling in all places, even the most remote; in all churches, even the most deserted; in all tabernacles, even the most poor—where it pleases his Father that he should dwell.

He loved mankind. The proof of love is to make great sacrifices for those who are loved. Now, what sacrifices did not the new Adam make? From being rich, he became poor; from being happy, he became sad; from being the Almighty King, he became a little child. He was made man like us, laden with all our miseries. Last of all, he laid down his life for us. Not a name of love that he did not take: he called himself our father, our brother, our friend, our spouse, our servant; and he realized the full meaning of all these names. He loved all men—but especially the poor, the lowly, the sick, the sinful—his friends and his enemies: from the summit of his cross he asked pardon for his murderers. Thus did the new Adam love during his mortal life.

Thus does he continue to love in the Eucharist. It was to be always with us that he made himself a prisoner in his sacrament. He remains there day and night, his hands full of graces, his heart burning with love, addressing these sweet words to men: "Come to me, all ye that are in misery or pain, and I will refresh you." Never did a mother nourish her child with her flesh: more tender than the most tender of mothers, the new Adam does this for each one of us, whenever we wish it. He loves all men, even those who offend him, even those who insult him in his temple. From the depth of his tabernacle he could send forth his thunderbolts, and he is silent. Children of the new Adam, how much should we love him!

This love of the new Adam for God and for men also regulates our love in regard to creatures. Our Lord vouchsafed to make use of them, but only to promote the glory of God his Father and the salvation of men his brethren. He availed himself of the whole universe to offer it to his Father, and to refer to him all that it had received from him. He sanctified the earth by dwelling on it, and by bedewing it with his tears and his blood. All those creatures that helped to make him suffer, he employed as so many instruments to satisfy the justice of God. All those that his Father had placed in his hands, he employed to make known that he was God as well as his Father, and thus to dissipate the darkness of paganism, and to dethrone the devil, who was everywhere causing himself to be adored instead of God.

The new Adam also made use of the universe to instruct men. He drew comparisons from nearly all creatures, in order to familiarize us with the most important and sublime truths. Sometimes he called our attention to the seed scattered on the ground, in order to acquaint us with the abuse that is made of the Word of God; sometimes to the good grain and the chaff in the barn, in order to show us how the good and the bad are mixed together in the Church; sometimes to the birds of the air or the lilies of the field, in order to illustrate for us the tender cares of providence.

Finally, with regard to himself, the new Adam only made use of creatures insofar as they were strictly necessary for his wants. He was born in a stable, and, wrapped in a few miserable swathing bands, laid on a little straw in a manger; he lived on alms or by the labor of his hands: he never possessed anything. What our Lord preached then he still preaches in the Eucharist. By changing bread and wine into his body and blood, he made the whole universe contribute to the glory of his Father and the salvation of men. We know that all creatures, heaven and earth, the sun and the stars, water, air, fire, and rain, the four seasons, heat and cold, all the elements, lend their aid in producing a crumb of bread and a drop of wine; and this bread and wine he turns by a miraculous change to the salvation of men and the glory of his Father.

Behold how the new Adam is the model of our thoughts and our affections—consequently, of our interior life; and let us not forget that we are bound to imitate him! No salvation for us if we have not the same thoughts and affections as he!

Jesus Christ, the model of our exterior life.—It is not enough that our thoughts and affections should be conformed to those of the Savior: our actions must also resemble his. We are therefore about to consider him as our general model in regard to conduct, no matter what our age or position. All men are divided into two classes: some command and others obey.

1. *Model of superiors.* Our Lord is the model of all superiors, that is, of all those whom he has raised above others, by making them the depositaries of a portion of his authority. He himself was the chief of all superiors, and his life may be summed up in five words, "He went about doing good."[1340] This life he continues in the tabernacle. It may be said of him today as formerly, "He goes about doing good." Behold the words which one ought to be able to say of every superior and to engrave on his tomb: "He went about doing good." It is only to do good to their fellow men that God has invested superiors with his authority. Now the good of man is his end; and his end is his salvation or the possession of God. To go about doing good, superiors must therefore regard as the first of their cares, and the most sacred of their duties, the salvation of their inferiors. Is it so?

2. *Model of inferiors.* Our Lord is the model of all inferiors, and his life may be summed up in five words, "He was subject to them,"[1341] that is, to Joseph and Mary. Obedience full,

entire, simple, constant in the sight of God: this is the great duty of inferiors. Behold the words which one ought to be able to say of every inferior, and to engrave on his tomb: "He was subject to them." This example of absolute submission the Savior continues to give in the Holy Eucharist. He submits to the priest with the same docility as to Joseph and Mary. The priest calls him from heaven, and he comes; tells him to remain in the tabernacle, and he remains there; asks him to visit the sick, and he visits them; begs him to give himself to the faithful, and he gives himself.

Model of all men. The new Adam is the model of all men in general:

1. *In their duties toward God.* Who was more religious than he, or where did his Father ever find a more perfect adorer? He loved his Father; he adored him in spirit and in truth; he drove out indignantly the profaners of the Temple; and his religious life may be summed up in a few words: "He was one with his Father, whose glory he always labored to procure, and he was obedient to him unto death, even the death of the cross."

Behold again the words which one ought to be able to say of each of us at our last breath, and to engrave on our tomb: "He loved God, for whose glory he always labored, and to whom he was subject unto death." One ought also to be able to add: "He was always ready to give his blood for him, if it were necessary." This example of religion the Savior does not cease to give in the Holy Eucharist. An adorer of his Father, a victim of obedience, a model of charity, he continues the life of religion which he began in Judea.

2. *In their duties toward one another.* And his life may be summed up in these words: "He loved men; he did them every kind of good; he even shed his blood for them." To love, to forgive, and to suffer—these are the things at which we also ought to aim, and from which others should frame the record of our lives. Admirable example, which the Savior continues to give in the Eucharist! There he continues to love men with a love carried even to excess, to passion, to foolishness, says St. Augustine. There he continues to forgive them and to ask mercy for them. There also he continues, mystically isolated, to suffer, in a sense, and to suffer without complaint.

3. *In their duties toward themselves.* Humility opposed to pride, chastity opposed to the love of pleasure, poverty opposed to the love of riches: these were the virtues which shone in the Person of the new Adam; these are the virtues which ought to shine in each of us. To resist pride, the love of pleasure, and the love of riches, is a sacred duty which each one of us ought to fulfill toward himself.

These examples of humility, chastity, and poverty, the Savior continues to offer us in the Sacrament of the Altar. If he annihilated himself in the mystery of the incarnation, must it not be acknowledged that in the mystery of the Eucharist he extends the humility of his incarnation still further, binding himself up whole and entire under the least particle of a consecrated host, and making himself smaller and lowlier on our altars than in the crib?[1342] The fathers of the Church were indeed right in calling this divine mystery "an extension of the incarnation," that is, an incarnation repeated more openly and, as it were, more extensively than the first. It is the perfection of the humility of the new Adam.

He was pure. He was a virgin. For his Mother, he would have the purest of virgins; for his foster-father, a virgin; for his beloved disciple, a virgin. He would permit his enemies to call him a blasphemer and a seditious man, to raise their wicked hands against him and to crucify him as a malefactor; but he would never permit them a word, a doubt, the shadow of a doubt, against his infinite purity.

Admirable chastity, which he causes to shine forth in all its splendor from the depth of his sanctuary! He wishes only to have virgin priests. He desires that all things around him should speak of the purity of angels. He is present in this sacrament with all his senses, and he makes no use of them: everything in him is divine. Yet more, he is present in it as the principle of all chastity: it is by drinking his adorable blood that we purify our blood, and that virginity germinates in our souls.

The Savior is also a model of the most perfect poverty in the Eucharist. He was poor in the crib and on the cross; but, in the Eucharist, is he not still poorer? Is it not a much poorer and more miserable state, to live only on credit, dependent on others, ill-lodged, meanly covered, badly received and worse treated—to be in sovereign dignity and to wear no badge of honor? At the crib, a miraculous star announces his glory and his birth; at Calvary, the perplexed stars and elements publish his divinity; but, in the Eucharist, all is silence. He rests in the most profound abasement. He is a King, and he hides his scepter and his crown. Such is his life in the Blessed Sacrament.

Jesus Christ, the model of all ages.—Our Lord is a perfect model for all ages. He traveled the whole course of human life, and left for every age an example to copy.

He was a little child, and, before being able to make use of his feet, he is presented in the Temple of Jerusalem, where he offers himself to his Father; and, at this early age, his life may be summed up in these words: "Then I said, Behold I come: in the head of the book it is written of me, that I should do thy will, O my God."[1343] Thus ought the life of every Christian child to be summed up. The first use of its reason ought to be an offering of itself and its whole life to the author of its existence. In the Eucharist, where the Savior daily becomes incarnate at the word of the priest, he still repeats, after the manner of his mysterious birth, the words: "Behold I come, O my God, to accomplish thy holy will."

In youth, he works and obeys; and his life may be summed up in these words, "I have been in labors from my childhood."[1344] He worked and obeyed in the sight of God. Behold the gospel of youth: a living gospel, always open before our eyes! As a matter of fact, the occupations of the Savior in the Eucharist are numerous and continual: to pray, to adore, to ask mercy, to speak to our hearts, to excite remorse, to encourage our timidity, to remove our errors, to throw light on our doubts, to console us in our sorrows—all this is his work, and he has been persevering at it during the last eighteen centuries in every quarter of the globe.

On reaching the age of maturity. He is weary. He allows himself neither rest nor quiet, because he has a great work to perform—the salvation of the world; and his life may be summed up in these words: "He was wearied with the toil of the day, and he spent the night in prayer."[1345] To pray and to work for the accomplishment of the will of God; behold the model, I will even say the condemnation of the age of maturity! This age no longer prays—no longer works for God, but for the world. "Business, business, business," that is to say, trifles, or castles of cards, which the breath of death overturns in a moment: these are the things that absorb all its attention, all its care, all its life. Yet the example of different conduct is not wanting.

Our Lord, in the Eucharist, gives it continually. From the depth of the tabernacle, his universal detachment cries out to us, "What doth it profit a man to gain the whole world, if he lose his own soul? Fool! this night thy soul shall be required of thee, and whose shall all these things be that thou hast gathered up?" Imitate your model. Work like him for your salvation. Seek first of all the kingdom of God, and everything else shall be added to you over and above.

The approach of death, far from making the new Adam relent in his zeal, only seemed to give him fresh ardor; and this portion of his life may be summed up in these words: "Having loved his own who were in the world, he loved them to the end."[1346] Never were his conversations more affecting or more instructive. Tender farewells, abundant blessings, kept falling from his divine mouth even to that supreme hour in which, the perfect model of a man to whom the world is no longer anything, while God is everything, he pronounced these words, the last that ought to be found on the lips of a dying Christian: "Father, into thy hands I commend my spirit!" Behold the model of all those whose last hour draws nigh! The close of their life ought to be summed up, like that of the Savior, in these words: "Having loved his own who were in the world, he loved them to the end."

Yes, to love them, but not as the son of the old Adam loves them. Instead of consecrating his last hours to edify and bless his own, and to recommend himself to that God before whom he is about to appear, he thinks only of the earth which he is about to leave. Certainly, our Lord is not to blame. Every day he presents to us in the Eucharist, as heretofore on Calvary, the model of a Christian death. In the sacrament of our altars, the Savior shows that he loves his own to the end; for, by daily immolating himself for them and for the glory of his Father, amid surroundings that speak only of the utmost destitution, he gives them a most touching lesson on detachment, mutual love, and confidence in God.

Jesus Christ, the model of all states.—Jesus Christ is not only the model of all ages, but also that of all states. As God has placed in every creature some marks of his divinity, some traces of his adorable perfections, so he has been pleased that every profession should represent some of the qualities and perfections of the new Adam. Accordingly, our Lord is the model of all states, since all are assembled in him; for he is man, showing himself man in every relation and in every condition. It is he who places all persons in their states, and he wishes that all persons in their states should share his dispositions and his sentiments.

He makes bishops and priests participators in his priesthood; for he is the sovereign priest, and he wishes that like him they should be called by God, and not by men, to this high dignity. He wishes that they should represent to the world his perfect sanctity, and that like him they should be holy, spotless, separated from sinners, humble, and more detached from creatures than the generality of Christians. He wishes that like him they should be the light of the world, the salt of the earth, the consolers of all the afflicted.

He wishes that like him they should bear the sins of the people, and do penance for them, without ever sharing in their corruption. He wishes that they should watch over all the sheep of the flock confided to their care, feeding them with the bread of the word and of the sacraments, ready to give their life in order to save them from sin and hell. All these examples he continually gives to priests in his Eucharistic life.

He makes kings participators in his royalty: for he is a King. This is a character which he took himself and which was given to him. He sat on the throne of David his father, and St. John saw him with this great name written on his garments: "King of kings and Lord of lords."[1347] He made use of his authority to destroy the kingdom of the devil and to establish the kingdom of God. And he wishes that the kings of the earth should make use of their authority for the same purpose, depending on him, and obeying his laws as he obeys the laws of his Father.

He wishes that, like him, the kings of the earth should govern their people according to the immutable rules of eternal justice and divine wisdom. He wishes that, like him, they should defend their subjects, protecting the innocent, and taking in hand the cause of the weak and the oppressed, without ever letting themselves be deceived for a moment by the flatteries of those who surround them. In a word, he wishes that they should be ready to die, if necessary, as he did, for the salvation of their people. All these examples he gives to kings in his Eucharistic life.

He makes fathers and mothers participators in his paternity. The new Adam contracted an ineffable alliance with the Church: he took the title of her spouse, and called her his spouse in return. He wishes that married persons should represent in their marriage the blessed union which exists between him and his Church. He wishes that husbands should love their wives as he loved the Church, delivering himself to death that he might sanctify it, and that he might leave it without spot or wrinkle. He wishes that wives should love their husbands as the Church loves him, and that they should be subject to them as the Church is subject to her divine spouse.

He wishes that, by a conformity of sentiments, like that which exists between him and the Church, husbands should have with their wives but one heart and one soul, in order to contribute to their mutual sanctification and to the sanctification of their family: thus honoring, in all their conduct, the alliance of the Son of God with our nature, the union of Jesus Christ with his Church.

He was pleased to take the character of father of Christians, and he is really such according to the Spirit. He chose to have adopted children, whose mother is the Church. He wishes that fathers and mothers should love their children with a holy love, as he and the Church love theirs. He wishes that they should take the utmost care of the spiritual life received by their children in baptism, or help them to recover it when unhappily it has been lost by sin, thus imitating his and the Church's tenderness. He wishes that fathers and mothers should teach their children to renounce themselves, to carry the cross daily, and to despise the goods of the world and what are called great fortunes, as he and the Church teach. All these examples the Savior gives unceasingly to parents in his Eucharistic life.

He wishes that the poor should represent his poverty. The new Adam was pleased to be born, to live, and to die poor. He was pleased to be the chief of the poor, the friend of the poor. He wishes that, after his example, the poor should endure their poverty lovingly and patiently, and that they should accept tranquilly all the pains attached to their condition. He wishes that, after his example, they should endeavor to earn their support by labor. If, when they have employed all their diligence, they still find themselves in want, he wishes that, after his example, they should receive, with gratitude and without being ashamed, the alms of their brethren. All these examples the Savior gives unceasingly to the poor in his Eucharistic life.

He wishes that virgins should represent his virginity. The new Adam, wishing to redeem the world, chose the state of virginity in preference to any other, as being not only the most holy, but the most suitable to his design of detaching men from the pleasures of the senses, the too ordinary source of the disorders that reign in the world. He wishes that virgins should learn from him how great a love they ought to have for this virtue, and in what manner they ought to live conformably to their state.

To make known to them how much he loves virginity, he was pleased that his body should be formed of the blood of a Virgin; and that, in the womb of this same Virgin, his body and soul should be consecrated to God his Father, to redeem mankind by the sacrifice of a virginal victim, all pure and spotless. He wishes that, after his example, virgins should regard themselves as consecrated to God, in order to serve him alone, to honor the infinite purity of his divine majesty, and to live like angels in a mortal body. All these examples the Savior gives unceasingly to virgins in his Eucharistic life.

He wishes that persecuted persons should represent his many virtues in the midst of persecution. The new Adam, whose doctrine and life were altogether opposed to those of the world, was despised, hated, persecuted by it. For his benefits, he received ingratitude; for his miracles, blasphemy; for his instructions, censure. He was opposed during his life and after his death; and he will continue to receive the same treatment till the end of time in the Eucharist and in all his members.

He left us his cross as an inheritance, and he wishes that we should carry it like him. He wishes that, after his example, we should be as calm in the midst of all our trials as a sheep that is led to the slaughter, and that we should no more open our mouth to complain than a lamb that is dumb before its shearer.[1348] He wishes that we should not attribute our sufferings to our persecutors, but to the power and the justice of God, saying as he himself said to Pilate, "You should not have any power over me, if it were not given you from above."[1349] He wishes that, after his example—did he not pray for his executioners?—we should only have blessings on our lips and charity in our hearts for those who injure us. All these examples the Savior gives us unceasingly in his Eucharistic life.

Lastly, the new Adam is the model of all men in their words and their actions; and his life may be summed up in these words: "He did all things well."[1350] He wishes that we should daily apply ourselves to do well whatever we do: on this he makes our perfection and salvation depend. Now to perform our actions in a manner meritorious for heaven, there are four conditions necessary: a) a state of grace; b) purity of intention; c) goodness of actions; and d) suitable circumstances.

Thus, the first fruit of our union with the new Adam is to make us live like him on earth, to make us perfect as our heavenly Father is perfect, and by this means to secure our happiness as far as happiness is compatible with the miseries inseparable from our exile.

The second is to make us live by his glorious life in heaven. The consummation of man in God for all eternity: this is the great end of the new Adam's life, the sublime term of all things. What this life of glory, of which grace is the beginning, will be, we shall make an effort to show in the General Summary, placed at the end of the catechism.

PRAYER

O my God! who art all love, I thank thee for having been pleased to pass through all states in order to sanctify them, and to teach me how to comport myself therein; grant me the grace to fulfill all the duties of my particular vocation, that I may have the happiness of sharing in thy glory for eternity.

I am resolved to love God above all things, and my neighbor as myself for the love of God; and, in testimony of this love, I will perform my actions well every day.

Lesson 57: What Destroys Our Union with the New Adam

Sin in general.—One thing alone broke the primitive union of man with God, and drew down a deluge of evils on the world: it was sin. This union was reestablished by the new Adam, and cemented by his divine blood. One thing alone can break this union anew: it is sin. The Savior did not fail to instruct his apostles on a matter of so much importance. His whole life, his labors, his sufferings, his death, his sacraments, all proclaim aloud this truth: that the Son of Man came into the world only to banish sin and to prevent its return. It remains for us, after his example, to speak to you of this dreadful evil, much less to acquaint you with its nature than to inspire you with a horror of it.

Sin is a willful disobedience to the law of God, or, as St. Augustine says, "a word, an action, or a desire contrary to the eternal law."[1351] We say *sin*, and not *vice*, because there is a great difference between the two. Sin is an act; vice is a habit. The three terms, *word, action, desire*, comprise different sorts of sins, whose instruments they point out: the tongue, the hand, the heart. We say "contrary to the eternal law," in order to show the unchangeable rule of good and evil. As a matter of fact, this eternal law is the principle of all natural, positive, divine, and human laws. All take their value and their force from their harmony with the eternal law, which is nothing else than the eternal will of God, essentially right and proper.

Original and actual sin.—We distinguish two kinds of sin: original and actual. Original sin is that which may be traced to the origin of the human race, which was committed by our first parents in the terrestrial paradise, and with which we are born defiled. The nature and the grievousness of this sin, as well as its transmission to all the posterity of Adam, were explained and proved in the first part[1352] of the catechism.

Mortal and venial sin.—Actual sin is that which we commit of our own free will: it is divided into mortal and venial. Mortal sin is that which kills the soul, by depriving it of the life of grace, and making it deserving of hell. Venial sin does not deprive the soul of the friendship of God, but lessens its fervor. This sin is called venial, that is to say, pardonable, because it is less unworthy of pardon than mortal sin. Both may be committed in thought, word, deed, and omission.

Nothing is more common than venial sin, even among Christians. Thoughts of self-complacency; idle words; little lies; a slight want of patience with children and servants, and of gentleness with the poor; distractions; railleries; resentments; sensuality; petty jealousies; laziness in rising, in obeying, in fulfilling one's duties: all these are so many venial sins, of which an account must be rendered to God, and for which atonement must be made in this life or in the next.

The distinctions of actual sin are founded on formal passages of scripture, on the teaching of the fathers, and on the doctrine of the Church. St. Paul evidently refers to mortal sin when he says, "The wages of sin is death; sinners shall not possess the kingdom of God."[1353] As for venial sin, the scripture clearly points it out in these words: "If we say that we have no sin, we deceive ourselves, and the truth is not in us."[1354] This expression, which, in its generality, embraces all mankind, cannot extend to mortal sin, since the apostles—among the apostles, St. John particularly—were not guilty thereof. In the same sense we must understand what St. James says, that "we all commit many sins,"[1355] as well as the gospel text in which our Lord lays down several degrees of punishment for sins against charity.[1356]

What is required to make a mortal sin.—There are three things necessary to make a mortal sin: advertence, consent, and grave matter.

1. *Advertence.* Advertence, taken in general, is the attention bestowed on anything. The object of advertence, in the present case, is not an action in itself, but its goodness or its badness: these things are very different. We may act with much reflection, without thinking whether that which we do is right or wrong. Examples: a man may willingly use meat on a Friday, without recollecting that it is a day of abstinence; or, recollecting quite well that the day is a Sunday, mistake or forget the hour of hearing Mass. In both cases an excuse is supplied by forgetfulness, inattention, want of advertence. To sin mortally, full advertence is necessary, and one must actually have paid attention, at least in a confused manner, to the malice of the action, or to the danger of sinning, or to the obligation of inquiring about this danger, or at all events one must have perceived the evil in the beginning, when placing the cause of the improper action that followed.

2. *Consent.* To commit a mortal sin, perfect consent of the will is necessary. "There is no sin," says St. Thomas, "that has not the will as its principle."[1357] Now, the will may act in three ways, relatively to the object presented to it by the understanding: a) it may positively consent to sin; b) it may positively resist; c) it may neither consent nor resist, but remain neutral. A person sins by consenting; and does not sin by resisting, provided the resistance is positive and absolute. As for him who remains neutral, it is probable that he sins to some extent, but his sin is only venial, if, in addition, the danger of consenting is not proximate.[1358]

This is the reason why, when there is question of carnal delectations, one is bound under pain of mortal sin to resist them positively, because these movements, when violent, easily draw on the consent of the will, if it does not positively resist.[1359] The consent may exist either directly in itself, when one actually adheres to sin, or indirectly in the cause, that is to say, when one places a cause really bad, and perceives, at least confusedly, the evils that may proximately result. For example, a man becomes drunk, foreseeing, as experience has taught him, that in the state of drunkenness he will commit great sins. He is responsible for the sins that he will commit, though at the moment of being guilty of them, he has no longer the use of reason.

3. *Grave matter.* It is necessary that the precept which one transgresses should be grave, and known as such. It is so known by the intention of the legislator; or by the severity of the punishments in store for those who violate it; or by the teaching of holy scripture, of the Church, or of tradition. As we cannot arrive easily at this knowledge on every occasion, we ought to take it as a rule of our conduct to avoid with the utmost care whatever we know to be a sin.[1360]

Enormity of mortal sin.—To know, at least imperfectly, the enormity of mortal sin, we must consider it in itself, in its effects, and in its punishments.

1. *In itself.* Mortal sin is a rebellion against God, and a monstrous ingratitude. But who is God, and what is his power? In the beginning, nothing of what we now see existed: no heaven, no earth, no mountains, no rivers, no animals, no plants. God spoke, and all things were made. With the same facility that he created the universe, he governs it; and all creatures obey him. He tells the sun to rise every day, and it rises. He tells the planets to make their long circuits through space, without ever turning aside from the line traced out for them by his almighty hand, and the planets pursue their course with exemplary regularity.

He calls the stormy winds, and they fly from the ends of the earth, and they throw the ocean into confusion, and huge waves rise like mountains, threatening men with destruction. He tells the stormy winds to be still, and they are stilled; he tells the furious sea to return to its bed, and the sea, obedient as a lamb under the hand of a shepherd, goes back to the abyss. He tells the earth to bring forth plants and fruits of every kind, and the earth is loaded with riches as various as our wants and our desires. At the least sign of his thought, numberless heavenly spirits fall prostrate at the foot of his throne, and say, "We are here." He speaks, and the cherubim, the seraphim, the angels, the archangels, execute his will with the rapidity of lightning.

This great God commands, and all creation hastens to render homage to him, all is submissive to him. I make a mistake: in the midst of the glorious concert, one voice is heard saying, "I will not obey." Who then is the audacious being that raises the standard of revolt against the eternal, omnipotent God? It is man!!!—man, a vile heap of rottenness; man, a poor, weak, miserable being, that lives only for a day, and, short as the time is, lives only by divine mercy! This is the being that dares to set the Almighty at defiance!

See how insolently man utters his blasphemies against God! "I know very well that you impose laws on all nature, and that all nature obeys you. But as for me, I will not obey you. I despise your laws, your promises, and your threats. I will think whatever I like, love whatever I like, do whatever I like, live as I like." This is the language used by the sinner, as often as he commits a mortal sin.

Mortal sin is not only an open rebellion against God, but it is a monstrous ingratitude. Who is the being that dares to say to God, I will not obey? It is man, laden with the weight of God's benefits, all covered with the sacred blood that saved him. It is man, for whom God created the world and sacrificed his Son. And what is most criminal is that man makes use of the very benefits of God to outrage him. Air, water, fire, light, clouds, plants, fruits, animals, metals, are God's creatures. This mind, this heart, this imagination, this soul, these eyes, these ears, this tongue, these feet, these hands, this body, man holds from God, and he makes use of them to outrage God!!! Ungrateful wretch—most fitting name for the sinner! Ingratitude is his crime, a crime that in all hearts excites horror and indignation. What we have said will suffice to give you a faint idea of the enormity of mortal sin, considered in itself.

2. *In its effects.* Mortal sin deprives us of the friendship of God, robs us of our past merits, and shuts heaven against us. Who can tell all that happens in an unfortunate soul from the moment that it falls into mortal sin? Beautiful as an angel, bright as the aurora, it becomes black as night, hideous as Satan. Its robe of innocence is torn away. The august Trinity no longer dwells in it: troops of fiends find their home there instead. Its name is blotted out of the book of life. Let it die in this state, and it is buried for eternity in a lake of fire.

We pity the countryman whose crops have been destroyed by hail, the mariner whose ship has been swallowed up by the waves: what pity does not the unfortunate soul deserve, which has lost its merits, its paradise, its God! True, if it has recourse to the sacrament of penance and obtains pardon for its fault, its merits will revive; but, so long as it remains an enemy of God, its merits will be lost to it. Yet more, it cannot acquire any new merits: whatever it does in the state of mortal sin is valueless for heaven.

3. *In its punishments.* To perceive the enormity of mortal sin, a very simple reflection is enough. God is just, infinitely just: he cannot punish sin more than it deserves. God is good, infinitely good: his mercy continually leads him to punish sin less than it deserves. Now, during six thousand years God has been deluging the world with calamities, and all to punish mortal sin. But this is nothing. To punish mortal sin God has prepared an eternal hell, in which the sinner shall be given over to torments the very thought of which makes us shudder.

What passes all imagination is that God, out of a hatred of sin, made his own Son die on a cross between two criminals! See the punishments of mortal sin! And God is just, and God is good—infinitely just and infinitely good! What then is mortal sin? We do not think of it: we commit it without any scruple, and, after committing it, we sleep tranquilly! We who have shed so many tears over trifles, scarcely shed one over our sins! Henceforth, at least, let it be said of us as was said of a holy bishop in the early ages, "This man fears nothing but sin."

Evil of venial sin.—From such a frightful picture of mortal sin, let us conclude that venial sin is no small evil. Like mortal sin, it is a rebellion against God, and an ingratitude. To estimate the greatness of this evil, which is committed with as much ease as one would drink a cup of water, let us here call to mind the teachings of faith. Cast your eyes over the world! See the numbers of sick people who languish on their beds of sorrow in hospitals and private dwellings! See all the cemeteries filled with human generations heaped on one another! See the multitudes of heretics and heathens who know not God or who know him amiss! Open purgatory, and see all the dear souls that sigh for deliverance from its flames! Go down to the gates of hell, and cast a look on the myriad piles of victims that groan in its fiery dungeons! Well, though to cure all the sick on earth, to raise all the dead to life, to convert all heretics and heathens, to liberate all the souls in purgatory, and to save all the damned, nothing more were needed than a single venial sin, a little lie, one should not be guilty of it. To deny this is to abandon the faith.

Let us go still further. See how God, who is infinitely just, punished venial sin in his most faithful servants! Moses and Aaron, two brothers so worthy of the great mission which God has confided to them—Moses to whom God spoke as a friend to a friend, Aaron the head of his priesthood—these two eminent servants of God commit a venial sin: they hesitate a moment when striking a rock in the desert. For this single fault, they will be prevented from entering the promised land. The land, after which they have been sighing for so many years, at whose borders they have just arrived by so many fatigues and tribulations, they will see with their eyes, that their regret may be increased, but they shall never set foot on it. David, a king according to God's own heart, allows himself to be moved by a feeling of vanity. It is enough. A terrible scourge, which in three days will carry off seventy thousand people, shall be the punishment of this single fault—a fault the like of which we perhaps commit often every day.

Such is the irreconcilable opposition that exists between the sanctity of God and sin. I am not surprised that the saints had so great a horror of venial sin that they would rather part with life than commit it. "I can die," said a holy bishop of Africa, in the midst of his torments, "but I cannot lie."

What ought especially to make us fear venial sin is that it leads to mortal sin. No one becomes a great sinner or a great saint suddenly: the end is reached by insensible degrees. Speaking according to truth, we must admit that, if ever we committed a mortal sin, we prepared the way for it by some venial sin. Among the sins called venial, there is one in particular that almost infallibly leads to mortal: it is the habitual neglect or omission of daily prayer. The body cannot live without food; the same with the soul. Now, the food of the soul, its daily bread, is morning and evening prayer. O my God! be pleased to inspire all those who read these lines with a steadfast resolution never to commit a single venial sin deliberately, however trivial it may appear!

The capital sins.—Among actual sins there are seven, called "capital," because they are, as it were, the poisoned sources of many others. All sins together are represented by the seven-headed beast of which St. John speaks in the Apocalypse. The seven heads of this frightful monster are the seven capital sins. All other sins depend on these, as the members of the body depend on the head.

The capital sins are pride, covetousness, lust, envy, gluttony, anger, and sloth.

1. *Pride.* Pride is an inordinate esteem of oneself, which makes a person prefer himself to others, and, instead of referring all that he is and all that he has to God, makes him refer all to himself. Though pride may be regarded as the origin of all other sins, and though it is mixed up with them,[1361] yet there are some that flow directly from it.

From pride spring: presumption, which is a desire to do what exceeds a person's strength or capacity; ambition, which is an inordinate anxiety to be honored; disobedience, which is a want of submission toward those to whom submission is due; hypocrisy, which makes a person pretend to have piety that he has not, or to have more piety than he has; incredulity, which makes a person unwilling to submit his reason to the teaching of the Church; obstinacy, which makes a person hold to his own opinion in spite of the well-grounded remarks of those who differ from him; boasting, which consists in praising oneself, one's merits, one's labors, one's success; haughtiness, which is an imperious manner of dealing with the neighbor, speaking to him in an overbearing and disdainful tone; vanity, which leads a person to glory in dress, figure, skill, or other advantages real or pretended.[1362] These are the children of pride: they are worthy of such a parent.

Pride is a great sin, since it made the devils. It is most injurious to God, since it tends to rob him of his glory. It ought to be most hateful to men, whom it degrades. It is directly opposed to the example of our Lord. It is a most dangerous sin: it turns aside the course of grace. God resists the proud, and lets them fall into the most humiliating sins. Pride may be regarded as the source of all other sins, and as the ordinary sign of reprobation.

The antidote of pride is humility. Humility is a virtue, founded on self-knowledge, which makes us do ourselves justice, that is to say, which makes us esteem ourselves at no more than we are worth. Now, we are nothing, we have nothing, we can do nothing: everything comes to us from God, everything in us belongs to him. We are therefore pure nothingness: Of what then can we be proud? Pride lives only on ignorance. Let us learn to know ourselves well, and we shall be humble. With this view let us often address to ourselves, and seriously, the following questions: In regard to body and soul, what have I been? what am I? what shall I be?

Humility is a virtue absolutely necessary for salvation. To obtain it we must ask it, and above all endeavor to practice it: in our thoughts, by never raising ourselves above any person; in our words, by always observing a modest tone of voice and never saying anything that might turn to our praise; and in our actions, by avoiding display and often performing lowly duties.

2. *Covetousness.* Covetousness is an inordinate attachment to the goods of earth. Treachery, fraud, wrangling, perjury, unrest, hard-heartedness, are the sad offspring of this vice. A person is known to be swayed by covetousness when he desires the goods of another; when the pleasure of having money is the only motive of what he does; when he rejoices immoderately in the possession of temporal goods or is afflicted excessively at their loss; when he strives to acquire or to retain temporal goods by unjust means; when he does not give to the poor what is superfluous; when he is not disposed to lose all that he possesses rather than offend God. Hence it comes that St. Paul terms covetousness a kind of idolatry.[1363]

Covetousness is a great sin. It is contrary to the love which we should have for God: it turns us aside from his service, since a man cannot have two masters. "There is nothing more wicked," says the Holy Ghost, "than the love of money, and no one more criminal than the avaricious man."[1364] Hence such a one is detested by God and by his fellow men.

The antidote of covetousness is charity toward the neighbor, manifested especially in almsgiving. Almsgiving is a very necessary virtue: according to our manner of practicing it, our Lord will regulate his sentence on the day of judgment.

3. *Lust.* Lust is that frightful sin whose very name ought to be forgotten by Christians, and which the rebelliousness of our passions prevents us from defining. The causes of this sin are pride, good-cheer, idleness, disregard for the poor: we spoke of its occasions when explaining the sixth commandment. The consequences of lust are blindness of mind, hardness of heart, ruin of health, disorder in domestic affairs, suicide, final impenitence. Watchfulness, mortification, flight of occasions, prayer, devotion to the Blessed Virgin, and especially meditation, and frequent confession and Communion, are the great remedies for this vice.

4. *Gluttony.* Gluttony follows impurity, of which it is often the cause. It consists in an inordinate love of eating and drinking, whether one indulges to excess or with sensuality. It is not the pleasure or relish found in food that characterizes gluttony: it is the want of moderation. A person may be guilty of gluttony in five ways: a) by eating before the proper hour, especially on fast days; b) by seeking out too costly dishes, having regard to one's condition; c) by eating or drinking too much; d) by taking food greedily, after the manner of beasts; e) by looking for too much delicacy in cookery.[1365]

The sins that arise from gluttony are brutishness of mind, vain joy, intemperate speech; very often lust, and its sad consequences. Of all the modes of sinning by gluttony, the most shocking, the most unworthy of man, that which places man below the level of irrational animals, is drunkenness. The drunkard exposes himself to the danger of committing a thousand sins: he becomes the disgrace of society, ruins his prospects, shortens his days, is cursed by heaven. Mortification is the great remedy for drunkenness. What an excellent habit it is, never to let any day pass without depriving oneself of something at meals in honor of our Lord's privations at Bethlehem, in Egypt, and at Nazareth!

5. *Envy.* Envy holds the fifth place among the monsters that tyrannize over us and defile our souls. It is a sadness at another's good, as if this were a misfortune for us, or a joy at another's misfortune, as if this were a good for us. The daughters of envy are falsehood, calumny, detraction, evil interpretation. Whoever abandons himself to this

vice imitates the devil, who, jealous of the happiness of our first parents, drew them into sin, and who continually labors to render us miserable. He imitates Cain, who, not being able to endure the advantages enjoyed by his brother Abel, killed him. He imitates the Jews, who, being envious of the splendor of the virtues and the miracles set before their eyes by our Lord, crucified him.

To cure himself of envy, a person should exercise fraternal charity, and consider that envy is much more hurtful to the envious than to the envied, because the envious pine away in secret anguish, and God often makes use of the sins of the envious to elevate those of whom they are jealous. The envy of the devil made us lose the terrestrial paradise, and our Lord was sent on earth to open for us the celestial paradise. The brethren of Joseph sold him out of envy, and God made use of their crime to elevate Joseph and to make him their master. Saul persecuted David out of envy, and God deprived Saul of his kingdom and gave it to David. It is also necessary to have recourse to humility, to mortification, to detachment from the goods of this world; for these virtues keep the heart from being enslaved by an immoderate love of honors, pleasures, or riches, which are the usual objects of envy.

6. *Anger.* Anger is an impetuous and inordinate movement of the soul, which leads us to take revenge, and to repel with violence whatever displeases us. We say an "inordinate movement," because there is a holy, just, and reasonable anger. Such was that of Moses against the Israelites who adored the golden calf at the foot of Sinai. Such was that of our Lord when he drove out of the Temple those scandalous troops of buyers and sellers who had changed the holy place into a den of thieves. But when anger is not caused by the motive of the glory of God or the advantage of the neighbor, or when it exceeds its just bounds, it is a frightful crime, which gives birth to hatreds, quarrels, injuries, murders, heart-burnings, family disturbances.

The disorder of anger consists in three things: a) in wishing to avenge oneself on him who is innocent and who has done us no wrong; b) in wishing to avenge oneself by private authority; c) in wishing to avenge oneself out of hatred and not out of a zeal for justice. A pagan philosopher advised, as a remedy for anger, that one should repeat the alphabet or drink a cup of cold water before speaking. As for us Christians, we have another remedy: it is a look at the crucifix, a thought of the gentleness of our divine master during his passion.

7. *Sloth.* Sloth comes in to terminate this dreadful catalogue of sins. Sloth is a disgust that makes us neglect our duty rather than go to the trouble of performing it. It is mortal as often as it leads us to fail in a grave obligation. The sins that it produces are contempt of the commandments, abandonment to vice, despair, and hatred of those who exhort us to forsake evil and to do good. There is a spiritual sloth, which leads us to neglect the duties of a Christian: and how many spiritual sluggards are there at the present day! The way to avoid it is to follow a good rule of life, approved of by a prudent confessor.

Sins against the Holy Ghost.—Besides the capital sins, which, as we have just seen, ought to inspire us with the greatest fear, there are others for which we can never have sufficient horror; on each one of them appears the name of the sin against the Holy Ghost. This deadly tree is divided into six branches: namely, despair of salvation; expectation of salvation without merit; impugning the known truth; envy at another's spiritual good; obstinacy in sin; and final impenitence. They are called sins against the Holy Ghost, because they are committed out of pure malice. We say that to sin out of malice is to sin against the Holy Ghost, because to the Holy Ghost is attributed goodness, which is the opposite of malice.

The sin against the Holy Ghost which our Lord says shall not be forgiven in this world nor the next[1366] is generally believed to be that of final impenitence, or despair in the mercy of God. Experience actually proves that those who are guilty of them very seldom return to penance. This, however, must be understood as of an extreme difficulty. It is thus that, when we say that a sickness is incurable, we do not mean that it can never possibly be cured, but that it is very seldom cured and is usually not cured.

How much we ought to fear sins against the Holy Ghost, which are daily becoming more and more common on earth! In effect, is it rare to see men and even women who live obstinate in evil, and who continue indifferent about all the duties of religion, in spite of the instructions of the ministers of the gospel, and even of the solemn warnings of God himself, such as plagues, famines, and revolutions? Is it rare to see persons who, in their conversations, their writings, and their speeches, attack religion, though its truth is as evident as the sun?[1367]

Sins that cry to heaven for vengeance.—Among the crimes of which man, becoming intensely wicked with his degradation, renders himself guilty, there are some that cannot be excused on any pretext. We number four such: willful murder; sinning against nature; oppression of the poor, especially of widows and orphans; and defrauding the laborer of his wages. We say that they cry to heaven for vengeance, because the injustice of these sins is so manifest, so crying, that nothing can hide or palliate it. To have an idea of the enormity of these crimes, it is enough to read in the scripture the terrible punishments with which God threatens those who are guilty of them.[1368]

We have now shown in what sin consists, and the different ways in which it may destroy our union with the new Adam. Must we not tremble to think that the germ of this frightful evil lives within us, that we bring it with us into the world, that it makes continual efforts to burst forth and to ruin us, by separating us from our Savior? Yes, the germ of sin is within us. All the capital sins themselves, the sources of so many others, take their rise in our own passions. These passions are like trees, and sin is their fruit. Does the fruit offend you? Cut down the trees that bear it.

Passions.—Now, the passions are three in number: the love of honors, the love of riches, and the love of pleasures. It is these that are called the three concupiscences. They are like three large wounds left on the human race by the original fall. Here you find the reason why the new Adam, the great physician of mankind, was pleased to be born, to live, and to die poor, humble, suffering. This lowliness, at which the world is scandalized, is the most splendid proof of his profound wisdom and his infinite goodness: it is the balm that he applies to our wounds.

As for us, if we wish to maintain our union with him, let us crush in our breasts the fatal germs of sin, which alone can destroy it. Let us crush them from our childhood: later on may be too late. These three great passions manifest themselves at a very early period in youth. First, pride, or the love of honors. The child is disobedient, insolent, surly, when his capricious wishes are not humored. After a while, he is delighted with little preferences and flatteries. All this does not appear very bad, nor even very dangerous; but, for my part, I say that this affection is a young viper, which he cherishes in his bosom, and which, unless great care is taken, will very soon attain to its full growth, and when an opportunity offers, will tear out his entrails. Aman wished to be honored and flattered. It was with impatience he saw that Mardochai did not bend his knee before him. He ended by trying to wash away in the blood of a whole people this supposed insult.

Next, the love of riches. Children are attached to a multitude of little things, to furniture, to dress, to ornaments. All this does not appear very bad, nor even very dangerous; but, for my part, I say that this affection is a young viper, which they cherish in their bosoms, and which, unless great care is taken, will very soon attain to its full growth, and, when an opportunity offers, will tear out their entrails. Judas, who began by loving a little money, ended by selling his master.

Lastly, the love of pleasures. You are fond of whatever flatters your body: a long sleep, choice food, a soft bed; in a word, whatever pleases taste, sight, smell, or touch. All this does not appear to you very bad, nor even very dangerous; but, for my part, I tell you that this inordinate affection is a young viper, which you cherish in your bosom, and which, unless you take great care, will very soon attain to its full growth, and, when an opportunity offers, will tear out your entrails. See that woman whose name the gospel records in letters of blood, Herodias: she first loved amusement, and she ended by asking the head of John the Baptist. Inquire of all those who have committed great crimes, and they will tell you that it was by little beginnings and small steps that they came to have no scruple in abandoning themselves to the most dreadful excesses.

PRAYER

O my God! who art all love, I thank thee for having made known to me the grievousness and malice of mortal sin; preserve me from ever falling into it.

I am resolved to love God above all things, and my neighbor as myself for the love of God; and, in testimony of this love, I will never deliberately commit a venial sin, however trivial it may appear.

Lesson 58: What Perpetuates Our Union with the New Adam

If a physician announced that he had discovered a remedy which would infallibly cure some of the numberless diseases that afflict poor humanity from the cradle to the grave, he should forthwith become the object of general gratitude. From all quarters, people would eagerly have recourse to him: journeys, fatigues, expenses, all would appear nothing in comparison with one's cure.

Enlightened by faith, we have acted the part of this physician, by pointing out in the preceding lesson the particular remedies for the various diseases of the soul. Oh, that all men would have recourse to these remedies with the same eagerness and confidence as they would have recourse to the corporal remedy of which we have spoken! Our word is not our own, but the infallible word of God. Our remedies are not our own, but the remedies of the heavenly physician, who came on earth to cure all that are sick.

But if a physician proved that he possessed a remedy which would infallibly cure all diseases, I leave you to think how earnestly persons in the most distant regions would flock to consult him, how generously they would reward him for his trouble, and how gratefully they would remember him who had changed their cruel pains into all the delights of health. Well, in the spiritual order, that is to say, in the order in which diseases are far more dangerous, this physician exists: he is our Lord. This universal remedy is in his hands: he offers it to us; he offers it to us *gratis*. To receive it, there is no need of journeys or fatigues: it is enough to wish to have it. This remedy, which has the twofold advantage of being preventive and curative, he gives us in the following formula: "My son, in all thy works remember thy last end, and thou shalt never sin."[1369]

General remedies for sin: The four last things.—The great panacea for all our ills is therefore the consideration of the four last things: death, judgment, hell, and heaven. They are called "last," because death is the end of life, and the last thing to happen to us in this world; the final judgment is the last of all judgments pronounced by our own conscience, by human tribunals, by God himself—hence, it is without appeal; hell is the last evil to befall the wicked—an evil of which they can never lessen the rigor, shorten the duration, or change the nature; and heaven is the last good reserved for the servants of God—an inalienable, superabundant, unmixed, and endless good. Such is the universal remedy prepared by the infallible physician.

As for the manner of using this remedy, it consists in two things: a) in faith, and b) in the habitual thought of this remedy.

First, we must believe in the reality of the four last things. Nothing is easier. It is enough to call to mind the splendid proofs which we have given on the matter in the course of the catechism, and which are to be found in the gospel, as well as in all other books of religion; then, the universal belief of all peoples, even pagans, who have always admitted eternal rewards and punishments after this life; finally, the necessity of this belief, which is such that to deny it is to deny the distinction between good and evil, to render society impossible among men, to deny the wisdom and justice of God, to deny God himself, in a word, to plunge into madness.

But to believe these great truths with a vague faith is not enough: we must believe them with a lively faith, and act in accordance with our faith. Now, it is by habitual recollection that our faith in regard to these four great realities will effectually regulate our conduct. This is the second thing to be done, in order to profit of the divine remedy. "In all thy works," says the heavenly physician, "remember thy last end, and thou shalt never sin."

In all thy works. Why "in all thy works"? Because there is not one in which our soul may not receive the germ of a disease: vanity, self-love, self-interest, cupidity, sensuality; "in all our works," because there is not one which may not lead us to eternal happiness, if well done; "in all our works," because this succession of ordinary occupations in thought, word, and deed, makes up our hours, our days, our months, our years, our life, and prepares us for heaven or for hell.

Remember. The way to perform our actions well and to direct our life well is to keep our eyes continually fixed on the end to which we tend, like the seaman who, wishing to reach an island lost in the distance, hardly turns aside his eyes for a moment from the compass or the polestar. "Remember": and, for this purpose, watch over your inward and outward senses, lest a variety of distractions should come to weaken in or to efface from your mind the salutary thought of your destiny, and you should be left to walk by the deceitful glare of the maxims of the world, the suggestions of the devil, or the judgments of your passions. "Remember": and, for this purpose, set every morning before your eyes the four last things, pondering over them in a meditation suited to your age and employments; let your thoughts return to them occasionally during the course of the day; and weigh them once more in your heart before you retire to rest. In order to facilitate the application of such a precious remedy, let us here give a model of the meditation just proposed.

1. *Death.* You can divide the consideration of it into four points. The first, that death is most certain, that no one can escape it: I shall die. The second, that the hour of death is most uncertain, that many persons die when they least think of it: I know not when I shall die; all I know is that I may die soon; it only requires a moment to die. The third, that death puts an end to all the projects and enterprises of life, that then is seen all the vanity of this world: I shall be divested of all, separated from all, forgotten by all.[1370] The fourth, that at death we repent of the evil which we have done and the good which we have not done, that it is therefore the height of folly to do what we shall most assuredly regret having done: how sorry I shall be to have abused so many graces!

2. *Judgment.* You can also divide the consideration of judgment into four points. The first, that the object of the judgment will be a thing of the utmost importance, supreme happiness or supreme misery: it will be decided whether I shall be a saint or a reprobate. The second, that the judgment will be conducted by the sovereign judge, who knows all things, and whom no person can resist: my secret faults, my hidden faults, will be brought to light, and will cover me with confusion, if I neglect to do penance for them.

The third, that the judgment will be held in presence of the assembled nations of the earth, so that no person can conceal himself: I shall be there—I myself—I shall be seen, I shall be known, I shall be called by my name. The fourth, that there will be no hope of escaping the sentence of the divine justice: I shall be immovably settled in my place by the omnipotence of God.

3. *Hell.* You can also divide the consideration of hell into four points. The first, its dimensions. It is a pit of immeasurable breadth, length, height, and depth. It is broad, because it contains all kinds of torments imaginable for soul and body; it is long, because all its pains are eternal; it is high, because all its pains are raised to the highest degree; and it is deep, because all its pains are real, unmixed with the least solace. Do I feel myself capable of dwelling forever in its devouring flames?

The second, its inhabitants. Hell is the abode of devils, the implacable enemies of men, whom it will be their delight to torment and insult; the abode of murderers, robbers, profligates, shameless wretches, bad children, bad parents, cursing and reproaching one another. Would this company appear very agreeable to me?

The third, its torments. They are of two kinds: the pain of loss and the pain of sense. The pain of loss, that is, the privation of the sovereign good: I have lost God, I have lost him through my own fault, I have lost him for a trifle, I have lost him beyond remedy. The pain of sense, that is, corporal affliction: I am buried in a pool of fire, I am penetrated with fire as salt meat is penetrated with salt,[1371] I touch nothing but fire, I breathe nothing but fire, I cannot have the slightest prospect of obtaining the least drop of water to lessen the heat or to quench the thirst that will torment me forever and ever.

The fourth, the way to it. The way to hell is sin: venial sin first, which, by weakening, disposes the soul to mortal falls; then mortal sin, which opens the gates of hell, marks out a place there, and only awaits the stroke of death to plunge the unfortunate victim into the fiery abyss. If I were to die this moment, where should I go?[1372]

4. *Heaven.* You can also divide the consideration of heaven into four points. The first, its dimensions. It is broad, because it contains all goods imaginable, and even unimaginable, for soul and body; it is long, because all its goods are eternal; it is high, because all its goods are most noble, far exalted above all known or supposed goods; and it is deep, because all its goods are real, unmixed with the least evil. And will I do nothing to obtain them?

The second, its inhabitants. Heaven is the bright abode of the Holy Trinity, of our Lord's humanity, of the Blessed Virgin, of the angels and saints, that is to say, of all that is most beautiful, most amiable, most perfect. What is any earthly magnificence in comparison with this?

The third, its joys. They are of two kinds: those of the soul and those of the body. The joys of the soul: to see, to possess, to love the sovereign good. The joys of the body: eternal life, eternal health, eternal beauty, eternal youth. Does all this whisper nothing to my heart, so eager for perishable goods, in which I find not one of the characteristics of true goods?

The fourth, the way to it. The way to heaven is fidelity in little things, for it is written: "He who is faithful in little things shall be faithful also in great things."[1373] This little action, which I perform at the present moment, if I perform it well, becomes a new ring in that long chain whose farther end rests in the hands of God, and which will guide me safely to the abode of everlasting happiness.

Thou shalt never sin. Do this, and "thou shalt never sin." "Thou shalt never sin," that is to say, according to the explanation of St. Denis, never mortally, seldom venially. The promise of God is formal, and, to make it more certain by contrast, the infallible oracle assures us that the cause of all the sins that defile the earth and fill hell is the want of meditation.[1374] "Thou shalt never sin": the testimony of experience leaves no doubt on the matter. The consideration of the four last things, says St. Augustine, is the destruction of pride, the extinction of jealousy, the banishment of lust, the foundation of virtue, the royal road to endless bliss.[1375]

If you read the history of the Church, it will teach you that the thought of the four last things has prevented more crimes and converted more sinners than all the preachers in the world. Who does not know the decisive influence of this salutary remedy on St. Chrysostom, St. Augustine, St. Jerome, St. Marcellus, St. Bernard, St. Ignatius, St. Francis Xavier, St. Aloysius Gonzaga, St. Francis Borgia, and a host of others?

The thought of the four last things is a sovereign remedy for preserving or raising us from sin, for enabling us to break bad and to contract good habits; but the cure is not complete. The Christian is what he ought to be only when his good habits have become the rule of his conduct. In effect, to maintain a temporal and to arrive at an eternal union with our Lord, it is not enough not to do evil: we must do good. It is not enough to be without vices: we must have virtues. Otherwise, we should expose ourselves to the sentence passed on the barren fig tree and the unprofitable servant. Now, how can virtues be practiced if they are not known? We proceed, therefore, to give an idea of them, sufficient for us to make our life truly Christian, and to render our union with our Lord permanent.

Virtues in general.—Man may be considered in regard to himself and in regard to God. Considered in regard to himself, man appears before us with his understanding and will. Considered in regard to God, man appears before us as one destined for the possession of God. Hence it is that we distinguish three kinds of virtues: intellectual virtues, moral virtues, and theological virtues.

But first, what is virtue in general? The word *virtue* means "strength," because, to do good, we must overcome ourselves, we must have strength. "Virtue," says St. Thomas, "is a good quality or a good habit of the soul, which makes us live conformably to right reason; or a habit which so perfects us that we may do good."[1376] Virtue is infused, that is to say, deposited in our soul by God himself, without concurrence on our part—as faith, hope, and charity in baptism; or acquired, that is to say, developed by repeated acts of our will supported by grace—as patience, mortification, and obedience.[1377]

Intellectual virtues.—The intellectual virtues are habits which perfect the mind. We distinguish three principal ones: wisdom, knowledge, and understanding.[1378]

Wisdom. Wisdom is a virtue by which our mind sees effects in their highest causes. In the material order, the man perfected by this virtue is like a spectator placed on the summit of a lofty mountain, who sees an immense extent of the earth, who sees the thunderbolts forming in the murky clouds, who sees the waters gathering into the deep subterranean caverns that feed the springs and streams, in a word, who sees in their causes those phenomena of which the ordinary man only knows the existence.

In the moral order, the man perfected by this virtue sees all events, the rise and fall of empires, the revolutions and tendencies as well as the punishments and rewards of peoples, in the cause of causes, the providence of God. What a degree of superiority does wisdom communicate to man! What ineffable delights does it procure for him! We need no longer be surprised that Solomon asked nothing else from the Lord, and that all good things, as he tells us, came to him together with it.[1379]

Prayer, the reading of good books, purity of heart, and meditation are the chief means to acquire this divine wisdom, which will preserve us from worldly, blind, accursed wisdom, the mortal enemy of God and man.[1380] Oh, how rare, consequently how necessary, is wisdom! Let us therefore beseech the Lord to grant it to us, saying with Solomon, "Give me wisdom, which sitteth by thy throne, that it may labor with me, and that I may know what is pleasing to thee."[1381]

Knowledge. Knowledge is a virtue by which our mind sees things in their effects, in their consequences, and in their closest bearings on the human race. Man, perfected by knowledge, values, judges, discusses, analyses, foresees: he traces effects to their causes, consequences to their principles, and, by chains of reasoning, forms systems which lead to important discoveries, as well in the material as in the moral order. Hence, it may be said that the wise man sees from above, and the learned man from below. The former descends from causes to effects; the latter ascends from effects to causes.[1382]

If nothing is more dangerous than a little learning, nothing is more estimable, or, at times, more useful, than true learning. Every one of us is bound, according to the condition in which God has placed him, to become solidly learned, that is to say, to acquire all the information necessary for the fulfillment of his duties toward God, toward himself, and toward the neighbor. Never was it permitted anyone to let his mind stagnate in ignorance: just as it is not permitted the tiller to leave his field uncultivated, or the servant to leave his master's talent unproductive. God condemns willful ignorance, while he promises a magnificent reward to those who perfect their mind by knowledge.[1383] The chief means to acquire knowledge are recollection, study, and docility.

Understanding. The third intellectual virtue is understanding. This is a habit which perfects our mind, and renders it capable of comprehending the principles of things, such as they are in themselves, abstracting from their consequences.[1384] The man endowed with this admirable virtue sees the pure truth: like a noble eagle, which, it is said, fixes its steady gaze, unwearied and undismayed, on the bright disc of the sun. Nothing clearer than his word, nothing surer than his glance, nothing more convincing than his declaration.

How necessary is understanding for us, to dispel the mists that the sophisms of others or our own passions raise at the present day—more than ever before—in regard to the most important principles, the truths essential to the existence of religion, of society, of the family! Such is, according to the oracle of the Holy Spirit, the special effect of this virtue, which we ought not to cease to ask of God, and to form within us by disengagement from the empire of sense and self-interest, and by the habit of reflection.[1385]

Wisdom, knowledge, and understanding are the three great virtues which perfect our mind. All three tend to the same end. That which distinguishes them from one another is not the similarity of their nature, but the order of their excellence. Thus, knowledge depends on understanding, and these two depend on wisdom, which contains them both, inasmuch as it reaches to the conclusions of all sciences, as well as to the principles from which they flow.[1386]

Moral virtues.—Moral virtues are those which, dealing with our inclinations and propensities, perfect our will by the practice of good, by the right use of reason. If they lead us to act through a natural motive, they are nothing but purely human virtues, fruitless for salvation. If they derive their motive from faith, they become supernatural, Christian, meritorious for eternal life.[1387] All the moral virtues do not occupy the same rank. There are four of them, namely: prudence, justice, fortitude, and temperance, which are called "cardinal virtues," because they are, as it were, the principles or sources of many other virtues. In effect, prudence governs the mind; justice governs the will; fortitude governs the irascible appetite; and temperance governs the concupiscible appetite.[1388]

Prudence. Prudence is a practical knowledge of what ought to be done and what ought to be avoided.[1389] Its office is to show us, in all that we say or do, the end to which we ought to tend and the means suitable thereto, modified by circumstances of time, place, and the like, so that our work may be good in every particular. This is the reason why prudence is called the mistress of virtues: it is, among them, what the eye is in the body, what salt is in meat, what the sun is in the universe. Nothing is more needed. It is formally commanded us by our Lord. It is the true science of the saints.[1390]

Prudence acts on all the faculties of the soul, which it obliges to help it in attaining its end: on the memory, which brings forward, at its command, the experience of others and our own experience, the faults of others and our own faults, that we may be put on our guard against new mistakes—also, the occasions of evil, that we may avoid them; on the understanding, which it enlightens in regard to the end that we ought to desire, and in regard to men and their dispositions; and on the will, which it guides to worthy operations.

The particular virtues which are referable to prudence, or which, as daughters, are born of it, are: foresight, which guesses the result and knows beforehand the means to succeed; circumspection, which, weighing everything attentively, leaves nothing to chance; discernment, which, after examining the pros and cons, chooses the wisest part, and the means best calculated to attain the desired end; and docility, which leads one to distrust self and to follow the counsels of the wise.

There are two kinds of vices opposed to prudence: some by defect, others by excess.

The former are five in number: a) precipitation, which consists in running to everything that presents itself—this vice is the cause of many faults, more or less grave according to circumstances; b) inconsideration, which judges, decides, acts without a sufficiently careful examination; c) inconstancy, which makes one change, without any serious reason, a resolution taken after mature thought; d) negligence, which makes one omit means proper for the execution of a project decided on; e) imprudence, which makes one take no heed of dangers, or warnings, but hasten to false steps, often to the occasions of sin and even to grievous sins.

The latter are also five in number: a) the prudence of the flesh, by which one directs his conduct according to the views and desires of corrupt nature; b) cunning, which is the art of finding out means to deceive the neighbor; c) deceit, which, by word or deed, sets such perfidious means to work; d) fraud, which is the result of cunning and deceit in positive facts, such as the employment of false measures or money in trade; e) too much solicitude about temporal things. What a pity it is to see so many worldly-wise people, who, referring everything to their own interests, are not at all scrupulous in regard to the nature of their projects or their choice of means! A day will come when it will be seen that they were the most imprudent of men, having lost the sovereign good for the sake of trifles.

As for the means of acquiring Christian prudence, the only prudence of which there is question here, and which essentially consists in the will to make everything subservient to one's salvation, in the will to lose everything rather than lose one's soul, the first is to ask it of God; the second is to take counsel of wise, upright, and discreet persons; the third is to inquire of oneself before performing any action, "What relation does this action bear to my eternal salvation?"

Justice. Justice is a virtue which leads us to give everyone his due.[1391] Its office is to maintain the stability of contracts, which is the foundation of tranquility, of public and private peace. In effect, if everyone could be satisfied with that which belongs to him, without desiring the goods of others, there would be neither war nor discord. This virtue, absolutely necessary, obliges individuals to give to their souls what pertains to their souls, and to their bodies what pertains to their bodies—food, medicine, etc.; to sell at a fair price; to keep to their engagements; and to repair the wrongs that they have inflicted.

It obliges the rulers of peoples to do justice to every person: it is for this end that they are invested with power;[1392] to distribute employments, dignities, and honors, according to merit, and not by favor. It obliges the nations to observe the rules of equity in their dealings with one another; not to make war without sufficient motives; and to respect even in a just war the laws of humanity, such as Christianity has established among civilized peoples. It obliges man to render to God the homage which is due to him; hence, the fundamental precept of our divine master: "Render to Caesar the things that are Caesar's, and to God the things that are God's."[1393]

As for the vices opposed to the virtue of justice, they are of two kinds: some by excess, others by defect.[1394] The first are: superstition, which falsifies the worship due to God, and fanaticism, which distorts it; also, usury, which oversteps one's rights in regard to the goods of others, and prodigality, which does the same in regard to one's own. The second are: irreligion, with which are connected impiety and indifference; hardness of heart and sourness of speech toward our parents; disobedience toward our superiors; ingratitude toward our benefactors; falsehood toward our equals; enmity toward our friends; lastly, and to repeat all in one word, injustice from every point of view.

Since it is necessary for all the world to practice justice, under pain of damnation, it is no less necessary to know the means of arriving at this virtue. The first is prayer; the second, detachment from temporal goods; the third, almsgiving; and the fourth, humility: for pride and selfishness are the direct cause of irreligion, dishonesty, and all other vices opposed to justice, considered in its full extent.

Fortitude. Fortitude is a virtue which enables us to overcome all the obstacles that oppose us in the practice of good and the endurance of evil.[1395] Its first office is to make us undertake and accomplish generously, in spite of dangers and difficulties, whatever is required of us by our duties toward God, toward the neighbor, and toward ourselves. Christian men and women, who daily trample on the repugnances of nature, on the seductions of the flesh and the world, in order to observe the gospel; religious and priests, who devote themselves, whether at home or abroad, to the spiritual and corporal welfare of mankind; soldiers, who face toil, hardship, and death: all these are so many models of active fortitude. Its second office is to make us bear, with Christian resignation, all sorts of persecutions, calumnies, afflictions, and temptations, rather than offend God: it goes so far as to make us accept death, when this is necessary for salvation. The martyrs are so many models of passive fortitude.

This virtue is indispensable to the Christian. "No one," says the gospel, "shall be crowned, unless he has fought well. The kingdom of heaven suffers violence: it is only those who vanquish themselves that shall bear it away."[1396]

The virtues which spring from fortitude and which add perfection to it are: confidence, which makes one believe himself able to encounter the perils and to surmount the difficulties that will be met with in reasonable undertakings; magnanimity, which inclines one to perform considerable works, worthy of great honor; magnificence, which leads one to hand out his money, with prompt and noble mind, for all the expenses necessary to attain a desired success; perseverance, which helps one to do good to the end, in spite of all the vexations with which his path is strewn; patience, which makes one calmly and serenely meet sickness or misfortune.

The vices opposed to fortitude are likewise of two kinds: by excess and by defect. By excess: rashness, which, without necessity, without calculating the means of success, makes one go forward to dangers; audacity, which makes one act similarly in regard to obstacles; presumption, which makes one undertake that which is above his strength. By defect: fear, pusillanimity, cowardice, sloth, human respect, which make one give way before difficulties and throw down his arms without a struggle, or almost without a struggle.

If we wish to acquire fortitude, as we are bound to do, we must have recourse to the following means: prayer, and the assiduous consideration of the lives of our Lord, the apostles, the martyrs, and so many other models of courage in labor and of resignation in suffering.

Temperance. Temperance is a virtue which makes man moderate in the use of the pleasures of this life.[1397] The office of temperance is not to interdict all sorts of pleasures, but to regulate their use in accordance with reason and the law of God. Viewing temperance thus, there is no one so blind as not to see the necessity of this virtue. The obligation to practice it is written under the various names of mortification, abstinence, continence, and sobriety, in every page of the scriptures, in every part of the history of our Lord and the saints.

The principal virtues which depend on temperance are: abstinence, which makes one observe moderation in the use of food and in the pleasure attached thereto, and above all teaches fidelity to the laws of fasting and abstinence established by the Church; sobriety, which makes one observe moderation in the use of drink, especially intoxicating drink; chastity, which restrains within the bounds of duty the inclination to carnal pleasure; bashfulness, which is a virtuous shame, inspiring an avoidance and abhorrence of looks, familiarities, actions capable of wounding chastity; modesty, which maintains order in one's inward and outward movements.[1398]

It also makes us practice humility, which, by a knowledge of our miseries, keeps us little in our own eyes, prevents us from rebelling against providence, and makes us refer to God alone all the good that we do; meekness, which tempers the ardor of the soul, drives away anger and impatience, settles us in a profound peace, and disposes us to treat the neighbor kindly at all times; clemency, which moderates external justice as far as reason permits, leading us to mitigate the punishments deserved by the guilty, and even to pardon them altogether, in consideration of their repentance or for some other legitimate cause.

The principal vices opposed to temperance are as follows. By defect: insensibility, which consists in abstaining, heedless of the order of God, from things necessary for life, for health, for the fulfillment of the duties of one's state, through a fear of taking the natural pleasure which is found therein. This fault is not common; hence, our Lord and the saints continually exhort us to mortification. By excess: intemperance, which is an inordinate love of pleasure, leading us into excesses in drinking, in eating, and in satisfying the senses. This vice draws in its train gluttony, drunkenness, impurity, and many other sins.

As for the means of acquiring temperance, we shall always point out prayer, the examples of our Lord and the saints, and the thought of the temporal and eternal evils that follow intemperance, such as disgrace, beastliness, want, disease, impenitence, and special punishments for all eternity.

Theological virtues.—The third class of virtues comprises the three theological virtues: faith, hope, and charity. Perfecting man in his relations with God, they produce, animate, and crown all the other virtues, to which they communicate their merit and value.[1399] These three virtues having been explained elsewhere, it remains for us to show the relations which they have with the other virtues, and the relations which all the virtues have with one another.

It is necessary, therefore, to know that all the moral virtues are so intertwined with one another that we cannot have a single one of them in its perfection without having all the others in a more or less elevated degree. In effect, perfect virtue is a firm and constant love of order, which makes us invariably seek and do what is conformable to reason enlightened by faith. Now, this love evidently contains all the other virtues, since, for example, a person cannot be perfectly just if he fails in regard to fortitude, temperance, or prudence: that is to say, if, in a point of fortitude, temperance, or prudence, he fails in a firm and constant love of order. It is the same with the other moral virtues, which, however, may exist, one without another, in a state of imperfection.

It is also necessary to know that all the virtues are, in a certain degree, necessary to salvation. Hence, no one can be saved if he does not, in a degree proportioned to his age, his condition, his education, possess wisdom, knowledge, understanding, prudence, justice, fortitude, temperance, faith, hope, and charity, and all the secondary virtues of which these virtues are the mothers.[1400]

To maintain the contrary would be to pretend that a barren tree is a good tree; that a slothful servant is a good servant; that the disciple of a God, the model of all virtues, is a good disciple, though he does not imitate him or make any account of his precepts. This would be to give the lie direct to all the saints, who, by the twofold preaching of their books and their examples, have taught us the necessity of virtue.

It is, moreover, necessary to know that all the intellectual and moral virtues, apart from the theological virtues, are worth nothing for salvation. In effect, these virtues, taken by themselves, can only help us to do a good that is natural, human, purely rational, which, having nothing heavenly in it, will never lead us to God, our last end. To have this precious advantage, they should be animated and ennobled by the three great virtues of the supernatural order, which tend directly to God. We must remark here, too, that not only the intellectual and moral virtues, but even faith and hope, are unable to lead us to heaven without charity. Charity is therefore the fruitful mother who brings forth all true virtues, and the august queen who exalts and crowns them. Without her, no more virtues worthy of the name; with her, all virtues in a degree sufficient to arrive at everlasting happiness.[1401]

Let us make a summary of this magnificent system of virtues, as it itself is a summary of the whole doctrine of the divine restorer of fallen man.

As there are ten commandments on which depend and to which refer all others, so there are ten great virtues on which depend and to which refer all others.

As there are three commandments which relate to God, and seven which relate to ourselves and the neighbor, so there are three virtues which relate to God, and seven which relate to ourselves and the neighbor.

As the ten commandments relate to the precept of charity, so all the virtues relate to charity, which is their beginning and their end. Thus the first three virtues, called intellectual virtues, perfect our mind and render it capable of discovering truth; the next four, called moral or cardinal virtues, perfect our will and render it capable of doing good; the last three, called theological virtues, perfect both our mind and our will and render them capable, respectively, of entering into an intimate acquaintance with God and doing supernatural good: consequently, they lead us to supreme happiness, which is union with God by charity in this world and in the next.

Hence, all the virtues are intertwined with one another, and the final end of all together is to develop man in God amid the storms of this life, until he is borne away to rejoice in him amid the delights of eternity; for heaven is love. Can you imagine anything more admirable, more blessed, more worthy of God and man?

The better to understand and appreciate this marvelous connection of all the virtues with one another, let us make use of a striking contrast and remark that all the vices are also connected with one another, and that their final end is to degrade man, by making him the slave of evil, amid the conflicts of this life, until they drag him down to the torments of a miserable eternity: for hell is hatred.

Hatred or love, hell or heaven: these are the closing words of the doctrine of our divine master, as they are the highest explanation of man and life, of time and eternity.

The Church: Its foundation.—The Son of God, who came on earth to instruct the human race, had specially consecrated the forty days after his resurrection to initiate the apostles in the secrets of his doctrine and to give them a perfect understanding of the scriptures. The end for which the eternal Word had vouchsafed to be born, to live, and to die; the necessity of the union of all men with him by faith, hope, and charity; the indispensable condition and means of this union, grace and prayer; the end of this union in time, the imitation of his life, and in eternity, the participation of his glory; the only cause capable of destroying this holy union and delivering us over again to the slavery of the devil, sin; the remedies for sin, the four last things and the virtues: all these things were known to the apostles, and they were in a state to instruct the world concerning them. What had the new Adam still to do before ascending into heaven?

On the one hand, all the generations that should come into this world were called to a union with him, as the only principle of their regeneration and salvation; on the other, the Savior could no longer instruct men in person—his earthly mission was accomplished. To perpetuate the work of redemption, and to render its benefits accessible to all people even till the end of time, he substitutes another for himself: he chooses a vicar. The plenitude of power which he received from his Father, he will confide to him; on him he will place the care of extending and consummating the great work which he himself has just begun. Never will man be raised to a higher dignity; never will a more formidable responsibility be laid on a mortal!

Who shall be this lieutenant for the Son of God? O abyss of mercy and wisdom! it shall be he who thrice denied his master at the voice of a maidservant! All that is most weak for the work that is most important! A reed to uphold the world! A great sinner to be the teacher of the faith and the father of Christians! In a word, the vicar of the new Adam shall be St. Peter.

Consecration of St. Peter.—Nothing more sublime, and, at the same time, more touching than the circumstances of his ordination. Let us hear the account thereof. A few days before ascending into heaven, the Savior, being in the midst of his apostles, cast his eyes on Simon Peter and addressed these mysterious words to him: "Simon, son of John, lovest thou me more than all these others here?" Neither Peter nor any of his companions could foresee the object of a question so unexpected.

What is its meaning? When a king wishes to confide some very high office to one of his subjects, he asks him for a guarantee, he requires security. This guarantee, this security, must be proportioned to the greatness of the charge. So our Lord acts. This divine pastor, who has just shed his blood for his sheep, is on the point of leaving them: he has resolved to confide them to the guidance and guardianship of his disciple, Peter. Before honoring him with these sublime functions, he asks him for a guarantee, he requires security. But what guarantee or security can he expect from a poor fisherman, with no other fortune than his boat and his nets? The greatest and best that man can offer—love; but love reaching to heroism; love ready to be immolated for the service of its master and for the interests of the charge confided to it. Such is the guarantee, such the security, which the Son of God requires of his disciple.

Hence, in addressing to St. Peter the question, "Lovest thou me more than the others?" he seems to say to him, "I am about to give a greater mark of my confidence to thee than to any of the others. Wilt thou give me in return a stronger pledge of thy inviolable fidelity? Lovest thou me, that is to say, art thou disposed, and more disposed than any of the others to sacrifice for me and my flock thy health, thy strength, thy life itself?" St. Peter answers with humility, "Lord! thou knowest that I love thee." It is only after obtaining this assurance that the divine pastor says to him, "Feed my lambs."

Penetrated with gratitude, Peter feels the exceeding great honor which his good master has done him. Then the Savior, to make him understand well the full extent of his engagements, asks him a second time, "Simon, son of John, lovest thou me?" "Yea, Lord!"

answers Peter as before, "thou knowest that I love thee." And Jesus says to him, "Feed my lambs." The Savior's lambs are the simple faithful.

If Peter was only to be charged with the guardianship and guidance of the lambs, the assurances that he had given would have sufficed. But he was to be charged with the care both of lambs and sheep, the flocks and the pastors. This additional function, which puts a finishing stroke to the confidence of the master and the glory of the disciple, requires a new pledge. The Savior asks therefore for the third time, "Simon, son of John, lovest thou me?"

One should be to Jesus that which Peter was, the first of the apostles, to feel as deeply as he did how bitter and disquieting such a question, so often repeated, seemed; the saddest recollections burst upon his mind. Peter loved much: his only fear now was that he did not love enough. Troubled and abashed, he answers with tearful eyes, "Lord! there is nothing unknown to thee: thou knowest that I love thee." The trial is over, and all the pledges are obtained. The Savior, satisfied, says to him, "Feed my sheep."

This expression was very short, but how deep was its meaning, and how abundantly it compensated the apostle for the transitory alarm that he had just experienced! It is not merely the guardianship and guidance of tender lambs, a figure of the simple faithful, that Jesus confides to Peter: at this moment, the individual pastors of the different flocks, represented by the sheep, become in regard to Peter a portion of the general flock, entrusted to his vigilance and subjected to his authority. Every shepherd must feed his own flock, and all the flocks, together with the shepherds, must meet in one fold, under the crook of the common shepherd.

Thus was consecrated the first of the popes. An immense dignity in exchange for an immense love: such were the conditions of this sublime contract, entered into between the Creator and his creature, the master and his disciple!

By the words of Jesus, Peter was constituted his vicar throughout the whole extent of his kingdom: the bishop of bishops; the father of fathers; the bishop, not merely of one particular see, the center of Catholic unity, but the bishop of the Universal Church; the prince of pastors, or, what is the same in regard to the nature of his dignity, the servant of the servants of God. Such is still at the present day, and such shall ever be, in the minds of all the faithful and of all Catholic pastors, the successor of Peter and the vicar of Jesus Christ.

Hence it is that, by a religious instinct common to all the members of the Church, our souls are penetrated on hearing the name of the sovereign pontiff with that feeling of profound veneration, blended with confidence and tenderness, which highborn children owe to their father. We all say, "our holy father the pope," because, all in general and each one in particular, we are his children. Woe to us if we change these sentiments or abandon this language! There is hardly any more certain sign of the decay of the faith in families, or of an approaching defection among peoples, than the lessening of this respect and the cooling of this love.

Nothing, therefore, was more august than the dignity with which the Savior honored Peter, that he might transmit it to his successors; but it laid tremendous obligations on him. Jesus did not wish that he should be ignorant of them. He explained to him clearly how far this love, which he had asked of him as a pledge of his fidelity, should lead him. He said, "Peter, when thou wast young, thou didst gird thyself, and didst go whithersoever it pleased thee. When thou growest old, thou shalt stretch out thy hands: another shall gird thee, and shall lead thee whither thou wouldst not go." The Savior was announcing to Peter the kind of death by which he should one day glorify God, namely, crucifixion.

Peter was not afflicted. More touched by the honor of dying on a cross after the example of his good master than by the glory of governing the Church, he never forgot this tender prophecy. Thirty years afterward, when, being more than sixty years old, he sighed for the accomplishment of the oracle, he wrote thus to the faithful, by whom he was loved and revered as a father: "My children, I hasten to exhort and instruct you, while I am surrounded with this mortal flesh. I am old: I shall soon quit the tabernacle of my body, as Jesus Christ our Lord hath been pleased to make known to me."[1402]

The Son of God, addressing himself next to all the apostles in general, says to them with as much love as majesty: "All power is given to me in heaven and on earth. Go: teach all nations. Fear not: I will be with you all days, even to the consummation of the world." His earthly mission is ended. The Church is founded. Nothing remains for him but to return to his Father, in order to send the vivifying Spirit that shall animate the mystical body just formed by him.

Ascension of the Savior.—After promising his apostles that the Paraclete shall descend on them, shall suddenly change them into new men, and shall make them capable of serving him as witnesses in Jerusalem, in Judea, in Samaria, in Galilee, and to the ends of the earth, Jesus sets out, and, passing through the village of Bethania, leads them to the Mount of Olives. Arrived at this place, lately the scene of his humiliations and immediately to be the scene of his glory, the divine master extends his hand, blesses them, and gently rises in the air. Their eyes follow him, till a bright cloud glides under his feet and serves him as a triumphant chariot on which he ascends to the highest heavens. The blessed Jerusalem opens its gates, and, amid the acclamations of all the celestial host, he advances, the firstborn among his brethren, the chief of the human race, to take, in our name, possession of eternal glory, surrounded by which he sits, and our humanity with him, on a sublime throne, at the right hand of his Father.

There, the supreme pontiff, the mediator, the advocate, the spouse of the Church, he watches over us, pleads our cause, guides the ship across the shoals until he brings it with all its passengers to the heavenly shore. He will intercede for us, and will let the immortal barque of Peter sail on until the time granted the human race to rehabilitate itself is ended. Then he will come again to separate forever those who shall have quitted this world purified, from those who, having abused their opportunity, shall have quitted it more defiled than they entered it. This is the formidable truth which he causes to be announced at the same hour to his apostles, and by them to the whole world.

While the apostles kept their eyes still turned heavenward, behold! two angels, under the appearance of men, robed in white, appeared at their side, and said to them, "Ye men of Galilee, why stand ye here looking up to heaven? This Jesus, who hath just departed from you, shall one day return with the same power that he hath displayed in ascending before you." At these words, the apostles adore once more their divine master, and return to Jerusalem. With the Blessed Virgin, they enter the upper chamber, and begin that retreat, the model of all others, which shall be terminated by such a number of prodigies, so glorious for the Savior and so consoling for us.

PRAYER

O my God! who art all love, I thank thee for having caused me to be born in the bosom of the Catholic Church; grant me the grace to live and die virtuously in it.

I am resolved to love God above all things, and my neighbor as myself for the love of God; and, in testimony of this love, I will become a member of the Society for the Propagation of the Faith.

Endnotes

1 Vatican I, Dogmatic Constitution *Dei Filius de fide catholica*, Ch. 4

2 Pope Benedict XIV, Apostolic Constitution *Etsi minime*, n. 13

3 Cf. Pope St. Pius X, Encyclical *Acerbo nimis*, n. 27

4 Gaume's catechism spans Volumes X-XIII of the Tradivox series.

5 See Fleury, *Manners of the Israelites.*

6 See Pluquet, *Dict. des Hérés.*, disc. prelim.

7 The Sanhedrim was the great council or senate of the Jews. It was composed of three chambers, almost on the same plan as our courts of justice: that of the scribes or doctors of the law; that of the priests; and that of the ancients. Each chamber was usually composed of twenty-three members, who, with the pontiff and the nasi—or president of the whole Sanhedrim—made altogether seventy-one persons, as God had ordained by Moses. The great council, thus composed, was the supreme tribunal of the Jews, even of those who were scattered among the Gentiles.

8 Cf. Dn 9:26; Os 3

9 Cf. Acts 5:36ff

10 Cf. Josephus, *War of the Jews*, Bk. 6, Ch. 5, n. 4

11 Pluribus persuasio inerat, antiquis sacerdotum litteris contineri, eo ipso tempore fore, ut valesceret oriens, profectique Judaea rerum potirentur (Tacitus, *Histories*, Bk. 5, n. 13).

12 Percrebuerat Oriente toto vetus et constans opinio, esse in fatis, ut eo tempore Judaea profecti rerum potirentur (Suetonius, *The Twelve Caesars*, "On Vespasian," n. 4).

13 Virgil, in his fourth eclogue, has only invested with the charms of poetry the oracle of the Sibyl of Cumae. Is it not very remarkable that this Sibyl describes the reign of the Messias almost in the same terms as the prophet Isaias? It is to her oracles that St. Justin the Martyr sends the pagans, in order to be prepared for the mysteries of Christianity. In proportion as the time for the arrival of the Desired of Nations drew nigh, an extraordinary light arose throughout the world. It seemed like the first rays of the Star of Jacob, which was about to appear. Cicero announces the speedy establishment of an eternal universal law, the law of all nations and all times: under one only master, who should be God himself. *Nec erit alia lex Romae*, he says, *alia Athenis, alia nunc, alia posthac; sed omnes gentes, et omni tempore una lex et sempiterna et immortalis continebit, unusque erit communis quasi magister et imperator omnium Deus* (Cicero, *De Republica*, Bk. 3; *apud Lactant., Divin. Inst.*, Bk. 6, Ch. 8. See *Redemption of the Human Race*, by Schmidt; *Le Christ devant le siécle, etc.*).

14 Mr. Maurice

15 Cf. Volney, *les Ruines*, Ch. 22, n. 13

16 Cf. Talmud, Ch. 11

17 Heaven and earth were in harmony to announce, each in its language, the fullness of time, and the most solemn hour of the general redemption. To the voice of prophets and traditions was joined the voice of the stars. In his *Symbolique des Songes*, M. Schuberr, professor at Munich, establishes by a multitude of astronomical calculations that the stars predicted in their manner the coming of our Lord Jesus Christ; that it was according to their revolutions that the Sabbatical year, or year of pardon and renovation, was reckoned; and that they renewed their course as often as the earth was renewed by penance. He shows that all the peoples of antiquity understood this language of the stars, and were acquainted with the great event, the great reconciliation, which they announced. See also *Vie de Notre-Seigneur Jésus Christ*, by Dr. Sepp.

18 Mt 2:5-6

19 Cf. Ps 71

20 Cf. Nm 18

21 See Chrysostom, *On Matthew*, Ch. 2.

22 The gospel gives us no details regarding the sojourn of the Holy Family in Egypt. A tradition states that, at the moment when the Son of God set foot on this idolatrous land, all its idols were overthrown. St. Brigit, whose revelations we may, on the authority of sovereign pontiffs, piously believe, assures us that the Holy Family often stood in need of bread. Oh, how touching is this thought!

23 Herod carried his barbarous suspicions so far that he put to death several of his near relations. Among them was one of his own sons, still young. "It was on account of this occurrence," says Macrobius, a

pagan author, "that the emperor Augustus jocosely remarked that it was better to be Herod's pig than his son, alluding to the law of the Jews, which prohibited the use of swine's flesh" (*Saturnalia*, Ch. 4).

24 God avenged on this wicked prince the death of John the Baptist, and the derision shown to our Lord. Being accused of an attempt to excite some rebellions in Judea, and unable to justify himself before Caligula, he was banished with Herodias to Lyons. According to tradition, Herod died miserably in this city, and Herodias still more miserably in Spain.

25 Why "thy father"? Joseph was not the father, according to the flesh, of Jesus, who had no other father than God; but God had transferred his rights to Joseph. He occupied the place of a father in regard to Jesus Christ; he was charged with the care of maintaining his childhood and bringing him up. As the husband of Mary, he had also the right to be called the father of this well-beloved Son: he shared authority and care with her.

26 Filius hominis non venit ministrari, sed ministrare (Mt 20:28). Nemo ambigat Dominum Jesum, cum adhuc in puerili esset aetate, obsequia praestitisse Mariae ipsique Josepho (Laurence Justinian, *On Obedience*, Ch. 8). Saepe focum, crebroque cibum parat officiosus, vasa lavat, bajulat undam de fonte, nuncque domum scopit (Jean Gerson, *In Joseph.*, Bk. 3).

27 Pliny and other ancient writers mention a kind of locust used as food by the poorer classes in the East. It was about four inches long, and as thick as one's finger.

28 Remark how carefully the evangelist specifies the date: such, assuredly, is not the style of impostors.

29 Cum dicitur Deus homo, vel in excelsum montem, vel in sanctam civitatem a diabolo assumptus, mens refugit, humanae hoc audire aures expavescunt. Qui tamen non esse incredibilia ista cognoscimus, si in illo et alia facta pensamus. Certe iniquorum omnium caput diabolus est, et hujus capitis membra sunt omnes iniqui. An non diaboli membrum fuit Pilatus? An non diaboli membra Judaei persequentes et milites crucifigentes Christum fuerunt? Quid ergo mirum, si ab illo permisit in montem duci, qui se pertulit etiam a membris illius crucifigi? Non est ergo indignum Redemptore nostro quod tentari voluit qui venerat occidi. Justum quippe erat, ut sic tentationes nostras suis tentationibus vinceret, sicut mortem nostram venerat sua morte superare (Gregory the Great, *Homily on Matthew*).

30 Following the Greek, these words of the Savior present another sense, which appears to us preferable: "Woman, what is it to thee and to me?" O thou, woman by excellence! thou, who art a Mother without ceasing to be a Virgin, of what importance can it be to thee or to me that they have no more wine? Thou knowest that this stimulant of the passions is not needed for the only generation that is worthy of God, worthy of thee, worthy of me. "My hour is not yet come": although the hour of performing miracles is not yet come for me, still as thou hast spoken the word, it is enough—I will perform one beforehand for the sake of my Mother. Thus, in the first part of his answer, the Savior reveals the sublime dignity of Mary, while, in the second, he renders homage to his own omnipotence.

31 Why changers in the porches of the Temple? The law obliged the Jews, dispersed throughout the world, to pay the Temple tax. This was an annual sum of half-a-crown a head, destined to defray the expenses of the Temple and the priests. When coming to Jerusalem, the Jews used to bring the money that circulated in the countries in which they dwelt. It was necessary to change this money for Jewish money, otherwise it would not be received. Hence, the changers. The Temple tax was the "Peter's pence" of the Jews.

32 Among the Jews, those who collected the taxes were called publicans. They were a most odious class to the Jews, who, believing themselves free, because descended from Abraham, looked upon them as little better than public robbers. Perhaps they really were so in secret.

33 We have seen the Savior pray before instructing, and, after instructing, confirm his doctrine by miraculous deeds. At every step of his public life we meet the same economy. Oh, what an example for masters and superiors!

34 The literal translation of the words *Dic tantum verbum*, etc. presents an admirable meaning, altogether in harmony with the words that the centurion will soon utter, *Dic tantum verbo:* Speak only by thy word, command only by thy word, and, like a faithful and healthy messenger, it will go, it will execute thy commission, it will heal my servant; for thou art almighty, and he who can do everything does whatever he desires by a word, notwithstanding distance or difficulty. *Nihil enim*, says St. Augustine, *medium est inter opus Dei atquae praeceptum, quia in praecepto est opus...quia voluntas Dei potestas est* (*Homily on Luke*, Bk. 5, n. 1).

35 In the scripture, the word *gates* often means "powers." This is the reason: it was at the gates of cities that the magistrates and other authorities, in a word, the powers used anciently to assemble to dispense justice. The terms became synonymous in the course of time.

36 "I represent him to myself," says a pious author, "as one of our poor beggars, whom hunger has disfigured and poverty stripped, who have only a few rags half-covering them and falling to pieces, who are hardly able to live on the trifling alms that they snatch by their entreaties from the passersby."

37 To understand the words of the sacred writer, "because he was the high priest of that year," we must recollect that Annas and Caiphas were both high priests, and that they were such for their whole lives; but they only acted in this capacity alternately. He who entered the holy of holies on the feast of Expiation was the pontiff for the current year. Neither of them ever lost the dignity of pontiff, though they exercised the functions of their office in turn.

38 He was called Iscariot, from the village of Iscarioth, in the tribe of Ephraim, not far from Samaria, where he was born.

39 The death of Jesus was near. Mary, in pouring this perfume on him, acquitted herself of a duty which piety and custom always desired to have fulfilled toward the dead before their burial, as if she foresaw that she should be hindered from doing so after the Savior's death.

40 On the universal practice of prayer before and after meals, see our *Traité du signe de la croix*. To dispense oneself from this duty is to violate a law of humanity.

41 The Savior had often taught his disciples in private. Yet he could say with truth that he had said nothing in secret, since the doctrine which he taught in private was the same as that which he taught in public. We easily understand that it was substantially the same, and that he only developed it more fully in his familiar conversations with his apostles.

42 The prophecy is fulfilled even at the present day. The empress St. Helen caused the clay of the Field of Blood to be removed to Rome. It serves as a cemetery for pilgrims: you may see it close to St. Peter's, behind the buildings of the Holy Office.

43 Pilate gained little by sacrificing the innocent to his ambition. About a year after the Savior's death he took a quantity of money from the treasury of the Temple to construct an aqueduct. The people were stirred up against him, and Pilate employed extreme measures to quell the sedition. He had recourse to still more horrible cruelties against the inhabitants of Samaria, who complained of them to Tiberius. On these complaints he was ordered to Rome, where he arrived in the year 37 of the Christian era, in the beginning of the reign of Caligula. Exiled to Pavia, or, according to another tradition, to the neighborhood of Vienne in Dauphiné, he killed himself, two years afterward, in despair. Thus, Judas who betrayed, and Pilate who condemned, the Savior, perished by suicide.

44 Tradition gives the name of Dimas to the good thief, and many chapels have been dedicated under his invocation. See our *Histoire du bon Larron*.

45 The paradise of which the Savior here speaks was the bosom of Abraham, or limbo, which was a place of rest for the just wholly purified, and might be regarded as a place of felicity begun. Our Lord, descending thither, filled it with essential beatitude.

46 The most general opinion is that this darkness really extended over the whole earth. We shall cite a few testimonies on the matter. The first is that of St. Denis the Areopagite...He writes to St. Polycarp in reply to the reproaches made against him by his old friend Apollophanes, who says that he has been employing, in a manner not very sincere, the testimonies of pagan authors to destroy paganism. "Apollophanes," he remarks, "ought to remember what passed when we were together in Egypt. As we were one day near the city of Heliopolis, we suddenly saw the moon coming to meet the sun—although it was not the time of the conjunction—and causing a great eclipse; and afterward, about the ninth hour of the day, we saw it leave the place which it occupied before the sun, and go to a place directly opposite in the heavens...This is what you can remind him of. And you, Apollophanes, contradict me if you dare—me, who accompanied you on the occasion, and who saw and admired the wondrous sight with you. Finally, at that moment Apollophanes, like a man beside himself, exclaimed, addressing me, as if he had really discovered the meaning of what was occurring: 'My dear Denis, there are changes in divine things.'"[a]

On the other hand, St. Denis exclaimed: "Either the author of nature is suffering or the machine of the universe is about to be destroyed." It is not surprising that St. Denis, though then a pagan, should have thought that the author of nature was suffering. To have this idea in his mind it sufficed for him to have read what Plato says of the sufferings of the God whom the world expected.

If the darkness was the effect of an eclipse, it was not less miraculous; for the Jewish Pasch, at the time of which Jesus Christ suffered death, was celebrated only at full moon. Now, everyone knows that an eclipse of the sun never happens when the moon is at the full. May it not have been owing to a vague but traditional knowledge of the darkness which should take place at the Savior's death, that pagan peoples were always seized with such alarm at the sight of eclipses?

In another letter, addressed to Apollophanes himself, at this time converted to Christianity, St. Denis speaks in these terms: "I am about to remind you of what occurred when we were together at Heliopolis in Egypt. I was then twenty-five years of age, and you were probably about the same. One Friday, about the hour of sext, or noon, we saw the moon coming suddenly and placing itself in front of the sun, and causing an eclipse which filled us with terror. I asked you at the time what you thought of this prodigy, and you made use in reply of an expression which shall never be effaced from my mind... You said: 'There are changes, my dear Denis, in divine things.' I took an exact note of the year and the period of the year at which this prodigy occurred; and, comparing what I had seen with what Paul afterward taught me regarding the matter, I surrendered to that truth to which you also have so happily surrendered."[b]

Let us now give the testimony of Phlegon, who was emancipated by the emperor Adrian. This author was a pagan; he wrote, in sixteen books, a history of the Olympiads from their origin until about the year of Jesus Christ 140. Now, he says that in the fourth year of the 102nd Olympiad, which should end about the middle of the year 33 of the vulgar era, or the year of the death of Jesus Christ, there was an eclipse of the sun, the greatest that had ever been seen: the obscuration being such that at the hour of noon one might see the stars in heaven. He adds that at the same time there was a very great earthquake in Bithynia, which overthrew nearly the whole city of Nice.[c]

Thallus, a Greek historian, speaks to the same effect as Phlegon. The time at which this Thallus lived is not precisely known; but St. Justin and Tertullian having quoted him, it is supposed that he must have been a contemporary of Phlegon's, if not more ancient.

The books of the two last-mentioned authors would seem to be the sources to which Tertullian and the martyr St. Lucian of Antioch were accustomed to refer the pagans in order to find therein a proof of the miraculous darkness which occurred at the death of the Savior.

[a] Dionysius Areopagite, Bk. 2, p. 7, ep. 91

[b] *In vita Dionys. apud Corder.*, t. 2, p. 273

[c] Cf. *Apud Euseb. Chronic.*, p. 188, edit. Scalig

47 In the center of the space before the cathedral of Puzzuoli we have seen the celebrated white marble pedestal, adorned with fourteen figures, which represent the fourteen cities of Asia Minor, overthrown by the earthquake that took place at the time of our Lord's death, and rebuilt by Tiberius. Thus, the profane monument of Puzzuoli is a palpable proof of the truth of the gospel narrative.

48 Jn 10:18

49 Ex 12:46

50 Zac 12:10

51 Jn 12:32

52 The shroud was also of linen. Hence the practice at the Holy Sacrifice of the Mass, of laying the body of our Lord on a linen cloth, to the exclusion of every other material. This is a remark made by St. Jerome nearly fourteen hundred years ago.

53 Yet the apostles obeyed and went into Galilee, to the mountain on which Jesus expressly directed them to meet him. *Undecim autem discipuli abierunt in Galilaeam in montem ubi constituerat illis Jesus* (Mt 28:16). A difficulty arises here. It was not in the province that bears the name of Galilee that Jesus showed himself to his apostles, either on the day of his resurrection or eight days afterward. Far from going at this time into a province whose frontier was nearly forty miles distant, the apostles did not quit the neighborhood of the capital during the solemnity. They were here on the evening of the resurrection, and they saw Jesus here, as he had promised them. They were also here eight days afterward, and it was here that Jesus showed himself to them for the second time before they set out for Galilee.

The difficulty would appear great, and one could hardly reconcile the letter of the text with the course of events. Yet the happy discovery of an ancient commentator, a bishop of Coimbra, appears to us to clear the matter up in a satisfactory manner. He had visited the places. He had examined everything. He had studied the difficulties of the text, and he solves them thus:*

"It is not necessary to believe that the Galilee to which Jesus Christ commanded his apostles to go, and to which he should precede them in order to show himself to them, was the province of Galilee. The Galilee of which there is question here was a mountain near the Mountain of Olives. For, on leaving Jerusalem by the Valley of Josaphat, one meets with three high mountains. That of Olives is in the middle, and is the loftiest of the three. To say nothing of the one which is seen on the right, there lies on the left a third, which bears the name of the Mountain of Galilee. On this mountain the Galileans had built themselves an ample habitation in which to reside when their affairs called them to Jerusalem; and thus it received the name of the Mountain of Galilee, which it preserves to this day. Hither did Jesus proceed to meet his apostles, and to render them witnesses of the truth of his resurrection." (See *Mémoires de Trévoux*, art. 95, Oct., 1729.)

* *Soarius. episc. Conimb., apud Baradium*, Ch. 6, *de Apparitione Christi in monte Galilaea*, Lugd., 1622, p. 449.

54 The proof of the resurrection may be formulized thus:

Jesus Christ is truly the Son of God, if he rose from the dead as he foretold; and he truly rose from the dead, if the apostles, in believing and preaching his resurrection, were not deceived or did not deceive. Now, they were not deceived and did not deceive.

They were not deceived. The resurrection of the Savior was a palpable fact, a fact which fell under the senses. It was not once only that the Savior appeared to the apostles, but many times; it was not in a dream nor in a passing manner that he showed himself to them, but in broad daylight, during forty consecutive days. They speak to him. They see him with their eyes. They touch him with their hands. They eat with him. They are assembled in full numbers when he appears. They at first refuse to believe it, and it is only on the evidence, or, so to speak, on the palpability of the fact that they yield. They declare throughout the whole world that they have seen him risen; they maintain it without ever contradicting themselves, and they lay down their lives to confirm their testimony. The apostles, therefore, had all desirable proofs of the resurrection of their master. Therefore, they were not deceived.

They did not deceive. a) They had nothing to gain by an imposition. On man's side, they had everything to fear—hatred, contempt, the vengeance of the laws; on God's side, the punishments reserved for impostors and blasphemers. b) Even though they should have had some interest to serve by an imposition, they could not succeed, because they would have had no solid proof to give of the resurrection of their master. The Jews, the pagans, the whole world, would refuse to believe them. Yet the Jews, the pagans, the whole world, believed and still believe in the resurrection. This great miracle, this evident proof of the divinity of Jesus Christ, awakened the admiration of men, and led them to renounce idolatry, and to embrace and defend, even at the risk of their lives, a religion which enters into contest with all the passions. Therefore, the apostles did not deceive.

On the other hand, they were not deceived. Therefore, the Savior truly rose from the dead; therefore, he is truly the Son of God; therefore, his religion is divine; therefore, under pain of damnation, it is necessary to believe what it teaches and to practice what it commands.

See, on the proofs of the resurrection, Duvoisin, *Démonstr. évang.*; Bergier, art. *Résurrection*; Bourdaloue, M. Frayssinous, etc.

In the *Bibliothèque des Pères*, by M. Guillon, Origène, t. 2, p. 64, 87, 93; Chrysostom, t. 14, p. 453, 461, 483; t. 15, p. 40, 67, 86.

55 Let us conclude the history of the mortal life of our Lord with the portraits of his Person and divinity traced by two very different hands, by two men not to be suspected of much partiality—Rousseau and Napoleon.

"I acknowledge," says the philosopher of Geneva, "that the majesty of the scriptures astonishes me. The sanctity of the gospel speaks to my heart. How insignificant are the books of the philosophers, with all their pomp, when put in comparison with this! Can it be that a book at once so simple and so sublime is the work of men? Does it breathe the tone of an enthusiastic or an ambitious sectary? What gentleness! What purity of manners! What a touching grace in its instructions! What an elevation in its maxims! What profound wisdom in its discourses! What presence of mind! What elegance and precision in its answers! What a dominion over the passions! Where is the man, where is the wise man, who knows how to act, to suffer, and to die, without weakness, without ostentation? When Plato painted his imaginary just man, overwhelmed with all the opprobriums of crime, and worthy of all the rewards of virtue, he painted Jesus Christ to perfection. The resemblance is so striking that all the fathers of the Church have perceived it, and no one can mistake it…

"How prejudiced and blind must one be to dare compare the son of Sophroniscus with the Son of Mary! What a distance between these two! Socrates, dying without ignominy, had little trouble in maintaining his dignity to the end; and if this easy death did not render honor to his life, it would be doubted whether Socrates, with all his spirit, was anything else than a sophist. But where did Jesus find among his acquaintances that pure and elevated morality of which he alone could give a lesson and an example? From the midst of the most furious fanaticism is heard the loftiest wisdom, and from a people wholly materialized comes forth the simplicity of the most heroic virtues. The death of Socrates, calmly philosophizing with his friends, is the sweetest that can be desired. The death of Jesus, in a sea of torments, outraged, mocked, cursed by a whole people, is the most horrible that can be feared. Socrates, taking the poisoned cup, blesses him who, weeping, presents it. Jesus, in the height of his most dreadful sufferings, prays for his cruel executioners.

"Yes, if the life and death of Socrates are those of a sage, the life and death of Jesus are those of a God. Shall we say that the history of the gospel was invented for amusement? No, it was not thus invented: the facts concerning Socrates, of which no one doubts, are less firmly supported than those concerning Jesus Christ. This, in the main, would only be to elude the difficulty, not to remove it. How far more unreasonable to imagine a number of persons combining to make up this book, than that one should furnish in his life its subject! Never did Jewish authors possess either its tone or its morality. The gospel has characteristics of truth so great, so striking, so perfectly inimitable, that the inventor, if such an individual could have existed, would be a more wonderful man than the hero."

Let us now hear the illustrious captive of St. Helena. As a general was one day discussing with him the divinity of our Lord, Napoleon replied:

"I have a knowledge of men, General, and I tell you that Jesus is not a mere man. Shallow minds imagine that they perceive a resemblance between Christ and the founders, conquerors, and gods of empires. This resemblance does not exist: between Christianity and every other religion the distance is infinite.

"The first comer will decide the question as I do, if he has a proper knowledge of things, and has had some experience of men. Who is there among us, General, that, beholding the different worships of nations, cannot tell their authors to the face: 'No, you are neither gods yourselves nor agents of the divinity. You have no mission from heaven. You are formed of the same slime as the rest of mortals; you are made with all the passions, and with all the vices that are their inseparable companions, so that it has been necessary to deify them with you. Your temples and priests themselves proclaim your origin. Are fables, and abominations, and rotten wood, the religions and the gods that are to be put in comparison with Christianity?'

"For my part, I say: No.

"In Lycurgus, Numa, Confucius, Mahomet, and the rest, I behold legislators, but nothing that reveals the divinity: even they themselves did not carry their pretensions so high. They excelled in their time, as I myself have done but in no respect did they appear divine beings. So far from it, I observe many affinities between them and me—I discover in them weaknesses and errors and other resemblances that bring them near to me and to humanity in general.

"It is not so with Christ. Everything about him astonishes me: his mind exceeds and his will confounds my feeble understanding. Between him and anyone else in the world there is no comparison. He is a being apart. His birth—his life—his death—the depth of his doctrine, which touches the greatest difficulties and is the most admirable solution of them—his mysterious singularity—his empire—his onward march through centuries and kingdoms—all is a mystery, which plunges me into a reverie from which I cannot recover; a prodigy, whose existence I cannot deny and cannot explain.

"Here I see nothing that speaks of man.

"You refer to Caesar and Alexander, their conquests, and the enthusiasm which they could enkindle in the heart of the soldier to draw him with them into daring expeditions; but in all this we need only behold the reward of the soldier's love, the ascendancy of genius, the glory of victory, the natural result of military discipline, the work of an experienced commander. But how many years did the Empire of Caesar last? How long did the enthusiasm of the soldiers of Alexander continue? The fame of these great leaders rose and fell with the chances of war. If victory had left them, do you doubt that admiration for them would have ceased? I ask you, did the military influence of Caesar and Alexander end with their lives—yes or no?

"Can you conceive a departed hero making conquests with an army wholly devoted to his memory? Can you conceive a phantom having soldiers without pay or prospects in this world, and inspiring them to the endurance of all kinds of privations? The body of Turenne was yet warm when his army fled before Montecuculli; and I—my armies forget me who am yet alive, as the Carthaginian army forgot Hannibal! Such is the power that falls to us great men! A single battle lost hurls us to the ground and robs us of our friends! How many a Judas have I seen near me!

"And now for my last argument: there is no God in heaven if a man has been able to conceive and execute with full success the design of usurping the divine worship by taking the name of God. Jesus is the only one who has attempted it. He alone has said clearly, has affirmed calmly: I am God—an expression very different from this one: I am a god. There is no mention in history of any other individual who gave himself the title of God in an absolute sense...How, then, has a Jew—whose existence is more certain than that of any other man who flourished in his time—a carpenter's son, been able, alone, to announce himself as God, the being of beings, the Creator of all things?

"He claims for himself all kinds of adoration. He builds his worship with his hands, not making use of stones, but men...And how, by a prodigy surpassing all other prodigies, does he seek the love of men, that is, the thing in the world most difficult to obtain, and all at once succeed?...I hence conclude his divinity. Alexander, Caesar, and Hannibal failed. They conquered the world; they have not gained a friend. I am, perhaps, the only person in our days who has any love for Hannibal, Caesar, or Alexander... It is true we love our children; but how many ungrateful children! Do your children, General, love you? You love them, but you are not sure of their love in return.

"Christ speaks, and henceforth the generations of men belong to him by closer and stronger bonds than those of blood, by a union more sacred and necessary than any other whatsoever...All those who sincerely believe in him feel that superior love of which the great destroyer, time, can neither waste the strength nor limit the duration. This is what I, Napoleon, admire most, because I have thought of it much: it proves absolutely to me the divinity of Christ...

"I enamored the multitudes who died for me. Would to God that I could form any comparison between the enthusiasm of my soldiers and the ardor of Christian charity, which are as different as their causes! But there was a necessity for my presence, for a word of mine, for my accent, for the electric flash of my look; then the sacred fire was kindled in hearts. Without a doubt I possess the secret of that magic power which rouses the mind; but I am not able to communicate it to anyone: none of my generals have learned it of me. Neither am I able to eternize my name and my love in hearts.

"Now that I am in St. Helena,...now that I am chained alone on this rock, who wages war and conquers empires for me? Where are the partners of my misfortunes? Does anyone think of me? Who in Europe troubles himself with my concerns? Who remains faithful to me? Where are my friends? Yes, two or three of you, whose fidelity will immortalize you, share my exile."

Here the voice of the emperor assumed a tone of melancholy, irony, and touching sadness, as he continued: "Yes, my existence shone with all the brilliancy of the diadem, with all the brilliancy of sovereignty; and yours, General, reflected that brilliancy, as the dome of the Invalides reflects the rays of the sun...But changes have come. The gilding has little by little disappeared: the rain of misfortune, with which I am every day drenched, and the storm of insults, which every day sweeps over me, have removed the last particles of it...We are only lead, General, and in a little while I shall be clay.

"Such is the destiny of great men, the Caesars and the Alexanders! We are forgotten; and the name of a conqueror, like that of an emperor, is useful only for a college theme! Our exploits fall under the rod of a pedant, who magnifies or annihilates us!...Yet a moment, and this shall be my lot...Assassinated by the English oligarchy, I die before my time, and my corpse shall soon be laid in the earth to become the food of worms...This is the approaching fate of the great Napoleon...What an abyss between my misery and the glory of Christ, who, still living everywhere throughout the world, is preached, incensed, loved, and adored by men!...Is this to die? Such was the death of Christ, the death of God!"

The emperor was silent, and the general was silent too. At length the former added: "If you do not understand that Jesus Christ is God—well, General, I cannot help you!"*

* *Sentim. de Napoléon sur le Christ*, Ch. 4—This noble plea is composed of various remarks that fell from the emperor in several conversations.

56 But cannot a person say with J. J. Rousseau: "I only know this miracle, like the rest, through men. Who witnessed this miracle? Men. Who have related it to me? Men. Always men between God and me! Would it not be more simple that God should speak to myself?"

It well became this haughty sophist to adopt an insulting tone against the God who had given him not only existence but the talents which he abused in the most revolting blasphemies! How did Rousseau know the existence, the conquests, the tragic end of Caesar, unless by the testimony of the generations appearing during the last eighteen centuries? Between these events and him there were many men: Did he on this account consider himself dispensed from the necessity of believing them, or rather would he not have been regarded as a madman if he did not believe them? He would desire that God should speak to himself; and why to him rather than to anyone else?

Did he suppose that the fire of his imagination was a title of preference in the eyes of him who esteems virtue and innocence in the highest degree? It would, therefore, be necessary that God should manifest himself by special revelations to every individual of the human species, that he should continually interfere with the natural order of things, and that he should multiply miracles beyond number, rendering them so common that they would lose all the splendor and force of miracles, and consequently be useless. For here would terminate the pretensions of a proud and foolish wisdom (M. Frayssinous, *Conférence sur la Résurrection*).

57 Cf. Chrysostom: *Cur in Pentecost. Acta leguntur*. (See M. Guillon, t. 14, Ch. 9, p. 464; and Origen, t. 2, p. 88, 89.)

58 Cf. 1 Cor 15:6

59 It is held as certain that the Blessed Virgin was the first visited by our Lord. (See Canisius, *De Maria V. Deipara*.)

60 This is the opinion of St. Jerome, St. Augustine, Theophylactus, etc.

61 To see and to believe are very different things; we believe that which we do not see, we do not believe that which we see. Hence, St. Thomas, who saw and touched Jesus Christ risen, had not, properly speaking, any faith in the resurrection, while we have this faith, we who believe in the resurrection of Jesus Christ without having seen him. Herein we are declared by Jesus Christ to be more blessed than Thomas, and even than all the other apostles, who only gave their assent to the dogma of the resurrection on the testimony of their eyes and their hands. Still Thomas made a most noble act of faith in confessing the divinity of his master, because he did not see it, and it was only by the revelation of the heavenly Father that he could, like Peter, know it.

62 Dubitatum est ab illis, ne dubitaretur a nobis (Leo the Great, *Sermon 71, qui est de Ascensions Domini*, I, Ch. 1).

63 J. J. Rousseau, *Lettre de la Montagne*

64 See *Eclaircissements sur les Sacrifices*, by M. de Maistre.

65 Cf Isaias, passim

66 Jn 1:29

67 Cf. 1 Jn 3:8

68 Sine sanguinis effusione non fit remissio (Heb 9:22).

69 Qui cum in forma Dei esset, non rapinam arbitratus est esse se aequalem Deo, sed semetipsum exinanivit, formam servi accipiens, in similitudinem hominum factus, et habitu inventus ut homo (Phil 2:6-7).

70 Et Verbum caro factum est (Jn 1:14). Eum, qui non noverat peccatum, pro nobis peccatum fecit, ut nos efficeremur justitia Dei in ipso (2 Cor 5:21).

71 Ego autem in medio vestrum sum, sicut qui ministrat (Lk 22:27).

72 Ps 21:7

73 Ipse se tantum humiliavit, ut ultra non posset; propter quod Deus tantum exaltavit, ut ultra non posset (Anselm).

74 Quaelibet satisfactio Christi suffecisset ad redemptionem, propter infinitam dignitatem personae (Aquinas, *Quodlibetal Questions*, Q. II, q. 1, a. 2).

75 Virum dolorum (Is 53:3).

76 Assumpsit dolorem in summo, vituperationem in summo (Cf. *Summa Theologiae*, III, q. 46, a. 6).

77 Propter quod et Deus exaltavit illum, et donavit illi nomen quod est super omne nomen: ut in nomine Jesu omne genu flectatur caelestium, terrestrium, et infernorum (Phil 2:9–10).

78 The plenitude of grace and truth that inundated our Lord by reason of the hypostatic union did not permit him to be subject to ignorance or concupiscence.

79 Omnia autem ex Deo qui nos reconciliavit sibi per Christum: et dedit nobis ministerium reconciliationis. Quoniam quidem Deus erat in Christo, mundum reconcilians sibi... (2 Cor 5:18-19).

80 Nam expectatio creaturae revelationem filiorum Dei expectat; vanitati enim creatura subjecta est non volens, sed propter eum qui subjecit eam in spe, quia et ipsa creatura liberatur a servitute corruptionis, in libertatem gloriae filiorum Dei. Scimus enim quod omnis creatura ingemiscit, et parturit usque adhuc (Rom 8:19-22).

81 Augustine, *On Original Sin*, Ch. 28

82 Jn 15ff

83 Cf. Rom 5:1; 1 Cor 15; Eph 4

84 Sicut revera homines nisi ex semine Adae propagati nascerentur, non nascerentur injusti, cum ea propagatione per ipsum dum concipiuntur propriam injustitiam contrahunt: ita, nisi in Christo renascerentur, nunquam justificarentur, cum ex renascentia per meritum passionis ejus, gratia qua justi fiunt, illis tribuatur (Council of Trent, Session 6, "Decree on Justification," Ch. 3).

85 Gal 5:2

86 Acts 4:12

87 Cf. Chrysostom, *Sermon, De Parascev.*

88 Et nos ipsi primitias spiritus habentes, et ipsi intra nos gemimus adoptionem filiorum Dei expectantes, redemptionem corporis nostri. Spe enim salvi facti sumus (Rom 8:23).

89 Yet the Savior, who, by offering himself to his Father at the very moment of original sin, had obtained for us the grace of this trial, was pleased in his infinite goodness to render it by coming into the world much less painful, much less hazardous than it was before his incarnation. This is one of the great advantages of the new law over the old.

A word regarding this touching mystery. By his coming, our Lord wonderfully diminished the consequences of sin. We have seen what he did to remedy ignorance and concupiscence. Since the time of his coming, a fuller and richer light has shone upon the world. The thick darkness of idolatry has disappeared. Virtues of the noblest character, little understood by heathens—chastity, humility, charity under all its forms—have been practiced in all their perfection by millions of the human family in every age, rank, and country. Consider, also, that the most abundant graces continually flow to the world by the seven channels that run from heaven to earth, the seven sacraments of the law of charity.

In regard to temporal evils, he proportionally ameliorated the condition of the physical man: a) for the law of universal hatred which reigned before his coming he substituted the law of universal charity; b) he abolished slavery—the sale, abandonment, and murder of children—the combats of gladiators, authorized by law among pagan peoples; c) he proscribed polygamy and divorce, which, making woman the vilest of creatures, condemned half the human race to degradation and tears; d) he made the poor, the sick, the imprisoned, sacred beings; e) he inspired the most tender compassion for all kinds of human miseries; f) he attacked those irregular passions which are the source of a multitude of diseases—a fundamental but neglected truth, which he proclaimed repeatedly, when he said to the sick whom he had healed: "Go, you are now cured, but sin no more, lest some worse thing happen you"; g) he rendered sufferings amiable by making known their true value; h) he surrounded death with hopes and consolations; i) he communicated to our bodies, by the august sacrament of the Eucharist, the tangible germ of a glorious resurrection. Were we to ask for anything more, would it not be to wish for eternity in time, heaven on earth, home in exile?

90 Cf. Rohrbacher, *De la Grace et de la Nature*, p. 39

91 Cf. Eph 1:10-23; Col 1:16-20

92 Acts 9:4

93 Mt 25:35ff

94 Lk 10:16

95 Mt 25:40

96 1 Cor 15:49; Cf. 2 Cor 3:18; Heb 2:14

97 See endnote 59, taken from St. Thomas, on p. 349 of Volume X of the Tradivox series.

98 Sicut fuit vetus Adam effusus per totum hominem et totum occupavit, ita modo totum obtineat Christus qui totum creavit, totum redemit, totum et glorificabit (Bernard, *Sermon 4, De Adv.*, n. 2-3).

99 See Introduction, "Union of man with the new Adam," p. 26-27 of Volume X of the Tradivox series.

100 Cf. Council of Trent, Session 6, Can. 3

101 Jn 3:18

102 Cf. Alphonsus Liguori, *Homo apost.*, t. 1; *Tract. 4*, n. 13

103 Cf. Rom 10:10

104 1 Cor 13:2

105 Mk 16:16

106 Heb 11:6

107 Dedit eis potestatem filios Dei fieri, his qui credunt in nomine ejus (Jn 1:12).

108 Ut credatis quia Jesus est Filius Dei: et ut, credentes, vitam habeatis in somine ejus (Jn 20:31).

109 Censores divinitatis haeretici (Tertullian, *Contra Marcion*, Bk. 2, Ch. 2).

110 Nonne cum omni fiducia de Deo dicere poterimus: Domine, si error est, a te ipso accepimus; nam ista in nobis tantis signis et prodigiis confirmata sunt, et talibus, quae nonnisi per te fieri possunt (Ricard. a S. Vict., *De Trinit.*, Bk. 1, Ch. 1). Quisquis adhuc prodigia ut credat inquirit, magnum est ipse prodigium, qui mundo credente non credit (Augustine, *City of God*, Bk. 22, Ch. 8, n. 1).

111 Mt 18:3

112 For proofs hereof, see Hermias, *De Irrisione philosophorum*; and Barruel, *Les Helviennes*.

113 The large *Traité de la Religion*, by Bergier, t. 3, 4, and 9, and Pere Crasset, on *La Foi Victorieuse*, may be consulted in regard to the mysteries.

114 *Histoire ecclésiastique*

115 Jb 38:11

116 Cf. Jn 17:11, 22

117 Cf. Rousseau, *Lettres de la Montagne*, p. 34

118 Cf. Bergier, t. 9, p. 9

119 Tertullian, *De Corona Militis*, Ch. 3

120 See Tertullian, quoted above; Lactantius, *The Divine Institutes*, Bk. 4, Ch. 26; Basil, *On the Holy Ghost*, Ch. 25; Gregory of Nyssa, *Life of St. Gregory Thaumaturgus*, Vol. 2, p. 980; Chrysostom, *Homily 55 on Matthew*;

Augustine, *City of God*, Bk. 22, Ch. 8; Ignatius of Antioch, *Epistle to the Philadelphians*; our *Treatise on the Sign of the Cross*, etc.

121 Augustine, *City of God*, Bk. 22, Ch. 8

122 Porro, cum in mensa sederis, coeperisque frangere panem, ipso ter consignato signo Crucis...gratias age (Athanasius, *De Virginitate*, n. 13).

123 Ne ergo Christi crucem erubescamus, sed si quis alius abscondat, tu palam ad frontem obsignato, ut daemones regium signum intuentes, tremuli procul aufugiant. Signo autem isto utere, tum edens ac bibens, tum sedens ac cubans, de lecto surgens, loquens, ambulans, et, ut semel dicam, in omni negotio...Non pudeat igitur nos crucifixum confiteri, sed in fronte confidenter signaculum crucis digitis imprimatur, et in aliis omnibus crux fiat: in panibus comedendis, et in poculis bibendis, et in egressu et ingressu, ante somnum, recumbendo et surgendo, eundo et quiescendo. Magna haec custodia, quae propter pauperes gratis datur: sine labore propter infirmos, cum a Deo sit haec gratia signum fidelium, et timor daemonum: triumphavit enim de illis in hoc signo: Ostenta illud audacter, quando enim viderint crucem recordantur Crucifixi. Metuunt enim qui contrivit capita draconis. Neque propterea quod est gratuitum condemnas hoc signavulum; sed ideo magis venerare benefactorem (Cyril of Jerusalem, *Catechetical Lecture* 4, n. 14, 18).

124 Rufinus, in his *Explanation of the Creed or Symbol*—found among the works of St. Cyprian—says: *Symbolum dici potest et indicium et collatio, hoc est quod plures in unum conferunt. Id enim Apostoli fecerunt in his sermonibus, in unum conferendo quod unusquisque senserit: indicium autem per quod agnosceretur ille qui Christum vere secundum apostolicas regulas praedicaret. Proinde discessuri ad praedicandum, istud unanimitatis et fidei suae indicium posuerunt, ut si quis occurreret forte de quo dubitaretur, interrogatus Symbolum agnosceretur an esset hostis an socius: quemadmodum symbola quaedam vel secreta verborum signa militibus ad eos dignoscendos traduntur.*

Similia apud Maximum *Taurinensem* in *Homily, De traditione ac expositione Symboli.*

On the necessity of the Symbol, St. Thomas speaks thus: *Necessarium fuit fidei veritatem in unum colligi, ut facilius posset omnibus proponi, ne aliquis per ignorantiam fidei a veritate deficeret. Et ab hujusmodi sententiarum fidei collectione nomen Symboli est acceptum...Veritas fidei in sacra scriptura diffuse continetur et variis modis et in quibusdam obscure; ita quod ad eliciendum fidei veritatem ex sacra scriptura requiritur longum studium et exercitium, ad quod non possunt pervenire omnes illi quibus necessarium est cognoscere fidei veritatem, quorum plerique aliis negotiis occupati studio vacare non possunt, et ideo necessarium fuit ut ex sententiis sacrae scripturae aliquid manifestum summarie colligeretur...quod quidem non est additum sacrae scripturae, sed potius ex sacra scriptura assumptum* (*Summa Theologiae*, II-II, q. 1, a. 9).

125 Editor's note: The Athanasian Creed, also known as *Quicumque Vult*, may be found in Volume VI of this series.

126 Ps 115:15

127 Editor's note: See Volume X of the Tradivox series.

128 De apostolis possumus dicers: Credimus Paulo, sed non credimus in Paulum; credimus Petro, sed non credimus in Petrum...Quid est ergo credere in Deum? Credendo amare, credendo diligere, credendo in eum ire, et ejus membris incorporari (Augustine, *Tractate 29 on John*, n. 6).

129 Necessarium est homini accipere per modum fidei non solum ea quae sunt supra rationem, sed etiam ea quae per rationem cognosci possunt. Et hoc propter tria. Primo quidem, ut citius homo ad veritatis divinae cognitionem perveniat. Scientia enim ad quam pertinet probare Deum esse et alia hujusmodi de Deo, ultimo hominibus addiscenda proponitur, praesuppositis multis aliis scientiis. Et sic non nisi post multum tempus vitae suae homo ad Dei cognitionem perveniret. Secundo, ut cognitio Dei sit communior. Multi enim in studio scientiae proficere non possunt, vel propter hebetudinem ingenii; vel propter alias occupationes et necessitates temporalis vitae; vel etiam propter torporem addiscendi. Qui omnino a Dei cognitione fraudarentur nisi proponerentur eis divina per modum fidei. Tertio modo, propter certitudinem. Ratio enim humana in rebus divinis est multum deficiens, cujus signum est quia philosophi, de rebus humanis naturali investigatione perscrutantes, in multis erraverunt et sibi ipsis contraria senserunt. Ut ergo esset indubitata et certa cognitio apud homines de Deo, oportuit quod divina eis per modum fidei traderentur, quasi a Deo dicta, qui mentiri non potest (*Summa Theologiae*, II-II, q. 2, a. 4, c.).

130 Dt 32:6; Cf. Mal 2:10

131 Rom 8:15

132 1 Jn 3:1

133 Rom 8:17

134 Rom 8:29

135 Cf. Heb 2:11

136 Mt 17:19

137 Jas 1:6-7

138 Lk 12:5

139 Lk 1:49

140 Jn 1:3

141 Gn 1:2

142 Ps 32:6

143 Lk 1:31. On the respect due to the name of Jesus, see "Feast of the Circumcision," Volume IV [i.e., Volume XIII of the Tradivox series].

144 Cf. Lv 8:30; 1 Kgs 10:1

145 Cf. Lk 1:33

146 Cf. Bellarmine, *Dottrina Cristiana*, p. 22

147 Is 53:8

148 The Profession of Faith of the Council of Trent

149 1 Cor 2:2

150 Jn 1:1, 14

151 Cf. *Catechism of the Council of Trent* [see p. 75 of Volume VII of the Tradivox series], and our *Traité du Saint-Esprit*, t. 1

152 Cf. Natal. Alexand., *De Symbol.*, p. 154

153 Cf. Bellarmine, *Dottrina Cristiana*, p. 29; Natal. Alexand., *De Symbol.*, p. 162

154 Sicut anima rationalis et caro unus est homo: Ita Deus et homo unus est Christus (The Athanasian Creed).

155 Nec solius carnis mater est, sed hominis Dei, sicut alias matres solius corporis genitrices nemo recte dixerit, quamvis animam non pariant: concipiunt enim et pariunt hominem anima corporeque constantem (Cyril, *Epistle, Ad Monach.*).

156 Lk 1:31-32; Cf. Lk 1:35

157 Cf. Lk 1:43

158 Cf. Gal 4:4

159 Si quis non confitetur Emmanuelem verum Deum esse, et ob id sanctam Virginem Deiparam, genuit enim ilia incarnatum Dei Verbum secundum carnem, anathema sit. (See Canisius, *De Maria V. Deipara*, Bk. 3, Ch. 19; Natal. Alexand., *De Symbol.*, p. 162; and all theologians.)

160 Cf. Augustine, *De Diversis Quaestionibus Octoginta Tribus*, q. 11; *Summa Theologiae*, III, q. 31, a. 4, c.

161 Cf. Natal. Alexand., *De Symbol.*

162 Cf. Bellarmine, *Dottrina Cristiana*, p. 26

163 We speak elsewhere of the time, place, and circumstances of Mary's divine childbearing.

164 Nova nativitate genitus est, conceptus a virgine, natus ex virgine, sine paternae carnis concupiscentia, sine maternae integritatis injuria; quia futurum hominum Salvatorem talis ortus decebat, qui et in se haberet humanae substantiae naturam, et humanae carnis inquinamenta nesciret (Leo the Great, *Sermon 2, De Nativ.*; Natal. Alexand., *De Symbol.*).

165 Gn 3:16

166 Cf. Jn 1:13; Rom 6:4

167 Dolor meus in conspectu meo semper (Ps 37:18).

168 Quis tibi imputabitsi perierint omnes nationes terrae? (Cf. Ws 12:12).

169 Cf. Lk 24:7; 9:22; 24:26

170 Cf. *Summa Theologiae*, III, q. 46, a. 6, c.

171 Etsi Christus pro omnibus mortuus sit, non omnes tamen mortis ejus beneficium recipiunt; sed ii duntaxat quibus meritum passionis ejus communicatur (Council of Trent, Session 6, "Decree on Justification," Ch. 3).

172 Cf. Bellarmine, *Dottrina Cristiana*, p. 35.

173 Cf. Tacitus, *The Annals*, Bk. 15

174 This is the remark of Eusebius of Caesarea in his *Ecclesiastical History*, Bk. 2, Ch. 2. It is justified by facts. Thus, we see that Pliny the Younger wrote to Trajan about what he had done in Asia against the Christians, etc.

175 Justin Martyr, *Second Apology*, Ch. 35, 48

176 Tertullian, *Apology*, Ch. 5. On the latter important fact, some very interesting details will be found in our work *Les Trois Rome*.

177 Tertullian, *Apology*, Ch. 21

178 Eusebius, *Ecclesiastical History*, Bk. 2, Ch. 2

179 Cf. See Sandini, *Hist. Familiae Sacrae*, Ch. 15

180 See our *Histoire des Catacombes*, p. 20-100.

181 Bellarmine, *Dottrina Cristiana*, p. 26

182 Deus conditor ac Redemptor noster claustra inferni penetrans, electorum exinde animas eduxit; nos illo ire non patitur, unde jam alios descendendo liberavit. Hi vero qui ante ejus adventum in hunc mundum venerunt, quantamlibet justitiae virtutem haberent, e corporibus educti in sinu coelestis patriae statim recipi nullo modo poterant; quia nondum ille venerat qui inferni claustra sua descensione solveret et justorum animas in perpetua jam sede collocaret (Gregory the Great, *Moralia in Job*, Bk. 13, Ch. 43).

Omnia etenim traxit qui de electis suis apud inferos nullum reliquit. Omnia abstulit, utique electa; neque enim infideles quosque et pro suis criminibus aeternis suppliciis deditos, ad veniam Dominus resurgendo reparavit; sed illos ex inferni claustris rapuit, quos suos in fide et actibus recognovit. Unde etiam recte per Osee dicit: "Ero mors tua, O mors; ero morsus tuus, inferne!" (Gregory the Great, *Homily 12 on the Gospels*).

In ultimo per novissimum omnes, qui ab initio discipuli, emundati et abiuti quae sunt mortis, in vitam venient Dei...Sicut Jeremias dicit: "Rememoratus est Dominus sanctus Israel mortuorum suorum, qui praedormierunt in terra defossionis," et descendit ad eos, uti evangelizaret eis salutare suum ad salvandum eos...Passio ejus expergefactio est dormientium discipulorum, propter quos et descendit in inferiora terrae (Irenaeus, *Against Heresies*, Bk. 4, Ch. 22).

Praedicavit Dominus iis quoque qui erant apud inferos...si qui sunt collocati apud inferos, ipsi sunt qui divinam audierunt virtutem et vocem; nam quis sanae mentis, et justorum et peccatorum animas esse existimaverit in una condemnatione injustitiae, maculem inurens Providentiae? Quid vero? an non significant Dominum annuntiasse evangelium, et iis (Cf. 1 Pt 3:19-20), qui perierant in diluvio, vel potius vincti fuerant, et iis qui in praesidio continebantur et custodia?...Dominus nulla alia de causa descendit ad inferos, quam ut annuntiaret evangelium...Anima ergo Christi animabus praedicavit evangelium (Clement of Alexandria, *The Stromata*, Bk. 6, ,p. 637).

Ob id porro deificata anima ad inferos descendit, ut quemadmodum his qui in terra versabantur, "Justitiae Sol" ortus erat, ita etiam illis qui subtus terram in tenebris et umbra mortis sedebant, illuceret. Ac sicut iis qui in terra erant, pacem, captivis remissionem, caesis visum evangelizaverat, atque illis quidem qui crediderant salutis auctor exstiterat; incredulos autem infidelitatis arguerat; sic etiam iis qui in inferno erant: ut ipsi "omne genu flecteretur, coelestium, terrestrium, et infernorum" (Phil 2:10). Hoc pacto, solutis illis qui ab omni aevo tenebantur, ipse rursus a morte ad vitam rediit, viam nobis ad resurrectionem sternens (John Damascene, *An Exposition of the Orthodox Faith*, Bk. 3, Ch. 22; Cf. Augustine, *City of God*, Bk. 20; Tertullian, *On the Soul*, Ch. 55; Justin Martyr, *Dialogue with Trypho*; Athanasius, *in illud: Omnia mihi tradita sunt*, p. 105; Cyril of Jerusalem, *Catechetical Lecture 4*; Gregory of Nyssa, *Oration 1, in Christi resurrectione*; Ambrose, *De Incarnat. Domini*, Ch. 5, n. 40; *et omnes sancti Patres*).

183 Lk 23:43

184 Cf. Bellarmine, *Dottrina Cristiana*

185 Ps 138:15; Eph 4:9

186 Cf. Jon 2; Mt 12:40

187 Ps 97:1

188 Quamvis autem in scripturis interdum legamus Christum Dominum a Patre suscitatum esse; hoc ad eum ut ad hominem referendum est; quemadmodum illa rursus ad eumdem ut Deum spectant quibus significatur eum sua virtute resurrexisse (*Catechism of the Council of Trent* [see p. 100 of Volume VII of the Tradivox series]).

189 Apoc 1:5; Cf. 1 Cor 15:20

190 Rom 6:9

191 1 Cor 15:21-22

192 *Si quis post acceptam justificationis gratiam, cuilibet peccatori poenitenti ita culpam remitti et reatum aeternae poenae deleri dixerit, ut nullus remaneat reatus poenae temporalis exsolvendae vel in hoc saeculo, vel in futuro in purgatorio, antequam ad regna coelorum aditus patere possit, anathema sit* (Council of Trent, Session 6, Can. 30).

Si quis dixerit totam poenam simul cum culpa remitti semper a Deo, satisfactionemque. poenitentium non esse aliam quam fidem, qua apprehendunt Christum pro eo satisfecisse, anathema sit (Council of Trent, Session 14, Can. 12).

Si quis dixerit missae sacrificium tantum esse laudis, et gratiarum actionis, aut nudam commemorationem sacrificii in cruce peracti, non autem propitiatorium; vel soli prodesse sumenti; neque pro vivis et defunctis, pro peccatis, poenis, satisfactionibus, et aliis necessitatibus offeri debere, anathema sit (Council of Trent, Session 22, Can. 3).

Nothing wiser than these decrees. The council did not decide whether or not purgatory is a particular prison in which souls are confined; in what manner they are purified—whether by fire or otherwise; what is the severity or the duration of their punishment; to what extent they are relieved by the prayers and good works of the living and by the Holy Sacrifice of the Mass; whether this sacrifice effects their deliverance *ex opere operato* or otherwise, and whether it benefits all in general or only those for whom it is specially offered. Every theologian may hold his own views on these different questions; but, as they are not dogmas of faith, matters of absolute certainty, no one is obliged to follow him (Holden, *De Resol. fid.*, Bk. 2, Ch. 6, § 1 and 2; Veron, *Regul. fid. Cathol.*, Ch. 2, § 3, n. 5, and § 6; Bossuet, *Exposit. de la Foi*, art. 8; Bergier, art. *Purgatoire*).

193 2 Mc 12:45-46

194 Cf. Josephus, *War of the Jews*, Ch. 91; M. Drach, *De la Prière pour les morts chez les Juifs.*

195 Cf. Mt 12:31

196 *Apostolic Constitutions*, Bk. 6, Ch. 30

197 Cf. Tertullian, *De Corona Militis*, Ch. 3

198 Cyprian, *Epistle 9*

199 Chrysostom, *Homily 59, to the People of Antioch*

200 Augustine, *Sermon 172*

201 Cf. Augustine, *De Haeresibus*, n. 53, 75

202 Isidore, *Book of the Divine Offices*, Ch. 315

203 Cyril of Jerusalem, *Catechetical Lecture 23*, n. 9

204 Calvin, *Institutes of the Christian Religion*, Bk. 3, Ch. 5, n. 70

205 Dispute at Leipsic, July 6, 1519

206 See Bergier, art. *Liturgis.*

207 The liturgy in the collection of prayers, rites, and ceremonies which pertain to the divine worship.

208 *Perpétuité de la Foi*, t. 5, p. 610; *Discussion amicale*, t. 2, p. 257; Morin, *Prière pour les morts*; *Histoire de l'Acad. des inscrip.*, t. 2, p. 121

209 Cf. Plato, *Gorgias*

210 Cf. Virgil, *Aeneid*, Bk. 6, v. 33

211 Cf. Justin Martyr, *Second Apology*

212 Cf. Tertullian, *De Spectaculis*, Ch. 3

213 Cf. *Hist. de l'Acad. des inscript.*, t. 2

214 *Hist. de l'Acad. des inscript.*, t. 1, p. 270; t. 2, p. 124

215 2 Mc 12:46

216 Cf. Bergier, art. *Purgatoire*

217 Abd 1:15

218 *Fêtes Chrét.*

219 Sic igitur Christas ascendit in coelum propria virtute, primo quidem, virtute divina; secondo, virtute animae glorificatae, moventis corpus prout vult (*Summa Theologiae*, III, q. 57, a. 3).

220 Cf. *Summa Theologiae*, III, q. 57, a. 2

221 Quam mirifico mysterio noster Jesus Christus vel tactu corporis sui, vel transitu gloriae suae, omnem ad momentum creaturam sanctificat, vivificat et illustrat: aquas enim consecrat dum baptizatur; terram

sanctificat dum sepelitur; mortuos suscitat dum resurgit; coelestia glorificat dum ascendit ad coelum, et sedet ad dexteram Patris (Augustine, *Sermon 17, De Temp.*; Cf. Suares, t. 3, p. 3, dist. 5, sect. 2).

222 Cf. Eph 1:20-22

223 Cf. Bellarmine, *Dottrina Cristiana*, p. 45

224 Ad dexteram Dei dicitur honoris et felicitatis inenarrabilis celsitudo (Augustine, *Sermon 214*).

225 Jn 14:3

226 1 Jn 2:1-2

227 Ascendit super omnes caelos, ut impleret omnia (Eph 4:10).

228 Solemnitas haec, consummatio et adimpletio est reliquarum solemnitatum, et felix clausula totius itinerarii Filii Dei (Bernard, *Sermon 2, De Ascens.*). Dominicarum festivitatum omnium complementum (Epiphanius, *Oration, De Christi Assumpt.*).

229 Cf. *Mémoires sur saint Alphonse de Liguori*, t. 3, p. 728

230 Lessons 16ff

231 In cogitationibus enim impii interrogatio erit (Ws 1:9). Perversae enim cogitationes separant a Deo (Ws 1:3; Mt 15:19). Omne verbum otiosum quod locuti fuerint homines, reddent rationem de eo in die judicii. Ex verbis enim tuis justificaberis, et ex verbis tuis condemnaberis (Mt 12:36-37). Esurivi enim et non dedistis mihi manducare, etc. (Mt 25:42). Maledictus qui facit opus Dei negligenter (Cf. Jer 48:10). Omnes enim nos manifestari oportet ante tribunal Christi, ut referat unusquisque propria corporis, prout gessit, sive bonum, sive malum (2 Cor 5:10).

232 Cf. Mt 25:31ff

233 Cf. Jl 3

234 Jn 5:27

235 Acts 10:42

236 The thought that the iniquity of scandal-givers does not end with their lives, and that they are really responsible for the consequences of their scandal till the end of the world, is one of the best calculated to inspire the faithful with a lively horror of this diabolical sin. The *Catechism of the Council of Trent*, having the approbation of the Church, tells us positively that the torments of those who are condemned on account of scandal will go on increasing daily till the end of ages, in proportion as new crimes, occasioned by their pernicious example, will be committed in the world. It is only at the last judgment, therefore, that, the measure of their crimes being filled up, the sentence of their condemnation and punishment can be finally pronounced.

You may conclude hence how miserable must be the fate of the authors and abettors of heresies and schisms, of those who inundate society with abominable books, and of scandal-givers in general.

On the other hand, good example will every day bring forth new fruits of merit and reward for those who have given it, and the last judgment alone will determine the degree of their happiness and glory in heaven. So we are taught by the *Catechism of the Council of Trent*. Can anything be more consoling? (*Note de monseigneur l'évêque de Montauban, trad. du Catéch, du Conc. de Trente*).

237 Cf. Jl 3:2

238 Tunc veniet unicuique dies ille, cum venerit ille dies, ut talis hinc exeat, qualis judicandus est illo die. Ac per hoc vigilare debet omnis Christianus, ne imparatum eum inveniat Domini adventus: imparatum invenerit dies ille quem imparatum invenerit vitae hujus ultimus dies (Augustine, *Sermon 49, De Temp.*; *Sermon 16, De Verbis Domini*).

239 Et praedicabitur hoc evangelium regni in universo orbe, in testimonium omnibus gentibus; et tunc veniet consummatio (Mt 24:14).

240 Ne quis vos seducat ullo modo: quoniam nisi venerit discessio primum (2 Thes 2:3).

241 Discessio scilicet populorum a suis principibus et praesertim a romano Imperio et a romano Pontifice... Tunc denique a fide et a Christo (Menoch., Cornelius a Lapide, Ambrose, etc., etc.).

242 ...Et revelatus fuerit homo peccati, filius perditionis, qui adversatur, et extollitur supra omne quod dicitur Deus (2 Thes 2:3-4).

243 Cf. Rom 11:23-32

244 See the development and proof of this matter in our *Introduction à l'Histoire de la Famille*, p. 149-190.

245 Cf. Mt 24:3ff. On the space necessary to contain all men, even supposing them to rise from the dead with the same dimensions as they bore during life, see *Catéch. philosoph.*, by Feller, p. 563. This space is smaller than might at first be imagined.

246 Lk 21:28

247 Clothed, it is believed, with aerial bodies, so as to be visible to all eyes.

248 Illuminabit abscondita tenebrarum, et manifestabit consilia cordium (1 Cor 4:5). Spes hypocritae peribit (Jb 8:13).

249 Et ibunt hi in supplicium aeternum, justi autem in vitam aeternam (Mt 25:34-46).

250 ...Sedit aeternumque sedebit, infelix Theseus (Virgil, *Aeneid*, Bk. 6, v. 345).

251 Plato, *Phaedo*

252 Plato, *Gorgias*. It would be as easy as possible to multiply texts on this subject from profane authors. (See all the *Démonst. évangél.*) It is necessary, however, to observe that the dogma of eternal punishment has been altered both in Plato and Virgil: the latter has merely arranged in verse the errors of the former on pantheism and metempsychosis.

253 Mt 25:41; Cf. Mk 9:43, 45, 47

254 *Iniqui voluissent utique, si potuissent, sine fine vivere, ut potuissent sine fine peccare. Ostendunt enim quia in peccato semper vivere cupiunt, qui nunquam desinunt peccare dum vivunt. Ad magnam ergo justitiam judicantis pertinet ut nunquam careant supplicio, qui in hac vita nunquam voluissent carere peccato...Omnipotens Deus quia pius est, miserorum cruciatus non pascitur; quia vero justus est, ab iniquorum ultione in perpetuum non sedatur* (Gregory the Great, *Dialogues*, Bk. 4, Ch. 44). *Angeli vero mali in nihil moventur, nisi in ordine ad finem peccati superbiae ipsorum; et ideo in omnibus peccant mortaliter, quaecumque propria voluntate agunt* (*Summa Theologiae*, I-II, q. 89, a. 4, c.). The same must be said of the reprobate.

255 Vermis qui in damnatis ponitur, non debet intelligi esse materialis, sed spiritualis, qui est conscientiae remorsus, qui dicitur vermis, in quantum oritur ex putredine peccati, et animam affligit, sicut corporalis vermis ex putredine ortus affligit pungendo (*Summa Theologiae*, III-Sup., q. 97, a. 2).

256 Mt 19:28

257 1 Cor 6:3

258 See the texts of the fathers in Cornelius a Lapide (Cf. Mt 19:28; 1 Cor 6:3).

259 Mt 28:19

260 Acts 5:3, 4

261 1 Jn 5:7. On all that regards the Holy Ghost, see our *Traité du Saint-Esprit*, 2 vols., oct.

262 See *Summa Theologiae*, I, q. 36, a. 1-4; Hist. de l'Eglise, *Concile de Florence*, p. 547.

263 Labbe, *Act. concile*, etc.

264 It is forbidden, as is well known, to represent the Holy Ghost otherwise than under the form of a dove or a tongue of fire. (See Ferraris, verb. *Spirit. sanctus.*)

265 Nemo potest dicere, Dominus Jesus, nisi in Spiritu Sancto (1 Cor 12:3).

266 *Omnis qui dicit verbum in Filium hominis, remittetur illi; ei autem qui in Spiritum Sanctum blasphemaverit, non remittetur* (Lk 12:10; Cf. Mt 12:32; Mk 3:29). When explaining sin in general, we speak of sin against the Holy Ghost, and what must be understood by the impossibility of obtaining pardon for it.

267 See Antoninus, *Chronicon Partibus Tribus Distincta*, Pt. 3, tit. 2, Ch. 13; Bellarmine, *De Christ.*, Bk. 2, Ch. 1, n. 30.

268 Cf. *Hist. univ. de l'Eglise*, quinzième siècle; *Traité du Saint-Esprit*, ii, ad fin.

269 Spiritus sapientiae et intellectus, Spiritus consilii et fortitudinis, Spiritus scientiae et pietatis...Spiritus timoris Domini (Is 11:2-3).

270 Cf. Cyprian, *On the Lapsed*; Augustine, *Sermon, De Tim. Domini*; Gregory the Great, *Homily 19 on Ezechiel*

271 *Quantum ad secundum, scilicet quod dona ista sint necessaria ad salutem, probatur, quia supremum donorum et infimum sunt necessaria, ergo et intermedia. Nam dicitur de sapientia: Neminem diligit Deus, nisi qui cum sapientia habitat vel graditur* (Cf. Ws 7:28); *et de timore dicitur: Sine timore Domini nemo poterit justificari* (Cf. Ecclus 1:28). *Ergo et alia necessaria.* (Id., *ubi supra.*) St. Thomas develops this argument admirably. Here are the words with which he concludes: *In ordine ad finem ultimum supernaturalem, ad quem ratio movet secundum quod est aliqualiter et imperfecte formata per virtutes theologicas, non sufficit ipsa motio rationis, nisi desuper adsit instinctus et motio Spiritus Sancti, secundum illud* (Rom 8:14, 17): "*Qui Spiritu Dei aguntur, hi filii Dei sunt...et haeredes,*" *et in*

Psalm 142:10, *dicitur:* "*Spiritus tuus bonus deducet me in terram rectam*"; *quia scilicet in haereditatem illius terrae beatorum nullus potest pervenire, nisi moveatur et deducatur a Spiritu Sancto. Et ideo ad illum finem consequendum, necessarium est homini habere donum Spiritus Sancti* (*Summa Theologiae*, I-II, q. 68, a. 2, c.).

Sunt autem ipsa septem dona connexa ad invicem, ut unum non possit haberi sine altero (Antoninus, *id.*, *id.*, § 5.) *Sicut vires appetitivae disponuntur per virtutes morales in comparatione ad regimen rationis, ita omnes vires animae disponuntur per dona in comparatione ad Spiritum Sanctum moventem. Spiritus autem sanctus habitat in nobis per charitatem, secundum illud* (Rom 5:5): "*Charitas Dei diffusa est in cordibus nostris per Spiritum Sanctum, qui datus est nobis*"; *sicut et ratio nostra perficitur per prudentiam. Unde sicut virtutes morales connectuntur sibi invicem in prudentia, ita dona Spiritus Sancti connectuntur sibi invicem in charitate; ita scilicet quod qui charitatem habet, omnia dona Spiritus Sancti habet, quorum nullum sine charitate haberi potest* (*Summa Theologiae*, I-II, q. 68, a. 5, c.).

Gratia ista septiformis, id est septem donorum, amittitur per quodlibet mortale peccatum. Et ideo statutum fuit antiquitus, ut pro quodlibet mortali imponeretur poenitentia septennis ut patet (Cf. *Summa Theologiae*, II-II, q. 1). *Praedicandum est scilicet, sicut per peccatum abjicit a se septiformem gratiam Spiritus Sancti, ita per septennem poenitentiam satisfaciat et recuperet eam* (Antoninus, tit. 10, Ch. 1).

272 Dona sunt quidam habitus perficientes hominem ad hoc quod prompte sequatur instinctum Spiritus Sancti...Animus hominis non movetur a Spiritu Sancto, nisi ei secundum aliquem modum uniatur: sicut instrumentum non movetur ab artifice nisi per contactum aut per aliquam unionem. Prima autem unio hominis est per fidem, spem, et charitatem. Unde istae virtutes praesupponuntur ad dona, sicut radices quaedam donorum. Unde omnia dona pertinent ad has tres virtutes, sicut quaedam derivationes praedictarum virtutum (*Summa Theologiae*, I-II, q. 68, a. 4).

273 *Haec dona sunt septem Spiritus missi in omnem terram contra septem Spiritus nequam de quibus dicitur* (Cf. Mt 12:43-45): "*Vadit Spiritus immundus et assumit septem Spiritus nequiores se et ingressi habitant ibi.*" *Donum timoris expellit superbiam...Donum pietatis expellit Spiritum invidiae...Spiritus scientiae repellit Spiritum irae...Spiritus consilii fugat Spiritum avaritiae...Spiritus fortitudinis illuminat Spiritum tristem inertiae, quae propter taedium laboris subterfugit viriliter bona operari...Spiritus intellectus removet Spiritum gulae...Spiritus sapientiae obruit Spiritum, luxuriae...*(*Sum. Theol.*, tit. 10, Ch. 1, § 4; de Donis Spir. sanct., edit. Venet. 1681). See St. Bernard also, t. 1, p. 23, 43, edit. Paris, 1843.

274 Not that these two Spirits are equal. Far from it: there is an infinite distance between them. One is the Holy Ghost—God. The other is simply a creature—the devil, to whom God, in his adorable wisdom, has left a great deal of power.

275 Neque enim est ullum omnino donum absque Spiritu Sancto ad creaturam perveniens (Basil, *De Spirit. Sanct. oper.*, t. 3, p. 66).

276 Sapientia non habitabit in terra suaviter viventium (Cf. Jb 28:13).

277 Animalis autem homo non percipit ea quae Dei sunt (1 Cor 2:14).

278 Cf. Prv 26:14; Ecclus 33:29

279 We explained them in the "Public Life of the Messias," when treating of the Sermon on the Mount. *Beatitudo est ultimus finis humanae vitae...Ad finem autem beatitudinis movetur aliquis, et appropinquat per operationes virtutum, et praecipue per operationes donorum, si loquamur de beatitudine aeterna, ad quam ratio non sufficit, sed in eam inducit Spiritus Sanctus, ad cujus obedientiam et sequelam per dona perficimur. Et ideo beatitudines distinguuntur quidem a virtutibus et donis, non sicut habitus ab eis distincti, sed sicut actus distinguuntur ab habitibus* (*Summa Theologiae*, I-II, q. 69, a. 1, c.). *Plus requiritur ad rationem beatitudinis quam ad rationem fructus. Nam ad rationem fructus sufficit quod sit aliquid habens rationem ultimi et delectabilis. Sed ad rationem beatitudinis ulterius requiritur quod si aliquid perfectum et excellens. Unde omnes beatitudines possunt dici fructus, sed non convertitur. Sunt enim fructus quaecumque virtuosa opera in quibus homo delectatur; sed beatitudines dicuntur solum perfecta opera, quae etiam ratione suae perfectionis magis attribuuntur donis quam virtutibus* (*Summa Theologiae*, I-II, q. 10, a. 2, c.).

280 Bonorum enim laborum gloriosus est fructus (Ws 3:15).

281 Gal 5:22-23

282 Gal 5:19-21. See St. Thomas (*Summa Theologiae*, I-II, q. 70, a. 4, c.).

283 Cf. *Summa Theologiae*, I-II, q. 69-70

284 Cf. 2 Pt 1:4; Jn 3:1; Eph 1:13

285 Qui comincia la seconda parte del *Credo:* perchè la prima parte appartiene a Dio, la seconda alla Chiesa, sposa di Dio (Bellarmine, *Dottrina Cristiana*, p. 53). *Rectus confessionis ordo poscebat, ut Trinitati subjungeretur Ecclesia, tanquam habitatori domus sua, et Deo templum suum, et conditori civitas sua* (Augustine, *Enchiridion*, Ch. 56).

286 Cf. Natal. Alexand., *De Symbol.*, p. 310

287 Erunt duo in carne una, non in duobus, nec in tribus. Propterea relinquet homo patrem et matrem suam et adhaerebit uxori suae, certe non uxoribus. Quod testimonium Paulus edisserens refert ad Christum et Ecclesiam, ut primus Adam in carne, secundus in Spiritu monogamus sit. Et una Eva mater cunctorum viventium, et una Ecclesia parens omnium Christianorum; sicut illam maledictus Lamech in duas divisit uxores, sic hanc haeretici et plures lacerant Ecclesias, quae, juxta Apocalypsim Joannis, Synagoga magis diaboli appellandae sunt, quam Christi conciliabula (Jerome, *Epistle 123*, n. 12).

288 Congregazione d'uomini, i quali si battezzano, e fanno professione della fede e legge di Christo, sotto l'ubbidienza del sommo Pontefice Romano (Bellarmine, *Dottrina Cristiana*, p. 54). With this definition agree the following ones, taken from the fathers and theologians: *Ecclesia plebs sacerdoti adunata; pastori suo grex adhaerens* (Cyprian, *Epistle 69, ad Florent. Pupian.*). *Ecclesia est populus Dei toto orbe terrarum diffusus* (Augustine, *On the Catechizing of the Uninstructed*, Ch. 3). *Ecclesia est catholicorum congregatio* (Nicol., I, *Dist. 4, De Consecrat.*). *Ecclesia est congregatio fidelium* (Aquinas, passim).

289 Ut scias quomodo oporteat te in domo Dei conversari, quae est Ecclesia Dei vivi, columna et firmamentum veritatis (1 Tm 3:15).

290 Cf. Cornelius a Lapide, *in hunc loc.*

291 Cf. 2 Cor 11; Apoc 21

292 Cf. Eph 1; Col 1

293 Ecclesia enim non metaphorice duntaxat Christi corpus est, quomodo terrena civitas, respublica, aut exercitus corpus unum dicuntur, propter unitatem regiminis, consiliorumque in eumdem finem conspirantium communionem; vere namque, realiter et proprie Christi corpus est, ut colligitur ex apostolo (1 Cor 12:12): "Sicut enim," inquit, "corpus unum est, et membra habet multa, unum tamen corpus sunt: ita et Christus." Quae verba S. Augustinus exponens (*On Merit and the Forgiveness of Sins, and the Baptism of Infants*, Bk. 1, Ch. 31), ait: "Non dixit, 'ita et Christi,' sed 'ita est Christus': unum Christum appellans caput et corpus." Quod quidem incredibile videri non debet: "Si enim divina substantia longe distantior atque incomparabili diversitate sublimior, potuit propter nos ita suscipere humanam substantiam, ut una persona fieret, quanto credibilius alii homines sancti et fideles ejus fiunt cum homine Christo unus Christus!" Quod principium centies repetit Augustinus, praesertim (in *Expositions on the Psalms*): "Totus Christus caput et corpus est. Caput et membra unus Christus" (Natal. Alexand., *De Symbol.*).

294 Abbraccia tutti i fedeli, che sono sparsi per tutto il mondo, e non solamente quelli che ora vivono, ma ancora quelli che furono dal principio del mondo, e quelli che saranno sin alla fine del mondo (Bellarmine, *Dottrrina Cristiana*, p. 56).

295 Per varia tempora, per varias aetates, quasi per septem dies magnae hebdomadae totius temporis in praesenti militat (Ecclesia). Ita ut primus dies sit actus ab Adam usque ad Noe; secundus a Noe usque ad Abraham; tertius ab Abraham usque ad David; quartus a David usque ad transmigrationem Babylonis; quintus a transmigratione usque ad Christum; sextus a Christo usque ad Antichristum; septimus ab Antichristo usque ad finem mundi. Haec Ecclesia per vineam designata est in parabola a Christo dicta (Cf. Mt 20). Ab Abel justo usque ad ultimum electum qui nasciturus est in fine mundi, quot sanctos protulit tot quasi palmites misit, inquit (Gregory the Great, *Homily*; Antoninus, *Summa Theologica Moralis*, III, "Prolog.," p. 4. See also Augustine, *Epistle 102*, q. 3; Aquinas; Natal. Alexand., *De Symbol.*).

296 Dicitur etiam Ecclesia inchoasse aliquando ab adventu Spiritus Sancti in discipulos in die Pentecostes; et hoc non simpliciter, sed quantum ad plenitudinem in discipulorum personis et gratiis et quantum ad dilatationem ejus per orbem et fidem explicitam articulorum quae in veteri testamento fuerat implicita, eadem tamen substantia, ut ait Aug. (Antoninus, *Summa Theologica Moralis*, III, "Prolog.," p. 4).

297 Council of Florence, 1438; Council of Trent, Sesson 6, "Decree on Reformation," Ch. 1; Sesson 14, "Doctrine on the Sacrament of Penance," Ch. 7

298 Mt 16:18-19

299 Jn 21:15, 16, 17

300 Lk 22:31-32

301 Cf. Bossuet, *Serm. sur l'unité de l'Eglise*

302 Mt 28:18

303 Mt 28:19-20

304 See Filassier, p. 301.

305 Cf. Mt 22

306 Cf Mt 25:12

307 Mk 16:16

308 Cf. Lk 12:4-7

309 Cyprian, *On the Unity of the Church*, n. 6

310 See the texts in Natal. Alexand., *De Symbol.*, p. 320.

311 In the social order, the same maxim is also the *raison d'etre* of all political parties. Who profess it more boldly, who sanction it more terribly, than Socialists and Communists? Does not every clique endeavor to cry but louder than the others: "I alone possess the truth. Out of my teaching, my philosophy, my policy, that is to say, out of my bosom, there is no salvation for society"?

312 Cf. *Catechism of the Council of Trent* [see p. 128-144 of Volume VII of the Tradivox series]

313 See the censure of *Emile* by the Sorbonne.

314 Christus dilexit Ecclesiam et seipsum tradidit pro ea (Eph 5:25. See Natal. Alexand., *De Symbol.*, p. 329).

315 Omnes homines vult salvos fieri et ad agnitionem veritatis venire (1 Tm 2:4). Non est in alio aliquo salus. Nec enim aliud nomen est sub caelo datum hominibus, in quo oporteat nos salvos fieri (Acts 4:12).

316 Cf. Mi 4; Is 60

317 In nullum quippe nomen religionis, seu verum, seu falsum, coagulari homines possunt, nisi aliquo signaculorum vei sacramentorum visibilium consortio colligantur (Augustine, *Contra Faustum*, Bk. 19, Ch. 11). Nulla securitas unitatis, nisi ex promissis Dei Ecciesia declarata, quae super montem constituta, abscondi non potest; et ideo necesse est ut omnibus terrarum partibus nota sit (Augustine, *Contra Epistolam Parmeniani*, Bk. 3, Ch. 5). Ecclesia vera neminem lateat (Augustine, *Answer to Petilian the Donatist*, Bk. 2, Ch. 32).

318 Si quis autem videtur contentiosus esse: nos talem consuetudinem non habemus, neque Ecclesia Dei (1 Cor 11:16).

319 Cf. Jn 10

320 Cf. Jn 17:10, 11, 16

321 Eph 5:27; Cf. Mt 28:19

322 Irenaeus, *Against Heresies*, Bk. 1, Ch. 10, n. 2

323 This was said, in 1820, by Harms de Kiel.

324 See Bossuet, *Variations*; Cobbett, *Reformation*; Letters of P. Scheffmacher, etc.

325 See the account of the celebrated protestant traveler, Tavernier.

326 See the *Development of Christian Doctrine*, by the celebrated Dr. Newman, an Anglican minister recently converted.

327 See Jauffret, p. 288.

328 Cyprian, *On the Unity of the Church*, n. 5

329 See the monumental proofs hereof in our *Histoire des Catacombes*.

330 Bossuet, *Prem. instr. past, sur les promesses de l'Eglise*, n. 35. "There has always been," continues the same bishop, "one unfortunate fact against them, which they have not been able to hide: I mean their novelty. No one can change the bygone ages, or give them predecessors, or show them in possession. The Catholic Church alone fills all preceding centuries by a succession that cannot be denied. The law comes before the gospel; Moses and the patriarchs are in a direct line with Jesus Christ. To be expected, to come, to be recognized by a posterity that should last as long as the world: these are the characteristics of the Messias in whom we believe. He was yesterday, he is today, and he shall be forever and ever" (*Disc. sur l'Hist. universelle*, p. ii, toward the end).

331 Translator's note: The illustrious Pius IX died on Feb. 7, 1878, and was succeeded by his present Holiness Leo XIII, elected on Feb. 20.

332 Cf. Tertullian, *Prescription against Heretics*. See the texts of the fathers on the notes of the Church in Natal. Alexand., *De Symbol.*

333 Cf. Mt 10:22; Mk 13:13; Lk 21:17

334 Cf. 1 Jn 1

335 Unus panis et unum corpus multi sumus, qui de uno pane et de uno calice participamus (Cf. 1 Cor 10:17).

336 Voluntatem timentium se faciet et deprecationem eorum exaudiet (Ps 144:19).

337 Peccatores Deus non exaudit (Jn 9:31; Cf. *Summa Theologiae*, II-II, q. 83, a. 16).

338 Cf. Montagne, *Tractate, De Gratia*; Ferraris, art. "Merit. et Peccat."; *Summa Theologiae*, II-II, q. 113, etc.

339 See the celebrated Spanish catechism, by P. Cajetan, *of the Pious Schools*.

340 Cf. Augustine, *De Vera Religione*, Ch. 5-6; *Tractate 32 on John*; Ambrose, *On the Duties of the Clergy*, Bk. 1, Ch. 29

341 Cf. Augustine, *On the Care of the Dead*

342 Cf. 1 Cor 12:2; Eph 4:7; Rom 12:6

343 Haec et enim voluntas Dei sanctificatio vestra (1 Thes 4:3).

344 Cf. 1 Cor 5; Baronius, art. 55, 998, etc.

345 De Ségur; De la Baume, etc.

346 Et nunc, reges, intelligite, erudimini, qui judicatis terram (Ps 2:10).

347 Ego sum, ego sum ipse qui deleo iniquitates tuas (Is 43:25).

348 Non minor potestas necessaria est ad hominem ex impio justum reddendum, et animam a morte peccati suscitandam, quam ad mundi creationem, et corpora a morte suscitanda; ad haec autem infinitam et immensam Dei vim requiri certum est; potestas dimittendi peccata, antequam Deus homo fieret, nulli creatae naturae a Deo concessa est. Primus omnium Christus Salvator noster, ut homo, cum idem verus Deus esset, hoc munus a Patre accepit (Natal. Alexand., *De Symbol.*, p. 339).

349 Ut sciatis quia Filius hominis habet potestatem in terra dimittendi peccata, ait paralytico: Surge, tolle grabatum tuum, et vade in domum tuam (Mt 9:6).

350 Jn 20:22, 21, 23

351 Ipsa proprie Spiritum Sanctum pignus accepit, sine quo non remittuntur ulla peccata, ita ut quibus remittuntur consequantur vitam aeternam (Augustine, *Enchiridion*, Ch. 65). In typo unitatis Petro dedit potestatem, ut id solvetur in terris quod ille solvisset...Igitur pax Ecclesiae dimittit peccata, et ab Ecclesiae pace alienatio tenet peccata...Petra tenet, petra dimittit; columba tenet, columba dimittit; unitas tenet, unitas dimittit (Augustine, *On Baptism, against the Dontatists*, Bk. 3, Ch. 17-18). Cf. S. Fulgent., etc.

352 Cf. Augustine, *Enchiridion*, Ch. 64

353 Quodcumque solveris super terram, erit solutum et in caelis (Mt 16:19).

354 Non dico tibi usque septies, sed usque septuagies septies (Mt 18:22). Cf. Cornelius a Ladipe, *in hunc loc.*; Augustine, *Enchiridion*, Ch. 64, 83

355 Nemo sibi dicat: Occulte poenitentiam ago; apud Deum ago; novit Deus, qui omnia agnoscit, quae in corde ago. Ergo sine causa dictum est: Quae solveritis in terra, soluta erunt in coelo. Ergo sine causa, sunt claves datae Ecclesiae Dei. Frustramus evangelium Dei, frustramus verba Christi: promittimus quod ille negat (Augustine, *Homily* 29, Ch. 3, lib. L. *Homil.*; Cf. Council of Trent, Session 23, "The True and Catholic Doctrine, Touching the Sacrament of Order," Ch. 4).

356 Peccatum veniale non contrariatur habituali gratiae vel charitati, sed retardat actum ejus in quantum nimis inhaeret homo bono creato, licet non contra Deum. Et ideo ad hoc quod peccatum veniale tollatur, non requiritur quod infundatur aliqua habitualis gratia, sed sufficit aliquis motus gratiae vel charitatis ad ejus remissionem...et hoc modo per Eucharistiam et extremam unctionem et universaliter per omnia sacramenta novae legis, in quibus confertur gratia, peccata venialia remittuntur (*Summa Theologiae*, III, q. 87, a. 2-3; Aquinas, *Opusculum, De Symb.*). Editor's note: See p. 74 of Volume VI of the Tradivox series.

357 Cf. Ferraris, *Biblioth.*, art. *Peccatum*, 305, n. 51

358 In pueris non est nisi peccatum originale, quod non consistit in actuali deordinatione voluntatis, sed in quadam habituali deordinatione naturae...; et ideo remittitur eis peccatum...per infusionem gratiae et virtutum, non autem cum actuali. Sed adulto, in quo sunt actualia peccata, quae consistunt in deordinatione actuali voluntatis, non remittuntur peccata, etiam in baptismo, sine actuali immutatione voluntatis, quod fit per poenitentiam (*Summa Theologiae*, III, q. 86, a. 2, rep. 1). Licet ad remissionem peccati venialis non requiratur nova infusio habitualis gratiae, requiritur tamen aliquis gratiae actus, qui non potest esse in eo qui subjacet peccato mortali...Sed peccatum mortale excludit totaliter habitum gratiae, sine quo nullum peccatum, mortale vel veniale, remittitur (*Summa Theologiae*, III, q. 87, a. 4, rep. 2-3).

359 Sacramentalia sic appellantur, vel ex eo quod soleant adhiberi ad sacramenta efficienda, vel ministranda; vel ex eo quod aliqualem sequantur et imitentur virtutem sacramentorum (Ferraris, art. *Peccatum*, p. 306).

360 Per sacramentalia remittuntur peccata venialia ex opere operato, remote tamen, et mediate, quatenus nempe per preces Ecclesiae junctas rebus sacramentalibus, dum iis pie utimur, movetur Deus (etsi non

infallibiliter), ut in nobis excitet pios illos motus, quibus adnexa est remissio venialium, partim ex opere operantis, quatenus homo iis sacramentalibus pie utitur in remedium ac remissionem peccatorum suorum cum piis motibus displicentiae peccatorum, conversionis in Deum, amoris, adorationis, et hujusmodi (Ferraris, art. *Peccatum*, p. 305).

361 *Summa Theologiae*, III, q. 87, a. 3, c.

362 Cf. Ferraris, p. 306; *De Poenit.*, dist. 3

363 Cf. Ibid.

364 Cf. Ibid. See, in reference to the sacramentals, our *Traité de l'ean benite.*

365 This is not the place to speak of the punishments imposed on the souls in purgatory for venial faults. St. Augustine tells us that the sufferings of these souls surpass all that can be endured in this world: *Gravior erit ille ignis, quam quidquid homo potest pati in hac vita.* Let us only say a word of the punishment of original sin in children who die without baptism. Among the different opinions of theologians, we adopt that of St. Thomas, St. Bonaventure, St. Gregory of Nyssa, St. Augustine, Vasquez, Suarez, Solas, De Lessius, Bécan, Ariaga, etc. According to this opinion, children who die without baptism do not suffer any pain of sense, and will not suffer any after the last judgment; they only suffer, and will only suffer, the pain of loss, that is, the privation of the intuitive vision of God, but without any inward or outward grief—in other terms, without any sorrow or sadness on account of the loss of beatitude. This does not prevent the fact of dying without baptism being a great, an everlasting misfortune for the child (Ferraris, art. *Peccatum*, p. 307).

366 Cf. Bellarmine, *Dottrina Cristiana*, p. 60

367 Rom 8:11

368 Corpus resurgens erit idem numero, sed alio modo se habens, quia fuit mortale, et surget in immortalitate (*Summa Theologiae*, III-Sup., q. 79, a. 1, rep. 1).

369 Cf. Jb 19:25-27

370 1 Cor 15:53

371 Non esset resurrectio proprie, nisi idem homo repararetur (*Summa Theologiae*, III-Sup., q. 79, a. 2, c.).

372 The ablest philosophers, such as Leibnitz, Clarke, Niewentit, etc., remark with reason that, to secure the sameness of a resuscitated body, it is not necessary that it should exactly recover all the particles of matter of which it was previously composed. The original mold (*stamen originale*), they say, which, by nutrition, receives foreign matters, to which it gives a form, is, properly speaking, the fundamental and essential element of the human body: it does not change by losing or acquiring these accessory particles of matter. Hence it follows: a) that the figure and physiognomy of a man do not change essentially in his growth or development; b) that the human body can never exceed a certain size, whatever nourishment may be given it; and c) that it is impossible to restore by nutrition one mutilated member. Accordingly, a man is judged by common sense to have the same body at thirty as at fifteen, because the original mold and organic conformation are not essentially changed: every body has its peculiar cast, which can belong to no other (Bergier, art. *Résurrection.* See also *Summa Theologiae*, III-Sup., q. 80, a. 5).

373 Et ideo reducetur humana natura per resurrectionem ad statum ultimae perfectionis, qui est in juvenili aetate, ad quam terminatur motus crementi, et a qua incipit motus decrementi (*Summa Theologiae*, III-Sup., q. 81, a. 1, c.). Rationabilius est dicere quod auctor qui naturam condidit, in resurrectione naturam corporis integre reparabit. Unde quidquid defectus vel turpitudinis ex corruptione, vel debilitate naturae, sive principiorum naturalium in corpore fuit, totum in resurrectione removebitur; sicut febris, lippitudo et similia: defectus autem qui ex naturalibus principiis in humano corpore naturaliter consequuntur, sicut ponderositas, passibilitas et similia in corporibus damnatorum erunt; quos defectus ab electorum corporibus gloria resurrectionis excludet (*Summa Theologiae*, III-Sup., q. 86, a. 1, c.).

374 Augustine, *City of God*, Bk. 22, Ch. 14-20; and *Summa Theologiae*, III, q. 81ff. St. Augustine thinks that the martyrs will bear on their bodies the marks of their wounds. This will be no deformity. On the contrary, it will add to the splendor and lustre of these glorious champions of the faith (Cf. *City of God*, Bk. 22, Ch. 19).

375 Cf. Jb 19:25-27

376 Dn 12:2

377 Jn 11:24

378 *Boun-Dehesch*, Vol. 2, p. 411. According to the learned, the book from which this passage has been taken was written at least five hundred years before the Christian era.

379 Cf. Augustine, *City of God*, Bk. 22, Ch. 28

380 Cf. Jn 5:25-29

381 Cf. 1 Cor 15

382 Cf. 1 Thes 4:12

383 Tertullian, *Apology*, Ch. 48. See also the admirable treatise by the same father, *On the Resurrection of the Flesh*.

384 Cf. Jn 5:28-29

385 1 Cor 15:51-52

386 See the development of this argument in Tertullian, *On the Resurrection of the Flesh*; Augustine, *City of God*, Bk. 22, Ch. 5

387 Propria fides est Christianorum resurrectio mortuorum. Hanc resurrectionem in seipso caput nostrum Christus ostendit, et exemplum fidei nobis praestitit, ut hoc sperent membra in se quod praecessit in capite (Augustine, *Sermon 241*, otherwise, *Sermon 143, De Temp.*). See the passages of the fathers in Natal. Alexand., *De Symbol.*

388 Augustine, *City of God*, Bk. 22, Ch. 5

389 Cf. Jn 5:28-29

390 1 Cor 15:52

391 Cf. Mt 24:31. (See Cornelius a Lapide, *On 1 Corinthians*, Ch. 15, v. 52; *On 1 Thessalonians*, Ch. 2, v. 15.)

392 Jn 5:25, 28-29

393 Cf. 1 Cor 15:51, 22,

394 Cf. Bellarmine, *Dottrina Cristiana*, p. 62.

395 Is 25:8

396 Os 13:14

397 Cf. 1 Cor 15:26

398 Apoc 21:4

399 1 Cor 15:42

400 Mt 13:43

401 Cf. Phil 3:21

402 1 Cor 15:41

403 Cf. Augustine, *City of God*, Bk. 2, Ch. 18, 20; Bk. 22, Ch. 2; Jerome, *On Isaias*, Ch. 60

404 1 Cor 15:44. See St. Thomas, who enters into the most minute details regarding the state of risen bodies (Cf. *Summa Theologiae*, q. 82, a. 4, and the questions following). See also the general summary at the end of Volume IV of the catechism [i.e., Volume XIII of the Tradivox series].

405 Cf. 1 Thes 4:12

406 See Natal. Alexand., *De Symbol.*, p. 354ff.

407 Et ibunt hi in supplicium aeternum, justi autem in vitam aeternam (Mt 25:46). Justorum animae in manu Dei sunt, et non tanget illos tormentum mortis (Ws 3:1).

408 Cf. Augustine, *City of God*, Bk. 19

409 Cf. 1 Cor 2:9

410 Cf. Apoc 7:16; 21:4

411 Mt 25:21

412 On the manner in which we shall see God, see Natal. Alexand., *De Symbol.*, p. 370.

413 Cf. 1 Jn 3:2

414 1 Cor 2:9. (See further particulars regarding our future state in the last lesson of the catechism, Volume IV [i.e., Volume XIII of the Tradivox series].)

415 Et sic dotes tres respondent tribus virtutibus theologicis; scilicet visio fidei; spei vero comprehensio…; charitati vero fruitio vel delectatio (*Summa Theologiae*, III-Sup., q. 95, a. 5, c.).

416 Aureola est quoddam privilegiatum praemium privilegiatae victoriae respondens, etc. (*Summa Theologiae*, III-Sup., q. 96, a. 11, c.).

417 Soto (In iv *dist.* 49).

418 Cf. Apoc 14, *Gloss. in hunc loc.*

419 Cf. Augustine, *Sermon 1, De Sanctis*

420 Cf. Dn 13:3

421 Cf. Rom 10:10

422 Mt 10:32-33

423 Confitentur se nosse Deum, factis autem negant (Ti 1:16).

424 *Puto quod prima salutis initia, et ipsa fundamenta fides est; profectus vero et augmenta aedificii spes est; perfectio autem et culmen totius operis charitas est, et ideo major omnium dicitur charitas* (Origen, *On Romans*, Ch. 4). Origen does not mean, any more than we, to say hereby that faith is the first grace: a condemned proposition.—*Fides absolute praecedit spem. Objectum enim spei...proponitur nobis per fidem, per quam nobis innotescit quod ad vitam aeternam possumus pervenire, et quod ad hoc paratum est nobis divinum auxilium...In via generationis spes est prior charitate...Spes enim introducit charitatem inquantum aliquis sperens remunerari a Deo, accenditur ad amandum Deum et servandum praecepta ejus. Sed, secundum ordinem perfections, charitas prior est naturaliter, et ideo adveniente charitate, spes perfectior redditur, quia de amicis maxime speramus* (*Summa Theologiae*, II-II, q. 17, a. 7, c.; a. 8, c.).

425 Editor's note: See Volume X of the Tradivox series.

426 Cf. *Summa Theologiae*, II-II, q. 22, a. 1, c.

427 Cf. 1 Par 10:14

428 Cf. 1 Tm 6:17

429 Heb 11:6

430 Spe salvi facti sumus (Rom 8:24).

431 Cf. Mayol., *Praeambul. ad Decal.*, q. 2, p. 836

432 Ecclus 5:6-7

433 Perpetrare flagitium aliquod, mors animae est; sed desperare est descendere in infernum (Isidore, *De Summo Bono*, Bk. 2, Ch. 14).

434 See our *Histoire du bon Larron.*, one vol., duod.

435 See Augustine, *On Psalm 38*, n. 9.

436 Spes incedit usque ad interiora velaminis (Cf. Heb 6:19).

437 Proprium et principale objectum spei est beatitudo aeterna...Quaecumque alia bona non debemus a Deo petere nisi in ordine ad beatitudinem aeternam (*Summa Theologiae*, II-II, q. 17, a. 2, c.; rep. 2).

438 Quia et divina gratia Dei sit et largitio quodammodo ipsius divinitatis (Cassian, *De Incarn. Chr.*, Bk. 2, Ch. 6). Sic igitur per hoc, quod dicitur homo gratiam Dei habere, significatur quiddam supernaturale in homine a Deo proveniens (*Summa Theologiae*, I-II, q. 110, a. 1, c.).

439 Editor's note: See Volume XIII of the Tradivox series.

440 See our *Traité du Saint-Esprit*, t. 2.

441 Donum supernaturale creaturae intellectuali gratis a Deo concessum intuitu meritorum Christi Domini, in ordine ad vitam aeternam (Montag., *De Grat.*, art. 2).

442 Donum gratiae excedit omnem facultatem naturae, cum nihil aliud sit quam quaedam participatio divinae naturae, quae excedit omnem aliam naturam; et ideo impossible est quod aliqua creatura gratiam causet. Sic enim necesse est quod solus Deus deificet communicando consortium divinae naturae per quamdam similitudinis participationem, sicut impossibile est quod aliquid igniat, nisi solus ignis (*Summa Theologiae*, I-II, q. 112, a. 1, c.). Gratia quae est accidens est quaedam similitudo divinitatis participata in homine (*Summa Theologiae*, III, q. 2, a. 10, rep. 1). Assumptio quae fit per gratiam adoptionis terminatur ad quamdam participationem divinae naturae secundum assimilationem ad bonitatem illius, secundum illud 2 Pt 1:4: *Divinae consortes naturae* (*Summa Theologiae*, III, q. 3, a. 4, rep. 3). Ex dictis hucusque, colliges et S. Thoma aliisque post ipsum cummuniter theologis, supernaturalitatem primario et essentialiter consistere, tum in excellentia supra ordinem, exigentiam, et vires activas, tum physicas tum intentionales cujuslibet naturae tam creatae quam creabilis; id est, quod supernaturale dicitur, a nulla natura creata produci, aut intuitione cognosci potest; tum in mira Dei, ut in se est, communicatione, id est, in eximia quadam cum ipso Deo, qualis in se est spectato, conjunctione et unione; aut realis et physica, qualis est hypostatica unio; aut intentionali proxima, qualis est visio beatifica, aut intentionali mediata, et minus proxima, qualia sunt gratia sanctificans, virtutes theologicae, aliaque hujusmodi dona, quae ad assequendam ipsius Dei, sicut in se est, possessionem ex natura sua ordinantur, ac per se disponunt (Montag., *De Grat.*, a. 2).

443 Cum omne bonum meritum nostrum non in nobis faciat nisi gratia; cum Deus coronat merita nostra, nihil aliud coronat quam munera sua (Augustine, *Epistle 194*, otherwise *Epistle 105*, n. 19).

444 De plenitudine ejus omnes nos accepimus (Jn 1:16).

445 Gratia enim est qua praedestinati vocamur, justificamur, glorificamur (Augustine, *Epistle 117*).

446 Participes enim Christi effecti sumus, si tamen initium substantiae ejus usque ad finem firmum retineamus (Heb 3:14).

447 Si quis dixerit sine praevenientis Spiritus Sancti inspiratione atque adjutorio, hominem credere, sperare, diligere, aut poenitere posse sicut oportet ut ei justificationis gratia conferatur, anathema sit (Council of Trent, Session 6, Can. 3).

448 Oratio est gratiae certificatio (Augustine, *On the Grace of Christ*, Ch. 26, n. 27). Deus enim est qui operatur in vobis et velle et perficere (Phil 2:13). Nemo potest dicere, Domine Jesus, nisi in Spiritu Sancto (1 Cor 12:3).

449 Si quis dixerit justificatum sine speciali auxilio Dei in accepta justitia perseverare posse,...anathema sit (Council of Trent, Session 6, Can. 22).

450 Council of Trent, Session 6, Can. 13

451 1 Cor 15:10; Cf. Council of Trent, Session 6, "Decree on Justification," Ch. 11. Non ego autem, sed gratia Dei mecum, id est, non solus, sed gratia Dei mecum, ac per hoc nec gratia Dei sola, nec ipse solus, sed gratia Dei cum illo (Augustine, *On Grace and Free Will*, Ch. 5, n. 12).

452 Non quod sufficients aimus aliquid cogitare a nobis, quasi ex nobis; sed sufficients nostra ex Deo est (2 Cor 3:5). Deus impossibilia non jubet sed jubendo monet facere quod possis…et adjuvat ut possis (Council of Trent, Session 6, Can. 2).

453 Cf. *Summa Theologiae*, I-II, q. 113, a. 3

454 Vos semper Spiritui Sancto resistitis (Acts 7:51; Cf. Council of Trent, Sessions 4-6).

455 See p. 200 of Volume X of the Tradivox series.

456 Unicuique datur manifestatio Spiritus ad utilitatem (1 Cor 12:7).

457 Gratia habitualis justificans ea est qua homo formaliter justus evadit, dum ei quoddam esse divinum communicatur, et suo modo divinae fit particeps naturae (Montag., *De Grat.*, p. 810).

458 Momentanea illustratio intellectus, et motio voluntatis, qua Deus in nobis sine nobis efficit, ut scilicet bene velimus et bene agamus (Montag., *De Grat.*, p. 819).

459 Cf. *Summa Theologiae*, I-II, q. 110, a. 2

460 Augustine, *On Nature and Grace*, Ch. 29

461 Christus tanquam caput in membra, et tanquam vitis in palmites, in ipsos justificatos jugitur virtutem influit, quae virtus bona eorum opera semper praecedit, et comitatur, et subsequitur, et sine qua nullo pacto Deo grata et meritoria esse possunt (Council of Trent, Session 6, "Decree on Justification," Ch. 16).

462 Cf. 2 Cor 5

463 Malos non perire quia boni esse non potuerunt, sed quia boni esse noluerunt (Third Council of Valence, Can. 2).

464 Si quis dixerit justificatum, vel sine speciali auxillo Dei in accepta justitia perseverare posse, vel cum eo non posse, anathema sit (Council of Trent, Session 6, Can. 22).

465 Cf. Libermann, *Theol.*, t. 4, p. 33ff

466 Justitia importat rectitudinem quamdam ordinisin ipsa interiori dispositione hominis, prout scilicet supremum hominis subditur Deo, et inferiores vires animae subduntur supremae, scilicet rationi…Haec autem justitia…fit in homine secundum rationem motus, qui est de contrario in contrarium, et secundum hoc justificatio importat transmutationem quamdam de statu injustitiae aut statum justitiae praedictae (*Summa Theologiae*, I-II, q. 113, a. 1, c.). Effectus divinae dilectionis in nobis, qui per peccatum tollitur, est gratia, qua homo fit dignus vita aeterna, a qua peccatum mortale excludit, et ideo non posset intelligi remissio culpae, nisi adesset infusio gratiae (*Summa Theologiae*, I-II, q. 113, a. 2, c.). Si quis dixerit homines justificari vel sola imputatione justitiae Christi, vel sola peccatorum remissione, exclusa gratia et charitate, quae in cordibus eorum per Spiritum Sanctum diffundatur, atque illis inhaereat, aut etiam gratiam, qua jutificamur, esse tantum favorem Dei, anathema sit (Council of Trent, Session 6, Can. 11-13; Montag., *De Grat.*, p. 1066). In eo qui habet usum liberi arbitrii non fit motio a Deo ad justitiam absque motu liberi arbitrii; sed ita infundit donum gratiae justificantis quod etiam simul cum hoc movet liberum arbitrium ad donum gratiae acceptandum in his qui sunt hujus motionis capaces (*Summa Theologiae*, I-II, q. 113, a. 3, c.).

467 Opus propter quod Deus homini praemium rependere debet (Montag., *De Grat.*, p. 110).

468 Meritum de condigno est opus liberum, bonum, ab homine viatore et justo, ex actu vel imperio charitatis factum, et ideo in Deum ut summum bonum virtualiter saltem relatum, cui ex justitia (licet non rigorosa, ut aiunt) et ex gratuita Dei promissione vita aeterna a Deo debetur (Montag., *De Grat.*, p. 1115).

469 Cf. 1 Cor 13

470 Bonum gratiae unius majus est quam bonum naturae totius universi (*Summa Theologiae*, I-II, q. 113, a. 9, rep. 2).

471 Gal 2:20

472 Ferraris, verb. *Orat.*

473 Rom 10:13-14

474 Lk 11:9; Mt 7:7

475 Jas 4:2. See the authorities in Ferraris, art. *Cratio*; *Summa Theologiae*, II-II, q. 83, a. 2.

476 Cf. Lk 18:1

477 Cf. Col 4:2

478 1 Thes 5:17

479 Eph 6:18

480 Quisquis non orat Deum assidue, nec divino ejus colloquio cupit assidue frui, is mortuus est...Animae mors est non provolvi coram Deo (Chrysostom, *De Orando Deo*, Bk. 1).

481 Hic censeo habere locum doctrinam quam de praecepto divino poenitentiae suo loco tradidi, et pro his divinis praeceptis affirmativis, ut charitatis, et similibus censeo esse generalem et necessariam, nimirum obligare haec praecepta, ut actus eorum non multo tempore differantur, sed aliquoties in vita fiant, quoties videlicit ad rectam et honestam vitam instituendam prudenti arbitrio judicatum fuerit...Credo tam necessariam esse orationem ad rectitudinem vitae, ut non sit remittenda dilatio unius anni, nec fortasse unius mensis. Quod usus ipse fidelium satis confirmat, etc. (Montag., *De Grat.*, t. 17, Ch. 10, 86).

482 Lk 18:1

483 Cf. Cornelius a Lapide, *On Luke*, Ch. 18

484 Sine intermissione orare quid est aliud quam beatam vitam quae nulla quam nisi aeterna est...? Sine intermissione desiderate. Semper ergo hanc a Domino Deo desideremus, et oramus semper (Augustine, *Epistle 130*, Ch. 9). Semper orat, qui semper secundum Deum operatur. Semper orat, qui semper bene agit (Cornelius a Lapide, *On Luke*, Ch. 18, 2; Cf. *Summa Theologiae*, II-II, q. 83, a. 14).

485 Cf. Ferraris, art. *Orat.*, n. 10

486 Cf. Dn 6; Ps 54

487 Cf. 3 Kgs 8; 2 Par 6-7; Basil, *On Psalm 28*; Chrysostom, *Homily 36 on 1 Corinthians*; Augustine, *Tractate 1 on John*

488 Cf. Ferraris, art. *Orat.*, 115, 13; Montag., *De Grat.*, p. 1001-1002

489 Ambrose, *Of Cain and Abel*, Bk. 1, Ch. 6

490 Cf. *Summa Theologiae*, II-II, q. 83, a. 5-6

491 Cf. Pope Nicholas, *Responses to the Questions of the Bulgars*

492 Cf. 1 Cor 11:5; Cornelius a Lapide, *in hunc loc.*

493 Cf. *Summa Theologiae*, II-II, q. 84, a. 3

494 Cf. Mt 21:22

495 Cf. Jas 1:6

496 Si fides deficit, oratio perit (Augustine, *Sermon 36, De Verbis Domini*).

497 Pro certo non exaudiendum se supplicans quisque non dubitet, cum dubitaverit se exaudiri; signum futurae impetrationis esse, quando Spiritus Sanctus movet ad petendum cum magna fiducia, et quasi securitate impetrandi (Cassian, *Coll.* 9, Ch. 32).

498 Jesus significat Salvatorem...ac per hoc quodcumque petimus adversus utilitatem salutis, non petimus in nomine Salvatoris (Augustine, *Sermon 36, De Verbis Domini*).

499 Ecclus 35:21

500 Quomodo te audiri postulas, cum teipsum non audias? (Cyprian, *On the Lord's Prayer*, n. 31).

501 Quid est voce psallere, mente autem domum aut forum circuire, nisi homines fallere at Deum irridere? (Council of Treves, Ch. "De Hor.").

502 Cf. Mt 15:22-28

503 Cf. Lk 11:5ff

504 Lk 18:1

505 Cf. *Tract de Orat.*, Ch. 100, t. 17, p. 1064

506 Cf. Lk 11. Si peccatores non exaudiret Deus, frustra publicanus dixisset: Domine, propitius esto mihi peccatori (Augustine, *Tractate 44 on John*, n. 13).

507 Oratio principaliter innititur fidei, non quantum ad efficaciam merendi, quia sic innititur principaliter charitati; sed quantum ad efficaciam impetrandi, quia per fidem homo habet notitiam omnipotentiae divinae et misericordiae, ex quibus oratio impetrat quod petit (*Summa Theologiae*, II-II, q. 83, a. 15, rep. 3). Oratio sine gratia gratum faciente meritoria non est...et tamen etiam oratio quae impetrat gratiam gratum facientem procedit ex aliqua gratia, quasi ex gratuito dono, quia ipsum orare est quoddam donum Dei, ut Augustinus dicit, in lib. *De Dono Perseverantiae*, Ch. 23 (*Summa Theologiae*, II-II, q. 83, a. 15, rep. 1).

508 Orandum est ut sit mens sana in corpore sano (Juvenal, *Satire 10*, n. 356).

509 Ponuntur quatuor conditiones, quibus concurrentibus semper aliquis impetrat quod petit: ut scilicet pro se petat, necessaria ad salutem, pie et perseveranter (*Summa Theologiae*, II-II, q. 83, a. 15, rep. 2).

510 Supradictis quatuor conditionibus, oratio semper infallibiliter impetrat, et si non impetrat, provenit ex defectu alicujus ex dictis conditionibus, ut omnes ipsas egregie complectens dicit S. Basilius, *Serm. de orand. Deum;* ideo quando petis, et non accipis, est quia perperam postulasti, vel infideliter, leviter, vel non conferentia tibi, vel destitisti (Ferraris, art. *Orat.*, n. 27).

511 Orationem vero peccatoris ex bono naturae desiderio procedentem Deus audit, non quasi ex justitia, quia peccator hoc non meretur, sed ex pura misericordia, observatis tamen quatuor praemissis conditionibus, ut scilicet pro se petat, necessaria ad salutem, pie et perseveranter (*Summa Theologiae*, II-II, q. 83, a. 16, c.).

512 Fideliter supplicans Deo pro necessitatibus hujus vitae, et misericorditer auditur, et misericorditer non auditor. Quid enim infirmo sit utile, magis novit medicus quam aegrotus (Prosper, *Sententia ex Augustine*). Non nos hortaretur ut peteremus, nisi dare vellet; nunquam oranti beneficia denegat, qui ut orantes non deficiant, sua pietate instigat (Augustine, *Sermon 5, De Verbis Domini*; Cf. Chrysostom, *On Luke*, Ch. 18. See also St. Ephrem, etc.).

513 Cf. Jer 12:11

514 Is 44:19

515 Omnis profectus spiritualis ex meditatione procedit (Rufinus, *On Psalm 36*).

516 Absque meditationis exercitio, nullus, secluso miraculo Dei, ad Christianae religionis normam attingit (Gerson, *De Med. consid.*, n. 7).

517 Alphonsus Liguori, *The Great Means of Salvation and of Perfection*, Pt. 3, Ch. 1

518 Cf. Francis de Sales, *Introduction to the Devout Life*, Pt. 2, Ch. 9

519 Mt 15:8

520 Triplex est attentio quae orationi vocali potest adhiberi; una quidam qua attenditur ad verba, ne quis in eis erret; secunda, qua attenditur ad sensum verborum; tertia, qua attenditur ad finem orationis, scilicet ad Deum et ad rem pro qua oratur, quae quidem est maxime necessaria, et hanc etiam possunt habere idiotae (*Summa Theologiae*, II-II, q. 83, a. 13, c.). Prima est attentio ad verba quibus petimus, deinde ad petitionem ipsam; et quaecumque earum attentionum adsit, non est repetenda inattenta oratio (Aquinas, *Sentences*, IV, d. 15, q. 4, a. 2, qa. 5, ad qa.).

521 Cf. *Summa Theologiae*, II-II, q. 83, a. 12

522 Duplex est oratio, communis et singularis: communis quidem oratio est quae per ministros Ecclesiae in persona totius fidelis populi Deo offertur, etc. (*Summa Theologiae*, II-II, q. 83, a. 12, c.).

523 Editor's note: See Volume XIII of the Tradivox series.

524 Oratio vero singularis est quae offertur a singulari persona cujuscumque sive pro se, sive pro aliis orantis (*Summa Theologiae*, II-II, q. 83, a. 12, c.).

525 Cf. Mt 6

526 In oratione dominica non solum petuntur omnia quae recte desiderare possumus, sed etiam eo ordine quo desideranda sunt; ut sic haec oratio non solum instruat postulare, sed etiam sit infirmativa totius nostri affectus (*Summa Theologiae*, II-II, q. 83, a. 9, c.).

527 *Summa Theologiae*, II-II, q. 83, a. 9, c.

528 Regula postulandi fidelibus a coelesti jurisperito data (Augustine, *Exposition on Psalm 142*).

529 E la più necessaria di tutte (Bellarmine, *Dottrina Cristiana*, p. 71; Cf. Council of Rome, Can. 2). *Nisi qui has duas sententias (Symbolum et Orationem Dominicam) et memoriter tenuerit et ex toto corde crediderit, et in oratione saepissime frequentaverit, catholicus esse non poterit* (Syn. Remens., vi, Can. 7. See also the Fourth Council of Toledo, Can. 9; Augustine, *Enchiridion*, Ch. 71; Cyprian, *On the Lord's Prayer*). One is obliged by the necessity of precept to know, at least as regards their substance, a) the Apostles' Creed in full; b) the Lord's Prayer; c) the precepts of the decalogue; d) such of the commandments of the Church as are common to all the faithful; e) the sacrament of baptism, which each of the faithful may have occasion to administer, and the sacraments of penance and the Eucharist, which we are bound to receive at least once a year. As for the other sacraments, an explicit faith is necessary only for those who receive them. But the knowledge of these different articles has its degrees: it may be more or less perfect, more or less extensive. Still it is not permitted to be entirely ignorant of them. It is only want of capacity that can excuse from mortal sin (Monseigneur Gousset, *Theol. Mor.*, t. 1, p. 129).

530 Quoniam victuri sumus in isto saeculo, ubi quis non vivit sine peccato, ideo remissio peccatorum non est in sola ablutione sacri baptismatis, sed etiam in Oratione Dominica et quotidiana. In ilia invenietis quasi quotidianum baptismum vestrum (Augustine, *Sermon 213, De Temp.*; Cf. *Enchiridion*, Ch. 81).

531 Ante omnia pacis doctor atque unitatis magister singillatim noluit et privatim precem fieri, ut quis cum precatur, pro se tantum precetur...Publica est nobis et communis oratio; et quando oramus, non pro uno, sed pro toto populo oramus, quia totus populus unum sumus. Deus pacis et concordiae magister, qui docuit unitatem, sic orare unum pro omnibus voluit, quomodo in uno omnes portavit (Cyprian, *On the Lord's Prayer*).

532 Ipsum intelligimus sine qualitate bonum, sine quantitate magnum, sine indigentia creatorem, sine situ praesentem, sine habitu omnia continentem, sine loco ubique totum (Augustine, *On the Trinity*, Bk. 5, Ch. 1).

533 Verba enim ilia, quae tertiae petitioni adjuncta sunt: 'Sicut in caelo et in terra,' ad quamlibet primarum trium petitionum referri posse docet Concilii Tridentini Catechismus, ut sic intelligamus: Sanctificetur nomen tuum in caelo et in terra; adveniat regnum tuum sicut in caelo et in terra; fiat voluntas tua sicut in caelo et in terra." (Natal. Alexand., *De Orat. Dom.*, p. 1322). Editor's note: For this quote from the *Catechism of the Council of Trent*, see Volume VII of the Tradivox series, p. 528-529.

534 In his verbis quotidie fideles Christi petunt ut perseverent in eo quod esse coeperunt (Augustine, *On Rebuke and Grace*, Ch. 10).

535 Cf. Mt 6

536 Ps 144:13; Cf. Est 13:9-11

537 Augustine, *On Psalm 118*; Cf. Bellarmine, *Dottrina Cristiana*, p. 79

538 Mt 19:17

539 Phil 2:8

540 Is 6:3; Cf. Apoc 4:8

541 Acts 9:6

542 Ps 56:8

543 Jb 1:21

544 Mt 26:39

545 Omnes enim, quando oramus, mendici Dei sumus, ante januam magni patris familias stamus, imo et prosternimur, et supplices ingemiscimus, aliquid volentes accipere (Augustine, *Sermon 15, De Verbis Domini*).

546 Et quid eget dives? Audeo dicere, ipso pane quotidiano eget dives. Quare enim abundant illi omnia? unde, nisi quia Deus dedit? quid habebit, si Deus subtrahat manum suam? Nonne multi dormierunt dives, et sur rexerunt pauperes? et quod illi non deest misericordiae Dei est, non potentiae ipsius (Augustine, *Sermon 36, De Divers.*).

547 Neque qui plantat est aliquid, neque qui rigat, sed qui incrementum dat, Deus (1 Cor 3:7).

548 Cf. Cyril of Jersualem, *Catechetical Lecture 23*, n. 15

549 *Panem nostrum quotidianum da nobis hodie, Eucharistiam tuam, quotidianum cibum* (Augustine, *Sermon 58*). Hence St. Matthew calls this bread "supersubstantial," above every substance.

550 Cibus noster quotidianus in hac terra serrac Dei est, qui semper erogatur Ecclesiis (Augustine, *Sermon 56*). Quid vobis plus esse videtur, verbum Dei an corpus Christi? Si verum vultis respondere, hoc utique dicere debetis, quod non sit minus verbum Dei quam corpus Christi, et ideo quanta sollicitudine observamus, quando nobis corpus Christi ministratur, ut nihil ex ipso de nostris manibus in terram cadat; tanta sollicitudine observemus, ne verbum Dei, quod nobis erogatur, dum aliud aut cogitamus aut loquimur, de corde nostro depercat; quia non minus reus erit qui verbum Dei negligenter audierit, quam ille cui corpus Christi in torram cadere negligentia sua per miserit (Caesarius of Arles, *Sermon 95 in append. Augustin.*, 300).

551 Panis vitae Christus est, et panis hic omnium non est, sed noster est; et quomodo dicimus Pater noster, quia intelligentium et credentium Pater est; sed et panem nostrum vocamus, quia Christus noster (qui ejus corpus contingimus) panis est (Cyprian, *On the Lord's Prayer*, n. 18).

552 Cf. Auct., *Oper. imperf. in* Ch. 6 *Matt.*

553 Panem nostrum dicimus, et tamen ut detur oramus. Noster quippe fit cum accipitur, qui tamen Dei est, quia ab illo datur (Gregory the Great, *Moralia in Job*, Bk. 24, Ch. 7, n. 13).

554 1 Tm 6:8

555 Cf. Mt 6

556 Bellarmine, *Dottrina Cristiana*, p. 88

557 Conducit Dominica Oratio ad impetrandum etiam lethalium peccatorum veniam, cum peccator, deposito hujusmodi criminum affectu, sinceroque dolore compunctus quod Deum offenderit…ait: "Pater, peccavi in caelum," etc. (Natal. Alexand., *De Orat. Domin.*, p. 1358).

558 Cf. 1 Cor 4:4

559 Cf. 1 Jn 1:10

560 Cf. Council of Trent, Session 6, Can. 23

561 Si soli debent dicere: Dimitte nobis, etc., qui diligunt inimicos, nescio quid faciam, nescio quid dicam… Dicturus enim vobis sum: Si non diligitis inimicos vestros, nolite orare? non audeo, imo, ut diligatis, orate. Sed numquid vobis dicturus sum: Si non diligitis inimicos vestros, nolite in Oratione Dominica dicere: Dimitte nobis debita nostra, sicut et nos dimittimus debitoribus nostris? Puta quia dico: Nolite orare? Si non dixeritis, non dimittuntur; si dixeritis, et non feceritis, non dimittuntur. Ergo dicendum est et faciendum, it dimittantur (Augustine, *Sermon 5*, otherwise *Sermon 56*).

562 Cf. Mt 6:15; 18:35

563 Eph 4:26

564 Cf. Cyril of Jerusalem, *Catechetical Lecture 23*, n. 17-18; Ambrose, *On the Sacraments*, Bk. 5, Ch. 4; Augustine, *Epistle 121*, Ch. 11

565 Cf. 2 Cor 12:7ff

566 Plantas nutriunt venti, et tentatio confirmat animae fortitudinem (Nilus of Sinai).

567 Ecclus 34:9

568 Beatus vir qui suffert tentationem, quoniam cum probatus fuerit accipiet coronam vitae (Jas 1:12).

569 Deus enim intentator malorum est, ipse autem neminem tentat (Jas 1:13).

570 Cf. 1 Cor 10:13

571 Cf. Cyprian, *On the Lord's Prayer*

572 Propter sanctiorem auctoritatem…servata est antiquitas (Augustine, *On Christian Doctrine*, Bk. 2, Ch. 11).

573 Absolutis precibus et gratiarum actione, quilibet de populo qui adest, faustis vocibus acclamat: Amen (Justin Martyr, *Second Apology*).

574 Cf. Bellarmine, *Dottrina Cristiana*, p. 95

575 Opus est mediatore ad mediatorem Christum, nec alter nobis utilior quam Maria (Bernard, *Sermon, De Assumpt.*, final one).

576 Lk 1:28

577 Lk 1:42

578 Cf. Council of Ephesus

579 Cf. *Lives of the Saints*, September 24

580 Cf. Bernard, *Sermon 2, sup. Miss.*—Quemadmodum continua respiratio non solum est signum vitae, sed etiam causa; sic sanctissimum Mariae nomen, quod in Dei servorum ore assidue versatur, simul

argumentum est, quod vera vita vivant, simul etiam hanc vitam ipsam efficit et conservat, omnemque eis laetitiam et opem ad omnia impertitur (Germanus, bishop of Constantinople, *in Orat. de Deip. Virg.*).

581 Bene plena, quia caeteris per partes praestatur, Mariae vero se tota infudit plenitudo gratiae (Jerome, *De Assumpt.*). Beata Virgo dicta est plena gratia, non ex parte ipsius gratiae, quia non habuit gratiam in summa excellentia (sicut Christus) qua potest haberi, nec ad omnes effectus gratiae, sed dicitur fuisse plena gratia per comparationem ad ipsam, quia scilicet habebat gratiam sufficientem ad statum illum ad quem erat electa a Deo, ut esset scilicet Mater Dei; et similiter Stephanus dicitur plenus gratia quia habebat gratiam sufficientem ad hoc quod esset idoneus minister et testis Dei, ad quod erat electus, et eadem ratione dicendum est de aliis. Harum tamen plenitudinum una est plenior alia, secundum quod aliquis est divinitus praeordinatus ad altiorem vel inferiorem statum (*Summa Theologiae*, III, q. 7, a. 10; Cf. Canisius, *De Maria V. Deipara*, Bk. 3, Ch. 6).

582 Cf. Bellarmine, *Dottrina Cristiana*, p. 97

583 Cf. Augustine, *On Nature and Grace*, Ch. 6

584 Dominus (*Filius*) tecum non tantum gratia, sed etiam natura, ex te factus homo; non tantum consensione voluntatis, sed etiam conjunctione carnis (Bernard, *Sermon 3, sup. Miss.*; Cf. Chrysostom, *Sermon 143*).

585 Cf. Rom 11

586 Lk 11:27

587 Sancta Dei Ecclesia eidem immortales gratias egit, quod vindex exstitisset Filii deitatis et Matris ejus honoris, utriusque praeconia illis vocibus celebrans, quas a sanctis sciret frequentatas esse Patribus, ubique locorum "Matrem Dei Mariam" omnium ore cantans, laudans atque praedicans. Tunc et additamentum illud accepisse creditur Angelica Salutatio: "Sancta Maria, Mater Dei, ora pro nobis," etc. Quod omnium Fidelium ore dici, ac frequentius repeti, et tanquam prima quaedam elementa piis parentibus una ferme cum lacte infantibus propinari consuevit: ut fieret secundum illum propheticum, "Ex ore indantium et lactentium perfecisti laudem tuam" (Ps 8:3; Mt 21:16), illuferentque superbo draconi pueruli (Baronius, *Anno* 431, t. 5, p. 457, n. 176, A).

588 Omnipotentia supplex.

589 Sileat misericordiam tuam, Virgo Beata, si quis eat qui invocatam te in necessitatibus suia sibi meminerit defuisse (*Sermon, De Nativ. B. Mar.*). Memorare, O piissima, etc.

590 Cf. *Raccolta d'indulgenze*, 258.

591 Cf. *Sup.*, 18; Bellarmine, *Dottrina Cristiana*, p. 100

592 See the explanation of the Hail, Holy Queen, in Canisius, *De Maria V. Deipara*, Bk. 5, Ch. 13 and in St. Alphonsus Liguori, *Glories of Mary*.

593 Ferraris, art. *Litan.*—Cum autem nemo ab historicis litaniarum auctor quamvis vetustissimus asseratur, quin eo antiquior litaniarum usus inveniatur, merito ab apostolis eas ducere originem censendum est (Quart., *Tract. Litan.*, Sect. 1, n. 4; Dilich., *Dict. Liturg.*, art. *Litan.*).

594 See the history of this occurrence in our work, *Les Trois Rome*.

595 Ferraris, art. *Litan.*—A quo litaniae primum fuerint institutae adhuc mihi est inexploratum, vetustissimum sane morem fuisse in Ecclesia litanias peragere certissimuin est (Baronius, *Annot*, ad *Martyrol.*, 25th April).

596 *Litaniis non possunt inseri alii Sancti praeter ibi descriptos* (Ferraris, art. *Litan.*).

On the 18th April, 1860, the Congregation of the Holy Office issued the following decree on the subject of litanies: *Litaniae omnes, praeter antiquissimas et communes, quae in Breviariis, Missalibus, Pontificalibus et Ritualibus continentur, et praeter Litanias de B. M. V. quae in sacra aede Lauretana decantari solent, non edantur sine revisione et adprobatione ordinarii, nec publice in ecclesiis, publicis oratoriis, et processionibus recitentur absque licentia et adprobatione Sacrorum Rituum Congregationis.* It follows hence a) that it is forbidden to publish particular litanies without episcopal revision and approbation;* b) that litanies, so approved by the ordinary, are only for private use; c) that, to introduce them into any public office, they must first be approved by the Congregation of Rites.

* It ought to be so with other prayers.

597 Ferraris, art. *Orat.*

598 Consentaneum visum est de sanctissimis Ecclesiae sacramentis agere, per quae omnia vera justitia vel incipit, vel coepta augetur, vel amissa reparatur (Council of Trent, Session 7, "Decree on the Sacraments," Proem.).

599 Eucharistia est...omnium sacramentorum finis. Per sanctificationes enim omnium sacramentorum fit praeparatio ad suscipiendam vel consecrandam Eucharistiam...sacramentum sacramentorum, quia sacramentis omnibus consummatam perfectionem confert (Cf. *Summa Theologiae*, III, q. 73, a. 3, c.).

600 Augustine, *City of God*, Bk. 10, Ch. 5; Cf. Augustine, *Epistle 2*. (See also Jerome, *On Amos*, Ch. 1, v. 1; Cyprian, *Epistle 15*; *On Baptism*; Ambrose, *On Baptism*.)

601 *Conférencier d'Angers*, t. 4, p. 7

602 Aliud oculis, aliud menti exhibet (Chrysostom, *Homily 7 on 1 Corinthinans*).

603 Cf. *Summa Theologiae*, III, q. 62, a. 2

604 Cf. *Summa Theologiae*, III, q. 63, a. 2-3

605 1 Pt 2:2

606 Cf. Augustine, *On Baptism, against the Donatists*, Bk. 1; *Summa Theologiae*, III, q. 63, a. 5—Si quis dixerit in tribus sacramentis, baptismo scilicet, confirmatione et ordine, non imprimi characterem in anima, hoc est signum quoddam spiritale et indelebile, unde et iterari non possunt, anathema sit (Council of Trent, Session 7, "On the Sacraments in General," Can. 9).

607 Ex opere operato.

608 Omnia sacramenta tribus perficiuntur, videlicet rebus tanquam materia, verbis tanquam forma, et persona ministri conferentis sacramentum, cum intentione faciendi quod facit Ecclesia: quorum si aliquod desit, non perficitur sacramentum.

609 Cf. Augustine, *Tractate 80 on John*

610 Augustine, *Tractate 2 on John*; *Tractate 6 on John*

611 Si quis dixerit in ministris, dum sacramenta conficiunt et conferunt, non requiri intentionem saltem faciendi quod facit Ecclesia, anathema sit (Council of Trent, Session 7, "On the Sacraments in General," Can. 11).

612 Cf. Heb 5

613 Cf. Council of Trent, Session 7, "On the Sacraments in General," Can. 10

614 Cf. Basil, *De Spiritu Sancto*; Council of Trent, Session 7, "On the Sacraments in General," Can. 13

615 Cf. 1 Cor 4

616 Auctor sacramentorum quis est, nisi Dominus Jesus? De coelo ista sacramenta venerunt (Ambrose, *On the Sacraments*, Bk. 4, Ch. 4).

617 Dominus noster Jesus Christus sacramentis numero paucissimis, observatione facillimis, significatione praestautissimis, societatem novi populi colligavit (Augustine, *Epistle 54 to Januarius*, n. 1).

618 Cf. Tertullian, *On the Resurrection of the Flesh*, Ch. 7

619 Cf. Justin Martyr, *Second Apology*

620 Cf. Tertullian, *Prescription against Heretics*, Bk. 40-41

621 Cf. Augustine, *Epistle 54 to Januarius*; *Answer to Petilian the Donatist*, Bk. 3, Ch. 14

622 Cf. Augustine, *Of the Good of Marriage*, Ch. 18, 24

623 Cf. Innocent I, *Epistle ad Decent.*; Chrysostom, *On the Priesthood*, Bk. 3

624 See *Pérpetuité de la Foi*.

625 Council of Trent, Session 7, "On the Sacraments in General," Can. 1

626 In quo omnes peccaverunt (Rom 5:12).

627 Divinae consortes naturae (2 Pt 1:4).

628 Gal 2:20

629 Si incorporeus esses, nuda ipse dona incorporea tradidisset tibi; quoniam vero corpori conjuncta est anima, in sensibilibus intelligenda tibi traduntur (Chrysostom, *Homily 83 on Matthew*).

630 Cf. Augustine, *Contra Faustum*, Bk. 19, Ch. 2

631 See the work of the celebrated Huet, bishop of Avranches: *Quaestiones Alnetanae*. It shows that there are found among every people some vestiges or rudiments of the seven sacraments.

632 Filii Dei...ego dixi: Dii estis (Jn 10:34; Ps 81:6). Sancti estote, quia ego sanctus sum (Lv 11:44).

633 Cf. Council of Trent, Session 7, "On the Sacraments in General," Can. 1; Council of Florence, Session 8, "Bull of Union with the Armenians"; *Summa Theologiae*, III, q. 65, a. 1

634 Cf. *Summa Theologiae*, III, q. 65, a. 1

635 Cf. Council of Trent, Session 7, "On Baptism"

636 Cf. Tertullian, *De Corona Militis*, Ch. 3

637 …Inquantum scilicet alicujus cor per Spiritum Sanctum movetur ad credendum et diligendum Deum, et poenitendum de peccatis; unde etiam dicitur baptismus poenitentiae (*Summa Theologiae*, III, q. 66, a. 11, c.).

638 Alia duo baptismata includuntur in baptismo aquae, qui efficaciam habet et ex passione Christi, et ex Spiritu Sancto, et ideo per hoc non tollitur unitas baptismatis…conveniunt cum baptismo aquae non quidem quantum ad rationem signi, sed quantum ad effectum baptismatis; et ideo, non sunt sacramenta (*Summa Theologiae*, III, q. 66, a. 11, rep. 1-2).

639 Cf. 1 Cor 14:40

640 Cf. *Conférencier d'Angers*, t. 8, p. 73

641 (Patrinus) non est de necessitate sacramenti; sed unus solus potest in aqua baptizare, necessitate imminente (*Summa Theologiae*, III, q. 67, a. 7).

642 Cf. Const. ap. Tertullian, *On Baptism*, Bk. 1, etc.

643 1 Pt 2:2

644 Cf. *Summa Theologiae*, III, q. 67, a. 7

645 Dionysius, *De Eccl. Hierosolym.*, Ch. 7, p. 3; Cf. *Summa Theologiae*, III, q. 68, a. 8

646 Cf. Gregory Nazianzus, *Oration, in Nat. Salv. circa finem*; Augustine, *Sermon 19, De Temp.*; *Sermon 37, De Temp.*

647 Jn 3:5

648 Cf. *Apostolic Canons*, Can. 50

649 Cf. Council of Trent, Session 5, Can. 5; Augustine, *Against Two Letters of the Pelagians*, Bk. 1, Ch. 13; Gregory the Great, *Register of Epistles*, Bk. 9; Councils of Vienne and Florence, *in mater. Sacram.* On the effects of original sin, see Volume I of this catechism, Lesson 16 [i.e., Volume X of the Tradivox series].

650 Cf. Augustine, *On Merit and the Forgiveness of Sins, and the Baptism of Infants*, Bk. 1, Ch. 39; Ambrose, *On Romans*, Ch. 2; *Summa Theologiae*, III, q. 69, a. 7; Gregory the Great, *Register of Epistles*, Bk. 7, Epistle 24

651 Cf. Council of Trent, Session 5, "Decree concerning Original Sin"

652 Cf. Council of Vienne, *De Summa Trinit. et Fide Cathol.*; Council of Trent, Session 6, "Decree on Justification," Ch. 7, 9

653 Si quis of the *chapt. Veniens de Presbyt. non baptiz.*

654 Augustine, *Tractate 11 on John*, n. 6; Cf. Council of Trent, Session 7, "On Baptism," Can. 11, 13

655 Ad verba aliena sanatur qui ad factum alienum vulneratur (Augustine, *Sermon 14, De Verbis Apostolis*, Ch. 2).

656 Lk 12:48

657 Cf. Ambrose, *On the Mysteries*; Chrysostom, *Homily 21, to the People of Antioch*

658 Jn 3:5

659 Council of Trent, Session 5, Can. 3; Cf. *Summa Theologiae*, III, q. 68, a. 1

660 Cf. Basil, *Homily, in fam. et siccitat*; Chrysostom, *Homily 72*

661 Cf. *Apostolic Constitutions*, Bk. 8, Ch. 32

662 Cf. Eusebius, *Life of Constantine*, Bk. 4, Ch. 61; Gregory Nazianzen, *Oration 20*; Socrates, *Historia Ecclesiastica*, Bk. 5, Ch. 17—*Impressuros baptismum jejuniis et pervigiliis orare oportet cum confessione omnium retro delictorum* (Tertullian, *On Baptism*, Ch. 28).

663 Sacramentary of St. Gelasius, of St. Gregory, Roman Ordo; Cf. Ambrose, *On the Mysteries*, Ch. 5; Cyril of Jerusalem, *Catechetical Lecture 20*; Jerome, *On John*, Bk. 12, Ch. 65; Optatus of Milevis, *Against the Donatists*, Bk. 5, against Parmenian

664 Cf. Constantine's baptistery, Anast., *in Sylvest.*

665 Such are those of Parma and Florence.

666 See *The Martyrdom of St. Genesius.*

667 Gregory the Great, *Oration, De Baptis.*

668 Cf. Tertullian, *De Corona Militis*, Ch. 3

669 Cf. Fleury, t. 7, p. 367

670 1 Pt 2:2

671 On the sacraments, see *Catechism of the Council of Trent*; Fleury, *Hist. Eccles.*, Bk. 1-10; Cyril of Jerusalem, *Catechism*; Chardon, *History of the Sacraments*, etc.

672 Cf. Baronius, *Anno* 259

673 Cf. Theodoret, *Sermon 5, De Graecor. affect. curand.*

674 The pagan reaction which has been felt in Europe, since the time of the Renaissance, on ideas, on manners, on literature, on the arts, has procured us these ridiculous names. The "heroes" of profane antiquity, fabulous gods and goddesses, flowers, fruits, and herbs have in turn seen their names borne by young Christians of both sexes in the eighteenth and nineteenth centuries. At the present day the names of the saints are returned to; but still they are a good deal disfigured. People say Lizzie, Nellie, Pollie: it would be too great a venture to say Elizabeth, Helen, Mary. The history of names has a deeper signification than might be imagined. See our work, *La Revolution*, t. 4.

675 See, in reference to the salt, our *Traité de l'eau bénite.*

676 Cf. Ambrose, *On the Sacraments*, Bk. 1, Ch. 1

677 See on this subject Tertullian, *De Corona Militis*, Ch. 24; Basil, *De Spiritu Sancto*, Ch. 27; Cyril of Jerusalem, *Catechetical Lecture 19*; Chrysostom, *Homily 21, to the People of Antioch*; Gregory Nazianzen, *Sermon On Baptism*, n. 40; Ambrose, *On the Mysteries*, Ch. 2; *On the Sacraments*, Bk. 1; Jerome, *On 1 Timothy*; *On Amos*; Augustine, *Epistle 149.*

678 Cf. Ambrose, *De Spiritu Sancto*, Ch. 10; Gregory the Great, *Register of Epistles*, Bk. 1, Epistle 129; *On Colossians*, Ch. 2

679 These linens were called *sabana.*

680 Cf. Baronius, *Anno* 481

681 See *Esprit des Cérémonies*, etc.

682 *Recherches philosophiques sur les Chinois*, a work not suspected of favoring Christianity, t. 1, p. 63; Cf. Torrens, *Reise nach China*, etc. More recent documents speak of 70,000 children being annually given over to death throughout the whole of China. See *Annals of the Holy Childhood.*

683 Augustine, *On Baptism, against the Donatists*, Bk. 3, Ch. 16; Cyprian, *Epistle 71*; Ambrose, *On the Sacraments*, Bk. 3, Ch. 2

684 See p. 227 of Volume VII of the Tradivox series.

685 Et in hoc unguento sacramentum chrismatis vultis interpretari, quod quidem in genere visibilium signaculorum sacramentum est sicut ipse baptismus (Augustine, *On Psalm 102*).

686 De his super quibus rogastis nos vos informari, utrum majus sit sacramentum manus impositio episcoporum, an baptismus, scitote utrumque magnum esse sacramentum (Melchiades, *De Consecr.*, dist. 5, Ch. 3). See other texts in Drouin, *De Re sacramentaria.*

687 Council of Trent, Session 7, "On Confirmation," Can. 1

688 Secundum sacramentum est confirmatio, cujus materia est chrisma confectum ex oleo, quod nitorem significat conscientitae, et balsamo, quod odorem significat bonae famae (Council of Florence, Session 8, "Bull of Union with the Armenians").

689 Quod itaque extra controversiam est, hoc dicatur, nimirum in Ecclesia Latina confirmationis sacramentum conferri adhibito sacro chrismate, sive oleo olivarum, balsamo commixto et ab episcopo benedicto, ductoque signo crucis per sacramenti ministrum in fronte suscipientis, dum idem minister formae verba pronuntiat (Encyclical *Ex Quo*, n. 52). See Ferraris, art. *Confirm.*; Alphonsus Liguori, *Tract. de Confirm.*, etc.

690 The balm of Peru is of a whitish yellow color, rather thick and odoriferous, and of a sharp bitter taste. The balm of Carthagena is of a greenish yellow color, a little thick, of a very pleasing smell and taste, not sharp or bitter like most of the others. The balm of Brazil is at first liquid, but, as it grows old, it becomes thick like honey; its color is a pale yellow, its taste somewhat bitter, and its odor sweet. The balm of Canada is yellowish, almost transparent, more or less liquid, and approaching turpentine somewhat in its taste and smell. In fine, the balm of Judea, the balm of Mecca, the balm of Syria, the balm of Galaad, which are all the same, are white, of a strong and excellent perfume, of a bitter taste, and so light that they do not sink in water; they are taken from a tree called the balm-tree (*amyris opobalsamum*), whose height is about that of a cherry tree.

The balm of Judea is the most ancient known, and, by its properties, the most recommended. Though the Church has not appointed any particular species of balm for the holy chrism, it is evident that the balm of Judea will always merit the preference. (See a most interesting dissertation entitled: *De opobalsami specie, ad sacrum chrisma conficiendum requisita*, Naples, octavo, by Michael d'Amato; and our *Traité de l'eau bénite.*)

691 See *Hist. des Sacrements—de la Confirm.*

692 Cyril of Jerusalem, *Catechetical Lecture 21*, n. 3

693 Cf. *Summa Theologiae*, III, q. 72, a. 12

694 2 Cor 2:15

695 *Summa Theologiae*, III, q. 72, a. 2, c. See also Fabian, *Epistle 3 to the Bishops of the East*; Augustine, *On Psalm 44*; *On Psalm 91*; *On the Trinity*, Bk. 13, Ch. 26; Gregory the Great, *Can.*, Ch. 1; Council of Laodicea, Can. 48; Second Council of Carthage, Can. 2; Third Council of Carthage, Can. 39; Dionysius, *Ecclesiastical Hierarchy*, Ch. 2, 4. On oil, see Ambrose, *On Psalm 118*; *De Spiritu Sancto*, Ch. 3; Cyprian, *Epistle 30*.

696 Cf. *Catechism of the Council of Trent* [see p. 232 of Volume VII of the Tradivox series]; Council of Florence, Session 8, "Bull of Union with the Armenians."

697 Cf. *Summa Theologiae*, III, q. 62, a. 4

698 Cf. *Summa Theologiae*, III, q. 72, a. 9

699 *Jure ordinario*—for the power of confirming is often delegated to simple priests: in missions, for example.

700 Cf. *Summa Theologiae*, III, q. 72, a. 11

701 Ut confirmati decedentes, majorem gloriam consequuntur, sicut et hic majorem obtinent gratiam (*Summa Theologiae*, III, q. 72, a. 8). Quod scite perpendentes Suarez, Layman, Diana, Gotonius, Juenin, Sylvester, Maurus, Roncaglia, et cardinalis Gottus, ab ipso citati, aliique plurimi affirmant. Sancte, ac licite, etiam juxta praesentem disciplinam, sacro chrismate inungi pueros ante septennum, cum aut praevidetur futura diutina absentia episcopi, aut idem versantur in discrimine vitae, aut alia urget necessitas, seu justa causa (Ferraris, art. *Confirm.*, n. 60).

702 Council of Trent, Session 7, "On the Sacraments in General," Can. 1

703 Council of Trent, Session 7, "On Confirmation," Can. 1

704 Acts 8:17

705 Cf. Drouin, *De Re sacramentaria*

706 Cf. *Conférencier d'Angers*, t. 7, p. 179

707 Ambrose, *On the Mysteries*, Ch. 7. See what we have said on the ninth article of the Creed, and particularly in our *Traité du Saint-Esprit*.

708 Cf. Acts 5:41

709 *Summa Theologiae*, III, q. 72, a. 1, c.

710 See the Council of Elvere, Can. 38, 48; and, in modern times, the Councils of Milan, Rouen, Bordeaux, Tours, Reims, etc.

711 Cf. *Summa Theologiae*, III, q. 72, a. 1—Quamvis continuo transituris sufficiant regenerationis beneficia, victuris tamen necessaria sunt confirmationis auxilia (Melchiades, *Epistle to the Bishops of Spain*; *Summa Theologiae*, III, q. 72, a. 8, obj. 4).

712 See explanation of the eighth article of the Creed.

713 Cf. *Hist. des Sacrements*, t. 1

714 Cf. Acts 8:14-15, 17

715 Tertullian, *On Baptism*, Ch. 7-8; *On the Resurrection of the Flesh*, Ch. 8; Cyprian, *Epistle 70*

716 Innocent I, *Epistle ad Decentium Eugub.*, Ch. 3

717 Cf. Ibid.

718 Manuscript pontifical of Archbishop Egbert, who lived about the eighth century.

719 Roman Ordo, written about the eighth century.

720 Cf. Cyprian, *Epistle 70*; Basil, *De Spiritu Sancto*, Ch. 17; Optatus of Milevis, *De Schis.*, Bk. 6

721 Cf. Cyril of Jerusalem, *Catechetical Lecture 21*, n. 3

722 Cf. Roman Ordo

723 Egbert's Pontifical, 8th century; Council of Wigorne and Cologne, 1280

724 Cf. Council of Chartres, 1526

725 Cf. Council of Cologne, cited above

726 Si multitudo confirmandorum id exigerit, dispositis illis per ordinem super gradus presbyterii, vel alibi, pontifex, stans cum mitra, illos confirmat per ordinem genuflexos, et uno ordine confirmato, illi surgunt, at alii genuftectunt et confirmantur, et sic usque in finem (*Roman Pontifical*).

727 Cf. *Roman Pontifical*

728 Quemadmodum enim si quis ceram cerae conjunxerit, utique alteram in altera invicemque immeasse videbit; eodem quoque opinor modo, qui Salvatoris nostri Christi carnem sumit, ac ejus pretiosum sanguinem bibit, ut ipse ait, unum quiddam cum eo reperitur (Cyril of Alexandria, *On John*, Ch. 5, n. 56). See also the other passages of the fathers, quoted in the Introduction to the catechism.

729 Cf. Justin Martyr, *Second Apology*; Irenaeus, *Against Heresies*, Bk. 4, Ch. 34; Chrysostom, *Homily 27 on Matthew*; Augustine, *Contra Adversarium Legis et Prophetarum*, Bk. 1, Ch. 18

730 Cf. 1 Cor 10:21; Ambrose, *De Elia et Jejunio*, Ch. 10; Augustine, *Tractate 47 on John*

731 Cf. *Homily 24 on 1 Corinthians*

732 Cf. Jerome, *On Matthew*, Ch. 15; Chrysostom, *On the Priesthood*, Bk. 6

733 Cf. Tertullian, *On the Resurrection of the Flesh*, Ch. 8; Cyril of Jerusalem, *Catechetical Lecture 23*; Jerome, *Epistle 14, to Heliodorus*; Augustine, *On the Trinity*, Bk. 3, Ch. 4; Cyprian, *On the Lapsed*

734 See *Perpétuité de la Foi* and *Discussion amicale*.

735 Cf. Council of Trent, Session 13

736 Cf. Council of Florence, Session 8, "Bull of Union with the Armenians"

737 Jn 6:56-57, 59

738 Cf. 1 Cor 11

739 Cf. Ambrose, *On the Sacraments*, Bk. 4, Ch. 9; Chrysostom, *Homily 60, to the People of Antioch*; *Homily 61, to the People of Antioch*; Augustine, *On Psalm 33*; Cyril of Alexandria, *On John*, Bk. 4, Ch. 13-14; Bk. 10, Ch. 13; Justin Martyr, *Second Apology*; Irenaeus, *Against Heresies*, Bk. 3; Dionysius, *Ecclesiastical Hierarchy*, Ch. 3; Hilary, *On the Trinity*; Jerome, *Epistle to Damasus*; John Damascene, *An Exposition of the Orthodox Faith*, Bk. 4, Ch. 14; Fourth Lateran Council; Council of Florence; Council of Trent; etc.

740 Lk 22:19; Cf. Council of Trent, Session 22, "Doctrine on the Sacrifice of the Mass," Ch. 1

741 Cyril of Jerusalem, *Catechetical Lecture 22*, n. 6, 9

742 See Renaudot, *Perpétuité de la Foi*; de Trevern, *Discussion amicale*, Turlot, *Catech.*, etc.

743 Council of Trent, Session 13, Can. 1

744 Cf. *Summa Theologiae*, III, q. 79, a. 3. Nullus habet gratiam ante susceptionem hujus sacramenti, nisi ex voto ipsius, vel per seipsum, sicut adulti; vel voto Ecclesiae, sicut pueruli, sicut supra dictum est (*Summa Theologiae*, III, q. 79, a. 1, rep. 1). Potest igitur hoc sacramentum operare remissionem peccatorum dupliciter: uno modo non perceptum actu, sed voto...Alio modo etiam perceptum ab eo qui est in peccato mortali, cujus conscientiam et affectum non habet: forte enim primo non fuit sufficienter contritus, sed devote et reverenter accedens consequetur per hoc sacramentum gratiam charitatis, quae contritionem perficiet, et remissionem peccati (*Summa Theologiae*, III, q. 79, a. 3, c.).

745 Jn 6

746 Augustine, *Confessions*, Bk. 7, Ch. 10

747 Council of Trent, Session 13, "Decree concerning the Most Holy Sacrament of the Eucharist," Ch. 2.—Unde et Ambrosius dicit quod "iste panis quotidianus sumitur in remedium quotidianae infirmitatis." Res autem hujus sacramenti est charitas, non solum quantum ad habitum, sed etiam quantum ad actum, qui excitatur in hoc sacramento, per quod peccata venialia solvuntur. Unde manifestum est quod virtute hujus sacramenti remittuntur peccata venialia (*Summa Theologiae*, III, q. 79, a. 4, c.).

748 Ambrose, *On the Sacraments*, Bk. 4, Ch. 6, n. 28

749 *Summa Theologiae*, III, q. 79, a. 6, c.

750 Cf. *Summa Theologiae*, III, q. 79, a. 5

751 Cyril of Alexandria, *On John*, Bk. 4

752 Cyprian, *Epistle 54*

753 Cf. *Summa Theologiae*, III, q. 79, a. 2

754 Augustine, *Tractate 26 on John*, n. 26

755 *Summa Theologiae*, III, q. 79, a. 1, rep. 3

756 Jn 6:55

757 Cf. Jb 19:25-27

758 Cf. Tertullian, *Apology*, Ch. 39

759 Lk 22:15

760 Non est igitur in mea potestate, sed in tua. Si volueris, me totum accipise (Jerome, *On Psalm 80*).

761 Cf. *Summa Theologiae*, III, q. 80, a. 1

762 Cf. 2 Pt 1:4

763 Jn 6:54

764 Cf. Council of Trent, Session 21, "Decree on Communion under Both Species, and the Communion of Infants," Ch. 4

765 Manifestum est quod omnes tenentur saltem spiritualiter manducare Eucharistiam, quia hoc est Christo incorporari...Spiritualis autem manducatio includit votum seu desiderium percipiendi hoc sacramentum (*Summa Theologiae*, III, q. 80, a. 11, c.).

766 Sicut ex fide Ecclesiae credunt, sic ex intentione Ecclesiae desiderant Eucharistiam (*Summa Theologiae*, III, q. 73, a. 3, c.).

767 Cf. Council of Trent, Session 13

768 Francis de Sales, *Introduction to the Devout Life*, Pt. 2, Ch. 20-21, edit. 1651—*Licet tepide*, says St. Bonaventure, *tamen confidens misericordia Dei fiducialiter accedas; quia qui se indignum reputat, cogitet quod tanto magis eget medico, quanto senserit se aegrotum. Neque ideo quaeris te jungere Christo, ut tu eum sanctifices, sed ut tu sanctificeris ab illo...Neque praetermittenda est Sancta* Communio, *si quandoque non sentit homo specialem devotionem, cum se ad illam praeparare studeat, vel in ipsa perceptione, vel post forte minus devotus se sentit quam vellet*. (See Alphonsus Liguori, *Manual of Confessors*, n. 290ff.)—*Iste panis quotidianus est, accipe quotidie, ut quotidie tibi prosit* (Augustine, *Sermon 28, De Verbis Domini*).—*Sic vive ut quotidie merearis accipere* (*Summa Theologiae*, III, q. 80, a. 10, c.).—*Quia semper pecco, debeo semper habere medicinam* (Ambrose, *On the Sacraments*, Bk. 4, Ch. 6, n. 28).—*Quotidie peccas, quotidie sume* (Augustine).—*Unus sit tibi dolor hac esca privari* (Chrysostom).

769 Cf. Gregory Nazianzen; Fleury, t, 4, p. 244

770 Palladius, *Hist. Eccl.*, Ch. 29

771 Cf. *Cérém. Amb.*, Bk. 1

772 In the third part of the catechism [i.e., Volume XII of the Tradivox series], we shall see with what respect certain religious communities prepared the matter of the august sacrifice.

773 Cf. Evagrius, *Ecclesiastical History*, Bk. 4, Ch. 35

774 Cf. Gregory of Tours, *Glory of Martyrs*, Bk. 1, Ch. 10

775 Cf. Nicephorus, *Church History*, Bk. 17, Ch. 25

776 Cf. Bona., *Reg. liturg.*, Bk. 2, Ch. 17

777 Cf. Ibid.

778 Summus pontifex cum solemniter celebrat sedeus communicat (Bona., *Reg. liturg.*, Bk. 2, Ch. 6, 17, p. 490).

779 Cyril of Jerusalem, *Catechetical Lecture 23*, n. 22

780 Gregory of Tours, *Glory of Martyrs*, Bk. 1, Ch. 31

781 Cf. Burchard, Bk. 5, Ch. 6

782 Cf. Council of Constance, Session 13

783 Perfectio hujus sacramenti non est in usu fidelium, sed in consecratione materiae. Et ideo nihil derogat perfectioni hujus sacramenti, si populus sumat corpus sine sanguine, dummodo sacerdos consecrans sumat utrumque (*Summa Theologiae*, III, q. 80, a. 12, rep. 2).

784 Cf. Bossuet, *Traité de la Comm. sous les deux espèces*, p. 165 et suiv.

785 Cf. Cornelius a Lapide, *in hunc loc*

786 Acts 2:46

787 Justin Martyr, *First Apology*, Ch. 65

788 Cf. Apud Sur., Jan. 7

789 Cf. Clement of Alexandria, *The Stromata*, Bk. 1

790 Basil, *Letter 93*

791 Cf. p. 289, ultim. edit.

792 Cf. *De Gest. S. Ludov.*

793 Cf. Bona., *Reg. liturg.*, Ch. 17, n. 5

794 Cf. Council of Toledo, Can. 14; Council of Saragossa, Can. 3

795 Cf. Eusebius, *Ecclesiastical History*, Bk. 5, Ch. 24

796 The metropolitan church of Reims contains a vestige of this ancient and venerable usage.

797 Cf. Anast. Bibliot., *in Sylvestro*

798 Ut sit Deus omnia in omnibus (1 Cor 15:28).

799 Idem Deus qui operatur omnia in omnibus (1 Cor 12:6).

800 Cf. Vaubert, *Dévotion a Jésus Christ.*, t. 1, 93

801 Per hoc sacramentum stat Ecclesia, fides roboratur, viret et viget Christiana religio et divinus cultus.

802 *Epistle 54*

803 Extracts from the registers of the state council of the Republic of Geneva, from 1585 to 1792.—Calvin managed to have himself forbidden to visit the hospital of the plague-stricken; and many ministers refused to go there, saying that they would sooner go to the devil (*Frag. biographiques des registres de la ville*, May 1, 1543, p. 10).

804 Charles Borromeo, *Acts of the Church of Milan*, Fifth Provincial Council, Pt. 2, Ch. 4

805 Cf. *Annal. de la Prop. de la Foi*, n. 59, 462. Translator's note: Since the above was written, the penal settlements of Australia have been abolished.

806 See *Dogme générateur de la pieté*, etc., by Mgr. Gerbet. It is interesting to know in detail the apostolic labors of these so-called missionaries. One of them fills up the record of his weeks thus:

"10th, worked at the forge; finished some window-frames.

"12th, sowed vegetables.

"13th, acted as mason.

"14th, mended a wheel-barrow, planted some trees, and cut away several feet of vines.

"16th, Sunday, we had a good congregation. Sermon listened to attentively. It was on the words, 'Blessed are they that mourn, for they shall be comforted.' May that sadness of which one never repents become more general among our poor Bechuanas!

"17th, fixed a wagon wheel, which was about to break.

"26th and 28th, worked at lintels."

This interesting and edifying letter from one of the missionaries whom the protestant propaganda maintains at the South of Africa was published by the protestant journal of the *Evangelical Missions* in its number for August, 1841.

The missionary ends his report with a piece of news which cannot fail to excite the interest and the sympathy of his readers:

"I have the pleasure to inform you that, on the 19th of this month, my wife was happily delivered of a little boy, who will be baptized John Eugene. The mother and child are doing well thanks be to our God and Father!—J. Lange."

807 Charge, 1842

808 This expression, full of simple candor, comes from a young protestant. Delighted with her visit one day to a hospital kept by French nuns, she said to them: "I would like very much to be what you are; but I feel that our religion does not go so far."

809 Cf. Lettres édifiantes

810 In Catholic language, the word *penance* has three meanings. First, a virtue by which man repents of his sins: the contrary vice is called impenitence, and consists in being unwilling to repent of one's sins and in wishing to persevere in them. The second, a penalty which man imposes on himself, to satisfy God for the evil which he has committed: thus we say that a man does great penance when he greatly afflicts his body by fasting and other austerities. The third, a sacrament, which our Lord instituted to forgive the sins of those who, having lost sanctifying grace and detested their faults, desire to return to the friendship of God. It is in this last sense that we are about to explain it.

811 Cf. Council of Trent, Session 14, "Doctrine on the Sacrament of Penance," Ch. 3; "On the Most Holy Sacrament of Penance," Can. 4

812 Cf. *Catechism of the Council of Trent* [see p. 292-293 of Volume VII of the Tradivox series]; *Summa Theologiae*, III, q. 84, a. 1

813 Ubi emendatio nulla, ibi poenitentia falsa (Tertullian, *De Paenitentia*, Ch. 2).

814 Versetur ante oculos nostros imago futuri judicii, et ascendat homo adversum se, ante faciem suam, atque constituto in corde judicio, adsit accusans cogitatio, et testis conscientia, et carnifex cor. Inde quidam sanguis animi confitentis per lacrymas profluat, postremo ab ipsa mente talis sententia proferatur, ut se indignum homo judicet participem corporis et sanguinis Domini (Augustine, cited by Aquinas in his *Pauline Commentaries*, on 1 Corinthians 11, Lectio 7, n. 704).

815 Contritio, quae primum locum inter dictos poenitentis actus habet, animi dolor ac detestatio est de peccato commisso, cum proposito non peccandi de caetero (Council of Trent, Session 14, "Doctrine on the Sacrament of Penance," Ch. 4).

816 Ibid.

817 See Drouin, *De Re sacramentaria*, art. *Contrit.*—*Admonendi sunt qui admissa deserunt, neque tamen plangunt ne jam retaxatas aestiment culpas quas, etsi agendo non multiplicant, nullis tamen fletibus mundant* (Gregory the Great, *Pastoral Rule*, Bk. 3, Ch. 30).

818 Cf. Alphonsus Liguori, *Homo apost.*, Tract. 16, n. 11-16

819 *Méthode de Saint-Sulpice*, p. 273

820 Cf. Jl 2:12-13

821 Dolor de peccatis mortalibus commissis debet esse summus, non intensive, sed appretiative, ita ut poenitens nihil magis detestetur quam peccatum, et velit potius omnia mala mundi perpeti, quam mortaliter Deum offendere (*Communis. vid.*, Ferraris, *Poenit. sacra.*, n. 33).

822 Some timid persons, not actually feeling this disposition to suffer all—death itself, for example—rather than commit one mortal sin, allow their minds to be disturbed with the fear that they have not contrition. It must be observed to them that the grace of undergoing these terrible trials not being actually necessary for them, it is not surprising that they do not perceive in themselves the sensible disposition to endure such sufferings. They should for the time being dispose themselves to make all the sacrifices that God actually requires of them, and for the others, rely upon his grace, which will never fail them in the hour of need. God is faithful and will never permit you to be tempted above your strength.

823 Cf. Augustine, *De Vera et Falsa Poenitent.*, Ch. 9—Ad valorem sacramenti requiritur dolor supernaturalis et universalis, saltem virtualiter respectu omnium peccatorum mortalium; unde si de uno solo mortali scienter non habeatur, nec scienter velit haberi dolor, peccatur gravissime et nullum redditur sacramentum, quia deficit materia proxima necessaria, quae est dolor reconciliativus cum Deo, qui saltem implicite et virtualiter debet includere detestationem omnium mortalium, etiam invincibiliter oblitorum, aut inculpabiliter ignoratorum (Ferraris, *Poenit. sacr.*, art. 11, n. 31).

824 Cf. Council of Trent, Session 14, "Doctrine on the Sacrament of Penance," Ch. 6; Session 6, Can. 2

825 Propositum debet esse absolutum, firmum, efficax et universale, se extendens ad omnia mortalia in posterum evitanda...Ad contritionem requiritur explicitum ac formale propositum vitae melioris (Ferraris, *Poenit. sacra.*, n. 33; Bellarmine, *De Poenit.*, Bk. 2, Ch. 6).

826 Cf. Alphonsus Liguori, *Theologia Moralis*, Bk. 6, n. 445

827 Vir duplex animo inconstans est in omnibus viis suis (Jas 1:8).

828 Lk 10:16

829 Vult et non vult piger. Sicut ostium vertitur in cardine suo, ita piger in lectulo suo. Vae duplici corde! (Prv 13:4; 26:14; Ecclus 2:14).

830 Os bilingue detestor (Prv 8:13).

831 Council of Trent, Session 14, "On the Most Holy Sacrament of Penance," Can. 7

832 See another fact in P. Lejeune, t. 9, *Sermon 240, on Confession*, at the end.

833 Jn 20:22-23. See the explanation of these words at the tenth article of the Creed.

834 See *Recherches sur la confession aurioulaire*, by M. Guillois, p. 61.

835 Confessio pure facienda est: quia non est pars una peccatorum dicenda, et altera reticenda, neque levia confitenda et gravia diffitenda: Nec alter accusandus et ipse excusandus, sed cum justo dicendum est: "Non declines, cor meum, in verba malitiae ad excusandas excusationes in peccatis." Haec enim sunt verba malitiae qua gravior vel pejor esse non possit...Proh dolor! sub humilitatis pallio sunt nonnulli superbiam inducentes, et putantes se posse vitare oculos judicis cuncta cernentis (*Sermon, De S. And.*

apost., t. 5, p. 1412, n. 9, edit, Paris, 1839; *Sermon, Domin. in psalm.*; p. 1172, n. 4; *Sermon 1, in fact. om. sanct.; Exhort. ad mil. Templi*, n. 12).

836 Ite, ostendite vos sacerdotibus; id est, per humilem oris confesaionem veraciter manifestate omnes interioris leprae vestrae maculas, ut mundari possitis (*S. Anselmi opera*, èdit. Colon., p. 176).

837 Sicut in baptismo originalia, ita in confessione remittuntur peceata actualia, etc., *in Elucidario.*—Ergo per utriusque sacramenti conditio, paret necessitas, atque hinc S. Praesul maritum sororis suae Jerosolymam transmigraturum sic admonebat (Bk. 3, Epistle 71): "Facite confessionem omnium peccatorum ab infantia vestra, quantum recordari potestis."

838 See D. Denis de Sainte-Marthe, *Erreurs des Calvinistes sur la Confession*; Bellarmine, le P. Alexandre. Collet, *De Poenitentia*; le *Traité historique de la Confession* de M. Boileau; les *Lettres* du P. Scheffmacher.

839 ...Illos ad confessionem provoco, sine qua nullus remissione peccatorum potietur (*Scal. Grad.* 4).

840 *Spiritualis filii, ego confessionem tuam primario et praecipue non recipio, nec tibi absolutionem concedo, sed per me Deus...Revela igitur et declara coram SS. Angelis, nihilque mihi cela eorum quae a te clam facta sunt, velut si Deo occulta cordium cognoscenti confitereris...* (*Apud Morin., de Poenit.*). Then follows a detailed interrogation on all sins, even to the most secret.

841 Habent quidem et terrestres principes vinculi potestatem, verum corporum solum. Id autem quod dico sacerdotum vinculum ipsam etiam animam contingit (Chrysostom, *On the Priesthood*, Bk. 3, Ch. 5).—Imitemur et nos hanc mulierem Samaritanam et ob propria peccata non erubescamus...qui enim homini detegere peccata erubescit, neque confiteri vult, neque poenitentiam agere, in illa die judicii, non coram uno vel duobus, sed universo terrarum orbe spectante traducetur (Chrysostom, *Homily, De mul. Samarit.*).

842 Nemo sibi dicat: Occulte ago, apud Deum ago: novit Deus qui mihi ignoscat, quid in corde meo ago. Ergo sine causa dictum est: 'Quae solveritis in terra soluta erunt et in coelo'? Ergo sine causa sunt claves datae Ecclesiae Dei? Frustramus evangelium, frustramus verba Christi, promittimus vobis quod ille negat (Augustine, *Sermon 392, inter Homily 1*).

843 Erat gaudens cum gaudentibus, flens cum flentibus; si quidem quotiescumque illi aliquis ad percipiendam poenitentiam lapsus suos confessus esset, ita flebat, ut et illum flere compelleret; causas autem criminum quas illi confitebantur nulli nisi Domini soli, apud quem intercedebat, loquebatur (Paulinus, *Life of Ambrose*, n. 39).

844 Necessario, iis peccata aperiri debent, quibus credita est dispensatio mysteriorum Dei (Basil, *The Shorter Rules*, q. 288).

845 *Coll. Select. Patr.*, t. 9

846 Sola igitur catholica Esclesia est quae verum cultum retinet...Sed quia singuli quique coetus haereticorum se potissimum esse Christianos, et suam esse Catholicam Ecclesiam putant, sciendum est illam esse veram in qua est confessio et poenitentia, quae peccata et vulnera, quibus subjecta est imbecillitas carnis, salubriter curat (Lactantius, *The Divine Institutes*, Bk. 4, Ch. 17, 30).

847 Si revelaverimus peccata nostra non solum Deo sed his qui possunt mederi vulneribus nostris atque peccatis, delebuntur peccata nostra (Origen, *Homily 32 on Leviticus*; *Homily 17 on Luke*; Cf. Origen, *Homily 2 on Psalm 37*).

848 Plerosque tamen hoc confessionis opus ut publicationem sui aut suffugere, aut de die in diem differre praesumunt, pudoris magis memores quam salutis; velut illi qui in partibus verecundioribus corporis contracta vexatione, conscientiam medentium vitant; et ita cum verescentia sua pereunt, grande plane emolumentum verecundiae, occultatio delicti pollicetur! Videlicet, si quid humanae notitiae subduxerimus, proinde et Deum celabimus? Adeoque existimatio hominum et conscientia Dei comparantur? An melius est damnatum latere, quam palam absolvi? (Tertullian, *De Paenitentia*, Ch. 10, 12).

849 Quamdiu sumus in hoc mundo, malorum quae in carne gessimus ex toto corde poeniteat, ut a Domino solvemur, dum poenitentiae tempus suppetit; postquam enim e mundo migravimus, non amplius possumus ibi exomologesim aut poenitentiam adhuc agere (Clement of Rome, *Second Epistle to the Corinthians*, n. 8).

850 Cf. 1 Jn 1:9; Jas 5:16—The monuments of the catacombs also render testimony to the antiquity of confession. (See, on the confessionals of apostolic times, our *Histoire des Catacombes*, p. 217.)

851 Cf. Acts 19:18

852 Cf. Grotius, Rosenmüller, etc. (See the *Catéch. de Constance*, t. 3, p. 572.)

853 For further development, see *Discussion amicale*, t. 2, p. 180ff.

854 See M. Drach's dissertation on *Confession among the Jews*.

855 See *Recherches sur la confession auriculaire*, by M. Guillois. This work is approved by Mgr. Bouvier, bishop of Mans: the approbation is dated 9th July, 1836.

856 Cf. *Zend-Avesta*, t. 2, p. 28ff

857 Mt 5:17

858 Cf. *Catechism of the Council of Trent* [see p. 306ff of Volume VII of the Tradivox series]

859 Cf. Council of Trent, Session 14, "Doctrine on the Sacrament of Penance," Ch. 2

860 Cf. Nm 14

861 2 Kgs 12:13-14

862 Cf. Council of Trent, Session 14, "Doctrine on the Sacrament of Penance," Ch. 8

863 Docet sancta Synodus Sacramenti Poenitentiae formam in qua praecipue ipsius vis sita est, in illius ministri verbis positam esse: Ego te absolvo, etc. (Council of Trent, Session 14, "Doctrine on the Sacrament of Penance," Ch. 3).

864 Cf. Council of Trent, Session 14, "Doctrine on the Sacrament of Penance," Ch. 6; "On the Most Holy Sacrament of Penance," Can. 10

865 Cf. Council of Trent, Session 14, "Doctrine on the Sacrament of Penance," Ch. 7

866 Jn 20:22-23

867 Cf. Council of Trent, Session 14, "Doctrine on the Sacrament of Penance," Ch. 1

868 Cf. Lk 24

869 Non enim (opera per peccatum mortificata) habent vim perducendi in vitam aeternam...solum secundum quod actu existunt, sed etiam postquam actu esse desinunt, secundum quod remanent in acceptatione divina (*Summa Theologiae*, III, q. 89, a. 5, c.).

870 Per poenitentiam remittuntur peccata. Remissio autem peccatorum non potest esse nisi per infusionem gratiae. Unde relinquitur quod per poenitentiam homini gratia infundatur; ex gratia autem consequuntur omnes virtutes gratuitae, sicut ex essentia animae fluunt omnes potentiae, ut in secunda parte habitum est. Unde relinquitur quod per poenitentiam omnes virtutes restituantur (*Summa Theologiae*, III, q. 89, a. 1, c.).

871 Cf. *Summa Theologiae*, III, q. 89, a. 3, c.

872 Cf. Council of Trent, Session 14, "Doctrine on the Sacrament of Penance," Ch. 2; "On the Most Holy Sacrament of Penance," Can. 6

873 Secunda tabula post naufragium est poenitentia (*Epistle 130*, n. 9; *Summa Theologiae*, III, q. 84, a. 6).

874 Ps 84:11

875 Cf. Mt 11:28

876 In many Catholic countries it is the custom to place inscriptions on the confessionals. All breathe mercy and clemency, of which the holy tribunal is the seat and the priest the minister. A celebrated protestant, well known by his strong prejudices against the Roman Church, could not help admiring these inscriptions. He took the trouble of writing down those which he met on the confessionals of Italy. Here they are, as we find them in his works: "Go, show yourself to the priest." "I will go to my father, and say to him: Father, I have sinned." "They shall be loosed in heaven." "Return, O my soul! into thy rest." "Go in peace, and sin no more." "He who hears you hears me." "Come to me, all ye who groan under the burden of your miseries." "The just man will reprove me with mercy." "See whether there is any way of iniquity in me, and bring me back into the road of heaven." "To hear the sighs of the captive" (Addison, Remarks on several parts of Italy, p. 31).

877 To feel all the effects that it produces on the soul, try to substitute for it, as some persons do unthinkingly, the worldly word *Sir*.

878 Cf. *Catechism of the Council of Trent* [see p. 306ff of Volume VII of the Tradivox series]

879 Marmontel

880 Silvio Pellico, *Mes Prisons*

881 M. de Maistre.

882 Totum hoc institutum divina sapientia dignum esse negari non potest, et si quid aliud hoc certe in Christiana religione praeclarum et laudabile est, quod et Sinenses ac Japonenses sunt admirati: nam et a peccatis multos deterret confitendi necessitas, eos maxime qui nondum obdurati sunt, et lapsis magnam consolationem praestat, ut adeo putem pium, gravem et prudentem confessarium magnum Dei organum

esse ad animarum salutem; prodest enim consilium ejus ad regendos affectus, ad animadvertenda vitia nostra, ad vitandas peccatorum occasiones, ad restituendum ablatum, et reparandum damnum datum, ad dubia eximenda, ad erigendam mentem afflictam, ad omnia denique mala aut tollenda aut mitigenda; et cum fideli amico vix quidquam in rebus humanis praestantius reperiatur quanti est, cum ipsa sacramenti divini inviolabile religione, ad fidem servandam opemque ferendam adstringi? (Leibnitz, *System theologicum, de Confessione*).

883 Indulgentia est gratia, qua certo aliquo opere, quod concedens praescribit, praestito, debita Deo poena temporalis (non autem culpa) extra sacramentum, sacrificium et martyrium, per applicationem satisfactionum Christi et sanctorum remittitur (Alphonsus Liguori, *Theologia Moralis*, Bk. 6, Tract. 4, n. 531; Ferraris, art. *Indulg.*).

884 Mt 16:19

885 Cf. 1 Cor 5

886 2 Cor 2:10

887 They were authorized by the canons of the Councils of Nice, Ancyra, Lerida, etc. St. Basil, St. Chrysostom, etc., approve of this conduct.

888 Cf. Cyprian, *Epistles 10-13*; *Epistle 23*

889 Cf. Session 25, "Decree Concerning Indulgences"

890 Cf. Augustine, *De Libero Arbitrio*, Bk. 3, Ch. 9-10; *On the Nature of Good*, Ch. 7; Anselm, *Cur Deus Homo*, Bk. 1, Ch. 2, 20, 23-24

891 Unigenitus Dei Filius...pretioso sanguine nos redemit, quem in ara crucis innocens immolatus, non guttam sanguinis modicam, quae tamen propter unionem ad Verbum pro redemptione totius humani generis suffecisset, sed copiose, velut quoddam profluvium noscitur effudisse...Quantum ergo exinde ut nec supervacua, inanis et superflua tantae effusionis miseratio redderetur, thesaurum militanti ecclesiae acquisivit, volens suis thesaurizare filiis plus Pater, ut sic sit infinitus thesaurus hominibus quo qui usi sunt, Dei amicitiae participes sunt effecti. Quem quidem thesaurum, non in sudario repositum, non in agro absconditum, sed per B. Petrum coeli clavigerum, ejusque successores, suos in terris vicarios, commisit fidelibus salubriter dispensandum, et propriis et rationalibus causis, nunc pro totali, nunc pro partiali remissione poenae temporalis pro peccatis debitae, tam generaliter, quam specialiter (prout cum Deo expedire cognoscerent) vere poenitentibus et confessis misericorditer applicandum (Clement VI, *Extravag. Unigenitus*, etc.).

892 Cf. *Extravag. Unigenitus*, etc.

893 Indulgentia plenaria ea est quae non tantum poenitentiam injunctam per confessarium, vel canones, aut secundum hos injungi debitam, sed etiam omnem purgatorii poenam tollit (Alphonsus Liguori, *Theologia Moralis*, Tract. 4, n. 535, p. 264; Cf. Ferraris, art. *Indulg.*, art. 3, p. 231).

894 Cf. *Raccoltà di indulgenze*, etc. (Roma, 1841, p. 16).

895 Cf. Ferraris, art. *Indulg.*, p. 232

896 Cf. Ferraris, art. *Indulg.*, p. 221

897 Cf. *Raccoltà*, etc. (Pref., p. xvi).

898 Indulgentia alia est partialis, qualis est unius, vel aliquot annorum; item septenae, quadragenae, etc. Per quas non significatur tolli tantam durationem purgatorii, sed tantam poenam remitti, quanta deleretur per jejunium unius, aut aliquot annorum, aut quadraginta dierum in pane et aqua, secundum canones olim imponi solitum (Alphonsus Liguori, *Theologia Moralis*, n. 536; Cf. Ferraris, p. 223).—We may remark with St. Antoninus that the number seven is often employed about indulgences, in opposition to the seven deadly sins.

899 Cf. Ferraris, p. 228—*Etsi in opere praestito non habueris intentionem consequendi indulgentias...et videtur certum si habueris interpretativam* (Alphonsus Liguori, *Theologia Moralis*, n. 5, 34, p. 261).—The interpretative intention consists in a disposition to gain indulgences, without there being any intention, actual, virtual, or even implicit, on the part of the will (Mgr. Gousset, t. 1, p. 20. See *Raccoltà*, etc., p. 23).

900 In some dioceses, by virtue of an apostolic indult, persons who confess twice a month may gain them.

901 Cf. *Raccoltà*, p. 19

902 Cf. *Raccoltà*, p. 552

903 Quasi pannus menstruatae universae justitiae nostrae (Is 64:6).

904 Iniquitates meae supergressae sunt caput meum (Ps 37:5).

905 Delicta quis intelligit? (Ps 18:13).

906 See also, regarding what occurs on the day of the plenary indulgence at Notre-Dame des Auges, the *Vie de saint François d'Assise*, by M. Chavin. 182.

907 See Ferraris, art. *Jubil.*

908 Cf. Lv 25; Nm 10

909 Joannes card. monachus testatur in cit. extravagante antiquorum, quod ex ipsius Bonifacii ore audivit: se ad hujusmodi constitutionem edendam impulsum esse quia vulgatum est quod talis indulgentia in annis centesimis a nativitate Christi olim concedi solebat (Ferraris, art. *Annus sanotus*).

910 On the ceremonies that accompany the opening of the jubilee, see *Les Trois Rome*, t. 1, p. 296.

911 When putting the tiara on the pope's head, the cardinal says: *Accipe thiaram tribus coronis ornatam, et scias te esse patrem principum et regum, rectorum orbis, in terra vicarium Salvatoris Domini nostri Jesu Christi, cui honor et gloria in saecula saeculorum.*

912 For further details, see *Les Trois Rome.*, t. 3, Jeudi-Saint.

913 Translator's note: There are several excellent little handbooks on Indulgences. See *Christian Instructed in the Nature and Use of Indulgences*, by Rev. F. A. Maurel; *Holy Indulgences*, by Rev. M. Comerford; and *Raccolta of Indulgences*, by Fr. Ambrose St. John.

914 Cf. Council of Trent, Session 14, "On the Sacrament of Extreme Unction," Ch. 2

915 Council of Trent, Session 14, "On the Sacrament of Extreme Unction," Can. 1

916 The first is given in baptism, the second in confirmation, the third in holy orders, and the fourth in extreme unction.

917 We will explain them in the fourth part of the catechism [i.e., Volume XIII of the Tradivox series].

918 Cf. *Summa Theologiae*, III-Sup., q. 31, a. 1

919 Cf. Council of Trent, Session 14, "On the Sacrament of Extreme Unction," Can. 1

920 Mk 6:13

921 Cf. Jn 21:25

922 Cf. Leo the Great, *Sermon 1, De Ascensione*

923 Jas 5:14-15

924 See the *Apologies* of St. Justin and Tertullian.

925 Cf. Origen, *Homily 2 on Leviticus*

926 *Si quis poenitentiam petens, dum sacerdos venerit, fuerit officio linguae privatus, constitutum est ut si idonea testimonia habuerit, quod ipse poenitentiam petiisset, et ipse per motus aliquos suae voluntatis aliquod signum facere potest, sacerdos impleat omnia sicut supra circa aegrotantem poenitentem scriptum est, id est orationem dicat et ungat cum oleo sancto, et Eucharistiam ei donet, etc.* (Nat., p. 15, Decret., Ch. 35).—See other texts in Drouin, *De Re sacramentaria*, and in Sainte-Beuve, *De Extr. Unct.*

927 Eusebius, *Epistle, ad Decent.*

928 *Summa Theologiae*, III-Sup., q. 30, a. 1

929 Cf. Aquinas, *Summa Contra Gentiles*, IV, Ch. 73

930 Cf. Council of Trent, Session 14, "On the Sacrament of Extreme Unction," Can. 2

931 Quia ratio operans nunquam inducit secundarium effectum, nisi secundum quod expedit ad principalem; ideo ex hoc sacramento non semper sequitur corporalis sanatio, sed quando expedit ad sanationem spiritualem; et tunc semper eam inducit, dummodo non sit impedimentum ex parte recipientis (Aquinas, *Summa Theologiae*, III-Sup., q. 30, a. 2, c.).

932 Cf. Bellarmine, *Dottrina Cristiana*, p. 198

933 Extrema unctio iterum conferri potest, si infirmus, postquam revaluisse videbatur, in periculum mortis recidat (Ferraris, art. *Extr. Unct.*, n. 37).

934 Cf. Spanish catechism by P. Cajetano, etc.

935 Nullum praeceptum exstat extremam unctionem recipiendi, cum ad salutem necessaria non sit (Cf. Aquinas, *Sentences*, IV, d. 23, q. 1, *et alii communiter*).—Unde non suscipere hoc sacramentum per se loquendo, secluso scandalo et contemptu, non est peccatum mortale, et multo minus peccant mortaliter domestici, si id non procurent (*Communiter*, Ferraris, art. *Extr. Unct.*, n. 38-39).

936 Cf. Council of Trent, Session 14, "On the Sacrament of Extreme Unction," Ch. 3

937 Cf. Councils of Rheims and Troyes, *apud Sainte-Beuve, de Extr. Unct.*

938 Cf. Cesarius, *App. oper.*; Augustine, *Sermon 279*

939 Cf. *Monastic. Anglic.*, t. 2, p. 775

940 Cf. D. Martène, *De Antiq. eccl. rit.*, t. 2, Ch. 7, art. 4

941 Cf. Delaunoy, *De Sacr. unctionis infirmorum*, p. 554

942 Cf. *Hist. des Sacr.*, t. 4

943 Ad renes: haec autem unctio omittitur semper in feminis et etiam in viris, qui, ob infirmitatem, vix aut sine periculo moveri non possunt (*Rituale Romanum*).

944 Principia peccandi in nobis sunt eadem quae et principia agendi, quia peccatum consistit in actu. Principia autem agendi in nobis sunt tria: primum est dirigens, scilicet vis cognoscitiva; secundum est imperans, scilicet vis appetitiva; tertium est exsequens, scilicet vis motiva...Ideo inunguntur loca quinque sensum... propter cognoscitivam; renes propter appetitivam; pedes propter motivam, etc. (*Summa Theologiae*, III-Sup., q. 32, a. 6, c.).

945 See Jauffret, *Du Culte public.*

946 Cf. Drouin, *De Re sacramentaria*; Chardon, *Hist. des Sacraments*, t. 6, etc.

947 Cf. Augustine, *Contra Epistolam Parmeniani*, Bk. 2, Ch. 13

948 Cf. Chrysostom, *On the Priesthood*, Bk. 3, Ch. 42

949 Cf. Jerome, *Dialogue against the Luciferians*

950 Cf. Leo the Great, *Epistle 81, to Dioscorus*

951 Sozomen, *Church History*, Bk. 7, Ch. 10

952 Council of Trent, Session 23, Can. 3

953 Status Ecclesiae est medius inter statum naturae et gloriae. Sed in natura invenitur ordo, quo quaedam aliis superiora sunt, et similiter in gloria, ut patet in angelis. Ergo in Ecclesia debet esse ordo...Deus sua opera in sui similitudinem producere voluit, quantum possibile fuit, ut perfecta essent et per ea cognosci posset, et ideo ut in suis operibus repraesentaretur, non solum secundum quod in se est, sed etiam secundum quod aliis influit, hanc legem naturalem imposuit omnibus, ut ultima per media perficerentur, et media per prima, ut Dionysius dicit. Et ideo ut ista pulchritudo Ecclesiae non deesset, posuit ordinem in ea, ut quidam aliis sacramenta traderent. Suo modo Deo in hoc assimilati, quasi Deo cooperatores, sicut et in corpore naturali quaedam membra aliis influunt (*Summa Theologiae*, III-Sup., q. 34, a. 1).

954 Editor's note: The essential matter required for valid sacramental ordination was given further precision under Pope Pius XII (cf. *Sacramentum Ordinis*, 1947) as being specifically the *impositio manus* (laying on of hands), long occurring in the Roman Rite amid the conferral of liturgical instruments (*traditio instrumentorum*) as described here.

955 Cf. Ferraris, art. *Ordo*, n. 49

956 Mt 4:19

957 Cf. Council of Trent, Session 23, Can. 4

958 Lk 22:19

959 Mt 28:18-20

960 Jn 20:21-23

961 Mt 18:18

962 Cf. Maximus of Turin

963 Cf. Peter Damian, *Sermon*

964 Lk 10:16

965 Cf. Zac 2:8

966 Here may be cited all the recent letters of missionaries in Oceania (Cf. *Annales de la Provagation de la Foi*, n. 56).

967 Lk 23:28

968 Cf. Council of Trent, Session 23, "Decree on Reformation," Ch. 12

969 Cf. Dionysius, *Ecclesiastical Hierarchy*, Ch. 6, Pt. 2; Augustine, *Sermon 17 ad patres in eremo*; Jerome, *On Ezechiel*, Ch. 44; Rabanus Maurus, *De Institutione Clericorum*; Bede, *Ecclesiastical History of the English Church*, Bk. 5, Ch. 22

970 Cf. Aristophanes, *The Birds*; *The Clouds*, Bk. 7

971 Cf. Cyprian, *Epistle 77*

972 Cf. Heb 5:4

973 See M. Thirat, *Esprit des cérémonies de l'Eglise*, p. 141.

974 Council of Trent, Session 23, "The True and Catholic Doctrine, Touching the Sacrament of Order," Ch. 2

975 Cf. Letters of Pope St. Cornelius in 251; Fourth Council of Carthage in 398

976 These different ministers, dedicated to the worship of God and the service of the Church, are comprised under the name of "clerics" or "clerks." This term denotes that they have been chosen by the Lord, that they are his portion, and that he is their inheritance.

977 *Summa Theologiae*, III-Sup., q. 37, a. 2, c.

978 Cf. *Esprit des Cérémonies*, p. 149

979 Cf. *Esprit des Cérémonies*, p. 153

980 Cf. *Esprit des Cérémonies*, p. 146

981 The most celebrated and trustworthy of the protestant historians of modern Germany, Henry Luden, surnamed the father of German history, does not hesitate to make the following declaration in the eighth volume of his history of the German people, published in 1833: "Always and everywhere, it is ecclesiastical celibacy that purchases us whatever we have, whatever we are. To it we owe our intelligence, the cultivation of the mind, the progress of the human race."

See also Cobbett, *History of the Reformation in England*, and the Abbé Jager, *Du Célibat ecclésiastique*, *Mémoires de* Modène, n. 47-48, 283.

982 Thus were called properties given to the Church of Rome.

983 See the Letters of St. Gregory.

984 It seems that the touching or handing of the chalice and paten is the whole matter of the order of subdeaconship in the Latin Church. Eugenius IV teaches so in the decree to the Armenians: *Subdiaconatus confertur per calicis vacui cum patena vacua superposita traditionem*. In the Greek Church, the matter of the subdeaconship is the imposition of hands which the bishop makes on the head of the person to be ordained, and the form is the prayer which he recites at the same time: there is nothing else discoverable in their euchologies, either ancient or modern, to which the names of matter and form can be applied. "Cela ne doit pas faire une difficulté," dit le *Conférencier d'Angers*, t. 11, p. 229. "Puisque c'est l'Eglise qui a institué cet ordre, il n'a dépendu que d'elle de lui assigner la matière et la forme qu'elle a crues convenables au ministère auquel elle destinait les Sous-Diacres; il a même été en son pouvoir de les changer pour en substituer d'autres, ou d'y en ajouter de nouvelles si elle le jugeait á propos."

985 Cf. Isidore, *De Ecclesiasticis Officiis*, Bk. 3, Ch. 8

986 Ambrose, *On the Duties of the Clergy*, Bk. 1, Ch. 42

987 Cf. Jerome, *Epistle 147 to Sabinianus*; Justin Martyr, *Second Apology*; Cyprian, *On the Lapsed*

988 Cf. Cyprian, *Epistle 12*

989 Cf. Acts 6:6

990 See the history of an ordination among the negroes of Africa, and the impression which it produced: *Annales de la Propagation de la Foi*, n. 120, p. 332, May, 1848.

991 See Kubichon: *Actions du Clergé dans les sociétés modernes.*

992 Gn 1:28

993 Gn 2:23

994 Cf. Tertullian, *On Monogamy*; *Prescription against Heretics*, Ch. 40; Ambrose, *On Abraham*, Bk. 1, Ch. 7; Augustine, *De Fide et Operibus*, Ch. 7; *Of the Good of Marriage*, Ch. 24; Tertullian, *Ad Uxorem*, Ch. 9; Ambrose, *Epistle 25, ad Vigil.*; Fourth Council of Carthage, Can. 13; Origen, *Tractate 7 on Matthew*; Athan., *Epistle, ad Ammonium*; Chrysostom, *Homily 56 on Genesis*; Augustine, *On Marriage and Concupiscence*, Bk. 1, Ch. 19, etc.

995 Divinum sacramentum esse atque unum ex illis septem quae Christus et Apostoli Ecclesiae tradiderunt (*Censur., orient. eccl.*, Ch. 7).

996 Cf. Council of Trent, Session 24

997 Praescripsit (sancta synodus)...Parochus, viro et muliere interrogatis, et eorum mutuo consensu intellecto, vel dicat: Ego vos in matrimonium conjungo, in nomine Patris, et Filii, et Spiritus Sancti; vel aliis utatur verbis, juxta receptum uniuscujusque provinciae ritum...qui aliter quam praesente parocho, vel alio sacerdote de ipsius paroc hi seu ordinarii licentia, et duobus vel tribus testibus, matrimonium contrahere attentabunt; eos sancta synodus ad sic contrahendum omnino inhabiles reddit; et hujusmodi contractus irritos et nullos esse decernit, prout eos prae senti decreto irritos facit et annulat (Council of Trent, Session 24, Ch. 1; Cf. Alphonsus Liguori, *Theologia Moralis*, Bk. 6, Tract. 6, n. 897; Ferraris, art. *Matr.*, n. 28).

998 Cf. Eph 5:32

999 Cf. Council of Trent, Session 24, "Doctrine on the Sacrament of Matrimony"

1000 Sacramenta vivorum aliquando primam gratiam conferre possunt, scilicet cum aliquis putans non esse in statu peccati mortalis, vel existimans se contritum accedit cum attritione ad sacramentum (Alphonsus Liguori, *Theologia Moralis*, Bk. 6, n. 6). See also Mgr. Gousset, *Theolog. Moral.*, t. 2, n. 22.

1001 Bonum quod habent nuptiae tripartitum est: fides, proles, sacramentum. In fide attenditur ne praeter vinculum conjugale cum altero, vel altera concubatur. In prole, ut amanter suscipiatur, benigne nutriatur, religiose educetur. In sacramento, ut conjugium non separetur, ut dimissus aut dimissa nec causa prolis alteri conjungatur (Augustine, *De Genesi ad Litteram*, Bk. 9, Ch. 7).

1002 Cf. Council of Trent, Session 24, "Doctrine on the Sacrament of Matrimony"

1003 Mt 19:5

1004 1 Cor 7:4

1005 Gn 3:12

1006 1 Pt 3:1ff

1007 Cf. 1 Tm 2:15

1008 Such is the meaning attached by theologians to these words of St. Paul: *Sacramentum hoc magnum est, ego autem dico in Christo et in Ecclesia.* (See Filassier, t. 1.)

1009 Cf. Tb 6:17-18

1010 Cf. 1 Cor 7:2; *Catechism of the Council of Trent* [see p. 367 of Volume VII of the Tradivox series]

1011 Cf. Phil., *De Special Leg.*

1012 Cf. Pliny, *Natural History*, Bk. 33, Ch. 1

1013 Hence it is that Tertullian calls this ring *annulus pronubus.*

1014 This word comes from the German.

1015 A friend of ours, the late learned and lamented Dr. Boudin, head physician of the military hospital at Vincennes, shows, in a work on consanguinity in marriage, the dangers to which families who marry within the degrees prohibited by the Church expose themselves. Marriages thus contracted give 28, 30, or 32 percent of deaf-mutes, while in other marriages the average is only 2 percent.

1016 See our developments on this subject in *l'Histoire de la société domestique*, t. 2, Ch. 11, p. 105 et suiv.

1017 Cf. 1 Cor 7

1018 Cf. Ignatius of Antioch, *Epistle to Polycarp*; Tertullian, *Ad Uxorem*

1019 Cf. Gregory Nazianzen, *Epistle 57*

1020 Cf. Ambrose, *De Virgin.*, Ch. 15

1021 Cf. Chrysostom, *Homily 9 on 1 Corinthians*

1022 See *Génie du Christ.*, t. 1, Ch. 10; Augustine, *Sermon 332*; *Sermon 51.*

1023 I conceive the unity, the indissolubility, and consequently the consecration of marriage by the impossibility of otherwise finding conjugal happiness, paternal authority, the education of children, or even honor or wealth. The mere prospect of the possibility of a divorce would suffice to make the best of married persons but an indifferent or even a degraded character, and the happiest alliance horrible (Madrolle, *Démonst. Eucharistique.*)

1024 Translator's note: In Anglo-Saxon the word *gospel* means "good spell" or "good news."

1025 Cf. *Summa Theologiae*, I-II, q. 62, a. 1, c.

1026 Ego ero merces tua magna nimis (Cf. Gn 15:1).

1027 1 Jn 4:8, 16

1028 Ipsa essentia divina charitas est...ita etiam charitas qua formaliter diligimus proximum est quaedam participatio divinae charitatis...Deus est vita effective et animae per charitatem et corporis per animam, sed formaliter charitas est vita animiae, sicut et anima vita corporis (*Summa Theologiae*, II-II, q. 23, a. 2, rep. 1-2).

1029 *Summa Theologiae*, II-II, q. 23, a. 6, c. Charitas comparatur fundamento et radici, in quantum ex ea sustentantur et nutriuntur omnes aliae virtutes (*Summa Theologiae*, II-II, q. 23, a. 8, rep. 2).

1030 Augustine, *Of the Morals of the Catholic Church*, Ch. 15, n. 25

1031 Cf. *Summa Theologiae*, I, q. 95, a. 4

1032 Cf. 1 Cor 13

1033 Bernard, *De Diligendo Deo*, Ch. 1

1034 Mt 10:37

1035 Jn 12:25

1036 Ps 118:112

1037 Cf. Heb 3

1038 Mt 19:17

1039 Cf. 1 Cor 9:24-25

1040 Si quis dixerit justificatum peccare dum intuitu mercedis aeternae bene operatur, anathema sit (Council of Trent, Session 6, Can. 31).

1041 Illicitum esse diligere Deum amore simpliciter mercenario, secus vero amore mercedis (Mayol., *Praeamb. ad Decal.*, q. 3; Scot., *In.* 3, dist. 27, n. 2).

1042 Apoc 4:8; Cf. Is 6:3

1043 Ex communi consensu sapientum verus actus amoris est dicere: Deus meus, quia es bonitas infinita, quia es infinite bonus, amo te super omnia...Et ideo desiderium possidendi Dei, qui est ultimus quidem noster finis, est proprius actus charitatis, imo perfectior aliis; nam possessio Dei est charitas consummata (Alphonsus Liguori, *Theologia Moralis*, Bk. 2, n. 24).

1044 1 Cor 2:9

1045 Non colitur Deus nisi amando (Augustine, *Epistle 140*, Ch. 18, n. 45).

1046 Dt 6:5-8

1047 Mt 19:17; Cf. 1 Jn 3:24

1048 Mt 22:37-38; Cf. Mt 19:17

1049 Cf. Mt 22:37-40

1050 Cf. Rom 8:35, 38-39

1051 Gal 2:20

1052 Ab aliquibus odio Deus haberi potest, in quantum scilicet apprehenditur peccatorum prohibitor et poenarum inflictor...Odium Dei est pessimum peccatum hominis (*Summa Theologiae*, II-II, q. 34, a. 1, c.; a. 2, s.c.).

1053 Proximus noster est omnis, qui in vita beata nobiscum esse potest (Cf. Augustine, *On the Catechizing of the Uninstructed*, Ch. 26, n. 50).

1054 Dilectio hominis ad seipsum est sicut exemplar dilectionis quae habetur ad alterum, sed exemplar potius est quam exemplatum; ergo homo ex charitate magis debet diligere seipsum quam proximum (*Summa Theologiae*, II-II, q. 26, a. 4, s.c.).

1055 Cf. Ferraris, art. *Virtus*, n. 60

1056 Cf. Origen, *Homily 3 on Canticle of Canticles*; Alphonsus Liguori, t. 4, n. 14, 15; *Summa Theologiae*, II-II, q. 26, a. 6-13

1057 Natura non tollitur per gloriam, sed perficitur. Ordo autem charitatis...ex ipsa natura procedit. Omnia enim naturaliter plus se quam alia amant. Ergo iste ordo remanebit in patria...continget in patria quod aliquis sibi conjunctum pluribus modis diliget; non enim cessabunt ab animo beati honestae dilectionis causae. Tamen omnibus istis rationibus praefertur incomparabiliter ratio dilectionis quae sumitur ex propinquitate ad Deum (*Summa Theologiae*, II-II, q. 26, a. 13, s.c.; c.).

1058 1 Jn 4:20

1059 Mt 22:39

1060 Cf. 1 Jn 3:18

1061 Cf. Mt 6:15; 18:35

1062 Lk 23:34

1063 Jn 13:15

1064 Cf. Ferraris, art. *Virtus*, n. 54. Specialia signa dilectionis per se loquendo non tenemur praestare inimicis ex praecepto charitatis, sed solum ex consilio: communis. Unde non tenemur inimicos aegrotos invisere, moestos consolari, egentibus succurrere, pecunias mutuare, hospitio vel convivio excipere, ad familiare colloquium admittere, obviam factos salutare et hujusmodi. Dicitur per se loquendo, quia ob varias circumstantias accidentarias saepius obligamur inimicis exhibere signa aliqua vel beneficia specialia charitatis (Ibid.).

1065 Mt 18:15-17

1066 Cf. 1 Tm 6:1

1067 Adhibeantur poenae non recuso, non interdico, sed ammo amantis, animo diligentis, animo corrigentis (Augustine, *Sermon 13*, n. 8).

1068 On fraternal correction, see Origen, *Commentary on Romans*, Bk. 9, Ch. 12; Augustine, *Sermon 82, De Verb. Evangel.*, on Mt 18:4, n. 7; *Sermon 383, De Amore Hominis*; *Epistle 211*; Gregory the Great, *Pastoral Rule*, Bk. 2, Ch. 6; *Exposition on the Gospel of Luke*, Bk. 8; Chrysostom, *Homily 30 on Hebrews*, Ch. 12; *Homily 31 on Hebrews*, Ch. 12; *Homily, De Profectu Evangelii.*

1069 Prv 14:34

1070 Tb 4:7-9; Cf. Ecclus 4:1ff; Dn 4:24

1071 Cf. Lk 11:41; Jas 2:13

1072 Cf. Alphonsus Liguori

1073 Passages from the fathers on almsdeeds: Augustine, *On Psalm 75*, n. 9; *Enchiridion*, Ch. 32, n. 19; *Sermon 62, De Verbis Domini*, Ch. 2, n. 12; *Tractate 1 on John*, n. 12; Chrysostom, *Homily, De Divite, De Lazaro*; Cyprian, *De Opere et Eleemosynis*; *Summa Theologiae*, III, q. 22, a. 5; Ambrose, *On the Duties of the Clergy*, Bk. 2, Ch. 16, n. 36, 77-78; Ch. 30, n, 148-150, 158. See also Turlot, *Catéch.*, p. 543.

1074 Editor's note: See Volume X of the Tradivox series.

1075 Mt 25:40

1076 The families most lavish of their goods in favor of the poor, and of their blood on battlefields for the defense of justice, have always been the most honored, the most lasting, and the most mighty: a delightful subject for history.

1077 On the social necessity of almsgiving, see our work *l'Europe en* 1848.

1078 On the internal and external effects of charity, see *Summa Theologiae*, II-II, q. 27, 33.

1079 On all these evils, see *Summa Theologiae*, II-II, q. 34-43.

1080 Cf. Mt 11:28-30

1081 Non erat unde se homo habere dominum cogitaret, nisi aliquid ei juberetur ef aliquid prohiberetur (Augustine, *On Genesis*, Ch. 2, etc., etc.).

1082 See the proof and development of this fact in our work *l'Europe en* 1848.

1083 Cf. Council of Trent, Session 6, Can. 2. Deus jubendo monet et facere quod possis et petere quod non possis, et adjuvat ut possis (Augustine, *On Nature and Grace*, Ch. 43). Nunquam instat praecepto, quin praecurrat auxilio (Leo the Great).

1084 Nos insensate…ambulavimus vias difficiles, etc. (Ws 5:4, 7).

1085 Ego sum Dominus Deus tuus qui eduxi te de terra Aegypti, de domo servitutis: non habebis deos alienos coram me (Ex 20:2-3).

1086 Cf. Gn 41:40-41

1087 Jb 31:26-28. See our treatise *Du Signe de la Croix.*

1088 3 Kgs 19:18

1089 Religio est virtus moralis per quam homines exhibent cultem et honorem Deo tanquam omnium creatori eb supremo Domino debitum (Alphonsus Liguori, Tract. 4, n. 14.)

1090 Cf. *Summa Theologiae*, II-II, q. 81, a. 5-6

1091 Cf. *Summa Theologiae*, II-II, q. 81, a. 7

1092 Cf. *Summa Theologiae*, II-II, q. 83, a. 2-3

1093 Quia ex duplici natura compositi sumus…duplicem adorationem Deo offerimus: scilicet spiritualem, quae consistit in interiori mentis devotione; et corporalem, quae consistit in exteriori corporis humiliatione (*Summa Theologiae*, II-II, q. 84, a. 2, c.). Deo reverentiam et honorem exhibemus non propter seipsum, quia ex seipso est gloria plenus, cui nihil a creatura adjici potest, sed propter nos, quia videlicet per hoc quod Deum reveremur et honoremus, mens nostra ei subjicitur, et in hoc perfectio ejus consistit; quaelibet enim res perficitur per hoc quod subditur suo superiori, sicut corpus per hoc quod vivificatur ab anima, aer per hoc quod illuminatur a sole (*Summa Theologiae*, II-II, q. 81, a. 7, c.).

1094 Cf. *Summa Theologiae*, II-II, q. 85, a. 1-4. A more detailed explanation of these matters will be given in the fourth part of the catechism [i.e., Volume XIII of the Tradivox series].

1095 Pertinet ad jus naturale ut homo, ex rebus sibi datis a Deo, aliquid exhibeat ad ejus honorem (*Summa Theologiae*, II-II, q. 86, a. 4, c.).

1096 Cf. *Summa Theologiae*, II-II, q. 88, a. 5

1097 See Ferraris, art. *Libri Prohib.*

1098 Studiosa voluntas emendi pretio temporali aliquod spirituale, vel spirituali annexum (Alphonsus Liguori, *Homo apost.*, Tract. 4). Pretium dividitur in munus a manu, pecunia est; munus a lingua, laus; munus ab obsequio, servitium. (See Ferraris, art. *Simonia*, art. 1, n. 26-28.)

1099 See Cicero, *On the Nature of the Gods*, Bk. 3; *On Divination*, Bk. 2, n. 149; and our *Treatise on the Holy Ghost.*

1100 See the history of Ochozias in the first chapter of the fourth book of Kings.

1101 Lv 19-20. *Flectere si nequeo superos, Acheronta movebo*, the pagans used to say.

1102 *Magnetismus animalis, somnambulismus ac spiritismus in suo complexu nil aliud sunt quam paganae superstitionis atque imperii daemonis instauratio* (*De Virtute Religionis*, auct. P. Perrone, 1866, p. 351). *Animadvertendum hic sedulo est, auctores catholicos a nobis allegatos (inter quos Em. Card. Gousset), qui mitius visi sunt de magnetismi usu scripsisse, ea aetate, seu annis illis sua edidisse commentaria, quando nondum detecta plene erat magnetismi vafrities* (*Id.*, p. 256). See also our *Traité du Saint-Esprit*, t. 1.

1103 Pro regula autem discernendi, an somnia sint a Deo, vel a daemone, observandum an somnium impellat ad opus bonum, vel malum, aut praesumptuosum. Item an post somnium homo se sentiat perturbatum et minus promptum ad opera pietatis, vel alacrem et promptum, tunc enim potest prudenter censere somnium esse a Deo. Communiter et ut plurimum in similibus in quibus tacitum tantum est pactum, venialiter tantum peccari docent doctores…Recte tamen notat Delrio esse semper rem valde periculosam juxta illa, (somnia) actiones suas dirigere, etiam non credendo (Alphonsus Liguori, Tract. 1, n. 9).

1104 Si homines rudes bona fide et ex devotione aliquem ritum ab Ecclesia non receptum observent, aliquando in sua simplicitate relinquendos esse dum difficulter abdueantur ab eo quod bona fide a suis majoribus acceperunt (Alphonsus Liguori, Tract. 1, n. 17).

1105 Cf. Gn 32:26; Rom 5:14; 4 Kgs 1:13; 4:37, etc.

1106 See M. Drach's *Dissert. sur l'inv. des Saints dans la Synag.*

1107 Leibnitz, *Théodicée*, p. 170

1108 Irenaeus, *Against Heresies*, Bk. 5, Ch. 19

1109 Ephrem, *Homily on Ezechiel*, n. 7; *On Lamentations*

1110 Origen, *Praep. Evang.*, Bk. 13, Ch. 7

1111 Eusebius, *Sermon, De Laud. B. Mar. Virg.*

1112 Cf. Lk 15:7

1113 Cf. Apoc 15:3. See *Summa Theologiae*, III-Sup., q. 92, a. 3; Gregory the Great, *Moralia in Job*, Bk. 12; Cyril of Jerusalem, *Catechetical Lecture 17*; Augustine, *On the Care of the Dead*, Ch. 15

1114 Cf. Augustine, *Sermon 2 on St. Stephen*; *Sermon 4 on St. Stephen*

1115 Cf. Jb 42; Gn 20

1116 Aquinas, *Sentences*, IV, d. 45, q. 3, a. 2.8

1117 Cf. Council of Trent, Session 25

1118 Cf. *Foi de nos pères*, by M. de Bussière, p. 196

1119 Cf. Ex 13:19; Ecclus 49:18; 4 Kgs 13:21; Ecclus 48:14; 4 Kgs 23:17-18; Mt 9:20, etc.

1120 See our *Histoire des Catacombes.*

1121 Cf. Ambrose, *Epistle 85*; *On Jeremiah*, Ch. 91; Augustine, *City of God*, Bk. 22, Ch. 8

1122 Augustine, *City of God*, Bk. 22, Ch. 8

1123 Cf. 4 Kgs 13:21

1124 Nihil est tam absurdi quod non dicatur ab aliquo philosopho.

1125 See the *Moniteur* of the 14th Nov., 1793, on the feast of the goddess Reason; also, our *Histoire de la Révolution*.

1126 Non assumes nomen Dei tui in vanum. Nee enim habebit insontem Dominus eum qui assumpserit nomen Domini Dei sui frustra (Ex 20:7).

1127 Mt 12:34; Lk 6:45

1128 Theodoret, *Questions on the Octateuch*, q. 42 on Exodus

1129 There is an indulgence of twenty-five days for each time that one pronounces the sacred names of Jesus and Mary.

1130 Assumere Deum in testem dicitur jurare, quia quasi pro jure introductum est, ut quod, sub invocatione divini testimonii dicitur, pro vero habeatur (*Summa Theologiae*, II-II, q. 89, a. 1, c.).

1131 Cf. Gn 21, 24, 25, 31, 47; Ex 22; Is 19, 45, 66; 1 Cor 15; 2 Cor 1; Rom 9; Lk 1; Acts 2; Heb 6, etc.

1132 Dominum tuum timebis et per nomen ejus jurabis (Cf. Dt 6:13).

1133 Jurationi non assuescat os tuum; multi enim casus in illa...Vir multum jurans implebitur iniquitate, et non discedet de domo ejus plaga (Ecclus 23:9, 12).

1134 Mt 5:34

1135 Apostolus, in epistolis suis jurans, ostendit quomodo accipiendum esset quod dictum est: "Dico vobis non jurare omnino," ne scilicet jurando ad facilitatem jurandi perveniatur, et ex facilitate jurandi ad consuetudinem, et a consuetudine in perjurium decidatur (Augustine, *On Lying*, Ch. 15, n. 28). Monet Dominus non jurare, non quia peccatum est verum jurare, sed quia est gravissinium peccatum falsum jurare, quo citius cadit qui jurare consuevit (Hilary, *Epistle 89*).

1136 Cf. Chrysostom, *On Matthew*, Ch. 7

1137 Cf. Mt 5:37

1138 Ibid.

1139 Cf. Augustine, *On the Sermon on the Mount*, Bk. 1, Ch. 17

1140 Jurabis, vivit Dominus, in veritate, in judicio et in justitia (Jer 4:2).

1141 Perjurium est mendacium juramento firmatum (*Summa Theologiae*, II-II, q. 98, a. 1, s.c.).

1142 Cf. *Summa Theologiae*, II-II, q. 98, a. 2, c.

1143 *Neque hic excusat levitas materiae; quia sive haec sit gravis, sive levis, seria, sive jocosa, aequaliter tamen Deo testificari falsum repugnat; et tale juramentum dicitur perjurium* (Alphonsus Liguori, *Theologia Moralis*, Bk. 3, n. 146). Hence, the proposition condemned by Innocent XI, in 1679: *Vocare Deum in testem mendacii levis, non est tanta irreverentia propter quam velit aut possit damnare hominem.*

1144 Videtis quam ista detestanda sit bellua, et de rebus humanis exterminanda (Augustine, *Sermon 180, De Verbis Apostoli Jacobi*, Ch. 2).

1145 Cf. Code pénal, art. 361

1146 Cf. *Summa Theologiae*, II-II, q. 91, a. 1. On the utility of singing the divine praises, see *Summa Theologiae*, II-II, q. 91, a. 2.

1147 Essai sur le blasphème.

1148 Qui blasphemaverit nomen Domini morte moriatur (Lv 24:16).

1149 Theodoret, *Questions on the Octateuch*, q. 33

1150 Non minus peccant qui blasphemant Christum regnantem in caelis, quam qui crucifixerunt ambulantem in terris (Augustine, *On Matthew*, Ch. 26).

1151 Cf. *Cod. Just. Collat, vi in Authent.*, tit. 5, etc.

1152 Cf. Bellarmine, *Dottrina Cristiana*, p. 124

1153 Cf. *Summa Theologiae*, II-II, q. 88, a. 5

1154 Non obligat votum factum cum semiplena animadversione, vel deliberatione (Alphonsus Liguori, *Theologia Moralis*, Bk. 3, n. 196).

1155 Dt 23:21; Cf. Dt 23:22-23

1156 Cf. *Summa Theologiae*, II-II, q. 88, a. 8

1157 Cf. Mgr. Gousset, *Théologie Morale*, t. 1, 221

1158 Mt 19:21

1159 Mt 8:20; Cf. Lk 11

1160 Cf. Mt 25; 1 Cor 7; *Summa Theologiae*, II-II, q. 155, a. 4

1161 Cf. Mt 16:24; 19:21

1162 Phil 2:8

1163 Cf. *Summa Theologiae*, II-II, q. 188, a. 6

1164 See Platus on the *Fruits of Religion*.

1165 Editor's note: See Volume XII of the Tradivox series.

1166 Cf. Council of Trent, Session 25, "On Regulars and Nuns," Ch. 15

1167 Translator's note: A very useful book for parents, showing them how to watch over and to foster the vocation of their children, is *The Child*, by the late bishop of Orleans. Another for children, is *The Choice of a State of Life*, by the late bishop of Bruges. Both have been translated into English.

1168 Sola causa qua non licet obedire parentibus (Bernard, *Epistle, ad Eliam*, n. 91).

1169 Remotis impedimentis verae religionis per primum et secundum praeceptum decalogi, consequens fuit ut tertium praeceptum poneretur, per quod homines in vera religione fundarentur (*Summa Theologiae*, II-II, q. 122, a. 4, c.).

1170 We shall make them known in the fourth part of the catechism [i.e., Volume XIII of the Tradivox series].

1171 Memento ut diem sabbati sanctifices (Ex 20:8).

1172 Cf. Nm 15:32-36

1173 It was on April 22, 1842, that P. Ang. de Masaccio was placed by the Church among the number of the saints.

1174 Cf. *Summa Theologiae*, II-II, q. 122, a. 4

1175 Diem dominicam ob venerabilem resurrectionem Domini nostri Jesu Christi, non solum in Pascha celebramus, verum etiam per singulas hebdomadas ipsius diei imaginem frequentamus (Innocent I, *Epistle, ad Decentium*). Ideo dies iste dicitur Domini, quia in eo tantum Domini Dei nostri cultui vacandum nobis est (Augustine).

1176 Cf. Apoc 1:10

1177 1 Cor 16:2

1178 Cf. Chrysostom, *Homily 13 on 1 Corinthians*; Ambrose, *On First Corinthians*; Theophylactus; *Apostolic Constitutions*, Bk. 8, Ch. 33; *Apostolic Canons*, Can. 64; Ignatius of Antioch, *Epistle to the Magnesians*; Justin Martyr, *Second Apology*; Tertullian, *Apology*, Ch. 15; *De Corona Militis*, Ch. 3; *On Idolatry*, Ch. 14; Cyprian, *Epistle 33*; Clement of Alexandria, *The Stromata*, Bk. 5, Ch. 14; Origen, *Homily 7 on Exodus*

1179 1 Kgs 25:31

1180 Cf. Alphonsus Liguori, *Theologia Moralis*, Bk. 3, n. 276

1181 Cf. Ibid.

1182 Acts that pertain to courts of justice are also forbidden; such as to institute lawsuits, to deliver summonses, to execute sentences. Necessity or custom alone can excuse judiciary acts.

1183 Cf. Alphonsus Liguori, *Theologia Moralis*, Bk. 3, n. 286; *Théologie Morale*, by Mgr. Gousset, t. 1, p. 250

1184 Cf. *Théologie Morale*, by Mgr. Gousset, t. 1, p. 251

1185 Amissionem militiae praescriptionemque patrimonii sustinebit, si quis unquam hoc die festo spectaculis interesset, aut cujuscumque judicis apparitor, praetextu negotii publici vel privati, haec quae hac lege statuta sunt, credidit emeranda (Baronius, Anno 469).

1186 Cf. Ex 16:23; 20:8; 8:2; 12:31; 14:17; 34:21; Lv 19:3; 23:3; Nm 15:32; 28:9; Dt 5:12; Is 56:2, 23; Jer 17:21, 27; Ez 20:12; 22:8; 2 Esd 13:16, 22; Mt 12:10; 1 Cor 16:2; Heb 4:4, 10, etc., etc.

1187 See our *Traité de la profanation du Dimanche*.

1188 Cf. *Théologie Morale*, t. 1, p. 253-254

1189 Cf. *Théologie Morale*, t. 1, p. 256

1190 It is a grievous fault for those who, being ignorant of the Christian doctrine, and, moreover, having no one to teach them, do not assist, when they can, at instructions.

1191 Several theologians regard it as a venial sin to be absent from vespers.

1192 Editor's note: See Volume XII of the Tradivox series.

1193 We shall speak of the social advantages of the Mass in the third part of the catechism [i.e., Volume XII of the Tradivox series].

1194 Cf. Council of Trent, Session 23

1195 Cf. Tim., *Hierosol. Orat. de Proph.*

1196 In qualibet missa invenitur omnis fructus quem Christus operatus est in cruce. Quidquid est effectus dominicae passionis, est effectus hujus sacrificii (Cf. Aquinas, *Commentary on Isaiah*, Ch. 6, Lect. 5).

1197 Cf. *Théologie Morale*, t. 1, p. 242

1198 Mk 10:36

1199 Cf. Billuart., *De Relig.*, dissert, 6, art. 5

1200 Cf. Alphonsus Liguori, *Theologia Moralis*, Bk. 4, n. 310

1201 Cf. *Théologie Morale*, t. 1, p. 241

1202 Cf. *Théologie Morale*, t, 1, p. 246

1203 Cf. Mt 22:35-40

1204 Honora patrem tuum et matrem tuam, ut sis longaevus super terram, quam Dominus Deus tuus dabit tibi (Ex 20:12).

1205 Praecepta decalogi ordinantur ad dilectionem Dei et proximi. Inter proximos autem maxime obligamur parentibus; et ideo immediate post praecepta ordinantia nos in Deum ponitur praeceptum ordinans nos ad parentes, qui sunt particulare principium nostri esse, sicut Deus est universale principium: et sic est quaedam affinitas hujus praecepti ad praecepta primae tabulae (*Summa Theologiae*, II-II, q. 122, a. 5).

1206 Cf. Ibid.

1207 Acts 5:29

1208 Lk 2:51

1209 Cf. Tb 5:23

1210 Cf. *Annal.*, n. 124, p. 189

1211 Augustine, *Confessions*, Bk. 9, Ch. 12, n. 30

1212 Cf. *Catechism of the Council of Trent* [see p. 436-437 of Volume VII of the Tradivox series]. No other natural cause can be assigned for the power of the Romans and the stability of their empire than respect for paternel authority: it is the same with the Chinese.

1213 Prv 19:26; Prv 30:17; Cf. Ex 21:17; Lv 20:9; Prv 17:2; Prv 20:20

1214 1 Tm 5:8; Cf. *Théologie Morale*, t. 1, p. 267

1215 Cf. 1 Kgs 2-4

1216 Cf. Augustine, *City of God*, Bk. 22

1217 *Annales de la Propag. de la Foi*, n. 124, p. 191

1218 Cf. *Annales*, n. 123, p. 126

1219 Cf. *Théologie Morale*, t. 1, p. 268

1220 Cf. *Théologie Morale*, t. 1, p. 269

1221 In tota anima tua time Dominum, et sacerdotes illius sanctifica. In omni virtute tua dilige eum qui te fecit, et ministros ejus non derelinquas. Honora Dominum ex tota anima tua, et honorifica sacerdotes (Ecclus 7:31-33).

1222 Cf. 1 Pt 2; Rom 13. Coram cano capite consurge, et honora personam senis, et time Dominum Deum tuum (Lv 19:32). Seniorem ne increpaveris (1 Tm 5:1).

1223 Cf. Eph 6:9; Col 4:1

1224 Cf. Augustine, *Sermon 94, De Sanctis*

1225 Cf. *Théologie Morale*, t. 1, p. 269

1226 Non occides (Ex 20:13).

1227 Cf. Gn 9:5-6

1228 Vim vi repellere omnes leges omniaque jura permittunt (Cf. *Summa Theologiae*, II-II, q. 64, a. 7, c.).

1229 Cf. *Théologie Morale*, t. 1, p. 273

1230 Legis hujus verbis non ita praescriptum: ne alium occidas; sed simpliciter: ne occidas (*Catechism of the Council of Trent* [see p. 442 of Volume VII of the Tradivox series]).

1231 Lactantius, *The Divine Institutes*, Bk. 2, Ch. 18

1232 *Esprit, Maximes, et Principes de J. J. Rousseau*

1233 Mt 5:21-22

1234 Mt 5:23-24

1235 Mt 18:7

1236 Mt 18:6

1237 Convenienter dicitur quod dictum vel factum minus rectum, praebens occasionem ruinae, sit scandalum (*Summa Theologiae*, II-II, q. 43, a. 1, c.).

1238 Non semper est scandalum, si peccas coram aliis, sed tantum quando, attentis circumstantiis tam personae agentis, tam coram quibus fit actus, potest probabiliter timeri ne per hunc actum trahantur ad peccatum, qui alias peccaturi non essent (Alphonsus Liguori, *Theologia Moralis*, Bk. 2, n. 43).

1239 Augustine, *De Past.*, Ch. 4; Cf. Augustine, *Tractate 42 on John*, n. 11

1240 The statistics of criminal justice show that, during the year 1845 alone, sixteen thousand offenders escaped the arm of justice.

1241 Translator's note: The reader will notice that some of the author's remarks, in treating of the commandments, apply more particularly to France than to other countries.

1242 Frequentior atque abundantior confessionum materia, propter quam major animarum numerus ad infernum delabitur (Alphonsus Liguori, *Theologia Moralis*, Bk. 3, n. 413).

1243 Cf. *Théologie Morale*, t, 1, p. 285

1244 Cf. Francis de Sales, *Introduction to the Devout Life*, Pt. 4, Ch. 3

1245 In cogitationibus impii interrogatio erit (Ws 1:9).

1246 De corde exeunt cogitationes malae (Mt 15:19).

1247 Perversae enim cogitationes separant a Deo (Ws 1:3).

1248 On the sin of luxury, see Bellarmine, *Dottrina Cristiana*, p. 142, etc.; *Summa Theologiae*, II-II, q. 154, a. 1; Mayol., *De Sexto Decal. Praecepto*, p. 535.

1249 Nolite inebriari vino in quo est luxuria (Eph 5:18).

1250 Juvenes…ut sobrii sint (Ti 2:6). Vinum et adolescentia prima sunt arma daemonum, et duplex incentivum voluptatis. Quid oleum flammae adjicimus? vini mero aestuans facile despumat in libidinem (Jerome, *Epistle 22 to Eustochium*, n. 8).

1251 Cf. Mt 5:29-30

1252 Editor's note: See Volume XII of the Tradivox series.

1253 Manners of the early Christians.

1254 Lam 3:51; Cf. Ecclus 14:9

1255 Jer 9:21

1256 1 Pt 3:3-4

1257 1 Tm 2:9

1258 Cf. *Vie de Saint Eloi*

1259 Jerome, *Letter 125 to Rusticus*, n. 11

1260 Omnem malitiam docuit otiositas (Cf. Ecclus 33:29).

1261 Cf. Cyprian, *De Bono Pudicit.*

1262 For a description of this frightful death, see *Les Trois Rome*, t. 2.

1263 Ipsa consuetudo balandi de paganorum observatione remansit (Caesarius of Arles, *Homily*).

1264 Nemo saltat sobrius, nisi forte insanit, neque in solitudine, neque in convivio moderato atque honesto... Saltatio omnium vitiorum est postremum, quibus relictis, omnino esse non potest (Cicero, *Oration for Lucius Murena*, Ch. 6, n. 12).

1265 Cum saltatrice non sis assiduus, nec audias illam, ne forte peress in efficacia illius (Ecclus 9:4).

1266 Decalvabit Dominus verticem filiarum Sion, et crimen earum nudabit (Is 3:17).

1267 Si Dei haec sunt verba, et vera, et divinitus inspirata, ut vera sunt, nefas sane fuerit Christianis quae dicimus agere.

1268 Sacrarium Veneris...arx omnium turpitudinum.

1269 Officinam obscenitatis.

1270 Gymnasium publicum incontinentiae, scholaque luxuriae.

1271 Nequitiarum chorus...quid enim ibi verecundiae potest esse ubi saltatur?

1272 Melius est die dominica arare quam choreas ducere.

1273 Chorea mundana est circulus, cujus centrum est diabolus et circumferentia angeli ejus circumstantes; et ideo rarum aut nunquam sine peccato fit.

1274 Cf. Francis de Sales, *Introduction to the Devout Life*, Pt. 3, Ch. 33

1275 Volumus has publicas saltationes de medio tolli sub anathematis poena.

1276 Ex choreis nihil unquam nisi libidinosum...inane spectaculum, honestis invisum oculis, viro indignum... Veneris praeludium; hic ludus multorum stuprorum causa fuit.

1277 Cf. *Théologie Morale*, t. 1, p. 293 et suiv. Whirling dances, such as are practiced at the present day, are not only contrary to all rules of modesty, but are most injurious to health. This is the opinion of the ablest physicians.

1278 Non furtum facies...non concupisces bonum proximi tui,...non servum, non ancillain, non bovem, non asinum, nec omnia quae illius sunt (Ex 20:15, 17).

1279 It was on account of his contempt for this principle that the author of a recent work on *Property* succeeded in proving nothing, or in proving quite the contrary of what he attempted. Not troubling himself with a divine right, he places the fundamental right of property in the natural wants of man. "A careful observation of human nature," he says, "is the method to follow in order to discover and demonstrate the rights of man," p. 16-17. Now, in this careful observation, the author finds the right of property. Well, take your choice: either the profound statesman proved in his book, by means of a careful observation of the nature of man, that property is an indispensable want of man's existence, a law of man, and consequently a natural right; or he did not prove it. In the first case, therefore, every man, by the law of his nature, has a right, not to labor, but to property: which is communism. In the second, therefore, the author has not established the right of property.

1280 Cf. *Institutes*, Bk. 4, tit. 1

1281 Fur a furvo dictus est, id est a fusco; nam noctis utitur tempore (Isidore, *Etymologiae*, Bk. 10, lit. F; *Summa Theologiae*, II-II, q. 66, a. 3, s.c.).

1282 Aliam rationem peccati habet rapina, et aliam furtum; ergo propter hoc differunt specie (*Summa Theologiae*, II-II, q. 66, a. 4, c.).

1283 Jas 5:4

1284 Lv 19:35; Prv 20:23

1285 Ex 20:15

1286 1 Cor 6:10

1287 Cf. *Théologie Morale*, t. 1, p. 494

1288 Cf. Ibid.

1289 Cf. Ibid.

1290 Non remittitur peccatum nisi restituatur ablatum, cum restitui potest (Augustine, *Epistle 153*, Ch. 6, n. 20).

1291 Hb 2:6

1292 Cf. *Théologie Morale*, t. 1, p. 519

1293 Cf. Jas 3

1294 Non loqueris contra proximum tuum falsum testimonium (Ex 20:16).

1295 Qui loquitur veritatem in corde suo (Ps 14:3).

1296 Cf. *Summa Theologiae*, II-II, q. 70, a. 4

1297 Prv 6:16; Cf. Prv 6:19

1298 Prv 21:28

1299 Cf. Edict of Francis I, 1531.

1300 Non dubitat mentiri eum qui volens falsum enuntiat causa fallendi (Augustine, *On Lying*, Ch. 4).

1301 Cf. Mk 13:32

1302 Prv 12:22

1303 Jn 8:44

1304 Let us say with Cicero, *Amicus Plato, sed magis amica veritas.*

1305 See, on lies, the books of St. Augustine; also his *Manual to Laurentius.*

1306 Cf. Alphonsus Liguori, *Theologia Moralis*, Bk. 3, n. 973

1307 Cf. *Théologie Morale*, t. 1, p. 548

1308 Prv 24:9

1309 Cf. Prv 4:24

1310 Ps 56:5

1311 Cf. 1 Cor 6:9-10

1312 Prv 22:1

1313 Cf. Bernard, *Sermon 24 on Canticle of Canticles*; Chrysostom, *Homily to the People of Antioch*

1314 Cf. Prv 4:24

1315 Cf. *Summa Theologiae*, II-II, q. 73, a. 2

1316 Cf. Alphonsus Liguori, *Theologia Moralis*, Bk. 3, n. 980

1317 Cf. Jerome, *Epistle 125 to Rusticus*

1318 Cf. Alphonsus Liguori, *Theologia Moralis*, Bk. 3, n. 996

1319 Cf. Ibid.

1320 Ecclus 28:15

1321 Susurratio est majus peccatum quam detractio, et etiam quam contumelia quia "amicus est melior quam honor; et amari melius est quam honorari" (*Summa Theologiae*, II-II, q. 74, a. 2, c.).

1322 Ecclus 19:10

1323 Let us give the sadly eloquent figures that support our words. It appears from the latest statistics published by the Keeper of the Seals:

1. That, according as instruction is propagated from year to year, the number of offenses increases in a like proportion.

2. That, in the number of these offenses or crimes, the class of accused, knowing how to read and write, enters as more than a fifth above the class of accused, completely illiterate; and that the class of accused, having received a high degree of instruction, enters as more than three times as many as the class of accused, completely illiterate. In other words, when 25,000 individuals of the totally illiterate class furnish five accused, 25,000 individuals of the class knowing how to read and write furnish more than six, and 25,000 individuals of the class having received superior instruction furnish more than fifteen.

3. That the degree of perversity in crime and the chance of escaping the pursuit of justice increase in a direct ratio with the amount of instruction.

4. That the districts in which instruction is most widely diffused are those which present the greatest number of crimes, that is to say, those wherein morality extends in an inverse ratio with instruction.

5. That relapses are more frequent among the accused who have received instruction than among those who cannot read or write.

1324 Jn 20:21; Mt 28:18; 18:18; Lk 10:16; Mt 18:17

1325 Gregory the Great, *Epistle 6 to Anastasius Aug.*

1326 Discourse at the consecration of the bishop of Cologne.

1327 Briefs of March 10, 1791, to Louis XVI and the bishops of the National Assembly.

1328 Cf. *Theol. Dogm.*, t. 1, p. 663

1329 The first, when speaking of holidays—in the fourth part of the catechism [i.e., Volume XIII of the Tradivox series]; the second, when speaking of the third precept of the decalogue; the fifth and the sixth, when speaking of Lent and Quarter Tense.

(Translator's note: The following are the commandments of the Church, as usually read in France:

1. Les fêtes tu sanctifieras, qui te sont de commandement.
2. Les dimanches messe ouïras, et les fêtes pareillement.
3. Tous tes péchés confesseras, a tout le moins une fois l'an.
4. Ton Créateur tu recevras, au moins à Pàques humblement.
5. Quatre-temps, vigiles, jeûneras, et le carême entièrement.
6. Vendredi, chair ne mangeras, ni le samedi mêmement.

It will be seen that they differ a little from those found in some other countries. This is not to be wondered at. The Church, having the powers to make laws, has also the power to modify them according to circumstances.)

1330 Ingulphus, abbot of Croyland

1331 Cf. Chron. de S. Denis; Chron. de Rouen, *apud Labb.*, t. 1, *Biblioth. nova.*

1332 Cf. William of Malmesbury, v. 3, *De Gestis Angborum*, Ch. 5; *Hist. des Sacrements*, t. 2, c. 6

1333 Optaret quidem sancta synodus, etc. (Council of Trent, Session 22, "Doctrine on the Sacrifice of the Mass," Ch. 6).

1334 See their sentiments, as collected in the *Treatise on Frequent Communion* by St. Liguori.

1335 See what we have said in Lessons 16 and 17 of this second part of the catechism.

1336 Magnus de caelo descendit medicus, quia magnus in terra jacebat aegrotus (Augustine, *Sermon 59, De Verbis Domini*).

1337 Lucerna pedibus meis verbum tuum (Ps 118:105).

1338 Cf. Phil 3:21

1339 Christianus alter Christus.

1340 Acts 10:38

1341 Lk 2:51

1342 Latet divinitas, latet humanitas; sola patent viscera caritatis (Bernard).

1343 Heb 10:7

1344 Ps 87:16

1345 Cf. Jn 4:6; Lk 6:12

1346 Jn 13:1

1347 Apoc 19:16

1348 Cf. Acts 8:32

1349 Jn 19:11

1350 Mk 7:37

1351 Peccatum est dictum, vel factum, vel concupitum contra legem aeternam (Augustine, *Contra Faustum*, Bk. 22, Ch. 27).

1352 Editor's note: See Volume X of the Tradivox series.

1353 Rom 6:23. See also Gal 5:20; Apoc 21:8; Ws 1:15-16.

1354 1 Jn 1:8

1355 Jas 3:2

1356 Cf. Mt 5. See also St. Augustine, *On Nature and Grace*, Ch. 30; Council of Trent, Session 6, Can. 2, 23, 25.

1357 Voluntas est principium peccatorum (*Summa Theologiae*, I-II, q. 74, a. 1, c.).

1358 Cf. Alphonsus Liguori, *De Peccat.*, n. 6

1359 Cf. Ibid.

1360 Nisi habeatur expressa auctoritas sacrae scripturae aut canonis, seu determinationis Ecclesiae, vel evidens ratio, nonnisi periculosissime peccatum mortale determinatur (Antoninus, *Summa Theologica Moralis*, I, tit. 2, Ch. 11).

1361 Initium omnis peccati est superbia (Ecclus 10:15).

1362 Superbia nominatur ex hoc quod aliquis per voluntatem tendit supra id quod est. Unde dicit Isidorus, (*Etymologiae*, Bk. 10, lit. S): "Superbus dictus est, quia super vult videri quam est" (*Summa Theologiae*, II-II, q. 162, a. 1, c.).

1363 Cf. Eph 5:5

1364 Avaro nihil scelestius (Ecclus 10:9).

1365 Praepropere, laute, nimis, ardenter, studiose (*Summa Theologiae*, II-II, q. 148, a. 4, obj. 1).

1366 Cf. Mt 12:32

1367 Cf. Gn 4:10; Ex 12; Jas 5

1368 Cf. Ibid.

1369 Fili...in omnibus operibus tuis, memorare novissima tua, et in aeternum non peccabis (Ecclus 7:40).

1370 Omnia si perdas, animam servare memento.

1371 Omnia victima igne salietur (Mk 9:48).

1372 Cf. Bellarmine, *Dottrina Cristiana*, p. 246

1373 Qui in minimis fidelis est, et in majori fidelis est (Cf. Lk 16:10).

1374 Desolatione desolata est omnis terra, quia nullus est qui recogitet corde (Jer 12:11).

1375 Consideratio hujus sententiae, destructio est superbiae, extinctio invidiae, medela malitiae, effugatio luxuriae, evacuatio vanitatis et jactantiae, constructio disciplinae, perfectio sanctimoniae, praeparatio salutis aeternae (Augustine, *De Speculo Peccati*, Ch. 1; Cornelius a Lapide, *in hunc loc.*). Hence, one cannot circulate too widely or read too often the little book entitled, *Think well on't.*

1376 *Summa Theologiae*, I-II, q. 55, a. 4; q. 58, a. 3

1377 Cf. Ferraris, art. *Virtus*, n. 6-7

1378 Virtus intellectualis est per quam intellectus perficitur ad considerandum verum: hoc enim est bonum opus ejus...ponit has solum tree virtutes intellectuales, scilicet sapientiam, scientiam, et intellectum (*Summa Theologiae*, I-II, q. 57, a. 2, c.; s.c.).

1379 Omnia bona venerunt mihi pariter cum illa (Ws 7:11).

1380 Cf. 1 Cor 3:19; Jas 3:15

1381 Da mihi sedium tuarum assistricem sapientiam...ut mecum sit at mecum laboret, ut sciam quid acceptum sit apud te (Ws 9:4, 10).

1382 Cf. *Summa Theologiae*, I-II, q. 57, a. 2

1383 Cf. Prv 15:24; 17:27; Ecclus 21:20, 26; 40:31

1384 Cf. *Summa Theologiae*, I-II, q. 57, a. 2

1385 Cf. Bar 3:14; Ecclus 39:8

1386 Si quis recte consideret, istae tres virtutes non ex aequo distinguuntur ab invicem, sed ordine quodam... scientia dependet ab intellectu sicut a principaliori; et utrumque dependet a sapientia sicut a principalissimo, quae sub se continet et intellectum et scientiam, ut de conclusionibus scientiarum dijudicans, et de principiis earumdem (*Summa Theologiae*, I-II, q. 57, a. 2, rep. 2).

1387 Cf. *Summa Theologiae*, I-II, q. 58, a. 3

1388 Cf. Bellarmine, *Dottrina Cristiana*, p. 209

1389 Cf. Ferraris, art. *Virt.*, n. 88-89

1390 Scientia sanctorum prudentia (Prv 9:10). Estote ergo prudentes sicut serpentes et simplices sicut columbae (Mt 10:16).

1391 Justitia...ea virtus est quae sua cuique distribuit (Augustine, *City of God*, Bk. 19, Ch. 21).

1392 Hence the saying of a woman among the people to the emperor Trajan: *Aut jus dicito, aut imperator esse desinito.*

1393 Mt 22:21

1394 Cf. *Summa Theologiae*, II-II, q. 66

1395 Fortitudo est considerata periculorum susceptio et laborum perpessio (*Summa Theologiae*, II-II, q. 123, a. 2, c.).

1396 Cf. 2 Tm 2:5; Mt 11:12

1397 Temperentia est virtus refraenans ac moderans inordinatos appetitus, et concupiscentias ac voluptates corporis quibus praesertim gustus et tactus afficitur (Ferraris, art. *Virt.*, n. 130).

1398 Cf. *Summa Theologiae*, II-II, q. 160, a. 1; Ferraris, art. *Virt.*, n. 131

1399 Cf. 1 Cor 13

1400 Omnes virtutes morales, sive cardinales, sive eis adjunctae, sunt its inter se connexae, ut nulla prorsus absque caeterarum comitatu obtineri possit in statu perfecto (Ferraris, art. *Virt.*, n. 91; Cf. Augustine, *Epistle 167*). Virtutes si sint disjunctae, non possunt esse perfectae secundum rationem virtutis, quia nec prudentia vera est, quae justa et temperans et fortis non est (Gregory the Great, *Moralia in Job*, Bk. 22, Ch. 1, n. 2; Cf. *Summa Theologiae*, I-II, q. 65, a. 1). Potest tamen una (virtus moralis) sine caeteris aliis esse in statu imperfecto (Ferraris, art. *Virt.*, n. 91).

1401 Cf. *Summa Theologiae*, I-II, q. 65, a. 2-3. For a further development of this matter, see the excellent work entitled *Traité des Vertus Chrétiennes*, by the abbé Busson, canon of Besançon.

1402 Cf. 2 Pt 1:13-14

ABOUT THIS SERIES

Tradivox was first conceived as an international research endeavor to recover lost and otherwise little-known Catholic catechetical texts. As the research progressed over several years, the vision began to grow, along with the number of project contributors and a general desire to share these works with a broader audience.

Legally incorporated in 2019, Tradivox has begun the work of carefully remastering and republishing dozens of these catechisms which were once in common and official use in the Church around the world. That effort is embodied in this *Tradivox Catholic Catechism Index*, a multi-volume series restoring artifacts of traditional faith and praxis for a contemporary readership. More about this series and the work of Tradivox can be learned at www.Tradivox.com.

SOPHIA INSTITUTE

Sophia Institute is a nonprofit institution that seeks to nurture the spiritual, moral, and cultural life of souls and to spread the Gospel of Christ in conformity with the authentic teachings of the Roman Catholic Church.

Sophia Institute Press fulfills this mission by offering translations, reprints, and new publications that afford readers a rich source of the enduring wisdom of mankind.

Sophia Institute also operates the popular online resource Catholic Exchange.com. *Catholic Exchange* provides world news from a Catholic perspective as well as daily devotionals and articles that will help readers to grow in holiness and live a life consistent with the teachings of the Church.

In 2013, Sophia Institute launched Sophia Institute for Teachers to renew and rebuild Catholic culture through service to Catholic education. With the goal of nurturing the spiritual, moral, and cultural life of souls, and an abiding respect for the role and work of teachers, we strive to provide materials and programs that are at once enlightening to the mind and ennobling to the heart; faithful and complete, as well as useful and practical.

Sophia Institute gratefully recognizes the Solidarity Association for preserving and encouraging the growth of our apostolate over the course of many years. Without their generous and timely support, this book would not be in your hands.

www.SophiaInstitute.com
www.CatholicExchange.com
www.SophiaInstituteforTeachers.org

Sophia Institute Press® is a registered trademark of Sophia Institute.
Sophia Institute is a tax-exempt institution as defined by the Internal Revenue Code, Section 501(c)(3). Tax ID 22-2548708.